Fundamentals of Abnormal Psychology and Modern Life

ROBERT C. CARSON Duke University

JAMES N. BUTCHER University of Minnesota

SUSAN MINEKA Northwestern University

Allyn and Bacon

Boston ▪ London ▪ Toronto ▪ Sydney ▪ Tokyo ▪ Singapore

Series Editor: *Rebecca Pascal*
Development Editor: *Joan Tinsley*
Senior Marketing Manager: *Caroline Croley*
Editorial-Production Administrator: *Susan Brown*
Editorial-Production Service: *Lifland et al., Bookmakers*
Composition and Prepress Buyer: *Linda Cox*
Manufacturing Buyer: *Megan Cochran*
Cover Administrator: *Linda Knowles*
Interior Design: *Carol Somberg*
Electronic Composition: *Publishers' Design and Production Services, Inc.*

A Pearson Education Company
75 Arlington Street
Boston, MA 02116

Internet: www.ablongman.com

Between the time Website information is gathered and then published, it is not unusual for some sites to have closed. Also, the transcription of URLs can result in unintended typographical errors. The publisher would appreciate notification where these occur so that they may be corrected in subsequent editions.

Library of Congress Cataloging-in-Publication Data
Carson, Robert C.
Fundamentals of abnormal psychology and modern life / Robert C. Carson, James N. Butcher, Susan Mineka
p. cm
Includes bibliographical references and index.
ISBN 0-321-03425-2
1. Psychology, Pathological. 2. Psychiatry. I. Butcher, James Neal. II. Mineka, Susan.
RC454 .C2733 2002
616.89—DC21
2001022690

Credits appear on p. 566, which constitutes a continuation of the copyright page.

Printed in the United States of America
10 9 8 7 6 5 4 3 VHP 06 05 04 03

Brief Contents

Contents

Single episode in partial remission (specify if: with prominent negative symptoms)/single episode in full remission
Other or unspecified pattern

Paranoid type
Disorganized type
Catatonic type
Undifferentiated type
Residual type

Schizophreniform disorder
Specify if: without good prognostic features/with good prognostic features
Schizoaffective disorder
Specify type: bipolar type/depressive type
Delusional disorder
Specify type: erotomanic type/grandiose type/jealous type/persecutory type/somatic type/mixed type/unspecified type
Brief psychotic disorder
Specify if: with marked stressor(s)/without marked stressor(s)/with postpartum onset
Shared psychotic disorder
Psychotic disorder due to [indicate the general medical condition]
With delusions
With hallucinations
Substance-induced psychotic disorder
Specify if: with onset during intoxication/with onset during withdrawal
Psychotic disorder NOS

MOOD DISORDERS
Code current state of major depressive disorder or bipolar I disorder as mild, moderate, severe without psychotic features, severe with psychotic features (mood congruent or mood incongruent), in partial remission, in full remission, or unspecified
Depressive disorders
Major depressive disorder
Single episode
Recurrent
Dysthymic disorder
[specify if: early onset/late onset; with atypical features]
Depressive disorder NOS
Bipolar disorders
Bipolar I disorder
Single manic episode [specify if: mixed]
Most recent episode hypomanic
Most recent episode manic
Most recent episode mixed
Most recent episode depressed
Most recent episode unspecified
Bipolar II disorder [specify (current or most recent episode): hypomanic/depressed]
Cyclothymic disorder
Bipolar disorder NOS
Mood disorder due to [indicate the general medical condition]
Substance-induced mood disorder [specify further]
Mood disorder NOS

ANXIETY DISORDERS
Panic disorder without agoraphobia
Panic disorder with agoraphobia
Agoraphobia without history of panic disorder
Specific phobia [specify type: animal type/natural environment type/blood-injection-injury type/situational type/other type]
Social phobia [specify if: generalized]
Obsessive-compulsive disorder [specify if: with poor insight]
Posttraumatic stress disorder [specify if: acute/chronic; with delayed onset]
Acute stress disorder
Generalized anxiety disorder
Anxiety disorder due to [indicate the general medical condition]
Substance-induced anxiety disorder [give more information]
Anxiety disorder NOS

SOMATOFORM DISORDERS
Somatization disorder
Undifferentiated somatoform disorder
Conversion disorder [specify type: with motor symptom or deficit/with sensory symptom or deficit/with seizures or convulsions/with mixed presentation]
Pain disorder
Associated with psychological factors
Associated with both psychological factors and a general medical condition [specify if: acute/chronic]
Hypochondriasis [specify if: with poor insight]
Body dysmorphic disorder
Somatoform disorder NOS

FACTITIOUS DISORDERS
[Four disorders]

DISSOCIATIVE DISORDERS
Dissociative amnesia
Dissociative fugue
Dissociative identity disorder
Depersonalization disorder
Dissociative disorder NOS

SEXUAL AND GENDER IDENTITY DISORDERS
Sexual dysfunctions
The following specifiers apply to all primary sexual dysfunctions: lifelong type/acquired type; generalized type/situational type; due to psychological factors/due to combined factors
Sexual desire disorders
Hypoactive sexual desire disorder
Sexual aversion disorder
Sexual arousal disorders
Female sexual arousal disorder
Male erectile disorder
Orgasmic disorders
Female orgasmic disorder
Male orgasmic disorder
Premature ejaculation
Sexual pain disorders
Dyspareunia (not due to a general medical condition)
Vaginismus (not due to a general medical condition)
Sexual dysfunction due to a general medical condition [specify further]
Substance-induced sexual dysfunction
Sexual dysfunction NOS
Paraphilias
Exhibitionism
Fetishism
Frotteurism
Pedophilia [specify if: sexually attracted to males/females/both]
Sexual masochism
Sexual sadism
Transvestic fetishism [specify if: with gender dysphoria]
Voyeurism
Paraphilia NOS
Gender identity disorders
Gender identity disorder
In children
In adolescents or adults
[specify if: sexually attracted to males/females/both/neither]
Gender identity disorder NOS

EATING DISORDERS
Anorexia nervosa [specify type: restricting type/binge-eating/purging type]
Bulimia nervosa [specify type: purging type/nonpurging type]
Eating disorder NOS

SLEEP DISORDERS
Primary sleep disorders
Dyssomnias
Primary insomnia
Primary hypersomnia [specify if: recurrent]
Narcolepsy
Breathing-related sleep disorder
Circadian rhythm sleep disorder [specify type]
Dyssomnia NOS
Parasomnias
Nightmare disorder
Sleep terror disorder
Sleepwalking disorder
Parasomnia NOS [and eight other disorders]

IMPULSE-CONTROL DISORDERS NOT ELSEWHERE CLASSIFIED
Intermittent explosive disorder
Kleptomania
Pyromania
Pathological gambling
Trichotillomania
Impulse-control disorder NOS

ADJUSTMENT DISORDERS
Adjustment disorder with depressed mood/anxiety/with mixed anxiety and depressed mood/with disturbance of conduct/with mixed disturbance of emotions and conduct

PERSONALITY DISORDERS
Note: These are coded on Axis II
Paranoid personality disorder
Schizoid personality disorder
Schizotypal personality disorder
Antisocial personality disorder
Borderline personality disorder
Histrionic personality disorder
Narcissistic personality disorder
Avoidant personality disorder
Dependent personality disorder
Obsessive-compulsive personality disorder
Personality disorder NOS

OTHER CONDITIONS THAT MAY BE A FOCUS OF CLINICAL ATTENTION
Psychological factors affecting medical condition [six factors]

MEDICATION-INDUCED MOVEMENT DISORDERS
[Seven disorders]

RELATIONAL PROBLEMS
[Five problems]

PROBLEMS RELATED TO ABUSE AND NEGLECT
[Five problems]

ADDITIONAL CONDITIONS THAT MAY BE A FOCUS OF CLINICAL ATTENTION
[Thirteen conditions]

ADDITIONAL CODES
Unspecified mental disorder (nonpsychotic)
No diagnosis or condition on Axis I
Diagnosis or condition deferred on Axis I
No diagnosis on Axis II
Diagnosis deferred on Axis II

Preface

Many of you are familiar with *Abnormal Psychology and Modern Life* as the "Coleman" text that you used in your undergraduate abnormal psychology class. This textbook has been providing an introduction to abnormal psychology since 1948, when James Coleman authored the first edition. Since the sixth edition in 1980, Bob Carson and Jim Butcher have focused diligently on updating this classic text, expanding its research focus to reflect the many changes in the field over two decades. Susan Mineka came on board the author team in 1996, adding her own research expertise to help create the most comprehensive and accessible text for today's students.

We, the author team, have now turned our attention to providing a new version of this classic text, offering another option for educating your students about this exciting field. *Fundamentals of Abnormal Psychology and Modern Life* is a briefer, more accessible text, which still retains the timely, dynamic coverage of the field that is a hallmark of *Abnormal Psychology and Modern Life.*

Fundamentals of Abnormal Psychology and Modern Life contains 15 chapters in a more streamlined presentation. It also features enhanced pedagogical tools to help your students better process the information as they read each chapter.

ORGANIZATION

The organization of this text provides a framework for understanding the field as a whole. This framework helps enhance student comprehension and serves as a handy reference for future study or research.

Chapter 1, Abnormal Psychology Over Time, sets forth a framework for understanding abnormal behavior, discussing the definition and classification of abnormal behavior, describing scientific research in abnormal psychology, and presenting a variety of historical perspectives. This leads into the discussion in Chapter 2, Causal Factors and Viewpoints in Abnormal Behavior. Throughout this chapter, the reader is made aware of the diversity of the field and the interaction of biological, psychosocial, and sociocultural factors. The ideal of achieving an integrative biopsychosocial approach to understanding the causes of mental disorders is emphasized. Chapter 3, Clinical Assessment and Treatment, includes both biologically and psychologically based therapies. Students are also introduced to the question of how one measures success in psychotherapy. Chapters 4 through 14 can be considered the core of the text. Here the clinical pictures, causal factors, and treatments and outcomes are examined for each category of disorders. Chapter 4 examines stress and adjustment disorders and is followed by chapters on panic and anxiety-based disorders; mood disorders and suicide; somatoform and dissociative disorders; psychological compromises of physical health and eating disorders; personality disorders; substance-related disorders; sexual variants, abuse, and dysfunctions; the schizophrenias; brain disorders and other cognitive impairments; and disorders of childhood and adolescence. The final chapter, Chapter 15, Contemporary Issues in Abnormal Psychology, introduces new conceptions and strategies concerning the prevention of mental disorders, using as a timely example the prevention of alcohol and drug abuse among adolescents.

The list below provides a more specific overview of each chapter. In keeping with the rapidly developing knowledge about biological influences on the entire spectrum of behavioral abnormalities, this text discusses such factors in numerous places.

- **Chapter 1,** Abnormal Psychology Over Time, discusses the classification of abnormal behavior, historical views of such behavior, and the process of conducting psychological research. The impact of the DSM (*Diagnostic and Statistical Manual*) taxonomic format on the field at large is highlighted.
- **Chapter 2,** Causal Factors and Viewpoints in Abnormal Psychology, includes coverage of contemporary psychodynamic perspectives, such as object relations, interpersonal, and attachment theories, with a focus on current research supporting these perspectives. Biological, psychosocial, and sociocultural viewpoints and causal factors are explored in depth.
- **Chapter 3,** Clinical Assessment and Treatment, covers biologically and psychologically based treatment approaches and considers the question of how to measure success in psychotherapy.
- **Chapter 4,** Stress-Related Disorders, contains a broadened interpretation of the biological changes that take place when a person experiences severe stress.

- **Chapter 5,** Panic, Anxiety, and Their Disorders, discusses anxiety disorders with increased attention to the nature and function of worry in generalized anxiety disorder, and to the role of attempted thought suppression in obsessive-compulsive disorder. Also, treatment approaches for the various anxiety disorders are addressed contiguously with the disorders to highlight how each treatment rationale is tailored to the primary features of the specific disorder.
- **Chapter 6,** Mood Disorders and Suicide, explores the relationship of mood disorders to creativity, using as examples famous persons in the arts including composers, artists, and poets. The chapter concludes with extensive coverage of suicide, including its prevention and intervention.
- **Chapter 7,** Somatoform and Dissociative Disorders, draws out certain similarities and interrelations between these two categories of mental disorders.
- **Chapter 8,** Psychological Compromises of Physical Health and Eating Disorders, includes extensive coverage of the eating disorders to reflect the increasingly widespread occurrence of these dangerous disorders among young women.
- **Chapter 9,** Personality Disorders, features special coverage of borderline and antisocial disorders, including new treatment approaches for the latter.
- **Chapter 10,** Substance-Related Disorders, offers a thorough update on the use and abuse of alcohol and drugs, in addition to a broadened interpretation of the biological impact of alcohol on the brain.
- **Chapter 11,** Sexual Variants, Abuse, and Dysfunctions, focuses on sexual disorders and features new biological treatments for male sexual dysfunction. The controversy surrounding "Megan's laws"—including legal and ethical issues concerning the release of convicted sex offenders—is discussed in a new "Highlight" feature.
- **Chapter 12,** The Schizophrenias, pays particular attention to new research evidence on these severe disorders, which continues to be produced at an extraordinary rate. The chapter also closely examines the competing neurodegenerative and neurodevelopmental perspectives.
- **Chapter 13,** Brain Disorders and Other Cognitive Impairments, includes discussion of traumatic brain injury, Alzheimer's disease, and mental retardation.
- **Chapter 14,** Disorders of Childhood and Adolescence, features discussion of autism and overall prevention programs for helping children and adolescents.
- **Chapter 15,** Contemporary Issues in Abnormal Psychology, covers recent developments concerning strategies for the prevention of mental disorders. The prevention of alcohol and drug abuse among adolescents is featured.

HELPFUL FEATURES AND PEDAGOGY

The extensive research base and accessible organization of this book are supported by high-interest features and helpful pedagogy to further engage students and support learning.

- **Chapter Outline.** Each chapter begins with a detailed outline that introduces the content and provides an overview of what is to come. This and the extensive chapter summary found at the end of each chapter are excellent tools for study and review.
- **Learning Objectives.** Each chapter opens with a set of learning objectives to help students focus on the most important points to be discussed. These learning objectives are also stressed in the Instructor's Manual, Test Bank, Study Guide, and Companion Website for consistency in teaching and learning.
- **Marginal Glossary.** Key terms are defined in the text when they are introduced and the definitions are highlighted at the bottom of the text pages for ease of studying.
- **In Review Questions.** A set of questions appears after each main text section, providing regular opportunities for self-assessment as students read and further reinforcing their learning.
- **Highlight Features.** These special sections expand on topics of particular interest, focusing on applications of research to everyday life, current events, and the latest research methodologies, technologies, and findings.
- **Unresolved Issues.** Selected chapters include end-of-chapter sections that demonstrate how far we have come and how far we have to go in our understanding of psychological disorders. The topics covered here provide insight into the future of the field.
- **Case Studies.** Extensive case studies of individuals with various disorders appear throughout the book, set off in color. Some are brief excerpts; others are detailed analyses. These cases bring disorders to life, while reminding students of the human factor that is so intimately a part of the subject matter of this text.

- **Patient Art.** Reproductions of artwork by individuals who have experienced various mental disorders are featured on chapter-opening pages, with brief biographical sketches of the artists. These images also help illuminate the human side of psychological disorders.

INTEGRATED RESEARCH ON MULTICULTURAL AND CROSS-CULTURAL ISSUES

Coverage of multicultural and cross-cultural issues in abnormal psychology has been integrated into many chapters. For example, Chapter 1 provides a general overview of cultural influences on the definition of abnormality. Chapter 2 includes an entire section on the sociocultural viewpoint and causal factors, including discussion of John Weisz's research on how cultural factors affect both the expression and the prevalence of symptoms. Chapter 5 discusses general sociocultural causal factors for anxiety disorders, focusing on cultural differences in sources of worry and considering *taijin kyofusho*. Chapter 6 discusses cross-cultural differences in depressive symptoms. Chapter 8 includes coverage of sociocultural factors in physical disease. Chapter 9 includes a section on sociocultural causal factors in personality disorders. Chapter 10 discusses sociocultural factors in alcohol abuse and dependence. Chapter 11 includes extensive discussion of cultural influences on sexual practices and standards. Chapter 12 covers sociocultural causal factors in schizophrenia, and Chapter 13 discusses cultural-familial mental retardation.

HELPFUL ANCILLARY MATERIALS

The following items are available to support learning and teaching with *Fundamentals of Abnormal Psychology and Modern Life*:

- **Student Study Guide with Practice Tests.** The Study Guide includes learning objectives, study questions, quizzes, and key terms for each chapter of the text, with an emphasis on stimulating critical thinking.
- **Student Practice Test Booklet.** A free set of practice tests is available with the purchase of a new textbook. This booklet includes 25 multiple-choice questions per chapter with answers and answer justification. Please ask your Allyn and Bacon sales representative for the appropriate ISBN to order this booklet packaged free with each textbook.
- **On the Net: Abnormal Psychology.** This helpful resource provides direct routes to research on various mental disorders, contacts with support services, and Web locations of mental health and professional organizations. It makes searches on the Internet more efficient and provides activities that demonstrate the wide range of related online resources.
- **Instructor's Manual** (Frank Prerost, Midwestern University). The Instructor's Manual provides chapter overviews, learning objectives, lists of key terms, abstracts with discussion questions, suggested readings, discussion and lecture ideas, suggested films, and ideas for activities and projects with student handouts, to support and extend each chapter of the textbook.
- **Test Bank.** The Test Bank contains over 100 multiple-choice questions, 15 essay questions, and 20 short answer questions per chapter. This collection of test questions can be edited using Allyn and Bacon's state-of-the-art computerized testing system.
- **Computerized Testing System.** Allyn and Bacon Test Manager is an integrated suite of testing and assessment tools for Windows and Macintosh. You can use Test Manager to create professional-looking exams in just minutes by selecting questions from the existing database, editing questions, and/or adding your own. Course management features include a class roster, gradebook, and item analysis. Test Manager also has everything you need to create and administer online tests. For first-time users, there is a guided tour of the entire Test Manager system and screen wizards to walk you through each area.
- **Transparencies.** A collection of four-color transparencies is available upon adoption, to help extend visual learning beyond the textbook.
- **PowerPoint Presentation CD-ROM.** A collection of preassembled PowerPoint slides highlighting key concepts in each chapter is available for easy use in your lectures. These slides include images from the text and links to the Companion Website and electronic Instructor's Manual files for flexibility in customization.
- **Patient Interview Videotape.** A videotape of patient interviews is available upon adoption of this text.
- **Additional Videotapes.** A collection of custom video segments highlighting issues related to diagnoses and treatment is available upon adoption of this text. Videos from "The World of Abnormal Psychology," a telecourse produced by the Annenberg/CPB Project in conjunction with Toby Levine Communications, Alvin H. Perlmutter, and Allyn and Bacon, are also

available to qualified adopters. Please contact your local Allyn and Bacon sales representative, or visit the Allyn and Bacon Website for more information.

- **Companion Website.** *Fundamentals of Abnormal Psychology and Modern Life* is supported by a free, extensive Companion Website with unique interactive case studies to allow students to apply what they have learned in the text. This Website also includes practice tests, annotated Web links, updated information on current events, matching activities, and other helpful study aids for each chapter of the textbook. Visit www.abacon.com/carson for more information.
- **Interactive Companion Website.** This text will be supported by an extensive PIN-protected Website that provides additional resources for each section of each chapter. These resources include Web links, Web activities, video clips, audio clips, case studies, matching exercises, fill-in-the-blank exercises, practice tests, and much more. Ask your Allyn and Bacon sales representative for more information.
- **Course Management.**Allyn and Bacon offers a range of course management options. Please ask your Allyn and Bacon sales representative for more information.

ACKNOWLEDGMENTS

We want to single out for special praise and appreciation our development editor, Joan Tinsley, a highly experienced editor of psychology textbooks. Joan's editorial wisdom and her enthusiasm for the project are central to whatever success this book enjoys.

We would also like to thank the many reviewers who have contributed helpful comments on this new textbook and on *Abnormal Psychology and Modern Life*, from which it was derived.

Patricia Slocum, College of DuPage
Steen Halling, Seattle University
Stephen Kahoe, El Paso Community College
Michael Hirt, Kent State University
Steve Nida, Franklin University
Eric Cooley, Western Oregon University

Norman Anderson, National Institute of Mental Health and Duke University Medical Center
John Bates, Indiana University
Alfred Baumeister, Vanderbilt University
Mitchell Berman, University of Southern Mississippi
Ira Berstein, University of Texas at Arlington
Bruce Bongar, Pacific Graduate School of Psychology
Robert F. Bornstein, Fordham University–Lincoln Center
Linda Bosmajian, Hood College
Kenneth Bowers, University of Waterloo
Thomas G. Bowers, Penn State–Harrisburg
Wolfgang Bringmann, University of Southern Alabama
Alan Butler, University of Maine
James Calhoun, University of Georgia
Caryn Carlson, University of Texas at Austin
Dennis Carmody, St. Peter's College
Alan Carr, University College Dublin
Kathleen Carroll, Yale University School of Medicine
Lee Anna Clark, University of Iowa
David Cole, University of Notre Dame
Bruce Compas, University of Vermont
Robert Deluty, University of Maryland Baltimore County
Joan Doolittle, Anne Arundel Community College
John Exner, Rorschach Workshops
Kenneth L. Farr, University of Texas at Arlington
Anthony F. Fazio, University of Wisconsin, Milwaukee
Gary Ford, Stephen F. Austin State University
Don Fowles, University of Iowa
Sol Garfield, Washington University
Carlton Gass, Veterans Administration Medical Center–Miami
Paul Goldin, Metropolitan State of Denver
Ethan Gornstein, Columbia University
Lisa Green, Baldwin-Wallace College
Susan Hardin, University of Akron
March Henley, Delaware County Community College
Karen Horner, Ohio State University
William Iacono, University of Minnesota
Ira Iscoe, University of Texas at Austin
Fred Johnson, University of the District of Columbia
Gary Johnson, Normandale Community College
John Junginger, SUNY Binghamton
John Kihlstrom, Yale University
Marlyne Kilbey, Wayne State University
David Kosson, Chicago Medical School
Dennis Kreinbrook, Westmoreland County Community College
Michael J. Lambert, Brigham Young University
Connie Lanier, Central Piedmont Community College
Marvin W. Lee, Shenandoah University
Gerard Lenthall, Keene State College
Gloria Leon, University of Minnesota

Arnold LeUnes, Texas A&M University
Richard Lewine, Emory University
Patrick Logue, Duke University Medical Center
Steven R. Lopez, UCLA
Lester Luborsky, University of Pennsylvania
Donna K. McMillan, St. Olaf College
Edwin Megargee, Florida State University
Dorothy Mercer, Eastern Kentucky University
Linda Montgomery, University of Texas of the Permian Basin
Eileen Palace, Tulane University Medical School
Dimitri Papageorgis, University of British Columbia
David L. Penn, Louisiana State University
John Poppleston, Akron University
Charles Prokop, Florida Institute of Technology
Paul Retzlaff, University of Northern Colorado
Clive Robins, Duke University Medical Center
William B. Scott, College of Wooster
Kenneth Sher, University of Missouri
Jerome Small, Youngstown State University
Gregory Smith, University of Kentucky
Cheryl L. Spinweber, University of California–San Diego
Kathleen Stafford, Court Diagnostic Clinic, Hudson, Ohio
Brian Stagner, Texas A&M University
Louis Stamps, University of Wisconsin–La Crosse
Veronica Stebbing, University College Dublin
Patricia Sutker, Veterans Medical Center–New Orleans
Alexander Troster, University of Kansas Medical Center
Samuel Turner, Medical University of South Carolina
Linda Van Egeren, Department of Veterans Affairs Medical Center–Minneapolis
Frank W. Weathers, UMASS Boston
Charles Wenar, Ohio State University
Fred Whitford, Montana State University
Jennifer Wilson, Duke University Medical Center
Richard Zinbarg, University of Oregon

About the Authors

Robert Carson, a native New Englander, received his undergraduate degree in psychology at Brown University. His graduate training, culminating in a PhD in clinical psychology, occurred at Northwestern University. He has been a member of both the medical and arts and sciences faculties at Duke University since 1960. In the course of that tenure, he served as head of Duke Medical Center's Division of Medical Psychology and as director of the doctoral clinical program in the Department of Psychology, and as chair of that department. He has taught psychology to undergraduates virtually uninterruptedly since his senior year at Brown, and in 1993–1994 was named a Distinguished Teacher in Duke University's Trinity College. Also, partly in recognition of his teaching contributions, he was appointed a G. Stanley Hall Lecturer by the American Psychological Association for 1989. Dr. Carson's scholarly interests are focused on the interpersonal dimensions of psychopathology, although he claims to work hard at remaining a generalist and avoiding excessive specialization.

James N. Butcher was born in West Virginia. He enlisted in the Army when he was 17 years old and served in the airborne infantry for 3 years, including a 1-year tour in Korea during the Korean War. After military service, he attended Guilford College, graduating in 1960 with a BA in psychology. He received an MA in experimental psychology in 1962 and a PhD in clinical psychology from the University of North Carolina at Chapel Hill. He was awarded Doctor Honoris Causa from the Free University of Brussels, Belgium, in 1990. He is currently professor of psychology in the Department of Psychology at the University of Minnesota and was associate director and director of the clinical psychology program at the university for 19 years. He was a member of the University of Minnesota Press's MMPI Consultative Committee, which undertook the revision of the MMPI in 1989. He was formerly the editor of *Psychological Assessment*, a journal of the American Psychological Association, and serves as consulting editor or reviewer for numerous other journals in psychology and psychiatry. Dr. Butcher has been actively involved in developing and organizing disaster response programs for dealing with human problems following airline disasters. He organized a model crisis intervention disaster response for the Minneapolis–St. Paul Airport and organized and supervised the psychological services offered following two major airline disasters: Northwest Flight 255 in Detroit, Michigan, and Aloha Airlines on Maui. He is a fellow of the American Psychological Association and the Society for Personality Assessment. He has published 40 books and more than 175 articles in the fields of abnormal psychology, cross-cultural psychology, and personality assessment.

Susan Mineka, born and raised in Ithaca, New York, received her undergraduate degree in psychology from Cornell University, graduating *magna cum laude*. She received a Ph.D. in experimental psychology from the University of Pennsylvania in 1974, and later completed a formal clinical retraining program from 1981 to 1984. She taught at the University of Wisconsin–Madison and the University of Texas at Austin before moving to Northwestern University in 1987. She has taught a wide range of undergraduate and graduate courses, including introductory psychology, learning, motivation, abnormal psychology, and cognitive-behavioral therapy. Her current research interests include cognitive and behavioral approaches to understanding the etiology, maintenance, and treatment of anxiety and mood disorders. She is currently a fellow of both the American Psychological Association and the American Psychological Society. She has served as editor of the *Journal of Abnormal Psychology* (1990–1994) and is currently on the editorial boards of several of the leading journals in the field. She was also president of the Society for the Science of Clinical Psychology (1994–1995) and president of the Midwestern Psychological Association (1997). She also served on the American Psychological Association's Board of Scientific Affairs (1992–1994, chair 1994) and on the executive board of the Society for Research in Psychopathology (1992–1994). During 1997–1998, she was a fellow at the Center for Advanced Study in the Behavioral Sciences at Stanford University.

CHAPTER ONE

Abnormal Psychology Over Time

George Widener, *Untitled* (1998), mixed media. Widener joined the U.S. Army at age 17 and traveled worldwide. After his military service ended, he studied engineering, but soon experienced emotional problems that were eventually diagnosed as depression. Widener believes that his depression arose in part as a reaction to a perceived lack of meaning in scientific endeavors. Turning to art, he taught himself to draw as a means of self-therapy.

LEARNING OBJECTIVES

After reading this chapter, you should be able to:

- Explain why it is so difficult to define "abnormal behavior," and describe different approaches to such a definition.
- Summarize the key concepts associated with classifying abnormal behavior, and identify three major approaches to classification.
- Describe the methodologies used to determine the rate of mental disorder in a population and the results of recent major epidemiological studies.
- Discuss how mental disorders were viewed during the Middle Ages.
- Describe the inhumane treatment received by mental patients in early "insane asylums" and the resulting humanitarian reforms.
- Explain how a biological link was established between the brain and mental disorder and how the understanding of psychological factors evolved.
- Discuss the methodologies and issues involved in research in abnormal psychology.

Abnormal behavior is a part of our common experience. Virtually all of us have had at least some experience with individuals whose behavior might be considered "abnormal." Our awareness of abnormal behavior may be based, for example, on encounters with a person on the street who talks agitatedly to no obvious listener, with the parent of a friend who had to go into an alcohol or drug rehabilitation program, with the neighbor who was afraid to go outside, or with the athlete who had to be hospitalized for an eating disorder. We hear about some multiple murder on the news and wonder how someone could do such a thing.

It is the purpose of this book to help you gain a better understanding of the variety of psychological problems that any of us may experience. It is easy to judge the loud and obnoxious drunk down the street or the youngster who seems constantly in conflict with authority, parental or otherwise. Understanding them, trying to figure out why they behave as they do, is quite another and usually far more challenging matter. As you will see, one of the themes reappearing throughout this book is that because people with and without psychological problems are all different and the influences on them complex and varied as well, there are few, if any, simple and straightforward explanations for abnormalities of behavior. Our hope is to increase your understanding so that when you encounter people exhibiting abnormal behavior or go through periods of psychological difficulty in your own life, you'll be prepared to raise potentially productive questions as to what is going on, rather than merely to judge the behavior or to feel overwhelmed by the problems you may be having.

In this chapter, we will look first at the ways abnormal behavior can be defined and classified. The issues here are probably more complex and controversial than you might expect. Having established this framework, we will consider some basic information about the occurrence of behavioral abnormalities in the population at large. Then we will look back briefly—before we look forward—to see how abnormal behavior has been viewed and treated from the early times to the present. Finally, we will examine how researchers study abnormal behavior—the methods psychologists and other mental health professionals use to uncover the information presented in subsequent chapters of the book.

This chapter is designed to give you a sense of the field as a fascinating work still very much in progress. As you will see time and again, this is not a field for those who want only cold, hard facts. Simple facts by themselves—such as that there are genetic contributions to a particular disorder—do not always yield very useful conclusions. Human behavior is fascinating because it is complexly organized. This is no less true for those experiencing psychological difficulties. Often, what we are looking for are patterns within the fabric created by a host of various simple facts, but even that level of insight remains sometimes out of reach.

Let's turn now to some cases from our files, the stories of three individuals with whom we have dealt as clinicians.

These presumably "normal" persons crossing an intersection in New York City are a highly varied group despite the common situation they share. People with psychological problems are no less different one from the other in their reactions to the various influences impinging on them.

Their cases describe the problematic behavior they exhibited, with only modest alteration to preserve anonymity. During the course of this book, we will flesh out more of the questions and potential answers such behaviors raise.

Case Study A Case of Suicide • Albert G., a 62-year-old professor at a small college in the Midwest, was immensely popular and well regarded by everyone who knew him. Students flocked to his classes; his professional colleagues sought his consultation and scholarly views; and he wrote, when his moods permitted, with penetrating insight and unusual candor. With such high praise and with obvious success, why did he kill himself—a victim of deep personal despair? He had lived a very organized and conscientious life, always concerned about how he was viewed by others. He lived alone but had several close friends. Still no one had been aware of the depth of his despondent moods. The suicide left everyone in the community wondering about the psychological forces that could prompt someone as seemingly well-adjusted as Albert to end his life.

Case Study Alcohol Shatters a Life • Sue D., a 38-year-old attorney, acknowledged to her treatment group that she did not know how long she had had a problem with alcohol and tranquilizer abuse. She had become painfully aware of her problems on an evening when she had gone to dinner with some friends and had lingered afterward in the restaurant bar to have a few drinks. She had drunk a great deal more than she had intended (as was often the case) and had gotten into a heated argument with other patrons and the manager of the bar. Sue explained how the situation had deteriorated. Objects had been thrown, the police had been called, and she had been arrested for public drunkenness and abuse of police officers. The police then had taken her to a detoxification center at the county hospital—the same hospital where she served as chief counsel. Sue told her group that the hospital administrator had been incensed, and her law firm partners had been embarrassed and outraged. Sue had been given the option of leaving the law firm or seeking treatment; she had chosen the latter and had begun a new phase of her life. She had entered a treatment program and was trying to understand how she had allowed her life to shatter as it had.

Case Study Donald G.'s Insulting Voices • Donald G. was 33 years old when one of us became professionally involved with him. Although he was of relatively high measured intelligence, he had never been employed for more than a few days at a time and lived in a sheltered community setting—except for brief, but frequent, periods of rehospitalization because of periods of marked agitation in which he reported hearing voices heaping insulting and abusive comments upon him. Donald appeared awkward, moderately inappropriate in introducing extraneous content into his conversations, and painfully unsure of himself in most social situations. The voices had made their appearance quite suddenly and without obvious provocation at age 17 after a brief period of social withdrawal. At that time he was stubbornly insistent that the voices were coming, with malicious intent, from within a neighbor's house and were being transmitted electronically to the speakers of the family television set. More recently he had conceded that he somehow produces them within himself. During periods of deterioration, he might be heard arguing vehemently with the voices, but for the most part he was now able to ignore them, though they are reportedly never entirely absent for sustained periods.

Prior to his breakdown, Donald had lived a relatively normal middle-class life, was reasonably popular among peers, had maintained passing grades in school, and had shown considerable athletic prowess, although his parents and teachers had often complained that he seemed inattentive and preoccupied. There was no evidence of his ever having abused drugs. Donald's prognosis (the likelihood that he would ever regain a full measure of functioning) was considered "guarded" by his professional caregivers.

As will be seen in this and subsequent chapters, there is no shortage of ideas purporting to explain the seemingly senseless behavioral distortions depicted in these accounts. Some of these ideas are promising, in the sense of having considerable scientific support, and some remain untested. Because so much about abnormal behavior and mental distress remains unexplained, another important goal of this book is to teach you how to discriminate among qualitative levels of supporting evidence. But first, we must deal with the elemental problem of trying to define our field of inquiry.

WHAT DO WE MEAN BY ABNORMAL BEHAVIOR?

To assess, treat, and prevent abnormal behavior such as that depicted above, we must first decide what is normal and what is abnormal and specify criteria for distinguishing one from the other. But making such formal distinctions is, in practice, far from easy. A number of factors complicate the task of defining "abnormal behavior."

First, the concepts of "abnormal behavior," "mental disorder," and "mental illness" have tended to merge in recent decades, with a focus on the *medical aspects* of "ab-

The almost incredible skill professional athletes display is highly "abnormal" in a literal and statistical sense. Yet we do not consider it abnormal behavior because that term is applied mainly to undesirable behavioral deviations.

normality"; but the course of mental disorders is not the same as that of medical diseases as ordinarily conceived.

Second, in any attempt to define "abnormal behavior," we must grapple with *valuational considerations:* The word *abnormal* literally means "away from the normal." But we do not usually employ the word *abnormal* for those high-end behaviors that are better than, or superior to, normal performance; genius is rarely if ever addressed in textbooks of abnormal psychology, whereas mental retardation almost always is. Even when we limit abnormality to the "subnormal" range, there remains the need to focus on a deviation from some specified norm. But what is the norm? For psychological disorders, we have no ideal, or even universally normal, model of human mental and behavioral functioning to use as a basis of comparison.

It is here that a third factor—*cultural influences*—further complicates the definition: Norms differ across societies. Does that mean that abnormal behavior is behavior that deviates from the norms of the society in which it is enacted? (See, e.g., Gorenstein, 1992; Sarbin, 1997; Scheff, 1984; Ullmann & Krasner, 1975.) On the surface, the answer might seem "yes"; but, although social and cultural contexts are obviously important, taking this position to its extreme would lead to the jarring conclusion that, for example, a Nazi concentration camp commandant of the early 1940s was acting "normally" in ordering and presiding over the cold-blooded murders of tens of thousands of men, women, and children of a group officially designated to be despised. In fact, from this point of view, actions to save the victims—such as Oscar Schindler's famous list of Jews exempt from gassing and cremation—might be taken as pathologically self-endangering. Clearly, a definition leading to such conclusions would be inadequate.

Despite the evident difficulties, the need to have a consensual understanding about what is to be considered abnormality is, in certain contexts, quite compelling. These contexts include, for example, legal cases, matters concerning health insurance coverage, clinical decisions as to whether to undertake treatment, and the writing of abnormal psychology textbooks. We need, in other words, some sort of working definition of the subject matter that is to occupy our attention.

The DSM Definition of Mental Disorder

Among practicing clinicians, the gold standard for defining mental disorder and its subclasses has become the American Psychiatric Association's *Diagnostic and Statistical Manual of Mental Disorders (DSM),* whose fourth edition (DSM-IV) was published in 1994 and revised (DSM-IV-TR) in 2000. Here is how the DSM-IV defines mental disorder:

> [A mental disorder] is conceptualized as a clinically significant behavioral or psychological syndrome or pattern that occurs in an individual and that is associated with present distress (a painful symptom) or disability (impairment in one or more areas of functioning) or with a significantly increased risk of suffering death, pain, disability, or an important loss of freedom. In addition, this syndrome or pattern must not be merely an expectable and culturally sanctioned response to a particular event, for example, the death of a loved one. Whatever its original cause, it must currently be considered a manifestation of a behavioral, psychological, or biological dysfunction in the individual. Neither deviant behavior (e.g., political, religious, or sexual) nor conflicts that are primarily between the individual and society are mental disorders unless the deviance or conflict is a symptom of a dysfunction in the individual, as described above. (American Psychiatric Association, 1994, pp. xxi–xxii)

The term *syndrome* refers to a group of clinical observations or symptoms that tend to co-occur. For example, feelings of despondency, lowered self-esteem, and preoccupation with negative thoughts constitute important parts of a depressive syndrome.

A noteworthy characteristic of this DSM definition is that it does not refer to the causes of a mental disorder. It also carefully rules out, among other things, certain otherwise questionable behaviors that are culturally sanctioned, such as (depressive) grief following the death of a significant other, and it is careful also to assert that mental disorders are always the product of "dysfunctions," dysfunctions that in turn always reside in individuals. In other words, there are no mentally disordered groups per se, although such a concept might arguably apply where some significant proportion of a group's members *individually* qualify as mentally disordered.

Although widely accepted, the DSM definition of mental disorder has by no means gone unchallenged. The value considerations involved in notions like *distress, disability,* and *increased risk* as well as the need to define the term *dysfunction* have all been raised as weaknesses of the definition, which is also regarded by many professionals as unduly tortuous and cumbersome.

Mental Disorder as Maladaptive Behavior

We suggest that a less cumbersome yet more encompassing definition of "abnormal behavior" focuses on whether the behavior fosters or threatens individual and group well-being. According to this criterion, **abnormal behavior** is *maladaptive behavior.* Even behavior that conforms strictly to contemporary societal values is abnormal, mentally disordered, if it seriously interferes with functioning and is self-defeating in its consequences.

In keeping with the above perspective as well as with the comprehensive aims of this book, *we define behavior as abnormal, a manifestation of mental disorder, if it is both persistent and in serious degree contrary to the continued well-being of the individual and/or that of the human community of which the individual is a member.* This "working definition" contains, of course, an explicit value judgment that ties the definition of mental disorder to the persistent enactment of behavior that produces harmful consequences for self and/or others.

Abnormal or disordered behavior defined in this manner includes the more traditional categories of mental disorders—such as alcoholism and schizophrenia—as well as, for example, self-destructive behaviors designed to establish a counterfeit "identity," promotion of intergroup hostility, destructive assaults on the environment in which all of us must live, irrational violence, and political corruption, regardless of whether such actions are condemned or condoned by a given society or subculture. All of these actions represent maladaptive behavior that impairs individual or group well-being. Typically, they sooner or later lead to personal distress among those attracted to their temporary or illusory benefits, and they often bring about destructive group conflict as well.

IN REVIEW

- What are three factors that complicate the task of defining "abnormal behavior"?
- What are two broad perspectives on defining "abnormal behavior"?

CLASSIFYING ABNORMAL BEHAVIOR

In abnormal psychology, classification involves the attempt to delineate meaningful subvarieties of maladaptive behavior. Like defining abnormal behavior, classification of some kind is a necessary step toward introducing order into our discussion of the nature, causes, and treatment of such behavior. It is intended to enable communication about particular clusters of abnormal behavior in agreed-upon and relatively precise ways. For example, we cannot conduct research on what might cause eating disorders unless we begin with a more or less clear definition of the behavior under examination; otherwise, we would be unable to select for intensive study persons whose behavior displays the aberrant eating patterns we hope to understand. There are other reasons for diagnostic classifications, too, such as gathering statistics on how common are the various types of disorder or meeting the needs of medical insurance companies (which insist on having formal diagnoses before they will authorize payment of claims).

Reliability and Validity

A classification system's usefulness depends largely on its reliability and validity. **Reliability** is the degree to which a measuring device produces the same result each time it is used to measure the same thing. If your scale showed a significantly different weight each time you stepped on it

abnormal behavior Maladaptive behavior detrimental to an individual and/or a group.

reliability Degree to which a measuring device produces the same result each time it is used to measure the same thing, or when two or more different raters use it.

Even though a test may be reliable—produce the same results on repeat occasions—it may not predict the characteristics we are interested in. For example, this test of strength might be reliable over several trials but not validly predict arm strength.

over some brief period, you would consider it a fairly unreliable device for measuring your body mass. In the context of classification, reliability is an index of the extent to which different observers can agree that a person's behavior fits a given diagnostic class. If observers cannot agree, it may mean that the classification criteria are not precise enough to determine whether the suspected disorder is present or absent.

validity Extent to which a measuring instrument actually measures what it purports to measure.

categorical approach Approach to classifying abnormal behavior that assumes that (1) all human behavior can be divided into the categories "healthy" and "disordered" and (2) there exist discrete, nonoverlapping classes or types of disorders.

dimensional approach Approach to classifying abnormal behavior that assumes that a person's typical behavior is the product of differing strengths or intensities of several definable dimensions, such as mood, emotional stability, aggressiveness, gender, identity, anxiousness, interpersonal trust, clarity of thinking and communication, social introversion, and so on.

prototypal approach Approach to classifying abnormal behavior that assumes the existence of prototypes of behavior disorders that, rather than being mutually exclusive, may blend into others with which they share many characteristics.

The classification system must also be *valid*. **Validity** refers to the extent to which a measuring instrument actually measures what it is supposed to measure. In the case of mental disorder classification, validity is defined by the degree to which a diagnosis accurately conveys something clinically important about the person whose behavior fits the category, such as helping to predict the future course of the disorder. If, for example, a person is diagnosed as having schizophrenia, as was Donald G. (described in one of the case studies at the beginning of the chapter), we should be able to infer from that classification some fairly precise characteristics that differentiate the person from others considered normal, or from those suffering from other types of mental disorder. Thus, the diagnosis of schizophrenia implies a disorder of unusually stubborn persistence, with recurrent episodes being common.

Differing Models of Classification

There appear to be three basic approaches for classifying abnormal behavior: categorical, dimensional, and prototypal (Widiger & Frances, 1985).

A **categorical approach,** similar to the diagnostic system of general medical diseases, assumes that (1) all human behavior can be divided into the categories "healthy" and "disordered" and (2) within the latter, there exist discrete, nonoverlapping classes or types of disorders having a high degree of within-class homogeneity in both "symptoms" displayed and the underlying organization of the disorders.

In contrast, a **dimensional approach** assumes that a person's typical behavior is the product of differing strengths or intensities of behavior along several definable dimensions, such as mood, emotional stability, aggressiveness, gender identity, anxiousness, interpersonal trust, clarity of thinking and communication, social introversion, and so on. The important dimensions, once established, are the same for everyone. In this conception, people differ from one another in their configuration or profile of these dimensional traits (each ranging from very low to very high), not in terms of behavioral indications of a corresponding "dysfunctional" entity presumed to underlie and give rise to the disordered pattern of behavior. "Normal" could be discriminated from "abnormal," then, by precise statistical criteria applied to dimensional intensities among unselected people in general, most of whom may be presumed to be close to average, or mentally "normal."

Finally, a **prototypal approach** assumes the existence of conceptual entities (*prototypes*) depicting idealized combinations of characteristics, ones that more or less regularly occur together in a less than perfect or standard way at the level of actual observation. Prototypes are part of our everyday thinking and experience; we can all readily generate in our mind's eye an image of a dog, while recognizing that we have never seen nor ever will see two identical dogs. Thus, a member of a prototypally defined group has at least some of the more central characteristics of the defined prototype, but typically not all of them. Also, some characteristics may be shared among differing prototypes—for example, many animals other than dogs have tails.

As we shall see, the DSM diagnostic criteria defining the various recognized classes of mental disorder, while explicitly intended to create categorical entities, more often than not result in prototypal ones. The central features of the various identified disorders are often somewhat vague, as are the boundaries purporting to separate one disorder from another. Much evidence suggests that a strict categorical approach to identifying differences among types of human behavior, whether normal or abnormal, may well be an unattainable goal (e.g., Carson, 1996b; Lilienfeld & Marino, 1995). Bearing this in mind as we proceed may help you avoid some confusion. For example, we commonly find that two or more identified disorders regularly occur together in the same psychologically disordered individual, a situation known as **comorbidity.** Does this really mean that such a person has two or more entirely separate and distinct disorders? In the typical instance, probably not.

DSM Classification of Mental Disorders

We have already introduced the *Diagnostic and Statistical Manual of Mental Disorders (DSM).* We return to it here because, in addition to attempting to define what is to be considered a mental disorder, this manual specifies what subtypes of mental disorder are currently officially recognized and provides a set of defining criteria for each. First introduced in 1952 as a means of standardizing diagnostic practices, the DSM has been revised over the years to be a less subjective and more "operational" document, which carefully details the exact observations that must be made for a diagnostic label to be assigned. In a typical case, a specific number of signs and symptoms from a designated list must be present before a diagnosis can be made. **Symptoms** generally refer to the patient's subjective descriptions, the complaints she or he presents about what is wrong. **Signs,** on the other hand, refer to objective observations the diagnostician may make either directly (e.g., the patient's inability to look another person in the eye) or indirectly (e.g., the results of pertinent tests administered by a psychological examiner). For a given diagnosis to be made, the diagnostician must observe the particular criteria—the symptoms and signs—asserted to define that diagnosis. Insisting that particular criteria be met enhances diagnostic reliability. On the other hand, many argue that the criteria have become so precise and rigid that *validity* has been diminished.

The Five Axes of DSM-IV-TR DSM-IV-TR evaluates an individual according to five foci, or **axes.** (The five axes are reprinted in full on the front endpapers of this book.) The first three axes assess an individual's present clinical status or condition:

Axis I. *The particular clinical syndromes or other conditions that may be a focus of clinical attention.* This would include schizophrenia, generalized anxiety disorder, major depression, and substance dependence. Axis I conditions are roughly analogous to the various illnesses and diseases recognized in general medicine.

Axis II. *Personality disorders.* A very broad group of disorders, discussed in Chapter 9, that encompasses a variety of problematic ways of relating to the world, such as histrionic personality disorder, paranoid personality disorder, or antisocial personality disorder. The last of these, for example, refers to an early-developing, persistent, and pervasive pattern of disregard for accepted standards of conduct, including legal ones. Axis II provides a means of coding for long-standing maladaptive personality traits that may or may not be involved in the development and expression of an Axis I disorder. Mental retardation is also diagnosed as an Axis II condition.

Axis III. *General medical conditions.* Listed here are any general medical conditions potentially relevant to understanding or management of the case. Axis III of DSM-IV-TR may be used in conjunction with an Axis I diagnosis qualified by the phrase, "Due to [a specifically designated]" general medical condition—for example, where a major depressive disorder is conceived as resulting from unremitting pain associated with some chronic medical disease.

comorbidity Occurrence of two or more identified disorders in the same psychologically disordered individual.

symptoms Patient's subjective description of a physical or mental disorder.

signs Objective observations of a patient's physical or mental disorder by a diagnostician.

axes (of DSM) Five foci used in DSM to evaluate an individual—the first three for assessing the person's present clinical status or condition and the other two for assessing broader aspects of the person's situation.

On any of these first three axes where the pertinent criteria are met, more than one diagnosis is permissible, and in fact encouraged. That is, a person may be diagnosed as having multiple psychiatric syndromes, such as panic disorder and major depressive disorder; disorders of personality, such as dependent or avoidant; or potentially relevant medical problems, such as cirrhosis (liver disease often caused by excessive alcohol use) and overdose, cocaine. The last two DSM-IV-TR axes are used to assess broader aspects of an individual's situation.

Axis IV. *Psychosocial and environmental problems.* This group deals with the stressors that may have contributed to the current disorder, particularly those that have been present during the prior year. The diagnostician is invited to use a checklist approach for various categories of *impinging life problems*—family, economic, occupational, legal, etc. For example, the phrase "problems with primary support group" may be included where a family disruption is judged to have contributed to the disorder.

Axis V. *Global assessment of functioning.* This is where clinicians note how well the individual is coping at the present time. A 100-point rating scale, the *Global Assessment of Functioning (GAF) Scale,* is provided for the examiner to assign a number summarizing a patient's overall functionability.

Axes IV and V, first introduced in DSM-III, are significant additions. Knowing the frustrations and demands a person has been facing is important for understanding the context in which the problem behavior has developed. Knowing someone's general level of functioning conveys important information not necessarily contained in the entries for other axes and indicates how well the individual is coping with his or her problems. Some clinicians, however, object to the routine use of these axes for insurance forms and the like on the grounds that such use unnecessarily compromises a patient's right to privacy by revealing, for example, a recent divorce (Axis IV) or a suicide attempt (Axis V). Because of such concerns, Axes IV and V are now considered optional for diagnosis and in fact are rarely used in most clinical settings.

As an example of an extended DSM-IV-TR diagnosis, let us consider the case of Albert G., the college professor described at the beginning of this chapter. Immediately before his suicide, his multiaxial diagnosis might have been as follows:

- *Axis I*
  Major depressive disorder
- *Axis II*
  Obsessive-compulsive personality disorder
- *Axis III*
  None
- *Axis IV*
  No primary support group
  Social environment problem: living alone
- *Axis V*
  Global functioning: 20 (some danger of hurting self)

Main Categories of Axis I and Axis II Disorders

The different Axis I and II disorders are identified in the previously noted listing of DSM-IV-TR diagnoses appearing on the endpapers of this book. They also serve as the means by which the clinical material in this book is organized. These diagnoses may be regarded for purposes of clarity as fitting into several broad etiological (major causal) groupings, each containing several subgroupings:

- *Disorders secondary to gross destruction or malfunctioning of brain tissue,* as in Alzheimer's dementia and a wide range of other conditions based on permanent or reversible organic brain pathology. These disorders are described in Chapter 13.
- *Substance-related disorders,* involving problems such as habitual drug or alcohol abuse. These are discussed in Chapter 10.
- *Disorders of psychological or sociocultural origin having no known brain pathology* as a primary causal factor. This is a very large group that includes a majority of the mental disorders discussed in this book, among them anxiety disorders (Chapter 5), somatoform and dissociative disorders (Chapter 7), psychophysiologic disorders (Chapter 8), psychosexual disorders (Chapter 11), and the Axis II personality disorders (Chapter 9). Traditionally, this group also includes severe mental disorders for which a specific organic brain pathology has not been demonstrated—such as major mood disorders (Chapter 6) and schizophrenia (Chapter 12), although it appears increasingly likely that they may be caused at least in part by certain types of aberrant brain functioning.
- *Disorders usually arising during childhood or adolescence,* including a broad group of disorders, featuring cognitive impairments such as mental retardation and specific learning disabilities (Chapter 13), and a large variety of behavioral problems, such as attention-deficit/hyperactivity disorder, which constitute deviations from the expected or normal path of development (Chapter 14).

In referring to mental disorders, several qualifying terms are commonly used. **Acute** is used to describe disorders of relatively short duration, usually under 6 months, such as transitory adjustment disorders (Chapter 4). In some contexts, it also connotes behavioral symptoms of high intensity. **Chronic** refers to long-standing and often permanent disorders, such as Alzheimer's dementia and some forms of schizophrenia. The term can also be applied generally to low-intensity disorders, since long-term difficulties are often of this sort. **Mild, moderate,** and **severe** are terms relating to varying points on a dimension of severity or seriousness. **Episodic** and **recurrent** are used to describe unstable disorder patterns that tend to come and go, as with some mood and schizophrenic conditions.

The Problem of Labeling The psychiatric diagnoses of the sort typified by the DSM system are not uniformly revered among mental health professionals (e.g., see Carson, 1997; Sarbin, 1997). Not even all psychiatrists are content with them (e.g., see Guze, 1995; Lidz, 1994; Tucker, 1998; Wilson, 1993). One important and frequently voiced criticism is that a psychiatric diagnosis is little more than a label applied to a defined category of socially disapproved or otherwise problematic behavior. (Recall our discussion of the value considerations intrinsic to defining "mental disorder.")

The diagnostic label does not describe a person, nor necessarily any underlying pathological condition ("dysfunction") the person harbors, but rather some behavioral pattern associated with that person's current level of functioning. Yet once a label has been assigned, it may close off further inquiry. It is all too easy—even for professionals—to accept a label as an accurate and complete description of an individual rather than of that person's current behavior. When a person is labeled "depressed" or "schizophrenic," others will be more likely to make certain assumptions about that person that may or may not be accurate. In fact, a diagnostic label can make it hard to look at the person's behavior objectively, without preconceptions about how he or she will act.

The pejorative and stigmatizing implications of many psychiatric labels can mark people as second-class citizens with severe limitations, often presumed to be permanent (Jones et al., 1984; Link et al., 1987). They can also have devastating effects on a person's morale, self-esteem, and relationships with others. The person so labeled may decide he or she "is" the diagnosis and adopt the latter, so to speak, as a life "career."

Clearly, it is important and in the disordered person's best interests for mental health professionals to be circumspect in the diagnostic process, in their use of labels, and in ensuring confidentiality with respect to both. A related change has taken place over the past 50 years regarding the person who goes to see a mental health professional. For years, the traditional term for such a person has been *patient,* which is closely associated with a med-

Gladys Burr (shown here with her attorney) is a tragic example of the dangers of labeling. Involuntarily committed by her mother (apparently because of some personality problems) in 1936 at the age of 29, Ms. Burr was diagnosed as psychotic and was later declared to be mentally retarded. Though a number of IQ tests administered from 1946 to 1961 showed her to be of normal intelligence, and though a number of doctors stated that she was of normal intelligence and should be released, she was confined in a residential center for the mentally retarded or in a state boarding home until 1978. Though a court did give her a financial reward in compensation, surely nothing can compensate for 42 years of unnecessary and involuntary commitment.

acute (disorder) Term used to describe a disorder of sudden onset, usually with intense symptoms.

chronic (disorder) Term used to describe a long-standing or frequently recurring disorder, often of progressing seriousness.

mild (disorder) Term used to describe a disorder of a low order of severity.

moderate (disorder) Term used to describe a disorder of an intermediate order of severity.

severe (disorder) Term used to describe a disorder of a high degree of seriousness.

episodic (disorder) Term used to describe a disorder that tends to abate and to recur.

recurrent (disorder) Term used to describe a disorder pattern that tends to come and go.

ically sick person and a passive stance, waiting (patiently) for the doctor's cure. Today, many such professionals, especially those trained in nonmedical settings, prefer the term *client* because it implies more responsibility and participation on the part of an individual for bringing about his or her own recovery. We shall be using these terms interchangeably in this text.

IN REVIEW

- Why is a classification system needed in abnormal psychology?
- What is the meaning of *reliability* and *validity* in reference to such a classification system?
- What are the three basic approaches for classifying abnormal behavior?
- Describe some of the problems associated with labeling.

THE EXTENT OF ABNORMAL BEHAVIOR

How many people actually have diagnosable psychological disorders today? The frequency or infrequency of particular disorders is an important consideration for a number of reasons. For one, researchers in the mental health field need to have a clear understanding of the nature and extent of abnormal behaviors in various groups of people because this may provide clues about their causes. For example, if only men and women who play ice hockey end up with a given disorder, then something about the sport—its tolerance of hostile aggression, its training, or its equipment—is a likely source of the problem. Additionally, mental health planners need to have a clear picture of the nature and extent of psychological problems within the citizenry in order to determine how resources, such as funding of research projects or services provided by community mental health centers, can be most effectively allocated.

epidemiology Study of the distribution of diseases, disorders, or health-related behaviors in a given population. Mental health epidemiology is the study of the distribution of mental disorders.

prevalence The proportion of active cases of a disorder that can be identified in a population at a given point in, or during a given period of, time.

incidence Occurrence (onset) rate of a given disorder in a given population.

Appearances are sometimes deceiving. Much real mental disorder is not obvious, and the frankly bizarre does not always signify abnormality. Modern epidemiological researchers employ trained interviewers and refined assessment techniques to determine the presence or absence of various mental disorders in the population of interest.

Before we can discuss the extent of mental disorders in society, we must clarify how psychological problems are counted. **Epidemiology** is the study of the distribution of diseases, disorders, or health-related behaviors in a given population. Mental health epidemiology refers to the study of the distribution of mental disorders. A key component of an epidemiological survey is determining the magnitude of the problem being studied—how frequently a particular disorder becomes a problem. There are several ways of doing this. The term **prevalence** refers to the proportion of active cases in a population that can be identified at a given point in, or during a given period of, time. For example, *point prevalence* refers to the estimated proportion of actual, active cases of the disorder in a given population at any instant in time. Prevalence is to be distinguished from **incidence,** which refers to the *occurrence*

TABLE 1.1 LIFETIME AND 12-MONTH PREVALENCE OF MAJOR TYPES OF DISORDER AS REPORTED IN THE NATIONAL COMORBIDITY SURVEY

	Male		Female		Total	
	Lifetime %	12-month %	Lifetime %	12-month %	Lifetime %	12-month %
Any mood disorder	14.7	8.5	23.9	14.1	19.3	11.3
Any anxiety disorder	19.2	11.8	30.5	22.6	24.9	17.2
Any substance abuse disorder	35.4	16.1	17.9	6.6	26.6	11.3
Nonaffective psychosis*	0.6	0.5	0.8	0.6	0.7	0.5
Any NCS-assessed disorder	48.7	27.7	47.3	31.2	48.0	29.5

*Includes schizophrenia, schizophreniform disorder, schizoaffective disorder, delusional disorder, and atypical psychosis.
Source: Kessler et al., 1994, p. 12.

(onset) rate of a given disorder in a given population, often expressed as a cumulative ratio of onsets per unit population over some time period—say 1 year. For example, schizophrenia is estimated to have an *incidence* in the United States as high as 2 per 1000 persons per year (Tien & Eaton, 1992). Incidence rates include recovered cases as well as people who may have died in the past year. Increasingly employed in the contemporary literature is a measure termed **lifetime prevalence,** which is the proportion of living persons in a population ever having had the disorder up to the time of epidemiological assessment; it, too, includes recovered cases. For example, the *lifetime prevalence* for schizophrenia (and schizophrenia-like) disorders is estimated at 0.7 percent of the noninstitutionalized U.S. population (Kessler et al., 1994). Its *point prevalence* is thought to be in the range of 0.2 to 2.0 percent (American Psychiatric Association, 1994).

Two major national mental health epidemiology studies, with direct and formal diagnostic assessment of participants, have been carried out in the United States in recent years. One, the Epidemiologic Catchment Area (ECA) study, concentrated on sampling the citizens of five communities: Baltimore, New Haven, St. Louis, Durham (NC), and Los Angeles (Myers et al., 1984; Regier et al., 1988; Regier et al., 1993). The other, the National Comorbidity Survey (NCS), was more extensive in sampling the entire U.S. population and had a number of sophisticated methodological improvements as well (Kessler et al., 1994). Since the main results of the two studies are fairly similar, we focus here on the NCS.

Table 1.1 summarizes the NCS findings with respect to 12-month and lifetime prevalence estimates (percentage of persons affected) among noninstitutionalized American male and female adolescents and adults (ages 15–54) for the various broad categories of Axis I disorders considered. It is important to note that the NCS study largely excluded Axis II (personality) disorders.

By any reasonable measure, these are sobering statistics. They tell us that at some time in their lives roughly half of the U.S. population between 15 and 54 will have had a diagnosable Axis I mental disorder, a quarter to a third of them within any one year. An astounding 35 percent of males will at some time in their lives have abused substances to the point of qualifying for a mental disorder diagnosis, and nearly one-quarter of women will have qualified for a serious mood disorder (mostly major depression). These NCS figures confirmed much other epidemiologic data in showing declining rates for most disorders with age progression and higher socioeconomic status.

The percentages of the NCS study also show a familiar pattern of gender differences. Women tend to be diagnosed as having more mood and anxiety disorders than men. The opposite pattern holds for substance-related disorders and for antisocial personality disorder. These trends may reflect assessment bias or actual gender differences. Both possibilities will be examined more fully as we address the separate disorders in later chapters of the book.

A final finding of note from the NCS study was the widespread occurrence of comorbidity among diagnosed disorders. Specifically, 56 percent of the respondents with a history of at least one disorder also had two or more additional disorders (for example, a person who drinks excessively may also be depressed and have an anxiety disorder). These persons with a history of three or more

lifetime prevalence The proportion of living persons in a population who have ever had a disorder up to the time of the epidemiological assessment.

comorbid disorders, estimated to be one-sixth of the U.S. population, or some 43 million people, tended to have disorders in the more severe ranges and would appear to represent a special group of unusually high psychological vulnerability.

As was true of NCS respondents, most people with significant psychological problems are not now hospitalized in large state or county psychiatric institutions. Various surveys indicate that admission to mental hospitals has decreased substantially over the past 45 years. The development of medications that control the more socially disruptive symptoms of some severe disorders is one reason for this change. The dramatic decline in the use of public mental hospitals has been accompanied by a steady rise in admissions to private psychiatric hospitals and to psychiatric facilities in general hospitals, most of them also privately sponsored (Kiesler & Simpkins, 1993; Lee & Goodwin, 1987). Because of their high costs, stays in private inpatient facilities tend to be much shorter than those in large public institutions. This trend away from use of the latter, often referred to as *deinstitutionalization*, will be discussed more extensively in Chapter 15.

People with psychological problems are now more likely to receive treatment in outpatient facilities such as community mental health centers (Narrow et al., 1993). However, evidence suggests that only about 25 percent of those with psychological problems actually receive any professional treatment at all (Regier et al., 1993; Robins et al., 1984). Of persons receiving any kind of help for their problems, about 40 percent rely on voluntary support networks, such as family, friends, and organized clubs that provide supportive information on coping as well as social interaction with other ex-patients (Narrow et al., 1993). The overall trends in the management of mental health problems are thus toward increased privatization, decreased duration of inpatient stays, and increased use of both professional and nonprofessional resources within the community.

IN REVIEW

- What is epidemiology?
- Compare and contrast the concepts of *prevalence* and *incidence*.
- What is the difference between point prevalence and lifetime prevalence?

exorcism Religiously inspired treatment procedure designed to drive out evil spirits or forces from a "possessed" person.

HISTORICAL VIEWS OF ABNORMAL BEHAVIOR

Our current views and treatments of abnormal behavior have a long history shaped by the prevailing attitudes of past times and the advances of science. Here we will trace that history in order to better understand the present. In a broad sense, we will see an evolution from beliefs we consider today as superstition to those based on scientific awareness—from a focus on supernatural causes to a knowledge of natural causes.

If we think, however, that we have now arrived at a knowledgeable and humane approach to treating the mentally ill, we should think again. We are still bound by culturally conditioned constraints and beliefs. For many, attitudes toward people who are different are still formed, at least in part, by superstition and fear. Even today one can find superstition and nonscientific thinking influencing the way people behave.

Demonology, Gods, and Magic

References to abnormal behavior in early writings show that the Chinese, Egyptians, Hebrews, and Greeks often attributed such behavior to a demon or god who had taken possession of a person. This belief is not surprising if we remember that "good" and "bad" spirits were widely used to explain lightning, thunder, earthquakes, storms, fires, sickness, and many other events that otherwise seemed incomprehensible. It was a simple and logical step to extend this theory to peculiar and incomprehensible behavior as well.

Although some instances of possession were thought to involve good spirits, most were considered to be the work of an angry god or an evil spirit, particularly when a person became excited or overactive and engaged in behavior contrary to religious teachings. Among the ancient Hebrews, for example, such possessions were thought to represent the wrath and punishment of God. Moses is quoted in the Bible as saying, "The Lord shall smite thee with madness." Apparently this punishment was thought to involve the withdrawal of God's protection and the abandonment of the person to the forces of evil.

The primary type of treatment for demonic possession was **exorcism,** which included various techniques for casting an evil spirit out of an afflicted person. These techniques varied considerably but typically included magic, prayer, incantation, noisemaking, and the use of various horrible-tasting concoctions, such as purgatives made from sheep's dung and wine. More severe measures, such as starving or flogging, were sometimes used in extreme cases to make the body of a possessed person such an unpleasant place that an evil spirit would be driven out.

Early Greek and Roman Thought

In the Greek temples of healing during the Golden Age of Greece (450–400 B.C.), considerable progress was made in the understanding and treatment of mental disorders. Interestingly, this progress was made in spite of the fact that Greeks of this time considered the human body sacred and thus little could be learned of human anatomy or physiology. During this period, the Greek physician Hippocrates (460–377 B.C.), often referred to as the father of modern medicine, received his training and made substantial contributions to the field.

Hippocrates denied that deities and demons intervened in the development of illnesses and insisted that mental disorders had natural causes and required treatments like other diseases. He believed that the brain was the central organ of intellectual activity and that mental disorders were due to brain pathology. He also emphasized the importance of heredity and predisposition and pointed out that injuries to the head could cause sensory and motor disorders.

Hippocrates' (460–377 B.C.) belief that mental disease was the result of natural causes and brain pathology was revolutionary for its time.

Hippocrates classified all mental disorders into three general categories—mania, melancholia, and phrenitis (brain fever)—and gave detailed clinical descriptions of the specific disorders included in each category. He relied heavily on clinical observation, and his descriptions, based on daily clinical records of his patients, were surprisingly thorough. Hippocrates considered dreams to be important in understanding a patient's personality. On this point, he was a harbinger of a basic concept of modern psychodynamic psychotherapy.

The treatments advocated by Hippocrates were far in advance of the exorcistic practices then prevalent. For the treatment of melancholia, for example, he prescribed a regular and tranquil life, sobriety and abstinence from all excesses, a vegetable diet, celibacy, exercise short of fatigue, and bleeding if indicated. He also believed in the importance of the environment and often removed his patients from their families.

Hippocrates' emphasis on the natural causes of diseases, clinical observation, and brain pathology as the root of mental disorders was truly revolutionary. Like his contemporaries, however, Hippocrates had little knowledge of physiology; he believed in the existence of four bodily fluids, or humors—blood, black bile, yellow bile, and phlegm. Although the concept of humors went far beyond demonology, it was too crude physiologically to be of much therapeutic value. Yet in its emphasis on the importance of bodily balances to mental health, it may be seen as a precursor of today's focus on the need for biochemical balances to maintain normal brain functioning and good health.

Hippocrates' work was continued by some of the later Greek and Roman physicians. Particularly in Alexandria, Egypt (which became a center of Greek culture after its founding in 332 B.C. by Alexander the Great), medical practices developed to a high level, and the temples dedicated to Saturn were first-rate sanatoriums. Pleasant surroundings were considered of great therapeutic value for mental patients, who were provided with constant activities, including parties, dances, walks in the temple gardens, rowing along the Nile, and musical concerts. Physicians of this time also used a wide range of therapeutic measures, including dieting, massage, hydrotherapy, gymnastics, and education, as well as some less desirable practices, such as bleeding, purging, and mechanical restraints.

One of the most influential Greek physicians was Galen (A.D. 130–200), who practiced in Rome. Although he elaborated on the Hippocratic tradition, he did not contribute much that was new to the treatment or clinical descriptions of mental disorders. Rather, he made a number of original contributions concerning the anatomy of

HIGHLIGHT 1.1

Procreation—A Risk Factor for Disorder?

Hippocrates believed that hysteria (the appearance of physical illness in the absence of organic pathology) was restricted to women and was caused by the uterus wandering to various parts of the body, pining for children. For this "disease," Hippocrates recommended marriage as the best remedy.

Sounds a bit foolish, right? Yet for centuries, the reproductive role of women has been associated with various psychological "disorders." These off-target views of women throughout history may be due in part to the fact that women have often been victimized by broader social attitudes centering on issues of gender and procreation. Add to that the fact that most of those writing the history have been men, who may not have sufficiently understood women's experiences. With more women entering higher education, another perspective on history, particularly with respect to social influences on mental disorders in women, has begun to bring more balance to the ways women have been and are viewed (Tomes, 1994). One can still find today, however, attitudes and expectations about social roles that result in a great deal of uncertainty and anxiety in women. ■

the nervous system. (These findings were based on dissections of animals because human autopsies were still not allowed.) Galen also maintained a scientific approach to the field, dividing the causes of psychological disorders into physical and mental categories. Among the causes he named were injuries to the head, alcoholic excess, shock, fear, adolescence, menstrual changes, economic reverses, and disappointment in love.

Roman medicine reflected the characteristic pragmatism of the Roman people. Roman physicians wanted to make their patients comfortable and thus used pleasant physical therapies, such as warm baths and massage. They also followed the principle of *contrariis contrarius* (opposite by opposite)—for example, having their patients drink chilled wine while they were in a warm tub.

Views During the Middle Ages

During the Middle Ages, the more scientific aspects of Greek medicine survived in the Islamic countries of the Middle East. The outstanding figure in Islamic medicine was Avicenna from Arabia (c. 980–1037), called the "prince of physicians" (Campbell, 1926) and author of *The Canon of Medicine,* perhaps the most widely studied medical work ever written. In his writings, Avicenna frequently referred to hysteria, epilepsy, manic reactions, and melancholia; in his treatment of the mentally ill, he was patient and humane.

In sharp contrast, the Middle Ages in Europe (from about 500 to 1500), often characterized as the Dark Ages, were largely void of scientific thinking about the mentally disturbed. Mental disorders became quite prevalent, especially toward the end of the period when medieval institutions, social structures, and beliefs began to change drastically. The contributions of Hippocrates and the later Greek and Roman physicians were soon lost in the welter

Galen (A.D. 130–200) believed that psychological disorders could have either physical causes, such as injuries to the head, or mental causes, such as disappointment in love.

Islamic physician Avicenna (c. 980–1037) approached the treatment of mental disorders with humane practices unknown to Western medical practitioners of the time.

As the notion spread in the Middle Ages that madness was caused by satanic possession, exorcism became a treatment of choice.

of popular superstition, and most of the physicians of Rome returned to some sort of belief in demonology as an underlying factor in abnormal behavior. Monasteries served as refuges and places of confinement for the mentally disturbed. "Treatment" consisted of prayer, holy water, sanctified ointments, the breath or spittle of the priests, the touching of relics, visits to holy places, and mild forms of exorcism.

During the last half of the Middle Ages in Europe, there emerged a peculiar trend involving **mass madness**—the widespread occurrence of group behavior disorders that were apparently cases of hysteria. Whole groups of people were affected simultaneously. In isolated rural areas, there were outbreaks of *lycanthropy,* a condition in which people believed themselves to be possessed by wolves and imitated their behavior. Dancing manias (epidemics of raving, jumping, dancing, and convulsions) were reported as early as the tenth century. One such episode, occurring in Italy early in the thirteenth century, was known as *tarantism,* because it was attributed to the tarantula's bite, which allegedly made individuals unwilling victims of the tarantula's spirit. The dancing became the "cure" and was the precursor of the dance known today as the tarantella. This dancing mania later spread to Germany and the rest of Europe, where it was known as *St. Vitus's dance.*

Mass madness occurred periodically into the seventeenth century but apparently reached its peak during the fourteenth and fifteenth centuries, a period noted for social oppression, famine, and pestilence (epidemic diseases). During this period, Europe was ravaged by a plague known as the Black Death, which killed millions (some estimates say 50 percent of the European population died) and severely disrupted social organization. Undoubtedly, many of the peculiar cases of mass madness were related to the fear and mysticism engendered by the terrible events of this period. People simply could not believe that frightening catastrophes such as the Black Death could have natural causes and thus could be within human power to control, prevent, or even create.

The Resurgence of Scientific Questioning in Europe

During the latter part of the Middle Ages and the beginning of the Renaissance, scientific questioning reemerged, and the superstitious beliefs that had slowed the understanding and therapeutic treatment of mental disorders began to be challenged. For example, Paracelsus, a Swiss

mass madness Widespread occurrence of group behavior disorders that are apparently cases of hysteria.

HIGHLIGHT 1.2

Mass Madness—Still With Us After All These Years?

Today, so-called mass hysteria occasionally occurs during periods of widespread public fear and stress; the affliction usually mimics some type of physical problem, such as fainting spells or convulsive movements. In 1982, for example, after a nationwide story about some Chicago-area residents poisoned by Tylenol capsules, California health officials reported a sudden wave of illness among some 200 people who drank soda at a high school football game. No objective cause for the illness could be found, and officials speculated that most sufferers had been experiencing a kind of mass hysteria related to the Tylenol incident (United Press International, 1982).

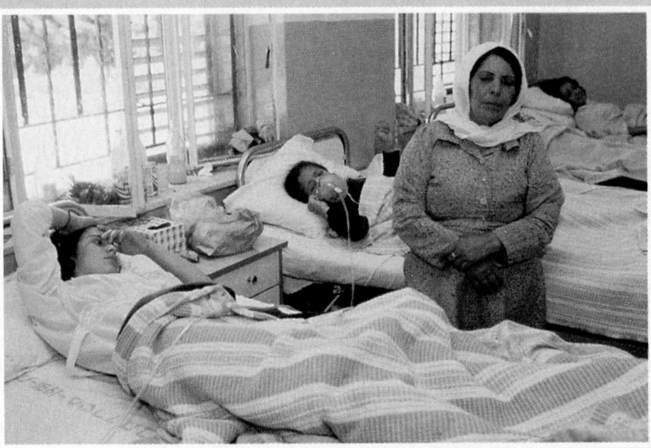
The illness experienced by a group of West Bank Palestinian schoolgirls in 1983 may have been a modern instance of mass hysteria.

And in 1983, several West Bank Palestinian girls all developed the same mysterious physical symptoms. Although Arab leaders at first suspected that the girls had been the victims of an Israeli poison plot, it was later thought that psychological factors had played an important role in the appearance of their symptoms. ■

physician (1490–1541), criticized the superstitious beliefs about possession; he insisted that the dancing mania was not a possession but a form of disease, and that it should be treated as such. He also postulated a conflict between the instinctual and spiritual nature of human beings, formulated the idea of psychic causes for mental illness, and advocated treatment by "bodily magnetism," later called *hypnosis* (Mora, 1967). Although Paracelsus rejected demonology, his view of abnormal behavior was colored by his belief in astral influences (*lunatic* is derived from the Latin word *luna,* or "moon"). He was convinced that the moon exercised a supernatural influence over the brain—an idea that persists among some people today.

Johann Weyer (1515–1588), a German physician and writer, was one of the first physicians to specialize in mental disorders; although ostracized by his peers and the Church for his progressive views, he is now considered the founder of modern psychopathology. Also, Teresa of Avila (1515–1582), a Spanish nun who was later canonized, made an extraordinary conceptual leap that has influenced thinking to the present day. Teresa, in charge of a group of cloistered nuns who had become hysterical and were therefore in danger from the Spanish Inquisition, argued convincingly that her nuns were not possessed but rather were "as if sick" (*comas enfermas*). Apparently, she did not mean that they were sick of body; rather, in the expression "as if," we have what is perhaps the first suggestion that a mind can be ill just as a body can. It was a momentous suggestion, which apparently began as a kind of metaphor but was, with time, accepted as fact: People came to see mental illness as an entity, and the "as if" dropped out of use (Sarbin & Juhasz, 1967).

In the face of these and other advocates of science, who continued their testimonies throughout the next two centuries, demonology and superstition gave ground. These advocates gradually paved the way for the return of observation and reason, which culminated in the development of modern experimental and clinical approaches.

The Establishment of Asylums and Shrines

From the sixteenth century on, special institutions called **asylums,** meant solely for the care of the mentally ill, grew in number. The early asylums were begun as a way of removing from society troublesome individuals who could

asylums Institutions meant solely for the care of the mentally ill.

not care for themselves. Although scientific inquiry into abnormal behavior was on the increase, most early asylums, often referred to as "madhouses," were not pleasant places or hospitals but primarily residences or storage places for the insane. The unfortunate residents lived and died amid conditions of incredible filth and cruelty.

One of the most notorious of these asylums was St. Mary of Bethlehem at London, which had been a monastery and was officially made into an asylum by Henry VIII in 1547. Its name was soon contracted to "Bedlam," and it became widely known for its deplorable conditions and practices. The more violent patients were exhibited to the public for one penny a look, and the more harmless inmates were forced to seek charity on the streets of London. Even as late as 1830, new patients had their heads shaved, were dressed in straitjackets, put on sparse diets, compelled to swallow some active purgative, and placed in dark cells. If these procedures did not quiet unruly or excited patients, more severe measures, such as starvation, solitary confinement, cold baths, and other torture-like methods, were used (Bennett, 1947). Other asylums were established across Europe and also in North America and Mexico, where, more often than not, the treatment of mental patients was no better than in the European institutions.

There were a few bright spots in this otherwise bleak situation. Out of the more humane Christian tradition of prayer, laying on of hands ("holy touch"), and visits to shrines, there arose several great shrines where treatment by kindness and love stood out in marked contrast to prevailing conditions. The shrine at Geel in Belgium, visited since the thirteenth century, is probably the most famous of these. Pilgrimages to Geel were organized for the mentally sick; many of the patients stayed on to live with the local inhabitants, and the colony of Geel has continued its work into modern times (Aring, 1974, 1975a; Belgian Consulate, personal communication, 1994).

Humanitarian Reform and Changing Attitudes

Clearly, by the late eighteenth century, most mental hospitals in Europe and America were in great need of reform. The humanitarian treatment of patients received great impetus from the work of Philippe Pinel (1745–1826) in France. In 1792, shortly after the first phase of the French Revolution, Pinel was placed in charge of La Bicêtre in Paris. In this capacity, he received the grudging permission of the Revolutionary Commune to remove the chains from some of the inmates as an experiment to test his views that mental patients should be treated with kindness and consideration—as sick people, not as vicious beasts or criminals. Had his experiment proved a failure, Pinel might have lost his head, but fortunately it was a great success. Chains were removed; sunny rooms were provided; patients were permitted to exercise on the hospital grounds; and kindness was extended to these poor beings, some of whom had been chained in dungeons for

This painting shows Philippe Pinel supervising the unchaining of inmates at La Bicêtre hospital. Pinel's experiment represented both a great reform and a major step in devising humanitarian methods of treating mental disorders.

30 years or more. The effect was almost miraculous. The previous noise, filth, and abuse were replaced by order and peace.

Pinel was later given charge of La Salpêtrière hospital, where the same reorganization was instituted with similar results. La Bicêtre and La Salpêtrière hospitals thus became the first modern hospitals for the care of the insane.

At about the same time that Pinel was reforming La Bicêtre, an English Quaker named William Tuke (1732–1822) established the York Retreat, a pleasant country house where mental patients lived, worked, and rested in a kindly religious atmosphere (Narby, 1982). This retreat represented the culmination of a noble battle against the brutality, ignorance, and indifference of the time.

In the United States, the revolution in the treatment of mental patients was reflected in the work of Benjamin Rush (1745–1813), the founder of American psychiatry, who incidentally had been one of the signers of the Declaration of Independence. While associated with the Pennsylvania Hospital in 1783, Rush encouraged more humane treatment of the mentally ill; wrote the first systematic treatise on psychiatry in America, *Medical Inquiries and Observations upon the Diseases of the Mind* (1812); and was the first American to organize a course in psychiatry. But even he did not escape entirely from established beliefs of his time. His medical theory was tainted with astrology, and his principal remedies were bloodletting and purgatives. In addition, he invented and used a device called the "tranquilizing chair," which was probably more torturous than tranquil for patients. The chair was thought to lessen the force of the blood on the head while relaxing the muscles. Despite these limitations, we can consider Rush an important transitional figure between the old era and the new.

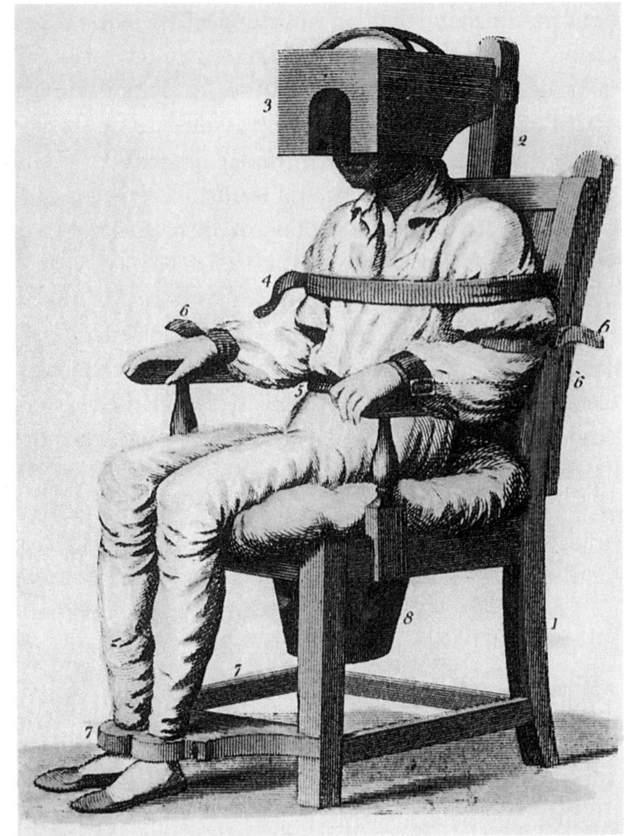

This is similar to the "tranquilizing chair" developed by Benjamin Rush around 1800. An agitated patient was strapped in until he or she became more docile.

During the early part of this period of humanitarian reform, the use of **moral management**—a wide-ranging method of treatment that focused on a patient's social, individual, and occupational needs—became relatively widespread. This approach, which stemmed largely from the work of Pinel and Tuke, began in Europe during the late eighteenth century and in America during the early nineteenth century. Rees (1957) described the approach this way:

> The insane came to be regarded as normal people who had lost their reason as a result of having been exposed to severe psychological and social stresses. These stresses were called the moral causes of insanity, and moral treatment aimed at relieving the patient by friendly association, discussion of his difficulties, and the daily pursuit of purposeful activity; in other words, social therapy, individual therapy, and occupational therapy. (pp. 306–307)

Moral management achieved a high degree of effectiveness—all the more amazing because it was done without the benefit of the antipsychotic drugs used today and because many of the patients were probably suffering from syphilis, the then-incurable disease of the central nervous system. In the 20-year period between 1833 and 1853, Worcester State Hospital's discharge rate for patients who had been ill for less than 1 year before admission was 71 percent. Even for patients with a longer preadmission disorder, the discharge rate was 59 percent (Bockhoven, 1972).

Despite its reported effectiveness in many cases, moral management was nearly abandoned by the latter part of the nineteenth century. The reasons were many and varied. Among the more obvious ones were the ethnic prejudice that came with the rising immigrant population, leading to tension between staff and patients; the failure of the movement's leaders to train their own replacements;

moral management Wide-ranging method of treatment that focused on a patient's social, individual, and occupational needs.

and the overextension of hospital facilities, reflecting the misguided belief that bigger hospitals would differ from smaller ones only in size.

Two other reasons for the demise of moral management—advances in biomedical science and the **mental hygiene movement,** which advocated treatment that focused almost exclusively on the physical well-being of hospitalized mental patients—are, in retrospect, truly ironic.

Advances in biomedical science contributed not only to the demise of moral management but also to the rise of the mental hygiene movement by fostering the notion that all mental disorders would eventually yield to biological explanations and biologically based treatments (Luchins, 1991). Thus, the psychological and social environment of a patient was considered largely irrelevant; the best one could do was keep the patient comfortable until a biological cure was discovered.

In this environment, the mental hygiene movement grew. Dorothea Dix (1802–1887), a New England schoolteacher and champion of the poor and "forgotten" people in prisons and mental institutions, raised millions of dollars to build suitable hospitals not only in the United States but in Canada, Scotland, and several other countries. She is credited with establishing 32 mental hospitals, an astonishing record considering the ignorance and superstition that still prevailed concerning mental illness. But here the irony enters: Although the creature comforts of patients may have improved under the mental hygienists, the patients received no help for their mental problems and thus were condemned subtly to helplessness and dependency. Also, as numbers of large mental hospitals were established, trained staff became scarce; and as patient populations increased, in part because of the focus on custodial care rather than a cure, overcrowding resulted, and conditions worsened.

Needless to say, the anticipated biological cure-all did not arrive. By the end of the nineteenth century, the mental hospital or asylum—"the big house on the hill"—with its fortress-like appearance, had become a familiar landmark in America. In it, mental patients lived under relatively harsh conditions despite the inroads made by moral management and the good intentions of the mental hygiene movement. To the general public, however, the asylum was an eerie place, and its occupants a strange and frightening lot. Little was done by the resident psychiatrists—at the time called *alienists* because they treated the "alienated," or insane—to educate the public so as to reduce the general fear and horror of insanity. A principal reason for this silence, of course, was that early psychiatrists had little actual information to impart.

Dorothea Dix (1802–1887) was a tireless reformer who made great strides in changing public attitudes toward the mentally ill.

Gradually, however, important strides were made toward changing the general public's attitude toward mental patients. In America, the pioneering work of Dix was followed by that of Clifford Beers (1876–1943), whose book *A Mind That Found Itself* was published in 1908. Beers, a Yale graduate, described his own mental collapse and told of the bad treatment he received in three typical institutions of the day. He also explained his eventual recovery in the home of a friendly attendant. Although chains and other torture devices had long since been given up, the straitjacket was still widely used as a means of "quieting" excited patients. Beers himself experienced this treatment and later described what such painful immobilization of the arms means to an overwrought mental patient. After Beers recovered, he began a campaign to make people realize that such treatment was no way to handle the sick. He soon won the interest and support of many

mental hygiene movement Movement that advocated a method of treatment that focused almost exclusively on the physical well-being of hospitalized mental patients.

Clifford Beers (1876–1943) used his own experiences of incarceration in mental institutions to wage a campaign for public awareness about the need for changes in attitudes toward and treatment of mental patients.

public-spirited individuals, including the eminent psychologist William James and the "dean of American psychiatry," Adolf Meyer.

IN REVIEW

- What aspects of Hippocrates' alternative approach to mental disorders were truly revolutionary?
- What is mass madness? Give some examples of this phenomenon.
- Describe the historical development of humanitarian reform, and identify some of the reasons why it occurred.

THE BEGINNING OF THE MODERN ERA

While the mental hygiene movement was gaining ground in the United States during the latter years of the nineteenth century, technological discoveries both at home and abroad were shaping the field of abnormal psychology. In this context, three major themes have evolved, which frame and influence our contemporary perspective of abnormal psychology as a scientific, or experimentally oriented, field of endeavor. These themes concern (1) a biological connection, (2) a psychological component, and (3) an experimental psychological foundation.

Establishing a Biological Link Between the Brain and Mental Disorder

With the emergence of modern experimental science in the early part of the eighteenth century, knowledge of anatomy, physiology, neurology, chemistry, and general medicine increased rapidly. These advances led to the gradual identification of the biological, or organic, pathology underlying many physical ailments. Scientists began to focus on diseased body organs as the cause of physical ailments. It was only another step to the assumption that mental disorder was an illness based on the pathology of an organ—in this case, the brain. The first systematic presentation of this viewpoint was made by the German psychiatrist Wilhelm Griesinger (1817–1868). In his textbook *The Pathology and Therapy of Psychic Disorders*, published in 1845, Griesinger insisted that all mental disorders could be explained in terms of brain pathology.

General Paresis and Syphilis A major biomedical breakthrough finally came with the discovery of the organic factors underlying *general paresis* (syphilis of the brain) and ultimately a treatment for it. One of the most serious mental illnesses of the day, general paresis produced paralysis and insanity and typically caused death within 2 to 5 years. The discovery of a cure for general paresis took nearly a century of research, beginning in 1825 when French physician A. L. J. Bayle differentiated the condition as a specific type of mental disorder. Many years later, in 1897, the Viennese psychiatrist Krafft-Ebing conducted experiments that established the relationship of general paresis to syphilis. It was almost a decade later, in 1906, when von Wassermann developed a blood test for syphilis; finally, in 1917, Wagner-Jauregg, chief of the psychiatric clinic of the University of Vienna, introduced the malarial fever treatment of syphilis in which the high fever associated with malaria killed off the spirochete (the bacterium that causes syphilis). Although today penicillin is an effective and simpler treatment for syphilis, the malarial treatment represented, for the first time in history, a clear-cut conquest of a mental disorder by medical science.

The field of abnormal psychology had come a long way—from superstitious beliefs to scientific proof of how brain pathology can cause a specific disorder. This breakthrough raised great hopes in the medical community that organic bases would be found for many other mental disorders—perhaps for all of them. And, to be sure, other successes followed. The brain pathology in cerebral arteriosclerosis and in the senile dementias was established by Alois Alzheimer and other investigators. Eventually, in the twentieth century, the organic pathologies underlying the toxic mental disorders (disorders caused by toxic substances such as lead), certain types of mental retardation, and other mental illnesses were discovered.

It is important to note here that although the discovery of the organic bases of mental disorders may have addressed the *how* behind causation, it did not, in most cases, address the question of *why*. This situation still holds true to some extent to this day. For example, although we know what causes certain "presenile" mental disorders—brain pathology—we do not yet know why some individuals are afflicted and others are not. Nonetheless, we can predict quite accurately the courses of these disorders. This ability is due not only to a greater understanding of the organic factors involved but also, in large part, to the work of a follower of Griesinger, Emil Kraepelin.

The Beginnings of a Classification System Emil Kraepelin (1856–1926) played a dominant role in the early development of the biological viewpoint. His textbook *Lehrbuch der Psychiatrie,* published in 1883, not only emphasized the importance of brain pathology in mental disorders but also made several related contributions that helped establish this viewpoint. The most important of these contributions was his system of classification of mental disorders, which became the forerunner of today's DSM system (discussed earlier in this chapter). Kraepelin noted that certain symptom patterns occurred together regularly enough to be regarded as specific types of mental disease. He then proceeded to describe and clarify these types of mental disorders, working out a scheme of classification that is the basis of the DSM system. The integration of the clinical material underlying this classification was a herculean task and represented a major contribution to the field of psychopathology.

Kraepelin saw each type of mental disorder as distinct from the others and thought that the course of each was as predetermined and predictable as the course of measles. Thus, the outcome of a given type of disorder could presumably be predicted even if it could not yet be controlled. Such conclusions led to widespread interest in the accurate description and classification of mental disorders.

Biologically based thinking represented the first great advance of modern science toward the understanding and treatment of mental disorders. Not all of the consequences of this early thinking were positive, however. Because the disorders best understood in terms of the then-available knowledge were those in which brain damage or deterioration was a central feature (as in general paresis), there naturally developed an expectation that all abnormal behavior would eventually be explained by reference to gross brain pathology. To be sure, organic mental disorders do occur (and we will consider them in Chapter 13), but the vast majority of abnormal behavior is not clearly associated with physical damage to brain tissue. Nonetheless, the **medical model**—a conceptual model that is inappropriate for much abnormal behavior—became stubbornly entrenched by these early but limited successes. It is important to note that the medical-model orientation is not limited to biological viewpoints on the nature of mental disorder. It is also extended into psychosocial theorizing by the adoption of a symptom/underlying-cause point of view. This point of view assumes that abnormal behavior, even though it may be psychological (rather than biological) in nature, is a symptom of some sort of underlying, internal pathology, or "illness"—just as a fever is a symptom of an underlying infection. As we will see shortly, Freud, who was a physician, took this approach in developing his psychoanalytic theory of abnormal behavior.

Establishing the Psychological Basis of Mental Disorder

Despite the emphasis on biological research, understanding of the psychological factors in human behavior was progressing, too. In late eighteenth- and early nineteenth-century France, the roots of a belief in psychological causation can be found in a somewhat unexpected place—the study of *hypnosis,* an induced state of relaxation in which a person is highly open to suggestion, especially in relation to hysteria.

Mesmerism Franz Anton Mesmer (1734–1815) was an Austrian physician who further developed Paracelsus' ideas about the influence of the planets on the human body; he believed that the planets affected a universal magnetic fluid in the body, the distribution of which determined health or disease. In attempting to find cures for mental disorders, Mesmer concluded that all people possessed magnetic forces that could be used to influence the

medical model Conceptual view of disordered behavior as a symptom of a disease process, rather than a pattern representing faulty learning or cognition.

Mesmer believed that the distribution of magnetic fluid in the body was responsible for determining health or disease. He further thought that all people possessed magnetic forces that could be used to influence the distribution of fluid in others, thus effecting cures. In this painting of his therapy, Mesmer is standing on the far right, holding a wand. Although he was eventually branded a fraud by his colleagues, his theories did demonstrate most of the phenomena later connected with the use of hypnosis.

distribution of the magnetic fluid in other people, thus effecting cures.

Mesmer put his views into practice in Vienna and various other cities, but it was in Paris in 1778 that he gained a broad following. There he opened a clinic in which he treated all kinds of diseases by "animal magnetism." In a dark room, patients were seated around a tub containing various chemicals, and iron rods protruding from the tub were applied to the affected areas of the patients' bodies. Accompanied by music, Mesmer appeared in a lilac robe, passing from one patient to another and touching each one with his hands or his wand. By this means, Mesmer was reportedly able to remove hysterical anesthesias and paralyses. He also demonstrated most of the phenomena later connected with the use of hypnosis.

Eventually branded a charlatan by his medical colleagues, Mesmer was forced to leave Paris and quickly faded into obscurity. His methods and results, however, were at the center of scientific controversy for many years—in fact, **mesmerism**, as his technique came to be known, was as much a source of heated discussion in the early nineteenth century as psychoanalysis became in the early twentieth century. This discussion led to a renewed interest in hypnosis itself as an explanation of the "cures" that took place.

mesmerism Treatment technique based on "animal magnetism" (hypnosis), formulated by Anton Mesmer.

Nancy School Group of physicians in nineteenth-century Europe who accepted the view that hysteria was a sort of self-hypnosis.

The Nancy School Later, Ambrose August Liébeault (1823–1904) and Hippolyte Bernheim (1840–1919), working in Nancy, France, developed the hypothesis that the hysteria they saw in patients was a sort of self-hypnosis. The physicians who accepted this view ultimately came to be known as the **Nancy School.** But not everyone agreed with this perspective. Jean Charcot (1825–1893), who was head of La Salpêtrière hospital in Paris and the leading neurologist of his time, had been experimenting with some of the phenomena described by the mesmerists. As a result of his research, Charcot disagreed with the findings of the Nancy School and insisted that degenerative brain changes led to hysteria. He was eventually proved wrong, but work on this problem by so outstanding a scientist did a great deal to awaken medical and scientific interest in hysteria.

The dispute between Charcot and the Nancy School was one of the major debates of medical history, during which many harsh words were spoken on both sides. The adherents of the Nancy School finally triumphed, representing the first recognition of a psychological cause for a mental disorder. This recognition spurred more research on the behavior underlying hysteria and other disorders. Soon it was suggested that psychological factors were also involved in anxiety states, phobias, and other mental problems. Eventually, Charcot himself was won over to the new point of view and did much to promote the study of psychological factors in various mental disorders.

The debate over whether mental disorders are caused by biological or psychological factors continues to this day. The outcome of the dispute between Charcot and the Nancy School represented a major step forward for psychology, however. Toward the end of the nineteenth century, it was clear that mental disorders could have either psychological bases or biological bases, or both. With this recognition, a major question remained to be answered: How do the psychologically based mental disorders actually develop?

The Beginnings of Psychoanalysis The first systematic attempt to answer this question was made by Sigmund Freud (1856–1939), who during five decades of observation, treatment, and writing developed a comprehensive theory of psychopathology that emphasized the inner dynamics of unconscious motives (often referred to as *psychodynamics*) and came to be known as the **psychoanalytic perspective.** The methods Freud used to study and treat patients came to be called **psychoanalysis.**

Freud was a brilliant young Viennese neurologist who received an appointment as lecturer on nervous diseases at the University of Vienna. In 1885, he went to study under Charcot and later became acquainted with the work of Liébeault and Bernheim at Nancy. He was impressed by their use of hypnosis with hysterical patients and came away convinced that powerful mental processes could remain hidden from consciousness.

On his return to Vienna, Freud worked in collaboration with another physician, Josef Breuer (1842–1925), who had introduced an interesting innovation in the use of hypnosis with his patients. Unlike hypnotists before him, Freud directed his patients to talk freely about their problems while under hypnosis. The patients usually displayed considerable emotion, and on awakening from their hypnotic states felt a significant emotional release, which was called a **catharsis.** This simple innovation in the use of hypnosis proved to be of great significance: It not only helped patients discharge their emotional tensions by discussing their problems, but it also revealed to the therapist the nature of the difficulties that had brought about certain symptoms. The patients, on awakening, saw no relationship between their problems and their hysterical symptoms.

It was this approach that led Freud to conceptualize the **unconscious**—that portion of the mind that contains experiences of which a person is unaware—and with it the belief that processes outside of a person's awareness can play an important role in the determination of behavior. In 1893, Freud and Breuer published their joint paper *On the Psychical Mechanisms of Hysterical Phenomena,* which was one of the great milestones in the study of the dynamics of the conscious and unconscious. Freud soon discovered, moreover, that he could dispense with hypnosis entirely. By encouraging patients to say whatever came into their minds without regard to logic or propriety, Freud found that the patients would eventually overcome inner obstacles to remembering and would discuss their problems freely. Two related methods allowed him to understand patients' conscious and unconscious thought processes. One method, **free association,** involved having patients talk freely about themselves, thereby providing information about their feelings, motives, and so forth. A

Psychoanalysis was introduced to North America at a famous meeting at Clark University in Worcester, Massachusetts, in 1909. Among those present were (back row) A. A. Brill, Ernest Jones, and Sandor Ferenczi; (front row) Sigmund Freud, G. Stanley Hall, and Carl Jung.

psychoanalytic perspective Theory of psychopathology, initially developed by Freud, that emphasizes the inner dynamics of unconscious motives.

psychoanalysis Methods Freud used to study and treat patients.

catharsis Discharge of emotional tension associated with something, such as talking about past traumas.

unconscious In psychoanalytic theory, a major portion of the mind that is a hidden mass of instincts, impulses, and memories, is not easily available to conscious awareness, and yet plays an important role in behavior.

free association Psychoanalytic method for probing the unconscious by having patients talk freely about themselves, their feelings, and their motives.

second method, **dream analysis,** involved having patients record and describe their dreams. These techniques helped analysts and patients gain insights and achieve a more adequate understanding of emotional problems. Freud devoted the rest of his long and energetic life to the development and elaboration of psychoanalytic principles. His views were formally introduced to American scientists in 1909, when he was invited to deliver a series of lectures at Clark University by the eminent psychologist G. Stanley Hall, who was then president of the university. These lectures created a great deal of controversy and helped popularize psychoanalytic concepts to scientists as well as the general public.

Freud's lively and seminal views earned a substantial following over his long career and continue to be influential even today—more than a hundred years after he began writing. More will be said of these views in Chapter 2.

Establishing an Experimental Research Tradition

The origins of much of the scientific thinking in contemporary psychology lie in early efforts to objectively study psychological processes. Although the early work of experimental psychologists did not bear directly on clinical practice or today's understanding of abnormal behavior, this tradition was clearly influential a few decades later in molding the thinking of the psychologists who brought these rigorous attitudes into the clinic.

The Early Psychological Laboratories In 1879, Wilhelm Wundt (1832–1920) established the first experimental psychology laboratory at the University of Leipzig. While studying the psychological factors involved in memory and sensation, Wundt and his colleagues devised many basic experimental methods and strategies. Early contributors to the empirical study of abnormal behavior were directly influenced by Wundt; they followed his experimental methodology and also used some of his research strategies to study clinical problems. For example, a student of Wundt's, J. McKeen Cattell (1860–1944), brought Wundt's experimental methods to the United States and used them to assess individual differences in mental processing.

Another of Wundt's students, Lightner Witmer (1867–1956), combined research with application and established the first American psychological clinic at the University of Pennsylvania. Witmer's clinic focused on the problems of mentally deficient children, in terms of both research and therapy. Witmer, considered to be the founder of clinical psychology (McReynolds, 1996, 1997), was influential in encouraging others to become involved in the new profession. One of these researchers, William Healy (1869–1963), founded the Chicago Juvenile Psychopathic Institute (later called the Institute of Juvenile Research) and was the first to view juvenile delinquency as a symptom of urbanization, not as a result of inner psychological problems. In so doing, he was among the first to seize upon a new area of causation—environmental, or sociocultural, factors.

By the first decade of the twentieth century, psychological laboratories and clinics were burgeoning, and a great deal of research was being generated (Reisman, 1991). The rapid and objective communication of scientific findings was perhaps as important in the development of modern psychology (or any science) as the collection and interpretation of research findings.

The Behavioral Perspective Within the framework of experimental psychology, the **behavioral perspective,** organized around the theme of the central role of learning in human behavior, emerged to challenge the supremacy of the psychoanalytic perspective on abnormal behavior. Although the behavioral perspective was initially developed through research in the laboratory rather than through clinical practice with disturbed individuals, its implications for explaining and treating maladaptive behavior soon became evident.

The origins of the behavioral view of abnormal behavior and its treatment are tied to experimental work on the form of learning known as **classical conditioning.** This work began with the discovery of the conditioned reflex by Russian physiologist Ivan Pavlov (1849–1936). Around the turn of the century, Pavlov demonstrated that dogs would gradually begin to salivate to a nonfood stimulus, such as a bell, after the stimulus had been regularly accompanied by food.

Pavlov's discoveries in classical conditioning excited a young American psychologist, John B. Watson (1878–1958), who was searching for objective ways to study hu-

dream analysis Psychoanalytic method involving the recording, description, and interpretation of a patient's dreams.

behavioral perspective A theoretical viewpoint organized around the theme that learning is central in determining human behavior.

classical conditioning A basic form of learning in which a neutral stimulus is paired repeatedly with an unconditioned stimulus (US) that naturally elicits an unconditioned response (UR). After repeated pairings, the neutral stimulus becomes a conditioned stimulus (CS) that elicits a conditioned response (CR).

Ivan Pavlov (1849–1936), a pioneer in demonstrating the part conditioning plays in behavior, is shown here with his staff and some of the apparatus used to condition reflexes in dogs.

man behavior. Watson reasoned that if psychology were to become a true science, it must abandon the subjectivity of inner sensations and other "mental" events, which were the focus of psychoanalysis, and limit itself to what could be objectively observed. What better way to do this than to observe systematic changes in behavior brought about simply by rearranging stimulus conditions? Watson thus changed the focus of psychology to the study of overt behavior, an approach he called **behaviorism.**

B. F. Skinner (1904–1990) formulated the concept of operant conditioning, in which reinforcers could be used to make a response more or less probable and frequent.

Watson challenged the psychoanalysts and the more biologically oriented psychologists of his day by suggesting that abnormal behavior was the product of unfortunate, inadvertent earlier conditioning and could be modified through reconditioning. Watson's approach placed heavy emphasis on the role of the social environment in conditioning personality development and behavior, both normal and abnormal.

While Pavlov and Watson were studying antecedent stimulus conditions and their relation to behavioral responses, E. L. Thorndike (1874–1949) and subsequently B. F. Skinner (1904–1990) were exploring a different kind of conditioning—one in which the consequences of behavior influence behavior. Behavior that operates on the environment may be instrumental in producing certain outcomes, and those outcomes, in turn, determine the likelihood that the behavior will be repeated on similar occasions. For example, Thorndike studied how cats could learn a particular response, such as pulling a chain, if that response was followed by food reinforcement. This type of learning came to be called *instrumental conditioning* and was later renamed **operant conditioning** by Skinner. In this context, it is proposed that certain behaviors (e.g., drinking alcohol or using drugs) may be instrumental in producing a maladaptive human response (e.g., psychological addiction) over time.

behaviorism School of psychology that formerly restricted itself primarily to the study of overt behavior.

operant (instrumental) conditioning Form of learning in which a particular response is reinforced and becomes more likely to be repeated on similar occasions.

IN REVIEW

- How did early experimental science help to establish brain pathology as a causal factor in mental disorders?
- Compare the views of the Nancy School with those of Charcot. How did this debate influence modern psychology?
- Evaluate the impact of the work of Freud and Watson on psychology today.

RESEARCH IN ABNORMAL PSYCHOLOGY

We turn now to some of the research strategies in use today, which have evolved from the work of early experimental researchers in psychology. You are probably already familiar with scientific methods in general and their uses in various areas of psychology. Certain issues and problems arise in applying these methods to understanding the nature, causes, and treatment of abnormal behavior; thus, some review is appropriate before we move on. Our review will be organized around the major approaches used in studying abnormal behavior: (1) direct observation of behavior, (2) hypotheses about behavior, (3) sampling and generalization, (4) correlation and causation, (5) experimental strategies, (6) case studies, and (7) retrospective and prospective strategies.

Observation of Behavior

As in virtually all other sciences, the bedrock of research in abnormal psychology is observation. The focus of such observations includes the overt actions of an organism, certain of its measurable internal states and behaviors (e.g., its physiological processes), and at the human level verbal reports about inner processes or events. It is the last of these sources of information that is by far the most troublesome and yet often the most interesting and potentially useful. For example, mental events are fundamentally *private* events, impossible to confirm objectively. Science normally demands such confirmation by others as a means of ensuring accuracy in the observations made. This constraint on public accessibility to important, primary "data" has been a source of considerable difficulty for the discipline of psychology in general and abnormal psychology in particular.

In the field of abnormal psychology, researchers must inevitably be concerned with inner processes such as thoughts, feelings, and interpretations of external events, for much of the theoretical bedrock of the field relates precisely to these private happenings. It follows that these researchers are to a remarkable extent dependent on subjects' reporting of their otherwise inaccessible inner experiences. As a result, much research effort has gone into the development of specialized techniques, such as precisely calibrated rating scales, for maximizing accurate or consistent reporting of such experiences.

Similar, although somewhat less problematic, considerations apply to observations of the overt behavior of research subjects, many of whom in this field are members of particular diagnostic groupings. These observations must be reliable if they are to serve as a useful basis for deriving inferences about the organization and underpinnings of the behavior being investigated. Hence, it has become routine in such investigations to employ observers who are trained to watch and record behavior systematically, using scientifically developed techniques.

Forming Hypotheses About Behavior

To make sense of observed behavior, all of us, including researchers, generate *hypotheses,* more or less plausible ideas to explain something—in this case, behavior. All empirical sciences use hypotheses, although these hypotheses appear to be more closely tied to observable phenomena in the more established physical sciences. For example, the concept of electricity is actually hypothetical. Scientists have only observed the effects of this presumed entity, but these effects are extremely reliable and predictable; hence, we believe in the real existence of electricity. Most people have less confidence in a construct such as repressed memories, as we shall see in later chapters.

These considerations are particularly important in the study of abnormal behavior. Almost by definition, abnormal behavior is difficult to fathom. It is extraordinary, and our minds are therefore attracted to extraordinary explanations of it—to extraordinary hypotheses. Whether these hypotheses can account satisfactorily for abnormal behavior is open to question, but it is clear that we need them in order to begin to understand. Behavior never explains itself, whether it is normal or abnormal.

Much of the subject matter of abnormal psychology is built on competing hypotheses that account more or less adequately for observed behavior declared to be disordered. These hypotheses are important because they frequently determine the therapeutic approaches used to treat disorders. For example, suppose we are confronted with someone who washes his or her hands 60 to 100 times a day, causing serious injury to the skin and underlying tissues. If we conclude that this behavior is a result of subtle neurological damage, we would try to discover the

The man shown here in the custody of a police officer had made a bloody and murderous attack on numerous passengers of a Long Island Railroad train. Many differing hypotheses purport to explain such deranged behavior, but none is at present sufficient in itself to do so. Our best guess is that an interaction of genetic, biological, psychosocial, developmental, and environmental factors operate together in some probably unique and still obscure fashion.

nature of the individual's disease in the hope of administering a cure. If we view the behavior as the symbolic cleansing of sinful thoughts, we would try to unearth and address the sources of the person's excessive scrupulousness. If we regard the hand-washing symptom as merely the product of unfortunate conditioning or learning, we would devise a means of counterconditioning to eliminate the problematic behavior. These different approaches reflect different viewpoints of the causes of the abnormal behavior and are discussed in detail in Chapter 2. Without such viewpoints and the hypotheses they lead to, we would be left with no means of grasping abnormal behavior, and few clues as to what should be done to change it.

Sampling and Generalization

Research in abnormal psychology is concerned with gaining enhanced understanding and, where possible, control of (that is, the ability to alter in predictable ways) abnormal behavior. Although we can occasionally get important leads from the intensive observation of a single case of a given disorder, such a strategy rarely yields enough information to allow us to reach firm conclusions. The basic difficulty with this strategy is that we cannot know whether our observations pertain to the disorder, to unrelated characteristics of the person with the disorder, to some combination of these factors, or even to characteristics of our own, of the observers. We need to study a larger group in order to know which of our observations are generalizable.

Using Groups to Identify Common Factors We generally place greater reliance on research studies using groups of individuals who show roughly equivalent abnormalities of behavior. Typically, several people in such studies share one characteristic (the problematic behavior) while varying widely on others. We can then infer that anything else they have in common, such as having a chronically depressed parent, may be related to the behavioral abnormality—provided, of course, that the characteristic is not widely shared by people who do not have the abnormality.

If we wanted to research the problem of major psychological depression, for example, a first step would be to determine criteria for identifying persons believed to be affected by the condition. DSM-IV-TR provides a set of such criteria, among them unrelievable sadness, diminished or absent pleasure response, fatigue, and sleep disturbances. We would then need to find people who fit our criteria, using a technique called **sampling,** in which we would select as subjects a limited number of depressed persons who appear to be *representative* of the much larger group of individuals having major depressive disorder. That is, our sample should mirror the larger group in terms of disorder severity and duration as well as any potentially important demographics such as average age, gender, and marital status. Ideally, the sample would be *randomly selected* from the larger depressed population, which is tantamount to ensuring that every person in that population has an equal chance of being included in our study sample. Without such a procedure, potential biases in sample selection could lead to erroneous conclusions about the larger group we wish to study. For example, if our research group of depressed people consisted only of college-educated members of the middle to upper-middle class, we might be tempted to attribute some characteristic—say, a tendency to drink wine with dinner—to depression sufferers that is in fact not true of depressed people in general, such as those less educated or from a different socioeconomic group.

Criterion and Control Groups Suppose we had a hypothesis that stress led to depression. We would need to be certain that the levels of prior stress experienced by our

sampling The process of selecting a representative subgroup from a defined population of interest.

depressed subjects were not similar to findings about groups suffering other mental disorders or the general population. If everyone experienced the same amount of stress, then prior stress would not be useful in telling us anything about depression per se. Researchers use a **control group,** a sample of people who do *not* exhibit the disorder being studied but who are comparable in all other respects to the **criterion group,** members of which do exhibit the disorder. Typically, the control group is psychologically "normal" according to specified criteria. We can then compare the two groups in certain areas—such as reported prior stress experienced—to determine if they differ. They would in fact almost certainly differ if only because of chance factors, but we have powerful statistical techniques to determine whether or not such observed differences are truly significant. If we found, for example, that the depressed individuals had significantly more prior stress than the normals, we might be tempted to pursue our hypothesis further and consider that the experience of unusual stress is causally related to the onset of major depression. Entertaining this hypothesis assumes, of course, that the people in our study have reported their stressful experiences accurately, a sometimes dubious assumption. Depression, for example, might cause people to review past innocuous (factually unstressful) events in a negative light. At most, in fact, we would have found an association, or *correlation,* between *reported* prior stress and the experience of major depression.

Though a dysfunctional family relationship may be correlated with some forms of abnormal behavior, it is not necessarily a causal factor because there may be many other ways of accounting for a particular mental disorder.

The Difference Between Correlation and Causation

In the above example (which happens to depict an actual circumstance in the scientific literature on depression), we could not legitimately conclude from our findings alone that the experience of severe prior stress *causes* the onset of major depression. There are simply too many alternative ways to account for such an association, including the possibility that depressed persons are more prone than others to remember stressful events in their immediate pasts. Correlation—in this case, between higher levels of reported stress and depression—does not imply causation.

The mere **correlation,** or association, of two or more variables can never by itself be taken as evidence of **causation**—that is, a relationship in which one of the associated variables (i.e., stress) *causes* the outcome of the other (i.e., depression). This is an important caveat to bear in mind, especially so in the field of abnormal psychology. Many studies in abnormal psychology show that two (or more) things regularly occur together, such as poverty and retarded intellectual development or depression and reported prior stressors. For example, at one time it was thought that marijuana *caused* juvenile delinquency because so many young offenders smoked it. Yet most of these juveniles also grew up in high crime neighborhoods with abundant models of adult criminal behavior. When marijuana smoking among youths moved into the well-to-do suburbs, the correlation between it and juvenile delinquency dropped precipitously. In other words, any causal relationship was probably one involving the quality of neighborhoods, not the smoking of pot. Correlated variables may well be related to one another in some kind of causal context, but the relationship can take a variety of forms:

Variable *a* causes variable *b* (or vice versa).

Variable *a* and variable *b* are both caused by variable *c*.

Variables *a* and *b* are both involved in a complex pattern of variables influencing *a* and *b* in similar ways.

control group Group of subjects who do not exhibit the disorder being studied but who are comparable in all other respects to the criterion group; also, a comparison group of subjects who do not receive a condition or treatment whose effects are being studied.

criterion group Group of subjects who exhibit the disorder under study.

correlation The tendency of two variables to covary. With positive correlation, as one variable goes up, so does the other; with negative correlation, as one variable goes up the other goes down.

causation Relationship in which one of two (or more) associated variables causes the other(s).

Even though correlational studies may not be able to pin down causal relationships, they can be a powerful and rich source of inference. They often suggest causal hypotheses and occasionally provide crucial data that confirm or refute these hypotheses. In abnormal psychology, they can be particularly useful to epidemiological research, which attempts to establish the pattern of occurrence of certain disorders (in this case, mental disorders) in different times, places, and groups of people. Where we find significant variations in the incidence or prevalence of a disorder, we ask why. For example, why is it (as noted earlier) that women experience a much higher rate of depression than men in the United States? This question has prompted a great deal of research, as will be seen in Chapter 6.

Experimental Strategies in Abnormal Psychology

Correlational research has the character of taking things as they are and determining covariations among observed phenomena. Do things vary together in a direct, corresponding manner, as with female gender and increased risk of depression; in an inverse manner, as with high socioeconomic status and generally less risk of mental disorder; or are the variables in question perhaps entirely independent of one another, such that a given state or level of one variable fails to predict reliably anything about that of another, as with handedness and mental disorder? And, as just noted, the documentation of covariations (associations) between variables may still leave us perplexed as to the causal pattern producing them.

Scientific research is most rigorous, and its findings most reliable, when it employs the full power of the **experimental method.** In such cases, scientists control all factors, except one, that could have an effect on a variable or outcome of interest; they then actively manipulate that one factor, often referred to as the **independent variable.** If the outcome of interest, often called the **dependent variable,** is observed to change as the manipulated factor is changed, that factor can be regarded as a cause of the outcome. For example, if a proposed treatment is provided to a given group of patients but withheld from an otherwise completely comparable one, and if the former group experiences positive changes significantly in excess of the latter group, then a powerful causal inference can be made regarding the treatment's efficacy.

Unfortunately, the experimental method cannot be applied to many problems of abnormal psychology. There are both practical and ethical reasons for this. Suppose, for example, we wanted to do an experiment to evaluate the hypothesis that stressful events can cause major depression. Our ideal experimental approach would be to choose at random two groups of normal adults for a longitudinal study—a study in which the same subjects are followed over a prolonged period of time. The individuals in one group would be subjected in systematic fashion to a rigorous program of contrived (but believable) stressful harassment, such as repeated breakdown of their computers' hard drives, resulting in loss of data already entered. Subjects in the other (control) group would spend the same amount of time in some comparable but smooth-running activity. Naturally occurring stressors in both groups would be monitored as well to ensure that the experimental (stressed) group was in fact more stressed. Some weeks or months later, the subjects of both groups would be assessed as to symptoms meeting DSM-IV-TR criteria for major depressive disorder—for example, persistently depressed mood, diminished interest or pleasure in usual activities, significant weight loss, sleep disturbance, etc. If the group of stressed subjects had significantly more occurrences of major depressive episodes than the controls did, our causal hypothesis would be confirmed: Prior stress causes depression. But it would of course be ethically unacceptable to treat people in a manner that is deliberately callous, destructive, and potentially dangerous (e.g., depressive episodes enhance the risk of suicide), even though the experiment itself would be methodologically sound.

Many variables of potential importance in abnormal behavior cannot be manipulated in the active way the experimental method demands, quite apart from the constraints ethical considerations may impose. Fortunately, we have made great progress in the statistical control of variables that do not yield to the classic form of experimental control. Statistical controls allow us in effect to "adjust" for otherwise uncontrolled (or uncontrollable) variables.

Animal Research The experimental method is sometimes used in causal research with animals, though here, too, ethical considerations apply. Such animal studies are

experimental method Rigorous scientific procedure by which hypotheses are tested.

independent variable Factor whose effects are being examined and which is manipulated in some way while other variables are held constant.

dependent variable In an experiment, the factor that is observed to change with changes in the manipulated (independent) variable.

Analogue studies in which generalizations are made from laboratory models to the real world may fail to make convincing connections. Results of testing—using rats, mice, dogs, or monkeys, for example, in a laboratory setting—may not hold up when extended to humans.

conceptual simulations, so to speak, of the processes thought to be involved in the development of abnormal human behavior. Experiments of this kind are generally known as **analogue studies**—studies in which a researcher attempts to emulate the conditions hypothesized as leading to abnormal behavior. These experiments attempt to establish the causes of maladaptive behavior by inducing a model of the behavior in subhuman species. The major scientific problem is, of course, to establish commonality between the contrived behavior and the real thing as it occurs naturally in the course of human development.

A case in point is Martin Seligman's research on the hypothesis that *learned helplessness* is a cause of depression in humans (Seligman, 1975). Laboratory experiments with dogs had demonstrated that, when subjected to repeated experiences of painful, unpredictable, inescapable electric shock, these dogs lost their ability to learn a simple escape routine to avoid further shock. They just sat and endured the pain. This observation led Seligman to argue that human depression (which he equated with the reaction of the helpless dogs) is a reaction to the experience of one's behavior having no effect on one's environment. As a result, animals or people "learn" that they are helpless to do anything. Experiments attempting to induce learned helplessness in humans and to determine if that state would produce mild and reversible depressions were sometimes disappointing. Human subjects did not always respond with helplessness to noncontingency situations, many of them actually showing enhanced effort following the frustrating experiences (see the February 1978 issue of *Journal of Abnormal Psychology,* Vol. 87).

Reacting to these disappointing results, Seligman and his colleagues (Abramson, Seligman, & Teasdale, 1978) modified the learned helplessness theory of depression. They suggested that a noncontingency experience should have a depression-inducing effect only on those persons prone to interpret failure-to-cope experiences in a negative way—specifically by attributing them to personal (internal) characteristics that are pervasive (global) and relatively permanent (stable). ("I'm such a clod; I never get anything right and I never will.") This idea has fared considerably better in subsequent research, which will be reviewed in Chapter 6. Curiously, the original concept of learned helplessness may be a better model of human anxiety disorders than of depression, as will be seen in Chapter 5.

In this case, despite the earlier disappointment, which illustrates the hazards involved in generalizing too readily from laboratory models to the real world, the learned helplessness analogue study generated much research and thereby clarified certain aspects of an important psychopathological problem relating to depression. In addition, its range of application has turned out to be probably considerably broader than was originally anticipated. We count that as a successful outcome.

Research on the Efficacy of Therapy The necessarily limited role of the experimental method in research on *causes* of abnormal behavior does not extend to research on *treatment,* where it has proved indispensable. It is a relatively simple and straightforward matter to set up a study in which a proposed treatment is given to a designated group of patients and withheld from a similar group of patients. Should the treated group show significantly more improvement than the latter, we can have confidence in the treatment's efficacy. It is nonetheless true that we may still not know why the treatment works, although investigators are becoming increasingly sophisticated about teasing out the mechanisms whereby therapeutic change is induced (e.g., see Hollon, DeRubeis, & Evans, 1987; Kazdin, 1994b).

Special techniques must usually be employed in treatment research to ensure that the two groups are in fact comparable in every respect except the presence or absence of the proposed active treatment agent. Once a treatment has proved effective, it can subsequently be employed for members of the original control group, leading to improved functioning for everyone.

analogue studies Studies in which a researcher attempts to emulate the conditions hypothesized as leading to abnormality.

An alternative research design may call for a comparison of two (or more) treatments in different equivalent groups. Typically, in this type of study, the efficacy of one of the treatments, the control condition, has already been proved. Such comparative outcome research has much to recommend it and is being increasingly employed (VandenBos, 1986).

Clinical Case Studies

Most disorders are still studied individually, using the traditional clinical case study method. A **case study** is an in-depth examination of an individual or family that draws from a number of data sources, including interviews and psychological testing. The clinical investigator, who is usually also a patient's therapist, intensively observes an individual's behavior and searches background facts that may be influencing the case. A case study includes a set of hypotheses about what is causing the problem and a guide to treatment planning. For example, the therapist may develop a hunch that the patient was taught inordinate levels of fearfulness by overconcerned parents, the effects of which are now contributing to the patient's clinical condition. The therapist must then decide on how to confirm or disconfirm this hypothesis of disruptive parental influence, which if confirmed at some reasonable level of probability will necessitate therapeutic attention to overcoming the damaging effects of parental depiction of the world in excessively dangerous terms. These hypotheses and therapeutic strategies may be revised as necessary, based on a patient's response to treatment interventions. This strategy is sometimes called an *N equals 1 experiment* (with *N* referring to the number of subjects in the experiment), especially when the precise relationships between successive treatment interventions (or their withdrawal) and patient responses are systematically monitored.

Much can be learned when skilled clinicians use the case study method, but the information acquired is often relevant only to the individual being studied and may be flawed, especially if we seek to apply it to other cases involving an apparently similar abnormality. When there is only one observer and one subject, and when the observations are made in a relatively uncontrolled context, the conclusions we can draw are very narrow and may be mistaken.

Retrospective Versus Prospective Strategies

The classic method of trying to uncover the probable causes of abnormal behavior has involved a **retrospective strategy** (i.e., looking backward), in which we start with present disordered behavior and work back from there to try to reconstruct the client's developmental history in the hope of determining what went wrong during its course. Our source material is limited to the patient's recollections and such other data as we may be able to unearth in diaries, records, memories of other family members, etc. The retrospective strategy involves many pitfalls. Memories are faulty and selective, tending to emphasize items that confirm the client's already adopted view of his or her situation. Apart from the fact that a disordered person may not be the most accurate or objective source of information, such a strategy invites investigators to discover what they expect to discover about the background factors theoretically linked to a disorder. For example, it is now clear that many false memories of ritual satanic abuse during childhood were implanted by therapists overzealously believing this to be a source of certain types of disorder (Spanos, 1996). Even outside observers of a client are likely to engage in 20/20 hindsight, reinterpreting the person's past behavior in light of his or her present problems.

Prospective strategies focus on individuals who have a higher-than-average likelihood of becoming psychologically disordered *before* abnormal behavior shows up. We can have much more confidence in our hypotheses about the causes of a disorder if we have been tracking various influences and measuring them ahead of time. When our hypotheses correctly predict the behavior a group of individuals will develop, we are much closer to establishing a causal relationship. In a typical instance, children sharing a risk factor known to be associated with relatively high rates of subsequent breakdown (such as having been born to a schizophrenic mother) are studied over the course of years. Those who do break down are compared with those who do not in the hope that crucial differentiating factors will be discovered.

As a group, researchers in abnormal behavior have learned there are few easy answers. In fact, the study of behavioral abnormalities has enriched the discipline of psychology by enhancing our understanding of how enormously complex the origins of human behavior really are.

case study An in-depth examination of an individual or family that draws from a number of data sources, including interviews and psychological testing.

retrospective strategy Research method that tries to uncover the probable causes of individuals' abnormal behavior by looking backward from the present.

prospective strategy Research method that focuses on individuals who have a higher-than-average likelihood of becoming psychologically disordered and studies them before abnormal behavior is observed.

IN REVIEW

- What is the difference between correlation and causation? Why is this important in the study of abnormal behavior?
- Why is the experimental method sometimes inappropriate for research in abnormal psychology? Why can analogue studies sometimes be used instead?
- What is a clinical case study? Why is it easy to draw erroneous conclusions from this method of research?
- What are the advantages and disadvantages of retrospective and prospective research strategies in abnormal psychology?

UNRESOLVED ISSUES: *The DSM*

As we have seen, the DSM is the current standard for defining what a mental disorder is and for differentiating among its supposed subtypes. It is a far from perfect system, as even its principal authors acknowledge (Frances et al., 1991). It is clear that the increasingly "operational" DSM approach has helped clinicians achieve respectable levels of reliability in the diagnostic process, particularly where structured diagnostic interviews are employed. However, the validity of the diagnoses in the current DSM remains the subject of controversy. Recent editions of the DSM have tended to sacrifice validity to improve interdiagnostician agreement, or reliability. But having diagnosticians agree on assignment of patients to a diagnosis of questionable validity or meaning does not in and of itself constitute an exceptional level of progress.

It is difficult to satisfy simultaneously the dual requirements of reliability and validity in diagnosing mental disorders. This is due to the enormous complexity of the factors underlying and determining human behavior. It is also due, according to many observers, to our having chosen an inadequate model for organizing our observations of behavioral abnormalities.

The Definitional Problem

The problems begin right at the beginning—in the DSM definition of "mental disorder." As you will recall, this definition requires that problematic behavior must be "a symptom of a dysfunction in the individual" if it is to qualify as an instance of mental disorder. What does this expression mean? The problematic behavior cannot itself be the "dysfunction" for that would be like saying mental disorders are due to mental disorders.

Identifying this flaw in the definition, Jerome Wakefield (1992a, 1992b, 1997) has proposed that "dysfunction" be interpreted as referring to some underlying mechanism that fails to perform according to "design." There are various logical and philosophical problems with this proposed solution (e.g., see Bergner, 1997; Carson, 1997; Lilienfeld & Marino, 1995). Its most glaring deficiency is an obvious one: With rare exception, no such defectively operating mechanisms have ever been precisely identified. Moreover, to imagine that we might some day be able to pinpoint a distinctive underlying dysfunction for each of the nearly 300 DSM diagnoses seems extremely farfetched.

The Overlap/Comorbidity Problem

Consistent with the adopted medical disease metaphor, the DSM attempts to treat mental disorder as consisting of a large number of discrete (nonoverlapping) categories, much the way medical/physical diseases are categorized and diagnosed. This insistence on a categorical format for mental disorder diagnoses that are primarily prototypal in nature is a source of much confusion and misdirected effort in the field at large. The DSM categories establish groupings that are neither internally homogeneous nor cleanly separated at the boundaries.

The DSM-IV made clear in its Introduction (American Psychiatric Association, 1994, pp. xv–xxv) that its primary purpose was to facilitate in a pragmatic manner clinical and research objectives. Unfortunately, it has proved difficult to limit the DSM's influence to this pragmatic aim. In many contexts, including legal ones, DSM categories become reified (i.e., assumed to constitute concrete, real phenomena, as ordained by nature) to unintended levels, thereby encouraging unwarranted inferences about the origins of mentally disordered behavior—for example, that these must always be exotic and wholly different from the origins of normal behavior.

The Expanding Horizons of "Mental Disorder"

Because there is no truly objective means for setting the limits of the concept of mental disorder and because it is in the economic and other interests of mental health professionals to designate larger and larger segments of human behavior as within the purview of "mentally disordered," there is constant pressure to include in the DSM more and more kinds of socially undesirable behavior. For example, one proposal was to include "road rage" (anger at other drivers) as a newly discovered mental disorder in the next edition of the DSM (Sharkey, 1997). There is considerable informal evidence that the steering committee responsible for the production of DSM-IV worked hard to fend off a large number of such frivolous proposals, and in fact they largely succeeded in curtailing additional diagnoses beyond those appearing in the previous edition (DSM-III-R) by adopting stringent criteria for inclusion. Nevertheless, this promises to be an uphill battle. Mental health professionals, like the members of other professions, tend to view the world through a lens that enhances the importance of phenomena relating to their own expertise. In addition, inclusion of a disorder in the DSM is a prerequisite for health insurers' reimbursement of services rendered.

It is thus in the interests of the public at large to keep a wary eye on proposed expansions of the "mentally disordered" domain. It is conceivable that failure to do so could eventually lead to a situation wherein almost anything but the most bland, conformist, and conventional of behaviors may be declared a manifestation of mental disorder. By that point, the concept will have become so indiscriminate as to lose most of its scientifically productive meaning.

Though some mental health professionals have serious reservations about the prevailing classificatory and diagnostic procedures, most do not recommend that these procedures be summarily abandoned or ignored. While far from ideal, they constitute the standard language of the field for both formal (especially research-based) and informal communication. Familiarity with the system in use is thus vital for the serious student. We hope, however, that this discussion has given you a more sophisticated perspective on the classificatory issues facing the field.

SUMMARY

WHAT DO WE MEAN BY ABNORMAL BEHAVIOR?

- The formal definition of "mental disorder," as offered in the *Diagnostic and Statistical Manual of Mental Disorders (DSM),* has certain problems that limit its clarity (what are these imputed "dysfunctions"?) and objectivity (who shall decide what is "harmful"?).
- There is probably no perfect or value-free solution to the definitional problem, but this book uses a working definition emphasizing behavioral maladaptiveness. Importantly, this perspective does not locate all mental disorder within individuals.

CLASSIFYING ABNORMAL BEHAVIOR

- There are problems with the categorical classification system adopted in the DSM. Notably, the categories result in neither within-class homogeneity nor between-class discrimination, leading to very high levels of comorbidity among disorders.
- Reliability and validity are key to any classification system, and, though not without its weaknesses, the DSM has improved diagnostic reliability and is essential to clinical practice and serious study in the field.
- One potential solution to the classification problem would be to dimensionalize the phenomena of mental disorder. Another would be to adopt a prototypal approach to their organization, which is what the DSM in fact provides without acknowledging that it does so.

THE EXTENT OF ABNORMAL BEHAVIOR

- Epidemiology is the study of the distribution of diseases, disorders, or health-related behaviors in a given population. Mental health epidemiology refers to the study of the distribution of mental disorders. Epidemiological researchers need a classification system that can help them determine the nature and extent of psychological problems within given populations.
- The prevalence of a disorder can be measured as point prevalence (the estimated proportion of actual, active cases of the disorder in a given population at any instant in time) or lifetime prevalence (the proportion of living persons in a population ever having had the disorder up to the time of the epidemiologic assessment).

- Encountering seemingly abnormal behavior is a common experience for nearly all of us, which is not surprising in light of prevalence rates indicating that about half of all Americans will at some time in their lives have a diagnosable Axis I mental disorder.

HISTORICAL VIEWS OF ABNORMAL BEHAVIOR

- Understanding of abnormal behavior over the centuries has not proceeded smoothly or uniformly; the steps forward have been uneven and irregular. Furthermore, unusual, even bizarre, views or beliefs have often sidetracked researchers and theorists.
- The dominant social, economic, and religious views of the times have had a profound influence on how people view abnormal behavior, as have advances in the physical and biological sciences. The twentieth century saw a general movement away from superstition and "magic" toward reasoned, scientific studies.
- In the ancient world, superstitions weakened as a result of the emergence of medical concepts in many places, such as Egypt and Greece; many of these concepts were developed and refined by Roman physicians.
- With the fall of Rome near the end of the fifth century A.D., most Europeans returned to superstitious views, which dominated popular thinking about mental disorders for over a thousand years.
- In the fifteenth and sixteenth centuries, it was still widely believed, even by scholars, that mentally disturbed people were possessed by evil spirits.
- During the latter stages of the Middle Ages and the early Renaissance, a spirit of scientific questioning reappeared in Europe, and several noted physicians spoke out against inhumane treatments, arguing that "possessed" individuals were actually "sick of mind" and should be treated as such.
- With the recognition of a need for the special treatment of disturbed people came the founding of various asylums toward the end of the sixteenth century. However, institutionalization resulted in isolation and maltreatment of mental patients. Slowly, this situation was recognized, and in the eighteenth century, further efforts were made to help afflicted individuals by providing them with better living conditions and humane treatment.
- The nineteenth century witnessed a number of scientific and humanitarian advances. The work of William Tuke in England and Benjamin Rush and Dorothea Dix in the United States prepared the way for several important developments in contemporary abnormal psychology: the gradual acceptance of mental patients as afflicted individuals who needed and deserved professional attention; the application of biomedical methods to the treatment of disorders; and the growth of scientific research on the biological, psychological, and sociocultural roots of abnormal behavior.

THE BEGINNING OF THE MODERN ERA

- In the early part of the eighteenth century, knowledge of anatomy, physiology, neurology, chemistry, and general medicine increased rapidly. These advances led to the identification of the biological, or organic, pathology underlying many physical ailments.
- In the nineteenth century, technological discoveries and advances in the biological sciences aided the understanding and treatment of disturbed individuals. A major biomedical breakthrough, for example, came with the discovery of the organic factors underlying general paresis (syphilis of the brain), one of the most serious mental illnesses of the day.
- The development of a psychiatric classification system by Kraepelin played a dominant role in the early development of the biological viewpoint. Kraepelin's work (a forerunner of the DSM system) helped establish the importance of brain pathology in mental disorders.
- The first major steps toward understanding psychological factors in mental disorders were taken by Sigmund Freud. During five decades of observation, treatment, and writing, he developed a theory of psychopathology, known as psychoanalysis, that emphasized the inner dynamics of unconscious motives. Over the last half century, other clinicians have modified and revised Freud's theory, evolving new psychodynamic perspectives.
- The end of the nineteenth and the beginning of the twentieth century also saw experimental psychology evolve into clinical psychology. Behaviorism emerged as an explanatory model in abnormal psychology. The behavioral perspective is organized around a central theme—that learning plays an important role in human behavior. Although this perspective was initially developed through research in the laboratory, unlike psychoanalysis, which emerged out of clinical practice with disturbed individuals, it has been shown to have important implications for explaining and treating maladaptive behavior.

RESEARCH IN ABNORMAL PSYCHOLOGY

- The best way to avoid misconception and error is to adopt a scientific approach to the study of abnormal behavior. This involves, among other things, a focus on research and research methods, including an appreciation of the distinction between what is observable and what is hypothetical or inferred.

- Research on mental disorders, if it is to produce valid results, must be done on people who are truly representative of the diagnostic groups to which they purportedly belong—a requirement that is often difficult to satisfy.
- It is crucial to remember that correlation between variables does not establish a causal relationship between them.
- Researchers use the experimental method and the prospective research strategy to resolve questions of causality, but these approaches are not always appropriate and may not always be effective.
- The individual case study, despite its weaknesses, remains a frequently used research technique in abnormal psychology.

KEY TERMS

abnormal behavior (p. 5)
reliability (p. 5)
validity (p. 6)
categorical approach (p. 6)
dimensional approach (p. 6)
prototypal approach (p. 6)
comorbidity (p. 7)
symptoms (p. 7)
signs (p. 7)
axes (of DSM) (p. 7)
acute (p. 9)
chronic (p. 9)
mild (p. 9)
moderate (p. 9)
severe (p. 9)
episodic (p. 9)
recurrent (p. 9)
epidemiology (p. 10)
prevalence (p. 10)
incidence (p. 10)
lifetime prevalence (p. 11)
exorcism (p. 12)
mass madness (p. 15)
asylums (p. 16)
moral management (p. 18)
mental hygiene movement (p. 19)
medical model (p. 21)
mesmerism (p. 22)
Nancy School (p. 22)
psychoanalytic perspective (p. 23)
psychoanalysis (p. 23)
catharsis (p. 23)
unconscious (p. 23)
free association (p. 23)
dream analysis (p. 24)
behavioral perspective (p. 24)
classical conditioning (p. 24)
behaviorism (p. 25)
operant (instrumental) conditioning (p. 25)
sampling (p. 27)
control group (p. 28)
criterion group (p. 28)
correlation (p. 28)
causation (p. 28)
experimental method (p. 29)
independent variable (p. 29)
dependent variable (p. 29)
analogue studies (p. 30)
case study (p. 31)
retrospective strategy (p. 31)
prospective strategy (p. 31)

CHAPTER TWO

Causal Factors and Viewpoints in Abnormal Psychology

Gale L. Bell, *Spaghetti #2* (1996), markers. Bell received her BFA from The Maryland Institute, College of Art. Because a learning disability interferes with her processing of language, she uses art as an alternative means of expression.

LEARNING OBJECTIVES

After reading this chapter, you should be able to:

- Explain how diathesis-stress models of the etiology of abnormal behavior and the concepts of protective factors and resilience are related.
- Summarize the causal factors of abnormal behavior according to the biological viewpoint, including neurotransmitter and hormonal imbalances, genetic vulnerabilities, constitutional liabilities, brain dysfunction, and physical deprivation or disruption.
- Outline the major psychosocial approaches to abnormal behavior, including the psychodynamic, behavioral, and cognitive-behavioral perspectives.
- Explain the concepts of schemas and self-schemas.
- Describe the effects of various psychosocial causal factors, including early deprivation or trauma (parental deprivation, institutionalization, abuse, etc.), inadequate parenting styles, marital discord and divorce, and problems with peer relationships.
- Describe the sociocultural viewpoint, and explain how sociocultural causal factors contribute to abnormal behavior.
- Explain why the biopsychosocial viewpoint may best fulfill the need for a more unified viewpoint.

We saw in the last chapter that speculation about the causes of abnormal behavior goes back very far in human history. From early times, those who observed disordered behavior grappled with the question of its cause. Hippocrates, for example, suggested that an imbalance in bodily humors produced abnormal behavior. To other observers, the cause was possession by demons or evil spirits. Later, bodily dysfunction was suggested as a cause.

Each attempt at identifying a cause brought with it a theory, or model, of abnormal behavior. For example, Hippocrates' theory, a type of disease model, posited the existence of four bodily humors that were connected with certain kinds of behavior. More recently, several important schools of thought have developed elaborate models to explain the origins of abnormal behavior and to suggest how it might be treated. We will discuss several of these theoretical perspectives, or viewpoints, in this chapter, giving attention to the causal and risk factors each has identified.

We will first consider biological viewpoints, which emphasize genetic and organic conditions that impair brain and bodily functioning and lead to psychopathology. Next, we will move on to psychosocial viewpoints: the psychodynamic perspectives focus on intrapsychic conflicts that lead to anxiety; the behavioral perspective, on faulty learning; and the cognitive-behavioral perspective, on types of information processing that lead to distorted thinking. We will look briefly, too, at the sociocultural viewpoint, which focuses on pathological social conditions and the importance of differing cultural backgrounds in shaping both vulnerability to psychopathology and the form psychopathology may take.

CAUSES AND RISK FACTORS FOR ABNORMAL BEHAVIOR

There are a multitude of reasons for studying what causes people to behave maladaptively. If we knew the causes for given disorders, we might be able to prevent conditions that lead to them and perhaps reverse conditions that maintain them. We could also classify and diagnose disorders better if we clearly understood their causes rather than relying on clusters of symptoms, as we usually do now.

Although understanding the causes of abnormal behavior is clearly a desirable goal, it is enormously difficult to achieve because human behavior is so complex. Even relatively simple human behavior, such as speaking or writing a single word, is the product of thousands of prior events—the connections among which are not always clear. Attempting to understand a person's life in causal terms is a task of enormous magnitude. As a result, many researchers in the behavioral sciences now prefer to speak of risk factors (variables correlated with an abnormal outcome) rather than of causes. Still, understanding causes remains the ultimate goal.

In abnormal psychology especially, we seldom find simple cause-and-effect sequences in which one factor alone causes a disorder. Instead, we usually deal with multiple interacting causal factors when studying the **etiology,** or causal pattern, believed to culminate in a disorder. Some of these factors may occur relatively early in life yet may not show their effects for many years; in such cases, the causal factor is assumed to *predispose* the person to develop the disorder. Other factors may occur shortly before the occurrence of the symptoms of the disorder; these factors are thought to prove too much for a person and *trigger* the disorder. Both these types of causal factors are at the heart of **diathesis-stress models** of abnormal

etiology Causal pattern underlying abnormal behavior.

diathesis-stress models Views of abnormal behavior as the result of stress operating on an individual with a biological, psychosocial, or sociocultural predisposition toward developing a specific disorder.

A child growing up under conditions of adversity may be protected from problems later in life if he or she has a warm and supportive relationship with some adult—in this case, a grandmother. Encouraging children to ask questions, taking the time to listen to their problems and concerns, and trying to understand the conflicts and pressures they face are the important elements of such a supportive and protective relationship.

behavior (Meehl, 1962), in which a *diathesis* leaves an individual predisposed or *vulnerable* to developing a disorder and *stress* is the trigger that taxes or exceeds the individual's personal resources and results in abnormal behavior. The diathesis underlying a disorder can derive from biological, psychosocial, and/or sociocultural causal factors.

In recent years, attention has focused not only on diatheses that leave a person vulnerable to disorder, but also on **protective factors,** influences that modify a person's response to an environmental stressor, making it less likely that he or she will experience the adverse consequences of the stressor (Masten & Coatsworth, 1995, 1998; Rutter, 1985). Protective factors most often lead to **resilience,** the ability to adapt successfully to even very difficult circumstances. One important protective factor in childhood is having a family environment in which at least one parent is warm and supportive, allowing the development of a good attachment relationship between child and parent (Hetherington & Parke, 1993; Masten & Coatsworth, 1998). Other protective factors include good mothering and school achievement (Hetherington & Parke, 1993; Masten & Coatsworth, 1995, 1998; Rutter, 1987a). Some protective factors have nothing at all to do with experiences, but are simply some quality or attribute of a person, such as having an easy temperament, high self-esteem, or high intelligence. Moreover, girls are less vulnerable than boys to many psychosocial stressors such as parental conflict and to physical hazards for reasons that are not yet well understood (Rutter, 1982).

protective factors Influences that modify a person's response to an environmental stressor, making it less likely that the person will experience the adverse effects of the stressor.

resilience The ability to adapt successfully to even very difficult circumstances.

Furthermore, protective factors are not necessarily positive experiences. Indeed, sometimes exposure to stressful experiences that are dealt with successfully can promote a sense of self-confidence or self-esteem and thereby serve as a protective factor; thus, some stressors paradoxically promote coping. This has sometimes been referred to as a "steeling" or "inoculation" effect and is more likely to occur with moderate than with mild or extreme stressors (Hetherington, 1991; Rutter, 1987a).

In sum, we can distinguish between causes of abnormal behavior that lie within and are part of the biological makeup or prior experience of a person (diatheses, or vulnerabilities or predispositions) and those that pertain to current challenges in a person's life (stressors). Typically, neither the diathesis(es) nor the stressor(s) is by itself sufficient to cause a disorder; but, in combination, they can sometimes push the individual to behave abnormally. As we shall see in the sections that follow, different models of abnormal behavior identify different diatheses and different stressors as the route to abnormality, and different protective factors as the route to resilience in the face of adversity.

Clearly, diathesis-stress models need to be considered within the broad framework of *multicausal developmental models*. Specifically, in the course of development, a child may acquire a variety of cumulative risk factors that may interact with each other in determining risk for psychopathology. These risk factors also interact, however, with a variety of protective processes, and sometimes with stressors, to determine whether the child develops in a normal and adaptive way, as opposed to showing signs of maladaptive behavior and psychopathology in childhood, in adolescence, or in adulthood. It is also important to note, however, that to understand what is abnormal one must always have a good understanding of normal human development. This has been the focus of the rapidly growing field of **developmental psychopathology,** which focuses on determining what is abnormal at any point in development by comparing and contrasting it with normal and expected changes that occur in the developmental process. For example, an intense fear of the dark in a 3- to 5-year-old child may not be considered abnormal, given that most children have at least one specific fear into early adolescence (Barlow, 1988). However, an intense fear of the dark in a high school or college-aged student would be considered abnormal.

IN REVIEW

- What is meant by a diathesis-stress model of abnormal behavior?
- Define *protective factors* and *resilience.* Give examples of each.
- Explain why diathesis-stress models are essentially multicausal developmental models.

MODELS OR VIEWPOINTS FOR UNDERSTANDING ABNORMAL BEHAVIOR

Students are often perplexed by the fact that, in the behavioral sciences, there are several competing explanations for the same thing. In general, the more complex the phenomenon being investigated, the greater the number of viewpoints that develop in an attempt to explain it. Inevitably, not all these viewpoints are equally valid. As you will see, the applicability of a viewpoint is often determined by the extent to which it helps an observer understand a given phenomenon, and its validity is usually determined by whether it can be supported through empirical research.

The viewpoints to be discussed here help us understand disorders on three fronts: their clinical pictures (their symptoms), their causal factors, and their treatments. In each case, these viewpoints help professionals organize the observations they have made, provide a system of thought in which to place the observed data, and suggest areas of focus for treatment and research. It is important to remember, however, that each of these viewpoints is a theoretical construction devised to orient psychologists in the study of abnormal behavior. As a set of hypothetical guidelines, each viewpoint speaks to the importance and integrity of its own position, often to the exclusion of other explanations. Unfortunately, these viewpoints may thus "blind" their adherents to other conceptualizations until some new insight is achieved that resolves the problems left unsolved. These new insights constitute *paradigm shifts,* fundamental reorganizations of how people think about an entire field of science (Kuhn, 1962). For example, the sun was thought to revolve around the earth until Copernicus proposed the radical idea that the earth revolved around the sun, causing a major paradigm shift in astronomy and physics.

As we saw in Chapter 1, Sigmund Freud helped shift the focus of abnormal psychology from biological illness or moral infirmity to unconscious mental processes within the person. In recent years, there seem to have been two paradigm shifts occurring in parallel in the study of abnormal behavior. First, a newer and slightly different biological viewpoint is having a significant impact and is the dominant force in psychiatry. Second, the behavioral and cognitive-behavioral viewpoints have become the dominant paradigms among most empirically oriented clinical psychologists.

In recent years, many theorists have come to recognize the need for a more integrative **biopsychosocial viewpoint** that acknowledges that biological, psychosocial, and sociocultural factors all interact and play a role in psychopathology and treatment. This viewpoint was first articu-

developmental psychopathology Field of psychology that focuses on determining what is abnormal at any point in development by comparing and contrasting it with normal and expected changes that occur in the developmental process.

biopsychosocial viewpoint Integrative approach that acknowledges that biological, psychosocial, and sociocultural factors all interact and play a role in psychopathology and treatment.

lated in order to account for the effects of psychological and sociocultural factors on physical health and has become the dominant viewpoint in the fields of health psychology and behavioral medicine (see Chapter 8). However, it has also been extended to the study of mental disorders and treatments.

With this in mind, we turn now to the viewpoints themselves. Our survey will be descriptive, and we will not advocate one viewpoint over another. Rather, we will present information about the key ideas of each perspective, along with information about attempts to evaluate their validity. We will also describe the kinds of causal factors that each model tends to emphasize. As you will see, different models often have different perspectives on how and why a particular causal factor is involved in any given disorder.

People's behavior during alcohol intoxication is one good example of how a temporary biological condition can dramatically affect functioning—in this case, by allowing behavior that normally would be inhibited.

IN REVIEW

- What are the three traditional viewpoints that have dominated the study of abnormal behavior in recent years?
- What is the central idea of the more current biopsychosocial viewpoint?

THE BIOLOGICAL VIEWPOINT AND CAUSAL FACTORS

As we saw in the discussion of general paresis and its link to syphilis in Chapter 1, the biological viewpoint focuses on mental disorders as diseases, many of the primary symptoms of which are cognitive or behavioral rather than physiological or anatomical. Mental disorders are thus viewed as disorders of the central nervous system, the autonomic nervous system, or the endocrine system that are either inherited or caused by some pathological process. At one time people holding this viewpoint hoped to find simple biological explanations; however, today most recognize that such explanations are unlikely to be so simple. Although their focus remains on the genetic, biochemical, and other biological processes that have become imbalanced and are disrupting behavior, many now allow for other causal factors (e.g., psychological and sociocultural) to play a role as well.

As noted in Chapter 1, the disorders first recognized as having biological or organic components were those associated with gross destruction of brain tissue. These disorders were neurological diseases—that is, they resulted from the disruption of brain functioning by physical or chemical means and often involved psychological or behavioral aberrations. However, neurological damage does not necessarily result in abnormal behavior.

Similarly, the bizarre thought content of delusions and other abnormal mental states is probably never, in itself, the direct result of brain damage. For example, memory loss can often be accounted for by structural damage to the brain, but it is not so apparent how such damage produces the sometimes bizarre content of the person's thoughts or behavior. Thus, we can understand how the loss of neurons in general paresis can lead to difficulties in executing certain tasks, but the fact that a person claims to be Napoleon is not likely to be the result simply of a loss of neurons. Such behavior must be the product of some sort of functional integration of different neural structures, some of which have been "programmed" by personality and learning based on past experience.

Today we know that many conditions (for example, brain inflammation or high fever) temporarily disrupt the information-processing capabilities of the brain without inflicting permanent damage or death to the nerve cells involved. In these cases, normal functioning is altered by the context (especially the chemical context) in which the nerve cells operate. The most familiar example occurs during alcohol intoxication, when disruptive or otherwise inappropriate behavior that would normally be inhibited is sometimes indulged in. In sum, many processes short of brain damage can affect the functional capacity of the brain and thus change behavior.

We will focus here on five categories of biological causal factors that seem particularly relevant to the development of maladaptive behavior: (1) neurotransmitter and hormonal imbalances in the brain, (2) genetic vulner-

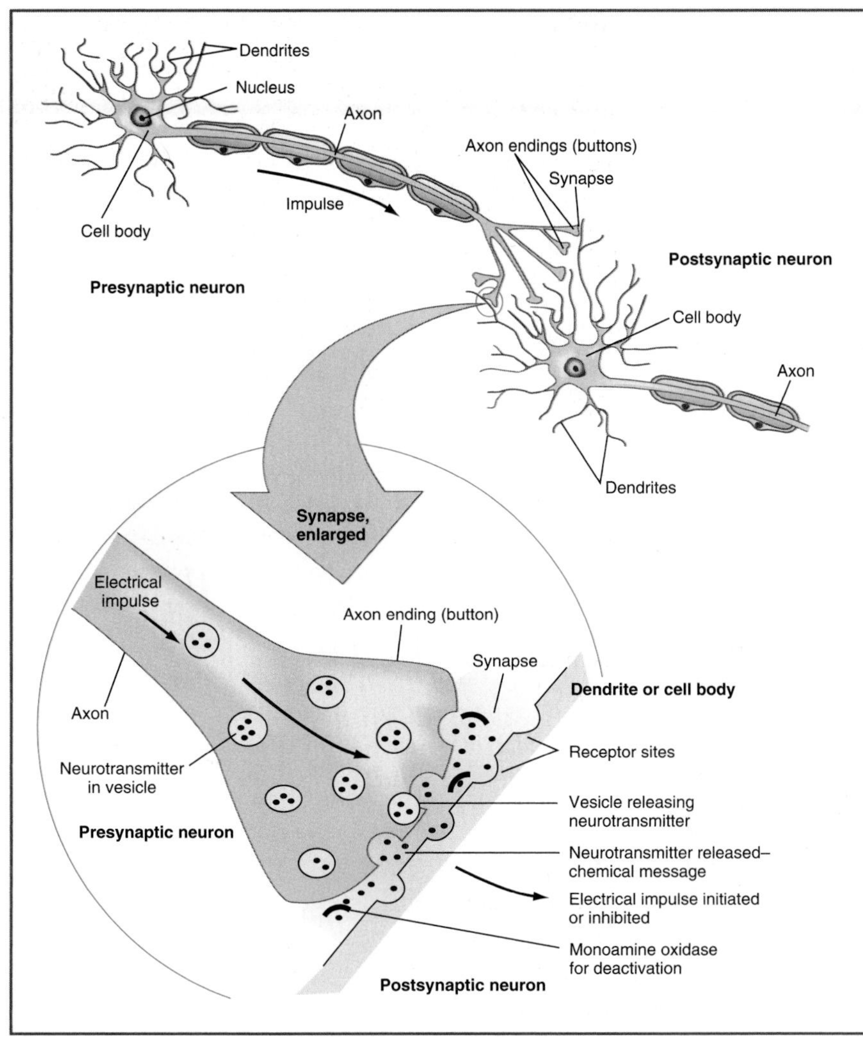

FIGURE 2.1
NEUROTRANSMISSION AND ABNORMAL BEHAVIOR
A nerve impulse, which is electrical in nature, travels from the cell body of a neuron (nerve cell) down the axon. Although there is only one axon for each neuron, each axon has branches at the end, called *axon endings,* or *terminal buttons.* When a nerve impulse reaches the axon ending, synaptic *vesicles* containing *neurotransmitters* travel to the presynaptic membrane of the axon and release neurotransmitters into the *synapse.* The released neurotransmitters then act on the postsynaptic membrane of the *dendrite* of the receiving neuron, which has specialized places called *receptor sites* where the neurotransmitters pass on their chemical message. The receptor sites then initiate the receiving cell's response. This is the essence of *neural transmission,* which occurs in the body's multitude of neurons. Neurotransmitters can carry either an excitatory or an inhibitory message—that is, some neurotransmitters cause postsynaptic neurons to fire and other neurotransmitters inhibit firing.

abilities, (3) constitutional liabilities, (4) brain dysfunction and neural plasticity, and (5) physical deprivation or disruption. Each of these categories encompasses a number of conditions that influence the quality and functioning of our bodies and our behavior. They are not necessarily independent of each other, and they often occur in varying combinations in different people.

Neurotransmitter and Hormonal Imbalances

In order for the brain to function adequately, neurons or nerve cells, need to be able to communicate effectively with one another. The site of communication from the axon of one neuron to the dendrites or cell body of another neuron is the **synapse** (or *synaptic cleft*)—a tiny, fluid-filled space between neurons. These interneuronal (or transsynaptic) transmissions are accomplished by chemical substances called **neurotransmitters** that are released into the synapse by the presynaptic neuron when a nerve impulse occurs (see Figure 2.1). There are many different kinds of neurotransmitters; some increase the likelihood that the postsynaptic neuron will "fire" (produce an impulse), while others inhibit the impulse. Whether the neural message is successfully transmitted to the postsynaptic neuron depends, among other things, on the concentration of certain neurotransmitters within the synaptic cleft.

Imbalances of Neurotransmitters The belief that *neurotransmitter imbalances* in the brain can result in ab-

synapse Site of communication from the axon of one neuron to the dendrites or cell body of another neuron—a tiny, fluid-filled space between neurons.

neurotransmitters Chemical substances that are released into a synapse by the presynaptic neuron when a nerve impulse occurs and increase or decrease the probability that the postsynaptic neuron will fire.

normal behavior is one of the basic tenets of the biological perspective today. Sometimes psychological stress can bring on neurotransmitter imbalances. These imbalances can be created in a variety of ways (see Figure 2.1). For example, there may be excessive production and release of a neurotransmitter into the synapses, causing a functional excess in levels of that neurotransmitter. Alternatively, there may be dysfunctions in the normal processes by which neurotransmitters, once released into the synapse, are deactivated. Ordinarily, this deactivation occurs in one of two ways. After being released into the synaptic cleft, a neurotransmitter either is deactivated by enzymes (such as monoamine oxidase) present in the synapse or, more commonly, is reabsorbed or sucked back into the presynaptic axon button, a process called *re-uptake*. Dysfunctions can create neurotransmitter imbalances either when the deactivation enzymes present in the synapse are deficient or when there is a slowing of the ordinary process of re-uptake. Finally, there may also be problems with the receptors in the postsynaptic neuron, which may be either abnormally sensitive or abnormally insensitive.

As we will see, different mental disorders are thought to stem from different patterns of neurotransmitter imbalances and from altered sensitivities of receptor sites. It is not surprising then that many medications used to treat various disorders are believed to operate through correcting these imbalances. For example, certain medications act to increase or decrease the concentrations of pertinent neurotransmitters in the synaptic cleft. They may do so by affecting the actions of the enzymes that ordinarily break down the neurotransmitter in the synapse, or by blocking the re-uptake process, or by altering the sensitivity of the receptor sites. For instance, the widely prescribed antidepressant Prozac appears to slow down the re-uptake process of the neurotransmitter serotonin (see Chapter 6).

Although there are dozens of different kinds of neurotransmitters, there are four that have been most extensively studied in relationship to psychopathology: (1) norepinephrine, (2) dopamine, (3) serotonin, and (4) GABA. The first three are all part of a class of neurotransmitters called *monoamines* because each is synthesized from a single amino acid (*monoamine* means "one amine"). Dopamine and norepinephrine are most closely related to one another (both are called *catecholamines*) because they are both synthesized from a common amino acid. Norepinephrine has been implicated as playing an important role in the emergency reactions our bodies show when we are exposed to an acutely stressful or dangerous situation, as will be discussed more extensively in Chapters 4 and 5. Dopamine has been implicated in a number of disorders, including schizophrenia. Serotonin has been found to have important effects on the way we process information from our environment (e.g., Spoont, 1992) and seems to play a role in emotional disorders such as anxiety and depression as well as in suicide, as we will see in Chapters 5 and 6. Finally, GABA (short for gamma-aminobutryic acid) was the most recently discovered of the neurotransmitters, and it is strongly implicated in anxiety, as will be discussed in Chapter 5.

hormones Chemical messengers that are secreted by the endocrine glands and affect various parts of the brain and body.

Hormonal Imbalances Some forms of psychopathology have also been linked to *hormonal imbalances*. **Hormones** are chemical messengers secreted by a set of endocrine glands in our bodies. Each of the endocrine glands produces and releases its own set of hormones, which travel through the bloodstream and affect various parts of the brain and body. Our central nervous system is linked to the endocrine system (in what is known as the *neuroendocrine system*) by the effects of the hypothalamus on the pituitary gland (see Figure 2.2), which is the mas-

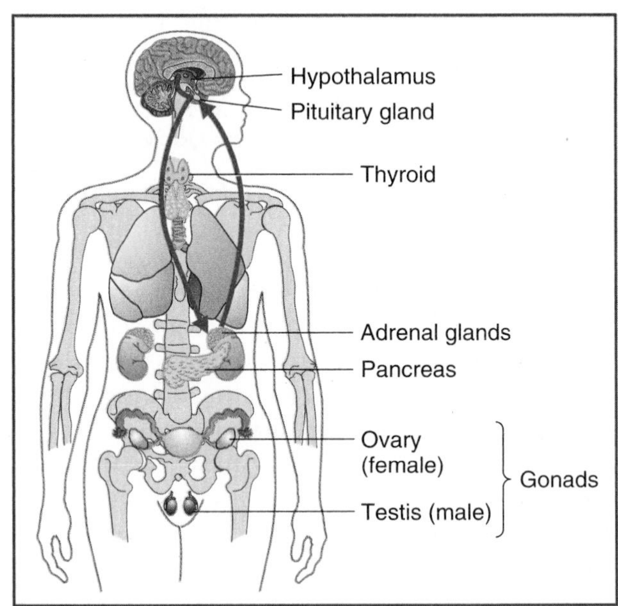

FIGURE 2.2
THE ENDOCRINE SYSTEM
This figure illustrates some of the major glands of the endocrine system, which produce and release hormones into the bloodstream. The hypothalamic-pituitary-adrenal-cortical axis is also shown (green arrows). The hypothalamus and pituitary are closely connected, and the hypothalamus periodically sends signals to the pituitary (the master gland), which in turn sends messages to the cortical part of the adrenal glands (above the kidneys) to release epinephrine and the stress hormone cortisol.

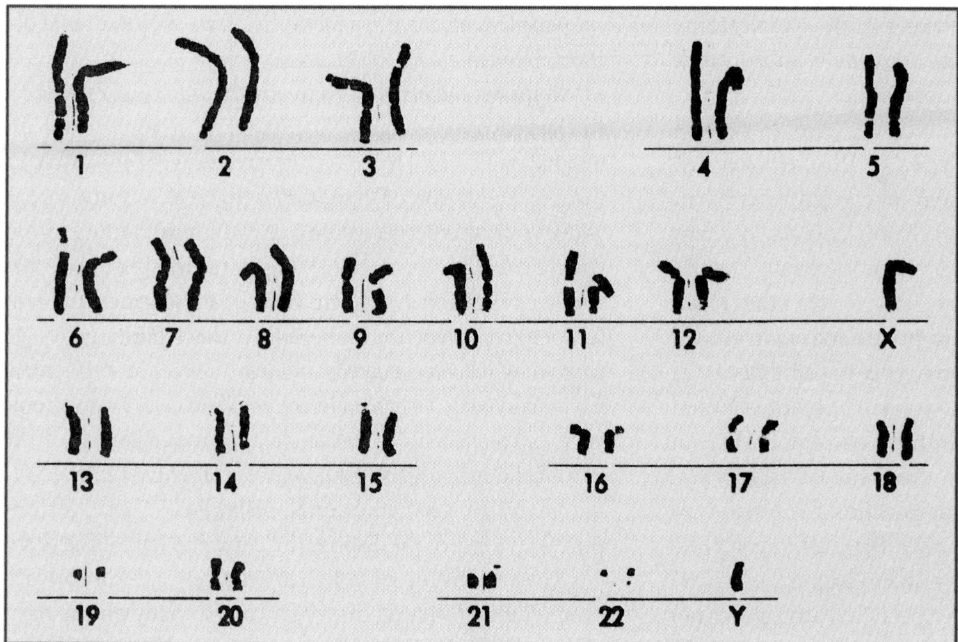

FIGURE 2.3
HUMAN CHROMOSOME PAIRS
Normal human cells have 23 pairs of chromosomes; one of each pair is inherited from the mother and one from the father. Twenty-two of these chromosome pairs are called *autosomes*; their biochemical action determines general anatomical and physiological characteristics. The remaining pair, the *sex chromosomes,* determine an individual's sex. In a female, both of the sex chromosomes—one from each parent—are designated as X chromosomes. In a male (shown here), the sex chromosome from the mother is an X chromosome, but that from the father is a Y chromosome.
Source: From T. D. Gelehrter, F. S. Collins, and D. Ginsburg, *Principles of Medical Genetics.* Copyright © 1998. Reprinted by permission of Lippincott/Williams & Wilkins.

ter gland of the body and produces a variety of hormones that regulate or control the other endocrine glands. One particularly important set of interactions occurs in the *hypothalamic-pituitary-adrenal-cortical axis.* Activation of this axis involves messages sent from the hypothalamus to the pituitary, which then stimulates the cortical part of the adrenal gland (located on top of the kidney) to produce epinephrine (adrenaline) and the stress hormone cortisol. As we will see, malfunction of this system has been implicated in various forms of psychopathology. Sex hormones are produced by the gonadal glands, and imbalance in these (such as the male hormones, or *androgens*) can also contribute to maladaptive behavior.

Genetic Vulnerabilities

The biochemical processes described above are themselves affected by *genes,* the long molecules of DNA (deoxyribonucleic acid) that are present at various locations on *chromosomes,* the chainlike structures within a cell nucleus (see Figure 2.3). Research in developmental genetics has shown that abnormalities in the structure or number of the chromosomes are associated with a wide range of malformations and disorders. For example, Down syndrome is a type of mental retardation (also associated with certain recognizable facial features) in which there is a trisomy (a set of three chromosomes instead of a pair) for chromosome 21. The extra chromosome is the primary cause of this disorder (see Chapter 13).

Many recent studies suggest that genetic vulnerabilities may play an important predisposing causal role in a number of different disorders—such as depression, schizophrenia, and alcoholism (e.g., Plomin, DeFries, McClearn, & Rutter, 1997). It is important to note here that genetic influences rarely express themselves in a simple and straightforward manner. This is because behavior, unlike some physical characteristics such as eye color, is not determined exclusively by genetic endowment: Rather than being a simple outcome of the information encoded in DNA, gene "expression" is instead the end product of an intricate process that may be influenced by internal (e.g., intrauterine) and external environmental factors. In other words, it is a product of the organism's interaction with the environment. Very often, genetic sources of vulnerability do not manifest themselves until later in life—adolescence or adulthood—and their effects are usually more subtle than those of chromosomal abnormalities.

The Relationship of Genotypes to Phenotypes A person's total genetic endowment is referred to as his or her **genotype.** Except for identical twins, no two humans ever begin life with the same genetic endowment. The observed structural and functional characteristics that result from an interaction of the genotype and the environment are referred to as a person's **phenotype.** In some cases, the genotypic vulnerability present at birth will not manifest its effect on the phenotype until much later in life. In many cases, the genotype may shape the environmental experiences the person has, thus affecting the phenotype in yet another very important way. For example, a child who may be genetically predisposed to aggressive behavior may be rejected by his or her peers in early grades because of aggressive behavior. Such rejection may lead the child to go on to associate with similarly aggressive and delinquent peers in later grades, leading to an increased likelihood of developing a full-blown pattern of delinquency in adolescence. When the genotype shapes the environmental experiences a child has in this way, we refer to the phenomenon as a **genotype-environment correlation** (Plomin et al., 1997). Another example occurs in extraverted children who seek the company of others, thereby enhancing their own tendencies to be sociable.

In addition, people with different genotypes may be differentially sensitive or susceptible to their environments; this susceptibility is known as a **genotype-environment interaction.** For example, people who are at genetic risk for depression have been shown to be more likely to respond to stressful life events by becoming depressed than are people without the genetic risk factors (Kendler et al., 1995; Plomin et al., 1997).

It appears likely that many of the most interesting (if still largely obscure) genetic influences on normal and abnormal behavior typically operate *polygenically,* that is, through the action of many genes together in some sort of additive or interactive fashion (e.g., Plomin, 1990; Plomin et al., 1997; Torgersen, 1993). A genetically vulnerable person has inherited a large number of these genes that collectively represent faulty heredity. These faulty genes, in turn, may lead to structural abnormalities in the central nervous system, to errors in the regulation of brain chemistry, or to excesses or deficiencies in the reactivity of the autonomic nervous system, which is involved in mediating many of our emotional responses. These various processes serve to predispose the person to later difficulties.

The few instances in which relatively straightforward predictions of mental disorders can be made on the basis of known laws of inheritance (e.g., involving only one gene) involve gross neurological impairment. In such cases, abnormal behavior arises in part as a consequence of a central nervous system malfunction, as in Huntington's disease; such conditions are covered in Chapter 13.

Methods for Studying Genetic Influences Although advances have been made in identifying faulty genetic endowment (including locating genes responsible for certain physical anomalies), we are not yet able to isolate specific gene defects responsible for mental disorders. Therefore, most of the information we have on the role of genetic factors in mental disorders is based not on studies of genes but on studies of people who are related to one another. There are three primary methods that are used in *behavior genetics,* the field that focuses on studying the heritability of mental disorders (as well as other aspects of psychological functioning): (1) the family history method, (2) the twin method, and (3) the adoption method.

The **family history method** requires that an investigator observe samples of relatives of each *proband* or *index case* (the subject, or carrier, of the trait or disorder in question) in order to see whether the incidence increases in proportion to the degree of hereditary relationship. In addition, the prevalence of the trait in a normal population is compared (as a control) with its prevalence among the relatives of the index cases. The central limitation of this method is that people who are more closely related genetically also usually tend to share more similar environments, making it difficult to disentangle genetic and environmental effects.

The **twin method** is the second approach used to study genetic influences on abnormal behavior. *Identical,*

genotype A person's total genetic endowment.

phenotype The observed structural and functional characteristics that result from the interaction of a person's genotype and the environment.

genotype-environment correlation The phenomenon whereby a person's genotype can shape his or her environmental experiences.

genotype-environment interaction Differential sensitivity or susceptibility to their environments among people having different genotypes.

family history method The use of patterns of a trait or disorder among first- and second-degree relatives to study possible genetic influences.

twin method The use of identical and nonidentical twins to study genetic influences on abnormal behavior.

This set of identical twins from Bouchard's University of Minnesota study of the relative roles of genetics and environment provides some striking support for the prominence of genetic influences on personality traits and attitudes (Bouchard et al., 1990). Jim Springer (left) and Jim Lewis (right) were separated four weeks after their birth in 1940. They grew up 45 miles apart in Ohio. After they were reunited in 1979, they discovered they had some eerie similarities: Both chain-smoked Salems, both drove the same model blue Chevrolet, both chewed their fingernails, and both had dogs named Toy. Further, they had both vacationed in the same neighborhood in Florida. When tested for such personality traits as sociability and self-control, they responded almost identically.

or *monozygotic,* twins share the same genetic endowment because they develop from a single zygote, or fertilized egg. Thus, if a given disorder or trait were completely heritable, one would expect the **concordance rate**—the percentage of twins sharing the disorder or trait—to be 100 percent. That is, if one identical twin had a particular disorder, the other twin would as well. There are virtually no forms of psychopathology where the concordance rates for identical twins are this high, and so we can safely conclude that virtually no disorders are completely heritable. However, as we will see, there are relatively high concordance rates for identical twins in some common and severe forms of psychopathology. These concordance rates are particularly meaningful when they differ from those found for nonidentical twins. *Nonidentical,* or *dizygotic,* twins do not share any more genes than do nontwin siblings with the same parents because they develop from two different fertilized eggs. One would therefore expect the concordance rate for a disorder to be much lower for nonidentical than for identical twins if the disorder has a strong genetic component because nonidentical twins have much less genetic similarity. So, evidence for genetic transmission of a trait or a disorder can be obtained by comparing the concordance rates between identical and nonidentical twins. For most of the disorders we will discuss, concordance rates are much lower for nonidentical twins than for identical twins.

The third method used to study genetic influences is the **adoption method.** In one variation on this method, the biological parents of individuals who have a given disorder (and who were given up for adoption shortly after birth) are traced and compared with the biological parents of individuals without the disorder (who were also adopted shortly after birth) to determine their rates of disorder. If there is a genetic influence, one expects to find a higher rate of the disorder in the biological relatives of those with the disorder than in those without the disorder. In another variation, one compares the rate of disorder in the adopted-away offspring of biological parents with a disorder with that seen in the adopted-away offspring of normal biological parents. If there is a genetic influence, then there should be a higher rate of disorder in the adopted-away offspring of the biological parents with the disorder.

Although each of these methods alone has its pitfalls of interpretation, if the results from studies using all three strategies converge, one can draw reasonably strong conclusions about the genetic influence on a disorder (Plomin et al., 1997; Rutter, 1991a). However, heritability studies also allow for testing the influence of environmental factors and even for differentiating "shared" and "nonshared" environmental influences (Plomin & Daniels, 1987; Plomin et al., 1997). *Shared environmental influences* are those that affect all children in a family similarly, such as overcrowding or poverty and sometimes family discord. *Nonshared environmental influences* are those in which different children in a family differ. These include experiences at school,

concordance rate The percentage of twins sharing a disorder or trait.

adoption method Comparison of biological and adoptive relatives of individuals who have or do not have a given disorder in order to assess genetic versus environmental influences.

as well as some features of upbringing in the home that may not be the same for all children, for example, when a parent treats one child in a qualitatively different way from another. An example of the latter occurs when parents who are quarreling and showing hostility to one another draw some children into the conflict but others are able to remain outside it (Rutter, Silberg, & Simonoff, 1993). For many important psychological characteristics and forms of psychopathology, nonshared influences appear to be more important—that is, experiences that are specific to a child may do more to influence his or her behavior and adjustment than experiences shared by all children in the family (Plomin et al., 1997; Rutter, 1991a).

Common Misconceptions About Genetic Influences

People have abundant misconceptions and stereotypes about studies of genetic influences on behavior and psychopathology. Several of the more important misconceptions are discussed here (Plomin et al., 1997; Rutter, 1991a; Rutter, Silberg, & Simonoff, 1993):

- *Strong genetic effects mean that environmental influences must be unimportant.* This is a misconception because even with traits or disorders that have a strong genetic influence, environmental factors can have a major impact on the level of the trait or disorder. Height, for example, is strongly genetically determined and yet nutritional factors have a very large effect on the actual height a person attains.
- *Genes provide a limit to potential.* To the contrary, one's potential can change if one's environment changes. One example involves children born to socially disadvantaged parents who are adopted and reared with socially advantaged parents. Their mean IQ is about 12 points higher than those reared in the socially disadvantaged environment (Plomin et al., 1997).
- *Genetic effects diminish with age.* Although many people assume that genetic effects should be maximal at birth (with environmental influences getting stronger with increasing age), it is now evident that this is not true (Plomin, 1986). As one example, for height, weight, and IQ, dizygotic twins are more alike than are monozygotic twins at birth, but over time dizygotic twins show greater differences than do monozygotic twins. Moreover, other genetic effects do not appear until much later in life, as in Huntington's disease, for example, to be discussed in Chapter 13.
- *Disorders that run in families must be genetic, and those that do not run in families must not be genetic.* Many examples contradict these misconceptions. For example, juvenile delinquency and conduct disorder tend to run in families, and yet this seems to be due primarily to environmental influences (McGuffin & Gottesman, 1985). Conversely, autism is such a rare disorder that it doesn't appear to run in families (only about 3 percent of the siblings of those with autism also have the disorder), and yet there seems to be a very powerful genetic effect (Plomin et al., 1997; Rutter, 1991b).

temperament Individual pattern of emotional and arousal responses to stimuli and characteristic ways of self-regulation that is considered to be primarily hereditary or constitutional.

Constitutional Liabilities

The term *constitutional liability* is used to describe any detrimental characteristic that is either innate or acquired so early—often prenatally—and in such strength that it is functionally similar to a genetic characteristic. We will briefly describe the role of several constitutional factors in the etiology of maladaptive behavior.

Physical Handicaps Included in the category of constitutional liabilities are physical handicaps such as low birth weight (5 pounds or less), which is associated with later mental disorders (including learning disabilities and emotional and behavioral disturbances). Approximately 6 to 7 percent of all babies born in the United States have a low birth weight (Barnard, Morisett, & Spieker, 1993; Kopp & Kaler, 1989). Low birth weight is most often associated with premature births but can also occur in full-term births. Prenatal conditions that can lead to premature birth and to low birth weight include nutritional deficiencies, disease, exposure to radiation, drugs, severe emotional stress, or the mother's excessive use of alcohol or tobacco.

Early intervention programs for the mothers of low birth weight infants, as well as for the infants, can be quite effective, at least in the short term, in preventing some of the early problems often associated with low birth weight (e.g., Hetherington & Parke, 1993). However, long-term interventions may be necessary to prevent the many difficulties often associated with *very* low birth weight.

Temperament **Temperament,** which involves not only reactivity but also characteristic ways of self-regulation, can also be a constitutional liability. When we say that babies differ in temperament, we mean that they differ in systematic ways in their emotional and arousal responses to various stimuli and in their tendency to approach, withdraw, or attend to various situations (Rothbart & Ahadi, 1994). These behaviors are regarded as constitutional rather than genetic because they are probably due to more

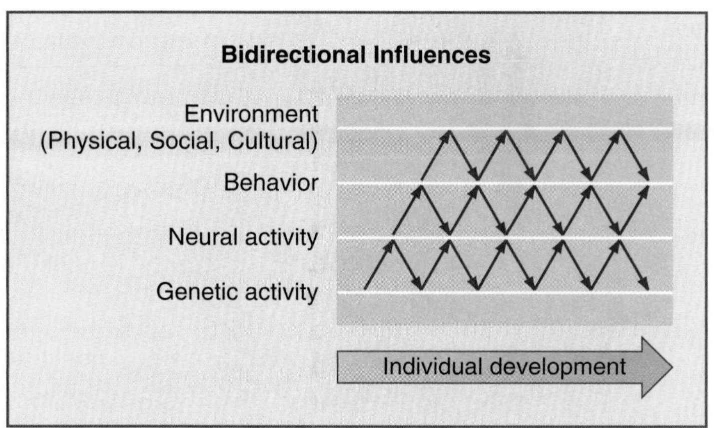

FIGURE 2.4
BIDIRECTIONAL INFLUENCES
A systems view of psychobiological development.
Source: Gilbert Gottlieb, from *Individual Development and Evolution: The Genesis of Novel Behavior.* New York: Oxford University Press, 1992. Copyright © 1992 by Oxford University Press. Reprinted with permission.

than genetic influences alone; prenatal and postnatal environmental factors may also play a role in their development (Kagan, 1994).

Early temperament is thought to be the substrate from which the personality develops because of its profound effects on a variety of important developmental processes (Rothbart & Ahadi, 1994). For example, a child with a fearful temperament has many opportunities for the classical conditioning of fear to situations in which fear is provoked. Later the child may learn to avoid entering those feared situations, and recent evidence suggests he or she may be especially likely to learn to fear social situations (Kagan, 1997), which is a risk factor for the development of anxiety disorders later in childhood and probably in adulthood (Biederman et al., 1990; Hirshfeld et al., 1992; Kagan, 1994, 1997). Conversely, 2-year-old children who show little fear of anything may have difficulty learning moral standards for their behavior from parents or society (Rothbart & Ahadi, 1994), and they have been shown to exhibit more aggressive and delinquent behavior at age 13 (Schwartz, Snidman, & Kagan, 1996).

Brain Dysfunction and Neural Plasticity

Significant damage of brain tissue places a person at risk for psychopathology, but specific brain lesions are rarely a primary cause of psychiatric disorder (Eisenberg, 1990). The incidence of such damage increases notably among the elderly, mostly because of the aging process itself (often resulting in Alzheimer's disease) or associated cardiovascular insufficiency, both of which will be discussed in Chapter 13. Subtle deficiencies of brain function are now implicated in many of the disorders that we will discuss throughout this book. Advances in our understanding of how these abnormalities in brain structure and function contribute to psychopathology have been increasing at a rapid pace in the past decade with the increased availability of sophisticated new neuroimaging techniques to study the function and structure of the brain. These and other kinds of techniques have been showing that genetic programs for brain development are not as rigid and deterministic as was once believed (e.g., Nelson & Bloom, 1997). For example, the formation of new neural connections (or synapses) after birth is dramatically affected by the experiences a young organism has (e.g., Greenough & Black, 1992). Rats reared in enriched environments (as opposed to isolation) show heavier and thicker cell development in certain portions of the cortex (as well as more synapses per neuron).

This research on neural and behavioral plasticity, in combination with that noted earlier on genotype-environment correlations, makes it clear why developmental psychopathologists have been devoting increasing attention to a **developmental systems approach,** which acknowledges not only that genetic activity influences neural activity, which in turn influences behavior, which in turn influences the environment, but also that these influences are bidirectional. As illustrated in Figure 2.4, various aspects of our environment (physical, social, and cultural) influence our behavior, which in turn affects our neural activity, and this in turn can even influence genetic activity (Gottlieb, 1992; Gottlieb, Wahlsten, & Lickliter, 1998).

Physical Deprivation or Disruption

Through a remarkable set of complex processes, the digestive, circulatory, and other bodily functions work to maintain the body's physiological equilibrium and inte-

developmental systems approach View of abnormal behavior that acknowledges that genetic activity influences neural activity, which in turn influences behavior, which in turn influences the environment, and that these influences are bidirectional.

gration. Insufficient rest, inadequate diet, or working too hard when ill can interfere with this equilibrium and thus with a person's ability to cope, predisposing him or her to a variety of problems. For example, prisoners have sometimes been broken by nothing more persuasive than the systematic prevention of sleep or deprivation of food over a period of several days. Experimental studies of volunteers who have gone without sleep for periods of 72 to 98 hours show increasing psychological problems as the sleep loss progresses—including disorientation for time and place and feelings of depersonalization.

Even relatively mild sleep deprivation if chronic can have adverse emotional consequences in children and adolescents. For example, Carskadon (1990) argued that performance lapses associated with excessive sleepiness in teens can in turn lead to an increased vulnerability to accidents, to the use of caffeine and alcohol, and to mood and behavior problems.

Prolonged food deprivation also affects psychological functioning. In particular, severe weight loss may have long-term psychological consequences. One group of former World War II and Korean War POWs who had lost 35 percent or more of their original body weight while in captivity were tested 30 years later; they performed more poorly on a variety of tests of cognitive functioning than did other former POWs who had not lost this much weight (Sutker, Galina, & West, 1990, 1995). In addition, Polivy and colleagues (1994) found that former POWs who had lost a great deal of weight as POWs reported higher than expected levels of binge eating for many years thereafter.

Perhaps the most tragic deprivation is seen in young children who are malnourished. Severe malnutrition impairs physical development and lowers resistance to disease. It also stunts brain growth, results in markedly lowered intelligence, and enhances risk for disorders such as attention-deficit disorder (which leads to attentional problems, increased distractibility, and interference with school performance) (Galler, 1984; Lozoff, 1989). In Western countries such as the United States, recent evidence has been accumulating that malnutrition is more common in families where the mother is traditionally passive in childcare; if these mothers are taught to give their infants nutritional supplements (assuming they are available), many of the adverse effects of early malnutrition can be reversed as the babies gain more energy and are more open to the socialization process which is so important for normal intellectual growth (Sameroff, 1995).

Finally, healthy mental development depends on a child's receiving adequate amounts of stimulation from the environment. In addition to psychological vulnerabilities that can be induced by too little stimulation, which will be discussed later, the *physical* development of the brain is adversely affected by an unstimulating environment. Conversely, many animal studies demonstrate that enhanced biological development is produced by conditions of special stimulation such as enriched and complex environments in which many different activities can be engaged in. The enhancements include positive changes in brain chemistry and structural changes in many parts of the brain such as increases in numbers of synapses and dendrites (Diamond, 1988; Nelson & Bloom, 1997; Swain et al., 1995).

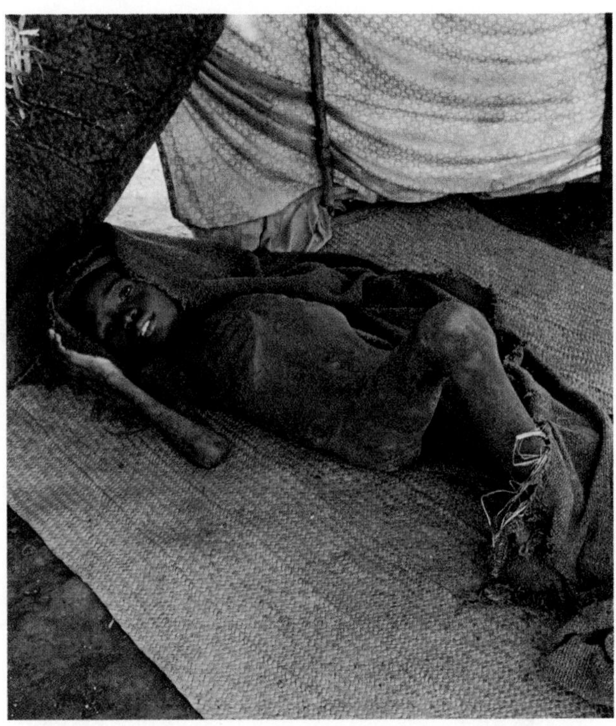

Children who are severely malnourished show stunted growth and lowered intelligence. This makes them vulnerable to attentional problems and, hence, impaired school performance. An unstimulating environment has also been shown to stunt brain development.

The Impact of the Biological Viewpoint

Biological discoveries have profoundly affected the way we think about human behavior. We now recognize the important role of biochemical factors and innate characteristics, many of which are genetically determined, in both normal and abnormal behavior. In addition, since the 1950s, we have a host of new drugs that can dramatically alter the severity and course of certain mental disorders—particularly the more severe ones such as schizophrenia, bipolar disorder, and major depression. In some ways, biological treatments seem to have more immediate results than other available therapies, and the hope is that they may in most cases lead to a "cure-all"—immediate results with seemingly little effort. All these new developments have brought a great deal of attention to the biological viewpoint, not only in scientific circles but also in the popular media. As a result, more and more types of abnormal behavior are being discussed and treated as if they were like medical illness.

However, as Gorenstein (1992) has argued, there are several common errors in the way many people interpret the meaning of recent biological advances. For instance, it is illusory to think—as some prominent biological researchers have—that establishing biological differences between, for example, schizophrenics and nonschizophrenics in and of itself substantiates that schizophrenia is an illness. All behavioral traits, such as introversion versus extraversion or high versus low sensation seeking, are characterized by distinctive biological characteristics, and yet we do not label these traits as illnesses. Thus, Gorenstein argues, the decision about what constitutes a mental illness or disorder must ultimately still rest on subjective opinion regarding the functional effects of the disordered behavior. Establishing the biological substrate does not bear on this issue because all behavior—normal and abnormal—has a biological substrate.

The second important misconception discussed by Gorenstein (1992) concerns the idea held by some that most, if not all, mental disorders are biological conditions with biological causes. Given that all our cognitions and behavior are ultimately reducible to a set of biological events occurring in the brain, it is a mistake to distinguish between psychological and biological causes in this way. As Gorenstein argues, psychological causes can be distinguished from biological causes "only prior to their entry into the central nervous system" (p. 123). This is because once a psychological cause has had its effect on a person, the effect of that psychological event is also mediated through the activities of the central nervous system. In actuality, then, if there is some observed dysfunction of the nervous system, this dysfunction could as well have arisen from psychosocial as from biological causes.

At a more general level, we must remind ourselves again that few, if any, mental disorders are independent of people's personalities or of the problems they face in trying to live their lives. We will examine viewpoints that emphasize these psychosocial and sociocultural considerations in the pages that follow, keeping in mind that the ultimate challenge will be to integrate these varying perspectives into a theoretically consistent biopsychosocial perspective on psychopathology.

IN REVIEW

- Describe the sequence of events involved in the transmission of nerve impulses, and explain how imbalances of neurotransmitters might produce abnormal behavior.
- What is the relationship of genotypes and phenotypes, and how can genotypes shape and interact with the environment?
- Summarize the three major methods used to study genetic influences on abnormal behavior.
- Give two examples of constitutional liabilities, and describe the role they can play in abnormal behavior.
- What kinds of brain dysfunctions tend to be implicated in abnormal behavior?
- What kinds of physical deprivations or disruptions can contribute to abnormal behavior?
- What common errors are made in interpreting the meaning of recent biological advances?

THE PSYCHOSOCIAL VIEWPOINTS

There are several psychosocial interpretations of abnormal behavior, reflecting a wide range of opinions regarding how to best understand humans not just as biological organisms but also as people with motives, desires, perceptions, etc. We will examine in some depth three psychosocial perspectives: psychodynamic, behavioral, and cognitive-behavioral. There are also two other perspectives that have been less influential in the study of abnormal behavior. One is the humanistic perspective, which focuses on freeing people from disabling assumptions and attitudes so that they can live fuller lives. Its emphasis is thus on growth and self-actualization rather than on curing diseases or alleviating disorders. The other is the existential perspective, which is less optimistic than the humanistic approach and emphasizes the difficulties inherent in self-fulfillment. In Chapter 3, we will consider the humanistic-existential approaches to psychotherapy—which focus on fostering growth toward a socially constructive and personally fulfilling way of life.

The three psychosocial viewpoints considered here represent distinct and sometimes conflicting orientations, but they are in some ways complementary. All of them emphasize the importance of early experience and an awareness of social influences and psychological processes within an individual, hence the term *psychosocial* as a de-

HIGHLIGHT 2.1

The Humanistic and Existential Perspectives

The Humanistic Perspective

The *humanistic perspective* views human nature as basically "good." It emphasizes present conscious processes—paying less attention to unconscious processes and past causes—and places strong emphasis on people's inherent capacity for responsible self-direction. Humanistic psychologists think that much of the empirical research designed to investigate causal factors is too simplistic to uncover the complexities of human behavior. Thus, the humanistic perspective tends to be as much a statement of values—how we ought to view the human condition—as it is an attempt to account for human behavior, at least among persons beset by personal problems.

This perspective is concerned with processes about which we have as yet little scientific information—love, hope, creativity, values, meaning, personal growth, and self-fulfillment. Although not readily subject to empirical investigation, certain underlying themes and principles of humanistic psychology can be identified—including the self as a unifying theme and a focus on values and personal growth.

In using the concept of self as a unifying theme, humanistic psychologists emphasize the importance of individuality. Among humanistic psychologists, Carl Rogers (1902–1987) developed the most systematic formulation of the *self-concept,* based largely on his pioneering research into the nature of the psychotherapeutic process. Rogers (1951, 1959) stated his views in a series of propositions that may be summarized as follows:

- Each individual exists in a private world of experience of which the *I, me,* or *myself* is the center.
- The most basic striving of an individual is toward the maintenance, enhancement, and actualization of the self.
- An individual reacts to situations in terms of the way he or she perceives them, in ways consistent with his or her self-concept and view of the world.
- A perceived threat to the self is followed by a defense—including a tightening of perception and behavior and the introduction of self-defense mechanisms.
- An individual's inner tendencies are toward health and wholeness; under normal conditions, a person behaves in rational and constructive ways and chooses pathways toward personal growth and self-actualization.

Humanistic psychologists emphasize that values and the process of choice are key in guiding our behavior and achieving meaningful and fulfilling lives. Each of us must develop values based on our own experiences and evaluations rather than blindly accepting the values of others; otherwise, we deny our own experiences and lose touch with our own feelings. To evaluate and choose for ourselves requires developing a clear sense of our own identity—who we are, what sort of person we want to become, and why. Only in this way can we become *self-actualizing,* meaning that we are achieving our full potential.

According to the humanistic view, psychopathology is essentially the blocking or distortion of personal growth and the natural tendency toward physical and mental health. Psychotherapists who adhere to the humanistic perspective focus on freeing people from disabling assumptions and attitudes so that they can live fuller lives. The emphasis is thus on growth and self-actualization rather than on curing diseases or alleviating disorders.

The Existential Perspective

The *existential perspective* resembles the humanistic view in its emphasis on the uniqueness of each individual, the quest for values and meaning, and the existence of freedom for self-direction and self-fulfillment. However, it takes a less optimistic view of human beings and places more emphasis on the irrational tendencies and the difficulties inherent in self-fulfillment—particularly in a modern, bureaucratic, and dehumanizing mass society. In short, living is much more of a "confrontation" for the existentialists than for the humanists. Existential thinkers are especially concerned with the inner experiences of an individual in his or her attempts to understand and deal with the deepest human problems. There are several basic themes of existentialism:

- *Existence and essence.* Our existence is a given, but what we make of it—our essence—is up to us.
- *Choice, freedom, and courage.* Our essence is created by our choices, because our choices reflect the values on which we base and order our lives.
- *Meaning, value, and obligation.* The will-to-meaning is a basic human characteristic to find satisfying values and guide one's life by them; important, too, are our obligations to each other.
- *Existential anxiety and the encounter with nothingness.* Nonbeing, or nothingness, which in its final form is death, is the inescapable fate of all human beings. The awareness of our inevitable death and its implications for our living can lead to existential anxiety—a deep concern over whether we are living meaningful and fulfilling lives.

Thus, existential psychologists focus on the importance of establishing values and acquiring a level of spiritual maturity worthy of the freedom and dignity bestowed by one's humanness. It is the avoidance of such central issues that creates corrupted, meaningless, and wasted lives. Much abnormal behavior, therefore, is seen as the product of a failure to deal constructively with existential despair and frustration. ■

scriptive label. After describing these different psychosocial viewpoints, we will consider a variety of psychosocial causal factors known to be associated with abnormal behavior and discuss how some of the psychosocial models explain their effects.

The Psychodynamic Perspectives

As discussed in Chapter 1, Sigmund Freud founded the psychoanalytic school, which emphasized the role of unconscious processes in the determination of both normal and abnormal behavior. A key concept here is the *unconscious.* Freud thought that the conscious part of the mind represents a relatively small area, while the unconscious part, like the submerged part of an iceberg, is the much larger portion. In the depths of the unconscious are the hurtful memories, forbidden desires, and other experiences that have been repressed—that is, pushed out of consciousness. However, unconscious material continues to seek expression and comes out in fantasies, dreams, slips of the tongue, and so forth, as well as when a person is under hypnosis. Until such unconscious material is brought to awareness and integrated into the conscious part of the mind—for example, through psychoanalysis—it may lead to irrational and maladaptive behavior.

The Structure of Personality: Id, Ego, and Superego

The actual techniques of psychoanalysis as a form of treatment for mental disorders are based on the general principles underlying Freud's theory of personality. Freud theorized that a person's behavior results from the interaction of three key components of the personality, or psyche: the id, ego, and superego. The **id** is the source of instinctual drives and the first personality structure to appear in infancy. These drives are inherited and considered to be of two opposing types: (1) *life instincts,* which are constructive drives primarily of a sexual nature and which constitute the **libido,** the basic energy of life; and (2) *death instincts,* which are destructive drives and tend toward aggression, destruction, and eventual death. Freud used the term *sexual* in a broad sense to refer to almost anything pleasurable, from eating to painting. The id operates on the **pleasure principle,** engaging in completely selfish and pleasure-oriented behavior, concerned only with the immediate gratification of instinctual needs without reference to reality or moral considerations. Although the id can generate mental images and wish-fulfilling fantasies, referred to as **primary process thinking,** it cannot undertake the realistic actions needed to meet instinctual demands.

Consequently, after the first few months of life, a second part of the personality, as viewed by Freud, develops—the ego. The **ego** mediates between the demands of the id and the realities of the external world. For example, during toilet training, the child learns to control a bodily function to meet parental-societal expectations, and it is

id In psychoanalytic theory, the reservoir of instinctual drives and the first personality structure to appear in infancy.

libido In psychoanalytic theory, the basic constructive energy of life, made up of the instinctual drives of the id, which are primarily sexual in nature.

pleasure principle Demand that an instinctual need be immediately gratified, regardless of reality or moral considerations.

primary process thinking Generation by the id of mental images and wish-fulfilling fantasies in response to instinctual needs.

ego In psychoanalytic theory, the rational part of the personality that mediates between the demands of the id, the constraints of the superego, and the realities of the external world.

The demands of the id are evident in early childhood. According to Freud, babies pass through an oral stage, in which sucking is a dominant pleasure.

the developing ego that takes the role of mediating between the physical needs of the body/id and the need to find an appropriate place and time. The basic purpose of the ego is to meet id demands, but in such a way as to ensure the well-being and survival of the individual. This role requires the use of reason and other intellectual resources in dealing with the external world, as well as the exercise of control over id demands. The ego's adaptive measures are referred to as **secondary process thinking,** and the ego operates on the **reality principle.** Freud viewed id demands, especially sexual and aggressive strivings, as inherently in conflict with the rules and prohibitions imposed by society.

secondary process thinking Reality-oriented rational processes used by the ego in dealing with the external world and exercising control over id demands.

reality principle Awareness of the demands of the environment and adjustment of behavior to meet those demands.

superego In psychoanalytic theory, the part of the personality that embodies ethical or moral dimensions (attitudes); the conscience.

intrapsychic conflicts Inner mental struggles resulting when the id, ego, and superego are striving for different goals.

ego-defense mechanisms Irrational protective measures, usually unconscious and reality-distorting, used by the ego to discharge or soothe anxiety rather than coping directly with the anxiety-provoking situation; also called *defense mechanisms.*

psychosexual stages of development According to Freudian theory, five periods during development from infancy through puberty, each characterized by a dominant mode of achieving sexual pleasure: the oral stage, the anal stage, the phallic stage, the latency stage, and the genital stage.

Freud postulated that, as a child grows and gradually learns the rules of parents and society regarding right and wrong, a third part of the personality gradually emerges from the ego—the **superego.** The superego is the outgrowth of the child's internalizing of the taboos and moral values of society. It is essentially what we refer to as the *conscience*; it is concerned with right and wrong. As the superego develops, it becomes an inner control system that deals with the uninhibited desires of the id. The superego operates through the ego system and strives to compel the ego to inhibit desires that are considered wrong or immoral. Because the ego mediates between fulfilling the desires of the id, the demands of reality, and the moral constraints of the superego, it is often called the *executive branch of the personality.*

Freud believed that the interplay of id, ego, and superego is of crucial significance in determining behavior. Often inner mental struggles arise because the three subsystems are striving for different goals. These conflicts are called **intrapsychic conflicts** and, if unresolved, lead to mental disorder.

Anxiety, Defense Mechanisms, and the Unconscious

The concept of anxiety (generalized feelings of fear and apprehension) is prominent in the psychoanalytic viewpoint because it is an almost universal symptom of neurotic disorders. Indeed, Freud believed that anxiety played a key causal role in most of the forms of psychopathology that will be discussed in this book. Sometimes the anxiety is overtly experienced, and sometimes it is repressed and then transformed into and manifested in other overt symptoms.

Anxiety is a warning signal of impending real or imagined dangers as well as a painful experience, and it forces an individual to take corrective action. Often, the ego can cope with objective or realistic anxiety through rational measures. However, when the source of anxiety is unconscious intrapsychic conflict, the ego unconsciously resorts to irrational protective measures that are referred to as **ego-defense mechanisms.** Some of the more common ones are described in Table 2.1. These defense mechanisms may discharge or soothe anxiety, but they do so by helping a person push painful ideas out of consciousness (such as by "forgetting" a dental appointment) rather than by dealing directly with the problem. These mechanisms result in a distorted view of reality, although some are clearly more adaptive than others.

Psychosexual Stages of Development In addition to his concept of the structure of personality, Freud also conceptualized five **psychosexual stages of development** that

TABLE 2.1 EGO-DEFENSE MECHANISMS

Mechanism	Example
Denial of reality: Protecting the self from an unpleasant reality by the refusal to perceive or face it.	A smoker concludes that the evidence linking cigarette use to health problems is scientifically worthless.
Displacement: Discharging pent-up feelings, often of hostility, on objects less dangerous than those arousing the feelings.	A woman harassed by her boss at work initiates an argument with her husband.
Fixation: Attaching oneself in an unreasonable or exaggerated way to some person, or arresting emotional development on a childhood or adolescent level.	An unmarried, middle-aged man still depends on his mother to provide his basic needs.
Projection: Attributing one's unacceptable motives or characteristics to others.	An expansionist-minded dictator of a totalitarian state is convinced that neighboring countries are planning to invade.
Rationalization: Using contrived "explanations" to conceal or disguise unworthy motives for one's behavior.	A fanatical racist uses ambiguous passages from Scripture to justify his hostile actions toward minorities.
Reaction formation: Preventing the awareness or expression of unacceptable desires by an exaggerated adoption of seemingly opposite behavior.	A man troubled by homosexual urges initiates a zealous community campaign to stamp out gay bars.
Regression: Retreating to an earlier developmental level involving less mature behavior and responsibility.	A man whose self-esteem has been shattered reverts to childlike "show-off" behavior and exhibits his genitals to young girls.
Repression: Preventing painful or dangerous thoughts from entering consciousness.	A mother's occasional murderous impulses toward her hyperactive 2-year-old are denied access to awareness.
Sublimation: Channeling frustrated sexual energy into substitutive activities.	A sexually frustrated artist paints wildly erotic pictures.

Source: Based on A. Freud (1946); American Psychiatric Association (1994), pp. 751–753.

we all pass through from infancy through puberty. Each stage is characterized by a dominant mode of achieving libidinal (sexual) pleasure.

Oral stage: During the first 2 years of life, the mouth is the principal erogenous zone; an infant's greatest source of gratification is sucking, a process that is necessary for feeding.

Anal stage: From age 2 to 3, the anus provides the major source of pleasurable stimulation during the time when toilet training is often going on and there are urges both for retention and elimination.

Phallic stage: From age 3 to 5 or 6, self-manipulation of the genitals provides the major source of pleasurable sensation.

Latency stage: From age 6 to 12, sexual motivations recede in importance as a child becomes preoccupied with developing skills and other activities.

Genital stage: After puberty, the deepest feelings of pleasure come from sexual relations.

Freud believed that appropriate gratification during each stage is important if a person is not to be stuck or fixated at that level. For example, he maintained that an infant who does not receive adequate oral gratification may be prone to excessive eating or drinking in adult life.

The Oedipus Complex and the Electra Complex In general, each stage of development places demands on an individual and arouses conflicts that Freud believed must be resolved. One of the most important conflicts occurs during the phallic stage, when the pleasures of self-stimulation and accompanying fantasies pave the way for the **Oedipus complex.** Oedipus, according to Greek mythology, unknowingly killed his father and married his mother. Each young boy, Freud thought, symbolically re-

Oedipus complex Desire for sexual relations with his mother and hatred of his father that a boy feels during the phallic stage of psychosexual development.

lives the Oedipus drama. He longs for his mother sexually and views his father as a hated rival; however, each young boy also fears that his father will take revenge on the son's lust by cutting off his penis. This **castration anxiety** forces the boy to repress his sexual desire for his mother and his hostility toward his father. Eventually, if all goes well, the boy identifies with his father and comes to have nonsexual affection for his mother.

The **Electra complex** is the female counterpart of the Oedipus complex and is also drawn from a Greek tragedy. It is based on the view that each girl desires to possess her father and to replace her mother. Freud also believed that each girl at the phallic stage experiences penis envy, wishing that she could be more like her father and brothers. Her emergence from the complex occurs when she comes to identify with her mother, and she settles for a promissory note: One day she will have a man of her own who can give her a baby—which unconsciously serves as a type of penis substitute.

For either sex, resolution of this conflict is considered essential if a young adult is to develop satisfactory heterosexual relationships. The psychoanalytic perspective holds that the best we can hope for is a compromise among our warring inclinations, and to realize as much instinctual gratification as possible with minimal punishment and guilt. This perspective thus presents a deterministic view of human behavior that minimizes rationality and freedom of self-determination. On a group level, it interprets violence, war, and related phenomena as the inevitable products of the aggressive and destructive instincts present in human nature.

Newer Psychodynamic Perspectives In seeking to understand his patients and develop his theories, Freud was chiefly concerned with the workings of the id, its nature as a source of energy, and the manner in which this id energy could be channeled or transformed. He also focused on the superego but paid relatively little attention to the importance of the ego. Later theorists developed some of Freud's basic ideas in three somewhat different directions. One new perspective was started by his daughter Anna Freud (1895–1982), who was much more concerned with how the ego performed its central functions as the "executive" of personality. She and some of the more influential of the second generation of psychodynamic theorists refined and elaborated on the ego-defense mechanisms and put the ego in the foreground, giving it an important organizing role in personality development (see Table 2.1). This school became known as **ego psychology.** A second new direction was taken by theorists who focused on very early aspects of the mother-infant relationship, and the third new psychodynamic perspective focused on social determinants of behavior and on the importance of people's interpersonal relationships. All three of these new perspectives dropped the original emphasis of traditional (Freudian) psychoanalytic theory on the primacy of libidinal energies and intrapsychic conflicts. The term *psychodynamic* generally refers to any of these second-generation theories that stem from Freud's original psychoanalytic theory in some important way and yet also depart from it in significant ways.

Object-Relations Theory **Object-relations theory** emphasizes the importance of the pre-Oedipal phase to personality development and psychopathology. This approach focuses on neither the id nor the ego, but rather on

Anna Freud (1895–1982) elaborated the theory of ego-defense mechanisms and pioneered the psychoanalytic treatment of children.

castration anxiety As postulated by Freud, the anxiety a young boy experiences when he desires his mother while at the same time fearing that his father may harm him by cutting off his penis; this anxiety forces the boy to repress his sexual desire for his mother and his hostility toward his father.

Electra complex Excessive and possessive emotional attachment (love) of a daughter for her father; the female counterpart of the Oedipus complex.

ego psychology Psychodynamic perspective that gives the ego an important organizing role in personality development.

object-relations theory Psychodynamic perspective that emphasizes the importance of an infant's or young child's interactions with real and imagined other people (objects), as well as how children make symbolic representations of important people in their lives.

According to object-relations theorists, children incorporate, or *introject,* symbolic aspects of important people in their lives (such as their parents) and then carry this representation with them as part of their developing personalities.

the objects toward which the infant and young child has directed the id impulses and which he or she has *introjected* (incorporated) into his or her personality. *Objects* in this context refer to the symbolic representations of other persons in the infant's or child's environment, most often parents. The concept of **introjection** refers to an internal process in which the infant or child incorporates symbolically, through images and memories, important people in his or her life. For example, the child might internalize the image of a parent's scowling face. Later, this *inner object,* the symbol or representation of the outer object, can influence how a person experiences events and behaves. We should note, too, that very young children do not differentiate between self and object (Mahler, 1976). Only gradually do children gain an internal representation of self as distinct from representation of other objects, a process of *separation-individuation* that is essential for the achievement of personal maturity.

Although there are many variations on object-relations theory, what they share is a focus on an infant's or young child's interactions with external and internal (real and imagined) other people, as well as on the relationships between the real and imagined objects. These theorists have developed the general notion that internalized objects can have various conflicting properties—such as exciting or attractive versus hostile, frustrating, or rejecting—and that these objects can also split off from the central ego and maintain independent existences, thus giving rise to inner conflicts. For example, a child might internalize the image of a punishing father; that image becomes a harsh self-critic. An individual experiencing such splitting among internalized objects is, so to speak, "the servant of many masters" and cannot therefore lead an integrated, orderly life.

In recent years, many American analysts have become advocates of the object-relations point of view. Among them is Otto Kernberg (b. 1928), noted especially for his studies of both borderline and narcissistic personalities (see Chapter 9). Kernberg's view is that the borderline personality, whose chief characteristic is instability (especially in personal relationships), is an individual who is unable to achieve a full and stable personal identity (self) because of an inability to integrate and reconcile pathological internalized objects.

The Interpersonal Perspective From an **interpersonal perspective,** abnormal behavior is best understood by analyzing a person's relationships, past and present, with other people. This perspective evolved as theorists took psychoanalytic theory to task for its neglect of crucial social factors. For example, Alfred Adler (1870–1937) emphasized social rather than inner determinants of behavior, noting that people are inherently social beings strongly motivated by the desire to belong to and participate in a group. Erich Fromm (1900–1980) focused on the orientations or dispositions (exploitative, for example) that people adopted in their interactions with others; he believed that these orientations to the social environment were the bases of much psychopathology. Karen Horney (1885–1952) independently developed a similar view and, in particular, vigorously rejected Freud's demeaning psychoanalytic view of women (for instance, the idea that women experience penis envy). According to Horney, "femininity" was a product of the culturally determined social learning that most women experienced. Erik Erikson (1902–1994) elaborated and broadened Freud's psychosexual stages into

introjection Internal process by which an infant or child incorporates symbolically, through images and memories, important people in his or her life.

interpersonal perspective Psychodynamic perspective that focuses on a person's relationships, past and present, with other people.

more socially oriented concepts, describing crises or conflicts that occurred at eight stages, each of which could be resolved in a healthy or unhealthy way. For example, during what Freud called the oral stage, when a child is preoccupied with oral gratification, Erikson believed that a child's real development centered on learning either "basic trust" of his or her social world or "basic mistrust." Although these crises are never fully resolved, failure to develop toward the appropriate pole of each crisis handicaps an individual during later stages. Trust, for instance, is needed for later competence in many areas of life.

Harry Stack Sullivan (1892–1949) offered a comprehensive and systematic theory of personality that was explicitly interpersonal. Sullivan (1953) maintained that the concept of personality had meaning only when defined in terms of a person's characteristic ways of relating to others. He argued that personality development proceeded through various stages involving different patterns of interpersonal relationships that shape the self-concept. Early in life, for example, a child becomes socialized mainly through interactions with parents. Somewhat later, peer relationships become increasingly important. In young adulthood, intimate relationships are established, culminating typically in marriage. Failure to progress satisfactorily through these various stages paves the way for maladaptive behavior.

Sullivan was concerned with the anxiety-arousing aspects of interpersonal relationships during early childhood (in contrast to Freud's emphasis on anxiety as a signal of unconscious conflict). Because an infant is completely dependent on parents and siblings for meeting all needs, a lack of love and care leads to insecurity and what can be an overwhelming sense of anxiety. He defined security as the freedom from anxiety. He also believed that anxiety about anxiety is fundamental to much psychopathology.

Finally, there are two more recent focuses of the interpersonal perspective. The first is **interpersonal accommodation,** a process through which two people develop patterns of communication and interaction that enable them to attain common goals, meet mutual needs, and build a satisfying relationship (Benjamin, 1982, 1993; Carson, 1979; Wiggins, 1982). When communication and interpersonal accommodation fail and a particular relationship does not meet the needs of one or both partners, it is likely to be characterized by conflict, dissension, and eventually dissolution. The second more recent focus of the interpersonal perspective is Bowlby's **attachment theory,** which emphasizes the importance of early experience with attachment relationships—especially that of parenting—to the development of secure attachments. The quality of one's attachment relationships plays an active role in shaping one's development throughout childhood, adolescence, and adulthood (Bowlby, 1969, 1973, 1980; Carlson & Sroufe, 1995). Attachment theory has become an enormously influential theory in child psychology and child psychiatry, as well as adult psychopathology.

interpersonal accommodation Process through which two people develop patterns of communication and interaction that enable them to attain common goals, meet mutual needs, and build a satisfying relationship.

attachment theory Idea put forth by Bowlby that the quality of one's attachment relationships plays an active role in shaping one's development throughout the lifespan.

Impact of the Psychodynamic Perspective In historical perspective, Freudian psychoanalysis can be seen as the first systematic approach to show how human psychological processes can result in mental disorders. Much as the biological perspective had replaced superstition with organic pathology as the suspected cause of mental disorders, the psychoanalytic perspective replaced brain pathology with intrapsychic conflict and exaggerated ego defenses as the suspected cause of at least some mental disorders.

Freud greatly advanced our understanding of both normal and abnormal behavior. Many of his original concepts have become fundamental to our thinking about human nature and behavior, including his emphasis on the role of unconscious motives and defense mechanisms, the importance of early childhood experiences in later personality adjustment and maladjustment, and the importance of sexual factors in human behavior and mental disorders. He also demonstrated that certain abnormal mental phenomena occur in attempts to cope with difficult problems and are simply exaggerations of normal ego-defense mechanisms. This realization that the same psychological principles apply to both normal and abnormal behavior dissipated much of the mystery and fear surrounding mental disorders.

Freud's psychoanalytic perspective has come under attack, however, for failing to recognize sufficiently the scientific limits of personal reports of experience as the primary mode of obtaining information and for a lack of scientific evidence to support many of its explanatory assumptions or the effectiveness of traditional psychoanalysis. In addition, Freudian theory has been criticized for an overemphasis on the sex drive, for a demeaning view of women, for pessimism about basic human nature, for exaggerating the role of unconscious processes, and for failing to consider motives toward personal growth and fulfillment.

The second generation of psychodynamic theorists has done much to improve the scientific efforts to measure concepts such as a person's core (yet unconscious) conflictual relationships. Progress has also been made in understanding the process of how psychodynamic therapy works and in documenting its effectiveness for certain problems (e.g., Crits-Christoph, 1992; Henry et al., 1994). For interpersonal psychotherapy especially, major progress has been made in determining ways to assess reliably interpersonal functioning (Benjamin, 1982, 1993), as well as in determining which aspects of the therapeutic process are important for successful outcomes (e.g., Henry & Strupp, 1994; Koss & Shiang, 1994). A number of important studies have documented its effectiveness in the treatment of disorders such as depression and bulimia, an eating disorder discussed in Chapter 8 (e.g., Fairburn et al., 1993; Klerman et al., 1994). In addition, Bowlby's attachment theory has generated an enormous amount of research supporting many of its basic tenets about normal and abnormal child development and adult psychopathology (e.g., Carlson & Sroufe, 1995).

The Behavioral Perspective

The behavioral perspective arose in the early twentieth century in part as a reaction against the unscientific methods of psychoanalysis. Behavioral psychologists believed that the study of subjective experience—through the techniques of free association and dream analysis—did not provide acceptable scientific data, because such observations were not open to verification by other investigators. In their view, only the study of directly observable behavior and of the stimuli and reinforcing conditions that control it could serve as a basis for understanding human behavior, normal or abnormal.

Although this perspective was initially developed through research in the laboratory rather than through clinical practice with disturbed patients, its implications for explaining and treating maladaptive behavior soon became evident. As discussed in Chapter 1, the roots of the behavioral perspective came from Ivan Pavlov's study of classical conditioning and from Edward Thorndike's study of instrumental conditioning (later renamed operant conditioning by B. F. Skinner). In the United States, John Watson did much to promote the behavioral approach to psychology with his book *Behaviorism* (1924).

Learning—the modification of behavior as a consequence of experience—provides the central theme of the behavioral approach. Because most human behavior is learned, the behaviorists addressed themselves to the question of how learning occurs. They focused on the effects of environmental conditions (stimuli) on the acquisition, modification, and possible elimination of various types of response patterns—both adaptive and maladaptive.

Classical Conditioning

A specific stimulus may come to elicit a specific response through the process of **classical conditioning.** For example, although food naturally elicits salivation, a stimulus that reliably precedes the presentation of food will also come to elicit salivation. In this case, food is the *unconditioned stimulus* (UCS), and salivation is the *unconditioned response* (UCR). A stimulus that precedes food delivery and eventually elicits salivation is called a *conditioned stimulus* (CS). Conditioning has occurred when presentation of the conditioned stimulus alone elicits salivation—now the *conditioned response* (CR). Pavlov, for instance, sounded a bell (the soon-to-be conditioned stimulus) just before he presented food (the unconditioned stimulus) to his dogs (Pavlov, 1927). After a number of bell-food pairings, the dogs salivated (the conditioned response) to the bell (the conditioned stimulus) alone. The dogs learned that the bell was a reliable predictor of food delivery and came to respond to it in a similar fashion.

The hallmark of classical conditioning is that a formerly neutral stimulus—the CS—acquires the capacity to elicit biologically adaptive responses through repeated pairings with the UCS. However, we also now know that this process of classical conditioning is not as blind or automatic as was once thought. Rather, it seems that animals (and people) actively acquire information about which CSs allow them to predict, expect, or prepare for a biologically significant event (the UCS). Indeed, only those CSs that provide reliable and nonredundant information about the occurrence of a UCS will acquire the capacity to elicit CRs (Hall, 1994; Rescorla, 1988). For example, if UCSs occur as often without being preceded by a CS as they do with one, conditioning will not occur; in such a case, the CS does not provide reliable information about the occurrence of the UCS. Figure 2.5 (on the next page) illustrates this process.

classical conditioning A basic learning process in which a neutral stimulus is paired repeatedly with an unconditioned stimulus (US) that naturally elicits an unconditioned response (UR); after repeated pairings, the neutral stimulus becomes a conditioned stimulus (CS) that elicits a conditioned response (CR).

FIGURE 2.5
CLASSICAL CONDITIONING
Before conditioning, the CS has no capacity to elicit fear, but after being repeatedly followed by a painful UCS that elicits fear, the CS gradually acquires the capacity to elicit fear as a CR. If there are also interspersed trials in which the UCS occurs but is not preceded by the CS, conditioning does not occur because in this case the CS does not have good predictive power about the occurrence of the UCS.

Classical Conditioning

Prior to conditioning:
Conditioned stimulus (neutral) (CS) ....Orientation response to light
(Light)
Unconditioned stimulus (UCS).......................Unconditioned response (UCR)
(Painful stimulus) (Pain and fear)

During conditioning:
Conditioned stimulus (light) (CS)
\+ ....Conditioned response (fear) (CR)
Unconditioned stimulus (UCS)
(painful stimulus)

Following conditioning:
Conditioned stimulus (alone) (CS) ....Conditioned response (fear) (CR)

Classically conditioned responses are well maintained over time; that is, they are not simply forgotten. However, if a CS is repeatedly presented without the UCS, the CR will gradually extinguish. This process, known as **extinction,** should not be confused with unlearning because the learned response may return at some future point in time (a phenomenon Pavlov called **spontaneous recovery**). Moreover, a somewhat weaker CR may also still be elicited in different environmental contexts than that in which the extinction process took place (Bouton, 1994; Bouton & Nelson, 1997). Thus, any extinction of fear that has taken place in a therapist's office may not necessarily generalize completely and automatically to other contexts outside the therapist's office. As we will see, these principles of extinction and spontaneous recovery have important implications for many forms of behavioral treatment.

The chief importance of classical conditioning in abnormal psychology is the fact that many physiological and emotional responses can be conditioned, including those relating to fear, anxiety, and sexual arousal, as well as those stimulated by drugs of abuse. Thus, for example, one can learn a fear of the dark if fear-producing stimuli (such as frightening dreams or fantasies) occur regularly during conditions of darkness, or one can acquire a fear of snakes if bitten by a snake.

extinction Gradual disappearance of a conditioned response that is no longer being reinforced.

spontaneous recovery The return of a learned response at some time after extinction has occurred.

instrumental (operant) conditioning Learning of a response through reinforcement of the response, either by receiving something that is rewarding or by escaping from something that is unpleasant.

reinforcement The delivery of a reward or pleasant stimulus or the escape from an aversive stimulus.

Instrumental Conditioning In **instrumental** (or **operant**) **conditioning,** an individual learns how to achieve a desired goal. The goal in question may be to obtain something that is rewarding or to escape from something that is unpleasant. Essential here is the concept of **reinforcement,** which refers to the delivery of a reward or a pleasant stimulus, or to the escape from an aversive stimulus. New responses are learned and tend to recur if they are reinforced. Although it was originally thought that instrumental conditioning, like classical conditioning, consisted of simple strengthening of a stimulus-response connection, it is now believed that the person learns a response-outcome expectancy (Mackintosh, 1983), and if sufficiently motivated for that outcome (e.g., being hungry), the person will make the response (e.g., opening the refrigerator) that he or she has learned produces the outcome (e.g., finding something to eat).

Initially a high rate of reinforcement may be necessary to establish an instrumental response, but lesser rates are usually sufficient to maintain it. In fact, an instrumental response appears to be especially persistent when reinforcement is intermittent—when the reinforcing stimulus does not invariably follow the response—as demonstrated by gambling, where occasional wins seem to maintain high rates of response. However, when reinforcement is consistently withheld over time, the conditioned response—whether classical or instrumental—gradually extinguishes. In short, the subject eventually stops making the response.

A special problem arises in extinguishing a response in a case in which a subject has been conditioned to anticipate an aversive event and to make an instrumental response to avoid it. For example, a boy who has nearly drowned in a swimming pool may develop a fear of water and a *conditioned avoidance response* in which he consistently avoids all large bodies of water. When he sees a pond, lake, or swimming pool, he feels anxious; running away and avoiding contact lessens his anxiety and is thus reinforcing. As a result, his avoidance response is highly resistant to extinction. It also prevents him from having experiences with water that could bring about extinction of his fear. In later discussions, we will see that conditioned avoidance responses play a role in many patterns of abnormal behavior.

As we grow up, instrumental learning becomes an important mechanism for discriminating between what will prove rewarding and what will prove unrewarding—and thus for acquiring the behaviors essential for coping with our world. Unfortunately, there is no guarantee that what we learn will always be useful. We may learn to value things that seem attractive in the short run, such as cigarettes or alcohol, but that can actually hurt us in the long run, or we may learn coping patterns such as helplessness, bullying, or other irresponsible behaviors that are maladaptive rather than adaptive in the long run.

Generalization and Discrimination In both classical and instrumental conditioning, when a response is conditioned to one stimulus or set of stimulus conditions, it can be evoked by other, similar stimuli; this process is called **generalization.** A person who fears bees, for example, may generalize that fear to all flying insects. A process complementary to generalization is **discrimination,** which occurs when a person learns to distinguish between similar stimuli and to respond differently to them based on which ones are followed by reinforcement. According to the behavioral perspective, complex processes like perceiving, forming concepts, and solving problems are all based on this basic discriminative learning process.

The concepts of generalization and discrimination have many implications for the development of maladaptive behavior. Although generalization enables us to use past experiences in sizing up new situations, the possibility always exists of making inappropriate generalizations—as when a troubled adolescent fails to discriminate between friendly and hostile "joshing" from peers. In some instances, a vital discrimination seems to be beyond an individual's capability—as when a bigoted person deals with others as stereotypes rather than as individuals—and may lead to inappropriate and maladaptive behavior.

Observational Learning Human and nonhuman primates are also capable of learning through observation alone—that is, without directly experiencing an unconditioned stimulus (for classical conditioning) or a reinforcement (for operant conditioning). For example, as we will see in Chapter 5, children can acquire fears simply through observing a parent or peer behaving fearfully with some object or situation that the child was not initially afraid of. In this case, the fear of the parent or peer is experienced vicariously and becomes attached to the formerly neutral object (Mineka & Cook, 1993). With respect to observational operant learning, Bandura did a classic series of experiments in the 1960s on how children will observationally learn various novel aggressive responses toward a large Bobo doll after they have observed models being reinforced for these responses (Bandura, 1969). Although the children themselves were never directly reinforced for showing these novel aggressive responses, they nonetheless showed them when given the opportunity to interact with the Bobo doll themselves. The possibilities for observational conditioning of both classical and operant responses greatly expand our opportunities for learning both adaptive and maladaptive behavior.

Impact of the Behavioral Perspective By means of relatively few basic concepts, behaviorism attempts to explain the acquisition, modification, and extinction of nearly all types of behavior. Maladaptive behavior is viewed as essentially the result of (1) a failure to learn necessary adaptive behaviors or competencies, such as how to establish satisfying personal relationships; or (2) the learning of ineffective or maladaptive responses. Maladaptive behavior is thus the result of learning that has gone awry and is defined in terms of specific, observable, undesirable responses.

The behavioral approach has been heralded for its precision and objectivity, for its wealth of research, and for its demonstrated effectiveness in alleviating certain disorders. A behavior therapist specifies what behaviors are to be changed and how they are to be changed—for example, eliminating undesirable reactions such as those that occur in phobias or learning desirable behaviors such as better social skills. Later, the effectiveness of the therapy can be evaluated objectively by the degree to which the stated goals have been achieved. On the other hand, the behav-

generalization Process by which a response that has been conditioned to one stimulus can be elicited by other, similar stimuli.

discrimination Process by which an individual learns to distinguish between and respond differently to two or more similar stimuli.

ioral perspective has been criticized for being concerned only with symptoms. However, this criticism is considered unfair by many contemporary behavior therapists given that successful symptom-focused treatment often ends up having very positive effects on other aspects of a person's life (e.g., Borkovec, Abel, & Newman, 1995; Telch et al., 1995). The behavioral perspective has also been criticized for ignoring other issues that may be important for those seeking help, such as searching for a sense of self-direction or meaning in life. Yet others have argued that it oversimplifies human behavior and cannot explain all of its complexities. This latter criticism, however, stems at least in part from misunderstandings about the complexities of current developments in behavioral approaches, which will be discussed in Chapter 5 (e.g., Mineka & Zinbarg, 1996). Whatever its limitations, the behavioral perspective has had and continues to have a tremendous impact on contemporary views of human nature, behavior, and psychopathology.

The Cognitive-Behavioral Perspective

Since the 1950s psychologists, including some learning theorists, have focused on cognitive processes and their impact on behavior. Cognitive psychology involves the study of basic information-processing mechanisms, such as attention and memory, as well as higher mental processes, such as thinking, planning, and decision making. The current emphasis within psychology as a whole on understanding all of these facets of normal human cognition originally began as a reaction against the relatively mechanistic nature of the traditional radical behavioral viewpoint, including its failure to attend to the importance of mental processes—both in their own right and for their influence on emotions and behavior.

Albert Bandura (b. 1925), a learning theorist who developed a cognitive-behavioral perspective, placed considerable emphasis on the cognitive aspects of learning. Bandura stressed that human beings regulate their behavior by internal symbolic processes—thoughts. That is, they learn by *internal reinforcement.* We prepare ourselves for difficult tasks, for example, by visualizing what the consequences would be if we did not perform them. Thus, we take our automobiles to the garage in the fall and have the antifreeze checked because we can "see" ourselves stranded on a road in winter. We do not always require external reinforcement to alter our behavior patterns; our cognitive abilities allow us to solve many problems internally. Bandura (1974) went so far as to say that human beings have "a capacity for self-direction" (p. 861). Bandura later developed a theory of self-efficacy—the belief that one can achieve desired goals (1977a, 1986). He posited that cognitive-behavioral treatments work in large part by improving self-efficacy.

Albert Bandura (b. 1925) stressed that people learn more by internal than external reinforcement. They can visualize the consequences of their actions rather than rely exclusively on environmental reinforcements.

cognitive-behavioral perspective A theory of abnormal behavior that focuses on how thoughts and information processing can become distorted and lead to maladaptive emotions and behavior.

More generally, the **cognitive-behavioral perspective** on abnormal behavior focuses on how thoughts and information processing can become distorted and lead to maladaptive emotions and behavior. Unlike behaviorism, with its focus on overt behavior, the cognitive view treats thoughts as "behaviors" that can be studied empirically and that can become the focus of attention in therapy. For example, a woman who is depressed and is asked to express the thoughts running through her head might respond with "I can never do anything right" or "No one will ever love me."

In addition, by studying the patterns of distorted information processing exhibited by people with various forms of psychopathology, investigators have illuminated the mechanisms that may be involved in the maintenance of certain disorders. For example, depressed individuals show memory biases favoring memories for negative information relative to those for positive or neutral information. Such biases are likely to help reinforce or maintain one's current depressed state (e.g., Mathews & MacLeod, 1994; Mineka & Zinbarg, 1998).

Attributions, Attributional Style, and Psychopathology *Attribution theory* has also contributed significantly to the cognitive-behavioral approach (Anderson, Krull, & Weiner, 1996; Fiske & Taylor, 1991; Heider, 1958). **Attribution** simply refers to the process of assigning causes to things that happen. We may attribute causes to external events, such as rewards or punishments ("He did it for the money"), or we may assume that the causes are internal—that they derive from traits within ourselves or others ("He did it because he enjoys it").

Attribution theorists have been interested in whether different forms of psychopathology are associated with *dysfunctional attributional styles,* characteristic ways that an individual may tend to make attributions for bad events or for good events. For example, depressed people tend to attribute bad events to internal, stable, and global causes ("I failed the test because I'm stupid" as opposed to "I failed the test because the teacher was in a bad mood and graded it unfairly"). However inaccurate our attributions may be, they become important parts of our view of the world and can have significant effects on our emotional well-being. They can also make us see other people and ourselves as unchanging and unchangeable, leading us to be inflexible in our relationships (Abramson, Seligman, & Teasdale, 1978; Buchanan & Seligman, 1995).

Cognitive Therapy Another pioneering cognitive theorist, Aaron Beck (b. 1921), adapted the concept of schemas from cognitive psychology (e.g., Neisser, 1967, 1982). A **schema** is an underlying representation of knowledge that guides current processing of information and often leads to distortions in attention, memory, and comprehension. According to Beck (1967; Beck & Emery, 1985; Beck, Freeman, et al., 1990), different forms of psychopathology are characterized by different maladaptive schemas that have developed as a function of adverse early learning experiences. They lead to the distortions in thinking characteristic of certain disorders such as anxiety, depression, and personality disorders.

Fundamental to Beck's perspective is the idea that the way we interpret events and experiences determines our emotional reactions to them. Suppose, for example, that you are sitting in your living room and hear a crash in the adjacent dining room. You remember that you left the window open in that room, and you conclude that a gust of wind must have knocked over your favorite vase that was sitting on the table. What would your emotional reaction be? Probably you would be annoyed or angry with yourself for having either left the window open or left the vase out (or both!). But suppose, on the other hand, you conclude that a burglar must have climbed in the open window. What would your emotional reaction be then? In all likelihood, you would feel frightened. Thus, your interpretation of the same event (hearing a crash in the next room) determines your emotional reaction to it.

Aaron Beck (b. 1921) pioneered the development of cognitive theories of depression, anxiety, and personality disorders. He also developed highly effective cognitive-behavioral treatments for these disorders.

Beck, generally considered the founder of cognitive therapy, has had the greatest impact on the development of cognitive-behavioral treatment approaches to various forms of psychopathology. Following Beck's lead, cognitive-behavioral theoreticians and clinicians have simply shifted their focus from overt behavior itself to the underlying cognitions assumed to be producing that behavior. The issue then becomes one of altering the maladaptive cognitions, including the underlying maladaptive schemas. For example, cognitive-behavioral clinicians are concerned with their clients' self-statements—with what the clients say to themselves by way of interpreting their experiences. People who interpret what happens in their lives as a negative reflection of their self-worth are likely to feel depressed; people who interpret a sensation that their heart is racing as meaning they may have a heart attack and may die are likely to have a panic attack. Cognitive-behavioral clinicians use a variety of techniques designed to alter whatever negative cognitive biases the client harbors (e.g., see Beck, Hollon, et al., 1985; Hollon & Beck, 1994).

attribution Process of assigning causes to things that happen.

schema An underlying representation of knowledge that guides current processing of information and often leads to distortions in attention, memory, and comprehension.

Some interpret terrifying scenes in a horror movie and the sensations of their heart pounding as a sign of excitement and having a good time; others interpret the same scenes and sensations as if something dangerous and scary is *really* happening. Cognitive-behavioral psychologists emphasize that the way we interpret an event can dramatically color our emotional reactions to it.

The Impact of the Cognitive-Behavioral Perspective

Today, the cognitive-behavioral perspective is highly influential, both because of the successes it has had in developing effective treatments for many disorders and because of the insights it has provided into the importance of distorted cognitions in understanding abnormal behavior. Many researchers and clinicians have found support for the principle of altering human behavior through changing the way people think about themselves and others. Many traditional behaviorists, however, remained skeptical of the cognitive-behavioral viewpoint (e.g., Wolpe, 1988, 1993). B. F. Skinner (1990), in his last major address, remained true to behaviorism. He questioned the move away from principles of operant conditioning and toward cognitive behaviorism. He reminded his audience that cognitions are not observable phenomena and, as such, cannot be relied on as solid empirical data. Although Skinner is gone, this debate will surely continue.

What the Adoption of a Perspective Does and Does Not Do

Each of the psychosocial perspectives on human behavior—psychodynamic, behavioral, and cognitive-behavioral—has and will continue to contribute to our understanding of psychopathology. Yet each perspective depends on generalizations from limited observations and research. Therefore, it is important to emphasize that adopting one perspective or another has important consequences: It influences our *perception* of maladaptive behavior, the *types of evidence* we look for, and *the way in which we are likely to interpret data*. For example, in attempting to explain a complex disorder such as alcoholism, the more traditional psychodynamic viewpoint focuses on intrapsychic conflict and anxiety that the person attempts to reduce through the intake of alcohol; the more recent interpersonal variant on the psychodynamic perspective focuses on difficulties in a person's past and present relationships that contribute to drinking; the behavioral viewpoint focuses on faulty learning of habits to reduce stress (drinking alcohol) and environmental conditions that may be exacerbating or maintaining the condition; and the cognitive-behavioral viewpoint focuses on maladaptive thinking, including deficits in problem solving and information processing such as irrational beliefs about the need for alcohol to reduce stress.

In the next section, we will discuss a range of psychosocial causal factors that have been implicated in the origins of maladaptive behavior. We will also illustrate how some of these different viewpoints provide contrasting (or sometimes complementary) explanations for how the causal factors exert their effects. In later chapters, we will discuss relevant concepts from all these viewpoints as they relate to different forms of psychopathology, and in many instances, we will contrast different ways of explaining and treating the same disorder.

IN REVIEW

- Describe the interaction of the id, ego, and superego in Freud's theory of personality, and explain how anxiety is implicated in abnormal behavior.
- Contrast the newer psychodynamic approaches—ego psychology, object-relations theory, and the interpersonal perspective—with the earlier Freudian perspective. *(continued)*

- What is the central theme of the behavioral perspective?
- How do classical and instrumental conditioning, generalization and discrimination, and observational learning contribute to the origins of abnormal behavior?
- What is the focus of the cognitive-behavioral perspective?
- What are the roles of attributions and schemas according to the cognitive-behavioral perspective?

PSYCHOSOCIAL CAUSAL FACTORS

We begin life with few built-in patterns and a great capacity to learn from experience. What we do learn from our experiences may help us face challenges resourcefully and lead to resilience in the face of future stressors. Unfortunately, some of our experiences may be much less helpful in later life, and we may be deeply influenced by factors in early childhood over which we have no control. *Psychosocial causal factors* are those developmental influences that may handicap a person psychologically, making him or her less resourceful in coping with events.

In this section, we will examine the psychosocial factors that make people vulnerable to disorders or that may precipitate disorders. After briefly examining the central role played by our perceptions of ourselves and our world, which derive from our schemas and self-schemas, we will review specific influences that may distort the cognitive structures on which good psychological functioning depends. We will focus on four categories of psychosocial causal factors that exemplify those that have been studied: (1) early deprivation or trauma, (2) inadequate parenting styles, (3) marital discord and divorce, and (4) maladaptive peer relationships. Such psychosocial factors typically do not operate alone. They interact with one another, with particular genetic and constitutional factors, and with particular settings or environments.

Our Views of the World and of Ourselves: Schemas and Self-Schemas

Each of the different viewpoints uses somewhat different terminology to describe the nature of the basic assumptions we make about ourselves and our worlds. However, for the sake of simplicity and because it is perhaps the dominant research-oriented approach today, we will use terminology from the cognitive-behavioral perspective to describe these assumptions that make up our frames of reference—our *schemas* about other people and the world around us, and our *self-schemas,* or ideas that we have about our own attributes. Because what we can learn or perceive directly through our senses can provide only an approximate representation of "reality," we need cognitive frameworks to fill in the gaps and make sense out of what we can observe and experience.

As already noted, a *schema* is an organized representation of prior knowledge about a concept or about some stimulus that helps guide the processing of current information (Alloy & Tabachnick, 1984; Fiske & Taylor, 1991). Our schemas about the world around us and about ourselves are our guides, one might say, through the complexities of living in the world as we understand it. We all have schemas about other people (for example, expectations that they are lazy or ambitious, or that they are very career-oriented or very marriage-minded), as well as schemas about social roles (for example, expectations about what constitute appropriate behaviors for a widow) and about events (for example, what comprise appropriate sequences of events for particular situations, such as coping with a loss) (Fiske & Taylor, 1991).

Our self-schemas—our frames of reference for what we are, what we might become, and what is important to us—influence our choice of goals and our confidence in being able to attain them. A key element of this older woman's self-schema was that she could accomplish her lifelong goal of obtaining a college education once her children were grown in spite of the fact that she was nearly 40 years older than the average college student.

Our **self-schemas** include our views on what we are, what we might become, and what is important to us, as well as our notions of the various roles we occupy or might occupy in our social environment, such as woman, man, student, parent, physician, American, older person, and so on. The various aspects of a person's self-schema also can be construed as his or her *self-identity*.

Why Schemas Are So Important Schemas about the world and self-schemas are vital to our ability to engage in effective and organized behavior. They guide and streamline our processing of information, allowing us to focus on what is most relevant and important. However, they are also sources of psychological vulnerabilities because some of our schemas or certain aspects of our self-schemas may be distorted and inaccurate. In addition, some schemas—even distorted ones—are held with conviction, making them resistant to change. This occurs in part because we are usually not completely conscious of our schemas. In other words, although our daily decisions and behavior are largely shaped by these frames of reference, we may be unaware of the assumptions on which they are based—or even of having made assumptions at all. We think that we are simply seeing things the way they are and often do not consider the fact that other pictures of the "real" world might be possible or that other rules for "right" might exist.

New experiences tend to be worked into our existing cognitive frameworks, or schemas, even if the new information has to be reinterpreted or distorted to make it fit—a process known as **assimilation.** We tend to cling to existing assumptions and reject or change new information that contradicts them. **Accommodation**—changing existing cognitive frameworks to make it possible to incorporate discrepant information—is a more difficult and threatening process, especially when important assumptions are challenged. Accommodation is, of course, a basic goal of psychosocial therapies—an explicit one in the case of the cognitive and cognitive-behavioral variants, but one that is deeply embedded in virtually all other approaches as well. The fact that accommodation is such a difficult process often makes major therapeutic change hard to accomplish.

self-schemas Our views of what we are, what we might become, and what is important to us.

assimilation Process of working new experiences into existing cognitive frameworks (schemas) even if the new information has to be reinterpreted or distorted to make it fit.

accommodation Process of changing existing cognitive frameworks to make possible the incorporation of discrepant information.

Because of differences in temperament, abilities, and experiences, children differ enormously in what kinds of schemas they develop, in what kinds of ways they learn to categorize their experiences, in what kinds of competencies, values, and goals they have, and in how they learn to deal with their impulses and regulate their behavior (e.g., Mischel, 1990, 1993). These learned variations make some children far better prepared than others for further learning and personal growth.

Predictability and Controllability A good example of how the events making up one child's experiences may be vastly different from those of another is whether the events are *predictable* or *controllable*. At one extreme are children who grow up in stable and lovingly indulgent environments, buffered to a large extent from the harsher realities of the world; at the other extreme are children whose experiences consist of constant exposure to unpredictable and uncontrollable frightening events or even unspeakable cruelties. Such different childhood experiences have corresponding effects on adult schemas about the world and about the self: Those at the one extreme suggest a world that is uniformly loving, unthreatening and benign, which of course it is not; those at the other evoke a jungle in which safety and perhaps even life itself are constantly in the balance. Given a preference in terms of likely outcomes, most of us would opt for the former of these sets of experiences. However, these actually may not be the best blueprint for engaging the real world, because it may be important to encounter some stressors and learn ways to deal with them in order to gain a sense of control (Seligman, 1975) or self-efficacy (Bandura, 1977a, 1986).

Exposure to multiple uncontrollable and unpredictable frightening events is likely to leave a person vulnerable to *anxiety*, a central problem in a number of the mental disorders to be discussed in this book (e.g., Barlow, 1988; Mineka, 1985a; Mineka & Zinbarg, 1996, 1998). A clinically anxious person is someone whose schemas include strong possibilities that terrible things over which he or she has no control may happen unpredictably, and that the world is a dangerous place. If the uncontrollable experiences of a child are highly traumatic (as in repeated physical or sexual abuse), he or she may not even develop a coherent self-schema. A fragmented self-schema, whatever its origin—and it is frequently traumatic—invites the development of abnormal behaviors. On this the psychosocial viewpoints all concur; they differ primarily in the mechanisms through which they hypothesize these abnormal behaviors develop.

Early Deprivation or Trauma

Experiences of early deprivation or trauma may leave children with deep and sometimes irreversible psychic scars. The deprivation of needed resources normally supplied by parents or parental surrogates is one such circumstance. The needed resources range from food and shelter to love and attention.

We can interpret the consequences of parental deprivation according to the various psychosocial viewpoints discussed earlier: Such deprivation might result in fixation at the oral stage of psychosexual development (Freud); it might interfere with the development of basic trust (Erikson); it might stunt the development of the child's capacity for relatively anxiety-free exchanges of tenderness and intimacy with others (Sullivan); it might retard the attainment of needed skills because of a lack of available reinforcements (Skinner); or it might result in the child's acquiring dysfunctional schemas and self-schemas in which relationships are represented as unstable, untrustworthy, and without affection (Beck). Any of these viewpoints might be the best way of conceptualizing the problems that arise in a particular case, or some combination of them might be superior to any single one.

Institutionalization In some cases, infants and young children are raised in an institution, where, compared with an ordinary home, there is likely to be less warmth and physical contact; less intellectual, emotional, and social stimulation; and a lack of encouragement and help in positive learning. The long-range prognosis for children suffering early and prolonged parental deprivation through institutionalization is considered unfavorable (e.g., Quinton & Rutter, 1988; Rutter, 1990). Many show maladaptive personality development and are at risk for psychopathology. Institutionalization later in childhood of a child who has already had good attachment experiences is not so damaging (Rutter, 1987a, 1987b). However, even among those institutionalized at an early age, some show resilience and do well in adulthood. One important protective factor found to influence this outcome is whether the child went from the institution into a harmonious family or a discordant one, with better outcomes occurring among those who entered harmonious homes (Rutter, 1990). Other influential protective factors include having some good experiences at school, whether in the form of social relationships or athletic or academic successes, and having a supportive marital partner in adulthood; these successes probably contribute to a better sense of self-esteem or self-efficacy (Quinton & Rutter, 1988; Rutter, 1985, 1990).

In February 1994, during a drug raid, Chicago police discovered 19 children in this freezing, squalid cockroach-infested apartment. The stove in the kitchen did not work, and children were found sharing food with dogs off the floor. The six adults in the apartment were charged with child neglect, and child abuse charges were also considered. Growing up in such a setting may predispose children to later psychological problems.

Deprivation and Abuse in the Home Most infants subjected to parental deprivation are not separated from their parents, but rather suffer from inadequate care at home. In these situations, parents typically neglect or devote little attention to their children and are generally rejecting. In a minority of cases, it also involves cruel and abusive treatment. In the United States, approximately 2 million reports of abuse and neglect are made annually, and over half are found to be accurate (Cicchetti & Toth, 1995a).

The effects of deprivation and rejection may be very serious. For example, Bullard and his colleagues (1967) delineated a "failure to thrive" syndrome that "is a serious disorder of growth and development [that] significantly compromises the health and sometimes endangers the life of the child" (p. 689). The problem is fairly common in low-income families, with estimates at about 6 percent of children born at medical centers serving low-income families (Lozoff, 1989). Such children are thought to be at risk for behavior problems and delays in development (Sameroff, 1995). The syndrome may sometimes occur in a child who has become severely depressed (Attie & Brooks-Gunn, 1995), and it may sometimes occur in children whose parents find them oppositional or "bad" and have difficulty feeding them (Sameroff, 1995). However, it is also now clear that this syndrome often has prenatal origins; a disproportionate number of children diagnosed with it had low birth weights (Lozoff, 1989).

Outright parental abuse (physical or sexual or both) of children has also been associated with many other negative effects on development, although some studies have suggested that, at least among infants, gross neglect may be worse than having an abusive relationship. Abused children often have a tendency to be overly aggressive (both verbally and physically), have difficulties in linguistic development, and have significant problems in emotional and social functioning, including depression and anxiety and impaired relationships with peers, who tend to avoid or reject them (e.g., Cicchetti & Toth, 1995a, 1995b; Emery & Laumann-Billings, 1998).

Abused and maltreated infants and toddlers are also likely to develop atypical patterns of attachment—most often a disorganized and disoriented style of attachment, characterized by bizarre, disorganized, and inconsistent behavior with the caregiver (Bowlby, 1969, 1973, 1980; Cicchetti & Toth, 1995a; Crittenden & Ainsworth, 1989). A significant portion of these children will continue to show "confused" patterns of relating to their mother up to at least age 13. The enduring effects of physical abuse are supported by reviews that concluded that childhood physical abuse predicts both familial and nonfamilial violence in adolescence and adulthood, especially in abused males (Cicchetti & Toth, 1995a; Emery & Laumann-Billings, 1998; Malinosky-Rummell & Hansen, 1993). Physical abuse was also found to be associated with self-injurious and suicidal behaviors, as well as anxiety, depression, personality disorders, lower IQ and reading ability, and physiological disturbances (Cicchetti & Toth, 1995a).

A significant proportion of parents who reject or abuse their children have themselves been the victims of parental rejection or abuse. Their early history of rejection or abuse clearly had damaging effects on their schemas and self-schemas, and probably resulted in a failure to internalize good models of parenting. Kaufman and Zigler (1989) estimated that there is about a 30 percent chance of this pattern of intergenerational transmission of abuse (see also Cicchetti & Toth, 1995a).

Nevertheless, maltreated children—whether the maltreatment comes from abuse or from deprivation—can improve to at least some extent when the caregiving environment improves (Cicchetti & Toth, 1995a; Emery & Laumann-Billings, 1998). Moreover, there is always a range of effects, and those who did not show the negative outcomes tended to have one or more protective factors, such as a good relationship with some adult during childhood, a higher IQ, positive school experiences, or physical attractiveness, among others.

Other Childhood Traumas Most of us have had one-time traumatic experiences that temporarily shattered our feelings of security, adequacy, and worth and influenced our perceptions of ourselves and our environment. The term *psychic trauma* is used to describe any aversive (unpleasant) experience that has harmful psychological effects on an individual. The following illustrates such an incident:

Case Study An Adopted Child • I believe the most traumatic experience of my entire life happened one April evening when I was 11. I was not too sure of how I had become a member of the family, although my parents had thought it wise to tell me that I was adopted. That much I knew, but what the term "adopted" meant was something else entirely. One evening after my step-brother and I had retired, he proceeded to explain it to me—with a vehemence I shall never forget. He made it clear that I wasn't a "real" member of the family, that my parents didn't "really" love me, and that I wasn't even wanted around the place. That was one night I vividly recall crying myself to sleep. That experience undoubtedly played a major role in making me feel insecure and inferior.

Traumas of this sort are apt to leave psychological wounds that may never completely heal. As a result, later stress that reactivates these wounds may be particularly difficult for an individual to handle; this often explains why one person has difficulty with a problem that is not especially stressful to another.

In another example of the effects of early trauma, Bowlby (1960, 1973, 1980) found that children from 2 to 5 years of age who are separated from their parents during prolonged periods of hospitalization not only suffer from short-term or acute effects of the separation, but can also suffer long-term effects of insecure attachment. As adults, they may have increased vulnerability to stressors. However, as with other early traumatic experiences, the long-term effects of separation depend heavily on the support and reassurance given a child by parents or other significant persons, which is most likely if the child has a secure relationship with at least one parent (Carlson & Sroufe, 1995; Lease & Ollendick, 1993; Main & Weston, 1981). Thus, not all children who experience even a parent's death exhibit discernible long-term effects (Brown, Harris, & Bifulco, 1985; Rutter, 1985).

Inadequate Parenting Styles

Even in the absence of severe deprivation, neglect, or trauma, many kinds of deviations in parenting can have profound effects on a child's subsequent ability to cope with life's challenges, and thus create vulnerability to various forms of psychopathology. Therefore, although their explanations vary considerably, the psychosocial viewpoints on abnormal behavior all focus attention on the behavioral tendencies a child acquires in the course of early social interaction with others—chiefly parents or parental surrogates.

You should keep in mind that a parent-child relationship is always bidirectional: As with any continuing relationship, the behavior of each person affects the behavior of the other. Some children are easier to love than others; some parents are more sensitive than others to an infant's needs. For example, Rutter and Quinton (1984b) found that parents tended to react with irritability, hostility, and criticism to children whose temperaments made them prone to negative moods and low on adaptability. These kinds of reactions may set such children at risk for psychopathology because they become "a focus for discord" in the family (Rutter, 1990, p. 191). Because parents find it difficult and stressful to deal with babies who are high on negative emotionality, many of these infants may be more prone to developing avoidant styles of attachment than are infants who are not high on negative emotionality (Rothbart, Posner, & Hershey, 1995).

Parental Psychopathology In general, it has been found that parents who have various forms of psychopathology, including schizophrenia, depression, antisocial personality disorder, and alcoholism, tend to have children who are at greater risk for a wide range of developmental difficulties. Although some of these effects undoubtedly have a genetic component, many researchers believe that genetic effects cannot account for all the adverse effects that parental psychopathology has on children. For example, the children of seriously depressed parents are at enhanced risk for disorder (Cicchetti & Toth, 1995b, 1998; Gotlib & Avison, 1993), at least partly because depression makes for unskillful parenting—notably including inattentiveness to a child's many needs (Gelfand & Teti, 1990) and ineffectiveness in managing and disciplining the child (Cicchetti & Toth, 1995b, 1998). In addition, children of alcoholics have elevated rates of truancy and substance abuse and a greater likelihood of dropping out of school, as well as higher levels of anxiety and depression and lower levels of self-esteem (Chassin, Rogosch, & Barrera, 1991; Gotlib & Avison, 1993), although many children of alcoholics do not have such difficulties.

Again, in spite of the profound effects that parental psychopathology can have on children, it should be noted that many children raised in such families do just fine because of a variety of protective factors that may be present. For example, a child who is living with a parent with a serious disorder but who also has a warm and nurturing relationship with the other parent, or with another adult outside the family, has a significant protective factor. Other important protective factors that promote resilience include having good intellectual skills or social and academic competence and being appealing to adults (Masten & Coatsworth, 1995, 1998).

Parenting Styles: Warmth and Control In the absence of parental psychopathology, there are still differences in parenting styles that can have a significant impact on a child's development and increase the risk of psychopathology. Four types of parenting styles seem to be related to different developmental outcomes for children: (1) authoritative, (2) authoritarian, (3) permissive-indulgent, and (4) neglectful-uninvolved. These styles vary in the degree of *parental warmth* (amount of support, encouragement, and affection versus shame, rejection, and hostility) and in the degree of *parental control* (extent of discipline and monitoring versus being largely unsupervised) (Emery & Kitzmann, 1995; Maccoby & Martin, 1983).

Authoritative Parenting The *authoritative style* is one in which the parents are both very warm and very careful to set clear limits and restrictions regarding certain kinds of behaviors, but also allow considerable freedom within certain limits. This style of parenting is associated with the most positive early social development, with the children tending to be energetic and friendly and showing development of general competencies for dealing with others and with their environments (Baumrind, 1975, 1993; Emery & Kitzmann, 1995). When followed into adolescence in a longitudinal study, children of authoritative parents continued to show positive outcomes.

Authoritarian Parenting Parents with an *authoritarian style* are high on control but low on warmth, and their children tend to be conflicted, irritable, and moody (Baumrind, 1975, 1993). When followed into adolescence, these children had more negative outcomes, with the boys doing particularly poorly in social and cognitive skills. If authoritarian parents also use overly *severe discipline* in the form of physical punishment—as opposed to the withdrawal of approval and privileges—the result tends to be increased aggressive behavior on the part of the child (Emery & Kitzmann, 1995; Eron et al., 1974; Patterson, 1979). Apparently, physical punishment provides a model of aggressive behavior that the child emulates and incorporates into his or her own self-schema (Millon & Davis, 1995).

Permissive-Indulgent Parenting A third parenting style is the *permissive-indulgent style,* in which parents are

This father, who is helping his child with homework, has an authoritative parenting style. He has a warm and supportive relationship with his son, but also sets clear limits and restrictions—for example, about how much homework must be done before his son is allowed to watch TV.

high on warmth but low on discipline and control. This style of parenting is associated with impulsive and aggressive behavior in children (Baumrind, 1967; Hetherington & Parke, 1993; Sears, 1961). Overly indulged children are characteristically spoiled, selfish, inconsiderate, and demanding. Unlike rejected and emotionally deprived children, indulged children enter readily into interpersonal relationships, but they exploit people for their own purposes in the same way that they have learned to exploit their parents (Millon & Davis, 1995). Overly indulged children also tend to be impatient and to approach problems in an aggressive and demanding manner (Baumrind, 1971, 1975). In short, they have self-schemas with significant "entitlement" features. Confusion and difficulties in adjustment may occur when "reality" forces them to reassess their assumptions about themselves and the world.

Neglectful-Uninvolved Parenting Finally, parents who are low on both warmth and control represent the *neglectful-uninvolved style.* This style of parental uninvolvement is associated with disruptions in attachment during childhood (Egeland & Sroufe, 1981), and with moodiness, low self-esteem, and conduct problems later in childhood (Baumrind, 1991; Hetherington & Parke, 1993). The children of uninvolved parents also have problems with peer relations and with academic performance (Hetherington & Parke, 1993).

When examining only the effects of restrictiveness (ignoring the warmth variable), research has shown that restrictiveness can serve as a protective factor for children growing up in high-risk environments, as defined by a combination of family occupation and education level, minority status, and absence of a father (Baldwin, Baldwin, & Cole, 1990). Among high-risk children, those who did well in terms of cognitive outcome (IQ and school achievement) tended to have more restrictive and less democratic parents. Restrictiveness was also particularly helpful in families living in areas with high crime rates.

Inadequate, Irrational, and Angry Communication

Parents sometimes discourage a child from asking questions and in other ways fail to foster the information exchange essential for helping the child develop essential competencies. Inadequate communication may take a number of forms. Some parents are too busy or preoccupied with their own concerns to listen to their children and to try to understand the conflicts and pressures they are facing. As a consequence, these parents often fail to give needed support and assistance, particularly when there is a crisis. Other parents have forgotten that the world often looks different to a child or adolescent—rapid social change can lead to a communication gap between generations. In other instances, faulty communication may take more deviant forms in which messages become completely garbled because a listener distorts, disconfirms, or ignores a speaker's intended meaning. Finally, children are often exposed to high levels of anger and conflict, which can lead to their becoming distressed and emotionally aroused. The anger can occur in the context of marital discord, abuse, or parental psychopathology, and it is often associated with psychological problems in children (Emery & Kitzmann, 1995; Schneider-Rosen & Cicchetti, 1984).

Marital Discord and Divorce

Disturbed parent-child interactions, such as parental rejection, are rarely found in severe form unless the total familial context is also abnormal. Thus, disturbed family structure is an overarching risk factor that increases an individual's vulnerability to particular stressors. We will distinguish between intact families in which there is significant marital discord and families that have been disrupted by divorce or separation.

Marital Discord Whatever the reasons for marital discord, when it is long-standing, it is likely to be frustrating, hurtful, and generally damaging in its effects on both adults and their children (Emery & Kitzmann, 1995). More severe cases of marital discord may expose children to one or more of the stressors we have already discussed: child abuse or neglect, the effects of living with a parent with a serious mental disorder, authoritarian or neglectful-uninvolved parenting, and spouse abuse. Interestingly, one recent study found that children could be buffered against many of the damaging effects of marital conflict if one or both parents had the following characteristics: warmth, proneness to giving praise and approval, and ability to inhibit rejecting behavior toward their children (Katz & Gottman, 1997).

Divorce or Other Separation In many cases, a family is incomplete as a result of divorce, separation, death, or some other circumstance. In the United States, nearly one half of marriages end in divorce and today it is estimated that 50 to 60 percent of children will live at some point in single parent families (Hetherington, Bridges, & Insabella, 1998).

Effects of Divorce on Parents Unhappy marriages are difficult, but ending a marital relationship can also be enormously stressful for the adults, both mentally and physically. Divorced and separated persons are overrepresented among psychiatric patients, although the direction of the causal relationship is not always clear. In their comprehensive review of the effects of divorce on adults, Amato and Keith (1991a) concluded that it is a major source of psychopathology, as well as physical illness, death, suicide, and homicide.

Effects of Divorce on Children Divorce can have traumatic effects on children, too. Feelings of insecurity and rejection may be aggravated by conflicting loyalties and, sometimes, by the spoiling the children receive while staying with one of the parents. Not surprisingly, some children do develop serious maladaptive responses. Temperamentally difficult children are likely to have a more difficult time adjusting than are temperamentally easy children (Hetherington, Stanley-Hagan, & Anderson, 1989). Delinquency and a wide range of other psychological problems are much more frequent among children and adolescents from divorced families than among those from intact families, although it is likely that a contributing factor here is prior or continuing parental strife (Chase-Lansdale, Cherlin, & Kiernan, 1995; Rutter, 1979). Finally, a number of studies have demonstrated that there may well be long-term effects of divorce on adaptive functioning into adulthood; many studies have found that young adults from divorced families have lower educational attainment, lower incomes, lower life-satisfaction, and an increased probability of being on welfare, having children out of wedlock, and having their own marriages end in divorce (Amato & Keith, 1991b; Chase-Lansdale et al., 1995; Hetherington et al., 1998).

Nevertheless, many children adjust quite well to the divorce of their parents. Indeed, a quantitative review of 92 studies on parental divorce and the well-being of children conducted on 13,000 children since the 1950s concluded that the average negative effects of divorce on children are actually quite modest in size (Amato & Keith, 1991a; see also Chase-Lansdale et al., 1995; Hetherington et al., 1998), as are the negative effects that persist into adulthood (Amato & Keith, 1991b). They also found that the effects seem to be decreasing over the past 50 years (particularly since 1970), perhaps because the stigma of divorce is decreasing (Amato & Keith, 1991a, 1991b).

The effects of divorce on children are often more favorable than the effects of remaining in a home torn by marital conflict and dissension (Emery & Kitzmann, 1995; Hetherington et al., 1998). At one time, it was thought that the detrimental effects of divorce might be minimized if a successful remarriage provided an adequate environment for child rearing. Unfortunately, however, on average, children living with a parent and a step-parent are no better off than children living with a single parent, although this is more true for girls than for boys.

Maladaptive Peer Relationships

Another important set of relationships outside the family—those involving age-mates, or peers—usually begins in the preschool years. Children at this age are hardly masters of the fine points of human relationships or diplomacy. Empathy—the appreciation of another's situation, perspective, and feelings—is at best only primitively developed, as can be seen in a child who turns on and rejects a current playmate when a more favored candidate arrives. The child's own immediate satisfaction tends to be the primary goal of any interaction, and there is only an uncertain recognition that cooperation and collaboration may

Juvenile socializing is a risky business in which a child's hard-won prestige in a group is probably perceived as being constantly in jeopardy. Actually, reputation and status in a group tend to be stable, and a child who has been rejected by peers is likely to continue to have problems in peer relationships.

bring even greater benefits. A substantial minority of children seem somehow ill-equipped for the rigors and competition of the school years, most likely by virtue of temperamental factors and psychosocial deficits in the family climate. A significant number of these children withdraw from their peers; a large number of others (especially among males) adopt physically intimidating and aggressive lifestyles. The neighborhood bully and the menacing schoolyard loner are examples.

A child who fails to establish a satisfactory relationship with peers during the developmental years is deprived of a crucial set of background experiences and is at higher-than-average risk for a variety of negative outcomes in adolescence and adulthood (Burks, Dodge, & Price, 1995; Coie & Cillessen, 1993; Kupersmidt, Coie, & Dodge, 1990). Peer social problems in childhood have been linked to later problems with depression, school dropout, and delinquency. Some of these effects may be causal, but peer social problems may also be early markers of disorders that have a heritable component but do not become full-blown until later in adolescence or adulthood. In actuality, what is often going on is that the peer social problems are indeed in part reflecting some heritable diathesis, but in turn are also serving as stressors that make it more likely that the underlying vulnerability will lead to full-blown disorder later on (Parker et al., 1995).

Fortunately, there is another side to this coin. If peer relations have their developmental hazards, they can also be sources of key learning experiences that stand an individual in good stead for years, perhaps for a lifetime. For a resourceful youngster, the give-and-take, the winning and losing, the successes and failures of the school years provide superb training in coming to grips with the real world and with his or her developing self—its capabilities and limitations, its attractive and unattractive qualities. The experience of intimacy with another, with a friend, has its beginning in this period of intense social involvement. If all has gone well in the early years, a child emerges into adolescence with a considerable repertoire of social knowledge and skills—often known as *social competence*. Practice and experience in intimate communication with others makes possible a transition from attraction, infatuation, and mere sexual curiosity to genuine love and commitment. Such resources can be strong protective factors against frustration, demoralization, despair, and mental disorder (Masten & Coatsworth, 1998).

IN REVIEW

- What are four categories of psychosocial causal factors that can contribute to the development of abnormal behavior?
- Why are schemas and self-schemas so important for understanding abnormal behavior and its treatment? How are they related to the processes of assimilation and accommodation?
- How do the variables of parental warmth and parental control vary among the authoritative, authoritarian, permissive-indulgent, and neglectful-uninvolved parenting styles? What kinds of influences do these parenting styles tend to have on children's development?

THE SOCIOCULTURAL VIEWPOINT AND CAUSAL FACTORS

By the beginning of the twentieth century, sociology and anthropology had emerged as independent scientific disciplines and were making rapid strides toward understanding the role of sociocultural factors in human development and behavior. Early sociocultural theorists include such notables as Ruth Benedict, Abram Kardiner, Margaret Mead, and Franz Boas. Their investigations and writings showed that individual personality development reflected the larger society—its institutions, norms, values, and ideas—as well as the immediate family and other groups. Studies also made clear the relationship between sociocultural conditions and mental disorders—between the particular stressors in a society and the types of mental disorders that typically occur in it. Further studies showed that the patterns of both physical and mental disorders in a given society could change over time as sociocultural conditions changed. These discoveries added new dimensions to modern perspectives on abnormal behavior (Westermeyer & Janca, 1997).

Uncovering Sociocultural Causal Factors Through Cross-Cultural Studies

The sociocultural viewpoint is concerned with the impact of the social environment on mental disorder, but the relationships between maladaptive behavior and sociocultural factors such as poverty, discrimination, or illiteracy are complex. It is one thing to observe that a person with a psychological disorder has come from a harsh environment. It is quite another thing, however, to show empirically that the environmental circumstances have a causal relationship to the disorder. Part of the problem relates to the impossibility of conducting controlled experiments. Investigators cannot ethically rear children with similar genetic or biological traits in diverse social or economic environments in order to find out which variables affect development and adjustment.

Nevertheless, individuals raised in different societies and exposed to very different environments have provided "laboratories" of sorts. Epidemiological research, the study of the incidence and distribution of physical and mental disorders in a population, has been able to implicate not only the social conditions and risk factors that are correlated with high incidences of given disorders, but also the groups for whom the risk of pathology is especially high—for example, refugees from other countries (Cohler, Stott, & Musick, 1995; Vega & Rumbaut, 1991). Although it is difficult with sociocultural research to identify true causal factors, the information it provides is a first step toward developing hypotheses about causal processes and formulating prevention and treatment programs.

Universal and Culture-Specific Disorders Research supports the view that many psychological disturbances—in both adults and children—are universal, appearing in most cultures studied (Al-Issa, 1982; Butcher, 1996a; Kleinman, 1988; Verhulst & Achenbach, 1995). For example, although the incidences and symptoms vary, the pattern of behaviors we call schizophrenia (Chapter 12) can be found among almost all peoples, from the most primitive to the most technologically advanced. Recent studies have also shown that certain psychological symptoms, as measured by the Minnesota Multiphasic Personality Inventory (MMPI-2; see Chapter 3), were consistently found among similarly diagnosed clinical groups in many other countries (e.g., Butcher, 1996a).

Culture can influence not only what mental disorders develop, if any, but also *how* they are experienced. Stress is often a precipitant of depression in Western cultures. However, in Taiwan and the People's Republic of China, people who are under stress tend to experience physical problems such as fatigue or weakness.

Nevertheless, sociocultural factors also appear to influence which disorders develop, the forms they take, and their courses. For example, Kleinman (1986, 1988) traced the ways in which Chinese people (in Taiwan and in the People's Republic of China) deal with stress differ from those of Westerners. He found that in Western societies depression was a frequent reaction to individual stress. In China, on the other hand, he noted a relatively low rate of reported depression. Instead, the effects of stress were more typically manifested in physical problems, such as fatigue, weakness, and other complaints. Kleinman and Good (1985) surveyed the experience of depression across cultures. Their data show that important elements of depression in Western societies—for example, the acute sense of guilt typically experienced—do not appear in other cultures. They also point out that the symptoms of depression (or dysphoria), such as sadness, hopelessness, unhappiness, lack of pleasure in the things of the world and in social relationships, have dramatically different meanings in different societies. For Buddhists, seeking

TABLE 2.2 CULTURE-BOUND SYNDROMES

Name of Disorder	Culture	Description
Amok	Malaysia (also observed in Laos, the Philippines, Polynesia, Papua New Guinea, Puerto Rico)	A disorder characterized by sudden, wild outbursts of violent aggression or homicidal behavior in which an afflicted person may kill or injure others. This rage disorder is usually found in males who are rather withdrawn, quiet, brooding, and inoffensive prior to the onset of the disorder. Episodes are often precipitated by a perceived slight or insult. Several stages have been observed: Typically in the first stage the person becomes more withdrawn; then a period of brooding follows in which a loss of reality contact is evident. Ideas of persecution and anger predominate. Finally, a phase of automatism or *Amok* occurs, in which the person jumps up, yells, grabs a knife, and stabs people or objects within reach. Exhaustion and depression usually follow, with amnesia for the rage period.
Koro	Southeast Asia (particularly Malaysia) and China	A fear reaction or anxiety state in which a man fears that his penis will withdraw into his abdomen and he may die. This reaction may appear after sexual overindulgence or excessive masturbation. The anxiety is typically very intense and of sudden onset. The condition is "treated" by having the penis held firmly by the patient or by family members or friends. Often the penis is clamped to a wooden box.
Taijin kyofusho (TKS)	Japan	A relatively common psychiatric disorder in Japan in which an individual develops a fear of offending or hurting other people through being awkward in social situations or because of an imagined physical defect or problem. The excessive concern over how a person presents himself or herself in social situations is the salient problem.
Zar	North Africa and Middle East	A person believes he or she is possessed by a spirit and may experience a dissociative episode during which shouting, laughing, singing, or weeping may occur. The person may also show apathy and withdrawal, not eating or working.

Source: Based on American Psychiatric Association (1994); Chowdhury (1996); Hatta (1996); Kiev (1972); Kirmayer (1991); Kirmayer, Young, & Hayton (1995); Lewis & Ednie (1997); Sheung-Tak (1996); Simons & Hughes (1985).

pleasure from things of the world and social relationships is the basis of all suffering; a willful disengagement is thus the first step on the road to salvation. For Shi'ite Muslims in Iran, grief is a religious experience, associated with recognition of the tragic consequences of living justly in an unjust world; the ability to experience dysphoria fully is thus a marker of depth of personality and understanding. Several examples of abnormal behavior that appear only in certain cultures are presented in Table 2.2.

Culture and Overcontrolled Versus Undercontrolled Behavior Fascinating issues are also raised by recent studies of childhood psychopathology in different cultures. In cultures such as that of Thailand, adults are said to be highly intolerant of *undercontrolled behavior* such as aggression, disobedience, and disrespectful acts by their children. Children are explicitly taught to be polite and deferential and to inhibit any expression of anger. This raises interesting questions about whether childhood problems of undercontrolled behavior would be lower in Thailand than in the United States, where such behavior seems to be tolerated to a greater extent. Conversely, it also raises the question of whether problems of *overcontrolled behavior,* such as shyness, anxiety, and depression, would be overrepresented in Thailand relative to the United States.

Two cross-national studies (Weisz, Suwanlert, et al., 1987, 1993) have confirmed that Thai children and adolescents do indeed have a greater prevalence of overcontrolled problems than do American children. Although there were no differences in the rate of undercontrolled problems between the two countries, there were differences in the kind of undercontrolled behaviors reported. For example, Thai adolescents had higher scores than American adolescents on indirect and subtle forms of undercontrol not involving interpersonal aggression, such as having difficulty concentrating or being cruel to animals; American adolescents, on the other hand, had higher scores than Thai adolescents on undercontrolled behaviors such as fighting, bullying, and disobeying at school (Weisz, Suwanlert, et al., 1993). However, these findings are further complicated by the fact that Thai and American parents differ a good deal in which problems they will bring for treatment. In general, Thai parents seem less likely than American parents to refer their children for psychological treatment (Weisz & Weiss, 1991; Weisz et al., 1997). This may be in part because of their Buddhist belief in the transience of problems and their optimism that their child's behavior will improve. Alternatively, Thai parents may not refer their children with undercontrolled problems for treatment simply because these problems are so unacceptable that they are embarrassed to make them public (Weisz et al., 1997).

Causal Factors Within the Sociocultural Environment

In much the same way that we receive a genetic inheritance that is the end product of millions of years of biological evolution, we also receive a sociocultural inheritance that is the end product of thousands of years of social evolution. Because each group fosters its own cultural patterns by systematically teaching its offspring, all its members tend to be somewhat alike—to conform to certain basic personality types. Children reared among headhunters become headhunters; children reared in societies that do not sanction violence learn to settle their differences in nonviolent ways. The more uniform and thorough the education of the younger members of a group, the more alike they will become. Thus, in a society characterized by a limited and consistent point of view, there are not the wide individual differences typical in a society like ours, where children have contact with diverse, often conflicting, beliefs. Even in our society, however, there are certain core values that most of us consider essential.

Subgroups within a general sociocultural environment—such as family, sex, age, class, occupational, ethnic, and religious groups—foster beliefs and norms of their own, largely by means of social roles that their members learn to adopt. Expected role behaviors exist for a student, a teacher, an army officer, a priest, a nurse, and so on. Because most people are members of various subgroups, they are subject to various role demands, which also change over time. In fact, an individual's life can be viewed as a succession of roles—child, student, worker, spouse, parent, and senior citizen. When social roles are conflicting, unclear, or uncomfortable, or when an individual is unable to achieve a satisfactory role in a group, healthy personality development may be impaired.

The extent to which role expectations can influence development is well illustrated by masculine and feminine roles in our own society and their effects on personality development and on behavior. In recent years, a combination of masculine and feminine traits (androgyny) has often been claimed to be psychologically ideal for both men and women. Many people, however, continue to show evidence of having been strongly affected by traditional assigned masculine and feminine roles. Moreover, there is accumulating evidence that the acceptance of gender-role assignments has substantial implications for mental health. In general, studies show that low "masculinity" is associated with maladaptive behavior and vulnerability to disorder in either biological sex, possibly because this condition tends to be strongly associated with deficient self-esteem (Carson, 1989). Baucom (1983), for example, showed that high-feminine-sex-typed (low-masculinity) women tend to reject opportunities to lead in group problem-solving situations. He likens this effect to learned helplessness, which has in turn been suggested as a causal factor in anxiety (Barlow, 1988; Mineka, 1985a; Mineka & Zinbarg, 1996) and depression (Abramson et al., 1978; Seligman, 1975). Given findings like these, it should not be too surprising that women show much higher rates of anxiety and depressive disorders (see Chapters 5 and 6).

Other Pathogenic Social Influences

There are many sources of pathogenic social influences, some of which stem from socioeconomic factors and others from sociocultural factors regarding role expectations and the destructive forces of prejudice and discrimination. We will look at some of the more important ones here.

Low Socioeconomic Status and Unemployment In our society, an inverse correlation exists between socioeconomic status and the prevalence of abnormal behavior—the lower the socioeconomic class, the higher the incidence of abnormal behavior (e.g., Kessler et al., 1994). The strength of the correlation seems to vary with different types of disorder, however. For example, antisocial personality disorder is strongly related to social class, occurring three times as frequently in the lowest income

In our society, the lower the socioeconomic class, the higher the incidence of abnormal behavior. The conditions under which lower-class youngsters are reared tend to inhibit the development of coping skills. Many individuals, however, emerge from low socioeconomic environments with strong, highly adaptive personalities and skills.

category as in the highest income category, whereas depressive disorders occur only about 50 percent more often in the lowest income category as in the highest income category (Kessler et al., 1994).

We do not understand all the reasons for the more general inverse relationship. There is evidence that some people with mental disorders slide down to the lower rungs of the economic ladder and remain there because they do not have the economic or personal resources to climb back up (Gottesman, 1991). These people will often have children who also show abnormal behavior for a whole host of reasons, including biological factors such as increased risk for prenatal complications leading to low birth weight. At the same time, more affluent people are better able to get prompt help or to conceal their problems. In addition, it is almost certainly true that people living in poverty encounter more, and more severe, stressors in their lives than do people in the middle and upper classes, and that they usually have fewer resources for dealing with them. Thus, the tendency for some forms of abnormal behavior to appear more frequently in lower socioeconomic groups may be at least partly due to increased stress in the people at risk (Gottesman, 1991; Hobfoll et al., 1995).

Children from families of lower socioeconomic status also tend to have more problems. A number of studies have documented a strong relationship between the poverty status of parents and lower IQs in children at least up to 5 years of age, with persistent poverty having the most adverse effects (Duncan, Brooks-Gunn, & Klebanov, 1994; McLoyd, 1998). Such adverse effects of poverty seem to be a function of many factors associated with it, including poor physical health or low birth weight, higher risk of prenatal exposure to drugs, higher risk of lead poisoning, and less cognitive stimulation in the home environment (McLoyd, 1998). Children from families of low socioeconomic status assessed while in preschool also show more acting out and aggressive behaviors over the next 4 years (Dodge, Pettit, & Bates, 1994). Nevertheless, findings from a longitudinal study of inner-city boys in Boston showed that in spite of coming from a high-risk socioeconomic background, many of them did very well and showed upward mobility. Resilience here was best indicated by childhood IQ and adequate childhood functioning in school, family, and peer relationships (Felsman & Valliant, 1987; Masten & Coatsworth, 1995).

In addition to studying the effects of poverty on children, other studies have examined the effects of unemployment per se on adults and children. Such studies have repeatedly found unemployment—with its financial hardships, self-devaluation, demoralization, and emotional distress—to be associated with enhanced vulnerability and elevated rates of abnormal behavior (Dew, Penkower, & Bromet, 1991; Dooley & Catalano, 1980). In fact, unemployment can be as damaging psychologically as it is financially.

In particular, rates of depression, marital problems, and somatic complaints increase during periods of unemployment, but usually normalize following reemployment (Dew et al., 1991; Jones, 1992). It is not simply that those who are mentally unstable tend to lose their jobs. These effects occur even when mental health status before unemployment is taken into account. Not surprisingly, the wives of unemployed men are also adversely affected, with higher levels of anxiety, depression, and hostility, which seem to be at least partially caused by the distress of the unemployed husband (Dew, Bromet, & Schulberg, 1987). In addition, children can be seriously affected. In the worst cases, the unemployed fathers engage in child abuse; many studies have documented an association between child abuse and father's unemployment (Cicchetti & Lynch, 1995; Dew et al., 1991). Maternal unemployment can also have adverse effects—especially if the mother is single. For example, McLoyd (1998) found that single African-American mothers who were unemployed (relative to those who were employed) showed more frequent punishment of their adolescent children, which in turn led to cognitive distress and depressive symptoms in the adolescents.

Disorder-Engendering Social Roles An organized society, even an "advanced" one, sometimes asks its members to perform roles in which the prescribed behaviors either are deviant themselves or may produce maladaptive reactions. Soldiers who are called upon by their superiors (and ultimately by the society) to deliberately kill and maim other human beings may subsequently develop serious feelings of guilt. They may also have latent emotional problems resulting from the horrors commonly experienced in combat, and hence be vulnerable to disorder. As a nation, we are still struggling with the many problems of this type that have emerged among veterans of the Vietnam War (Kulka et al., 1990), as discussed in Chapter 4. Feelings of guilt over atrocities committed were especially pronounced in Vietnam veterans.

Prejudice and Discrimination Based on Race, Ethnicity, and Gender Vast numbers of people in our society have been subjected to demoralizing stereotypes and overt discrimination in areas such as employment, education, and housing. We have made progress in race relations since the 1960s, but the lingering effects of mistrust and discomfort among various ethnic and racial groups can be clearly observed on almost any college campus. For the most part, students socialize informally only with members of their own subcultures, despite the attempts of many well-meaning college administrators to break down the barriers. The tendency of students to avoid crossing these barriers limits their educational experiences and probably contributes to continued misinformation about, and prejudice toward, others. Prejudice against minority groups may play a role in the increased prevalence of certain mental disorders these groups sometimes show (Cohler et al., 1995; Kessler et al., 1994).

We have made progress in recognizing the demeaning and often disabling social roles our society has historically assigned to women. Again, though, much remains to be done. As already noted, many more women than men suffer from various emotional disorders, notably depression and many anxiety disorders. Mental health professionals believe that this higher prevalence is a consequence of both the vulnerabilities (such as passivity and dependence) intrinsic to the traditional roles assigned to women and the special stressors with which many modern women must cope (being full-time mothers, full-time homemakers, and full-time employees) as their traditional roles rapidly change. However, it should also be noted that working outside the home has also been shown to be a protective factor against depression, at least under some circumstances (e.g., Brown & Harris, 1978).

Social Change and Uncertainty The rate and pervasiveness of change today are different from anything our ancestors ever experienced. All aspects of our lives are affected—our education, our jobs, our families, our leisure pursuits, our finances, and our beliefs and values. Constantly trying to keep up with the numerous adjustments demanded by these changes is a source of considerable stress. Simultaneously, we confront inevitable crises as the earth's consumable natural resources dwindle and as our environment becomes increasingly noxious with pollutants. Certain neighborhoods have increasing problems with drugs and crime. No longer are Americans confident that the future will be better than the past or that technology will solve all our problems. Sometimes this results in despair, demoralization, and a sense of helplessness, which are well-established predisposing conditions for abnormal reactions to stressful events (Dohrenwend et al., 1980; Seligman 1990, 1998).

The Impact of the Sociocultural Viewpoint

With the gradual recognition of sociocultural influences, what was previously an almost exclusive concern with individuals has broadened to include societal, communal, familial, and other group settings as contributory factors in mental disorders. Sociocultural research has led to programs designed to improve the social conditions that foster maladaptive behavior and mental disorder and to community facilities for the early detection, treatment, and long-range prevention of mental disorder. In Chapter 15, we will examine some clinical facilities and other programs—both governmental and private—that have been established as a result of community efforts.

The sociocultural viewpoint has been criticized for its lack of scientific rigor. Clearly, it is not possible to achieve the degree of control of a laboratory experiment when studying the sociocultural environment. Nonetheless, there is strong evidence of cultural influences on abnormal behavior, and this area of research may yet answer many questions about the origins and courses of behavior problems (Cohler et al., 1995; Marsella et al., 1985). Several researchers have suggested that cross-cultural research can enhance our knowledge of the *range of variation* that is possible in human behavioral and emotional development, as well as generating ideas about what causes normal and abnormal behavior, which can later be tested more rigorously in the laboratory (Weisz et al., 1997).

Even so, many professionals may fail to adopt an appropriate cultural perspective when dealing with mental illness. Many cross-cultural researchers have noted a reluctance of "mainstream" psychologists and psychiatrists to incorporate the cross-cultural perspective in their research and clinical practices even when their subjects or patients are from diverse cultures (e.g., Clark, 1987; Cohler et al., 1995; Kleinman, 1988). This is in spite of increasing research showing that patients may do better when treated by therapists from their own ethnic group (or at least by someone familiar with the patient's culture) (Sue et al., 1991; Tharp, 1991; Yeh, Takeuchi, & Sue, 1994). In a shrinking world, with instant communication and easy transportation, it is crucial for scientists and professionals to take a world view. In fact, Kleinman and Good (1985) consider cultural factors so important to our understanding of depressive disorders that they have urged the psychiatric community to incorporate another axis in the DSM diagnostic system to reflect cultural factors in psychopathology. Although this has not yet happened, the authors of DSM-IV (1994) did include an appendix in which they specified the ways in which cultural factors should be considered when making psychiatric diagnoses.

Ultimately, of course, the potential impact of the sociocultural viewpoint will only be realized when it is integrated with both biological and psychosocial perspectives (and the same point applies to these other perspectives as well). As noted early in this chapter, such a unified perspective, called the *biopsychosocial viewpoint*, acknowledges the interaction of biological, psychosocial, and sociocultural causal factors in the development of abnormal behavior. This biopsychosocial model is being extended to the study of many disorders because it fits well with the conclusion that most disorders, especially those occurring beyond childhood, are the result of many causal factors—biological, psychosocial, and sociocultural. Moreover, the particular combination of causal factors for any person may be unique, or at least not widely shared by large numbers of people with the same disorder. For example, some children may become delinquent because of a genetic predisposition for antisocial behavior, while others may become delinquent because of sociocultural environmental influences, such as living in an area with a large number of gangs. In any case, we can achieve a scientific understanding of many of the causes of abnormal behavior even if we cannot predict such behavior with exact certainty for each individual.

IN REVIEW

- What are some examples of universal and culture-specific disorders?
- What cultural factors help account for differences in overcontrolled and undercontrolled behavior problems in Thai versus American children?
- Identify some pathogenic social influences, and explain how they contribute to abnormal behavior.

SUMMARY

CAUSES AND RISK FACTORS FOR ABNORMAL BEHAVIOR

- The occurrence of abnormal or maladaptive behavior is usually considered to be the joint product of a person's vulnerability (diathesis) to disorder and of certain stressors that challenge his or her coping resources.
- The concept of protective factors is important for understanding why some people affected by both a diathesis and a stressor do not develop a disorder, but instead show resilience.

MODELS OR VIEWPOINTS FOR UNDERSTANDING ABNORMAL BEHAVIOR

- At present, there are many different viewpoints concerning the symptoms, causes, and treatment of abnormal behavior.
- Biological, psychosocial, and sociocultural factors all play a role in psychopathology, and thus a biopsychosocial viewpoint may be the best one.

THE BIOLOGICAL VIEWPOINT AND CAUSAL FACTORS

- The modern biological approach to mental disorders has focused a good deal on the biochemistry of brain functioning, as well as on more subtle forms of brain dysfunction.
- Biologically based vulnerabilities include genetic endowment (including chromosomal irregularities), constitutional liabilities, brain dysfunction and neural plasticity, and physical deprivation or disruption.
- Investigations in this area show much promise for advancing our knowledge of how the mind and the body interact to produce maladaptive behavior.

THE PSYCHOSOCIAL VIEWPOINTS

- The psychosocial viewpoints of abnormal behavior, which emphasize human psychology rather than biology, vary widely in their focus and influence.
- The source of the psychodynamic perspective is Freudian psychoanalytic theory, which emphasizes libidinal energies and intrapsychic conflict.
- Newer psychodynamic perspectives still focus somewhat on inner, often unconscious, forces but are heavily influenced by object-relations theory, the quality of very early (pre-Oedipal) mother-infant relationships, or social and interpersonal determinants of behavior.
- The behavioral perspective on abnormal behavior, which was rooted in the desire to make psychology an objective science, has established itself as a major force in the field.
- Behaviorism focuses on the role of learning in human behavior and views maladaptive behavior as the result of either failing to learn appropriate behaviors or learning maladaptive behaviors.
- Initially a reaction against the behavioral perspective, the cognitive-behavioral perspective attempts to incorporate the complexities of human cognition in a rigorous, information-processing framework.
- Adherents of the cognitive-behavioral viewpoint attempt to alter maladaptive thinking and improve a person's abilities to solve problems and to plan.

PSYCHOSOCIAL CAUSAL FACTORS

- Psychosocial factors can also play a role in making people vulnerable to psychological problems.
- People's schemas and self-schemas clearly affect the way they process information and the kinds of values and attributions concerning the world they have. The efficiency, accuracy, and coherence of a person's schemas and self-schemas appear to provide an important protection against breakdown.
- Sources of psychosocially determined vulnerability include early social deprivation or severe emotional trauma, inadequate parenting styles, marital discord and divorce, and maladaptive peer relationships.

THE SOCIOCULTURAL VIEWPOINT AND CAUSAL FACTORS

- The sociocultural viewpoint is concerned with the social environment as a contributor to mental disorder, but the effects of sociocultural factors are complex.
- The prevalence of some disorders and the forms they take vary widely among different cultures. Unfortunately, we know little of the specific factors involved in these variations.
- In our own culture, certain prescribed roles, such as those relating to gender, appear to make some individuals more predisposed to disorder than others.
- Low socioeconomic status is also associated with greater risk for various disorders.
- To obtain a comprehensive understanding of the complex interactions that result in mental disorder, we must integrate the sociocultural viewpoint with the biological and psychosocial viewpoints to obtain an integrative perspective or a biopsychosocial viewpoint.

KEY TERMS

etiology (p. 37)
diathesis-stress models (p. 37)
protective factors (p. 38)
resilience (p. 38)
developmental psychopathology (p. 39)
biopsychosocial viewpoint (p. 39)
synapse (p. 41)
neurotransmitters (p. 41)
hormones (p. 42)
genotype (p. 44)
phenotype (p. 44)
genotype-environment correlation (p. 44)
genotype-environment interaction (p. 44)
family history method (p. 44)
twin method (p. 44)
concordance rate (p. 45)
adoption method (p. 45)
temperament (p. 46)
developmental systems approach (p. 47)
id (p. 51)
libido (p. 51)
pleasure principle (p. 51)
primary process thinking (p. 51)
ego (p. 51)
secondary process thinking (p. 52)
reality principle (p. 52)

superego (p. 52)
intrapsychic conflicts (p. 52)
ego-defense mechanisms (p. 52)
psychosexual stages of development (p. 52)
Oedipus complex (p. 53)
castration anxiety (p. 54)
Electra complex (p. 54)
ego psychology (p. 54)
object-relations theory (p. 54)
introjection (p. 55)
interpersonal perspective (p. 55)
interpersonal accommodation (p. 56)
attachment theory (p. 56)
classical conditioning (p. 57)
extinction (p. 58)
spontaneous recovery (p. 58)
instrumental (operant) conditioning (p. 58)
reinforcement (p. 58)
generalization (p. 59)
discrimination (p. 59)
cognitive-behavioral perspective (p. 60)
attribution (p. 61)
schema (p. 61)
self-schemas (p. 64)
assimilation (p. 64)
accommodation (p. 64)

CHAPTER THREE

Clinical Assessment and Treatment

George Widener, *Bulgarian Series: January Protest,* mixed media. Widener joined the U.S. Army at age 17 and traveled worldwide. After his military service ended, he studied engineering, but soon experienced emotional problems that were eventually diagnosed as depression. Widener believes that his depression arose in part as a reaction to a perceived lack of meaning in scientific endeavors. Turning to art, he taught himself to draw as a means of self-therapy.

LEARNING OBJECTIVES

After reading this chapter, you should be able to:

- Describe the basic elements of clinical assessment, including its nature and purpose and the relationship between diagnosis and treatment.
- Summarize the various techniques used to assess the structure and function of the brain.
- Compare structured and unstructured interviews as means of assessing psychosocial functioning.
- Discuss various tools for the clinical observation of behavior and identify the advantages of each.
- Explain the difference between projective and objective personality tests, and give examples of each type.
- Summarize some ethical issues and other considerations affecting the integration of assessment data for use in planning or changing treatment.
- Describe early attempts at biological intervention, and identify those that are still considered effective.
- Identify four major types of drugs commonly used to treat mental disorders, and discuss their applications, modes of action, and effectiveness.
- State the overall assumptions and goals of psychotherapy.
- Describe the basic goals and techniques of classical psychoanalysis, and trace the developments in psychodynamic therapy since Freud.
- Describe the principles and techniques of various behavior therapies and cognitive-behavioral therapies.
- Understand the assumption underlying humanistic-experiential therapies.
- Discuss the difficulties associated with attempting to evaluate the effectiveness of psychotherapy.

As we have seen, mental disturbances are likely to be the product of a complex set of contributing factors, many of which may not be apparent either immediately or after many months of intense scrutiny in the course of psychotherapy. Thus, diagnosis should be an ongoing process that accompanies, rather than only preceding, treatment.

clinical assessment Procedure in which a clinician uses psychological tests, observation, and interviews to develop a summary of a client's symptoms and problems in order to understand their nature and extent.

A diagnosis is usually a prerequisite, at least in the form of a "diagnostic impression," before any clinical services can be provided to the person seeking them. The key for the clinician is to be ready to make adjustments as necessary to accommodate new and changing assessments over the course of treatment.

In this chapter, we will review some of the physical and psychological assessment procedures widely used by clinicians and show how the data obtained can be integrated into a coherent clinical picture for use in diagnosis and in decision making about referral and treatment. We will then review the range of biological and psychologically based therapies that are available. Finally, we will conclude with a discussion of treatment outcomes, which will bring us full circle to assessment. Comparison of posttreatment assessment results with those from pretreatment is an essential feature in evaluating the effectiveness of various therapies.

CLINICAL ASSESSMENT

When a client first meets with a clinician, he or she usually presents a complaint—a description of the behavioral, emotional, or physical discomfort that has prompted him or her to seek help. This initiates the process of **clinical assessment,** a procedure by which the clinician—using psychological tests, observation, and interviews—develops a summary of the client's symptoms and problems in an attempt to understand their nature and extent. The information gained from assessment paves the way for clinical diagnosis, typically according to the DSM system (see Chapter 1), and for determination of treatment.

For the mental health practitioner, few clinical assessments are routine, and adequate techniques for confirming initial impressions may prove elusive. With rare exceptions, the "lab work" often essential to medical assessment is irrelevant. Psychological disorders usually lack identifying biological characteristics. Furthermore, they are always interlaced with the personalities of the individuals suffering them and usually with the entire surrounding social fabric.

The Dynamics of Clinical Assessment

What does a clinician need to know? First, of course, the presenting problem must be identified. Are there indications of self-defeating behavior? Is there any evidence of recent deterioration in cognitive functioning? Are there excesses in behavior, such as eating or drinking too much? Are there notable deficits, for example, in social skills? How appropriate is the person's behavior? Is the person manifesting behavior that would be acceptable in some contexts but often displaying it when it is plainly unresponsive to the situation or to reasonable social expectations? How pervasively has the problem affected the individual's social roles and interactions? Excesses, deficits, and appropriateness are key dimensions to be noted if the clinician is to understand the particular problem that has brought the individual to the clinic or hospital. In addition, what is the duration of the current complaint? Is it a situational problem precipitated by some environmental stressor such as divorce or unemployment, a manifestation of a more pervasive and long-term disorder, or is it perhaps some combination of the two? How is the person dealing with the problem? What, if any, prior help has been sought? Is the individual using available personal and environmental resources in a good effort to cope?

For most clinical purposes, arriving at a formal diagnostic classification is much less important than having a basic understanding of the individual's history, intellectual functioning, personality characteristics, and environmental pressures and resources. That is, an adequate assessment includes much more than a diagnostic label. To help the clinician in making these determinations, the DSM-IV-TR classification includes guidelines for rating both the severity of the stressors in a person's current environment and the level of a person's overall adjustment in meeting the demands of a complex social environment (see Chapter 1 and the endpapers of this book).

The diverse and often conflicting bits of information about the individual's personality traits, behavior patterns, environmental demands, and so on must then be integrated into a consistent and meaningful picture. Some clinicians refer to this picture as a **dynamic formulation,** because it not only describes the current situation but includes hypotheses about what is driving the person to behave in maladaptive ways. At this point in the assessment, the clinician should have a plausible explanation—for example, for why a normally passive and mild-mannered man suddenly flew into a rage and started breaking up furniture.

The formulation should allow the clinician to develop hypotheses about the client's future behavior as well. What is the likelihood of improvement or deterioration if the person's problems are left untreated? Which behaviors should be the initial focus of change, and what treatment methods are likely to be most efficient in producing this change? How much change might reasonably be expected from a particular type of treatment?

Where feasible, decisions about treatment are made collaboratively with the consent and approval of the individual. In cases of severe disorder, however, they may have to be made without the patient's participation or, in rare instances, even without consulting responsible family members.

In many clinical settings, assessment and diagnosis may involve a number of participants who take differing roles in the process and who gather data helpful to a comprehensive evaluation of the client's situation from several theoretical perspectives and many different sources. These participants may include family members, friends, school officials (if the client is a child or adolescent), and mental health professionals and representatives of social agencies with which the client may have had prior contact. The client is "staffed" in a meeting attended by all these contributors in an attempt to process and integrate all the available information, arrive at a consensus diagnosis, and plan the initial phase of treatment intervention. See Table 3.1 for a brief summary of the training and professional identities of the mental health personnel who might participate in such assessment teams, although the most likely to be present would be a psychiatrist, clinical psychologist, social worker, and psychiatric nurse.

Of course, the nature and comprehensiveness of clinical assessments vary according to the client's problem and the treatment agency's facilities. Our survey will include a discussion of neurological and neuropsychological assessment, the clinical interview, behavioral observation, and personality assessment through the use of projective and objective tests.

Assessment of the Physical Organism

In some situations or with certain psychological problems, a medical evaluation is necessary to determine if physical abnormalities may be causing or contributing to the problem. In addition to a general physical, the medical examination may include special examinations aimed at assessing the structural (anatomical) and functional (physiological) integrity of the brain as a behaviorally significant physical system (Rozensky, Sweet, & Tovian, 1997).

The Neurological Examination Because brain pathology is sometimes involved in or suspected to underlie some mental disorders, a specialized neurological examination may be given in addition to the general medical examination. This examination may include an

dynamic formulation Integrated evaluation of an individual's personality traits, behavior patterns, environmental demands, and the like intended to describe the person's current situation and to hypothesize about what is driving the person to behave in maladaptive ways.

TABLE 3.1 PERSONNEL IN MENTAL HEALTH

Professional

Clinical Psychologist: PhD in psychology, with both research and clinical skill specialization. One-year internship in a psychiatric hospital or mental health center. Or, PsyD in psychology (a professional degree with more clinical than research specialization) plus one-year internship in a psychiatric hospital or mental health center.

Counseling Psychologist: PhD in psychology plus internship in a marital- or student-counseling setting; normally, a counseling psychologist deals with adjustment problems pertaining to education, marriage, or occupation, not involving severe mental disorder.

School Psychologist: Ideally, a person having doctoral training in child-clinical psychology, with additional training and experience in academic and learning problems. At present, many school systems lack the resources to maintain an adequate school psychology program.

Psychiatrist: MD with residency training (usually three years) in a psychiatric hospital or mental health facility; specializes in the diagnosis and treatment of mental disorders.

Psychoanalyst: MD or PhD plus intensive training in the theory and practice of psychoanalysis.

Psychiatric Social Worker: MSW, or PhD with specialized clinical training in mental health settings.

Psychiatric Nurse: RN certification plus specialized training in the care and treatment of psychiatric clients. Nurses can attain MA and PhD in psychiatric nursing.

Occupational Therapist: BS in occupational therapy plus internship training with physically or psychologically handicapped individuals, helping them make the most of their resources.

Pastoral Counselor: Ministerial background plus training in psychology. Internship in mental health facility as a chaplain.

Paraprofessional

Community Mental Health Worker: Person with limited professional training who works under professional direction; usually involved in crisis intervention.

Alcohol- or Drug-Abuse Counselor: Limited professional training but trained in the evaluation and management of alcohol- and drug-abuse problems.

In a clinic or hospital setting, assessment data are usually evaluated in a staff conference attended by members of an interdisciplinary team—including, for example, a clinical psychologist, a psychiatrist, a social worker, and a psychiatric nurse. Sharing findings may lead to a diagnostic classification for a patient and a course of treatment. Staff decisions can have far-reaching consequences for patients: thus, it is important that clinicians be aware of the limitations of assessment.

electroencephalogram (EEG) to assess brain-wave patterns in awake and sleeping states. An EEG is a graphic record of the brain's electrical activity. It is obtained by placing electrodes on the scalp and amplifying the minute brain-wave impulses from various areas of the brain; these amplified impulses drive oscillating pens whose deviations are traced on a strip of paper moving at a constant speed. Much is known about the normal pattern of brain-wave impulses in waking and sleeping states and under various conditions of sensory stimulation. Significant divergences from the normal pattern can thus reflect abnormalities of brain function, such as might be caused by a brain tumor or other lesion.

When an EEG reveals a *dysrhythmia* in the brain's electrical activity, other specialized techniques may be used in an attempt to arrive at a more precise diagnosis of the problem. The ability to identify structural abnormalities in the brain was revolutionized with the invention of **computerized axial tomography,** known as a **CAT scan.** This procedure relies on the use of X-rays to reveal images of parts of the brain, which a neurologist can then study to determine the localization and extent of anomalies in the brain's structure.

CAT scans have been increasingly replaced by **magnetic resonance imaging (MRI)** as the technique of choice in detecting structural (anatomical) anomalies in the central nervous system, particularly the brain. The images of the interior of the brain obtained with MRI are typically sharper than CAT scans because of the former's superior ability to differentiate subtle variations in soft tissue. In addition, the MRI procedure is normally far less complicated to administer, and it does not (like CAT) subject the patient to ionizing radiation or protracted exposure to X-rays. Essentially, MRI involves the precise measurement of variations in magnetic fields that are caused by the differing water content of various organs and parts of organs. The anatomical structure of a cross section at any given plane through an organ such as the brain can be computed and depicted graphically with great structural differentiation and clarity. MRI thus makes possible, without the use of X-rays, visualization of all but the most minute abnormalities of brain structure. It has been particularly useful in confirming degenerative brain processes, as manifested, for example, in enlarged cerebrospinal fluid spaces within the brain. Therefore, MRI studies have considerable potential to illuminate the contribution of brain anomalies to "nonorganic" psychoses, such as schizophrenia.

To determine functional abnormalities, neurologists can use a scanning technique called **positron emission tomography** (which yields a **PET scan**). This technique provides a metabolic portrait by tracking natural compounds, like glucose, as they are metabolized by the brain or other organs. By showing areas of differential metabolic activity, the PET scan can reveal problems that are not immediately apparent anatomically and thus has the potential to lead to important discoveries about the organic processes underlying disorders and provide clues to more effective treatments (Zametkin & Liotta, 1997). Drawbacks of this procedure, however, are that the pictures are not that clear, and the procedure itself requires the injec-

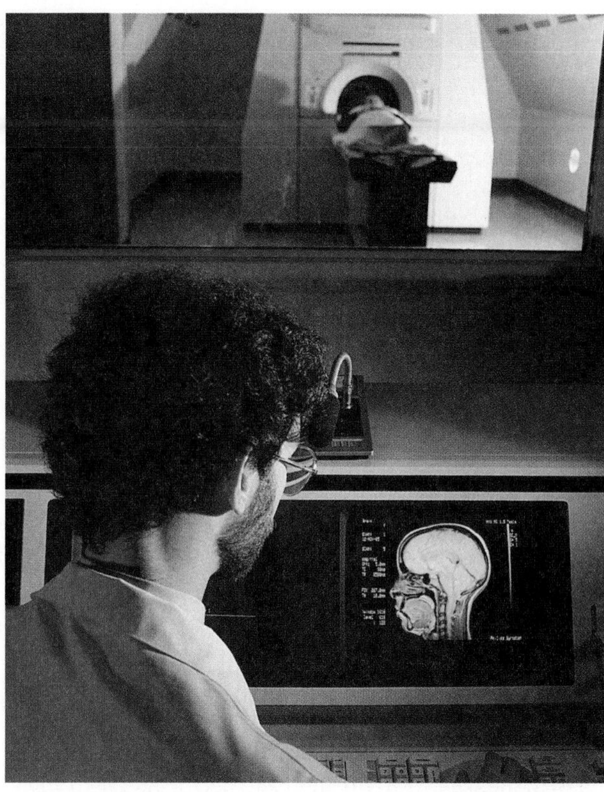

Until relatively recently, knowledge of human brain functioning was acquired only through anatomical studies and inferences from behavior. However, rapidly evolving neuroimaging technology, as shown in this picture, has been providing more detailed information about both the structure and the functioning of the human brain.

electroencephalogram (EEG) Graphic record of the brain's electrical activity, obtained by placing electrodes on the scalp and recording the brain-wave impulses from various brain areas.

computerized axial tomography (CAT scan) Radiological technique used to locate and assess structural abnormalities in the brain.

magnetic resonance imaging (MRI) Scanning technique involving measurement of variations in magnetic fields that allows visualization of the anatomical features of internal organs, including the central nervous system and particularly the brain.

positron emission tomography (PET scan) Scanning technique that monitors metabolic processes in the brain or other organs to appraise functioning.

TABLE 3.2 THE HALSTEAD-REITAN NEUROPSYCHOLOGICAL TEST BATTERY FOR ADULTS

Test	Purpose
Halstead Category Test	Measures the ability to learn and remember material and can provide clues as to a subject's judgment and impulsivity.
Tactual Performance Test	Measures a subject's motor speed, response to the unfamiliar, and ability to learn and use tactile and kinesthetic cues.
Rhythm Test	Measures attention and sustained concentration through an auditory perception task.
Speech Sounds Perception Test	Determines whether a subject can identify spoken words.
Finger Oscillation Task	Measures the speed at which a subject can depress a lever with the index finger.

tion of short-lived radioactive atoms, which is worrisome to many clinicians.

An even newer neuroimaging technique known as **functional MRI (fMRI)** holds great promise for studying psychopathology (Bigler, 1996). In its most common form, fMRI measures changes in local oxygenation (i.e., blood flow) of specific areas of brain tissue, which in turn depend on neuronal activity in those specific regions. Ongoing psychological activity, such as sensations, images, and thoughts, can thus be "mapped," at least in principle, revealing the specific areas of the brain that appear to be involved in their neurophysiological mediation. Not only is fMRI less invasive than PET, the images obtained are also much clearer.

The Neuropsychological Examination Behavioral and psychological impairments due to organic brain abnormalities may become manifest before any organic brain lesion is detectable by scanning or other means. In these instances, reliable techniques are needed to measure any alteration in behavioral or psychological functioning that has occurred because of the organic brain pathology. This need is met by a growing cadre of psychologists specializing in **neuropsychological assessment,** which involves the use of an expanding array of testing devices to measure a person's cognitive, perceptual, and motor performance as clues to the extent and location of brain damage (Grant & Adams, 1996; Spreen & Strauss, 1998). These measures provide information without the risks attendant to more invasive neurological procedures.

Depending on a patient's case history and other available information, neuropsychologists may focus their assessment by using measures that address specific abilities or disorders, such as memory (Psychological Corporation, 1997b) or dementia (Storandt & VandenBos, 1994), for example. In other instances, neuropsychologists may administer a more general test battery to a patient. Data from a battery of standardized tasks, particularly perceptual-motor ones, can give valuable clues not only about any cognitive and intellectual impairment following brain damage but also about the location of the brain damage. The most widely used test battery for this purpose is the Halstead-Reitan Neuropsychological Test Battery (Reitan & Wolfson, 1985), which is composed of several tests and variables from which an "index of impairment" can be computed (see Table 3.2). Though it typically takes 4 to 6 hours to complete and requires substantial administrative time, this battery is being used increasingly in neuropsychological evaluations to measure a subject's behavioral and psychological functioning in a number of areas (Reitan & Wolfson, 1985). It yields a great deal of useful information about an individual's cognitive and motor processes that is not available through other means (La Rue & Swanda, 1997).

Psychosocial Assessment

Psychosocial assessment attempts to provide a realistic picture of an individual in interaction with his or her social environment. This picture includes relevant information concerning the individual's personality makeup and present level of functioning, as well as information about the stressors and resources in his or her life. Psychosocial

functional MRI (fMRI) Scanning technique that measures changes in local oxygenation (blood flow) to specific areas of brain tissue, which in turn depend on neuronal activity in those specific regions, allowing the mapping of psychological activity such as sensations, images, and thoughts.

neuropsychological assessment Use of psychological tests that measure a person's cognitive, perceptual, and motor performance to obtain clues to the extent and location of brain damage.

Whether one uses a structured or unstructured interview, it is important for those using this form of psychological assessment to have their goals clearly in mind, to attempt to establish a comprehensive list of symptoms and problems the person wishes to explore, and to pay attention to the kind of relationship that is being established in the interview.

assessment procedures include interviewing, clinical observations, and a number of projective and objective psychological tests, which we will review in this section.

Interviews and behavioral observation are relatively direct attempts to determine a person's beliefs, attitudes, and problems. Psychological tests, on the other hand, are a more indirect means of assessing psychological characteristics.

Assessment Interviews An assessment interview, often considered the central element of the assessment process, usually involves a face-to-face interaction in which a clinician obtains information about various aspects of a patient's situation, behavior, and personality makeup. Assessment interviews are of two general types: unstructured and structured. In the **unstructured interview,** the clinician follows no preexisting plan with respect to content and sequence of the probes introduced. The clinician asks questions as they occur to him or her, in part based on the responses to previous questions. In the **structured interview,** the clinician probes the client in a manner that is highly controlled. Guided by a sort of master plan (that sometimes goes as far as specifying the examiner's exact wording), the clinician is typically seeking to discover if the person's symptoms and signs "fit" diagnostic criteria that are precise and "operational." There are a number of structured diagnostic interviews available. In clinical and research situations, for example, a popular instrument has been the Structured Clinical Interview for DSM Diagnosis (SCID), which yields diagnoses carefully attuned to the DSM diagnostic criteria.

The research data show that, in general, structured interviews are far more reliable than unstructured ones (Garb, 1989; Taylor & Meux, 1997). On the other hand, every rule has its exceptions, and there are many skilled clinicians who prefer unstructured interviews for obtaining an overall understanding of patient functioning.

Considering the subjectivity of much of the interviewing process, it should not be surprising that efforts have been made to computerize and presumably better structure the process and make it more reliable. A number of computer programs with highly sophisticated branching subroutines are available for specific interviewing purposes. For example, programs exist that record a client's alcohol- and drug-abuse history (Allen & Skinner, 1987) and take a client's social history (Giannetti, 1987); there is even a computer-based diagnostic interview program that allows the clinician to follow the hierarchical structure of DSM and ask the appropriate questions until the most appropriate diagnostic category is reached (First, Williams, & Spitzer, 1997). All these programs are fairly easy to administer and can provide a wealth of reliable and useful data.

Despite the progress made in reducing subjective factors by computerizing or otherwise making various aspects of the assessment process relatively automatic, it is important to understand that excessive reliance on such techniques can introduce error. The complexity of human behavior is bound to produce many exceptions to any rule. In the final analysis, therefore, there is probably no adequate substitute for expert clinical judgment.

The Clinical Observation of Behavior One of the traditional and most useful assessment tools a clinician has is direct observation of a patient's characteristic behavior—personal hygiene, emotional responses, and any signs of depression, anxiety, aggression, hallucinations, or delusions he or she may manifest (Cone, 1999). Ideally, clinical observation takes place in the natural environment (such as classroom or home), but it is more likely to occur upon admission to a clinic or hospital (Leichtman, 1995). For example, a brief description is usually made of a patient's behavior at hospital admission, and more detailed observations are made periodically on the ward.

unstructured interview Assessment interview in which the clinician follows no preexisting plan with respect to content and sequence of questions to the client.

structured interview Assessment interview in which the clinician questions the client in a manner that is highly controlled.

In addition to making their own observations, many clinicians enlist their patients' help by providing instruction in **self-monitoring**—self-observation and objective reporting of behavior, thoughts, and feelings as they occur in various natural settings. Such a method can be a valuable aid in determining the kinds of situations, possibly previously unrecognized, in which maladaptive behavior is likely to be evoked, and numerous studies also show self-monitoring to have therapeutic benefits in its own right. Alternatively, a patient may be asked to fill out a more or less formal self-report or checklist concerning problematic reactions experienced in various situations. Many instruments have been published in the professional literature and are commercially available to clinicians. Assuming that the right questions are asked and that people are willing to disclose information about themselves and capable of doing so accurately, the results can have a crucial bearing on treatment planning—for example, by providing essential information for structuring a behavioral or cognitive-behavioral treatment intervention.

The use of **rating scales** in clinical observation and in self-reports can help not only to organize information but also to encourage reliability and objectivity (Aiken, 1996). That is, the formal structure of a scale is likely to keep observer inferences to a minimum. The most useful rating scales commonly used are those that enable a rater to indicate not only the presence or absence of a trait or behavior but also its prominence (Streiner & Norman, 1995). One of the rating scales most widely used for recording observations in clinical practice and in psychiatric research is the Brief Psychiatric Rating Scale (BPRS), which provides a structured and quantifiable format for rating clinical symptoms, such as somatic concern, anxiety, emotional withdrawal, guilt feelings, hostility, suspiciousness, and unusual thought patterns. A similar but more specifically targeted instrument, the Hamilton Rating Scale for Depression (HRSD), has become almost the standard for selecting clinically depressed research subjects and also for assessing the responses of such subjects to various treatments (see Otto, Fava, et al., 1997). Helpful as these scales may be, they are more widely used for research situations than for making treatment or diagnostic decisions in clinical practice.

self-monitoring Observing and recording one's own behavior, thoughts, and feelings as they occur in natural settings.

rating scales Structured assessment devices for organizing information obtained from clinical observation and self-reports to encourage reliability and objectivity.

intelligence tests Tests used to measure an individual's level of intellectual capability.

A psychologist administers the WISC-III, an intelligence test that provides information about how well a child performs on a variety of cognitive challenges. An individually administered test such as this can require considerable time—often 2 to 3 hours—to give, score, and interpret; thus, it is appropriate to use these types of tests primarily when intelligence testing is considered critical to the diagnosis.

Intelligence Tests To measure an individual's intellectual abilities, a clinician can choose from a wide range of **intelligence tests.** The Wechsler Intelligence Scale for Children–Revised (WISC-III) and the current edition of the Stanford-Binet Intelligence Scale are widely used in clinical settings for measuring the intellectual abilities of children. Probably the most commonly used test for measuring adult intelligence is the Wechsler Adult Intelligence Scale–Revised (WAIS-III) (Psychological Corporation, 1997a). It includes both verbal and performance material and consists of 11 subtests.

Individually administered intelligence tests—such as the WISC-III, the WAIS-III, and the Stanford-Binet—typically require 2 to 3 hours to administer, score, and interpret. In many clinical situations, there is not sufficient time or funding to use these tests. In cases where intellectual impairment or organic brain damage is thought to be central to a patient's problem, intelligence testing may be the most crucial part of the assessment procedure. Moreover, information about cognitive functioning can provide valuable clues as to a person's intellectual resources in dealing with problems (Zetzer & Beutler, 1995). Yet in many clinical settings and for many clinical cases, gaining a thorough understanding of a client's problems and initiating a treatment program do not require knowing the kind of detailed information about intellectual functioning these instruments provide. In these cases, intelligence testing is not recommended.

Projective Personality Tests There are a great many tests designed to measure personal characteristics other than intellectual facility. It is customary to group these personality tests into projective and objective types. **Projective tests** are unstructured in that they rely on various ambiguous stimuli, such as inkblots or pictures, rather than explicit verbal questions, and the person's responses are not limited to the "true," "false," or "cannot say" variety. An assumption underlying the use of projective tests is that in trying to make sense out of vague, unstructured stimuli, individuals "project" into their responses their own problems, motives, and wishes (Lerner, 1995). Such responses are akin to the childhood pastime of detecting familiar scenes in cloud formations, with the important exception that the stimuli are in this case fixed and largely the same for all subjects. The fact that the stimuli remain the same permits determination of the normative range of responses to the test materials, which in turn can be used to identify objectively deviant responding. Thus, projective tests are aimed at discovering the ways in which an individual's past learning and personality structure may lead him or her to organize and perceive ambiguous information from the environment. Prominent among the several projective tests in common use are the Rorschach Test, the Thematic Apperception Test, and various sentence-completion tests.

The Rorschach The **Rorschach Test** is named after the Swiss psychiatrist Hermann Rorschach, who initiated experimental use of inkblots in personality assessment in 1911. The test uses ten inkblot pictures, to which a subject responds in succession after being instructed somewhat as follows (Exner, 1993):

> People may see many different things in these inkblot pictures; now tell me what you see, what it makes you think of, what it means to you.

Use of the Rorschach Test in clinical assessment has declined over the years, in part because its use is complicated and requires considerable training but more so because its results can be unreliable. For example, interpreters might disagree on the symbolic significance of a client's response "a house in flames." One clinician might interpret this particular response as suggesting great feelings of anxiety, whereas another might see the response as suggesting a desire on the part of the client to set fires. Another reason for the Rorschach's decline may be because today's mental health facilities generally require specific behavioral descriptions rather than descriptions of deep-seated personality dynamics, such as those that typically result from interpretation of Rorschach Test results. Attempts are being made to address these criticisms by moving beyond the original discursive and free-wheeling

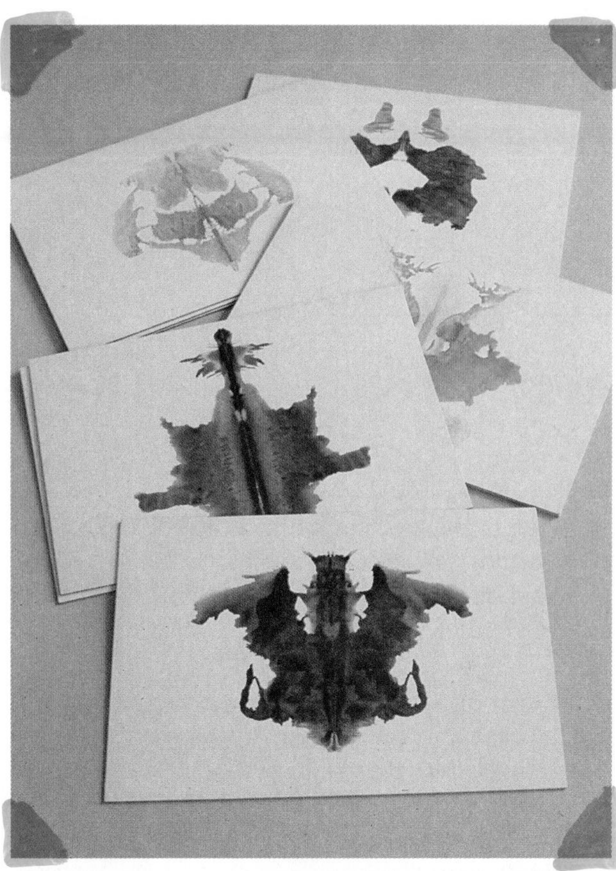

The Rorschach Test, which uses inkblots similar to those illustrated here, is a well-known projective test.

projective tests Unstructured personality tests that use various ambiguous stimuli that an individual is encouraged to interpret and from which his or her personality characteristics can be analyzed.

Rorschach Test Projective personality test consisting of ten inkblot pictures to which an individual responds with associations that come to mind; analysis of these responses enables a clinician to infer personality characteristics.

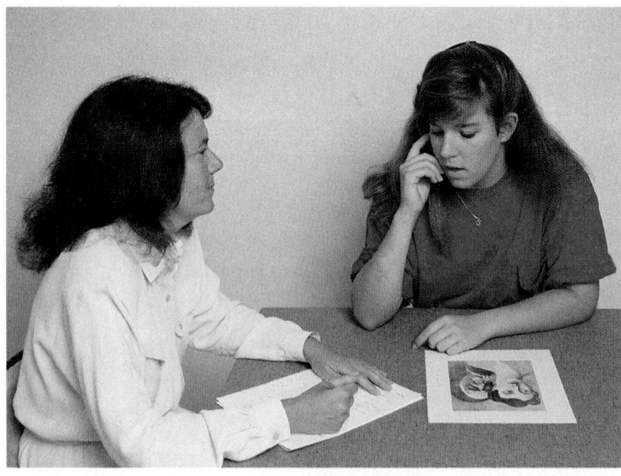

The Thematic Apperception Test (TAT) asks a subject to develop stories about the people depicted in a series of drawings. The person's stories about the people shown in the cards are thought to reflect his or her personality characteristics, motives, beliefs, attitudes, problems, and symptoms.

interpretive approaches and objectifying Rorschach interpretations by clearly specifying test variables and empirically exploring their relationship to external criteria, such as clinical diagnoses (Exner, 1995).

The Thematic Apperception Test The **Thematic Apperception Test (TAT)** was introduced in 1935 by its coauthors, C. D. Morgan and Henry Murray of the Harvard Psychological Clinic, and it is still widely used in clinical practice (Rossini & Moretti, 1997). The TAT consists of a series of simple pictures, some highly representational and others quite abstract, about which a subject is instructed to make up stories. The content of the pictures, much of it depicting people in various contexts, is highly ambiguous as to actions and motives, so that subjects tend to project their own conflicts and worries into it. Although there are formal scoring and interpretation systems available for TAT evaluation, little evidence shows that they make a clinically significant contribution; instead, most clinicians simply make a qualitative and subjective determination of how the story content reflects the person's underlying traits, motives, and preoccupations. Such interpretations often depend as much on "art" as on "science," and there is much room for error in such an informal procedure.

Not surprisingly, the TAT has been criticized for its reliability and validity. Still, some clinicians skilled in its use are capable of making astonishingly accurate assessments from TAT stories. Another drawback is that the TAT can take considerable time to administer and interpret. Finally, the TAT has been criticized for the "dated" quality of its test stimuli: The pictures, developed in the 1930s, appear quaint to many contemporary subjects, who have difficulty identifying with the characters shown in them.

Sentence-Completion Test Another projective procedure that has proved useful in personality assessment is the **sentence-completion test.** There are a number of such tests designed for children, adolescents, and adults (e.g., see Novy, Blumentritt, et al., 1997). Such tests consist of the beginnings of sentences that a subject is asked to complete, such as "I wish . . . ," "My mother . . . ," "Sex . . . ," "I hate . . . ," and "People . . . ".

Sentence-completion tests, linked somewhat to the free-association method, are slightly more structured than the Rorschach and most other projective tests. They help examiners pinpoint important clues to an individual's problems, attitudes, and symptoms through the content of his or her responses. Interpretation of the item responses, however, is generally subjective and unreliable. Despite the fact that the test stimuli (the sentence stems) are standard, interpretation is usually done in an ad hoc manner and without benefit of norms.

In sum, projective tests have an important place in many clinical settings, particularly those that attempt to obtain a comprehensive picture of a person's psychodynamic functioning and have the necessary trained staff to conduct extensive individual psychological evaluations. The great strengths of projective tests—their unstructured nature and their focus on the unique aspects of personality—are at the same time their weaknesses because they make interpretation subjective, unreliable, and difficult to validate. Moreover, projective tests typically require a great deal of time to administer and advanced skill to interpret—both scarce quantities in many clinical settings.

Objective Personality Tests

Objective tests are structured—that is, they typically use questionnaires, self-inventories, or rating scales in which questions or items are carefully phrased and alternative responses are specified as choices. They therefore involve a far more controlled format than that of projective tests and thus are

Thematic Apperception Test (TAT) Projective personality test consisting of a series of simple pictures about which an individual is instructed to make up stories; analysis of the stories gives a clinician clues about the person's conflicts, traits, personality dynamics, and the like.

sentence-completion test Projective personality test utilizing incomplete sentences that a person is to complete; analysis of the responses enables a clinician to infer personality dynamics.

objective tests Structured personality tests, such as questionnaires, self-inventories, or rating scales, used in psychological assessment.

more amenable to objectively based quantification. One virtue of such quantification is precision, which in turn enhances the reliability of test outcomes.

The MMPI One of the major objective tests for personality assessment is the **Minnesota Multiphasic Personality Inventory (MMPI),** now called the **MMPI-2** after a revision in 1989. It has become the most widely used personality test for both clinical assessment and psychopathology research (Butcher, 1996b; Lees-Haley, Smith, et al., 1996). We will examine it in some depth here because it is, in many ways, the prototype and the standard of this class of instruments.

Several years in development, the MMPI was introduced for general use in 1943 by Starke Hathaway and J. C. McKinley. The original MMPI was a kind of self-report instrument consisting of 550 items covering topics ranging from physical condition and psychological states to moral and social attitudes. Subjects were encouraged to answer either "true" or "false." Subjects' answers were then analyzed based on several standardized scales (which we'll discuss below). In response to criticism in later years, the MMPI items were modernized, and new items were written to address additional problem areas. Two separate pools of items were established: an adult form, designated MMPI-2 (Butcher et al., 1989), and an adolescent form, designated MMPI-A (Butcher et al., 1992).

The pool of items for the original MMPI was administered to a large group of normal individuals (informally called the "Minnesota normals") and several quite homogeneous groups of patients having particular psychiatric diagnoses. (It is important to note that for MMPI-2, the group sample was made considerably more representative of the American population—by including individuals from different racial and ethnic backgrounds, ages, and social classes—than was that for the original MMPI.) Answers to all the items were then item-analyzed to see which ones differentiated the various groups. On the basis of the findings, ten clinical scales were constructed, each consisting of the items that were answered by one of the patient groups in the direction opposite to the predominant response of the normal group (see Table 3.3). This rather ingenious method of scorable item selection, known as *empirical keying,* was original to the MMPI and doubtless accounts for much of the instrument's power. Note that it involves no subjective prejudgment about the "meaning" of a true or false answer to any item; that meaning resides entirely in whether or not the answer is the same as that given by patients with varying diagnoses. Should an examinee's pattern of true/false responses closely approximate that of a particular pathological group, it is a reasonable inference that he or she shares other psychiatrically significant characteristics with that group—and may in fact be a member of that group "psychologically."

Each of the ten clinical scales thus measures tendencies to respond in psychologically deviant ways. Raw scores on these scales are compared with the corresponding scores of the normal population, many of whom did (and do) answer a few items in the critical direction, and the results are plotted on the standard MMPI profile form (see Figure 3.1). By drawing a line connecting the scores for the different scales, a clinician can construct a profile that shows how far from normal a patient's performance is on each of the scales. The Schizophrenia Scale, for example (to reiterate the basic strategy), is made up of the items that schizophrenic patients consistently answered in a way that differentiated them from normal individuals. People who score high (relative to norms) on this scale, though not necessarily schizophrenic, often show propensities typical of the schizophrenic population. For instance, high scorers on this scale may be socially inept and withdrawn and have peculiar thought processes; they may have diminished contact with reality and, in severe cases, delusions and hallucinations.

The MMPI-2 also includes a number of validity scales to detect whether a patient has answered the questions in a straightforward, honest manner. For example, there is one scale that detects lying or claiming extreme virtue as well as several scales to detect faking or malingering. Extreme endorsement of the items on any of these scales may invalidate the test, while lesser endorsements frequently contribute important interpretive insights. In addition to the validity scales and the ten clinical scales, a number of "special" problem scales have been devised—for example, to detect problems of substance abuse, marital distress, and post-traumatic stress disorder.

Clinically, the MMPI-2 is used in several ways to evaluate a patient's personality characteristics and clinical problems. Perhaps the most typical use of the MMPI-2 is as a *diagnostic standard.* As we have seen, the individual's profile pattern is compared with profiles of known patient groups. If the profile matches that of a group, information about patients in this group can suggest a broad *descriptive diagnosis* for the person under study. Another approach to MMPI interpretation, *content interpretation,* is used to supplement the empirical correlates. Here, a clinician focuses on the content themes in a person's response to the inventory. For example, if an individual endorses an un-

Minnesota Multiphasic Personality Inventory (MMPI/MMPI-2)
Widely used and empirically validated scale for personality assessment.

TABLE 3.3 THE SCALES OF THE MMPI-2

Validity Scales

Cannot say score (?)	Measures the total number of unanswered items
Lie scale (L)	Measures the tendency to claim excessive virtue or to try to present an overall favorable image
Infrequency scale (F)	Measures the tendency to falsely claim or exaggerate psychological problems in the first part of the booklet; alternatively, detects random responding
Infrequency scale (FB)	Measures the tendency to falsely claim or exaggerate psychological problems on items toward the end of the booklet
Defensiveness scale (K)	Measures the tendency to see oneself in an unrealistically positive way
Response Inconsistency	Measures the tendency to endorse items in an inconsistent or random manner (VRIN)
Response Inconsistency	Measures the tendency to endorse items in an inconsistent true or false manner (TRIN)

Clinical Scales

Scale 1	*Hypochondriasis* (Hs)	Measures excessive somatic concern and physical complaints
Scale 2	*Depression* (D)	Measures symptomatic depression
Scale 3	*Hysteria* (Hy)	Measures hysteroid personality features such as a "rose-colored glasses" view of the world and the tendency to develop physical problems under stress
Scale 4	*Psychopathic deviate* (Pd)	Measures antisocial tendencies
Scale 5	*Masculinity-femininity* (Mf)	Measures gender-role reversal
Scale 6	*Paranoia* (Pa)	Measures suspicious, paranoid ideation
Scale 7	*Psychasthenia* (Pt)	Measures anxiety and obsessive, worrying behavior
Scale 8	*Schizophrenia* (Sc)	Measures peculiarities in thinking, feeling, and social behavior
Scale 9	*Hypomania* (Ma)	Measures unrealistically elated mood state and tendencies to yield to impulses
Scale 0	*Social introversion* (Si)	Measures social anxiety, withdrawal, and overcontrol

Special Scales

Scale APS	*Addiction Proneness Scale*	Assesses the extent to which the person matches personality features of people in substance use treatment
Scale AAS	*Addiction Acknowledgment Scale*	Assesses the extent to which the person has acknowledged substance abuse problems
Scale MAC-R	*Mac Andrew Addiction Scale*	An empirical scale measuring proneness to become addicted to various substances
MDS	*Marital Distress Scale*	Assesses perceived marital relationship problems

usually large number of items about fears, a clinician might well conclude that he or she is preoccupied with fear.

Overall, the authors of MMPI-2 have retained the central elements of the original instrument but have added a number of features and refinements to it, including provision for systematic "content" profile analysis. The revised versions have been validated in several clinical studies (Archer, Griffin, & Aiduk, 1995; Brems & Lloyd, 1995; Butcher, Rouse, & Perry, 1998; M. E. Clark, 1996). As was the authors' intent, the scales of MMPI-2 correlate highly with those of the original MMPI, and practitioners are able, with little change in their interpretive approaches, to use the revised instrument in the same way they did the original.

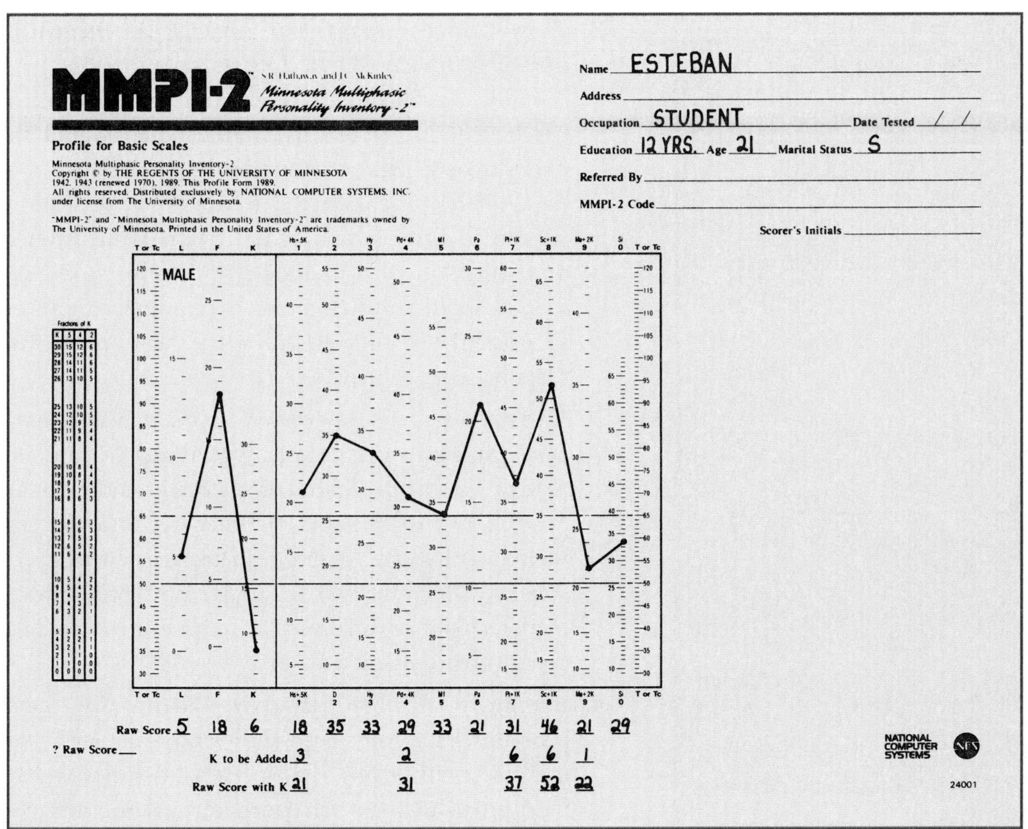

MMPI-2™ S.R. Hathaway and J.C. McKinley *Minnesota Multiphasic Personality Inventory-2™*

Profile for Basic Scales

Minnesota Multiphasic Personality Inventory-2
Copyright © by THE REGENTS OF THE UNIVERSITY OF MINNESOTA
1942, 1943 (renewed 1970), 1989. This Profile Form 1989.
All rights reserved. Distributed exclusively by NATIONAL COMPUTER SYSTEMS, INC. under license from The University of Minnesota.

"MMPI-2" and "Minnesota Multiphasic Personality Inventory-2" are trademarks owned by The University of Minnesota. Printed in the United States of America.

Name ESTEBAN
Address
Occupation STUDENT Date Tested / /
Education 12 YRS. Age 21 Marital Status S
Referred By
MMPI-2 Code
Scorer's Initials

MALE

Raw Score 5 18 6 18 35 33 29 33 21 31 46 21 29
? Raw Score
K to be Added 3 2 6 6 1
Raw Score with K 21 31 37 52 22

NATIONAL COMPUTER SYSTEMS

24001

FIGURE 3.1 AN MMPI-2 PROFILE
This profile suggests a pattern of serious mental disorder—probably schizophrenia.

Advantages of Objective Personality Tests Self-report inventories, such as the MMPI-2, have a number of advantages over other types of personality tests. They are cost-effective, highly reliable, and objective; they can also be scored and interpreted, and even administered, by computer. A number of general criticisms, however, have been leveled against the use of self-report inventories. As we have seen, some clinicians consider them to be too mechanistic to accurately portray the complexity of human beings and their problems. Also, because these tests require a person to read, comprehend, and answer verbal material, patients who are illiterate or confused cannot complete them. Furthermore, the individual's cooperation is required in self-report inventories, and it is possible that he or she may distort answers to create a particular impression. The validity scales of the MMPI-2 are a direct attempt to deal with this last criticism.

Integrating Assessment Data

Clinicians in individual private practice normally assume the often arduous task of integrating assessment data on their own. Or, as noted earlier in this chapter, the job may be done by a team of professionals in a clinic or hospital setting. In either case, the goal is to integrate all the assessment information at hand to see whether the findings complement each other and form a definitive clinical pic-

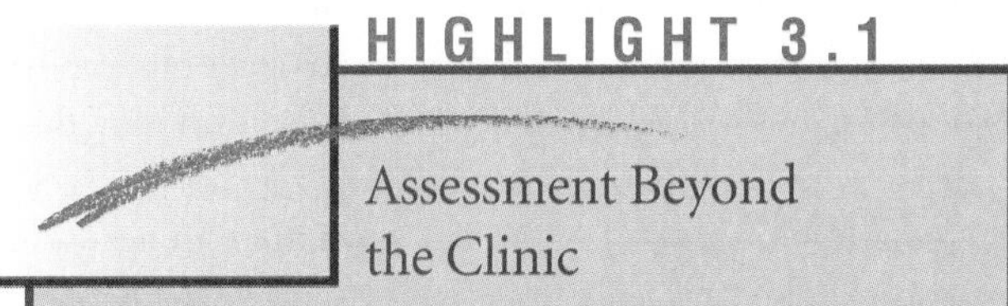

HIGHLIGHT 3.1

Assessment Beyond the Clinic

Psychological tests are widely used in settings other than clinical assessment situations. For example, tests such as the MMPI-2, because of their objectivity in describing personality, are widely used in courts for answering questions such as whether an individual is competent to stand trial or whether a personal injury claimant is suffering from stress following an alleged injury. Another nonclinical setting in which personality assessment is widely used is for personnel screening for jobs that require emotionally stable people, such as airline pilots, police officers, and nuclear power plant workers. ■

HIGHLIGHT 3.2

iassesstoo.com

Possibly the most dramatic recent innovation in clinical assessment involves the widespread use of computers in the administration, scoring, and interpretation of psychological tests. It is now possible to obtain immediate interpretation of psychological test results, either through an interactive software program or by using a modem to access a computer network that interprets tests. In the past few years, rapid developments have been taking place in the area of computerized assessment. It is conceivable that within the next few years most clinical assessments will involve computers in some capacity, either for administration, scoring, and interpretation or for completing an entire test battery. Of course, mental health professionals will still play a major role in determining the appropriateness and adequacy of the computer's diagnostic output. ■

ture or whether gaps or discrepancies exist that necessitate further investigation. This integration may lead to a tentative diagnostic classification for a client or patient. Two important considerations of assessment integration are ethics and efficacy.

Ethical Issues in Assessment The decisions made on the basis of assessment data may have far-reaching implications for the people involved. A staff decision may determine whether a depressed person will be hospitalized or remain with his or her family or whether an accused person will be declared competent to stand trial. Thus, a valid decision, based on accurate assessment data, is of far more than theoretical importance. Because of the impact that assessment can have on the lives of others, it is important that those involved keep several issues in mind when evaluating test results:

1. *Potential cultural bias of the instrument or the clinician.* There is the possibility that psychological tests may not elicit valid information from a patient from a minority group (Gray-Little, 1995). A clinician from one sociocultural background (for example, a middle-class white American) may have trouble assessing objectively the behavior of someone from another background (such as a Southeast Asian refugee).
2. *Theoretical orientation of the clinician.* Assessment is inevitably influenced by a clinician's assumptions, perceptions, and theoretical orientation. For example, a psychoanalytically oriented professional would be likely to view behaviors as reflecting underlying motives, whereas a behavioral clinician would be likely to see the behavior in the context of the immediate or preceding stimulus situation. If the differing assessments should lead to treatment recommendations of significantly differing efficacy for a client's problems, these biases could have serious repercussions.
3. *Underemphasis on the external situation.* Many clinicians overemphasize personality traits as the cause of patients' problems without giving due attention to the possible role of stressors or other circumstances in their life situations. An undue focus on a patient's personality, which may be encouraged by some assessment techniques, can divert attention from potentially critical environmental factors.
4. *Insufficient validation.* Many psychological assessment procedures have not been sufficiently validated. For example, unlike many of the personality scales, widely used procedures for behavioral observation and behavioral self-report have not been subjected to strict psychometric validation. The tendency on the part of clinicians to accept the results of these procedures at face value has recently been giving way to a broader recognition of the need for more explicit validation.
5. *Inaccurate data or premature evaluation.* There is always the possibility that some assessment data—and any diagnostic label or treatment approach based on them—may be inaccurate. Some risk is always involved in making predictions for an individual on the basis of group data or averages. Inaccurate data or premature conclusions not only may lead to a misunderstanding of a patient's problem, but may close off attempts to get further information, with possibly grave consequences for the patient.

Incorporating Psychological Test Data into Therapy

The importance of using assessment data not only to diagnose a client but also to determine the best treatment and evaluate the progress of therapy may seem obvious. It is surprising, then, to note that many psychotherapists and psychotherapy researchers do not routinely use assessment techniques (Ben-Porath, 1997; Nelson & Adams, 1997). Research has provided clear evidence of the likely beneficial effects of psychological assessment in the treatment process (Ben-Porath, 1997; Finn & Tonsager, 1997; Harkness & Lilienfield, 1997; Haynes, Leisen, & Blaine,

1997; Nelson & Adams, 1997). The extensive research has had relatively little impact on the way therapy is conducted, however.

Interestingly, there is growing evidence to indicate that the results of psychological tests can, when sensitively shared with clients, bring about remarkable personality change and insight in clients (Miller & Rollnick, 1991); Finn and Tonsager (1997) and Newman and Greenway (1997) have shown that personality information from tests given to clients early in the intervention can bring about improved self-esteem and a lowering of psychological symptoms. Test feedback alone produced therapeutic results that were comparable to or better than those of therapy without psychological test feedback.

Furthermore, new assessment data collected during the course of therapy can provide feedback on the effectiveness of the therapy and serve as a basis for making needed modifications in an ongoing treatment program. Clinical assessment data are also critical to evaluating the final outcome of therapy and in comparing the effectiveness of different therapeutic and preventive approaches.

So why do many trained psychotherapists begin and continue their treatment without incorporating objective psychological information into the process? A simple lack of training in assessment techniques could be one explanation. Theoretical bias, another. And the cost of assessment could be still another reason for not including assessment information in the treatment process. Unfortunately, assessment may be the easiest aspect of the clinical process to dispense with under the fiscal realities of managed care. This is ironical, of course. Since assessment has been shown to impact outcome positively, it might in the long run reduce mental health costs, or at least better ensure the mental health of clients. With this in mind, we turn now to an examination of biologically and psychologically based therapies.

IN REVIEW

- What is the difference between diagnosis and clinical assessment? What components must be integrated into a dynamic formulation?
- Compare and contrast five important neurological procedures. What makes each one particularly valuable?
- What are the assumptions behind the use of projective tests? How do they differ from objective tests?
- What are some advantages of objective personality tests?
- What are some ethical issues clinicians should be aware of when evaluating patients' test results?

BIOLOGICALLY BASED THERAPIES

Today, both biological and psychological treatment approaches are used in attempts to help individuals overcome psychopathology. We will examine psychological approaches in the next section; here, we will consider some biological methods that have evolved for the treatment of mental disorders. In general, we will see that as more has been learned in the various subfields of medicine, biological treatments have gone from rather invasive bodily procedures to less risky ones, yielding in large part to prescription medicines designed to address a given problem. The specificity of the newer treatments usually means that they have fewer potentially damaging side effects.

Early Attempts at Biological Intervention

The history of biological intervention records some interesting, though by today's standards often extreme and primitive, methods of treating mental illness by altering bodily processes. Some have been widely used in several periods of history. For example, ridding the body of unwanted substances by purging (with laxatives and emetics) was a typical treatment in ancient Rome, during the medieval period, and during the eighteenth century (Agnew, 1985). In fact, purging was so widespread during some periods, particularly the eighteenth century, that it was a common practice not only in medicine but among the population in general. Other seemingly more barbaric techniques, such as bleeding, have been widely used as treatments of the mentally disordered as well as for a broad range of physical diseases.

By 1917, with the discovery that general paresis, or syphilis of the brain, could be curbed by intentionally infecting a patient with malaria (the consequent fevers were lethal to the spirochete), the stage was set for the development of extraordinarily bold but often hazardous new biological treatments. Two treatments that emerged during this period are now known as electroconvulsive therapy and neurosurgery.

Electroconvulsive Therapy Early efforts to induce convulsions involved the use of camphor and insulin, both of which proved dangerous and generally disappointing. In 1938, two Italian physicians, U. Cerletti and L. Bini, after visiting a slaughterhouse and seeing animals rendered unconscious by electric shock, induced convulsions

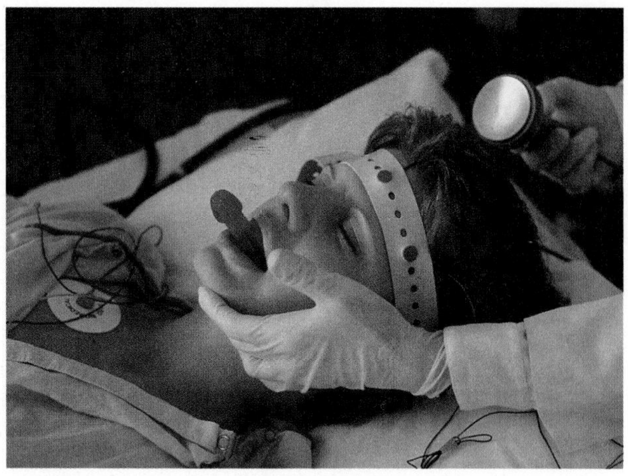

A patient administered electroconvulsive therapy (ECT) today is given an anesthetic and muscle-relaxant premedication to prevent violent contractions. In the days before such medication was available, the initial seizure was sometimes so violent as to fracture vertebrae.

by passing an electric current through a patient's head. This method, which became known as **electroconvulsive therapy (ECT),** is effective in alleviating severe depressive and manic episodes, and is still used today, albeit in a less intrusive way.

Although ECT is known to be effective, the mechanism by which it works has never been adequately explained. Some researchers believe that the therapeutic effect is brought about by changes in the levels of certain neurotransmitters or by changes in receptor sensitivity, but the mechanism of action remains a mystery (Abrams, 1997; Gitlin, 1996). However, at least one important study has shown that specific neural systems must be activated for the treatment to be effective (Sackheim et al., 1993).

In *bilateral ECT,* a low- or high-energy electric current of brief pulses is passed from one side of a patient's head to the other for up to about 1.5 seconds. The patient immediately loses consciousness and undergoes marked muscle contractions (Abrams, 1997; Gitlin, 1996). Today, anesthetics and muscle-relaxant premedications are used to prevent violent contractions, and careful, continuous monitoring during the procedure lowers side effects and risk. In the days before such medications were available, the initial seizure was sometimes so violent as to fracture vertebrae, one of several potential complications of this therapy.

After awakening several minutes after ECT, the patient has amnesia for the period immediately preceding the therapy and is usually somewhat confused for the next hour or so. Normally, a treatment series consists of less than a dozen sessions, although occasionally more are needed (Gitlin, 1996). With repeated treatments, usually administered three times weekly, the patient gradually becomes disoriented, a state that usually clears after termination of the treatments.

A newer variation, called *unilateral ECT,* limits the flow of current to only one side of the brain, typically the nondominant side (the right, for most people); evidence shows that this less intrusive technique lessens distressing side effects (such as memory impairment) without decreasing therapeutic effectiveness if higher-energy electrical currents are used. However, other studies suggest that unilateral ECT may not be as effective as the bilateral form, and so many experts recommend starting with unilateral and switching to bilateral after five or six treatments if no improvement is seen (Abrams, 1997; Gitlin, 1996).

Many authorities support the use of ECT as the only effective way of dealing with some severely depressed and suicidal patients—especially if they have not responded to several different antidepressant medications. However, the use of ECT is considered controversial by many others, especially because today there is such an abundance of effective alternative approaches—such as antidepressant medications. Moreover, memory impairment resulting from ECT can remain for some months (Gitlin, 1996). However, earlier concerns that ECT might produce structural damage to the brain have been laid to rest, and it is now clear that properly administered ECT does not produce any structural damage to the brain (Devanand et al., 1994; Gitlin, 1996).

Neurosurgery Brain surgery used in the treatment of functional or central nervous system disorders has sometimes been called *psychosurgery,* though many prefer the term **neurosurgery,** because it does not imply that the "psyche" is being operated upon (Mindus et al., 1993). In the mid 1930s, **prefrontal lobotomy,** in which the frontal lobes of the brain are severed from the deeper centers underlying them, became a widely used neurosurgical procedure for treating the mentally ill. This operation, which

electroconvulsive therapy (ECT) Method of treatment that passes electric currents through the head to produce convulsions and unconsciousness and is used primarily to alleviate severe depressive and manic episodes; also known as *electroshock therapy.*

neurosurgery Brain surgery used in the treatment of functional or central nervous system disorders.

prefrontal lobotomy Surgical procedure used before the advent of antipsychotic drugs in which the frontal lobes of the brain are severed from the deeper centers underlying them, resulting in permanent structural changes in the brain.

HIGHLIGHT 3.3

A Case in Point: The Tragedy of Prefrontal Lobotomy

Rosemary Kennedy, sister of President John F. Kennedy and Senators Robert and Edward Kennedy, was born mentally retarded. Though doctors recommended that she be institutionalized, the family rebelled against the suggestion, and with their considerable financial and familial resources, and the help of a special governess and many private tutors, Rosemary made great strides and lived an accomplished if sheltered life. She participated fully in the Kennedy family's activities, and even developed the social skills needed to be presented successfully as a debutante and later to the King and Queen at Buckingham Palace when her father, Joseph Kennedy, was ambassador to England. All this, and still no one outside the family noticed Rosemary's mental retardation, which the family had kept hidden because of the considerable stigma associated with it at the time.

When the family returned to the United States from England around the beginning of World War II, 21-year-old Rosemary's behavior deteriorated, perhaps because of her increasing frustration about not being able to do all the things her siblings were able to do and having to leave the school in England where she had felt successful. She became quite violent and frequently ran away from home or her convent school. There was considerable concern for her safety, and Joseph Kennedy—without his wife Rose's knowledge—turned to the medical experts of the time, searching for a solution.

These experts convinced Joe that the miracle treatment lay in prefrontal lobotomy. Rosemary Kennedy became one of the thousands submitted to that "desperate" cure. In Rosemary's case, the surgery was a tragic failure—all her previous accomplishments were wiped out, leaving little of her former personality and adaptive ability intact: "You could see by looking at her that something was wrong, for her head was tilted and her capacity to speak was almost entirely gone. There was no question now that she could no longer take care of herself and that the only answer was an institution" (Ann Gargan King, a cousin, as reported by Goodwin, 1988, p. 744). ■

results in permanent structural changes in the brain of the patient, stands as a dubious tribute to the extremes to which professionals have sometimes been driven in their search for effective treatments for the psychoses. In the two decades between 1935 and 1955 (after which the new antipsychotic drugs became widely available), tens of thousands of mental patients in this country and abroad were subjected to prefrontal lobotomy and related neurosurgical procedures. In fact, in some settings, as many as 50 patients were treated in a single day (Freeman, 1959). As is often the case with newly developed therapeutic techniques, initial reports tended to be enthusiastic, downplaying complications (including a 1 to 4 percent death rate) and undesirable side effects, such as a permanent inability to inhibit impulses and an unnatural "tranquility" characterized by undesirable shallowness or absence of feeling.

The advent of the major antipsychotic drugs led to a widespread decrease in the use of neurosurgery, especially prefrontal lobotomy. Such operations are rare today, and when they are performed, more advanced techniques result in substantially less permanent damage to the brain and thus fewer side effects. Even so, contemporary use of neurosurgery in the treatment of severe mental disorders is recommended only for patients who have not responded to all other forms of treatment considered standard for the disorder over a period of 5 years and who are experiencing extreme and disabling symptoms. Patients are accepted for neurosurgical treatment only if they are rationally capable of understanding the procedure and provide informed consent (Rauch & Jenike, 1998).

Psychopharmacological Methods of Treatment

One of the goals of **psychopharmacology**—the science of determining which drugs work to alleviate which mental disorders and why they do so—remained elusive until the mid-1950s, at which point, a genuine revolution in the treatment of the more severe disorders occurred with the

psychopharmacology Science of determining which drugs alleviate which mental disorders and why they do so.

HIGHLIGHT 3.4

A New Era Arrives...

Although the benefits of the antipsychotic drugs, or neuroleptics, have often been exaggerated, it is difficult to convey the truly enormous influence they have had in altering the environment of the typical mental hospital. One of the authors, as part of his training, worked several months in the maximum security ward of one such hospital just before the introduction of this type of medication in 1955. The ward patients fulfilled the common stereotypes of individuals "gone mad." Bizarreness, nudity, wild screaming, and an ever-present threat of violence pervaded the atmosphere. Fearfulness and a nearly total preoccupation with the maintenance of control characterized the staff's attitude. Such an attitude was not unrealistic in terms of the frequency of serious physical assaults by patients, but it was hardly conducive to the development or maintenance of an effective therapeutic program.

Then, quite suddenly—within a period of perhaps a month—all of this dramatically changed. The patients began receiving the new antipsychotic medication chlorpromazine. The ward became a place in which one could get to know one's patients on a personal level and perhaps even initiate programs of *milieu therapy,* a form of psychosocial therapy in which the entire facility is regarded as a therapeutic community, and the emphasis is on developing a meaningful and constructive environment in which the patients participate in the regulation of their own activities. A new era in hospital treatment had arrived, aided enormously and in many instances actually made possible by the development of these extraordinary drugs. ■

discovery of a drug (chlorpromazine) that actually treated the symptoms of schizophrenia. This breakthrough was followed by the discovery of drugs for treating the anxiety-based disorders and antidepressants and lithium salts for treating mood disorders.

In this section, we will look at these four types of chemical agents, now commonly used in therapy for mental disorders: (1) antipsychotic drugs, (2) antidepressant drugs, (3) antianxiety drugs (minor tranquilizers), and (4) lithium (as well as other mood-stabilizing drugs). These drugs are sometimes referred to as *psychotropic* (literally, mind-turning or mind-altering), in that their main effect is on an individual's mental life. As we examine drugs used in therapy, it is important to remember that people differ in how rapidly they metabolize drugs—that is, in how quickly their bodies break down the drugs once ingested. What this means is that people differ, too, in the dosage of a drug they need to experience the desired therapeutic effect. Determining correct dosage is a critical factor of drug therapy because too much or too little of a drug can be ineffective and (in the case of too much) even life-threatening, depending on the individual. (Table 3.4 presents a summary of drugs commonly used for therapy.)

antipsychotic drugs Group of drugs that produce a calming effect in many patients as well as alleviating or reducing the intensity of psychotic symptoms, such as delusions and hallucinations; also called *neuroleptics.*

Antipsychotic Drugs The traditional **antipsychotic drugs** as a group are called *neuroleptics,* or sometimes *major tranquilizers,* but this latter term is somewhat misleading for they do more than tranquilize. They are used for the major disorders, such as the schizophrenias and psychotic mood disorders. Although they do indeed produce a calming effect on many patients, their unique quality is that of somehow alleviating or reducing the intensity of psychotic symptoms, such as delusions (false beliefs) and hallucinations (misperceptions). In some cases, in fact, a patient who is already excessively "tranquil" (for example, withdrawn or immobile) becomes active and responsive to the environment under treatment with these drugs.

With the remarkable early successes of *chlorpromazine* (trade name Thorazine), the first of the *phenothiazine* family of drugs for treating schizophrenia, in the early 1950s, other pharmaceutical companies began to manufacture and market their own variants of the drug. Virtu-

TABLE 3.4 DRUGS COMMONLY USED FOR THERAPY

Class	Generic Name	Trade Name	Used to Treat	Effects and Side Effects
Antipsychotic				
(a) Low-potency dopamine blockers	chlorpromazine thioridazine mesoridazine	Thorazine Mellaril Serentil	Psychotic (especially schizophrenia) symptoms, such as extreme agitation, delusions, and hallucinations; aggressive or violent behavior	Somewhat variable in achieving intended purpose of suppression of psychotic symptoms. Side effects, such as dry mouth, are often uncomfortable. In long-term use may produce motor disturbances, such as Parkinsonism and tardive dyskinesia.
(b) Middle-potency dopamine blockers	perphenazine kixaoube molindone thiothixene trifluoperazine	Trilafon Loxitane Moban Navane Stelazane		
(c) High-potency dopamine blockers	haloperidol fluphenazine	Haldol Prolixin		
(d) Atypical	clozapine	Clozaril	Schizophrenia	Suppresses psychotic thinking. Side effects include sedation, seizure, hypotension, fever, vomiting.
	risperidone	Risperdal	Schizophrenia	Like clozapine, it suppresses psychotic thinking, but appears to produce fewer negative side effects.
Antidepressant and Mood-Altering				
(a) Tricyclics (TCAs) and related drugs	imipramine amitriptyline desipramine nortriptyline protriptyline doxepin trimipramine clomipramine	Tofranil Elavil Norpramin Aventyl Vivactil Sinequan Surmontil Anafranil	Relatively severe depressive symptoms, especially of psychotic severity and unipolar in type; some also used in treatment of panic disorder, OCD, and bulimia	Somewhat variable in alleviating symptoms, and noticeable effects may be delayed up to 3–5 weeks. Side effects may cause discomfort. Not safe in overdose.
(b) Monoamine oxidase (MAO) inhibitors	phenelzine tranylcypromine selegiline	Nardil Parnate Eldepryl	Depression, panic disorder, and social phobia	Multiple side effects—some of them dangerous. Use of MAO inhibitors requires dietary restrictions.
(c) Selective serotonin reuptake inhibitors (SSRIs)	fluoxetine fluvoxamine sertraline paroxetine	Prozac Luvox Zoloft Paxil	Depressive symptoms, OCD, panic disorder, bulimia	Effects take about 3 weeks. Side-effect profile is favorable, though some nausea, insomnia, and sexual dysfunction have been reported.

(continued)

TABLE 3.4 (CONTINUED)

Class	Generic Name	Trade Name	Used to Treat	Effects and Side Effects
(d) Atypical antidepressants	trazodone	Desyrel	Depression	Less likelihood of response than TCAs. Not much used today. Minimal risk of overdose. Side effects include cognitive slowing.
	bupropion venlafaxine nefazodone	Wellbutrin Effexor Serzone	Depression	Used with patients who have not responded to TCAs or SSRIs. Relatively few side effects and relatively safe in overdose.
(e) Antimanic (bipolar) or mood stabilizers	lithium carbonate	Eskalith Lithane Lithonate	Manic episodes and some severe depressions, particularly recurrent ones or those alternating with mania	Usually effective in resolving manic episodes, but highly variable in effects on depression, probably because the latter is a less homogeneous grouping. Multiple side effects unless carefully monitored; high toxicity potential.
	carbamazepine	Tegretol	Bipolar disorder—especially manic episodes	Effective in treating bipolar disorders. Neurotoxic side effects have been noted, including unsteady gait, tremor, ataxia, and increased restlessness.
	valproate	Depakote	Bipolar disorder—especially manic episodes	Fewer side effects than lithium. Often used with bipolar patients who cannot take lithium.
Antianxiety				
(a) Propanediols (rarely used today)	meprobamate	Equanil Miltown	Nonpsychotic personality problems in which anxiety, tension, or panic attacks are prominent features; also used as anticonvulsants and as sleep-inducers (especially flurazepam, triazolan, and temazepan)	Somewhat variable in achieving intended purpose of tension reduction. Used often to treat alcohol withdrawal symptoms. Side effects include drowsiness and lethargy.
(b) Benzodi-azepines	diazepam chlordiazepoxide flurazepam oxazepam clorazepate alprazolam clonazepan triazolan temazepan lorazepan	Valium Librium Dalmane Serax Tranxene Xanax Klonopin Halcion Restoril Ativan		
(c) New anxiolytics	buspirone	Buspar	Generalized anxiety disorder	Effects take 1–4 weeks to occur. Not useful in treating acute anxiety. Not addictive or sedating. No addiction potential.

Sources: Based on data from Bohn (1993); Dunner (1993); Gitlin (1996); Keck & McElroy (1998); Nathan & Gorman (1998); Preskorn & Burke (1992); Tacke (1990).

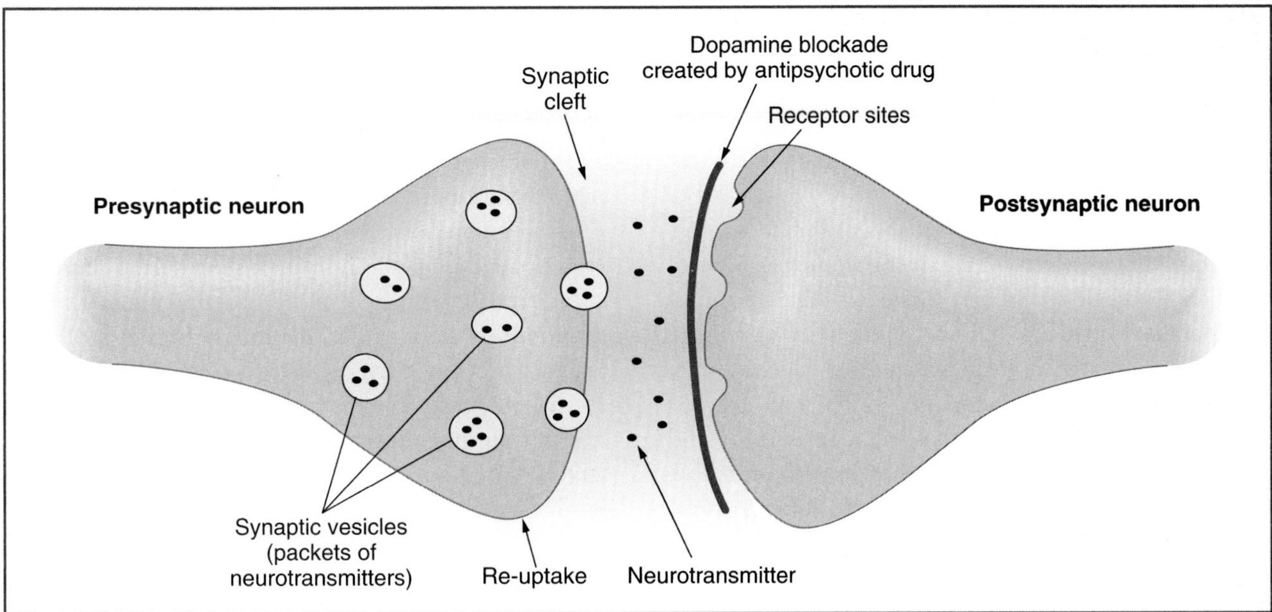

FIGURE 3.2 ANTIPSYCHOTICS AS DOPAMINE RECEPTOR SITE BLOCKERS
Source: Adapted from Gitlin (1996), p. 287.

ally all these antipsychotics accomplish a common biochemical effect—namely, they block dopamine receptor sites in neurons (see Figure 3.2). However, they vary significantly in the potency of the dopamine blockade they produce.

Most studies have found that approximately 60 percent of schizophrenic patients treated with some traditional antipsychotic medication show a near complete remission of extreme symptoms within 6 weeks (compared to only about 20 percent of those treated with a placebo); still, 20 to 30 percent seem resistant to these medications (Sheitman et al., 1998). Moreover, these drugs are useful in treating other disorders that have psychotic symptoms. With persistent use or at high dosages, however, all these preparations have varying degrees of troublesome side effects, such as dryness of the mouth and throat, sedation, and weight gain; some even have side effects that mimic the classic symptoms of Parkinson's disease: tremor of extremities, muscle tightening, akinesia (characterized by a decrease in spontaneous movements), and akathisia (motor restlessness characterized by fidgety, purposeless movements) (Gitlin, 1996). One particularly troublesome side effect of long-term antipsychotic drug treatment is the development of *tardive dyskinesia*—a disfiguring disturbance of motor control, particularly of the facial muscles (e.g., involuntary thrusting movements of the tongue, chewing movements, lip smacking, eyeblinking), which, in a minority of cases, can be progressive and irreversible.

Many of the side effects of taking antipsychotics may be relieved by substituting another drug of the same class, by switching to a different class of drug, or by reducing the dosage (Sheitman et al., 1998). Recent research with treatment-resistant schizophrenics has focused on possible alternative drugs—now generally known as the *atypical antipsychotics*. For example, in approximately 30 percent of patients who have failed to respond to at least three traditional neuroleptics, *clozapine*, the first widely hailed atypical antipsychotic to be developed, suppresses psychotic thinking without as many of the negative side effects, including tardive dyskinesia, associated with traditional antipsychotic medications (Gitlin, 1996; Sheitman et al., 1998). However, clozapine has its own serious side effect—about 1 percent of patients develop an immunodeficiency that has resulted in several deaths—and careful blood-monitoring is a must to protect the patient. Several newer but less well studied atypical antipsychotic drugs (i.e., risperidone, sertindole, quetiapine, and olanzapine) are promising in that they seem to act similarly to clozapine but without the life-threatening risk to the immune system.

Antidepressant Drugs The first **antidepressant drugs** made their appearance shortly after the introduction of

antidepressant drugs Drugs that are used primarily to elevate mood and relieve depression.

chlorpromazine in the late 1950s, and their initial discoveries were quite serendipitous. Although many of these drugs were developed and first used as antidepressants, they have also been found to be effective with other disorders, including bulimia and even some anxiety disorders and personality disorders.

The first antidepressants, the *monoamine oxidase (MAO) inhibitors,* were initially being studied as a treatment for tuberculosis and were found to elevate the mood of tuberculosis patients (Gitlin, 1996). They were later shown to be effective in treating depressed patients. They inhibit the activity of monoamine oxidase, an enzyme present in the synaptic cleft that helps break down the monoamine neurotransmitters (such as serotonin and norepinephrine) that have been released into the cleft. MAO inhibitors are not widely used today, largely because of the dietary restrictions that must be imposed on patients taking them and because of a number of unpleasant side effects. They are used primarily in cases of atypical depression that are characterized by hypersomnia and overeating and that have not responded well to other types of antidepressant medications (Nemeroff & Schatzberg, 1998).

Mike Wallace, from CBS's hugely successful program *60 Minutes,* is one of many public figures who has been open with the public about his experience with depression.

Another group of antidepressants, the *tricyclics (TCAs),* inhibit the re-uptake of norepinephrine and serotonin (to a lesser extent) once they have been released into the synapses. Although the immediate short-term effect of tricyclics is to increase the availability of norepinephrine and serotonin in the synapses, the long-term effect of these drugs (when they begin to have their clinical effects after 3 to 5 weeks) is to produce functional *decreases* in available norepinephrine and serotonin (Gitlin, 1996; Thase & Howland, 1995). It is also known that when the tricyclics have been taken for several weeks, they alter a number of other aspects of cellular functioning, including how receptors function and how cells respond to activation of receptors and synthesis of neurotransmitters. Because the timing of these alterations in cellular functioning parallels that in which these drugs exert their antidepressant effects, one or more of these changes are likely to be involved in mediating the antidepressant effects (see Figure 3.3).

Up until the 1990s, the tricyclics and their variants were used more often than the MAO inhibitors, because they were less toxic and did not require troublesome dietary restrictions. Still, the tricyclics also have unpleasant side effects, such as dry mouth, fatigue, dizziness, blurred vision, constipation, and occasional erectile dysfunction in men. Therefore, some patients do not continue taking the drug long enough for it to have its antidepressant effect.

A "second generation" of antidepressants began to be released in 1988 and has since come to dominate the market. These are the *selective serotonin re-uptake inhibitors (SSRIs),* which selectively inhibit the re-uptake of serotonin rather than inhibiting the re-uptake of both serotonin and norepinephrine, as is the case with the tricyclics. The SSRIs became the preferred class of antidepressant drugs in the 1990s because they are thought to be relatively "safe"; that is, they are easier to use, have fewer side effects, and are generally not fatal in overdose as the tricyclics can be. However, it should also be noted that the SSRIs are generally not considered to be more effective than the classic tricylic antidepressants—they are simply more acceptable and better tolerated by many patients.

Clinical trials with the SSRIs have reported that patients tend to improve after about 3 to 5 weeks of treatment with the drug. Commonly reported side effects of the SSRIs include nausea, diarrhea, nervousness, insomnia, and sexual dysfunction (ranging from decreased arousal to erectile dysfunction and/or delayed time to orgasm) (Gitlin, 1996; Nemeroff & Schatzberg, 1998).

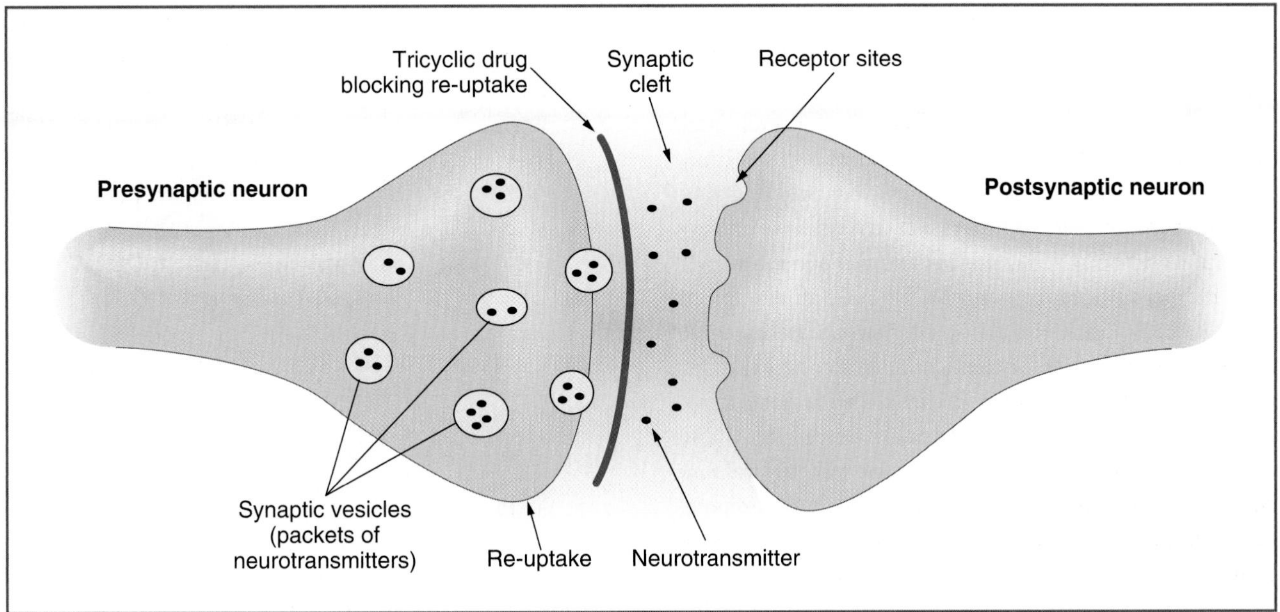

FIGURE 3.3 TRICYCLIC ANTIDEPRESSANTS AS RE-UPTAKE BLOCKERS
Source: Adapted from Gitlin (1996), p. 287.

Research on new antidepressants is fast-moving, and there are currently a number of new antidepressants that are not only quite different from each other but also from the more established medications. Many of these newer drugs hold promise because they appear to have fewer side effects (e.g., trazodone and bupropion) and to act more quickly than the SSRIs on severe major depression (e.g., nefazadone and venlafaxine), a factor that can be critical if the patient is suicidal.

Pharmacological treatment for depression often produces dramatic results. Improvement in response to antidepressant medications is in sharp contrast to the effects of antipsychotic medications, which apparently only suppress schizophrenic symptoms. This statement, however, must be tempered with the observation that persons suffering from severe depression, unlike people with severe schizophrenia, often respond to any treatment (such as a placebo drug) or even no treatment at all (Nemeroff & Schatzberg, 1998). However, depression is often a recurrent disorder, and so drugs have to be administered over long periods. If the drugs are discontinued when symptoms have just remitted, there is a high probability of relapse, probably because the underlying depressive episode is still present and only its symptomatic expression has been suppressed (Frank et al., 1990). Long-term administration of these drugs is often effective in preventing relapses as well as in preventing recurrent episodes in patients who are susceptible to recurrence (Gitlin, 1996; Nemeroff & Schatzberg, 1998).

Antianxiety Drugs The **antianxiety drugs,** also known as *anxiolytics* or *minor tranquilizers,* are used for a wide range of conditions in which tension and anxiety are significant components, including anxiety-based and psychophysiologic disorders. They are also used as supplementary treatment for certain neurological disorders to control such symptoms as convulsive seizures, but they have little place in the treatment of the psychoses. They are among the most widely prescribed drugs, a fact that has caused concern among some leaders in the medical and psychiatric fields because of their addictive potential and sedating effects.

The most popular class of antianxiety drugs today is the *benzodiazepines,* the first of which were released in the early 1960s. The benzodiazepines act by somehow selectively diminishing generalized anxiety while leaving adaptive behaviors largely intact. They are thus far superior to many other types of anxiety-reducing drugs, which tend to produce widespread negative effects on adaptive functioning. Nevertheless, all of the benzodiazepines have a basically sedative effect, and many patients treated with them complain of drowsiness and lethargy—not too surprising given that these drugs are also among those most commonly used to treat insomnia. Unfortunately, all of

antianxiety drugs Drugs that are used primarily for alleviating a wide range of conditions involving tension and anxiety; also called *anxiolytics.*

the benzodiazepines have the potential of inducing dependence when used unwisely or in excess (Gitlin, 1996; Roy-Byrne & Cowley, 1998). In addition, relapse rates following discontinuation of these drugs is extremely high (Roy-Byrne & Cowley, 1998). This is probably mostly because the drugs do not "cure" the individual; they treat only the symptoms of these disorders, which tend to be chronic conditions (although they do wax and wane in intensity).

The benzodiazepines probably exert their effects through stimulating the action of *gamma-aminobutyric acid (GABA),* an inhibitory neurotransmitter now thought to be functionally deficient in people with generalized anxiety (Gitlin, 1996; Roy-Byrne & Cowley, 1998). GABA ordinarily plays an important role in the way the brain inhibits anxiety in stressful situations. The benzodiazepines appear to enhance GABA activity in certain parts of the brain known to be implicated in anxiety.

The only new type of antianxiety medication that has been released since the early 1960s is buspirone (Buspar), which is completely unrelated to the benzodiazepines and is thought to act in complex ways on serotonergic functioning rather than on GABA activity. It has been shown to be as effective as the benzodiazepines in treating generalized anxiety disorder (Gitlin, 1996; Roy-Byrne & Cowley, 1998). The primary drawback to its use is that it takes 2 to 4 weeks for it to exert its anxiolytic effects, and therefore it is not useful in acute situations or in treating insomnia. Its primary advantage is that, unlike the benzodiazepines, it has no addictive potential and is not sedating.

Lithium and Other Mood-Stabilizing Drugs In the late 1940s in Australia, John Cade discovered that *lithium salts,* naturally occurring mineral compounds, were effective in treating manic disorders. Even though we still do not know how lithium works, there can be no doubt concerning its remarkable effectiveness in at least partially resolving about 70 percent of clearly defined manic states—usually within 7 to 10 days, although it is sometimes more effective when used in conjunction with an antipsychotic drug or a benzodiazepine (Keck & McElroy, 1998). In lithium, psychiatry may have achieved its first essentially preventive treatment method—although, for some patients maintained on the drug for lengthy periods, there may be serious complications, including thyroid dysfunction and occasional kidney damage, as well as memory and motor-speed problems (Gitlin, 1996). Nevertheless, discontinuation of lithium is also very risky, with estimates that the probability of relapse after withdrawal from it is 28 times higher than when on it, with about 50 percent of patients relapsing within 6 months (Keck & McElroy, 1998).

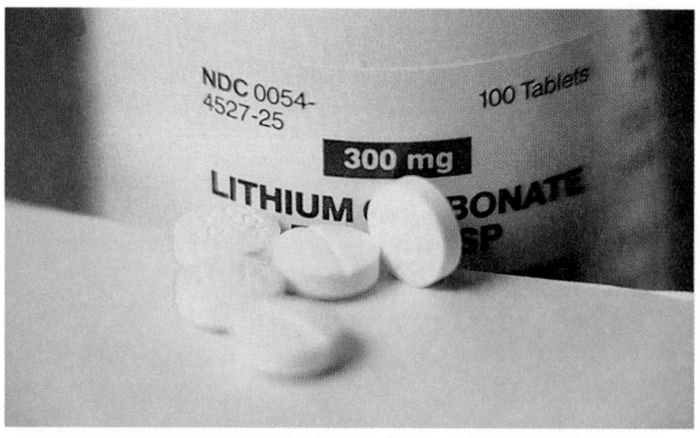

Lithium treatment requires careful monitoring of the dosage—too much can be lethal and too little is ineffective. There is no doubt, however, that the drug has been a boon to those people who have experienced repeated bouts with mania, depression, or both throughout their adult lives.

Lithium may appear to be a veritable wonder drug, but there are significant limitations to its use. First, if not used at the proper dosage, lithium can be toxic, causing such side effects as delirium or convulsions, and even death. At the same time, if lithium is to have any noticeable therapeutic effect, it must be used in quantities within the range of potential dangerousness, which varies among individuals. Thus, careful, ongoing monitoring of a patient's blood levels of lithium is a must. In some patients, lithium has some unpleasant side effects, such as lethargy, decreased motor coordination, gastrointestinal difficulties, increased thirst and urination, and weight gain.

Recently, two other drugs—carbamazepine and valproate—have also been used with considerable success to treat bipolar disorders, but they are probably less effective than lithium in the treatment of bipolar depressive episodes. Although they are not as toxic as lithium, they, too, have significant side effects.

IN REVIEW

- Why is there controversy surrounding the use of ECT? Despite such controversy, why is it still in use?
- What is a prefrontal lobotomy, and what effects does it have on a patient?
- What are the effects and side effects of antipsychotic drugs?
- What are the effects and side effects of antidepressant drugs?
- What are some of the overall advantages and disadvantages of pharmacological methods for treating behavior disorders?

Effective psychotherapy requires a good "working alliance," another term for a good therapeutic relationship.

PSYCHOLOGICALLY BASED THERAPIES

Most of us have experienced a time or situation when we were dramatically helped by talking things over with a relative or friend. As a noted psychoanalyst, Franz Alexander (1946), pointed out long ago, formal psychotherapy as practiced by a mental health professional has much in common with this familiar experience. Most therapists, like all good listeners, rely on a repertoire of receptiveness, warmth, empathy, and they take a nonjudgmental approach to the problems their clients present. Most, however, also introduce into the relationship psychological interventions that are designed to promote new understandings or behaviors, or both, on the client's part. The fact that these interventions are deliberately planned and systematically guided by certain theoretical preconceptions (of the kind discussed in Chapter 2) is what distinguishes **psychotherapy**—the professional treatment of mental disorders by psychological methods—from more informal helping relationships. As we will see, it is these theoretical differences that largely distinguish a given type of psychotherapy from the others.

The belief that people with psychological problems can change—can learn more adaptive ways of perceiving, evaluating, and behaving—is the conviction underlying all psychotherapy. The outcome of psychotherapy will normally be dependent on whether the client and therapist are successful in achieving a productive "working alliance" (Horvath & Greenberg, 1994; Krupnick et al., 1996). Provided there is this firm footing to the client-therapist relationship, it can withstand painful self-disclosure and the almost inevitable trials and tribulations associated with the induction of a new worldview, a more functional emotional reactivity, and a revised and expanded repertoire of behaviors by the client.

The client's major contribution to the therapeutic relationship is his or her motivation. Almost as important as motivation is a client's *expectation* of receiving help. This expectancy is often sufficient in itself to bring about substantial improvement (Fisher & Greenberg, 1997a; Frank, 1978; Lambert, Shapiro, & Bergin, 1986).

To the therapeutic relationship, the therapist brings a variety of professional skills and methods intended to help individuals see themselves and their situations more objectively—that is, to gain a different perspective. Besides helping provide a new perspective, most therapy situations also offer a client a protected setting in which he or she is helped to practice new ways of feeling and acting, gradually developing both the courage and the ability to take responsibility for acting in more effective and satisfying ways.

Effective therapy depends, at least to some extent, on a good match between client and therapist (Talley, Strupp,

psychotherapy Professional treatment of mental disorders by psychological methods.

HIGHLIGHT 3.5

Another Enduring Effect of Slavery

Because of the history of slavery and continued overt and subtle racism, oppression, and discrimination in the United States, the psychotherapy involving African-American clients and white mental health professionals may pose special problems around the issue of rage. Rage is said to be a common, everyday experience among many African-Americans, yet the larger society has a very low tolerance for its expression. Unexpressed rage leads to despair and the mental health consequences thereof. The white therapist, who may have little personal acquaintance with rage and who may share the larger culture's proscriptions regarding it, may have a hard time recognizing its signs or dealing effectively with it in his or her African-American clients—thus failing to engage what may be a central issue in these clients' lives (see Hardy & Laszloffy, 1995). ■

& Morey, 1990). Hence, a therapist's own personality is necessarily a factor of some importance in determining therapeutic outcomes, quite aside from his or her background and training or the particular formal treatment plan adopted (Beutler, Machado, & Neufeldt, 1994; Blatt, Sanislow, et al., 1996; Lambert, 1989). For example, a therapist who inadvertently but unfailingly takes charge in finding solutions for clients' problems will have considerable difficulty in working with people presenting serious difficulties in the area of inhibited autonomy, as in the case of extremely dependent people.

In an increasingly multicultural and socioeconomically disparate society, it is becoming increasingly important to consider how cultural and ethnic differences may affect the client-therapist relationship and therapy outcomes (Sue, Zane, & Young, 1994). Overall, there is as yet no solid evidence that psychotherapeutic outcomes are diminished when client and therapist are of different race or ethnicity (Beutler et al., 1994; Sue, Zane, & Young, 1994). However, Atkinson (1983) and Atkinson, Furlong, and Poston (1986) found that African-American clients experience greater rapport and satisfaction with African-American than with white therapists, and other evidence suggests that they may be more amenable to self-disclosure when the therapist is also African-American (Jackson & Kirschner, 1973). Similarly, Mexican-Americans state a strong preference for therapists sharing their ethnic background and express the view that such therapists are more "credible" than Anglo therapists would be (Lopez, Lopez, & Fong, 1991; Ponce & Atkinson, 1989). In another study, the significance of the client-therapist ethnic match for Mexican-American clients in the Los Angeles area appeared to depend on whether or not English was the client's primary language—if it was not, the clients had better outcomes when the therapist was also of Mexican-American heritage (Sue et al., 1991).

Despite general agreement among psychotherapists on the importance of the client-therapist relationship, professionals can and do differ in their assessments and treatments of psychological disorders. As we saw in Chapter 2, the differing viewpoints on human motivation and behavior lead to quite different appraisals of exactly what "the problem" is and how a person should be helped to overcome it. We will explore here some of the most widely used and accepted psychological treatment approaches: psychodynamic therapies, behavior therapies, cognitive and cognitive-behavioral therapies, humanistic-experiential therapies, and therapies for interpersonal relationships.

Psychodynamic Therapies

A **psychodynamic therapy** is any psychological treatment approach that focuses on individual personality dynamics, usually from a psychoanalytic or some psychoanalytically derived perspective (see Chapter 2). In keeping with Freud's fascination with the principles of thermodynamics, the underlying model relates to the channeling and transformations that occur in the "energy" contained in human drives and motives. The therapy is mainly practiced in two basic forms: classical psychoanalysis, and psychoanalytically oriented psychotherapy.

Classical Psychoanalysis As developed by Freud and his immediate followers, *classical psychoanalysis* is an intensive (at least three sessions per week), long-term procedure for uncovering repressed memories, thoughts, fears, and conflicts presumably stemming from problems in early psychosexual development—and helping individuals come to terms with these in light of the realities of adult life. Usually a client lies in a relaxed position on a couch and gives a running account of all the thoughts,

psychodynamic therapy Any psychological treatment that focuses on individual personality dynamics, usually from a psychodynamic or some psychodynamically derived perspective.

In classical psychoanalysis, the patient lies in a relaxed position, facing away from the psychoanalyst. The idea behind this is that in this position he or she is better able to let thoughts go and say whatever comes to mind without trying to gauge the therapist's reactions. The therapist, too, is able to listen more freely for themes and patterns in the material when relieved of the conventions of face-to-face contact.

feelings, and desires that come to mind as one idea leads to another. The therapist normally takes a position behind the client so as not to in any way distract or disrupt the client.

It is thought that gaining insight into repressed material frees individuals from the need to keep wasting their energies on repressing the urge to "let go" and on other defense mechanisms. Instead, they can bring their personality resources to bear on consciously resolving the anxieties that prompted the repression in the first place. Freed from the effort of keeping threatening thoughts out of consciousness (so the theory states), they can turn their energies to better personality integration and more effective living.

Four basic techniques are characteristic of classical psychoanalysis:

1. *Free association.* The psychoanalytic technique in which the client says whatever comes into his or her mind, regardless of how personal, painful, or seemingly irrelevant it may be, is called **free association.** The goal is to explore the contents of the preconscious, that part of the mind thought to contain derivatives of repressed unconscious material, which if properly "interpreted" can lead to its uncovering. Analytic interpretation involves a therapist's tying together a client's often disconnected ideas, beliefs, and actions into a meaningful explanation to help the client gain insight into the relationship between his or her maladaptive behavior and the repressed (unconscious) events and fantasies that drive it.
2. *Analysis of dreams.* This is a technique based on the idea that repressive defenses are lowered when a person is asleep, and forbidden desires and feelings may find a symbolic outlet in dreams. A dream has both **manifest content,** which is the dream as it appears to the dreamer, and **latent content,** which is composed of the actual motives that are seeking expression but are so painful or unacceptable that they are disguised. The therapist attempts to uncover these disguised meanings by studying the images that appear in the manifest content of a client's dream and his or her preconscious associations to them.
3. *Analysis of resistance.* During the process of free association or of associating to dreams, an individual may evidence **resistance**—an unwillingness or inability to talk about certain thoughts, motives, or experiences (Strean, 1985). Because resistance prevents painful and threatening material from entering awareness, its sources must be identified if an individual is to face the problem and learn to deal with it in a realistic manner.
4. *Analysis of transference.* As client and therapist interact, the relationship between them may become complex and emotionally involved. Often clients carry over and apply to their therapist attitudes and feelings that they had in their relations with a parent or other person close to them in the past, a process known as **transference.** Thus clients may react to the analyst as they did to that earlier person and feel the same love, hostility, or rejection that they felt long ago. Once transference is understood, the client can "relive" the past pathogenic relationship with the therapist *in* the therapeutic setting and work to overcome the feelings of hostility and self-devaluation that may have stemmed from it.

free association Psychoanalytic method for probing the preconscious by having a client say whatever comes into his or her mind.

manifest content In psychoanalytic theory, the meaning of a dream as it appears to the dreamer, which masks the latent content.

latent content In psychoanalytic theory, the actual motives of a dream that are seeking expression but are so painful or unacceptable that they are disguised by the manifest content of the dream.

resistance In psychoanalysis, the person's unwillingness or inability to talk about certain thoughts, motives, or experiences.

transference In psychoanalysis, the process whereby clients project onto the therapist attitudes and feelings they had in a past relationship with a parent or other person close to them.

The resolution of the transference is said to be the key element in effecting a psychoanalytic "cure." It can be jeopardized by **countertransference,** however, a process in which the therapist reacts in accord with the client's transferred attributions rather than objectively, thus increasing the likelihood that the client will merely repeat in the therapeutic relationship the typical relationship difficulties characterizing his or her adult life. To avoid countertransference, all psychoanalysts must themselves undergo psychoanalysis before they begin independent practice.

Psychodynamic Therapy Since Freud The original version of psychoanalysis is practiced only rarely today. Arduous and expensive in terms of time, money, and emotional commitment, classical psychoanalysis may take several years before both analyst and client are satisfied that all major issues in the client's life have been satisfactorily resolved. In *psychoanalytically oriented psychotherapy,* therapy is still loosely based on psychoanalytic concepts, but therapists typically schedule less frequent sessions, such as once per week, and sit face-to-face with the client instead of having the latter recline on a couch with the analyst out of sight behind them. Likewise, the relatively passive stance of the analyst (primarily listening to the client's free associations, and rarely offering interpretations) is replaced with an active conversational style, in which the therapist attempts to clarify distortions and gaps in the client's construction of the origins and consequences of his or her problems, thus challenging client "defenses" as they present themselves. It is widely believed that this more direct approach significantly shortens total treatment time.

Whether contemporary psychodynamic approaches to therapy focus on *object relations* ("objects" in psychoanalytic jargon are other people) or *attachment* or *self psychology,* they all tend to have a strongly *interpersonal* focus (e.g., Benjamin, 1996b; Crits-Christoph & Connolly, in press; Frank & Spanier, 1995; Horowitz, 1996; Kiesler, 1996). They emphasize, in other words, what traditional Freudians would consider transferential and countertransferential phenomena, with the important extension of this concept to virtually all of a disturbed person's relationships. First articulated in this country by Harry Stack Sullivan (see Chapter 2), the central idea is that all individuals at all times involuntarily invoke schemas acquired from their earliest interactions with others, such as parents, in interpreting what is going on in their current relationships. Where those earlier relationships have had problematic features, such as rejection or abuse, their "introjected" characteristics may distort in various ways an individual's ability to process accurately and objectively the information contained in current interpersonal transactions. Thus, the formerly abused or rejected person may come to operate under the implicit (unconscious) assumption that the world is generally rejecting and/or abusive. The mistrust stemming from this belief negatively affects current relationship possibilities—in the worst instances, possibly even leading (because of the reactions of others to the client's wariness, reticence, or counteraggression) to a further confirmation for that client of the world's being a nasty if not dangerous place, an instance of self-fulfilling prophecy (e.g., see Carson, 1982; Wachtel, 1993).

countertransference In psychoanalysis, the process in which the therapist reacts in accord with the client's transferred attributions rather than objectively.

Interpersonally oriented psychodynamic therapists vary considerably in their time focus, whether they concentrate on remote events of the past or on current ("the here and now") interpersonal situations and impasses—including those of the therapy itself—or some balance of the two. Probably, as already suggested, most seek to expose, bring to awareness, and modify the effects of the remote developmental sources of the difficulties the client is currently experiencing. Psychodynamic therapies generally retain, then, the classical psychoanalytic goal of understanding the present in terms of the past. What they ignore are the psychoanalytic notions of staged libidinal energy transformations and of entirely internal (and impersonal) drives that are channeled into psychopathological symptom formation.

Evaluating Psychodynamic Therapies Classical psychoanalysis is routinely criticized for being time-consuming and expensive; for being based on a questionable, stultified, and sometimes cultlike approach to human nature; for neglecting a client's immediate problems in the search for unconscious conflicts in the remote past; and for inadequate proof of its general effectiveness (see Smith, Glass, & Miller, 1980; Wallerstein, 1989). Nevertheless, many people do feel that they have profited from psychoanalysis—particularly in terms of greater self-understanding, relief from inner conflict and anxiety, and improved interpersonal relationships. Psychoanalytically oriented psychotherapy remains the treatment of choice for many individuals who are seeking extensive insight into themselves and broad-based personality change. In trying to reconcile these contrasting observations, we may be confronting two different standards of evaluating therapeutic outcomes: on the one hand, *efficacy* (involving maximally rigorous controlled research designs), and on the other, *effectiveness* (a looser but probably overall more realistic standard). This distinction has become prominent in the literature only in the last few years (Seligman, 1995).

Turning our attention to the usually far briefer versions of interpersonal psychodynamic therapies, the situation appears brighter—even under an efficacy standard (see Anderson & Lambert, 1995). In general, the demonstrated results of this type of therapy are quite impressive. We would single out in particular the interpersonal therapy model developed by Klerman and colleagues (1984), originally targeted for the problem of depression, where it has demonstrated value (Frank & Spanier, 1995). It has also been shown to be a promising treatment for bulimia nervosa (Fairburn et al., 1993), and it is currently being investigated in other clinical contexts as well.

The greatest contribution of the interpersonal approach may be its role in the developing movement toward "integration" of the various forms of therapy. Numerous contemporary investigators and clinicians have pointed to the multiple ways in which interpersonal issues play a central role in psychodynamic, behavioral, cognitive, and even psychopharmacological therapies (e.g., Beutler, 1992; Blatt, Zuroff, et al., 1996; Lazarus, 1997a, 1997b; Linehan, 1993; Safran, 1990a, 1990b; Wachtel, 1997).

Behavior Therapies

Although the use of conditioning techniques in therapy has a long history, it was not until the 1960s that **behavior therapy**—the use of therapeutic procedures based originally on the principles of classical and operant conditioning—really came into its own. A behavior therapist specifies in advance the precise maladaptive behaviors to be modified and the adaptive behaviors to be achieved, as well as the specific learning principles or procedures to be used in producing the desired results.

Instead of exploring past traumatic events or inner conflicts, behavior therapists attempt to modify problem behaviors directly by extinguishing or counterconditioning maladaptive reactions, such as anxiety, or by manipulating environmental contingencies—that is, by the use of reward, suspension of reward, or, occasionally, punishment to shape overt actions. Indeed, for the strict behaviorist, "personality" does not exist except in the form of a collection of modifiable habits. Behavior therapy techniques seem especially effective in altering maladaptive behavior when a reinforcement is administered contiguous with a desired response, and when a person knows what is expected and why the reinforcement is given. The ultimate goal, of course, is not only to achieve the desired responses but to bring them under the control and self-monitoring of the individual. We will elaborate briefly on the key techniques of behavior therapy.

Joseph Wolpe is shown here conducting systematic desensitization therapy to reduce a client's anxiety. The client, in a relaxed state, is told to imagine the weakest item on her hierarchy of anxiety-producing stimuli. If she feels anxious, she is instructed to stop imagining and relax again.

Guided Exposure *Guided exposure* is the technique behavior therapists have developed to ensure the *unlearning* of certain maladaptive reactions. One method of guided exposure is **systematic densensitization,** which is aimed at teaching a person to relax or behave in some other way that is inconsistent with anxiety while in the presence (real or imagined) of the anxiety-producing stimulus (Wolpe, 1958). It may therefore be considered a type of counterconditioning procedure.

The term "systematic" refers to the carefully graduated manner in which the person is exposed to the feared stimulus: The client first constructs an anxiety hierarchy of imagined scenes graded as to their capacity to elicit anxiety; then, actual therapy sessions consist of repeatedly imagining the scenes in the hierarchy under conditions of deep relaxation, beginning with the items at minimum anxiety and gradually working toward those rated in the more extreme ranges. A session is terminated at any point

behavior therapy Use of therapeutic procedures based originally on the principles of classical and operant conditioning.

systematic desensitization Behavior therapy technique aimed at teaching a person to relax or behave in some other way that is inconsistent with anxiety while in the presence (real or imagined) of the anxiety-producing stimulus.

when the client reports experiencing significant anxiety, the next session resuming at a lower point in the hierarchy. Treatment continues until all items in the hierarchy can be imagined without notable discomfort, at which point the client's real-life difficulties will typically have shown substantial improvement. The usual duration of a desensitization session is about 30 minutes, and the sessions are often given two to three times per week. The overall therapy program may, of course, take a number of weeks or even months.

As in the case of psychodynamic therapy, the original systematic desensitization model has now been largely supplanted by briefer and more direct techniques. One variation involves the use of a tape recorder to enable a client to carry out the desensitization process at home. Another utilizes group desensitization procedures—as in marathon desensitization groups, in which the entire program is compressed into a few days of intensive treatment.

By the mid-1980s, it had become apparent that the central ingredient to systematic desensitization was in fact "exposure" to the heretofore avoided anxiety-provoking stimuli, the remaining components being seen largely as facilitating that exposure. Therapists began to explore a variety of quite direct approaches to having clients repeatedly experience the actual—not merely imaginal—internal stimuli (e.g., heartbeat irregularities) or external stimuli (e.g., high places) that had been identified as producing anxiety reactions. Such an approach is often referred to as **in vivo exposure** (as opposed to **in vitro,** or imaginal, **exposure**).

In vivo exposure seems to have advantages with respect to both efficiency and efficacy over in vitro exposure whenever it is possible to identify in concrete terms those situations evoking anxiety and to induce the client to confront them directly (Barlow, 1988, 1993; Emmelkamp, 1994; Nathan & Gorman, 1998; Roth & Fonagy, 1996). For example, in vivo procedures are particularly effective in treating phobias such as agoraphobia (fear of heights). Some technologically oriented therapists have even begun to experiment with computerized virtual reality as a means of exposing clients to scenes that would be unwise, inconvenient, or impossible to recreate in real life (e.g., Rothbaum et al., 1995a, 1995b, 1996). The technique appears to have considerable promise.

In vivo exposure is a technique that involves placing an individual in a real-life anxiety-arousing situation with the goal of extinguishing the conditioned avoidance of the anxiety-provoking stimulus, as well as anxiety itself. For example, a client with a fear of heights may be taken to the top of a tall building to demonstrate that the feared consequences do not occur.

in vivo exposure Exposure to anxiety-provoking stimuli that takes place in a real-life situation, as opposed to a therapeutic or laboratory setting.

in vitro exposure Exposure to anxiety-provoking stimuli that takes place in a therapeutic or laboratory setting.

aversion therapy Form of behavior therapy aimed at modifying undesirable behavior by using punishment.

Aversion Therapy **Aversion therapy** involves modifying undesirable behavior by the old-fashioned method of punishment. Punishment may involve either the removal of highly desired reinforcers or the use of aversive stimuli, but the basic idea is to reduce the "temptation value" of stimuli that elicit undesirable behavior. Aversion therapy has been used in the treatment of a wide range of maladaptive behaviors, including smoking, drinking, overeating, drug dependence, gambling, sexual deviance, and bizarre psychotic behavior. Probably the most commonly used aversive stimuli today are drugs having noxious effects, such as those that induce nausea and vomiting when a recovering alcoholic ingests alcohol.

Another variant of aversion therapy is called *covert, or vicarious, sensitization,* in which an attempt is made to induce unpleasant feelings such as disgust or fear in association with tempting stimuli (Maletsky, 1998). For example, Weinrot and Riggan (1996) describe a procedure in which adolescent sexual offenders view specially prepared videotapes that graphically depict plausible consequences of engaging in deviant behavior, such as being raped during prison confinement or being shamed and rejected by opposite-sex peers who know of the offense.

Aversion therapy is primarily a way of stopping maladaptive responses for a brief period of time; it is unlikely that the behavior will be permanently relinquished unless alternative forms of gratification are learned during the therapy. Therefore, it is critical to substitute for the maladaptive behavior new, more adaptive patterns of behavior that will prove reinforcing in themselves.

Modeling As the name implies, **modeling** involves the learning of skills through imitating another person, such as a parent or therapist, who performs the behavior to be acquired. A younger client may be exposed to behaviors or roles in peers who act as assistants to the therapist and then be encouraged to imitate and practice the desired new responses. For example, modeling may be used to promote the learning of simple skills, such as self-feeding by a profoundly mentally retarded child, or more complex ones, such as being more effective in social situations by a shy, withdrawn adolescent. In work with children, especially, effective decision making and problem solving may be modeled where the therapist "thinks out loud" about everyday choices that present themselves in the course of therapy (Kendall, 1990; Kendall & Braswell, 1985).

Modeling and imitation are used with other types of therapy. For example, in an early classic work, Bandura (1964) found that live modeling of fearlessness combined with instruction and guided exposure was the most effective treatment for snake phobia, resulting in the elimination of phobic reactions in over 90 percent of the cases treated.

Systematic Use of Reinforcement Often referred to as *contingency management,* systematic programs involving the management of reinforcement to suppress (extinguish) unwanted behavior or to elicit and maintain effective behavior have achieved notable success, particularly but by no means exclusively in institutional settings.

The suppression of problematic behavior may be as simple as removing the reinforcements supporting it, provided, of course, that the latter can be identified. Response shaping, token economies, and behavioral contracting are among the most widely used of such techniques.

Positive reinforcement is an effective technique for managing behavior problems, with food or other treats or privileges often used as reinforcers. This autistic child is being reinforced for some positive behavior by being stroked with a feather tickler.

Response Shaping Positive reinforcement is often used in **response shaping**—that is, in establishing by gradual approximation a response that is actively resisted or is not initially in an individual's behavioral repertoire. This technique has been used extensively in working with children's behavior problems. For example, in a now classic case of a 3-year-old autistic child who refused to wear eyeglasses, the therapist first trained the boy to expect a bit of candy or fruit at the sound of a toy noisemaker. Then training was begun with empty eyeglass frames. The boy was first reinforced with the candy or fruit for picking them up, then for holding them, then for carrying them around, then for bringing the frames closer to the eyes, etc. Though successive approximations, the boy finally learned to wear his glasses with their corrective lenses (Wolf, Risley, & Mees, 1964).

Token Economies Approval and other intangible reinforcers may be ineffective in many behavior modification programs, especially those dealing with severely maladaptive behavior. In such instances, programs called

modeling Learning of skills by imitating another person who performs the behavior to be acquired.

response shaping Behavior therapy technique using positive reinforcement to establish by gradual approximation a response that is actively resisted or is not initially in a person's behavioral repertoire.

token economies may be preferable, in which appropriate behaviors are rewarded with tangible reinforcers in the form of tokens that can later be exchanged for desired objects or privileges (Kazdin, 1980). In ground-breaking work with hospitalized individuals with schizophrenia, for example, Ayllon and Azrin (1968) found that using the commissary, listening to records, and going to movies were considered highly desirable activities by most of the patients. Consequently, these activities were chosen as reinforcers for socially appropriate behavior. To participate in any of them, a patient had to earn a number of tokens by demonstrating appropriate ward behavior.

Token economies have been used to establish adaptive behaviors ranging from elementary actions, such as eating and making one's bed, to the daily performance of responsible hospital jobs. In the latter instance, the token economy resembles the outside world where an individual is paid for his or her work in tokens (money) that can later be exchanged for desired objects and activities. The use of tokens as reinforcers for appropriate behavior has a number of distinct advantages: (1) the number of tokens earned depends directly on the amount of desirable behavior shown; (2) tokens, like money in the outside world, may be made a general medium of currency in terms of what they will "purchase" and hence are not readily subject to satiation and tend to maintain their incentive value; (3) tokens can reduce the delay that often occurs between appropriate performance and reinforcement; (4) the number of tokens earned and the way in which they are "spent" are largely up to the individual; and (5) tokens tend to bridge the gap between the institutional environment and the demands and system of payment that will be encountered in the outside world.

The ultimate goal in token economies, as in other programs involving initially extrinsic reinforcement, is not only to achieve desired responses but to bring such responses to a level where their adaptive consequences will be reinforcing in their own right—intrinsically reinforcing. For example, extrinsic reinforcers may be used initially to help children overcome reading difficulties, but once a child becomes proficient in reading, this skill will presumably provide intrinsic reinforcement as the child comes to enjoy reading for its own sake.

Behavioral Contracting A technique called **behavioral contracting** is used in some types of psychotherapy and behavior therapy to identify the behaviors that are to be changed and to maximize the probability that these changes will occur and be maintained (Nelson & Mowry, 1976). By definition, a *contract* is an agreement between two or more parties—such as a therapist and a client, a parent and a teenager, or a husband and a wife—that governs the nature of an exchange. In therapy, this agreement, often in writing, specifies a client's obligations to change as well as the responsibilities of the other party to provide something the client wants in return, such as tangible rewards, privileges, or therapeutic attention. Behavior therapists frequently make behavioral contracting an explicit focus of treatment, thus helping establish the treatment as a joint enterprise for which both parties have responsibility.

Sometimes a contract is negotiated between a disruptive child and a teacher, specifying that the child will maintain or receive certain privileges as long as he or she behaves in accordance with the contract. Another common application of contracting is in behavioral couples therapy, where the principles governing the exchange of "reinforcements" between the distressed parties is formally negotiated and sometimes even committed to writing (e.g., Cordova & Jacobson, 1993).

Formal therapeutic contracts are not long-term solutions to regulating interpersonal behavior. Rather, like aversion therapy, contracts provide an opportunity to interrupt self-sustaining dysfunctional behavior for a time, thus permitting the emergence of new responses that may prove more adaptive and satisfying.

Biofeedback and Relaxation Training The process of teaching a person to influence his or her own physiological processes is referred to as **biofeedback.** It involves several steps: (1) monitoring the physiological response that is to be modified (perhaps blood pressure or skin temperature); (2) converting the information to a visual or auditory signal; and (3) providing a means of prompt feedback—indicating to a subject as rapidly as possible when the desired change is taking place (Blanchard & Epstein, 1978). Given this feedback, the subject may then seek to reduce his or her emotionality, as by lowering the skin temperature. For the most part, biofeedback is oriented to reducing the reactivity of some organ system in-

token economies Behavior modification programs often used in hospital or institutional settings, in which patients are rewarded for appropriate behaviors with reinforcers in the form of tokens that can later be exchanged for desired objects or privileges.

behavioral contracting Positive reinforcement technique that uses a contract, or formal agreement, often between members of a couple or family, to identify the behaviors to be changed and to specify the rewards or privileges that will follow.

biofeedback Behavioral treatment technique in which a person is taught to influence his or her own physiological processes.

nervated by the autonomic nervous system—very often a physiological component of the anxiety response.

The importance of the autonomic nervous system in the development of abnormal behavior has long been recognized. However, although there is general agreement that many physiological processes can be regulated to some extent by learning, the application of biofeedback procedures to alter abnormal behavior has produced equivocal results. The effects of biofeedback procedures are generally small and often do not generalize to situations outside the laboratory, where the biofeedback devices are not present (Blanchard & Young 1973, 1974). There is good evidence nevertheless that tension headache victims may respond quite favorably to biofeedback (E. Blanchard, 1994). Also, Flor and Birbaumer (1993) demonstrated a rather impressive effect of muscle tension biofeedback in the control of musculoskeletal pain of the back and jaw, an effect that was still present at a 24-month follow-up. The latter study, however, did not include a relaxation training comparison group. Where that comparison has been made, biofeedback usually has not been shown to be any more effective than relaxation training, leading to the suggestion that biofeedback may simply be a more elaborate (and usually more costly) means of teaching clients how to relax (e.g., Blanchard et al., 1980). Relaxation training itself continues to amass a very creditable record in the treatment of various medical conditions, as shown in a quantitative review by Carlson and Hoyle (1993), as well as various mental disorders where anxiety is a substantial component (Nathan & Gorman, 1998; Roth & Fonagy, 1996).

Evaluating Behavior Therapies Compared with psychodynamic and other psychotherapies, behavior therapies appear to have three distinct advantages. First, their treatment approach is precise. The target behaviors to be modified are specified, the methods to be used are clearly delineated, and the results can be readily evaluated (Marks, 1982). Second, explicit learning principles form a sound basis for effective interventions because of their demonstrated scientific validity (Borkovec, 1997; Kazdin & Wilson, 1978). Third, the economy of time and cost is quite good. Not surprisingly, then, the overall outcomes achieved with behavior therapies compare very favorably with those of other approaches (Nathan & Gorman, 1998; Roth & Fonagy, 1996; Smith et al., 1980). Behavior therapies usually achieve results in a short period of time because they are generally directed to specific symptoms, leading to faster relief of a client's distress and to lower costs.

As with other approaches, the range of effectiveness of behavior therapies is not unlimited; they work better with certain kinds of problems than with others. Generally, the more pervasive and vaguely defined the client's problem, the less likely that a behavior therapy will be useful. For example, behavior therapies appear to be less frequently used to treat Axis II personality disorders, whose symptoms are less specific. On the other hand, behavioral techniques are the backbone of modern approaches to treating sexual dysfunctions, as will be discussed in Chapter 11. Quantitative reviews of therapeutic outcomes confirm the expectation that behavior therapies have a particular value in the treatment of anxiety disorders, to which the powerful exposure techniques can be brought to bear (Andrews & Harvey, 1981; Chambless et al., 1998; Clum, Clum, & Surls, 1993; Nathan & Gorman, 1998). The extensive quantitative review conducted by Smith and colleagues (1980) reveals the less expected finding of a relatively good outcome record with the psychoses. Thus, although behavior therapies are not a cure-all, they have earned in a relatively brief period a highly respected place among the available psychosocial treatment approaches.

Cognitive and Cognitive-Behavioral Therapies

As we have seen, early behavior therapists focused on observable behavior; they regarded the inner thoughts of their clients as not really part of the causal chain. Eventually, however, some behavior therapists began to reappraise the importance of "private events"—thoughts, perceptions, evaluations, and self-statements—seeing them as processes that mediate the effects of objective stimulus conditions and thus help determine behavior and emotions (Borkovec, 1985; Mahoney & Arnkoff, 1978).

Out of this reappraisal evolved the **cognitive** or **cognitive-behavioral therapies** (terms for the most part used interchangeably), which are characterized by two main themes: (1) the conviction that cognitive processes influence emotion, motivation, and behavior; and (2) the use of cognitive and behavior-change techniques in a pragmatic (hypothesis-testing) manner. We consider three approaches: (1) the rational emotive behavior therapy of Albert Ellis, (2) the stress-inoculation training of Donald Meichenbaum, and (3) the cognitive therapy of Aaron Beck.

Rational Emotive Behavior Therapy One of the earliest developed of the behaviorally oriented cognitive

cognitive therapy Another term for *cognitive-behavioral therapy.*

cognitive-behavioral therapy Any therapy based on altering dysfunctional thoughts and cognitive distortions.

Cognitive-behavioral therapy is geared toward uncovering and changing the faulty beliefs and unrealistic assumptions that can warp our perceptions of ourselves and events and contribute to depression and other disorders.

therapies was the rational emotive therapy (now called **rational emotive behavior therapy,** or **REBT**) of Albert Ellis (1958, 1973, 1975, 1989; Ellis & Dryden, 1997). Ellis (1970) proposed that one or more core irrational beliefs, reproduced in Table 3.5, are specific to and at the root of most psychological maladjustment. In Ellis's view, many of us have learned these unrealistic beliefs, which then cause us to expect too much of ourselves and to behave irrationally and ineffectively; this then leads to the recognition of failure and the emotional response of self-devaluation.

rational emotive behavior therapy (REBT) Type of cognitive-behavioral therapy focusing on changing a client's irrational beliefs, on which maladaptive emotional responses and thus behavior are presumed to depend.

stress-inoculation training (SIT) A cognitive-behavioral treatment approach that focuses on altering the self-statements an individual makes in stress-producing situations.

TABLE 3.5 ELLIS'S CORE IRRATIONAL BELIEFS

One should be loved by everyone for everything one does.

Certain acts are awful or wicked, and people who perform them should be severely punished.

It is horrible when things are not the way we would like them to be.

If something may be dangerous or fearsome, one should be terribly upset about it.

It is better to avoid life problems, if possible, than to face them.

One needs something stronger or more powerful than oneself to rely on.

One should be thoroughly competent, intelligent, and achieving in all respects.

Because something once affected one's life, it will indefinitely affect it.

One must have perfect and certain self-control.

Happiness can be achieved by inertia and inaction.

We have virtually no control over our emotions and cannot help having certain feelings.

The task of rational emotive behavior therapy is to restructure the individual's belief system and self-evaluation, especially with respect to the irrational "shoulds," "oughts," and "musts" that are preventing a more positive sense of self-worth and a creative, emotionally satisfying, and fulfilling life. Several methods are used to teach the client to identify and dispute the beliefs that are producing the negative emotional consequences.

Rational emotive behavior therapists also use behaviorally oriented techniques, usually to help clients practice living in accord with their new beliefs and philosophy. They typically give homework assignments to encourage clients to have new experiences and break negative chains of behavior. Clients might be instructed to reward themselves by an external reinforcer, such as a food treat, after working 15 minutes at disputing their beliefs, or they might reinforce themselves with private self-statements such as "You are doing a really good job." Embracing such a belief, incidentally, will probably have positive effects whether or not it is factually true (Bandura, 1986; Taylor & Brown, 1988).

Stress-Inoculation Therapy A second cognitive-behavioral approach to treatment is **stress-inoculation therapy (SIT)**—a type of self-instructional training focused on altering the self-statements an individual routinely makes in stress-producing situations, in order to improve functioning under stressful conditions (Meichenbaum, 1985, 1993). Like other cognitive-behavioral therapies, stress-inoculation therapy assumes that a person's problems result from maladaptive beliefs that are leading to negative emotional states and maladaptive behavior, familiar elements in the causal chain cognitive theorists have posited.

Stress-inoculation therapy usually involves three stages. First is *cognitive preparation*, in which client and therapist together explore the client's beliefs and attitudes about problem situations and identify the self-statements that produce maladaptive behavior. Second is *skill acquisition and rehearsal*, in which more adaptive self-statements are learned and practiced. For example, a person attempting to cope with the "feeling of being overwhelmed" would rehearse reassuring self-statements aimed at overcoming those feelings (e.g., "When fear comes, just pause," "Label your fear from 0 to 10 and watch it change," "Just think about something else." [Meichenbaum, 1974, p. 16]). Finally, the third phase of stress-inoculation therapy, *application and practice*, involves applying the new coping strategies. The client attempts easier situations first and only gradually tries more stressful situations as he or she feels confident of mastering them.

Beck's Cognitive Therapy The basic assumption underlying Aaron Beck's cognitive therapy approach is that maladaptive behaviors result from the clients' illogical thinking about themselves, the world they live in, and the future. Originally developed for the treatment of depression (Beck et al., 1979; Hollon & Beck, 1978), Beck's therapy has since been extended to anxiety disorders, eating disorders and obesity, conduct disorder in children, personality disorders, substance abuse, and even chronic fatigue syndrome.

In Beck's cognitive therapy, clients do not change their beliefs by debate and persuasion as is common in rational emotive behavior therapy; rather, therapist and client together identify the client's beliefs and expectations and formulate them as hypotheses to be tested. They then design ways in which the client can check out these hypotheses in the real world. These disconfirmation experiments are planned to give the individual successful experiences, thereby interrupting the destructive sequence previously described. They are arranged according to difficulty, so that the least difficult (or risky) tasks will be accomplished successfully before the more difficult ones are attempted.

In the treatment of depression, a client and a therapist may schedule the client's daily activities on an hour-by-hour basis. Such activity scheduling is an important part of therapy with depressed individuals because reducing such clients' inactivity interrupts their tendencies to ruminate about themselves. An important part of the arrangement is the scheduling of pleasurable events, because many depressed clients have lost the capacity for gaining pleasure from their own activities. Both the scheduled pleasurable activities and the rewarding experiences that derive from carrying out the behavioral experiments tend to increase an individual's satisfaction and positive mood. In addition, the client is encouraged to discover and change underlying dysfunctional assumptions or depression-inducing schemas that may be leading to self-defeating tendencies. Because these dysfunctional schemas are seen as creating the person's vulnerability to depression, this phase of treatment is considered essential in ensuring resistance to relapse when the client faces stressful life events in the future.

Evaluating Cognitive-Behavioral Therapies It is important to understand that the intellectual status of cognitive therapy is not without controversy. The exact nature of the relationship between emotion, cognition, and behavior still remains far from clear. Can it be, for example, that thoughts cause emotions and behavior? Aaron Beck acknowledges that disordered cognitions are *not* a cause of abnormal behavior or emotions, but rather are an intrinsic (yet alterable) element of such behavior and emotions (Beck & Weishaar, 1989). If the critical cognitive components can be changed, according to this view, then the behavior and maladaptive emotions will change.

In spite of the ongoing debate about the nature of the relationship between cognitions and behavior, the therapies that have evolved from the cognitive approach have become popular today. Ellis's rational emotive behavior therapy, for example, has enjoyed widespread attention. Research suggests, however, that it may not be the best choice of therapy for most diagnosed clinical populations but, instead, may be most useful in helping generally healthy people cope better with everyday stress and perhaps prevent them from developing full-blown anxiety or depressive disorders (Haaga & Davison, 1989, 1992).

Stress-inoculation therapy has been successfully used with a number of clinical problems, including anger, pain, Type A behavior, and mild forms of anxiety. This approach is particularly suited to increasing the adaptive capabilities of individuals who have shown a vulnerability to developing problems in certain stressful situations. In addition, with its focus on improving general coping skills, stress-inoculation therapy may be useful for preventing behavior disorders (e.g., Meichenbaum & Jaremko, 1983).

A review of research evaluating Beck's type of cognitive therapy suggests that it is extremely effective in alleviating many different types of disorders (see Hollon & Beck, 1994, for a comprehensive review). In the case of depression, considerable evidence suggests that cognitive therapy is arguably at least comparable to drug treatment, in all but the most severe cases (e.g., psychotic depression). Moreover, it has superior long-term advantages: Several studies have shown that relapse was less likely during the first and second years of posttreatment if a client had been treated with cognitive therapy, whether or not there was also treatment with antidepressant drugs (Craighead, Craighead, & Ilardi, 1998).

The combined use of cognitive and behavior therapy approaches is now quite routine. Although some disagreement continues about whether the effects of cognitive treatments are actually the result of cognitive changes, it does appear that cognitive change is the best predictor of long-term outcome, at least for depression and panic disorder (Hollon, Evans, & DeRubeis, 1990). We anticipate that in the next few years more attention will be devoted to these important questions about how cognitive-behavioral therapies work. (See the Fall 1997 issue of *Behavior Therapy* [vol. 28, no. 4] for related interesting discussions by experts in the field.) Indeed, these questions have assumed increased importance in light of the striking and widely documented success of this mode of therapy.

HIGHLIGHT 3.6

All Together Now—Therapy in Groups

All the major systematic approaches to psychotherapy that we have discussed—psychoanalysis, behavior therapy, and so on—have been applied in group as well as individual settings. Group therapy traditionally involved a relatively small group of clients in a clinic or hospital setting. The degree of structure and of client participation in the group process varies in different types of groups. Most often, groups are informal, and many follow the format of encounter groups, in which the interpersonal interactions may become quite intense as members try to speak candidly and deal with their problems. Occasionally, more or less formal lectures or visual materials are presented to clients as a group—for example, a group of alcoholic clients may be shown a film depicting the detrimental effects of excessive drinking—with a group discussion afterward. Although this approach by itself has not proved effective in combating alcoholism, it is often a useful adjunct to other forms of group therapy. ■

Humanistic-Experiential Therapies

The humanistic-experiential therapies (also known as humanistic-existential therapies) see psychopathology as stemming in many cases from problems of alienation, depersonalization, loneliness, and a failure to find meaning and genuine fulfillment. Problems of this sort, it is held, are not likely to be solved either by delving into forgotten memories (the psychodynamic approach) or by correcting specific maladaptive behaviors (the behavioral approach).

The humanistic-experiential therapies are based on the assumption that we have both the freedom and the responsibility to control our own behavior—that we can reflect on our problems, make choices, and take positive action. Humanistic-experiential therapists feel that a client must take most of the responsibility for the direction and success of therapy, with a therapist merely serving as counselor, guide, and facilitator. These therapies may be carried out with individual clients or with groups of clients. Although humanistic-experiential therapies differ among themselves in details, their central focus is always that of expanding a client's "awareness."

Client-Centered Therapy The **client-centered therapy** (or **person-centered therapy**) of Carl Rogers (1902–1987) focuses on the natural power of the organism to heal itself (Rogers, 1951, 1961, 1966). Rogers saw psychotherapy as a process of removing the constraints and hobbling restrictions that often impede therapy. These constraints, he believed, grow out of unrealistic demands that people place on themselves when they believe, as a condition of self-worth, that they should not have certain kinds of feelings, such as hostility. By denying that they do in fact have such feelings, they lose touch with their own genuine experience; the result is lowered integration, impaired personal relationships, and various forms of maladjustment.

The primary objective of this form of therapy is to help clients accept and be themselves. To this end, client-

client-centered (person-centered) therapy Nondirective type of humanistic-experiential therapy developed chiefly by Carl Rogers, which focuses on the natural power of the organism to heal itself—to help clients accept and be themselves.

centered therapists establish a psychological climate in which clients can feel unconditionally accepted, understood, and valued as people. Within this context, the therapist employs *nondirective* techniques such as empathic reflecting or restatement of the client's descriptions of life difficulties. If all goes well, clients begin to feel free to explore their real feelings and thoughts and to accept them as parts of themselves. As their self-concept becomes more congruent with their actual experiencing, they become more self-accepting and more open to new experience and new perspectives; in short, they become better-integrated people.

In contrast to most other forms of therapy, in client-centered therapy, the therapist does not give answers or interpret what a client says; rather, he or she simply listens attentively and acceptingly to what the client wants to talk about, interrupting only to restate in different words what the client is saying. Such restatements, without any judgment or interpretation by the therapist, are meant to help the client clarify further the feelings and ideas that he or she is exploring.

Newer forms of humanistic therapies still adhere to Rogers's emphasis on an active self (client) and the importance of unconditional positive regard from the therapist. They "shortcut" the therapeutic process by at times having the therapist go beyond simple clarification to directly confront a client with specific maladaptive modes of self-presentation upon which he or she may be relying. It is still the client's search and the client's insights that are seen as central in therapy, however.

Existential Therapy The existential perspective, like the client-centered, emphasizes the importance of the human situation *as perceived by an individual.* Existentialists are deeply concerned about the "human predicament," the alienation and depersonalization of individuals in contemporary society and the lack of meaning in peoples' lives. They see in human beings, however, a unique ability to reflect on and question their existence, which confronts them with the responsibility for "being"—for deciding what kind of person to become, for establishing their own values, and for actualizing their potentialities.

Existential therapists follow no rigidly prescribed procedures but emphasize the uniqueness of each individual and his or her "way of being in the world." They stress the importance of being aware of one's own existence—challenging an individual directly with questions concerning the meaning and purpose of existence—and of the therapeutic encounter, the complex relationship established between two human beings interacting in the therapeutic situation as they both try to be open and "authentic." Besides being authentic themselves, it is the task of existential therapists to keep a client focused on the here and now—on what the client is choosing to do, and therefore to be, at the moment. This sense of immediacy, of the urgency of experience, is the touchstone of existential therapy and sets the stage for the individual to clarify and choose between alternative ways of being.

Gestalt Therapy In German, the term *gestalt* means "whole," and gestalt therapy places considerable importance on the need to integrate thought, feeling, and action into one's self-awareness. Gestalt therapy was developed by Frederick (Fritz) Perls (1967, 1969) as a means of doing this.

According to Perls, we all unknowingly carry the excess baggage of unfinished or unresolved traumas and conflicts, which we then tend to reenact in our relations with other people. In gestalt therapy, which is commonly used in a group setting, the therapist works intensively with one person at a time, attempting to help identify the aspects of the individual's self or world that are not being acknowledged in awareness. Individuals may be asked to act out fantasies or dreams concerning their feelings and conflicts. By having to express themselves in front of the group and being denied the use of their usual techniques for avoiding self-awareness, gestalt therapy clients are said to be brought to an "impasse," at which point they must confront their feelings and conflicts and "take care of unfinished business," a euphemism for working through unresolved conflicts.

Evaluating Humanistic-Experiential Therapies The humanistic-experiential therapies have been criticized for their lack of highly systematized models of human behavior and its specific aberrations, their lack of agreed-upon therapeutic procedures, and their vagueness about what is supposed to happen between client and therapist. These very features, however, are seen by many proponents of this general approach as contributing to its strength and vitality.

Modern-era, controlled research on the outcomes produced by the humanistic-experiential therapies is relatively sparse; when such outcomes are compared with those of behavioral and cognitive-behavioral therapies, they tend to be inferior (Greenberg, Elliott, & Lietaer, 1994). These therapies appear unsuitable for individuals experiencing severe mental disorders, such as schizophrenia (Rogers et al., 1967). But these therapies—with their emphasis on achieving self-growth and self-awareness—do have considerable appeal for those who are experiencing mild problems of maladaptive behavior.

Therapy for Interpersonal Relationships

Many problems brought to practitioners are explicitly relationship problems. That is, the presenting complaint is not so much about dissatisfaction with oneself or one's own behavior as about the inability to achieve satisfactory accords with significant others. A common example is marital distress. The maladaptive behavior is in these instances shared between the members of the relationship; it is, to use the contemporary term, "systemic" (Gurman, Kniskern, & Pinsof, 1986), or, in other words, the product of a "system," one that may be amenable to both understanding and change. Problems deriving from the in-place system require therapeutic techniques that focus on relationships as much as or more than on individuals. In this section, we will explore the growing fields of couples and family therapy as examples of this type of multiple-client intervention. In general, these therapies, when placed in the context of helping individuals to change, focus on altering the reactions of the interpersonal environment to the behavior of each involved person. It is important to note that couples and family therapies can be conducted from any of the perspectives discussed in this chapter and in Chapter 2 (see the review by Alexander, Holtzworth-Munroe, & Jameson [1994] for examples).

Couples Counseling (Marital Therapy) In **couples counseling**, or **marital therapy**, the couple is typically seen together, and therapy can include a wide range of procedures that focus on clarifying and improving the couple's interactions and relationships. Most therapists emphasize mutual need gratification, social role expectations, communication patterns, and similar interpersonal factors.

Not surprisingly, happily married couples tend to differ from unhappily married couples in remaining best friends, talking more to each other, keeping channels of communication open, using more problem-solving behavior, making more use of nonverbal communication, and showing more sensitivity to each other's feelings and needs (e.g., Margolin & Wampold, 1981).

One of the difficulties in couples therapy is the intense emotional involvement of the partners, which makes it difficult for them to perceive and accept the realities of their relationship. Often, each of the partners can see clearly what is "wrong" with the other but cannot identify his or her own attitudes and behaviors that are contributing to the relationship impasse. To help correct this problem, videotape recordings have been used increasingly to recapture crucial moments of intense interaction between the partners. By watching playbacks of these tapes after immediate tensions have diminished, the partners can gain a fuller awareness of the nature of their interactions. For example, a husband may realize for the first time that he tries to dominate rather than listen to his wife and consider her needs and expectations, or a wife may realize that she is continually undermining her husband's feelings of worth and self-esteem.

Behavioral marital therapy, which often utilizes a contractual approach, has been used to bring about desired changes in marital relationships; the partners, for example, may be taught to reinforce instances of desired behavior while withdrawing reinforcement for undesired behavior. Other approaches include training the partners to use Rogerian nondirective techniques in listening to each other and helping each other clarify and verbalize their feelings and reactions.

How generally effective is couples therapy at resolving relationship crises and promoting more effective marriages or intimate partnerships? In one study comparing behavioral with insight-oriented psychodynamic marital therapy, neither proved superior to the other, but both significantly outperformed a waiting-list control condition (Snyder & Wills, 1989). In another study, 54.6 percent of partners who underwent couples therapy were still married at the time of a 5-year follow-up, as opposed to 29 percent of partners who had undergone individual therapy (Cookerly, 1980). All forms of therapy were associated with significantly better results at keeping marriages together than is characteristic of general population norms (Christensen & Heavey, 1999).

Finally, couples therapy has been successfully used as an adjunct in the treatment of individual problems, such as depression, phobias, alcohol abuse, and sexual dysfunction (Alexander et al., 1994; Jacobson, Holtzworth-Munroe, & Schmaling, 1989; Roth & Fonagy, 1996; Shadish et al., 1993). Behavioral marital therapy, in particular, has been found to be a valuable adjunctive approach in the treatment of major depression among clients who are also experiencing marital discord (Craighead, Craighead, & Ilardi, 1998).

Of course, the motivational factor makes the interpretation of outcome assessments of couples therapy somewhat difficult. People strongly motivated to stay in their relationships are more likely to give couples therapy a serious try; such motivation may itself make for partnership longevity or, perhaps, tolerance of partner abnormality.

couples counseling Form of interpersonal therapy involving sessions with both members of the couple present and emphasizing mutual need gratification, social role expectations, communication patterns, and similar interpersonal factors.

marital therapy Another term for *couples counseling*.

Treatment of the entire family may be desirable where abnormal behavior patterns in individuals are maintained by family dynamics.

Family System Therapy A **family system approach** makes the assumption that the within-family behavior of a particular family member is to a large extent under the influence of the behaviors and communication patterns of other family members. Considered from such a viewpoint, the problem or disorder shown by an "identified client" is often only a symptom of a larger family problem. A careful study of the family of a disturbed child, for example, may reveal that the child is merely reflecting the pathology of the family unit. As a result, most family therapists share the view that the family—not simply the designated "client"—must be directly involved in therapy if lasting improvement is to be achieved.

Probably the most widely used approach to family therapy is the **conjoint family therapy** of Virginia Satir (1967), whose focus is on improving faulty communications, interactions, and relationships among family members and on fostering a family system that better meets the needs of each member. Another approach to resolving family disturbances is called **structural family therapy** (Minuchin, 1974). This approach, explicitly based on systems theory, holds that, if the family context can be changed, then the individual members will behave more supportively and less pathogenically toward each other.

Structural family therapy is focused on present interactions and requires an active but not directive approach on the part of a therapist. Initially, the therapist gathers information about the family—a structural map of the typical family interaction patterns—thus discovering whether the family system has rigid or flexible boundaries, who dominates the power structure, who gets blamed when things go wrong, and so on. Armed with this understanding, the therapist then operates as an agent for altering the interactions among the members, which often entails changing such characteristics as overinvolvement, overprotectiveness, rigidity, and poor conflict resolution skills.

Structural family therapy has a quite good record of success in the treatment of anorexia nervosa (Dare & Eisler, 1997). It has also been used successfully in the treatment of bulimia nervosa (Schwartz, Barrett, & Saba, 1983), childhood psychosomatic disorders (Minuchin et al., 1975), and narcotics addiction (Stanton & Todd, 1976).

Like problems experienced by couples, maladaptive family relationships associated with various types of clinical problems in identified clients have been successfully

family system approach Treatment approach that makes the assumption that the within-family behavior of a particular family member is largely influenced by the behaviors and communication patterns of other family members.

conjoint family therapy Approach to family therapy that focuses on improving communications, interactions, and relationships among family members and on fostering a family system that better meets the needs of each member.

structural family therapy Approach to family therapy that focuses on analyzing and altering the patterns of interaction among family members to help them behave more supportively and less pathogenically toward each other.

overcome by behaviorally oriented therapies (Nathan & Gorman, 1998; Roth & Fonagy, 1996). With this type of therapy, the therapist's primary task may be seen as reducing the negative effect of the family on the identified client as well as that of the client on other family members. "The therapist does this by actively manipulating the relationship (by instruction, role-playing, etc.) between members so that the relationship changes to a more positively reinforcing and reciprocal one" (Huff, 1969, p. 26).

In an early review of family therapy approaches, Gurman and Kniskern (1978) concluded that structural family therapy had had more impressive results than most other experientially and psychodynamically oriented approaches they had considered. By the time of a subsequent review 8 years later (Gurman et al., 1986), the conclusion had shifted somewhat to favor behavioral interventions—one measure of the tremendous momentum generated by behavioral approaches and now shared by the cognitive-behavioral ones. A quantitative review of outcomes by Shadish and colleagues (1993) supported the high standing accorded behavioral procedures in therapeutic work with families.

IN REVIEW

- What are the four basic techniques of psychoanalysis? How are they used in psychodynamic therapies?
- How do behavior therapies differ from psychodynamic therapies?
- What two main themes characterize all cognitive-behavioral therapies?
- What is the central focus of humanistic-experiential therapies?
- Describe two types of interpersonal therapy. What assumption underlies these approaches?

HOW DOES ONE MEASURE SUCCESS IN PSYCHOTHERAPY?

Evaluating the success of psychological treatment is a difficult enterprise for several reasons. At best, it is an inexact process, dependent on imperfect measurement and outcome data. A therapist may not be the best judge of a client's progress, since any therapist is likely to be biased in favor of seeing himself or herself as competent and successful; in addition, the therapist typically has only a limited observational sample, the client's in-session statements and behavior, from which to make judgments of overall change. Nor is a client necessarily a reliable source of information on therapeutic outcomes; clients not only may want to think they are getting better for various personal reasons, but they may report that they are being helped in an attempt to please the therapist. Family members may also be inclined to "see" the improvement they had hoped for, although they often seem to be more realistic than either the therapist or the client in their evaluations of outcome.

Clinical ratings by an independent observer are sometimes used in psychotherapy-outcome research to evaluate the progress of clients; these may be more objective than ratings by those directly involved in the therapy. Another widely used objective measure of client change is performance on various psychological tests. A client evaluated in this way takes a battery of tests before and after therapy, and the differences in scores are assumed to reflect progress or its lack, or occasionally even deterioration. Although such tests may indeed show changes, these may sometimes be artifactual, yielding a false impression that some real change has been documented (Speer, 1992). Also, the particular tests are not necessarily valid predictors of changes, if any, the therapy may induce, nor of how the client will behave in real life. Without follow-up assessment, they can also provide little information on how enduring any change is likely to be.

Objectifying and Quantifying Change

Generalized terms such as *recovery, marked improvement,* and *moderate improvement,* often used in outcome research in the past, are open to considerable differences in interpretation. Today, there is a strong trend toward using more quantitatively precise modes of measuring change. Even under the best of measurement circumstances, however, there is always the possibility that improvement will be attributed to the particular form of treatment used, when it is in fact a product of placebo effects, other events in a client's life, or even of spontaneous change.

Would Change Occur Anyway?

In this context, it is pertinent to ask what happens to disturbed people who do not obtain formal treatment. In view of the many ways that people can help each other, it is not surprising that often considerable improvement occurs without professional therapeutic intervention. Relevant here is the observation that treatment offered by professional therapists has not, in general, been clearly demonstrated to be superior in outcome to nonprofessionally administered therapies (Christensen & Jacobson, 1994). Also, some forms of psychopathology, such as manic and depressive episodes and some instances of schizophreniform disorder, appear to run a fairly brief

HIGHLIGHT 3.7

Eclecticism and the Integration of Psychotherapies

The various "schools" of psychotherapy described in this chapter used to be more in opposition to one another than they are today. There seems to be a movement toward a relaxation of boundaries and a willingness among therapists to explore differing ways of approaching clinical problems, a process sometimes called *multimodal therapy* (Lazarus, 1981, 1985, 1997b). When asked what their orientation is, most psychotherapists today will reply "eclectic," which usually means that they try to borrow and combine concepts and techniques from various schools, depending on what seems best for the individual case. This inclusiveness even extends to efforts to combine individual and family system therapies (e.g., Feldman, 1992; E. Wachtel, 1994) and biological and psychosocial approaches (e.g., Feldman & Feldman, 1997; Klerman et al., 1994; Pinsof, 1995).

The goal to integrate the psychotherapies has captured the interest of many researchers and writers (e.g., Gold & Stricker, 1993; Goldfried, Greenberg, & Marmar, 1990; Norcross & Goldfried, 1992; P. Wachtel, 1997). But determining exactly how to do it remains elusive, and may even be unattainable. If a grand, overriding theory of psychotherapy does emerge from the efforts of the psychotherapy integrationists or from other sources, our guess is that it will be accompanied by dramatic new insights about the nature of mental disorders. At present, we still know too little that is ironclad about the "inner workings" of both disorders and their treatments, which is what permits radically differing conceptions to thrive side-by-side. ■

course with or without treatment, and there are many other instances in which disturbed people improve over time for reasons that are not apparent.

Even if many emotionally disturbed persons tend to improve over time without psychotherapy, it seems clear that psychotherapy can often accelerate improvement or ensure desired behavior change that might not otherwise occur (Lambert & Bergin, 1994; Telch, 1981). Most researchers today would agree that psychotherapy is more effective than no treatment, and indeed the evidence confirms this strongly. The chances of an average client benefiting significantly from psychological treatment are, overall, impressive (Lambert & Bergin, 1994).

Can Therapy Be Harmful?

Some client-psychotherapist relationships, perhaps as many as 10 percent, apparently result in the client's being worse off than if psychotherapy had never been undertaken (Lambert & Bergin, 1994). Obvious ruptures of the therapeutic alliance—in which client and therapist become embroiled in a mutually antagonistic and downwardly spiraling course—account for only a portion of the failures. In other instances, the match of therapist and client just isn't right. Certain therapists, probably for reasons of personality, just do not do well with certain types of client problems (Lambert, 1989; Lambert & Bergin, 1994).

A special case of therapeutic harm is the problem of sex between therapist and client, typically seduction of a client (or former client) by a therapist, which is considered unethical conduct. Given the frequently intense and intimate quality of therapeutic relationships, it is not surprising that sexual attraction arises. What is distressing is the apparent frequency with which it is manifested in exploitive and unprofessional behavior on the part of therapists—all the more so in light of the fact that virtually all authorities agree that such liaisons are nearly always destructive of good client functioning in the long run (Pope, Sonne, & Holroyd, 1993). Recognizing that this reprehensible behavior cannot be stopped in all cases, any prospective client seeking therapy needs to be sufficiently wary to determine that the therapist chosen is one of the large majority committed to high ethical and professional standards.

IN REVIEW

- What sources of information are used to evaluate the effectiveness of psychological treatment? What are their limitations?
- What are some reasons why psychotherapy could be harmful in a small percentage of cases?

SUMMARY

CLINICAL ASSESSMENT

- Clinical assessment is one of the most important and complex tasks facing mental health professionals. The extent to which a person's psychological problems are understood and appropriately treated depends largely on the adequacy of the clinical assessment.
- Because many psychological problems have physical components, either as causal factors or as symptom patterns, it is often important to include a medical examination in the psychological assessment. In cases where organic brain damage is suspected, a neurological test—such as an EEG or a CAT, PET, or MRI scan—aids in determining the site and extent of structural or functional anomaly.
- Psychosocial assessment methods are techniques for gathering relevant psychological information for clinical decisions about patients. The most widely used and most flexible psychosocial assessment techniques are the clinical interview and behavior observation, which attempt to assess an individual's beliefs, attitudes, and symptoms directly.
- Psychological tests, in contrast, attempt to measure aspects of personality indirectly using standardized stimuli.
- Two different types of personality tests have been developed: (1) projective tests, in which unstructured stimuli are presented to a subject, who then "projects" meaning or structure onto the stimuli, thereby revealing "hidden" motives, feelings, and so on; and (2) objective tests, or personality inventories, in which a subject is required to read and respond to itemized statements or questions. Objective personality tests provide a cost-effective means of collecting a great deal of personality information rapidly.

BIOLOGICALLY BASED THERAPIES

- One biologically based therapy is electroconvulsive therapy (ECT). Exactly how ECT works is not yet understood, but there is little doubt of its efficacy for certain patients, especially those suffering from severe depression. Nevertheless, some controversy about this method of treatment persists.
- The effective psychopharmacological methods of treatment include antipsychotic drugs (neuroleptics), which can diminish psychotic (especially schizophrenic) symptoms.
- Antidepressant medications are widely used to treat not only patients with severe depression, but also those with several anxiety disorders. Many anxiety-based and psychophysiologic disorders respond to antianxiety drugs. Finally, lithium is effective for controlling manic episodes.

PSYCHOLOGICALLY BASED THERAPIES

- Many psychologically based therapies have been developed to treat individuals with mental disorders. Several psychodynamic therapies have developed out of the psychoanalytic tradition. These approaches accept some elements of Freudian theory but diverge on key points, such as the length of time to be devoted to therapy or the role of primitive psychosexual drives in personality dynamics.
- A second major class of psychological interventions is behavior therapies. These approaches make use of a number of techniques, such as guided exposure, aversion therapy, modeling, reinforcement, behavioral contracting, and biofeedback and relaxation training.
- Cognitive or cognitive-behavioral therapies apply behavior therapy methods to private events—that is, thoughts or cognitions. This approach attempts to modify a person's self-statements and constructions of events to change his or her behavior. Cognitive-behavioral therapies have been used for a wide variety of clinical problems, ranging from depression to anger control.
- Several other psychologically based treatment methods have been referred to as humanistic-experiential therapies. One of the earliest of these approaches is the client-centered therapy of Carl Rogers.
- In addition to individual treatment approaches, multiple-client interventions exist for problematic interpersonal relationships. Couples counseling and family therapy typically assume that a person's problems lie partly in his or her interactions with others. Consequently, the focus of treatment is to change the ways in which partners or family members interact.

HOW DOES ONE MEASURE SUCCESS IN PSYCHOTHERAPY?

- Evaluation of the success of psychotherapy in producing desired changes in clients is difficult. Two standards for doing so have evolved: efficacy and effectiveness. Research in psychotherapy, however, has shown that most treatments are more effective than no treatment at all.

- Therapy can sometimes go awry, causing psychological deterioration. This possibility brings up larger questions involving ethical issues that therapists must confront.

KEY TERMS

clinical assessment (p. 80)
dynamic formulation (p. 81)
electroencephalogram (EEG) (p. 83)
computerized axial tomography (CAT scan) (p. 83)
magnetic resonance imaging (MRI) (p. 83)
positron emission tomography (PET scan) (p. 83)
functional MRI (fMRI) (p. 84)
neuropsychological assessment (p. 84)
unstructured interview (p. 85)
structured interview (p. 85)
self-monitoring (p. 86)
rating scales (p. 86)
intelligence tests (p. 86)
projective tests (p. 87)
Rorschach Test (p. 87)
Thematic Apperception Test (TAT) (p. 88)
sentence-completion test (p. 88)
objective tests (p. 88)
Minnesota Multiphasic Personality Inventory–Second Edition (MMPI-2) (p. 89)
electroconvulsive therapy (ECT) (p. 94)
neurosurgery (p. 94)
prefrontal lobotomy (p. 94)
psychopharmacology (p. 95)
antipsychotic drugs (p. 96)
antidepressant drugs (p. 99)
antianxiety drugs (p. 101)
psychotherapy (p. 103)
psychodynamic therapy (p. 104)
free association (p. 105)
manifest content (p. 105)
latent content (p. 105)
resistance (p. 105)
transference (p. 105)
countertransference (p. 106)
behavior therapy (p. 107)
systematic desensitization (p. 107)
in vivo exposure (p. 108)
in vitro exposure (p. 108)
aversion therapy (p. 108)
modeling (p. 109)
response shaping (p. 109)
token economies (p. 110)
behavioral contracting (p. 110)
biofeedback (p. 110)
cognitive therapy (p. 111)
cognitive-behavioral therapy (p. 111)
rational emotive behavior therapy (REBT) (p. 112)
stress-inoculation training (SIT) (p. 112)
client-centered (person-centered) therapy (p. 114)
couples counseling (p. 116)
marital therapy (p. 116)
family system approach (p. 117)
conjoint family therapy (p. 117)
structural family therapy (p. 117)

CHAPTER FOUR

Stress-Related Disorders

Joan Bowman, *Illumination,* watercolor. Bowman, a native Texan, lives with post-traumatic stress disorder. Both a poet and a visual artist, she learned to paint in art therapy. Her work, she says, is about the heart and its cleansing.

LEARNING OBJECTIVES

After reading this chapter, you should be able to:

- Define *stressor, stress,* and *coping strategies,* and discuss factors that increase or decrease a person's vulnerability to stress.
- Contrast the two major categories of stress responses, and outline the possible physical and psychological negative effects of severe stress.
- Characterize the elements of the DSM diagnosis of adjustment disorder, and list some factors that increase the risk of adjustment disorder.
- List the DSM diagnostic criteria for acute stress disorder and post-traumatic stress disorder, and contrast the two disorders.
- Summarize the major features of people's reactions to catastrophic events, including rape, combat, and severe threats to safety and security.
- Summarize the approaches that have been used to treat or prevent stress disorders and evaluate their effectiveness.

It is probably not necessary to point out that life can be stressful. Everyone faces a different mix of adjustive demands in life, and any one of us may break down if the going gets tough enough. Under conditions of overwhelming stress, even a previously stable person may develop temporary (transient) psychological problems and lose the capacity to gain pleasure from life (Berenbaum & Connelly, 1993). This breakdown may be sudden, as in the case of a person who has gone through a severe accident or fire, or it may be gradual, as in the case of a person who is involved in a deteriorating marriage or other intimate relationship and has been subjected to prolonged periods of tension and challenges to his or her self-esteem. Most often, a person recovers once a stressful situation is over, although in some cases there may be long-lasting damage to self-concept and an increased vulnerability to certain types of stressors. Today's stress can be tomorrow's vulnerability. In the case of a person who is quite vulnerable to begin with, of course, a stressful situation may precipitate more serious and lasting psychopathology.

In Chapter 2, we focused on the diathesis, or vulnerability, half of the diathesis-stress model of abnormal behavior. We saw that our vulnerabilities, whether biological or psychological, can predispose us to develop abnormal behavior. In this chapter, we will focus on the role of stress as a precipitating causal factor in abnormal behavior. We will see that, at times, the impact of stress depends not only on its severity, but on a person's preexisting vulnerabilities as well. It is important to remember here that many of the factors that contribute to diatheses are also sources of stress. This is especially true of psychosocial factors, such as emotional deprivation, inadequate parenting, and the like. In this chapter, our focus will be on the precipitating nature of stress; in Chapter 2, we focused on its predisposing nature. As you read this chapter, however, keep in mind that people are different in the way they perceive, interpret, and cope with stress and traumatic events.

Research findings and clinical observations on the relationship between stress and psychopathology are so substantial that the role of stressors in symptom development is formally emphasized in diagnostic formulations. In DSM-IV-TR (American Psychiatric Association, 2000), for example, a diagnostician can specify on Axis IV the specific psychosocial stressors facing a person. The Axis IV scale is particularly useful in relation to three Axis I categories: adjustment disorder, acute stress disorder, and post-traumatic stress disorder (acute, chronic, or delayed). These disorders involve patterns of psychological and behavioral disturbances that occur in response to identifiable stressors. The key differences between them lie not only in the severity of the disturbances but also in the natures of the stressors and the time frames during which the disorders occur. In these disorders, the stressors supposedly can be identified as causal factors and specified on Axis IV.

In this chapter, we will first look at what stress is, the factors that affect it, and how we react to it. We will then examine severe, catastrophic stress situations that precipitate the development of post-traumatic stress disorder. In the last part of the chapter, we will look at attempts made by mental health workers to intervene in the stress process either to prevent stress reactions or to limit their intensity and duration once they have developed.

WHAT IS STRESS?

Life would be simple indeed if all of our needs were automatically satisfied. In reality, however, many obstacles, both personal and environmental, prevent this ideal situation. We may be too short for professional basketball or have less money than we need. Such obstacles place adjustive demands on us and can lead to stress. The term *stress* has typically been used to refer both to the adjustive demands placed on an organism and to the organism's internal biological and psychological responses to such demands. To avoid confusion, we will refer to adjustive demands as **stressors,** to the effects they create within an

stressors Adjustive demands placed on an individual or group.

Living in extreme poverty with insufficient life resources can be a powerful stressor in a person's life at any age, but especially for children. The trauma of sudden and powerful natural disasters can also produce intense stress, particularly among young people like the boy shown in the aftermath of a devastating storm that took his home and most of his possessions.

organism as **stress,** and to efforts to deal with stress as **coping strategies.** Note that separating these constructs is somewhat arbitrary, as Neufeld (1990) has pointed out: Stress is a by-product of poor or inadequate coping. For the purpose of study, however, making the distinction between stress and stressors can be of help. What is important to remember in the long run is that the two concepts—stress and coping—are interrelated and dependent on each other.

All situations, positive and negative, that require adjustment can be stressful. Thus, according to Canadian physiologist Hans Selye (1956, 1976a), the notion of stress can be broken down further into **eustress** (positive stress) and **distress** (negative stress). (In most cases, the stress experienced during a wedding would be eustress; during a funeral, distress.) Both types of stress tax a person's resources and coping skills, though distress typically has the potential to do more damage.

Factors Predisposing a Person to Stress

Although no two people are faced with exactly the same pattern of stressors, a number of factors predispose individuals to experience stress, including the following:

stress Effects created within an organism by the application of a stressor.

coping strategies Efforts to deal with stress.

eustress Positive stress.

distress Negative stress, associated with pain, anxiety, or sorrow.

crisis A stressful situation that approaches or exceeds the adaptive capacities of an individual or group.

The Nature of the Stressor A number of characteristics of the stressor itself can influence a person's predisposition to stress; these characteristics include the stressor's significance, intensity immediacy, cumulative effect, and duration. Although most minor stressors—such as misplacing one's keys, for example—may be dealt with as a matter of course, stressors that involve important aspects of one's life—such as the death of a loved one, a divorce, a job loss, or a serious illness—tend to be highly stressful.

From time to time, most of us experience stressors that are especially acute (sudden and intense). The term **crisis** is used to refer to any time when a stressful situation approaches or exceeds the adaptive capacities of a person or group. Crises are often especially stressful because the stressors are so potent that the coping techniques we typically use do not work.

Not surprisingly, encountering a number of stressors at the same time can leave one vulnerable, a fact of which many working mothers are fully aware. Furthermore, stressors often appear to have a cumulative effect (Singer, 1980); a married couple may maintain amicable relations through a long series of minor irritations or frustrations only to dissolve the relationship in the face of one last straw of a precipitating stressor.

The Person's Perception of the Stressor The different reactions people have to environmental events is due in part to the way they perceive the situation; a person who feels overwhelmed and is concerned that he or she will be unable to deal with a stressor is more likely to experience negative consequences from the situation than is a person who feels able to manage it. For example, recovery from the stress resulting from major surgery can be markedly facilitated when a patient is given realistic expectations beforehand (e.g., Leventhal, Patrick-Muller, & Leventhal, 1998).

The Individual's Stress Tolerance The term **stress tolerance** refers to a person's ability to withstand stress without becoming seriously impaired. People vary greatly in overall vulnerability to stressors; some individuals have difficulty handling even relatively minor stress. For example, when a person is faced with uncontrollable stressors (such as being sexually abused at an early age), he or she tends to become vulnerable or highly sensitized to later assault or abuse.

A Lack of External Resources and Social Supports The lack of external supports, whether social and family support or even material support, can make a given stressor more potent and weaken a person's capacity to cope with it. For example, a divorce or the death of a mate evokes more stress if a person feels alone and unloved than if he or she surrounded by caring people.

Responding to Stress

In general, increased levels of stress threaten a person's well-being and produce automatic, persistent attempts to relieve the tension. In short, stress forces a person to do something. What is done depends on many influences. Clearly, the many characteristics of the stressor itself (noted above) influence a person's response to stress. But sometimes inner factors such as a person's frame of reference, motives, competencies, or tolerance for stress play the dominant role in determining his or her coping strategies. For example, a person who has successfully handled adversity in the past may be better equipped to deal with similar problems in the future (Major et al., 1997; Masten & Coatsworth, 1998). (See the discussion on resilience in Chapter 2.) At other times, environmental conditions such as social demands and expectations are of primary importance. Any stress reaction, of course, reflects the interaction of inner strategies and outer conditions, some more influential than others but all working together to make the person react in a certain way. Ironically, some people *create* stress for themselves. Recent studies have shown that stressful situations might be in part related to or produced by the person's cognitions. For example, if you're feeling depressed or anxious already, you may perceive a friend's canceling a movie date as more stressful than if you are not depressed or anxious. That is, a vicious cycle occurs, causing some people to generate the life events that in turn produce their psychological adjustment problems (Simons et al., 1993).

In reviewing certain general principles of responding to stress, it is helpful to conceptualize three interactional levels: (1) on a biological level, there are immunological defenses and damage-repair mechanisms; (2) on a psychological and interpersonal level, there are learned coping patterns, self-defenses, and support from family and friends; and (3) on a sociocultural level, there are group resources, such as labor unions, religious organizations, and law-enforcement agencies.

The failure of coping efforts on any of these levels may seriously increase a person's vulnerability on the other levels. For example, a breakdown of immunological defenses may impair not only bodily functioning, but psychological functioning as well; chronically poor psychological coping patterns may lead to other diseases; or the failure of a group on which a person depends may seriously interfere with his or her ability to satisfy basic needs. The impact of stress on bodily functioning and physical disorder will be discussed more fully in Chapter 8.

In responding to stress, a person is confronted with two challenges: (1) to meet the requirements of the stressor, and (2) to protect the self from psychological damage and disorganization. When a person feels competent to handle a stressful situation, a **task-oriented response** is typical—that is, behavior is directed primarily at dealing with the requirements of the stressor. Typically, this response means that the person objectively appraises the situation, works out alternative solutions, decides on an appropriate strategy, takes action, and evaluates feedback. The steps in a task-oriented response—whether the actions turn out to be effective or ineffective—are generally flexible enough to enable a person to change course.

When a person's feelings of adequacy are seriously threatened by a stressor, a **defense-oriented response** tends to prevail—that is, behavior is directed primarily at protecting the self from hurt and disorganization, rather than at resolving the situation. Typically, the person using a defense-oriented response has forsaken more productive task-oriented action in favor of an overriding concern

---

stress tolerance A person's ability to withstand stress without becoming seriously impaired.

task-oriented response Behavior directed primarily toward dealing with the requirements posed by a stressor.

defense-oriented response Behavior directed primarily at protecting the self from hurt and disorganization, rather than at resolving the stressful situation.

Two ways that we may choose to deal with a stressful situation are through a task-oriented response, in which we try to resolve the situation, or through a defense-oriented response, in which we protect ourselves from psychological damage and disorganization. The couple weeping and holding each other in this photo have witnessed a fire in a Bronx discotheque that left 87 dead. They cannot change or resolve the situation. Their reactions are defense-oriented, used to help them cope with the hurt of an overwhelming stressor

for maintaining the integrity of the self, however ill-advised and self-defeating the effort may prove to be.

There are two common types of defense-oriented responses. The first consists of responses such as crying, repetitive talking, and mourning, which seem to function as psychological damage-repair mechanisms. The second type consists of the so-called ego- or self-defense mechanisms introduced in Chapter 2. These mechanisms, including such responses as denial and repression, relieve tension and anxiety and protect the self from hurt and devaluation. For example, the person who fears that his or her own difficulties with intimacy and warmth may have caused a relationship to end might cope defensively by projecting blame on the other person. Ego-defense mechanisms such as these protect a person from external threats, such as failures in work or relationships, and from internal threats, such as guilt-arousing desires or actions.

These defense mechanisms are ordinarily used in combination rather than singly, and they are often combined with task-oriented behavior. Ego-defense mechanisms are considered maladaptive when they become the predominant means of coping with stressors and are applied in excess (Erickson, Feldman, Shirley, & Steiner, 1996).

personality (psychological) decompensation Lowering of adaptive psychosocial functioning in the face of sustained or severe stressors.

IN REVIEW

- Distinguish among stressors, stress, and coping strategies.
- How can the nature of the stressor, the individual's perception of it, his or her stress tolerance, and his or her external resources and supports modify the effects of stress?
- What are the differences between task-oriented and defense-oriented responses to stress?
- Name two ego-defense mechanisms that are examples of defense-oriented responses to stress.

THE EFFECTS OF SEVERE STRESS

As was noted earlier, our reactions to stress can give us competencies we need and would not develop without being challenged to do so. Stress can be damaging, however, if certain demands are too severe for our coping resources or if we believe and act as if they are. Severe stress can exact a high cost in terms of lowered efficiency, depletion of adaptive resources, wear and tear on the biological system, and, in extreme cases, severe personality and physical deterioration—referred to as **personality** or **psychological decompensation**—or even death.

On a physiological level, severe stress may result in alterations that can impair the body's ability to fight off in-

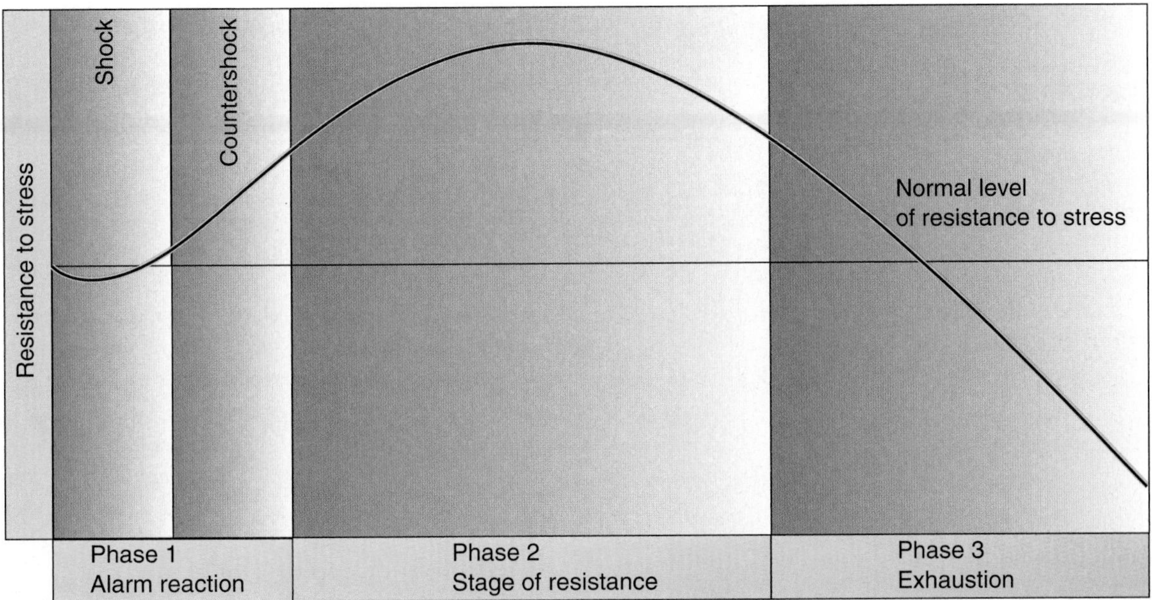

FIGURE 4.1
SELYE'S GENERAL ADAPTATION SYNDROME (GAS)
The general adaptation syndrome (GAS), shown in the diagram above, graphically illustrates a typical person's general response to stress. In the first phase (alarm reaction), the person shows an initial lowered resistance to stress or shock. If the stress persists, the person shows a defensive reaction or resistance (resistance phase) in an attempt to adapt to stress. Following extensive exposure to stress, the energy necessary for adaptation may be exhausted, resulting in the final stage of the GAS—collapse of adaptation (exhaustion phase).

vading bacteria and viruses. On a psychological level, the perception of threat leads to an increasingly narrow perceptual field and rigid cognitive processes. For example, a person exposed to the trauma of war for a prolonged period of time may find it impossible to make realistic plans for the future. It thus becomes difficult or impossible for the person to see the situation objectively or to perceive the alternatives actually available. This process often appears to be part of suicidal behavior.

Biological Effects of Stress

Persistent or severe stress (trauma) can markedly alter a person's physical health, as will be detailed in Chapter 8. It is difficult to specify the exact biological processes underlying an organism's response to traumatic situations. However, a model that helps explain the course of biological decompensation under excessive stress is the **general adaptation syndrome,** introduced by Selye (1956, 1976b). This explanatory view has been supported by research in the field (Chrousos & Gold, 1992; Mazure & Druss, 1995). Selye found that the body's reaction to sustained and excessive stress typically occurs in three major phases: (1) *alarm reaction,* in which the body's defensive forces are "called to arms" by the activation of the autonomic nervous system; (2) *stage of resistance,* in which biological adaptation is at the maximum level in terms of bodily resources used; and (3) *exhaustion,* in which bodily resources are depleted and the organism loses its ability to resist, allowing further exposure to stress to lead to illness and death. A diagram of this general adaptation syndrome is shown in Figure 4.1.

When individuals are under severe stress, to the point of decompensation, natural maintenance mechanisms attempt to repair damage and reorganize normal functioning—that is, to return the organism's *homeostasis,* the "balanced" state in which the organism finds itself when basic biological needs are being met. If the stress has resulted in extensive damage, this restorative process is often a matter of helping people reorganize the adaptive processes, defenses, and routines that they had before the trauma caused their disorganization. However, individuals may not be as effective in dealing with routine problems as they were before the trauma.

general adaptation syndrome A three-stage model that helps explain the course of a person's biological decompensation under excessive stress and that consists of alarm reaction, resistance, and exhaustion.

Chronic frustration and anger are frequent accompaniments of modern life and can cause repeated activation of the sympathetic nervous system. This in turn can cause health and other problems.

What are the long-term biological effects of trauma? Over the past 20 years, a great deal of research has been devoted to exploring the link between stress and physiological changes in human beings. Here we will briefly examine two major physiological effects of stress. In Chapter 8, we will explore more fully several physical disorders such as heart disease and cancer that have likely been influenced, or partially caused, by psychological factors.

Stress and the Sympathetic Nervous System Ever since the pioneering work of Cannon (1915), psychologists have been aware of the important role the sympathetic nervous system (SNS) plays in response to stressful or dangerous situations. When the organism is faced with danger, the sympathetic nervous system discharges adrenaline, preparing the organism for "flight or fight" as follows: (1) Heart rate increases, and blood flow (and blood pressure) to the large muscles increases to provide the organism with the capability of reacting to physical threats; (2) pupils dilate so that more light enters the eye; (3) the skin constricts to limit blood loss in the event of injury; and (4) blood sugar increases to provide more ready energy. Through this biological reaction, the organism is made ready for "emergency" physical effort.

After we have had our sympathetic nervous systems activated and are biologically ready for physical combat, what happens after the physical threat vanishes? Most of us probably believe that even after a very stressful experience, rest can completely restore us. However, this is not the case. It appears that, over time, there is a degree of wear and tear on the system with employment of the stress response. In his pioneering studies of stress, Selye found this evidence:

> Experiments on animals have clearly shown that each exposure leaves an indelible scar, in that it uses up reserves of adaptability, which cannot be replaced. It is true that immediately after some harassing experience, rest can restore us almost to the original level of fitness by eliminating acute fatigue. But the emphasis is on the word *almost.* Since we constantly go through periods of stress and rest during life, even a minute deficit of adaptation energy every day adds up—it adds up to what we call aging. (1976a, p. 429)

Moreover, once the stress response has been activated over long periods or in an extreme manner, it becomes more difficult to return to homeostasis—it is difficult to shut off the organism's natural stress response.

Studies of the impact of overactivation of the sympathetic nervous system on traumatized populations suggest that these individuals have a heightened responsivity (e.g., increased subjective distress, blood pressure, heart rate, and epinephrine levels) to trauma-related cues even years after the traumatic situation (e.g., Baum et at., 1983; McFall, Murburg, Ko, et al., 1990; Yehuda et al., 1992). These findings suggest that the stress response can have significant impact on the individual's cardiovascular system. Severe trauma and persistent stress can increase the individual's blood pressure to the point that arteriosclerotic damage can occur in the heart and blood vessels, placing the individual at risk for hypertension, heart attack, and stroke (see Chapter 8).

Stress and the Immune System Stress can also impact the organism through the hypothalamic-pituitary-adrenal glands and produce a serious endocrine imbalance that takes a major toll on the organism's immune system. The hypothalamus releases hormones that stimulate the pituitary to release other hormones that regulate many bodily functions, such as tissue and bone growth and reproduction. Stress, operating through the hypothalamic-pituitary-adrenal system, can result in a suppression of the immune system (Cacioppo, 1994), making the organism vulnerable to diseases to which it would normally be immune. Although no one really knows why the immune system is suppressed during periods of stress, this emergency response probably served a protective function in the evolution of our species in that it may have prevented individuals from developing autoimmune diseases (Sapolsky, 1994). However, it is clear that the suppression of the immune system under chronic stress can have dire long-range health consequences—a susceptibility to external diseases. The relatively new field of **psychoneuroimmunology** has as its focus the effects of stressors on the immune system. Having a lowered immune system response can mean that the individual is vulnerable to catching communicable diseases as well as being vulnerable to major mental health problems such as depression (Yehuda, Teicher, Trestman, et al., 1996).

Stress appears to affect the immune system by elevating corticosteroid levels. This decreases lymphocyte metabolism and reduces the organism's immunity to disease (Mazure & Druss, 1995; Yehuda, 1998). Several studies (e.g., Boscarino, 1996) have reported alterations in cortisol levels for combat veterans with post-traumatic stress disorder (PTSD); for example, low cortisol after stress predicts who will develop PTSD. Interestingly, the alterations often reported are lowered levels of cortisol rather than higher levels, as predicted by Selye's model. Recently, Yehuda and colleagues (1998) reported lower levels of cortisol among rape victims with severe avoidance and symptoms of severe injury but not among all rape victims. Not all of the answers are in hand yet, but these inconsistent findings likely result from habituation or hypersensitivity of the stress-adapted organism to the hormone (Southwick et al., 1997).

Psychological Effects of Long-Term Stress

Personality decompensation in the face of trauma is somewhat easier to specify. It appears to follow a course resembling that of biological decompensation and may in fact involve specific biological responses:

1. *Alarm and mobilization.* First, a person's resources for coping with trauma are alerted and mobilized. Typically involved at this stage are emotional arousal, increased tension, heightened sensitivity, greater alertness (vigilance), and determined efforts at self-control. At the same time, the person undertakes various stress responses that may be task-oriented or defense-oriented, or a combination of the two, in attempts to meet the emergency. During this stage, symptoms of maladjustment may appear, such as continuous anxiety and tension, gastrointestinal upset or other bodily diseases, and lowered efficiency, signs that the mobilization of adaptive resources is inadequate.
2. *Resistance.* If trauma continues, a person is often able to find some means for dealing with it and able to maintain some adjustment to life. Trauma resistance may be achieved temporarily by concerted, task-oriented responses; the use of ego-defense mechanisms may also be intensified during this period. Even in the resistance stage, however, indications of strain may exist. For example, psychophysiologic symptoms such as acute stomach distress and mild reality distortions such as hypersensitivity to sounds may occur during the late phases of this stage. In addition, the person may become rigid and cling to previously developed defenses rather than trying to reevaluate the traumatic situation and work out more adaptive responses.
3. *Exhaustion.* In the face of continued excessive trauma, a person's adaptive resources are depleted and the coping strategies called forth in the stage of resistance begin to fail. As the stage of exhaustion begins, the individual's ability to deal with continuing stress is substantially lowered, and exaggerated and inappropriate defensive measures may be employed to deal with the situation. The latter reaction may be characterized by psychological disorganization and a break with reality, involving delusions and hallucinations. These delusions appear to represent increasingly disorganized thoughts and perceptions, along with desperate efforts to salvage psychological integration and self-integrity by restructuring reality. Metabolic changes that impair normal brain functioning may also be involved in delusional and hallucinatory behavior. Eventually, if the excessive stress continues, the process of decompensation proceeds to a stage of severe psychological disorganization, perhaps involving continuous uncontrolled violence, apathy, stupor, and even death. Siegel (1984) found this pattern among 31 hostage victims whose cases he analyzed. Those who had been held under conditions of isolation, visual deprivation, physical restraint, physical abuse, and threat of death typically experienced hallucinations.

IN REVIEW

- Describe the three phases of Selye's general adaptation syndrome. Compare them with the three stages of personality decompensation.
- What is the effect of stress on the sympathetic nervous system?
- What is the effect of stress on the immune system?

psychoneuroimmunology Field of study whose focus is on the effects of stressors on the immune system

ADJUSTMENT DISORDER: REACTIONS TO COMMON LIFE STRESSORS

A person whose response to a common stressor such as divorce, childbirth, losing a job, or even getting married is maladaptive and occurs within 3 months of the stressor can be said to have an **adjustment disorder.** The person's reaction is considered maladaptive if he or she is unable to function as usual or if the reaction is excessive, considering the nature of the particular stressor. In adjustment disorder, the person's maladjustment lessens or disappears when (1) the stressor has subsided or (2) the individual learns to adapt to the stressor. Should the symptoms continue beyond 6 months, DSM-IV-TR recommends that the diagnosis be changed to some other mental disorder. As will be evident in the discussion below, the reality of adjustment disorders does not always adhere to such a strict time schedule.

Clearly, not all reactions to stressors are adjustment disorders. What seems to push a normal reaction into this category is the inability to function as usual, and yet this criterion is true for many other disorders (such as anxiety disorder) as well. We will not resolve this uncertainty any time soon; it is perhaps more important to recognize that adjustment disorder is probably the least stigmatizing and mildest diagnosis a therapist can assign to a client, and it is frequently used by therapists for insurance purposes so that a client's medical records do not contain more severe diagnoses (even though such a diagnosis may be warranted at some later time).

adjustment disorder A disorder in which a person's response to a common stressor is maladaptive and occurs within 3 months of the stressor.

acute stress disorder (ASD) Disorder following a traumatic event that involves three or more dissociative symptoms (sense of numbing or detachment, reduction in awareness of surroundings, derealization, depersonalization, and/or dissociative amnesia) and that occurs within 4 weeks of the event and lasts for a minimum of 2 days and a maximum of 4 weeks.

post-traumatic stress disorder (PTSD) Disorder that involves the same symptoms as acute stress disorder and occurs following an extreme traumatic stress but in which the person shows symptoms that last longer than 4 weeks.

disaster syndrome Common reactions of many victims of a major catastrophe during the traumatic experience as well as the initial reactions after it and long-lasting complications.

ACUTE AND POST-TRAUMATIC STRESS DISORDERS: REACTIONS TO CATASTROPHIC EVENTS

The DSM-IV-TR provides two major classifications—acute stress disorder (ASD) and post-traumatic stress disorder—for reactions to stressors that are unusually severe (involving intense fear), including, for example, a life-threatening situation, the destruction of one's home, seeing another person mutilated or killed, or being the victim of physical violence. Importantly, these are the only disorders described in this book for which there is a clear-cut precipitant as a necessary cause. The person's response to the severe stressor typically involves intense fear, helplessness, or horror and increased anxiety and impairment as the person persistently re-experiences the traumatic event in spite of efforts to avoid stimuli that may bring back memories of it. In addition, the person may experience impaired concentration and memory, as well as feelings of depression.

Clearly, these disorders include elements of anxiety—generalized feelings of fear and apprehension—but the anxiety bears such a close relationship to the experience of major stress that these disorders are classed as stress-related. Chapter 5 will cover the anxiety disorders.

Distinguishing Between Acute Stress Disorder and Post-Traumatic Stress Disorder

The differences between the two classifications largely relate to the severity of the symptom patterns and the timing of their occurrence. **Acute stress disorder (ASD)** occurs within 4 weeks of the traumatic event and lasts for a minimum of 2 days and a maximum of 4 weeks (see Table 4.1). During or following the distressing event, the person experiences three or more of the following dissociative symptoms: a sense of numbing or detachment, a reduction in awareness of his or her surroundings, derealization, depersonalization, and dissociative amnesia (an inability to recall important aspects of the trauma).

If the symptoms of acute stress disorder last longer than 4 weeks, the appropriate diagnosis is **post-traumatic stress disorder (PTSD),** which is not diagnosed unless the symptoms last for at least 1 month (see Table 4.2). Post-traumatic stress disorder can be further specified in terms of when the symptoms begin. If the symptoms begin

TABLE 4.1 ACUTE STRESS DISORDER (ASD)

In order to receive an Acute Stress Disorder diagnosis, the individual needs to meet the following criteria as adapted from the DSM-IV-TR:

- The person has been exposed to a traumatic situation in which both of the following conditions were present: He or she experienced, witnessed, or was confronted with an event that involved actual or threatened death or serious injury, or a serious threat to the physical integrity of self or others. The person's response also involved the feeling of intense fear, helplessness, or horror.
- During or following the distressing event, the person has three (or more) of the following dissociative symptoms:
  1. A subjective sense of numbing, detachment, or absence of emotional responsiveness
  2. A reduction in awareness of his or her surroundings (e.g., "being in a daze")
  3. Derealization
  4. Depersonalization
  5. Dissociative amnesia (i.e., inability to recall an important aspect of the trauma)
- The person persistently reexperiences the trauma by at least one of the following symptoms: recurrent images of the trauma, thoughts, dreams, illusions, flashback episodes, or a sense of reliving the experience, or persistent distress on exposure to reminders of the traumatic event.
- The person shows a marked avoidance of stimuli that arouse recollections of the trauma (e.g., thoughts, feelings, conversations, activities, places, or people).
- The person has marked symptoms of anxiety or increased arousal (e.g., difficulty sleeping, irritability, poor concentration, hypervigilance, exaggerated startle response, motor restlessness).
- The disturbance following the trauma causes clinically significant distress or impairment in social, occupational, or other important areas of functioning or impairs the individual's ability to pursue some necessary task, such as obtaining necessary assistance or mobilizing personal resources by telling family members about the traumatic experience.
- The disturbance lasts for a minimum of 2 days and a maximum of 4 weeks and occurs within 4 weeks of the traumatic event.
- The disturbance is not due to the direct physiological effects of a substance (e.g., a drug of abuse, a medication) or a general medical condition, is not better accounted for by Brief Psychotic Disorder, and is not merely an exacerbation of a preexisting Axis I or Axis II disorder.

Source: American Psychiatric Association, 2000.

within 6 months of the traumatic event, then the reaction is considered to be *acute*. If symptoms begin more than 6 months after the traumatic event, the reaction is considered to be *delayed*. The delayed version of PTSD is less well defined and more difficult to diagnose than the type that emerges shortly after the precipitating incident. Some authorities have questioned whether a delayed reaction should be diagnosed as PTSD at all; instead, some would categorize such a reaction as some other anxiety-based disorder. It is important to keep in mind that the criteria for PTSD specify that the reaction must last for at least 1 month.

A **disaster syndrome** appears to characterize the reactions of many victims of major catastrophes in which great loss or public suffering has occurred. This syndrome may be described in terms of the reactions during the traumatic experience, the initial reactions after it (the acute post-traumatic stress), and the long-lasting or late-arising complications (the chronic or delayed post-traumatic stress).

his wife's hand, but an explosion from within literally blew her out of his hands and pushed him back and down onto the wing. He reached the runway, turned to go back after her, but the plane blew up seconds later.

[Five months later] Martin was depressed and bored, had wild dreams, a short temper and became easily confused and irritated. "What I saw there will terrify me forever," he says. He told [the psychologist who interviewed him] that he avoided television and movies, because he couldn't know when a frightening scene would appear. (From Perlberg, 1979, pp. 49–50.)

Dealing with the consequences of natural disasters can require great efforts at adaptation, as shown by the people in this flood. Some studies have shown that as many as 20 percent of children exposed to a disaster may suffer adjustment disorders in the aftermath.

In some instances the guilt of the survivors seems to center on the belief that they deserved to survive no more or perhaps even less than those who died. As one flight attendant explained after the crash of a Miami-bound jet in the Florida Everglades that took many lives, "I kept thinking, I'm alive. Thank God. But I wondered why I was spared. I felt, It's not fair" (*Time,* Jan. 15, 1973, p. 53).

Extreme post-traumatic symptoms following serious accidents are not uncommon. Blanchard, Hickling, Barton, and Taylor (1996) followed up a group of motor vehicle accident victims, who had sought medical attention as a result of their accidents. They found that one-third of those who initially met PTSD diagnostic criteria had not experienced a reduction in symptoms at a 12-month follow-up. In a review and comparison of all published disaster research in which estimates of post-disaster psychopathology were included, on average, 17 percent of victims showed psychological adjustment problems in the aftermath of the disaster (Rubonis & Bickman, 1991). This figure is similar to the finding of La Greca, Silverman, Vernberg, and Prinstein (1996) that 18 percent of the children studied after Hurricane Andrew had symptoms of PTSD. Green and colleagues (1992) and Green and Lindy (1994) followed up 193 victims of the tragic Buffalo Creek flood 14 years later, finding that symptoms of past and present PTSD were diagnosable in a significant portion of the sample.

A person's traumatic reaction state may be more complicated in cases of severe loss. For example, following the Oakland/Berkeley firestorm in which 24 people died and 3125 others lost their homes, Koopman, Clasesen, and Spiegel (1997) reported that those who experienced major loss (like their home) were likely to experience a series of stressful changes. Similarly, those who become disabled find that their lives have markedly changed. An individual who becomes paralyzed in an automobile accident in which his wife is killed not only has to deal with the grief over losing a close relationship but must do so during a long period of rehabilitation and severely changed life. The psychological effects of disability compensation may also complicate the recovery. Personal damage lawsuits tend to prolong post-traumatic symptoms because of the difficulties of litigation (Egendorf, 1986; Okura, 1975).

Causal Factors in Post-Traumatic Stress

Most people function relatively well in catastrophes, and, in fact, many behave with heroism (Rachman, 1990). Whether or not someone develops PTSD depends on a number of factors. Some research suggests that personality seems to play a role in reducing vulnerability to stress when the stressors are severe (Clark, Watson, & Mineka, 1994). At high levels of traumatic exposure, the nature of the traumatic stressor itself appears to account for most of the stress-response variance (e.g., Ursano, Boydstun, & Wheatley, 1981); however, there appears to be greater likelihood of PTSD among women than among men (Breslau, Davis, et al., 1997). In other words, everyone has a breaking point, and at sufficiently high levels of stress, the average person can be expected to develop some psychological difficulties (which may be either short-lived or long-term) following a traumatic event.

In all cases of post-traumatic stress, conditioned fear—the fear associated with the traumatic experience—appears to be a key causal factor. Thus, prompt psychotherapy following a traumatic experience is considered important in preventing conditioned fear from establishing itself and becoming resistant to change.

We will now explore several precipitants of PTSD, examining both the immediate and long-range effects of each type of traumatic experience, including rape, military combat, imprisonment as a POW or in a concentration camp, and severe threats to safety and security.

The Trauma of Rape

Rape involves the act of forcing someone to engage in sexual intercourse against his or her will—a situation that can inflict severe trauma on a victim. In our society, rape occurs with an alarming frequency. In most cases, the victim is a woman. Rape is the most frequent cause of PTSD in women (Kessler, Sonnega, Bromet, Hughes, & Nelson, 1995). In Chapter 11, we consider the pathology of rapists; our concern in this chapter is with a victim's response to rape, which can vary depending on a number of factors. In *stranger rape*—a rape in which the victim does not know the offender—the victim is likely to experience strong fear of physical harm and death. In *acquaintance rape,* the reaction is apt to be slightly different (Ellison, 1977; Frazier & Burnett, 1994). In such a situation, the victim may feel not only fear but also betrayal by someone she had trusted. She may feel more responsible for what happened and experience greater guilt. She may also be more hesitant to seek help or report the rape to the police out of fear that she will be held partially responsible for it.

Factors Influencing the Experience of Post-Traumatic Stress after Rape The age and life circumstances of a victim may also influence her reaction (Adam, Everett, & O'Neal, 1992). For a young child who knows nothing about sexual behavior, rape can lead to sexual scars and confusion, particularly if the child is encouraged to forget about the experience without thoroughly talking it over first (Browne & Finkelhor, 1986). For young adult women, rape can increase the conflicts over independence and separation that are normal in this age group. In an effort to be helpful, parents of these victims may encourage various forms of regression, such as moving back to the family home, which may prevent mastery of this developmental phase. Married rape victims with children face the task of explaining their experience to their children. Sometimes the sense of vulnerability that results from rape leaves a woman feeling temporarily unable to care for her children.

Husbands and boyfriends, if unsympathetic to what a woman is undergoing after being raped, can negatively influence a rape victim's adjustment by their attitudes and behavior. Rejection, blaming, uncontrolled anger at the offender, or insistence on a quick resumption of sexual activity can serve to increase the victim's negative feelings.

McCann, Sakheim, and Abrahamson (1988) found that the experience of rape affected women in five areas of life functioning. First, physical disturbances, including hyperarousal or anxiousness (typical symptoms of PTSD), were common. One study found that women who had a history of sexual assault tended to see themselves as in poorer health (Golding, Cooper, & George, 1997). Second, women who had been sexually assaulted tended to experience emotional problems, such as anxiety, depressed mood, and low self-esteem. Fierman and colleagues (1993) found that prior trauma, particularly sexual abuse, physical abuse, and rape, were prominent in the life histories of patients seeking treatment at an anxiety clinic. Falsetti and colleagues (1995) reported that 94 percent of their sample of women with panic disorders had histories of criminal victimization. Third, following rape, women tended to report cognitive dysfunction, including disturbed concentration and the experience of intrusive thoughts (Valentiner, Foa, Riggs, & Gershuny, 1996). Fourth, many women reported engaging in atypical behavioral acts, such as aggressive or antisocial actions and substance abuse, after being raped. Finally, many women who experienced rape tended to report having interference in their social relationships, including sexual problems, intimacy problems, and further victimization in sexual relationships. All these symptoms reflect those of PTSD.

Long-Term Effects Whether a rape victim will experience serious psychological problems depends to a large extent on her past coping skills and level of psychological functioning. A previously well-adjusted woman usually will regain her prior equilibrium, but rape can precipitate severe pathology in a woman with psychological difficulties (Meyer & Taylor, 1986). Victims' perceptions as to whether they are able to control future circumstances influence the recovery process. Women who tended to blame themselves or thought more about *why* the rape occurred were slower to recover from the trauma than those who believed that future assaults were less likely (Frazier & Schauben, 1994). When problems do continue, or when they become manifest later in delayed PTSD, they are likely to involve anxiety, depression, withdrawal, and heterosexual relationship difficulties (Gold, 1986; Koss, 1983; Meyer & Taylor, 1986).

Counseling Rape Victims Many crisis centers have specialized rape counseling services, such as hotlines and trained paraprofessionals who provide general support for victims, both individually and in groups. Many crisis centers also have victim advocacy services in which a trained volunteer accompanies a woman who has been raped to a hospital or police station, helps her understand the procedures, and assists her with red tape. The advocate may also accompany the victim to meetings with legal representatives and to the trial, experiences that tend to temporarily reactivate the trauma of the rape.

The Trauma of Military Combat

It has been estimated that in World War II, 10 percent of Americans in combat developed combat exhaustion (the term used for acute stress disorder during World War II). However, the actual incidence is not known because many soldiers received supportive therapy at their battalion aid stations and were returned to combat within a few hours. In fact, combat exhaustion was the single greatest cause of loss of personnel during that war (Bloch, 1969). During the Korean War, the incidence of combat exhaustion dropped from an initial high of over 6 percent to 3.7 percent; 27 percent of medical discharges were for psychiatric reasons (Bell, 1958). In the Vietnam War, the figure dropped to less than 1.5 percent for combat exhaustion, with a negligible number of discharges for psychiatric disorders (Allerton, 1970; Bourne, 1970).

However, research has shown a high prevalence of stress for Vietnam veterans. Though combat exhaustion, or acute stress disorder, was not as great a factor as in previous wars, combat-related stress apparently manifested itself later and was clearly related to combat *experience*, not fatigue (Goldberg et al, 1990). A further analysis found that men who had experienced high levels of combat had a greater prevalence of post-traumatic stress symptoms than those who had had lower levels of combat exposure (Bremner, Southwick, & Charney, 1995).

Clinical Picture in Combat-Related Stress The specific symptoms of combat-related stress disorders vary considerably, depending on the type of duty, the severity and nature of the traumatic experience, and the individual's personality.

One study evaluated the self-reports of 251 Vietnam veterans, grouping them according to three levels of experienced stress: (1) exposed to combat; (2) exposed to abusive violence in combat; and (3) participated in abusive violence in combat (Laufer, Brett, & Gallops, 1985). They found that post-traumatic symptoms, including intrusive imagery, hyperarousal, numbing, and cognitive disruption, were associated with exposure to combat violence. Participation in abusive violence was most highly associated with more severe pathologies marked by cognitive disruptions, such as depression. The researchers concluded that the clinical picture of PTSD varies according to the stressors experienced. Combat involvement is also not the only stressor in a war zone. Soldiers involved in grave registration duties (i.e., handling corpses) had high rates of PTSD symptoms such as anger, anxiety, and somatic complaints compared with soldiers not assigned to such duties (McCarroll, Ursano, & Fullerton, 1995). Moreover, some people entering the military are more vulnerable to developing stress-related symptoms than others.

Despite these variations, however, the general clinical picture was surprisingly uniform for soldiers who developed combat stress in different wars. The first symptoms were increasing irritability and sensitivity, sleep disturbances, and recurring nightmares. A recent empirical study of the emotional components of PTSD in combat veterans found anger and anger-control problems to be a strong component in their post-traumatic stress (Chemtob et al.,

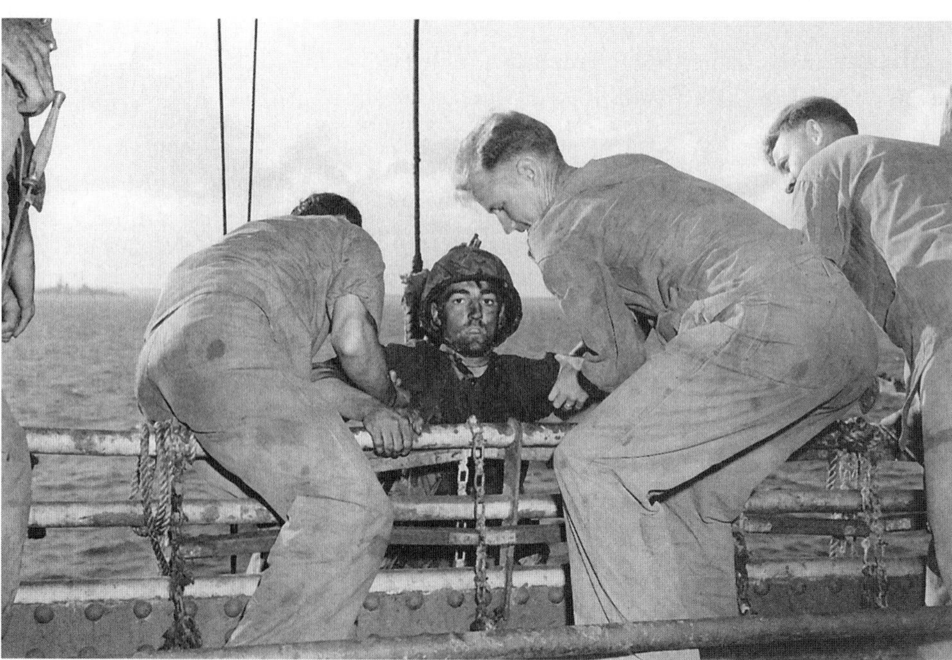

It has been estimated that in World War II, 10 percent of Americans in combat developed combat exhaustion. The stress of combat clearly took its toll on this Marine, who had just finished two days of heavy fighting in the Pacific.

HIGHLIGHT 4.2

The High Emotional Cost of Peacekeeping

Peacekeeping missions to strife-torn countries have been launched as humanitarian efforts designed to serve only peaceful purposes—to protect the civilian population by placing neutral forces between warring factions and to provide security for relief efforts to the civilian population. However, the duties and responsibilities of the personnel involved in these deployments can be very ambiguous, and "mission creep" can actually embroil the peacekeepers in intense conflict for which they were unprepared. Indeed, some "non-combat" military assignments such as in Somalia and Bosnia can be as stressful as wartime experience and can result in tragedies that can be highly traumatic for those involved.

A tragic example came about when young men and women in the military were sent on a humanitarian mission to feed thousands of starving civilians in Somalia. Some armed Somali militants did not accept the outside help and aggressively resisted the peacekeeping efforts. On June 5, 1993, 24 Pakistani peacekeepers were killed when their mission was "expanded" to include closing down a radio station being used by one of the factions for anti-UN propaganda. Then in October 1993, 18 American soldiers were killed in an expedition to capture one of the Somali warlords. Television broadcasts provided vivid accounts of the action and horrible pictures of some of the American soldiers' bodies being dragged through the streets in defiance of the UN presence. The mission was altered substantially after these incidents.

Many of those deployed in this humanitarian mission experienced significant stress as a result of their assignment. Some also experienced PTSD symptoms in the months following their deployment. Recent studies by Litz and colleagues (Litz, Orsillo, Friedman, Ehlich, et al., 1997; Litz, King, King, et al., 1997) reported the prevalence of PTSD symptoms among military personnel who were deployed on the peacekeeping mission to Somalia. They surveyed 3461 active duty personnel, finding that 8 percent of the soldiers showed PTSD symptoms at a 5-month follow-up. ■

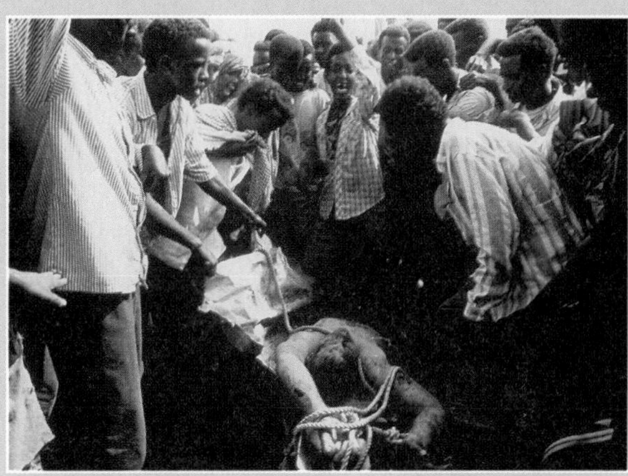

Even peacekeeping missions can prove as stressful or as tragic as wartime duty, as shown in this horrible scene of an American soldier's body being dragged through the streets of Mogadishu.

1994). Many veterans experience, at times, overwhelming anger over minor events that for some is difficult to control. Such maladaptive behaviors may require intervention even years after the stress of military combat has faded (Chemtob, Novaco, Hamada, & Gross, 1997).

The recorded cases of combat-related stress among soldiers in various wars show that the common symptom usually has been the feeling of overwhelming anxiety. In comparison, it is interesting to note that most physically wounded soldiers have shown less anxiety or less combat exhaustion than non–physically wounded soldiers, except in cases of permanent mutilation. Apparently, a wound, in providing an acceptable escape from a stressful combat situation, removes the source of anxiety.

Prisoners of War and Holocaust Survivors Among the most stressful and persistently troubling wartime experiences is that of being a prisoner of war (Beal, 1995; Page, Engdahl, et al., 1997). Although some people have been able to adjust to the stress (especially if part of a supportive group), the past shows us that the toll on most prisoners is great. About 40 percent of the American prisoners in Japanese POW camps during World War II died during their imprisonment; an even higher number of prisoners of Nazi concentration camps died. Survivors of Nazi concentration camps often sustained residual organic and psychological damage along with a lowered tolerance for stress of any kind. Symptoms were often extensive and commonly included anxiety, insomnia, headaches, irritability, depression, nightmares, impaired sexual potency, and functional diarrhea (which occurs in any situation of stress, even relatively mild stress). Such symptoms were attributed not only to the psychological stressors but also to biological stressors, such as head injuries, prolonged malnutrition, and serious infectious diseases (Sigal et al., 1973; Warnes, 1973).

Among returning POWs, the effects of the psychological trauma they had suffered were often masked by the feelings of relief and jubilation that accompanied release from confinement. Even when there was little evidence of residual physical pathology, however, survivors of POW camps commonly showed impaired resistance to physical illness, low frustration tolerance, frequent dependence on alcohol and drugs, irritability, and other indications of emotional instability (Chambers, 1952; Goldsmith & Cretekos, 1969; Hunter, 1978; Strange & Brown, 1970; Wilbur, 1973).

In a retrospective study of psychological maladjustment symptoms following repatriation, Engdahl and colleagues (1993) interviewed a large sample of former POWs and found that half of them reported symptoms that met standard criteria for PTSD in the year following their release from captivity; nearly a third met PTSD criteria 40 to 50 years after their wartime experiences, indicating the marked persistence of the effects of this type of trauma.

Another measure of the toll taken by the prolonged stress of being in a POW or concentration camp is the higher death rate after return to civilian life. Among returning World War II POWs from the Pacific area, Wolff (1960) found that, within the first 6 years, nine times as many died from tuberculosis as would have been expected in civilian life, four times as many from gastrointestinal disorders, over twice as many from cancer, heart disease, and suicide, and three times as many from accidents. Many problems of adjustment and post-traumatic symptoms can be found in POWs many years after their release (Sutker & Allain, 1995). Bullman and Kang (1997) found an increased risk of death due to external causes (for example, from overdose and accidents) associated with PTSD in Vietnam veterans.

Some of the lingering problems experienced by former POWs might be a direct result of harsh treatment and starvation during captivity. Sutker and colleagues (1992) conducted a study of memory and cognitive performance of POW survivors and found that those who experienced the greatest trauma-induced weight loss, defined as greater than 35 percent of their pre-captive weight, performed significantly worse on memory tasks than those who experienced less weight loss.

HIGHLIGHT 4.3

Living in a War Zone

Just being in a war zone with the ever-present possibility that a shell can explode and kill or injure anyone in the area is a frightening experience (Zeidner, 1993). In fact, civilians living in war zones are also at risk for PTSD. Studies of 492 Israeli elementary school children who were exposed to SCUD missile attacks during the war with Iraq found that higher stress responses occurred in areas that were hit by missiles (Schwarzwald et al., 1993). In another study, the anxiety levels of the civilians exposed to the threat of attack were significantly higher during the war than when they were retested when the war was over (Weizman et al., 1994). Moreover, anxiety was higher during the evenings (when the SCUD attacks usually occurred) than during the day. ■

Causal Factors in Wartime Stress Problems In a wartime situation, with the continual threat of injury or death and repeated narrow escapes, a person's ordinary coping strategies are relatively useless. The adequacy and security the person has known in the relatively safe and dependable civilian world are completely undermined. At the same time, we must not overlook the fact that most soldiers subjected to combat have not become psychiatric casualties, although most of them have evidenced severe fear reactions and other symptoms of personality disorganization that were not serious enough to be incapacitating. In addition, many soldiers have tolerated almost unbelievable stress before they have broken, while others have become casualties under conditions of relatively slight combat stress or even as noncombatants—for example, during basic training.

In order to understand traumatic stress reactions to combat, we need to look at factors such as constitutional predisposition, personal maturity, loyalty to one's unit, and confidence in one's officers, as well as the actual stress experienced.

Temperament Do constitutional differences in sensitivity, vigor, and temperament affect a soldier's resistance to combat stress? They probably do, but little actual evidence supports this assumption. We have more information about the conditions of battle that tax a soldier's emotional and physical stamina. Add other factors that often occur in combat situations, such as severe climatic conditions, malnutrition, and disease, to the strain of continual emotional mobilization, and the result is a general lowering of a person's physical and psychological resistance to all stressors.

Psychosocial Factors A number of psychological and interpersonal factors may contribute to the overall stress experienced by soldiers and predispose them to break down under combat. Such factors include reductions in personal freedom, frustrations of all sorts, and separation from home and loved ones. Central, of course, are the many stresses arising from combat, including constant fear, unpredictable and largely uncontrollable circumstances, the necessity of killing, and prolonged harsh conditions.

Personality (which is shaped by temperamental differences beginning in infancy) is an important determinant of adjustment to military experiences. Personality characteristics that lower a person's resistance to stress or to particular stressors may be important in determining his or her reactions to combat. Personal immaturity sometimes stemming from parental overprotection is commonly cited as making a soldier more vulnerable to combat stress. Worthington (1978) found that American soldiers who experienced problems readjusting after they returned home from the Vietnam War also tended to have had greater difficulties before and during their military service than soldiers who adjusted readily. In their study of the personality characteristics of Israeli soldiers who had broken down in combat during the Yom Kippur War, Merbaum and Hefez (1976) found that over 25 percent reported having had psychological treatment prior to the war. Another 12 percent had experienced difficulties previously in the 6-day Israeli-Arab war of 1967. Thus, about 37 percent of these soldiers had clear histories of some personality instability that may have predisposed them to break down under combat stress. On the other hand, of the other soldiers who broke down, over 60 percent had not shown earlier difficulties and would not have been considered to be at risk for such breakdown.

A background of personal maladjustment does not always make a person a poor risk for withstanding combat stress. Some people are so accustomed to anxiety that they cope with it more or less automatically, whereas soldiers who are feeling severe anxiety for the first time may be terrified by the experience, lose their self-confidence, and go to pieces.

Sociocultural Factors Several sociocultural factors play an important part in determining a person's adjustment to combat. These general factors include clarity and acceptability of war goals, identification with the combat unit, esprit de corps, and quality of leadership.

Many factors may contribute to traumatic reactions to combat—constitutional predisposition, personal immaturity, compromised loyalty to one's unit, diminished confidence in one's officers, as well as the actual stress experienced. Thus, although combat situations completely undermine a person's ordinary coping strategies, some soldiers can tolerate great stress without becoming psychiatric casualties, while others may break down under only slight combat stress.

An important consideration is how clear and acceptable the war's goals are to a person. If the goals can be concretely integrated into the soldier's values in terms of his or her "stake" in the war and the worth and importance of what he or she is doing, this will help support the soldier psychologically. Another important factor is a person's identification with the combat unit. In fact, the stronger the sense of group identification, the less chance that a soldier will break down in combat. Feelings of *esprit de corps* influence a person's morale and adjustment to extreme circumstances. Finally, the quality of leadership and confidence in one's unit are of vital importance in a soldier's adjustment to combat. If a soldier respects his or her leaders, has confidence in their judgment and ability, and can accept them as relatively strong parental or sibling figures, the soldier's morale and resistance to stress are bolstered. On the other hand, lack of confidence or dislike of leaders is detrimental to morale and to combat stress tolerance.

It also appears that returning to an unaccepting social environment can increase a soldier's vulnerability to post-traumatic stress. For example, in a 1-year follow-up of Israeli men who had been psychiatric war casualties during the Yom Kippur War, Merbaum (1977) found that they not only continued to show extreme anxiety, depression, and extensive physical complaints, but in many instances appeared to have become more disturbed over time. Merbaum hypothesized that their psychological deterioration had probably been due to the unaccepting attitudes of the community; in a country so reliant on the strength of its army for survival, considerable stigma is attached to psychological breakdown in combat. Because of the stigma, many of the men were experiencing not only isolation within their communities, but also self-recrimination about what they perceived as failure on their own part. These feelings exacerbated the soldiers' already stressful situations. In a more recent follow-up study of Yom Kippur War veterans, Solomon and Kleinhauz (1996) reported that residual PTSD symptoms (intrusive thinking and avoidance) were present in war veterans compared with controls 18 years after the war ended.

Long-Term Effects In some cases, soldiers who have experienced combat exhaustion may show symptoms of post-traumatic stress for sustained periods of time. In cases of delayed PTSD, some soldiers who have stood up exceptionally well under intensive combat situations have experienced post-traumatic stress only upon their return home, often in response to relatively minor stresses that they had handled easily before. Evidently, these soldiers suffered long-term damage to their adaptive capabilities, in some cases complicated by memories of killing enemy soldiers or civilians as well as feelings of guilt and anxiety (Haley, 1978; Horowitz & Solomon, 1978).

In a study of Vietnam returnees, Strange and Brown (1970) compared combat and noncombat veterans who were experiencing emotional difficulties. The combat group showed a higher incidence of depression and of difficulties in close interpersonal relationships. They also showed a higher incidence of aggressive and suicidal threats but did not actually carry them out. In a later study of Vietnam veterans who were making a satisfactory readjustment to civilian life, DeFazio, Rustin, and Diamond (1975) found that the combat veterans reported certain symptoms twice as often as the noncombat veterans. The nature and extent of delayed PTSD are somewhat controversial (Burstein, 1985). Reported cases of delayed PTSD among Vietnam combat veterans are often difficult to relate explicitly to combat stress because these people may also have other significant adjustment problems. People with adjustment difficulties may erroneously attribute their present problems to specific incidents from their past, such as experiences in combat. The wide publicity recently given to delayed PTSD has made it easy for clinicians to find a precipitating cause in their patients' backgrounds. Indeed, the frequency with which this disorder has recently been diagnosed in some settings suggests that its increased use is as much a result of its plausibility and popularity as of its true incidence.

Severe Threats to Personal Safety and Security

Some of the most traumatic and psychologically disabling circumstances a person can experience involve those in which a drastic threat to personal security must be faced. Even living in a modern, civilized society is no guarantee of having uninterrupted peaceful pursuit of our dreams and ambitions. All too often in the modern world we hear about tragic sociopolitical circumstances that require large populations to leave their homeland and join a scattered trail of refugees to some unknown place with horribly lawless and inhumane treatment.

This section briefly describes some extreme situations that are among the most stressful circumstances for anyone to cope with, and that often result in long-range psychological adjustment problems for the victims. We will examine three traumatic circumstances: (1) forced relocation; (2) being held hostage; and (3) torture. Although such circumstances are extreme and unlikely for most of us to encounter, they are all too frequent in our oftentimes turbulent world.

Forced Relocation It is estimated that more than 16 million refugees exist in today's world, mostly from developing countries, with only about 11 percent of them relocating in developed nations such as the United States and Canada (Westermeyer, Williams, & Nguyen, 1991). Most refugees move between third-world countries. For example, more than 1.5 million Kurdish refugees from Iraq have either fled to Iran or live near the Iraq-Turkey border in makeshift living quarters, and there are countless numbers of Rwandan refugees living in Zaire.

In the United States, recent refugees have come from many countries—Ethiopia, the former Soviet Union, Iran, Cuba, Haiti, Laos, Vietnam, Cambodia, and Somalia. The Southeast Asians who began arriving in the United States after 1975 perhaps had the most difficult adjustment. Although many of these people were functioning well in their homeland and in time became successful and happy American citizens, others have had difficulty adjusting (Carlson & Rosser-Hogan, 1993; Clarke, Sack, & Goff, 1993; Westermeyer, Williams, & Nguyen, 1991). Refugees who have low self-esteem tend to be the ones who have the most difficulty adjusting to new cultures (Nesdale, Rooney, & Smith, 1997). For example, a 10-year longitudinal study of Hmong refugees from Laos found that many refugees had made considerable progress in their acculturation (Westermeyer, Neider, & Callies, 1989). Many had improved economically—about 55 percent were employed, with incomes approaching those of the general population. The percentage of the refugees initially living on welfare had dropped from 53 to 29 percent after 10 years. As a group, psychological adjustment had also improved, with symptoms of phobia, somatization, and low self-esteem showing the most positive changes. Considerable problems remained, however. Many refugees still had not learned the language, some seemingly had settled permanently onto the welfare rolls, and some showed symptoms such as anxiety, hostility, and paranoia that changed little over the period studied. Although many refugees adapted to their new culture, many were still experiencing considerable adjustment problems even after 10 years in the United States (Hinton, Tiet, et al., 1997; Westermeyer, 1989) or in other countries such as Norway (Hauff & Vaglum, 1994).

Many adults who emigrate—especially those forced to leave their homes—experience a high degree of stress and psychological adjustment problems. However, even greater degrees of stress can occur with their children (Rousseau, Drapeau, & Corin, 1996). In a study of Chinese migrants to Canada, Short and Johnston (1997) found that the degree of stress in children was often buffered by greater adjustment in the parents. Their study highlighted the importance of measuring stress levels of adults and implementing strategies to alleviate their "settlement concerns" in order to lower the level of stress for children.

The Trauma of Being Held Hostage Hostage taking seems to increase each year. Not only are politically driven hostage-taking situations becoming more frequent, but kidnappings in the United States for economic or other motives also seem on the rise. Clearly, such situations can produce disabling psychological symptoms in victims (Allodi, 1994). The following case describes a man who experienced a horrifying ordeal that left him with intense symptoms of anxiety and distress for months following the incident.

Case Study **Abduction and Its Aftermath** • Mr. A. was a married accountant, the father of two, in his early thirties. One night, while out performing an errand, he was attacked by a group of youths. These youngsters made him get into their car, and took him to a deserted country road.

There they pulled him from the car and began beating and kicking him. They took his wallet, began taunting him about its contents (they had learned his name, his occupation, and the names of his wife and children), and threatened to go to his home and harm these family members. Finally, after brutalizing him for several hours, they tied him to a tree, one youth held a gun to his head, and after he begged and pleaded for his life, the armed assailant pulled the trigger. The gun was empty, but at the moment the trigger was pulled the victim defecated and urinated in his pants. Then the youths untied him and left him on the road.

This man slowly made his way to a gas station he had seen during his abduction, and called the police. [One of the authors] was called to examine him, and did so at intervals for the next 2 years. The diagnosis was PTSD. He had clearly experienced an event outside the range of normal human experience, and was at first reexperiencing the event in various ways: intrusive recollections, nightmares, flashbacks, and extreme fear upon seeing groups of unsavory looking youths. He was initially remarkably numb in other respects: He withdrew from the members of his family and lost interest in his job. He felt generally estranged and detached. He expected to die in the near future. There were also symptoms of increased psychophysiologic arousal: poor sleeping, difficulty concentrating, exaggerated startle response, and when he first spoke [with the author] about his abduction in detail, he actually soiled himself at the moment he described doing so during the original traumatic experience.

This man received treatment during the next 2 years from another psychiatrist, consisting of twice-weekly intensive individual psychotherapy sessions and the concurrent administration of a tricyclic antidepressant. The individual psychotherapy consisted of discussions that focused on the sense of shame and guilt this man felt over his behavior during his abduction. He wished he had been more stoic and had not pleaded for his life. With the understanding help of his psychotherapist, he came to see that he could accept responsibility for his behavior during his captivity, that his murderous rage at his abductors was understandable, as was his desire for revenge, and that his response to his experience was not remarkable compared with what others might have done and felt. Eventually he began to discuss his experience with his wife and friends, and by the end of the 2 years over which [the author] followed him, he was essentially without symptoms, although he still became somewhat anxious when he saw groups of tough-looking youths. Most importantly, his relationship with his wife and children was warm and close, and he was again interested in his work. (From Sonnenberg, 1988, p. 585.)

Many Burmese political dissidents who later escaped to Thailand experienced torture before their escape.

Psychological Trauma Among Victims of Torture Among the most highly stressful experiences human beings have reported have been those inhuman acts perpetrated upon them by other human beings in the form of systematic torture.

Most of what is known about the psychological consequences of torture comes from anecdotal reports by victims. In an effort to understand the psychological factors involved, the long-term consequences of torture, and possible rehabilitation strategies, Başoğlu and colleagues (1994) conducted a unique empirical study in which 55 former Turkish prisoners who were political activists were compared with 55 political activists who were not tortured. The researchers found that although the victims of torture were for the most part not extremely psychiatrically disturbed compared with the controls, the victims of imprisonment and torture did experience significant symptoms of PTSD related to being uprooted, being a refugee, living in a repressive political environment, and living through related traumatic events. Moreover, Başoğlu and his colleagues also found evidence sufficient to conclude that torture induces psychological effects independent of other stressors. Interestingly, these researchers found that traumatic experience from torture had a differential impact depending on the manner in which torture was applied—that is, whether the torture was perceived by the victim as uncontrollable and unpredictable (Başoğlu & Mineka, 1992). Victims who were able to assert some element of cognitive control over the circumstances (for example, who were able to predict and ready themselves for the pain they were about to experience) tended to be less affected over the long term. The researchers came to this conclusion:

> Prior knowledge of and preparedness for torture, strong commitment to a cause, immunization against traumatic stress as a result of repeated exposure, and strong social supports appear to have protective value against PTSD in survivors of torture. (p. 76)

In a further follow-up study of torture victims, Başoğlu, Mineka, and colleagues (1997) found additional support for the idea that psychological preparedness for trauma is an extremely important protective factor for lessening the psychological effects of torture.

IN REVIEW

- What are the severe stressors associated with acute and post-traumatic stress disorders, and how do these two groups of stressors differ?
- What are the main differences between acute stress disorder and post-traumatic stress disorder?
- What are the three stages of disaster syndrome? At which stage might PTSD develop?
- Differentiate between acute and delayed PTSD. What is controversial about the frequency of diagnosis of the latter?

HIGHLIGHT 4.4

Unpredictable and Uncontrollable Stressors

For the past 30 years, extensive research with animals has shown that two of the most important determinants of how an organism responds to stress are whether the stressors are unpredictable or uncontrollable or both. An unpredictable stressor occurs without warning and its nature may be unforeseen. With an uncontrollable stressor, there is no way to respond to reduce its impact, such as by escape or avoidance. In general, both people and animals are more stressed by unpredictable and uncontrollable stressors than by stressors that are of equal physical magnitude but that are either predictable or controllable or both (e.g., Mineka & Zinbarg, 1996).

There are many parallels in the symptoms of PTSD and the behavioral and physiological consequences of unpredictable and uncontrollable stressors in animals (e.g., Başoğlu & Mineka, 1992; Foa, Zinbarg, & Rothbaum, 1992; Friedman & Yehuda, 1995; Mineka & Zinbarg, 1996). It is known, for example, that uncontrollable stressors stimulate some brain systems and increase levels of central and peripheral norepinephrine (Friedman & Yehuda, 1995; Southwick, Yehuda, & Morgan, 1995). This led PTSD researchers to hypothesize that administration of a drug called *yohimbine* (a naturally occurring substance) to persons with PTSD might increase their symptoms, because yohimbine is known to activate noradrenergic neurons. Consistent with this hypothesis, Southwick and colleagues (1995) found that 40 percent of a group of 20 Vietnam veterans with PTSD experienced flashbacks. In addition, the veterans with PTSD showed increases in other symptoms, such as intrusive traumatic thoughts, emotional numbing, and grief.

Uncontrollable stressors are also known to cause stress-induced analgesia (SIA), or diminished sensitivity to pain, in animals. Formerly neutral conditioned stimuli that are paired with uncontrollable stressors can also become conditioned to elicit this analgesia. This SIA is known to work through the production of endogenous, or internally produced, opiatelike substances in the brain (Southwick et al., 1995; van der Kolk & Saporta, 1993). PTSD researchers now believe that many of the symptoms of emotional numbing seen in people with PTSD may be caused by this same kind of SIA, rather than being a psychological defensive reaction against remembering the trauma. Consistent with this are results from a study by Pitman and his colleagues (1990) in which veterans with and without PTSD who watched a film depicting combat in Vietnam (certainly a conditioned stimulus for trauma) were later given a pain sensitivity test. Those with PTSD showed reduced pain sensitivity relative to those without PTSD. Those with PTSD also showed a relative blunting of emotional responses to the film. This and other studies support the idea that the symptoms of emotional numbing in PTSD stem from the opioid-mediated SIA that has developed because of the experience with uncontrollable stressors.

If unpredictable and uncontrollable stressors are most likely to produce PTSD, which of the people who experience such stressors will be most likely to develop PTSD? Again, researchers have turned to the animal literature for answers (e.g., Mineka & Zinbarg, 1996). For example, it is known that prior experience with uncontrollable stressors can sensitize the organism—that is, make it more susceptible to the negative consequences of later experiences with uncontrollable trauma. Several studies of PTSD have confirmed that this is indeed the case, with victims of childhood abuse being more susceptible to PTSD in response to both sexual and nonsexual assault in adulthood (see Foa et al., 1992; Mineka & Zinbarg, 1996). In addition, soldiers who had been physically abused in childhood were more likely to develop PTSD during the Vietnam war (Post, Weiss, & Smith, 1995).

Considerable research now supports the hypotheses that perceptions of uncontrollability and unpredictability play an important role in the development and maintenance of PTSD symptoms. Moreover, the animal literature showing that prior experiences with uncontrollable stressors may sensitize an organism to the negative effects of subsequent experience with other uncontrollable stressors has led to important new findings regarding which individuals may be most susceptible to PTSD. ■

TREATMENT AND PREVENTION OF STRESS DISORDERS

In general, the more stable and better-integrated a personality and the more favorable a person's life situation, the more quickly he or she will recover from a severe stress reaction. Many people who experience a disaster benefit from at least some psychological counseling, no matter how brief, to begin coping with their experiences (Shelby & Tredinnick, 1995). Brom, Kleber, and Defares (1989) conducted a controlled study of the effectiveness of brief therapy with people experiencing PTSD and found that treatment immediately following the traumatic event significantly reduced the PTSD symptoms. Sixty percent of the treated persons showed improvement, while only 26 percent of the untreated group improved. The researchers also found, however, that treatment did not benefit everyone and that some people maintained their PTSD symptoms even after therapy was terminated.

Treatment is often required, too, for disaster area workers. Many people called to the scene of a disaster to assist victims later experience PTSD themselves. Epstein, Fullerton, and Ursano (1998) found that workers who provide support to bereaved families of disaster victims are at risk for increased illness, psychiatric symptoms, and negative psychological well-being for up to 18 months following the disaster. They also reported that individuals with lower levels of education, those who had exposure to grotesque burns, and those who had strong feelings of numbness following exposure were more likely to experience later psychological symptoms following an air disaster.

Supportive therapy and proper rest (induced by sedatives if necessary) usually can alleviate symptoms that lead to PTSD (Everly, 1995; Morgan, 1995). Repetitive talking about the experience and constantly reliving it in fantasies or nightmares may serve as built-in repair mechanisms to help a person adjust to the traumatic event.

The treatment of stress-related psychological problems is most effective when intervention is applied early or as soon as possible following the traumatic events. We will describe some medications that have been considered useful in providing relief from the symptoms of PTSD; however, pharmacotherapy works best in the context of psychological treatment. We will also describe effective approaches to reduction of symptoms related to stress.

Stress Prevention or Reduction

In some situations, it may be possible to prevent maladaptive responses to stress by preparing a person in advance to deal with the stress. This approach to stress management has been shown to be effective in cases where the person is facing a known traumatic event, such as major surgery or the breakup of a relationship. In these cases, a professional attempts to prepare the person in advance to better deal with the stressful event through developing more realistic and adaptive attitudes about the problem.

The use of cognitive-behavioral techniques to help people manage potentially stressful situations or difficult events has been widely explored (Beech, Burns, & Sheffield, 1982; MacDonald & Kuiper, 1983; Meichenbaum & Cameron, 1983). This preventive strategy, often referred to as **stress-inoculation training,** prepares people to tolerate an anticipated threat by changing the things they say to themselves before the crisis. A three-stage process is employed. The first stage provides information about the stressful situation and about ways people can deal with such dangers. In the second stage, self-statements that promote effective adaptation—for example, "Don't worry, this little pain is just part of the treatment"—are rehearsed. In the third stage, the person practices making such self-statements while being exposed to a variety of ego-threatening or pain-threatening stressors, such as unpredictable electric shocks, stress-inducing films, or sudden cold. This last phase allows the person to apply the new coping skills learned earlier.

Treatment of Post-Traumatic Stress Symptoms

Medications Several medications are used to provide relief for intense PTSD symptoms. Antidepressants are sometimes helpful in improving symptoms of depression, intrusion, and avoidance (Marshall & Klein, 1995; Shaley, Bonne, & Eth, 1996). However, since the symptoms can fluctuate over a brief period of time, careful monitoring of medications or dosages is required. The use of medications tends to be focused on specific symptoms—for example, intrusive distressing symptoms or nightmares, images of horrible events, startle reaction, and so forth. Vargas and Davidson (1993) concluded that psychotherapy along with medications was more effective in improving PTSD symptoms than medications taken alone.

Crisis Intervention Therapy A brief problem-focused counseling approach referred to as **crisis intervention** (see Chapter 15) may aid a victim of a traumatic event in re-

stress-inoculation training Preventive strategy that prepares people to tolerate an anticipated threat by changing the things they say to themselves before the crisis.

crisis intervention Problem-focused counseling approach that tries to provide psychological help to an individual or group after the stressful event is over.

adjusting to life after the stressful situation has ended. In brief crisis-oriented therapy with people in a crisis situation, the disaster victims are given emotional support and encouraged to talk about their experiences during the crisis (Cigrang, Pace, & Yasuhara, 1995). People who are able to deal with their emotional reactions during the crisis are better able to adjust to life circumstances following the disaster (Chemtob, Tomas, Law, & Cremniter, 1997).

Direct Therapeutic Exposure One behaviorally oriented treatment strategy that has been used effectively with PTSD clients is *direct therapeutic exposure* (Fairbank et al., 1993). In this approach, the client is exposed or reintroduced to stimuli that have come to be feared or associated with the traumatic event (McIvor & Turner, 1995). This procedure involves repeated or extended exposure, either in vivo or in the imagination, to objectively harmless but feared stimuli for the purpose of reducing anxiety (Fairbank et al., 1993).

Exposure to stimuli that have come to be associated with fear-producing situations might also be supplemented by other behavioral techniques in an effort to reduce the symptoms of PTSD. For example, the use of traditional behavioral therapy methods such as relaxation training and assertiveness training might also be found to be effective in helping a client deal with the anxiety following a traumatic event.

The following case shows the effectiveness of this approach.

Case Study **Therapy for an Angry Vet with PTSD** • A male veteran diagnosed with PTSD and substance abuse was enrolled in a treatment program and received anger management treatment. He began attending the anger management groups in May 1992 and continues to attend a drop-in anger management support group regularly.

John is a 45-year-old, divorced, Hispanic, Vietnam veteran, with a 25-year history of alcohol and heroin dependence. He grew up in Texas, graduated from high school, and served in the Navy from July 1969 to April 1971. During his tour in Vietnam, John saw significant combat, including friendly and hostile incoming fire. He took part in amphibious invasions and engaged the enemy in fire fights. John saw many of his comrades killed, including his best friend who was killed only a few feet away from him by an exploding land mine. He also witnessed many atrocities, including the killing of Vietnamese civilians.

John began using alcohol and heroin while in Vietnam. Following his discharge, he experienced symptoms of depression, fearfulness, hypervigilance, and isolation. John began to increase his alcohol and heroin use in an attempt to decrease these feelings. Although trained as a welder, John was unable to hold steady employment. Prior to his entry into treatment for PTSD, he was hospitalized on several occasions for depression and two suicide attempts. John was arrested more than 30 times for assault and disorderly conduct.

In 1990, John began outpatient treatment in the Post-Traumatic Stress Disorder Clinic at the San Francisco Veterans Affairs Medical Center. He engaged in group psychotherapy and received pharmacotherapy; however, he continued to abuse alcohol and heroin and displayed significant behavioral difficulties, including occasional assaults. In December 1991, John was hospitalized in the inpatient PTSD program following an escalation of angry outbursts, including an incident in which, apparently without provocation, he swung a stick at a man he encountered on a walk.

At the time of his admission to both the treatment program and the anger management group in May 1992, John reported that he had not used alcohol or other drugs for a month. He complained, however, of intrusive thoughts and memories, nightmares, flashbacks, sleep disturbance, poor concentration, and frequent outbursts of anger.

During his initial sessions in the anger management group, John reported high levels of irritability and anger, and very low frustration tolerance. On one occasion, he destroyed personal property during an episode of rage. Over the course of several weeks in the group, John became skilled at monitoring his anger by using the anger meter and identifying the physical, emotional, and situational cues that led to his escalation of anger. He also became aware of his hostile self-talk and began to use anger management strategies, such as time-out and an exercise program, to control his anger effectively. By the eighth week of treatment, John was regularly practicing assertiveness techniques, such as conflict resolution. His improvement is exemplified by an incident that occurred during his tenth week of treatment. John reported that he had become angered when he learned that his landlord had let his ex-wife into his apartment without his permission. Rather than acting out aggressively against the landlord or destroying property, John spoke directly to his landlord, resolving the incident assertively.

John has continued to make significant progress. He completed the 12-week group and continues to attend an anger management support group for clients in the program. He has maintained his abstinence throughout his treatment in the program. He has become significantly less isolated, having formed friendships with group members, and has enrolled in a work training program. He has progressed from angry outbursts and violently acting out to taking brief time-outs and assertively resolving conflicts. John is now more confident in his ability to negotiate difficult situations, can identify anger-provoking situations, and can manage his anger effectively with specific cognitive and behavioral techniques. (From Reilley, Clark, Shopshire, Lewis, & Sorensen, 1994, p. 406.)

IN REVIEW

- What strategies are useful for prevention or reduction of maladaptive responses to stress?
- Describe three treatment approaches for patients with PTSD.

UNRESOLVED ISSUES: *The Abuse of PTSD and Other Stress-Related Diagnoses*

This chapter has addressed the role of stress in producing psychological disorders. A considerable amount of research has substantiated the link between severe stress or trauma and subsequent psychological problems. People may react to stressful situations in ways that are quite disabling. Many symptoms of PTSD can interfere with psychological functioning, at least for a time, and can require considerable adaptive effort to overcome.

In recent years, alleged psychological disability as a result of PTSD has been used in both civil and criminal cases (Slovenko, 1994). PTSD has been used as a defense in court cases to justify criminal acts according to the not guilty by reason of insanity plea (see Chapter 15). The following case illustrates the sometimes loose connection between PTSD and deviant behavior.

Case Study • In January 1987, an employee of an air cargo company, who had been fired from his job the day before, returned to the office dressed in army fatigues and carrying a sawed-off shotgun. He chased several employees away from the office and took his former supervisor hostage. He held his supervisor at gunpoint for about 1½ hours, making him beg for his life. During this time, he fired about 21 shots at desks, computers, and windows, destroying a great deal of property. Once the hostage-taking situation ended, the former employee was arrested on charges of property destruction and assault with a deadly weapon. He reportedly claimed that he was extremely distraught and was suffering from PTSD. He explained that he had just seen the movie *Platoon,* which brought back horrible memories of Vietnam and resulted in his becoming enraged. However, a check of his background and military records showed that he had never been in Vietnam and had actually spent his service time in a low-stress noncombat environment.

There have been a number of similar incidents in which alleged PTSD symptoms have been incorporated into the legal defense strategy of individuals facing felony convictions. For example, one dramatic case is of a World War II POW veteran who killed his daughter's estranged husband. He later claimed that he committed this act because of the "ghosts of the past." He claimed that he was afraid for his life when his son-in-law approached him, and he shot him because he thought he was going to be "beaten to death" (*Los Angeles Times,* Sept. 8, 1997).

The frequent sensational nature and resulting publicity of some cases may give the impression that the use of the PTSD defense is on the increase. A study of insanity plea defendants showed that concerns over widespread abuse of the PTSD insanity defense are unfounded because the defense is not used as frequently as is often supposed. Appelbaum and colleagues (1993) found that of 8163 defendants pleading insanity between 1980 and 1986, only 28 (0.3 percent) had been given PTSD diagnoses. People with a PTSD diagnosis employing the insanity defense were, however, more likely to be able to avoid pretrial detention than those in the control group of non-PTSD defendants (Appelbaum et al., 1993).

The PTSD syndrome is more frequently being used in civil court cases, such as those involving compensation and personal injury. For example, in one case (*Albertson's Inc.* v. *Workers' Compensation Appeals Board of the State of California,* 1982), a bakery employee was awarded damages because her boss's comments to her caused her great embarrassment. The court concluded that job harassment was a sufficient cause of psychological damage and stress, and it was thus compensable. In another case, a police officer filed a compensation claim because his job had created a great deal of stress for him. The police officer was not awarded a stress-related disability; the court ruled that when a person accepts a job as a police officer, he or she accepts the stress that accompanies it. The court did, however, award compensation payments for his physical disability (ulcers) that resulted from the stressful job (*Egeland* v. *City of Minneapolis,* 1984).

Establishing legal justification for the stress defense is an interesting exercise, often involving considerable imagination if not out-and-out mythmaking. Whether a stressor is causally linked to a specific psychological disorder, thereby warranting compensation in disability cases or commanding leniency in criminal trials, is often difficult to substantiate and usually involves expert witness testimony by psychiatrists or psychologists. In most situations, both sides in a case rely on expert testimony to support their side. However, the most important factor, from the standpoint of legal precedent, is that there must be sufficient evidence that the alleged stressor was clearly related to the behavior in question.

Seeking psychological damages for alleged stress, whether justified or contrived, will probably continue as a legal strategy in court cases. Earlier, it was thought that the stressor needed to be so extreme as to be "outside the range of normal experience." However, changes in DSM-IV eliminated this requirement. The modified criteria for PTSD can form the basis of a disease claim in situations where a mental stimulus (thoughts and memories) can cause a mental or occupational disease. Because symptoms of stress disorders are not uniform, and disabilities following stressful events are not easily predictable, it is likely that the problem of clearly establishing causal links between stressors and claimed symptoms will continue to plague our courts.

SUMMARY

WHAT IS STRESS?

- Many factors influence a person's response to stressful situations. The impact of stress depends not only on its severity but also on the person's preexisting vulnerabilities.
- A number of factors predispose individuals to experience stress: the nature of the stressor, the person's perception of the stressor, the person's stress tolerance, and the availability of external resources and social supports.
- In attempting to deal with stressful events, a person may react with task-oriented or defense-oriented responses.

THE EFFECTS OF SEVERE STRESS

- The effects of extreme or prolonged stress on a person can include extensive physical and psychological problems.
- A model that helps explain the course of biological decompensation under excessive stress is the general adaptation syndrome, introduced by Selye. This states that the body's reaction to sustained and excessive stress occurs in three major phases: alarm reaction, stage of resistance, and exhaustion.
- The course of personality decompensation in the face of severe stress or trauma is similar to biological decompensation and includes alarm and mobilization, resistance, and exhaustion.

ADJUSTMENT DISORDER: REACTIONS TO COMMON LIFE STRESSORS

- The DSM classifies people's problems in response to stressful situations under two general categories: adjustment disorders and stress disorders.
- A person whose response to a common stressor is maladaptive and occurs within 3 months of the stressor can be said to have an adjustment disorder.

ACUTE AND POST-TRAUMATIC STRESS DISORDERS: REACTIONS TO CATASTROPHIC EVENTS

- Intense psychological problems in response to trauma or excessively stressful situations (such as rape, military combat, imprisonment, being held hostage, forced relocation, and torture) may be categorized as acute stress disorder (ASD) or post-traumatic stress disorder (PTSD).
- Stress disorders may involve a variety of symptoms, including intrusive thoughts and repetitive nightmares about the traumatic events, intense fear, avoidance of stimuli associated with it, and increased arousal manifested as anxiety, chronic tension, irritability, insomnia, impaired concentration and memory, and depression.
- If the symptoms begin 6 months or more after the traumatic event, the diagnosis is delayed PTSD.
- Many factors contribute to breakdown under excessive stress, including the intensity of the stress, the duration of the traumatic event, the person's preexisting biological makeup and personality adjustment, and the ways in which the person manages problems once the stressful situation is over.

TREATMENT AND PREVENTION OF STRESS DISORDERS

- Stress-inoculation therapy can prepare people to manage stressful situations, and crisis intervention can help people recover from traumatic experiences and readjust.

- Several medications are also used to provide relief for intense PTSD symptoms, including antidepressants.
- In many cases, PTSD symptoms recede as the stress diminishes, especially if the person is given supportive psychotherapy. In extreme cases, however, there may be residual damage or prolonged maladjustment.

UNRESOLVED ISSUES: THE ABUSE OF PTSD AND OTHER STRESS-RELATED DIAGNOSES

- Post-traumatic stress disorder has been used in criminal cases to explain deviant behavior and, more frequently, in civil cases to justify compensation for preceived damages.
- The extent to which this psychological disorder has been successfully used in court has varied. In some situations, especially when extreme trauma has been involved, the maladaptive behavior is readily explainable in terms of the traumatic event. In other situations, however, a causal link between maladaptive behavior and a traumatic event has been difficult to establish.

KEY TERMS

stressors (p. 123)
stress (p. 124)
coping strategies (p. 124)
eustress (p. 124)
distress (p. 124)
crisis (p. 124)
stress tolerance (p. 125)
task-oriented response (p. 125)
defense-oriented response (p. 125)
personality (psychological) decompensation (p. 126)
general adaptation syndrome (p. 127)
psychoneuroimmunology (p. 129)
adjustment disorder (p. 130)
acute stress disorder (ASD) (p. 130)
post-traumatic stress disorder (PTSD) (p. 130)
disaster syndrome (p. 131)
stress-inoculation training (p. 144)
crisis intervention (p. 144)

CHAPTER FIVE

Panic, Anxiety, and Their Disorders

Nicole Aimee Macaluso, *August Day of 1998*, painted low relief. Macaluso is a Chicago native whose father worked in the arts. She suffers from both panic attacks and manic depressive disorder. Her paintings express the idea of time, often by assembling several perceptions or vignettes in a single canvas.

LEARNING OBJECTIVES

After reading this chapter, you should be able to:

- Distinguish between fear and anxiety.
- Identify the major features and causal factors, as well as the treatment approaches, for specific and social phobias.
- Give the diagnostic criteria for panic disorder with and without agoraphobia, and summarize the different causal factors and treatment approaches for these conditions.
- Describe the symptoms, causal factors, and treatments for generalized anxiety disorder.
- Characterize obsessive-compulsive disorder, and summarize its causal factors and treatment.
- Provide several examples of sociocultural differences in anxiety disorders.

As noted in Chapter 4, even stable, well-adjusted people may break down if forced to face extensive combat stress, torture, or devastating natural disaster. But for some people, everyday problems can be disturbing. Faced with the normal demands of life—socializing with friends, waiting in line for a bus, being on an airplane, touching a doorknob—they experience the arousal of serious fear or anxiety. In the most severe cases, people with anxiety problems may be unable to leave their homes or may spend much of their time in maladaptive behavior, such as constant hand washing.

Anxiety—a general feeling of apprehension about possible danger—was in Freud's formulation a sign of an inner battle or conflict between some primitive desire (from the id) and prohibitions against its expression (from the ego and superego). This anxiety seemed evident to Freud in clients who were obviously fearful and nervous. Today, the DSM has identified a group of disorders that share obvious symptoms and features of anxiety as the *anxiety disorders*, which will be the focus of this chapter.

Historically, anxiety disorders were considered to be examples of **neurotic behavior,** which involved the exaggerated use of avoidance behaviors (such as not leaving home) or defense mechanisms (such as rationalizing that making a trip by car is "more convenient" than confronting the feared airplane ride). Although neurotic behavior can be quite maladaptive and self-defeating, a neurotic person is not out of touch with reality, incoherent, or dangerous.

The idea of **neurosis** has a long history and is still used in psychodynamic professional circles, and in casual conversation by the general public. Freud challenged earlier long-held beliefs that neurosis was due to neurological malfunction and argued instead that it was caused by intrapsychic conflict. To Freud, neuroses were *psychological disorders* that resulted when there was anxiety, which was a sign of intrapsychic conflict. As already noted, this anxiety was sometimes very evident, as in clients who were obviously fearful or anxious. To complicate matters, however, Freud also believed that the anxiety might *not* be obvious, either to the person involved or to others, if psychological defense mechanisms were able to deflect or mask it. Yet, in his view, it was still causing the neurotic behavior in such cases. For example, Freud believed that many of his patients' physical complaints (such as temporary blindness or paralysis) were caused by anxiety—chiefly about sexual or aggressive feelings with which they were uncomfortable. In such cases, Freud's ideas required inferring that anxiety somehow existed in the mind and caused neurotic behavior even though it could not be observed or measured.

The DSM avoids such inferences about the causes of disorders. Therefore, although we still hear and use the term *neurosis,* DSM-IV-TR separates what used to be officially called "neuroses" into different categories based on their symptoms, which can be observed and measured. People with anxiety disorders, which we shall be considering in this chapter, show prominent symptoms of anxiety. Most of the other disorders that Freud considered neuroses, but that did not involve obvious anxiety symptoms, have been reclassified and will be discussed in Chapter 7 (the somatoform and dissociative disorders). One final category of neurotic disorders (depressive neurosis) is now included with the other mood disorders, which will be discussed in Chapter 6.

We begin by discussing the nature of fear and anxiety as emotional states, which have an extremely important adaptive value but to which humans at times seem all too vulnerable. We will then move on to discuss each of the anxiety disorders as described in DSM-IV-TR and their causal factors and optimal modes of treatment.

THE FEAR AND ANXIETY RESPONSE PATTERNS

The task of defining *fear* and *anxiety* is difficult; there has never been complete agreement whether the two emotions

neurotic behavior Exaggerated use of avoidance behaviors or defense mechanisms in response to anxiety.

neurosis Term used historically to characterize maladaptive behavior resulting from intrapsychic conflict and marked by prominent use of defense mechanisms.

are indeed distinct from each other. Historically, the most common way of distinguishing between fear and anxiety has been to ask whether there is a clear and obvious source of danger that would be regarded as real by most people. When the source of danger is obvious, the experienced emotion has been called *fear*. With anxiety, however, people frequently cannot specify clearly what the danger is. Intuitively, anxiety seems to be experienced as an unpleasant inner state in which a person is anticipating some dreadful thing happening that is not entirely predictable from the actual circumstances.

In recent years, many prominent researchers have proposed a more fundamental distinction between fear, or panic, and anxiety (e.g., Barlow, Chorpita, & Turovsky, 1996; Gray, 1991; Gray & McNaughton, 1996). According to these theorists, **fear** or **panic** is a basic emotion that involves the activation of the "fight-or-flight" response of the sympathetic nervous system, allowing us to respond quickly when faced with any imminent threat such as a dangerous predator or someone with a pointed and loaded gun. Fear has three components: (1) cognitive/subjective components ("I feel afraid"), (2) physiological components (such as increased heart rate and heavy breathing), and (3) behavioral components (a strong urge to escape) (Lang, 1968, 1971). These components are only "loosely coupled" (Lang, 1985), which means that someone might show, for example, physiological and behavioral indications of fear without much of the subjective component, or vice versa. For the fear response to serve its adaptive purpose of enabling us to escape or avoid danger, it must be activated with great speed. Indeed, subjectively, we often seem to go from a normal state to a state of intense fear almost instantaneously.

Fear or panic is a basic emotion that occurs in many higher animals and humans. It is usually associated with a distinctive facial expression, such as that shown here, and involves activation of the fight-or-flight response of the sympathetic nervous system. This response allows the organism to react quickly when faced with a dangerous situation, such as being threatened by a predator. In humans who are having a panic attack, there is no external threat; panic occurs because of some misfiring of this response system.

Anxiety, in contrast to fear, is best thought of as a complex blend of emotions and cognitions that is much more diffuse than fear. At the cognitive/subjective level, anxiety involves negative mood, worry about possible future threat or danger, self-preoccupation, and a sense of being unable to predict the future threat or to control it if it occurs (Barlow, 1988; Barlow et al., 1996). Rather than involving the activation of the fight-or-flight response itself, as occurs with fear, anxiety involves preparing for that response should it become necessary ("Something awful may happen, and I had better be ready for it if it does"). Like fear, anxiety involves not only cognitive/subjective components, but also physiological and behavioral components. At a physiological level, anxiety involves a state of chronic overarousal that may reflect a state of readiness for dealing with danger should it occur (preparation for, or priming of, the fight-or-flight response). At a behavioral level, anxiety may involve a strong tendency to avoid situations where the danger or threat might be encountered, but there is no immediate urge to flee associated with anxiety, as there is with fear (Barlow, 1988; Barlow et al., 1996). Although anxiety is often adaptive in mild or moderate degrees, it is maladaptive when it becomes chronic and severe, as we generally see in people diagnosed with anxiety disorders.

Although there are many threatening situations that provoke fear or anxiety unconditionally, many sources of fear and anxiety are learned. Human and animal experi-

fear A basic emotion that involves the activation of the "fight-or-flight" response of the sympathetic nervous system.

panic A basic emotion that involves the activation of the "fight-or-flight" response of the sympathetic nervous system.

anxiety A general feeling of apprehension about possible danger; much more diffuse than fear.

mentation going back many decades has established that the basic fear and anxiety response patterns are highly conditionable. That is, previously neutral and novel stimuli that are repeatedly paired with, and reliably predict, aversive events (such as various kinds of physical or psychological trauma) can acquire the capacity to elicit fear or anxiety themselves. For example, a girl who sees and hears her father physically abuse her mother in the evening may become anxious as soon as she hears her father's car arrive in the driveway at the end of the day. In such situations, a wide variety of initially neutral stimuli may accidentally come to serve as cues that something threatening and unpleasant is about to happen. These neutral stimuli may consist not only of external cues, but also of internal bodily sensations such as stomach or intestinal contractions or heart palpitations. As a result of such pairings, these conditioned stimuli can themselves become fear- or anxiety-provoking. In addition, thoughts and mental images become capable of eliciting the fear or anxiety response pattern. In this scenario, virtually any type of novel stimulus (external, mental, or internal bodily sensations) that reliably precedes and predicts an aversive event can be expected to acquire the tendency to elicit fear or anxiety. For example, the girl whose father beats her mother might well come to feel anxious even when thinking about her father.

IN REVIEW

- Compare and contrast fear or panic with anxiety, making sure to note that both emotions involve three response systems but differ with respect to time orientation.
- Explain the significance of the fact that both fear and anxiety can be classically conditioned.

anxiety disorder Any mental disorder characterized by unrealistic, irrational fear or anxiety of disabling intensity; DSM-IV-TR recognizes seven types of anxiety disorder: phobic disorders (specific or social), panic disorder (with or without agoraphobia), generalized anxiety disorder, obsessive-compulsive disorder, and post-traumatic stress disorder.

phobia Persistent and disproportionate fear of some specific object or situation that presents little or no actual danger to a person.

specific phobias Persistent or disproportionate fears of other species (snakes, spiders), aspects of the environment (high places, water), or situations (being in airplanes or elevators).

social phobia Fear of social situations, in which a person might be exposed to the scrutiny of others and might act in a humiliating or embarrassing way.

OVERVIEW OF THE ANXIETY DISORDERS

An **anxiety disorder,** as the term suggests, has an unrealistic, irrational fear or anxiety of disabling intensity at its core and also as its principal and most obvious manifestation. DSM-IV-TR recognizes seven primary types of anxiety disorder: phobic disorders of the "specific" or "social" type, panic disorder with or without agoraphobia, generalized anxiety disorder, obsessive-compulsive disorder, and post-traumatic stress disorder (discussed in Chapter 4).

Anxiety disorders are relatively common, affecting more than 23 million Americans each year and costing the United States $46.6 billion in 1990 in direct and indirect costs (nearly one-third of the nation's total mental health bill of $148 billion) (National Institutes of Mental Health, 1998). In the National Comorbidity Survey, the most recent large epidemiological study, anxiety disorders as a group were the most common kind of disorder for women, affecting approximately 30 percent of the female population at some point in life, and the second most common kind of disorder for men, affecting approximately 19 percent of the male population at some point in life (Kessler et al., 1994). Twelve-month prevalence rates were 23 percent for women and 12 percent for men. In terms of specific anxiety disorders, phobias were the second most common psychiatric disorder reported for women (with major depression being the most common) and the fourth most common for men (behind alcohol abuse, alcohol dependence, and major depression). It is also very common for a person diagnosed with one anxiety disorder to be diagnosed with one or more additional anxiety disorders, as well as with a mood disorder.

We begin our discussion of anxiety disorders with the phobic disorders. A **phobia** is a persistent and disproportionate fear of some specific object or situation that presents little or no actual danger to a person. In DSM-IV-TR, there are three main categories of phobias: (1) specific phobia, (2) social phobia, and (3) agoraphobia. **Specific phobias** (formerly known as *simple phobias*) may involve fears of other species (snake and spider phobias being the most common) or fears of various aspects of the environment, such as water, heights, or tunnels. **Social phobia** involves fear of social situations (such as public speaking, eating in restaurants, or attending parties) in which a person is exposed to the scrutiny of others and is afraid of acting in a humiliating or embarrassing way. Traditionally, *agoraphobia* was thought to involve, somewhat paradoxically, a fear of both open and enclosed spaces. However, as discussed later, it is now understood that agoraphobia most often stems from anxiety about having a panic attack in situations where escape might prove difficult or embarrassing. The apparent paradox is resolved in this view because escape may be difficult from both open and enclosed spaces. Because it is no longer considered to be closely related to the specific phobias, we will discuss agoraphobia in the context of panic disorder, as is done in DSM-IV-TR.

IN REVIEW

- What is the central feature of all anxiety disorders; that is, what do they have in common?
- What are the central features of the three major kinds of phobias?

SPECIFIC PHOBIAS

A person is diagnosed as having a specific phobia if he or she shows strong and persistent fear triggered by the presence of (or anticipation of an encounter with) a specific object or situation. The level of fear must also be excessive or unreasonable relative to the actual danger posed by the object or situation. When individuals with specific phobias encounter a phobic stimulus, they almost always show an immediate fear response that often resembles a panic attack except that there is a clear external trigger (American Psychiatric Association, 1994, p. 410). This fight-or-flight response, discussed earlier, prepares the person to escape from the situation. Phobics also go to great lengths to avoid encounters with their phobic stimulus, or sometimes even seemingly innocent representations of it, such as a photograph. To qualify for a diagnosis of phobia, the avoidance of the feared situation, or the distress experienced in the feared situation, must also interfere significantly with normal functioning or produce marked distress.

Table 5.1 lists some common specific phobias and their objects, clearly illustrating the wide variety of stimuli and situations around which specific phobias may be centered. In DSM-IV-TR, five subtypes of specific phobias are listed: (1) animal subtype (e.g., snakes or spiders); (2) natural environment subtype (e.g., heights or water); (3) blood-injection-injury subtype (discussed below); (4) situational subtype (e.g., airplanes or elevators); (5) atypical subtype (e.g., choking or vomiting). Some of these specific phobias involve very exaggerated fears of things that many of us fear to some extent, such as darkness, fire, disease, spiders, and snakes. Others, such as phobias of water or

People with claustrophobia may find elevators so frightening that they go to great lengths to avoid them. If for some reason they have to take an elevator, they will be very frightened and may have thoughts about the elevator falling, the doors never opening, or there not being enough air to breathe.

TABLE 5.1 COMMON SPECIFIC PHOBIAS

Name of Phobia	Focus of Fear
Acrophobia	Heights
Algophobia	Pain
Astraphobia	Thunderstorms, lightning
Claustrophobia	Enclosed places
Hydrophobia	Water
Monophobia	Being alone
Mysophobia	Contamination or germs
Nyctophobia	Darkness
Ochlophobia	Crowds
Pathophobia	Disease
Pyrophobia	Fire
Zoophobia	Animals or some particular animal

dogs, involve situations or stimuli that do not elicit fear in most people. Many of us have at least a few minor irrational fears, but in phobic disorders such fears are intense and interfere significantly with everyday activities. For example, claustrophobic persons may go to great lengths to avoid entering a small room or an elevator, even if this means climbing many flights of stairs or turning down jobs that might require them to take an elevator. This avoidance is a cardinal characteristic of phobias; it occurs both because the phobic response itself is so unpleasant and because the phobic person makes an irrational appraisal of the likelihood that something terrible will happen.

The following case is typical of specific phobia.

Case Study A Pilot's Wife's Fear of Heights and Enclosed Spaces • Mary, a married mother of three, was 47 at the time she first sought treatment for both claustrophobia and acrophobia. She reported having been intensely afraid of enclosed spaces and of heights since her teens. She remembered having been locked in closets by her older siblings when she was a child; the siblings also confined her under blankets to scare her, and added to her fright by showing her pictures of spiders after releasing her from under the blankets. She traced the onset of her claustrophobia to those traumatic incidents, but she had no idea why she was afraid of heights. While her children had been growing up, she had been a housewife and had managed to live a fairly normal life in spite of her two specific phobias. However, her children were now grown and she wanted to find a job outside her home. This was proving to be very difficult, however, because she could not take elevators and was not comfortable being on anything other than the first floor of an office building because of her fear of heights. Moreover, her husband had for some years been working for an airline, which entitled him to free airline tickets for himself and his wife. The fact that she could not fly (primarily because of her claustrophobia but to some extent because of her acrophobia as well) had become a sore point in her marriage because they both wanted to be able to take advantage of these free tickets to see faraway parts of the United States and Europe. Thus, although she had had these phobias for many years, they had only become truly disabling in recent years, as her life circumstances had changed and she could no longer easily avoid heights or enclosed spaces.

Although people who suffer from phobias usually know that their fears are somewhat irrational, they say that they cannot help themselves. If they attempt to approach the phobic object or situation, they are overcome with fear or anxiety, which may vary from mild feelings of apprehension and distress (usually while still at some distance) to a full-fledged activation of the fight-or-flight response very similar to a panic attack. Regardless of how it begins, phobic avoidance behavior tends to be reinforced by the reduction in anxiety that occurs each time the feared object or situation is avoided. In addition, phobias may sometimes be maintained (usually without the sufferer's awareness) in part by secondary gains (benefits derived from being disabled), such as increased attention, sympathy, and some control over the behavior of others. For example, a phobia for driving may result in a homemaker being able to escape from responsibilities outside the home, such as grocery shopping or transporting children to and from school.

blood-injection-injury phobia Persistent and disproportionate fear of the sight of blood or injury or the possibility of having an injection, causing a drop in heart rate and blood pressure.

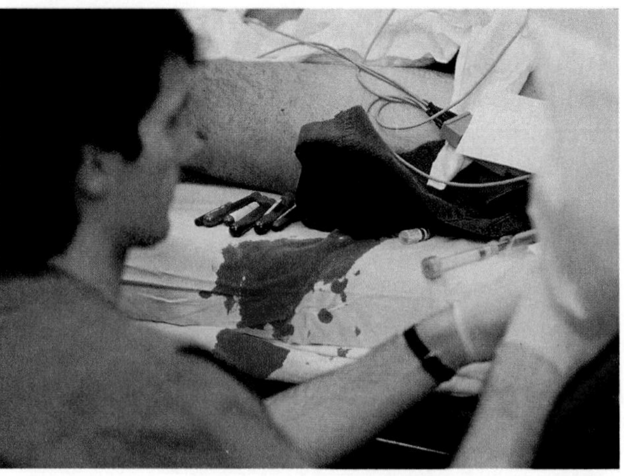

People with blood-injection-injury phobia are terrified of being confronted with scenes involving blood or injury and often faint if they do encounter such a scene. Such people go to great lengths to avoid doctors and hospitals, sometimes to the extent of avoiding necessary medical treatments.

Blood-Injection-Injury Phobia

One category of specific phobias that probably occurs in about 3 to 4 percent of the population has a number of interesting and unique characteristics (Öst & Hellström, 1997; Page, 1994). In **blood-injection-injury phobia**, the afflicted person shows a unique physiological response when confronted with the sight of blood or injury or the possibility of having an injection. Rather than showing the simple increase in heart rate and blood pressure that is seen when most phobics encounter their phobic object or situation, these people show an initial acceleration, followed by a dramatic drop in both heart rate and blood pressure. This is frequently accompanied by nausea, dizziness, and fainting (Öst & Hellström, 1997).

Interestingly, blood-injection-injury phobics show this unique physiological response pattern only in the presence of blood and injury stimuli; in the presence of other feared objects, they show the more typical physiological pattern characteristic of the fight-or-flight response (see Öst & Hugdahl, 1985). This category of phobia also has a strong familial component, with as many as two-thirds of blood-injection-injury phobics having at least one first-degree relative who also has this phobia. Whether this reflects a genetic effect or common environmental experiences shared by members of the same family is still unclear (Neale et al., 1994; Page & Martin, 1998). From an evolutionary and functional standpoint, this unique physiological response pattern may have evolved for a specific purpose: By fainting, a person being attacked might inhibit further attack (Marks & Nesse, 1991).

Age of Onset and Gender Differences

Specific phobias are quite common, especially in women. Results of the National Comorbidity Survey revealed a lifetime prevalence rate of over 16 percent for women and nearly 7 percent for men (Kessler et al., 1994; Magee et al., 1996). The relative sex ratios vary considerably according to the type of specific phobia. For example, about 90 to 95 percent of people with animal phobias are women, but the sex ratio is less than two to one for blood-injection-injury phobia. The average age of onset for different types of specific phobias also varies widely. Animal phobias usually begin in childhood (they are actually equally common in boys and girls, but boys tend to "outgrow" them), as do blood-injection-injury phobias, dental phobias, and natural environment phobias such as those for heights and water. However, other phobias, such as claustrophobia, tend to begin in adolescence and early adulthood (American Psychiatric Association, 1994; Öst, 1987).

Psychosocial Causal Factors

There are a variety of psychosocial causal factors that have been implicated in the origins of specific phobias. For example, according to the *psychodynamic view* of the origins of phobias, phobias represent a defense against anxiety that stems from repressed impulses from the id. Because it is too dangerous to "know" such a repressed impulse, the anxiety is displaced onto some external object or situation that has some symbolic relationship to the real object of the anxiety. There is, however, no good evidence to support this view, and so greater attention has focused on an alternative view from the behavioral perspective that sees phobias as examples of learned behavior.

Phobias as Learned Behavior Specifically, there are many instances in which the principles of classical conditioning appear to account for the acquisition of irrational fears and phobias. As noted earlier, the fear response has been shown in countless experiments to be readily conditioned to previously neutral stimuli when they are paired with traumatic or painful events. Moreover, from the principles of classical conditioning, we would also expect that, once acquired, phobic fears would *generalize* to other similar objects or situations. Recall, for example, that in Mary's case her generalized claustrophobia had probably been caused by multiple incidents as a child when her siblings locked her in closets and confined her under blankets to scare her.

Direct traumatic conditioning may be especially common in the onset of dental phobia (Kent, 1997), claustrophobia (Rachman, 1997), and accident phobia (Kuch, 1997). However, it is not the only way in which people can learn irrational fears. Indeed, much human learning, including the learning of fears, is observational. Simply watching a phobic person behaving fearfully with his or her phobic object can be distressing to the observer and can result in fear being transmitted from one person to another through a process of *vicarious* or *observational classical conditioning*. Thus, merely observing the fear of another in a given situation may cause the observer to acquire a fear of that situation.

Confidence that vicarious conditioning of intense fears can indeed occur has been greatly increased by animal research, using rhesus monkey subjects. In these experiments, Mineka and Cook and their colleagues (e.g., 1984, 1991, 1993) showed that laboratory-reared monkeys who were not initially afraid of snakes rapidly developed a phobic-like fear of snakes simply through observing a wild-reared monkey behaving extremely fearfully with snakes. Moreover, the monkeys could also learn to be afraid simply through watching a videotape of the wild-reared monkey model behaving fearfully with snakes—suggesting that the mass media may play a role in vicariously conditioning fears and phobias in people (Cook & Mineka, 1990).

Conditioning models for the acquisition of phobias have often been criticized because at first glance they do not appear to account for why so many people who undergo traumatic experiences do *not* develop intense or persistent fears or phobias. In other words, given all the traumas people undergo, why don't more people develop phobias (Rachman, 1990)? Much of the answer to this

Monkeys who watch a model monkey (such as the one shown here) behaving fearfully with a live boa constrictor will rapidly acquire an intense fear of snakes themselves. Fears can thus be learned vicariously, without any direct traumatic experience.

A person who has good experiences with a potentially phobic stimulus, such as the young woman romping here with her dog, is likely to be immunized from later acquiring a fear of dogs even if she has a traumatic encounter with one.

question seems to stem from differences in life experiences that affect the outcome of a given instance of vicarious or direct conditioning. The traditional view was that phobias originate from simple instances of traumatic conditioning or avoidance learning that occurred more or less in a vacuum in a person's life. Instead, we now know that many experiences that occur *before, during,* and *after* a given instance of traumatic or observational conditioning affect how much fear is experienced, conditioned, or maintained over time. For example, research suggests that many positive experiences with friendly dogs *before* experiencing a dog bite will probably keep the bite victim from developing a dog phobia (e.g., Mineka & Cook, 1986). Events that occur *during* a conditioning experience, as well as before it, are also important in determining the level of fear that is conditioned. For example, experiencing an inescapable and uncontrollable event, such as being attacked by a dog that one cannot escape being bitten by, is expected to condition fear much more powerfully than experiencing the same intensity of trauma that is escapable or to some extent controllable (Mineka, 1985a; Mineka & Zinbarg, 1996). In addition, the experiences that a person has *after* a conditioning experience may affect whether the conditioned fear is maintained or strengthened. For example, even verbal information that later alters one's interpretation of the dangerousness of a previous trauma (for example, being told "You're lucky to be alive because the man who held you up at the bank last week is a known killer") can be sufficient to cause the level of fear to be increased (Davey, 1997). These examples all show that the factors involved in the origins and maintenance of fears and phobias are more complex than suggested by the traditional conditioning view.

Recently it has been suggested that *cognitive* variables may help maintain phobias once they have been acquired. Not only are people with phobias constantly on the alert for their phobic objects or situations or other stimuli relevant to those, but they also markedly overestimate the probability that feared objects or situations have been or will be followed by aversive events. This cognitive bias may help maintain or strengthen phobic fears with the passage of time (Davey, 1997; Mineka, 1992; Öhman & Mineka, 2001; Tomarken, Sutton, & Mineka, 1995).

Biological Causal Factors

Genetic and Temperamental Causal Factors First, there are several studies suggesting a modest genetic contribution to the development of specific phobias (Fyer et al., 1995; Kendler et al., 1992b). Second, genetic and temperamental or personality variables are known to affect the speed and strength of conditioning of fear (Eysenck, 1965; Gray, 1987; Pavlov, 1927). That is, people are more or less likely to acquire phobias depending on their temperament or personality. Indeed, Kagan and his colleagues have found that children defined as *behaviorally inhibited* (excessively timid, shy, etc.) at 21 months old were at higher risk for the development of multiple specific phobias at 7 to 8 years old than were uninhibited children (32 percent versus 5 percent). The average number of reported fears in the inhibited group was three to four per child (Biederman et al., 1990).

Evolutionary Causal Factors Our evolutionary history has affected which stimuli we are most likely to come to fear. For example, people are much more likely to have phobias of snakes, water, heights, and enclosed spaces than of bicycles, guns, or cars, even though the latter objects may be at least as likely to be associated with trauma. It seems that primates and humans may be prepared evolutionarily to rapidly associate certain kinds of objects—such as snakes, spiders, water, and enclosed spaces—with aversive events (e.g., Öhman, 1996; Öhman & Mineka, 2001; Seligman, 1971). This *preparedness* to acquire certain fears especially readily seems to exist because there may have been a selective advantage in the course of evolution for those primates and humans who rapidly acquired fears of certain objects or situations that posed real threats to them. Thus, "prepared" fears are not inborn or innate but rather are easily acquired or especially resistant to extinction. Öhman and Mineka (2001) have recently summarized numerous lines of evidence supporting this position. Their review also shows that learning to fear such prepared stimuli has several unique characteristics. For example, prepared fear learning, relative to fear learning about more arbitrary stimuli, can occur more automatically without conscious awareness. and it is more resistant to higher cognitive influences (such as trying to talk oneself out of the phobia).

People are more likely to acquire fears of objects or situations that once posed a threat to our evolutionary ancestors than of objects that did not exist in our early evolutionary history (such as cars and knives). Such prepared fears include a fear of heights.

Treating Specific Phobias

The behavior therapy most commonly used in the treatment of specific phobias involves controlled *exposure* to the stimuli or situations that elicit phobic fear. Clients are gradually placed—symbolically or under "real life" conditions—in those situations they find most frightening. Clients are encouraged to expose themselves (either with the aid of a therapist or a friend, or alone) to their feared situations for long enough periods of time that their fear begins to subside. It is often found that a variant on this procedure known as *participant modeling* is even more effective than exposure alone. With participant modeling, developed by Bandura in the 1960s, the therapist models ways of interacting with the phobic object or situation in calm and nonfearful ways (Bandura, 1969, 1977a, 1997b). These techniques enable clients to learn that the feared stimuli are not as frightening as they had thought and that their anxiety, albeit unpleasant, is not harmful and will gradually dissipate (Craske & Rowe, 1997; Foa & Kozak, 1986; Mineka & Thomas, 1999). Exposure-based treatment is widely considered to be the treatment of choice for specific phobias (Craske & Rowe, 1997), and research has shown that for certain phobias, such as small animal phobias, flying phobia, and blood-injection-injury phobia, it can often be highly effective when conducted in a single long session (up to 3 hours) (Öst, 1997).There are no effective pharmacological treatments for specific phobias.

An example of the use of exposure therapy comes from the treatment of Mary, the housewife whose acrophobia and claustrophobia were described earlier.

One variation on exposure therapy is called *participant modeling.* Here the therapist models how to touch and pick up a live tarantula and encourages the spider-phobic client to imitate her behavior. This treatment is graduated, with the client's first task being simply to touch the tarantula from the outside of the cage, then to touch the tarantula with a stick, then with a gloved hand, then with a bare hand, and finally to let the tarantula crawl over his hand. This is a highly effective treatment, with the most spider-phobic clients being able to reach the top of the hierarchy within 60 to 90 minutes.

Case Study **Mary's Treatment** • Treatment consisted of 13 sessions of graduated exposure exercises in which the therapist first accompanied Mary into mildly fear-provoking situations, and then gradually into more and more fear-provoking situations. Mary also engaged in homework doing these exposure exercises by herself. The prolonged in vivo ("real life") exposure sessions lasted as long as necessary for her anxiety to subside. Initial sessions focused on her claustrophobia and getting her to be able to ride for a few floors in an elevator, first with the therapist and then alone. Later she took longer elevator rides in taller buildings. Exposure for the acrophobia consisted of walking around the periphery of the inner atrium on the top floor of a tall hotel, and later spending time at a mountain vista overlook. The top of the claustrophobia hierarchy consisted of taking a tour of an underground cave. After 13 sessions, Mary successfully took a flight with her husband to Europe and climbed to the top of many tall tourist sites there.

IN REVIEW

- What are the five subtypes of specific phobias listed in the DSM?
- How does blood-injection-injury phobia differ from the other specific phobias?
- Describe the original classical conditioning explanation for the origins of specific phobias, and identify the primary criticisms of this hypothesis.
- Explain how behavioral and biological (genetic and evolutionary) explanations have improved and expanded the basic conditioning hypothesis of phobia acquisition.
- Describe the most effective treatment for specific phobias.

SOCIAL PHOBIA

Social phobia was identified as a distinct form of phobia only in the late 1960s (Marks, 1969). Fear of negative evaluation by others may be the hallmark of social phobia (Hope & Heimberg, 1993). As currently conceptualized in DSM-IV-TR, social phobia has two subtypes: specific and generalized. People with *specific social phobias* have disabling fears of one or more discrete social situations (e.g., public speaking, urinating in a public bathroom, or eating or writing in public) in which they fear they may be exposed to the scrutiny of others and may act in an embarrassing or humiliating manner. Because of their fears, they either avoid these situations or endure them with great distress. Intense fear of public speaking is the single most common specific social phobia. Individuals with *generalized social phobia* have significant fears of most social situations (including both public performance situations *and* situations requiring social interactions) and often also receive a diagnosis of avoidant personality disorder (see Chapter 9) (e.g., Skodol et al., 1995; Turner, Beidel, & Townsley, 1992). That these phobias are truly *social* becomes clear when one observes that these people have no difficulty performing the same acts (e.g., speaking, urinating, or eating) when alone.

The diagnosis of social phobia is very common, with estimates from the recent National Comorbidity Survey that about 11 percent of men and 15 percent of women qualify for a diagnosis of social phobia at some point in their lives (Kessler et al., 1994). Unlike specific phobias, which most often originate in childhood, social phobias typically begin during adolescence or early adulthood (Hope & Heimberg, 1993; Wells & Clark, 1997). Over half of individuals with social phobias suffer from one or more additional anxiety disorders at some point in their lives (e.g., panic disorder, generalized anxiety disorder, specific phobia, or PTSD). Approximately 40 percent also suffer from a depressive disorder at some point (Magee et al., 1996). Moreover, approximately one-third also abuse alcohol in order to reduce their anxiety and help them face their feared situations (for example, drinking *before* going to a party) (Magee et al., 1996).

The case of Paul is typical of social phobia (except that not all social phobics have full-blown panic attacks, as Paul did, in their feared situations).

Case Study **A Surgeon's Social Phobia** • Paul was a single white male in his mid-30s when he first presented for treatment at an anxiety clinic. He was a surgeon who reported a 13-year history of social phobia. He had very few social outlets because of his persistent concerns that people would notice how nervous he was in social situations, and he had not dated in many years for the same reasons. He was convinced that people would perceive him as foolish or crazy, and particularly worried that people would notice how his jaw tensed up when around other people. He frequently chewed gum in public situations because he thought that this kept his face from looking distorted. Importantly, he had no particular problems talking with people in professional situations. He was, for example, quite calm talking with patients before and after surgery. During surgery, when his face was covered with a mask, he also had no trouble carrying out surgical tasks and no trouble interacting with the other surgeons and nurses in the room. The trouble began when he left the operating room and had to make small talk with the other doctors and nurses. He frequently had panic attacks in social situations where he had to make eye contact and social chit-chat. During the panic attacks, he experienced heart palpitations, fears of going crazy, and a sense of his mind "shutting down." The most specific trigger for these fears and panic attacks was making eye contact in social situations. Because the panic attacks occurred only in social situations, he was diagnosed as having social phobia rather than panic disorder.

Paul reported that his social phobia and panic had begun about 13 years earlier at a time when he was under a great deal of stress. His family's business had failed, his parents had divorced, and his mother had had a heart attack. It was in this context of multiple stressors that a personally traumatic incident probably triggered the onset of his social phobia. One day, he had come home from medical school to find his best friend in bed with his fiancée. It was about one month later that he had his first panic attack and started avoiding social situations.

Interaction of Psychosocial and Biological Causal Factors

Social phobias involve learned behaviors that have been shaped by evolutionary factors. Such learning is most likely to occur in people who are genetically or temperamentally at risk.

Social Phobias as Learned Behavior Like specific phobias, social phobias often seem to originate out of simple instances of *direct* or *vicarious classical conditioning*, such as experiencing or witnessing a perceived social defeat or humiliation or being or witnessing someone else being the target of anger or criticism (Öst & Hugdahl, 1981; Townsley et al., 1995). Other research suggests that generalized social phobics may be especially likely to have grown up with parents who were socially isolated and who devalued sociability, thus providing ample opportunity for vicarious learning of social fears (Bruch, 1989; Rosenbaum et al., 1994).

Social Fears and Phobias in an Evolutionary Context Social fears and phobias by definition involve fear of members of one's own species; this is in contrast, for example, to animal fears and phobias, which involve fear of potential predators. Öhman and his colleagues have theorized that social fears and phobias evolved as a by-product of dominance hierarchies that are a common social arrangement among primates (Öhman, Dimberg, & Öst, 1985). Dominance hierarchies are established through aggressive encounters between members of a social group, and a defeated individual typically displays fear and submissive behavior but only rarely attempts to escape the situation completely. Thus, these investigators argue, it is not surprising that social phobics are more likely to endure being in their feared situation than to run away and escape it, as animal phobics are likely to do. They further note that it is probably not coincidental that social phobias most often originate in adolescence and early adulthood, which is also when dominance conflicts are most prominent.

Humans may also have an *evolutionarily based predisposition* to acquire fears of social stimuli that signal dominance and aggression from other humans. These social stimuli include facial expressions of anger or contempt (Öhman, 1996; Öhman, Dimberg, & Esteves, 1989). Conditioning of fears to such prepared social stimuli can occur automatically without conscious awareness and is resistant to higher cognitive influences. Such findings may help to account for the seemingly irrational quality of social phobias, in that the emotional reaction can be activated without a person's awareness of any threat.

Infants and young children who are easily distressed are sometimes high on the temperamental variable called *behavioral inhibition*. Such infants show an increased risk of developing social phobia in adolescence.

Genetic and Temperamental Factors As with specific phobias, not all persons who undergo or witness traumatic social humiliation or defeat go on to develop full-blown social phobias. Some research suggests that there is a modest genetic contribution to social phobia (Kendler et al., 1992b), but more research is needed before the contributions of genetic and environmental variables can be disentangled.

The *temperamental variable* that appears to be of greatest importance is behavioral inhibition. Infants who are easily distressed by unfamiliar stimuli are at increased risk for becoming fearful during childhood and show increased risk of developing social phobia by adolescence (Kagan, 1997). Another longitudinal study found that children between ages 8 and 12 who were high on behavioral inhibition, defined as being very shy and fearful and wary of strangers, were much more likely to have a less positive and less active social life in young adulthood, and the men were also more likely to be emotionally distressed (Gest, 1997).

Perceptions of Uncontrollability Exposure to *uncontrollable stressful events* (such as Paul finding his fiancée in bed with his best friend) may play an important role in the development of social phobia. Perceptions of uncontrollability often lead to submissive and unassertive behavior such as that characteristic of socially anxious or phobic persons. This may be especially likely if the perceptions of uncontrollability stem from an actual social defeat, which is known in animals to lead to both increased submissive behavior and increased fear (Mineka & Zinbarg, 1995). Consistent with this finding is the observation that social phobics have a diminished sense of personal control over events in their lives; they are particularly prone to beliefs that control over events is primarily determined by "powerful others" (Cloitre et al., 1992).

Cognitive Variables In recent years, increased attention has also been paid to the role that *cognitive factors* play in the onset and maintenance of social phobia. Beck and colleagues (1985) suggested that social phobics tend to expect that other people will reject or negatively evaluate them, leading to a sense of vulnerability in the presence of others who might potentially pose a threat. These *danger schemas* (see Chapter 2) of social phobics lead them to be hypervigilant for cues that people around them are negative or critical, leading them to spend a great deal of their time paying attention to and evaluating possible negative evaluations by others (Clark, 1997). In addition, the schemas of social phobics may also include expectations that their own inept social behavior will lead to disastrous consequences, which interferes with their ability to interact in as skillful a fashion as they might if they were not so preoccupied. This in turn may lead to a vicious circle in which their somewhat awkward behavior may indeed lead others to react to them in a less friendly fashion, thus confirming their expectations (Clark, 1997; Wells & Clark, 1997).

Treating Social Phobia

In contrast to specific phobias, social phobias can sometimes be treated with medications. There have been some promising results with the use of beta-blockers (drugs often used to treat high blood pressure) such as Inderal on an occasional basis—especially for the performance anxiety shown by actors or musicians (Gitlin, 1996). These medications seem to work because they help control peripheral autonomic arousal symptoms such as trembling hands or voice. However, it appears that other categories of drugs are more effective for full-blown social phobia (Den Boer, Vilet, & Westenberg, 1996). These include several types of antidepressants and some antianxiety, or *anxiolytic,* drugs. One negative factor associated with the use of medication for treating social phobia, which tends to be a chronic condition, is that relapse rates upon discontinuation of the drug tend to be quite high (Hayward & Wardle, 1997; Potts & Davidson, 1995).

But the original and still the most efficacious treatments for social phobia involve behavior therapy and cognitive-behavioral therapy. Behavioral treatments were developed first and generally involve prolonged exposure to social situations that evoke fear, usually in a graduated manner—in a fashion parallel to exposure therapy for specific phobias. More recently, as research has revealed the underlying distorted cognitions that characterize social phobia, cognitive techniques have been added to these behavioral techniques, generating a form of cognitive-behavioral therapy. The therapist attempts to help clients with social phobia identify their underlying negative automatic thoughts ("I've got nothing interesting to say" or "No one is interested in me"), which are often irrational and generally involve discrete predictions about what will happen to them in various social situations. After helping clients understand that these automatic thoughts often involve cognitive distortions, the therapist then helps the clients change these inner thoughts and beliefs through logical reanalysis. A distinct advantage that behavioral and cognitive-behavioral therapy techniques have over medication is that they produce much more long-lasting improvement, with very low relapse rates; indeed, clients often continue to improve after treatment is over.

An example of successful combined treatment can be seen in the case of Paul, the surgeon with social phobia described earlier.

Case Study **Paul's Treatment** • Since the onset of his social phobia 13 years earlier, Paul had taken a tricyclic antidepressant at one point, which had helped stop his panic attacks. However, he continued to fear them intensely and still avoided social situations; thus, the medication had little effect on his social phobia. He had also been in supportive psychotherapy, which helped his depression at the time but not his social phobia or his panic. At the time he came for treatment at an anxiety clinic, he was not on any medication or receiving any other form of treatment. Treatment at the clinic consisted of 14 weeks of cognitive-behavior therapy. By the end of treatment, he was not panicking at all and was quite comfortable in most social situations he had previously avoided. He was seeing old friends that he had avoided for years because of his anxiety, and was beginning to date. Indeed, he even asked his female therapist for a date during the last treatment session!

IN REVIEW

- Distinguish between specific and generalized social phobia.
- Identify the psychosocial and biological causal factors of social phobia, and explain how they interact.
- Describe the major treatment approaches used for social phobias.

PANIC DISORDER WITH AND WITHOUT AGORAPHOBIA

Diagnostically, **panic disorder** is defined and characterized by the occurrence of "unexpected" panic attacks that often seem to come "out of the blue." According to the DSM-IV definition, the person must have experienced recurrent unexpected attacks and must have been persistently concerned about having another attack or worried about the consequences of having another attack (e.g., of "losing control" or "going crazy") for at least a month. To qualify as a full-blown panic attack, an episode must involve abrupt onset of at least 4 of 13 symptoms, such as shortness of breath, heart palpitations, sweating, dizziness, depersonalization (a feeling of being detached from one's body) or derealization (a feeling that the external world is strange or unreal), fear of dying, and fear of "going crazy" or of "losing control." Such attacks are often "unexpected" or "uncued" in the sense that they do not appear to be provoked by identifiable aspects of the immediate situation. Indeed, they sometimes occur at times when they might be least expected, such as during relaxation or during sleep (known as *nocturnal panic*). In other cases, however, the panic attacks are said to be "situationally predisposed" in that they are more likely to occur in particular situations, such as while the person is driving a car or in a crowd. The stark terror of a panic attack typically subsides within a matter of minutes.

Given that 10 out of the 13 possible symptoms of a panic attack are somatic, it is not too surprising that many people experiencing such an attack do not identify it as a panic attack, but instead think they are, for example, having a heart attack. As many as 90 percent of these people may show up repeatedly at emergency rooms or at their physicians' offices for what they are convinced is a medical problem—usually cardiac, respiratory, or neurological (Hirshfeld, 1996). Unfortunately, a correct diagnosis of the problem is often not made for years, in spite of numerous costly medical tests that produce normal results. Such delays in reaching the correct diagnosis, and the waste of time and money on unnecessary medical tests, are avoided if the person sees a physician who is familiar with the condition or who refers the person to a mental health professional (Hirshfeld, 1996; Katon, 1994). This is important because panic disorder causes considerable impairment in social and physical functioning (approximately equal to that caused by major depression; Hirshfeld, 1996) and because panic disorder can contribute to the development of, or exacerbation of, a variety of medical problems (Schmidt & Telch, 1997). Finally, evidence has been accumulating that 30 to 60 percent of persons who experience a chest pain syndrome, but who have normal coronary arteries (no evidence of heart disease), actually have a previously undiagnosed panic disorder. Thus, patients complaining of chest pain but showing no evidence of coronary artery disease should be given a psychiatric interview to determine whether they have panic disorder (Carter, Servan-Schreiber, & Perlstein, 1997).

panic disorder A mental disorder characterized by the occurrence of repeated, unexpected panic attacks, often accompanied by intense anxiety about having another one.

Distinguishing Features Between Panic and Anxiety

The two features of panic attacks that distinguish them from other types of anxiety are their characteristic brevity and their intensity. In a panic attack, the symptoms develop abruptly and usually reach a peak intensity within 10 minutes; the attacks usually subside in 20 to 30 minutes and rarely last more than an hour. Periods of anxiety, by contrast, do not usually have such an abrupt onset, are generally more long-lasting, and have symptoms that are not as intense. In terms of the distinction drawn at the beginning of the chapter between fear and anxiety, it is important to note that a number of influential contemporary researchers of panic believe that a panic attack is simply the activation of the fight-or-flight response of the sympathetic nervous system (Gray, 1987; Gray & McNaughton, 1996), which is identified with the emotion of fear for some theorists (e.g., Barlow, 1988; Barlow et al., 1996). Barlow refers to a panic attack as a "false alarm" for which there is no obvious trigger, as opposed to the "true alarm" that occurs when one confronts a grizzly bear or the "learned alarm" that occurs when one encounters a phobic object. Thus, for Barlow, the primary feature that distinguishes the panic attacks occurring in panic disorder from the phobic responses seen when specific and social phobics encounter their feared object or situation is simply whether there is an identifiable external trigger. As discussed earlier, anxiety, in contrast to phobic fear and panic, is a more complex and diffuse blend of emotions and cognitions, including high levels of negative affect, worry about future threat, and a sense of preparation for dealing with danger should it occur.

The case of Mindy Markowitz is typical of someone who has panic disorder without agoraphobia.

Case Study **An Art Director's Panic Attacks** • Mindy Markowitz is an attractive, stylishly dressed 25-year-old art director for a trade magazine, who comes to an anxiety clinic after reading about the clinic program in the newspaper. She is seeking treatment for "panic attacks" that have occurred with increasing frequency over the past year, often two or three times a day. These attacks begin with a sudden intense wave of "horrible fear" that seems to come out of nowhere, sometimes during the day, sometimes waking her from sleep. She begins to tremble, is nauseated, sweats profusely, feels as though she is choking, and fears that she will lose control and do something crazy, like run screaming into the street.

Mindy remembers first having attacks like this when she was in high school. She was dating a boy her parents disapproved of, and had to do a lot of "sneaking around" to avoid confrontations with them. At the same time, she was under a lot of pressure as the principal designer of her high school yearbook, and was applying to Ivy League colleges. She remembers that her first panic attack occurred just after the yearbook went to press and she was accepted by Harvard, Yale, and Brown. The attacks lasted only a few minutes, and she would just "sit through them." She was worried enough to mention them to her mother; but because she was otherwise perfectly healthy, she did not seek treatment.

Mindy has had panic attacks intermittently over the 8 years since her first attack, sometimes not for many months, but sometimes, as now, several times a day. There have been extreme variations in the intensity of the attacks, some being so severe and debilitating that she has had to take a day off from work.

Mindy has always functioned extremely well in school, at work, and in her social life, apart from her panic attacks and a brief period of depression at age 19 when she broke up with a boyfriend. She is a lively, friendly person who is respected by her friends and colleagues both for her intelligence and creativity and for her ability to mediate disputes.

Mindy has never limited her activities, even during the times that she was having frequent, severe attacks, although she might stay home from work for a day because she was exhausted from multiple attacks. She has never associated the attacks with particular places. She says, for example, that she is as likely to have an attack at home in her own bed as on the subway, so there is no point in avoiding the subway. Whether she has an attack on the subway, in a supermarket, or at home by herself, she says, "I just tough it out." (From Spitzer et al., 1994.)

Severe agoraphobics are often fearful of venturing out of their homes into public places, in part because of fear of having a panic attack in a place from which escape might prove physically difficult or psychologically embarrassing. They may even become housebound unless accompanied by a spouse or trusted companion.

Agoraphobia

Historically, agoraphobia was thought to involve a fear of the *agora,* the Greek word for public places of assembly (Marks, 1987). And, indeed, the most commonly feared and avoided situations for agoraphobics include streets and crowded places such as shopping malls, movie theaters, and sports arenas. Standing in line can be particularly difficult. However, agoraphobics also usually fear one or more forms of travel, and commonly avoid cars, buses, airplanes, and subways. What is the common theme that underlies this seemingly diverse cluster of fears? It is thought that **agoraphobia** usually develops as a complication of having panic attacks (which can be quite terrifying) in one or more of the situations just mentioned. Agoraphobics, concerned they may have a panic attack or get sick, are anxious about being in places or situations from which escape would be physically difficult or psychologically embarrassing, or in which immediate help would be unavailable in the event that something bad happened (American Psychiatric Association, 2000). In cases of moderate severity, these people may even be uncom-

agoraphobia Intense fear of being in places or situations from which escape would be physically difficult or psychologically embarrassing, or in which immediate help would be unavailable in the event that something bad happened.

fortable venturing outside their homes alone, doing so only with significant anxiety. In very severe cases, agoraphobia is a terribly disabling disorder in which a person cannot go beyond the narrow confines of home, or even particular parts of the home.

The case of Anne Watson is in many respects typical of panic disorder with agoraphobia.

Case Study **A Mother with Panic Disorder with Agoraphobia** • Ms. Watson, married mother of two and age 45 at her first clinic contact, experienced her first panic attack some 2 years earlier, several months after the sudden death of an uncle to whom she had been extremely close while growing up. While returning home from work one evening, she had the feeling that she couldn't catch her breath. Immediately thereafter her heart began to pound, she broke out in a cold sweat, and she had a sense of unreality. Feeling immobilized by a leaden quality in her legs, she became certain she would pass out or die before she could reach home. Soliciting help from a passerby, she was able to engage a cab, directing the driver to take her to the nearest hospital emergency room. Her ensuing physical examination revealed no abnormalities apart from a slightly elevated heart rate, which subsided to normal limits before the examination was completed. She regained composure rapidly and was able to return home on her own.

Four weeks later, after the incident had been all but forgotten, Ms. Watson had a second similar attack while at home preparing a meal. Four more occurred in the next several weeks, all of them surprises, and she began to despair about discovering their source. She also noticed that she was becoming anxious about the probability of additional attacks. Consultation with the family physician yielded a diagnosis of "nervous strain" and a prescription for antianxiety medication. The medication made Ms. Watson calmer, but seemed to have no effect on the continuing panics. She discovered alcohol was even more effective than the medication in relieving her tension and began to drink excessively, which only increased the worry and concern of her husband.

As the attacks continued, Ms. Watson began to dread going out of the house alone. She feared that while out she would have an attack and would be stranded and helpless. She stopped riding the subway to work out of fear she might be trapped in a car between stops when an attack struck, preferring instead to walk the 20 blocks between her home and work. She also severely curtailed her social and recreational activities—previously frequent and enjoyed—because an attack might occur, necessitating an abrupt and embarrassing flight from the scene. When household duties and the like required brief driving excursions, she surreptitiously put these off until she could be accompanied by one of the children or a neighbor. Despite these drastic alterations of lifestyle and her growing unhappiness and desperation, however, she remained her normal self when at home or when her husband accompanied her away from home. (Adapted from Spitzer et al., 1983.)

Agoraphobia Without Panic Although agoraphobia is a frequent complication of panic disorder, it can also occur in the absence of prior full-blown panic attacks. In such cases, a common pattern is that of a gradually spreading fearfulness in which more and more aspects of the environment outside the home acquire threatening properties. Cases of agoraphobia without panic are extremely rare in clinical settings. When they are seen, there is often a history of what are called *limited symptom attacks* (with fewer than four symptoms) or of some other unpredictable somatic ailment such as epilepsy or colitis in which the person may fear sudden physical incapacitation (Barlow, 1988; McNally, 1994). However, cases of agoraphobia without panic are not uncommon in epidemiological studies (e.g., Eaton & Keyl, 1990; Kessler et al., 1994). The reasons for this are unclear at the present time, and little research attention has yet been directed toward understanding agoraphobia without panic. Some believe that in many cases this disorder would more appropriately be characterized as a kind of specific phobia if correct diagnostic procedures were used (McNally, 1994).

Prevalence and Age of Onset

Panic disorder with and without agoraphobia affects many people. For example, the National Comorbidity Survey found approximately 3.5 percent of the adult population had panic disorder at some time; 1.5 percent also had agoraphobia. Approximately another 5 percent qualified for a diagnosis of agoraphobia without panic. The same study found that, like the prevalence of social phobia, the prevalence of panic disorder seems to be increasing in younger generations (Magee et al., 1996).

The age of onset for panic disorder with or without agoraphobia is most often between 15 and 24, especially for men, but it can also begin when people, especially women, are in their 30s and 40s (Eaton et al., 1994; Hirshfeld, 1996). Once it begins, it tends to have a chronic course, although the intensity of symptoms often waxes and wanes over time (Ehlers, 1995; Wolfe & Maser, 1994). The prevalence of panic disorder without agoraphobia is about twice as common in women as in men (Eaton et al., 1994). Agoraphobia also occurs more frequently in women than in men; indeed, severe cases are about four times more common in women than in men (e.g., Bekker, 1996;

Reich, Noyes, & Troughton, 1987). The most common explanation of this finding is a sociocultural one. That is, in our culture (and many others as well), it is more acceptable for women experiencing panic to avoid the situations they fear or to depend on having a trusted companion accompany them when they enter their feared situations. Men who experience panic are more likely to "tough it out" because of societal expectations.

Comorbidity with Other Disorders

Persons with panic disorder with or without agoraphobia often have one or more additional diagnoses, including generalized anxiety disorder, social phobia, specific phobia, depression, and alcohol abuse (Brown, 1996; Craske & Barlow, 1993; Magee et al., 1996). Current estimates are that 30 to 50 percent of persons with panic disorder will experience a serious depression at some point in their lives (Gorman & Coplan, 1996). Not uncommonly, they may also meet criteria for dependent or avoidant personality disorder (a personality disorder is diagnosed when a person has personality traits that are inflexible and maladaptive and that cause significant impairment or distress; see Chapter 9) (Craske & Barlow, 1993). There is also considerable controversy over whether clients with panic disorder show an increased risk of suicidal ideation and suicide attempts. Reviews have concluded that there is little evidence that panic disorder, by itself, increases the risk for suicide, although it may do so indirectly by increasing the risk for depression and substance use, both of which are risk factors for suicide (e.g., Hornig & McNally, 1995; Warshaw et al., 1995).

The Timing of a First Panic Attack

Although panic attacks themselves appear to come "out of the blue," their initial appearance frequently follows feelings of distress (Lelliott et al., 1989) or some highly stressful life circumstance, such as the loss of a loved one, loss of an important relationship, loss of a job, or criminal victimization (see Falsetti et al., 1995, for a review; Manfro et al., 1996). Indeed, according to averages across many studies, approximately 80 to 90 percent of clients report their first panic attack as having occurred after one or more negative life events.

Nevertheless, not all individuals who have a panic attack following a stressful event go on to develop full-blown panic disorder. In fact, occasional panic attacks occur in many people who do not have panic disorder or agoraphobia. Indeed, current estimates are that 7 to 30 percent of adults have experienced at least one panic attack in their lifetime, but most have not gone on to develop full-blown panic disorder. Occasional panic attacks also commonly occur in persons who have other anxiety disorders and/or major depression (Barlow, Brown, & Craske, 1994; Brown, 1996). Given that panic attacks occur much more commonly than does panic disorder, we are led to an important question: What causes full-blown panic disorder to develop in only a subset of these people? Several prominent and very different theories about the causes of panic disorder have addressed this question.

Biological Causal Factors

There is good evidence that panic disorder has a heritable component. For example, monozygotic twins are somewhat more likely to be concordant for the diagnosis than are dizygotic twins (Kendler et al., 1992b, 1993a, 1995). However, it should also be emphasized that the heritability that does exist is modest. Moreover, evidence suggests that there is overlap in the genetic vulnerability factors for panic disorder and phobias (Kendler et al., 1995), meaning that people genetically at risk for one are also at risk for the other.

A variety of research findings have also led biological psychiatrists to hypothesize that panic disorder results from one or more biochemical abnormalities in the brains of clients with the disorder. For example, Klein (1981, 1993) and others (e.g., Sheehan, 1982, 1983) have argued that panic attacks are alarm reactions that are caused by biochemical dysfunctions. This biochemical dysfunction hypothesis appears to be supported by numerous studies over the past 35 years that have shown that clients with panic disorder are much more likely to experience panic attacks when they are exposed to a variety of *biological challenge procedures* than are normal controls or controls with other mental disorders. These biological challenge procedures (ranging from taking various drugs to inhaling air with altered amounts of carbon dioxide) put stress on certain neurobiological systems, which in turn produce intense physical symptoms (such as increased heart rate and blood pressure), often culminating in a panic attack for clients with panic disorder (but generally not for people without panic disorder).

Panic and the Brain One biological theory implicates a particular area of the brain—the locus coeruleus in the brain stem (see Figure 5.1)—and a particular neurotransmitter—norepinephrine—which is centrally involved in brain activity in this area. For example, Redmond (1985) showed that electrical stimulation of the locus coeruleus in monkeys leads to a response that strongly resembles a panic attack; moreover, destruction of this area leaves monkeys seemingly unable to experience fear even in the

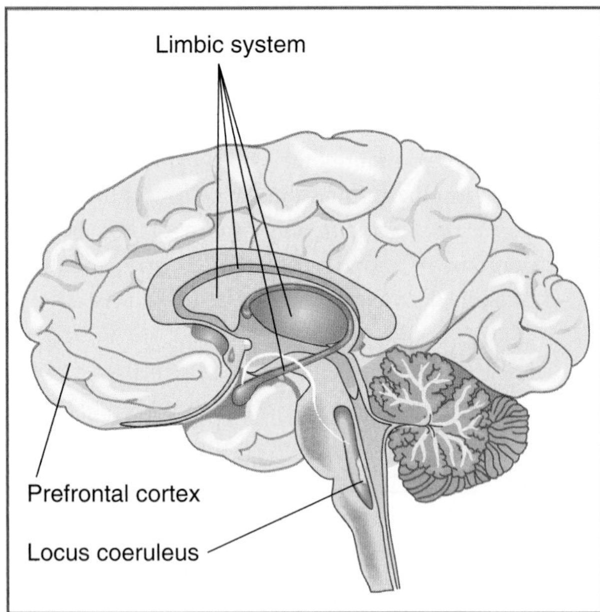

FIGURE 5.1 A BIOLOGICAL THEORY OF PANIC, ANXIETY, AND AGORAPHOBIA
According to one theory (Gorman et al., 1989), panic attacks may arise from abnormal activity in the locus coeruleus, a small area in the brain stem. The anticipatory anxiety that people develop about having another panic attack is thought to arise from activity in the limbic system. Phobic avoidance, a learned response, may involve activity of the prefrontal cortex.

presence of real danger. In addition, some of the drugs once commonly used in the treatment of panic disorder—the tricyclic antidepressants such as imipramine and the monamine oxidase inhibitors—are also known to decrease norepinephrine function (Goddard, Woods, & Charney, 1996; Redmond, 1985). Thus, it is possible that abnormal norepinephrine activity in the locus coeruleus may play a causal role in panic attacks (e.g., Goddard et al., 1996).

More recently, another brain structure in the midbrain—the central periaqueductal gray—has also been implicated as playing a central role in the generation of panic attacks (Gray & McNaughton, 1996). Moreover, because of recent evidence that drugs that selectively affect another neurotransmitter—serotonin—are very useful in the treatment of panic disorder, attention has been drawn to the likelihood of alterations in serotonin transmission in causing panic disorder, along with alterations in norepinephrine transmission.

interoceptive fears Fears focused on various internal bodily sensations.

But panic attacks are only one component of panic disorder. As we have seen, persons with panic disorder also experience anticipatory anxiety about the possible occurrence of another attack, and those with agoraphobia also engage in phobic avoidance behavior. It seems likely that different brain areas are involved in these different aspects of panic disorder. The panic attacks themselves may arise from activity in the locus coeruleus in the brain stem (and/or the central periaqueductal gray in the midbrain) and involve "storms of autonomic nervous system activity" (Gorman et al., 1989, p. 150). In people who have one or more panic attacks and who go on to develop significant anticipatory anxiety about having another, the limbic system (a part of the brain below the cortex that is very involved in emotional behavior) generates this anxiety, which often involves a vague sense that future attacks may occur and be dangerous (see Figure 5.1). Because there are well-defined pathways between the locus coeruleus and the limbic system, Gorman and colleagues (1989) proposed that panic attacks may produce generalized or anticipatory anxiety by lowering the threshold for stimulation of anxiety from the limbic system. Finally, they argue that the phobic avoidance seen with agoraphobia is truly a learned phenomenon that is controlled by the prefrontal cortex, which is the part of the brain involved in learning (see Figure 5.1). Gray and McNaughton (1996) have also summarized evidence for the role of the limbic system in anticipatory anxiety (see also Charney, Grillon, & Bremner, 1998).

Cognitive and Behavioral Causal Factors

Interoceptive Conditioning Model One early hypothesis about the origins of panic disorder with agoraphobia was the "fear of fear" hypothesis in which agoraphobics come to fear the experience of a panic attack because it is so terrifying (Goldstein & Chambless, 1978). More recent elaborations of this model have argued that panic disorder involves **interoceptive fears**—that is, fears focused on various internal bodily sensations. These fears may have come about through a process of interoceptive conditioning in which various internal bodily sensations that have been associated with panic attacks acquire the capacity to provoke panic themselves. For example, heart palpitations may occur at the beginning of a full-blown attack; because they become predictors of the rest of the attack, they may acquire the capacity to provoke panic (Antony & Barlow, 1996; Bouton, Mineka, & Barlow, 2001; van den Hout, 1988). According to the most recent version of this conditioning model, panic attacks also allow the conditioning of *anxiety* to internal or external cues that are associated with panic, thus explaining the origins of anticipatory anxiety and agoraphobic fear. Moreover, people with certain genetic, temperamental, or cognitive-behavioral vulnerabilities will show stronger conditioning of anxiety and panic, explaining why only a subset of those who have panic attacks go on to develop panic disorder (Bouton et al., 2001).

Cognitive Model Beck and Emery (1985) and Clark (1986, 1988, 1997) also proposed a *cognitive* model of panic. According to this model, clients who experience panic attacks are hypersensitive to their bodily sensations and are very prone to giving them the direst possible interpretation. Clark refers to this as a tendency to catastrophize about the meaning of bodily sensations. For example, a client might notice that his heart is racing and conclude that he is having a heart attack. That very frightening thought causes many more physical symptoms of fear or anxiety, which provides further fuel for the catastrophic thoughts, leading to a vicious cycle culminating in a panic attack. Or if someone feels dizzy and interprets this as meaning that she is going to faint or that she may have a brain tumor, this interpretation could culminate in a panic attack through the same kind of vicious cycle (see Figure 5.2). It should be noted that the person is often not aware of making these catastrophic interpretations; rather, the thoughts are often just barely out of the realm of awareness (Rapee, 1996). These "automatic thoughts," as Beck calls them, are in a sense the triggers of panic.

One fascinating study consistent with the cognitive model of panic creates particular difficulties for any purely biological model. In this study, a biological challenge procedure (infusion of sodium lactate) was used, and the idea was to see if a brief explanation of what to expect in a panic provocation study could prevent panic (Clark, 1997). Clients with panic disorder either were given a brief but detailed explanation of what physical symptoms to expect from their infusion of sodium lactate, along with a rationale for why they should not worry about these symptoms, or were given minimal explanation. Clients with the cognitive rationale showed less strong physiological responses to the sodium lactate infusion (for example, their heart rate did not increase as much as did that of control clients). Moreover, the clients with the cognitive rationale about what to expect were significantly less likely to panic in response to the sodium lactate infusion than were the control clients (30 percent versus 90 percent). The cognitive model does not deny a role for biological or genetic factors in producing a vulnerability to panic, but it asserts that cognitive variables play a much more immediate and prominent causal role in initiating panic attacks. Specifically, according to the cognitive model, sodium lactate infusion (like other biological challenge procedures that tend to provoke panic) produces arousal, thereby mimicking the physiological cues that normally precede a panic attack, or serve as a sign of some other impending catastrophe (Margraf, Ehlers, & Roth, 1986a, 1986b). Panic disorder clients, who already start at a higher level of arousal and who are very familiar with these early warning cues, apparently frequently misinterpret these symptoms as the beginning of a panic attack. As proposed by Clark and Beck, such a misinterpretation would be expected to lead to a full-blown attack in many panic disorder clients but not in normal controls, who do not make such misinterpretations.

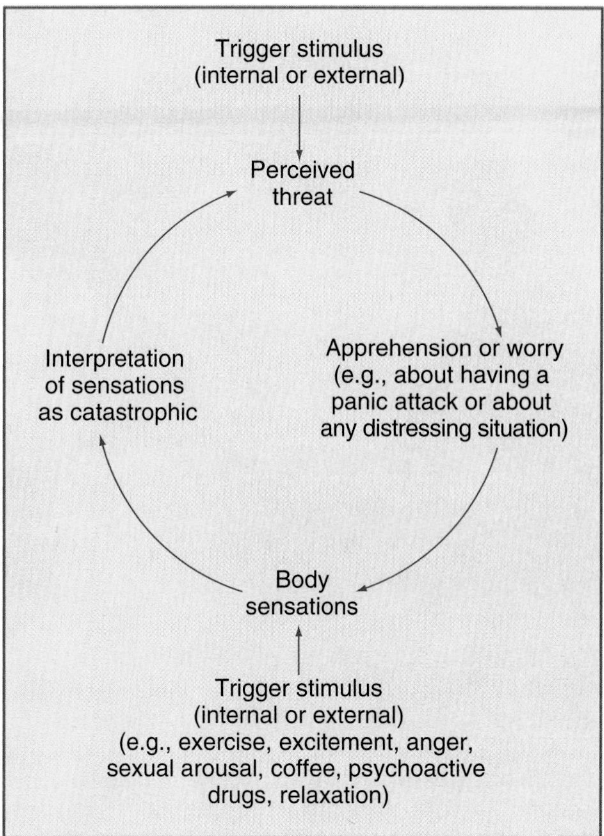

FIGURE 5.2 THE PANIC CIRCLE
Any kind of perceived threat may lead to apprehension or worry, which is accompanied by various bodily sensations. According to the cognitive model of panic, if a person then catastrophizes about the meaning of his or her bodily sensations, this will raise the level of perceived threat, thus creating more apprehension and worry, as well as more physical symptoms, which fuel further catastrophic thoughts. This vicious cycle can culminate in a panic attack. The initial physical sensations need not arise from the perceived threat (as in the top of the circle), but may come from other sources (such as exercise, anger, or psychoactive drugs).
Source: Reprinted from *Behavior Research and Therapy, 24,* D. M. Clark, "A cognitive approach to panic," 461–470, © 1986, with permission from Elsevier Science.

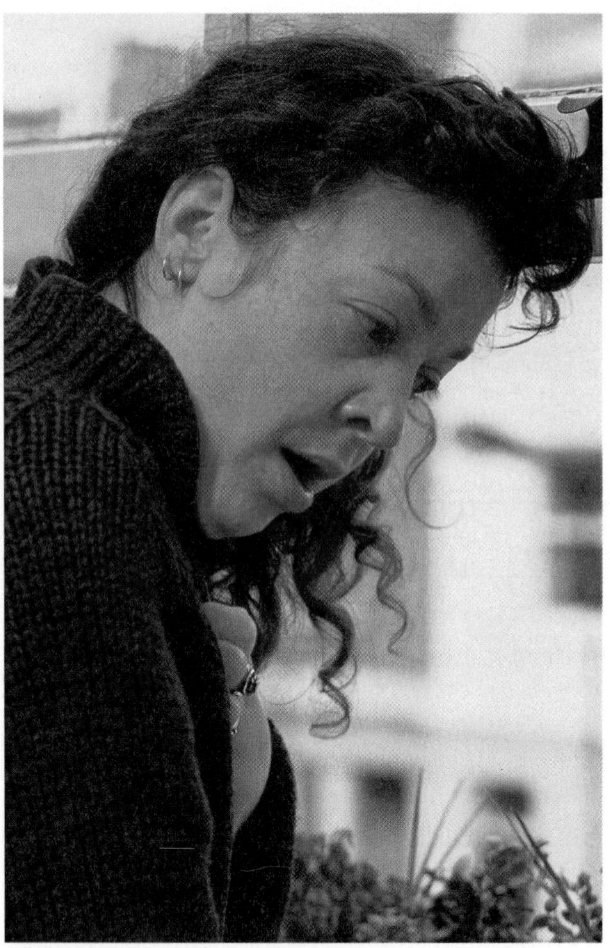

The tendency to catastrophize about bodily sensations, such as having difficulty catching one's breath, may play an important role in the spiraling of anxiety or worry into a panic attack. But how this tendency develops is not yet well understood.

The key difference between the cognitive model and the interoceptive conditioning (or "fear of fear") model is the importance to the cognitive model of the *meaning* the person places on bodily sensations, which causes panic attacks to occur when the person makes catastrophic interpretations about certain bodily sensations. Such catastrophic cognitions are not necessary with the interoceptive conditioning model (Antony & Barlow, 1996; Bouton et al., 2001). Both the interoceptive conditioning and cognitive models cite similar background experiences as creating a vulnerability to developing panic disorder once panic attacks have occurred. One source of vulnerability may come from learning experiences prior to a first attack, such as observing parents model illness-related behavior or having panic attacks (Ehlers, 1993). Another possibility is that the tendency to catastrophize or show conditioned anticipatory anxiety could develop after the first attack because of the way doctors and significant others respond to that attack (Bouton et al., 2001; Clark, 1997).

Finally, there are also many studies that underscore the fact that people with panic disorder have *cognitive biases* that affect the way they process threatening information. Such people are not only more prone to interpreting ambiguous bodily sensations as threatening (Clark, 1997); they also show a bias to remember threatening information (McNally, 1994, 1996; see also Becker, Rinck, & Margraf, 1994). There is also evidence that their attention is particularly drawn to threatening information, especially information about physical threats, and that they are especially good at detecting their own heartbeats (Ehlers & Breuer, 1996). Whether these information-processing biases play a causal role in panic disorder is unclear, but they are certainly likely to help maintain the disorder once it has begun.

Perceived Control and Anxiety Sensitivity Other cognitive and behavioral explanations of panic disorder and agoraphobia have looked at a number of different factors. For example, some research suggests that having a sense of perceived control in a situation where a panic attack might occur may block panic (e.g., Sanderson, Rapee, and Barlow, 1989). Moreover, the fact that clients experience the panic attacks as largely *unpredictable and uncontrollable* may help maintain them (see Antony & Barlow, 1996; Bouton et al., 2001; Mineka & Zinbarg, 1996).

In addition, several researchers propose that people who have high levels of preexisting *anxiety sensitivity* (a high level of belief that certain bodily symptoms may have harmful consequences) are more prone to developing panic attacks and perhaps panic disorder (Cox, 1996; McNally, 1994; Reiss & McNally, 1985). For example, someone high on anxiety sensitivity would endorse statements like this: "When I notice that my heart is beating rapidly, I worry that I might have a heart attack." We know that people with panic disorder score higher on a measure of anxiety sensitivity than do people with other anxiety disorders (e.g., Taylor, 1995). Several good prospective studies have also shown that people high in anxiety sensitivity are indeed more prone to developing panic attacks and perhaps panic disorder.

For example, Schmidt, Lerew, and Jackson (1997) followed over 1400 young adults undergoing basic military training for 5 weeks. The study design was excellent for testing a diathesis-stress model for the onset of panic attacks, because people with varying levels of the diathesis were all followed and studied during a period of high levels of unpredictable and uncontrollable stress, when panic attacks often begin (e.g., Pollard, Pollard, & Corn, 1989).

Schmidt and colleagues found that high levels of anxiety sensitivity predicted the development of spontaneous panic attacks during this highly stressful period. For example, of those scoring in the top 10 percent on the Anxiety Sensitivity Index (Peterson & Reiss, 1987), 20 percent experienced at least one panic attack during the 5 weeks of basic training; only 6 percent of the remaining study participants had a panic attack in the same time period. In addition, it was noteworthy that anxiety sensitivity also served as a risk factor for functional impairment of peer and supervisory relationships, for poor physical health, and for poor overall performance.

In summary, research into both biological and psychological factors involved in panic disorder has provided important insights into this disorder since it was first identified as a distinct disorder. It seems unlikely that research from either perspective alone will ever be able to provide a complete account of this disorder, and attempts at synthesizing and integrating findings from both perspectives are anticipated.

Treating Panic Disorder and Agoraphobia

Medications Many clients with panic disorder (with or without agoraphobia) are prescribed drugs in the benzodiazepine category, such as Xanax. These individuals frequently show some symptom relief (even in the acute situation of having an attack) with these minor tranquilizers (known as anxiolytics, or antianxiety drugs), and some are able to function more effectively. However, the effects are generally much smaller (when compared with the effects of a placebo) than is generally recognized by the public. These drugs also tend to lose their effectiveness after a number of weeks (Barlow, 1988). The anxiolytic drugs can also have quite undesirable side effects, such as drowsiness and sedation, which lead to impaired cognitive and motor performance. Furthermore, it is not uncommon for a patient to develop an increasing tolerance for and persistent dependence on one of these drugs, which have considerable addictive potential. Withdrawal from these drugs can be slow and difficult, and very often precipitates relapse unless it is carried out very gradually (for example, over a period of 2 to 4 months) (e.g., Ballenger, 1996). In addition, many people expect too much of a treatment that merely reduces symptoms without affecting the underlying problem, and the masking of their symptoms may discourage them from seeking needed psychotherapy that may have more long-lasting effects.

The other category of medications that are useful in the treatment of panic disorder and agoraphobia is the antidepressants. These drugs have both advantages and disadvantages when compared with anxiolytics. One major advantage is that they are not addictive. However, one disadvantage is that they take several weeks before they have any beneficial effects and so are not useful for the acute situation in which a person having a panic attack or extreme anxiety comes to a doctor. Troublesome side effects (such as dry mouth and blurred vision or interference with sexual arousal) can also be a serious problem with the antidepressants. Thus, a large number of clients refuse to take these drugs or stop taking them because of the side effects (Wolfe & Maser, 1994), or simply because many have an almost phobic-like response to the idea of taking any medication (Ballenger, 1996). Moreover, relapse rates are quite high once the drugs are discontinued.

Behavioral and Cognitive-Behavioral Treatments
The original behavioral treatment for agoraphobia that was developed in the early 1970s involved prolonged exposure, often with the help of a therapist or family member, to feared situations. Such exposure-based treatments proved quite effective, generally helping about 60 percent of agoraphobic clients show clinically significant improvement. These results, which left approximately 40 percent not improved to a clinically significant degree, led to further research designed to improve success rates (McNally, 1994).

One possible limitation of exposure-based treatments was that they had not targeted panic attacks per se. In the mid-1980s, two new techniques were developed in response to increasing recognition of the centrality of panic attacks to this condition. One of these techniques involves a variant on exposure known as *interoceptive exposure*. Given the prominent fears that people with panic disorder have of their bodily sensations, the idea is that fear of these internal sensations should be treated in the same way as fear of external agoraphobic situations is treated—namely, through prolonged exposure to those internal sensations so that the fear may extinguish. Thus, clients are asked to do a variety of exercises (such as hyperventilating, shaking their head from side to side, running in place, holding their breath, ingesting caffeine, etc.) that bring on physical sensations they may fear. Whichever exercises bring on the sensations that most resemble the symptoms the client experiences during panic attacks are then targeted for practice so that extinction of the anxiety that accompanies these physical sensations may occur.

The second kind of technique developed in the mid-1980s were cognitive techniques, which recognized the significance of catastrophic automatic thoughts to at least the maintenance of panic disorder. These cognitive-behavioral treatments, which target not only agoraphobic

HIGHLIGHT 5.1

Cognitive-Behavioral Therapy for Panic Disorder

The cognitive-behavioral model of panic disorder has been responsible for the formulation of a new treatment that has been shown to be highly effective in over a dozen different studies in at least four countries (Barlow et al., 2000; Wolfe & Maser, 1994). Although the treatments used in the different research studies vary somewhat, there are many common threads that identify each as a form of cognitive-behavior therapy.

In one version, there are three aspects to the treatment (Barlow & Craske, 1994). Clients are first taught about the cognitive model of panic through the use of numerous examples from their own experiences with panic, as well as the experiences of other people with the disorder. Through learning about the panic circle (see Figure 5.2), they come to see how their tendency to catastrophize about the meaning of their bodily sensations is likely to spiral initially low levels of anxiety into full-blown panic. Clients are taught to identify their own automatic thoughts during panic attacks, as well as during anxiety-provoking situations. They are then taught about the logical errors that people who have panic disorder are prone to making and asked to subject their own automatic thoughts to a logical reanalysis. For example, a person who fears having a heart attack is asked at the first sign of heart palpitations to examine the evidence that this might be true (e.g., asking him when the doctor last told him that his heart was perfectly healthy), to assess the likelihood of having a heart attack at age 30, etc. In later sessions, the cognitive part of the treatment is focused on teaching people how to *decatastrophize*—that is, to learn how to decide what the worst possible outcome might be if they did have a panic attack (e.g., if they had a panic attack while driving, they might have to pull their car over to the side of the road until the attack subsided). Once they learn to decatastrophize, the entire experience of panic usually becomes less terrifying, although still quite unpleasant.

The second part of the treatment may involve teaching people with panic disorder several techniques that lower their overall level of physical arousal and tension. These techniques include deep muscle relaxation and breathing from the diaphragm. By learning these techniques, they can reduce the number of physical symptoms of anxiety (from which panic attacks tend to spiral) and also gain a sense of control over their level of arousal and anxiety.

The third part of the treatment involves exposure to feared situations and feared bodily sensations. Because of the importance of interoceptive fears (fears of bodily sensations), clients are asked to do a variety of exercises with the therapist that bring on different bodily sensations. These include hyperventilating, breathing through a straw, shaking one's head from side to side, jogging in place, holding one's breath for a minute, etc. After each exercise, clients describe the sensations produced, how similar these sensations are to those they experience during panic, and how scary those sensations are. Whichever exercises produce symptoms most similar to those they experience during panic attacks are targeted for practice. The idea is that if clients practice these exercises, their anxiety about these sensations will gradually extinguish. Clients who have extensive agoraphobic avoidance also begin to expose themselves to their feared situations for long enough that their anxiety begins to extinguish. ■

avoidance but also panic attacks per se, generally seem to produce better results than were obtained with the original exposure therapy techniques, which focused exclusively on exposure to external (exteroceptive) situations (Clark, 1996, 1997; McNally, 1994). However, at least two studies showed that combining interoceptive and exteroceptive exposure may produce results as good as those of a treatment package that adds cognitive techniques (Margraf & Schneider, 1991; Telch, 1995). Indeed, in most of the studies conducted using one of the variants on these treatments, 75 to 95 percent of people with panic disorder were panic-free at the end of 8 to 14 weeks of treatment, and gains were well maintained at 1-year follow-up (Clark, 1996).

What about the combination of medication and cognitive-behavioral therapy? In the short term, this may produce a superior result to either type of treatment alone (as has been found in some but not all studies). However, in the long term, once medication has been tapered, clients who have been on medication, even when they also received behavioral or cognitive-behavioral treatment, seem to show a greater likelihood of relapse (Barlow et al., 2000; Marks et al., 1993), perhaps because they have attributed their gains to the medication rather than to their personal efforts (Başoğlu et al., 1994).

IN REVIEW

- Describe the major diagnostic features of both panic disorder and agoraphobia, and explain how they are thought to be related.
- What biological causal factors have been implicated in panic disorder?
- Compare and contrast the interoceptive conditioning and cognitive models of panic.
- Explain how anxiety sensitivity may be involved in the development of panic disorder.
- Describe the major treatment approaches for panic disorder and their relative advantages and disadvantages.

GENERALIZED ANXIETY DISORDER

People with generalized anxiety disorder, unlike those with other anxiety disorders, do not have effective anxiety-avoidance mechanisms. Thus, although victims of other anxiety disorders can to some extent allay their anxieties through avoidance behaviors, victims of generalized anxiety disorder experience seemingly unavoidable feelings of threat and anxiety.

Generalized anxiety disorder (GAD) is characterized by chronic excessive worry about a number of events or activities. This state was originally described as *free-floating anxiety* because it was not anchored to a specific object or situation, as the specific and social phobias are. DSM-IV-TR criteria specify that the worry must occur more days than not for at least 6 months and that it must be experienced as difficult to control. Its content cannot be exclusively related to the worry associated with a concurrent Axis I disorder, such as the possibility of having a panic attack. The subjective experience of excessive worry must also be accompanied by at least three of the following six symptoms: (1) restlessness or feelings of being keyed up or on edge, (2) a sense of being easily fatigued, (3) difficulty concentrating or mentally going blank, (4) irritability, (5) muscle tension, and (6) sleep disturbance.

General Characteristics

The general picture of people suffering from generalized anxiety disorder is that they live in a relatively constant state of tension, worry, and diffuse uneasiness. The fundamental process is one of *anxious apprehension,* which is defined as a future-oriented mood state in which a person attempts to be constantly ready to deal with upcoming negative events (Barlow et al., 1996; Brown, O'Leary, & Barlow, 1993). This mood state is characterized by high levels of negative affect, chronic overarousal, and a sense of uncontrollability (Barlow et al., 1996). Although anxious apprehension is also part of other anxiety disorders (e.g., the agoraphobic is anxious about future panic attacks and about dying; the social phobic is anxious about possible negative social evaluation), it is the essence of GAD, leading Barlow and others to refer to this disorder as the "basic" anxiety disorder (Wells & Butler, 1997).

In addition to their excessive levels of worry and anxious apprehension, people with GAD often have difficulty concentrating and making decisions, dreading to make a mistake. They may engage in certain subtle avoidance activities such as procrastination or checking, but these are generally not very effective in reducing anxiety. They also tend to show a marked vigilance for possible signs of threat in their environment. Commonly, they complain of muscle tension, especially in the neck and upper shoulder region, and sleep disturbances, including insomnia and nightmares.

No matter how well things seem to be going, people with GAD are apprehensive and anxious. Their nearly constant worries leave them continually upset, uneasy, and discouraged. In one study, their most common spheres of worry were found to be family, work, finances, and personal illness (Roemer, Molina, & Borkovec, 1997). Not only do these patients have difficulty making decisions, but after they have managed to make a decision, they worry endlessly over possible errors and unforeseen circumstances that may prove the decision to be wrong and lead to disaster. Even after going to bed, people suffering from GAD are not likely to find relief from their worries. Often, they review each mistake, real or imagined, recent or remotely past. When they are not reviewing and regretting the events of the past, they are anticipating all the difficulties that may arise in the future. They have no

generalized anxiety disorder (GAD) A mental disorder characterized by chronic excessive worry about a number of events or activities, with no specific threat present, and accompanied by at least three of the symptoms of restlessness, fatigue, difficulty concentrating, irritability, muscle tension, and sleep disturbance.

TABLE 5.2 GENDER DIFFERENCES IN THE ANXIETY DISORDERS: LIFETIME PREVALENCE ESTIMATES

Disorder	Prevalence in Men (%)	Prevalence in Women (%)	Ratio
Specific phobias	6.7	15.7	2.34
Social phobia	11.1	15.5	1.4
Panic disorder	0.8	2.0	2.5
Generalized anxiety disorder	3.6	6.6	1.8
Obsessive-compulsive disorder	2.0	2.9	1.45
Post-traumatic stress disorder	5	10.4	2.08

Note: Because these figures are from different studies and may not be strictly comparable, they should be taken as approximations of current estimates of gender differences.
Sources: Barlow, 1988; Eaton et al., 1994; Karno et al., 1988; Kessler et al., 1994; Magee et al., 1996.

appreciation of the logic most of us use in concluding that it is pointless to torment ourselves about possible outcomes over which we have no control. Although it may seem at times that people with GAD are actually looking for things to worry about, it is their feeling that they cannot control their tendency to worry.

Prevalence and Age of Onset

Generalized anxiety disorder is a relatively common condition; estimates are that it is experienced by approximately 3 percent of the population in any 1-year period and by 5 percent at some point in life (Kessler et al., 1994). This makes it slightly more common than panic disorder with or without agoraphobia. GAD is approximately twice as common in women as in men (a somewhat less dramatic difference than is seen with many specific phobias or with severe agoraphobia). (See Table 5.2 for summaries of gender differences in the different anxiety disorders.) Age of onset is often difficult to determine: 60 to 80 percent of clients report that they remember having been anxious nearly all their lives; many others report a slow and insidious onset (Rapee & Barlow, 1993; Wells & Butler, 1997).

Although GAD is quite common, most people with this disorder do manage to function in spite of their high levels of worry and anxiety; perhaps because of this, they are less likely to come to clinics for psychological treatment than are people with panic disorder or major depression, which are frequently more debilitating conditions. Although individuals suffering from GAD may not present for psychological treatment as often as do clients with certain other conditions, they do show up in physicians' offices with medical complaints (such as muscle tension or fatigue) at very high rates; indeed, like people with panic disorder, they are generally considered to be overusers of health care resources (Roy-Byrne & Katon, 1997; Schweizer & Rickels, 1997).

Comorbidity with Other Disorders

Generalized anxiety disorder often co-occurs with other Axis I disorders, especially other anxiety and mood disorders. The most common co-occurring anxiety disorders are panic disorder with agoraphobia, social phobia, and specific phobia (Wittchen et al., 1994). In addition, many people with GAD experience occasional panic attacks without qualifying for a full-blown diagnosis of panic disorder (Barlow, 1988). Many of these people show mild to moderate depression as well as chronic anxiety (Brown et al., 1993; Schweizer & Rickels, 1996; Wells & Butler, 1997). This finding is not unexpected in view of their generally gloomy outlook on the world. Nor is it surprising that excessive use of tranquilizing drugs, sleeping pills, and alcohol often complicates the clinical picture in people with GAD.

The following case is fairly typical of generalized anxiety disorder.

Case Study **A Graduate Student with GAD** • John was a 26-year-old single graduate student in the social sciences at a prestigious university. Although he reported that he had had problems with anxiety nearly all his life, even as a child, the past 7 to 8 years since he had left home and gone to college had been worse. During the past year, his anxiety had seriously interfered with his functioning. He reported worries about several different spheres of his life. He was very concerned about his own health and that of his parents. During one incident a few months earlier, he had thought that his heart was beating slower than usual, and he had experienced some tingling sensations; this led him to worry that he might die. In another incident, he had heard his name being paged over a loudspeaker in an airport and worried that someone at home must be dying. He was also very worried about his future because he had had trouble completing his master's thesis on time, given his high level of anxiety. He also worried excessively about getting a bad grade even though he had never had one during four years at a prestigious Ivy League university or at his equally prestigious graduate institution. In classes, he worried excessively about what the professor and other students thought of him and tended not to talk unless the class was small and he was quite confident about the topic. Although he had a number of friends, he had never had a girlfriend because of his shyness about dating. He had no problem talking or socializing with women as long as it was not defined as a dating situation. He worried that he should only date a woman if he was quite sure it could be a serious relationship from the outset. He also worried excessively that if a woman did not want to date him, it meant that he was boring.

In addition to his worries, John reported muscle tension and easy fatiguability. He also reported great difficulty concentrating and a considerable amount of restlessness and pacing. When he couldn't work, he spent a great deal of time daydreaming, which worried him because he didn't seem able to control it. At times he had difficulty falling asleep if he was particularly anxious, but at other times he slept excessively, in part to escape from his worries. He frequently experienced dizziness and palpitations, and in the past had had full-blown panic attacks. Overall, he reported frequently feeling paralyzed and unable to do things.

Both of John's parents were professionals; his mother was also quite anxious and had been treated for panic disorder. He was obviously extremely bright and had managed to do very well in school in spite of his lifelong problems with anxiety. But as the pressures of finishing graduate school and starting his career loomed before him, and as he got older and still had never dated, the anxiety became severe enough that he sought treatment.

Psychosocial Causal Factors

The Psychoanalytic Viewpoint According to the psychoanalytic viewpoint, generalized or free-floating anxiety results from an unconscious conflict between ego and id impulses that is not adequately dealt with because the person's defense mechanisms have broken down. Freud believed that it was primarily sexual and aggressive impulses that had been either blocked from expression or punished upon expression that led to free-floating anxiety. Defense mechanisms may be overwhelmed when a person experiences frequent and extreme levels of anxiety, which might happen if expression of id impulses was frequently blocked (e.g., under periods of prolonged sexual deprivation). In other cases, adequate defense mechanisms may never have developed. According to the psychoanalytic view, the primary difference between specific phobias and free-floating anxiety is that the defense mechanisms of repression and displacement are operative in the phobias, whereas these defense mechanisms are not operative in free-floating anxiety.

Classical Conditioning to Many Stimuli According to early behavioral formulations, generalized anxiety stems from classical conditioning of anxiety to many environmental cues in the same general way that a phobia is conditioned to a specific stimulus. Thus, the primary difference between phobias and generalized anxiety is simply the number of environmental cues that have become sources of anxiety (Wolpe, 1958). This purely behavioral formulation has not fared well as psychologists' understanding of generalized anxiety has evolved. As noted earlier, the essence of GAD is now thought to be anxious apprehension or worry about a variety of negative things that may happen, rather than a fear of many external or internal stimuli, as the purely behavioral view would have us believe (Barlow et al., 1996; Borkovec, 1985, 1994).

The Role of Unpredictable and Uncontrollable Events Uncontrollable and unpredictable aversive events are much more stressful than are controllable and predictable aversive events, and so it is perhaps not surprising that the former also create more fear and anxiety (Barlow, 1988; Barlow et al., 1996; Mineka, 1985a; Mineka & Zinbarg, 1996). This has led researchers to hypothesize that people with GAD may have a history of experiencing many important events in their lives as unpredictable and/or uncontrollable. For example, having a boss or spouse who has unpredictable and uncontrollable bad moods and temper tantrums for seemingly trivial or nonexistent reasons might lead to a person being in a chronic state of anxiety. Perhaps this history of unpredictability and uncontrollability contributes to their seeming inability to control their worries. Conversely, research shows that early experiences with control and mastery can immunize to some extent against the harmful effects of exposure to stressful situations, and, by analogy, perhaps against the development of generalized anxiety (see Chorpita & Barlow, 1998; Mineka, Gunnar, & Champoux, 1985; Mineka & Zinbarg, 1996).

In addition, perhaps some of the tension and hypervigilance (the sense of always looking for signs of threat) that persons with GAD experience may stem from their lacking *safety signals* in their environment. If a person has primarily had experience with predictable stressors (e.g.,

It is possible that some of the chronic tension and hypervigilance that individuals with generalized anxiety disorder experience may stem from their lacking safety signals in their environment. Without such safety signals, such as knowing when their boss or spouse will or will not be angry with them, they may never be able to relax and feel safe.

on Mondays the boss is always in a bad mood and is likely to be highly critical), he or she can predict when something bad is likely to happen through the occurrence of a cue or signal (Monday at work); for such a person, the absence of that signal (Tuesday through Friday at work) implies *safety*. But if another person has experienced many unpredictable or unsignaled stressors (e.g., the boss or a parent is in a bad mood and highly critical on random days of the week), he or she will not have developed safety signals for when it is appropriate to relax and feel safe, leading to a sense of relatively chronic anxiety (Mineka, 1985a; Mineka & Zinbarg, 1996; Seligman & Binik, 1977). Thus, a relative lack of safety signals may help account for why people with GAD feel constantly tense and vigilant for possible threats.

The Content of Anxious Thoughts Another prominent line of research on *cognitive* factors involved in generalized anxiety disorder focuses both on the content of anxious cognitions and on the effects that anxiety has on the processing of threatening information. Beck and Emery (1985) summarized evidence showing that clients with GAD tend to have images and automatic thoughts revolving around physical injury, illness or death, loss of control, failure and inability to cope, rejection, and mental illness. Common automatic thoughts included "I will make a fool of myself," "People will laugh at me," "What if I fail?" "I won't have time to do a good job," and "I'll never be as capable as I should be" (Beck & Emery, 1985, p. 106). It is generally thought that these negative automatic thoughts are fueled by underlying maladaptive assumptions or schemas about the world, which these individuals have developed in the course of growing up. Common maladaptive assumptions that clients with GAD may have include "Any strange situation should be regarded as dangerous," "It is always best to assume the worst," "My survival depends on my always being competent and strong," and "My security and safety depend on anticipating and preparing myself at all times for any possible danger" (Beck & Emery, 1985, p. 63).

The Nature and Function of Worry As research has clarified the central role that worry plays in GAD, some investigators have examined the benefits people with GAD think they derive from worrying, as well as the actual functions the process of worrying seems to serve. The five most common benefits of worrying people with GAD cite are (1) superstitious avoidance of catastrophe ("worrying makes it less likely that the feared event will occur"); (2) actual avoidance of catastrophe ("worrying helps to generate ways of avoiding or preventing catastrophe"); (3) avoidance of deeper emotional topics ("worrying about most of the things I worry about is a way to distract myself from worrying about even more emotional things, things that I don't want to think about"); (4) coping and preparation ("worrying about a predicted negative event helps me to prepare for its occurrence"); (5) motivating device ("worrying helps to motivate me to accomplish the work that needs to be done") (Borkovec, 1994, pp. 16–17).

Exciting developments in the understanding of the functions worrying actually serves for individuals with GAD have given new insights into why the worrying is so self-sustaining and why it is perceived as so uncontrollable. When people with GAD worry, their emotional and physiological response to aversive imagery is actually suppressed. This suppression of emotional and physiological responses serves to reinforce (that is, increase the probability of) the process of worrying. Because worrying suppresses physiological responding, it also serves to keep the person from fully experiencing or processing the topic that is being worried about, and it is known that such full processing is necessary if extinction of the anxiety is to occur (Borkovec, 1994). Thus, the threatening meaning of the topic being worried about is maintained.

Moreover, although worrying serves an immediate dampening function for physiological arousal, it is also associated with a longer-term maintenance of emotional disturbance. There is some evidence that attempts to control thoughts and worry may paradoxically lead to increased experience of intrusive thoughts and enhanced perception of being unable to control them (Wells & Butler, 1997).

Cognitive Biases for Threatening Information In addition to having frequent thoughts with threatening content, people with GAD process threatening information in a biased way. Many studies have shown that generally anxious people tend to have their attention drawn toward threat cues when there is a mixture of threat and nonthreat cues in the environment. Nonanxious people show, if anything, the opposite bias, tending to have their attention drawn away from threat cues (see Mathews & MacLeod, 1994; Mineka & Nugent, 1995; Mineka et al., 1998, for reviews). Moreover, this differing perception of threat cues occurs at a very early stage of information processing, even before the information has entered the person's conscious awareness. This automatic, unconscious attentional bias seems to have the effect of reinforcing or even enhancing the person's current emotional state. That is, if one is already anxious and one's attention is automatically drawn toward threat cues in the environment, this would only seem to make the anxiety worse. Generally anxious people also have a much stronger tendency to interpret ambiguous information in a threatening way than do nonanxious individuals. For example, when clinically anxious subjects read a series of ambiguous sentences (e.g., "The doctor examined little Emma's growth" or "They discussed the priest's convictions"), they are more likely to remember the threatening meaning of the sentences than are nonanxious controls (Eysenck et al., 1991; Williams, Watts, MacLeod, & Mathews, 1997).

In summary, several cognitive variables seem to promote the onset of generalized anxiety disorder as well as its maintenance. Experience with unpredictable and/or uncontrollable life events may promote both current anxiety, as well as a vulnerability to anxiety in the presence of future stressors (Barlow et al., 1996; Mineka, 1985a; Mineka & Zinbarg, 1996). In addition, schemas that one develops early in life about how to cope with strange and dangerous situations and about how to survive may leave one prone to developing automatic thoughts focused on possible threats. The content of such thoughts surely helps to maintain anxiety, as does the process of worrying itself. Finally, for anxiety-prone people, anxiety affects the processing of threatening information in such a way that they automatically pay attention to threatening cues in their environment. Moreover, they are prone to interpret ambiguous information in a threatening manner.

Biological Causal Factors

Genetic Factors Although evidence regarding genetic factors in GAD is mixed, it does seem likely that there is a modest heritability, as for the other anxiety disorders (Kendler et al., 1992a; MacKinnon & Foley, 1996; Plomin et al., 1997). Indeed, scientists have identified a specific gene related to anxiety and neuroticism. This was one of the first identifications of a specific gene that affects an important human personality trait—specifically, who is prone to anxiety and other negative moods and who is prone to a more stable, laid-back attitude (Lesch et al., 1996). But these same scientists have emphasized that the size of the relationship between this gene and neuroticism is quite small, accounting for only about 4 percent of the variance in people's neuroticism levels. Nevertheless, these findings are considered very important because people with high levels of neuroticism are known to be at increased risk for both anxiety and depressive disorders (Clark, Watson, & Mineka, 1994).

A Functional Deficiency of GABA In the 1950s, certain drugs were found to reduce anxiety. This category of drugs, the benzodiazepines, includes some of today's most widely prescribed psychoactive drugs (e.g., Valium, Librium, and most recently Xanax). The discovery of the marked effects that these drugs have on generalized anxiety was followed in the 1970s by the finding that the drugs probably exert their effects through stimulating the action of gamma-aminobutyric acid (GABA), a neurotransmitter later strongly implicated in generalized anxiety (Redmond, 1985). It appears that highly anxious people have a kind of functional deficiency in GABA, which ordinarily plays an important role in the way the brain inhibits anxiety in stressful situations. The benzodiazepines appear to reduce anxiety by increasing GABA activity in certain parts of the brain known to be implicated in anxiety, such as the limbic system. Whether the functional deficiency in GABA seen in anxious people causes their anxiety or occurs as a consequence of it is not yet known, but it does appear that this functional deficiency promotes the maintenance of anxiety.

More recently, researchers have discovered that another neurotransmitter—serotonin—is also involved in modulating anxiety. However, the exact mechanisms remain unknown and are likely to be very complicated (Glitz & Balon, 1996). At present, it seems that GABA, serotonin, and perhaps norepinephrine all play a role in anxiety, but the ways in which they interact remain unknown.

Neurobiological Differences Between Panic and Anxiety It is important to reemphasize here that the neurobiological factors implicated in panic attacks and generalized anxiety are *not* the same (Charney, Grillon, & Bremner, 1998; Gray & McNaughton, 1996). As was noted at the outset of this chapter, contemporary theorists draw a distinction between fear, or panic, and anxiety that is far more fundamental than the old one that anxiety is simply fear without a known source. Fear and panic involve the activation of the fight-or-flight response, and the brain area(s) and neurotransmitter that seem most strongly implicated in the emotional response are the locus coeruleus in the brain stem and/or the central periaqueductal gray in the midbrain and the neurotransmitter norepinephrine. Generalized anxiety, or anxious apprehension, is a more diffuse emotional state involving arousal and a preparation for a possible impending threat, and the brain area and neurotransmitter that seem most strongly implicated are the limbic system and GABA (Gorman et al., 1989; Redmond, 1985). More recently, some involvement of serotonin has been suggested for both emotional states, but this neurotransmitter quite probably acts in somewhat different ways in the two states.

Treating Generalized Anxiety Disorder

As already noted, many clients with generalized anxiety disorder are seen by family physicians rather than by mental health professionals; they are seeking relief from their "nerves" or anxieties and/or their various functional (psychogenic) physical problems. Most often in such cases, drugs from the benzodiazepine (anxiolytic) category such as Valium are used—or misused—for tension relief and for relaxation; they also reduce subjective anxiety and may reduce emotional reactivity to new stressors. As was noted earlier concerning panic disorder, these drugs are generally not as effective as is believed by the general public, and their effectiveness often wears off after a few weeks of continuous medication. Moreover, they are quite habit-forming and difficult to taper. However, there is one new drug—buspirone—that is from a different category but also seems effective. It has an advantage over the benzodiazepines in not being addictive, but it has the disadvantage that a therapeutic response may take several weeks (Glitz & Balon, 1996). Several types of antidepressant medications have also been shown to be useful in the treatment of GAD (Gitlin, 1996).

Cognitive-behavioral therapy for generalized anxiety disorder has also become increasingly effective as refinements in the techniques are made. This therapy usually involves a combination of behavioral techniques such as training in deep muscle relaxation with cognitive restructuring techniques aimed at reducing worry and its negative content. Although GAD initially appeared to be among the most difficult of the anxiety disorders to treat, advances have been made, and a number of studies have shown very effective treatment outcomes for 60 to 70 percent of persons with the condition (Wells & Butler, 1997).

Case Study Cognitive-Behavioral Therapy for John's GAD • The case of John, the graduate student with GAD discussed earlier, serves as an example of the success of cognitive-behavioral therapy with this condition. Before seeking treatment with a cognitive-behavioral therapist, he had seen someone at a student counseling center for several months the previous year but hadn't found the "talk therapy" very useful. He had heard from his mother that cognitive-behavioral therapy might be useful and had sought a referral for such treatment. He was in treatment for about 6 months, during which time he found training in deep muscle relaxation helpful in reducing his overall level of tension. In addition, cognitive restructuring helped reduce his worry levels considerably; indeed, he reported that he was worrying much less about all spheres of his life. He still had problems with procrastinating when he had deadlines, but this too was improving. He also began socializing more frequently and had tentatively begun dating when treatment ended (for financial reasons). He was better able to see that if a woman didn't wish to go out with him again, this did not mean that he was boring but simply that they might not be a good match.

IN REVIEW

- What are the key characteristics of generalized anxiety disorder, and what is its typical age of onset?
- Describe the role of unpredictable and uncontrollable events in the development of GAD, and explain other cognitive factors in GAD.
- Explain the function that worrying may actually serve for people with GAD and how this may help maintain the disorder.
- What are the major biological causal factors of GAD?
- Compare and contrast the biological and cognitive-behavioral treatments for GAD.

obsessive-compulsive disorder (OCD) An anxiety disorder characterized by the persistent occurrence of unwanted and intrusive thoughts or distressing images, usually accompanied by compulsive behaviors designed to neutralize the obsessive thoughts or distressing images or to prevent some dreaded event or situation.

OBSESSIVE-COMPULSIVE DISORDER

Diagnostically, **obsessive-compulsive disorder (OCD)** is defined by the persistent occurrence of unwanted and intrusive obsessive thoughts or distressing images; these are

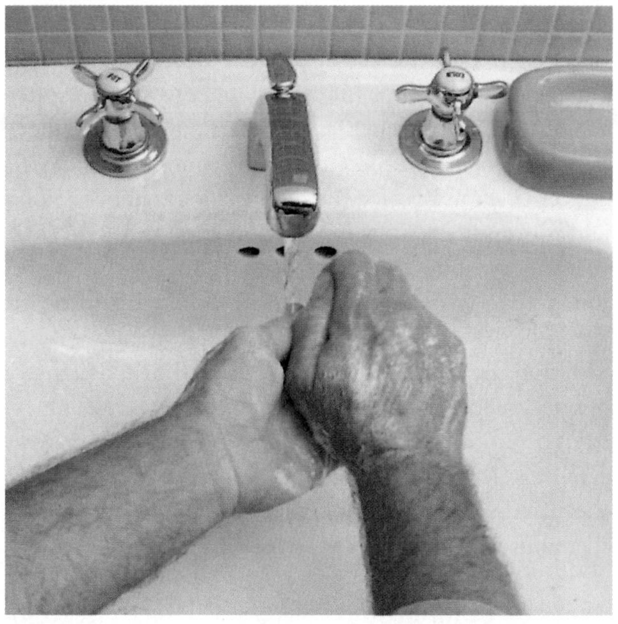

Many of us show some compulsive behavior, but people with obsessive-compulsive disorder feel compelled to repeatedly perform some act in response to an obsession in order to reduce the anxiety or discomfort created by the obsession. Although the person may realize that the behavior is excessive or unreasonable, he or she does not feel able to control the urge. Obsessive-compulsive washers may spend hours a day washing and may even use abrasive cleansers to the point that their hands bleed.

usually accompanied by compulsive behaviors designed to neutralize the obsessive thoughts or distressing images or to prevent some dreaded event or situation. More specifically, according to DSM-IV-TR, **obsessions** are persistent and recurrent intrusive thoughts, images, or impulses that are experienced as disturbing and inappropriate. People who have obsessions try to ignore or suppress them or to neutralize them with some other thought or action. **Compulsions** can be either overt repetitive behaviors (such as hand washing, checking, or ordering) or covert mental acts (such as counting, praying, or saying certain words silently). A person with obsessive-compulsive disorder usually feels driven to perform the compulsive behavior in response to an obsession, and there are often very rigid rules regarding how the compulsive behavior should be performed. In addition, the person must recognize that the obsession is the product of his or her own mind rather than being imposed from without (as might occur in schizophrenia). Finally, the DSM-IV-TR diagnosis requires that the seemingly involuntary behavior must cause the person marked distress, consume excessive time (over an hour a day), or interfere with occupational or social functioning.

The following is a fairly typical case of severe obsessive-compulsive disorder.

Case Study **An Artist's Obsessions with Confessing •** Mark was a 28-year-old single male with severe obsessions about causing harm to others, including committing crimes. The obsessions were accompanied by lengthy and excessive checking rituals. At the time he came to an anxiety disorder clinic, he was no longer able to live by himself, and had been forced to move back home with his parents after having lived for several years on his own since college. His obsessions about harming others or confessing to crimes were so severe that he was virtually confined to his room and could only leave it if he had a tape recorder with him so that he would have a record of any crimes he confessed to. The clinic was several hours' drive from his home; his mother usually had to drive. One day when he drove, he began obsessing that he had caused an accident at an intersection and felt compelled to spend several hours driving and walking around all parts of that intersection to find evidence of the accident. He could not speak on the phone for fear of confessing some crime that he had not committed, and he could not mail a letter for the same reason. He also could not go into a store alone or into public bathrooms, where he feared he might write a confession on the wall.

Mark was a very bright young man with considerable artistic talent. He had finished college at a prestigious school for people interested in the arts and had begun a successful career as an artist when the obsessions began in his early 20s. At first they were focused on the possibility that he would be implicated in some crime that he had not committed; only later did they evolve to the point that he was actually afraid that he might commit a crime and confess to it. The checking rituals and avoidance of all places where such confessions might occur eventually led to his having to give up his career and his own apartment and move back in with his family.

Prevalence and Age of Onset

Although obsessive-compulsive disorder was once thought to be extremely rare (e.g., a 1974 review by Black estimated the prevalence at 0.05 percent), estimates from the Epidemiologic Catchment Area study indicate that it is much

obsessions Persistent and recurrent intrusive thoughts, images, or impulses that a person experiences as disturbing and inappropriate but has difficulty suppressing.

compulsions Overt repetitive behaviors (such as hand washing, checking, or ordering) or more covert mental acts (such as counting, praying, or saying certain words silently) that a person feels driven to perform in response to an obsession.

more prevalent than was once thought (see Antony, Downie, & Swinson, 1998). Specifically, the average 1-year prevalence rate of OCD in this composite sample was 1.6 percent, and the average lifetime prevalence was 2.5 percent (Robins & Regier, 1991); these figures appear to be similar in other cultures studied (Gibbs, 1996). Divorced (or separated) and unemployed people were somewhat overrepresented (Karno et al., 1988), which is not surprising given the difficulties that this disorder creates for interpersonal and occupational functioning. More recent results show there is only a small gender difference, making OCD different from most of the rest of the anxiety disorders in this regard. Although the disorder generally begins in late adolescence or early adulthood, it is not uncommon in children, where its symptoms are strikingly similar to those in adults (March & Leonard, 1998; Valleni-Basile et al., 1994). Childhood onset is often associated with greater severity. In most cases, the disorder has a gradual onset but tends to be chronic once it becomes serious, although the severity of symptoms usually waxes and wanes in intensity over time (e.g., Rasmussen & Eisen, 1991).

Characteristics of Obsessive-Compulsive Disorder

Current estimates are that over 90 percent of those who come for treatment for obsessive-compulsive disorder experience both obsessions and compulsions. When mental rituals or compulsions such as counting or praying are included as compulsive behaviors, this figure jumps to 98 percent. In 90 percent of cases, the compulsions are seen as functionally related to the obsessions (Riggs & Foa, 1993). For example, it can be predicted that someone with an obsession about dirt and contamination will have washing rituals.

Most of us have experienced minor obsessive thoughts, such as whether we remembered to lock the door or turn the stove off. In addition, most of us occasionally engage in repetitive or stereotyped behavior, such as checking the stove or the lock on the door or stepping over cracks on a sidewalk. In OCD, however, the thoughts are much more persistent and distressing and generally appear irrational or excessive to the individual, and, along with the associated compulsive acts, they interfere considerably with everyday behavior. Nevertheless, research indicates that normal and abnormal obsessions and compulsive behaviors exist on a continuum, with the primary differences being the frequency and intensity of the obsessions and the degree to which the obsessions and compulsions are troubling and to which they are resisted (Gibbs, 1996; Salkovskis & Kirk, 1997).

Types of Obsessive Thoughts Obsessive thoughts may center on a variety of topics. A recent review concluded that the content of obsessions consists most often of contamination fears, fears of harming self or others, and pathological doubt. Other fairly common themes are concerns about or need for symmetry, sexual obsessions, and obsessions concerning religion or aggression. These themes are quite consistent cross-culturally and across the lifespan (Gibbs, 1996). Obsessive thoughts involving themes of violence or aggression might include a wife's idea that she might poison her husband or a daughter's mental image of pushing her mother down a flight of stairs. Even though such obsessive thoughts are only very rarely carried out in action, they remain a source of often excruciating torment to someone who is plagued with them but in no way wants to cause such harm.

Types of Compulsions People with OCD feel compelled to perform repeatedly acts that often seem pointless and absurd even to them and that they in some sense do not want to perform. These compulsive acts are of five primary types: cleaning, checking, repeating, ordering/arranging, and counting (Antony, Downie, & Swinson, 1998), with many patients showing multiple kinds of rituals. For a smaller number of patients, the compulsion is to perform various everyday acts such as eating or dressing extremely slowly (primary obsessional slowness); for others, the compulsion is to have things exactly symmetrical or "evened up" (Rasmussen & Eisen, 1991). Washing rituals vary from relatively mild ritual-like behavior, such as spending 15 to 20 minutes washing one's hands after going to the bathroom, to more extreme behavior, such as washing one's hands with disinfectants for hours every day to the point that the hands bleed. Checking rituals also vary from relatively mild, such as checking all the lights, appliances, and locks two or three times before leaving the house, to very extreme, such as going back to an intersection where one thinks one may have run over a pedestrian and spending hours checking for any sign of the imagined accident, as Mark did. Both cleaning and checking rituals are often performed a specific number of times and thus also involve counting. Compulsive rituals are sometimes covert or cognitive in nature, involving feelings and thoughts. The performance of the compulsive act or the ritualized series of acts usually brings a feeling of reduced tension and satisfaction (Rachman & Hodgson, 1980; Salkovskis & Kirk, 1997).

Consistent Themes Given the many different ways in which it presents itself, OCD seems more homogenous than one might expect (Rasmussen & Eisen, 1991). Certain factors seem consistent across nearly all the different clinical presentations: (1) anxiety is the affective symptom (except with primary obsessional slowness); (2) nearly all people afflicted with OCD fear that something terrible will happen to themselves or others for which they will be responsible; and (3) compulsions usually reduce the anxiety, at least in the short term.

Another consistent theme across different cases of OCD is its characterization as a "what if" illness (Rasmussen & Eisen, 1991). Most clients with this disorder are continually worried about the possibility that something terrible will happen. "If there is a one in a million chance that something terrible will happen, they somehow convince themselves that it will happen to them ... [e.g.] 'The very fact that it is within the realm of possibility, however unlikely, that I will stab my baby, or poison my child, is enough to terrify me so that I can think of nothing else no matter how hard I try.'" (Rasmussen & Eisen, 1991, p. 37). This tendency to judge risks unrealistically seems to be a very important feature of OCD.

Comorbidity with Other Disorders Like the rest of the anxiety disorders, obsessive-compulsive disorder frequently co-occurs with mood and other anxiety disorders. Depression is especially common, with estimates suggesting that as many as 67 percent of those with OCD may experience major depression at some time in their life (Gibbs, 1996). Given the chronic and debilitating nature of OCD, it is not too surprising that many develop depression at least partly in response to having OCD. The anxiety disorders with which OCD most often co-occurs are social phobia, panic disorder, and specific phobia (e.g., Antony et al., 1998). The most common personality disorders (see Chapter 9) in people with OCD are dependent and avoidant. Indeed, Baer and colleagues (1992) found that about 25 percent of 55 OCD clients met criteria for either avoidant or dependent personality disorder, with a subset having both (Summerfeldt, Huta, & Swinson, 1998).

Another disorder that has been studied extensively only in the past decade—**body dysmorphic disorder (BDD)**—also co-occurs rather commonly with OCD (12 percent of patients with OCD also had body dysmorphic disorder in one large study) and is thought by most researchers in this area to be a closely related disorder (e.g., Phillips, 1996; Simeon et al., 1995).

Psychosocial Causal Factors

Until recently, the dominant theories of the origins of obsessive-compulsive disorder were the psychoanalytic and behavioral views.

Psychoanalytic Viewpoint According to Freud's psychoanalytic view, a person with OCD has been unable to cope with the instinctual conflicts of the Oedipal stage and either has never advanced beyond this stage or has regressed back to an earlier stage of psychosexual development. Specifically, such a person is thought to be fixated in the anal stage of development (about 2 years of age), when children are thought to derive sensual pleasure from defecating, both as physical release and as a creative act ("Mommy, see what I made!"). This is also the time at which parents are attempting to toilet train their children, which involves learning to control and delay these urges. If parents are too harsh and make the child feel bad and dirty about soiling himself or herself, they may instill rage in the child, as well as guilt and shame about these drives. According to this theory, the intense conflict that may develop between impulses from the id to let go and those from the ego to control and withhold leads to the development of certain defense mechanisms that may ultimately produce obsessive-compulsive symptoms. Unfortunately, there has been virtually no empirical research documenting any of the major tenets of this theory, and the treatment that stems from it has not proved to be useful in treating OCD.

The Behavioral Viewpoint The behavioral view of obsessive-compulsive disorder derives from O. H. Mowrer's two-process theory of avoidance learning (1947). According to this theory, neutral stimuli become associated with aversive stimuli through a process of classical conditioning and come to elicit anxiety. For example, touching a doorknob or shaking hands might become associated with the "scary" idea of contamination. Once having made this association, the person may discover that the anxiety produced by shaking hands or touching a doorknob may be reduced by an activity such as hand washing. Washing his or her hands extensively then reduces the person's anxiety, and the washing response is reinforced, making it more likely to occur again in the future when anxiety about contamination is evoked in other situations (Rachman & Shafran, 1998). Once learned, such avoidance responses are extremely resistant to extinction (Mineka & Zinbarg, 1996; Salkovskis & Kirk, 1997). This model has been very useful in helping us understand what factors may help to maintain obsessive-compulsive behavior, and it has also been useful in generating an effective form of treatment. However, it has not been as helpful in explaining why peo-

body dysmorphic disorder (BDD) A mental disorder characterized by obsession with some perceived flaw or defect in a person's appearance

HIGHLIGHT 5.2

Mirror, Mirror on the Wall . . .

Body dysmorphic disorder (BDD) is officially classified in DSM-IV-TR as a somatoform disorder (see Chapter 7), but most researchers and clinicians consider it to be more closely related to OCD. Katharine Phillips (1996) has carefully described the condition in *The Broken Mirror: Understanding and Treating Body Dysmorphic Disorder,* a book written for people who suffer from this disorder as well as for their families and clinicians. People with BDD are obsessed with some perceived flaw or flaws in their appearance. They may focus on almost any body part: Their skin has blemishes, their breasts are too small, their face is too thin (or too fat) or disfigured by blood vessels that others find repulsive, etc. Some of the more common locations for perceived defects are skin (65%), hair (50%), nose (38%), eyes (20%), legs/knees (18%), chin/jaw (13%), breasts/chest/nipples (12%), stomach/waist (11%), and lips (11%) (Phillips, 1996). These are not the ordinary concerns that most of us have about our appearance; they are far more extreme, leading in many cases to complete preoccupation and significant emotional pain. For example, many BDD sufferers are afraid to date or go to parties because they do not want people to see them with their perceived defect. In severe cases, they may become so isolated that they never leave the house. In most cases, others do not see the defect that the person with BDD focuses on, or if they do, they see only a very minor defect within the normal range.

Another common feature of people with BDD is that they frequently seek reassurance from friends and family about their defects but the reassurances almost never provide more than very temporary relief. They also frequently seek reassurance for themselves by checking their appearance in the mirror countless times a day. They also commonly compare their body parts with those of others and scrutinize others very carefully. They frequently try to camouflage their perceived defect through clothing or makeup or by maintaining unusual postures. It is also quite common that they engage in excessive grooming behavior (for example, spending hours fixing their hair or applying makeup). People with BDD commonly make their way into the office of a dermatologist or plastic surgeon. An astute doctor will not do the requested procedure and may instead make a referral to a psychologist or psychiatrist. All too often, though, the patient does get what he or she requests—and unfortunately is almost never satisfied with the outcome, often having repeated surgeries.

People with body dysmorphic disorder often seek plastic surgery for what they perceive to be serious flaws in their appearance. In *First Wives Club,* the actress Goldie Hawn played a woman who is unhappy with her lips, wishing them to be fuller in shape. She has plastic surgery to make them fuller, and yet is still quite unhappy with the outcome, as is typical of individuals with body dysmorphic disorder who undergo such surgery.

At this point, the similarities to OCD should be fairly obvious. People with BDD, like those with OCD, have prominent obsessions and engage in a variety of ritualistic-like behaviors such as reassurance seeking, mirror checking, camouflaging, etc. As was true with OCD in the past, most people suffering from BDD never seek psychological or psychiatric treatment. Rather, they suffer silently, or they go to dermatologists or plastic surgeons (Phillips, 1996). Reasons for this secrecy and shame include worries that others will think they are superficial, silly, or vain, and that if they mention their perceived defect, others will notice it and focus more on it.

Part of the reason more people with BDD are now seeking treatment is because the disorder has received a good deal of media attention in the past decade, including being discussed on some daily talk shows, where it is sometimes called "imaginary defect disorder." Phillips and others (1996) estimate that it is not a rare disorder, perhaps affecting 1 to 2 percent of the general population and up to 8 percent of people with depression. Like OCD, it occurs only slightly more often in women than men. It commonly co-occurs with a mood disorder, social phobia, or obsessive-compulsive disorder (Veale et al., 1996). As increasing attention is focused on this disorder, hopefully the secrecy and shame often surrounding it will decrease and more people will seek treatment.

The same kinds of treatment that work for OCD are also the treatments of choice for BDD. In the case of medications, it is clearly the drugs that work on serotonin (clomipramine and the selective serotonin-reuptake inhibitors) that are most effective. In the case of behavior therapy, a variant of the exposure and response prevention treatment used for OCD is most effective for BDD (Phillips, 1996). ■

ple with OCD develop obsessions in the first place or why they have such abnormal assessments of risk.

OCD and Preparedness Just as the conditioning view of phobias has been revitalized through the addition of the preparedness concept, which puts phobias in the evolutionary context of fears that may have been adaptive for our early ancestors, so too has our understanding of obsessive-compulsive disorder increased through looking at it in an evolutionary context. For example, the preparedness concept is also relevant to understanding the nonrandom distribution of obsessive thoughts and compulsive rituals (De Silva, Rachman, & Seligman, 1977). For example, thoughts about dirt and contamination associated with compulsive washing are so common as to make their occurrence seem nonrandom. The overall consensus seems to be that humans' obsessions with dirt and contamination and certain other potentially dangerous situations did not arise out of a vacuum but rather have deep evolutionary roots (Mineka & Zinbarg, 1996).

In addition, some theorists have argued that the displacement activities that many species of animals engage in under situations of conflict or high arousal bear a significant resemblance to the compulsive rituals seen in obsessive-compulsive disorder (Holland, 1974; Mineka, 1985a; Mineka & Zinbarg, 1996; Winslow & Insel, 1991). Displacement activities often involve grooming (for example, a bird preening his feathers) or nesting under conditions of high conflict or frustration, and may therefore be related to the grooming (e.g., washing) or tidying rituals seen in people with OCD, which are often provoked by anxiety, discomfort, or distress brought about by obsessive thoughts or images.

The Role of Memory Cognitive factors have also been implicated in obsessive-compulsive disorder. Sher, Frost, and Otis (1983; see also Sher et al., 1989), for example, have shown that people with checking compulsions show poor memory for their behavioral acts, such as "Did I check to see if the stove was off?" Having a poor memory for one's actions could easily be seen as contributing to the repetitive nature of checking rituals. More recently, there is increasing evidence that people with OCD do indeed have impairments in their nonverbal memory but not their verbal memory (Trivedi, 1996). They also have low confidence in their memory ability (Gibbs, 1996; Trivedi, 1996).

The Effects of Attempting to Suppress Obsessive Thoughts It has been shown that when normal people attempt to suppress unwanted thoughts (for example, "Don't think about white bears"), they may find a paradoxical increase in those thoughts later (Wegner, 1994). Moreover, two other studies with normal subjects showed that thought suppression during a negative mood produced a connection between the thought and the negative mood. When the negative mood occurred again later, the thought was more easily experienced, or when the thought was later experienced, the mood returned (Wenzlaff, Wegner, & Klein, 1991). These researchers concluded that if people try not to think of something, "unintentionally they bond that thought to their mood such that each will later make the other return" (p. 507).

Given that people with normal and abnormal obsessions differ primarily in the degree to which their thoughts are resisted and found unacceptable, a major factor contributing to the frequency of obsessive thoughts and negative moods may be these attempts to suppress them, leading to paradoxical increases. For example, when OCD clients were asked to record intrusive thoughts in a diary, both on days when they were told to try to suppress those thoughts and on days without instructions to suppress, the OCD clients reported approximately twice as many intrusive thoughts on the days they were attempting to suppress them (Salkovskis & Kirk, 1997; Trinder & Salkovskis, 1994). This is similar to the paradoxical effect that attempts of people with generalized anxiety disorder to control worry may lead to an increase in intrusive thoughts.

Biological Causal Factors

In the past 20 years, there has been an explosion of research investigating the possible biological basis for obsessive-compulsive disorder. Some studies have sought to discover whether there is a genetic contribution to this disorder. Others have explored whether there are structural brain abnormalities or abnormalities in specific neurotransmitter systems associated with it. The accumulating evidence from all three kinds of studies is that biological causal factors are probably more clearly implicated in the causes of OCD than in any of the other anxiety disorders.

Genetic Influences Genetic studies have included both twin studies and family studies. Evidence from twin studies reveals a moderately high concordance rate for OCD in monozygotic twins and a lower rate in dizygotic twins. A recent review of 14 published studies included 80 pairs of monozygotic twins, of whom 54 were concordant for the diagnosis of OCD, and 29 pairs of dizygotic twins, of whom 9 were concordant. This is consistent with a moderate genetic heritability (Billett, Richter, & Kennedy, 1998). Most family studies have also found substantially higher rates of OCD in first-degree relatives of OCD clients than would be expected based on current estimates of the population prevalence of OCD; about 10 percent of first-degree relatives have diagnosable OCD (Pauls et al., 1995).

Abnormalities in Brain Function The search for structural abnormalities in the brains of OCD clients has also been intense in the past 15 years, but the results of seven major studies have not revealed a consistent pattern of such abnormalities (Brody & Baxter, 1996; Cottraux & Gérard, 1998; Trivedi, 1996). In addition, as major advances have been made in techniques used to study the *functioning* of brain structures, attempts have been made to determine whether some brain structures may show functional abnormalities, even if they do not show structural abnormalities per se. Findings from at least a half-dozen studies using positron emission tomography (PET) scans have shown that clients with OCD have abnormally active metabolic levels in the orbital prefrontal cortex, the caudate nucleus, and the cingulate cortex. Some of these studies have also shown some normalization of at least some of these abnormalities with successful treatment, with either medication or behavior therapy (see Brody & Baxter, 1996; Cottraux & Gérard, 1998; Trivedi, 1996). There are also findings that implicate abnormalities in the functioning of the basal ganglia (Cottraux & Gérard, 1998), although it is possible that this may be true for only a subset of clients with OCD (Piggot, Myers, & Williams, 1996).

The Role of Serotonin Pharmacological studies of obsessive-compulsive disorder intensified with the discovery that a drug called Anafranil (clomipramine) is often effective in the treatment of this disorder. Clomipramine is closely related to other tricyclic antidepressants (see Chapter 6) but is more effective than they are in the treatment of OCD (Murphy et al., 1996). It seems very likely that clomipramine is more effective than the other tricyclics with OCD because it has greater effects on the neurotransmitter serotonin, which is now strongly implicated in OCD. This is also in keeping with the fact that several other antidepressant drugs such as fluoxetine (Prozac), which also have relatively selective effects on serotonin, have also been shown to be about equally useful in the treatment of OCD (Dolberg et al., 1996a, 1996b; Murphy et al., 1996). Indeed, OCD is quite different from the other anxiety and mood disorders in that it most clearly shows a preferential response to drugs that affect serotonin. The other anxiety and mood disorders respond to a wider range of drugs (Dolberg et al., 1996a, 1996b; Murphy et al., 1996).

The exact nature of the dysfunction in serotonergic systems in OCD is as yet unclear (see Gross, Sasson,

Chopra, & Zohar, 1998; Murphy et al., 1996). In general, the complex picture that seems to be emerging is that increased serotonin activity and increased sensitivity of some brain structures to serotonin may be involved in OCD symptoms. However, it is also becoming clear that dysfunction in serotonergic systems cannot by itself fully explain this complex disorder. Other neurotransmitter systems and functional abnormalities in certain brain structures also seem to be involved (e.g., Hollander et al., 1992).

In summary, there is a substantial body of evidence implicating biological causal factors in OCD. This evidence comes from genetic studies, from studies of structural brain functioning, and from psychopharmacological studies. Although the exact nature of these factors and how they are interrelated are not yet understood, major research efforts are currently underway and are sure to enhance our understanding of this very serious and disabling disorder in the next decade.

Treating Obsessive-Compulsive Disorder

As mentioned in the preceding section, research shows that medications that affect the neurotransmitter serotonin seem to be the only class of medications studied to date that have reasonably good effects in treating persons with OCD. These selective serotonin-reuptake inhibitors (such as clomipramine, or Anafranil, and fluoxetine, or Prozac) appear to reduce the intensity of the symptoms of this disorder, with approximately 50 to 70 percent of OCD clients showing at least a 25 percent reduction in symptoms (relative to 4 to 5 percent with a placebo) (Dolberg et al., 1996a, 1996b; Koran et al., 1996). Some clients may show greater improvement than this, but approximately 30 to 50 percent do not show what is considered to be clinically significant improvement.

A major disadvantage of drug treatment for OCD, as for other anxiety disorders, is that relapse rates are very high (approximately 90 percent) following discontinuation of the drug (Dolberg et al., 1996a, 1996b). Thus, many clients who do not seek alternative forms of behavior therapy that have more long-lasting benefits may have to stay on these drugs indefinitely, given that OCD, like other anxiety disorders, tends to be a chronic condition if left untreated.

A behavioral treatment involving a combination of exposure and (compulsive) response prevention may be in the long run the most effective approach to the difficult problem of treating OCD (e.g., Foa, Franklin, & Kozak, 1998; Steketee, 1993). This treatment involves having the client with OCD repeatedly expose himself or herself to stimuli that will provoke the obsession (such as touching the bottom of a shoe or a toilet seat in a public bathroom for someone with compulsive washing), and then preventing the client from engaging in his or her compulsive rituals, which ordinarily would be engaged in to reduce the anxiety/distress provoked by the obsession. Preventing the rituals is essential so that the client can see that the anxiety created by the obsession will dissipate naturally if enough time is allowed to pass. This treatment tends to help clients who stick with it, with most showing a 50 to 70 percent reduction in symptoms (Steketee, 1993). On average, about 50 percent are much improved or very much improved, and another 25 percent are moderately improved. These results are generally considered superior to those obtained with medication (Foa et al., 1998).

The successful use of this treatment in the case of Mark, the young artist with severe OCD, is described here briefly.

Case Study **Mark's Treatment** • Mark was initially treated with medication and with exposure and response prevention. He found the side effects of the medication (clomipramine) intolerable and gave it up within a few weeks. For the behavioral treatment, he was directed to get rid of the tape recorder and was given a series of exercises in which he exposed himself to feared situations where he might confess to a crime or cause harm to others, including making phone calls, mailing letters, and entering stores and public bathrooms (all things he had been unable to do). Checking rituals (including the tape recorder) were prevented. Although the initial round of treatment was not especially helpful, in part because of the distance and difficulty of getting to treatment, he did eventually commit to more intensive treatment by moving to a small apartment closer to the clinic and did quite well.

Finally, because OCD in its most severe form is such a crippling and disabling disorder, psychiatrists have begun in recent years to reexamine the usefulness of certain neurosurgical techniques for the treatment of severe intractable OCD (which may be found in as many as 10 percent of people diagnosed with OCD) (Mindus, Rasmussen, & Lindquist, 1994). Before such surgery is even contemplated, the person must have had severe OCD for at least 5 years and not responded to any of the known treatments discussed so far (both behavior therapy and several medications). Several studies have shown that a significant number of cases that were intractable with all other known treatments do respond quite well to neurosurgery designed to destroy brain tissue in one of the areas implicated in this condition (Pigott & Seay, 1998).

IN REVIEW

- Summarize the major symptoms of obsessive-compulsive disorder.
- Explain how the behavioral view of OCD has been revitalized by the addition of the concept of preparedness.
- How have cognitive factors been implicated in OCD?
- What are the major biological causal factors of OCD?
- Evaluate the biological and behavioral treatment approaches for OCD.

GENERAL SOCIOCULTURAL CAUSAL FACTORS FOR ANXIETY DISORDERS

Cross-cultural research suggests that although anxiety is a universal emotion and anxiety disorders probably exist in all human societies, there are many differences in the prevalence and in the form of expression of these disorders in different cultures (Good & Kleinman, 1985; Kirmayer, Young, & Hayton, 1995).

Cultural Differences in Sources of Worry

In the Yoruba culture of Nigeria, there are three primary clusters of symptoms associated with generalized anxiety: (1) worry, (2) dreams, and (3) bodily complaints. The sources of worry are very different than those in Western society, however, and they focus on creating and maintaining a large family and on fertility. Dreams are a major source of anxiety because they are thought to indicate that one may be bewitched. Somatic complaints are also unusual from a Western standpoint. Common ones include "Occasionally I experience heat sensation in my head," "I have the feeling of something like water in my brain," "Things like ants keep on creeping in various parts of my brain," and "I am convinced some types of worms are in my head" (Ebigbo, 1982; Good & Kleinman, 1985). Nigerians with this syndrome also often have paranoid fears of malevolent attack by witchcraft (Kirmayer et al., 1995). In India, there are also many more worries about being possessed by spirits and about sexual inadequacy than are seen in generalized anxiety in Western cultures (Carstairs & Kapur, 1976; Good & Kleinman, 1985).

Another culture-related syndrome that occurs in places like China is *koro,* which for men involves intense acute fear that their penis is shrinking into the body and that when this process is complete, the sufferer will die (see Table 2.2). For women, the fear is that their nipples are retracting and their breasts are shrinking. Koro tends to occur in epidemics—especially in cultural minority groups whose survival is threatened. It occurs in a cultural context in which there are concerns about male sexual potency (Kirmayer et al., 1995).

Taijin Kyofusho

There is also some evidence that the form that certain anxiety disorders take has actually evolved so as to fit within certain cultural patterns. A good example is the Japanese disorder *taijin kyofusho* (TKS), which is related to the Western diagnosis of social phobia. Like social phobia, it refers to a fear of interpersonal relations or a fear of social situations (Kirmayer, 1991; Kleinknecht, Dinnel, & Kleinknecht, 1997; Tseng et al., 1992). However, Westerners with social phobia are afraid of social situations where they may be the object of scrutiny or criticism. By contrast, most people with TKS have a single dominant symptom, which in the past was a fear of blushing but currently seems to be most often a fear of making eye contact—symptoms not mentioned in the DSM description of social phobia (Kirmayer, 1991). Body dysmorphic disorder—the fear that some part of the body is defective or malformed (discussed earlier)—also commonly occurs in TKS sufferers, who have a morbid fear of embarrassing or offending others through their inappropriate behavior or their perceived physical defects. That is, they may think that their blushing or making eye contact, or their emitting an offensive odor, or their imagined deformity, is causing others significant discomfort. This fear of bringing shame on others or offending them is what leads to social avoidance (Kleinknecht et al., 1997).

Kirmayer (1991; Kirmayer et al., 1995) has argued that the pattern of symptoms that occurs in *taijin kyofusho* has clearly been shaped by cultural factors. Japanese children are raised to be highly dependent on their mothers and to have a fear of the outside world, especially of strangers. As babies and young children, they are praised for being obedient and docile. There is also a great deal of emphasis in Japanese culture on implicit communication—being able to guess another's thoughts and feelings and being sensitive to them. People who make too much eye contact are likely to be considered to be aggressive and insensitive, and children are taught to look at the throat of someone with whom they are conversing rather than into the eyes. The society is also very hierarchical and structured, and many subtleties in language and facial communication are used to communicate one's response to social status.

Kirmayer compares the effects of such Japanese cultural patterns on the symptoms seen in *taijin kyofusho* with the effects of Western cultural patterns on the symptoms seen in social phobia:

> The delusional fear of harming others through one's tense or inappropriate social behavior is rooted in Japanese concerns about the social presentation of self. Other-centered group conformity puts the individual on stage at all times and transforms ordinary awkwardness into a more serious social or moral failing. In Western society, where individuality is emphasized, concern with the feelings of the other does not reach a comparable intensity and so does not promote the formation of rigid preoccupations with injuring or offending others. (Kirmayer, 1991, p. 24)

At a more general level, cross-cultural researchers have noted that recognition of the cognitive component of most anxiety disorders leads one to expect many cross-cultural variations in the form that these disorders take. Anxiety disorders can be considered to be, at least in part, disorders of the interpretive process. Because culture influences the categories and schemas that people use to interpret their symptoms of distress, there are bound to be significant differences in the form that anxiety disorders take in different cultures (e.g., Good & Kleinman, 1985; Kirmayer et al., 1995).

IN REVIEW

- What are some examples of cultural differences in sources of worry?
- How is *taijin kyofusho* related to social phobia, and what kinds of cultural forces seem to have shaped it?

SUMMARY

THE FEAR AND ANXIETY RESPONSE PATTERNS

- Fear or panic is a basic emotion that involves activation of the fight-or-flight response of the autonomic nervous system.
- Anxiety is a more diffuse blend of emotions that includes high levels of negative affect, worry about possible threat or danger, and the sense of being unable to predict threat or to control it if it occurs.
- The anxiety disorders involve maladaptive behavior patterns that appear to have anxiety or panic or both at their core.

SPECIFIC PHOBIAS

- Specific phobias involve an intense and irrational fear of specific objects or situations, accompanied by a good deal of avoidance behavior. When confronted with the feared stimulus, the phobic person often shows activation of the fight-or-flight response.
- Many sources of fear and anxiety are believed to be acquired through conditioning or other learning mechanisms, although some people are more predisposed than others to acquire such responses.
- We seem to have a biologically based preparedness to acquire fears of objects or situations that posed a survival threat to our early ancestors.
- Behavior therapy involving controlled exposure to the stimuli or situations that elicit phobic fear is the preferred treatment for specific phobias. Participant modeling is an especially effective variant on this procedure.

SOCIAL PHOBIA

- In social phobia, a person has disabling fears of one or more social situations, usually because of fears of negative evaluation by others or of acting in an embarrassing or humiliating manner.
- We also seem to have an evolutionarily based predisposition to acquire fears of social stimuli signaling dominance and aggression from other humans, including facial expressions of anger or contempt, although some people are more predisposed to do so than others.
- Social phobics are also preoccupied with negative self-evaluative thoughts that tend to interfere with their ability to interact in a socially skillful fashion.
- Although medications such as antidepressants and anxiolytics are sometimes used to treat social phobia, behavioral and cognitive-behavioral treatments are most effective. Also, relapse rates are lower than with drug treatment.

PANIC DISORDER WITH AND WITHOUT AGORAPHOBIA

- In panic disorder, a person experiences unexpected panic attacks that often create a sense of stark terror, which usually subsides in a matter of minutes.
- Many people who experience panic attacks develop anxious apprehension about experiencing another one because the attacks can be so terrifying; many also develop agoraphobic avoidance of situations in which

they fear that they might have an attack and would find it difficult to escape or would be especially embarrassed.

- The interoceptive conditioning model of panic disorder states that when people with certain predispositions have one or more panic attacks, this occasions the conditioning of both panic and anxiety to internal (interoceptive) cues. Anticipatory anxiety and agoraphobic anxiety can also be conditioned to external cues.
- The cognitive model of panic disorder states that this condition may develop in people who are prone to making catastrophic misinterpretations of their bodily sensations.
- Biological theories of panic disorder emphasize that the disorder may result from biochemical abnormalities in the brain as well as abnormal activity of the neurotransmitter norepinephrine and probably also serotonin. Panic attacks may arise in the brain areas called the locus coeruleus and the central periacqueductal gray.
- Anxiolytics such as Xanax are effective in the short term for treating panic disorder (with or without agoraphobia), but these drugs are somewhat sedating and addictive and relapse rates upon their discontinuation are high. Antidepressants are safer in the long term, but they have some unpleasant side effects and take several weeks to show their effects. Exposure-based behavioral treatment, including interoceptive and exteroceptive exposure, has shown good success rates with persons suffering panic attacks. Cognitive-behavioral therapy is also highly effective for treating panic disorders.

GENERALIZED ANXIETY DISORDER

- In generalized anxiety disorder, a person has chronic and excessively high levels of worry about a number of events or activities and responds to stress with high levels of psychic and muscle tension.
- Generalized anxiety disorder may occur in people who have had extensive experience with unpredictable and/or uncontrollable life events.
- People with generalized anxiety disorder seem to have danger schemas, leading to images and automatic thoughts centered on illness, loss of control, inability to cope, etc.
- The neurobiological factors implicated in generalized anxiety disorder are a functional deficiency in the neurotransmitter GABA, which is involved in inhibiting anxiety in stressful situations, and the limbic system in the brain. Thus, different neurotransmitters and brain areas are involved in panic attacks and generalized anxiety.
- Generalized anxiety disorder may respond to treatment with medications such as buspirone, antidepressants, or anxiolytics. However, cognitive-behavioral therapy focusing on deep muscle relaxation and cognitive restructuring is the most effective treatment in the long run.

OBSESSIVE-COMPULSIVE DISORDER

- In obsessive-compulsive disorder, a person experiences unwanted and intrusive distressing thoughts or images that are usually accompanied by compulsive behaviors designed to neutralize those thoughts or images; checking and cleaning rituals are most common.
- Genetic studies, studies of structural brain functioning, and psychopharmacological studies have provided evidence that biological causal factors seem to be involved in obsessive-compulsive disorder.
- Once this disorder begins, the temporary anxiety-reducing qualities of the compulsive behaviors may help to maintain it.
- Medications that are selective serotonin-reuptake inhibitors have reasonably good effects in treating persons with obsessive-compulsive disorder; however, relapse rates are high following discontinuation of the drugs. A behavioral treatment involving a combination of exposure and response prevention is the most effective approach.

GENERAL SOCIOCULTURAL CAUSAL FACTORS FOR ANXIETY DISORDERS

- There are cross-cultural differences in topics that anxious people worry about.
- *Taijin kyofusho* is a disorder that occurs in the Japanese culture and is related to the Western diagnosis of social phobia. The central symptom is a fear of eye contact or a fear of blushing. This disorder has clearly been shaped by cultural factors in Japan, a very hierarchical and structured society where there is a great deal of emphasis on implicit communication.

KEY TERMS

neurotic behavior (p. 150)
neurosis (p. 150)
fear (p. 151)
panic (p. 151)

anxiety (p. 152)
anxiety disorder (p. 152)
phobia (p. 152)
specific phobias (p. 152)
social phobia (p. 152)
blood-injection-injury phobia (p. 154)
panic disorder (p. 162)
agoraphobia (p. 163)
interoceptive fears (p. 166)
generalized anxiety disorder (GAD) (p. 171)
obsessive-compulsive disorder (OCD) (p. 176)
obsessions (p. 177)
compulsions (p. 177)
body dysmorphic disorder (BDD) (p. 179)

CHAPTER SIX

Mood Disorders and Suicide

James Hoyt, *Portrait* (1980), oil on canvas. Born in Aberdeen, Maryland, Hoyt started drawing as a child and studied painting and draftsmanship in school. In early adulthood, he was misdiagnosed as having schizophrenia. This diagnosis was later changed to bipolar disorder, which has been treated successfully, allowing him to enjoy a productive life.

LEARNING OBJECTIVES

After reading this chapter, you should be able to:

- Describe the prevalence and onset patterns of mood disorders, and distinguish between unipolar and bipolar disorders.
- Summarize the symptoms and causal factors for the unipolar disorders.
- Summarize the symptoms and causal factors for the bipolar disorders.
- Describe the treatments that have been shown to be effective with mood disorders.
- Summarize the risk factors for suicide.
- Describe the key features of suicide prevention and intervention programs.

Most of us get depressed from time to time. Failing an exam, not getting into one's first-choice college or graduate school, or breaking up with a romantic partner are all examples of events that can precipitate a depressed mood in many people. However, **mood disorders** involve much more severe alterations in mood, and ones that last for much more prolonged periods of time. In such cases, the disturbances of mood are intense and persistent enough to be clearly maladaptive, often leading to serious problems in relationships and work performance. In fact, it was estimated that depression ranked fourth among 150 health conditions in terms of "disease-burden" to American society in 1990—that is, total direct costs (such as for treatment) and indirect costs (such as days missed at work, disability, premature deaths, etc.). Moreover, the forecast was that by 2020, depression would be the single leading cause of death (Murray & Lopez, 1996). Consider the following case.

Case Study **A Very Successful "Total Failure"** • A prominent businesswoman, Margaret, in her middle years, noted for her energy and productivity, was unexpectedly deserted by her husband for a younger woman. Following her initial shock and rage, she began to have uncontrollable weeping spells and doubts about her business acumen. Decision making became an ordeal. Her spirits rapidly worsened, and she began to spend more and more time in bed, refusing to deal with anyone. Her alcohol consumption increased to the point that she was seldom entirely sober. Within a period of weeks, serious financial losses were incurred owing to her inability, or refusal, to keep her affairs in order. She felt she was a "total failure," a self-attribution that was entirely resistant to alteration by a review of her considerable achievements; indeed, her self-criticism gradually spread to all aspects of her life and her personal history. Finally, members of her family, having become alarmed, essentially forced her to accept an appointment with a clinical psychologist.

Was something "wrong" with Margaret, or was she merely experiencing normal human emotions due to her husband's departure? The psychologist concluded that she was suffering from a mood disorder and initiated treatment. The diagnosis, based on the severity of the symptoms and the degree of impairment, was major depressive disorder.

When significant mood change brings about behavior that seriously endangers a person's welfare, psychologists and other mental health professionals conclude that the person has a mood disorder. Mood disorders are diverse in nature, as is illustrated by the many types of depression recognized in DSM-IV-TR and listed in Table 6.1. Nevertheless, in all mood disorders (formerly called *affective disorders*), extremes of emotion, or *affect*—soaring elation or deep depression—dominate the clinical picture. Other symptoms are also present, but the abnormal mood is the defining feature.

WHAT ARE MOOD DISORDERS?

The two key moods involved in mood disorders are **mania,** characterized by intense and unrealistic feelings of excitement and euphoria, and **depression,** which involves feelings of extraordinary sadness and dejection. Some people with mood disorders experience both of these kinds of moods at one time or another, but others experience only depression. Mania and depression are often conceived to be at opposite ends of a mood continuum, with normal mood in the middle. However, in some cases, a patient may have symptoms of mania and depression more or less at the same time, showing rapidly alternating moods such as sadness, euphoria, and irritability, all within the same episode of illness.

mood disorders Mental disorders characterized by disturbances of mood that are intense and persistent enough to be clearly maladaptive.

mania Emotional state characterized by intense and unrealistic feelings of excitement and euphoria.

depression Emotional state characterized by feelings of extraordinary sadness and dejection.

IN REVIEW

- What is the major difference between unipolar disorders and bipolar disorders, and how prevalent are the two types of mood disorder?
- How do the prevalence rates of unipolar and bipolar disorders differ between the sexes and over the lifespan?

UNIPOLAR MOOD DISORDERS

Sadness, discouragement, pessimism, and hopelessness about being able to improve matters are familiar feelings to most people. Depression is unpleasant while it lasts, but for most of us, it usually does not last long. Sometimes it seems almost to be self-limiting, turning off after a period of days or weeks. Sometimes we may experience it as having been in some sense useful: We were stuck, and now we can move on; our new perspective may open unexpected possibilities.

This scenario contains hints that may be significant to a general understanding of depression. For example, mild depression may actually be adaptive in the long run; much of the "work" of depression seems to involve facing images, thoughts, and feelings that one would normally avoid; and depression may sometimes be self-limiting. These considerations suggest that the capacity for depression may be "normal"—even desirable—if the depression is brief and mild. They also suggest the idea of normal depressions—depressions that can be expected to occur in anyone undergoing painful but common life events, such as significant personal, interpersonal, or economic losses. An example is the grieving process that follows the loss of a close relative.

There are other less obvious situations that can also provoke depressive feelings. For example, "success" depressions have been observed in politicians following election to public office after a difficult campaign and in novelists and actors who experience a big success. Many college students also experience mild or serious depression during their years of supposed freedom and carefree personal growth. Some of these depressions are in the normal range, but some can be very serious and require clinical attention, as will be described later. Moreover, even though the birth of a child is usually seen as a happy event, "postpartum blues" are very common in women following childbirth. These depressed feelings are within the normal range of mood variation (Hobfoll et al., 1995; O'Hara et al., 1990, 1991) and should be distinguished from true postpartum depression (discussed later) in which a woman experiences a major depression following the birth of a child.

Mild to Moderate Depressive Disorders

The point at which mood disturbance becomes a diagnosable mood disorder is a matter of clinical judgment. Severe mood disorders are obviously abnormal. However, a gray area also exists in which a distinction between normal and abnormal is more difficult to establish. DSM-IV-TR includes two main categories for depressions of mild to moderate severity: *dysthymia* and *adjustment disorder with depressed mood*. These are both considered in the following subsections.

Dysthymia To qualify for a diagnosis of **dysthymia,** a person must have a persistently depressed mood, more days than not, for at least 2 years (1 year for children and adolescents). In addition, dysthymics must have at least two of the following six symptoms when depressed: (1) poor appetite (or overeating), (2) sleep disturbance, (3) low energy level, (4) low self-esteem, (5) difficulties in concentration or decision making, and (6) feelings of hopelessness. That is, they experience moderate levels of depression over a chronic period of at least 2 years; moreover, they are not psychotic (out of touch with reality). The average duration of dysthymia is 5 years but it can persist for 20 years or more (Keller, Hirschfeld, & Hanks, 1997). Normal moods may briefly intercede, but they last at most from a few days to a few weeks. Indeed, this occurrence of intermittently normal moods seems to be the primary characteristic distinguishing dysthymia from major depression, since the average number of symptoms endorsed by patients from the two categories does not appear to differ (Klein, Riso, & Anderson, 1993). Thus, individuals with dysthymia do not really show less severe symptoms than do major depressives; the difference is simply that they do not necessarily have the symptoms every day. No identifiable precipitating event or condition need be present, although such circumstances are frequently observed for depression of this general type (e.g., Roth & Mountjoy, 1997).

Dysthymia is quite common, with a lifetime prevalence of nearly 5 percent for men and 8 percent for women

dysthymia Moderately severe mood disorder characterized by a persistently depressed mood (more days than not) lasting for at least 2 years and by additional symptoms such as poor appetite, sleep disturbance, low energy level, low self-esteem, difficulty in concentrating, and feelings of hopelessness.

HIGHLIGHT 6.1

Loss and the Grieving Process

We usually think of grief as a normal psychological process a person goes through following the death of a loved one—a process that appears to be more damaging for men than women (Stroebe & Stroebe, 1983). Grief has certain characteristic qualities. Indeed, Bowlby (1980) observed that there are usually four phases of response to the loss of a spouse or close family member:

1. Numbing and disbelief that may last from a few hours to a week and may be interrupted by outbursts of intense distress, panic, or anger.
2. Yearning and searching for the dead person, which may last for months or occasionally for years.
3. Disorganization and despair.
4. Some level of reorganization.

In the second phase (which resembles anxiety more than depression), the grieving person may show great restlessness, insomnia, and preoccupation with the dead person; anger is also very common in this phase and is entirely normal. The intensity of the yearning and search gradually diminishes. The third phase of disorganization and despair sets in when the person finally accepts the loss as permanent and finds it is necessary to discard old patterns of thinking, feeling, and acting, including establishing a new identity (e.g., as a widow or widower). During this phase, the person may meet the criteria for a major depression. Gradually, however, most people pass into the fourth phase and begin to rebuild their lives. The ability to respond to the external world is gradually regained, sadness abates, zest returns, and a person emerges into a more productive engagement with the challenges of life.

This has generally been considered to be the "normal" pattern. The process of grieving following bereavement (suffering the loss of a loved one) is normally completed within a year (Clayton, 1982). Some people, however, become stuck somewhere in the middle of the sequence, and if depressive symptoms persist beyond the first year after loss, therapeutic intervention may be called for. This persistence of grieving is often called *chronic grief* and may occur in 10 to 20 percent of bereaved individuals (Jacobs, 1993; Middleton et al., 1996).

We usually think of grief as the psychological process a person goes through following the death of a loved one. This man is grieving at his wife's grave. Grief may accompany other types of loss as well, including separation or divorce, or loss of a pet.

Social scientists working with bereaved individuals around the world suggest that the bereaved person maintains a continued connection to the deceased person that may change over time but that persists indefinitely: "While the death is permanent and unchanging, the process is not. . . . The resolution of grief involves continuing bonds that survivors maintain with the deceased and . . . these continuing bonds can be a healthy part of the survivor's ongoing life" (Silverman & Klass, 1996, pp. 18–22). ■

(Kessler et al., 1994). The following case, which shows obvious self-sustaining features, is typical of this disorder.

Case Study **A Dysthymic Junior Executive** • A 28-year-old junior executive was referred by a senior psychoanalyst for "supportive" treatment. She had obtained a master's degree in business administration and moved to California a year and a half earlier to begin work in a large firm. She complained of being "depressed" about everything: her job, her husband, and her prospects for the future.

She had previously had extensive psychotherapy. She had seen an "analyst" twice a week for 3 years while in college, and a "behaviorist" for a year and a half while in graduate school. Her complaints were of persistent feelings of depressed mood, inferiority, and pessimism, which she claims to have had since she was 16 or 17 years old. Although she did reasonably well in college, she constantly ruminated about those students who were "genuinely intelligent." She dated during college and graduate school, but claimed that she would never go after a guy she thought was "special," always feeling inferior and intimidated. Whenever she saw or met such a man, she acted stiff and aloof, or actually walked away as quickly as possible, only to berate herself afterward and then fantasize about him for many months. She claimed that her therapy had helped, although she still could not remember a time when she didn't feel somewhat depressed.

Just after graduation, she had married the man she was going out with at the time. She thought of him as reasonably desirable, though not "special," and married him primarily because she felt she "needed a husband" for companionship. Shortly after their marriage, the couple started to bicker. She was very critical of his clothes, his job, and his parents; and he, in turn, found her rejecting, controlling, and moody. She began to feel that she had made a mistake in marrying him.

Recently, she has also been having difficulties at work. She is assigned the most menial tasks at the firm and is never given an assignment of importance or responsibility. She admits that she frequently does a "slipshod" job of what is given her, never does more than is required, and never demonstrates any assertiveness or initiative to her supervisors. She views her boss as self-centered, unconcerned, and unfair, but nevertheless admires his success. She feels that she will never go very far in her profession because she does not have the right "connections" and neither does her husband, yet she dreams of money, status, and power.

Her social life with her husband involves several other couples. The man in these couples is usually a friend of her husband. She is sure that the women find her uninteresting and unimpressive, and that the people who seem to like her are probably no better off than she.

Under the burden of her dissatisfaction with her marriage, her job, and her social life, feeling tired and uninterested in "life," she now enters treatment for the third time. (From Spitzer et al., 1994, pp. 110–111.)

Adjustment Disorder with Depressed Mood Basically, **adjustment disorder with depressed mood** is behaviorally indistinguishable from dysthymia. It differs from dysthymia in that it does not exceed 6 months in duration, and it requires the existence of an identifiable (presumably precipitating) psychosocial stressor in the client's life within 3 months before the onset of depression. The justification for making a clinical diagnosis is that the client is experiencing impaired social or occupational functioning, or that the observed stressor (see Chapter 4) would not normally be considered severe enough to account for the client's depression. There is a difficulty here because the diagnosis assumes that the person's problems will remit when the stressor ceases. Chronic cases that do not remit later need to be rediagnosed as dysthymia.

Despite some problems with the formal diagnostic criteria, there are doubtless many cases of relatively brief but moderately serious depression (involving definite maladaptive behavior) that occur in reaction to stressful circumstances. (Uncomplicated bereavement following loss of a loved one, by the way, would not be included under this diagnosis.) The following excerpt from a clinical interview involves an individual with adjustment disorder with depressed mood.

Case Study **Therapy Session: Divorcing and Depressed**

PATIENT: Well, you see, doctor, I just don't concentrate good, I mean, I can't play cards or even care to talk on the phone. I just feel so upset and miserable, it's just sorta as if I don't care any more about anything.

DOCTOR: You feel that your condition is primarily due to your divorce proceedings?

PATIENT: Well, doctor, the thing that upset me so, we had accumulated a little bit through my efforts—bonds and money—and he [sigh] wanted one half of it. He said he was going to San Francisco to get a job and send me enough money for support. So [sigh] I gave him a bond, and he went and turned

adjustment disorder with depressed mood Moderately severe mood disorder similar to dysthymia but not exceeding 6 months in duration and having an identifiable psychosocial stressor within 3 months before the onset of depression.

around and went to an attorney and sued me for a divorce. Well, somehow, I had withstood all the humiliation of his drinking and not coming home at night and not knowing where he was, but he turned and divorced me and this is something that I just can't take. I mean, he has broken my heart and broken everything, and I've been nothing but good to him. I just can't take it, doctor. There are just certain things that people—I don't know—just can't accept. I just can't accept that he would turn on me that way.

Major Depressive Disorder

The diagnostic criteria for **major depressive disorder** require that the person exhibit more symptoms than are required for dysthymia and the symptoms be more persistent (not interwoven with periods of normal mood). An affected person must experience either markedly depressed mood or marked loss of interest in pleasurable activities most of every day for at least 2 weeks. In addition, the person must experience at least four or more of the following symptoms during the same period: (1) fatigue or loss of energy; (2) insomnia or hypersomnia (that is, too little or too much sleep); (3) decreased appetite and significant weight loss without dieting (or, much more rarely, their opposites); (4) psychomotor agitation or retardation (a slowdown of mental and physical activity); (5) diminished ability to think or concentrate; (6) self-denunciation to the point of claiming worthlessness or guilt out of proportion to any past indiscretions; and (7) recurrent thoughts of death or thoughts of suicide.

Someone who has major depression is not only sad, but also shows a host of other symptoms such as feelings of worthlessness or guilt, diminished ability to think or concentrate, loss of energy, loss of appetite, and sometimes recurrent thoughts of death or suicide.

Most of these symptoms (at least five, including either sad mood or loss of interest or pleasure) must be present all day and nearly every day for 2 consecutive weeks before the diagnosis is applicable. The diagnosis of major depression is not made if a patient has ever experienced a manic or hypomanic episode; in such a case, the current depression is viewed as a depressive episode of bipolar disorder, which is discussed in the next section.

It should be noted that few, if any, depressions—including milder ones—occur in the absence of significant anxiety (Akiskal, 1997; Mineka, Watson, & Clark, 1998). Indeed, issues surrounding the co-occurrence of depression and anxiety at both the symptomatic and diagnostic levels have raised many questions and received an enormous amount of attention in recent years.

The following conversation between a therapist and a 34-year-old woman illustrates a major depression of moderate severity.

Case Study "I'm a Failure": A Case of Major Depression

THERAPIST: Good morning, how are you today?

PATIENT: [Pause] Well, okay I guess, doctor.... I don't know, I just feel sort of discouraged.

THERAPIST: Is there anything in particular that worries you?

PATIENT: I don't know, doctor... everything seems to be futile... nothing seems worthwhile any more. It seems as if all that was beautiful has lost its beauty. I guess I expected more than life has given. It just doesn't seem worthwhile going on. I

major depressive disorder Severe mood disorder in which only depressive episodes occur most of every day for at least 2 weeks and the person experiences other symptoms, such as fatigue, sleep disturbance, loss of appetite and weight, psychomotor agitation or retardation, difficulty in concentrating, self-denunciation, guilt, and recurrent thoughts of death or suicide.

HIGHLIGHT 6.2

Comorbidity of Anxiety and Mood Disorders

An overlap between symptoms of depression and those of anxiety occurs at all levels of analysis—patient self-report, clinician ratings, diagnosis, and family/genetic factors (Clark & Watson, 1991a, 1991b; Mineka et al., 1998). That is, persons who rate themselves high on a scale for symptoms of anxiety also tend to rate themselves high on a scale for symptoms of depression, and clinicians rating these same individuals do the same thing. Moreover, the overlap also occurs at the diagnostic level. One recent review of the literature estimated that just over half of the patients who receive a diagnosis of a mood disorder also receive a diagnosis of an anxiety disorder at some point in their lives, and vice versa (Mineka et al., 1998).

At present, the dominant theoretical approach to understanding the overlap between depression and anxiety is that most of the measures used to measure both sets of symptoms tap the broad mood and personality dimension of *negative affect,* which includes affective states such as distress, anger, fear, guilt, and worry (Clark & Watson, 1991a, 1991b; Clark et al., 1994; Tellegen, 1985; Watson et al., 1995a, 1995b). Depressed and anxious individuals generally cannot be distinguished from each other on the basis of their high level of negative affect. But researchers have also shown that anxiety and depression can be distinguished on the basis of a second dimension of mood and personality known as *positive affect,* which includes affective states such as excitement, delight, interest, and pride. Depressed persons tend to be characterized by low levels of positive affect, but anxious individuals are not. That is, only depressed individuals show the signs of fatigue and lack of energy and enthusiasm characteristic of low positive affect. Clark and Watson (1991b) have also shown that some anxious patients (especially panic patients), but not depressed people, tend to be characterized by high levels of yet another mood dimension known as *anxious hyperarousal,* symptoms of which include racing heart, trembling, dizziness, and shortness of breath. This tripartite model thus explains what features of anxiety and depression are common to both (high negative affect) and what features are distinct (low positive affect for depression and anxious hyperarousal for panic) (Mineka et al., 1998). Each of the other anxiety disorders has its own separate and relatively unique component as well (Brown, Chorpita, & Barlow, 1998; Mineka et al., 1998; Zinbarg & Barlow, 1996).

There are also several features of diagnostic comorbidity between anxiety and mood disorders that raise interesting questions. For example, there is usually a sequential relationship between the symptoms of anxiety and depression, both within an episode and between episodes. Bowlby (1973, 1980) described a biphasic response to separation and loss in which the first phase appears to be one of agitation and anxiety, followed by despair and depression. And, across a lifetime, individuals are more likely to experience an anxiety disorder first and a depressive disorder later, rather than vice versa (Alloy et al., 1990; Kessler, 1997b; Mineka et al., 1998). There is also differential comorbidity between depression and the various anxiety disorders, with panic disorder and obsessive-compulsive disorder being more likely than, for example, simple or social phobia to be accompanied by depression (Kessler et al., 1996; Mineka et al., 1998). ■

can't seem to make up my mind about anything. I guess I have what you would call the "blues."

THERAPIST: Can you tell me more about your feelings?

PATIENT: Well . . . my family expected great things of me. I am supposed to be the outstanding member of the family . . . they think because I went through college everything should begin to pop and there's nothing to pop. I . . . really don't expect anything from anyone. Those whom I have trusted proved themselves less than friends should be.

THERAPIST: Oh?

PATIENT: Yes, I once had a very good girlfriend with whom I spent a good deal of time. She was very important to me. . . . I thought she was my friend but now she treats me like a casual acquaintance [tears].

THERAPIST: Can you think of any reason for this?

PATIENT: Yes, it's all my fault. I can't blame them—anybody that is. . . . I am not worthy of them . . . I am worthless . . . nobody can love me. I don't deserve friends or success. . . .

THERAPIST: You don't deserve friends?

PATIENT: Well . . . I am just no good. I am a failure. I was envious of other people. I didn't want them to have more than I had and when something bad happened to them I was glad. . . . All my flaws stand out and I am repugnant to everyone. [Sighs] I am a miserable failure. . . . There is no hope for me.

As this conversation between a woman and her therapist illustrates, a person with major depression shows not only mood symptoms of sadness but also a variety of *cognitive* and *motivational* symptoms that are more severe than in milder forms of depression. In this case, the depressed woman shows various cognitive distortions, including being firmly convinced that she is a failure and that her family also thinks so. She vacillates between anger at her friends and family for not being trustworthy and self-hatred and self-blame. Because of her sense of hopelessness about her future, she shows no motivation to try to improve her situation. Her problems with friends who appear to no longer be close to her occur commonly with depression because, as we will see, most people do not like to be around depressed persons.

Subtypes of Major Depression Several subcategories of major depression have been defined according to the particular symptom patterns displayed. Such efforts are driven mostly by the hope of distinguishing causes and effective treatments for the different subtypes. One such subcategory in DSM-IV-TR is major depression of the **melancholic type.** This designation is applied when, in addition to meeting the criteria for major depression, a patient has either loss of interest or pleasure in almost all activities or does not react to usually pleasurable stimuli or desired events. In addition, the patient must also experience at least three of the following: (1) early morning awakenings, (2) depression being worse in the morning, (3) marked psychomotor retardation or agitation, (4) significant loss of appetite and weight, (5) inappropriate or excessive guilt, or (6) depressed mood that has a qualitative difference from the sadness experienced following a loss or during a nonmelancholic depression. This subtype of major depression is influenced more by genetic factors than are other forms of depression (Kendler, 1997). Also, patients with this subtype of depression may be more likely to respond to electroconvulsive treatment or to tricyclic antidepressant medications than to selective serotonin re-uptake inhibitors (see the discussion of treatment later in this chapter) (Gitlin, 1996; Roose et al., 1994).

Psychotic symptoms, characterized by loss of contact with reality and including delusions (false beliefs) or hallucinations (false sensory perceptions), may sometimes accompany the other symptoms of major depression. In such cases, a diagnosis of **severe major depressive episode with psychotic features** is made. Ordinarily, any delusions or hallucinations present are **mood-congruent psychotic features**—that is, they seem in some sense "appropriate" to serious depression because the content is negative in tone. Examples of mood-congruent delusions might involve themes of personal inadequacy, guilt, deserved punishment, death, disease, and so forth. For example, the delusional idea that one's internal organs have totally deteriorated—an idea sometimes held by severely depressed people—ties in with the mood of a despondent person. In contrast, the idea that one has been chosen by the Deity for a special mission to save humankind is inconsistent with the negative self-views normally seen in depression. The latter type of disordered or delusional thinking, which occurs more rarely, is termed a **mood-incongruent psychotic feature**—that is, it is inconsistent with the predominant mood. Psychotically depressed individuals are more likely to show some of the symptoms of melancholia and to have a poorer long-term prognosis than are nonpsychotic depressives (Coryell, 1997).

Sometimes major depression may have a **postpartum onset** (beginning within 4 weeks of a baby's birth). Although it used to be thought that postpartum major depression was quite common, it is now known that major depression occurs no more frequently in the postpartum period than would be expected in women of the same age and socioeconomic status who had not given birth (Hobfoll et al., 1995; O'Hara et al., 1990, 1991). So, although postpartum "blues" are quite common, the once firmly held notion that women were at especially high risk for significant depression in the postpartum period has not

melancholic type Subtype of major depression that involves loss of interest or pleasure in almost all activities and other symptoms, including early morning awakenings, worsening of depression in the morning, psychomotor agitation or retardation, loss of appetite and weight, inappropriate or excessive guilt, and sadness that is qualitatively different from the sadness usually experienced after a loss.

severe major depressive episode with psychotic features Major depression involving loss of contact with reality, often in the form of delusions or hallucinations.

mood-congruent psychotic features Delusional thinking that is consistent with a person's predominant mood.

mood-incongruent psychotic features Delusional thinking that is inconsistent with a person's predominant mood.

postpartum onset Beginning within 4 weeks of the birth of a baby.

been upheld. Typical postpartum depression is best understood as an adjustment disorder because it tends to be relatively mild and is resolved rather quickly (Brems, 1995).

Distinguishing Major Depression Discriminating major depression from other forms of depressive disorder is not always easy. Major depression may coexist with dysthymia in some people, a condition given the designation "double depression" (Keller & Shapiro, 1982; Keller, Hirschfeld, & Hanks, 1997). Double depressives are people who are moderately depressed on a chronic basis and who undergo increased problems from time to time, periods during which they manifest "major" depressive symptoms. Among clinical samples of individuals with dysthymia, the experience of double depression appears to be common. For example, in one clinical sample of dysthymics, 54 percent were in a major depressive episode at the time they sought treatment, and 75 percent reported a lifetime history of one or more major depressive episodes (e.g., Klein, Riso, & Anderson, 1993). Although nearly all double depressives appear to recover from their major depressive episode (at least for a while), less than half are likely to recover from the dysthymia as well (Keller et al., 1997).

Depression as a Recurrent Disorder When a diagnosis of major depression is made, it usually also specifies whether this is a *single* (initial) episode or a *recurrent* episode (one or more previous episodes have already occurred). This reflects the fact that depressive episodes are usually time-limited (with the average duration of an untreated episode being about 6 months, according to DSM-IV-TR). In a large untreated sample of depressed women, certain predictors that pointed to a longer time until spontaneous remission of symptoms were financial difficulties, obsessive-compulsive symptoms, severe stressful life events, and high genetic risk (Kendler, Walters, & Kessler, 1997). However, depressions often recur following a period of remission of symptoms of at least 2 months. **Recurrence** has been distinguished from **relapse,** where the latter term refers to the return of symptoms within a fairly short period of time and probably reflects the fact that the underlying episode of depression has not yet run its course (Frank et al., 1991; Keller et al., 1982). Relapse may commonly occur, for example, when pharmacotherapy is terminated prematurely after symptoms have remitted but before the underlying episode is really over (Hollon, DeRubeis, & Evans, 1996; Shelton et al., 1991).

Estimates of the recurrence of major depression vary widely: Based on an extensive review of nearly all studies done between 1970 and 1993, Piccinelli and Wilkinson (1994) estimated that 26 percent of patients experienced a recurrence within 1 year of recovery and 76 percent experienced a recurrence within 10 years of recovery. The same review estimated that approximately 10 to 12 percent show persistent depression over 5- and 10-year follow-up periods (see also Keller et al., 1997). There is also evidence that the probability of recurrence increases with the number of prior episodes. Conversely, the probability of recurrence seems to decrease the longer the person remains symptom-free.

Persons who experience recurrent depressions can be distinguished from those who experience only a single episode in a number of ways. Those with some form of recurrent depression show not only greater severity in terms of number and frequency of symptoms, but also many more suicide attempts, more work and social impairment, higher divorce rates, and higher rates of family members with a history of depression (Merikangas, Wicki, & Angst, 1994).

The traditional view has been that a person suffering from a recurrent major mood disorder is essentially normal between episodes. This view has been increasingly called into question as more research data have become available (Coryell & Winokur, 1982, 1992), and some have raised the possibility that major depressive episodes may leave "scars" that may leave a person at risk for future recurrences. Such scars might include fears about having another depression and continuing low-grade symptoms, including resignation, pessimism, or insecurity. Evidence for the scar hypothesis at this point is mixed (Klein et al., 1993; Rohde, Lewinsohn, & Seeley, 1990).

Seasonal Affective Disorder Some people who experience recurrent depressive episodes show a seasonal pattern, commonly known as **seasonal affective disorder.** To meet DSM-IV-TR criteria for recurrent major depression with a seasonal pattern, the person must have had at least two episodes of depression in the past 2 years, occurring at the same time of the year (most commonly, the fall or winter), and full remission from each episode must also have

recurrence A new occurrence of a disorder after a period of remission of symptoms lasting for at least 2 months.

relapse Return of the symptoms of a disorder within a fairly short period of time.

seasonal affective disorder Mood disorder involving at least two episodes of depression in the past 2 years, occurring at the same time of year (most commonly, fall or winter) and with full remission from each episode occurring at a certain time of year (most commonly, spring).

occurred at a certain time of year (most commonly, the spring). In addition, the person cannot have had other nonseasonal depressive episodes in the same 2-year period, and most of his or her lifetime depressive episodes must have been of the seasonal variety. Prevalence rates suggest that winter seasonal affective disorder is more common in people living at higher latitudes (northern climates) and in younger people. As will be discussed later, there has been a great deal of interesting research on this relatively recently identified subtype of depression.

We now turn to a discussion of the possible roles of biological, psychosocial, and sociocultural causal factors for unipolar mood disorders.

People who live in higher latitudes (northern climates for those in the northern hemisphere) are more likely to exhibit seasonal affective disorder in which depression occurs primarily in the fall and winter months and tends to remit in the spring or summer months.

Biological Causal Factors

It has long been known that a variety of diseases and drugs can affect mood, sometimes leading to depression, and sometimes to elation or even hypomania. Indeed, this idea goes back to Hippocrates, who hypothesized that depression was caused by an excess of "black bile" in the system (c. 400 B.C.). Many contemporary researchers have also sought to determine whether there is a biological basis for at least some of the depressive disorders. These investigators have considered genetic and constitutional factors as well as neurophysiological, neuroendocrinological, and biochemical alterations. A good deal of attention has also been focused on disturbances in many of our biological rhythms, including the effects of seasonal variations in light and darkness.

Hereditary Factors The prevalence of unipolar mood disorders is higher among blood relatives of persons with clinically diagnosed mood disorders than in the population at large (e.g., Plomin et al., 1997). Because of the difficulties of disentangling hereditary and environmental influences, however, a higher rate of a disorder among family members can never in itself be taken as conclusive proof of genetic causation. However, twin studies have also suggested that there may be a moderate genetic contribution to unipolar depression. Plomin and colleagues (1997) reviewed evidence from five studies showing that a monozygotic co-twin of a twin with unipolar major depression is about two to four times more likely to develop major depression than a dizygotic co-twin of a depressed twin. Overall, the case for some hereditary contribution to the causal factors for unipolar major depression is quite strong (Katz & McGuffin, 1993; Plomin et al., 1997). For example, several good studies estimate that genes contribute from 33 to 50 percent of the variance in the tendency to develop (that is, the liability for) unipolar depression.

The evidence for a genetic contribution is much less consistent for milder forms of unipolar depression such as dysthymia (Katz & McGuffin, 1993; Plomin et al., 1997; Roth & Mountjoy, 1997), and, indeed, some twin studies have not found any evidence of a genetic contribution to these milder but more chronic forms of unipolar depression. Thus, any genetic contribution to more minor depressive disorders is likely to be very modest at best (Roth & Mountjoy, 1997).

There is also considerable evidence from genetic and family studies of close relationships between anxiety disorders and depressive disorders (Clark & Watson, 1991a, 1991b; Kendler, 1996; Kendler et al., 1995; Mineka et al., 1998). Indeed, several very large twin studies and a recent review have shown that the liability for unipolar depression and generalized anxiety disorder actually comes from the same genetic factors, and which disorder develops is a result of whatever environmental experiences the person has (Kendler, 1996; Kendler et al., 1992d, 1995). By contrast, the genetic relationship between panic disorder and depression, and that between the other anxiety disorders and depression, are also significant but more modest in magnitude (Kendler et al., 1995; Mineka et al., 1998).

Biochemical Factors Starting in the 1960s, the view that depression may arise from disruptions in the delicate balance of neurotransmitter substances that regulate and mediate the activity of the brain's nerve cells, or neurons, has received a great deal of attention. Neurotransmitters, released by the activated presynaptic neuron, mediate the transfer of nerve impulses across the synaptic cleft from one neuron to the next in a neuronal pathway; they may either stimulate or inhibit the firing of the next neuron in the chain (see Figure 2.1 on p. 41).

A large body of evidence suggests that various biological therapies often used to treat severe mood disorders—such as antidepressant drugs and electroconvulsive therapy—may affect the concentrations or the activity of neurotransmitters at the synapse and thus determine the extent to which particular brain pathways are relatively volatile or sluggish in conducting messages. In fact, the largely accidental discovery of these treatments (particularly the antidepressant drugs) and the initial explanations of how they work are what first encouraged the development of biochemical theories of the etiology of major depression.

Early attention in the 1960s and 1970s focused primarily on three neurotransmitter substances of the monoamine class—norepinephrine, dopamine, and serotonin—because researchers observed that antidepressant medications seemed to have the effect of increasing the availability of these neurotransmitters at the synapses. This observation led to the "monoamine hypothesis"—that depression was at least sometimes due to an absolute or relative depletion of one or all of these neurotransmitters at important receptor sites in the brain (Schildkraut, 1965). Some 30 years later, it became clear that the answer is more complicated than this straightforward hypothesis would suggest (e.g., Thase & Howland, 1995; Whybrow, 1997). For example, some studies have found exactly the opposite of what is predicted by the monoamine hypothesis—that is, net *increases* in norepinephrine activity in depressed patients (see Thase & Howland, 1995, for a review). Furthermore, even though the immediate short-term effects of antidepressant drugs are to increase the availability of norepinephrine and serotonin, the long-term effects of these drugs (when they actually begin to have their clinical effects 2 to 4 weeks later) are to produce functional *decreases* in available norepinephrine and serotonin.

In the past 15 to 20 years, research on the etiology of depression has shifted toward more integrative theories that either do not focus exclusively on biochemical systems or, to the extent that they do, focus more on the interactions of biochemical systems rather than on single neurotransmitters.

Neuroendocrine and Neurophysiological Factors

There has also been a good deal of research on the possible neurophysiological and neuroendocrine (hormonal) correlates of some distinguishable forms of mood disorder (Checkley, 1992; Thase & Howland, 1995). Ideas about hormonal influences on mood have a long history. One contemporary theory (e.g., Holsboer, 1992; Stokes & Sikes, 1987; Thase & Howland, 1995) has focused on the *hypothalamic-pituitary-adrenal axis,* and in particular on the hormone *cortisol,* which is excreted by the outermost portion of the adrenal glands and is regulated through a complex feedback loop (see Figure 2.2 on p. 42). Blood plasma levels of this substance are known to be elevated in from 50 to 60 percent of seriously depressed patients (Holsboer, 1992), suggesting a possible clue of etiological significance. Indeed, research has shown that the complex feedback loop involved in regulation of the entire hypothalamic-pituitary-adrenal axis (see Figure 2.2) is not operating properly in approximately half of seriously depressed patients (e.g., Shelton et al., 1991; Thase & Howland, 1995).

The other endocrine system that has relevance to depression is the *hypothalamic-pituitary-thyroid axis,* because it is known that disturbances to this axis are also linked to mood disorders (Checkley, 1992; Marangell et al., 1997; Thase & Howland, 1995). For example, people with low thyroid levels (a condition known as *hypothyroidism*) often become depressed. In addition, about 25 to 40 percent of depressed patients who have normal thyroid levels have abnormal regulation of this axis. Furthermore, administration of thyrotropin-releasing hormone (which through a complex sequence of steps leads to increased levels of thyroid hormone) improves the mood and the sense of motivation and coping for both normal and psychiatric subjects (Loosen, 1986; Shelton et al., 1991).

Other exciting neurophysiological research in the 1990s followed up on earlier neurological findings showing that lesions of the left (but not the right) anterior or prefrontal cortex (for example, from having a stroke in that region) often lead to depression (e.g., Robinson & Downhill, 1995). This led to the idea that perhaps depression in people without brain lesions in this region is nonetheless linked to lowered levels of brain activity there. (See Figure 6.1.) Several studies have supported this idea. When one measures the electroencephalographic (EEG) activity of both cerebral hemispheres in depressed patients, one finds that there is an asymmetry, or imbalance, in the EEG activity in the two anterior (prefrontal) regions. In particular, depressed persons show relatively low activity in the left hemisphere in these regions (Davidson, 1998; Henriques & Davidson, 1991). It also seems that this may be a risk marker for depression, since patients in remission show the same pattern (Henriques & Davidson, 1990), as do children at risk for depression (Tomarken, Simien, & Garber, 1994). Studies using brain-imaging techniques such as positron emission tomography (PET)

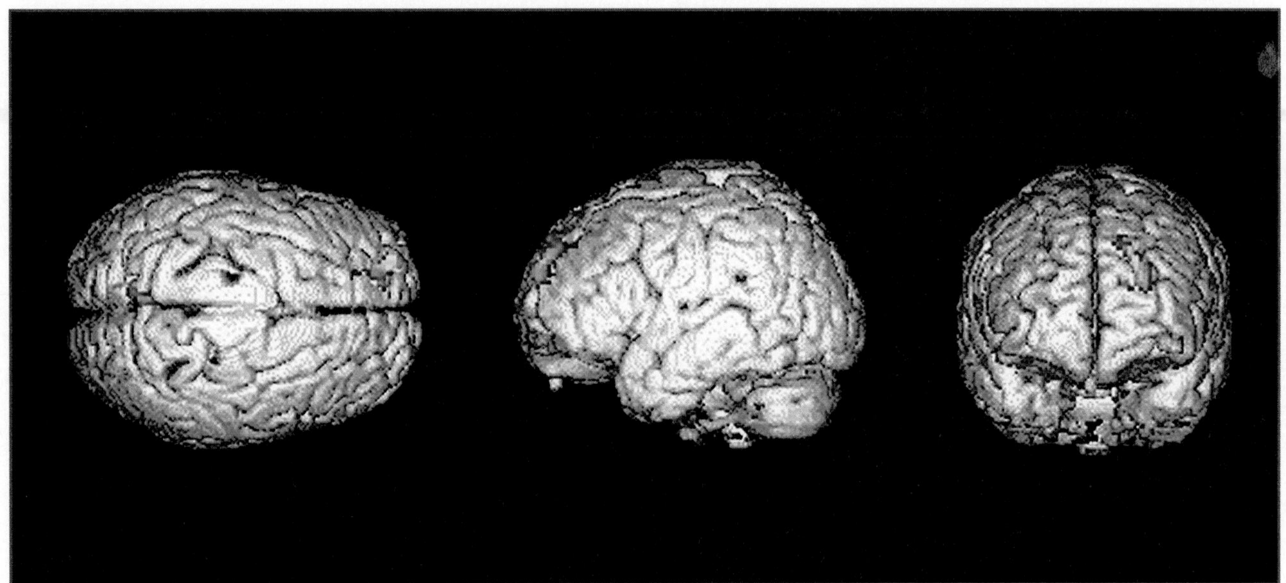

FIGURE 6.1 FUNCTIONAL MRI CHANGES IN PREFRONTAL ACTIVITY IN DEPRESSED PATIENTS
The red and yellow areas on these scans illustrate (in three different views) the increase in left prefrontal activation that occurred in a group of depressed patients following treatment compared to their activation pattern during an acute depressive episode. Thus, the red and yellow images depict where changes in cerebral blood in the left prefrontal area occurred in response to affective stimuli from before to after successful antidepressant treatment. The second scan was obtained 8 weeks following the first scan. Patients were treated with an antidepressant medication during those 8 weeks.
Source: Courtesy of Richard J. Davidson, University of Wisconsin–Madison.

also suggest that severely depressed patients show decreased metabolism in the anterior (prefrontal) regions of the cerebral hemispheres, especially on the left side (see Thase & Howland, 1995, for a review). Although this is a relatively new area of research, it seems to hold promise as a way of identifying persons at risk, both for an initial episode and for recurrent episodes.

Disturbances in Sleep and Other Biological Rhythms

Although findings of sleep disturbances in depressed patients have existed as long as depression has been studied, only relatively recently have some of these findings been linked to more general disturbances in biological rhythms. These links provide some of today's most interesting biologically based etiological hypotheses.

Sleep is characterized by five stages that occur in a relatively invariant sequence throughout the night (Stages 1 to 4 of non-REM sleep, and REM sleep). REM sleep (rapid eye movement sleep) is characterized by rapid eye movements and dreaming, as well as other bodily changes; the first REM period does not usually begin until near the end of the first sleep cycle, about 75 to 80 minutes into sleep. Depressed patients, especially those with melancholic features, show a variety of sleep problems, ranging from early morning awakening, periodic awakening during the night (poor sleep maintenance), and, for some, difficulty falling asleep. Such problems occur in about 80 percent of hospitalized depressed patients and about 50 percent of depressed outpatients. Moreover, research using EEG recordings has found that many depressed patients enter the first period of REM sleep after only 60 minutes or less of sleep (i.e., less than the typical 75 to 80 minutes) and also show greater amounts of REM sleep early in the night than are seen in nondepressed persons. Because this early period of the night is when most deep sleep (Stages 3 and 4) usually occurs, the depressed person also receives a lower than normal *amount* of deep sleep. These findings suggest disturbances in both the overall sleep-wake cycle and the REM sleep rhythm (Shelton et al., 1991; Thase & Howland, 1995). Some of these sleep disturbances remain even when the depression remits, and one study found that some of them are present in people who are at high genetic risk for depression (Lauer et al., 1995).

Circadian Rhythms Humans have other circadian (24-hour, or daily) rhythms besides those of the sleep cycle, including body temperature and secretion of cortisol, thyroid-stimulating hormone, and melatonin (a hormone secreted during the dark by the pineal gland at the base of the brain). Some of these circadian rhythms are controlled by two related central "oscillators," which act like internal biological clocks.

Research has found some abnormalities in all of these rhythms in depressed patients, although not all depressed patients show abnormalities in all the rhythms (Shelton et al., 1991; Thase & Howland, 1995). There is currently no agreement about the exact nature of the dysfunctions, but there seems to be increasing agreement that some kind of circadian rhythm dysfunction is not just a symptom of depression but may actually play a causal role in many of the clinical features of depression. Indeed, some theorists have even gone so far as to propose that the primary biological disturbance in depression is in the regulation of the circadian system, with alterations in neurotransmitters occurring as a secondary consequence to the disturbed rhythms (Goodwin & Jamison, 1990; Healy & Williams, 1988). All of these theories need considerably more research to determine how valid they are.

Sunlight and Seasons A rather different kind of rhythm abnormality or disturbance may be seen in the subtype of unipolar depression known as *seasonal affective disorder,* discussed earlier. In this subtype of mood disorder, most patients seem to be responsive to the total quantity of available light in the environment (Oren & Rosenthal, 1992), with a majority (but not all) becoming depressed in the fall and winter and normalizing in the spring and summer (Wehr et al., 1986; Whybrow, 1997). Research in animals has also documented that many seasonal variations in basic functions such as sleep, activity, and appetite are related to the amount of light in a 24-hour period (which except near the equator is much greater in summer than in winter). Depressed patients who fit the seasonal pattern usually show increased appetite and hypersomnia rather than decreased appetite and insomnia (Dalgleish, Rosen, & Marks, 1996). They also have clear disturbances in their circadian cycles, showing weaker 24-hour patterns than normal individuals (Teicher et al., 1997). There is a good deal of research on patients with seasonal affective disorder demonstrating the therapeutic use of controlled exposure to light, even artificial light (Dalgleish et al., 1996; Oren & Rosenthal, 1992). The mechanisms through which light therapy works for seasonal affective disorder are still not well understood, but it is quite possible that it may work by reestablishing normal biological rhythms (Fava & Rosenbaum, 1995).

Psychosocial Causal Factors

Psychological causal factors are also very important in most mood disorders. However, it is important to remember that biological and psychosocial approaches to understanding the mood disorders can be quite compatible, because in many ways they are simply working at different levels of analysis. As discussed in Chapter 2, psychological and behavioral factors implicated in causing depression ultimately are reducible to a set of biological events occurring in the brain and central nervous system, even if how this occurs is not yet completely understood.

Stressful Life Events as Causal Factors Psychosocial stressors are known to be involved in the onset of a variety of disorders, ranging from some of the anxiety disorders to schizophrenia, but nowhere has their role been more carefully studied than in the case of unipolar depression (e.g., Kessler, 1997a). Indeed, many investigators have been impressed with the high incidence of stressful life events that apparently serve as precipitating factors for unipolar depression (Kessler, 1997a). The most frequently encountered of these precipitating circumstances include the following:

- Situations that tend to lower self-esteem, such as being fired or failing an important exam.
- The thwarting of an important goal or the posing of an insoluble dilemma, such as being told the fellowship you were counting on to support you in graduate school is no longer available.
- Developing a physical disease or abnormality that activates ideas of deterioration or death, such as being diagnosed with cancer.
- Several stressors occurring in a series, such as the breakup of an important romantic relationship followed by doing poorly at school or work.
- Insidious stressors unrecognized as such by the affected person, such as living with a depressed or physically disabled person who needs a lot of care.

Perhaps not surprisingly, separations from people important in one's life (through divorce, for example) are strongly associated with depression (Kessler, 1997a). Another serious stressor that has been the focus of study only fairly recently is caregiving to a spouse with a debilitating disease such as Alzheimer's (formerly known as senility), which is known to be associated with the onset of both major depression and generalized anxiety disorder for the caregiver (e.g., Russo et al., 1995). Finally, depressed people sometimes generate stressful life events, in part as a by-product of their depressed state (e.g., Davila et al., 1995; Hammen, 1991). For example, depression is associated with poor interpersonal problem solving (such as resolving conflicts with a spouse or child), which in turn leads to higher levels of interpersonal stress, which in turn lead to further symptoms of depression. This problem-solving difficulty may also involve failure to keep up with routine tasks such as paying bills, which may result in getting in trouble with the telephone or electric company or the Internal Revenue Service.

Brown and Harris (1978) estimated that stressful life events played a causal role in the depression of about 50 percent of their subjects. In another sophisticated study, Dohrenwend and colleagues (1986) found that depressed patients had more negative life events of three types in the year before the onset of their depression than did nondepressed controls: physical illness and injury, fateful loss events (such as death or divorce), and events that disrupted the social network (such as having to move to a new state because of one's job). Kessler's review (1997a) of this literature also suggests that the relationship between stressful life events and depression is much stronger in people who have had one or more previous episodes than in those who are having their first onset.

Chronic Strains Whether mildly stressful events and chronic strains are also associated with the onset of depression is more controversial. Some of the most sophisticated studies have found that minor stressful events are not associated with the onset of clinical depression and chronic strains only occasionally are, but other studies have found such associations to exist (e.g., Bebbington et al., 1988; Dohrenwend et al., 1995; Lewinsohn, Hoberman, & Rosenbaum, 1988). One excellent review of the literature concluded that chronic stressors (such as poverty) and minor stressful events may be associated with an increase in depressive symptoms but probably not with major depression (Monroe & Simons, 1991).

Individual Differences in Responses to Stressors If we take the position—and the available research data seem to justify doing so—that some people are constitutionally more prone than others to develop mood disorders, then it would seem reasonable to suppose that such high-risk persons are more susceptible to the effects of severely stressful events. Some evidence has shown that, at least for women, those at genetic risk for depression not only experienced more stressful life events (Kendler & Karkowski-Shuman, 1997), but were also more sensitive to them (Kendler et al., 1995). That is, those at genetic risk are three times more likely than those not at genetic risk to respond to severely stressful life events with depression. However, there is also evidence for the idea that a large percentage of the population (perhaps half) is at risk for depression if exposed to one or more severely stressful life events (Monroe & Simons, 1991). For example, Brown and Harris (1978) found that among depressed women, more than 60 percent (compared with about 20 percent of nondepressed women) had experienced one or more such life events in the past 2 to 6 months. Looked at from a different perspective, with one severely stressful life event, the odds were about 50/50 of becoming depressed, with two such events, the odds were about 75/25 of becoming depressed, and with three or more such events, 100 percent of the women became depressed (although there was a very small sample in this category). This suggests that nearly any person who experiences a series of misfortunes can become clinically depressed.

If a woman living in poverty is already genetically at risk for depression, the stresses associated with living in poverty may be especially likely to precipitate a major depression.

How Stressors Act One way in which stressors may act is through their effects on biochemical and hormonal balances, and on biological rhythms. Whybrow (1997), in a summary of research in this area, suggested that psychosocial stressors may cause long-term changes in brain functioning and that these changes may play a role in the development of mood disorders. Essentially the same point has been made by other leading researchers in the field (Akiskal, 1979; Thase, Frank, & Kupfer, 1985; Thase & Howland, 1995).

Types of Diathesis-Stress Models for Unipolar Depression We can now turn to the more general question of how stress interacts with various types of vulnerability factors to produce depression. As noted in

solute certainty that an important bad outcome was going to occur (or that a highly desired good outcome was not going to occur). For some people, having such a hopelessness expectancy may by itself lead to depression, although this may be true for only a subset of depressives.

Research is currently testing this theory. A major longitudinal prospective study of college students who are hypothesized to be at high risk for unipolar depression because they have a pessimistic attributional style and have dysfunctional beliefs is beginning to yield evidence quite supportive of some of the major tenets of the theory (Alloy, Abramson, et al., 1999). For example, students in the high-risk group were seven times more likely to develop an episode of major depression in a 2-year follow-up period than were those in the low-risk group. Moreover, the high-risk students who also had a tendency to ruminate about their negative thoughts and moods were even more likely to become depressed than were the nonruminators. (See also Lynd-Stevenson, 1996, for related results.) Although this research is still preliminary, the hopelessness theory, like the other cognitive theories, is likely to remain a significant area of research for the foreseeable future.

People without social support networks are more prone to depression when faced with major stressors. Depressed people also have smaller and less supportive social support networks while they are depressed and to some extent even after their depression has remitted.

Interpersonal Effects of Mood Disorders Although there is no interpersonal theory of depression that is as clearly articulated as are the cognitive theories, there has nevertheless been a considerable amount of research in the past two decades on interpersonal factors in depression. As we will see, interpersonal problems and social skills deficits may well play a causal role in at least some cases of depression. In addition, depression creates many interpersonal difficulties—with strangers and friends as well as with family members (Hammen, 1991, 1995). We will start by discussing the way in which interpersonal problems can play a causal role in depression.

Lack of Social Support and Social Skills Deficits We noted earlier that Brown and Harris (1978) had found that women without a close confiding relationship were more vulnerable to depression. Since that time, many more studies have supported the idea that people who lack social support are more vulnerable to becoming depressed and that depressed individuals have smaller and less supportive social networks (e.g., Gotlib & Hammen, 1992; Holohan & Moos, 1991). These restricted social networks seem to precede the onset of depression, and although depressed persons may have more social contact when their symptoms remit, their social networks are still more restricted than those of never-depressed persons. In addition, many people suffering from depression have social skills deficits. For example, they seem to speak more slowly and monotonously and to maintain less eye contact; they are also poorer than nondepressed people at solving interpersonal problems (e.g., Gotlib & Hammen, 1992).

The Effects of Depression on Others Not only do depressed people have interpersonal problems, but their own behavior inadvertently seems to make these problems worse. For example, the behavior of a depressed individual often places others in the position of providing sympathy, support, and care. Such positive reinforcement does not necessarily follow, however. Depressive behavior can, and over time frequently does, elicit negative feelings and rejection in other people, including strangers, roommates, and spouses (Coyne, 1976; see also Gotlib & Hammen, 1992). In fact, merely being around a depressed person may induce depressed feelings or negative affect in others (Howes, Hokanson, & Loewenstein, 1985; Joiner & Metalsky, 1995) and may make a nondepressed person less willing to interact again with the depressed person. The ultimate result can be a downwardly spiraling relationship from which the nondepressed person finally withdraws, making the depressed person feel worse (e.g., Coyne, 1976; Joiner & Metalsky, 1995).

Marriage and Family Life Interpersonal aspects of depression have also been carefully studied in the context of marital and family relationships. Gotlib and Hammen (1992) reviewed evidence that between one-third and one-half of all couples experiencing marital distress include at least one partner with clinical depression. In addition, it is known that marital distress predicts a poor prognosis for a depressed spouse whose symptoms have remitted. That is, a person whose depression clears up is more likely to relapse if he or she has an unsatisfying marriage (Butzlaff & Hooley, 1998; Hooley & Teasdale, 1989).

As already noted, the high co-occurrence of marital distress and depression may sometimes occur because the depressed partner's behavior triggers negative affect in his or her spouse along the lines discussed above for strangers and roommates. But there is also evidence that marital distress can lead to depression, because marital distress often precedes a depressive episode and is frequently identified as a precipitant of depression and as a reason for seeking treatment (see Gotlib & Hammen, 1992). Thus the evidence suggests both that marital distress can lead to depression and that depression can lead to marital distress. Depression also all too often sets the occasion for marital violence.

The effects of one family member's depression extend to infants, children, and adolescents as well. Parental depression puts children at high risk for many problems, but especially for depression (Murray et al., 1996; Puig-Antich et al., 1989). For adolescent girls, it also increases the risk for conduct problems (Davies & Windle, 1997). There are many studies documenting the damaging effects of negative interactional patterns between depressed mothers and their children. For example, depressed mothers show more friction and have less playful, mutually rewarding interactions with their children (e.g., Murray & Cooper, 1997). Indeed, most evidence points to the maternal interactional style rather than the depressive symptoms per se as playing the most decisive role in the negative outcomes on infants and children (Murray & Cooper, 1997).

Summary of Psychosocial Causal Factors There are many different psychological theories regarding what causes unipolar depression, ranging from the psychodynamic to the cognitive and interpersonal. Some, such as Beck's cognitive theory and the reformulated helplessness and hopelessness theories, are clearly formulated as diathesis-stress models, where the diathesis is seen as cognitive in nature. The psychodynamic and interpersonal approaches both emphasize the importance of early experiential variables (such as the quality of the parent-child relationship) in determining vulnerability to depression. Each of these theories captures interesting aspects of the causal pathways to depression, and given the probable heterogeneity of unipolar depression, it is unlikely that any one theory will ever successfully explain all of the variance regarding who does and who does not become depressed when faced with comparable stressful life circumstances.

In a large proportion of couples experiencing marital distress, at least one of the partners is clinically depressed. Marital distress also predicts a relatively poor prognosis for the depressed partner.

Sociocultural Causal Factors

The prevalence of mood disorders seems to vary considerably among different societies: In some, mania is more frequent, while in others, depression is more common. However, it has been difficult to provide conclusive evidence of this difference because of various methodological problems, including widely differing diagnostic practices across cultures, and because of considerable cross-cultural variation in the symptoms of depression (Kaelber, Moul, & Farmer, 1995). Moreover, much of the research conducted in this area has not made clear-cut distinctions between unipolar and bipolar disorders, which also renders conclusions difficult. Nevertheless, we will review some of the sociocultural factors affecting depression.

Cross-Cultural Differences in Depressive Symptoms Marsella's (1980) early comprehensive review of the cross-cultural literature on depression left little doubt that this disorder often takes a different form from that customarily seen in American society and in other Western cultures. For example, in some non-Western cultures such as China, where rates of depression are low, the psychological symptoms of depression are often not present. Instead, people exhibit so-called somatic and vegetative manifestations, such as sleep disturbance, loss of appetite, weight loss, and loss of sexual interest (Kleinman, 1986; see also Goodwin & Jamison, 1990). Interestingly, in some such cultures, there is not even a concept of depression

HIGHLIGHT 6.4

Depression and Marital Violence

It has long been known that mood-disordered persons have an enhanced risk for engaging in violence, including family violence. Until fairly recently, however, virtually all of that enhanced risk was thought to be related to the lack of control and disinhibition associated with manic or hypomanic episodes. Continuing research has called that view into question and implicated depressive episodes in the occurrence of much violence, specifically domestic violence (e.g., Maiuro et al., 1988).

Men who attack their partners violently (some women attack men, but usually less violently, cf., Jacobson et al., 1994; O'Leary, 1995) commonly do so as a means of attempting, by inspiring fear in the partner, to control a situation that they perceive as threatening their "proprietary" assumptions about the partnership (e.g., Maiuro et al., 1988; Murphy, Meyer, & O'Leary, 1994; Wilson & Daly, 1996). Such men tend to be highly emotionally dependent on their partners, despite appearances to the contrary, and they tolerate poorly signs of a partner's autonomy. Their underlying sense of inadequacy fuels their desperate attempts to maintain control over the partnership. Too often, the result is a violent attack (Murphy, Meyer, & O'Leary, 1994).

Many men who experience marital distress and become depressed tend to be "unsuccessful," either chronically or in response to recent reversals of fortune. Self-perceived "failure," in terms of conventional male values such as providing for the economic needs of the family, is thus often present (Pan, Neidig, & O'Leary, 1994; Vinokur, Price, & Caplan, 1996). Moreover, as they get depressed, many men turn to alcohol or other disinhibiting drugs as a type of "self-medication" to reduce stress and relieve depression, thus making it even more likely that they will impulsively attempt a violent solution to end their acute despair (Leonard & Senchak, 1996; Pan, Neidig, & O'Leary, 1994). Like other dysfunctional reactions to a deteriorating relationship, this one, too, almost always makes matters worse.

The causal relationships among depression, marital distress, and familial violence thus appear to be mutually reinforcing and multidirectional in nature. In fact, the victims of physical abuse are themselves likely to become clinically depressed (O'Leary, 1995), thus diminishing their ability to take effective action. Once these behaviors are established as a pattern, it becomes extremely difficult, even with professional help, to disentangle cause from effect and to restore mutual understanding, respect, trust, and effective nonviolent functioning. Unfortunately, as pointed out by Fruzzetti (1996), the DSM, which recognizes disorders as exclusively "within" individuals, provides no adequate diagnostic recognition of this common scenario.

Contemporary research suggests that there is often evidence of problematic early attachment processes among the perpetrators and victims of domestic violence. Based on the work of Bowlby (1980) in England, psychologists have developed apparently good ways of measuring adults' attachment propensities (Griffin & Bartholomew, 1994), usually differentiating among three "levels" having significant implications for adult relationships. A person with a *secure* attachment pattern comfortably "connects with" and engages others at optimal levels of intimacy and mutual autonomy. *Insecure* attachment patterns include the *anxious-ambivalent* pattern, involving high intimacy needs mixed with anxiety and conflictful, unstable attachment, and the *avoidant* pattern, which involves an active distancing of the self from others. The general hypothesis is that partners with insecure attachment patterns, particularly the anxious-ambivalent variety, are at significantly increased risk for marital distress, depression, and domestic violence. In support of this hypothesis, Maiuro and colleagues (1988) found evidence of disturbed attachment patterns in a sample of domestically violent men. Moreover, Roberts, Gotlib, and Kassell (1996) have demonstrated what appears to be a causal relationship between attachment insecurity and the emergence of depressive symptoms. As already noted, depressive symptoms in the marital context are associated with a substantially enhanced risk of domestic violence, which sometimes proves deadly. ■

In some cultures, the concept of depression as we know it simply does not exist. For example, Australian aborigines who are "depressed" show none of the guilt and self-abnegation commonly seen in people from industrialized societies. They also do not show suicidal tendencies, but instead are more likely to vent their hostilities onto others rather than onto themselves.

that is reasonably comparable to our own. The psychological components that seem to be missing are the feelings of guilt and self-recrimination that are so commonly seen in the "developed" countries (Kidson & Jones, 1968; Lorr & Klett, 1968; Zung, 1969). In fact, among several groups of Australian aborigines, Kidson and Jones (1968) found not only an absence of guilt and self-recrimination in depressive reactions, but also no incidence of attempted or actual suicide. In connection with the latter finding, they stated, "The absence of suicide can perhaps be explained as a consequence of strong fears of death and also because of the tendency to act out and project hostile impulses" (p. 415). That is, these aborigines were more likely to vent their hostility onto others than onto themselves through suicide.

A Belief in Self-Sufficiency In spite of the difficulties of drawing definitive conclusions about cross-cultural differences, a number of interesting cross-cultural findings raise provocative questions about the kinds of factors that promote high versus low rates of mood disorders. For example, in early studies of East Africans, Carothers (1947, 1951, 1959) found manic disorders to be fairly common but depressive disorders relatively rare—the opposite of their incidence in the United States. He attributed the low incidence of depressive disorders to the fact that in traditional African cultures individuals have not usually been held personally responsible for failures and misfortunes. The culture of the Kenya Africans Carothers (1947, 1951, 1959) observed may be taken as fairly typical in this respect. Their behavior was largely group-determined, and therefore they were not confronted with problems of self-sufficiency, choice, and responsibility, which are so prominent in Western cultures. Setting high achievement goals was discouraged (so there was little room for disappointment or failure in this regard). They were humble toward the harsh environment they lived in and always expected the worst from it. Responsibility and blame for misfortunes were attributed to outside forces; because the individuals weren't personally responsible, there were few opportunities for self-devaluation. Needless to say, much has changed in Africa since Carothers made these observations, and more recent data suggest a quite different picture. In general, it appears that as societies take on the ways of Western culture, their members become more prone to developing Western-style mood disorders (Marsella, 1980).

Relieving Losses In the few societies relatively untouched by Western culture, such as the Kaluli, a primitive tribe in New Guinea studied by Scheiffelin (1984), it is still very difficult to detect any sign of depression. A summary of Scheiffelin's work by Seligman (1990) provides interesting suggestions regarding why this might be the case:

> Briefly, the Kaluli do not seem to have despair, hopelessness, depression, or suicide in the way we know it. What they do have is quite interesting. If you lose something valuable, such as your pig, you have a right to recompense. There are rituals (such as dancing and screaming at the neighbor who you think killed the pig) that are recognized by the society. When you demand recompense for loss, either the neighbor or the whole tribe takes note of your condition and usually recompenses you one way or another. The point I want to make here is that reciprocity between the culture and the individual when loss occurs provides strong buffers against loss becoming helplessness and hopelessness. I want to suggest that a society that prevents loss from becoming hopelessness, and that prevents sadness from becoming despair, breaks up the process of depression. Societies that promote, as ours does, the transition from loss to helplessness to hopelessness, promote depression. (Seligman, 1990, pp. 4–5)

Demographic Differences in the United States In our own society, the role of sociocultural factors in mood disorders is gradually becoming evident. Results from the large Epidemiological Catchment Area study conducted at multiple sites in the United States in the early 1980s were informative. In general, this study did not find any substantial racial differences, although the prevalence seemed to be slightly lower among blacks and Hispanics than among non-Hispanic whites (Regier et al., 1993). For unipolar disorders, there are a number of studies showing that the poor have higher rates of major depression and that single and divorced persons tend to have higher rates of unipolar depression than do those who are married, although, as we have already seen, marital distress is highly associated with depression (Kaelber et al., 1995).

IN REVIEW

- What are the major features that differentiate dysthymia, adjustment disorder with depressed mood, and major depressive disorder?
- What are three common subtypes of major depressive disorder?
- Distinguish between recurrence and relapse.
- Summarize the biological, psychosocial, and sociocultural causal factors for unipolar mood disorders.
- What is the role of stressful life events in unipolar depression, and how do different diathesis-stress models account for their effects?

BIPOLAR DISORDERS

As we have seen, despite their seeming opposition, depression and mania are sometimes closely related; and some people even experience both states simultaneously. As with the unipolar disorders, the severity of disturbance in bipolar disorders ranges from mild to moderate to severe. In the mild to moderate range, the disorder is known as *cyclothymia,* and in the moderate to severe range, the disorder is known as *bipolar disorder.*

Cyclothymia

As we have noted, mania is in some ways the opposite of depression. It is a state involving excessive levels of excitement, elation, or euphoria, often liberally mixed with inflated self-esteem or grandiosity and the assumption of great powers. Periods of intense irritability are also often intermixed (Whybrow, 1997). In its milder forms, this state is known as **hypomania.** It has long been recognized that some people are subject to cyclical mood changes with relative excesses of hypomania and depression that, though substantial, are not disabling. These, in essence, are the symptoms of the disorder known as **cyclothymia** (see Table 6.1).

The DSM-IV-TR definition of cyclothymia describes the pattern of symptoms like a less serious version of major bipolar disorder, minus certain extreme symptoms and psychotic features, such as delusions, and minus the marked impairment caused by full-blown manic or major depressive episodes. In the depressed phase of cyclothymia, a person's mood is dejected, and he or she experiences a distinct loss of interest or pleasure in usual activities and pastimes. In addition, the person may exhibit sleep irregularity (too much or too little); low energy levels; feelings of inadequacy; decreased efficiency, productivity, talkativeness, and cognitive sharpness; social withdrawal; restriction of pleasurable activities, including a relative lack of interest in sex; a pessimistic and brooding attitude; and tearfulness. An individual with cyclothymia does not, however, experience enough of the symptoms, or experience them persistently enough, to qualify for a diagnosis of major depression (similar to someone with dysthymia, except without the duration criterion).

Symptoms of the hypomanic phase of cyclothymia are essentially the opposite of the symptoms of dysthymia, except that the sleep disturbance is invariably one of an apparent decreased need for sleep. As in the case of bipolar disorder, no obvious precipitating circumstance may be evident for the abrupt change in mood, and an affected person may have significant periods between episodes in which he or she functions in a relatively adaptive manner. To qualify for a diagnosis of cyclothymia, however, there must be at least a 2-year span during which there are numerous periods with both hypomanic and depressed symptoms (only 1 year is required for adolescents and children).

The following case illustrates cyclothymia.

Case Study **A Cyclothymic Car Salesman** • A 29-year-old car salesman was referred by his current girlfriend, a psychiatric nurse, who suspected he had a mood disorder, even though the patient was reluctant to admit that he might be a "moody" person. According to him, since the age of 14, he has experienced repeated alternating cycles that he terms "good times and bad times." During a "bad" period, usually lasting 4 to 7 days, he oversleeps 10 to 14 hours daily, lacks energy, confidence, and motivation—"just vegetating," as he puts it. Often he abruptly shifts, characteristically upon waking up in the morning, to a 3-to-4-day stretch of overconfidence, heightened social awareness, promiscuity, and sharpened thinking—"things would flash in my mind."

hypomania Mild form of mania.

cyclothymia Mild mood disorder characterized by cyclical periods of hypomanic and depressive symptoms that are not disabling.

At such times, he indulges in alcohol to enhance the experience, but also to help him sleep. Occasionally the "good" periods last 7 to 10 days, but culminate in irritable and hostile outbursts, which often herald the transition back to another period of "bad" days. He admits to frequent use of marijuana, which he claims helps him "adjust" to daily routines.

In school, A's and B's alternated with C's and D's, with the result that the patient was considered a bright student whose performance was mediocre overall because of "unstable motivation." As a car salesman, his performance has also been uneven, with "good days" canceling out the "bad days"; yet even during his "good days," he is sometimes perilously argumentative with customers and loses sales that appeared sure. Although considered a charming man in many social circles, he alienates friends when he is hostile and irritable. He typically accumulates social obligations during the "bad" days and takes care of them all at once on the first day of a "good" period. (From Spitzer et al., 1994, pp. 155–156.)

In short, cyclothymia consists of mood swings that, at either extreme, are clearly maladaptive but of insufficient intensity to merit being designated as a major disorder.

Bipolar Disorder

Although recurrent cycles of mania and melancholia were recognized as early as the sixth century, it remained for Kraepelin, in 1899, to introduce the term *manic-depressive insanity* and to clarify the clinical picture. Kraepelin described the disorder as a series of attacks of elation and depression, with periods of relative normality in between, and a generally favorable prognosis. Today, DSM-IV-TR calls this illness **bipolar disorder.**

Bipolar disorder is distinguished from major depression by at least one episode of mania. Any given episode is classified as depressive, manic, or mixed, according to its predominant features. The depressed or manic classification is self-explanatory. A mixed episode is characterized by symptoms of both manic and major depressive episodes, whether the symptoms are intermixed or alternate rapidly every few days. Such cases were once thought to be relatively rare but are increasingly recognized as relatively common (Cassidy et al., 1998).

Even though a patient may be exhibiting only manic symptoms, the implicit assumption is that all mania-like behaviors must be part of cyclothymia or bipolar disorder. Thus, there are no officially recognized "unipolar" manic or hypomanic counterparts to dysthymia or major depression. Like unipolar major depression, bipolar disorder is typically a recurrent disorder. The recurrences can be seasonal in nature, in which case **bipolar disorder with a seasonal pattern** is diagnosed. Although most patients with bipolar disorder experience periods of remission when they are relatively symptom-free, as many as 20 to 30 percent continue to experience significant impairment (occupational and/or interpersonal) and mood lability. Moreover, a few chronic patients continue to meet diagnostic criteria over long periods of time, even years, sometimes despite the successive application of all standard treatments.

Features of Bipolar Disorder The features of the depressive form of bipolar disorder are usually clinically indistinguishable from those of major depression (e.g., American Psychiatric Association, 1994; Perris, 1992). The essential difference is that these depressive episodes alternate with manic ones. In about two-thirds of cases, the manic episodes either immediately precede or immediately follow a depressive episode; in other cases, the manic and depressive episodes are separated by intervals of relatively normal functioning. Before modern treatments were available, the periods of disorder often gradually lengthened over a person's lifetime, leaving the person in one phase or the other of the illness nearly all the time (Whybrow, 1997).

DSM-IV identified another a form of bipolar disorder called *Bipolar II disorder,* in which the person may not experience full-blown manic episodes, but has experienced clear-cut hypomanic episodes (as in cyclothymia). That this is indeed a distinct disorder is suggested by findings that Bipolar II disorder evolves into Bipolar I disorder (the type already described, with full-blown manic episodes—usually called simply "bipolar disorder") in less than 5 percent of cases (Coryell, Endicott, & Keller, 1987). If Bipolar II disorder were simply a milder early version of Bipolar I disorder, one would expect a much higher percentage of cases of Bipolar II to evolve into Bipolar I. Figure 6.3 illustrates the different kinds of patterns of manic and depressive episodes that can be seen in bipolar disorders.

Manic symptoms in bipolar disorder tend to be extreme, and there is significant impairment of occupational and social functioning. A person who experiences a manic episode has a markedly elevated, euphoric, and expansive mood, often interrupted by occasional outbursts of irritability or even violence—particularly when others refuse

bipolar disorder Severe mood disorder in which a person experiences both manic and depressive episodes.

bipolar disorder with a seasonal pattern Bipolar disorder in which recurrences are seasonal in nature.

Many highly creative people are believed to have had bipolar disorder, going through periods of intense productivity in their creative medium during manic phases and often through unproductive periods when clinically depressed. Two such individuals are the German composer Robert Schumann (1810–1856) and the English novelist Virginia Woolf (1882–1941). Schumann was committed to a mental asylum in 1854 and died there 2 years later. Woolf committed suicide by drowning herself.

to go along with the manic person's antics and schemes. This mood must persist for at least a week to qualify for a diagnosis. In addition, three or more of the following symptoms must also occur in the same time period: A notable increase in goal-directed activity may occur, which sometimes may appear as an unrelievable restlessness, and mental activity may also speed up, so that the person may evidence a "flight of ideas" or thoughts that "race." Dis-

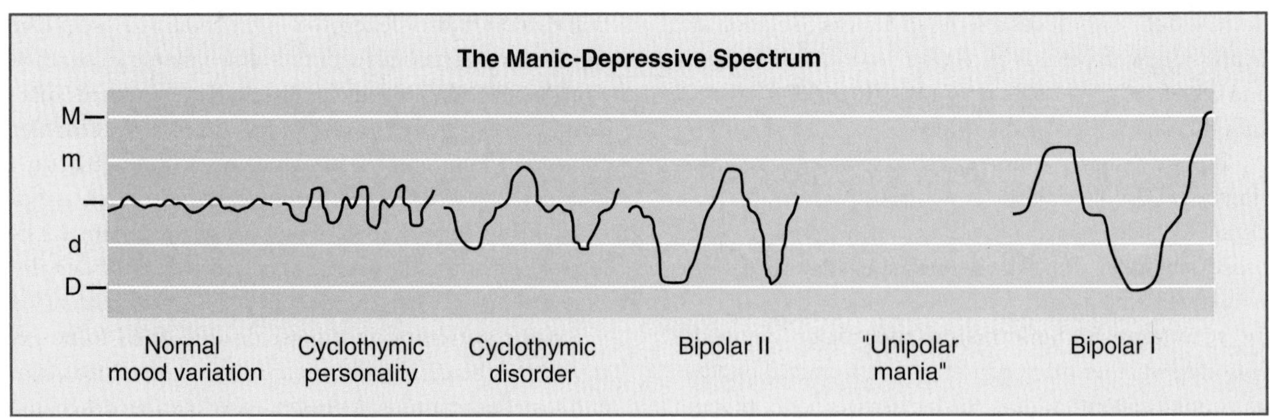

FIGURE 6.3 THE MANIC-DEPRESSIVE SPECTRUM

There is a spectrum of bipolarity in moods. All of us have our ups and downs, which are part of normal mood variation. People with a cyclothymic personality have more marked and regular mood swings, and people with cyclothymic disorder go through periods during which they meet the criteria for dysthymia (except for the 2-year duration), and other periods when they meet criteria for hypomania. People with Bipolar II disorder have periods of major depression as well as periods of hypomania. Unipolar mania is an extremely rare condition. Finally, people with Bipolar I disorder have periods of major depression and periods of mania. (Cyclothymic personality and "unipolar mania" are not officially recognized as diagnostic categories.)

Source: From Frederick K. Goodwin and Kay J. Jamison, *Manic Depressive Illness.* Copyright © 1990 Oxford University Press, Inc. Used by permission of Oxford University Press.

tractibility, high levels of verbal output in speech or in writing, and a severely decreased need for sleep may occur. In addition, inflated self-esteem is common and, when severe, becomes frankly delusional, so that the person harbors feelings of enormous grandeur and power. Personal and cultural inhibitions loosen, and the person may indulge in foolish ventures with a high potential for painful consequences, such as foolish business ventures, major spending sprees, and sexual indiscretions. Finally, as noted earlier, a study of 237 manic patients also revealed that during manic episodes some patients report intermixed symptoms of depressed mood, anxiety, guilt, and suicidal thoughts (Cassidy et al., 1998).

The following conversation illustrates a manic episode of moderate severity. The patient is a 46-year-old woman.

Case Study **Therapy Session with a Moderately Manic Patient**

DOCTOR: Hello, how are you today?

PATIENT: Fine, fine, and how are you, Doc? You're looking pretty good. I never felt better in my life. Could I go for a schnapps now. Say, you're new around here, I never saw you before—and not bad! How's about you and me stepping out tonight if I can get that sour old battleship of a nurse to give me back my dress. It's low cut and it'll wow 'em. Even in this old rag, all the doctors give me the eye. You know I'm a model. Yep, I was number one—used to dazzle them in New York, London, and Paris. Hollywood has been angling with me for a contract.

DOCTOR: Is that what you did before you came here?

PATIENT: I was a society queen . . . entertainer of kings and presidents. I've got five grown sons and I wore out three husbands getting them . . . about ready for a couple of more now. There's no woman like me, smart, brainy, beautiful, and sexy. You can see I don't believe in playing myself down. If you are good and know you're good, you have to speak out, and I know what I've got.

DOCTOR: Why are you in this hospital?

PATIENT: That's just the trouble. My husbands never could understand me. I was too far above them. I need someone like me with savoir faire you know, somebody that can get around, intelligent, lots on the ball. Say, where can I get a schnapps around here—always like one before dinner. Someday I'll cook you a meal. I've got special recipes like you never ate before . . . sauces, wines, desserts. Boy, it's making me hungry. Say, have you got anything for me to do around here? I've been showing these slowpokes how to make up beds, but I want something more in line with my talents.

DOCTOR: What would you like to do?

PATIENT: Well, I'm thinking of organizing a show, singing, dancing, jokes. I can do it all myself, but I want to know what you think about it. I'll bet there's some schnapps in the kitchen. I'll look around later. You know what we need here . . . a dance at night. I could play the piano, and teach them the latest steps. Wherever I go, I'm the life of the party.

This case is particularly illustrative of the inflated self-esteem characteristic of a manic person. The erotic suggestiveness and impatience with routine seen here are also common features of manic episodes.

Because a person who is depressed cannot be diagnosed as bipolar unless he or she has exhibited at least one manic episode in the past, many people with bipolar disorder whose initial episode or episodes are depressive will be misdiagnosed at first, and possibly throughout their lives (if no manic episodes are observed). Although estimates vary widely across studies, one review estimated that about 10 to 13 percent of people who have an initial major depressive episode will later have a manic or hypomanic episode and at that time will be diagnosed as having Bipolar I or II disorder (Akiskal et al., 1995).

Such unfortunate misdiagnoses are important because treatments of choice differ for unipolar and bipolar depression. Moreover, evidence suggests that some antidepressant drugs used to treat what is thought to be unipolar depression may actually precipitate manic episodes in patients who actually have as yet undetected bipolar disorder, thus worsening the course of the illness (Goodwin & Ghaemi, 1998; Whybrow, 1997). On the other hand, misdiagnosis is automatically prevented if a person first has manic symptoms: By the DSM definition, this would be a bipolar disorder.

On average, people with bipolar disorder suffer from more episodes during their lifetimes than do persons with unipolar disorder (although these episodes tend to be somewhat shorter). Indeed, according to DSM-IV, more than 90 percent of those who have had one manic episode go on to have further episodes (see also Coryell et al., 1995). As many as 5 to 10 percent of persons with bipolar disorder experience at least four episodes (either manic or depressive) every year, a pattern known as **rapid cycling.** In fact, those who go through periods of rapid cycling usually experience many more than four episodes a year; in

rapid cycling A pattern of bipolar disorder involving at least four manic or depressive episodes per year.

one treatment clinic for this condition, the average was 16 episodes a year (Whybrow, 1997). Rapid cycling is more common in women than men and is sometimes precipitated by taking certain kinds of antidepressants (Leibenluft, 1996; Whybrow, 1997). Fortunately, for many patients, rapid cycling is a temporary phenomenon and gradually disappears (Coryell et al., 1995).

Overall, the probabilities of "full recovery" from bipolar disorder (that is, being symptom-free for a period of 4 to 7 years) are discouraging. One 10-year prospective study of over 200 patients found that 24 percent had relapsed within 6 months of recovery, 77 percent had had at least one new episode within 4 years of recovery, and 82 percent had done so by 7 years (Coryell et al., 1995). Many of these recurrences occurred in spite of maintenance lithium therapy (discussed later).

Schizoaffective Disorder

Occasionally, clinicians are confronted with a patient whose mood disorder is as severe as those seen in major depression or bipolar disorder but whose mental and cognitive processes are so out of touch with reality as to suggest the presence of a schizophrenic psychosis (see Chapter 12). Such cases are likely to be diagnosed as **schizoaffective disorder** in DSM-IV-TR. To receive this diagnosis, a person must have a period of illness during which he or she meets criteria for both a major mood disorder (unipolar or bipolar) and at least two major symptoms of schizophrenia (such as hallucinations and delusions). However, during at least 2 weeks of the illness, the person must experience the schizophrenic symptoms in the absence of prominent mood symptoms, and he or she must meet criteria for a mood disorder for a substantial portion of the period of illness. In spite of its inclusion in the DSM, the diagnosis of schizoaffective disorder is a controversial one. Some clinicians believe that these persons are basically schizophrenic; others believe that they have primarily psychotic mood disorders; and still others consider schizoaffective disorder a distinct entity, with some good evidence supporting its validity as a separate category (Kendler et al., 1995).

The often severe disturbances of psychological functioning seen in these cases, such as mood-incongruent delusions and hallucinations, are indeed reminiscent of schizophrenic phenomena. Unlike schizophrenia, however, schizoaffective disorder tends to be highly episodic, with a relatively good prognosis for individual attacks and often with relatively lucid periods between episodes. Prognosis for full recovery for schizoaffective patients is probably better than for schizophrenic ones but considerably worse than for those with other mood disorders (Kendler et al., 1995; Winokur & Tsuang, 1996).

schizoaffective disorder Severe mood disorder accompanied by at least two major symptoms of schizophrenia, such as hallucinations and delusions.

Biological Causal Factors

As for the unipolar disorders, a host of causal factors have been posited for bipolar disorders over the past century. However, biological causal factors are clearly dominant, and the role of psychosocial causal factors has received significantly less attention in the literature.

Hereditary Factors Research shows that there is a significant genetic component to bipolar disorder, one that is stronger than for unipolar disorder. One summary of studies suggests that about 9 percent of the first-degree relatives of a person with a bipolar disorder can also be expected to have bipolar disorder (nine times the rate of the disorder in the general population) (Katz & McGuffin, 1993; Plomin et al., 1997). Twin studies also point to a genetic basis. One particularly good study by Bertelsen, Harvald, and Hauge (1977) estimated that monozygotic twins were over three times more likely to be concordant (67 percent) for a diagnosis of bipolar disorder than were dizygotic twins (20 percent). This study suggests that genes account for over 80 percent of the variance in the tendency to develop (that is, the liability for) bipolar disorder. This is higher than heritability estimates for unipolar disorder or any of the other major adult psychiatric disorders, including schizophrenia (Torrey et al., 1994).

Efforts to locate the chromosomal site of the gene or genes implicated in the transmission of bipolar disorder suggest that transmission is likely polygenic. Still no consistent support yet exists for any specific mode of genetic transmission of the bipolar disorders (e.g., Goodwin & Ghaemi, 1998; Plomin et al., 1997).

Biochemical Factors The early monoamine hypothesis for unipolar disorder discussed earlier was extended to bipolar disorder. The hypothesis was that if depression is caused by deficiencies of norepinephrine and/or serotonin, then perhaps mania is caused by excesses of these neurotransmitters. Although there is some evidence for increased norepinephrine activity during manic episodes, serotonin activity appears to be low in both depressive and manic phases. More recently, it has been suggested that norepinephrine, serotonin, and dopamine are all involved in regulating our mood states (Whybrow, 1997). Disturbances in the balance of these neurotransmitters seem to be the key to understanding bipolar disorder, a debilitating illness that can send its victims on an emotional rollercoaster, although exactly how is not yet clear (Goodwin & Jamison, 1990; Whybrow, 1997). Evidence for the role of dopamine stems in part from observations that addictive drugs often stimulate dopamine and the reward centers in the brain and produce manic-like behavior. Thus, in mania, both dopamine and norepinephrine appear to be elevated. This may explain why antipsychotic drugs (which lower dopamine levels) can be helpful in reducing the psychotic symptoms of mania (Whybrow, 1997).

Other Biological Causal Factors Some hormonal research on bipolar depression has focused on the hypothalamic-pituitary-adrenal axis. Bipolar patients, at least when depressed, show evidence of dysregulation of this axis, at about the same rate as do unipolar patients (Goodwin & Jamison, 1990). Many bipolar patients also have subtle but significant abnormalities in the functioning of the hypothalamic-pituitary-thyroid axis, and administration of thyroid hormone is known to make antidepressant drugs work better at times (Goodwin & Jamison, 1990; Whybrow, 1997). However, thyroid hormone (like some antidepressant drugs) can also precipitate manic episodes in bipolar patients (Wehr & Goodwin, 1987).

Considerable evidence also exists regarding disturbances in biological rhythms in bipolar disorder. During manic episodes, bipolar patients tend to sleep very little (seemingly by choice, not because of insomnia). During depressive episodes, they tend toward hypersomnia (too much sleep), but they do not appear to show the reduced latency to REM sleep seen in unipolar patients (Goodwin & Jamison, 1990; Whybrow, 1997). Bipolar disorder also sometimes shows a seasonal pattern, like unipolar disorder, suggesting disturbances of biological rhythms. Given the cyclic nature of the disorder itself, this focus on disturbances in biological rhythms holds promise for future integrative theories of the biological underpinnings of bipolar disorder. This is particularly true because bipolar patients seem especially sensitive to any changes in their daily cycles, which require resetting of their biological clocks (Whybrow, 1997).

With the modern technology of positron emission tomography (PET), it is possible to visualize variation in brain glucose metabolic rates in the same person when in both depressed and manic states. Whybrow (1997) summarized evidence from studies using PET and other neuroimaging techniques: Whereas blood flow to the left prefrontal cortex is reduced during depression, it is reduced in the right frontal and temporal regions during mania. During normal mood, blood flow across the two

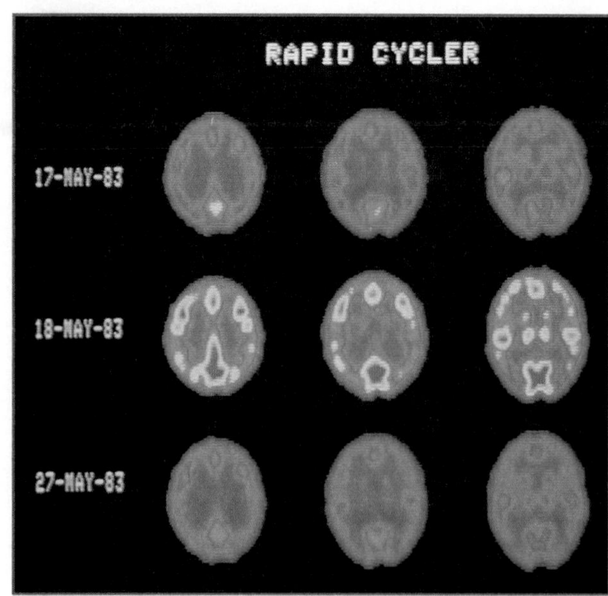

FIGURE 6.4 POSITRON EMISSION TOMOGRAPHY (PET) SCANS OF IDENTICAL PLANES OF THE BRAIN OF A RAPID-CYCLING BIPOLAR PATIENT

The top and bottom sets of scans were obtained on days when the patient was depressed; the middle set was obtained on a hypomanic day. Colors of scans correspond to glucose (sugar) metabolic rates in the respective brain areas, the reds and yellows representing high rates and the blues and greens low rates.

Source: Drs. Michael E. Phelps and John C. Mazziotta, UCLA School of Medicine

brain hemispheres is approximately equal. Thus, there are shifting patterns of brain activity during mania and during depressed and normal moods. Figure 6.4 presents PET scans of a person with rapid-cycling bipolar disorder, showing additional aspects of the differences in patterns of brain glucose metabolic rates during both manic and depressed phases.

Psychosocial Causal Factors

Stressful Life Events Early in the course of bipolar disorder, stressful life events preceding manic or depressive episodes may be precipitants, just as Kraepelin noted in his clinical observations (Goodwin & Jamison, 1990). It has long been argued that the manic and depressive episodes become more autonomous as the illness unfolds and do not usually seem to be precipitated by stressful events (e.g., Post, 1992). Some of these conclusions may be premature, however, given that most studies addressing this issue have relied on patients' memories of events before episodes, which may be unreliable (Johnson & Roberts, 1995). Several good prospective studies using the most sophisticated stress measurement techniques found a significant association between the occurrence of high levels of stress and the experience of manic, hypomanic, or depressive episodes. Moreover, stress seemed to play just as important a role in precipitating episodes for people who had had more episodes of illness as for those with fewer (Hammen, 1995; Swendsen et al., 1995). Indeed, one study even found that patients with more prior episodes were more likely to have episodes following major stressors than were patients with fewer prior episodes (Hammen & Gitlin, 1997).

How might stressful life events operate to increase the chance of relapse? One hypothesized mechanism is through the destabilizing effects that stressful life events may have on critical biological rhythms, which, as we already discussed, are strongly implicated in biological views on bipolar disorder. Although evidence in support of this idea is still preliminary, it appears to be a promising hypothesis (Johnson & Roberts, 1995).

One interesting example of the apparent role of aversive life events as precipitating causes in bipolar attacks has been described by Ellicott and colleagues (1990, p. 1997).

Case Study **Life Changes and Bipolar Disorder** • Mr. A., a 30-year-old man, had been given a diagnosis of Bipolar I disorder at age 21. He had had two manic episodes and multiple minor depressions and hypomanic episodes before treatment at the affective disorders clinic. After entering the study, he remained asymptomatic on a regimen of lithium carbonate and had no severely threatening life events (those rated four or five on the objective threat scale) during the first 6 months of observations. Then the patient reported a severely threatening event that involved a month-long financial investigation at his workplace. Directly afterward he experienced a mild subsyndromal depression, which spontaneously resolved after 18 days. Several weeks later, however, Mr. A reported three severely threatening events over the course of a month, two of which were employment-related changes that jeopardized his job, and one of which involved a major estrangement from his live-in girlfriend. One week after these events, he had a 2-week manic episode, which was controlled on an outpatient basis with an increased dose of lithium and which subsided into hypomania that persisted over 3 months.

There is also some evidence that personality and cognitive variables may interact with stress in determining the likelihood of relapse. For example, one study found that bipolar individuals who were highly introverted or obsessional were especially responsive to stress (Swendsen et al., 1995). Another found that students who had a pessimistic attributional style and also had negative life events showed an increase in depressive symptoms whether they were bipolar or unipolar depressives (Alloy, Reilly-Harrington, & Fresco, 1997).

Psychodynamic Views According to psychodynamic theorists, manic and depressive disorders may be viewed as two different but related defense-oriented strategies for dealing with severe stress. Manic persons try to escape their difficulties by a "flight into reality"—that is, they try to avoid the pain of their inner lives through outer-world distractions. With a tremendous expenditure of energy, a manic person tries to deny feelings of helplessness and hopelessness and to play a role of domineering competence. Once this mode of coping with difficulties is adopted, it is maintained until it has spent itself in emotional exhaustion, for the only other alternative is an admission of defeat and inevitable depression. Thus, as a manic episode proceeds, any defensive value it might originally have had is negated, for thought processes are speeded up to a point where an individual can no longer process incoming information with any degree of efficiency. This results in behavior that is highly erratic at best and incomprehensible at the extreme.

According to psychodynamic views of bipolar disorder, the shift from mania to depression may tend to occur when the defensive function of the manic reaction breaks down. Similarly, the shift from depression to mania may tend to occur when an individual, devalued and guilt-ridden by inactivity and an inability to cope, finally feels compelled to attempt some countermeasure, however desperate. Although the view of manic and depressive reactions as extreme defenses may seem plausible up to a point, it is difficult to account satisfactorily for the more extreme versions of these states without acknowledging the importance of biological causal factors. The effectiveness of biological treatment in alleviating severe episodes lends support to the importance of these factors.

Sociocultural Causal Factors

As noted earlier, a great deal of the research on sociocultural causal factors for mood disorders has not made clear-cut diagnostic distinctions between unipolar and bipolar mood disorders. Moreover, given that bipolar disorder is much more rare than unipolar disorder, all research focusing on depression was included in our earlier discussion of sociocultural factors in unipolar disorder. Here we discuss only research on demographic differences in bipolar disorder because this is the only work that has made a clear distinction between unipolar and bipolar disorders.

Demographic Differences in the United States A number of studies have shown that bipolar disorder is more common in the higher than in lower socioeconomic

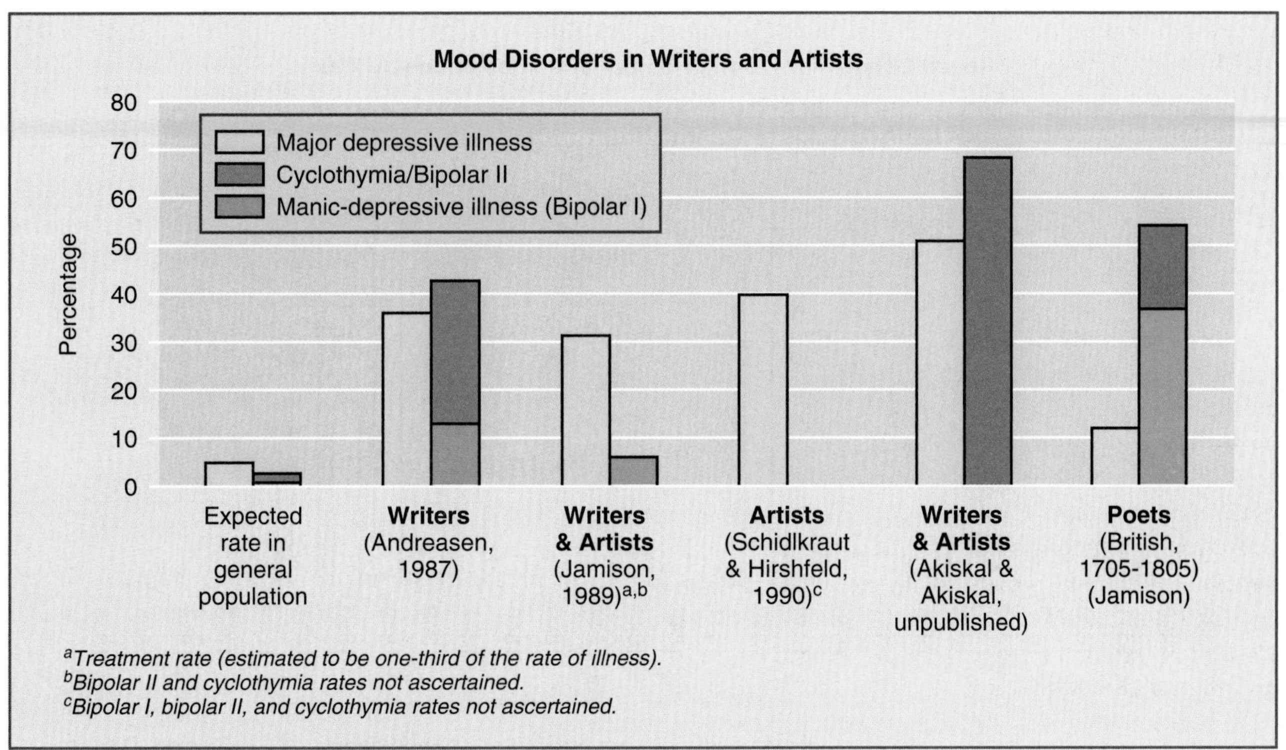

FIGURE 6.5 RATES OF MOOD DISORDERS IN WRITERS AND ARTISTS
Although it is difficult to determine reliable diagnoses of influential writers, poets, and artists (many of whom are long ago deceased), a number of psychological historians have compiled figures, such as these, which clearly indicate that such individuals are far more likely to have had a unipolar or bipolar mood disorder than the general population.
Source: Adapted from Jamison (1993).

classes (see Goodwin & Jamison, 1990); this is the opposite of what has been found for unipolar disorder (Kaelber et al., 1995). Moreover, some studies show that individuals with bipolar disorder also tend to have more education than do individuals with unipolar depression. In one study, relatives of bipolars (compared with relatives of unipolars) were found to have higher levels of occupational and educational achievement, with the differences being especially striking for those who themselves had bipolar disorder (Coryell et al., 1989). Some have suggested that this association of bipolar disorder with higher socioeconomic status might come about because some of the personality and behavioral correlates of bipolar illness, at least in hypomanic phases (such as outgoingness, increased energy, and increased productivity), may lead to increased achievement and accomplishment (Goodwin & Jamison, 1990; Jamison, 1993; Whybrow, 1997). Moreover, this is consistent with a good deal of evidence that both unipolar and bipolar disorders, but especially bipolar disorder, occur with alarming frequency in poets, writers, composers, and artists (Jamison, 1993). Jamison has also documented how the periods of productivity for a number of such famous individuals covary with the manic, or hypomanic, and depressive phases of their illness (see Figures 6.5 and 6.6).

Bipolar disorder, like unipolar disorder, is slightly more common in single and divorced persons (Boyd & Weissman, 1985). Moreover, perhaps even more so than with unipolar disorder, there is a good chance that bipolar disorder itself may contribute to divorce, although there is no good evidence on this point at present.

IN REVIEW

- Describe the symptoms and clinical features of cyclothymia and bipolar disorder.
- What distinguishes schizoaffective disorder from other severe mood disorders?
- Summarize the major causal factors (including biological and psychosocial) that have been implicated in bipolar disorders.
- What role does stress seem to play in bipolar disorder?

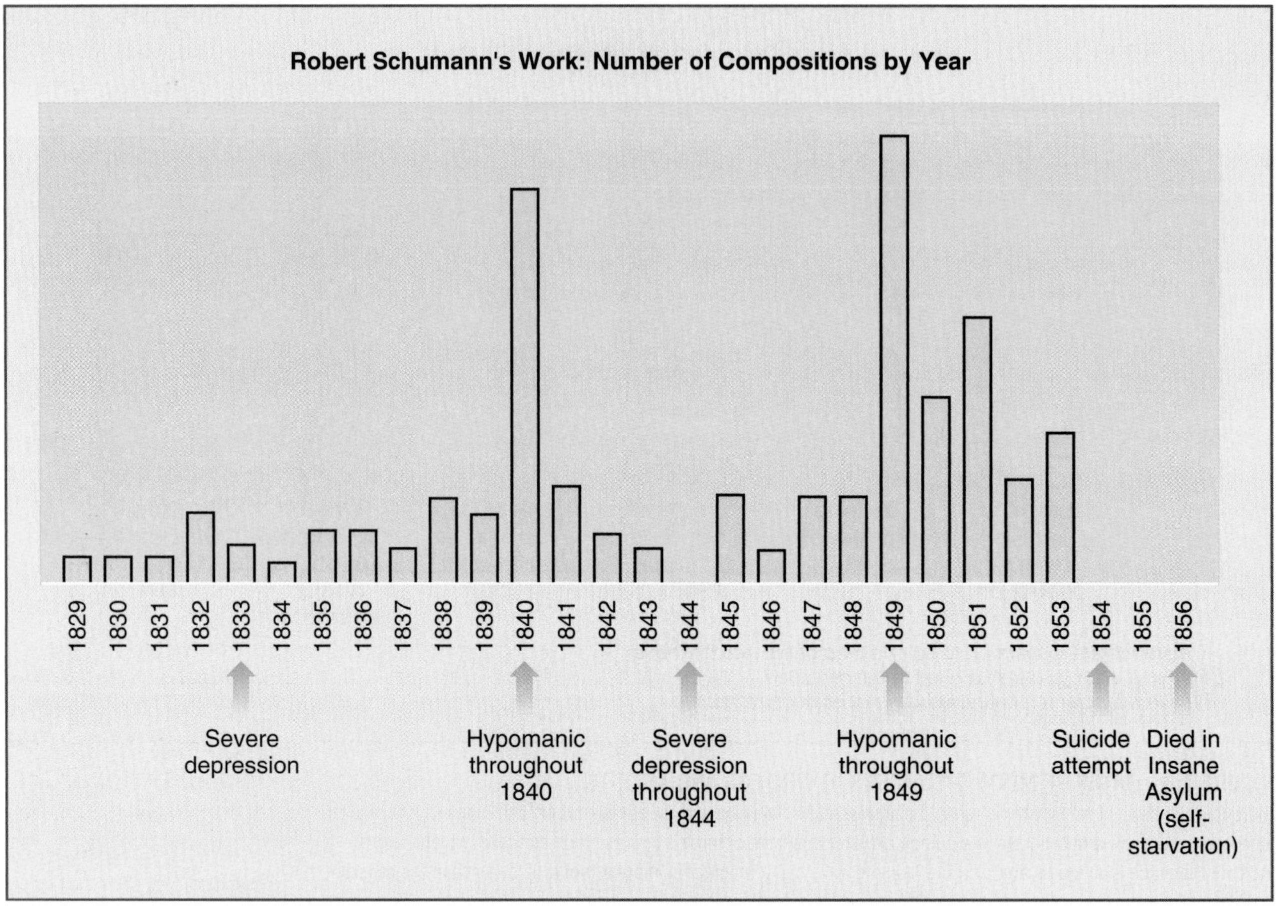

Robert Schumann's Work: Number of Compositions by Year

1829 1830 1831 1832 1833 1834 1835 1836 1837 1838 1839 1840 1841 1842 1843 1844 1845 1846 1847 1848 1849 1850 1851 1852 1853 1854 1855 1856

Severe depression

Hypomanic throughout 1840

Severe depression throughout 1844

Hypomanic throughout 1849

Suicide attempt

Died in Insane Asylum (self-starvation)

FIGURE 6.6 ROBERT SCHUMANN'S WORK: NUMBER OF COMPOSITIONS BY YEAR
Number of the German composer Robert Schumann's compositions by year as they covaried with manic and depressive phases of his bipolar disorder.
Source: Adapted from E. Slater and A. Meyer, "Contributions to a pathography of the musicians: Robert Schumann." In *Confinia Psychiatrica,* 2(1959), pp. 65–94. Reprinted by permission of Karger, Basel, Switzerland.

TREATMENTS AND OUTCOMES FOR MOOD DISORDERS

Many patients who suffer from mood disorders (especially unipolar disorders) never seek treatment, and without formal treatment, the great majority of manic and depressed patients will recover (at least temporarily) within less than a year. However, with the wide variety of treatments that are available today and the enormous amount of personal suffering and lost productivity that depressed and manic individuals endure, more and more people who experience these disorders are seeking treatment. This is an era in which there is greatly increased public awareness of the availability of effective treatments and there is somewhat less stigma associated with experiencing a mood disorder.

Pharmacotherapy and Electroconvulsive Therapy

Antidepressant, antipsychotic, and antianxiety drugs are all used in the treatment of unipolar and bipolar disorders. For most moderately to seriously unipolar depressed patients, including those with dysthymia (Kocsis et al., 1997), the drug treatment of choice from the 1960s to the 1990s was one of the standard antidepressants (called *tricyclics* because of their chemical structure), such as Tofranil (imipramine) (Gitlin, 1996; Nemeroff & Schatzberg, 1998). The efficacy of the tricyclics has been demonstrated in hundreds of studies comparing the response of depressed patients given these drugs with the response of patients given a placebo. Unfortunately, the tricyclics often have unpleasant side effects, such as dry mouth, constipation, sexual dysfunction, and weight gain, and many patients discontinue these drugs before they can have the antidepressant effect. In addition, if a patient has bipolar disorder (either known or not yet diagnosed because of no prior manic episode), treatment with an antidepressant can sometimes precipitate a manic episode or precipitate a rapid-cycling form of bipolar disorder (Nemeroff & Schatzberg, 1998).

Selective Serotonin Re-uptake Inhibitors For all these reasons, physicians have more often been prescribing the selective serotonin re-uptake inhibitors (SSRIs), a relatively new category of antidepressant drugs that tend to have many fewer side effects and are better tolerated by patients than are the tricyclics. Several of these, such as Prozac (fluoxetine) and Zoloft (sertraline), are now extremely popular among physicians in various specialties, not only for treating patients with significant unipolar depression but also for people with mild depressive symptoms (Gitlin, 1996; Nemeroff & Schatzberg, 1998). The primary negative side effects of the SSRIs are that many of them cause orgasmic problems or lowered interest in sexual activity.

Prescriptions for Prozac and other SSRIs are being written at a rate that many believe seems excessive. Should modest distress or unhappiness be an occasion for taking drugs? Or should it instead be an occasion for seriously examining one's life and perhaps seeking psychotherapy? There are many interesting and controversial questions about the ethics of prescribing drugs to essentially healthy people simply because those drugs may make them feel more energetic, outgoing, and productive than they have ever been. These have been discussed widely in the popular media since the publication of the controversial best-selling book *Listening to Prozac* (Kramer, 1993), written by a psychiatrist who describes his own dilemmas in deciding when and for how long to prescribe the drug for his patients (many of whom are not depressed).

The Course of Treatment with Antidepressant Drugs Unfortunately, antidepressant drugs usually require at least several weeks to take effect. Also, discontinuing the drugs when symptoms have remitted may result in relapse. Recall that the natural course of a depressive episode, if left untreated, is typically 6 to 9 months. Thus, if depressed patients take drugs for 3 to 4 months and then stop because they are feeling better, they are likely to relapse because the underlying depressive episodes were actually still present and only their symptomatic expression had been suppressed (Gitlin, 1996; Nemeroff & Schatzberg, 1998). Because depression tends to be a recurrent disorder, there are also increasing trends to continue patients for very long periods of time on the drugs in order to prevent recurrence. For example, Frank and colleagues (1990) continued patients on moderate doses of imipramine for 3 years and found that only about 20 percent showed a recurrence, compared with about 90 percent of those maintained on placebo for the same time period. Thus, when properly prescribed, these drugs are often effective for prevention as well as treatment in patients subject to recurrent episodes (Gitlin, 1996; Nemeroff & Schatzberg, 1998) (see also Chapter 3).

Lithium and Other Mood-Stabilizing Drugs Lithium has become widely used as a mood stabilizer in the treatment of both depressive and manic episodes of bipolar disorder. The term *mood stabilizer* is often used to describe lithium and related drugs because they have both antimanic and antidepressant effects—that is, mood-stabilizing effects in either direction. Lithium therapy is often effective in preventing cycling between manic and depressive episodes, and bipolar patients are frequently maintained on lithium over long time periods. Early studies indicated that lithium was considered an effective preventive for approximately 65 percent of patients suffering repeated bipolar attacks (Prien, 1992), but other studies present a more pessimistic picture, with several large studies finding only slightly over 33 percent of patients remaining free of an episode over a 5-year follow-up period. Nevertheless, maintenance on lithium clearly leads to having *fewer* episodes than are experienced by patients who discontinue the medication. In a quantitative study of patients discontinuing medication, the risk of having a new episode was 28 times higher per month when not on medication than when on medication (Nemeroff & Schatzberg, 1998).

Lithium therapy has some unpleasant side effects, such as lethargy, decreased motor coordination, and gastrointestinal difficulties in some patients. Long-term use of lithium has also been associated with kidney malfunction and sometimes permanent kidney damage (Gitlin, 1996; Goodwin & Jamison, 1990). Not surprisingly, these side effects, combined with the fact that many bipolar patients seem to miss the highs and the abundance of energy associated with hypomanic or manic episodes, sometimes reduce patients' compliance with this drug treatment.

More recently, evidence has also been emerging of the usefulness of another category of drugs known as the *anticonvulsants* (such as carbamazepine and valproate) in the treatment of bipolar disorder (Nemeroff & Schatzberg, 1998). These drugs may often be effective in patients who do not respond well to lithium or who have unacceptable side effects with it (Nemeroff & Schatzberg, 1998).

Both bipolar and unipolar patients who show signs of psychosis (hallucinations and delusions) may also receive *antipsychotic* medications (see Chapters 3 and 12) in conjunction with their antidepressant or mood-stabilizing drugs (Nemeroff & Schatzberg, 1998).

Electroconvulsive Therapy Because antidepressants often take 3 to 4 weeks to produce significant improvement, *electroconvulsive therapy* (ECT) is often used with severely depressed patients who may present an immediate and serious suicidal risk, including those with psychotic or melancholic features (Gitlin, 1996; Weiner & Krystal, 1994). ECT is also used with patients who have not responded to other forms of pharmacological treatment; it is frequently considered the treatment of choice for the elderly who often either cannot take antidepressant medications or do not respond well to them (Niederehe & Schneider, 1998). When selection criteria for this form of treatment are carefully observed, a complete remission of symptoms occurs after about six to twelve treatments (with two or three per week being typical), meaning that a majority of severely depressed patients can be vastly better in 2 to 4 weeks (Gitlin, 1996). Maintenance dosages of antidepressant and antianxiety drugs are then ordinarily used to maintain the treatment gains achieved, until the depression has run its course. ECT is also very useful in the treatment of manic episodes, with recent reviews of the evidence suggesting that it is associated with remission or marked improvement in 80 percent of manic patients (Gitlin, 1996; Mukherjee, Sackeim, & Schnur, 1994). However, maintenance on mood-stabilizing drugs following ECT is still usually required to prevent relapse (Gitlin, 1996).

Psychotherapy

In the best of circumstances, antidepressant medication or ECT used in the treatment of depression is combined with individual or group psychotherapy directed at helping a patient develop a more stable long-range adjustment. Considerable evidence also suggests that certain forms of psychotherapy for depression, alone or in combination with drugs, significantly decrease the likelihood of relapse within a 2-year follow-up period (Hollon & Beck, 1994; Hollon, DeRubeis, & Evans, 1996). Although these results are encouraging, no study has as yet followed patients for long enough to know whether these treatments are also effective in preventing recurrence—that is, a new depressive episode. Studies on the efficacy of combining drugs and psychotherapy have been reviewed by Klerman and colleagues (1994), who concluded that whether combined treatment is really superior to either kind of treatment alone is as yet unclear.

Proposed psychosocial treatments for unipolar depression have proliferated at an extraordinary rate over the years. In addition to depression-focused modifications of traditional therapies, a number of therapies have been developed that specifically address the problem of unipolar depression, and yet others specifically address the problems of people with bipolar disorder. By and large, these psychosocial therapies are intended for outpatient (nonpsychotic) treatment, but they are increasingly applied in inpatient settings as well (e.g., Craighead, Craighead, & Iladi, 1998; Thase et al., 1991).

Two of the best-known psychotherapies specific for unipolar depression are the cognitive-behavioral approach of Beck and colleagues (Beck et al., 1979) and the interpersonal therapy (IPT) program developed by Klerman, Weissman, and colleagues (Klerman et al., 1984). Both are usually relatively brief approaches (ten to twenty sessions) that focus on here-and-now problems rather than on the more remote causal issues that are often focused on in psychodynamic psychotherapy.

Cognitive-Behavioral Therapy Cognitive-behavioral techniques consist of highly structured, systematic attempts to teach people with unipolar depression to systematically evaluate their beliefs and negative automatic thoughts. They are also taught to identify and correct their biases or distortions of information processing and to uncover and challenge their underlying depressogenic assumptions. This form of therapy relies heavily on an empirical approach, in that patients are taught to treat their beliefs as hypotheses that can be tested through the use of behavioral experiments.

An example of challenging a negative automatic thought through a behavioral experiment can be seen in the following interchange between a cognitive therapist and a depressed patient.

Case Study **Therapy Session: "My Husband Doesn't Love Me Any More"**

PATIENT: My husband doesn't love me any more.

THERAPIST: That must be a very distressing thought. What makes you think that he doesn't love you?

PATIENT: Well, when he comes in in the evening, he never wants to talk to me. He just wants to sit and watch TV. Then he goes straight off to bed.

THERAPIST: OK. Now, is there any evidence, anything he does, that goes against the idea that he doesn't love you?

PATIENT: I can't think of any. Well, no, wait a minute. Actually it was my birthday a couple of weeks ago, and he gave me a watch which is really lovely. I'd seen them advertised and mentioned I liked it, and he took notice and went and got me one.

THERAPIST: Right. Now how does that fit with the idea that he doesn't love you?

PATIENT: Well, I suppose it doesn't really, does it? But then why is he like that in the evening?

THERAPIST: I suppose him not loving you any more is one possible reason. Are there any other possible reasons?

PATIENT: Well, he has been working very hard lately. I mean, he's late home most nights, and he had to go in to the office at the weekend. So I suppose it could be that.

THERAPIST: It could, couldn't it? How could you find out if that's it?

PATIENT: Well, I could say I've noticed how tired he looks and ask him how he's feeling and how the work's going. I haven't done that, I've just been getting annoyed because he doesn't pay any attention to me.

THERAPIST: That sounds like an excellent idea. How would you like to make that a homework task for this week? (From Fennell, 1989.)

Another example of trying to challenge a patient's underlying depressogenic assumption of having to be loved is seen in the following interchange.

Case Study **Therapy Session: "I Must Be Loved"**

PATIENT: Not being loved leads automatically to unhappiness.

THERAPIST: Not being loved is a "nonevent." How can a nonevent lead automatically to something?

PATIENT: I just don't believe anyone could be happy without being loved.

THERAPIST: This is your belief. If you believe something, this belief will dictate your emotional reactions.

PATIENT: I don't understand that.

THERAPIST: If you believe something, you're going to act and feel as if it were true, whether it is or not.

PATIENT: You mean if I believe I'll be unhappy without love, it's only my belief causing my unhappiness?

THERAPIST: And when you feel unhappy, you probably say to yourself, "See, I was right. If I don't have love, I am bound to be unhappy."

PATIENT: How can I get out of this trap?

THERAPIST: You could experiment with your belief about having to be loved. Force yourself to suspend this belief and see what happens. Pay attention to the natural consequences created by your belief. For example, can you picture yourself on a tropical island with all the delicious fruits and other food available?

PATIENT: Yes, it looks pretty good.

THERAPIST: Now, imagine that there are primitive people on the island. They are friendly and helpful, but they do not love you. None of them loves you.

PATIENT: I can picture that.

THERAPIST: How do you feel in your fantasy?

PATIENT: Relaxed and comfortable.

THERAPIST: So you can see that it does not necessarily follow that if you aren't loved, you will be unhappy. (From Beck et al., 1979, p. 260.)

The usefulness of cognitive-behavioral therapy has been amply documented in dozens of studies, including several studies with unipolar depressed inpatients and with patients diagnosed with depression of the melancholic type (Craighead et al., 1998; Hollon & Beck, 1994). It may have a special advantage in preventing relapse, although evidence of whether it can also prevent recurrence is not yet available (Hollon et al., 1996). It seems to be at least as effective as pharmacotherapy, even in the treatment of severe unipolar depression (DeRubeis, Gelfand, Tang, & Simons, 1999). Nevertheless, some have questioned whether adequate tests of the comparative efficacy of cognitive-behavioral therapy versus pharmacotherapy have yet been conducted (Hollon et al., 1996; Hollon & Beck, 1994).

Interpersonal Therapy The interpersonal therapy (IPT) approach has not yet been subjected to as extensive an evaluation as has cognitive-behavioral therapy. The findings of a carefully designed multi-site study sponsored by the National Institute of Mental Health, however, strongly supported its effectiveness in the treatment of unipolar depression, as well as that of cognitive-behavioral therapy. The question of whether IPT can be useful in long-term follow-up for individuals with severe recurrent unipolar depression has also been addressed (Craighead et al., 1998; Frank et al., 1990). Patients who received continued treatment with IPT once a month or who received continued medication were much less likely to have a recurrence than were those maintained on placebo over a 3-year follow-up period.

Family and Marital Therapy Of course, in any treatment program, it is important to deal with unusual stressors in a patient's life, because an unfavorable life situation may lead to a recurrence of the depression and may necessitate longer treatment. This point has been strongly supported by studies that extended to the unipolar and bipolar mood disorders the well-established finding that relapse in schizophrenia is correlated with certain noxious elements in family life (Butzlaff & Hooley, 1998; Hooley, 1998). Behavior by a spouse that can be interpreted by a former patient as criticism seems especially likely to produce relapse of depression. For example, some types of couples or family interventions directed at reducing the level of expressed emotion or hostility have been found to be very useful in preventing such relapses (e.g., Miklowitz, 1996). For bipolar disorder, family therapy in conjunction with medication significantly reduces the chance of relapse. In addition, for married people who are depressed and having marital discord, it has been shown that marital therapy (focusing on the marital discord rather than on the one partner's depression) is as effective as cognitive-behavioral therapy in reducing unipolar depression for the depressed spouse. The marital therapy had the further advantage of also producing greater increases in marital satisfaction than did the cognitive-behavioral therapy (Beach & O'Leary, 1992; Craighead et al., 1998; Jacobsen et al., 1991).

General Outcomes Even without formal therapy, as we have noted, the great majority of manic and depressed patients recover from a given episode within less than a year. With the modern methods of treatment discussed here, the general outlook has become increasingly favorable. Although relapses may occur in some instances, these can often be prevented by maintenance therapy—either through continuation of medication and/or through follow-up therapy sessions at regular intervals.

At the same time, the mortality rate for depressed patients appears to be significantly higher than that for the general population, partly because of the higher incidence of suicide, but some studies also indicate an excess of deaths due to natural causes as well (see Coryell & Winokur, 1992; Futterman et al., 1995), including coronary heart disease (Frasure-Smith, Lesperance, & Talajic, 1993, 1995). Manic patients also have a high risk of death, due to such circumstances as accidents (with or without alcohol as a contributing factor), neglect of proper health precautions, or physical exhaustion (Coryell & Winokur, 1992). Thus, although the development of more effective drugs and forms of psychotherapy have brought greatly improved outcomes for patients with mood disorders, the need clearly remains for still more effective treatment methods, both immediate and long-term. Also, a great need remains to study the factors that put people at risk for depressive disorders and to apply relevant findings to early intervention and prevention.

IN REVIEW

- Evaluate the effectiveness of antidepressant medications, electroconvulsive therapy, and mood-stabilizing drugs such as lithium in the treatment of unipolar and bipolar disorders.
- Describe the three major forms of psychotherapy that have been shown to be effective for treating depression.

SUICIDE

The risk of **suicide**—taking one's own life—is a significant factor in all depressive states. Although it is obvious that some people commit suicide for reasons other than depression, estimates are that about 50 percent of those who complete the act do so during or in the recovery phase of a depressive episode (Isacsson & Rich, 1997). Paradoxically, the act often occurs at a point when a person appears to be emerging from the deepest phase of the depressive attack. The risk of suicide is about 1 percent during the year in which a depressive episode occurs, but the lifetime risk for someone who has recurrent depressive episodes is about 15 percent (D. C. Clark, 1995). Put in a different way, depressed people are 20 times more likely than nondepressed people to commit suicide. Moreover, even when suicide is not associated with depression, it is still generally associated with some other psychiatric disorder; estimates are that over 90 percent of people who commit suicide are suffering some psychiatric disorder at the time (Isacsson & Rich, 1997).

Suicide now ranks among the ten leading causes of death in most Western countries. In the United States, it is the eighth or ninth leading cause of death, with estimates of more than 30,000 suicides each year (Silverman, 1997). Indeed, the problem may be much more serious than these figures suggest, because many self-inflicted deaths

suicide Taking one's own life.

are attributed in official records to other "more respectable" causes. Most experts agree that the number of actual suicides is at least two to four times higher than the number officially reported (O'Donnell & Farmer, 1995; Silverman, 1997). In addition to completed suicides, estimates suggest that more than 200,000 people attempt suicide each year and that nearly 3 percent of Americans have made a suicide attempt at some time in their lives (D. C. Clark, 1995).

Statistics, however accurate, cannot begin to convey the tragedy of suicide in human terms. As we will see, most people who commit suicide are ambivalent about taking their own lives. This irreversible choice is often made when they are alone and in a state of severe psychological distress and anguish, unable to see their problems objectively or to evaluate alternative courses of action. Thus, a basic humanitarian problem is that suicide involves the seemingly senseless death of a person who may be ambivalent about living or who does not really want to die. A second tragic concern arises from the long-lasting distress that such an action can cause among those left behind. As Shneidman (1969), a leading suicidologist, put it, "The person who commits suicide puts his psychological skeleton in the survivor's emotional closet" (p. 22). Studies of survivors show that loss of a loved one through suicide "is one of the greatest burdens individuals and families may endure" (Dunne, 1992, p. 222).

In the discussion that follows, we will focus on various aspects of the incidence and clinical picture of suicide, on factors that appear to be of causal significance, on degrees of intent and ways of communicating it, and on issues of treatment and prevention.

The Clinical Picture and the Causal Pattern

Who commits suicide? What are the motives for taking one's own life? What general sociocultural variables appear to be relevant to an understanding of suicide? These are the questions we will consider.

Who Attempts and Who Commits Suicide? Suicide *attempts* are primarily actions of young people; at least two-thirds of suicide attempters are under 35 (Hawton, 1992). In the United States, women are about three to four times as likely as men to attempt suicide. Rates of suicide attempts are also about four times higher in people who are separated or divorced than in people with any other marital status (D. C. Clark, 1995). Most attempts occur in the context of interpersonal discord or other severe life stress. The story is different, however, for *completed suicides;* three to four times more men than women die by suicide each year in the United States. The highest rate of completed suicides is in the elderly (65 and over). Although these rates had been coming down since 1930, especially for elderly men (Silverman, 1997), there was unfortunately a trend back upward during the 1980s and 1990s (see Figure 6.7). Among elderly victims, half or more suffer from a chronic physical illness that can lead either directly or indirectly (through depression) to the increased risk for suicide.

For women, the most commonly used method of suicide is drug ingestion; men tend to use methods more likely to be lethal, particularly gunshot, which may be a good part of the reason why completed suicides are higher among men. There is also some evidence from various Western countries, including the United States, that sug-

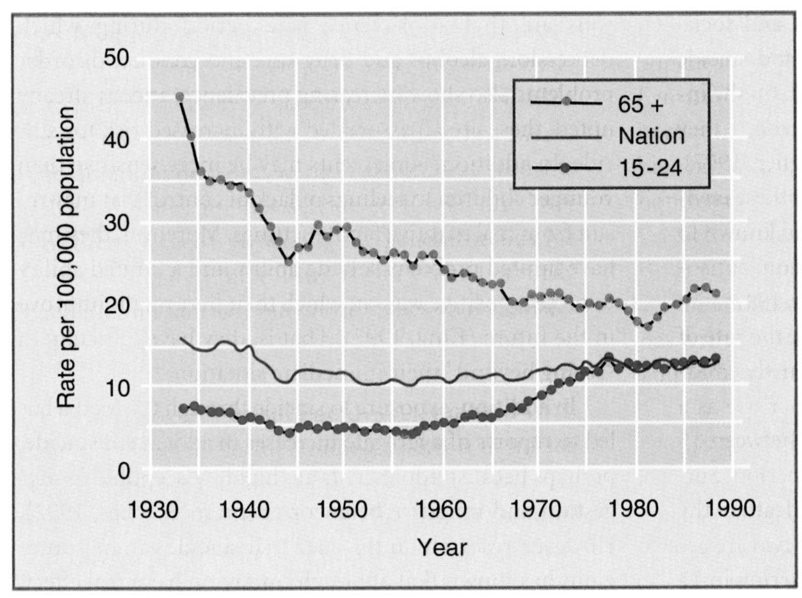

FIGURE 6.7
RATES OF SUICIDE FROM 1930 TO 1990
Rates of suicide in the elderly dropped dramatically since the 1930s, with a slight increase in the late 1980s. By contrast, rates of suicide in the 15–24 age range have increased dramatically over the same period.
Source: Adapted from McIntosh (1992).

tempt will be fatal, especially if the first attempt was a serious one (Hawton, 1992). Long-term follow-up of those who have made a suicide attempt show that about 7 to 10 percent will eventually die by suicide (D.C. Clark, 1995). Moreover, of people who do kill themselves, about 20 to 40 percent have a history of one or more previous attempts; however, nearly half of those who commit suicide have made no previous attempts (D.C. Clark, 1995).

Communication of Suicidal Intent Research has clearly disproved the tragic belief that those who threaten to take their lives seldom do so. A review of many studies conducted around the world that involved interviewing friends and relatives of people who had committed suicide revealed that more than 40 percent had communicated their suicidal intent in very clear and specific terms, and another 30 percent had talked about death or dying in the months preceding suicide. These communications were usually made to several people and occurred within a few weeks or months before the suicide (D.C. Clark, 1995). Nevertheless, it should also be remembered that such information is always gathered after the fact and most of those interviewed say the suicide came as a surprise.

It is also interesting that most of these communications of intent are to friends and family members and not to mental health professionals. Indeed, nearly 50 percent of people who die by suicide have never seen a mental health professional in their lifetime, and only 25 to 30 percent are under the care of one at the time of their death (Clark & Fawcett, 1992). This is generally true even of those with major depression. One study in Finland showed that only 45 percent of individuals with a diagnosis of major depression who had committed suicide were receiving any kind of psychiatric treatment at the time of death, and it was generally minimal and inadequate (Isometsä et al., 1994).

Indirect threats to friends and family members typically include references to being better off dead, discussions of suicide methods and burial, statements such as "If I see you again . . . ," and dire predictions about the future. Whether direct or indirect, communication of suicidal intent usually represents a warning and a cry for help. The person is trying to express distress and ambivalence about suicide. As several investigators have pointed out, many people who are contemplating suicide feel that living may be preferable if they can obtain the understanding and support of their family and friends. Failing to receive these after a suicidal threat, they go on to actual suicide.

Suicide Notes Several investigators have analyzed suicide notes in an effort to better understand the motives and feelings of people who take their own lives. In several large studies of completed suicides, it has been found that only about 15 to 25 percent left notes, usually addressed to relatives or friends (Maris, 1997). The notes, usually coherent and legible, were mailed, found on the person's body, or located near the suicide scene. In terms of emotional content, the suicide notes were categorized in one classic study into those showing positive, negative, neutral, and mixed affect (Tuckman, Kleiner, & Lavell, 1959). The emotional content of the notes was rated, in decreasing order of frequency, as positive, neutral, mixed, and negative.

An understanding of the reasons for or motives underlying note writing (or its absence) could possibly help make the bases of these variations clearer. For example, the motivation for writing a note with positive content may stem from the desire to be remembered positively. More specifically, statements of love and concern may be motivated by the desire to reassure the survivor of the worth of the relationship.

Suicide Prevention and Intervention

Preventing suicide is extremely difficult. One complicating factor is that most people who are depressed and contemplating suicide do not realize that their thinking is restricted and irrational and that they are in need of assistance. As we have seen, less than one-third voluntarily seek psychological help, and most of those who do probably do not receive adequate care. More are likely to visit a doctor's office with multiple vague complaints of physical symptoms, which go undetected by the doctor as symptoms of depression or alcoholism. Others are brought to the attention of mental health personnel by family members or friends who are concerned because the person appears depressed or has made suicide threats. The vast majority, however, do not receive the assistance they desperately need. As we have seen, most people who attempt suicide do not really want to die and give prior warning of their intentions; if a person's cry for help can be heard in time, it is often possible to intervene successfully.

Moreover, it is important to recognize that not everyone agrees that all suicides should be prevented. The question of whether people have a right to commit suicide presents complex and vexing ethical issues.

Currently, the main thrust of preventive efforts is on crisis intervention. Efforts are gradually being extended, however, to the broader tasks of alleviating long-term stressful conditions known to be associated with suicidal behavior and trying to better understand and cope with the suicide problem in high-risk groups (Hawton, 1992).

HIGHLIGHT 6.6

Do We Have a Right to Commit Suicide?

Most of us see the preservation of human life as a worthwhile value. Thus, in our society, suicide is generally considered not only tragic but "wrong." Efforts to prevent suicide, however, also involve ethical problems. If people wish to take their own lives, what obligation—or right—do others have to interfere? Not all societies have taken the position that others should interfere when someone wishes to commit suicide. For example, the classical Greeks believed in dignity in death, and people who were extremely ill could get permission from the state to commit suicide (Humphry & Wickett, 1986). In certain Western European countries such as the Netherlands today, the law also allows terminally ill people to be given access to drugs that they can use to commit suicide (Silverman, 1997).

By contrast, in the United States, there is heated debate about the right of people who are terminally ill or who suffer chronic and debilitating pain to shorten their agony. One group, the Hemlock Society, supports the rights of terminally ill people to get help in terminating their own life when they wish (called *assisted suicide* or *voluntary euthanasia*); the society also provides support groups for people making this decision. Several other groups press related issues at a legislative level. One physician in Michigan, Dr. Jack Kevorkian, has helped over 130 gravely ill people commit suicide and, in so doing, has tried to get Michigan to pass laws permitting such acts. Although he has as yet failed to do so and has been imprisoned a number of times, there has been increasing sympathy on the part of substantial numbers of people for this position (e.g., Silverman, 1997). Arguments against this position have included fears that the right to suicide might be abused. For example, people who are terminally ill and severely incapacitated might feel pressured to end their own lives rather than burden their families with their care, or the cost of their care in a medical facility or hospice. However, the Netherlands, where assisted suicide is legal, has not seen this happen, as advocates in this country point out.

But what about the rights of suicidal people who are not terminally ill and who have dependent children, parents, a spouse, or other loved ones who will be adversely affected, perhaps permanently (Lukas & Seiden, 1990), by their death? Here a person's "right to suicide" is not immediately obvious. The right to suicide is even less clear in the case of those who are ambivalent about taking their lives and who might, through intervention, regain their perspective and see alternative ways of dealing with their distress. As noted earlier, the great majority of people who attempt suicide either do not really want to die or are ambivalent about taking their lives; even for the minority who do wish to die, the desire is often a transient one. With improvement in a person's life situation and a lifting of depression, the suicidal crisis is likely to pass and not recur.

So should interventions be required whenever feasible? Here the dilemma further intensifies when intervention requires that a person be hospitalized involuntarily; when personal items, such as belts and sharp objects, are taken away; and when calming medication is more or less forcibly administered. Sometimes considerable restriction is needed to calm the individual. Not uncommonly, particularly in these litigious times, the responsible clinician feels trapped by threats of potential legal action. Undue restriction might lead to a civil rights suit, whereas failure to employ all available safeguards could, in the case of the patient's injury or death, lead to a potentially ruinous malpractice claim initiated by the patient's family (Fremouw, de Perczel, & Ellis, 1990). Currently, it appears that most practitioners resolve this dilemma by taking the most cautious and conservative course. Thus, many patients are hospitalized with insufficient clinical justification. Even where the decision to hospitalize is made on good grounds, however, preventive efforts may be fruitless, as truly determined persons may find a way to commit suicide even on a "suicide watch." ■

Crisis Intervention The primary objective of crisis intervention is to help a person cope with an immediate life crisis. If a serious suicide attempt has been made, the first step involves emergency medical treatment, usually in the emergency room of a general hospital or clinic. It appears, however, that only about 10 percent of suicide attempts are considered of sufficient severity to warrant intensive medical care. Most people who attempt suicide are referred, after initial treatment, to inpatient or outpatient mental health facilities (D.C. Clark, 1995; Comstock, 1992). This is important because, as already noted, the suicide rate for previous attempters is much higher than that for the population in general, and so it is apparent that those who have attempted suicide remain a relatively high-risk group.

When people contemplating suicide are willing to discuss their problems with someone at a suicide prevention center, it is often possible to avert an actual suicide attempt. Here the primary objective is to help these people regain their ability to cope with their immediate problems—and to do so as quickly as possible. Emphasis is usually placed on (1) maintaining contact with a person over a short period of time, usually one to six contacts; (2) helping the person realize that acute distress is impairing his or her ability to assess the situation accurately and to choose among possible alternatives; (3) helping the person see that other ways of dealing with the problem are available and preferable to suicide; (4) taking a highly directive and supportive role; and (5) helping the person see that the present distress and emotional turmoil will not be endless. When feasible, counselors may elicit the understanding and emotional support of family members or friends, and, of course, they may make use of any relevant community agencies. Admittedly, however, these are stopgap measures and do not constitute complete therapy.

It is important to distinguish between (1) individuals who have demonstrated relatively stable adjustment but have been overwhelmed by some acute stress (about 35 to 40 percent of people coming to the attention of hospitals and suicide prevention centers) and (2) individuals who have been tenuously adjusted for some time and in whom the current suicidal crisis represents an intensification of ongoing problems (about 60 to 65 percent of suicidal cases). For people in the first group, crisis intervention is usually sufficient to help them cope with the immediate stress and regain their equilibrium. For people in the second group, crisis intervention may also be sufficient to help them deal with the present problem, but since their lifestyle is one of "staggering from one crisis to another," they are likely to require more comprehensive therapy.

Since the 1960s, the availability of competent assistance at times of suicidal crisis has been expanded through the establishment of hotlines for suicide prevention centers. At present, there are several thousand such hotlines in the United States, but less than 200 are members of the American Association of Suicidology, raising questions about the quality of care offered by the majority (Seeley, 1997). These centers are geared primarily toward crisis intervention, usually via the 24-hour-a-day availability of telephone contact. Some centers, however, offer long-term therapy programs, and they can refer suicidal people to other community agencies and organizations for special types of assistance. Suicide prevention centers are staffed by a variety of personnel: psychologists, psychiatrists, social workers, clergy, and trained volunteers. Although there was initially some doubt about the wisdom of using nonprofessionals in the important first-contact role, experience has shown that the empathic concern and peer-type relationship provided by a caring volunteer can be highly effective in helping a person through a suicidal crisis. Unfortunately, the assessment of the effects of these centers has not revealed much impact on suicide rates, except perhaps in young women, who are the primary users (Hawton, 1992; Seeley, 1997).

One difficult problem with which suicide prevention centers must deal is that most people who use them do not follow up their initial contact by seeking additional help from the center or other treatment agencies. Therefore, some suicide prevention centers have made more systematic attempts to expand their services to better meet the needs of clients, for example, by introducing long-range after-care or maintenance-therapy programs. Unfortunately, one prospective study of nearly 300 suicide attempters randomly assigned to either an intensive psychosocial treatment program aimed at prevention of further attempts or a "care as usual" condition revealed no differences in further suicide attempts at a 1-year follow-up (van der Sande et al., 1997).

Focus on High-Risk Groups and Other Measures Many investigators have emphasized the need for broadly based preventive programs aimed at alleviating the life problems of people who are in high-risk groups for suicide. Few such programs have actually been initiated, but one approach has been to involve older men—a high-risk group—in social and interpersonal roles that help others. These roles may lessen their frequent feelings of isolation and meaninglessness. Among this group, such feelings often stem from forced retirement, financial problems, the death of loved ones, impaired physical health, and feelings of being unwanted.

Other measures to broaden the scope of suicide prevention programs include focusing efforts on the training of clergy, nurses, police, teachers, and other professional personnel who come in contact with many people in their communities. An important aspect of such training is to increase these individuals' alertness for, and sensitivity to, suicidal threats. For example, a parishioner might intensely clasp the hand of a minister after church services and say, "Pray for me." Because such a request is quite normal, a minister who is not alert to suicidal cries for help might reply with a simple "Yes, I will" and turn to the next person in line—only to receive the news a few days later that the parishioner has committed suicide.

IN REVIEW

- Which groups of people are most likely to attempt suicide, which groups are most likely to complete suicide, and what are some of the major precipitants of suicide?
- Summarize the psychosocial, biological, and sociocultural factors associated with suicide.
- How is suicidal ambivalence related to communication of suicidal intent?
- What are the goals of suicide intervention programs, and how successful do they seem to be?

SUMMARY

WHAT ARE MOOD DISORDERS?

- Mood disorders (formerly called *affective disorders*) are those in which extreme variations in mood—either low or high—are the predominant feature. We all experience such variations at mild to moderate levels occasionally, but for some people the extremity of a mood in either direction is clearly maladaptive and associated with a host of other symptoms.
- The large majority of people with mood disorders have some form of unipolar depression—dysthymia or major depression—involving a range of affective, cognitive, and motivational symptoms including persistent sadness, negative thoughts about the self and the future, and lack of energy or initiative to engage in formerly pleasurable activities. Basic biological functioning is often also altered—for example, the sleep pattern may be dramatically altered, or the person may become uninterested in food or eating.

UNIPOLAR MOOD DISORDERS

- For unipolar disorders, there are biological, psychosocial, and sociocultural causal factors. There is evidence of a modest genetic contribution to vulnerability for major depression. Severe depressions are also clearly associated with multiple interacting disturbances in the balance of neurotransmitters and hormones, as well as disruptions in circadian and seasonal rhythms.
- Among psychosocial theories of unipolar depression, Beck's cognitive theory and the reformulated helplessness and hopelessness theories are formulated as diathesis-stress models, where the diathesis is cognitive in nature (e.g., dysfunctional beliefs or pessimistic attributional style, respectively). Personality variables such as neuroticism may also serve as a diathesis for depression.
- Psychodynamic and interpersonal theories emphasize the importance of early experiences (especially early losses and the quality of the parent-child relationship) in setting up a predisposition for unipolar depression.
- Sociocultural research shows significant cross-cultural differences in the way depression manifests itself, as well as in how likely it is to occur following stressful life events.
- It is unlikely that any one theory will ever explain all of the pathways to unipolar depression, which is undoubtedly determired by multiple causal factors.

BIPOLAR DISORDERS

- In the much less common bipolar disorders (cyclothymia, and Bipolar I and II disorders), the person experiences episodes of both depression and mania (or hypomania). During manic or hypomanic episodes, the symptoms are essentially the opposite of those during depressive episodes.
- For bipolar disorders, biological causal factors play an even stronger role than they do for unipolar disorders. The genetic contribution to bipolar disorder is probably stronger than for any other major adult psychiatric disorder. Biochemical imbalances, neuroendocrine abnormalities, and disturbances in biological rhythms are also clearly implicated, although the exact nature of the abnormalities remains to be determined.
- Stressful life events may be involved in precipitating manic or depressive episodes, but it is unlikely that they play a truly causal role.

TREATMENTS AND OUTCOMES FOR MOOD DISORDERS

- Biologically based treatments, such as drugs or electroconvulsive therapy, are often used in the treatment of the more severe mood disorders, and are generally considered necessary in the treatment of bipolar disorder. Increasingly, however, some types of psychotherapy are also being used effectively with many cases of more severe unipolar disorders, as well as the milder forms of mood disorder. Considerable evidence suggests that recurrent depression is best treated by specialized forms of psychotherapy or by maintenance for prolonged periods on drugs, or a combination of the two.

SUICIDE

- Because suicide is a constant danger with depressive syndromes of any type or severity, an assessment of suicide risk is essential in the proper management of mood disorders; it also occurs frequently in people with schizophrenia and alcoholism.
- Biological causal factors for suicide include genetic vulnerability and alterations in serotonin functioning. Sociocultural causal factors include social and religious views toward death, group cohesiveness, and social disorganization.
- Suicide prevention programs generally consist of crisis intervention, often in the form of suicide hotlines. Although these are undoubtedly effective in averting some suicide attempts, the long-term success of treatment aimed at preventing suicide in those at high risk is much less clear.

KEY TERMS

mood disorders (p. 189)
mania (p. 189)
depression (p. 189)
unipolar disorders (p. 191)
bipolar disorders (p. 191)
dysthymia (p. 192)
adjustment disorder with depressed mood (p. 194)
major depressive disorder (p. 195)
melancholic type (p. 197)
severe major depressive episode with psychotic features (p. 197)
mood-congruent psychotic features (p. 197)
mood-incongruent psychotic features (p. 197)
postpartum onset (p. 197)
recurrence (p. 198)
relapse (p. 198)
seasonal affective disorder (p. 198)
depressogenic schemas (p. 206)
dysfunctional beliefs (p. 206)
negative automatic thoughts (p. 206)
negative cognitive triad (p. 206)
learned helplessness (p. 208)
attribution (p. 208)
hopelessness theory (p. 208)
hypomania (p. 214)
cyclothymia (p. 214)
bipolar disorder (p. 215)
bipolar disorder with a seasonal pattern (p. 215)
rapid cycling (p. 217)
schizoaffective disorder (p. 218)
suicide (p. 226)

CHAPTER SEVEN

Somatoform and Dissociative Disorders

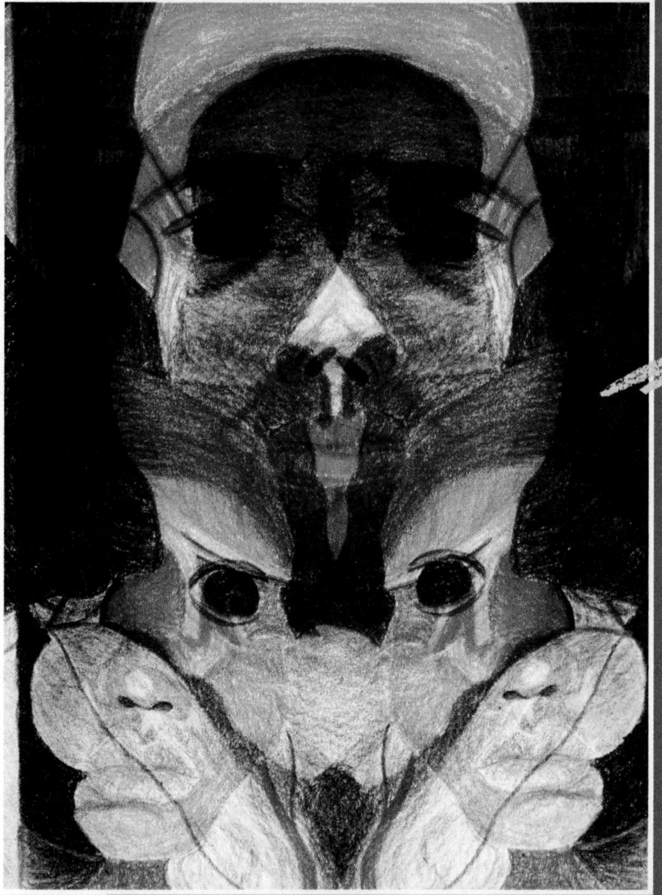

Carole Eskridge, *Starving Madona and Children #2,* pastels and photo. Eskridge worked hard in childhood to develop her artistic talent. As an adult, she was diagnosed with schizophrenia, after enduring emotional and behavioral problems that nearly destroyed her life. Eskridge now lives in Huntsville, Alabama, where she founded the Visionary Guild for Mentally Ill Artists.

LEARNING OBJECTIVES

After reading this chapter, you should be able to:

- Describe the major symptoms and causal factors of somatoform disorders.
- Identify the similarities and differences between somatization disorder and hypochondriasis.
- Describe the symptoms of conversion disorder and summarize its development.
- Discuss the effectiveness of various treatments for somatoform disorders.
- Describe the major symptoms and causal factors of dissociative disorders, and differentiate among dissociative amnesia and fugue, dissociative identity disorder, and depersonalization disorder.
- Identify the most appropriate treatments for the dissociative disorders, and list the limitations of biological and psychological treatments.

The disorders to be examined in this chapter may seem much less familiar and less readily grasped as merely exaggerated forms of everyday psychological phenomena such as feelings of depression or anxiety. Somatoform and dissociative processes appear to involve more complex and convoluted mental operations than those we have so far encountered. There is even growing empirical evidence (e.g., Nijenhuis et al., 1998; Pribor et al., 1993; Ross, 1997; Saxe et al., 1994; van der Kolk et al., 1996) of a significant link between dissociative tendencies on the one hand and the likelihood of experiencing somatoform symptoms on the other.

The **somatoform disorders** are a group of conditions involving physical complaints or disabilities that occur without any evidence of physical pathology to account for them. Despite the range of clinical manifestations—from blindness to paralysis—they share one key feature: All are expressions of psychological difficulties in the "body language" of medical problems that on careful examination cannot be documented to exist. Equally key to these disorders is the fact that the affected patients are *not* merely faking symptoms and attempting to deceive others; for the most part, they genuinely and sometimes passionately believe that something is terribly wrong with their bodies. They therefore show up in large numbers in the practices of primary care physicians, who then have the often difficult task of deciding how to manage their complaints.

The **dissociative disorders,** on the other hand, are conditions involving a disruption in a person's sense of personal identity. Included here are some of the more dramatic phenomena to be observed in the entire domain of psychopathology: people who cannot recall who they are or where they may have come from, or who split themselves into two or more individuals having independent "personalities" and autobiographical memories. The term *dissociation* refers to this type of splitting process, in which some part of the person's experience of self and the world becomes autonomous from and normally inaccessible to conscious appraisal and executive direction by the main, or "host," personality.

SOMATOFORM DISORDERS

Soma means "body," and somatoform disorders involve patterns in which individuals complain of bodily symptoms that suggest the presence of medical problems, but for which no organic basis can be found that satisfactorily explains the symptoms. Such individuals are typically preoccupied with their state of health and with various presumed disorders or diseases of bodily organs.

In our discussion, we will focus on four more or less distinct somatoform patterns: (1) somatization disorder, (2) hypochondriasis, (3) pain disorder, and (4) conversion disorder. Although all four involve the "neurotic" development or elaboration of physical disabilities, the patterns of causation and the most effective treatment approaches may differ somewhat. The diagnosis of undifferentiated somatoform disorder is reserved for those persistent (i.e., duration of at least 6 months) and unfounded complaints of insufficient clarity or intensity to meet criteria for a more specific somatoform disorder. DSM-IV-TR also includes a sixth syndrome under the somatoform rubric: body dysmorphic disorder, in which there is a preoccupation with some imagined defect in one's physical appearance. As noted in Chapter 5, this type of problem is best considered a variant of obsessive-compulsive disorder.

Somatization Disorder

Somatization disorder is characterized by multiple complaints of physical ailments that extend over a long period,

somatoform disorders Conditions involving physical complaints or disabilities that occur without any evidence of physical pathology to account for them.

dissociative disorders Conditions involving a disruption in a person's sense of personal identity.

somatization disorder A somatoform disorder characterized by multiple complaints of physical ailments that extend over a long period, beginning before age 30, that are inadequately explained by independent findings of physical illness or injury, and that lead to medical treatment or to significant life impairment.

beginning before age 30, and that are inadequately explained by independent findings of physical illness or injury and that lead to medical treatment or to significant life impairment. Not surprisingly, therefore, somatization disorder is relatively common among patients in primary medical care settings around the world (Gureje et al., 1997).

A diagnostician need not be convinced that these claimed illnesses actually existed in a patient's background history; the mere reporting of them is sufficient. DSM-IV-TR lists four types and levels of symptoms that must be present, at least to a minimal degree, to justify a diagnosis of somatization disorder.

1. *Four pain symptoms:* The patient must report a history of pain experienced with respect to at least four different sites or functions—for example, head, abdomen, back, joints, or rectum, or during menstruation, sexual intercourse, or urination.
2. *Two gastrointestinal symptoms:* The patient must report a history of at least two symptoms, other than pain, pertaining to the gastrointestinal system—such as nausea, bloating, diarrhea, multiple food intolerances, or vomiting when not pregnant.
3. *One sexual symptom:* The patient must report at least one reproductive system symptom other than pain—for example, sexual indifference or dysfunction, menstrual irregularity, or vomiting throughout pregnancy.
4. *One pseudoneurological symptom:* The patient must report a history of at least one symptom, not limited to pain, suggestive of a neurological condition—for example, any of various symptoms that mimic sensory or motor impairments (such as loss of sensation or involuntary muscle contraction in a hand) or that involve anomalies of consciousness or memory (for example, an episode of dissociative amnesia, to be described later).

The main features of somatization disorder are illustrated in the following case, which also involves a secondary diagnosis of depression.

Case Study A Woman and Her As-Yet-Undiscovered Illness • A 38-year-old married woman, the mother of five children, reports to a mental health clinic with the chief complaint of depression, meeting diagnostic criteria for major depressive disorder, the latest of several such episodes. Her marriage, which began at age 17, has been a chronically unhappy one; her husband is described as an alcoholic with an unstable work history, and there have been frequent arguments revolving around finances, her sexual indifference, and her complaints of pain during intercourse.

The history reveals that the patient had herself abused alcohol between ages 19 and 29, but has been abstinent since. She describes herself as nervous since childhood and as having been continuously sickly beginning in her youth; she believes she has a not-yet-discovered physical illness. She experiences chest pain and reportedly has been told by doctors that she has a "nervous heart." She sees physicians frequently for abdominal pain, having been diagnosed on one occasion as having a "spastic colon." In addition to M.D. physicians, she has consulted chiropractors and osteopaths for backaches, pains in her extremities, and a feeling of anesthesia in her fingertips. She was recently admitted to a hospital following complaints of abdominal and chest pain and of vomiting, during which admission she received a hysterectomy. Following the surgery, she has been troubled by spells of anxiety, fainting, vomiting, food intolerance, and weakness and fatigue. Physical examinations reveal completely negative findings.

The patient attributes her depression to hormonal irregularities, and she continues to seek a medical explanation of her other problems as well. (Adapted from Spitzer et al., 1994, pp. 404–405.)

Somatization disorder, formerly called *Briquet's syndrome* after the French physician who first described it, has not been as extensively researched as the other somatoform disorders. It is believed to be about ten times more common among women than among men, with a lifetime prevalence of up to 2 percent (American Psychiatric Association, 1994). Despite its significant prevalence in medical settings, therefore, its developmental course and specific etiology remain quite uncertain.

There is evidence of a familial linkage with antisocial personality disorder (see Chapter 9), one that could have some genetic basis. There is also some speculation, based on prevalence discrepancies for these two disorders between men and women, that a common underlying predisposition tends to lead to antisocial behavior in men and to somatization in women (Guze et al, 1986; Lilienfeld, 1992; Sigvardson et al., 1984). Both disorders also appear disproportionally prevalent among those of lower socioeconomic status (Lilienfeld, 1992). Even accepting the dubious assumption of an entirely genetic basis for family linkage, however, it is far from clear (1) how any genetic influence might encourage such outcomes, (2) why they should vary with gender, and (3) what is the role, if any, of low socioeconomic status in contributing to either disorder. Conceivably, the associations observed here may have the common theme of gross family disorganization, which is also known to be associated with various forms of child abuse.

Hypochondriasis

The differences between somatization disorder and **hypochondriasis** remain conceptually unclear, although the DSM diagnostic criteria for the two do allow a practical separation between them. Evidently, the two disorders (if they are in fact distinct) are closely related (see Noyes et al., 1993). The main differences seem to be that hypochondriasis may have its onset after age 30, and that the abnormal health concerns characteristic of hypochondriasis need not focus on any particular set of symptoms or on a profusion of them. A hypochondriacal person mostly focuses on the idea that he or she has a serious disease, such as tuberculosis or lung cancer, rather than claiming various symptoms or physical disabilities.

Hypochondriasis is one of the most frequently seen somatoform patterns, with a prevalence in general medical practice of between 4 and 9 percent. The disorder is characterized by multiple and stubbornly held complaints about possible physical illness even though no evidence of such illness can be found. Hypochondriacal complaints are usually not restricted to any physiologically coherent symptom pattern; rather, they express a preoccupation with health matters and unrealistic fears of disease. Although hypochondriacal people repeatedly seek medical advice, their concerns are not in the least lessened by their doctors' reassurances—in fact, they are frequently disappointed when no physical problem is found.

Major Characteristics Individuals with hypochondriasis may complain of uncomfortable and peculiar sensations in the general area of the stomach, chest, head, genitals, or anywhere else in the body. They usually have trouble giving a precise description of their symptoms, however. They may begin by mentioning pain in the stomach, which on further questioning is not really a pain but a gnawing sensation, or perhaps a feeling of heat, or of pressure, whose locus may now on more careful observation have migrated to a neighboring portion of the abdomen, and so on. The mental orientation of these individuals keeps them constantly on the alert for new symptoms, the description of which may challenge the capacity of mere language to communicate.

Hypochondriacal patients are likely to be avid readers of popular magazines on medical topics and are apt to feel certain that they are suffering from every new disease they read or hear about. They are major consumers of over-the-counter (and often virtually worthless) remedies touted in ads as being able to alleviate vaguely described problems such as "tired blood" or "irregularity." Tuberculosis, cancer, exotic infections, and numerous other diseases are readily self-diagnosed by these individuals.

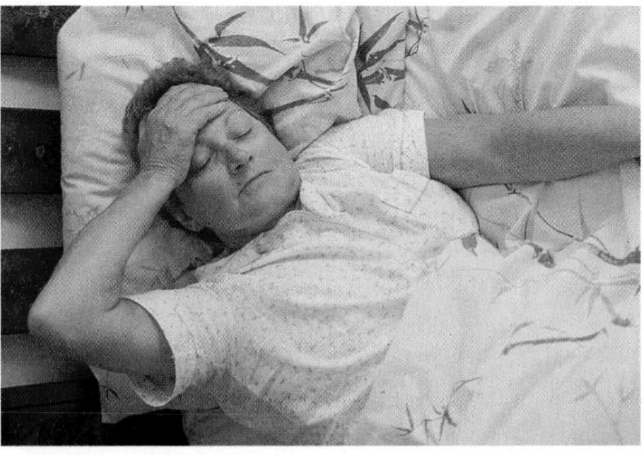

Hypochondriacal individuals are preoccupied with health matters and unrealistic fears of disease. They are convinced that they have symptoms of physical illness, but their complaints typically do not conform to any coherent symptom pattern, and they usually have trouble giving a precise description of their symptoms.

Such individuals are sure that they are seriously ill and cannot recover. Yet—and this is revealing—despite their exaggerated concerns over their health, they do not usually show the intense fear or anxiety that might be expected of those suffering from such horrible ills. In fact, they are usually in good physical condition. Nevertheless, they are sincere in their conviction that the symptoms they detect represent real illness. They are not **malingering**—consciously faking symptoms to achieve specific goals external to the medical context—although an attentive listener may get the impression that something more is being communicated in these complaints.

The following case captures a typical clinical picture in hypochondriasis and incidentally demonstrates that a high level of medical sophistication does not necessarily rule out a person's developing this disorder.

hypochondriasis A somatoform disorder characterized by the person's preoccupation with the fear that he or she has a serious disease, based on misinterpretations of bodily symptoms.

malingering Consciously faking symptoms of illness or disability to achieve some specific nonmedical goal.

Case Study A Radiologist's Abdominal Mass • This 38-year-old radiologist initiated his first psychiatric consultation following his 9-year-old son's accidentally discovering his father palpating (examining by touch) his own abdomen and saying to him, "What do you think it is this time, Dad?" The radiologist describes the incident and his accompanying anger and shame with tears in his eyes. He also describes his recent return from a 10-day stay at a famous out-of-state medical diagnostic center to which he had been referred by an exasperated gastroenterologist colleague who'd reportedly "reached the end of the line" with his radiologist patient. The extensive physical and laboratory examinations performed at the center had revealed no significant physical disease, a conclusion the patient reports with resentment and disappointment rather than relief.

The patient's history reveals a long-standing pattern of overconcern about personal health matters, beginning at age 13 and exacerbated by his medical school experience. Until fairly recently, however, he had maintained reasonable control over these concerns, in part because he was embarrassed to reveal them to other physicians. He is conscientious and successful in his profession and active in community life. However, he spends much of his leisure time at home alone in bed. His wife, like his son, has become increasingly impatient with his morbid preoccupation about life-threatening but undetectable diseases.

In describing his current symptoms, the patient refers to his becoming increasingly aware over the past several months of various sounds and sensations emanating from his abdomen and of his sometimes being able to feel a "firm mass" in its left lower quadrant. His tentative diagnosis is carcinoma (cancer) of the colon. He tests his stool for blood weekly and palpates his abdomen for 15 to 20 minutes every 2 to 3 days. He has performed several X-ray studies of himself in secrecy after hours at his office. Generally discouraged in demeanor, the patient brightens notably in describing a clinically insignificant finding of a urethral anomaly, the result of a laboratory test he had had performed on himself. (Adapted from Spitzer et al., 1994, pp. 88–90.)

As in this case, hypochondriacal persons often show a notable preoccupation with digestive and excretory functions. Some keep charts of their bowel movements, and most are able to give detailed information concerning diet, constipation, and related matters. Many, as suggested earlier, use a wide range of self-medications of the type frequently advertised on television. However, they do not show the losses or distortions of sensory, motor, and visceral functioning that occur in conversion disorder (to be discussed in a later section); nor do their complaints have the bizarre delusional quality—such as "insides rotting away" or "lungs drying up"—that occurs in some psychotic disorders.

More Than Meets the Eye? Most of us as children learn well the lesson that, when we are sick, special comforts and attention are provided and, furthermore, that we are excused from a number of responsibilities or at least are not expected to perform certain chores up to par. This lesson has been learned all too well by the hypochondriacal adult. Such an adult is in effect saying (1) I deserve more of your attention and concern, and (2) You may not legitimately expect me to perform as a well person would. Typically, these messages are conveyed with more than a touch of angry rebuke or whining, inconsolable demand.

These patients have, as a group, more deep-seated problems than merely a fear of disease; most also meet criteria for other Axis I psychiatric diagnoses (Barsky, Wyshak, & Klerman, 1992). Moreover, Barsky and colleagues (1994) have noted reports of significantly elevated psychological trauma, including violence and sexual abuse, in the childhood histories of hypochondriacal patients, compared with controls. These investigators also found that their hypochondriacal patients reported much childhood sickness and missing of school, suggesting that the pattern of communicating psychic distress by reference to physical malfunction was learned quite early.

In short, hypochondriasis may be viewed as a certain type of needful interpersonal communication as well as a disorder involving abnormal preoccupation with disease. Treatment of the latter in the absence of an appreciation of the former frequently produces clinical frustration, if not exasperation. In fact, it may be that the (understandable) impatience with which many physicians react to these patients has the unintended effect of maintaining or increasing their fears of abandonment and of an early demise from some terrible condition that remains undetected by an insufficiently caring physician (Kirmayer, Robbins, & Paris, 1994; Noyes et al., 1993).

HIGHLIGHT 7.1

Hypochondriasis and the "Real"-Illness Cure

What happens if a hypochondriacal patient becomes sick with a genuinely serious medical condition? Barsky and colleagues (1998) found that such a situation "sometimes ameliorated the hypochondriacal symptoms because it served to legitimize the patients' complaints, sanction their assumption of the sick role, and lessen the skepticism with which they had previously been regarded.... As one [patient] noted, 'Now that I know Dr. X is paying attention to me, I can believe him if he says nothing serious is wrong'" (p. 744). ■

Pain Disorder

Pain disorder is characterized by reported pain of sufficient duration and severity to cause significant life disruption and the absence of objective findings of medical pathology that would explain the experienced pain and behavior of the magnitude observed. DSM-IV-TR specifies two coded subdiagnoses: (1) pain disorder associated with psychological factors, and (2) pain disorder associated with both psychological factors and a general medical condition. The first subdiagnosis applies where any coexisting general medical condition is considered of minimal causal significance in the pain complaint; the second applies where the experienced pain is considered to be out of proportion to an established medical condition that might cause some pain. When general medical conditions are implicated in pain, they are coded on Axis III. Medically unexplained pain associated with sexual intercourse is diagnosed as dyspareunia, a sexual disorder (see Chapter 11).

The Subjectivity of Pain We have no way of gauging with certainty the actual extent of someone else's pain. Physicians and mental health professionals are reduced to rough estimates based on "pain behavior," which includes the patient's verbal report of feeling it as well as observations of grimacing, restricted mobility, "protective" movements, favoring the alternate limb, etc. However, simply because it is fundamentally impossible to assess pain with pinpoint accuracy, this does not justify the conclusion that a patient is faking or exaggerating his or her pain, although such judgments are regrettably frequent in clinical situations.

Pain disorder is fairly common among psychiatric patients (Katon, Egan, & Miller, 1985) and is more often diagnosed among women. There is considerable evidence that, even where some physical basis for pain is present, its experienced intensity is a function of the level of stress the patient is currently undergoing. For example, Schwartz, Slater, and Birchler (1994) reported a study in which chronic back pain patients subjected to a prior contrived stressful circumstance reported more pain and engaged in more nonverbal pain behavior than a comparable group exposed to an emotionally neutral prior circumstance.

The reported pain may be vaguely located in the area of the heart or other vital organs, or it may center in the lower back or limbs. (Tension headaches and migraines are not included here, since they involve demonstrable physiological changes, such as muscle contractions.) People with predominantly *psychogenic* (that is, psychologically caused) pain disorders may adopt an invalid lifestyle. They tend to "doctor-shop" in the hope of finding both a physical confirmation of their pain and some medication to relieve their suffering. This behavior continues even if several visits to doctors fail to indicate any underlying physical problem. Sadly enough, in many cases, patients with somatoform pain actually wind up being disabled—either through addiction to pain medication or through the crippling effects of surgery they have been able to obtain as treatment for their condition. The following case is illustrative.

Despite the thoroughly believable quality of this man's suffering, the experience of pain is always subjective and private. Pain does not exist in perfect correlation with observable tissue damage or irritation.

pain disorder A somatoform disorder characterized by reported pain of sufficient duration and severity to cause significant life disruption and the absence of medical pathology that would explain the experienced pain.

Case Study **Pain Disorder and Lost Youth** • An attractive, socially prominent, middle-aged woman developed a severe pain, increasing over time, in her right breast. Over a period of several years, she consulted numerous physicians in various specialties, none of whom was able to establish any objective medical reason for the pain, despite the employment of every known diagnostic procedure that might yield an answer; the painful breast was, so far as could be determined using the most advanced methods available, anatomically and physiologically normal. Increasingly desperate, she so pressured one of her physicians that he recommended she consider mastectomy (surgical removal of the breast), and she did in fact travel to a tertiary-care, university medical center to request this operation.

Fortunately, the surgeon to whom she was assigned was compassionate and psychologically sophisticated; he sensed that this pain was somehow associated with the woman's concerns about growing older and losing her sexual attractiveness, which had been central to her self-esteem and feelings of worth since adolescence. He skillfully diverted her to an experienced psychotherapist. In somewhat less than a year of work with this therapist, the patient was free of pain and in general far more comfortable with herself and her life.

Unnecessary, mutilating surgery was in this case averted; sometimes, in pain disorder, it is not.

Conversion Disorder

Conversion disorder, known originally as *hysteria,* involves a pattern in which symptoms of some physical malfunction or loss of control appear without any underlying organic pathology. These symptoms often mimic neurological disorders of one kind or another. Conversion disorder is one of the most intriguing and baffling patterns in psychopathology, and we still have much to learn about it.

As was mentioned in Chapter 1, the term *hysteria* was derived from the Greek word meaning uterus. It was thought by Hippocrates and other ancient Greeks that this disorder was restricted to women, and that it was caused by sexual difficulties, particularly by the wandering of a frustrated womb to various parts of the body because of sexual desires and a yearning for children. Thus, the uterus might lodge in the throat and cause choking sensations, or in the spleen, resulting in temper tantrums. Hippocrates considered marriage the best remedy for the affliction. Freud used the term *conversion hysteria* for this disorder because he believed that the symptoms were an expression of repressed sexual energy—that is, the unconscious conflict a person felt about his or her sexual desires was converted into a bodily disturbance. For example, a person's guilty feelings about masturbation might be solved by developing a paralyzed hand. This was not done consciously, of course, and the person was not aware of the origin or meaning of the physical symptom.

Escape and Secondary Gain In contemporary psychopathology, reactions of this type are no longer interpreted in Freudian terms as the conversion of sexual conflicts or other psychological problems into physical symptoms. Though still called *conversion disorder,* the physical symptoms are now usually seen as serving the rather obvious function of providing a plausible excuse, enabling an individual to escape or avoid an intolerably stressful situation without having to take responsibility for doing so. Relatedly, the psychoanalytic term **secondary gain,** which originally referred to advantages of the symptom(s) beyond the "primary gain" of neutralizing intrapsychic conflict, has also been retained. Generally, it is used to refer to any external circumstance, such as attention from loved ones or financial compensation, that tends to reinforce the maintenance of disability.

Decreasing Incidence Conversion disorder was once relatively common in civilian and especially in military life. In World War I, conversion disorder was the most frequently diagnosed psychiatric syndrome among soldiers; it was also relatively common during World War II. Conversion disorder typically occurred under highly stressful combat conditions and involved men who would ordinarily be considered stable. Here, conversion symptoms—such as paralysis of the legs—enabled a soldier to avoid an anxiety-arousing combat situation without being labeled a coward or being subjected to court-martial.

Today, conversion disorder constitutes only 1 to 3 percent of all disorders referred for mental health treatment. Interestingly enough, the decreasing incidence seems to be closely related to our growing sophistication about medical and psychological disorders: A conversion disorder apparently loses its defensive function if it can be readily shown to lack an organic basis. In an age that no longer believes in such phenomena as being "struck blind" or suddenly afflicted with an unusual and dramatic paraplegia, the cases that do occur increasingly simulate more exotic physical diseases that are harder to diagnose, such as convulsive seizures or seeming malfunction of internal organs. More commonly seen in contemporary cases of conversion disorder are symptoms not so obviously and directly related to the nature of the problem with which

conversion disorder A somatoform disorder in which symptoms of some physical malfunction or loss of control appear without any underlying organic pathology; originally called *hysteria.*

secondary gain Any external circumstance that tends to reinforce the maintenance of disability.

the patient, without awareness, is attempting to cope. The following case is illustrative.

Case Study **A Desperate Wife's Vertigo** • A 46-year-old housewife, mother of four children, was referred for psychiatric evaluation of her frequent and incapacitating attacks of dizziness accompanied by nausea, in the course of which the environment would take on a "shimmering" appearance and she would have the experience of "floating" and an inability to maintain her balance. Consultation with an internist, a neurologist, and an otolaryngologist had resulted in no satisfactory medical explanation for these experiences; she was, in fact, pronounced physically fit.

The patient readily admitted to some marital difficulties, chiefly revolving around her spouse's verbal abuse and excessive criticism of her and their children. Nevertheless, she declared that she very much loved and needed her husband, and she saw no connection between her "attacks" of dizziness and his occasionally unpleasant behavior.

Careful evaluation, however, revealed that her attacks almost always occurred in late afternoon, at about the time her husband returned from work, and when he was usually most grumpy and critical; she admitted that she dreaded his arrival because he would usually complain about the messiness of the house and the dinner she had planned. With the onset of her attacks, she normally would have to lie on a couch and would not feel "up" for doing anything until 7:00 or 8:00 P.M., with the result that her husband and the children would eat at local fast-food establishments. The patient would spend the rest of the evening watching TV, usually falling asleep and not returning to the couple's bedroom until 2:00 or 3:00 A.M. Meanwhile, the husband watched TV in the bedroom until *he* fell asleep. Communication between the couple was thus kept to a minimum. (Adapted from Spitzer et al., 1994, pp. 244–245.)

Here we see with particular clarity how "functional" a conversion disorder may be in the overall psychic economy of the patient, despite its imposing a certain cost in illness or disability.

The range of symptoms in conversion disorder is practically as diverse as for physically based ailments. In describing the clinical picture in conversion disorder, it is useful to think in terms of three categories of symptoms: (1) sensory, (2) motor, and (3) visceral.

Sensory Symptoms Any of the senses may be involved in sensory conversion reactions. The most common forms include loss or partial loss of sensitivity, excessive sensitivity, loss of sensitivity to pain, and exceptional sensations, such as tingling or heat.

Some idea of the range of sensory symptoms that may occur in conversion disorder can be gleaned from Ironside and Batchelor's (1945) classic study of hysterical visual symptoms among airmen in World War II. They found blurred vision, photophobia (extreme sensitivity to light), double vision, night blindness, a combination of intermittent visual failure and amnesia, deficient stereopsis (the tendency to look past an object during attempts to focus on it), restriction in the visual field, intermittent loss of vision in one eye, color blindness, jumbling of print during attempts to read, and failing day vision. They also found that the symptoms of each airman were closely related to his performance duties. Night fliers, for example, were more subject to night blindness, while day fliers more often developed failing day vision.

The other senses may also be subject to a wide range of problems. A puzzling and unsolved question about conversion blindness and deafness is whether affected persons actually cannot see or hear, or whether the sensory information is received but screened from consciousness. In general, the evidence supports the idea that the sensory input is registered but is somehow screened from explicit conscious recognition. Virtually all of the symptoms seen in conversion disorder can be reproduced on a temporary basis by hypnotic suggestion, particularly among highly hypnotizable subjects (Hilgard, 1994). Hypnotized subjects and conversion patients also share certain anomalies that suggest their sensory losses are not absolute. For example, hysterically blind persons rarely endanger themselves by walking into hazardous situations, and a normal subject hypnotically induced to be unable to see an object in his or her path will nevertheless avoid walking into it.

Motor Symptoms Motor conversion reactions also cover a wide range of symptoms, but only the most common are mentioned here.

Paralysis conversion reactions are usually confined to a single limb, such as an arm or a leg, and the loss of function is usually selective. For example, in writer's cramp, a person cannot write but may be able to use the same muscles in shuffling a deck of cards or playing the piano. *Tremors* (muscular shaking or trembling) and *tics* (localized muscular twitches) are common. Occasionally, symptoms include contractures, which usually involve flexing of the fingers and toes or rigidity of the larger joints, such as the elbows and knees. Paralyses and contractures frequently lead to walking disturbances. A person with a rigid knee joint may be forced to throw his or her leg out in a sort of arc as he or she walks.

The most common speech-related conversion disturbances are *aphonia,* in which an individual is able to talk only in a whisper, and *mutism,* in which he or she cannot speak at all. Interestingly enough, a person who can talk only in a whisper can usually cough in a normal manner. In true, organic laryngeal paralysis both the cough and the voice are affected. Aphonia is a relatively common conversion reaction that usually occurs after some emotional shock, whereas mutism is relatively rare. Occasionally, symptoms may involve convulsions, similar to those in epilepsy. People with such symptoms, however, show few of the usual characteristics of true epilepsy—they rarely, if ever, injure themselves in falls; their pupillary reflex to light remains unaffected; they are able to control excretory functions; and they rarely have attacks when others are not present.

Visceral Symptoms DSM-IV-TR recognizes four subtypes of conversion disorder according to the kinds of symptoms displayed: (1) sensory, (2) motor, (3) seizure or convulsion, and (4) "mixed." Traditionally, however, a number of other fairly common visceral symptoms, such as "lump in the throat" and choking sensations, coughing spells, difficulty in breathing, cold and clammy extremities, belching, nausea, and vomiting, seemingly referring to alterations in the functioning of internal organs, have also been considered to be basically conversion phenomena.

Actual organic symptoms may be simulated to an almost unbelievable degree. In a pseudoattack of acute appendicitis, a person not only may evidence lower abdominal pain and other typical symptoms, but also may have a temperature far above normal. Conversion-reaction cases of malaria and tuberculosis have also been cited in the literature. In the latter, for example, an individual may show all the usual symptoms—coughing, loss of weight, recurrent fever, and night sweats—without actual organic disease. Numerous cases of pseudopregnancy have been reported, in which menstruation may cease, the abdominal area and breasts may enlarge, and the woman may experience morning sickness.

Diagnosis of Conversion Disorder Because the symptoms in conversion disorder can simulate almost every known disease, accurate diagnosis can be a serious problem. However, in addition to specialized medical techniques, several criteria are commonly used for distinguishing between conversion disorder and true organic disturbances:

- *A certain unconcern* ("la belle indifférence"), *in that the patient describes what is wrong in a rather matter-of-fact way, with little of the anxiety and fear that would be expected in a person with a paralyzed arm or loss of sight.*
- *The frequent failure of the dysfunction to conform clearly to the symptoms of the particular disease or disorder simulated* (e.g., little or no wasting away or atrophy of a "paralyzed" limb occurs in paralyses that are conversion reactions, except in rare and long-standing cases).
- *The selective nature of the dysfunction* (e.g., individuals with conversion blindness do not usually bump into people or objects; "paralyzed" muscles can be used for some activities but not others).
- *Under hypnosis or narcosis (a sleep-like state induced by drugs) the symptoms can usually be removed, shifted, or reinduced at the suggestion of the therapist.*

Precipitating Circumstances In the development of a conversion disorder, the following chain of events typically occurs: The patient experiences (1) a desire to escape from some unpleasant situation; (2) and then a fleeting wish to be sick in order to avoid the situation (this wish, however, is suppressed as unfeasible or unworthy); and, finally, under additional or continued stress, (3) begins to show the appearance of the symptoms of some physical ailment. The individual typically sees no relation between the symptoms and the stress situation. The particular symptoms that occur are usually those of a previous illness or are copied from other sources, such as symptoms observed among relatives, seen on television, or read about in magazines.

Whatever specific factors may be involved in a given instance, the basic motivational pattern underlying most conversion disorders seems to be to avoid or reduce anxiety-arousing stress by getting sick—thus converting an unresolvable emotional problem into a face-saving physical one. Once this response is learned, it is maintained because it is repeatedly reinforced—by both anxiety reduction and whatever gains (sympathy and support or more material compensation) result from being disabled.

Distinguishing Conversion Disorder from Malingering/Factitious Disorder Sometimes, of course, persons do deliberately and consciously feign disability or illness. For these instances, DSM-IV-TR distinguishes between *malingering* and *factitious disorder* on the basis of the feigning person's apparent goals. As noted earlier, the malingering person is seen as seeking a specific outcome, such as an award of money or avoidance of an unwanted duty or obligation. In **factitious disorder,** the person's

factitious disorder A disorder in which a person feigns disability or illness in order to maintain the personal benefits the "sick role" may provide, including the attention and concern of medical personnel and/or family members.

HIGHLIGHT 7.2

Factitious Disorder by Proxy

News reports sometimes surface concerning seemingly doting parents who are suspected of deliberately making their child sick. Some of these individuals may be suffering from the bizarre and often deadly (to the child) *factitious disorder by proxy.* In this disorder, the parent administers widely available drugs (e.g., emetics, laxatives, diuretics, or stimulants or depressants) or illness-inducing chemicals (e.g., cleaning products) to his or her child in order to induce illness.

Those meeting the criteria for factitious disorder by proxy may themselves have a history of factitious disorder—now perhaps held in check by the proxy strategy. Not surprisingly, these individuals often have other problems, especially somatoform or personality disorders. As a group, they tend to have a fascination, or preoccupation, with things medical and are given to exaggeration, if not frank lying, about themselves and their life experiences. The disorder is commonly precipitated by life stressors, particularly marital conflict or disruption. Cases of this disorder are often discovered when parent and child make unduly frequent returns or increasingly urgent visits to the same hospital or clinic. If the perpetrator becomes aware of suspicions, however, she or he may abruptly terminate contact with the medical facility, only to show up at another one to restart the entire procedure. ■

goal is the more general one of maintaining the personal benefits the "sick role" may provide, including the attention and concern of medical personnel. Frequently these patients surreptitiously alter their own physiology—for example, by taking drugs—in order to simulate various real illnesses.

It is usually possible to distinguish between a conversion (or other somatoform) disorder and frank malingering or factitiously "sick" role-playing with a fair degree of confidence. Persons engaged in the latter strategies are consciously perpetrating frauds by faking the symptoms of diseases or disabilities, and this fact is reflected in their demeanor. Individuals with conversion disorder are usually dramatic and apparently naive; they are concerned mainly with the symptoms and willingly discuss them, often in excruciating detail. If inconsistencies in their behaviors are pointed out, they are usually unperturbed. Persons who are feigning symptoms, on the other hand, are inclined to be defensive, evasive, and suspicious; they are usually reluctant to be examined and slow to talk about their symptoms, lest the pretense be discovered.

The phenomenon of *mass hysteria,* as typified by outbreaks of Saint Vitus's dance and biting manias during the Middle Ages, is a form of conversion disorder that has become relatively rare in modern times. As we saw in Chapter 1, however, some outbreaks do still occur. In all cases, suggestibility clearly plays a major role—a conversion reaction in one person rapidly spreads to others for whom, one suspects, the appearance of having the imputed "condition" has some sort of psychic payoff.

Causal Factors in Somatoform Disorders

Knowledge of causal and risk factors for the somatoform disorders is relatively limited. For unknown reasons, they have not been the subject of a great deal of systematic research effort in recent years. We will summarize those findings that have been reasonably well established.

Biological Causal Factors The precise role of genetic and constitutional factors in somatoform disorders has not been clearly defined. Limited evidence suggests a modest genetic contribution to somatoform disorders generally (Cloninger et al., 1984; Guze et al., 1986; Noyes et al., 1997; Sigvardsson et al., 1984), but observed familial concordance for somatoform behaviors might also be the result of learning from exposure to somatizing parents or siblings (see Kreitman et al., 1965; Kriechman, 1987).

Some research has found that somatoform disorders involving nervous system and musculoskeletal symptoms show a pronounced tendency to be located on the left side of the body (Bishop, Mobley, & Farr, 1978; Galin, Diamond, & Braff, 1977; Stern, 1977). Since the right side of the brain generally controls the left side of the body, and vice versa, this suggests that the right cerebral hemisphere (which is known to be involved chiefly with nonverbal mental processes) may have some special importance in mediating these disorders.

Psychosocial Causal Factors Given the heterogeneous nature of somatoform disorders, emphasized in a review of pertinent research by Iezzi and Adams (1993), it should perhaps come as no surprise that these problems are often accompanied by other psychiatric disorders, notably depression and anxiety disorders (e.g., Boyd et al., 1984; Ebert & Martus, 1994). As a group, then, somatizing patients exhibit widespread difficulties in their emotional lives, exhibiting a pattern of negative affect and emotional vulnerability frequently referred to as *neuroticism* (Lipowski, 1988; see also Chapter 5). Neuroticism as a personality trait has been shown to include facets of anxiety, angry hostility, depression, self-consciousness, impulsiveness, and vulnerability (Costa & Widiger, 1994), a combination of characteristics often associated with medical complaints that prove on careful examination to be spurious (Costa & McCrae, 1987). However, the range of disorders for which neuroticism is a risk factor appears very broad. It is far from specific to disorders of the somatoform type.

Possibly somewhat more specific is a reported history of childhood abuse. There is increasing evidence (e.g., Barsky et al., 1994; Ross, 1997; Salmon & Calderbank, 1996) of a significant association between the development of somatizing symptom patterns and memories of having been seriously abused as a child. If confirmed, such an association would be one of several convergences with dissociative disorders (to be discussed later).

Another group of patients showing frequent somatoform patterns are those who seem unwilling or unable to communicate their personal distress in other than somatic language (Bach & Bach, 1995; Joucamaa et al., 1996). They tend to focus on and amplify body sensations almost to the exclusion of attending to their own subjective attitudes and feelings, which, if negative in character (as is often the case), are referred to some supposedly malfunctioning body part.

Sociocultural Causal Factors The prevalence of somatoform disorders appears to vary considerably among differing cultures (Isaac et al., 1995; Janca et al., 1995). There are several non-Western cultures (e.g., the Chinese) in which, unlike our own, frank expression of emotional distress is considered unacceptable. We would thus expect somatizing patterns to be relatively more common in these areas, and this expectation appears to be borne out (see Katon, Kleinman, & Rosen, 1982; Kirmayer, 1984).

The old diagnostic term *neurasthenia* (literally "weakened nerves"), referring to medically unexplained chronic complaints of physical weakness and fatigue, is still applied frequently by mental health practitioners in many other parts of the world, including China. It does not appear as an independent diagnosis in the DSM, although the inherently vague diagnosis of *undifferentiated somatoform disorder* may be employed for patients presenting with this clinical picture. Possibly the DSM authors wished to avoid confusion with the increasingly diagnosed *chronic fatigue syndrome,* the attributed causal roots of which remain in dispute. In any event, it appears that the idea of psychologically caused fatigue is less accepted here than in other parts of the world, probably with a consequent constraining effect on prevalence rates—some of it artifactual (if it's not in the DSM, it's not likely to be counted).

Treatment and Outcomes in Somatoform Disorders

Most authorities recommend caution in using medical (e.g., drug) interventions in the treatment of somatoform disorders. Where there is no alternative (many of these patients, convinced of the realness of their symptoms, adamantly refuse psychotherapy), antianxiety and antidepressant medication are sometimes useful in making the patient more comfortable. Drugs are rarely effective in achieving sustained relief of primary symptoms, and the antianxiety drugs in particular entail a substantial risk of inducing dependency. In many instances, the best treatment turns out to be no treatment at all, but rather the provision of support, reassurance, and nonthreatening explanations as to causal factors; frequent office visits and contrived medical reexaminations may be helpful in this general approach. With the exception of conversion disorder and pain syndromes, however, the prognosis for full

In many instances, the best treatment for somatoform disorders turns out to be no treatment at all. Providing support and reassurance, even with office visits and contrived examinations, may be the best treatment of all. The prognosis for full recovery from somatoform disorders is not encouraging.

weeks, or sometimes even years later, such persons may suddenly find themselves in strange places, not knowing how they got there and with apparently complete amnesia for their fugue periods. Their activities during their fugues may vary from merely going to a series of motion pictures to traveling across the country, entering a new occupation, or starting a whole new way of life.

The pattern in dissociative amnesia, it should be noted, is essentially similar to that in conversion disorder, except that instead of avoiding some unpleasant situation by becoming physically dysfunctional, a person avoids thoughts about the situation or in the extreme leaves the scene. Threatening information becomes inaccessible, apparently owing to some sort of "automatic" cognitive blockage (often described as *repression*). This is the "pure case" scenario. In other instances, there is evidence that the individual consciously suppresses the threatening information by avoiding (via distraction, etc.) thoughts and associative threads that may lead to its exposure in awareness; physically leaving the scene where threatening cues abound is one way of maintaining freedom from troublesome facts that might otherwise present themselves.

During a dissociative fugue, an individual appears normal and is able to engage in complex activities. Normally the activities chosen reflect a rather different lifestyle from the previous one, the rejection of which is usually obvious. Such behavior is well illustrated in the following case.

Case Study **A Middle Manager's Dissociative Fugue** • Burt Tate, a 42-year-old short-order cook in a small-town diner, was brought to the attention of local police following a heated altercation with another man at the diner. Questioned by the police, he gave his name as Burt Tate and indicated that he had arrived in town several weeks earlier. However, he could produce no official identification and could not tell the officers where he had previously lived and worked. No charges were proffered and no arrest made, but Burt was asked to accompany the officers to the emergency room of a local hospital so that he might be examined, to which he agreed.

Burt's physical examination was negative for evidence of recent head trauma or any other medical abnormality, and there was no indication of drug or alcohol abuse. He was oriented as to current time and place, but manifested no recall of his personal history prior to his arrival in town. He did not seem especially concerned about his total lack of a remembered past. He was kept in the hospital overnight for observation and discharged the following day.

Meanwhile, the police instituted missing-person search procedures and discovered that Burt matched the description of one Gene Saunders, a resident of a city some 200 miles away who had disappeared a month earlier. The wife of Mr. Saunders was brought to the town and confirmed the real identity of Burt, who, now noticeably anxious, stated that he did not recognize Mrs. Saunders.

Prior to his disappearance, Gene Saunders, a middle-level manager in a large manufacturing firm, had been experiencing considerable difficulties at work and at home. A number of stressful work problems, including failure to get an expected promotion, the loss through resignation of some of his key staff, failure of his section to meet production goals, and increased criticism from his superior—all occurring within a brief time frame—had upset his normal equanimity. He had become morose and withdrawn at home, and had been critical of his wife and children. Two days before he had left, he had had a violent argument with his 18-year-old son, who'd declared his father a failure and had stormed out of the house to go live with friends. (Adapted from Spitzer et al., 1989, pp. 215–216.)

dissociative identity disorder (DID) A dissociative disorder in which a person manifests at least two more or less complete systems of identity; formerly called *multiple personality disorder (MPD).*

host personality The original personality in a person with dissociative identity disorder.

Dissociative Identity Disorder

Dissociative identity disorder (DID), formerly *multiple personality disorder (MPD),* is a dramatic dissociative pattern, usually having identifiable stressor precipitants, in which a patient manifests at least two more or less complete *systems of identity.* When well-developed (many "alter" identities are quite fragmentary), each such system has distinctive emotional and thought processes and represents a separate entity having relatively stable characteristics. The individual may change from one identity to another at periods varying from a few minutes to several years, though shorter time frames are more common. One, the original personality, is normally the **host personality;** other identities are usually strikingly different from the host personality and often from one another; one may be carefree and fun-loving, and another quiet, studious, and serious. Needs and behaviors inhibited in the main or host personality are usually liberally displayed by the others. The case of Mary Kendall is illustrative.

Case Study **Mary, Marian, and Other Alters** • Mary, a 35-year-old divorced social worker, had a somewhat rare condition in her right forearm and hand, one of several general medical problems, that caused her chronic pain. Medical management of this pain had proven problematic, and it was decided to teach her self-hypnosis as a means whereby she might control it. She proved an excellent hypnotic subject and quickly learned effective pain-control technique.

Her hypnotist-trainer, a psychiatrist, described Mary's life in rather unappealing terms. She is said to be competent professionally but has an "arid" personal and social life. Although her brief marriage ended some 10 years ago, she evidences little interest in men and doesn't seem to have any close friends. She spends most of her free time doing volunteer work in a hospice, a type of supportive alternative care facility where terminally ill patients go to die.

In the course of the hypnotic training, Mary's psychiatrist discovered that she seemed to have substantial gaps in her memory. One phenomenon in particular was very puzzling: She reported that she could not account for what seemed an extraordinary depletion of the gasoline in her car's tank. She would arrive home from work with a nearly full tank, and by the following morning as she began her trip to work would notice that the tank was now only half-full. When it was advised that she keep track of her odometer readings, she discovered that on many nights on which she insisted she'd remained at home the odometer showed significant accumulations of up to 100 miles. The psychiatrist, by now strongly suspecting that Mary had a dissociative disorder, also established that there were large gaps in her memories of childhood. He shifted his focus to exploring the apparently widespread dissociative difficulties.

In the course of one of the continuing hypnotic sessions, the psychiatrist again asked about "lost time," and was greeted with a response in a wholly different voice tone that said, "It's about time you knew about me." Marian, an apparently well-established alter identity, went on to describe the trips she was fond of taking at night, during which she traveled to various scenic resort areas to "work out problems." It soon became apparent that Marian was extraordinarily abrupt and hostile, the epitome in these respects of everything the compliant and self-sacrificing Mary was not. Marian regarded Mary with unmitigated contempt, and asserted that "worrying about anyone but yourself is a waste of time."

In due course, some six other alter identities emerged, all rather saliently arranged in characteristic behavior along a dimension anchored at one end by traits of marked compliance/dependency and at the other by equally marked aggressiveness/autonomy. There was notable competition among the alters for time spent "out," and Marian was often so provocative as to frighten some of the more timid others, which included a 6-year-old child. When one of the hostile adult alters seriously threatened suicide, the alarmed therapist insisted on consulting the other identities, to which the intended suicidal alter responded with charges of violation of doctor-patient confidentiality!

Mary's history, as gradually pieced together, included memories of physical and sexual abuse by her father as well as others during her childhood. She also reported considerable feelings of guilt for not having protected her siblings from similar abuse. Her mother was described as not especially physically abusive but as having abdicated to a large extent the maternal role, forcing Mary from a young age to assume these duties in the family.

Four years of subsequent psychotherapy resulted in only modest success in achieving a true "integration" of these diverse trends in Mary Kendall's selfhood. (Adapted from Spitzer et al., 1994, pp. 56–57.)

The number of **alter identities** in DID patients varies, but in two substantial series of cases evaluated by questionnaire, it averaged an amazing 15 (Ross, 1989). The historical trend, in fact, seems to be one of increasing multiplicity, suggesting the operation of social factors, perhaps even some "competition" among these patients and/or their therapists in numbers of alters identified (Spanos, 1996; Spanos & Burgess, 1994). As already noted, the quality of alters' existence varies considerably from being robust, persistent, and complexly organized to being merely fragmentary, amorphous, and fleeting; for example, a given alter may never come "out" but only be referred to by other alters. Hence it is not entirely clear what these accounts may tell us. The fact that alters are usually strikingly different from the host, or primary, personality leads to the inference that the alters express rejected parts of the original self. Physical characteristics of alters are also highly varied, and alters have been known to include nonhuman species.

The Nature of Alters Alters are not in any meaningful sense of the word *personalities*. They are pretended, fragmented parts of a single person and serve as devices to manage otherwise unmanageable psychological distress:

> Alter personalities are highly stylized enactments of inner conflicts, drives, memories, and feelings.... The patient's conviction that there is more than one person in her is a dissociative delusion. (Ross, 1997, p. 144)

Certain roles are extremely common in the alter repertoires of DID patients. These include the roles of Child, Protector, and Persecutor; an Opposite Sex alter, who may share one of these other roles, is also present in most cases (Ross, 1989, 1997). Normally, alters know of the existence

alter identities Identities other than the host personality in a person with dissociative identity disorder.

and depersonalization disorder. For that reason, we shall concentrate here on suspected causal factors in DID.

Modifying to a considerable extent his previously expressed (1989) views emphasizing the almost unique importance of childhood traumatic abuse in the etiology of DID, Ross (1997) has more recently suggested four separate "pathways" that may lead to the emergence of the DID syndrome. The pathways are not mutually exclusive, and a given case may incorporate a mixture of two or more of them.

1. *The childhood abuse pathway:* This is the original and still widely held conception that DID arises from the child's attempts to cope with an overwhelming sense of hopelessness and powerlessness in the face of repeated traumatic abuse. Lacking other resources or routes of escape, the child creates "stable internal persons who are always available for attachment, safety, security, and nurturing" (Ross, 1997, p. 65).
2. *The childhood neglect pathway:* This is a variant form of the childhood abuse pathway in which the child is not physically or sexually abused so much as left to his or her own devices, perhaps being locked in closets or basements or left unattended over long periods of time. Here, mothers of such children are usually described as psychiatrically impaired themselves—with problems such as depression, schizophrenia, chronic alcohol abuse, or even DID.
3. *The factitious pathway:* Here the symptoms of DID are displayed as typically one of several "scams" the person employs in engaging the health care system. There is usually an elaborate medical-surgical history and often multiple prior psychiatric diagnoses. Ross (1997) regards the factitious pathway (when uncontaminated with others) as representing a more severe psychiatric problem than the abuse pathway.
4. *The iatrogenic pathway:* The term *iatrogenic* as used in general medicine means "treatment-induced." In including this pathway, Ross acknowledges the widespread evidence that some cases of DID arise as a consequence of incompetent and misguided treatment for misdiagnosed other types of disorder—most notably bipolar (Chapter 6), post-traumatic stress (Chapter 4), or mixed syndromes involving some dissociative elements.

Most of the available research purporting to shed light on the potential causes of DID has been oriented to "pure form" cases, which in the above scheme includes the first two trauma-based pathways. However, even that research is unevenly distributed and in certain areas quite sparse.

Biological Causal Factors There is no convincing evidence of a genetic contribution to pathological dissociation. The same conclusion is echoed in a twin study reported by Waller and Ross (1997). Nevertheless, future research may uncover a modest risk from this source. Certainly, it would be premature to rule out the possibility of a heightened innate dissociative capacity in patients experiencing these disorders (Braun & Sachs, 1985).

Psychosocial Causal Factors Evidence is building impressively in support of the notion that DID is largely a type of post-traumatic dissociative disorder (see Brown, 1994; Wolfe, Gentile, & Wolfe, 1989; Zelikovsky & Lynn, 1994). It is not difficult to imagine how the development of the partially independent (dissociated) subsystems that constitute alter identities could serve important adaptive and coping functions for individuals who were severely and repeatedly traumatized as children, by some sort of overall family pathology of abuse.

Figure 7.1 depicts the percentages of abuse reported by the victims in five separate studies involving a total of 843 DID patients. The reported sexual abuse in such studies, moreover, often goes well beyond inappropriate touching or fondling and includes attempted intercourse and oral/anal penetration (e.g., Ross et al., 1991).

The message of these data is amplified in a uniquely documented study of 12 convicted murderers diagnosed as having DID, 11 men and 1 woman. In this study, Lewis and colleagues (1997) searched medical, psychiatric, social service, school, military, and prison records, and records of interviews with family members and others, to determine the actual occurrence of prior abuse. In addition, they examined scars on the bodies of their subjects; 11 of the 12 had them, and they were mostly consistent with abuse reports. As determined by these methods, all 12 had been abused as children, and this abuse—both general and sexual—was notably severe. Interestingly, these victims are reported as not for the most part remembering their childhood abuse, or remembering it only partially when queried. Figure 7.2 summarizes these results. Unfortunately, this study did not include a control group of otherwise comparable murderers not evidencing DID symptomatology. Hence, we cannot be certain that the childhood abuse of these subjects is not as much (or more) associated with conviction for murder as it is with the development of DID; nor is it unreasonable to assume that dissociative experiences would be encouraged by lengthy incarceration. Still, it seems unwise to ignore entirely the information provided by this flawed but otherwise impressive and logistically demanding investigation.

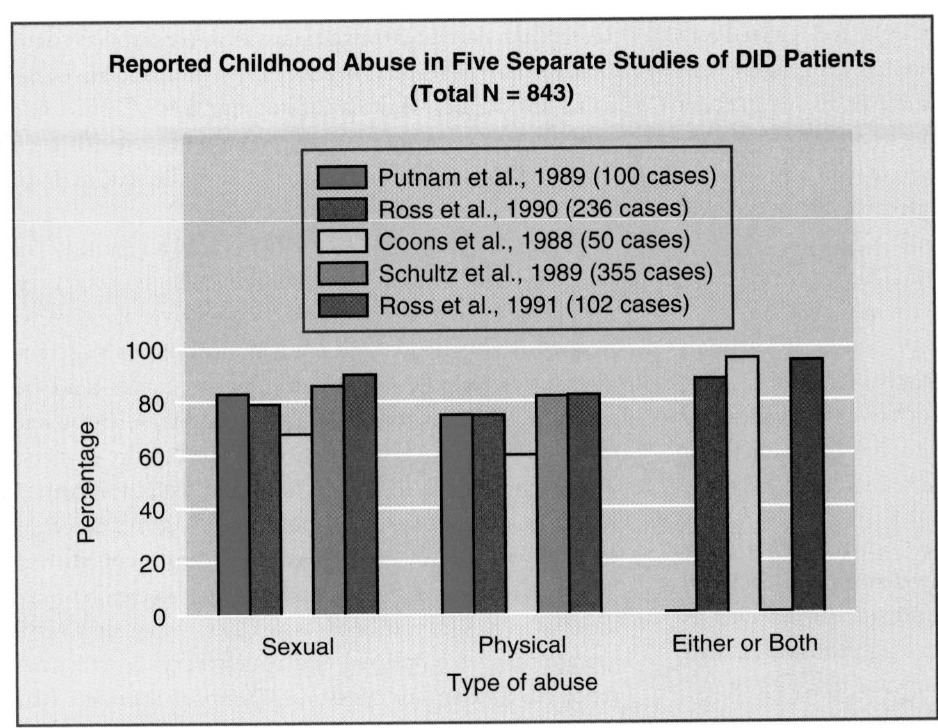

FIGURE 7.1
Results of Studies on Childhood Abuse as a Cause of DID

Case reports, notably including the rather famous one of Sybil, who is reported to have been repeatedly tortured and nearly killed by her psychotic mother (Schreiber, 1973), describe the cruelty that some DID patients suffered as children as gut-wrenching in its severity. However, reports of widespread sexual and other forms of childhood abuse as causal factors in DID, as well as in certain other disorders, have become a matter of controversy in recent years. In some cases, these reports are the result of false memories, which are in turn a product of highly leading and suggestive techniques by convinced but inadequately skilled psychotherapists (e.g., see Yapko, 1994). While this sort of thing has undoubtedly happened, and with tragic consequences to innocent families, it is also true that brutal abuse of children occurs too often and that it can have devastating effects on normal development, among other things probably encouraging pathological dissociation (see Nash et al., 1993; Trickett & Putnam, 1993).

Does DID occur in the absence of a history of severe childhood trauma? If we accept the seemingly reasonable notion of differing but often intersecting "pathways" lead-

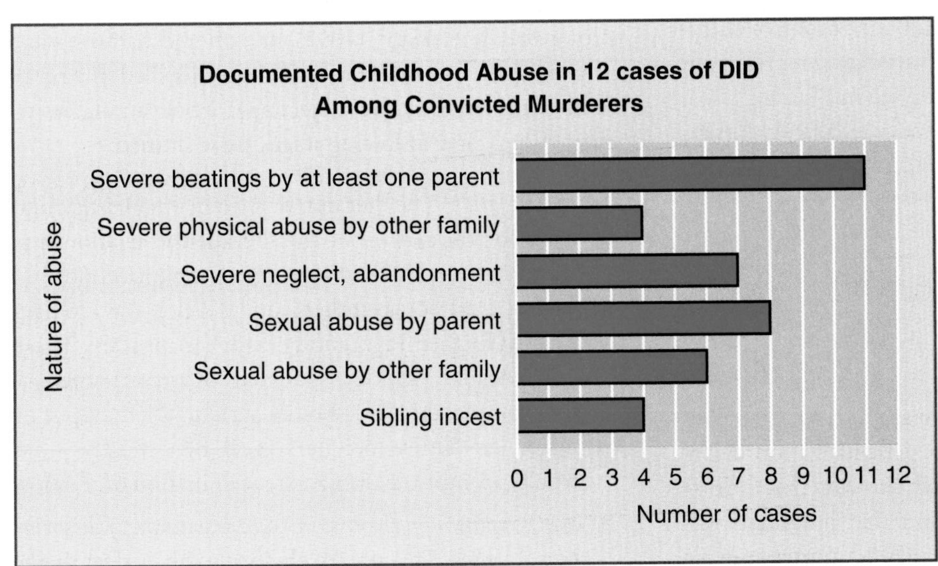

FIGURE 7.2
Some Evidence for a Link Between Childhood Abuse and Adult DID
Source: Adapted from Lewis et al., (1997), Table 2, pp. 1708–1709.

ing to the clinical manifestations of DID, as described earlier, then the appropriate answer would be "probably yes." We would expect in such cases, however, to see in these people evidence of other factors encouraging the development of dissociative tendencies, such as ease of hypnotizability (Butler et al., 1996) and a high capacity for personal absorption (inward focus of attention) and fantasy (Kihlstrom, Glisky, & Angiulo, 1994). The Dissociative Experiences Scale (Bernstein & Putnam, 1986), a self-administered questionnaire that taps into the absorption trait as well as episodes of dissociative experiences, has been widely used to measure dissociative tendencies and has garnered considerable support as a valid predictor of dissociative symptoms (Carlson & Armstrong, 1994).

Sociocultural Causal Factors There seems little doubt that the incidence and prevalence of dissociative disorders, especially their more dramatic forms such as DID, are strongly influenced by the degree to which such phenomena are either accepted as normal behavior or tolerated as legitimate mental disorders by the surrounding cultural context. And, as seen in our own society, such acceptance and tolerance are likely to vary over time.

Many seemingly related phenomena, such as spirit possession, occur in abundance in many different parts of the world where the local culture sanctions them (Krippner, 1994). Instances of what our dominant culture might regard as pathological dissociation are not always maladaptive and need not be construed in these negative, mental disorder terms. As Stanley Krippner puts it, "People can create personalities as required to defend themselves against trauma, to conform to cultural pressures, or to meet the expectations of a psychotherapist, medium, or exorcist. This malleability has both adaptive and maladaptive aspects" (1994, p. 358). Taking this perspective, we are again confronted with the stubborn problem of trying to disentangle issues of widely varying values from our definition of mental disorder, discussed in Chapter 1. Is it really so bad to fragment one's identity to cope with traumatic events? Or is some of our concern based on Western values of self and rationality?

Treatment and Outcomes in Dissociative Disorders

As with the causal factors, little is known about the treatment and outcomes in dissociative amnesias, fugues, and depersonalization disorder. For depersonalization disorder, as noted earlier, there is research showing that the disorder is resistant to treatment, but that judgment was based on only 30 cases and was mainly impressionistic rather than deriving from a rigorous and controlled quantitative analysis (Simeon et al., 1997). In dissociative amnesia and fugue, where a limited number of individual case reports are essentially all we have, the yield is even less. We therefore again concentrate on the treatment of DID.

Most therapists of DID patients set "integration" of the previously separate alters into the host personality as the primary goal of treatment. However, given the diverse, frequently destructive, and often amorphous or fragmentary qualities of alters, we are not sure we understand the meaning of the term as used in this context. A reasonable criterion of therapeutic success would be that the alters no longer emerge, or that they have markedly diminished power to assume executive control of the host's behavior or otherwise interfere with his or her adjustment efforts.

Most reports on the treatment of DID in the literature are treatment summaries of single cases, with widely varying approaches employed and widely varying outcomes reported. Ellason and Ross (1997) reported on a 2-year post-discharge follow-up of DID patients originally treated in a specialized inpatient unit. Fifty-four of 135 such patients were located and systematically assessed. These patients, especially those achieving "integration," generally showed marked improvements in various aspects of their lives. These results may suggest some reason for treatment optimism, but we must wonder about the clinical status of the other 81 "lost" patients, a substantial majority of those originally treated. On average, they may have done less well; that is, it is likely that the 54 ex-patients who were located form a sample biased in favor of good outcomes.

Given an apparent diversity of treatment approaches, it would be helpful from at least a research standpoint if some agreement could be reached on what characteristics a maximally promising treatment approach would have. Along this line, Kluft (1993) has offered a three-stage model for the treatment of DID, one endorsed in a more recent work on the same subject by Horevitz and Loewenstein (1994). The following stages are identified:

1. *Stabilization.* The therapist and client establish ground rules for the nature of the therapeutic relationship, share their understandings of the problem, explore issues of trust between them, and develop ways to help prevent further fragmenting in the face of stress. These ground rules include a statement of circumstances—for example, threats of bodily harm to the therapist or his or her family members made by any alter—that would prompt the immediate termination of therapy.
2. *Working through the trauma and resolution of dissociative defenses.* This phase, obviously the critical thera-

peutic one, is said to involve three essential tasks: (a) the client must begin to deal effectively with amnesia and the propensity to "switch" among differing identity states; (b) he or she must face and deal with dissociative memories, reconnecting them to real-life events; and (c) he or she must reestablish connections between distinct, seemingly separate, identity states.

3. *Postintegration therapy.* This is basically a stage of repair and compensation for the multiple deficiencies left in the wake of (often) years of pseudo-adjustment accomplished by means of dissociative strategies. Huge gaps may appear in the patient's skills, knowledge, and general functioning, and there is often a sense of profound loneliness and detachment, owing to the requirement to resume living in a world that is in many respects wholly unfamiliar. Also, patients are now feeling/acknowledging intensely painful memories they had before avoided. Grief concerning the "loss" of a comforting if very costly adjustment is frequently a complicating feature. This last phase of therapy is said to be often long (1 to 2 years) and arduous for both patient and therapist.

The general outline of this treatment plan makes a good deal of sense and deserves careful empirical evaluation. Unfortunately, it is by no means certain that the considerable funding needed to launch such a project will become available at any time in the foreseeable future.

IN REVIEW

- What are the similarities and differences between somatoform disorders and dissociative disorders?
- What are the four types of dissociative amnesia, and what distinguishes them?
- What are the symptoms of dissociative identity disorder, and why is this diagnosis controversial?
- Explain the nature of alter identities. What are some common alter "roles"?

UNRESOLVED ISSUES: DID and Childhood Trauma

In the 1990s, a chasm divided the ranks of mental health professionals with respect to the validity of the diagnosis of dissociative identity disorder and the related issue of "recovered memories" (i.e., memories not originally accessible) of childhood abuse, particularly sexual abuse, which were asserted to be a major causal factor in the production of severe adult dissociative pathology. Some DID patients have sued their parents for having inflicted abuse; some have also sued their therapists and psychiatric institutions for implanting memories of abuse they now believe did not occur. Some parents, on the other hand, have fought back, asserting that they have been falsely accused, and suing therapists for damages. As a result, many families have been torn apart by the fallout from this remarkable climate of suspicion, accusation, litigation, and unrelenting hostility. Although the validity of the DID diagnosis and the purported origins of the disorder in childhood abuse are basically separate questions, they have tended to become fused in the course of the debate among mental health professionals.

The controversy is rooted in disagreements about the nature, reliability, and malleability of human autobiographical memory. With rare exception, evidence for childhood abuse as a cause of DID is restricted to "recovered memories" of adult persons being treated for dissociative experiences. Treatment, according to the view of believers, dismantles the repressive defense and thus makes available to awareness an essentially accurate memory recording of the past abuse. Disbelievers counter with the scientifically well-supported argument that human memory of past events does not operate in this computer-like manner, retrieving with perfect accuracy an unadulterated record of information previously "input." Rather, human memory is constructive, and highly subject to modification or revision based on experiences of events happening after an original memory trace is established (Schacter, Norman, & Koustaal, 1998). Directly addressing the abuse issue, Kirsh, Lynn, and Rhue (1993) put it this way: "A traumatic history... consists not only of past childhood events but also of the person's interpretations, embellishments, and distortions of those events from the perspective of recent events, accomplishments, behaviors, and relationships that constitute life in the present" (p. 18).

There can be little doubt that, since the outset of the 1990s, many poorly trained therapists, uninformed with respect to how the human memory system works, bought into the notion that a suitably vigorous therapeutic approach could uncover a true and accurate record of the traumatic childhood experiences of their clients. Persuaded by a therapist's certainty and persistence, which were often accompanied by liberal use of confusion-inducing procedures such as hypnotic trance states, many clients did eventually "remember" such incidents, confirming the therapist's "expert" opinion.

Until there can be clear, unimpeachable evidence to compel a consensus among responsible members of both the clinical and the scientific communities, the most reasonable course is to insist that clinicians treating persons suspected of having dissociative reactions due to childhood trauma be held to the highest standards of professional practice. This involves a certain level of intellectual competence, or knowledge of the basic psychological processes likely to be involved when abuse is possibly an issue—such as memory functioning, developmental theory, and the nature and consequences of psychic trauma.

SUMMARY

- Originally considered to be subvarieties of the general class known as *neurotic disorders,* somatoform and dissociative disorders were recognized as separate and distinct general types of disorder in contemporary versions of the DSM. They share certain similarities, both being covert ways of avoiding psychological stress while denying personal responsibility for doing so. There are suggestions, as well, that the two kinds of disorders are both associated with traumatic childhood experiences, and are often comorbid.

SOMATOFORM DISORDERS

- Somatoform disorders are those in which psychological problems are manifested in physical disorders (or complaints of physical disorders) that mimic medical conditions but that cannot be found to result from corresponding organic pathology. These disorders include somatization disorder (chronic absence of a sense of physical wellness), hypochondriasis (anxious preoccupation with self-attributed disease), pain disorder (experienced pain disproportionate to objective findings of disease), and conversion disorder (relatively specific malfunction in the sensory, motor, or visceral functioning).
- Secondary gains, or external benefits that accrue to a person by virtue of being disabled, may complicate the picture in somatoform disorders and may interfere with treatment.
- While there are known risk factors for the development of these disorders, such as neuroticism, causal factors remain for the most part nonspecific. With the exceptions of pain disorder and conversion disorder, treatment prospects generally are not encouraging.

DISSOCIATIVE DISORDERS

- In dissociative disorders, the normal processes regulating awareness and the normal capacities of the mind apparently become disorganized, leading to various anomalies of consciousness and personal identity. These disorders include dissociative amnesia (with or without fugue), dissociative identity disorder (DID) (in which the individual may harbor a multitude of seemingly autonomous personalities or personality fragments), and the far more common depersonalization disorder (in which the person has a sense of lost connection with the self).
- The incidence or prevalence of diagnosed cases of DID has increased markedly over the last three decades, suggesting it is a disorder whose occurrence is strongly affected by sociocultural trends.
- Certain personality traits, such as the capacity for absorption, appear to facilitate dissociative experiences, and there is growing evidence that traumatic abuse in childhood is a specific risk factor for the development of dissociative disorders, especially DID.
- Treatment of dissociative disorders, especially DID, is regarded as difficult, and in well-established cases, the prospects for complete recovery may be quite limited.

UNRESOLVED ISSUES: DID AND CHILDHOOD TRAUMA

- The diagnosis of DID remains highly controversial among mental health professionals, as does the purported association between DID and traumatic childhood abuse.

KEY TERMS

somatoform disorders (p. 238)
dissociative disorders (p. 238)
somatization disorder (p. 238)
hypochondriasis (p. 240)
malingering (p. 240)
pain disorder (p. 242)
conversion disorder (p. 243)
secondary gain (p. 243)
factitious disorder (p. 245)
implicit memory (p. 248)
implicit perception (p. 248)
psychogenic (dissociative) amnesia (p. 249)
fugue (p. 249)
dissociative identity disorder (DID) (p. 250)
host personality (p. 250)
alter identities (p. 251)
depersonalization disorder (p. 252)
derealization (p. 253)

CHAPTER EIGHT

Psychological Compromises of Physical Health and Eating Disorders

Sue E. Clancy, *A Tree of Suppression.* Clancy is a photographer, painter, illustrator, writer, and pre-press technician who lives in Norman, Oklahoma. Her work uses a variety of media and addresses many themes, including the key role food plays in our culture and how attitudes and emotions surrounding it can give rise to eating disorders.

LEARNING OBJECTIVES

After reading this chapter, you should be able to:

- Discuss the influence of general health, attitudes, and coping styles on the risk of physical illness.
- Describe the focus of the field of psychoneuroimmunology and explain how stress affects the immune system.
- Discuss the relationship between hypertension and coronary heart disease and how they are affected by Type A behavior and other psychological factors.
- Summarize the biological, psychosocial, and sociocultural factors contributing to psychogenic illness.
- Describe several treatment approaches for psychogenic diseases.
- Compare and contrast the symptoms and diagnostic criteria for anorexia nervosa, bulimia nervosa, and binge eating disorder.
- Describe the typical personality patterns, cognitive styles, and family dynamics of anorexic and bulimic patients.

Traditionally, the medical profession has concentrated its efforts on understanding and influencing anatomical and physiological factors in disease. In psychopathology, on the other hand, interest centered primarily on the discovery and remedy of psychological factors associated with mental disorders. Today, we realize that both these approaches are limited: Although a disorder may be primarily physical or primarily psychological, it is always a disorder of the whole person—not just of the body or the psyche.

Today, the mind and body are seen more as a two-way street. Fatigue or a bad cold may lower tolerance for psychological stress; an emotional upset may lower resistance to physical disease; a woman's attempts to meet contemporary standards of beauty may plunge her into a dangerous confrontation with starvation; other maladaptive behaviors, such as excessive alcohol use, may contribute to the impairment of various organs, like the brain and liver. Furthermore, a person's overall life situation has much to do with the onset of a disorder, its nature, duration, and prognosis. Sociocultural influences also affect the types and incidence of disorders found in members of different cultures and gender and age groups. The ailments to which people are most vulnerable—whether physical, psychological, or both—are determined in no small part by when, where, and how they live. In short, an individual is a biopsychosocial unit.

Behavioral medicine is the broad interdisciplinary approach to the treatment of physical disorders that are thought to have psychosocial factors as major aspects in their causation and/or maintenance. The field thus includes professionals from many disciplines—including medicine, psychology, and sociology—who take into account biological, psychological, and sociocultural influences when considering a person's health. The emphasis, however, is essentially on the role psychological factors play in the occurrence, maintenance, and prevention of physical illness.

In this chapter, we address largely **psychogenic illnesses**—psychologically induced or maintained diseases. **Health psychology** is a psychological subspecialty within behavioral medicine that deals with psychology's contributions to the diagnosis, treatment, and prevention of psychological components of physical dysfunction. Some psychologists have adopted this as an area of major professional interest. Since the 1970s, the field has developed rapidly and has had a notable impact on virtually the entire range of clinical medicine (Belar, 1997; Hafen et al., 1996).

A behavioral medicine approach to physical illness examines the broad biopsychosocial context of the following problem areas (adapted from Gentry, 1984):

- The psychological factors, such as critical life events, characteristic behavior, and personality organization, that may predispose an individual to physical illness.
- The ways in which the negative effects of stress can be reduced by personal resources, such as coping styles, social supports, and certain personality traits.
- The biological mechanisms by which human physiology is altered by stressors, particularly those arising from maladaptive behavior, and the effects of stress on the immune, endocrine, gastrointestinal, and cardiovascular systems, among others.
- The psychological processes involved in the health choices individuals make with respect to such matters as hazardous lifestyles, health care decisions, and adherence to preventive regimens.

behavioral medicine Broad interdisciplinary approach to the treatment of physical disorders that are thought to have psychosocial factors as major aspects in their causation and/or maintenance.

psychogenic illness Any psychologically induced or maintained disease.

health psychology Subspecialty within behavioral medicine that deals with psychology's contributions to diagnosis, treatment, and prevention of psychological components of physical dysfunction.

Persistent negative affect has been shown to be associated with health endangerment.

The physiological arousal behind this cat's response, while useful for fleeing danger or defending against an aggressor, is not so useful to humans today and takes its toll on tissues and systems if it is not promptly discharged.

portant to note that a large body of evidence has implicated a component of this coping style as a significant risk factor for coronary heart disease. More generally, any type of chronic negative affect seems to enhance the risk of disease (Friedman & Booth-Kewley, 1987b; Hafen et al., 1996). Peterson and colleagues (1998), for example, reported a significantly elevated mortality rate among a group of intellectually gifted individuals who had, a half-century earlier, a tendency to treat negative events as catastrophes.

Psychological Stress and Autonomic Arousal

Our cave-dwelling ancestors needed the ability to rapidly prepare their bodies for the intense life-or-death struggles that were part of their daily existence. Nature provided this ability in the form of a rather elaborate apparatus for dramatically enhancing energy mobilization on a short-term basis. The events making this emergency reaction possible involve chiefly the sympathetic division of the autonomic nervous system. It was termed the *fight-or-flight response* in 1929 by the distinguished physiologist Walter B. Cannon (1871–1945), thus underscoring its apparent function in either fleeing danger or subduing an aggressor. In describing the fight-or-flight pattern, Cannon noted that, with the advance of civilization, these reactions have become obsolete to a degree. Today, because we are rarely able to flee or physically attack a threat (such as a noisy neighbor or traffic congestion), no effective avenue exists for the prompt discharge of the high states of physiological readiness that may be triggered in these situations. In Cannon's view (and in the view of many contemporary investigators), this state of affairs, when unduly repetitive or long-continued, produces tissue breakdown—that is, disease, such as high blood pressure (hypertension).

The arousal of the autonomic nervous system involves many component processes, some of them subtle or even silent in terms of being readily observed. With increasing levels of arousal, we can directly observe the more dramatic manifestations: increased breathing and heart rate, increased sweating, increased muscle tone, and flushing; a keen observer will note pupillary dilation, enhancing vision. With adequate instrumentation, we could also observe increased blood pressure, the dumping of sugar reserves into the blood, redistribution of blood pooled in the viscera to the peripheral or voluntary musculature, and enhanced secretion of powerful neurotransmitters. All of these changes are sometimes referred to collectively as the *alarm reaction* (Selye, 1976b), the first phase of a general adaptation syndrome described in Chapter 4. These changes are the body's response to a "battle stations" signal from the brain. Such a system did not evolve to deal with trifling circumstances, and it is hardly surprising that such widespread and potent effects, if not permitted to subside, might over time lead to organic pathology.

Coming to a similar conclusion, the early psychosomatic theorists, notably Flanders Dunbar (1943) and Franz Alexander (1950), reasoned that chronic *internal* sources of threat could place physical health in serious jeopardy. In other words, unremitting psychological stress of the type found in, for example, chronic anxiety disorders (Chapter 5) might actually cause physical damage to vital organs. These early theorists appear to have been largely on the right track, although—as so often happens in psychology and in science generally—many of their conceptions have proved inaccurate or oversimplified.

Psychosocial Factors and the Immune System

The link between prior stress and the occurrence of physical illness includes various types of disease not thought to involve excessive autonomic nervous system activity in their causal pattern. It includes certain forms of cancer, for example. These correlational observations suggest the involvement of a very generalized type of vulnerability that stress may also induce. Specifically, it suggests that stress may compromise immune functioning. Put another way, the harmful physical effects of stress may involve not only the "alarm" stage of the general adaptation syndrome, but the "resistance" one as well, which is the essential function of the immune system.

Studies examining the association between stress and immune functioning have established an association between the occurrence of presumably stressful circumstances (e.g., medical school exams) and diminished immune reactivity. Such immune system compromise would make a person more susceptible to infections, among other negative effects, although there is some evidence of substantial individual differences in this type of reactivity to stress (Manuck et al., 1991).

Elements of the Human Immune System While much remains to be learned about the details of immunologic functioning, particularly in regard to psychosocial influences, certain broad outlines are now fairly well understood.

The immune system is traditionally divided into two branches: humoral and cellular. The humoral branch refers to the activity of B-cells and the antibodies they produce. Cellular immune function, on the other hand, is mediated by T-cells, whose effects, while widespread, do not include antibody production. When an organism is invaded by an *antigen*—that is, a substance recognized as "foreign"—B-cells and T-cells become activated and multiply rapidly, deploying the various forms of counterattack mediated by each type of cell.

B-cells, which are formed in the bone marrow, perform their defensive function by producing antibodies that circulate in the blood serum. B-cell (or humoral immune) functioning is involved chiefly with detection of and protection against the more common varieties of bacterial infection. *T-cells* develop in the thymus and mediate immune reactions that, while slower, are both more extensive and more direct in character than those generated by B-cells. These include: (1) destruction of certain types of antigens, especially nonbacterial ones such as viruses and neoplasms (tumor cells); (2) regulation and, in certain instances, activation of the other, antibody-based division of the defense system; and (3) termination of the immune response when danger subsides. T-cells mainly generate an attack that is highly specific to a given invading antigen.

The protective activity of the B-cells and T-cells is supported and reinforced by other specialized components of the system—most notably natural killer cells, macrophages (literally, "big eaters"), and granulocytes. The front line of immune defense is thus contained within this highly differentiated system of white cells that circulate freely in the blood or remain as resident reinforcements in the lymph nodes. The immune system's response to antigen invasion is thus generalized and intricately orchestrated, requiring the intact functioning of numerous components. As will be seen, it is by now a virtual certainty that the brain is centrally involved in this control of immune system events.

Psychosocial Compromise of the Immune Response
As a disease of the immune system, AIDS provides a good illustration of the interrelationship between stress and the immune response. Though stress may not *cause* AIDS to be expressed in the HIV-positive person, it apparently weakens further the body's already compromised immune response (Kiecolt-Glaser & Glaser, 1988, 1992). For example, Antoni and colleagues (1990) reported preliminary results indicating that behavioral interventions, such as aerobic exercise, had positive psychological and immunocompetence effects among groups of uninfected high-risk and early-stage infected gay men. More recently, Kemeny and colleagues (1994) presented evidence suggesting that a depressed mood was associated with enhanced HIV-1

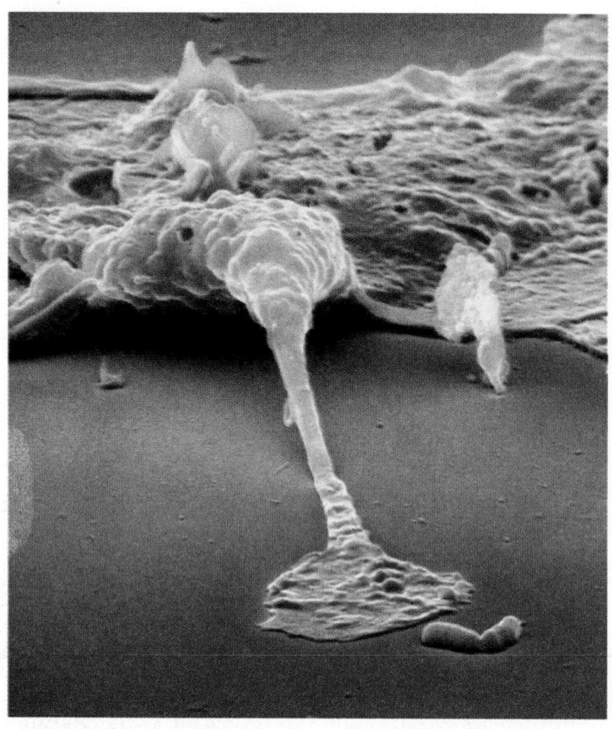

A macrophage reaches out to eat bacteria. Macrophages are important components of the immune system because they initiate the action of B-cells and T-cells against bacterial, or antigen, invasion.

activity among infected gay men, confirming in this group the more general point that psychological depression compromises immune function (Herbert & Cohen, 1993). It also enhances the likelihood of continued high-risk behavior in as yet uninfected men (Kalichman et al., 1997a). Since there are effective treatments for depression, notably including psychosocial ones such as cognitive-behavioral therapy (e.g., DeRubeis, 1997; Hollon et al., 1992), the current almost exclusive focus on pharmacological approaches in treating AIDS may be neglecting an important alternative.

Original correlational evidence of a stress-illness relationship has been fortified by studies permitting a stronger causal inference concerning the role of stress in reducing immunocompetence. Strauman, Lemieux, and Coe (1993) found that natural killer cell cytotoxicity (i.e., its power to eradicate an antigen) was significantly diminished with induced negative self-evaluations, an effect that was especially strong for persons who were determined to be anxious and/or dysphoric in mood before the experiment. In another experimental demonstration, stressful life events, self-perceived stress, and negative emotion—all assessed before exposure—significantly predicted which subjects would become ill with colds (Cohen, Tyrrell, & Smith, 1993).

As already suggested, depression or negative affect may turn out to have special significance with respect to the suppression of immune protection. A review of the evidence by Weisse (1992) indicated a strong association between dysphoric mood and compromised immune function, one that appears to be at least partially independent of specific situations or events that may have provoked depressed feelings; that is, the state of being depressed *in itself* adds something beyond any negative effects of the stressors precipitating this mood. Another review of the relevant research found that depressive affect was reliably associated with lowered numbers of white cells following foreign protein challenge, lowered natural killer cell activity, and lowered quantities of several varieties of circulating white cells (Herbert & Cohen, 1993). A possibly related finding is that health care use diminished with recovery from depressive disorders among members of a health maintenance organization (Von Korff et al., 1992).

The list of conditions demonstrated to be associated with diminished immune function is, in fact, a long one. Besides psychological depression, it includes sleep deprivation, marathon running, space flight, and death of a spouse (Schleifer, Keller, & Stein, 1985; Schleifer et al., 1989; Vasiljeva et al., 1989). Cacioppo and colleagues (1998) have recently added caregiving to a demented person such as an Alzheimer's patient (see Chapter 13) to the list. Immune responsiveness has been shown to vary with even normal, daily mood variations (Stone et al., 1987). A group of researchers at Ohio State University has repeatedly demonstrated the compromise of white blood cell proliferation, including diminished natural killer cell activity, among medical students undergoing the stress of academic examinations (Glaser et al., 1985, 1987). Natural killer cells are believed to play a key role in tumor surveillance and the control of viral infections.

Psychoneuroimmunology Indications of strong relationships between certain negative psychological states and diminished immune system functioning suggest some sort of central mediating mechanism that presides over the interaction. The obvious candidate for such a role is the central nervous system, specifically the brain. Such considerations have led to the development of the field of **psychoneuroimmunology,** which explores psychological

psychoneuroimmunology Field whose focus is on the impact of psychological factors, such as the effects of stressors, on the brain's control of the immune system via neural, neurochemical, and hormonal processes.

interactions in the brain's control of immune responsiveness by way of its control over neural, neurochemical, and endocrinological (hormonal) processes. Although still relatively new, the field has developed in a rapid and impressive manner (see Maier & Watkins, 1998, and Maier, Watkins, & Fleshner, 1994, for an overview).

Determining the Pathway for Brain Mediation Trying to determine how stressors—in particular, psychosocial or mental ones—may impair the immune response through some type of brain mediation has been one of the major challenges of psychoneuroimmunology (Antoni et al., 1990; Jemmott & Locke, 1984; Kiecolt-Glaser & Glaser, 1992; Maier & Watkins, 1998; Maier et al., 1994).

The Hypothalamic-Pituitary-Adrenocortical Axis Researchers initially focused on the hypothalamic-pituitary-adrenocortical (HPA) axis as the primary pathway. According to this hypothesis, the processing of stressful events in the brain causes hypothalamic activation of the pituitary, which, in turn, stimulates the adrenal cortex to secrete excessive levels of adrenocortical hormones, substances known to have powerfully negative (as well as some positive) effects on immune functioning. In fact, corticosteroids such as cortisone are used to treat diseases where suppression of the immune system is desired, such as rheumatoid arthritis, an "autoimmune" disease in which the immune system makes a mistake and attacks healthy tissue.

Other Neurochemicals and Immune Function Other research suggests that other pathways may include hormones (including growth hormone, testosterone, and estrogen) and a variety of more exotic neurochemicals (including the endorphins). And the link between psychosocial stressors and the immune system may be even more direct. The discovery of nerve endings in thymus, spleen, and lymph nodes, tissues literally teeming with white blood cells, suggests the possibility of direct neural control of immunologic agents. It is known, too, that white blood cell surfaces contain receptors for circulating neurochemicals (Rogers, 1989). We must assume that the presence of these receptors on these cells is not accidental and that the cells respond in some way to messages conveyed by brain-regulated substances in the bloodstream, such as various peptides.

Conditioned Immunosuppression Perhaps most unexpectedly, immunosuppression can be classically conditioned (Ader & Cohen, 1984; Maier et al., 1994)—that is, it can come to be elicited as an acquired response to previously neutral stimuli, just as Pavlov's dogs learned to salivate to a tone. Conceivably, even mental stimuli such as thoughts or images could thus come to activate immunosuppression if they were regularly paired with immunosuppressive events (operating as unconditioned stimuli). For example, the 1 to 3 years of immunosuppression believed to follow the death of a spouse (Hafen et al., 1996, p. 25) might be due to repeatedly evoked images of a lost and more pleasant past, images that became conditioned stimuli for immunosuppression through association with the latter during an earlier period of intense grieving.

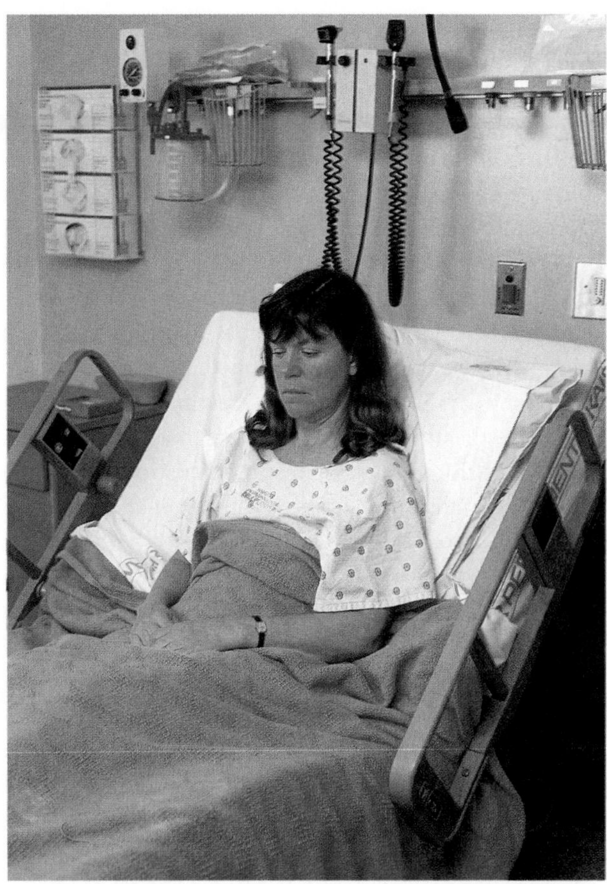

Just as stress can disrupt the immune system and make a person vulnerable to disease, so can being sick and the taxing of the immune system make a person vulnerable psychologically—to anxiety and depression, for example.

Immune Feedback Complicating the picture of the effects of psychosocial stressors on the immune system is the fact that the influences are bidirectional. Maier and colleagues (Maier et al., 1994; Maier & Watkins, 1998) present strong evidence that a person's behavior and psychological states do indeed affect immune functioning, but the status of immunologic defenses also feeds back to affect current mental states and behavioral dispositions by affecting the blood levels of circulating neurochemicals, which in turn modify brain states. Such a feedback loop might, for example, account for the frequently observed effect of stress in inducing psychological depression. That is, stressors may evoke immunosuppression, which could, in turn, result in chemical signals to the brain having the effect of inducing depressive thoughts and behavior.

Stressor Toxicity While efforts to relate specific stressors to specific physical diseases have not generally been successful, stress is becoming a key underlying theme in understanding the development and course of virtually all organic illness. Stress may serve as a predisposing, precipitating, or reinforcing factor in the causal pattern, or it may merely aggravate a condition that might have occurred anyway. Even stress that is treatment-related, as in aggressive therapy for certain cancers, may carry its own measure of risk for compromising defensive resources by seriously diminishing the patient's quality of life, as pointed out by Anderson, Kiecolt-Glaser, and Glaser (1994). Post-traumatic stress may continue to have destructive health effects long after the traumatic event, as suggested in the long-term problematic health histories of women (and men) who have been victims of sexual assault (Golding, 1994; Golding, Cooper, & George, 1997). Often stress appears to speed up the onset or increase the severity of a disorder and to interfere with the body's immunological defenses and other homeostatic repair functions. Presuming that we all have one organ system in our bodies that is relatively vulnerable, a high, chronic level of stress puts us at risk for a breakdown of that organ system, and perhaps others, sooner or later.

Lifestyle as a Factor in Health Endangerment

Increasing understanding of the biological mechanisms involved in our psychological and physiological states has meant that a great deal of attention is today being paid to the role of lifestyle in the development or maintenance of many health problems. Numerous aspects of the way we live are now considered influential in the development of some severe physical problems: diet (particularly overeating and consuming too many high-fat, low-fiber foods), lack of exercise, smoking cigarettes, family estrangement and divorce, excessive alcohol and drug use, constantly facing high-stress situations, and even ineffective ways of dealing with day-to-day problems are but a few of the many lifestyle patterns that are viewed as contributing causes.

Lifestyle factors—habits or behavior patterns presumably under our own control—play a major role in three of the leading causes of death in this country: coronary heart disease, automobile accidents, and alcohol-related deaths. Meanwhile, we continue to struggle with the AIDS epidemic. Despite widespread knowledge that use of the latex condom is an effective measure for preventing transmission of the HIV-1 retrovirus, very large numbers of sexually active persons (both homosexual and heterosexual) continue their high-risk behavior (Bryan, Aiken, & West, 1997; Carey et al., 1997; Fisher & Fisher, 1992; Kalichman, Kelly, & Rompa, 1997b; Kalichman et al., 1997a; Kelly & Murphy, 1992).

Even in cases where virtual proof of causation exists, such as cigarette smoking, it is difficult for many people to change their lifestyles to reduce their risk of disease—an incentive that may seem very remote for currently healthy people. Significant and lasting change is generally hard to accomplish, and this is especially true where available rewards are immediate and powerful, as in the case of addictions (Chapter 10). After having two heart attacks and surgery to remove a cancerous lung, one man continued to smoke two and a half packs of cigarettes a day, even though he frequently said, "I know these things are killing me a little at a time... but they have become so much a part of my life I can't live without them!"

IN REVIEW

- How does a person's attitude and outlook on life affect health maintenance and deterioration?
- How can optimism either help or hinder a person's ability to cope with illness? How does a deficit in optimism affect health outcomes?
- What physiological mechanisms are involved in autonomic nervous system arousal?
- Describe the relationship between stress and the immune system.

PSYCHOLOGICAL FACTORS AND CARDIOVASCULAR DISEASE

Diseases of the cardiovascular system (the heart and its connected tree of vessels through which its pumping action distributes and retrieves blood) remain the most serious health problem confronting Americans and their health care professionals in terms of deaths accounted for and disabilities experienced. The bulk of the difficulty consists of three interrelated clinical conditions: (1) hypertension (high blood pressure); (2) coronary heart disease (CHD), where arteries supplying blood to the heart muscle itself become clogged; and (3) stroke, where the same types of clogging affect arterial supply to the brain. Of these, we deal here with hypertension and CHD;

HIGHLIGHT 8.2

Suppressed Rage or Suppression of Something More Benign?

The classical psychoanalytic interpretation of hypertension is that affected people suffer from suppressed rage (e.g., Gentry et al., 1982; Spielberger et al., 1985). Although suppressed hostility might be expected to run high among inner-city residents, including African-Americans, the suppressed-rage hypothesis cannot be said to be firmly established with respect to all, or even necessarily a majority of, affected persons. Instead, McClelland (1979) found that individuals can be driven to high blood pressure and hypertension not so much by suppressed rage as by the need to inhibit the expression of certain power motives. In the case of African-Americans, any number of seemingly benign power motives—simply aspiring to a certain job, profession, or neighborhood—may qualify as acts poorly tolerated by a majority white society and thus needing to be inhibited. The result may be elevated blood pressure (Jorgensen et al., 1996). ■

stroke, which is in many ways similar to CHD in its etiology, is covered in Chapter 13.

Essential Hypertension

When a physiologically normal person is calm, his or her heartbeat is regular, pulse is even, blood pressure is relatively low, and visceral organs are well supplied with blood. With stress, however, the vessels of the visceral organs constrict, and blood flows in greater quantity to the muscles of the trunk and limbs—part of the fight-or-flight response described earlier. With the tightening of the tiny vessels supplying the visceral organs, the heart must work harder. As it beats faster and with greater force, the pulse quickens and blood pressure mounts. Usually, when the crisis passes, the body resumes normal functioning and the blood pressure returns to normal. Under continuing emotional strain, however, high blood pressure may become chronic.

Blood pressure below 140/90 is considered "normotensive"; blood pressure above 160/100 is considered unambiguously "high." (By convention, the first number given is the *systolic* pressure, that occurring when the heart contracts; the second is the *diastolic,* or between-beat, pressure.) Consistent readings between these extremes are designated "borderline," as is a pattern in which a person fluctuates between normotensive and high pressures (Turner, 1994). Much evidence indicates that borderline readings are a risk factor for the development of definite, sustained hypertension, a disease estimated to afflict over 40 million Americans.

Many clinicians and investigators hold the view that hypertension begins with a biological predisposition to high cardiovascular reactivity to stress (see, e.g., Tuomisto, 1997; Turner, 1994) and then, given untoward life circumstances, progresses through borderline to frank hypertension in the adult years. Other organic malfunctions known to induce hypertension account for only a small percentage of hypertension cases; the large remainder are given the designation **essential hypertension,** meaning no specific physical cause is known. Essential hypertension is often symptomless until its effects become manifest in medical complications. In addition to enhancing significantly the likelihood of CHD and stroke, it is often a causal factor in occlusive disease of the peripheral arteries, congestive heart failure (due to the heart's inability to overcome the resistance of constricted arteries), kidney failure, blindness, and a number of other serious physical ailments.

High blood pressure is thus an insidious and dangerous disorder. Ironically, it is both simple and painless to detect by means of the familiar inflated arm cuff, automated versions of which are widely available for self-testing at shopping centers and the like. The normal regulation of blood pressure, however, is so complex that when it goes awry in a particular case, identifying the causal factors can be extremely difficult (Herd, 1984). Kidney dysfunction, for example, may be a cause, an effect, or both, of dangerously elevated pressures.

Hypertension can also result from excessive sodium (e.g., salt) in the diet, or from excessive metabolic retention of sodium. Indeed, sodium may be part of the reason why the incidence of hypertension is about twice as high among African-Americans as among white Americans

essential hypertension High blood pressure that has no specific known physical cause.

Even though many Type As don't have coronary problems while some Type Bs do, personality makeup seems to play an important role in predisposing a person to illness—or to health, as suggested here.

personality—characterized in the literature as one possessing a high degree of "hardiness," or the ability to withstand stress and bounce back from it (e.g., Hafen et al., 1996). Research justifies the generalization that negative attitudes about oneself, the world (including its people), and the future are associated with higher levels of physical and mental illness (especially depression). But, as in the case of attempts to define the "coronary-prone" (Type A) personality, efforts to identify more specific types of association between personality characteristics and particular diseases tend to founder in the face of the variability of people and of the diseases they contract.

For example, although Kidson (1973) found hypertensive patients as a group to be significantly more insecure, anxious, sensitive, and angry than a nonhypertensive control group, a sizable number of the control-group members also showed these characteristics. As we have emphasized, the relationships between particular personality variables and disease processes, while often clearly important, tend to be complex and difficult to pin down (see Friedman, Hawley, & Tucker, 1994).

So even though personality makeup seems to play an important role, we still do not know why some people with predisposing personality characteristics do not develop a particular disease, nor can we account adequately for the wide range of personality types among people who suffer from the same medical condition. Usually, we can only conclude that particular personality factors are weakly but significantly correlated with the occurrence of certain illnesses.

Interpersonal Relationships as Sources of Protection Being "connected" with others in mutually supportive ways—as in well-functioning families—is a significant protective factor in maintaining physical health. Research strongly supports that conclusion and extends it beyond the confines of the family. Having a good social support system is a significant predictor of good health maintenance; by contrast, being alone and lonely is a predictor for multiple illnesses and death from multiple causes (Hafen et al., 1996). Death rates from physical disease are markedly higher in people who have recently undergone marital problems or divorce than in the general population (Bloom, Asher, & White, 1978; Burman & Margolin, 1989; Siegel, 1986). Loss of a spouse through death also puts the survivor at elevated risk for illness, but men are more adversely affected by the death of their wives than women are by the death of their husbands (Hafen et al., 1996; Stroebe & Stroebe, 1983).

Lynch (1977), in a book entitled *The Broken Heart*, argues convincingly that the relatively high incidence of heart disease in industrialized communities stems in part from the absence of positive human relationships. And Stanford University psychiatrist David Spiegel (1991) reported himself as "stunned" by finding that a group of seriously ill breast cancer patients who had been assigned to group therapy (and thus developed strong, mutually supportive ties) survived, on average, twice as long as a comparable group of women given only standard medical treatment.

The Learning of Illnesses Although Pavlov and many subsequent investigators have demonstrated that autonomic responses can be conditioned—as in the case of salivation—it was long assumed that people could not learn to control such responses "voluntarily." We now know that this assumption was wrong. Not only can autonomic reactivity be conditioned involuntarily via the classical Pavlovian model, but operant conditioning of the autonomic nervous system can also take place.

Thus, the hypothesis has developed that certain physical disorders may arise through accidental reinforcement of symptom and behavioral patterns. "A child who is repeatedly allowed to stay home from school when he has an upset stomach may be learning the visceral responses of chronic indigestion" (Lang, 1970, p. 86). Similarly, an adolescent girl may get little or no attention from being "good," but if she starves herself to the point of severe weight loss she may become the center of attention. If this pattern is continued, she might learn to avoid weight gain at all costs and correspondingly learn a profound aversion to food. The increasing alarm of her parents and others would presumably serve as a potent reinforcement for her to continue avoiding food.

Although causal factors other than conditioning are now thought to play a role in most cases of psychogenic illness, it seems clear that regardless of how a physical symptom may have developed, it may be elicited by suggestion and maintained by the reinforcement provided by *secondary gains,* indirect external benefits derived from the illness behavior. The role of suggestion was demonstrated by a classic study in which 19 of 40 volunteer asthmatic subjects developed asthma symptoms after breathing the mist of a salt solution that they were falsely told contained allergens, such as dust or pollen. In fact, 12 of the subjects had full-fledged asthma attacks. When the subjects then took what they thought was a drug to combat asthma (actually the same salt mist), their symptoms disappeared immediately (Bleeker, 1968). This study clearly shows the effect of suggestion on an autonomically mediated response. Why the other 21 subjects remained unaffected is not clear.

In short, it appears that some physical disorders may be acquired, maintained, or both in much the same way as other behavior patterns. Indeed, this finding is a basic tenet of behavioral medicine and health psychology, one aspect of which examines how various behavior modification and psychotherapeutic techniques can alter overt and covert reactions to physical disease processes (Blanchard, 1994; Bradley & Prokop, 1982; Gentry, 1984; Hafen et al., 1996; Stone et al., 1987; Williams & Gentry, 1977; see also the August 1992 [vol. 60, no. 4] special issue of the *Journal of Consulting and Clinical Psychology*).

Sociocultural Causal Factors

The incidence of specific disorders, both physical and mental, varies in different societies, in different strata of the same society, and over time. In general, what Cannon (1929) called "diseases of civilization" do not occur among nonindustrialized societies such as the aborigines of the Australian Western Desert (Kidson & Jones, 1968), the Navajo Indians of Arizona, or certain isolated groups in South America (Stein, 1970). As these societies are exposed to social change, however, gastrointestinal, cardiovascular, and other psychogenic diseases begin to make their appearances. There is evidence of change in the nature and incidence of such disorders in Japan, paralleling the tremendous social changes that have taken place there since World War II (Ikemi et al., 1974). For example, the incidence of hypertension and coronary heart disease have increased markedly with the post-war westernization of Japanese culture.

In general, it appears that any sociocultural conditions that markedly increase life stress tend to play havoc with the biological human organism and lead to an increase in disease as well as other physical and mental problems.

IN REVIEW

- What is the problem of specificity with respect to psychogenic diseases?
- What are three possible genetic contributions to disease, and how will genetic mapping help to unravel these?
- What personality characteristics appear to be associated with disease resistance?
- Explain how learning might be involved in the development of psychogenic illness.

TREATMENTS AND OUTCOMES FOR PSYCHOGENIC ILLNESSES

Though a particular environmental stressor may have been a key causal factor in the development of a physical illness, removal of this stressor, even combined with learning more effective coping techniques, may not be enough to bring about recovery if organic changes have taken place; such changes may have become chronic and irreversible.

Treatment of psychogenic physical illnesses must begin with a thorough assessment of the nature and seriousness of the organic pathology involved. Since the latter may prove progressive and/or life-threatening, immediate medical intervention may be necessary to curtail or reverse the pathological condition. Once the patient is sufficiently stabilized medically, wisdom dictates the need for a comprehensive intervention plan based on behavioral also that there is less comorbidity with other psychiatric disorders (Telch & Stice, 1998).

Prevalence of Eating Disorders

It is generally agreed that the prevalence of eating disorders, particularly bulimia nervosa, increased markedly over the last four decades of the twentieth century. Moreover, this increase appears to be "real," and not significantly the product of heightened sensitivity and, subsequently, diagnosis among clinicians, as is suspected for dissociative identity disorder (Chapter 7). The reasons for the increase are not fully understood, but most authorities point to changing norms regarding the "ideal" size and shape of women as one decisive factor. The female "curves" once almost uniformly admired by both men and women are now considered unattractive and undesirable, particularly by many women. Added to this external motivation is the fact that the personal security and solid self-esteem that would doubtless be powerful bulwarks against such influences are apparently not easy to acquire or maintain among adolescent girls and young women in our post-modern society—which we shall consider more fully below.

The point prevalences of the full syndromes among adolescent and young adult women in the United States are estimated to be between 0.5 and 1.0 percent for anorexia nervosa, and between 1.0 and 3.0 percent for bulimia nervosa (American Psychiatric Association, 1994). As we have seen, however, such specifically identifiable cases account for only some two-thirds of persons seeking help for eating disorders. We may thus conservatively estimate the point prevalence of all diagnosable eating disorders among postpubertal American females to be minimally 4.0 percent—that is, at least 4 in 100 such persons may be expected to have an eating disorder of sufficient severity to warrant clinical intervention.

Historically, these disorders have been largely confined to the white majority of middle to upper socioeconomic status. A variety of observations suggests that these disorders are becoming more prevalent among the less privileged. Nor is this phenomenon limited to the United States. Le Grange, Telch, and Tibbs (1998) recently reported widespread eating disorder difficulties among both Caucasian and non-Caucasian South African college students. Among American women of college age, 10 percent or more of them acknowledge some symptoms of eating disorder, which may or may not be severe enough to meet diagnostic criteria (G. Leon, personal communication, November 12, 1997; Heatherton et al., 1995). For some, this will prove a temporary condition, according to a 10-year follow-up of persons who were in college at initial assessment (Heatherton et al., 1997). At follow-up, the women in this study had experienced significant declines in disordered eating and increased satisfaction with their bodies, despite continuing preoccupation with losing weight. In contrast, many men in the study reported increased concern about their eating habits.

Generalized Risk and Causal Factors in Eating Disorders

In discussing the origins of eating disorders, it is useful to distinguish general vulnerabilities, or those characteristics that seem implicated in a variety of disordered outcomes, from those influences that appear to be relatively specific to the development of eating problems. In this section, we will first review those factors that appear to contribute to the prevalence of a range of problems, including eating disorders, among young women in our society. There appear to be a number of these risk factors that raise the overall likelihood of developing an eating disorder of some kind but are not specific to either eating (as opposed to other types of) disorders or to the particular form in which an eating disorder may be manifested, such as anorexia nervosa, bulimia nervosa, or BED. Following that, we will take up and review what is known or suspected about anorexia nervosa and bulimia nervosa in terms of specific elements of developmental history that may contribute to the disordered outcome. (To date, little of a reliable nature is known about the origins of BED.) It should be understood from the outset, however, that eating disorders (like most other disorders) are undoubtedly multi-determined, and therefore it is unlikely that compelling single factors as causes will be discovered.

Self-Ideal Body Image Discordance That there is a general sociocultural factor idealizing extremes of thinness in women in "advanced" Western cultures (and, by cultural diffusion, elsewhere) is beyond question. Nearly all instances of eating disorder in general begin with the "normal" dieting that is extremely common among young women in our culture. As several converging lines of evidence indicate (e.g., Fallon & Rozin, 1985; Rodin, 1993; Wiseman et al., 1992; Zellner, Harner, & Adler, 1989), one important product of these thinness pressures is that girls and women often develop highly intrusive and pervasive perceptual biases regarding how "fat" they are. Probably the most important of these are the perceptual discrepancies between the image the girl or young woman has of her own body and the "ideal" female form as represented in contemporary media. Such perceptual biases lead girls and women to believe that men prefer more slender shapes than they in fact do. Figure 8.1 illustrates this set of findings.

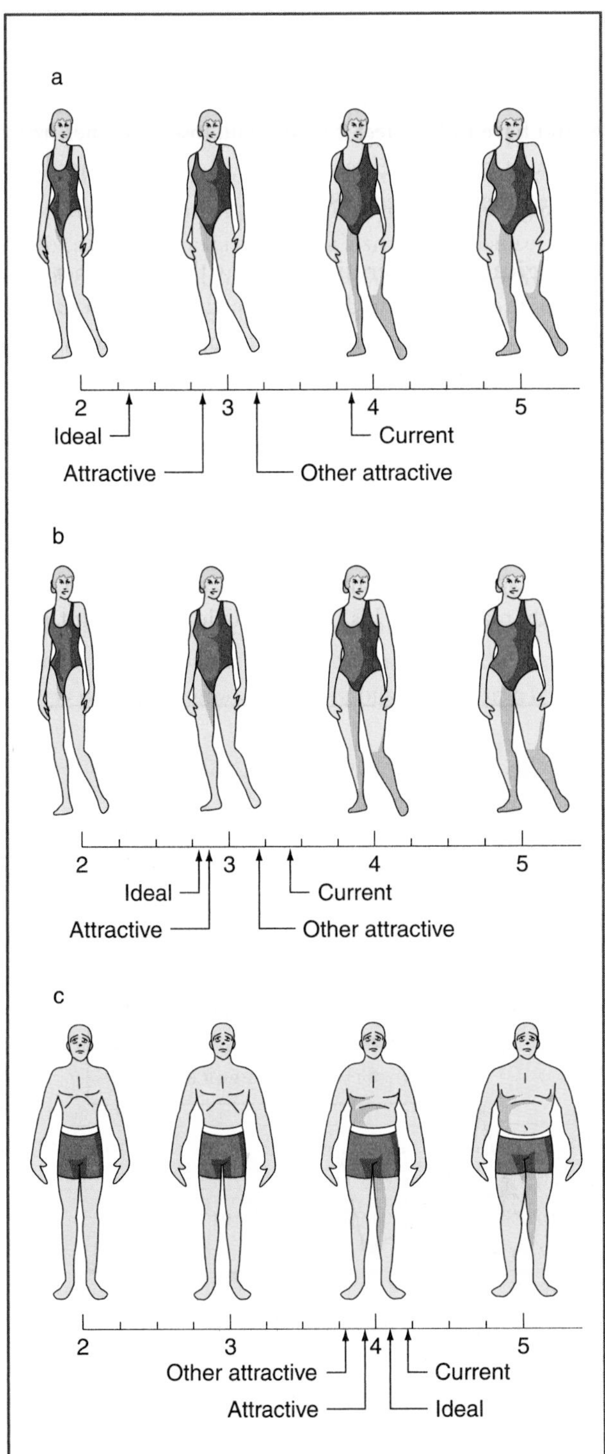

FIGURE 8.1 EATING DISORDER STATUS AND GENDER AS DETERMINANTS OF DESIRABLE BODY SHAPE
Indicated are mean ratings of women identified as having abnormal eating patterns (a), of women having normal eating patterns (b), and of a demographically comparable group of men (c). All subjects rated their "current" figure, their "ideal" figure, and the figure thought most attractive by the opposite sex (labeled "attractive"). Also included are the actual mean ratings of "most attractive" provided by opposite-sex subjects (labeled "other attractive").
Source: Zellner, Harner, & Adler (1989).

As the female ideal represented by models grows thinner, a young girl's sense of the discrepancy between her own real weight and her fantasized ideal grows, creating a loss of self-esteem as well as a desire to attain an ever-more impossible weight that can only be reached by compulsive dieting.

Most studies indicate that this phenomenon is quite specific to females, perhaps adding to (or being a significant cause of) the decreases in self-esteem mid-adolescent girls regularly experience. Young males—as a group—remain unaffected by any special slenderness value (perhaps because they are not the subjects of such concerted image-making). Somewhat curiously, and in marked contrast to anorexia nervosa and bulimia nervosa patients, most binge-eating disorder patients do not appear to overvalue thinness, although they do disparage their own bodies (Marcus, 1997).

Such widespread self-ideal discrepancies might be less disconcerting if most of the young women thus affected had a reasonable chance of attaining their body ideal by

Research has shown that the families of anorexic girls tend to be intolerant of disagreements and subtly undermining of daughters' efforts at autonomy, perhaps by being overly critical or through an abundance of advice. As a result, their daughters may be tempted to please their parents' perfectionism and exert their own will in the one area where they are clearly in control: their bodies.

ily; and to persevere, even in the absence of tangible reward" (Strober, 1997, p. 233). These qualities are almost the antitheses of what is required by the new demands placed on a girl with the advent of puberty or upon confronting numerous other developmentally normal life changes, such as going off to college, where being able to adapt easily to new situations is highly advantageous.

The personality antecedents of bulimia appear not to be as well articulated as in anorexia and more heterogeneous. The premorbid characteristics of many bulimia nervosa patients, however, are seen as similar to those noted above (e.g., Gleaves & Eberenz, 1993). Research on bulimics has found one subgroup sharing characteristics of emotional instability and impulsivity (Vitousek & Manke, 1994). Nearly all authorities agree that, like persons with anorexia nervosa, a large proportion of bulimia nervosa patients show a long-standing pattern of excessive perfectionism (Garner & Garfinkel, 1997), which appears to manifest itself in widespread negative self-evaluation (e.g., see Fairburn et al., 1997), particularly if the person perceives herself to be overweight (Joiner, Heatherton, & Keel, 1997a). Maturity fears (fears of becoming adult) may be another shared characteristic of both anorexia- and bulimia-disposed persons (Garner, Vitousek, & Pike, 1997; Joiner et al., 1997b).

Family Patterns Clinicians dealing with anorexia nervosa patients have for decades been impressed with certain problems that seem regularly to characterize the families out of which these distressed young women emerge, so much so that many advocate a family therapy approach to treatment intervention (Dare & Eisler, 1997). Anorexia nervosa patients usually describe their fathers as emotional absentees and their mothers as excessively dominant, intrusive, overbearing, and markedly ambivalent in dispensing affection. However, attempts to depict family characteristics associated with eating disorders must be subject to the general caution that these observations may sometimes be contaminated by the impact the eating disorder has on family functioning. That is, the causal connection, if any, might be in the other direction.

The portrait of families of anorexic patients painted by the research and clinical literature is generally consistent with the portrayal rendered by the girls and young women themselves. Families of anorexics are described as having limited tolerance for disharmonious affect or psychological tension; the parents emphasize propriety and rules, overly control their children and discourage autonomy, and have poor conflict resolution skills (Strober, 1997). In addition, many of these families evidence long-standing preoccupations regarding the desirability of thinness, dieting, and a good physical appearance (Garner & Garfinkel, 1997).

Hilde Bruch (1986) saw the anorexic person as attempting to camouflage an undeveloped and amorphous selfhood by being different, even unique, in a special and fiercely independent way. We can thus conceive of a typical developmental course in which the compliance and perfectionism of the pre-anorexic girl is an adaptation to the rigid rules and control of a family system intolerant of deviation or disharmony. In such a situation and without supportive parents, a daughter is left with little personal foundation, external support, or instrumental means to express the normal strivings for individuality and autonomy that are enhanced with the onset of adolescence. In this situation the daughter "rebels" in one of the few ways available in this family system—by becoming a super-perfect exemplar of the values of thinness and of propriety and restraint with respect to the indulgence of needs, even the very basic one of hunger. In effect, she "turns the tables" on the oppressive influences dominating her life. She retains this "autonomous" position with a stubborn fierceness and relentlessness that is routinely impressive even to clinicians with long experience in the field.

Findings about family patterns in bulimia nervosa suggest, again, a number of similarities with anorexia nervosa. For example, families of bulimic women are characterized by such risk factors as high parental expectations, dieting by other family members, and critical comment from other family members about shape, weight, or eating (Fairburn et al., 1997).

The parents of bulimic young women were found to be controlling, despite their overt intentions to be helpful or generous (Ratti, Humphrey, & Lyons, 1996). Such parental behaviors appear to encourage daughters to attack themselves, and the attack shows up as disparaged self-image (see, e.g., Benjamin, 1996b)—a propensity Wonderlich, Klein, and Council (1996) found abnormally present in their sample of bulimic women. These parental behaviors may also make daughters susceptible to "internalizing" dysfunctional thinness values (Mason & Chaney, 1996). In short, available knowledge suggests that both anorexic and bulimic individuals have a common problem of being deeply but ambivalently involved with their parents in power struggles concerning their autonomy and identity. Such problems are, of course, a notable adolescent developmental hurdle in our culture and so are far from exclusive to persons with eating disorders. The evidence suggests that there may be something special about the families of eating disordered women, in that they appear to fail in providing the support for autonomous functioning that would enable these young women to negotiate successfully the challenge of becoming, unambivalently, fully functioning independent persons.

Treatment of Eating Disorders

The therapeutic management of eating disorders is multifaceted, complicated in no small part by the fact that, in the case of anorexia, failure can result in the patient's death. Fortunately, there are a large number of procedures available, including hospitalization if the situation is desperate. These can be brought to bear to (1) stabilize the patient and (2) maximize chances for full and lasting recovery. Hospitalization permits control of the patient's environment, and of her food intake (if necessary by measures such as tube feeding), to an extent not possible in more natural settings. Ultimate success, however, depends on whether the patient becomes committed to change—which is not always to be assumed.

Treatment of Anorexia Nervosa Efforts to treat the psychological aspects of anorexia must frequently wait until the patient is renourished and her weight reestablished to a level that will ensure both survival and the ability to profit from an emotionally demanding psychological intervention. Not uncommonly, this involves hospitalization under conditions of rigorous dietary control and monitoring of progress toward a targeted range of weight gain (Andersen, Bowers, & Evans, 1997). Normally, this short-term effort is successful. What is less reliable is the anorexic person's ability to maintain these gains. This is, in fact, extremely doubtful without treatment that is also designed to modify or eradicate the psychological conditions fueling the anorexic behavior.

Many varieties of psychosocial intervention are potentially useful in reversing the problems underlying anorexia. Unfortunately, and unlike the situation with bulimia, there have been surprisingly few controlled studies to allow for a truly informed choice among these psychosocial treatments. This is probably due in large measure to the fact that successful treatment of anorexia, by whatever means, takes a long time. As we shall see, cognitive-behavioral therapy (CBT) (discussed earlier in this chapter and in Chapter 3) has proved very effective in treating bulimia, and because anorexia shares many similarities with bulimia, CBT is often attempted in cases of anorexia.

One highly detailed model for the application of CBT

techniques to anorexia emphasizes the *differences* between the average bulimic and anorexic patient (such as the frequently uncertain motivation and the pronounced social deficits of the anorexic), and builds into the treatment plan techniques for managing the special problems of the anorexic, such as her predictable distancing and distrust of the therapist (Garner, Vitousek, & Pike, 1997).

Treatment of Bulimia Nervosa One of the more dramatic successes of research in psychopathology and its treatment in recent decades has been the unmatched success of CBT in the treatment of bulimia nervosa. Multiple controlled studies of immediate post-treatment and long-term follow-up outcomes of CBT treatment of bulimia nervosa have established CBT as the clear treatment of choice for this disorder (e.g., Agras et al., 1992; Fairburn et al., 1993; Fichter et al., 1991; Leitenberg et al., 1994; Wilson & Fairburn, 1993, 1998; Wilson, Fairburn, & Agras, 1997). Such studies have included competitive comparisons with medication therapy (chiefly antidepressants) and generally show CBT to be clearly superior. In fact, combining these two approaches produces only a modest increment in effectiveness over that achievable with CBT alone (Wilson & Fairburn, 1998).

The behavioral component of CBT for bulimia is focused on normalizing eating patterns—ending bingeing and purging and teaching the person instead to eat small amounts more regularly. For example, the patient is put on a prescribed schedule for eating, one emphasizing temporal regularity rather than amounts eaten. The cognitive elements of CBT treatment address the dysfunctional thought patterns usually present in bulimia, such as the all-or-nothing thinking described above. For example, the tendency to divide all foods into "good" and "bad" categories is disputed by providing factual information and by arranging for the patient to demonstrate to herself that ingesting "bad" food does not inevitably lead to a total loss of control over eating.

Treatment of Binge-Eating Disorder Little of a systematic nature is known about effective treatment for binge-eating disorder (BED), probably because this is a heterogeneous and relatively neglected category of disorder. Undoubtedly, most instances have some overlap with both anorexia and bulimia. Hence clinicians have tended to try to adapt relevant aspects of the treatment of these disorders to the particular clinical picture presented by the BED patient. This is well illustrated in the approach advocated by Marcus (1997), who emphasizes the adaptation of already established CBT techniques for treatment of anorexia and bulimia nervosa to the special circumstances of the BED patient. Such patients are typically overweight and subject to chaotic eating patterns. They also typically have a variety of illogical and contradictory "rules" about food ingestion—for example, sharing with bulimics a rigid distinction between "good" and "bad" foods. They may also have stereotypical attitudes about the character flaws of overweight people and so lack the self-esteem that might motivate them to stop their bingeing.

Many BED patients are failed veterans of various diet plans based on unproven and sometimes nonsensical principles, adding to their burden of misinformation, confusion, and sense of failure. Significant depression is a common comorbid condition for binge eaters. Thus, a judiciously planned program of CBT, together with corrective and factual information on nutrition and weight loss, can be helpful to many of these people. Fairburn and Carter (1997) suggest the addition of selected self-help reading materials to such a therapeutic program.

IN REVIEW

- How do the prevalence rates for eating disorders vary according to socioeconomic status, gender, sexual orientation, and nationality?
- What are the major causal factors for anorexia nervosa and for bulimia nervosa?
- Compare the treatments for anorexia nervosa and bulimia nervosa, and account for the widespread use of cognitive-behavioral therapy.

SUMMARY

GENERAL PSYCHOLOGICAL FACTORS IN HEALTH AND DISEASE

- Research has clearly established and DSM has recognized that psychological factors influence the development of many physical disorders and play an important role in the course of disease processes.
- The relatively new field of behavioral medicine has its origins in the general recognition of psychological influences on physical illnesses and seeks to extend the conception of disease beyond the traditional medical preoccupation with the physical breakdown of organs and organ systems.

- The influence of psychological variables on health is readily apparent in excessive autonomic nervous system responses to stressor conditions, sometimes directly resulting in organ damage. There is also increasing evidence that psychosocial challenges, including negative emotional states, can impair the immune system's ability to respond, leaving a person more vulnerable to disease-producing agents.
- Damaging habits and lifestyle patterns—for example, cigarette smoking and high-risk sexual behavior—also enhance the risk for many physical diseases.

PSYCHOLOGICAL FACTORS AND CARDIOVASCULAR DISEASE

- The distressingly common diseases of hypertension and coronary heart disease seem to be linked to chronic negative emotions.
- The Type A behavior pattern, in particular, its hostility component, is well established as an independent risk factor for coronary heart disease.

GENERAL CAUSAL FACTORS IN PHYSICAL DISEASE

- Biological causal factors, including genetic vulnerabilities, excessive autonomic reactivity, and possible organ weaknesses, are, of course, key elements in the etiological patterns of psychogenic illnesses.
- General and specific psychosocial factors, including the extent and quality of relationships with others, have been shown to play a role in the development of many physical diseases.

TREATMENTS AND OUTCOMES FOR PSYCHOGENIC ILLNESSES

- Biological factors must be considered in the treatment of any physical disease, regardless of strong evidence of psychological contributions to its development.
- A common factor in many psychogenic diseases is the inadequacy of an individual's coping resources for managing stressful life circumstances.
- Cognitive-behavioral therapy shows much promise in alleviating the psychological problems contributing to many diseases.

EATING DISORDERS

- Adolescent and young adult eating disorders have reached epidemic proportions in the United States and elsewhere. These disorders occur chiefly in females and are thought to be due in large part to a media-supported and unrealistic standard that associates feminine attractiveness and beauty with excessive thinness.
- Although there are a number of eating disorders, the three most common ones are (1) anorexia nervosa, or severe food restriction with or without binge eating and purging; (2) bulimia nervosa, or frequent binge eating accompanied by inappropriate compensatory behaviors involving either purging or nonpurging methods; and (3) binge-eating disorder (BED), or frequent binge eating with little or no accompanying inappropriate compensatory behavior to limit weight gain.
- By far the most dangerous of the eating disorders is anorexia nervosa, because of its sometimes lethal consequences due to starvation as well as more directly suicidal behavior. The treatment of anorexia nervosa is especially difficult and often prolonged.
- Certain personality characteristics and family patterns, such as perfectionism and overcontrol, tend to be shared by eating-disorder patients.

KEY TERMS

behavioral medicine (p. 261)
psychogenic illness (p. 261)
health psychology (p. 261)
placebo effect (p. 263)
psychoneuroimmunology (p. 266)
essential hypertension (p. 269)
Type A behavior pattern (p. 270)
anorexia nervosa (p. 278)
bulimia nervosa (p. 278)
binge-eating disorder (BED) (p. 280)

10

CHAPTER NINE

Personality Disorders

Louise Dalip Bego, *Self Portrait* (1995), acrylic on canvas. In 1973, Bego suffered a traumatic brain injury in a car accident. The long-term effects of this injury have been memory loss, inexplicable outbursts of anger, and a personality transformation. Bego turned to painting as an outlet for her feelings of depression, fear, and rage. She has won several citations for her work in her home state of Michigan.

LEARNING OBJECTIVES

After reading this chapter, you should be able to:

- List the major symptoms of the various personality disorders and give several reasons why their diagnosis is difficult.
- Identify the three clusters into which the different personality disorders are grouped.
- Summarize what is known about the biological, psychosocial, and sociocultural causal factors of the personality disorders.
- Discuss the difficulties of treating individuals with personality disorders and describe approaches to treatment.
- Compare and contrast the symptoms and causal factors for psychopathy and antisocial personality disorder.
- Explain why it is difficult to treat psychopathy and antisocial personality disorder and describe the most promising of the current treatment approaches.

A person's broadly characteristic traits, coping styles, and ways of interacting in the social environment emerge during childhood and normally crystallize into established patterns by the end of adolescence or early adulthood. These patterns constitute the individual's personality—the set of unique traits and behaviors that characterize the individual. For most of us, our adult personality is attuned to the demands of society. In other words, we readily comply with societal expectations. In contrast, there are certain people who, although not necessarily displaying obvious symptoms of an Axis I disorder, nevertheless seem somehow ill equipped to become fully functioning members of society. For these individuals, personality formation has led to some traits that are so inflexible and maladaptive that they are unable to perform adequately at least some of the roles expected of them by their society.

These people may be diagnosed as having **personality disorders,** which were formerly known as *character disorders*. Personality disorders typically do not stem from debilitating reactions to stress, as in post-traumatic stress disorder or many cases of major depression. Rather, these disorders stem largely from the gradual development of inflexible and distorted personality and behavioral patterns, which result in persistently maladaptive ways of perceiving, thinking about, and relating to the world. These maladaptive approaches usually significantly impair at least some aspects of functioning and in some cases cause a good deal of subjective distress. For example, people with avoidant personality disorder are so shy and hypersensitive to rejection that they actively avoid most social interactions.

The category of personality disorders is broad, encompassing behavioral problems that differ greatly in form and severity. The milder cases involve people who generally function adequately but who would be described by their relatives, friends, or associates as troublesome, eccentric, or difficult to get to know. These individuals have characteristic ways of approaching situations and other people that make them have difficulties either in developing close relationships with others or in getting along with those with whom they have close relationships. However, they are often quite capable or even gifted in some ways. One especially severe personality disorder results in extreme and often unethical "acting out" against society that makes individuals less able to function in a normal setting; many are incarcerated in prisons or maximum security hospitals, although some are able to manipulate others and keep from getting caught.

Many people with personality disorders never come in contact with mental health agencies. Individuals with some personality disorders are identified through the correctional system or through court-ordered psychological evaluations stemming from family problems such as neglect or physical abuse. Others eventually show up in alcohol treatment programs or in psychiatric emergency rooms after a suicide attempt. There is not a great deal of solid evidence on the prevalence of most personality disorders. Weissman's (1993) comprehensive summary of epidemiological studies of all the personality disorders concluded that about 10 to 13 percent of the population meets the criteria for one or more personality disorders at some point in life. There are some suggestions that personality disorders may decrease after age 50. Not surprisingly, personality disorders are more common among psychiatric patients.

In DSM-IV-TR, the personality disorders are coded on a separate axis, Axis II (along with mental retardation; see Chapter 13), because they are regarded as being different enough from the standard psychiatric syndromes (which are coded on Axis I) to warrant separate classification. As already noted, the personality disorders of Axis II represent long-standing, deeply embedded personality traits that are thought to be inflexible and maladaptive and that cause social or occupational adjustment problems or personal distress. They are also extremely resistant to modification. Although a person might be diagnosed on Axis II only, some individuals can be diagnosed on both Axes I

personality disorders Mental disorders stemming from the gradual development of inflexible and distorted personality and behavioral patterns that result in persistently maladaptive ways of perceiving, thinking about, and relating to the world.

and II, which reflects the existence of both a currently active mental disorder and a more chronic, underlying personality disorder. For example, someone with avoidant personality disorder might also develop major depression.

CLINICAL FEATURES OF PERSONALITY DISORDERS

People with personality disorders often cause at least as much difficulty in the lives of others as in their own lives. Other people tend to find the behavior of individuals with personality disorders confusing, exasperating, unpredictable, and, in varying degrees, unacceptable—although it is rarely as bizarre or out of contact with reality as that of people with psychotic disorders. Some people with personality disorders experience a good deal of emotional suffering, although others do not, at least not obviously. The behavioral deviations shown by people with personality disorders are persistent and seem to be intrinsic to their personalities. These people have difficulty taking part in mutually respectful and satisfying social relationships. Whatever the particular trait patterns affected individuals have developed (obstinacy, covert hostility, suspiciousness, or fear of rejection, for example), these patterns color their reactions to each new situation and lead to a repetition of the same maladaptive behaviors. For example, a dependent person may wear out a relationship with someone, such as a spouse, by incessant and extraordinary demands, such as demanding never to be left alone; after that partner leaves, the person may go immediately into another dependent relationship and repeat the behavior. Thus, personality disorders are marked by considerable consistency over time, with no apparent learning from previous troubles.

In the past, these persistent disorders were thought to center on and evolve from personality characteristics referred to as *temperament* or *character traits,* suggesting the possibility of hereditary or constitutional influences. As discussed in Chapter 2, temperamental differences emerge early in infancy and involve differences in one's inborn disposition to react affectively to environmental stimuli—for example, being very shy and frightened by novel stimuli versus being more outgoing and not easily frightened. One way of thinking about temperament is that it lays the early foundation for the development of the adult personality, but it is not the sole determinant of adult personality. The possibility of genetic transmission of a liability for some of these disorders, particularly antisocial and schizotypal personality, has received strong support in the research literature (Nigg & Goldsmith, 1994).

However, environmental and social factors, particularly learning-based habit patterns and maladaptive cognitive styles, have also been identified as possible causal factors (Millon & Davis, 1995). Many of these maladaptive habits and cognitive styles may originate in disturbed parent-child attachment relationships, rather than deriving simply from temperamental differences. Early attachment relationships are thought by developmental psychologists to create models for children of what adult relationships should be like. If early models are not healthy, this may predispose a child to a pattern of personality development that can lead to the diagnosis of personality disorder later in life.

The DSM Criteria

The essential feature of a personality disorder is an enduring pattern of inner experience and behavior that deviates markedly from the expectations of the individual's culture. Some of the DSM criteria state that the stable and enduring pattern must be inflexible and pervasive across a broad range of personal and social situations and its onset can be traced back at least to adolescence or early adulthood. In addition, the pattern must be manifested in at least two of the following areas: cognition, affectivity, interpersonal functioning, and impulse control. Finally, it must also lead to clinically significant distress or impairment in important areas of functioning. Specific diagnostic criteria are also provided for each of the personality disorders (American Psychiatric Association, 1994, p. 630); these will be discussed later in this chapter.

Difficulties in Diagnosing Personality Disorders

A special caution is in order regarding the personality disorders. Perhaps more misdiagnoses occur here than for any other of the DSM categories. There are a number of reasons for this problem:

- *The personality disorder categories are not as sharply defined as most Axis I diagnostic categories.* For example, it may be difficult to diagnose reliably whether someone meets a criterion for dependent personality disorder such as "goes to excessive lengths to obtain nurturance and support from others" or "has difficulty making everyday decisions without an excessive amount of advice and reassurance from others" (e.g., Tryer, 1995). Because the criteria for personality disorders are defined by inferred traits or consistent patterns of behavior rather than by objective behavioral standards, more judgment is required on the part of

One of the problems with the diagnostic categories of personality disorders is that the exact same observable behaviors may be associated with different personality disorders and yet have different meanings with each disorder. For example, this woman's behavior and expression looking out this closed window could suggest the suspiciousness and avoidance of blame seen in paranoid personality disorder, or it could indicate the social withdrawal and absence of friends that characterize schizoid personality disorder, or it could indicate social anxiety about interacting with others because of fear of being rejected or negatively evaluated, as seen in avoidant personality disorder.

the clinician making the diagnosis than is the case for many Axis I disorders.

- *The diagnostic categories are not mutually exclusive.* People often show characteristics of more than one personality disorder (Tryer, 1995; Widiger & Sanderson, 1995). For example, someone might show the suspiciousness, mistrust, avoidance of blame, and guardedness of paranoid personality disorder, along with the withdrawal, absence of friends, and aloofness that characterize schizoid personality disorder. As a result, many clients diagnosed with one personality disorder also qualify for at least one other personality disorder. Widiger and Rogers (1989) found this to be the case 85 percent of the time; in some other studies, patients were given an average of four or more personality disorder diagnoses (Shea, 1995; Skodol et al., 1991). Furthermore, one of the most common diagnoses is a grab-bag category—"personality disorder not otherwise specified" (e.g., Tryer, 1995; Widiger & Corbit, 1995). Clearly, these individuals are not neatly fitting the prototypes that are described in DSM.
- *The assumption in DSM is that we can make a clear distinction between the presence and the absence of a personality disorder, but the personality characteristics that define these disorders are all dimensional in nature*—that is, they range from normal expressions to pathological exaggerations and can be found, on a smaller scale and less intensely expressed, in many normal people (Carson, 1996b; Clark & Livesley, 1994; Livesley et al., 1994; Widiger & Sanderson, 1995). For example, liking one's work and being conscientious about the details of one's job do not mean that one has obsessive-compulsive personality disorder, nor does being economically dependent automatically make a spouse a dependent personality. Applying categorical diagnostic labels to people who are in some cases functioning reasonably well is always risky; it is especially so when the diagnosis involves judgment about characteristics that are also common in normal people. In fact, researchers have tried, without success, to find discrete breaks in the personality dimensions—that is, points at which normal behavior becomes clearly distinct from pathological behavior (Widiger & Sanderson, 1995).

These problems can lead to unreliability of diagnoses, and they often do. This has left both clinicians and researchers somewhat dissatisfied with Axis II of DSM (Widiger & Sanderson, 1995). Someday, a more accurate way of diagnosing the personality disorders may be devised. In the meantime, however, the categorical system of symptoms and traits will continue to be used, with the recognition that it is more dependent on the observer's judgment than one might wish. Bearing these cautions in mind, we will look now at the elusive and often exasperating clinical features of the personality disorders. It is important to remember, however, that we will be describing the prototype for each personality disorder. In reality, it is rare for any individual to fit these "ideal" descriptions.

IN REVIEW

- What is the definition of a personality disorder?
- What are the general DSM criteria for diagnosing personality disorders?
- What are three reasons for the high frequency of misdiagnoses of personality disorders?

CATEGORIES OF PERSONALITY DISORDERS

DSM-IV-TR groups personality disorders into three clusters on the basis of similarities among them:

- *Cluster A* includes paranoid, schizoid, and schizotypal personality disorders. People with these disorders often seem odd or eccentric, showing unusual behavior ranging from distrust and suspiciousness to social detachment.
- *Cluster B* includes histrionic, narcissistic, antisocial, and borderline personality disorders. Individuals with these disorders have in common a tendency to be dramatic, emotional, and erratic. Their impulsive behavior, often involving antisocial activities, is more colorful, more forceful, and more likely to bring them into contact with mental health or legal authorities than the behaviors characteristic of disorders in the first cluster.
- *Cluster C* includes avoidant, dependent, and obsessive-compulsive personality disorders. In contrast to the disorders in the other clusters, anxiety and fearfulness are often part of these disorders, making it difficult in some cases to distinguish them from anxiety-based disorders. People with these disorders, because of their anxieties, are more likely to seek help.

See Table 9.1 for a summary of types of personality disorders.

Paranoid Personality Disorder

Individuals with **paranoid personality disorder** have a pervasive suspiciousness and distrust of others. They tend to see themselves as blameless and instead find fault for their own mistakes and failures in others—even to the point of ascribing evil motives to others. Such people are constantly expecting trickery and looking for clues to validate their expectations, while disregarding all evidence to the contrary. They are often preoccupied with doubts about the loyalty of friends, leading to a reluctance to confide in others. They also may be hypersensitive, as indicated by a tendency to read threatening meanings into benign remarks. They also commonly bear grudges and are quick to react with anger (Bernstein, Useda, & Siever, 1995; Widiger & Frances, 1994).

paranoid personality disorder Personality disorder characterized by pervasive suspiciousness and distrust of others.

It is important to keep in mind that individuals with paranoid personalities are not usually psychotic; that is, most of the time, they are in clear contact with reality, although they may experience transient psychotic symptoms (Thompson-Pope & Turkat, 1993). Another disorder, paranoid schizophrenia (to be discussed in Chapter 12) shares some symptoms with paranoid personality disorder. Individuals with paranoid schizophrenia have additional problems, however, including a more persistent loss of contact with reality and extreme cognitive and behavioral disorganization, such as delusions and hallucinations.

Case Study **A Paranoid Construction Worker** • A 40-year-old construction worker believes that his coworkers do not like him and fears that someone might let his scaffolding slip in order to cause him injury on the job. This concern followed a recent disagreement on the lunch line when the patient felt that a coworker was sneaking ahead and complained to him. He began noticing his new "enemy" laughing with the other men and often wondered if he were the butt of their mockery. He thought of confronting them, but decided that the whole issue might just be in his own mind, and that he might get himself into more trouble by taking any action.

The patient offers little spontaneous information, sits tensely in the chair, is wide-eyed and carefully tracks all movements in the room. He reads between the lines of the interviewer's questions, feels criticized, and imagines that the interviewer is siding with his coworkers. He makes it clear that he would not have come to the personnel clinic at all except for his need for sleep medication.

He was a loner as a boy and felt that other children would form cliques and be mean to him. He did poorly in school, but blamed his teachers—he claimed that they preferred girls or boys who were "sissies." He dropped out of school and has since been a hard and effective worker; but he feels he never gets the breaks. He believes that he has been discriminated against because of his Catholicism, but can offer little convincing evidence. He gets on poorly with bosses and coworkers, is unable to appreciate joking around, and does best in situations where he can work and have lunch alone. He has switched jobs many times because he felt he was being mistreated.

The patient is distant and demanding with his family. His children call him "Sir" and know that it is wise to be "seen but not heard" when he is around. At home he can never comfortably sit still and is always busy at some chore or another. He prefers not to have people visit his house and becomes restless when his wife is away visiting others. (From Spitzer et al., 1981, p. 37.)

This pervasive suspiciousness and mistrust of other people leave an individual with paranoid personality prone to numerous difficulties and hurts in interpersonal

TABLE 9.1 SUMMARY OF PERSONALITY DISORDERS

Personality Disorder	Characteristics	Prevalence	Gender Ratio Estimate
Cluster A			
Paranoid	Suspiciousness and mistrust of others; tendency to see self as blameless; on guard for perceived attacks by others	0.5–2.5%	males > females
Schizoid	Impaired social relationships; inability and lack of desire to form attachments to others	<1%	males > females
Schizotypal	Peculiar thought patterns; oddities of perception and speech that interfere with communication and social interaction	3%	males > females
Cluster B			
Histrionic	Self-dramatization; overconcern with attractiveness; tendency to irritability and temper outbursts if attention seeking is frustrated	2–3%	males = females
Narcissistic	Grandiosity; preoccupation with receiving attention; self-promotion; lack of empathy	<1%	males > females
Antisocial	Lack of moral or ethical development; inability to follow approved models of behavior; deceitfulness; shameless manipulation of others; history of conduct problems as a child	1%, females; 3%, males	males > females
Borderline	Impulsiveness, inappropriate anger; drastic mood shifts; chronic feelings of boredom; attempts at self-mutilation or suicide	2%	males > females (by 3:1)
Cluster C			
Avoidant	Hypersensitivity to rejection or social derogation; shyness; insecurity in social interaction and initiating relationships	0.5–1%	males = females
Dependent	Difficulty in separating in relationships; discomfort at being alone; subordination of needs in order to keep others involved in a relationship; indecisiveness	2%	males = females
Obsessive-compulsive	Excessive concern with order, rules, and trivial details; perfectionistic; lack of expressiveness and warmth; difficulty in relaxing and having fun	1%	males > females (by 2:1)

Source: APA, 1994; Weissman, 1993; Zimmerman & Coryell, 1990.

relationships. These difficulties typically lead the person to be continually "on guard" for perceived attacks by others.

Schizoid Personality Disorder

Individuals with **schizoid personality disorder** usually show an inability to form social relationships and a lack of interest in doing so. Consequently they typically do not have good friends, with the possible exception of close relatives. Such people are unable to express their feelings and are seen by others as cold and distant; they often lack social skills and can be classified as loners or introverts, with solitary interests and occupations (Widiger & Frances, 1994). They tend not to take pleasure in many activities, including sexual activity. They may even appear indifferent to praise or criticism from others. More generally, they are not very emotionally reactive (rarely experiencing strong positive or negative emotions), which contributes

schizoid personality disorder Personality disorder characterized by the inability to form social relationships or express feelings and lack of interest in doing so.

People with schizoid personality disorder are often loners interested in solitary pursuits, such as assembling odd collections of objects.

to their appearing cold and aloof (Widiger & Frances, 1994).

Early theorists considered a schizoid personality to be a likely precursor to the development of schizophrenia, but research on the possible genetic transmission of schizoid personality disorder has failed to establish either a link between the two disorders or a hereditary basis for schizoid personality (Kalus, Bernstein, & Siever, 1995). Still, schizoid personality disorder may show some links with the so-called negative symptoms of schizophrenia (see Chapter 12), which include anhedonia (an inability to experience pleasure or joy) and social withdrawal (Kalus et al., 1995).

The following case illustrates a fairly severe schizoid personality disorder in a man who had been functioning adequately as judged both by occupational criteria and by his own standards of "happiness." When he sought help, it was at the encouragement of his supervisor and his physician.

Case Study **A Schizoid Computer Analyst** • Bill D., a highly intelligent but quite introverted and withdrawn 33-year-old computer analyst, was referred for psychological evaluation by his physician, who was concerned that Bill might be depressed and unhappy. At the suggestion of his supervisor, Bill had recently gone to the physician because of rather vague physical complaints and his gloomy outlook on life. Bill had virtually no contact with other people. He lived alone in his apartment, worked in a small office by himself, and usually saw no one at work except for the occasional visits of his supervisor to give him new work and pick up completed projects. He ate lunch by himself and about once a week, on nice days, went to the zoo for his lunch break.

Bill was a lifelong loner; as a child, he had had few friends and always preferred solitary activities over family outings (he was the oldest of five children). In high school, he had never dated and in college had gone out with a woman only once—and that was with a group of students after a game. He had been active in sports, however, and had played varsity football in both high school and college. In college, he had spent a lot of time with one relatively close friend—mostly drinking. However, this friend now lived in another city.

Bill reported rather matter-of-factly that he had a hard time making friends; he never knew what to say in a conversation. On a number of occasions, he had thought of becoming friends with other people but simply couldn't think of the right words, so "the conversation just died." He reported that he had given some thought lately to changing his life in an attempt to be more "positive," but it never had seemed worth the trouble. It was easier for him not to make the effort because he became embarrassed when someone tried to talk with him. He was happiest when he was alone.

In short, the central problem of people with schizoid personality disorder is that they neither desire nor enjoy close relationships with other people. It is as though the needs for love, belonging, and approval failed to develop in these people—or if they had been there earlier in development, they had somehow disappeared at an early stage. The result is a profound barrenness of interpersonal experience.

Schizotypal Personality Disorder

Individuals with **schizotypal personality disorder** are not only excessively introverted with pervasive social and interpersonal deficits; they also have cognitive and percep-

schizotypal personality disorder Personality disorder characterized by excessive introversion, pervasive social and interpersonal deficits, cognitive and perceptual distortions, and eccentricities in communication and behavior.

tual distortions and eccentricities in their communication and behavior (Widiger & Frances, 1994). Although schizotypal and schizoid personalities are both characterized by social isolation and withdrawal, the two can be distinguished in that schizotypal personality—but not schizoid personality—also involves oddities of thought, perception, or speech. Although reality contact is usually maintained, highly personalized and superstitious thinking is characteristic of people with schizotypal personality, and under extreme stress, they may experience transient psychotic symptoms (Thompson-Pope & Turkat, 1993; Widiger & Frances, 1994). Indeed, they often believe that they have magical powers and may engage in magical rituals. Their oddities in thinking, talking, and other behaviors are similar to those often seen in more severe forms in schizophrenic patients; in fact, people with schizotypal personality disorder are sometimes first diagnosed as exhibiting simple or latent schizophrenia.

The prevalence of this disorder in the general population is estimated at about 3 percent (American Psychiatric Association, 1994). Unlike schizoid personality disorder, a genetic and biological association with schizophrenia has been clearly documented for schizotypal personality disorder (Kendler & Gardner, 1997; Meehl, 1990a; Nigg & Goldsmith, 1994). Indeed, several studies have documented that patients with schizotypal personality disorder (Siever, Bernstein, and Silverman, 1995), as well as college students with the disorder (Lencz et al., 1993), have a deficit in their ability to track a moving target visually that is also common in schizophrenia (see Chapter 12). They also show attentional deficits (Lees-Roitman et al., 1997) and working memory deficits (e.g., being able to remember a span of digits) common in schizophrenia (Squires-Wheeler et al., 1997). In fact, the term *schizotypal* is an abbreviation for "schizophrenic genotype" (Rado, 1956), and many consider it to be part of a spectrum of schizophrenia that often occurs in the first-degree relatives of schizophrenics (Kendler & Gardner, 1997; Nigg & Goldsmith, 1994). Moreover, teenagers who have a schizotypal personality type have been shown to be at increased risk for developing schizophrenia and schizophrenia-spectrum disorders in adulthood (Siever et al., 1995; Tyrka, Cannon, et al., 1995).

Case Study The Disconnectedness of a Schizotypal Woman • The patient is a 32-year-old unmarried, unemployed woman on welfare who complains that she feels "spacey." Her feelings of detachment have gradually become stronger and more uncomfortable. For many hours each day, she feels as if she were watching herself move through life, and the world around her seems unreal. She feels especially strange when she looks into a mirror. For many years, she has felt able to read people's minds by a "kind of clairvoyance I don't understand." According to her, several people in her family apparently also have this ability. She is preoccupied by the thought that she has some special mission in life, but is not sure what it is; she is not particularly religious. She is very self-conscious in public, often feels that people are paying special attention to her, and sometimes thinks that strangers cross the street to avoid her. She has no friends, feels lonely and isolated, and spends much of each day lost in fantasies or watching TV soap operas.

The patient speaks in a vague, abstract, digressive manner, generally just missing the point, but she is never incoherent. She seems shy, suspicious, and afraid she will be criticized. She has no gross loss of reality testing, such as hallucinations or delusions. She has never had treatment for emotional problems. She has had occasional jobs, but drifts away from them because of lack of interest. (From Spitzer et al., 1989, pp. 173–174.)

The distinguishing feature of a schizotypal personality is peculiar thought patterns, which are in turn associated with a loosening—although not a complete rupture—of ties to reality. The individual appears to lack some key integrative competence of the sort that enables most of us to "keep it all together" and move our lives toward some personal goals. As a result, many basic abilities, such as being able to communicate clearly, are never fully mastered, and the person tends to drift aimlessly and unproductively through the adult years.

Histrionic Personality Disorder

Excessive attention-seeking behavior and emotionality are the key characteristics of individuals with **histrionic personality disorder.** They tend to feel unappreciated if not the center of attention, and their lively, dramatic, and excessively extraverted styles often ensure that they can charm others into attending to them. But these qualities do not lead to stable and satisfying relationships because others tire of providing this level of attention. In seeking attention, people with this disorder are quite theatrical and emotional, as well as sexually provocative and seductive, in their appearance and behavior. Their style of speech may be dramatic but is also quite impressionistic

histrionic personality disorder Personality disorder characterized by excessive attention-seeking behavior, emotional instability, and self-dramatization.

People with histrionic personality disorder often engage in seductive and attention-seeking behavior—appearing in public in scanty clothing, for example.

and lacking in detail. They are often highly suggestible and consider relationships to be closer than they are. They may attempt to control their partner through seductive behavior and emotional manipulation, but they also show a good deal of dependence. They are usually considered to be self-centered, vain, and overconcerned about the approval of others, who see them as overly reactive, shallow, and insincere.

The prevalence of this disorder in the general population is estimated at 2 to 3 percent. Some studies have suggested that it is more common in women than men, but other studies have found no sex differences (American Psychiatric Association, 1994). Overdiagnosis in women may occur in Western cultures because many of the criteria for histrionic personality disorder (overdramatization, vanity, seductiveness, and overconcern with physical appearance) are more likely to be observed in women than in men. This automatically increases the chances that women might be diagnosed as having the disorder.

Case Study **A Secretary with Histrionic Personality Disorder** • Pam, a 22-year-old secretary, was causing numerous problems for her supervisor and coworkers. According to her supervisor, Pam was unable to carry out her duties without constant guidance. Seemingly helpless and dependent, she would overreact to minor events and job pressures with irritability and occasional temper tantrums. If others placed unwanted demands on her, she would complain of physical problems, such as nausea or headaches; furthermore, she frequently missed work altogether. To top it off, Pam was flirtatious and often demandingly seductive toward the men in the office.

As a result of Pam's frequent absenteeism and her disruptive behavior in the office, the supervisor and the personnel manager recommended that Pam be given a psychological evaluation and counseling in the Employee Assistance Program. She went to the first appointment with the psychologist but failed to return for follow-up visits. She was finally given a discharge notice after several incidents of temper outbursts at work.

Both Pam's physical complaints and her seductive behavior are examples of attention-seeking tactics commonly found in the histrionic personality pattern. When these tactics fail to bring about the desired result, irritability and temper outbursts often follow.

Narcissistic Personality Disorder

Individuals with **narcissistic personality disorder** show an exaggerated sense of self-importance, a preoccupation with being admired, and a lack of empathy for the feelings of others (Blais, Hilsenroth, & Castlebury, 1997). Ronningstam and Gunderson (1989) reported that grandiosity was the most generalizable and the most frequently used criterion for diagnosing narcissistic patients. The grandiosity of narcissistic patients is manifested by a strong tendency to overestimate their abilities and accomplishments, while often concurrently underestimating the abilities and accomplishments of others. Their sense of entitlement is frequently a source of astonishment to others, although they themselves seem to regard their lavish expectations as merely what they deserve. They behave in stereotypical ways (for example, with constant self-references and bragging) to gain the acclaim and recognition that feeds their grandiose expectations and their fantasies of unlimited success, power, beauty, or brilliance. Because they believe they are so special, they often think they can only be understood by other high-status people or should associate only with such people. These tactics, to those around them, appear to be excessive efforts to make themselves look good.

Narcissistic personalities share another central element—they are unwilling to take the perspective of others, to see things other than "through their own eyes." In this sense, all children start out as narcissists and only gradually acquire a perspective-taking ability. For reasons that are far from entirely understood, some children do not show normal progress in this respect, and indeed, in

narcissistic personality disorder Personality disorder characterized by an exaggerated sense of self-importance, a preoccupation with being admired, and a lack of empathy for the feelings of others.

extreme cases, show little or none. The latter may grow up to become adult narcissistic personalities. Along with showing a lack of empathy, narcissistic persons not uncommonly take advantage of others to achieve their own ends and often show arrogant, snobbish, or haughty behaviors and attitudes. Finally, they are often very envious of other people or believe that other people are envious of them (Gunderson, Ronningstam, & Smith, 1995). Not surprisingly, most of these people don't seek psychological treatment because they view themselves as nearly perfect and in no need of change.

Most researchers and clinicians believe that people with narcissistic personality disorder have a very fragile sense of self-esteem underneath all their grandiosity. This may be why they are often preoccupied with what others think, why they show such a great need for admiration, and why they are so preoccupied with fantasies of outstanding achievement. Not surprisingly, they are also very sensitive to criticism, which may leave them feeling humiliated, empty, or full of rage (Widiger & Frances, 1994).

Case Study **A Narcissistic Graduate Student** • A 25-year-old, single graduate student complains to his psychoanalyst of difficulty completing his Ph.D. in English literature and expresses concerns about his relationships with women. He believes that his thesis topic may profoundly increase the level of understanding in his discipline and make him famous, but so far he has not been able to get past the third chapter. His mentor does not seem sufficiently impressed with his ideas, and the patient is furious at him, but also self-doubting and ashamed. He blames his mentor for his lack of progress and thinks that he deserves more help with his grand idea—that his mentor should help with some of the research. The patient brags about his creativity and complains that other people are "jealous" of his insight. He is very envious of students who are moving along faster than he and regards them as "dull drones and ass-kissers." He prides himself on the brilliance of his class participation and imagines someday becoming a great professor.

He becomes rapidly infatuated with women and has powerful and persistent fantasies about each new woman he meets, but after several experiences of sexual intercourse feels disappointed and finds them dumb, clinging, and physically repugnant. He has many "friends," but they turn over quickly, and no one relationship lasts very long. People get tired of his continual self-promotion and lack of consideration of them. For example, he was lonely at Christmas and insisted that his best friend stay in town rather than visit his family. The friend refused, criticizing the patient's self-centeredness; and the patient, enraged, decided never to see this friend again. (From Spitzer et al., 1981, pp. 52–53.)

Compared with some of the other personality disorders, narcissistic personality disorder is thought to be relatively rare; it is estimated to occur in about 1 percent of the population. Given the overlapping features between histrionic and narcissistic personality disorders, Widiger and Trull (1993) attempted to summarize the major differences in this way: "The histrionic tends to be more emotional and dramatic than the narcissistic, and whereas both may be promiscuous, the narcissistic is more dispassionately exploitative, while the histrionic is more overtly needy. Both will be exhibitionistic, but the histrionic seeks attention, whereas the narcissistic seeks admiration" (p. 388).

Antisocial Personality Disorder

Individuals with **antisocial personality disorder** (ASPD) continually violate and show disregard for the rights of others through deceitful, aggressive, or antisocial behavior, typically without remorse or loyalty to anyone. They tend to be impulsive, irritable, and aggressive and show a pattern of generally irresponsible behavior. This pattern of behavior must have been occurring since the age of 15, and before 15, the person must have had symptoms of conduct disorder, a childhood and young adolescent disorder that includes persistent patterns of aggression toward people or animals, destruction of property, deceitfulness or theft, and serious violation of rules at home or in school (see Chapter 14). Antisocial personality disorder is much more common in men than in women, with a lifetime prevalence of about 3 percent in men and about 1 percent in women (e.g., Golomb et al., 1995; Robins et al., 1984). Because this disorder has been studied more fully than the others, it will be examined in some detail later in this chapter.

Case Study **A Thief with ASPD** • Mark, a 22-year-old, came to a psychology clinic on court order. He was awaiting trial for car theft and armed robbery. His case records revealed that he had a long history of arrests beginning at age 9, when he had been picked up for vandalism. He had been expelled from high school for truancy and disruptive behavior. On a number of occasions, he had run away from home for days or weeks at a time—always returning in a disheveled and "rundown" condition. He had never held a job for more than a few days at a time, even though his gen-

antisocial personality disorder (ASPD) Personality disorder characterized by continual violation of and disregard for the rights of others through deceitful, aggressive, or antisocial behavior, typically without remorse or loyalty to anyone.

erally charming manner enabled him to obtain work readily. He was described as a loner, with few friends. Though initially charming, Mark usually soon antagonized those he met with his aggressive, self-oriented behavior.

Mark was generally affable and complimentary during the therapy session. At the end of it, he enthusiastically told the therapist how much he'd benefited from the counseling and looked forward to future sessions. Mark's first session was his last. Shortly after it, he skipped bail and presumably left town to avoid his trial.

Criteria for narcissistic personality disorder also overlap with those for antisocial personality disorder. Widiger and Trull (1993) noted that the most basic distinction is that "the narcissist's exploitation would be more for the purpose of demonstrating domination, prestige, and superiority rather than for the personal, material gain of the antisocial personality" (p. 388).

Borderline Personality Disorder

Individuals with **borderline personality disorder** (BPD) show a pattern of behavior characterized by impulsivity and instability in interpersonal relationships, self-image, and moods. The term *borderline personality* has a long and rather confusing history (Widiger & Trull, 1993). Originally it was most often used to refer to a condition that was thought to occupy the "border" between neurotic and psychotic disorders (as in the term *borderline schizophrenia*). However, this sense of the term *borderline* later became identified with schizotypal personality disorder, which, as was noted earlier, is biologically related to schizophrenia. Since DSM-III, the term *borderline personality disorder* has been used for people who have "enduring personality features of instability and vulnerability" (Widiger & Trull, 1993, p. 372), and this disorder is no longer considered to be biologically related to schizophrenia.

People with borderline personalities show serious disturbances in basic identity. Their sense of self is highly unstable. Given this extremely unstable self-image, it is not surprising that they also have highly unstable interpersonal relationships. For example, they may make desperate efforts to avoid real or imagined abandonment, perhaps because their fears of abandonment are so intense. Feeling slighted, they might, for example, become verbally abusive toward loved ones or might threaten suicide over minor setbacks. Given such behaviors, it is not surprising that they commonly have a history of intense but stormy relationships, typically involving overidealizations of friends or lovers that later end in bitter disillusionment and disappointment (Gunderson, Zanarini, & Kisiel, 1995).

The mood of people with borderline personality disorder is also highly unstable. For example, they may display intense outbursts with little provocation and have difficulty controlling their anger. They tend to have a low tolerance for frustration, as well as chronic feelings of emptiness. Associated with the sense of emptiness is a common intolerance for being alone. Their extreme affective instability is reflected in drastic mood shifts and impulsive or erratic self-destructive behaviors, such as binges of eating, gambling, sex, substance abuse, or reckless driving. Suicide attempts, often flagrantly manipulative, are frequently part of the clinical picture (Soloff et al., 1994), and self-mutilation is one of the most discriminating signs for borderline personality (Widiger et al., 1986). Not uncommonly, the self-injurious behavior is associated with relief from anxiety or dysphoria, and research has documented that it may even be associated with analgesia (absence of the experience of pain in the presence of a theoretically painful stimulus) (Figueroa & Silk, 1997; Russ et al., 1994). Suicide attempts among those with borderline personality disorder are not always simply manipulative, with prospective studies suggesting that 3 to 9 percent of patients may ultimately complete suicide (Soloff et al., 1994).

Case Study Self-Mutilation in a Woman with Borderline Personality Disorder • A 26-year-old unemployed woman was referred for admission to a hospital by her therapist because of intense suicidal preoccupation and urges to mutilate herself with a razor. The patient was apparently well until her junior year in high school, when she became preoccupied with religion and philosophy, avoided friends, and was filled with doubt about who she was. Academically she did well, but later, during college, her performance declined. In college, she began to use a variety of drugs, abandoned the religion of her family, and seemed to be searching for a charismatic religious figure with whom to identify. At times, massive anxiety swept over her, and she found it would suddenly vanish if she cut her forearm with a razor blade.

Three years ago, she began psychotherapy, and initially idealized her therapist as being incredibly intuitive and empathic. Later she became hostile and demanding of him, requiring more and more sessions, sometimes two in one day. Her life centered on her therapist, by this time to the exclusion of everyone else. Al-

borderline personality disorder (BPD) Personality disorder characterized by impulsivity and instability in interpersonal relationships, self-image, and moods.

though her hostility toward her therapist was obvious, she could neither see it nor control it. Her difficulties with her therapist culminated in many episodes of her forearm cutting and suicidal threats, which led to the referral for admission. (From Spitzer et al., 1994, p. 233.)

Clinical observation of people with borderline personality disorder points strongly to a problem in achieving a coherent sense of self as a key predisposing causal factor. These people somehow fail to complete the process of achieving a coherent and stable self-identity, and this failure leads to complications in interpersonal relationships. Although people with borderline personality disorder are usually aware of their circumstances and surroundings, they may have relatively short or transient episodes in which they appear to be out of contact with reality and experience delusions or other psychotic-like symptoms, such as hallucinations, paranoid beliefs, body image distortions, or dissociative symptoms. Among inpatients with severe borderline personality disorder, the frequency and duration of psychotic symptoms may be greater (Gunderson et al., 1995). Among patients with dissociative symptoms, the risk for self-mutilation seems especially high (Brodsky, Cloitre, & Dulit, 1995).

Estimates are that about 2 percent of the population may qualify for the diagnosis of borderline personality disorder, although people with this disorder represent a disproportionate number of patients in both inpatient and outpatient clinical settings (Widiger & Trull, 1993). There are estimates that about 8 percent of outpatients and about 15 percent of inpatients seeking treatment have borderline personality disorder. Approximately 75 percent of individuals receiving this diagnosis are women.

Given its many and varied symptoms and problems with a sense of personal identity, it is not surprising that this personality disorder commonly co-occurs with a variety of Axis I disorders, ranging from mood and anxiety disorders (especially panic and PTSD) to substance use and eating disorders (Widiger & Trull, 1993). The relationship with mood disorders is especially strong, with about 50 percent of those with borderline personality disorder also qualifying for a mood disorder diagnosis at some time (Widiger & Trull, 1993). However, the depression experienced by the individual with borderline personality is apparently somewhat different from that of other depressives in that it is more often characterized by chronic feelings of loneliness (Soloff, Cornelius, & George, 1991; Westen et al., as cited in Gunderson & Philips, 1991). Furthermore, borderline personality patients are also much more likely than depressives to view their relationships with family and friends as hostile and noncohesive and to show more pervasive dysfunction in social relationships (Benjamin & Wonderlich, 1994; Sack et al., 1996). In addition, borderline patients with depression do not show as good a response as do other depressed patients to the most common classes of antidepressant medications (Gitlin, 1996; Gunderson & Philips, 1991).

There is also substantial co-occurrence of borderline personality disorder with other personality disorders—especially histrionic, dependent, antisocial, and schizotypal personality disorders. Nevertheless, Widiger and Trull (1993) noted that a prototypical case of borderline personality can be distinguished from cases of these other personality disorders in the following way: "The prototypic borderline's exploitative use of others is usually an angry and impulsive response to disappointment, whereas the antisocial's is a guiltless and calculated effort for personal gain. Sexuality may play a more central role in the relationships of histrionics than in borderlines, evident in the histrionic's tendency to eroticize situations, to compete with members of the same sex, and to be inappropriately seductive. The prototypic schizotypal lacks the emotionality of the borderline, and tends to be more isolated, odd and peculiar" (p. 377).

Avoidant Personality Disorder

Individuals with **avoidant personality disorder** have a pattern of extreme social inhibition and introversion leading to lifelong patterns of limited social relationships and reluctance to enter into social interactions. Because of their hypersensitivity to, and their fear of, criticism and rebuff, they do not seek out other people; yet they desire affection and are often lonely and bored. Unlike people with schizoid personality disorder, they do not enjoy their aloneness; their inability to relate comfortably to other people causes acute anxiety and is accompanied by low self-esteem and excessive self-consciousness. Because of their hypersensitivity to any sign of rejection or social derogation, they may readily see ridicule or disparagement where none was intended.

Case Study A Librarian with Avoidant Personality Disorder • Sally, a 35-year-old librarian, lived a relatively isolated life and had few acquaintances and no close personal friends.

avoidant personality disorder Personality disorder characterized by extreme social inhibition and introversion, limited social relationships, hypersensitivity to criticism and rejection, and low self-esteem and excessive self-consciousness.

From childhood on, she had been very shy and had withdrawn from close ties with others to keep from being hurt or criticized. Two years before she entered therapy, she had had a date to go to a party with an acquaintance she had met at the library. The moment they had arrived at the party, Sally had felt extremely uncomfortable because she had not been "dressed properly." She left in a hurry and refused to see her acquaintance again. It was because of her continuing concern over this incident that—2 years later—Sally decided to go into therapy, even though she dreaded the possibility that the psychologist would be critical of her.

In the early treatment sessions, she sat silently much of the time, finding it too difficult to talk about herself. After several sessions, she grew to trust the therapist, and she related numerous incidents in her early years in which she had been "devastated" by her alcoholic father's obnoxious behavior in public. Though she had tried to keep her school friends from knowing about her family problems, when this had become impossible, she instead had limited her friendships, thus protecting herself from possible embarrassment or criticism. When Sally first began therapy, she avoided meeting people unless she could be assured that they would "like her." With therapy that focused on enhancing her assertiveness and social skills, she made some progress in her ability to approach and talk with people.

The key difference between the loner with schizoid personality disorder and the loner with avoidant personality disorder is that the latter is hypersensitive to criticism, shy, and insecure. The schizoid personality is cold, aloof, and indifferent to criticism.

Sally's extreme need to avoid situations in which she might be embarrassed is the keynote of the avoidant personality. Life is full of risks; yet such people cannot face even the slightest risk of embarrassment or criticism. They want guarantees of success before they will participate—and if they cannot have them, they just will not play the game.

Some research suggests that avoidant personality may be at least partially a biologically based disorder, often starting in infancy or childhood, that is reinforced by environmental factors to become a highly stable and chronic behavioral pattern (e.g., Alden & Kapp, 1988; Kagan, 1997; Kagan, Reznick, & Snidman, 1988). The key difference between the loner with schizoid personality disorder and the loner with avoidant personality disorder is that the latter is hypersensitive to criticism, shy, and insecure, while the former is aloof, cold, and indifferent to criticism (Millon & Martinez, 1995). Another difficult distinction is that between dependent and avoidant personalities. In this case, dependent personalities have great difficulty separating in relationships because they have feelings of incompetence about functioning on their own, while avoidant personalities have problems initiating relationships because of fearing criticism or rejection (Millon & Martinez, 1995). In addition, the primary focus of the dependent personality is on being taken care of, whereas the primary focus of the avoidant personality is on avoidance of humiliation and rejection (American Psychiatric Association, 2000). It should also be noted, however, that these two disorders co-occur rather frequently.

Another major problem is in distinguishing avoidant personality disorder from generalized social phobia (Chapter 5). For example, numerous studies found substantial overlap between these two disorders, with a general conclusion that avoidant personality disorder may simply be a somewhat more severe manifestation of generalized social phobia (e.g., Alpert et al., 1997; Holt, Heimberg, & Hope, 1992; Millon & Martinez, 1995; Turner, Beidel, & Townsley, 1992). These findings led Widiger (1992) to suggest that these two disorders "may represent boundary conditions of the anxiety and personality disorders that involve essentially the same psychopathology" (p. 341). DSM-IV came to the same conclusion, noting that they overlap so extensively "that they may be alternative conceptualizations of the same or similar conditions" (American Psychiatric Association, 1994, pp. 663–664).

Dependent Personality Disorder

Individuals with **dependent personality disorder** show extreme dependence on other people, particularly a need to be taken care of, which leads to clinging and submissive behavior. They also show acute discomfort—even panic—at the possibility of separation or sometimes even simply having to be alone, often leading to excessive reliance on emergency medical services (Bornstein, 1992, 1997). These individuals usually build their lives around other people and subordinate their own needs and views to keep these people involved with them, often leading to indiscriminate selection of mates. They often fail to get appropriately angry with others because of a fear of losing their support, which means that they may remain in psychologically or physically abusive relationships. They have great difficulty making even simple everyday decisions without a great deal of advice and reassurance. This may be because they lack self-confidence and feel helpless even when they have actually developed good work skills or other competencies. They may function well as long as they are not required to be on their own.

Case Study **A Mother with Dependent Personality Disorder** • Sarah D., a 32-year-old mother of two and a part-time tax accountant, came to a crisis center late one evening after Michael, her husband of a year and a half, abused her physically and then left home. Although he never physically harmed the children, he frequently threatened to do so when he was drunk. Sarah appeared acutely anxious and worried about the future and "needed to be told what to do." She wanted her husband to come back and seemed rather unconcerned about his regular pattern of physical abuse. At the time, Michael was an unemployed resident at a halfway house for paroled drug abusers and was participating in a day treatment program that taught abstinence from all addictive substances through harassment and group cohesiveness. He was almost always in a surly mood and "ready to explode."

Although Sarah had a well-paying job, she voiced great concern about being able to make it on her own. She realized that it was foolish to be "dependent" on her husband, whom she referred to as a "real loser." (She had had a similar relationship with her first husband, who had left her and her oldest child when she was 18.) Several times in the past few months, Sarah had made up her mind to get out of the marriage but couldn't bring herself to break away. She would threaten to leave, but when the time came to do so, she would "freeze in the door" with a numbness in her body and a sinking feeling in her stomach at the thought of "not being with Michael."

As a result of their lack of confidence, dependent personalities passively allow other people to take over the major decisions in their lives—such as where they will live and work, what friends they will have, and even how they will spend their time. These individuals typically appear "selfless" and bland, since they usually feel they have no right to express even mild individuality. They are often preoccupied with a fear of being left to take care of themselves, and if one relationship ends, they will often seek out a new one with great urgency. It is quite common for people with dependent personality disorder to have a comorbid diagnosis of an anxiety disorder (especially social phobia, panic disorder, or generalized anxiety disorder) (Bornstein, 1995). Among patients with eating disorders, dependent personality disorder is also quite common.

Some features of dependent personality disorder overlap with those of borderline, histrionic, and avoidant personality disorders, but there are differences as well. For example, both those with borderline personality and those with dependent personality fear abandonment. However, individuals with borderline personality react with feelings of emptiness or rage if abandonment occurs, whereas individuals with dependent personality react to threatened abandonment with submissiveness and appeasement and after abandonment with an urgent seeking of a new relationship. Moreover, individuals with dependent personality do not have the pattern of intense and stormy relationships typical of those with borderline personality. Histrionic and dependent personalities both have strong needs for reassurance and approval. However, the style of the histrionic personality is much more gregarious, flamboyant, and actively demanding of attention, whereas the dependent personality is more docile and self-effacing. Finally, as already noted, the avoidant and dependent personalities share feelings of inadequacy and hypersensitivity, but the avoidant personality is more socially timid and avoids relationships rather than be rejected, whereas the dependent personality seeks out relationships with others, in spite of the fear of being rejected (Hirschfeld, Shea, & Weise, 1995).

dependent personality disorder Personality disorder characterized by extreme dependence on others, particularly a need to be taken care of, leading to clinging and submissive behavior.

Obsessive-Compulsive Personality Disorder

Perfectionism and an excessive concern with maintaining order characterize those individuals with **obsessive-compulsive personality disorder** (OCPD). They are also preoccupied with maintaining mental and interpersonal control through careful attention to rules and schedules. They are very careful in what they do so as not to make mistakes, and they will often repeatedly check for possible mistakes. Because the details they are preoccupied with are often trivial, they use their time poorly, leading to problems in finishing projects. They also tend to be devoted to work to the exclusion of leisure activities and may have difficulty relaxing or doing anything just for fun (Widiger & Frances, 1994).

According to current views, the central feature of people with obsessive-compulsive personality disorder is that they are excessively conscientious, which includes the disposition to be deliberate, disciplined, competent, achievement-striving, and organized as well as quite inflexible about moral or ethical issues (Widiger & Frances, 1994). At an interpersonal level, these individuals have difficulty delegating tasks to others and are quite rigid and stubborn. Not surprisingly, other people tend to view obsessive-compulsive personalities as rigid, stiff, and cold.

It was once thought that obsessive-compulsive personality disorder served as a diathesis for full-blown obsessive-compulsive disorder (discussed in Chapter 5). However, this is generally not considered to be the case today; instead, two other personality disorders—dependent and avoidant—are actually more commonly associated with obsessive-compulsive disorder (Pfohl & Blum, 1995). To underscore this distinction, recall that a person with full-blown obsessive-compulsive disorder suffers from the persistent intrusion of particular undesired thoughts or images (obsessions) that are a source of extreme anxiety or distress. The anxiety or distress can only be reduced through the performance of compulsive rituals (such as cleaning or checking), and much of the person's life may be absorbed by the time taken to perform these rituals over and over again. By contrast, people with obsessive-compulsive personality disorder have lifestyles characterized by overconscientiousness, inflexibility, and perfectionism, but without the presence of true obsessions or compulsive rituals. Although they may be anxious about getting all their work done in keeping with their exacting standards, they are not anxious about their compulsiveness itself, as individuals with obsessive-compulsive disorder usually are.

obsessive-compulsive personality disorder (OCPD) Personality disorder characterized by perfectionism and an excessive concern with maintaining order and control.

Case Study Alan, An Obsessive-Compulsive Personality • Alan appeared to be well suited to his work as a train dispatcher. He was conscientious, perfectionistic, and attended to minute details. However, he was not close to his coworkers, and, reportedly, they thought him "off." He would get quite upset if even minor variations to his daily routine occurred. For example, he would become tense and irritable if coworkers did not follow exactly his elaborately constructed schedules and plans. If he became tied up in traffic, he would beat the steering wheel and swear at other drivers for holding him up.

In short, Alan got little pleasure out of life and worried constantly about minor problems. His rigid routines were impossible to maintain, and he often developed tension headaches or stomachaches when he couldn't keep his complicated plans in order. His physician, noting the frequency of his physical complaints and his generally perfectionistic approach to life, referred him for a psychological evaluation. Psychotherapy was recommended to Alan, although the prognosis for significant behavioral change was considered questionable. He did not follow up on the treatment recommendation because he felt that he could not afford the time away from work.

Some features of obsessive-compulsive personality disorder overlap with some features of narcissistic, antisocial, and schizoid personality disorders, although there are also distinguishing features. For example, individuals with either obsessive-compulsive or narcissistic personality disorder may be highly perfectionistic, but the narcissistic individual is more grandiose and likely to believe he or she has achieved perfection, whereas the obsessive-compulsive personality is often quite self-critical. Individuals with narcissistic or antisocial personality disorder may also share the lack of generosity toward others that characterizes obsessive-compulsive personality disorder, but the former tend to indulge themselves, whereas obsessive-compulsives are equally unwilling to be generous with themselves and others. Finally, both the schizoid and the obsessive-compulsive personality may have a certain amount of formality and social detachment, but only the schizoid personality lacks the capacity for close relationships. The obsessive-compulsive personality has difficulty in interpersonal relationships because of excessive devotion to work and because of difficulty expressing emotions.

An Overview of Personality Disorders

Aaron Beck and his colleagues (Beck & Freeman, 1990; Pretzer & Beck, 1996) have proposed a useful integrative scheme that highlights some of the commonalties and differences among the personality disorders (see Table 9.2). Part of this scheme details how each personality disorder can be characterized by a distinct set of behavior patterns that are overdeveloped and another set of behavior patterns that are underdeveloped. In many cases, the deficient behaviors are somehow counterparts to the overdeveloped behaviors. In addition, Beck and colleagues also propose that each personality disorder is characterized by different core dysfunctional beliefs that people with each disorder have about themselves and the world around them. Modifying these dysfunctional beliefs is a key focus of Beck's cognitive therapy for personality disorders.

TABLE 9.2 TYPICAL OVERDEVELOPED AND UNDERDEVELOPED STRATEGIES AND CORE DYSFUNCTIONAL BELIEFS FOR SELECTED PERSONALITY DISORDERS

Personality Disorder	Overdeveloped Strategy	Underdeveloped Strategy	Core Dysfunctional Belief
Cluster A			
Paranoid	Vigilance	Serenity	Motives are suspect; don't trust anyone.
	Mistrust	Trust	Be on guard.
Schizoid	Autonomy	Intimacy	Others are unrewarding.
	Isolation	Reciprocity	Relationships are messy and undesirable
Cluster B			
Antisocial	Combativeness	Empathy	I'm entitled to break the rules.
	Exploitativeness	Reciprocity	Others are patsies, wimps.
	Predation	Social sensitivity	Others are exploitative.
Histrionic	Exhibitionism	Reflectiveness	People are there to admire me.
	Expressiveness	Control	I can go by my feeling.
	Impressionism	Systematization	People are there to serve me.
Narcissistic	Self-aggrandizement	Sharing	Since I'm special, I deserve special rules.
	Competitiveness	Group identification	I'm above the rules; I'm better than others.
Cluster C			
Avoidant	Social vulnerability	Self-assertion	It's terrible to be rejected, put down.
	Avoidance	Gregariousness	If people know the real me, they will reject me.
	Inhibition		I can't tolerate unpleasant feelings.
Dependent	Help seeking	Self-sufficiency	I need people to survive, be happy.
	Clinging	Mobility	I need a steady flow of support, encouragement.
Obsessive-compulsive	Control	Spontaneity	I know what's best; details are crucial.
	Responsibility	Playfulness	People should do better, try harder.

Source: From Beck and Freeman, *Cognitive Therapy of Personality Disorders*, pp. 42, 54–55.

A person with obsessive-compulsive personality disorder is highly perfectionistic, leading to serious problems finishing various projects. Such individuals are also excessively devoted to work. In addition, they are quite inflexible about moral and ethical issues and have difficulty delegating tasks to others. They are also inclined to be ungenerous with themselves and others.

IN REVIEW

- What are the general characteristics of the three clusters of personality disorders?
- Describe and differentiate among the following Cluster A personality disorders: paranoid, schizoid, and schizotypal.
- Describe and differentiate among the following Cluster B personality disorders: histrionic, narcissistic, antisocial, and borderline.
- Describe and differentiate among the following Cluster C personality disorders: avoidant, dependent, and obsessive-compulsive.

CAUSAL FACTORS IN PERSONALITY DISORDERS

Little is yet known about the causal factors in personality disorders, partly because these disorders have received consistent attention only since DSM-III was published in 1980 and partly because they are less amenable than other disorders to thorough study. One major problem in studying the causes of personality disorders stems from the high level of comorbidity among them, which makes it difficult to untangle which causal factors are associated with which disorder. For example, in a review of four studies, Widiger and colleagues found that 85 percent of patients who qualified for a diagnosis of one personality disorder also qualified for at least one more, and many qualified for several more (Widiger & Rogers, 1989; Widiger et al., 1991). An additional problem is that many people with personality disorders are never seen by clinical personnel. Typically, those who do come to the attention of clinicians or legal authorities have already developed a severe disorder, so that only retrospective (rather than prospective) study is possible—that is, trying to reconstruct the chain of events that may have led to the disorder.

Biological Causal Factors

Of possible biological factors, it has been suggested that infants' temperaments (high or low vitality, behavioral inhibition, and so on) may predispose them to the development of particular personality disorders. Given that most personality traits have been found to be moderately heritable (e.g., Carey & DiLalla, 1994), it is not surprising that there is increasing evidence for genetic contributions to certain personality disorders (Nigg & Goldsmith, 1994; Plomin et al., 1997). For example, some research suggests that genetic factors may be important for the development of paranoid personality disorder (Nigg & Goldsmith, 1994), schizotypal personality disorder (Nigg & Goldsmith, 1994), borderline personality disorder (Widiger & Trull, 1993), and antisocial personality disorder (Carey & Goldman, 1997).

In addition, some progress is being made in understanding the psychobiological substrate of at least some of the personality disorders (Depue, 1996; Hollander et al., 1994; Siever & Davis, 1991). For example, people with borderline personality disorder appear to be characterized by lowered functioning of the neurotransmitter serotonin, which may be why they show impulsive-aggressive behavior, including parasuicidal acts such as cutting their arms with a knife (Figueroa & Silk, 1997; Hollander et al., 1994). Patients with borderline personality disorder may also show disturbances in the regulation of noradrenergic neurotransmitters that are similar to those seen in chronic stress conditions such as PTSD (see Chapter 4). In particular, their hyperresponsive noradrenergic system may be related to their hypersensitivity to environmental changes (Figueroa & Silk, 1997). In addition, deficits in the dopamine systems may be related to a disposition toward transient psychotic symptoms (Kernberg, 1996).

Nevertheless, like the Axis I disorders, none of the personality disorders is entirely heritable, and none can be understood solely from a biological perspective. Thus, psychosocial and sociocultural causal factors must also play crucial roles in their origins, and an understanding of these disorders at a psychological level must supplement any understanding of their biological underpinnings. The ultimate goal would be to achieve a biopsychosocial perspective on the origins of each personality disorder, but we are far from that goal today.

Psychosocial Causal Factors

Early Learning Experiences Among psychosocial factors, early learning is usually assumed to contribute the most toward predisposing a person to develop a personality disorder, yet there is little research to support this belief. A significant number of studies have suggested that abuse and neglect in childhood may be related to the development of certain personality disorders. For example, in what is perhaps the largest and best-designed study to date, Zanarini and colleagues (1997) reported on the results of detailed interviews of over 350 patients with borderline personality disorder and over 100 with other personality disorders. Patients with borderline personality disorder reported significantly higher rates of abuse than did patients with other personality disorders: emotional abuse (73 versus 51 percent), verbal abuse (76 versus 52 percent), physical abuse (59 versus 34 percent), and sexual abuse (61 versus 32 percent). Overall, about 90 percent of patients with borderline personality disorder reported some type of childhood abuse and neglect. Although this and many other related studies are suggestive that borderline personality disorder (and perhaps other personality disorders as well) is associated with early childhood trauma, one notable shortcoming of the studies is that they rely on retrospective self-reports of individuals who are known for their exaggerated and distorted views of other people (Ruegg & Frances, 1995; Rutter & Maughan, 1997; see also Chapter 11). Moreover, although these rates of abuse and neglect may seem rather alarming, it is important to note that the majority of children who experience early abuse and neglect do not end up with serious personality disorders or psychopathology (Rutter & Maughan, 1997).

Psychodynamic Views Psychodynamic theorists such as Otto Kernberg (1984, 1996) and Heinz Kohut (1977) have also written a great deal about the origins of several of the personality disorders—most notably borderline, antisocial, histrionic, and narcissistic personality disorders. For example, with regard to narcissistic personality disorder, Kohut argued that all children go through a phase of primitive grandiosity during which they think that all events and needs revolve around them. For normal development beyond this phase to occur, according to him, parents must do some mirroring of the infant's grandiosity. This helps the child develop normal levels of self-confidence. Kohut argued, "However grave the blows may be to which the child's grandiosity is exposed by the realities of life, the proud smile of the parents will keep alive a bit of the original omnipotence, to be retained as the nucleus of the self-confidence and inner security about one's worth that sustain the healthy person throughout his life" (Kohut & Wolff, 1978, p. 182; from Widiger & Trull, 1993). Kohut further proposed that narcissistic personality disorder is likely to develop if parents are neglectful, devaluing, or unempathetic to the child; this individual will be perpetually searching for affirmation of this idealized and grandiose sense of self.

Although this theory has been very influential among psychodynamic clinicians, it unfortunately has no real empirical support. And, indeed, it is interesting to note

Otto Kernberg (b. 1928), shown on the left, is an influential psychoanalytic theorist who has written a great deal about borderline and narcissistic personality disorders. Heinz Kohut (1913–1981), another twentieth-century psychoanalytic thinker, theorized that poor parenting can cause narcissistic personality disorder by failing to build a child's normal self-confidence.

that Theodore Millon—a personality disorder researcher from the social learning perspective of Bandura—has argued quite the opposite. He believes that narcissistic personality disorder comes from parental overvaluation (Millon & Davis, 1996). For example, he has proposed that "these parents pamper and indulge their youngsters in ways that teach them that their every wish is a command and that they deserve prominence without even minimal effort" (Millon, 1981, p. 175; from Widiger & Trull, 1993). That theorists from these two quite different traditions (psychoanalytic and social learning) can come to such opposite conclusions illustrates the current poverty of knowledge regarding particular antecedents for these disorders. The only disorder for which there is a good deal of research on causal factors is antisocial personality disorder, which is discussed at length later in this chapter.

Another current variant on psychodynamic thinking about the origins of personality disorders stems from the interpersonal approach to psychopathology and psychotherapy (see Chapter 2). Benjamin's (1996a, 1996b) sophisticated empirical approach to understanding the psychopathology of both Axis I and Axis II disorders quantifies a patient's interpersonal and intrapsychic aspects of relationships and is beginning to yield important insights not only about the probable origins of personality disorders but also about how best to treat them.

Sociocultural Causal Factors

Sociocultural factors contributing to personality disorders are even less well defined. The incidence and form of psychopathology in general do vary somewhat with time and place, and the same may be true for personality disorders, although evidence on this point is sketchy at best. Moreover, some clinicians believe that personality disorders have increased in American society in recent years. If this claim is true, the increase may be related to changes in this culture's general priorities and activities. Is the increased emphasis on impulse gratification, instant solutions, and pain-free benefits leading more people to develop the self-centered lifestyles seen in more extreme forms in the personality disorders? Only further research can clarify this question.

IN REVIEW

- Why is relatively little known about the causal factors in personality disorders?
- What are some of the biological, psychological, and sociocultural factors that seem to be implicated in personality disorders?

TREATMENTS AND OUTCOMES FOR PERSONALITY DISORDERS

Individuals with personality disorders seem especially resistant to therapy. In addition, people who have both an Axis I disorder and a personality disorder do not, on average, do as well in treatment for their Axis I disorder as do patients without a comorbid personality disorder, especially if the treatment approach is not modified to account for the personality disorder (Pretzer & Beck, 1996). In part, this reduced success occurs because people with personality disorders, almost by definition, have rigid ingrained personality traits that often make them resist doing the things that would help improve their Axis I condition. Other reasons why personality disorders may complicate treatment of Axis I conditions is that people with personality disorders often have difficulties establishing and maintaining good therapeutic relationships with their therapists (Van Velzen & Emmelkamp, 1996).

In many cases, people with personality disorders are seen clinically as part of another person's treatment. For example, in couples counseling, a person identified as the "patient" may have a spouse or partner with a personality disorder. Or a child referred to a child guidance center may have a parent with a personality disorder. In these cases, of course, the problems of the so-called patient may be due in no small measure to the great strain caused by the family member with a personality disorder. A narcissistic father, who is so self-centered and demanding of attention from others that family relationships are constantly strained, leaves little room for small children to grow into self-respecting adults. Likewise, a mother with dependent personality disorder, whose typical manner of responding to others is to be highly submissive and clinging and fearful of separation, may create an unhealthy family atmosphere that distorts a child's development. After seeing a child in such a family context, a child or family therapist has often quickly concluded that psychological attention, if it is to be effective at all, must be focused on the parental relationships. The following case clearly illustrates this problem.

Case Study **The Child of a Father with Paranoid Personality Disorder** • Mrs. A. brought her 7-year-old son, Christopher, to a mental health center for treatment because he was fearful of going out and recently had been having bad nightmares. Mrs. A. sought help at the recommendation of the school social worker after Chris refused to return to school. She voiced a great deal of concern for Chris and agreed to cooperate in the treatment by attending parent effectiveness training sessions.... Her husband... adamantly refused to participate. Mrs. A described him as a "very proud and strong-willed man" who was quite suspicious of other people. She felt that he might be afraid people would blame him for Chris's problems. She reported that he had been having a lot of problems lately—he had seemed quite bitter and resentful over some local political issues and tended to blame others (particularly minorities) for his problems....

After several sessions of therapy, Mrs. A. confessed to her therapist that her husband's rigid and suspicious behavior was disrupting the family. He would often come home from work and accuse her of, for example, "talking with Jewish men." He was a domineering person who set strict house rules and enforced them with loud threats and intimidation. Both Mrs. A. and Chris were fearful of his tyrannical demands.... Mrs. A. also felt a great deal of sympathy for her husband because she felt that deep down inside he was frightened; she reported that he kept numerous guns around the house and several locks on the doors for protection against outsiders, whom he feared. Thus, it became clear that her husband had at least certain features of paranoid personality disorder and that this was creating a great deal of difficulty for the family.

Because many people with personality disorders—especially those in Cluster A and Cluster B—enter treatment only at someone else's insistence, they often do not believe that they need to change. These people typically put the responsibility for treatment on others and are adept at avoiding the focus of therapy themselves. In addition, their therapeutic relationships tend to be fragile or stormy. For those with personality disorders in Cluster B, the pattern of acting out, typical in their other relationships, is carried into the therapy situation, and instead of dealing with their problems at the verbal level, they may become angry at their therapist and loudly disrupt the sessions. When questioned about such inappropriate behavior, these people often drop out of treatment or become even more entrenched in defending their behavior.

Adapting Therapeutic Techniques to Specific Personality Disorders

In some situations, therapeutic techniques must be modified. For example, recognizing that traditional individual psychotherapy tends to encourage dependency in people who are already too dependent (such as those with dependent, histrionic, and borderline personality disorders), it is often useful to develop treatment strategies specifically aimed at altering a dependent person's basic lifestyle instead of fostering it. Patients with a Cluster C disorder, such as dependent or avoidant personality disorder, may be hypersensitive to any perceived criticism from the therapist and may quit prematurely for such reasons. In such cases, the therapist has to be extremely careful to make sure that this does not happen. One approach is to ask the patient for feedback about the therapist's behavior and attitude at the end of each session (Beck & Freeman, 1990). By letting the patient give feedback and by discussing possible changes for future sessions, the therapist appears nondefensive and yet also encourages and reinforces assertive criticism on the part of the patient.

Such specific therapeutic techniques are a central part of the relatively new cognitive approach to personality disorders (look again at Table 9.2) (Beck & Freeman, 1990; Pretzer & Beck, 1996). The cognitive approach assumes that the dysfunctional feelings and behavior associated with the personality disorders are largely the result of schemas that tend to produce consistently biased judgments, as well as tendencies to make cognitive errors in many types of situations. Recall that schemas involve specific rules that govern information processing and behavior. Changing the underlying dysfunctional schemas is at the heart of cognitive therapy for personality disorders, and doing so is particularly difficult because these schemas are held in place by behavioral, cognitive, and emotional elements. Nevertheless, through the usual cognitive techniques of monitoring automatic thoughts, challenging faulty logic, and assigning behavioral tasks intended to help challenge the patient's dysfunctional assumptions and beliefs, cognitive therapists may have made a significant step in advancing treatment for personality disorders. At this point, for most disorders there are only case studies or uncontrolled clinical studies, rather than controlled treatment studies, but the results are promising (Crits-Christoph, 1998; Pretzer & Beck, 1996).

In general, therapy for people with severe personality disorders may be more effective in situations such as inpatient settings where acting-out behavior can be constrained. In addition, many patients with borderline personality disorder are hospitalized for safety reasons because of their frequent suicidal behavior (Norton & Hinshelwood, 1996; Silk et al., 1994).

Treating Borderline Personality Disorder

Of all the personality disorders, there has probably been more attention paid to the treatment of borderline personality disorder, in part because treatment prognosis (probable outcome) for patients with this disorder is typically considered to be guarded because of their longstanding problems and extreme instability. Because borderline personality patients are usually difficult to manage as a result of their behavioral problems and acting-out tendencies, treatment often involves a judicious use of both biological and psychological methods (Gitlin, 1996).

Pharmacotherapy The use of drugs is especially controversial with this disorder because it is so frequently associated with suicidal behavior. Nevertheless, several reviews of the evidence for psychopharmacological treatment of borderline personality disorder have concluded that low doses of antipsychotic medication have modest but significant effects that are broad-based; that is, patients show some improvement in depression, anxiety, suicidality, rejection sensitivity, and occasional psychotic symptoms (Gitlin, 1996; Woo-Ming & Siever, 1998). These reviews also concluded that benzodiazepines (anxiolytics) and tricylic antidepressants are generally ineffective in the treatment of borderline personality disorder, but that antidepressant drugs from the same class as Prozac (SSRIs) are promising. Lithium may also be useful in reducing irritability, suicidality, and angry behavior (Woo-Ming & Siever, 1998). In general, the drugs are used as an adjunct to psychological treatment.

Psychological Treatments Traditional psychodynamic therapy for borderline personality disorder has been significantly modified and adapted for the particular problems of persons with this disorder. For example, Kernberg's (1985, 1996) form of psychodynamic psychotherapy for this disorder is much more directive than is typical psychodynamic treatment. The primary goal of treatment is seen as strengthening the weak egos of these individuals, with a particular focus on their primary defense mechanism of *splitting*, which leads them to black-and-white, all-or-none thinking, as well as to rapid shifts in their reactions to other people (including the therapist) as "all good" or "all bad." Although this treatment can be effective in some cases, it is expensive and time-consuming (often lasting a good number of years) and is only beginning to be subjected to controlled research.

Probably the most promising treatment for borderline personality disorder is Marsha Linehan's (1987, 1993) dialectical behavior therapy, a kind of behavior therapy that also incorporates some principles of client-centered therapy and is specifically designed for treating this disorder. Linehan believes that it is the inability to tolerate strong states of negative affect that is central to this disorder, and one of the primary goals of treatment is to encourage patients to accept this negative affect without engaging in self-destructive or other maladaptive behaviors. Accordingly, she has developed a problem-focused treatment based on a clear hierarchy of goals: (1) decreasing suicidal behavior; (2) decreasing behaviors that interfere with therapy, such as missing sessions, lying, and getting hospitalized; (3) decreasing escapist behaviors that interfere with a stable lifestyle, such as substance abuse; (4) increasing behavioral skills in order to regulate emotions, to increase interpersonal skills, and to increase tolerance for distress; and (5) other goals the patient chooses. Suicidal behaviors are the first target "simply because psychotherapy is not effective with dead patients" (Linehan, 1987, p. 329) and because this indicates that these behaviors are taken very seriously.

Dialectical behavior therapy combines individual and group components, with the group setting focusing more on the skills training for interpersonal skills, emotion regulation, and stress tolerance. This all occurs with a therapist who is taught to accept the patient for who he or she is, in spite of the patient's behaviors that make it so difficult to do so (such as bursts of rage, suicidal behaviors, missing appointments, etc.). Linehan makes a clear distinction between accepting the patient for who he or she is and approving of the patient's behavior. For example, a therapist cannot approve of self-mutilation, but he or she should indicate acceptance of that as part of a patient's problem.

Results from one important controlled study using dialectical behavior therapy were very encouraging (Linehan et al., 1991; Linehan, Heard, & Armstrong, 1993; Linehan et al., 1994). Borderline personality patients who received dialectical behavior therapy were compared with patients receiving treatment as usual in the community over a 1-year treatment period and a 1-year follow-up period. Patients who received dialectical behavior therapy showed greater reduction in self-destructive and suicidal behaviors, as well as in levels of anger, than did those in the treatment-as-usual group. They were also more likely to stay in treatment and to require fewer days of hospitalization than the control group. At follow-up, they were doing better occupationally and were rated as better adjusted in terms of interpersonal and emotional regulation skills than the control group. Although these results may seem modest in some ways, they are considered extraordinary by most therapists who work with this population.

Treating Other Personality Disorders

There has been less research on treating personality disorders other than borderline personality disorder. For example, among Cluster A disorders, schizotypal personality disorder has not yet found a promising treatment approach. Gitlin (1996) summarized evidence showing that low doses of antipsychotic drugs may result in modest improvements, but no treatment has yet produced anything approaching a cure for most people with this disorder (see also Woo-Ming & Siever, 1998). Other than uncontrolled studies or single cases, no systematic studies on treating people with either paranoid or schizoid personality disorder exist (Gitlin, 1996; Pretzer & Beck, 1996). There is also little more than uncontrolled studies or single cases documenting the effectiveness of either cognitive therapy or medication for the treatment of narcissistic, antisocial, or histrionic personality disorder in Cluster B (Gitlin 1996; Pretzer & Beck, 1996).

Treatment of some Cluster C personality disorders, such as dependent and avoidant personality disorders, has not been extensively studied but appears more promising than for many of the disorders in Clusters A and B (e.g., Mehlum et al., 1991). Winston and colleagues (1994), for example, found significant improvement in patients with Cluster C disorders using a form of short-term psychotherapy that is active and confrontational (see also Pretzer & Beck, 1996). There is also some evidence that one category of antidepressants is sometimes useful in treating avoidant personality disorder just as it is for treating generalized social phobia (with which this personality disorder is almost always comorbid) (Gitlin, 1996; Woo-Ming & Siever, 1998). Finally, there is suggestive evidence from case studies that several other classes of antidepressants may be useful in treating avoidant personality disorder (Woo-Ming & Siever, 1998).

IN REVIEW

- Why are personality disorders especially resistant to therapy?
- Under what circumstances do persons with personality disorders generally get involved in psychotherapy?
- What is the relevance of dysfunctional schemas to Beck and Freeman's cognitive approach to treatment of personality disorders?
- What is known about the effectiveness of treatments for specific personality disorders?

ANTISOCIAL PERSONALITY AND PSYCHOPATHY

As we have seen, the outstanding characteristics of people with antisocial personality disorder (ASPD) is their tendency to persistently disregard and violate the rights of others. They do this through deceitful, aggressive, or antisocial behavior, with little or no sign of remorse. Basically, these people have a lifelong pattern of unsocialized and irresponsible behavior, with little regard for safety—either their own or that of others. These characteristics bring them into repeated conflict with society. Only individuals 18 or older are diagnosed as antisocial personalities. According to the DSM, this diagnosis is made if the following criteria are met:

- *There have been at least three behavioral problems occurring after age 15,* such as repeatedly performing acts that are grounds for arrest, repeated deceitfulness, impulsivity or failure to plan for the future, irritability and aggressiveness, disregard for safety, consistent irresponsibility in work or financial matters, and lack of remorse.
- *There were at least three instances of deviant behavior before age 15,* such as aggression toward people or animals, destruction of property, deceitfulness or theft, and serious violation of rules (symptoms of conduct disorder—see Chapter 14).
- *The antisocial behavior is not a symptom of another mental disorder such as schizophrenia or a manic episode.*

Psychopathy and ASPD

The use of the term *antisocial personality disorder* dates back only to DSM-III in 1980, but many of the central features of this disorder have long been labeled **psychopathy,** or *sociopathy.* Psychopathy was first carefully described by Cleckley (1941, 1982) in the 1940s. In addition to the defining features that DSM lists for ASPD, psychopathy also includes such traits as lack of empathy, inflated and arrogant self-appraisal, and glib and superficial charm. With their strong emphasis on behavioral criteria that can be measured reasonably objectively, DSM-III and DSM-IV broke from the tradition of psychopathy researchers in an attempt to increase the reliability of the diagnosis (the level of agreement among clinicians on the diagnosis). However, much less attention has been paid to the validity of the ASPD diagnosis—that is, whether it measures a meaningful construct and whether that construct is the same as psychopathy.

psychopathy A condition involving the defining features of antisocial personality disorder as listed in DSM, as well as such traits as lack of empathy, inflated and arrogant self-appraisal, and glib and superficial charm.

Two Dimensions of Psychopathy Research over the past 20 years by Robert Hare and his colleagues suggests that ASPD and psychopathy are related but differ in significant ways. Hare (1980, 1991; Hart & Hare, 1997) developed the 20-item Psychopathy Checklist as a way for clinicians and researchers to diagnose psychopathy based on the Cleckley criteria. Extensive research with this checklist has shown that there are two related but separable dimensions of psychopathy, with each predicting different types of behavior. The first dimension involves the affective and interpersonal core of the disorder and includes traits such as lack of remorse, callousness, selfishness, and an exploitative use of others. The second dimension reflects behavior—the aspects of psychopathy making up an antisocial, impulsive, and socially deviant lifestyle. The second dimension is much more closely related to the DSM-III and DSM-IV diagnosis of ASPD than is the first dimension (Hare, Hart, & Harpur, 1991; Hart & Hare, 1997). Not surprisingly, therefore, it is typically found that a higher percentage of prison inmates qualify for a diagnosis of ASPD than for one of psychopathy. That is, a significant number of inmates show the antisocial, deviant, and aggressive behaviors that result in their meeting the criteria for a diagnosis of ASPD, but not enough of the selfish, callous, and exploitative behaviors to qualify for a diagnosis of psychopathy.

An additional implication is that the current conceptualization of ASPD may not cover what may be a substantial segment of the population that shows many of the features of the affective and interpersonal dimension of psychopathy but not as many features of the behavioral and antisocial dimension, or at least few enough that they do not get into trouble with the law. This group might include some unprincipled business professionals, high-pressure evangelists, and crooked politicians.

The issues surrounding these two diagnoses remain highly controversial. Many researchers are likely to continue studying the Cleckley/Hare diagnosis of psychopathy rather than the DSM diagnosis of ASPD. This is both because of the long and rich tradition of research on psychopathy and because the diagnosis of psychopathy has been shown to be a better predictor of a variety of important facets of criminal behavior than is the diagnosis of ASPD. For example, a diagnosis of psychopathy appears to be the single best predictor of violence (Hart, 1998; Hart & Hare, 1997). The controversy over the use of a diagnosis of psychopathy or a diagnosis of ASPD is not likely to be resolved soon, and, unfortunately, different researchers in this area make different choices, leading to some confusion when trying to interpret the research on causal factors. The sections that follow attempt to be clear which diagnostic category was being used in the various studies, because the causal factors may well not be identical.

However, whichever diagnosis is used, individuals with ASPD or with psychopathy are clearly a mixed group. Few of these people find their way into community clinics or mental hospitals. A larger number are confined in jail, but as already noted, a history of repeated legal or social offenses is certainly not sufficient justification for assuming that an individual is psychopathic or has ASPD. In addition, a large number of psychopathic individuals manage to stay out of correctional institutions, although they tend to be in constant conflict with authority. Unfortunately, studying these latter individuals is difficult because they are usually hard to find. One researcher (Widom, 1977) who wanted to study these individuals used an ingenious ad in local newspapers that read:

> Are you adventurous? Psychologist studying adventurous, carefree people who've led exciting, impulsive lives. If you're the kind of person who'd do almost anything for a dare and want to participate in a paid experiment, send name, address, phone, and short biography proving how interesting you are to . . . (p. 675)

When the individuals who responded were given a battery of tests, they turned out to be similar in personality makeup to institutionalized psychopaths. Unfortunately, little other work has been conducted on noninstitutionalized psychopaths.

The Clinical Picture in Antisocial Personality and Psychopathy

Often charming, spontaneous, and likable on first acquaintance, psychopaths and antisocial personalities are deceitful and manipulative, callously using others to achieve their own ends. Many of them seem to live in a series of present moments, without consideration for the past or future.

We will summarize characteristics that psychopaths and antisocial personalities tend to share and then describe a case that illustrates the wide range of behavioral patterns that may be involved. Although all the characteristics examined in the following sections are not usually found in a particular case, they are typical of psychopaths as described by Cleckley (1941, 1982). Many people with ASPD also share at least a subset of these characteristics, although they are not all criteria for the DSM diagnosis.

Inadequate Conscience Development Psychopaths appear unable to understand and accept ethical values except on a verbal level. They glibly claim to adhere to high moral standards that have no apparent connection with their behavior. In short, their conscience development is severely retarded or nonexistent, and they behave as if social regulations do not apply to them, leading to their frequently drifting into criminal activities. In spite of their retarded conscience, their intellectual development is typically normal. Moreover, there is some evidence that intelligence and education seem to serve as protective factors for adolescents who are at risk for adult psychopathy or antisocial personality (Hawkins, Arthur, & Olson, 1997). For example, several studies found that many adolescents with conduct disorder who are known to be predisposed to antisocial personality or psychopathy never get involved in criminal behavior because they are positively influenced by schooling. Thus, they presumably focus their energies on more socially accepted behaviors (e.g., White, Moffitt, & Silva, 1989).

Serial killer Ted Bundy exhibited antisocial behavior at its most extreme and dangerous. He showed the classic psychopathic traits of good looks, charm, and intelligence. But he was also highly manipulative and showed a total lack of remorse for his victims. Bundy's clean-cut image, which he used to get close to his victims—all young women whom he sexually abused and then murdered—was so convincing as to be chilling when the magnitude of his acts became apparent. Bundy was executed in Florida in 1989.

Irresponsible and Impulsive Behavior Psychopaths generally have a callous disregard for the rights, needs, and well-being of others. They have learned to take rather than earn what they want. Prone to thrill seeking and deviant and unconventional behavior, they often break the law impulsively and without regard for the consequences. They seldom deny themselves immediate pleasure for future gains or long-range goals.

Many studies have shown that antisocial personalities and perhaps psychopaths have high rates of alcoholism and other substance abuse or dependence disorders (e.g., Cloninger, Bayon, & Przybeck, 1997; Sher & Trull, 1994). Alcohol abuse is related to the antisocial or deviant behavior dimension of psychopathy, not to the interpersonal and affective dimension (Hemphill, Hart, & Hare, 1994). The relationship between antisocial behavior and substance abuse is sufficiently strong that some have questioned whether there may be a common factor leading to both alcoholism and antisocial personality.

Ability to Impress and Exploit Others Psychopaths are often charming and likable, with a disarming manner that easily wins friends. Typically, they have a good sense of humor and an optimistic outlook. Although frequent liars, they usually seem sincerely sorry if caught in a lie and promise to make amends—but will not do so. They are adept at exploiting other people. For example, many psychopaths engage in unethical sales schemes in which they use their charm and the confidence they inspire in others to make "easy money," but they are often able to convince other people—as well as themselves—that they are free of fault. Although initially able to win the liking and friendship of other people because of their ability to impress, psychopaths are seldom able to keep close friends. They seemingly cannot understand love in others or give it in return. Manipulative and exploitative in sexual relationships, psychopaths are irresponsible and unfaithful mates.

Hare, who has conducted more research on psychopathy than any other individual, recently characterized the prototypic psychopath in the following manner:

> Conceptualizing psychopaths as *remorseless predators* helped me to make sense of what often appears to be senseless behavior. These are individuals who, lacking in conscience and feelings for others, find it easy to use charm, manipulation, intimidation, and violence to control others and to satisfy their own social needs. They cold-bloodedly take what they want and do as they please, violating social norms and expectations without the slightest sense of guilt or regret. Their depredations affect virtually everyone at one time or another, because they form a significant proportion of persistent criminals, drug dealers, spouse and child abusers,

swindlers and con men.... They are well represented in the business and corporate world, particularly during chaotic restructuring, where the rules and their enforcement are lax and accountability is difficult to determine (Babiak, 1995). Many psychopaths emerge as "patriots" and "saviors" in societies experiencing social, economic, and political upheaval (e.g., Rwanda, the former Yugoslavia, and the former Soviet Union). They wrap themselves in the flag, and enrich themselves by callously exploiting ethnic, cultural, or racial tensions and grievances. (1998, pp. 128–129)

Psychopathy is well illustrated in the following classic case study published by Hare (1970).

Case Study **A Psychopath in Action** • Donald S., 30 years old, has just completed a 3-year prison term for fraud, bigamy, false pretenses, and escaping lawful custody. The circumstances leading up to these offenses are interesting and consistent with his past behavior. With less than a month left to serve on an earlier 18-month term for fraud, he faked illness and escaped from the prison hospital. During the 10 months of freedom that followed, he engaged in a variety of illegal enterprises; the activity that resulted in his recapture was typical of his method of operation. By passing himself off as the "field executive" of an international philanthropic foundation, he was able to enlist the aid of several religious organizations in a fund-raising campaign. The campaign moved slowly at first, and in an attempt to speed things up, he arranged an interview with the local TV station. His performance during the interview was so impressive that funds started to pour in. However, unfortunately for Donald, the interview was also carried on a national news network. He was recognized and quickly arrested. During the ensuing trial it became evident that he experienced no sense of wrongdoing for his activities. He maintained, for example, that his passionate plea for funds "primed the pump"—that is, induced people to give to other charities as well as to the one he professed to represent. At the same time, he stated that most donations to charity are made by those who feel guilty about something and who therefore deserve to be bilked.

While in prison he was used as a subject in some of the author's research. On his release he applied for admission to a university and, by way of reference, told the registrar that he had been one of the author's research colleagues! Several months later the author received a letter from him requesting a letter of recommendation on behalf of Donald's application for a job.

Background. Donald was the youngest of three boys born to middle-class parents. Both of his brothers led normal, productive lives. His father spent a great deal of time with his business; when he was home he tended to be moody and to drink heavily when things were not going right. Donald's mother was a gentle, timid woman who tried to please her husband and to maintain a semblance of family harmony. When she discovered her children engaged in some mischief, she would threaten to tell their father. However, she seldom carried out these threats because she did not want to disturb her husband and because his reactions were likely to be dependent on his mood at the time; on some occasions he would fly into a rage and beat the children and on others he would administer a verbal reprimand, sometimes mild and sometimes severe.

By all accounts Donald was considered a willful and difficult child. When his desire for candy or toys was frustrated he would begin with a show of affection, and if this failed he would throw a temper tantrum; the latter was seldom necessary because his angelic appearance and artful ways usually got him what he wanted. ... Although he was obviously very intelligent, his school years were academically undistinguished. He was restless, easily bored, and frequently truant. His behavior in the presence of the teacher or some other authority was usually quite good, but when he was on his own he generally got himself or others into trouble. Although he was often suspected of being the culprit, he was adept at talking his way out of difficulty.

Donald's misbehavior as a child took many forms including lying, cheating, petty theft, and the bullying of smaller children. As he grew older he became more and more interested in sex, gambling, and alcohol. When he was 14 he made crude sexual advances toward a younger girl, and when she threatened to tell her parents he locked her in a shed. It was about 16 hours before she was found. Donald at first denied knowledge of the incident, later stating that she had seduced him and that the door must have locked itself. He expressed no concern for the anguish experienced by the girl and her parents.... His parents were able to prevent charges being brought against him....

When he was 17, Donald ... forged his father's name to a large check, and spent about a year traveling around the world. He apparently lived well, using a combination of charm, physical attractiveness, and false pretenses to finance his way. During subsequent years he held a succession of jobs, never ... for more than a few months. Throughout this period he was charged with a variety of crimes, including theft, drunkenness in a public place, assault, and many traffic violations. In most cases he was either fined or given a light sentence.

A Ladies' Man. His sexual experiences were frequent, casual, and callous. When he was 22, he married a 41-year-old woman whom he had met in a bar. Several other marriages followed, all bigamous.... The pattern was the same: He would marry someone on impulse, let her support him for several months, and then leave. One marriage was particularly interesting. After being charged with fraud Donald was sent to a psychiatric institution for a period of observation. While there he came to the attention of a female member of the professional staff. His charm, physical attractiveness, and convincing promises to reform led her to intervene on his behalf. He was given a suspended sentence and they were married a week later. At first things went reasonably well, but when she refused to pay some of his gambling debts he forged her name to a check and left. He was soon caught and given an 18-month prison term. . . . He escaped with less than a month left to serve.

It is interesting to note that Donald sees nothing particularly wrong with his behavior, nor does he express remorse or guilt for using others and causing them grief. Although his behavior is self-defeating in the long run, he considers it to be practical and possessed of good sense. Periodic punishments do nothing to decrease his egotism and confidence in his own abilities. . . . His behavior is entirely egocentric, and his needs are satisfied without any concern for the feelings and welfare of others. (Reprinted with permission of Robert P. Hare, University of British Columbia, rhare@interchange.ubc.ca)

Causal Factors in Psychopathy and Antisocial Personality

Far more research has been conducted on the causes of psychopathy and antisocial personality than on any of the other personality disorders, so we are beginning to have a clearer picture of what some of the more important causal factors are. Contemporary research has variously stressed the causal roles of genetic factors, deficiencies in aversive emotional arousal, more general emotional deficits, the early learning of antisocial behavior as a coping style, and the influence of particular family and environmental patterns.

Because an antisocial person's impulsiveness, acting out, and intolerance of discipline tend to appear early in life, several investigators have focused on the role of biological factors as causative agents for psychopathic behaviors. The following three sections focus on some of these biological factors.

Genetic Influences Most behavior genetics research has focused on genetic influences on criminality rather than on psychopathy per se. There have been many studies using the twin method (comparing concordance rates between monozygotic and dizygotic twins), as well as a number of studies using the adoption method (rates of criminal behavior in the adopted-away children of criminals are compared with the rates of criminal behavior in adopted-away children of normals). The results of both kinds of studies show a modest heritability for antisocial or criminal behavior (e.g., Carey & Goldman, 1997; Nigg & Goldsmith, 1994), and at least one study reached similar conclusions for psychopathy (Schulsinger, 1972). However, researchers also note that strong environmental influences (to be discussed later) interact with genetic predispositions to determine which individuals with a predisposition become criminals or antisocial personalities (Carey & Goldman, 1997; Lykken, 1995; Rutter, 1996).

Deficient Aversive Emotional Arousal and Conditioning Research evidence indicates that psychopaths show deficient aversive emotional arousal; this condition presumably renders them less prone to fear and anxiety in stressful situations and less prone to normal conscience development and socialization. This lack of anxiety is more closely associated with the egocentric, callous, exploitative dimension of psychopathy than with the antisocial behavioral dimension (Frick, 1998; Lykken, 1995).

In an early classic study, for example, Lykken (1957) found that psychopaths showed deficient conditioning of anxiety when anticipating punishment and were slow at learning to stop responding in order to avoid punishment. As a result, psychopaths presumably fail to acquire many of the conditioned reactions essential to normal passive avoidance of punishment, conscience development, and socialization (Trasler, 1978). Hare has recently summarized work on this issue by stating, "It is the emotionally charged thought, images, and internal dialogue that give the 'bite' to conscience, account for its powerful control over behavior, and generate guilt and remorse for transgressions. This is something that psychopaths cannot understand. For them conscience is little more than an intellectual awareness of rules others make up—empty words" (1998, p. 112).

An impressive array of studies support this early work of Lykken showing that psychopaths are deficient in the conditioning of anxiety (e.g., Fowles & Missel, 1994; Hare, 1978, 1998; Lykken, 1995). Because such conditioning may underlie successful avoidance of punishment, this may also explain why their impulsive behavior goes unchecked. According to Fowles, the deficient anxiety conditioning seems to stem from psychopaths' having a deficient *behavioral inhibition system* (Fowles, 1980, 1993; Fowles & Missel, 1994; see also Newman, 1997). The behavioral inhibition system has been proposed by Gray (1987; Gray & McNaughton, 1996) to be the neural system underlying anxiety. It is also the neural system responsible for learning to inhibit responses to cues signaling punishment; this kind of *passive avoidance learning,* as it is termed, depends on conditioning of anxiety to the cue and the response, and then learning to avoid punishment by not making the response (for example, by not committing robbery one avoids punishment). Thus, deficiencies in this neural system are associated both with deficits in anxiety conditioning and, in turn, with deficits in learning to avoid punishment through passive avoidance (which seems to depend on conditioning of anxiety).

The second important neural system in Gray's model is the *behavioral activation system:* This system activates behavior in response to cues for reward (positive reinforcement), as well as to cues for *active avoidance* of threatened punishment (such as lying or running away to avoid punishment that one has been threatened with). According to Fowles's theory, the behavioral activation system is thought to be normal or possibly overactive in psychopaths, which may explain why they are quite focused on obtaining reward. Moreover, if they are caught in a misdeed, they are also very focused on actively avoiding threatened punishment (e.g., through deceit and lies or running away). This hypothesis of Fowles that psychopaths have a deficient behavioral inhibition system and a normal or possibly overactive behavioral activation system seems to be able to account for three features of psychopathy: (1) psychopaths' deficient conditioning of anxiety to signals for punishment, (2) their related difficulty learning to inhibit responses that may result in punishment (such as illegal and antisocial acts), and (3) their normal or hypernormal active avoidance of punishment (by deceit, lies, and escape behavior) when actively threatened with punishment (Fowles, 1993, p. 9; see also Hare, 1998b).

More General Emotional Deficits Researchers have also been interested in whether there are more general emotional deficits in psychopaths other than in the conditioning of anxiety (Fowles & Missel, 1994; Hare, 1998b). Psychopaths showed less significant physiological reactivity to distress cues (slides of people crying, obviously quite distressed) than did nonpsychopaths, confirming the idea that they are low on empathy (Blair et al., 1997). However, they were not underresponsive to unconditioned threat cues such as slides of sharks, pointed guns, or angry faces.

In a summary of research on emotional deficits in psychopathy, Hare stated, "Psychopaths . . . seem to have difficulty in fully understanding and using words that for normal people refer to ordinary emotional events and feelings. . . . It is as if emotion is a second language for psychopaths, a language that requires a considerable amount of . . . cognitive effort on their part" (1998, p. 115).

A Developmental Perspective It has long been known that these disorders generally begin early in childhood, especially for boys, and that the number of antisocial behaviors exhibited in childhood is the single best predictor of who develops an adult diagnosis of psychopathy or antisocial personality (Robins, 1978). The early antisocial symptoms include "theft, incorrigibility, running away from home, truancy, associating with other delinquent children, staying out past the hour allowed, discipline problems in school and school retardation" (Robins, 1978, p. 260), which today are associated with a diagnosis of conduct disorder. In addition, an earlier age of onset of such antisocial symptoms is associated with a greater likelihood of developing adult antisocial personality (Robins, 1991; Robins & Price, 1991).

Antisocial personality disorder in adulthood is always preceded by conduct disorder in adolescence (usually early-onset conduct disorder). However, not all adolescents with conduct disorder (especially late-onset conduct disorder) go on to become adult antisocial personalities.

Prospective studies have shown that it is children with an early history of *oppositional defiant disorder,* characterized by a pattern of hostile and defiant behavior toward authority figures that usually begins by the age of 6 years, followed by early-onset conduct disorder around age 9, who are most likely to develop antisocial personality disorder, psychopathy, or other serious problems as adults. By contrast, those who develop conduct disorder in adolescence do not usually become psychopaths or antisocial personalities but instead have problems limited to the adolescent years (Hinshaw, 1994; Moffitt, 1993a). As summarized by Hinshaw (1994), the typical pattern in the prepsychopath is as follows:

> For the prototypic "early onset" child, irritable, difficult temperamental style in infancy yields to harshly defiant, argumentative behavior during preschool; early indexes of fighting, lying, and petty theft by the beginning of grade

> school; assault and sexual precocity in preadolescence; robbery and substance abuse by midadolescence; and repetitive criminal activities, callous relationships, and spousal and child abuse in adulthood (Caspi & Moffitt, 1995; Moffitt, 1993a). Thus antisocial activities persist, but they change in form markedly with development. (p. 21)

The second early diagnosis that is often a precursor to adult psychopathy or ASPD is *attention-deficit/hyperactivity disorder* (ADHD). ADHD is characterized by restless, inattentive, and impulsive behavior, a short attention span, and high distractibility (see Chapter 14). When ADHD occurs with conduct disorder (which happens in 30 to 50 percent of cases), this leads to a high likelihood that the person will develop adult psychopathy (Lynam, 1996; McBurnett & Pfiffner, 1998). Indeed, Lynam (1996, 1997) has referred to children with both ADHD and conduct disorder as "fledgling psychopaths."

There is increasing evidence that genetic propensities leading to mild neuropsychological problems, such as those leading to hyperactivity or attentional difficulties, along with a difficult temperament, may be important predisposing factors for early-onset conduct disorder. The behavioral problems that these predisposing factors create have a cascade of pervasive effects over time. For example, Moffitt and Lynam (1994) presented this hypothesis:

> How might neuropsychological risk initiate a chain of events that culminates in antisocial disorders? One possibility is that such behavioral deficits evoke a chain of failed parent-child encounters.... Children with difficult temperaments and early behavior problems pose a challenge to even the most resourceful, loving, and patient families.... Children characterized by a "difficult temperament" in infancy are more likely to resist their mothers' efforts to control them. ... Children's oppositional behaviors often provoke and force adult family members to counter with highly punitive and angry responses.... Children who coerce parents into providing short-term payoffs in the immediate situation may thereby learn an interactional style that continues to "work" in similar ways in later social encounters and with different interaction partners.... The child with neuropsychological problems and difficult behavior may learn early to rely on offensive interpersonal tactics. If he generalizes antisocial tactics to other settings, his style may consolidate into a syndrome of conduct disorder. (pp. 245–247)

In addition, many other psychosocial and sociocultural contextual variables contribute to the probability that a child with the genetic or constitutional liabilities discussed above will develop conduct disorder, and later adult psychopathy or ASPD. Early research suggested that parental rejection, inconsistency, and abuse of the child may be precursers of psychopathy (e.g., Greer, 1964; Hare, 1970). More recent research has led to a more complete picture of the range of psychosocial and sociocultural causal factors involved in psychopathy. As summarized by Patterson and colleagues (Capaldi & Patterson, 1994; Dishion & Patterson, 1997), these include parents' own antisocial behavior, divorce and other parental transitions, low socioeconomic status, a poor neighborhood, and parental stress and depression. All of these contribute to poor and ineffective parenting skills—especially ineffective discipline, monitoring, and supervision. "These children are trained by the family directly in antisocial behavior by coercive interchanges and indirectly by lack of monitoring and consistent discipline" (Capaldi & Patterson, 1994, p. 169; see also Dishion & Patterson, 1997). This, in turn, all too often leads to association with deviant peers and the opportunity for further learning of antisocial behavior. Their mediational model of how all this occurs is illustrated in Figure 9.1.

In summary, individuals with psychopathy and antisocial personality show patterns of deviant behavior from early childhood, often at first in the form of oppositional defiant disorder and then in the form of early-onset conduct disorder (sometimes along with attention-deficit/hyperactivity disorder). Increasingly, our understanding of the causal factors suggests that varying combinations of biological, psychosocial, and sociocultural factors appear to be involved. In other words, this is one disorder for which a biopsychosocial approach is absolutely critical.

Sociocultural Causal Factors and Psychopathy

Cross-cultural research on psychopathy reveals that it is a disorder that occurs in a wide range of cultures, including nonindustrialized ones as diverse as the Inuit of northwest Alaska and the Yorubas of Nigeria. The Yorubas' concept of a psychopath is "a person who always goes his own way regardless of others, who is uncooperative, full of malice, and bullheaded" and the Inuit's concept is of someone whose "mind knows what to do but he does not do it.... This is an abstract term for the breaking of many rules when awareness of the rules is not in question" (Murphy, 1976, p. 1026; cited in Cooke, 1996, p. 23). Nevertheless, the exact manifestations of the disorder are based on cultural factors, and the prevalence of the disorder also seems to vary due to sociocultural influences that encourage or discourage its development.

Regarding the cross-cultural manifestations of the disorder, one of the primary symptoms for which cultural variations occur is the frequency of aggressive and violent behavior. Socialization forces have an enormous impact on the expression of aggressive impulses. Thus, it is not surprising that in some cultures, such as China, people we

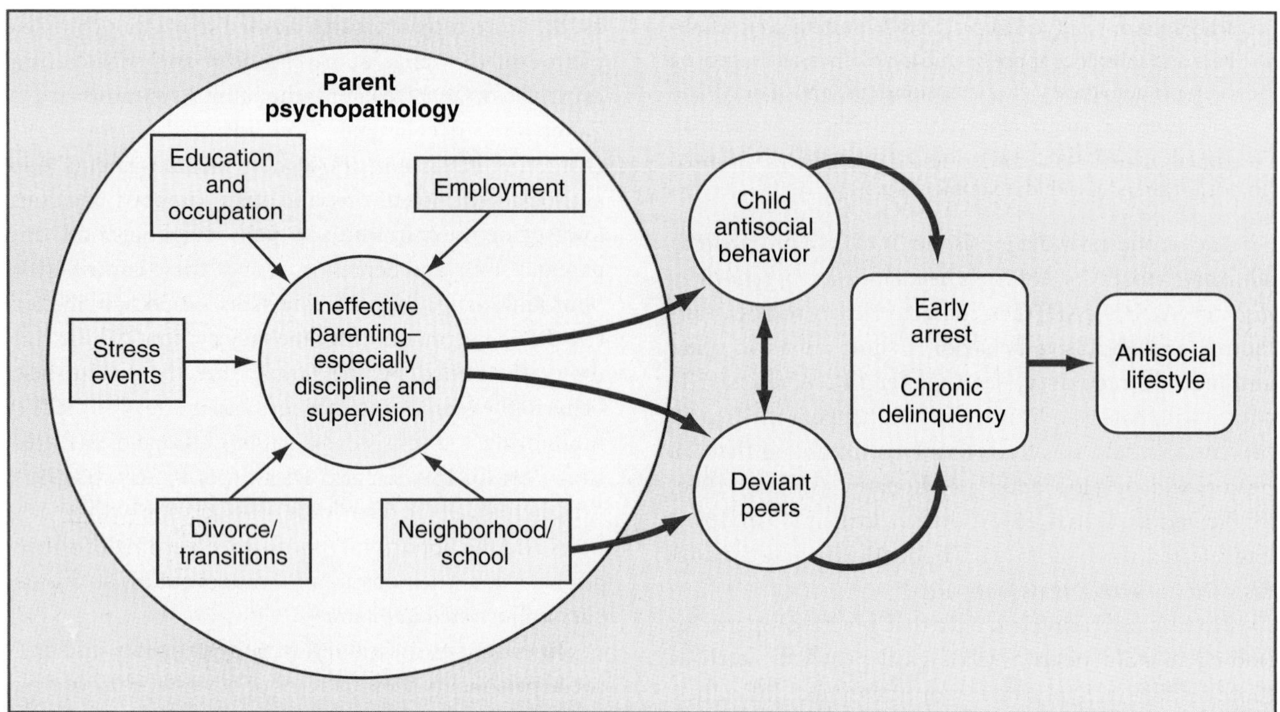

FIGURE 9.1 A MODEL FOR THE ASSOCIATION OF FAMILY CONTEXT AND ANTISOCIAL BEHAVIOR
Each of the contextual variables in this model has been shown to be related to antisocial behavior in boys, which in turn is related to antisocial behavior in adult males. Antisocial behavior in girls is far less common and has also been found to be less stable over time, making it more difficult to predict.
Source: From D. M. Capaldi and G. R. Patterson, "Interrelated Influences of Contextual Factors on Antisocial Behavior in Childhood and Adolescence for Males." In *Progress in experimental personality and psychopathology research.* © 1994 Springer Publishing Company, Inc., New York 10012. Used by permission.

would call psychopaths may be much less likely to engage in aggressive, especially violent behavior than they are in most Western cultures (Cooke, 1996).

Moreover, cultures can be classified along a dimension distinguishing between individualistic and collectivist societies. Competitiveness, self-confidence, and independence from others is emphasized in relatively individualistic societies, whereas contributions to the group, acceptance of authority, and stability of relationships are encouraged in relatively collectivist societies (Cooke, 1996). Individualistic societies (such as our own) would be expected to be more likely to promote some of the behavioral characteristics that, carried to the extreme, result in psychopathy. These characteristics include "glibness and superficiality, grandiosity, promiscuity... together with a lack of responsibility within relationships" and "the competitiveness... associated not only with higher crime rates but also with increases in... deceptive, manipulative, and parasitic behavior" (Cooke, 1996, p. 27). Although the evidence bearing on this is minimal, it is interesting to note that estimates of the prevalence of antisocial personality in Taiwan, a relatively collectivist society, are much lower than those in the United States (approximately 0.1 to 0.2 percent versus 2 to 3 percent). This intriguing preliminary work on sociocultural factors contributing to both the symptomatology and the prevalence of psychopathy is in its infancy, but it is likely to provide important new insights into the origins of this disorder in the years to come.

Treating Psychopathy and Antisocial Personality Disorder

Because most people with psychopathic and antisocial personalities do not exhibit obvious overt signs of psychopathology and can function effectively in many respects, they seldom come to the attention of mental hospitals or clinics. Those who run afoul of the law may participate in rehabilitation programs in penal institutions, but they are rarely changed by them. Even if more and better therapeutic facilities were available, effective treatment would still be a challenging task.

Factors inherent in the psychopath's personality—the inability to trust, to feel as others do, to learn from experience, and to accept responsibility for one's actions—apparently make the prognosis for psychodynamic psychotherapy very poor (Lösel, 1998). In addition, therapists must be vigilant for the possibility that the psychopathic patient may attempt to manipulate them, and that the information provided about the patient's life is likely to contain distortions and fabrications (Lösel, 1998). Biological treatments for psychopathy—including electroconvulsive therapy and drugs—have not fared much better. There is some evidence to suggest that antipsychotic drugs that might be expected to reduce aggressive behavior in psychopaths who also show schizotypal symptoms may have beneficial effects on certain symptoms. Drugs such as lithium and carbamazepine, which are used to treat bipolar disorder, have also had some success in treating the aggressive impulsive behavior of violent criminals (Gitlin, 1996; Lösel, 1998). Finally, there have been some tentative but promising results using antidepressants from the SSRI category, which can sometimes reduce aggressive impulsive behavior and increase interpersonal skills (Lösel, 1998). However, none of these biological treatments have substantial impact on the disorder as a whole, and much work remains to be done to determine more clearly which medications are most promising and for which symptoms.

Cognitive-Behavioral Treatments Cognitive-behavioral therapists have developed multifaceted techniques that appear to offer some promise of more effective treatment for at least some psychopaths or antisocial personalities (Lösel, 1998; Rice & Harris, 1997). Common targets of cognitive-behavioral interventions for psychopathy or ASPD include the following:

- Increasing self-control, self-critical thinking, and social perspective-taking
- Victim awareness
- Anger management
- Changing antisocial attitudes
- Curing drug addiction
- Reducing contacts with antisocial peers and improving interactions with nonantisocial peers

Such interventions require a controlled situation in which the therapist can administer or withhold reinforcement and the individual cannot leave treatment (such as an inpatient or prison setting). The controlled situation seems necessary for treatment to succeed. The antisocial behavior typically involves a total lifestyle rather than a specific maladaptive behavior, like a phobia, that can be targeted for treatment. Without a controlled situation, the intermittent reinforcement of short-term gains and successful avoidance of punishments, combined with a lack of anxiety and guilt, leave an antisocial individual with little motivation to change. Punishment by itself is ineffective for changing antisocial behavior.

Beck and Freeman's (1990) cognitive treatment for personality disorders also offers an interesting approach that can be incorporated into the treatment of ASPD by focusing on improving social and moral behavior through examination of self-serving dysfunctional beliefs that psychopaths tend to have. These include "Wanting something or wanting to avoid something justifies my actions"; "I always make good choices"; "The views of others are irrelevant to my decisions, unless they directly control my immediate consequences"; and "Undesirable consequences will not occur or will not matter to me" (Beck & Freeman, 1990, p. 154). In cognitive therapy, the therapist tries to guide the patient toward higher and more abstract kinds of thinking using principles that are based on theories of moral and cognitive development. This is done through guided discussions, structured cognitive exercises, and behavioral experiments.

Case Study Cognitive Therapy with a Psychopath

THERAPIST: How well has the "beat-the-system" approach actually worked out for you over time?

BRETT: It works great... until someone catches on or starts to catch on. Then you have to scrap that plan and come up with a new one.

THERAPIST: How difficult was it, you know, to cover up one scheme and come up with a new one?

BRETT: Sometimes it was really easy. There are some real pigeons out there.

THERAPIST: Was it always easy?

BRETT: Well, no. Sometimes it was a real bitch.... Seems like I'm always needing a good plan to beat the system.

THERAPIST: Do you think it's ever easier to go with the system instead of trying to beat it in some way?

BRETT: Well, after all that I have been through, I would have to say yes, there have been times that going with the system would have been easier in the long run.... But... it's such a challenge to beat the system. It feels exciting when I come up with a new plan and think I can make it work. Going with the system might not even occur to me.

THERAPIST: So what you choose to do is dictated by how excited you feel about your idea, your plan?

BRETT: Yeah.

THERAPIST: Yet several of your plans have actually ended up costing you and creating hassles in the long run.

HIGHLIGHT 9.1

Prevention of Psychopathy and Antisocial Personality Disorder

Given the difficulties in treating conduct disorder and ASPD, there is an increasing focus on prevention programs oriented toward both minimizing some of the developmental and environmental risk factors and breaking some of the vicious cycles into which at-risk children seem to get themselves. Given the multifaceted developmental model described in the text, many different stages present targets for preventive interventions. For example, targeting the early family environment by teaching effective parental discipline and supervision is becoming increasingly popular. At-risk children whose families receive such interventions do better academically, are less likely to associate with delinquent peers, and are less likely to get involved in drug use. Such family or parent training can even be effective in reducing further antisocial behavior in children and adolescents already engaged in such behavior, although conducting the intervention with preschool children was more effective and less labor-intensive (Olds et al., 1986; Olds, Henderson, & Tatelbaum, 1994; see Reid & Eddy, 1997, for a review).

Other prevention efforts have targeted the school environment, or the school and family environments concurrently. These programs are targeted at children in high-risk schools (generally inner-city and poor) who already show poor peer relations and high levels of disruptive behavior. The focus with these children is on improving their interpersonal problem-solving skills, emotional awareness abilities, and self-control skills. Teachers are taught how to manage disruptive behavior, and parents are informed of the information their children are being given. Early results are promising in terms of reducing later conduct problems. Children are also less likely to be rated by peers as aggressive and more likely to be better liked and to show better reading skills (Coie, 1996; Reid & Eddy, 1997).

Although preventive interventions such as these can be costly, if they can prevent (or at least dramatically reduce) the extremely costly effects on society when at-risk children develop full-blown adult ASPD or psychopathy, the long-term benefits will outweigh the initial costs. ■

BRETT: Yeah.

THERAPIST: How does that fit with your goal of having an easy, carefree life where you don't have to work too hard?

BRETT: It doesn't. [pause] So how do I get the easy life, Doc?...

THERAPIST: Do you ever think about what all your choices are and weigh them out, according to what consequences each one would have?

BRETT: Not usually. Usually, I just go for beating the system.

THERAPIST: What do you think would happen if you thought about other options?...

BRETT: I don't know.

THERAPIST: Is there some situation that you are dealing with right now in your life that you have to come up with money for, and you have to figure out how you are going to do it?

BRETT: Yeah... how I'm going to afford to rent my apartment, the lease on the nightclub property, getting the place ready to open for business, and still pay my lawyer....

[Later in the session after discussing options]

THERAPIST: So it sounds like you have several options for dealing with your current financial situation. Most of the time in the past, you have dealt with financial demands by getting involved in some beat-the-system scheme.... This time, you have discussed several possibilities. Which do you think will be the easiest and best in the long run?

BRETT: Fix up the space at the club and move in.

(From Beck and Freeman, *Cognitive Therapy of Personality Disorders,* pp. 171–172. Copyright © 1990 Guilford Publications, Inc.)

Although cognitive therapy along such lines seems quite promising, there have been only case studies documenting its effectiveness (Davidson & Tryer, 1996). It seems unlikely that cognitive therapy by itself will be highly effective but when combined with some of the behavioral treatments described above, it may be quite useful.

How effective are the best of these multifaceted cognitive-behaviorally oriented treatment programs? In general, the effects to date are significant but only modest in size. However, these programs are somewhat more effective in treating young offenders (teenagers) than in treating older offenders, who are usually hard-core lifelong psychopaths. The available evidence suggests that psychopathy is probably more difficult to treat than ASPD (Lösel, 1998; Rice & Harris, 1997) and research on developing effective treatments is still in its very early stages.

Fortunately, many psychopathic and antisocial personalities improve after the age of 40 even without treatment, possibly because of weaker biological drives, better insight into self-defeating behaviors, and the cumulative effects of social conditioning. Such individuals are often referred to as "burned-out psychopaths" (Hare, McPherson, & Forth, 1988). However, Harpur and Hare (1994) have also shown that it is only the antisocial behavioral dimension of psychopathy that diminishes with age; the egocentric, callous, and exploitative affective and interpersonal dimension does not.

In view of the distress and unhappiness that psychopaths inflict on others and the social damage they cause, it seems desirable—and more economical in the long run—to put increased effort into the development of effective prevention programs. There is considerable ongoing longitudinal prevention research on children at risk for conduct disorder.

IN REVIEW

- List the three DSM criteria that must be met before an individual is diagnosed as an antisocial personality.
- What additional personality traits that define psychopathy are not included in the DSM criteria for antisocial personality disorder?
- Why do most individuals with antisocial personality disorder or psychopathy seldom come to the attention of mental hospitals and clinics?
- What are some characteristics that psychopaths and antisocial personalities share?
- What is known about the biological, psychosocial, and sociocultural causal factors of psychopathy and antisocial personality disorder?
- What treatments have been used for these disorders, and how successful have they been?

UNRESOLVED ISSUES: Axis II of DSM-IV-TR

While reading this chapter, you may have had some difficulty in forming a clear, distinctive picture of each of the personality disorders. It is quite likely that the characteristics and attributes of some of these disorders (such as schizoid personality disorder) seemed to blend with those of others (such as schizotypal or avoidant personality disorders). As discussed earlier, in most cases, people do not neatly fit these prototypes but instead qualify for more than one personality disorder.

These Axis II diagnoses are also quite unreliable, as noted earlier. One of the major problems is that the classifications on Axis II are dimensional in nature; that is, the data on which Axis II classifications are based are underlying personality traits on which people vary in terms of degree. For example, suspiciousness could be rated on a scale from 0 (extremely low) to 100 (extremely high). Where to place the cut-off point on this 0–100 scale specifying exactly what qualifies as fitting the diagnostic criterion for a personality disorder is arbitrary. Moreover, when cut-off points or thresholds for diagnoses are changed, as was done for several personality disorders when DSM-III was revised to DSM-III-R, this can have drastic effects in the apparent prevalence rates of particular personality disorders. For example, those revisions resulted in "an 800 percent increase in the rate of schizoid personality disorder and a 350 percent increase in narcissistic personality disorder" (Morey, 1988a, p. 575).

A second problem inherent in Axis II classifications is the fact that there are enormous differences in the kinds of symptoms shown by people who nevertheless obtain the same diagnosis (Clark, 1992; Widiger & Sanderson, 1995). For example, to obtain a DSM-IV-TR diagnosis of borderline personality disorder, a person has to meet five out of nine possible symptom criteria. This means that two people with this diagnosis might share only one symptom: one might meet criteria 1 through 5, and the other might meet criteria 5 through 9. By contrast, a third individual who met only criteria 1 through 4 would not be diagnosed with borderline personality disorder at all and yet surely would be more similar symptomatically to the first person than the first two people were to each other (Clark, 1992; Widiger & Sanderson, 1995).

For these and other reasons, both researchers and clinicians are somewhat dissatisfied with Axis II. Nevertheless, the developers of DSM-III made an important theoretical leap when they recognized the importance of weighing premorbid personality factors in the clinical picture and thus developed Axis II. Use of the Axis II concepts can lead to a better understanding of a case, particularly with regard to treatment outcomes. Strong, ingrained personality characteristics can work against treatment interventions. The use of Axis II forces a clinician to attend to these long-standing and difficult-to-change personality factors in planning treatment.

What can be done to resolve the difficulties with Axis II? Most researchers feel that the psychiatric community should give up on the categorical approach to classification in favor of a dimensional approach, with rating methods that would take into account the relative "amounts" of the primary traits shown by patients. Some of the resistance to such a dimensional approach to classification stems from the fact that medically oriented practitioners have a pronounced preference for categorical diagnosis. Moreover, there are fears that a dimensional approach to personality measurement might not be accepted because learning how to make and apply sound quantitative ratings might involve far too much time for most busy clinicians. Nevertheless, reviews of the evidence show that many clinicians are unhappy with the current categorical system, which is cumbersome when used properly because it requires assessment of nearly 80 diagnostic criteria for all the DSM-IV-TR personality disorders (Widiger, 1993; Widiger & Sanderson, 1995). Indeed, Widiger has argued persuasively that the use of a dimensional approach might require less time because it would reduce the redundancy and overlap that currently exist across the categories.

In sum, the ultimate status of Axis II in future editions of the DSM is uncertain. Many problems inherent in using categorical classes for essentially dimensional behavior (traits) have yet to be resolved, although they are now almost universally recognized. One of the primary reasons why a dimensional approach has not yet replaced the categorical system is that a number of different dimensional systems have been proposed, and there is as yet no clear evidence as to which one is best (Clark & Livesley, 1994; Livesley, 1995; Widiger & Sanderson, 1995).

SUMMARY

CLINICAL FEATURES OF PERSONALITY DISORDERS

- Personality disorders, in general, appear to be inflexible and distorted behavioral patterns and traits that result in maladaptive ways of perceiving, thinking about, and relating to the environment.

CATEGORIES OF PERSONALITY DISORDERS

- Three general clusters of personality disorders have been described in DSM: Cluster A includes paranoid, schizoid, and schizotypal personality disorders; individuals with these disorders seem odd or eccentric. Cluster B includes histrionic, narcissistic, antisocial, and borderline personality disorders; individuals with these disorders share a common tendency to be dramatic, emotional, and erratic. Cluster C includes avoidant, dependent, and obsessive-compulsive personality disorders; individuals with these disorders show fearfulness or tension, as in anxiety-based disorders.

CAUSAL FACTORS IN PERSONALITY DISORDERS

- There is relatively little research into the causes of many of the personality disorders. According to some evidence, constitutional and genetic factors play a role in borderline, paranoid, schizotypal, and antisocial personality disorders. However, none of the disorders is entirely heritable, and current work is directed at understanding which psychological factors also play a causal role.
- Some evidence suggests that early childhood abuse may play a role in causing borderline personality disorder, but prospective studies are needed to draw definitive conclusions about this relationship.

TREATMENTS AND OUTCOMES FOR PERSONALITY DISORDERS

- There is also relatively little research on treatments for personality disorders.
- Treatment of the Cluster C disorders, which include dependent and avoidant personality disorders, seems most promising. However, a new form of behavior therapy (dialectical behavior therapy) shows considerable promise for treating borderline personality disorder, which is in Cluster B. Cluster A disorders, such as schizotypal and paranoid personality disorders, are most difficult to treat.

ANTISOCIAL PERSONALITY AND PSYCHOPATHY

- One of the most problematic of the personality disorders is antisocial personality disorder, which is closely related to psychopathy. A person with psychopathy is callous and unethical, without loyalty or close relationships, but often with superficial charm and intelligence. Individuals with a diagnosis of ASPD or psychopathy engage in an antisocial, impulsive, and socially deviant lifestyle. The disorder often begins and is recognized in childhood or early adolescence, but only persons who are 18 or over are given the diagnosis of antisocial personality. Constitutional, learning, and adverse environmental factors seem to be important in causing these disorders. Some evidence suggests that genetic factors may also predispose an individual to develop these disorders.
- Psychopaths also show deficiencies in aversive emotional arousal and show poor conditioning of anxiety and passive avoidance, which seems to reflect an underactive behavioral inhibition system—the neural substrate for anxiety. They also seem to show more general emotional deficits.
- Treatment of psychopaths is difficult in part because they rarely see any need for change and tend to blame other people for their problems. Traditional psychotherapy is typically ineffective, but where control is possible, as in institutional settings, multifaceted cognitive-behavioral approaches have had some modest success.

KEY TERMS

personality disorders (p. 291)
paranoid personality disorder (p. 294)
schizoid personality disorder (p. 295)
schizotypal personality disorder (p. 296)
histrionic personality disorder (p. 297)
narcissistic personality disorder (p. 298)
antisocial personality disorder (ASPD) (p. 299)
borderline personality disorder (BPD) (p. 300)
avoidant personality disorder (p. 301)
dependent personality disorder (p. 303)
obsessive-compulsive personality disorder (OCPD) (p. 304)
psychopathy (p. 311)

HIGHLIGHT 10.1

Addictive Behavior of a Different Kind

Not all addictive disorders involve the use of substances with chemical properties that induce dependency. People can develop "addictions" to certain activities that can be just as life-threatening as severe alcoholism and just as damaging, psychologically and socially, as drug abuse. Two activities that can seem "addictive" in some cases are eating and gambling.

Hyperobesity—often called *morbid obesity*—is defined as being 100 pounds or more above ideal body weight. It can be a dangerous, life-threatening disorder, resulting in diabetes, musculoskeletal problems, high blood pressure, and other cardiovascular problems that may place a person at high risk for a heart attack. Although some cases of extreme obesity result from metabolic or hormonal disorders, most obese persons simply take in more calories than they burn.

Hyperobesity, as a disorder, may be placed in several diagnostic categories, depending on which characteristics are emphasized. A focus on the physical changes, for example, results in a view of hyperobesity as having both psychological and physical components. Many clinicians, however, view the central problem not as the excessive weight itself, but as the long-standing habit of overeating. Thus, hyperobesity resulting from gross, habitual overeating is considered to be more like the problems found in the personality disorders—especially those ingrained personality problems that involve loss of control over an appetite of some kind (Orford, 1985).

Pathological gambling, also known as *compulsive gambling,* is a progressive disorder characterized by continuous or periodic loss of control over gambling; a preoccupation with gambling and obtaining money for gambling; irrational behavior; and continuation of the gambling behavior in spite of adverse consequences (Rosenthal, 1992). Gambling appears to be a major national pastime, with some 50 percent of the U.S. population gambling at one time or another, on anything from Saturday night poker games to the outcome of sporting events. While most people can gamble occasionally, without it interfering with their lives, an estimated 6 to 10 million Americans get "hooked" on gambling. Both men and women appear to be vulnerable to pathological gambling. One recent study of slot machine "addicts" reported that there were no gender differences associated with this behavior (Ohtsuka, Bruton, et al., 1997).

Although pathological gambling does not involve a chemically addictive substance, it can be considered an addictive disorder because of the personality factors that tend to characterize compulsive gamblers, the difficulties attributable to their compulsive gambling, and the treatment problems involved. Like other addictions, pathological gambling is a behavior maintained by short-term gains despite long-term disruption of an individual's life. ■

occupational, or health problem. **Psychoactive substance dependence** is a more severe form of a substance-use disorder and usually involves a marked physiological need for increasing amounts of a substance to achieve the desired effects. *Dependence* means that an individual will show a tolerance for a drug or withdrawal symptoms when the drug is unavailable. **Tolerance**—the need for increased amounts of a substance to achieve the desired effects—results from biochemical changes in the body that affect the rate of metabolism and elimination of the substance from the body. **Withdrawal symptoms** are physical symptoms, such as sweating, tremors, and tension, that accompany abstinence from the drug.

Because alcohol is one of the most common and most researched of abused substances, we will begin with alcohol abuse and dependence. Much of our knowledge of long-term effects, causes, and addictive mechanisms for

psychoactive substance dependence A more severe form of substance-use disorder characterized by a marked physiological need for increasing amounts of the substance to achieve the desired affects.

tolerance The need for increased amounts of a substance to achieve the desired effects.

withdrawal symptoms Physical symptoms, such as sweating, tremors, and tension, that accompany abstinence from a drug.

Alcohol is associated with over half of the deaths and serious injuries suffered in automobile accidents in the United States each year.

these disorders apply to some degree to other substance-related disorders as well.

ALCOHOL ABUSE AND DEPENDENCE

The terms *alcoholic* and *alcoholism* have been subject to some controversy and have been used differently by various groups in the past. The term **alcoholic** is often used to refer to a person with a serious drinking problem, whose drinking impairs his or her life adjustment in terms of health, personal relationships, and occupational functioning. Likewise, the term **alcoholism** refers to a dependence on alcohol that seriously interferes with life adjustment. There is a trend today toward use of a more restrictive definition. For example, the World Health Organization no longer recommends the term *alcoholism* but prefers the term *alcohol dependence syndrome*—"a state, psychic and usually also physical, resulting from taking alcohol, characterized by behavioral and other responses that always include a compulsion to take alcohol on a continuous or periodic basis in order to experience its psychic effects, and sometimes to avoid the discomfort of its absence; tolerance may or may not be present" (1992, p. 4). However, because the terms *alcoholic* and *alcoholism* are still widely used in practice, we will continue to use them in this book.

The Prevalence, Comorbidity, and Demographics of Alcoholism

However defined, alcoholism is a major problem in the United States. A large NIMH epidemiological study found the lifetime prevalence for alcoholism in the United States to be 13.4 percent. One in seven people meet the criteria for alcohol abuse (Grant, 1997).

The potentially detrimental effects of excessive alcohol use—for an individual, his or her loved ones, and society—are legion. For one thing, heavy drinking is associated with vulnerability to injury (Shepherd & Brickley, 1996). The lifespan of the average alcoholic is about 12 years shorter than that of the average citizen, and alcohol ranks as the third major cause of death in the United States, behind coronary heart disease and cancer. Alcohol significantly lowers performance on cognitive tasks such as problem solving—and the more complex the task, the greater the impairment (Pickworth, Rohrer, & Fant, 1997). Organic impairment, including brain shrinkage, occurs in

alcoholic A person with a serious drinking problem, whose drinking impairs his or her life adjustment in terms of health, personal relationships, and occupational functioning.

alcoholism A dependence on alcohol that seriously interferes with life adjustment.

a high proportion of alcoholics (Errico, Parsons, & King, 1991; Lishman, Jacobson, & Acker, 1987), especially among *binge drinkers,* people who abuse alcohol following periods of sobriety (Hunt, 1993).

In addition to the serious problems excessive drinkers create for themselves, they also pose serious difficulties for others (Gortner, Gollan, & Jacobson, 1997). Alcohol abuse is associated with over half the deaths and major injuries suffered in automobile accidents each year in the United States (Brewer, Morris, et al., 1994), and with about 50 percent of all murders (Bennett & Lehman, 1996), 40 percent of all assaults, over 50 percent of all rapes (Seto & Barbaree, 1995), and 30 percent of all suicides. About one out of every three arrests in the United States is related to alcohol abuse. Violent offenders have higher rates of alcohol problems than the general population (Martin, 1992). In a survey of alcohol-related violence in Norway, Rossow (1996) reported that 3 percent of adults in the general population sample reported having taken part in a fight when they were intoxicated. These individuals were most often young people who drank frequently and visited public places to drink. Interestingly, in a study of substance abuse and violent crime in the United States, Dawkins (1997) found that alcohol was more frequently associated with both violent and nonviolent crime than were other drugs such as marijuana.

In recent years, substantial research has focused on the link between alcohol-abuse disorders and other disorders, such as depression, schizophrenia, and antisocial personality. Over 37 percent of alcohol abusers suffer from at least one other mental disorder (Rovner, 1990). Depression ranks high among the mental disorders occurring comorbidly with alcoholism, not surprisingly since alcohol is a depressant (Kranzler, Del Boca, & Rounsaville, 1997.) About 10 percent of alcoholics commit suicide (Miles, 1977), and over 18 percent are found to have a history of suicide attempts (Black et al., 1986). About half of the individuals with schizophrenia have either alcohol or drug abuse or dependency as well (Kosten, 1997). The relationship between antisocial personality disorder and alcohol abuse is strong (Harford & Parker, 1994; Kwapil, 1996), though by no means are the two completely overlapping; nor is it clear which (if either) disorder might cause the other (Carroll, Ball, & Rounsaville, 1993). High rates of substance abuse are found among antisocial personalities (Clark, Watson, & Reynolds, 1995). In a survey of eight alcohol treatment programs, Morganstern, Langenbucher, and others (1997) found that 57.9 percent of the patients had a personality disorder, with 22.7 percent meeting the criteria for antisocial personality disorder.

Alcoholism in the United States cuts across all age, educational, occupational, and socioeconomic boundaries. It is considered a serious problem in industry, in the professions, and in the military; it is found among such seemingly unlikely candidates as priests, airline pilots, politicians, surgeons, law enforcement officers, and teenagers. The once common image of the alcoholic as an unkempt resident of skid row is clearly inaccurate. Further myths about alcoholism are noted in Table 10.1.

Most problem drinkers are men, at about five times the frequency of women (Helzer et al., 1990). There do not appear to be important differences in rates of alcohol abuse between black and white Americans. It appears, too, that problem drinking may develop during any life period from early childhood through old age. One study reported that 64.9 percent of a sample of high school students indicated a moderate use of alcohol and 18.8 percent of the students reported a misuse of alcohol (Mann, Chassin, & Sher, 1987). Being married, having higher levels of education, and being older are associated with a lower incidence of alcoholism (Helzer et al., 1990). Surveys of alcoholism rates in different cultural groups in North America and Asia have found varying rates of alcoholism across diverse cultural samples (Caetano, Clark, & Tam, 1998).

The course of alcoholism can be both "erratic and fluctuating." A recent survey found that some alcoholics go through long periods of abstinence. Of 600 respondents in the study (most of whom were alcohol dependent), over half (56 percent) had periods of abstinence for 3 months and 16 percent reported a period of 5 years of abstinence (Schuckit et al., 1997). It is therefore important to keep in mind that the course of alcoholism can vary, even including periods of remission.

The Clinical Picture of Alcohol Abuse and Dependence

Although many investigators have maintained that alcohol is a dangerous systemic poison even in small amounts, others believe that moderate amounts are not harmful to most people. Some studies have even shown that small amounts of red wine can serve as a protective factor for coronary artery disease (Klasky, 1996). Whatever position one takes on this issue, virtually everyone can agree on the dangers of drinking too much (see Table 10.2). In this section, we will examine the physical and psychosocial effects of alcohol abuse and dependence.

Alcohol's Effects on the Brain Alcohol has complex and seemingly contradictory effects on the brain. At lower levels, alcohol stimulates certain brain cells and activates the brain's "pleasure areas," which release opium-like endogenous opioids that are stored in the body (Braun,

TABLE 10.1 SOME COMMON MISCONCEPTIONS ABOUT ALCOHOL AND ALCOHOLISM

Fiction	Fact
Alcohol is a stimulant.	Alcohol is actually both a nervous system stimulant and a depressant.
You can always detect alcohol on the breath of a person who has been drinking.	It is not always possible to detect the presence of alcohol. Some individuals successfully cover up their alcohol use for years.
One ounce of 86-proof liquor contains more alcohol than two 12-ounce cans of beer.	Actually, two 12-ounce cans of beer contain more than an ounce of alcohol.
Alcohol can help a person sleep more soundly.	Alcohol may actually interfere with sound sleep.
Impaired judgment does not occur before there are obvious signs of intoxication.	In fact, impaired judgment can occur long before motor signs of intoxication are apparent.
An individual will get more intoxicated by mixing liquors than by taking comparable amounts of one kind—e.g., bourbon, Scotch, or vodka.	It is the actual amount of alcohol in the bloodstream rather than the mix that determines intoxication.
Drinking several cups of coffee can counteract the effects of alcohol and enable a drinker to "sober up."	Drinking coffee does not affect the level of intoxication.
Exercise or a cold shower helps speed up the metabolism of alcohol.	Exercise and cold showers are futile attempts to increase alcohol metabolism.
People with "strong wills" need not be concerned about becoming alcoholics.	Alcohol is seductive and can lower the resistance of even the "strongest will."
Alcohol cannot produce a true addiction in the same sense that heroin can.	Alcohol has strong addictive properties.
One cannot become an alcoholic by drinking just beer.	One can consume a considerable amount of alcohol by drinking beer. It is, of course, the amount of alcohol that determines whether one becomes an alcoholic.
Alcohol is far less dangerous than marijuana.	There are considerably more individuals in treatment programs for alcohol problems than for marijuana abuse.
In a heavy drinker, damage to the liver shows up long before brain damage appears.	Heavy alcohol use can be manifested in organic brain damage before liver damage is detected.
The physiological withdrawal reaction from heroin is considered more dangerous than is withdrawal from alcohol.	The physiological symptoms accompanying withdrawal from heroin are no more frightening or traumatic to an individual than alcohol withdrawal. Actually, alcohol withdrawal is potentially more lethal than opiate withdrawal.
Everybody drinks.	Actually, 28 percent of men and 50 percent of women in the United States are abstainers.

1996; Van Ree, 1996). At higher levels, alcohol depresses brain functioning, inhibiting one of the brain's excitatory neurotransmitters, glutamate, which in turn slows down activity in parts of the brain. Inhibition of glutamate in the brain impairs the organism's ability to learn and affects the higher brain centers, impairing judgment and other rational processes and lowering self-control. As behavioral restraints decline, a drinker may indulge in the satisfaction of impulses ordinarily held in check. Some degree of motor uncoordination soon becomes apparent, and the drinker's discrimination and perception of cold, pain, and other discomforts are dulled. Typically, the drinker experiences a sense of warmth, expansiveness, and well-being. In such a mood, unpleasant realities are screened out, and the drinker's feelings of self-esteem and adequacy rise. Casual acquaintances become the best and most under-

TABLE 10.2 EARLY WARNING SIGNS OF DRINKING PROBLEMS

1. *Frequent desire*—increase in desire, often evidenced by eager anticipation of drinking after work and careful attention to maintaining supply.
2. *Increased consumption*—increase that seems gradual but is marked from month to month. An individual may begin to worry at this point and lie about the amount consumed.
3. *Extreme behavior*—commission of various acts that leave an individual feeling guilty and embarrassed the next day.
4. *"Pulling blanks"*—inability to remember what happened during an alcoholic bout.
5. *Morning drinking*—either as a means of reducing a hangover or as a "bracer" to help start the day.

A person who exhibits this pattern is well on the road to abusive drinking. The progression is likely to be facilitated if there is environmental support for heavy or excessive drinking from the person's spouse, job situation, or sociocultural setting.

standing of friends, and the drinker enters a generally pleasant world of unreality in which worries are temporarily left behind. Interestingly, a recent investigation by Sayette (1994) showed that when intoxicated people describe themselves they are more likely than are sober people to downplay their negative characteristics. That is, they tend to disclose fewer negative items in their speech in a self-protective effort.

When the alcohol content of the bloodstream reaches 0.10 percent (0.08 in some states), the individual is considered to be intoxicated, at least with respect to driving a vehicle. Muscular coordination, speech, and vision are impaired, and thought processes are confused. Even before this level of intoxication is reached, however, judgment becomes impaired to such an extent that the person misjudges his or her condition. For example, drinkers tend to express confidence in their ability to drive safely long after such action is, in fact, quite unsafe. When the blood-alcohol level reaches approximately 0.5 percent (this level differs somewhat among individuals), the entire neural balance is upset and the individual passes out. Unconsciousness apparently acts as a safety device, because concentrations above 0.55 percent are usually lethal (see Table 10.3).

In general, it is the amount of alcohol actually concentrated in the bodily fluids, not the amount consumed, that determines intoxication. The effects of alcohol, however, vary for different drinkers, depending on their physical condition, the amount of food in their stomach, and the duration of their drinking. In addition, alcohol users may gradually build up a tolerance for the drug so that ever-increasing amounts may be needed to produce the desired effects. Women metabolize alcohol less effectively than men and thus become intoxicated on smaller amounts of alcohol (Gordis et al., 1995). Drinkers' attitudes are important, too: Although actual motor and intellectual abilities decline in direct ratio to the blood concentration of alcohol, many people who consciously try to do so can maintain apparent control over their behavior, showing few outward signs of being intoxicated even after drinking relatively large amounts of alcohol.

Exactly how alcohol works on the brain is only beginning to be understood, but several physiological effects are common. The first is a tendency toward decreased sexual inhibition but, simultaneously, lowered sexual performance. As Shakespeare wrote in *Macbeth*, alcohol "provokes the desire, but it takes away the performance." An appreciable number of alcohol abusers also experience blackouts—lapses of memory. At first, these occur at high blood-alcohol levels, and a drinker may carry on a rational conversation or engage in other relatively complex activities but have no trace of recall the next day. For heavy drinkers, even moderate drinking can elicit memory lapses. Another phenomenon associated with alcoholic intoxication is the hangover, which many drinkers experience at one time or another. As yet, no one has come up with a satisfactory explanation or remedy for the symptoms of headache, nausea, and fatigue characteristic of the hangover.

The Physical Effects of Chronic Alcohol Use For individuals who drink to excess, the clinical picture is highly unfavorable (Maher, 1997). For one thing, the alcohol that is taken in must be assimilated by the body, except for about 5 to 10 percent that is eliminated through breath, urine, and perspiration. The work of assimilation

TABLE 10.3 ALCOHOL LEVELS IN THE BLOOD AFTER DRINKS TAKEN ON AN EMPTY STOMACH BY A 150-POUND MALE DRINKING FOR ONE HOUR

Amount of Beverage	Alcohol Concentration in Blood (Percentage)	Effects	Time for Alcohol to Leave the Body (Hours)
1 cocktail (1 1/2 oz. whiskey) *or* 5 1/2 oz. ordinary wine *or* 1 bottle beer (12 oz.)	0.025	Slight changes in feeling	1
2 cocktails *or* 11 oz. ordinary wine *or* 2 bottles beer	0.05	Feelings of warmth, mental relaxation	2
3 cocktails *or* 16 1/2 oz. ordinary wine *or* 4 bottles beer	0.07	Exaggerated emotion and behavior—talkative, noisy, or morose	4
4 cocktails *or* 22 oz. ordinary wine *or* 6 bottles beer	0.1	Clumsiness—unsteadiness in standing or walking	6
6 cocktails *or* 27 1/2 oz. ordinary wine *or* 1/2 pint whiskey	0.15	Gross intoxication	10

Note: Blood-alcohol level following given intake differs according to a person's weight, the length of the drinking time, and the person's sex.
Source: From *Time,* April 22, 1974. Copyright © 1974 Time, Inc.

is done by the liver, but when large amounts of alcohol are ingested, the liver may be seriously overworked and eventually suffer irreversible damage. In fact, from 15 to 30 percent of heavy drinkers develop cirrhosis of the liver, a disorder involving extensive stiffening of the blood vessels. About 40 to 90 percent of the 26,000 annual cirrhosis deaths every year are alcohol-related (DuFour, Stinson, & Cases, 1993). Alcohol-related cirrhosis is a problem in other countries as well. The Medical Council on Alcoholism in England (1997) reported an increase in liver disease in England and Wales, particularly in women. There is even some evidence that an alcoholic's brain could be accumulating diffuse organic damage even when no extreme organic symptoms are present (Lishman, 1990). As discussed in Chapter 13, researchers have found extensive alcohol consumption to be associated with an increased amount of neurological deficit in later life (Parsons, 1998).

Alcohol is also a high-calorie drug: There are 100 calories in 4 ounces of wine, 150 in a 12-ounce glass of beer, and 70 in an ounce of whiskey. A pint of whiskey—enough to make about eight to ten ordinary cocktails—provides about 1200 calories, which is approximately half the ordinary caloric requirement for a day (Bellerson, 1997; Flier, Underhill, & Lieber, 1995; Ray & Ksir, 1995). Thus, consumption of alcohol reduces a drinker's appetite for other food. Because alcohol has no nutritional value, the excessive drinker often suffers from malnutrition (Derr & Gutmann, 1994). Furthermore, heavy drinking impairs the body's ability to utilize nutrients, so the nutritional deficiency cannot be made up by popping vitamins. Alcoholics also experience increased gastrointestinal symptoms such as stomach pains (Fields et al., 1994).

For pregnant women, even moderate amounts of alcohol are believed to be dangerous to the developing fetus. Heavy drinking by a pregnant woman can result in physical and behavioral abnormalities in her child, a condition known as **fetal alcohol syndrome (FAS)** (Alison, 1994; see also Figure 10.1). For example, such infants have shown growth deficiencies, facial and limb irregularities, and central nervous system dysfunctions (Mattson & Riley, 1998; Mattson et al., 1998; Short & Hess, 1995).

fetal alcohol syndrome (FAS) A pattern of physical and behavioral abnormalities observed in some infants whose mothers consumed alcohol during pregnancy.

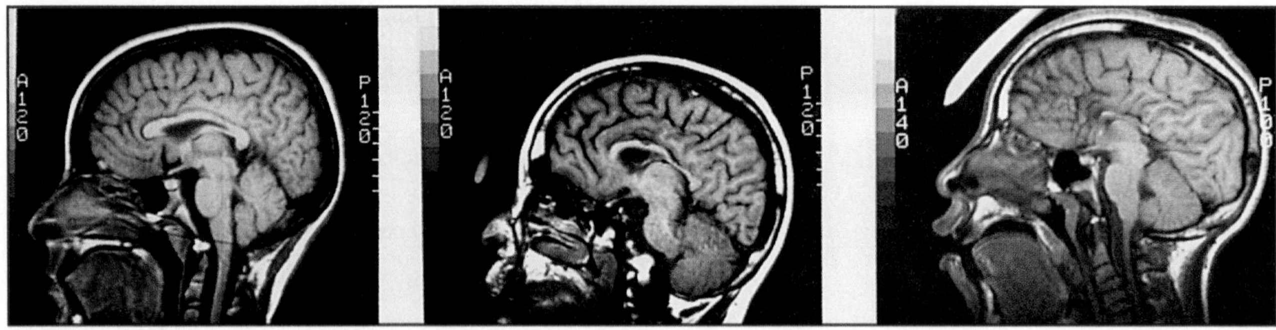

FIGURE 10.1 BRAIN DAMAGE IN TEENAGERS BORN WITH FETAL ALCOHOL SYNDROME
MRIs of three children: (left) Normal control, 13-year-old female; (center) FAS, 13-year-old male with focal thinning of the corpus callosum; (right) FAS, 14-year-old male with complete agenesis of the corpus callosum—the corpus callosum did not develop.
Source: Mattson, S. N., Jernigan, T. L., & Riley, E. P. (1994). MRI and prenatal alcohol exposure. *Alcohol Health & Research World, 18* (1), 49–52.

Fetal alcohol syndrome is also associated with the development of mental disorders in adults (Famy, Streissguth, & Unis, 1998). Although data on fetal alcohol syndrome are often difficult to obtain, estimates range from 1 to 3 per 1000 births (Abel, 1990) in the general population to 25 per 1000 births for women who are chronic alcoholics (Abel, 1988). Research in laboratory animals has confirmed the devastating neurological effects of alcohol exposure in utero (Hannigan, 1996). Interestingly, nearly all cases of fetal alcohol syndrome occur in the United States, even though some other countries have higher rates of alcohol use than the United States. In fact, the phenomenon of fetal alcohol syndrome has been referred to as an "American paradox" (Abel, 1998), as researchers have noted that the syndrome is strongly related to socioeconomic class.

Psychosocial Affects of Alcohol Abuse and Dependence In addition to various physical problems, an excessive drinker usually suffers from chronic fatigue, oversensitivity, and depression. Initially, alcohol may seem to provide a useful crutch for dealing with the stresses of life, especially during periods of acute stress, by helping screen out intolerable realities and enhancing the drinker's feelings of adequacy and worth. The excessive use of alcohol becomes counterproductive, however, resulting in lowered feelings of adequacy and worth, impaired reasoning and judgment, and gradual personality deterioration. Behavior typically becomes coarse and inappropriate, and the drinker assumes increasingly less responsibility, loses pride in personal appearance, neglects spouse and family, and becomes generally touchy, irritable, and unwilling to discuss the problem.

As judgment becomes impaired, an excessive drinker may be unable to hold a job and generally becomes unqualified to cope with new demands that arise. General personality disorganization and deterioration may be reflected in loss of employment and marital breakup. By this time, the drinker's general health is likely to have deteriorated, and brain and liver damage may have occurred.

Psychoses Associated with Alcoholism Several acute psychotic reactions fit the diagnostic classification of substance-induced disorders. These reactions may de-

The effects of fetal alcohol syndrome can be both dramatic and long-lasting. This child shows some of the permanent physical abnormalities characteristic of the syndrome: widely spaced eyes, short broad nose, underdeveloped upper lip, and receding chin.

HIGHLIGHT 10.2

How Much Drinking Endangers Fetal Health?

The HEW report warns pregnant women against drinking more than 1 ounce of alcohol per day or the equivalent (two 12-ounce cans of beer or two 5-ounce glasses of wine, for example). The amount of alcohol that can be ingested safely during pregnancy is not known, but it is clear that fetal alcohol syndrome is most likely among children of heavy alcohol users rather than light to moderate users (Kolata, 1981b). Nonetheless, the Surgeon General and many medical experts have concurred that pregnant women should abstain from using alcohol, as the "safest course" until safe levels of alcohol consumption can be determined (Raskin, 1993). ■

velop in people who have been drinking excessively over long periods of time or who have a reduced tolerance for alcohol for other reasons—for example, because of brain lesions. Such acute reactions usually last only a short time and generally consist of confusion, excitement, and delirium. There is some evidence to suggest that delirium might be associated with lower levels of thiamine in alcoholics (Holzbeck, 1996). These disorders are often called "alcoholic psychoses" because they are marked by a temporary loss of contact with reality. Two commonly recognized psychotic reactions will be briefly described.

Among those who drink excessively for a long time, a reaction known as *alcohol withdrawal delirium* (formerly known as *delirium tremens*) may occur. This reaction usually happens following a prolonged drinking spree when the person is in a state of withdrawal. Slight noises or sudden moving objects may cause considerable excitement and agitation. The full-blown symptoms include (1) disorientation as to time and place; (2) vivid hallucinations; (3) acute fear; (4) extreme suggestibility; (5) marked tremors of the hands, tongue, and lips; and (6) other symptoms, including perspiration, fever, a rapid and weak heartbeat, a coated tongue, and foul breath.

The delirium typically lasts from 3 to 6 days and is generally followed by a deep sleep. When a person awakens, few symptoms—aside from possible slight remorse—remain, but frequently the individual is badly scared and may not resume drinking for several weeks or months. Usually, however, drinking is eventually resumed, followed by a return to the hospital with a new attack. The death rate from withdrawal delirium as a result of convulsions, heart failure, and other complications once approximated 10 percent (Tavel, 1962). With drugs such as chlordiazepoxide, however, the death rate during withdrawal delirium and acute alcoholic withdrawal has been markedly reduced.

A second alcohol-related psychosis is the disorder referred to as *alcohol amnestic disorder* (formerly known as *Korsakoff's syndrome*). This condition was first described by the Russian psychiatrist Korsakoff in 1887 and is one of the most severe alcohol-related disorders (Oscar-Berman, Shagrin, Evert, & Epstein, 1997). The outstanding symptom is a memory deficit (particularly with regard to recent events), which is sometimes accompanied by falsification of events (confabulation). Persons with this disorder may not recognize pictures, faces, rooms, and other objects that they have just seen, although they may feel that these people or objects are familiar. Such people increasingly tend to fill in their memory gaps with reminiscences and fanciful tales that lead to unconnected and distorted associations. The memory disturbance itself seems related to an inability to form new associations in a manner that renders them readily retrievable. Such a reaction usually occurs in older alcoholics, after many years of excessive drinking. These patients have also been observed to show other cognitive impairments such as planning deficits (Joyce & Robbins, 1991) and intellectual decline.

Case Study A 48-Year-Old Homeless Veteran with Alcohol Amnestic Disorder • Averill B. was brought into the detoxification unit of a local county hospital by the police following an incident at a crowded city park. He was arrested because of his assaultive behavior toward others (he was walking through the crowded groups of sunbathers muttering to himself, kicking at people). At admission to the hospital, Averill was disoriented (did not know where he was), incoherent, and confused. When asked his name he paused a moment, scratched his head and said "George Washington." When asked about what he was doing at the park, he indicated that he was "marching in a parade in his honor."

Research with sophisticated brain-imaging techniques has found that patients with alcohol amnestic disorder show cortical lesions (Jernigan et al., 1991; Kopelman, 1991), but the exact significance of this finding is not clear. The symptoms of alcohol amnestic disorder are now thought to be due to vitamin B (thiamine) deficiency and other dietary inadequacies. But vitamin replacement therapy does not eliminate the symptoms (Lishman, 1990), so the damage may be more chronic. Some memory function appears to be restored after prolonged abstinence. However, some personality deterioration usually remains in the form of memory impairment, blunted intellectual capacity, and lowered moral and ethical standards.

Biological Causal Factors in Alcohol Abuse and Dependence

How does alcohol come to have such powerful effects—an overpowering hold that occurs in some people after only a few uses of the drug? Although the exact mechanisms are not fully agreed on by experts in the field, two important factors are apparently involved. The first is the ability of some drugs to activate areas of the brain that produce intrinsic pleasure and immediate, powerful reward. The second factor is the person's biological makeup, or constitution, which includes both genetic inheritance and the environmental influences (learning factors) that enter into the need to seek mind-altering substances to an increasing degree. The development of an alcohol addiction is a complex process involving many elements—constitutional vulnerability and environmental encouragement as well as the unique biochemical properties of the psychoactive substance.

The Neurobiology of Addiction Drugs differ in terms of their biochemical properties as well as how rapidly they enter the brain. There are several routes of administration—oral, nasal, and intravenous. Alcohol is usually drunk, the slowest route; cocaine, in contrast, is often self-administered by injection or taken nasally. Central to the neurochemical process underlying addiction is the role the drug plays in activating the "pleasure pathway." The **mesocorticolimbic dopamine pathway (MCLP)** is the center of psychoactive drug activation in the brain. The MCLP is made up of neurons in the middle portion of the brain known as the ventral tegmental area (see Figure 10.2) and connects to other brain centers such the nucleus accumbens and then to the prefrontal cortex. This neuronal system is involved in such functions as control of emotions, memory, and gratification. Research has shown that direct electrical stimulation of the MCLP produces great pleasure and has strong reinforcing properties (Liebman & Cooper, 1989). Alcohol is rewarding in that it produces euphoria by stimulating this area in the brain, changing the brain's normal functioning and activating the pleasure pathway. Drugs that activate the brain reward system obtain reinforcing action and, thereby, promote further use.

mesocorticolimbic dopamine pathway (MCLP) The center of psychoactive drug activation in the brain, made up of neurons in the ventral tegmental area and connected to other brain centers.

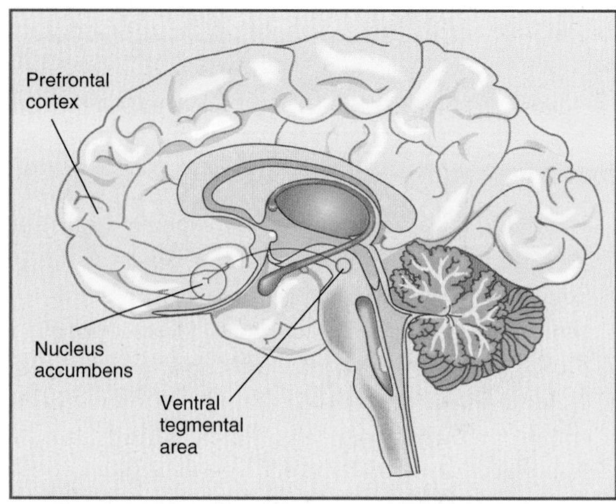

FIGURE 10.2 THE MESOCORTICOLIMBIC PATHWAY
The mesocorticolimbic pathway (MCLP), running from the ventral tegmental area to the nucleus accumbens to the prefrontal cortex, is central to the release of the neurotransmitter dopamine and in mediating the rewarding properties of drugs.
Source: Office of Technology Assessment (1993).

The exposure of the brain to such a drug changes its neurochemical structure and results in a number of behavioral effects. With continued use of the drug, neuroadaptation, or tolerance, and dependence develop.

Genetic Vulnerability The possibility of a genetic predisposition to developing alcohol-abuse problems has been widely researched. Alcoholism clearly tends to run in families (Dawson, Harford, & Grant, 1992). A review of 39 studies of families of 6251 alcoholics and 4083 nonalcoholics who had been followed over 40 years reported that almost one-third of alcoholics had at least one parent with an alcohol problem (Cotton, 1979). Likewise, a study of children of alcoholics by Cloninger and colleagues (1986) reported strong evidence for the inheritance of alcoholism. These investigators found that, for males, having one alcoholic parent increased the rate of alcoholism from 11.4 percent to 29.5 percent and having two alcoholic parents increased the rate to 41.2 percent. For females with no alcoholic parents, the rate was 5.0 percent; for those with one alcoholic parent, the rate was 9.5 percent; and for those with two alcoholic parents, it was 25.0 percent.

Research has shown that prealcoholic men show physiological patterns that differ from those of nonalcoholic men in several respects. Prealcoholic men tend to feel a greater reduction of stress with alcohol ingestion than do nonalcoholic men (Finn & Pihl, 1987; Finn, Sharkansky, et al., 1997). They also show different alpha wave patterns on EEG recordings (Stewart, Finn, & Pihl, 1990). Prealcoholic men were found to show larger conditioned physiological responses to alcohol cues than were individuals who were considered at a low risk for alcoholism, according to Earlywine and Finn (1990). These results suggest that prealcoholic men may be more prone to develop tolerance for alcohol than low-risk men.

In support of possible genetic factors in alcoholism, a Japanese team has shown that rats bred to lack a particular gene (FYN) stayed drunk longer than normal rats (Miyakawa et al., 1997). These rats were hypersensitive to the hypnotic effect of alcohol. In addition, some research has suggested that certain ethnic groups, particularly Asians and Native Americans, have abnormal physiological reactions to alcohol—a phenomenon referred to as "alcohol flush reaction." Fenna and colleagues (1971) and Wolff (1972) found that Asian and Eskimo participants showed a hypersensitive reaction, including flushing of the skin, a drop in blood pressure, heart palpitations, and nausea following the ingestion of alcohol. This physiological reaction is found in roughly half of all Asians (Chen & Yeh, 1997) and results from a mutant enzyme that fails to break down alcohol molecules in the liver during the metabolic process (Takeshita et al., 1993). Although cultural factors cannot be ruled out, the relatively lower rates of alcoholism among Asian groups might be related to the extreme discomfort associated with the alcohol flush reaction (Higuci et al., 1994).

Research has begun to accumulate that genetic factors contribute substantially to the development of alcohol preference. Research with animals, for example, has shown that strains of animals can be bred to have a very high preference for alcohol (McBride et al., 1992). Moreover, genetic factors are likely to be involved in increased susceptibility or sensitivity to the effects of drugs. For example, low doses of alcohol or other addictive substances might be more stimulating to some people as a result of inherited differences in the mesocorticolimbic dopamine pathway described earlier (Liebman & Cooper, 1989). It seems increasingly likely that inherited factors affect an individual's response to psychoactive substances such as alcohol.

Nevertheless, genetic factors alone are not the whole story, and the role they play in the development of alcoholism remains unclear. The genetic mechanism for the generally agreed upon observation that alcoholism is familial is insufficient to explain the behavior fully. That is, genetic transmission in the case of alcoholism does not follow the hereditary pattern found in other strictly genetic disorders.

Genetic Influences and Learning When we talk about familial or constitutional differences, we are not strictly limiting our explanation to genetic inheritance. Rather, learning factors appear to play an important part in the development of constitutional reaction tendencies. Having a genetic predisposition or biological vulnerability to alcoholism, of course, is not a sufficient cause of the disorder. The person must be exposed to the substance to a sufficient degree for the addictive behavior to appear. In the case of alcohol, almost everyone in America is exposed to the drug to some extent—in most cases through peer pressure, parental example, and advertising. The development of alcoholism involves living in an environment that promotes initial as well as continuing use of the substance. People become conditioned to stimuli and tend to respond in particular ways as a result of learning. There clearly are numerous reinforcements for using alcohol in our social environments and everyday lives. Furthermore, the use of alcohol in a social context is often a sufficient reason for many people to continue using the drug. However, research has also shown that psychoactive drugs such as alcohol contain *intrinsic* rewarding properties that provide pleasure in and of themselves—apart from the social context or the drug's operation to diminish worry or frustration. As we saw earlier, the drug stimulates pleasure centers in the brain, and once use begins, the substance develops a reward system of its own.

Psychosocial Causal Factors in Alcohol Abuse and Dependence

Not only do alcoholics become physiologically dependent on alcohol, they develop a powerful psychological dependence as well—they become socially dependent upon the drug to help them enjoy social situations. Because excessive drinking is ultimately so destructive to a person's total life adjustment, the question arises as to how psychological dependence is learned. A number of psychosocial factors have been advanced as possible answers.

Failures in Parental Guidance Stable family relationships and parental guidance are extremely important molding influences for children, and this stability is often lacking in families of alcoholics. Children who have parents who abuse alcohol or other drugs are vulnerable to developing substance abuse and related problems themselves. The experiences and lessons we learn from important figures in our early years have a significant impact, one way or another, on us as adults. Children who are exposed to negative role models early in their lives or experience other negative circumstances because the adults around them provide limited guidance often falter on the difficult steps they must take in life (Deming, Chase, & Karesh, 1996; Vega et al., 1993). These formative experiences can have a direct influence on whether a youngster becomes involved in maladaptive behavior such as alcohol or drug abuse. For example, parent substance use is associated with early adolescent drug use (Hops et al., 1996).

In one program of research aimed at evaluating the possibility that negative socialization factors might influence alcohol use, Chassin and colleagues (1993) replicated findings that alcohol abuse in parents was associated with substance use in adolescents. They then evaluated several possible mediating factors that can influence adolescents in initiating alcohol use. They found that parenting skills or parental behaviors were associated with substance use in adolescents. Alcoholic parents are less likely to keep track of what their children are doing, and this lack of monitoring often leads to an adolescent's affiliation with drug-using peers. In addition, Chassin and colleagues found that stress and negative affect (more prevalent in families with an alcoholic parent) were associated with alcohol use in adolescents. In a follow-up study, Chassin and colleagues (1996) reported that although lack of monitoring, stress, and negative affect are all contributors to adolescent alcohol abuse, there are likely to be other factors involved as well.

Psychological Vulnerability Is there an "alcoholic personality"—a type of character organization that predisposes a person to use alcohol rather than some other defensive pattern of coping with stress? An alcoholic personality has been described as an individual (usually an alcoholic's child) who has an inherited predisposition toward alcohol abuse and who is impulsive, prefers taking high risks, is emotionally unstable, has difficulty planning and organizing behavior, has problems in predicting the consequences of his or her actions, has many psychological problems, finds that alcohol is helpful in coping with stress, does not experience hangovers, and finds alcohol rewarding (Finn, 1990). In addition, these individuals expect a great deal of the world, require an inordinate amount of praise and appreciation, react to failure with marked feelings of hurt and inferiority, have low frustration tolerance, and feel inadequate and unsure of their abilities to fulfill expected male or female roles. Persons at high risk for developing alcoholism are significantly more impulsive and aggressive than those at low risk for abusing alcohol (Morey, Skinner, & Blashfield, 1984).

While such findings provide promising leads for understanding the causes of alcoholism, it is difficult to assess the role of specific personality characteristics in the development of the disorder. Certainly, many people with similar personality characteristics do not become alcoholics, and others with dissimilar ones do. The only characteristic that appears common to the backgrounds of most problem drinkers is personal maladjustment, yet most maladjusted people do not become alcoholics. An alcoholic's personality may be as much a result as a cause of his or her dependence on alcohol—for example, the excessive use of alcohol may lead to depression, or a depressed person may turn to the excessive use of alcohol, or both.

The excessive use of alcohol may lead to depression, or a depressed person may turn to the excessive use of alcohol.

The two psychopathological conditions that have been most frequently linked to addictive disorders are depression (Kranzler et al., 1997) and antisocial personality (Cadoret et al., 1985; Rounsaville, Kranzler et al., 1998). By far, most of the research has related antisocial personality with addictive disorders, with about 75 to 80 percent of the studies showing a strong association (Alterman, 1988), or conduct disorder with addictive disorders (Slutsky, Heath, et al., 1998). However, other diagnostic groups have also been found to co-occur with addictive disorders—for example, schizophrenia (Buckley et al., 1994); borderline personality (Miller et al., 1993b); anxiety disorders (Deas-Nesmith, Brady, & Campbell, 1998); and bipolar disorder (Mason & Ownby, 1998).

Some research has suggested that there may be gender differences in the association between depression and alcohol abuse. One group of researchers (Moscato, Russell, et al., 1997) found the degree of association between depression and alcohol abuse problems to be greater among women. In addition, some authorities have suggested that patients who are comorbid alcoholic-depressives may be exhibiting both disorders distinctly (Coryell et al., 1992).

Stress, Tension Reduction, and Reinforcement A number of investigators have pointed out that the typical alcoholic is discontented with his or her life and is unable or unwilling to tolerate tension and stress. For example, in a large sample of Norwegians, Watten (1995) found that there was a high degree of association between alcohol consumption and negative affectivity such as anxiety and somatic complaints. In other words, the subjects drank to relax. In this view, anyone who finds alcohol to be tension-reducing is in danger of becoming an alcoholic, even without an especially stressful life situation. However, as a sole explanatory hypothesis, the tension-reduction causal model is difficult to accept. For example, if this process were a main cause, we would expect alcoholism to be far more common than it is, since alcohol tends to reduce tension for most people who use it. In addition, this model does not explain why some excessive drinkers are able to maintain control over their drinking and continue to function in society while others are not.

Expectations of Social Success A number of investigators have been exploring the idea that cognitive expectation might play an important role both in the initiation of drinking and in the maintenance of drinking behavior once the person has begun to use alcohol (Connors, Maisto, & Derman, 1994; Marlatt, Baer, et al., 1998). Many people, especially young adolescents, expect that alcohol use will lower tension and anxiety and increase sexual desire and pleasure in life (Seto & Barbaree, 1995). In this view, often referred to as the *reciprocal influence model,* adolescents begin drinking as a result of expectations that alcohol will increase their popularity and acceptance by their peers. Research has shown that expectancies of social benefit can influence adolescents' decisions to start drinking and predict their consumption of alcohol (Christiansen et al., 1989).

This view—that adolescents' expectations that drinking will ease their feelings of social awkwardness might influence their drinking behavior—provides professionals with an important and potentially powerful means of deterring, or at least delaying, the onset of drinking among young people. From this perspective, alcohol use in teenagers can be countered by providing young people with more effective social tools and ways of altering these expectancies before drinking begins.

Time and experience do have a moderating influence over these alcohol expectancies. There is clear evidence to suggest that these expectancies become less influential over time or with age. In a longitudinal study of college drinking, Sher, Wood, and colleagues (1996) found that there was a significant decrease in outcome expectancy over time. Older students showed less expectation of the benefits of alcohol than beginning students.

The problem, of course, is that until they reach the point of having more realistic expectations about drinking, too many students participate in **binge drinking**, the practice of drinking large quantities of alcoholic beverages in a relatively short period of time, often with deadly consequences.

Case Study The Sometimes Tragic Consequences of College Fun • Scott K., an 18-year-old college freshman from a prestigious university in Boston, went to a party at an off-campus fraternity house he was pledging. During an evening that was filled with heavy drinking, Scott lapsed into unconsciousness and his heart stopped. Although he was rushed to the emergency room where medics attempted to revive him, it was too late—he died without regaining consciousness. His blood-alcohol level at the time was .41—an amount that is four times the legal limit for driving in the state. (From Goldberg, 1997.)

This tragic incident occurred just a few weeks after another college student in Louisiana died and 12 classmates had to be hospitalized for alcohol poisoning after an evening of drinking. Deaths due to alcohol poisoning, though seemingly more tragic when they occur among the young, are not uncommon. In fact, about 4000 people a year die of alcohol poisoning (Goldberg, 1997).

Marital and Other Intimate Relationships Excessive drinking often begins during crisis periods in marital or other intimate personal relationships, particularly crises that lead to hurt and self-devaluation. The marital relationship may actually serve to maintain the pattern of excessive drinking. In one case, a 36-year-old homemaker began to drink to excess during times of extreme marital distress, particularly when her husband of 3 years began staying out all night and physically abusing her when he came back home. In other cases, marital partners may behave toward each other in ways that promote or enable the spouse's excessive drinking. For example, a husband who lives with an alcoholic wife is often unaware of the fact that, gradually and inevitably, many of the decisions he makes every day are based on the expectation that his wife will be drinking. These expectations, in turn, may make the drinking behavior more likely. Thus, one important concern in many treatment programs today involves identifying the personality or lifestyle factors in a relationship that serve to promote, maintain, or justify the drinking behavior of an alcoholic.

Excessive use of alcohol is one of the most frequent causes of divorce in the United States (Fillmore et al.,

binge drinking The practice of drinking large quantities of alcoholic beverages in a relatively short period of time.

HIGHLIGHT 10.3

Binge Drinking in College

How extensive is college binge drinking? In spite of the fact that alcohol use is illegal for most undergraduates, binge drinking on campus is widespread (Rabow & Duncan-Schill, 1995). In fact, 44 percent of college students in the United States are binge drinkers, according to a survey by Wechsler and colleagues (1994). Goodwin (1992) reported that 98 percent of fraternity and sorority members drink some amount every week. College students in the United Kingdom have been shown to have an even higher rate of alcohol consumption, hangovers, blackouts, and missed classes than college students in the United States (Delk & Meilman, 1996), and 34 percent of respondents in Australia reported mixing alcohol and driving and having greater concerns about drinking to excess than students in Israel, the United States, and Singapore (Isralowitz, Borowski, et al., 1992).

Whether binge drinking episodes occur following off-campus parties or on one of the annual "breakaways" to Panama City or Atlanta, they are commonly associated with negative consequences. (Cities such as Fort Lauderdale, Florida, have discouraged these gatherings because of their adverse consequences.) In their survey, Wechsler and colleagues (1994) reported a strong positive relationship between the frequency of binge drinking and a number of alcohol-related problems. In fact, binge drinkers were nearly ten times more likely than non-binge drinkers to engage in unplanned sexual activity, use no protection when having sex, get into trouble with campus police, damage property, or get hurt after drinking. Men and women tended to report similar levels of these problems, except that men tended to engage in more property damage. Over 16 percent of the men and 9 percent of the women reported having gotten in trouble with the campus police. About 47 percent of the frequent binge drinkers but only 14 percent of the non-binge drinkers indicated that they had experienced five or more of the problems identified in the survey.

Interestingly, a follow-up survey of college drinking in 1997 (Wechsler et al., 1998) reported strikingly similar results—2 out of 5 students (about 42.7 percent) were considered binge drinkers, compared with 44.1 percent in the earlier study. ■

1994) and is often a hidden factor in the two most common causes—financial and sexual problems. The deterioration in alcoholics' interpersonal relationships, of course, further augments the stress and disorganization in their lives. The break-up of marital relationships can be a highly stressful situation for many people. The stress of divorce and the often erratic adjustment period that follows can lead to increased substance-abuse problems.

Sociocultural Factors

In a general sense, our culture has become dependent on alcohol as a social lubricant and a means of reducing tension. Thus, numerous investigators have pointed to the role of sociocultural as well as physiological and psychological factors in the high rate of alcohol abuse and dependence among Americans (Vega et al., 1993).

The effect of cultural attitudes toward drinking is well illustrated by Muslims and Mormons, whose religious values prohibit the use of alcohol, and by orthodox Jews, who have traditionally limited its use largely to religious rituals. The incidence of alcoholism among these groups is minimal. Interestingly, Europe and six countries that have been influenced by European culture—Argentina, Canada, Chile, Japan, the United States, and New Zealand—make up less than 20 percent of the world's population yet consume 80 percent of the alcohol (Barry, 1982). Alcohol abuse continues to be a problem in Europe, and it has been noted to have great consequence in terms of accidents (Lehto, 1995), crime (Rittson, 1995), increased liver disease (Medical Council on Alcoholism, 1997), and the extent to which young people are becoming involved in substance use problems (Anderson & Lehto, 1995). The French appear to have the highest rate of alcoholism in the world. In addition, France shows the highest prevalence rates among hospitalized patients: 18 percent of hospital patients (25 percent of males and 7 percent of females) were reported to have alcohol use disorders though only 6 percent of admissions were for alcohol problems (Reynaud, Leleu, et al., 1997). In Sweden, another country with

The cultural influences on alcoholism are clear when one looks at the extremely low incidence of alcoholism among orthodox Jews, whose religious values prohibit drinking except in religious services.

high rates of alcoholism, the proportion of hospital admissions attributed to alcohol was 13.2 percent for men and 1.1 percent for women (Andreason & Brandt, 1997). Thus, it appears that religious sanctions and social customs can determine whether alcohol is one of the coping methods commonly used in a given group or society.

The behavior that is manifested under the influence of alcohol appears to be influenced by cultural factors. Lindman and Lang (1994), in a study of alcohol-related behavior in eight countries, found that most subjects expressed the view that aggressive behavior frequently followed after drinking "many" drinks; however, the expectation that alcohol leads to aggression is related to cultural traditions and early exposure to violent or aggressive behavior.

In sum, we can identify many reasons why people drink—as well as many conditions that can predispose them to do so and reinforce drinking behavior—but the actual combination of factors that result in a person's becoming an alcoholic are still unknown.

Treatment of Alcoholism

Alcohol abuse and dependence are difficult to treat because many alcoholics refuse to admit that they have a problem or to seek assistance before they "hit bottom," and many who do go into treatment leave before therapy is completed. Di Clemente (1993) refers to the addictions as "diseases of denial." In a survey that included more than 60,000 treated alcoholics, Booth, Cook, and Blow (1992) reported that 11 percent left treatment against medical advice. When alcoholics are confronted with their drinking problem, they may react with denial or become angry at the "messenger" and withdraw from this person (Miller & Rollnick, 1991).

Complicating matters further is the presence of other mental disorders in alcohol or drug-abusing patients, a very important consideration when it comes to treatment. In order to ensure more effective treatment of these complicated problems, Brems and Johnson (1997) recommend that treatment of co-occurring mental health problems involve more cross-disciplinary collaboration, greater integration of substance abuse and mental health treatments, and sensitization of caregivers to the difficulties of treating patients with comorbid disorders. Given that the problems of alcoholism are often complex, requiring flexibility and individualization of treatment procedures, a multidisciplinary treatment approach appears to be most effective (Margolis & Zweben, 1998).

Also, an alcoholic's needs change as treatment progresses. Treatment program objectives usually include detoxification, physical rehabilitation, control over alcohol-abuse behavior, and development of an individual's realization that he or she can cope with the problems of living and lead a much more rewarding life without alcohol. Traditional treatment programs usually have as their goal abstinence from alcohol. However, some programs attempt to promote controlled drinking as a treatment goal for problem drinkers. No matter what the treatment method, however, relapse is common and is seen as part of the treatment and recovery process by many in the field.

Biological Treatment Approaches Biological approaches include a variety of treatment measures such as medications to reduce cravings, to ease the detoxification process, and to treat co-occurring mental health problems that are thought to potentially underlie the drinking behavior (Romach & Sellers, 1998).

Medications to Block the Desire to Drink Disulfiram (Antabuse), a drug that causes violent vomiting when followed by ingestion of alcohol, may be administered to prevent an immediate return to drinking (Chic et al., 1992). The primary value of drugs of this type seems to be their ability to interrupt the alcoholic cycle for a period of time, during which psychological therapy may be undertaken (Gorlick, 1993). Uncomfortable side effects may accompany the use of Antabuse; for example, alcohol-based after-shave lotion can be absorbed through the skin, resulting in illness. Moreover, the cost of Antabuse treatment, since it requires careful medical maintenance, is higher than for many other, more effective treatments (Holder et al., 1991).

Another type of medication that has been used in a promising line of research (Anton, 1996; Columbus, Allen, & Fertig, 1995) is *naltrexone,* an opiate antagonist that helps reduce the "craving" for alcohol that alcoholics experience by blocking the pleasure producing effects of alcohol. O'Malley, Jaffe, Rode, and Rounsaville (1996) have shown that naltrexone reduced the alcohol intake and lowered the incentive to drink in alcoholics, compared with a control sample who were given a placebo.

Medications to Lower the Side Effects of Acute Withdrawal The initial focus of treatment is on detoxification (the elimination of alcoholic substances from an individual's body), the treatment of withdrawal symptoms described earlier, and a medical regimen for physical rehabilitation. One of the primary goals in treatment of withdrawal symptoms is to reduce the physical symptoms characteristic of the syndrome, such as insomnia, headache, gastrointestinal distress, and tremulousness. Central to the treatment are the prevention of heart arrhythmias, seizures, delirium, and death (Bohn, 1993). These steps can usually best be handled in a hospital or clinic, where drugs such as Valium have largely revolutionized the treatment of withdrawal symptoms. Such drugs overcome motor excitement, nausea, and vomiting; prevent withdrawal delirium and convulsions; and help alleviate the tension and anxiety associated with withdrawal. Concern is growing, however, that the use of tranquilizers at this stage does not promote long-term recovery and may foster addiction to another substance. Accordingly, some detoxification clinics are exploring alternative approaches, including a gradual weaning from alcohol instead of a sudden cutoff. Maintenance doses of mild tranquilizers are sometimes given to patients withdrawing from alcohol to reduce anxiety and help them sleep. Such use of tranquilizers may be less effective than no treatment at all, however. Usually, patients must learn to abstain from tranquilizers as well as from alcohol, because they tend to misuse both. Further, under the influence of tranquilizers, patients may even return to alcohol use.

Medications to Treat Co-occurring Disorders Tranquilizing medications are also used in the treatment of alcoholism in ways other than easing withdrawal symptoms. For example, medications such as *desimpramine* are used to treat depression symptoms and alcohol consumption that are comorbid (Anton, 1996).

Psychological Treatment Approaches Detoxification is optimally followed by psychological treatment, including family counseling and the use of community resources relating to employment and other aspects of a person's social readjustment. Although individual psychotherapy is sometimes effective, the focus of psychosocial measures in the treatment of alcoholism more often involves group therapy, environmental intervention, behavior therapy, and the approach used by Alcoholics Anonymous and family groups such as Al-Anon and Al-Ateen.

Group Therapy In the confrontational give-and-take of group therapy, alcoholics are often forced to face their problems (perhaps for the first time) and their tendencies to deny or to minimize their involvement in their troubles when they describe them to a knowing audience of "peers." These group treatment situations can be extremely difficult for alcoholics who have been engrossed in denial of their own responsibilities, but they also provide the opportunity for alcoholics to see new possibilities for coping with circumstances that have led to their difficulties. Often, but by no means always, this problem recognition paves the way for learning more effective methods of coping and other positive steps toward dealing with the drinking problem.

In some instances, the spouses of alcoholics and even their children may be invited to join in group therapy meetings. In other situations, family treatment is itself the central focus of therapeutic efforts. In this case, the alcoholic is seen as a member of a disturbed family in which all the members have a responsibility for cooperating in treatment. Because family members are frequently the people most victimized by the alcoholic's addiction, they often tend to be judgmental and punitive, and the alcoholic, who has already passed harsh judgment on himself or herself, tolerates this further source of devaluation poorly. In other instances, family members may unwittingly encourage an alcoholic to remain addicted—for example, a man with a need to dominate his wife may find that a continually drunken and remorseful spouse best meets his needs.

Environmental Intervention As with other serious maladaptive behaviors, a total treatment program for alcoholism usually requires measures to alleviate a patient's aversive life situation. Environmental support has been shown to be an important ingredient to an alcoholic's recovery (Booth et al., 1992a, 1992b). As a result of their drinking, alcoholics often become estranged from family and friends and either lose or jeopardize their jobs; they are often lonely and may live in impoverished neighborhoods. Typically, the reaction of those around them is not as understanding or supportive as it would be if the alcoholic had a physical illness of comparable magnitude. Simply helping alcoholics learn more effective coping techniques may not be enough if their social environment remains hostile and threatening. For alcoholics who have been hospitalized, halfway houses—designed to assist them in their return to family and community—are often important adjuncts to their total treatment program.

The relapses and continued deterioration that alcoholics often experience are associated with their lack of close relationships with family or friends, as well as living in a stressful environment. In general, it appears unlikely that an alcoholic will remain abstinent after treatment unless the negative psychosocial factors that operated in the past also change for the better.

Behavior Therapy One interesting and often effective form of treatment for alcohol-abuse disorders is behavior therapy, of which several types exist. One is *aversive conditioning*, involving the presentation of a wide range of noxious stimuli accompanying alcohol consumption in order to suppress drinking behavior. For example, the ingestion of alcohol might be paired with an electric shock or a drug that produces nausea.

A variety of pharmacological and other deterrent measures can be used in behavior therapy after detoxification. One approach involves an intramuscular injection of emetine hydrochloride, an emetic. Before experiencing the nausea that results from the injection, a patient is given alcohol, so that the sight, smell, and taste of the beverage become associated with severe retching and vomiting. That is, a conditioned aversion to taste and smell of alcohol develops. With repetition, this classical conditioning procedure acts as a strong deterrent to further drinking—probably in part because it adds an immediate and unpleasant physiological consequence to the more general socially aversive consequences of excessive drinking.

Behavioral and cognitive-behavioral approaches often target behaviors that are thought to contribute to use of alcohol—for example, depression. Research has shown that cognitive-behavioral interventions can both improve the person's mood state and lower substance abuse (Brown, Evans, Miller, et al., 1997). Another behavioral approach that has shown substantial benefit has been behavioral couples therapy. More benefit at lower cost was found for behavioral couples therapy than for individual behavior therapy (Fals-Stewart, O'Farrell, & Birchler, 1997).

One contemporary procedure for treating alcoholics has been the cognitive-behavioral approach recommended by Alan Marlatt (1985) and Marlatt, Baer, and colleagues (1998). This approach combines cognitive-behavioral intervention strategies with social-learning theory and modeling of behavior. The approach, often referred to as a "skills-training procedure," is usually aimed at younger problem drinkers who are considered to be at risk for developing more severe drinking problems because of alcoholism in their family history or their heavy current consumption level. This approach relies on such techniques as increasing specific knowledge about alcohol, developing coping skills to be used in situations associated with increased risk of alcohol use, modifying cognitions and expectancies, and acquiring stress-management skills. This cognitive-behavioral approach clearly has intuitive appeal; however, its relative effectiveness has yet to be demonstrated. Holder and colleagues (1991) reported that this approach tends to be less effective than other skills-training procedures.

Self-control training techniques (Miller, Brown, et al. 1995), in which the goal of therapy is to get alcoholics to reduce alcohol intake without necessarily abstaining altogether, have a great deal of appeal for some drinkers. There is even a computer-based self-control training program that has been shown to reduce problem drinking in a controlled study (Hester & Delaney, 1997). It is difficult, of course, for individuals who are extremely dependent on the effects of alcohol to abstain totally from drinking. Thus, many alcoholics fail to complete traditional treatment programs. The idea that they might be able to learn to control their drinking and at the same time enjoy the continued use of alcohol might serve as a motivating element (Lang & Kidorf, 1990).

HIGHLIGHT 10.4

Controlled Drinking Versus Abstinence

The debate over whether alcoholics can learn to drink moderately has continued for decades. Miller and colleagues (1986), for example, evaluated the results of four long-term follow-up studies of controlled-drinking treatment programs; they concluded that controlled drinking was more likely to be successful in persons with less severe alcohol problems.

Some researchers (e.g., Dawe & Richmond, 1997; Heather, 1995; Kahler, 1995; Sobell & Sobell, 1995) uphold the efficacy of controlled-drinking programs, while others (e.g., Glatt, 1995) point to difficulties with alcoholics' ability to maintain control. Most workers in the field still assume that total abstinence should be the goal for all problem drinkers. Some groups, such as Alcoholics Anonymous, are adamant in their opposition to treatment programs whose aim is controlled drinking for alcohol-dependent individuals. ■

Alcoholics Anonymous Alcoholics Anonymous (AA) is a self-help counseling program in which both person-to-person and group relationships are emphasized. AA accepts both teenagers and adults with drinking problems, has no dues or fees, does not keep records or case histories, does not participate in political causes, and is not affiliated with any religious sect, although spiritual development is a key aspect of its treatment approach. To ensure anonymity, only first names are used. Meetings are devoted partly to social activities, but they consist mainly of discussions of the participants' problems with alcohol, often with testimonials from those who are successfully dealing with alcoholism. The term *alcoholic* is used by AA and its affiliates to refer either to persons who currently are drinking excessively or to people who have recovered from such problems but must, according to AA philosophy, continue to abstain from alcohol consumption in the future. That is, in the AA view, one is an alcoholic for life, whether or not one is drinking; one is never "cured" of alcoholism but is instead "in recovery."

An important aspect of AA's rehabilitation program is that it eases some personal responsibility by helping alcoholics see themselves not as weak-willed or lacking in moral strength, but rather simply as having an affliction—they cannot drink—just as other people may not be able to tolerate certain types of medication. With mutual help and reassurance from group members who have shared similar experiences, many alcoholics acquire insight into their problems, a new sense of purpose, greater ego strength, and more effective coping techniques. Continued participation in the group, of course, helps prevent the crisis of a relapse.

Affiliated movements, such as Al-Anon family groups and Al-Ateen (with over 35,000 groups in the United States and Canada), are designed to bring family members together to share common experiences and problems, to gain understanding of the nature of alcoholism, and to learn techniques for dealing with their own problems in the situation. There have also been some "spin-off" alcohol rehabilitation programs that follow this social-modeling approach, using peer-oriented treatment that evolved from the AA approach (Borkman, Kaskutas, Room, et al. 1998). These approaches may follow the AA model but include other treatment methods as well (Wallace, 1996).

The reported success of Alcoholics Anonymous is based primarily on anecdotal information rather than objective study of treatment outcomes because AA does not participate in external comparative research efforts. Brandsma, Maultsby, and Welsh (1980), however, included an AA program in their extensive comparative study of alcoholism treatments. The success of this treatment method with severe alcoholics was quite limited. One important finding was that the AA method had high drop-out rates compared with other therapies. About half of the people who come to AA drop out of the program within 3 months. On the positive side, however, a study by Morganstern, Labouvie, and colleagues (1997) reported that affiliation with AA after alcohol treatment was associated with better outcomes than was no involvement with AA, and a study by Tonigan, Toscova, and Miller (1995) found that AA involvement was strongly associated with success in outpatient samples.

Outcome Studies The outcome of treatment of alcoholism varies considerably, depending on the population studied and on the treatment facilities and procedures employed. Rates of success range from low for hard-core alcoholics to 70 to 90 percent where modern treatment and after-care procedures are used. Rounsaville and colleagues (1987) reported that psychopathology was influential in treatment outcomes for alcoholics. Alcoholics who were also diagnosed as having a personality or affective disorder tended to have poorer outcomes in alcohol treatment than did those for whom the diagnosis was simply alcoholism.

In their 4-year follow-up of a large group of treated alcoholics, Polich and colleagues (1981) found that alcoholics were difficult to treat regardless of the method used. Only 7 percent of the total sample (922 males) abstained from alcohol use throughout the 4-year period, and 54 percent continued to show alcohol-related problems. One interesting finding supports the view that some alcoholics may be able to learn to control their alcohol use without having to totally abstain from drinking—18 percent of the alcoholics in the sample had been able to drink without problems during the 6-month period before follow-up.

Treatment is most likely to be effective when an individual realizes that he or she needs help, when adequate treatment facilities are available, and when the individual attends treatment regularly. Having a positive relationship with the therapist was associated with better treatment outcome (Connors et al., 1997). One strategy is aimed at reinforcing treatment motivation and abstinence early in the treatment process by providing "check-up" follow-ups on drinking behavior. Miller, Benefield, and Tonigan (1993) reported that "Drinking Check-Up" sessions during the early stages of therapy resulted in a reduction of drinking for some clients in the first 6 weeks of therapy, as compared with clients who did not have the check-ups.

Some researchers have maintained that treatment for alcohol use and abuse disorders would be more effective if important patient characteristics were taken into account in providing therapy (Mattson, Allen, Longabaugh, et al., 1994). That is, patients with certain personality characteristics or with differing degrees of severity of their drinking problems might do better with a specific therapeutic approach. This view was evaluated in an extensive study of patient-treatment matching (referred to as Project MATCH) that was sponsored by the National Institute on Alcohol Abuse and Alcoholism (NIAAA). The findings were unexpected. For the three treatments studied—Twelve-Step Facilitation Therapy (an AA-type program), a cognitive-behavioral therapy, and a treatment technique referred to as Motivational Enhancement Therapy, which attempts to get clients to assume responsibility for helping themselves—matching the patient to a particular treatment did not appear to be related to an effective outcome (Babor, 1996; Project MATCH Group, 1997). The treatments studied all had equal outcomes. Gordis (1997) concluded that "it is likely that patients in competently run alcoholism treatment programs will do as well with one of the three treatments studied as with the others."

Relapse Prevention One of the greatest problems in the treatment of addictive disorders, such as alcoholism or any substance dependence problem, is maintaining abstinence or self-control once the behavioral excesses have been checked. Most alcohol treatment programs show high success rates in "curing" the addictive problems, but many programs show lessening rates of abstinence or controlled drinking at various periods of follow-up. Many treatment programs do not pay sufficient attention to the important element of maintaining effective behavior and preventing relapse into previous maladaptive patterns.

Given the fact that alcoholics are highly vulnerable to relapse, some researchers have focused on the importance of the need to help them remain abstinent. In one cognitive-behavioral approach, relapse behavior is a key factor in alcohol treatment (Marlatt, 1985; Marlatt & VandenBos, 1997). The behaviors underlying relapse are seen as "indulgent behaviors" that are based on an individual's learning history. When an individual is abstinent or has an addiction under control, he or she gains a sense of personal control over the indulgent behavior. The longer the person is able to maintain this control, the greater the sense of achievement—the self-efficacy or confidence—and the greater the chance that he or she will be able to cope with the addiction and maintain control. However, a person may violate this rule of abstinence through a gradual, perhaps unconscious, process, rather than through a sudden "falling off the wagon" that constitutes the traditional view of craving and relapse. In the cognitive-behavioral view, a person may inadvertently make a series of mini-decisions, even while maintaining abstinence, that begin a chain of behaviors making relapse inevitable. For example, an abstinent alcoholic who buys a quart of bourbon just in case his friends drop by is unconsciously preparing the way for relapse.

It is difficult for many people to remain abstinent from alcohol because of the luring appeal of advertisements and store displays. Given the fact that alcoholics are highly vulnerable to relapse, many experts believe that treatment should also include teaching the alcoholic to expect slips and not see them as huge failures, which can then provide the rationale for such thinking as "Well, I've blown my abstinence. I might as well go get drunk."

Another type of relapse behavior involves the "abstinence violation effect," in which even minor transgressions are seen by the abstainer to have drastic significance. The effect works this way: An abstinent person may hold that he or she should not, under any circumstance, transgress or give in to the old habit. Abstinence-oriented treatment programs are particularly guided by this prohibitive rule. What happens, then, when an abstinent man becomes somewhat self-indulgent and takes a drink offered by an old friend? He may lose some of the sense of self-efficacy, the confidence needed to control his drinking. Since the vow of abstinence has been violated, he may feel guilty about giving in to the temptation and rationalize that he "has blown it and become a drunk again, so why not go all the way?"

In relapse prevention treatment, clients are taught to recognize the apparently irrelevant decisions that serve as early warning signals of the possibility of relapse. High-risk situations such as parties or sports events are targeted, and the individuals learn to assess their own vulnerability to relapse. Clients are also trained not to become so discouraged that they lose their confidence if they do relapse. Some cognitive-behavioral therapists have employed a "planned relapse" phase in the treatment to supervise an individual's cognitive-behavioral strategies for getting through this important problem area. In other words, if patients are taught to expect a relapse, they are better able to handle it.

IN REVIEW

- What is the difference between alcohol abuse and alcohol dependence?
- What are the three major physiological effects of alcohol?
- Identify the physical, interpersonal, and social/occupational problems that can result from chronic alcohol abuse.
- What are five major psychosocial factors that may contribute to alcohol dependence?
- Describe four psychosocial interventions used to treat alcohol dependence.

DRUG ABUSE AND DEPENDENCE

Aside from alcohol, the psychoactive drugs most commonly associated with abuse and dependence in our society appear to be (1) narcotics, such as opium and its derivatives; (2) sedatives, such as barbiturates; (3) stimulants, such as cocaine and amphetamines; (4) antianxiety drugs, such as benzodiazepines; and (5) hallucinogens, such as LSD and PCP. (These and other drugs are summarized in Table 10.4.) Caffeine and nicotine are also drugs of dependence, and disorders associated with tobacco withdrawal and caffeine intoxication are included in the DSM-IV-TR diagnostic classification system.

An estimated 28 million people worldwide incur significant health risks by using various psychoactive substances other than alcohol, tobacco, and volatile solvents such as glue (World Health Organization, 1997). Though they may occur at any age, drug abuse and dependence are most common during adolescence and young adulthood (Smith, 1989) and vary according to metropolitan area, race and ethnicity, labor force status, and other demographic characteristics (Hughes, 1992).

The extent to which drug abuse has become a problem for society is reflected in a study of drug involvement among applicants for employment at a large teaching hospital in Maryland (Lange et al., 1994). Beginning in 1989 and covering a 2-year period, all applicants for employment were screened through a pre-employment drug screening program (individuals were not identified in the initial study). Of 593 applicants, 10.8 percent were found to have detectable amounts of illicit drugs in their tests. The most frequently detected drug was marijuana (55 percent of those tested positively), followed by cocaine (36 percent) and opiates (28 percent).

Among those who abuse drugs, behavior patterns vary markedly, depending on the type, amount, and duration of drug use; the physiological and psychological makeup of the individual; and, in some instances, the social setting in which the drug experience occurs. Thus, it appears most useful to deal separately with some of the drugs that are commonly associated with abuse and dependence in contemporary society.

Opium and Its Derivatives (Narcotics)

People have used opium and its derivatives for over 5000 years. Galen (A.D. 130–201) considered theriaca, whose principal ingredient was opium, to be a panacea:

> It resists poison and venomous bites, cures inveterate headache, vertigo, deafness, epilepsy, apoplexy, dimness of sight, loss of voice, asthma, coughs of all kinds, spitting of blood, tightness of breath, colic, the iliac poisons, jaundice, hardness of the spleen, stone, urinary complaints, fevers, dropsies, leprosies, the trouble to which women are subject, melancholy and all pestilences.

Even today, opium derivatives are still used for some of the conditions Galen mentioned.

TABLE 10.4 PSYCHOACTIVE DRUGS COMMONLY INVOLVED IN DRUG ABUSE

Classification	Drug	Effect
Narcotics	Opium and its derivatives	Alleviate physical pain
	Opium	Induce relaxation and pleasant reverie
	Morphine	Alleviate anxiety and tension
	Codeine	
	Heroin	
	Methadone (synthetic narcotic)	Treatment of heroin dependence
Sedatives	Alcohol (ethanol)	Reduce tension
		Facilitate social interaction
		"Blot out" feelings or events
	Barbiturates	Reduce tension
	Nembutal (pentobarbital)	
	Seconal (secobarbital)	
	Veronal (barbital)	
	Tuinal (secobarbital and amobarbital)	
Stimulants	Amphetamines	Increase feelings of alertness and confidence
	Benzedrine (amphetamine)	Decrease feelings of fatigue
	Dexedrine (dextroamphetamine)	Stay awake for long periods
	Methedrine (methamphetamine)	Increase endurance
	Cocaine (coca)	Stimulate sex drive
Antianxiety drugs (minor tranquilizers)	Librium (chlordiazepoxide)	Alleviate tension and anxiety
	Miltown (meprobamate)	Induce relaxation and sleep
	Valium (diazepam)	
	Xanax	
Psychedelics and hallucinogens	Cannabis	Induce changes in mood, thought, and behavior
	Marijuana	
	Hashish	
	Mescaline (peyote)	"Expand" one's mind
	Psilocybin (psychotogenic mushrooms)	Induce stupor
	LSD (lysergic acid diethylamide-25)	
	PCP (phencyclidine)	

Note: This list is by no means complete; for example, it does not include newer drugs, such as Ritalin, which are designed to produce multiple effects; it does not include the less commonly used volatile hydrocarbons, such as glue, paint thinner, gasoline, cleaning fluid, and nail-polish remover, which are highly dangerous when sniffed for their psychoactive effects; and it does not include the antipsychotic and antidepressant drugs, which are abused, but relatively rarely.

Opium is a mixture of about 18 chemical substances known as *alkaloids*. In 1805, the alkaloid present in opium in the largest amount (10 to 15 percent) was found to be a bitter-tasting powder that could serve as a powerful sedative and pain reliever; it was named **morphine** after Morpheus, god of sleep in Greek mythology. The hypodermic needle was introduced in America about 1856, allowing morphine to be widely administered to soldiers during the Civil War, not only to those wounded in battle but also to those suffering from dysentery. As a consequence, many Civil War veterans returned to civilian life addicted to the drug, a condition euphemistically referred to as "soldier's illness."

Scientists concerned with the addictive properties of morphine hypothesized that one part of the morphine

opium A narcotic that has powerful sedative and pain-killing effects but is extremely addictive; its derivatives are morphine, heroin, and codeine.

morphine Addictive psychoactive drug that is derived from opium and can serve as a powerful sedative and pain reliever.

HIGHLIGHT 10.5

Coffee Anyone?

The chemical compound *caffeine* is found in many commonly available drinks and even some foods. Although the consumption of caffeine is widely practiced and socially promoted in contemporary society, excessive caffeine intake can cause problems. The negative effects of caffeine consumption arise from intoxication rather than withdrawal. Unlike withdrawal from drugs such as alcohol or nicotine, withdrawal from caffeine does not produce severe symptoms; some people experience headaches, but they are usually mild.

Caffeine-induced organic mental disorder (also referred to as *caffeinism*), as described in DSM-IV-TR, involves symptoms of restlessness, nervousness, excitement, insomnia, muscle twitching, and gastrointestinal complaints. It follows the ingestion of caffeine-containing substances, such as coffee, tea, cola, or chocolate. The amount of caffeine that results in intoxication differs among individuals; however, consumption of over 1 gram of caffeine could result in muscle twitching, cardiac arrhythmia, agitation, and rambling thoughts. Consumption of 10 grams of caffeine can produce seizures, respiratory failures, and death. ■

molecule might be responsible for its analgesic properties (that is, its ability to eliminate pain without inducing unconsciousness) and another for its addictiveness. At about the turn of the twentieth century, it was discovered that if morphine was treated by an inexpensive and readily available chemical called acetic anhydride, it would be converted into another powerful analgesic called **heroin.** Leading scientists of the time agreed on the merits of heroin, and the drug came to be widely prescribed in place of morphine for pain relief and related medicinal purposes. However, heroin was a cruel disappointment, for it proved to be an even more dangerous drug than morphine, acting more rapidly and more intensely and being equally if not more addictive. Eventually, heroin was removed from use in medical practice.

As it became apparent that opium and its derivatives—including codeine, which is used in some cough syrups—were perilously addictive, the U.S. Congress enacted the Harrison Act in 1914. Under this and later acts, the unauthorized sale and distribution of certain drugs became a federal offense; physicians and pharmacists were held accountable for each dose they dispensed. Thus, overnight, the role of a chronic narcotic user changed from that of addict—which was considered a vice, but tolerated—to that of criminal. Unable to obtain drugs through legal sources, many turned to illegal ones, and eventually to other criminal acts as a means of maintaining their suddenly expensive drug supply.

During the 1960s, there was a rapid increase in heroin use, but since 1975 the actual number of heroin users has diminished steadily (Smith, 1989). Heroin-related hospital admissions decreased in recent years from 47 percent of total drug-related admissions to 37 percent (DAWN Project, 1996).

Effects of Morphine and Heroin Morphine and heroin are commonly introduced into the body by smoking, snorting (inhaling the powder), eating, "skin popping," or "mainlining"—the last two being methods of introducing the drug via hypodermic injection. *Skin popping* refers to injecting the liquefied drug just beneath the skin, and *mainlining* to injecting the drug directly into the bloodstream. In the United States, a young addict usually moves from snorting to mainlining.

Among the immediate effects of mainlined or snorted heroin is a euphoric spasm (the rush) lasting 60 seconds or so, which many addicts compare to a sexual orgasm. However, vomiting and nausea have also been known to be part of the immediate effects of heroin and morphine use. This rush is followed by a high, during which an addict typically is in a lethargic, withdrawn state in which bodily needs, including needs for food and sex, are markedly diminished; pleasant feelings of relaxation, euphoria, and reverie tend to dominate. These effects last from 4 to 6 hours and are followed—in addicts—by a negative phase that produces a desire for more of the drug.

heroin Psychoactive drug that is chemically derived from morphine and has the same ability to relieve pain but is even more intense and addictive.

HIGHLIGHT 10.6

Still Want That Cigarette?

The poisonous alkaloid *nicotine* is the chief active ingredient in tobacco; it is found in cigarettes, chewing tobacco, and cigars, and it is even used as an insecticide.

Strong evidence exists for a nicotine dependency syndrome, which almost always begins during the adolescent years and may continue into adulthood as a difficult-to-break and health-endangering habit. (Most quit-smoking programs average only about a 20 to 25 percent success rate.) The Surgeon General's report (USDHHS, 1994) estimated that 3.1 million U.S. adolescents and 25 percent of 17- to 18-year-olds are smokers.

Nicotine-induced organic mental disorder, as it is called in DSM-IV-TR, results from ceasing or reducing the intake of nicotine-containing substances after acquiring a physical dependence on them. The diagnostic criteria for this disorder include (1) the daily use of nicotine for at least several weeks and (2) the following symptoms after nicotine ingestion is stopped or reduced: craving for nicotine; irritability, frustration, or anger; anxiety; difficulty concentrating; restlessness; decreased heart rate; and increased appetite or weight gain. Several other physical symptoms often associated with withdrawal from nicotine are decreased metabolic rate, headaches, insomnia, tremors, increased coughing, and impairment of performance on tasks requiring attention. These withdrawal symptoms usually continue for several days to several weeks, depending on the extent of the nicotine habit. ■

The use of an opium derivative over a period of time usually results in a physiological craving for the drug. The time required to establish the drug habit varies, but it has been estimated that continual use over a period of 30 days is usually sufficient. Users then find that they have become physiologically dependent on the drug in the sense that they feel physically ill when they do not take it. In addition, users of an opium derivative gradually build up a tolerance to the drug so that increasingly larger amounts are needed to achieve the desired effects.

When people addicted to an opiate do not get a dose of the drug within approximately 8 hours, they start to experience withdrawal symptoms. The character and severity of these reactions depend on many factors, including the amount of the narcotic habitually used, the intervals between doses, the duration of the addiction, and especially the addict's health and personality.

Contrary to what some addicts believe, withdrawal from heroin is not always dangerous or even very painful. Many addicted people withdraw without assistance. Withdrawal can, however, be an agonizing experience for some people, with symptoms of runny nose, tearing eyes, perspiration, restlessness, increased respiration rate, and an intensified desire for the drug. As time passes, the symptoms may become more severe. Typically, a feeling of chilliness alternates with vasomotor disturbances of flushing and excessive sweating, vomiting, diarrhea, abdominal cramps, pains in the back and extremities, severe headache, marked tremors, and varying degrees of insomnia. Beset by these discomforts, an individual refuses food and water, and this, coupled with the vomiting, sweating, and diarrhea, results in dehydration and weight loss. Occasionally, symptoms may include delirium, hallucinations, and manic activity. Cardiovascular collapse may also occur and can result in death. If morphine is administered, the subjective distress experienced by the addict temporarily ends, and physiological balance is quickly restored.

Withdrawal symptoms will usually be on the decline by the third or fourth day and will have disappeared by the seventh or eighth day. As the symptoms subside, the person resumes normal eating and drinking and rapidly regains lost weight. After withdrawal symptoms have ceased, the individual's former tolerance for the drug is reduced; as a result, there may be a risk that the person might overdose by taking the former dosage.

Typically, the life of a narcotic addict becomes increasingly centered on obtaining and using drugs, so the addiction usually leads to socially maladaptive behavior as the individual is eventually forced to lie, steal, and associate with undesirable contacts to maintain a supply of drugs. Many addicts resort to petty theft to support their habits, and some female addicts turn to prostitution as a means of financing their addictions.

Along with the lowering of ethical and moral restraints, addiction has adverse physical effects on an individual's well-being. An inadequate diet, for example, may

vey on Drug Abuse (N = 17,747 in 1995) reported that they had used marijuana in the past (Bobashev & Anthony, 1998). In a survey of drug-related visits to the emergency room (DAWN Project, 1996), the number of visits related to marijuana use increased over 17 percent in both 1994 and 1995. There was a 200 percent increase in admissions since 1990. Many of these emergency room visits, as one might suspect, involved the use of other substances along with marijuana.

Effects of Marijuana The specific effects of marijuana vary greatly, depending on the quality and dosage of the drug, the personality and mood of the user, the user's past experiences with the drug, the social setting, and the user's expectations. However, considerable consensus exists among regular users that when marijuana is smoked and inhaled, a state of slight intoxication results. This state is one of mild euphoria distinguished by increased feelings of well-being, heightened perceptual acuity, and pleasant relaxation, often accompanied by a sensation of drifting or floating away. Sensory inputs are intensified. Often a person's sense of time is stretched or distorted, so that an event lasting but a few seconds may seem to cover a much longer span. Short-term memory may also be affected; for example, a person may notice a bite taken out of a sandwich but does not remember having taken it. For most users, pleasurable experiences, including sexual intercourse, are reportedly enhanced. When smoked, marijuana is rapidly absorbed into the bloodstream, and its effects appear within seconds to minutes but seldom last more than 2 to 3 hours.

Marijuana may lead to unpleasant as well as pleasant experiences. For example, if a person uses the drug while in an unhappy, angry, suspicious, or frightened mood, these feelings may be magnified. With higher dosages and with certain unstable or susceptible individuals, marijuana can produce extreme euphoria, hilarity, and overtalkativeness, but it can also produce intense anxiety and depression as well as delusions, hallucinations, and other psychotic-like behavior. Evidence suggests a strong relationship between daily marijuana use and the occurrence of self-reported psychotic symptoms (Tien & Anthony, 1990).

Marijuana's short-range physiological effects include a moderate increase in heart rate, a slowing of reaction time, a slight contraction of pupil size, bloodshot and itchy eyes, a dry mouth, and an increased appetite. Furthermore, marijuana induces memory dysfunction and a slowing of information processing (Mathew, Wilson, & Melges, 1992). Continued use of high dosages over time tends to produce lethargy and passivity. In such cases, marijuana appears to have depressant and hallucinogenic effects. The effects of long-term and habitual marijuana use are still under investigation, although a number of possible adverse side effects have been related to the prolonged, heavy use of marijuana. For example, marijuana use tends to diminish self-control. One study exploring past substance-use history in incarcerated murderers reported that among men who committed murder, marijuana was the most commonly used drug. One-third indicated that they had used the drug before the homicide, and two-thirds were experiencing some effects of the drug at the time of the murder (Spunt et al., 1994).

Marijuana has often been compared to heroin, but the two drugs have little in common with respect either to tolerance or to physiological dependence. Marijuana does not lead to physiological dependence, as heroin does, so discontinued use is not accompanied by withdrawal symptoms. Marijuana can, however, lead to psychological dependence, in which a person experiences a strong need for the drug whenever he or she feels anxious and tense. In fact, one study found that 16 percent of a sample of marijuana users reported having withdrawal-like symptoms such as nervousness, tensions, sleep problems, and appetite change (Weisbeck, Schuckit, et al., 1996).

Treatment of Marijuana Dependence Psychological treatment methods have been shown to be effective in reducing marijuana use in adults who are dependent on the drug (Zweben & O'Connell, 1992). One study compared the effectiveness of two treatments—Relapse Prevention (RP) and Support Group (SSP)—with marijuana-dependent adults (Stephens, Roffman, & Simpson, 1994). Both treatment conditions resulted in substantial reduction in marijuana use in the 12 months following treatment. As with other addictive drugs, there may be among the users many individuals with antisocial or "psychosis-prone" personalities (Kwapil, 1996); in these cases, treatment is hampered by the underlying personality disorder.

IN REVIEW

- What are the major physical and psychological effects of morphine and heroin use?
- What are three major causal factors in the development of opiate dependence?
- Describe the psychosocial and biological treatments for opiate dependency.

(continued)

- What are some physical and psychological effects of cocaine and amphetamine abuse? Describe some effects of withdrawal from these drugs.
- What are some effects of excessive barbiturate use and the subsequent withdrawal symptoms?
- Describe the psychological effects of using LSD.
- What are the short- and long-term effects of marijuana use?

UNRESOLVED ISSUES: The Genetics of Alcoholism

The origin of alcohol-abuse problems has puzzled researchers for some time. At different periods, various views have dominated. At times, authorities have tended toward the view that sociocultural factors (including sin and personal degradation) are the primary sources of alcohol abuse. One theme that has persisted, however, is the idea that some individuals are more prone to developing alcoholism than are others. Are some people genetically predisposed to alcohol abuse? Several avenues of research have shown the relevance of genetic factors in the development of alcoholism (Plomin et al., 1997).

Many experts today agree that genetic factors are likely to play an important role in developing sensitivity to the addictive power of drugs such as alcohol (Gardner, 1997; Hyman, 1994; Koob & Nestler, 1997). Research has shown that mice can be bred to have a sensitivity or preference for alcohol (Hyman, 1994). People, like mice, vary considerably in their preference for alcohol—some have an inherent liking for the drug, others a dislike for it. Research has shown that some people, such as the sons of alcoholics, have a high risk for developing problems with alcohol because of an inherent motivation or sensitivity to the drug (Conrod, Pihl, & Vassileva, 1998).

Research on the children of alcoholics who were adopted by other (nonalcoholic) families has also provided useful information bearing on the genetics of alcoholism. Studies have been conducted of alcoholics' children who were placed for adoption early in life and so did not come under the environmental influences of their biological parents. For example, Goodwin and colleagues (1973) found that children of alcoholic parents who had been adopted by nonalcoholic foster parents had nearly twice the number of alcohol problems by their late 20s as did a control group of adopted children whose real parents were not alcoholics. In another study, Goodwin and colleagues (1974) compared the sons of alcoholic parents who were adopted in infancy by nonalcoholic parents with those raised by their alcoholic parents. Both adopted and nonadopted sons later evidenced high rates of alcoholism—25 percent and 17 percent, respectively. These investigators concluded that being born to an alcoholic parent, rather than being raised by one, increased a son's risk of becoming an alcoholic. However, studies have not consistently found such a link for daughters of alcoholics (McGue, 1998).

Other researchers have attempted to determine if individuals who have a genetic "risk" for alcoholism—such as children of alcoholics—show signs of a predisposition toward alcoholism (McGue, Pickens, & Svikis, 1992). Evidence for increased alcoholism risk includes such factors as a decreased intensity of subjective feelings of intoxication, a smaller decrease in motor performance, and less body sway after alcohol ingestion. Along with these behavioral indices, increases in prolactin (a pituitary hormone) levels after low doses of alcohol have been thought to occur in individuals with a predisposition to alcohol abuse. Research into these risk factors in alcohol predisposition typically involves obtaining a sample of highly susceptible individuals, such as children of alcoholics, and a sample of controls, and then determining if certain variables (one or more of the risk factors) distinguish the groups. Research by Schuckit and Gould (1988) has shown that alcohol susceptibility indicators significantly separate sons of alcoholics from matched controls. Further evidence for a genetic basis in alcoholism has come from the search for underlying mechanisms for the transmission of alcohol abuse or susceptibility to alcoholism. Hoffman and Tabakoff (1996) have hypothesized that alcohol-induced changes in neuroreceptors might play a role in tolerance to alcohol and in alcohol dependency. They suggest that decreased dopamine, which occurs during withdrawal, might be involved in the individual's compulsion to initiate or to maintain drinking behavior.

The evidence on the genetic basis of alcoholism continues to be debated, however, and other experts are not convinced of the primary role of genetics in alcoholism.

Some have employed the evidence that genetic factors appear to play a stronger role in men than in women (Merikangas & Swendsen, 1997) to question the relative power of genetics as an explanatory factor in substance abuse. Searles (1991) points to the ambiguous evidence for the genetics of alcoholism and cautions against accepting genetic causal factors in the development of alcoholism. Negative results have been found in both adoptive studies and in studies designed to follow up the behavior of high-risk individuals. It is clear that the great majority of children who have alcoholic parents do not themselves become alcoholics—whether or not they are raised by their real parents. The successful outcomes—that is, children of alcoholics who make successful life adjustments—have not been sufficiently studied. In one study of high-risk children of alcoholics, a group of young men 19 to 20 years of age, who were presumably at high risk for developing alcoholism, were carefully studied for symptoms of psychopathology. Schulsinger and colleagues (1986) found no differences in psychopathology or alcohol-abuse behavior from a control sample similar to the general population. In another study of high-risk individuals, Alterman, Searles, and Hall (1989) failed to find differences in drinking behavior or alcohol-related symptoms between a group of high-risk subjects (those who had alcoholic fathers) and a group of non–high-risk subjects.

Although much evidence implicates genetic factors in alcoholism, the precise role these factors play in the etiology is still unknown. Available evidence suggests that they might be important as predisposing causes or they might contribute in combination with constitutional variables (such as susceptibility to the effects of alcohol) in the development of alcoholism. (So a constitutional predisposition to alcoholism could be acquired as well as inherited.) It is not known whether acquired biological conditions, such as endocrine or enzyme imbalances, increase an individual's vulnerability to alcoholism.

At present, it appears that the genetic interpretation of alcoholism remains an attractive hypothesis; however, additional research is needed. It is not likely that genetics alone will account for the full range of alcohol and drug problems. Social circumstances are still considered to be powerful forces in providing both the availability of and the motivation to use alcohol and other drugs. McGue (1998) has noted that the mechanisms of genetic influence should be viewed as compatible, rather than competitive, with psychological and social determinants of this disorder.

SUMMARY

ALCOHOL ABUSE AND DEPENDENCE

- Addictive behavior—such as alcohol or drug abuse—is one of the most widespread mental health problems facing society.
- Dependence occurs when an individual develops a tolerance for the substance or exhibits withdrawal symptoms when the substance is not available.
- Several psychotic reactions are associated with alcoholism, including alcohol withdrawal delirium and alcohol amnestic disorder.
- A number of causal factors are considered important in the development of alcoholism. Alcohol stimulates brain centers that produce euphoria—which then becomes a desired goal to attain. It is widely believed that genetic factors may play some role in susceptibility to alcoholism through such biological avenues as metabolic rate and sensitivity to alcohol.
- Psychosocial causal factors for alcoholism include failures in parental guidance, psychological vulnerability, stress, the desire for tension reduction, and crises in marital and other relationships. Although the existence of an "alcoholic personality" has been disavowed by most theorists, a variety of personality factors apparently play an important role in the development and expression of addictions.
- Sociocultural factors, such as different attitudes toward alcohol seen in different cultures, may also predispose individuals to alcoholism.
- Treatment approaches found to be effective for alcoholism include both medications and psychological treatments. Most treatment programs require abstinence; however, research has suggested that some alcoholics can learn to control their drinking while continuing to drink socially. This approach remains controversial. A source of help for some alcoholics is Alcoholics Anonymous; however, the extent of successful outcomes with this program has not been sufficiently studied. One of the major difficulties concerning response to treatment is relapse prevention.

DRUG ABUSE AND DEPENDENCE

- Drug-abuse disorders may involve physiological dependence on psychoactive drugs such as opiates or barbiturates; however, psychological dependence may also occur with any of the drugs that are commonly used today—for example, marijuana or cocaine.

- Possible causal factors for drug abuse problems include the influence of peer groups, the existence of a drug culture, and the availability of drugs as tension reducers or as pain relievers.
- Some recent research has explored a possible physiological basis for drug abuse. The discovery of endorphins, opiate-like substances produced by the brain and pituitary gland, has raised speculation that there may be a biochemical basis to drug addiction. The so-called pleasure pathway—the mesocorticolimbic dopamine pathway (MCLP)—has come under study in recent years as the possible brain site underlying addiction.
- The treatment of individuals who abuse drugs is generally difficult and often fails, for a number of reasons: The abuse may reflect a long history of psychological difficulties; interpersonal and marital distress may be involved; and financial and legal problems may be present. In addition, the addicted individual often denies that problems exist and is not motivated to work on them.
- Several biological and psychosocial approaches to the treatment of drug abuse have been developed. Medication to deal with withdrawal symptoms and treatment for malnutrition may be necessary. Psychological therapies, such as group therapy and behavioral interventions, may be effective with some drug abusers.
- Most drug abuse treatment programs show reasonably high success rates in the initial "curing" of addictive problems but lower success rates at follow-up. Recent research on relapse prevention has contributed new insights into the problems of self-control once addictive behaviors have been checked. Part of this approach involves making individuals aware of factors that can lead to relapse and preparing them to deal with such setbacks.

UNRESOLVED ISSUES: THE GENETICS OF ALCOHOLISM

- There is some evidence that genetic factors play a role in the development of alcoholism. However, more research is needed to clarify the precise role that genetics plays.

KEY TERMS

addictive behavior (p. 325)
psychoactive drugs (p. 325)
toxicity (p. 325)
psychoactive substance abuse (p. 325)
psychoactive substance dependence (p. 326)
tolerance (p. 326)
withdrawal symptoms (p. 326)
alcoholic (p. 327)
alcoholism (p. 327)
fetal alcohol syndrome (FAS) (p. 331)
mesocorticolimbic dopamine pathway (MCLP) (p. 334)
binge drinking (p. 337)
opium (p. 345)
morphine (p. 345)
heroin (p. 346)
endorphins (p. 348)
methadone (p. 349)
cocaine (p. 350)
amphetamine (p. 351)
barbiturates (p. 352)
hallucinogens (p. 352)
LSD (p. 352)
flashback (p. 353)
mescaline (p. 353)
psilocybin (p. 353)
marijuana (p. 353)
hashish (p. 353)

CHAPTER ELEVEN

Sexual Variants, Abuse, and Dysfunctions

George Widener, *The Shadow Gang.* Widener joined the U.S. Army at age 17 and traveled worldwide. After his military service ended, he studied engineering, but soon experienced emotional problems that were eventually diagnosed as depression. Widener believes that his depression arose in part as a reaction to a perceived lack of meaning in scientific endeavors. Turning to art, he taught himself to draw as a means of self-therapy.

LEARNING OBJECTIVES

After reading this chapter, you should be able to:

- Discuss several examples of sociocultural influences on sexual practices and cultural standards and values.
- Define, give examples of, and describe the clinical features of the following paraphilias: fetishism, transvestic fetishism, voyeurism, exhibitionism, sadism, and masochism.
- Describe the most effective treatments for paraphilias, and summarize their causal factors.
- Identify the clinical features of and describe the treatments for gender identity disorders (gender identity disorder of childhood and transsexualism).
- Discuss the controversies surrounding children's testimony regarding sexual abuse and adults' "recovered memories" of childhood sexual abuse.
- Review what is known about the frequency of different kinds of childhood sexual abuse and its perpetrators.
- List the major sexual dysfunctions, describe their general features, review etiological theories, and summarize the major approaches to treatment.

Loving, sexually satisfying relationships contribute a great deal to our happiness, but our understanding of them has advanced slowly, largely because they are so difficult for people to talk about openly and because funding for research is often hard to come by.

Loving, sexually satisfying relationships contribute a great deal to our happiness, and if we are not in such relationships, we are apt to spend a great deal of time, effort, and emotional energy looking for them. Sexuality is a central concern of our lives, influencing our choice of intimate partners and how happy we are with them and with ourselves.

In this chapter, we will first look at the psychological problems that make sexual fulfillment especially difficult for some people—the vast majority of them men—who develop unusual sexual interests that are difficult to satisfy in a socially acceptable manner. For example, exhibitionists are sexually aroused by showing their genitals to strangers, who are likely to be disgusted and frightened. Thus, exhibitionists' sexual expression often requires the discomfort of others, a situation that is not only socially unacceptable, but potentially traumatic to the unwilling viewer. Other sexual variants may be problematic primarily to the individual: Transsexualism, for example, is a disorder involving discomfort with one's biological sex and a strong desire to be of the opposite sex. Still other sexual variants, such as fetishism, in which sexual interest centers on some inanimate object or body part, involve behaviors that, although bizarre and unusual, do not clearly harm anyone. Perhaps no other topic covered in this book exposes the difficulties in defining boundaries between normality and psychopathology as clearly as variant sexuality does.

The second category of problems we will consider is sexual abuse, a pattern of pressured or forced sexual contact. Because sexual abuse has especially devastating social effects, we will devote a major section to this topic. During the past decade or so, there has been a tremendous increase in attention to the problem of sexual abuse of both children and adults (most adult victims being women). Research has addressed both the causes and consequences of this problem.

The third category of sexual difficulties examined in this chapter is sexual dysfunctions, which include problems that impede satisfactory performance of sexual acts. Premature ejaculation, for example, causes men to reach orgasm much earlier than they and their partners find satisfying. In addition, many women do not have orgasms during sexual intercourse, yet find intercourse enjoyable and satisfying. Another example of a sexual dysfunction is hypoactive sexual desire disorder, in which a man or woman shows little or no sexual drive or interest.

Much less is known about sexual deviations, abuse, and dysfunctions than is known about many of the other disorders we have considered thus far in this book, such as anxiety and depression. One major reason is the sex taboo. Although sex is an important concern for most people, many have difficulty talking about it openly. This makes it difficult to obtain knowledge about even the most basic facts, such as the frequency of various sexual practices, feelings, and attitudes. This is especially true when the relevant behaviors are socially ostracized; it is difficult both to ask people about such behaviors and to trust their answers. Another reason why sex research has progressed less rapidly is that many issues related to sexuality—including homosexuality, teenage sexuality, abortion, and childhood sexual abuse—are among the most divisive and controversial in our society, which can make it difficult to get funding for sex research. For example, although sex offenders are widely feared and millions of dollars are spent keeping convicted sex offenders behind bars every year, the National Institute of Mental Health spent only $1.2 million on sex offender research in 1993, compared with $125.3 million on depression (Goode, 1994).

Despite these significant barriers, we do know some things about sexual variants and dysfunctions. Clinical investigations have provided rich descriptions of many sexual variants. Etiological research on sexual dysfunctions and deviations, although in its infancy, has shown promise for some disorders, and we will examine these developments.

Before we turn to specific disorders, we will first consider sociocultural influences on sexual behavior and attitudes. Standards of sexual conduct vary across cultures and over time within a culture. Being aware of this variability at the outset will help you better appreciate the difficulties of classifying sexual practices as "abnormal" or "deviant."

SOCIOCULTURAL INFLUENCES ON SEXUAL PRACTICES AND STANDARDS

Although some aspects of sexuality and mating, such as men's greater emphasis on their partner's attractiveness, are universal across cultures (Buss, 1989), others are quite variable. For example, all known cultures have taboos against sex between close relatives, but attitudes toward premarital sex vary considerably (Frayser, 1985). Ideas about acceptable sexual behavior also change over time. Less than 100 years ago, for example, sexual modesty dictated that women's arms and legs were always hidden in public. Today, actors are shown nude in movies and sometimes even on television.

Despite the substantial variability in sexual attitudes and behavior in different times and places, many people typically behave as if the sexual standards of their time and place are obviously correct, and they are intolerant of sexual nonconformity. Sexual nonconformists are often considered evil or sick. And such judgments are not always arbitrary. There has probably never existed a society in which Jeffrey Dahmer, who was sexually aroused by killing men, then having sex with them, storing their corpses, and sometimes eating them, would be considered psychologically normal. Nevertheless, it is useful to be aware of historical and cultural influences on sexuality. When the expression or the acceptance of a certain behavior varies considerably across eras and cultures, we should at least pause to consider whether our own stance is the most appropriate one. Because the influences of time and place are so important in shaping sexual behavior and attitudes, we begin by exploring three cases that illustrate how opinions about "acceptable" and "normal" sexual behavior may change dramatically over time or differ dramatically from one culture to another.

Case 1: Degeneracy and Abstinence Theory

During the 1750s, the Swiss physician Simon Tissot developed *degeneracy theory,* the central belief of which was that semen is necessary for physical and sexual vigor in men and for masculine characteristics such as beard growth (Money, 1985, 1986). He based this theory on observations of human eunuchs and castrated animals. Of course, we now know that the loss of the male hormone testosterone, and not of semen, is responsible for relevant characteristics of eunuchs and castrated animals. Based on his theory, however, Tissot asserted that two practices were especially harmful: masturbation and patronizing prostitutes. Both of these practices not only wasted the vital fluid, semen, but also (in his view) overstimulated and exhausted the nervous system. Tissot also recommended that married people engage solely in procreative sex to avoid the waste of semen.

A descendant of degeneracy theory, *abstinence theory,* was advocated in the United States during the 1830s by the Reverend Sylvester Graham (Money, 1985, 1986). The three cornerstones of his crusade for public health were healthy food (Graham crackers were named for him), physical fitness, and sexual abstinence. Graham's most famous successor, Dr. John Harvey Kellogg, began practicing medicine in the 1870s. He ardently disapproved of masturbation and urged parents to be wary of signs that their children were indulging in it. He published a paper on the 39 signs of "the secret vice," which included, among others, weakness, early symptoms of consumption (TB), sudden change in disposition, lassitude, dullness of the eyes, premature and defective development, sleeplessness, fickleness, untrustworthiness, bashfulness, love of solitude, unnatural boldness, mock piety, and round shoulders. Kellogg, like Graham, was especially concerned with dietary health. He urged people to eat more cereals and nuts and less meat, because he believed that eating meat increased sexual desire. Thus, Kellogg's cornflakes were invented "almost literally, as anti-masturbation food" (Money, 1986, p. 186). As a physician, Kellogg was professionally admired and publicly influential, earning a fortune publishing books discouraging masturbation. Kellogg's recommended treatments for "the secret vice" were quite extreme. For example, he advocated that especially persistent masturbation in boys be treated by sewing the foreskin with silver wire, or as a last resort, circumcision without anesthesia. Persistent female masturbation was to be treated by burning the clitoris with carbolic acid.

Given the influence of physicians like Kellogg, it should perhaps come as no surprise that many people believed that masturbation caused insanity (Hare, 1962). This hypothesis started with the anonymous publication in the early eighteenth century in London of a book entitled *Onania, or the Heinous Sin of Self-Pollution*. It asserted that masturbation was a common cause of insanity. This idea probably arose from observations that many patients in mental asylums masturbated openly (unlike sane people, who are more likely to do it in private) and that the age at which masturbation tends to begin (at puberty, in early adolescence) precedes by several years the age when the first signs of insanity often begin (late adolescence and young adulthood) (Abramson & Seligman, 1977). The idea that masturbation may cause insanity appeared in some psychiatry textbooks as late as the 1940s.

Although abstinence theory and associated attitudes seem highly puritanical by today's standards, they have had a long-lasting influence on attitudes toward sex in American and other Western cultures. It was not until 1972 that the American Medical Association declared: "Masturbation is a normal part of adolescent sexual development and requires no medical management" (American Medical Association Committee on Human Sexuality, 1972, p. 40). Around the same time, the Boy Scout manual dropped its antimasturbation warnings. Nonetheless, in 1994, Jocelyn Elders was fired as U.S. Surgeon General for suggesting publicly that sex education courses should include discussion of masturbation.

Case 2: Ritualized Homosexuality in Melanesia

Melanesia is a group of islands in the South Pacific that has been intensively studied by anthropologists, who have uncovered cultural influences on sexuality there that are unlike any known in the West. Between 10 and 20 percent of Melanesian societies practice a form of homosexuality within the context of male initiation rituals that all male members of society must experience. The best studied society has been the Sambia of Papua New Guinea (Herdt & Stoller, 1990). Two beliefs related to Sambian sexual practices are *semen conservation* and *female pollution*. Like Tissot, the Sambians believe that semen is important for many things, including physical growth, strength, and spirituality. Furthermore, they believe that it takes many inseminations (and much semen) to impregnate a woman. Finally, they believe that semen cannot easily be replenished by the body and so must be conserved or obtained elsewhere. The female pollution doctrine refers to the belief that the female body is unhealthy to males, primarily due to menstrual fluids. At menarche, Sambian women are secretly initiated in the menstrual hut, which is forbidden to all males.

In order to obtain or maintain adequate amounts of semen, young Sambian males practice semen exchange with each other. Beginning as boys, they learn to practice fellatio (oral sex) in order to ingest semen. At first, they take only the oral role, but after puberty they can take the penetrative role, inseminating younger boys. Ritualized homosexuality among the Sambian men is seen as an exchange of sexual pleasure for vital semen. (It is interesting that although both the Sambians and Victorian-era Americans believed in semen conservation, their solutions to the problem were radically different.) When Sambian males are well past puberty, they begin the transition to heterosexuality. At this time, the female body is thought to be less dangerous because the males have ingested protective semen over the previous years. For a time, they have sex with women and still participate in fellatio with younger boys, but homosexual behavior stops after the birth of a man's first child. Most of the Sambian men make the transition to exclusive adult heterosexuality without problems. Those few who do not are (somewhat ironically) considered misfits.

In summary, ritualized homosexuality among the Melanesians is a striking example of the influence of culture on sexual attitudes and behavior. A Melanesian adolescent who refused to practice homosexuality would be viewed as abnormal, and such adolescents are apparently absent or rare. Homosexuality among the Sambians is not

HIGHLIGHT 11.1

Homosexuality as a Normal Sexual Variant

Although its current status as a normal sexual variant might suggest that no further mention of homosexuality is warranted in an abnormal psychology textbook, a more extensive discussion is given here for two reasons: First, American attitudes toward homosexuality remain highly ambivalent, at least in part because of uncertainty about the causes and correlates of sexual orientation (Schmalz, 1993); so it is important to clarify why it should not be considered pathological. Second, although homosexuality is not pathological, it is sometimes related to a condition that remains in DSM-IV-TR—gender identity disorder (discussed on pp. 371–374). Thus, some findings about homosexuality may apply to gender identity disorder as well.

How Common Is Homosexuality?

Large, well-done studies from the United States (Billy et al., 1993; Michael et al., 1994), France (ACSF Investigators, 1992), and England (Johnson et al., 1992) suggest that the rate of adult homosexual behavior in the overall population is between 2 and 6 percent, with the rate of exclusive male homosexuality between 1 and 2 percent. The analogous rates for female homosexuality are approximately half of those for males. Moreover, approximately 20 percent of men and women report having had at least one instance of sexual attraction to a member of their own sex after the age of 15 (Sell, Wypij, & Wells, 1995). Some people are bisexual, although this orientation may be even less common than exclusive homosexuality, especially since the onset of the AIDS epidemic in the mid-1980s (Masters, Johnson, & Kolodny, 1992). For many bisexuals, their homosexuality comes after they have established a heterosexual orientation (Weinberg, Williams, & Pryor, 1994).

What Causes Some People to Become Homosexual and Others Heterosexual?

One important study found no solid support for the psychoanalytic hypothesis that homosexuality is associated with dysfunctional parent-child relationships (Bell, Weinberg, & Hammersmith, 1981). The most striking finding of this study was that, on average, homosexual adults recalled substantially more sex-atypical behavior in their childhoods than did heterosexual adults. For example, gay men were much more likely

the same as homosexuality in contemporary United States, with the possible exception of those Sambian men who have difficulty making the heterosexual transition.

Case 3: Homosexuality and American Psychiatry

During the past half-century, the status of homosexuality has changed enormously both within psychiatry and psychology and for society in general. In the not-too-distant past, homosexuality was a taboo topic. Now, movies, talk shows, and TV sitcoms and dramas address the topic explicitly by including gay men and lesbians in leading roles. As we shall see, developments in psychiatry and psychology have played an important role in these changes.

Homosexuality as Sickness Reading the medical and psychological literature on homosexuality written before 1970 can be a jarring experience. Prior to that time, the predominant view was that homosexual people were mentally ill—and this was a relatively tolerant view compared with some earlier views that homosexuals were criminals in need of incarceration (Bayer, 1981). For example, in the sixteenth century, King Henry VIII of England declared "the detestable and abominable vice of buggery [anal sex]" a felony punishable by death, and it was not until 1861 that the maximum penalty was reduced to 10 years' imprisonment. Similarly, in the United States, laws were very repressive until recently, and even now homosexual behavior continues to be a criminal offense in some states.

Contrary to prevailing views in the late nineteenth and early twentieth centuries, several prominent theorists suggested that homosexuality was consistent with psychological normality. So although some psychoanalysts later became the most vigorous proponents of the disease position, Freud's own attitude toward homosexual people was remarkably progressive for the time and is well expressed in his touching "Letter to an American Mother" (1935):

than heterosexual men to recall playing with girls, cross-dressing, shunning sports, and wishing they were girls. Lesbians were also much more likely than heterosexual women to recall enjoying sports and wishing they were boys (see also Bailey & Zucker, 1995; Green, 1987). Nevertheless, it should be emphasized that many gay men and lesbians appear to have been sex-typical as children.

Observations that homosexual people have sexual orientations and other behaviors more typical of the opposite sex are consistent with one highly influential etiological hypothesis of sexual orientation—that homosexual people may have been subjected to early, possibly prenatal, hormonal influences more typical of those usually affecting the opposite sex (e.g., LeVay, 1991, 1993). Genetic factors have also been implicated in both male (Bailey & Pillard, 1991; Hamer et al., 1993) and female (Bailey et al., 1993) sexual orientation. For example, concordance rates for homosexuality were 52 percent for male monozygotic twins, compared with 22 percent for male dizygotic twins; the comparable figures for female homosexuality were 48 and 16 percent. These findings are consistent with a substantial role for heredity (Bailey & Pillard, 1991). But because approximately half of the monozygotic twin pairs in the genetic studies were discordant for sexual orientation, environmental factors are clearly also important (Bailey et al., 1993). The nature of the environmental influences is uncertain; these factors could be either biological (e.g., prenatal stress) or social (e.g., parental child-rearing philosophy). One clearly erroneous hypothesis about environmental influences is that homosexual adults seduce and "recruit" younger individuals to homosexuality (Bell et al., 1981).

Is Homosexuality a Sign of Mental Disturbance?

Nonpatient samples of homosexual and heterosexual subjects typically show little, if any, difference in psychological adjustment (Gagnon & Simon, 1973; Siegelman, 1979). There is some evidence that homosexual people do have higher rates of alcoholism and depression (Mosbascher, 1988; Pillard, 1988). However, it is likely that these elevated rates of alcoholism and depression are a consequence of the prejudice and stigmatization that these individuals often experience rather than being a consequence of having a homosexual orientation per se.

In summary, most research suggests that homosexuality is compatible with psychological normality. The exact causes of sexual orientation remain unclear, although recent evidence has increasingly implicated genetic and other biological variables. Researchers are actively pursuing these questions. ■

Dear Mrs....

I gather from your letter that your son is a homosexual. I am most impressed by the fact that you do not mention this term yourself in your information about him. May I question you, why you avoid it? Homosexuality is assuredly no advantage, but it is nothing to be ashamed of, no vice, no degradation, it cannot be classified as an illness; we consider it to be a variation of the sexual function produced by a certain arrest of sexual development. Many highly respectable individuals of ancient and modern times have been homosexuals, several of the greatest men among them (Plato, Michelangelo, Leonardo da Vinci, etc.). It is a great injustice to persecute homosexuality as a crime, and cruelty too....

By asking me if I can help, you mean, I suppose, if I can abolish homosexuality and make normal heterosexuality take its place. The answer is, in a general way, we cannot promise to achieve it....

Sincerely yours with kind wishes,

Freud

By the 1940s, psychoanalysts began to take a more pessimistic view of the mental health of homosexual people, viewing homosexuality as an escape from heterosexuality and therefore incompatible with mental health (e.g., Rado, 1962). They stressed the role of "highly pathologic parent-child relationships" (e.g., Bieber et al., 1962). In the case of male homosexuality, they believed domineering, emotionally smothering mothers and detached, hostile fathers prevented boys from identifying closely with their fathers, a step they hypothesized was necessary to normal psychological development. It may have been important that these psychoanalysts based their opinions primarily on their experiences seeing gay men in psychoanalytic therapy, who are likely to be more psychologically troubled than other gay men.

Around 1950, the view of homosexuality as sickness began to be challenged. Scientific blows to the pathology position included Alfred Kinsey's finding that homosexual behavior was much more common than had been previously believed, although we now know that his estimates

Despite the fact that homosexuality is considered a normal sexual variation, compatible with psychological normality, discrimination and violence against homosexuals remains a very significant problem today.

were too high (Kinsey, Pomeroy, & Martin, 1948; Kinsey et al., 1953). Perhaps the most influential studies were performed by Evelyn Hooker (1957). She demonstrated that trained psychologists could not distinguish the psychological test results of homosexual and heterosexual subjects.

Gay men and lesbians also began to challenge psychiatric orthodoxy. Beginning in the 1950s, homophile organizations encouraged frank discussion of the status of homosexuality and spawned committed opponents of the homosexuality-as-illness position. The 1960s saw the birth of the radical gay liberation movement, which took the more uncompromising stance that "gay is good." The decade closed with the famous Stonewall riot in New York City, sparked by police mistreatment of gay men, which provided a clear signal that homosexual people would no longer passively accept their status as second-class citizens. By the 1970s, openly gay psychiatrists and psychologists were working from within the mental health profession to change the orthodox position. Specifically, they wished to have homosexuality removed from the *Diagnostic and Statistical Manual of Psychiatric Disorders* (DSM-II).

In 1973, after acrimonious debate, the Board of Trustees of the American Psychiatric Association (APA) voted to remove homosexuality from DSM-II (APA, 1968). This move was opposed by some APA members, who argued that the board abandoned scientific principles because of political pressure. They prevailed on the APA to put the matter before its membership in a referendum, and in 1974 the membership voted 5,854 to 3,810, to remove homosexuality from DSM-II. This episode was both a milestone for gay rights and an embarrassment for psychiatry, and more generally, for advocates of psychodiagnosis. The spectacle of the psychiatric nomenclature being modified on the basis of a vote rather than the scientific consensus of experts appeared to confirm what psychodiagnosis' harshest critics, such as Thomas Szasz (1974), had been saying, that the label "mental illness" merely reflects the values of mental health professionals.

The authors of this book believe the APA made a correct decision in removing homosexuality from DSM-II, because the vast majority of evidence shows that homosexuality is compatible with psychological normality. Furthermore, the resolution of this issue by vote is not problematic. The classification of any behavior as psychopathology necessitates a value judgment that the behavior is undesirable. This value judgment is usually implicit and unchallenged—for example, few people, even among schizophrenic patients themselves, deny the impairment and pain caused by schizophrenia. Challenges by gay and lesbian people forced mental health professionals to confront the values question explicitly, and they made the correct determination that homosexuality is not a psychological disorder.

IN REVIEW

- What does each of the three examples of sociocultural influences on sexual practices and standards reveal about cultural differences and historical changes in what is considered acceptable and normal sexual behavior?
- How has the psychiatric view of homosexuality changed over time? Identify a few key historical events that propelled this change.

SEXUAL AND GENDER VARIANTS

We now turn to the problematic sexual variants included in DSM-IV-TR. There are two general categories: paraphilias and gender identity disorders.

The Paraphilias

The **paraphilias** are a group of persistent sexual behavior patterns in which unusual objects, rituals, or situations are required for full sexual satisfaction. Although mild forms of these behaviors probably have occurred in the lives of many normal people, a paraphilic person is distinguished by the insistence and relative exclusivity with which his or her sexuality focuses on the acts or objects in question—without which orgasm is often impossible. Paraphilias also frequently have a compulsive quality, with some paraphilic individuals requiring orgasmic release as often as four to ten times per day (Money, 1986, p. 133). Paraphilic individuals may or may not have persistent desires to change their sexual preferences. Some paraphilias require a partner, and a fortunate paraphilic individual may discover another person with a reciprocal paraphilia—as in sexual sadomasochism (discussed below)—which may then lead to a lasting, although by conventional standards somewhat bizarre, love affair. Fairly common is a situation in which a sexually normal person becomes unwittingly involved in a paraphilic person's ritualized sexual program, only gradually discovering that he or she is a mere accessory, a sort of stage prop, in the latter's sexual drama. Because nearly all paraphilic persons are male, we use masculine pronouns to refer to them.

DSM-IV-TR recognizes eight specific paraphilias: (1) fetishism, (2) transvestic fetishism, (3) voyeurism, (4) exhibitionism, (5) sexual sadism, (6) sexual masochism, (7) pedophilia, and (8) frotteurism (rubbing against a nonconsenting person). An additional category, paraphilias not otherwise specified, includes several rarer disorders such as telephone scatologia (obscene phone calls), necrophilia (sexual desire for corpses), and coprophilia (sexual arousal to feces). Of the DSM-specified paraphilias, we will discuss all but frotteurism, a category that is relatively new and not yet satisfactorily researched. Our discussion of pedophilia is postponed, however, until the later section on sexual abuse.

Fetishism In **fetishism,** sexual interest typically centers on some inanimate object, such as an article of clothing, or some nonsexual part of the body. As is generally true for the paraphilias, males are most commonly involved in cases of fetishism; reported cases of female fetishists are extremely rare (Mason, 1997). The range of fetishistic objects includes hair, ears, hands, underclothing, shoes, and perfume. The mode of using these objects to achieve sexual excitation and gratification varies considerably, but it commonly involves kissing, fondling, tasting, or smelling the objects. Fetishism does not normally interfere with the rights of others, except in an incidental way such as asking the partner to wear the object during sexual encounters. Many men have a strong sexual fascination for paraphernalia such as brassieres, garter belts, hose, and high heels. Although such men do not typically meet diagnostic criteria for fetishism, because the paraphernalia are not necessary or strongly preferred for sexual arousal (as is required to be diagnosed as having a fetish), they do illustrate the high frequency of fetish-like preferences among men.

To obtain the required object, a fetishistic person may commit burglary, theft, or even assault. Probably the articles most commonly stolen by fetishistic individuals are women's undergarments. In many cases, the excitement and suspense of the criminal act itself typically reinforce the sexual stimulation and sometimes actually constitute the fetish—the stolen article being of little importance. For example, one adolescent admitted entering many homes and said that the entering itself usually sufficed to induce an orgasm.

Frequently, fetishistic behavior consists of masturbation in association with a fetishistic object. One pattern of fetishism is illustrated by the case of a man whose fetish was women's shoes and legs:

> The fetishist in this case was arrested several times for loitering in public places, such as railroad stations and libraries, watching women's legs. Finally he chanced on a novel solution to his problem. Posing as an agent for a hosiery firm, he rented a large room, advertised for models, and took motion pictures of a number of women walking and seated with their legs displayed to best advantage. He then used these pictures to achieve sexual satisfaction through masturbation and found that they continued to be adequate for the purpose. (Adapted from Grant, 1953)

Most theories of the etiology of fetishism emphasize the importance of classical conditioning. It is not difficult to imagine how women's underwear, or their hair, legs,

paraphilias A group of persistent sexual behavior patterns in which unusual objects, rituals, or situations are required for full sexual satisfaction.

fetishism Sexual variant in which sexual interest centers on some inanimate object or nonsexual part of the body.

perfume, etc., might become eroticized by a close association with sex and the female body. It is important to emphasize, however, that differential experiences alone do not seem sufficient to explain why some men develop fetishes. Although perhaps most high-heeled shoe fetishists, for example, had a particularly arousing early sexual experience with a woman wearing high-heeled shoes, most men who had such an experience do not develop fetishes. It seems likely that this is because there are individual differences in conditionability of sexual responses, and those high in sexual conditionability are especially prone to developing one or more fetishes. We will later return to the role of conditioning in the development of paraphilias, in general.

Transvestic Fetishism The achievement of sexual arousal and satisfaction by "cross-dressing"—that is, dressing as a member of the opposite sex—is called **transvestic fetishism.** Typically, the onset of transvestism is during adolescence and involves masturbation while wearing female clothing or undergarments. Although some gay men dress "in drag" on occasion, they do not typically do this for sexual pleasure and hence are not transvestic fetishists. The vast majority of transvestites are heterosexual (Talamini, 1982). Buckner (1970) formulated a description of the "ordinary" male transvestite from a survey of 262 transvestites conducted by the magazine *Transvestia:*

> He is probably married (about two-thirds are); if he is married, he probably has children (about two-thirds do). Almost all of these transvestites said they were exclusively heterosexual—in fact, the rate of "homosexuality" was less than the average for the entire population. The transvestic behavior generally consists of privately dressing in the clothes of a woman, at home, in secret.... The transvestite generally does not run into trouble with the law. His cross-dressing causes difficulties for very few people besides himself and his wife. (p. 381)

This clinical picture has not changed since Buckner's report; nor, unfortunately, has the state of knowledge about the etiology of this disorder, about which very little is known (Zucker & Blanchard, 1997).

Case Study **A Transvestite's Dilemma** • Mr. A., a 65-year-old security guard, formerly a fishing-boat captain, is distressed about his wife's objections to his wearing a nightgown at home in the evening, now that his youngest child has left home. His appearance and demeanor, except when he is dressing in women's clothes, are always appropriately masculine, and he is exclusively heterosexual. Occasionally, over the past 5 years, he has worn an inconspicuous item of female clothing even when dressed as a man, sometimes a pair of panties, sometimes an ambiguous pinkie ring. He always carries a photograph of himself dressed as a woman.

His first recollection of an interest in female clothing was putting on his sister's bloomers at age 12, an act accompanied by sexual excitement. He continued periodically to put on women's underpants—an activity that invariably resulted in an erection, sometimes a spontaneous emission, sometimes masturbation, but never accompanied by fantasy. Although he occasionally wished to be a girl, he never fantasized himself as one. He was competitive and aggressive with other boys and always acted "masculine." During his single years he was always attracted to girls, but was shy about sex....

His involvement with female clothes was of the same intensity even after his marriage. Beginning at age 45, after a chance exposure to a magazine called *Transvestia,* he began to increase his cross-dressing activity. He learned there were other men like himself, and he became more and more preoccupied with female clothing in fantasy and progressed to periodically dressing completely as a woman. More recently he has become involved in a transvestite network, writing to other transvestites contacted through the magazine and occasionally attending transvestite parties. Cross-dressing at these parties has been the only time that he has cross-dressed outside his home.

Although still committed to his marriage, sex with his wife has dwindled over the past 20 years as his waking thoughts and activities have become increasingly centered on cross-dressing.... He always has an increased urge to dress as a woman when under stress; it has a tranquilizing effect.... For years his children served as a barrier to his giving free rein to his impulses. Following his retirement from fishing, and in the absence of his children, he finds himself more drawn to cross-dressing, more in conflict with his wife, and more depressed. (From Spitzer et al., 1994.)

As we have indicated, transvestic fetishism may complicate a relationship. However, like other kinds of fetishism, it causes overt harm to others only when accompanied by illegal acts such as theft or destruction of property. This is not always the case with the other paraphilias, many of which do contain a definite element of injury or significant risk of injury—physical or psychological—to one or more of the parties involved in a sexual encounter. Typically, these practices have strong legal sanctions against them. We will consider only the most common forms of these paraphilias: voyeurism, exhibitionism, sadism, and masochism.

transvestic fetishism Achievement of sexual arousal and satisfaction by dressing as a member of the opposite sex.

Studies have shown that men who cross-dress may actually feel less anxiety and shyness when in their female roles. Although a transvestic man may therefore enjoy venturing into the social roles of the other sex, he may also be markedly distressed by urges to do so, and, if married, his transvestism may also cause difficulties for his wife. Some cross-dressers seek out others of their kind to deal with their special problems in support groups like the one shown.

Voyeurism The synonymous terms **voyeurism** and *scotophilia* refer to the achievement of sexual pleasure through clandestine peeping. Voyeurism occurs as a sexual offense primarily among young men. These "Peeping Toms," as they are commonly called, usually observe females who are undressing or couples engaging in sexual relations. Frequently, they masturbate during their peeping activity.

How do young men develop this pattern? First, viewing the body of an attractive female seems to be quite stimulating sexually for many, if not most, men. In addition, the privacy and mystery that have traditionally surrounded sexual activities tend to increase curiosity about them. Second, if a young man with such curiosity feels shy and inadequate in his relations with the other sex, it is not too surprising for him to accept the substitute of voyeurism. In this way, he satisfies his curiosity and to some extent meets his sexual needs without the trauma of actually approaching a female, and thus without the rejection and lowered self-status that such an approach might bring. In fact, voyeuristic activities often provide important compensatory feelings of power and secret domination over an unsuspecting victim, which may contribute to the maintenance of this pattern. A voyeur does not normally seek sexual activity with those he observes. If a voyeur manages to find a wife in spite of his interpersonal difficulties, as many do, he is rarely well-adjusted sexually in his relationship with his wife, as the following case illustrates.

Case Study **A Peeping Tom** • A young married college student had an attic apartment that was extremely hot during the summer months. To enable him to attend school, his wife worked; she came home at night tired and irritable and not in the mood for sexual relations. In addition, "the damned springs in the bed squeaked." In order "to obtain some sexual gratification" the student would peer through his binoculars at the room next door and occasionally saw another young couple there engaged in erotic activities. This stimulated him greatly, and he thus decided to extend his peeping to a sorority house. During his second venture, however, he was reported and apprehended by the police. This offender was quite immature for his age, rather puritanical in his attitude toward masturbation, and prone to indulge in rich but immature sexual fantasies.

voyeurism Achievement of sexual pleasure through clandestine "peeping," usually watching females undressing and/or couples engaging in sexual activities.

Exhibitionism The term **exhibitionism** (*indecent exposure* in legal terms) describes the intentional exposure of the genitals to others (generally strangers) in inappropriate circumstances and without their consent. The exposure may take place in some secluded location, such as a park, or in a more public place, such as a department store, church, theater, or bus. In cities, an exhibitionist often drives by schools or bus stops, exhibits himself while in the car, and then drives rapidly away. In many instances, the exposure is repeated under fairly constant conditions, such as only in churches or buses, or in the same general vicinity and at the same time of day. In one case, a young man exhibited himself only at the top of an escalator in a large department store. The type of victim is usually also fairly consistent for an individual exhibitionist. For a male offender, the typical victim is ordinarily a young or middle-aged female who is not known to the offender, though children and adolescents may also be targeted disproportionately (Murphy, 1997). Exhibitionism is the most common sexual offense reported to the police in the United States, Canada, and Europe, accounting for about one-third of all sexual offenses (Murphy, 1997). According to some estimates as many as 20 percent of women may have been the target of either exhibitionism or voyeurism (Kaplan & Krueger, 1997; Meyer, 1995).

In some instances, exposure of the genitals is accompanied by suggestive gestures or masturbation, but more often there is only exposure. A significant minority of exhibitionists have also committed aggressive acts, sometimes including coercive sex crimes against adults or children (Murphy, 1997). Indeed, some research indicates that there may be a subclass of exhibitionists who may best be considered as having antisocial personality disorder, as described in Chapter 9 (Forgac & Michaels, 1982; Kaplan & Krueger, 1997).

It should be remembered that an exhibitionistic act takes place without the viewer's consent and may be emotionally upsetting, as is indeed the perpetrator's intent. This intrusive quality of the act, together with its explicit violation of propriety norms respecting "private parts," assures condemnation. Thus, society considers exhibitionism a criminal offense.

exhibitionism Intentional exposure of the genitals to others (generally strangers) in inappropriate circumstances and without their consent.

sadism Achievement of sexual stimulation and gratification by inflicting physical or psychic pain or humiliation on a sexual partner.

Sadism The term **sadism** is derived from the name of the Marquis de Sade (1740–1814), who for sexual purposes inflicted such cruelty on his victims that he was eventually committed as insane. Although the term's meaning has broadened to denote cruelty in general, we will use it in its restricted sense to mean the achievement of sexual stimulation and gratification by inflicting physical or psychic pain or humiliation on a sexual partner. A closely related pattern is the practice of "bondage and discipline" (B & D), which may include tying a person up, hitting or spanking, and so on, to enhance sexual excitement. These elements of a sadist's erotic interest suggest a psychological association with rape (Marshall & Barbaree, 1990a), discussed in a later section. The arousal of sadistic individuals thus heavily depends on the infliction of suffering, or the appearance of it, on their partners.

The pain may be inflicted by such means as whipping, biting, or pinching; the act may vary in intensity, from fantasy to severe mutilation and even murder. Mild degrees of sadism (and masochism, discussed below) are involved in the sexual foreplay customs of many cultures, and some couples in our own society—both heterosexual and homosexual—regularly engage in such practices. It is important to distinguish transient or occasional interest in sadomasochistic practices from sadism as a paraphilia. Surveys have found that perhaps 5 to 10 percent of men and women enjoy sadistic or masochistic activities occasionally (Baumeister & Butler, 1997). Paraphilic sadism and masochism, in which sadomasochistic activities are the preferred or exclusive means to sexual gratification, appear to be rare and, like all paraphilias, occur almost exclusively in men.

In some cases, sadistic activities lead up to or terminate in actual sexual relations; in others, full sexual gratification is obtained from the sadistic practice alone. A sadist, for example, may slash a woman with a razor or stick her with a needle, experiencing an orgasm in the process. The peculiar and extreme associations that may occur are shown by the case of a young man who entered a strange woman's apartment, held a chloroformed rag to her face until she lost consciousness, and branded her on the thigh with a hot iron. She was not molested in any other way.

On the other hand, many serial killers are also sexual sadists. One study characterized 20 sexually sadistic serial killers, responsible for 149 murders throughout the United States and Canada (Warren, Dietz, & Hazelwood, 1996). Most were white males in their late twenties or early thirties. Their murders were remarkably consistent over time, reflecting sexual arousal to the pain, fear, and panic of their victims. Choreographed assaults allowed them to carefully control their victims' deaths. Some of the men reported that the God-like sense of being in control of the life and death of another human being was especially exhilarating. The sample exhibited a number of other paraphilias, including fetishism and exhibitionism. Eighty-five percent of the sample reported consistent violent sexual fantasies, and 75 percent collected materials of a violent theme, including videotapes or pictures of their own sadistic acts or sexually sadistic pornography. The majority of the men also exhibited extensive antisocial behavior, suggesting that a lack of conscience contributed to their homicidal acts.

Notorious serial killers include Ted Bundy, who was executed in 1989. Bundy confessed to the murder of over 30 young women, almost all of whom fit a target type: women with long hair parted in the middle. Bundy admitted that he used his victims to re-create for him the covers of detective magazines or scenes from "slasher movies." Although many sadists have had chaotic childhoods, Bundy and some others have come from middle-class families and loving parents. Unfortunately, the causal factors involved in these extreme cases of sadism are not well understood.

Masochism The term **masochism** is derived from the name of the Austrian novelist Leopold V. Sacher-Masoch (1836–1895), whose fictional characters dwelt lovingly on the sexual pleasure of pain. As in the case of the term *sadism,* the meaning of *masochism* has been broadened beyond sexual connotations, so that it includes deriving pleasure from self-denial, from physical suffering as an act of atonement, such as that of religious flagellants, and from hardship and suffering in general. Here we restrict discussion to the sexual aspects of masochistic behavior.

In masochism, a person achieves sexual stimulation and gratification from the experience of pain and degradation in relating to a lover. Interpersonal masochistic activities require the participation of at least two people—one superior "disciplinarian" and one obedient "slave." Such arrangements are not uncommon in either heterosexual or homosexual relationships. Masochists do not usually want, or cooperate with, true sexual sadists, but with individuals willing to hurt or humiliate them within limits they set. Masochism appears to be much more common than sadism (Baumeister & Butler, 1997). Sadomasochistic activities, including bondage and discipline, are often performed communally, within "dungeons" in major cities. Such activities might involve men being bound and whipped by women called *dominatrixes* wearing tight leather or rubber outfits. These activities are playful rather than frightening, at least to the participants.

One particularly dangerous form of masochism, called *autoerotic asphyxia,* involves self-strangulation to the point of oxygen deprivation. Coroners in most major U.S. cities are familiar with cases in which the deceased is found hanged next to masochistic pornographic literature or other sexual paraphernalia. Accidental deaths attributable to this practice have been estimated to range between 250 and 1000 per year in the United States (Uva, 1995).

Case Study **Autoerotic Asphyxia** • A woman heard a man shouting for help and went to his apartment door. Calling through the door, she asked the man inside if he needed help.

"Yes," he said. "Break the door down."...

The woman returned with her two sons, who broke into the apartment. They found the man lying on the floor, his hands tied behind him, his legs bent back, and his ankles secured to his hands. A mop handle had been placed behind his knees. He was visibly distraught, sweating, and short of breath, and his hands were turning blue. He had defecated and urinated in his trousers. In his kitchen the woman found a knife and freed him.

When police officers arrived and questioned the man, he stated that he had returned home that afternoon, fallen asleep on his couch, and awakened an hour later only to find himself hopelessly bound. The officers noted that the apartment door had been locked when the neighbors broke in. The man continued his story.... When the officers filed their report, they noted that "this could possibly be a sexual deviation act." Interviewed the next day, the man confessed to binding himself in the position in which he was found.

A month later, the police were called back to the same man's apartment. A building manager had discovered him face down on the floor in his apartment. A paper bag covered his head like a hood. When the police arrived, the man was breathing rapidly with a satin cloth stuffed in his mouth. Rope was stretched around his head and mouth and wrapped his chest and waist....

Two years passed, and the man moved on to another job. He failed to appear for work one Monday morning. A fellow employee found him dead in his apartment. During their investigation, police were able to reconstruct the man's final minutes. On the preceding Friday, he had bound himself in the following manner: sitting on his bed and crossing his ankles, left over right, he had bound them together with twine. Fastening a tie around his neck, he then secured the tie to an 86-inch pole behind his back. Aligning the pole with his left side, the upper end crossing the front of his left shoulder, he placed his hands behind his bent legs and there, leaving his wrists 4 inches apart, secured them with a length of rope. He then tied the rope that secured his wrists to the

masochism Achievement of sexual stimulation and gratification from experiencing pain or degradation in relating to a lover.

pole and to an electric cord girdling his waist. Thus bound, he lay on his bed on his back and stretched his legs. By thus applying pressure to the pole, still secured to the tie around his neck, he strangled himself. In order to save himself, he might have rolled over onto his side and drawn up his legs; but the upper end of the pole pressed against the wall. He was locked into place. (From Spitzer et al., 1994.)

Men's vulnerability to paraphilias such as fetishism may be a result of their greater dependency on physical stimuli. This, in turn, makes them more likely to form sexual associations to nonsexual stimuli, such as women's legs or high-heeled shoes, quite possibly through a process of classical conditioning.

Causal Factors and Treatments for Paraphilias

Many paraphilic individuals have explanations for their unusual sexual preferences. For example, an amputee paraphilic (whose preference is a partner with a missing limb) recalled that his fascination with female amputees originated during adolescence. He was neglected emotionally by his cold family but heard a family member express sympathetic feelings for an amputee. He developed the wish that he would become an amputee and thus earn their sympathy. This story raises many questions. Emotionally cold families are not uncommon, and sympathy for amputees is nearly universal. Surely, not every male in a cold family who detects sympathy for amputees develops an amputee paraphilia. Such stories do not necessarily have any validity because people are often unaware of the forces that shape them (Nisbett & Wilson, 1977).

At least two facts about paraphilias are likely to be etiologically important. First, as we have already noted, almost all paraphiliacs are male. Second, people with paraphilias often have more than one (American Psychiatric Association, 1994; Maletzky, 1998). For example, the corpses of men who died accidentally in the course of autoerotic asphyxia are partially or fully cross-dressed in 25 to 33 percent of cases (Blanchard & Hucker, 1991). There is no obvious reason for the association between masochism and transvestism. Why should it be so?

Money (1986) has suggested that men's vulnerability to paraphilias is closely linked to their greater dependency on visual sexual imagery. Perhaps sexual arousal in men depends on physical stimulus features to a greater degree than it does in women, whose arousal may depend more on emotional context, such as being in love with a partner. If so, men may be more vulnerable than women to forming sexual associations to nonsexual stimuli.

The fact that men with one paraphilia often have others suggests that such men are especially vulnerable. Freund and Blanchard (1993) have suggested that the vulnerability is to errors in what they call *erotic target location*. According to this theory, although most men become heterosexual, they are not born with that orientation but instead must learn, through a process of classical conditioning, which stimuli together constitute a female sex partner, who is their target stimulus. This is the process of erotic target location. Perhaps certain men have nervous systems prone to errors in targeting, possibly allowing them to acquire these associations especially easily, which might also help to explain the incidence of multiple paraphilias. This theory is somewhat more useful in explaining paraphilias such as transvestism and certain fetishes (e.g., for women's underwear), in which the sexual stimuli are related to feminine characteristics, than it is for explaining others, such as masochism, in which the paraphilic target has no obvious association with normal sexual activities.

Treatments for Paraphilias Over the past 30 years, significant progress has been made in developing moderately effective treatments for the paraphilias, although research on treatment of these disorders generally lags behind that for most other disorders discussed in this book. One problem is that most people with paraphilias do not seek treatment for these conditions, but rather receive it only after they have been caught and detained in jail or prison. Thus, their motivations for change may often stem more from a desire to get released than from a genuine desire to change. Moreover, many do not readily admit all of their deviant behavior and do not consider a therapist an ally if, as is often the case, the therapist must report on the offender's progress to prison authorities or parole boards (Maletzky, 1998). Nevertheless, treatments that combine cognitive and behavioral elements have been shown to be moderately successful in effecting changes in deviant arousal and behavioral patterns in a significant number of cases. Moreover, there is increasing evidence suggesting that these treatments can result in significantly reduced rates of recidivism compared to those seen in untreated offenders, although further research is needed before these findings can be considered definitive.

One key component of treatment involves techniques commonly known as *aversion therapy*—in this case, aversive conditioning to deviant sexual fantasies. Although early treatments tended to use electric shock as the unconditioned stimulus, greater success has more recently been achieved using what is called *assisted covert sensitization,* which involves having the patient imagine a deviant sexual arousal scene. At the point where arousal is high, the patient imagines aversive consequences (simple covert sensitization) and a foul odor is introduced via an open vial or an automated odor pump to help condition a real aversion to these deviant scenes (hence the name assisted covert sensitization). Variations on this technique are now employed in most cognitive-behavioral treatment programs (Maletzky, 1998). Other important components of cognitive-behavioral treatment programs for paraphiliacs include social skills training (Maletzky, 1998; McFall, 1990) and restructuring of cognitive distortions that may be helping to maintain the deviant sexual arousal and behavior patterns. For example, men with exhibitionism often misattribute blame ("She kept looking at me like she was expecting it"), debase their victims ("She was just a slut anyway"), and minimize the consequences ("I never touched her, so I couldn't have hurt her").

In assessing treatment programs that combine these and other elements, a study of approximately 1500 offenders who had been followed for at least 1 year with very stringent criteria for success reported rather impressive results (Maletzky, 1998). Rates of success were the lowest for transvestic fetishism (nearly 79 percent) and were the highest for exhibitionism, voyeurism, and fetishism (approximately 95 percent). Nevertheless, much work remains to be done in this area, especially in light of the fact that these promising treatments are not yet widely available.

Gender Identity Disorders

Gender identity refers to one's sense of maleness or femaleness and may be distinguished from *gender role,* which refers to the masculinity and femininity of one's overt behavior (Money, 1988, p. 77). Of all behavioral traits, gender identity may have the strongest correlation with biological sex, but the correlation is imperfect. Some rare individuals feel extreme discomfort with their biological sex and strongly desire to change to the opposite sex. Indeed, some adults with gender identity disorders, often called *transsexuals,* do opt for expensive and complicated surgery to accomplish just that. In DSM-IV-TR, **gender identity disorder** is characterized by two components: (1) a strong and persistent **cross-gender identification,** which is the desire to be, or the insistence that one is, of the opposite sex; and (2) **gender dysphoria,** which is persistent discomfort about one's biological sex or the sense that the gender role of that sex is inappropriate (American Psychiatric Association, 2000). The disorder may occur in children or adults, both males and females.

Gender Identity Disorder of Childhood Boys with gender identity disorder show a marked preoccupation with traditionally feminine activities (Zucker & Bradley, 1995). They may prefer to dress in female clothing. They enjoy stereotypical games of girls, such as playing dolls or house (in which they usually play the mother), drawing pictures of beautiful girls, and watching TV programs with favorite female characters. They usually avoid rough-and-tumble play. They may express the desire to be a girl. Girls with gender identity disorder typically balk at parents' attempts to dress them in traditional feminine clothes such as dresses. They prefer boys' clothing and short hair, and they may be misidentified by strangers as boys. Their fantasy heros typically include powerful male figures, like Batman and Superman. They show little interest in playing dolls or dressing up and strong interest in sports. Although mere tomboys frequently have many or most of those traits, girls with gender identity disorder are distinguished by their desire to be a boy, or to grow up as a man. Boys with gender identity disorder are often ostracized as "sissies" by their peers. Young girls with gender identity disorder are treated more normally by their peers, as cross-gender behavior in girls is better tolerated (Zucker, Sanikhani, & Bradley, 1997). In clinic-referred gender identity disorder, boys outnumber girls five to one. An appreciable percentage of that imbalance may reflect

gender identity disorder Disorder characterized by strong and persistent identification with members of the opposite sex and persistent discomfort about one's biological sex or the sense that the gender role of that sex is inappropriate.

cross-gender identification The desire to be, or the insistence that one is, of the opposite sex.

gender dysphoria Persistent discomfort about one's biological sex or the sense that the gender role of that sex is inappropriate.

greater parental concern about femininity in boys than masculinity in girls.

The most common adult outcome of boys with gender identity disorder appears to be homosexuality rather than transsexualism (Bradley & Zucker, 1997). In Richard Green's (1987) study of 44 very feminine boys, only one sought sex change surgery as an adult. About three-quarters of the sample became gay or bisexual men who were evidently satisfied with their biological sex. There have been no prospective studies of girls with gender identity disorder. A recent analysis of retrospective reports of lesbians' sex-atypical behavior suggests that very masculine girls are more likely than other girls to become homosexual, but that most of them probably grow up as heterosexual women (Bailey & Zucker, 1995). Thus, the vast majority of children with gender identity disorder probably become homosexual or heterosexual adults, with only a small minority becoming transsexuals. If such children typically adjust well in adulthood, should they be considered to have a mental disorder?

One argument for considering children with atypical childhood gender identity to be disordered is that such children are often greatly distressed and thus should receive treatment. They suffer for two general reasons: First, by definition (i.e., current diagnostic criteria), they are unhappy with their biological sex. Second, as we have noted, they are likely to be mistreated by their peers and to have strained relations with their parents. An argument against considering such children as disordered is that the primary obstacle to their happiness is a society that is intolerant of cross-gender behavior. Thus, labeling children with atypical gender identity as "sick" shifts the blame from society, where it belongs. The diagnostic status of gender identity disorder of childhood therefore deserves serious debate.

Treatment Children with gender identity disorder are often brought by their parents for psychotherapy. Specialists attempt both to treat the child's unhappiness with his or her biological sex and to ease strained relations with parents and peers. Therapists try to improve peer and parental relations by teaching such children how to reduce their cross-gender behavior, especially in situations where it might cause interpersonal problems. Gender dysphoria is typically treated psychodynamically—that is, by examining inner conflicts. Controlled studies evaluating such treatment remain to be conducted.

transsexualism Gender identity disorder in adults who identify with members of the opposite sex (as opposed to accepting their own biological sex) and who strongly desire to (and often do) change their sex.

Transsexualism

Transsexualism is basically the adult form of gender identity disorder, and transsexuals show pronounced symptoms of both cross-gender identification and gender dysphoria. Many, perhaps most, transsexuals desire to change their sex, and surgical advances have made this goal partially feasible, although expensive. Transsexualism is apparently a very rare disorder. European studies suggest that approximately 1 per 30,000 adult males and 1 per 100,000 adult females seek sex reassignment surgery. Until recently, most researchers assumed that in all cases transsexualism was the adult version of childhood gender identity disorder. This is indeed often the case. That is, many transsexuals had gender identity disorder as children (despite the fact that most children with gender identity disorder do not become transsexual), and their adult behavior is analogous. This appears to be the case for all female-to-male transsexuals (i.e., individuals born female who become male). Virtually all such individuals recall being extremely tomboyish, with masculinity persisting unabated until adulthood. Most, but not all, female-to-male transsexuals are sexually attracted to women. One female-to-male transsexual had these recollections:

> [I have felt different] as far as I can remember. Three years old. I remember wanting to be a boy. Wearing boy's clothes and wanting to do all the things boys do. I remember my mother as I was growing up saying, "Are you ever going to be a lady? Are you ever going to wear women's clothing?" These kind of things as far back as I can remember. I can remember as I got a little older always looking at women, always wanting a woman... I feel like a man, and I feel like my loving a woman is perfectly normal. (Green, 1992, p. 102)

In contrast to female-to-male transsexuals, there are two kinds of male-to-female transsexuals—homosexual and autogynephilic transsexuals—and these types have very different causes and developmental courses (Blanchard, 1989). Homosexual transsexuals might be conceptualized as extremely feminine gay men who also wish to change their sex. They generally have had gender identity disorder since childhood and, as adults, wish to have sex with men. In contrast, autogynephilic transsexuals appear to have a paraphilia in which their attraction is to the image of themselves as a woman; they are typically attracted to women or men or both. Typically, they did not have gender identity disorder as children. This distinction between two types of male-to-female transsexuals is not currently made in the DSM. Although it may not be relevant for treatment purposes (both types of transsexuals are appropriate for sex reassignment surgery), it is fundamental for understanding the diverse psychology of this problem.

Dr. Richard Raskin (left), a physician and professional tennis player, became Renee Richards through transsexual surgery.

A *homosexual male-to-female transsexual* is a genetic male who describes himself as a woman trapped in a man's body and who is sexually attracted to men. Such feelings often date back to childhood. Such men seek a sex change operation in part so that, as women, they will have the ability to attract heterosexual male partners (Freund et al., 1974). Although homosexual transsexuals are attracted to members of their own genetic sex, they resent being labeled "gay" because they do not feel that they belong to their genetic sex (Adams & McAnulty, 1993). Nevertheless, from an etiological standpoint, homosexual transsexualism probably overlaps with ordinary homosexuality. What in rare cases causes gay men who are extremely feminine to want to change their sex is not yet well understood.

One adult homosexual male-to-female transsexual recalled the following:

> I used to like to play with girls. I never did like to play with boys. I wanted to play jacks. I wanted to jump rope and all those things. The lady in the schoolyard used to always tell me to go play with the boys. I found it distasteful. I wanted to play with the girls. I wanted to play the girl games. I remember one day the teacher said, "If you play with the girls one more day, I am going to bring a dress to school and make you wear it all day long. How would you like that?" Well, I would have liked it. (Green, 1992, p. 101)

Autogynephilic transsexualism (Blanchard, 1989, 1992) appears to occur only in genetic males, and its primary clinical feature is **autogynephilia,** a paraphilia characterized by sexual arousal at the thought or fantasy of being a woman (Blanchard, 1991, 1993). Indeed, autogynephilic transsexuals usually, but not always, report a history of transvestic fetishism. However, autogynephilic transsexualism has other symptoms as well. For example, unlike other transvestites, autogynephilic transsexuals fantasize that they have female genitalia. Perhaps because of this fantasy, their gender dysphoria is especially acute, motivating their desire for sex reassignment surgery. Autogynephilic transsexuals may report sexual attraction to women, to both men and women, or to neither. Research has shown that these subtypes of autogynephilic transsexuals are very similar to each other and differ from homosexual transsexuals in important respects beyond their sexual orientations (Blanchard, 1985, 1989, 1991). Unlike homosexual transsexuals, autogynephilic transsexuals do not appear to have been especially feminine in childhood or adulthood. Autogynephilic transsexuals typically seek sex-reassignment surgery much later than homosexual transsexuals (Blanchard, 1994). The causal factors for autogynephilic transsexualism probably overlap with those of other paraphilias but are not yet well understood.

Treatment Psychotherapy is usually not helpful in resolving transsexuals' gender dysphoria. The only treatment that has been shown to be effective is surgical sex reassignment. Initially, transsexuals awaiting surgery are given hormone treatment. Biological men are given estrogens to facilitate breast growth, skin softening, and shrinking of muscles. Biological women are given testosterone, which suppresses menstruation, increases facial and body hair, and deepens the voice. Typically, transsexuals must live for many months under hormonal therapy, and they generally must live for at least a year as the gender they wish to become. If they successfully complete the trial period, they undergo surgery and continue to take hormones indefinitely. In male-to-female transsexuals, the

autogynephilia A male paraphilia characterized by sexual arousal at the thought or fantasy of being a woman.

HIGHLIGHT 11.3

The Reliability of Children's Reports of Past Events

As more and more children have been brought forward to testify in court about alleged physical and sexual abuse by parents or other adults, researchers have become increasingly concerned about determining how reliable the testimony of children—especially that of young children—can be expected to be. Because abuse of children is distressingly common, children's reports of such abuse must always be taken seriously. Increasingly, however, doubt is being cast on the accuracy of young children's testimony, especially when they have been subjected to repeated interviews over many months, with highly leading questions, sometimes in a coercive atmosphere. Unfortunately, this appears to be the way in which children are sometimes treated before the trials in which they testify.

Stephen Ceci, a leading developmental psychologist studying this problem, summarized a series of experiments that casts grave doubt on young children's testimony if they have been exposed repeatedly to suggestive interviews over long intervals of time (Ceci, 1995). For example, Ceci summarized evidence that preschoolers have greater difficulty distinguishing between real and imagined acts (such as deciding whether they really touched their nose or only imagined touching it) than do older children or adults (Foley, Santini, & Sopasakis, 1989). Moreover, other research led Ceci to conclude that simply "repeatedly thinking about a fictitious event can lead some preschool children to produce vivid, detailed reports that professionals are unable to discern from their reports of actual events" (1995, p. 103).

In one important study called the "Sam Stone Study," Leichtman and Ceci (1995) interviewed preschool children four times over 10 weeks for details about a previously staged 2-minute visit by a stranger named Sam Stone to their day-care center. Some of the children were given no prior information about Sam Stone before his visit and were never asked suggestive questions during the four interviews; other children were given a stereotype about Sam Stone before his visit (such as that he was clumsy: "That Sam Stone is always getting into accidents and breaking things") and were also given leading questions during the four interviews (for example, "Remember that time Sam

Pedophilia frequently involves manipulation of the child's genitals. One study found sexual penetration occurred in more than half of cases and that use of physical force or violence occurred in 89 percent (Stermac, Hall, & Henskens, 1989). Although penetration and associated violence are often injurious to the child, the injuries are usually a by-product rather than a goal, as would be true for injuries inflicted by a sadist.

Studies investigating the sexual responses of pedophiles have achieved quite consistent results (Barbaree, 1990). Such studies tend to use a penile plethysmograph in order to directly measure erectile responses to sexual stimuli rather than relying on self-report. (A plethysmograph consists of an expandable band placed around the penis, connected to a recording device.) In general, men who have molested nonfamilial female children have shown greater sexual arousal to pictures of nude or partially clad girls than have matched nonoffenders. Interestingly, however, as a group, the offenders also responded strongly to adult women. Thus, deviant sexual preference alone may not explain why some men become pedophiles. Other factors include cognitive and nonsexual motivational factors. For example, child molesters are more likely than nonoffenders to believe that children will benefit from sexual contacts with adults and that children often initiate such contacts (Segal & Stermac, 1990). Motivationally, many pedophiles appear to desire mastery or dominance over another individual, and some idealize aspects of childhood such as innocence, unconditional love, and simplicity. Indeed, perhaps the most common type of pedophile is someone who is an interpersonally unskilled man drawn to children because he feels in control in relationships with them.

In the past few decades, there has been a dramatic increase in pedophilia among a group long considered to be highly trustworthy—the Catholic clergy. Although the majority of priests are innocent of sexual wrongdoing, the Catholic Church has admitted that a significant minority have committed sexual abuse, including pedophilia. At least 400 priests were charged with sexual abuse during the 1980s, and $400 million was paid in damages in the decade beginning in 1985 (Samborn, 1994). The most serious

Stone... spilled chocolate on that white teddy bear? Did he do it on purpose or by accident?"). One month later, after the four subsequent interviews were completed (about 14 weeks after Sam Stone's visit), all children were interviewed by a new interviewer who asked about two events that had not happened during Sam Stone's visit—whether he had soiled a teddy bear and/or ripped a book. For the children given no prior stereotype about Sam Stone and no leading questions during the initial four interviews, only 10 percent of the youngest preschoolers claimed that Sam Stone had been responsible for at least one of these two non-events, and, when gently challenged about this, only 2.5 percent stuck to the story that Sam had done these things. (Older preschoolers seldom committed such errors.) By contrast, for the younger preschoolers who were given a prior stereotype that Sam Stone was clumsy and who had been asked leading questions during the four interviews, a startling 72 percent of the youngest children claimed that Sam Stone had either soiled the teddy bear or ripped the book, or both. When gently challenged, 44 percent continued to claim that they had seen him do these things. Leichtman and Ceci tested the believability of these reports by showing the videotapes of some of the interviews to over 1000 researchers and clinicians who work with children. When asked which events actually occurred during Sam Stone's visit and asked to rate the children for the accuracy of their testimony, the majority of the professionals were highly inaccurate. Indeed, the videotape of the child who was least accurate was rated as being most credible, and the videotape of the child who was in reality most accurate was rated as least credible. Leichtman and Ceci (1995) concluded: "It is not that the members of these audiences were worse than anyone else at assessing which children gave accurate accounts, but that the accuracy of children's reports is extremely difficult to discern when children have been subjected to repeated erroneous suggestions over long retention intervals, especially when coupled with the induction of stereotypes" (p. 20).

In summary, although young children are sometimes capable of correct recall of what happened to them, they are also susceptible to a greater variety of sources of post-event distortion than are older children and adults. Nevertheless, even adults are susceptible to a variety of sources of post-event distortion, though to a lesser degree (Loftus, Feldman, & Dashiell, 1995; see also Chapter 7, pp. 257–258), and so the differences should be seen as a matter of degree rather than of kind (Ceci, 1995). ■

James R. Porter, a former Roman Catholic priest, was convicted of acts of pedophilia that had been committed many years earlier. His conviction occurred after a number of persons came forward with reports of his earlier abuse when they were members of his church as children.

scandal involved James R. Porter, then a 57-year-old father of four who was alleged to have sexually abused as many as 100 children when he was a priest in Massachusetts during the 1960s. Porter later admitted to his offenses and was convicted of molesting his children's baby-sitter in 1987. The Church settled a multimillion-dollar lawsuit with 25 men whom Porter had abused while a priest. Because of the scandals, there have been calls for the Church to take more aggressive steps to find, isolate, and treat abusive priests (Greeley, 1993).

Incest

Any culturally prohibited sexual relations (up to and including coitus) between family members, such as a brother and sister or a parent and child, is known as **incest.** Although a few societies have approved of incestuous relationships—at one time it was the established practice for Egyptian pharaohs to marry their sisters to prevent the royal blood from being "contaminated"—the incest taboo is virtually universal among human societies. Incest often produces children with mental and physical problems because biological relatives are much more likely than nonrelatives to share the same bad genes, and hence to have children with two sets of bad genes. For example, in one study, 15 of 38 offspring of incestuous unions had been admitted to hospitals for treatment of mental retardation (Jancar & Johnston, 1990). Presumably for this reason, many nonhuman animal species, and all known primates, avoid matings between close relatives. The mechanism for human incest avoidance appears to be lack of sexual interest in people to whom one is continuously exposed from an early age. For example, biologically unrelated children who were raised together in Israeli kibbutzim rarely marry or have affairs with others from their rearing group when they become adults (Shepher, 1971). Evolutionarily, this makes sense. In most cultures, children reared together will be biologically related siblings.

In our society, the actual incidence of incest is difficult to estimate because it usually comes to light only when reported to law enforcement or other agencies. It is almost certainly more common than is generally believed, in part, because many victims are reluctant to report the incest or do not consider themselves victimized (De Young, 1982; Maisch, 1972). Brother-sister incest is clearly the most common form of incest, even though it is rarely reported (Masters, Johnson, & Kolodny, 1992). The second most common pattern is father-daughter incest (Gebhard et al., 1965; Kinsey et al., 1948, 1953). Indeed, girls living with stepfathers are at especially high risk for incest, perhaps because there is less of an incest taboo among nonbiological relatives (Finkelhor, 1984; Masters et al., 1992; Russell, 1986). Mother-son incest is thought to be relatively rare. In occasional cases, multiple patterns of incest may exist within the same family, and some incestuous fathers victimize all of their daughters serially as they become pubescent.

Incestuous fathers tend to be of lower intelligence than other fathers, but they do not typically evidence serious psychopathology (Williams & Finkelhor, 1990). Indeed, they are often shy and conventional and claim devotion to their families (Masters et al., 1992). Most incestuous offenders are not pedophiles; only 20 to 30 percent have pedophilic arousal patterns (Langevin et al., 1985; Marshall, Barbaree, & Christophe, 1986). Most incestuous fathers have experienced substantial sexual dysfunction with their wives or adult partners. They have also tended to avoid child-care or nurturing activities that may otherwise have led them to treat their children as children, rather than sexual objects. The wives of men who commit incest were often sexually abused themselves as children, and in more than two-thirds of such cases, the wife often did not help or protect her child even if she knew about the incest (Masters et al., 1992).

incest Any culturally prohibited sexual relations between family members, such as a brother and sister or a parent and child.

rape Sexual activity that occurs under actual or threatened forcible coercion of one person by another.

Rape

The term **rape** describes sexual activity that occurs under actual or threatened forcible coercion of one person by another. In most states, legal definitions restrict forcible rape to forced intercourse or penetration of a bodily orifice by a penis or other object. *Statutory rape* is sexual activity with a person who is legally defined (by statute or law) to be under the age of consent (18 in most states). Statutory rape is considered to have occurred regardless of the apparent willingness of an underage partner. In the vast majority of cases, rape is a crime of men against women, although in prison settings, it is often men against men. As with childhood sexual abuse, several issues related to rape are scientifically and politically controversial. Two especially controversial questions are how frequently rape occurs and whether rape is primarily motivated by sex or aggression.

Prevalence of Rape It might seem to be fairly straightforward to estimate the prevalence of rape, but different studies have varied wildly in their estimates (Lynch, 1996). Figures may vary as a result of both the precise definition of "rape" used and the way in which the information is gathered (direct or indirect questions, for example). The FBI routinely gathers statistics on most major crimes reported to local law enforcement agencies throughout the country. The incidence of unreported rapes can be estimated from the National Crime Survey of the Bureau of Justice Statistics (BJS), which drew on a probability sample of 59,000 households. In this survey, respondents were asked whether they had experienced "forced or coerced sexual intercourse." Projecting to lifetime risk from this study leads to the estimate that approximately 5 to 7 percent of women will be victims of rape or attempted rape (Gilbert, 1992) during the course of their lives. However, another large study using a similar definition of rape provided an estimate that closer to 13 percent of women said that it had occurred sometime during their lives (Resnick et al., 1993), a much higher rate than the other study. The two surveys differed in a number of respects that may have contributed to the difference, but it is not clear which figure provides a more accurate lifetime estimate (Lynch, 1996).

Is Rape Motivated by Sex or Aggression? Traditionally, rape has been classified as a sex crime, and society has assumed that the rapist was motivated by lust. However, some feminist scholars have challenged this view, arguing instead that rape is motivated by the need to dominate, to assert power, and to humiliate a victim rather than by sexual desire for her (e.g., Brownmiller, 1975). Certainly from the perspective of the victim, rape is always an act of violence, whatever the rapist's motivation.

In spite of the fact that feminist writers have argued that rape is primarily a violent act, there are many compelling reasons why sexual motivation is often, if not always, a very important factor (e.g., L. Ellis, 1989; Palmer, 1988). For example, although rape victims include females of all ages and degrees of physical attractiveness, the age distribution of rape victims is not at all random but includes a very high proportion of women in their teens and early twenties. This age distribution is quite different from the distribution for other violent crimes, in which the elderly are overrepresented because of their vulnerability. In contrast, less than 5 percent of rape victims are over the age of 50 (Groth, 1979), supporting the interpretation that rapists prefer younger (and more attractive) victims. Furthermore, rapists usually cite sexual motivation as a very important cause of their actions (Smithyan, 1978, p. iv). Finally, as we shall see, at least some rapists share features of paraphiliacs, such as a characteristic arousal pattern to abnormal (in their case, rape) stimuli and multiple paraphilias (Abel & Rouleau, 1990). Paraphiliacs are typically highly sexually motivated. Thus, sexual desire is clearly a factor motivating many rapists.

Two prominent researchers studying sex offenders, Raymond Knight and Robert Prentky, have shown that all rapists actually have both aggressive and sexual motives, but to varying degrees. Two of the subtypes they have identified are motivated primarily by aggression, and two of the subtypes are motivated primarily by distorted sexual motives (Knight & Prentky, 1990; Knight, Prentky, & Cerce, 1994). In a study validating this classification system, Barbaree and colleagues (1994) found that the rapists of the sexual subtypes showed greater sexual arousal to taped scenes of rape than did rapists of the aggressive subtypes. Further research validating this classification system should be useful in helping to design better treatments for the different subtypes of rapists.

Rape and Its Aftermath Rape tends to be a repetitive activity rather than an isolated act, and most rapes are planned events. About 80 percent of rapists commit the act in the neighborhoods in which they reside; most rapes take place in an urban setting at night. The specific scene of the rape varies greatly, however. The act may occur on a lonely street after dark, in an automobile in a large shopping center's parking lot, or in the elevator or hallway of a building. Rapists have also entered apartments or homes by pretending to be making deliveries or repairs. About a third or more of all rapes involve more than one offender, and often they are accompanied by beatings. The remainder are single-offender rapes in which the victim and the offender may know each other; the closer the relationship, the more brutally the victim may be beaten.

In addition to the physical trauma inflicted on a victim, the psychological trauma may be severe, leading to what has been called a *rape trauma syndrome* (Burgess & Holmstrom, 1974) or post-traumatic stress disorder (Becker & Kaplan, 1991). One especially unfortunate factor in rape is the possibility of pregnancy; another is the chance of contracting a sexually transmitted disease. A rape may also have a negative impact on a victim's marriage or other intimate relationships. The situation is likely to be particularly upsetting to a husband or boyfriend if he has been forced to watch the rape, as is occasionally the case when a victim is raped by the members of a juvenile gang.

The concept of "victim-precipitated" rape, a favorite of defense attorneys and of some police and court jurisdictions, turns out on close examination to be a myth. According to this view, a victim (especially a repeated victim), although often bruised both psychologically and physically—if not worse—is regarded as the cause of the crime, often on such grounds as the alleged provocativeness of her clothing, her past sexual behavior, or her presence in a location considered risky (Stermac, Segal, & Gillis, 1990). The attacker, on the other hand, is treated as unable to quell his lust in the face of such irresistible provocation—and therefore not legally responsible for the act. A society as troubled as ours is by sexual assault can ill-afford this type of nonsensical and myth-based jurisprudence; in a century of combined clinical practice, none of the authors of this book has ever encountered a woman who desired to be raped or ever heard a convincing account of any such case. Despite evidence to the contrary, however, the harmful and dangerous concept that women want to be forced into sex is persistent and widespread (Segal & Stermac, 1990).

Rape, even at its least violent, is a bullying, intrusive violation of another person's integrity, selfhood, and personal boundaries that deserves to be viewed with more gravity—and its victims with more compassion and sensitivity—than is usually the case. Much still remains to be done in providing services to these victims (Koss, 1983), many of whom suffer from moderately severe post-traumatic stress disorder (see Chapter 4).

Alex Kelly, a young man from a wealthy family who certainly does not fit the stereotype of a rapist, was convicted in 1997 of raping a 16-year-old girl in 1986, and was sentenced to 16 years in prison. While awaiting his trial in 1987, Kelly fled the United States and spent 8 years as an international fugitive before being caught and returned to the United States for trial.

Rapists and Causal Considerations Based on information gathered by the FBI about arrested and convicted rapists, rape is usually a young man's crime. According to FBI *Uniform Crime Reports,* about 60 percent of all rapists arrested are under 25 years of age, with the greatest concentration in the 18-to-24 age group. Of the rapists who get into police records, about 30 to 50 percent are married and living with their wives at the time of the crime. As a group, they come from the low end of the socioeconomic ladder and commonly have a prior criminal record (Masters et al., 1992). About half were drinking heavily or drunk when they committed the rape. Seventy percent were strangers to the victims.

One subset of rapists, date rapists (that is, an acquaintance who rapes a woman typically in a context of a date or other social interaction) have a somewhat different demographic profile in that they are often middle- to upper-class young men who rarely have criminal records. However, these men, like incarcerated rapists, are also characterized by promiscuity, hostile masculinity, and an emotionally detached, predatory personality (i.e., the personality style of a psychopath) (Knight, 1997). What distinguishes them, primarily, is that incarcerated rapists show much higher levels of impulsive, antisocial behavior than do date rapists. In addition, impulsive, antisocial men are more likely to commit multiple, serious offenses leading to incarceration.

The case can be made that some rapists have a paraphilia—not different in its essentials from the paraphilias already discussed (Abel & Rouleau, 1990). Many rapists have many features of paraphiliacs. For example, they often report having recurrent, repetitive, and compulsive urges to rape. They typically try to control the urges, but the urges eventually become so strong that they act on them. Many rapists have other paraphilias. In one study of 126 rapists, for example, 28 percent had interest in exhibitionism and 18 percent in voyeurism (Abel & Rouleau, 1990). Most important, rapists have a characteristic pattern of sexual arousal (Abel & Rouleau, 1990; Lohr, Adams, & Davis, 1997). Most rapists are similar to normal nonoffending men in being sexually aroused by depictions of mutually satisfying, consensual intercourse. However, in contrast to normal men, many rapists are also sexually aroused by depictions of sexual assaults. Evidently, they are less sensitive to the inhibitory mechanisms that prevent most men from seeking sexual gratification coercively. A small minority of rapists, characterized by very violent assaults, are aroused more by assaults than sexual stimuli. They appear to be sexual sadists.

Rapists also show some deficits in their cognitive appraisals of women's feelings and intentions (Segal & Stermac, 1990). For example, they have difficulty decoding women's negative cues during social interactions. This could lead to inappropriate behaviors that women would experience as sexually intrusive. In one study, for example, rapists and nonrapist offenders were shown a series of vignettes of heterosexual couples interacting, and subjects were asked to guess which emotional cues were being portrayed. Rapists were significantly less accurate than the control groups (violent nonrapists and nonviolent nonrapists) in interpreting cues. Moreover, rapists were especially bad at reading women's cues, and errors associated with negative cues were most common (Lipton, McDonel, & McFall, 1987).

Conviction rates for rape are low, and most men who have raped are free in the community. In fact, one study (reported in Abel & Rouleau, 1990) found that 907 separate acts of rape were committed by only 126 nonincarcerated offenders, an average of 7 per offender. In the 1990s, new rape laws were adopted by a majority of states; many of these were based on the "Michigan model," which describes four degrees of criminal sexual conduct, with different punishment levels for different degrees of seriousness. In calling the offense "criminal sexual conduct" rather than "rape," the Michigan law also appropriately places the emphasis on the offender rather than the victim. Unfortunately, most sexual assaults are not reported, and of those that are, less than 10 percent result in conviction (Darke, 1990). Convictions often bring light sentences, and a jail term does not dissuade a substantial number of offenders from repeating their crimes. To repeat, the result is that the large majority of rapists are not in prison but out in our communities.

There is growing intolerance about sex offenders who repeat their crimes. The case of Willie Horton, who sexually assaulted a woman while out on parole, figured prominently in the defeat of Michael Dukakis in the 1988 presidential election (Dukakis, then Governor of Massachusetts, was accused of permitting the parole). But are such stories representative? Are sex offenders typically incurable? The efficacy of treatment for sex offenders is controversial, and this is the topic to which we now turn (e.g., Marshall, 1993; Marshall & Pithers, 1994; Quinsey et al., 1993).

Treatment and Recidivism of Sex Offenders

Therapies for sex offenders are very similar to those described earlier for the paraphilias, typically having at least one of the following three goals: to modify patterns of sexual arousal, to modify cognitions and social skills to allow more appropriate sexual interactions with adult partners, and/or to reduce sexual drive.

Psychotherapies Attempts to modify sexual arousal patterns usually involve aversion therapy, in which inappropriate sexual arousal to a paraphilic stimulus (such as a slide of a prepubescent girl for a pedophile) is paired with an aversive event, such as forced inhalation of noxious odors or a shock to the arm. But reducing deviant sexual arousal is probably insufficient. Deviant arousal patterns need to be replaced by arousal to acceptable stimuli (Maletzky, 1998; Quinsey & Earls, 1990). Most often investigators have attempted to pair the pleasurable stimuli of orgasm with sexual fantasies involving sex between consenting adults. For example, patients might be asked to masturbate while thinking of deviant fantasies; at the moment of ejaculatory inevitability, the patient switches his fantasy to a more appropriate theme. The moment of switching themes is gradually moved backward in time until, ideally, the patient can rely entirely on appropriate themes. Both therapies intended to reduce inappropriate sexual arousal, and those intended to increase nondeviant sexual arousal have been shown to be somewhat effective in the laboratory (Maletzky, 1998; Quinsey & Earls, 1990). But how well this therapeutic change generalizes to the prisoner's outside world may be problematic if his motivation wanes.

Cognitive restructuring therapy attempts to eliminate sex offenders' cognitive distortions, because these may play a role in sexual abuse (Maletzky, 1998). In addition, social-skills training aims to help sex offenders (especially rapists) learn to process social information from women more effectively (Maletzky, 1998; McFall, 1990). For example, some men read positive sexual connotations into women's neutral or negative messages, or they believe that women's refusals of sexual advances reflect "playing hard to get." Training typically involves interaction of patients and female partners, who can give the patients feedback on their response to their interaction. Cognitive treatment of sex offenders, as well as social-skills training, have shown some promise (Maletzky, 1998; Marshall & Barbaree, 1990b; McFall, 1990).

Recidivism (shifting back to one's original behavior after treatment) is a huge problem among sex offenders. Although some reviews of the treatment literature have reached positive conclusions (e.g., Marshall et al., 1991), some studies have also provided rather disturbing results about the long-term effectiveness of many psychosocial treatments of sex offenders (Emmelkamp, 1994; Rice, Quinsey, & Harris, 1991). For example, in one important study Quinsey and colleagues (1993) followed 136 child molesters for an average of 6 years following their release from imprisonment. Nearly half had committed another violent or sexual offense, and this rate of recidivism did not differ among the 50 men who had received aversion therapy and the 86 men who had not. Moreover, the degree of aversion that was conditioned during treatment was not a significant predictor of recidivism. Some studies have had somewhat more promising results, including Maletzky's (1998) important study of over 4000 rapists and pedophiles. Although this study unfortunately does not have an untreated control group, as the study by Quinsey and colleagues did, and to date only 1-year follow-up results have been reported for all the offenders, the success rates were very promising—75 percent for rapists, and 80 to 95 percent for different types of pedophiles. And this study used very stringent criteria for success (i.e., participants completed all treatment sessions, they reported no covert or overt deviant sexual behavior at the end of treatment or at the 1-year follow-up, they showed no deviant sexual arousal as measured with a penile plethsymograph at the end of treatment or follow-up, and they had no repeat legal charges).

Biological and Surgical Treatments The most controversial treatment for sex offenders involves castration, either surgical removal of the testes or the hormonal treatment sometimes called "chemical castration" (Besharov, 1992; Bradford, 1990; Money, 1986, pp. 135–145). Both surgical and chemical castration lower the testosterone level, which in turn lowers the sex drive, allowing the offender to resist more easily any inappropriate impulses. Recently, an uncontrolled study of the drug Lupron yielded dramatic results: 30 men with paraphilias reported an average of 48 deviant fantasies per week prior to therapy, and no such fantasies during treatment (Rosler & Witztum, 1998). Lupron is especially effective at reducing testosterone and has fewer bad side effects than other drugs, such as Depo-Provera. Studies of surgical castration of sex offenders conducted in Europe suggest similar results. These studies have typically included diverse categories of offenders, from pedophiles to rapists of adult women. Follow-up has sometimes exceeded 10 years. Recidivism rates of castrated offenders are typically less than 3 percent, compared with greater than 50 percent of uncastrated offenders (Berlin, 1994; Bradford, 1990; Green, 1992; Wille & Beier, 1989). However, many feel that the treatment is brutal and dehumanizing (Gunn, 1993). Interestingly, most recent cases have involved a request by the sex offender himself to be castrated in exchange for a lighter sentence.

Combination of Biological and Psychosocial Treatments Increasingly many treatment programs use a combination of hormone therapy and cognitive-behavioral treatments, with the hope that eventually the hormone treatment can be tapered off after the offender has learned techniques for impulse control (Maletzky, 1998). However, the single most important defect of nearly all available studies is the lack of randomly assigned controls who were equally motivated for treatment. Some have argued that denying treatment to sex offenders is unethical (e.g., Marshall et al., 1991). However, this could only be true if the treatment were effective, and it is unclear at this point whether it is. Research in this area is further complicated by the fact that the outcome variable in most studies is whether the man is reconvicted for another sex offense during the follow-up period. Because most sex offenses go unpunished (the offender is often never even caught, let alone convicted), using this as the outcome variable will exaggerate the apparent effectiveness of treatment and underestimate the dangerousness of sex offenders. Given the social importance of the questions of whether sex offenders can be helped and how likely they are to offend again, it is important that society devote the resources necessary to answer them.

Efficacy of Treatments It is obvious that the efficacy of treatment for sex offenders is controversial. Much work remains to be done and it is probably most accurate to say that at the present time we simply do not know how likely it is that various treatments will significantly reduce sex offenders' likelihood of recidivism (Maletzky, 1998; Quinsey et al., 1993), and the treatments that show promise are not yet widely in use.

It is possible both to acknowledge that sex offenders cause immense human suffering and to feel sympathy for their plight. Many sex offenders have been burdened with a deviant sexual arousal pattern that has caused them great personal and legal trouble. Consider the case of Scott Murphy, a convicted pedophile:

> He lives alone with a friend, works odd hours and doesn't go out of his way to meet neighbors. Ironically, Murphy has never been prouder of his behavior. He admits he'll never be cured and will always be attracted to young boys. But he says he is now making every attempt to steer clear of them: "I went from constantly living my whole life to molest kids to now living my whole life to not molest kids." It's a 24-hour-a-day job. On the highway, Murphy keeps at a distance to guarantee he makes no eye contact with the young passengers in school buses. When the Sunday paper arrives at home, he immediately throws out the coupon section because the glossy ads often depict attractive boy models. He refuses to leave the office when kids might be walking to or from school and got rid of his television so the sit-com images of young boys wouldn't distract him. (Popkin, 1994, p. 67)

HIGHLIGHT 11.4

Megan's Law

On July 29, 1994, 7-year-old Megan Kanka, from Hamilton Township, New Jersey, was walking home from her friend's house. Just before she reached her front door, a neighbor invited her to his house to see his new puppy. The neighbor, Jesse Timmendequas, 33, was a landscaper who had lived across the street for about a year. Unknown to Megan, Megan's parents, or anyone else in the neighborhood, he was also a twice-convicted child molester (and lived with two other convicted sex offenders). When Megan followed him inside, he led her to an upstairs bedroom, strangled her unconscious with his belt, raped her, and asphyxiated her with a plastic bag. Timmendequas then placed Megan's body in a toolbox, drove to a soccer field and dumped it near a portable toilet. Subsequently, Timmendequas was apprehended, convicted, and sentenced to death.

Megan's murder sparked outrage that dangerous sex offenders could move into a neighborhood without anyone there knowing about their presence. In response, the New Jersey state legislature passed Megan's Law, which mandated that upon release, convicted sex offenders register with police and that authorities notify neighbors of the offenders' presence by distributing flyers, alerting local organizations, and canvassing door-to-door. Similar laws have been passed in many other states, and it is now possible in California to examine a CD-ROM containing the name, picture, and legal history of convicted sex offenders in that state. Some states post sex offenders' identities on Web sites. Delaware will soon require sex offense convictions to be indicated on driver's licenses.

Although Megan's Laws have been enormously popular with state legislators and citizens, they have not been uncontroversial. Civil libertarians have objected to community notification requirements, which, they argue, endanger released offenders, who have paid their debt to society, and also prevent them from successfully integrating back into society. Although the various Megan's Laws are intended to protect potential victims rather than encourage harassment of sex offenders, the latter has occurred. For example, John Becerra, a convicted sex offender, moved into a two-story home in the New York City area in December 1995, hoping to begin a new life with his wife and their 9-year-old son. But he and his family found themselves the target of a persistent campaign of protests by their neighbors. Signs around the neighborhood warned, "Beware of Sex Offender," their car was vandalized, and rallies were held outside their home.

Although this kind of treatment is not condoned, it does happen, all too frequently. Are the benefits from such laws worth this cost? At this point, definitive data are not available, but some data have brought the effectiveness of Megan's Laws into question. One study in Washington state found that in the period before that state's Megan's Law, 22% of sex offenders who had been arrested committed another sex crime. After the law went into effect, the rate was quite similar at 19% (Schenk, 1998).

The recognition that some sex offenders have high recidivism rates and the uncertainty as to whether treatment helps have led some states to pass laws that require involuntary commitment of dangerous offenders to psychiatric facilities even after their sentence has been served. Leroy Hendricks was convicted five times of molesting children and admitted that only his death could guarantee that he would commit no further offenses. In 1994, Kansas prosecutors invoked state law to prevent his release after he served 10 years in prison, but this action was challenged as unconstitutional. The primary objection was that holding Hendricks after his sentence amounted to giving him a second punishment for the same offense. In 1997, the U.S. Supreme Court ruled narrowly (5-4) that people such as Hendricks can be held if they are considered mentally abnormal and are likely to commit new crimes.

In order to ensure that released sex offenders will not reoffend, some states have passed legislation requiring chemical or surgical castration for certain types of sex offenders because research shows lower recidivism rates with these treatments than with psychotherapies alone. For example, California now requires that repeat child molesters undergo chemical castration as a condition of parole. Michigan has passed a similar law applying to repeat rapists. Civil libertarians, such as the ACLU, have argued that such requirements violate the Constitution's ban on cruel and unusual punishment, because of potentially severe side effects. Furthermore, because the treatment may affect both sex drive and spermatogenesis, civil libertarians argue, it violates offenders' "reproductive privacy rights." ■

Society cannot allow Murphy to act on his sexual preference; nor can his past crimes be forgotten. Nevertheless, in deciding how to treat people like Scott Murphy, it is humane to remember that many of them have a tormented inner life.

IN REVIEW

- What are the short-term consequences of childhood sexual abuse, and why is knowledge about the long-term consequences more uncertain?
- What are the major issues surrounding children's testimony about sexual abuse and adults' recovered memories of sexual abuse?
- Define *pedophilia, incest,* and *rape,* and summarize the major clinical features of the perpetrators of these crimes.
- Identify the main goals of treatment of sex offenders, and describe the different treatment approaches.

SEXUAL DYSFUNCTIONS

Sexual dysfunction refers to impairment either in the desire for sexual gratification or in the ability to achieve it. It varies markedly in degree, but regardless of which partner is alleged to be dysfunctional, the enjoyment of sex by both parties in a relationship is typically adversely affected. Sexual dysfunctions occur in both heterosexual and homosexual couples. In some cases, they are caused by dysfunctional psychosexual adjustment and learning. In others, organic factors are most important. Both the explanation and treatment of sexual dysfunction have become more biologically oriented in recent years (Rosen & Leiblum, 1995).

There are four relatively distinct phases of the human sexual response (Masters & Johnson, 1966, 1970, 1975). Disorders can occur in any of the first three phases (American Psychiatric Association, 1994). The first phase is the **desire phase,** which consists of fantasies about sexual activity or a sense of desire to have sexual activity. The second phase is the **excitement phase,** during which there is generally both a subjective sense of sexual pleasure and physiological changes that accompany this subjective pleasure, including penile erection in the male and vaginal lubrication and enlargement in the female. The third phase is **orgasm,** during which there is a release of sexual tension and a peaking of sexual pleasure. The final phase is **resolution,** during which the person has a sense of relaxation and well-being. We will first describe the most common dysfunctions that accompany the first three phases and then discuss issues of causation and treatment. Table 11.1 summarizes the dysfunctions we will be covering here.

How common are sexual dysfunctions? It is obviously difficult to do large-scale research on such a sensitive topic. Nevertheless, the National Health and Social Life Survey (Laumann et al., 1994) assessed sexual problems during the previous year in 3,432 randomly selected Americans. Although they did not use DSM diagnostic criteria, the researchers inquired about similar problems. For women, the most common complaints were lack of sexual interest (33%) and inability to experience orgasm (24%). For men, climaxing too early (29%), anxiety about sexual performance (17%), and lack of sexual interest (16%) were reported most frequently. Altogether, 45% of men and 55% of women reported some dysfunction during the past year. Clearly, a high percentage of people will experience sexual dysfunction sometime during their lives.

Dysfunctions of Sexual Desire

Sexual Desire Disorders Researchers have delineated two types of sexual desire disorders. The first is **hypoactive sexual desire disorder.** It is a dysfunction in which either a man or a woman shows little or no sexual drive or interest. It is assumed in most cases that the biological basis of the sex drive remains unimpaired (see Schreiner-Engel et al., 1989), but that for some reason sexual motivation is blocked. Individuals with this disorder usually come to the attention of clinicians only at the request

sexual dysfunction Impairment either in the desire for sexual gratification or in the ability to achieve it.

desire phase First phase of the human sexual response, consisting of fantasies about sexual activity or a sense of desire to have sexual activity.

excitement phase Second phase of the human sexual response, in which there is generally a subjective sense of sexual pleasure and physiological changes, including penile erection in the male and vaginal lubrication and enlargement in the female.

orgasm Third phase of the human sexual response, during which there is a release of sexual tension and a peaking of sexual pleasure.

resolution Final phase of the human sexual response, during which a person has a sense of relaxation and well-being.

hypoactive sexual desire disorder Sexual dysfunction in which a person shows little or no sexual drive or interest.

TABLE 11.1 SEXUAL DYSFUNCTIONS

Dysfunctions	Characteristics
Dysfunctions of Sexual Desire	
Hypoactive sexual desire disorder	Little or no sexual drive or interest
Sexual aversion disorder	Total lack of interest in sex and avoidance of sexual contact
Dysfunctions of Sexual Arousal	
Male erectile disorder	Inability to achieve or maintain an erection (formerly known as impotence)
Female sexual arousal disorder	Nonresponsiveness to erotic stimulation both physically and emotionally (formerly known as frigidity)
Dysfunctions of Orgasm	
Premature ejaculation	Unsatisfactorily brief period between the beginning of sexual stimulation and the occurrence of ejaculation
Male orgasmic disorder	Inability to ejaculate during intercourse (also known as retarded ejaculation)
Female orgasmic disorder	Difficulty in achieving orgasm, either manually or during sexual intercourse
Sexual Pain Disorders	
Vaginismus	Involuntary muscle spasm at the entrance to the vagina that prevents penetration and sexual intercourse
Dyspareunia	Painful coitus; may have either an organic or a psychological basis

of their partners, who typically complain of insufficient sexual interaction. This fact exposes one problem with the diagnosis, because it is known that preferences for frequency of sexual contact vary widely among otherwise normal individuals. Who is to decide what is "not enough"? DSM-IV-TR explicitly indicates that this judgment is left to the clinician, taking into account the person's age and the context of his or her life. In extreme cases, clinical judgment is easier because sex actually becomes psychologically aversive, and the condition warrants a diagnosis of **sexual aversion disorder,** the second type of sexual desire disorder. With this disorder, the person shows extreme aversion to, and avoidance of, all genital sexual contact with a partner.

Depression may contribute to some cases of sexual desire disorders (Rosen & Leiblum, 1987). Although sexual desire disorders typically occur in the absence of obvious organic pathology, there is evidence that organic factors may sometimes play a role. Sexual arousal in both men and women depends on testosterone (Alexander and Sherwin, 1993; Sherwin, 1988). The increase in sexual desire problems with age may be in part attributable to declining levels of testosterone, but evidence regarding the utility of testosterone replacement therapy suggests that it is usually not beneficial except possibly in women whose ovaries have been removed (Segraves & Althof, 1998). Although there has been interest since antiquity in the possibility that a drug might be found to increase sexual desire, no effective aphrodisiacs exist.

Sexual desire disorder appears to be the most common female sexual dysfunction (Laumann et al., 1994). Despite this fact, it has inspired far less etiological and treatment research than have male dysfunctions, especially erectile disorder and premature ejaculation. One main reason for this disparity is doubtless the centrality that many men place on their ability to perform sexually. There has also been, until recently, a general neglect of female sexuality and an implicit societal attitude that women simply do not care much about sex.

Dysfunctions of Sexual Arousal

Male Erectile Disorder Inability to achieve or maintain an erection sufficient for successful sexual intercourse

sexual aversion disorder Sexual dysfunction in which a person shows extreme aversion to, and avoidance of, all genital sexual contact with a partner.

Sexual dysfunctions can occur at the desire, excitement, or orgasm phase of the sexual response cycle. Many people, if not most, will experience some sexual dysfunction sometime during their lives. If it becomes chronic or highly disturbing to one or both partners, it warrants treatment.

was formerly called *impotence.* It is now known as **male erectile disorder,** or *erectile insufficiency*. In lifelong erectile disorder, a man has never been able to sustain an erection long enough to accomplish a satisfactory duration of penetration. In acquired or situational erectile disorder, a man has had at least one successful experience of coitus but is presently unable to produce or maintain the required level of penile rigidity. Lifelong insufficiency is a relatively rare disorder, but it has been estimated that half or more of the male population has had some experience of erectile insufficiency on at least a temporary basis.

Masters and Johnson (1975; Masters et al., 1992) and Kaplan (1974, 1987) believed that erectile dysfunction is primarily a function of anxiety about sexual performance. In other reviews of the accumulated evidence, however, Barlow and colleagues (Beck & Barlow, 1984; Sbrocco & Barlow, 1996) have played down the role of anxiety per se—under some circumstances, it can actually enhance sexual performance in normally functioning men and women (Barlow, Sakheim, & Beck, 1983; Hoon, Wincze, & Hoon, 1977; Palace & Gorzalka, 1990; see Sbrocco & Barlow, 1996, for a review). For example, in one study, sexually functional male subjects in a laboratory experiment were made anxious by being told that there was a 60 percent chance of receiving electric shock while watching an erotic film unless they had an average-sized erection; these men actually showed more sexual arousal to the film than did men who were not threatened with shock (Barlow et al., 1983).

male erectile disorder Sexual dysfunction in which a man is unable to achieve or maintain an erection sufficient for successful sexual intercourse; formerly known as *impotence.*

Instead of anxiety per se, Barlow and colleagues emphasize that it is cognitive distractions frequently associated with anxiety that seem to interfere with sexual arousal in dysfunctional people. For example, one study found that nondysfunctional men who were distracted by non–anxiety provoking material to which they were listening on earphones while watching an erotic film showed less sexual arousal than did men who were not distracted (Abrahamson et al., 1985). Barlow and colleagues believe that sexually dysfunctional men and women get distracted by negative thoughts about their performance during a sexual encounter (such as "I'll never get aroused" or "She will think I'm inadequate"). Their research suggests it is this preoccupation with negative thoughts, rather than anxiety per se, that is responsible for inhibiting sexual arousal. Moreover, such self-defeating thoughts not only decrease pleasure but can also increase anxiety if the erection does not occur (Malatesta & Adams, 1993), and this in turn can fuel further negative self-defeating thoughts (Sbrocco & Barlow, 1996).

Erectile problems are a common consequence of aging. Prolonged or permanent erectile disorder before the

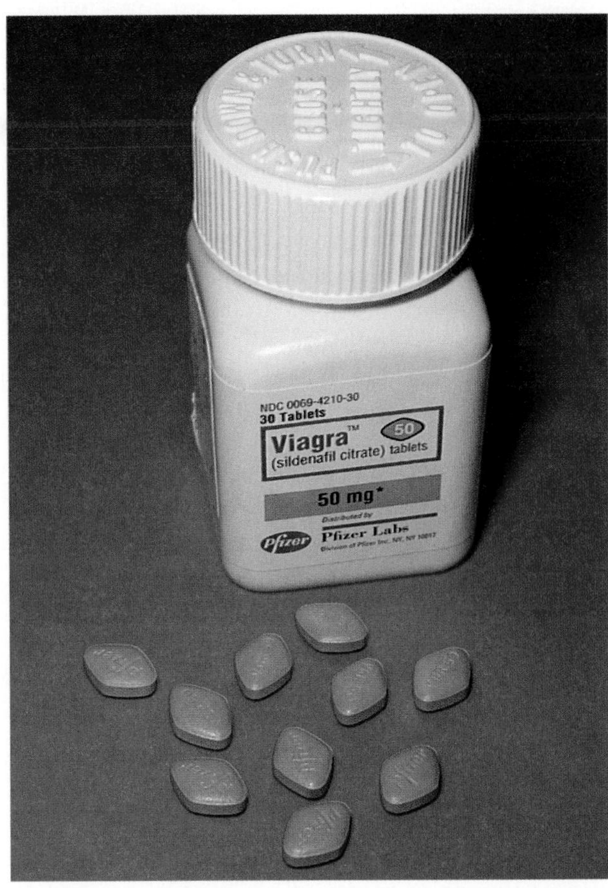

The drug Viagra works by making nitric oxide, the primary neurotransmitter involved in penile erection, more available. It is taken orally, about an hour before sexual activity. Unlike some other biological treatments for sexual dysfunction, Viagra only works if sexual desire is present.

age of 60 is relatively rare. One study found that more than half of married men over 70 had some erectile difficulties (Diokno, Brown, & Herzog, 1990). However, studies have also indicated that men and women in their 80s and 90s are often quite capable of enjoying intercourse (Kaplan, 1974; Malatesta & Adams, 1993; Masters et al., 1992). For example, in one study of 202 healthy men and women between ages 80 and 102, it was found that nearly two-thirds of the men and one-third of the women were still having sexual intercourse, although this was not generally their most common form of sexual activity (Bretschneider & McCoy, 1988).

Increased erectile dysfunction with age and erectile disorder in general are increasingly viewed as medical rather than psychological problems (Rosen, 1996). The most frequent cause of erectile disorder in older men is vascular disease, resulting in decreased blood flow to the penis or in diminished ability of the penis to hold blood to maintain an erection. Thus, hardening of the arteries, high blood pressure, and other diseases causing vascular problems are often causes of erectile disorder. Smoking, obesity, and alcohol abuse are associated lifestyle factors. For young men, one cause of erectile problems is having had *priapism,* or an erection that will not diminish, even after a couple of hours, and that is typically unaccompanied by sexual excitement. Priapism can occur as a result of prolonged sexual activity or disease or as the side effect of certain medications. Untreated cases result in erectile dysfunction approximately 50 percent of the time (Starck, Branna, & Tallen, 1994), and thus priapism should be treated as a medical emergency.

Distinguishing between psychogenic and organically caused erectile disorder for diagnostic purposes is at best a complicated process. The normal man has several erections per night, associated with periods of REM (rapid eye movement) sleep. Some researchers have suggested that organically based erectile disorder can be distinguished from psychogenically based erectile disorder by noting an absence of these nocturnal erections. However, it appears that many other factors must also be evaluated in order to establish a proper diagnosis (Malatesta & Adams, 1993), because the nocturnal penile erection procedure has been found, by itself, to produce unreliable results (Mohr & Beutler, 1990). In most cases, there are probably a combination of psychological and organic causal factors.

A variety of medical treatments have been employed, often when cognitive-behavioral treatments have failed. These include drugs such as yohimbine, injections of smooth muscle–relaxing drugs into the penile erection chambers (corpora cavernosa), and even a vacuum pump (Rosen, 1996). In extreme cases, penile implants may be used. These devices can be inflated to provide erection on demand. They are made of silicone rubber or polyurethane rubber. Such treatments have generally shown success in clinical trials, although they are rather extreme interventions that often evoke bothersome side effects (Rosen & Leiblum, 1995). Perhaps for these reasons, there has been immense interest in the revolutionary new drug Viagra (sildenafil). Viagra works by facilitating nitric oxide (that is, making it more available), the primary neurotransmitter involved in penile erection. Viagra is taken orally, at least 1 hour before sexual activity. Unlike some other biological treatments for erectile dysfunction, Viagra promotes erection only if sexual desire is present.

Clinical trials of Viagra have been impressive. In one double-blind study, over 70 percent of men receiving at least 50 mg of Viagra reported that their erections had improved, compared with fewer than 30 percent of men receiving a placebo (Carlson, 1997; see also Goldstein et al., 1998). Side effects are relatively uncommon and not serious (e.g., the most common side effect, headache, was reported by 11 percent of patients), provided that the person does not have serious preexisting heart problems, in which case Viagra can be very dangerous (even life-threatening). Based on these results, there has been immense public interest in the drug, and some analysts have predicted that Viagra may be the most commercially successful drug ever marketed. This is an indication of both the high prevalence of sexual dysfunction and the importance that people attach to sexual performance.

Female Sexual Arousal Disorder Formerly and somewhat pejoratively referred to as *frigidity,* **female sexual arousal disorder**—the absence of sexual arousal feelings and an unresponsiveness to most or all forms of erotic stimulation—is in many ways the female counterpart of erectile disorder. Its chief physical manifestation is a failure to produce the characteristic swelling and lubrication of the vulva and vaginal tissues during sexual stimulation, a condition that may make intercourse quite uncomfortable. To be diagnosed, the disturbance must cause the woman marked distress or interpersonal difficulty. The diagnosis of female sexual arousal disorder by itself is rare (Segraves & Segraves, 1991).

Although the causes of this disorder are not well understood, possible reasons for the inhibition of sexual feeling range from early sexual traumatization, to excessive and distorted socialization about the evils of sex, to dislike of, or disgust with, a current partner's sexuality. One reason progress toward understanding of this disorder may be slow is that female sexuality may be in some senses more complicated than male sexuality, and this complexity may slow progress toward etiological theories and interventions. For example, it appears that the correlation between subjective sexual arousal and physiological sexual arousal (i.e., genital response) is much lower for women than for men (Heiman, 1980; Laan & Everaerd, 1995). That is, it is not uncommon for women to feel unaroused sexually, but to have some genital response; the reverse also occurs frequently. This may complicate progress toward understanding female sexual arousal disorder (and other female sexual disorders) (Andersen & Cyranowski, 1995). Yet there is some indication that sexual arousal disorder in women is increasing rapidly (Beck, 1995). Hopefully, research on this disorder will increase commensurate with the importance and prevalence of the problem.

Given its relative rarity, it is not surprising that no treatment studies have been conducted. The widespread use of vaginal lubricants may effectively mask and treat the disorder in many women (Rosen & Leiblum, 1995). Some research suggests that under certain conditions, women's genital arousal can be increased by increasing their autonomic arousal—for example, via exercise or anxiety (Meston & Gorzalka, 1996; Palace, 1995). However, this work is still in its preliminary stages. Finally, there has been great interest in the possibility that Viagra will have positive effects for women analogous to its effects for men (Kolata, 1998). Female genital response probably depends in large part on the same neurotransmitter systems that underlie male genital response, and thus it is plausible that Viagra will be effective in women as well. Although therapeutic trials with women have begun in Europe, results of those trials are as of yet inconclusive.

female sexual arousal disorder Sexual dysfunction involving the absence of sexual arousal feelings and unresponsiveness to most or all forms of erotic stimulation.

premature ejaculation Persistent and recurrent onset of orgasm and ejaculation with minimal sexual stimulation, occurring before, at, or shortly after penetration and before the man wants it to.

Orgasmic Disorders

Premature Ejaculation **Premature ejaculation** refers to persistent and recurrent onset of orgasm and ejaculation with minimal sexual stimulation. It may occur before, at, or shortly after penetration but before the man wants it to. The consequences include failure of the partner to achieve satisfaction and, often, acute embarrassment for the prematurely ejaculating man, with disruptive anxiety about recurrence on future occasions. Men who have had this problem from their first sexual encounter often try to diminish sexual excitement, by avoidance of stimulation, self-distraction, and "spectatoring," or psychologically taking the role of an observer rather than a participant (Metz, Pryor, Nesvacil, Abuzzahab, & Koznar, 1997).

An exact definition of prematurity is necessarily somewhat arbitrary. For example, the clinician must consider the age of a client—the alleged "quick trigger" of the younger man being more than a mere myth (McCarthy, 1989). Indeed, approximately half of young men complain of early ejaculation (Frank, Anderson, & Rubenstein, 1978). Not surprisingly, premature ejaculation is most likely after a lengthy abstinence (Malatesta & Adams, 1993; Spiess, Geer, & O'Donohue, 1984). DSM-IV-TR acknowledges that many factors affect time to ejaculation by noting that the diagnosis is made only if ejaculation occurs before, at, or shortly after penetration and before the man wants it to. Premature ejaculation is the most prevalent male sexual dysfunction (Laumann et al., 1994; Segraves &

Althof, 1998). Indeed, some estimate that 15 to 20 percent of American men have at least a moderate degree of difficulty in controlling rapid ejaculation (Masters et al., 1992).

In sexually normal men, the ejaculatory reflex is to a considerable extent under voluntary control. They monitor their sensations during sexual stimulation and are somehow able, perhaps by judicious use of distraction, to forestall the point of ejaculatory inevitability until they decide to "let go" (Kaplan, 1987). Premature ejaculators are for some reason unable to use these techniques effectively to control their ejaculation. Explanations have ranged from psychological factors such as increased anxiety (Kaplan, 1987) to physiological factors such as increased penile sensitivity (Gospodinoff, 1989). Presently, however, no explanation has much empirical support.

For many years, sex therapists have primarily considered premature ejaculation to be psychogenically caused and highly treatable via behavioral therapy, such as the *pause-and-squeeze technique* (Masters & Johnson, 1970). This technique requires the man to monitor his sexual arousal during sexual activity. When arousal is intense enough that the man feels that ejaculation might occur soon, he pauses, and he or his partner squeezes the head of the penis for a few moments, until the feeling of pending ejaculation passes. Initial reports suggested that this technique was approximately 90 percent effective; more recent studies have reported a much lower overall success rate (Rosen & Leiblum, 1995; Segraves & Althof, 1998). Thus, for men with whom behavioral treatments have not worked, there has been increasing interest in possible use of pharmacological interventions. Antidepressants such as fluoxetine (Prozac) and clomipramine that block serotonin re-uptake have been found to prolong ejaculatory latency in men with premature ejaculation (Rowland & Slob, 1997; Segraves & Althof, 1998); some can be taken about 6 hours before anticipated intercourse, and others must be taken every day. Moreover, evidence suggests that the drugs work only as long as they are being taken, rather than providing a long-term cure (Segraves & Althof, 1998).

Male Orgasmic Disorder Sometimes called *retarded ejaculation* or *inhibited male orgasm,* **male orgasmic disorder** refers to a persistent delay in the ability to ejaculate or an inability to ejaculate during intercourse following a normal sexual excitement phase. Men who are completely unable to ejaculate are rare. About 85 percent of men who have difficulty ejaculating during intercourse can nevertheless achieve orgasm by other means of stimulation, notably through solitary masturbation (Masters et al., 1992). In milder cases, a man can ejaculate in the presence of a partner, but only by means of manual or oral stimulation (Kaplan, 1987).

Psychological treatments emphasize the reduction of performance anxiety, in addition to increasing genital stimulation (Rosen & Leiblum, 1995; Segraves & Althof, 1998). In other cases, retarded ejaculation can be related to specific physiological problems, such as multiple sclerosis, or to the use of certain medications. Although antidepressants that block serotonin re-uptake appear to be an effective treatment for premature ejaculation, they sometimes delay or prevent orgasm to an unpleasant extent in some men (Ashton, Hamer, & Rosen, 1997; Rosen & Leiblum, 1995). These side effects are common (Gitlin, 1996), but can often be treated pharmacologically (Ashton et al., 1997).

Female Orgasmic Disorder Many women who are readily sexually excitable and who otherwise enjoy sexual activity nevertheless experience **female orgasmic disorder** (formerly *inhibited female orgasm*)—persistent or recurrent delay in or absence of orgasm following a normal sexual excitement phase. Of these women, many do not routinely experience orgasm during sexual intercourse without direct supplemental stimulation of the clitoris; indeed, this pattern is so common that it is not generally considered dysfunctional. A small percentage of women are able to achieve orgasm only through direct mechanical stimulation of the clitoris, as in vigorous digital manipulation, oral stimulation, or the use of an electric vibrator. Even fewer are unable to have the experience under any known conditions of stimulation; this condition, called *lifelong orgasmic dysfunction,* is analogous to lifelong erectile insufficiency in males.

What causes female orgasmic disorder is not well understood, but a multitude of contributory factors have been hypothesized. For example, some women feel fearful and inadequate in sexual relations. A woman may be uncertain whether her partner finds her sexually attractive, and this may lead to anxiety and tension that interfere with her sexual enjoyment. Or she may feel inadequate because she is unable to have an orgasm or does so infrequently. Sometimes a nonorgasmic woman will pretend to have orgasms to make her sexual partner feel fully adequate. The longer a woman maintains such a pretense,

male orgasmic disorder A persistent delay in the ability to ejaculate or an inability to ejaculate during intercourse following a normal sexual excitement phase.

female orgasmic disorder Persistent or recurrent delay in or absence of orgasm following a normal sexual excitement phase.

however, the more likely she is to become confused and frustrated; in addition, she is likely to resent her partner for being insensitive to her real feelings and needs. This resentment in turn only adds to her sexual difficulties.

The diagnosis of orgasmic dysfunction is complicated by the fact that the subjective quality of orgasm varies widely among women, within the same woman from time to time, and depending on mode of stimulation. Thus, precise evaluations of occurrence and quality are difficult (Malatesta & Adams, 1993; Segraves & Althof, 1998). The criteria to be applied are also unclear in the vast middle range of orgasmic responsiveness in which most women's experiences actually fall (Masters et al., 1992; Segraves & Althof, 1998). The authors of this book believe that this question is best left to a woman herself to answer; if she is dissatisfied about her responsiveness, and if there is a reasonable likelihood that treatment will help, then she should seek it.

Regarding treatment, it is important to distinguish between lifelong and situational female orgasmic dysfunction. Treatment of the former, typically beginning with instruction and guided practice in masturbating to orgasm, has a high likelihood of success (Andersen, 1983; Segraves & Althof, 1998). In contrast, "situational" anorgasmia (where a woman may experience orgasm in some situations, with certain kinds of stimulation, or with certain partners, but not under the precise conditions she desires) often proves more difficult to treat, perhaps in part because it is often associated with relationship difficulties that may also be difficult to treat (Beck, 1992).

Dysfunctions Involving Sexual Pain

Vaginismus An involuntary spasm of the muscles at the entrance to the vagina (not due to a physical disorder) that prevents penetration and sexual intercourse is called **vaginismus.** Evidently these muscles are readily conditionable to respond with intense contraction to stimuli associated with impending penetration. In some cases, women who suffer from vaginismus also have sexual arousal disorder, possibly as a result of conditioned fears associated with earlier traumatic sexual experiences. In most cases, however, they show normal sexual arousal but are still afflicted with vaginismus (Masters et al., 1992). It is not always possible to identify the "unconditioned stimuli" presumed to have been involved in the acquisition of vaginismus (Kaplan, 1987), probably because the disorder is sometimes "overdetermined" in the sense of having multiple causal factors (Segraves & Althof, 1998). This form of sexual dysfunction is relatively rare, but, when it occurs, it is likely to be extremely distressing for both an affected woman and her partner, sometimes leading to erectile or ejaculatory dysfunction in the partner (Leiblum, Pervin, & Campbell, 1989; Segraves & Althof, 1998). Treatment of vaginismus typically involves a combination of banning intercourse, training of the vaginal muscles, and graduated self-insertion of vaginal dilators of increasing size. It generally appears to be effective (Rosen & Leiblum, 1995; Segraves & Althof, 1998).

Dyspareunia Painful coitus, or **dyspareunia,** can occur in men but is far more common in women (Lazarus, 1989). This is the form of sexual dysfunction most likely to have an obvious organic basis—for example, occurring in association with infections or structural pathology of the sex organs. It may sometimes have a psychological basis, however, as in the case of a woman who has an aversion to sexual intercourse and experiences her displeasure as intense physical discomfort; in such cases, the designation "functional" is used. Understandably, dyspareunia is often associated with vaginismus. Treatment of this problem usually requires addressing the specific organic or physiological problems that contribute to it, but often there may also be a conditioned psychological response that requires psychological intervention (Segraves & Althof, 1998).

vaginismus Involuntary spasm of the muscles at the entrance to the vagina that prevents penetration and sexual intercourse.

dyspareunia Painful coitus.

IN REVIEW

- Compare and contrast the symptoms of the dysfunctions of sexual desire, arousal, and orgasm in men and women.
- Why have common female sexual dysfunctions been studied less than male sexual dysfunctions?
- What are the most effective treatments for male erectile disorder and premature ejaculation and for female orgasmic disorder?

SUMMARY

SOCIOCULTURAL INFLUENCES ON SEXUAL PRACTICES AND STANDARDS

- Defining boundaries between normality and psychopathology in the area of sexual behavior may be more difficult than for any other topic covered in this book.
- There have been widespread sociocultural influences on what have been viewed as normal or aberrant sexual practices, making it difficult for psychologists to specify abnormal sexuality.
- Degeneracy theory and abstinence theory were very influential for long periods of time in the United States and many other Western cultures, leading to very conservative views on heterosexual sexuality. The hypothesis that masturbation can cause insanity was also influential for several centuries and appeared in some psychiatry textbooks until the 1940s.
- In contrast to Western cultures, among the Sambians of Melanesia, homosexuality is practiced by all adolescent males in the context of sexual initiation rites. In young adulthood, males make a rather abrupt transition to heterosexuality, in most cases without apparent difficulty.
- Until rather recently, homosexuality was viewed in many Western cultures as either criminal behavior or as a form of mental illness. However, since 1972, homosexuality is no longer considered by mental health professionals to be abnormal but is considered a normal sexual variant.

SEXUAL AND GENDER VARIANTS

- Paraphilias are sexual variants that involve persistent patterns of sexual behavior and arousal in which unusual objects, rituals, or situations are required for full sexual satisfaction. They almost always occur in males.
- The paraphilias include (1) fetishism (in which sexual interest centers on some inanimate object or nonsexual part of the body), (2) transvestic fetishism (in which sexual arousal and satisfaction result from cross-dressing), (3) voyeurism (in which sexual pleasure is achieved through clandestine peeping), (4) exhibitionism (in which sexual pleasure results from intentional exposure of the genitals to others in inappropriate circumstances and without their consent), (5) sadism (in which sexual arousal occurs through inflicting cruelty on one's sexual partner), (6) masochism (in which sexual arousal occurs when pain or degradation is inflicted on oneself), and (7) pedophilia (in which sexual attraction is directed toward prepubescent children).
- What causes paraphilias is not well understood. One theory is that males are vulnerable to problems in erotic target location. In this view, men are not born with an automatic attraction to either women or men but instead must learn which stimuli constitute a female or male sexual partner. Perhaps some men have nervous systems more prone to errors in targeting; this might explain why so many men with paraphilias have more than one.
- Gender identity disorders occur in both children and adults. Childhood gender identity disorder is characterized by cross-gender identification and gender dysphoria. Most boys who have this disorder grow up to have a homosexual orientation; a few become transsexuals. Retrospective studies suggest that some girls who have gender identity disorder become lesbians but that the majority become heterosexuals.
- Transsexualism is a very rare gender identity disorder in which an adult believes that he or she is trapped in the body of the wrong sex. There are two types of male-to-female transsexuals: homosexual transsexuals (who are attracted to the people of their same biological sex) and autogynephilic transsexuals (who may be attracted to people of either sex and whose gender dysphoria is related to a paraphilia).
- The only known effective treatment for transsexualism is a sex-change operation. Although its use remains highly controversial, it does appear to have fairly high success rates with people who are carefully diagnosed as being true transsexuals.

SEXUAL ABUSE

- Sexual abuse is sexual contact that involves coercion or at least one individual who cannot consent. There are three categories: pedophilia (another type of paraphilia), incest, and rape. All three kinds of abuse occur at alarming rates today, although it is difficult to estimate their true prevalence.
- Among the controversies surrounding how perpetrators of sexual abuse are identified are controversies about the accuracy of children's testimony and about the accuracy of adults' recovered memories of sexual abuse that often arise during psychotherapy.
- Pedophiles engage in sexual activity with prepubescent children, and quite commonly they are indifferent to the sex of the child.

- Incest involves culturally prohibited sexual relations among family members; it overlaps with pedophilia when adult family members sexually abuse children.
- Rape can occur between strangers or people who know each other; it involves force or threat of force.
- All sexual abuse can have serious short-term and long-term consequences for its victims. What leads people to engage in sexual abuse is poorly understood at this time.
- Treatment of sex offenders has not as yet proved highly effective in most cases, although promising research in this area is being conducted.

SEXUAL DYSFUNCTIONS

- A sexual dysfunction is an impairment either in the desire for sexual gratification or in the ability to achieve it.
- There are four phases of the human sexual response: the desire phase, the excitement phase, orgasm, and resolution. Dysfunctions can occur in any of the first three phases.
- Both men and women can experience hypoactive sexual desire disorder, in which they have little or no interest in sex. In more extreme cases, individuals may develop sexual aversion disorder, which involves avoidance of all sexual contact with a partner.
- Dysfunctions of the arousal phase include male erectile disorder and female arousal disorder. Male erectile disorder can occur for psychological or physiological reasons, or a combination of the two.
- Dysfunctions of orgasm include premature ejaculation and male orgasmic disorder (retarded ejaculation) for men and include female orgasmic disorder for women.
- There are also two sexual pain dysfunctions: vaginismus, which occurs in women, and dyspareunia (painful coitus), which occurs in women and occasionally in men.
- Remarkable progress has been made in the treatment of sexual dysfunctions, and the success rates of treatments for some of these dysfunctions are quite high.

KEY TERMS

paraphilias (p. 365)
fetishism (p. 365)
transvestic fetishism (p. 366)
voyeurism (p. 367)
exhibitionism (p. 368)
sadism (p. 368)
masochism (p. 369)
gender identity disorder (p. 371)
cross-gender identification (p. 371)
gender dysphoria (p. 371)
transsexualism (p. 372)
autogynephilia (p. 373)
sexual abuse (p. 374)
pedophilia (p. 377)
incest (p. 380)
rape (p. 380)
sexual dysfunction (p. 386)
desire phase (p. 386)
excitement phase (p. 386)
orgasm (p. 386)
resolution (p. 386)
hypoactive sexual desire disorder (p. 386)
sexual aversion disorder (p. 387)
male erectile disorder (p. 388)
female sexual arousal disorder (p. 390)
premature ejaculation (p. 390)
male orgasmic disorder (p. 391)
female orgasmic disorder (p. 391)
vaginismus (p. 392)
dyspareunia (p. 392)

CHAPTER TWELVE

The Schizophrenias

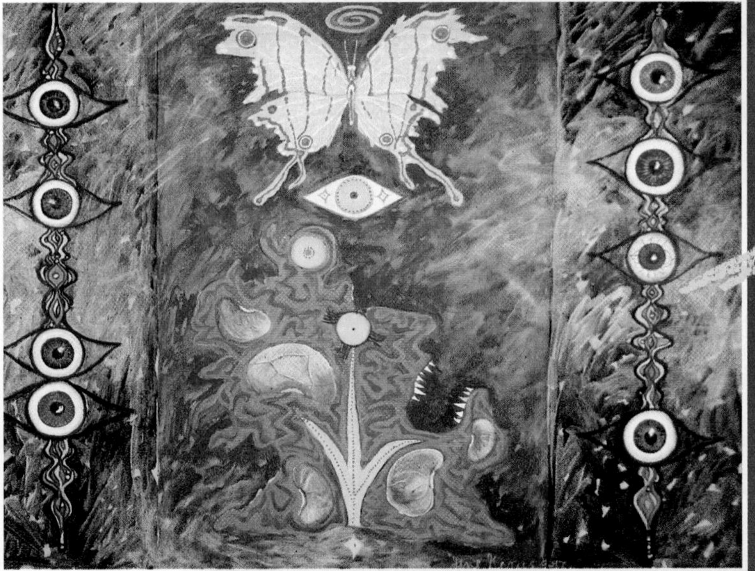

Jane A. Gerus, *Vision.* Originally from Cleveland, Ohio, Gerus moved to Minnesota to receive treatment for drug dependence. She was later hospitalized for schizophrenia and asthma. While hospitalized, Gerus used magic markers to produce her first pictures, capturing the vividness of her dreams and visions. Her paintings continue to reveal her inner world.

LEARNING OBJECTIVES

After reading this chapter, you should be able to:

- Summarize the history of the concept of schizophrenia.
- Discuss the prevalence rates and age of onset of schizophrenia in terms of gender and sociocultural differences.
- Describe the major symptoms of schizophrenia.
- List the DSM criteria for the diagnosis of schizophrenia.
- Compare and contrast the subtypes of schizophrenia.
- Summarize the biological, psychosocial, and sociocultural causal factors in schizophrenia.
- Describe and evaluate the major biological and psychosocial treatments for schizophrenia.

You probably already have some familiarity with the term *schizophrenia*. Its plural form, **the schizophrenias,** is used for this chapter's title in recognition of the growing consensus that what is meant by "schizophrenia" encompasses several differing types of relatively severe mental disorder. As the American Psychiatric Association (1997b) put it, "It is likely that schizophrenia is the final common pathway for a group of disorders with a variety of etiologies, courses, and outcomes" (p. 49).

Nevertheless, DSM-IV-TR provides diagnostic criteria only for "Schizophrenia," thus treating it as though it were a singular entity. To avoid confusion, therefore, and also for the sake of convenience, we frequently employ the singular form of the term in what follows. It should be understood, however, that the diagnostic criteria for the diagnosis of schizophrenia are probably a manifestation of an unknown number of differing pathological conditions sharing a "final common pathway"—a striking and essential feature, which is a significant loss of contact with reality, often referred to as **psychosis.**

The hallmark of the schizophrenias is thus a more or less sharp break with the world in which most less disturbed people live, a world that is rooted in a basic consensus about what is true and real in our shared experience. The typical person with schizophrenia is someone who has lost or become detached from a set of anchoring points fundamental to adequate mental integration and communication with the surrounding human environment. These individuals may, for example, claim to be God or assert that their brains are hooked up to the CIA via satellite, or they may appear "disconnected" from all meaningful interactions with other human beings. To those around the schizophrenic person during an active phase of the disorder, he or she appears alien, incomprehensible, unpredictable, and often frightening.

If we look more closely, trying to identify the component processes underlying this detachment from reality, we observe many differing psychological abnormalities in persons whose behavior meets criteria for the schizophrenia diagnosis. These include extreme oddities in action, thinking, perception, feeling, sense of self, and manner of relating to others, with the features displayed varying from one patient to another. This heterogeneity extends well beyond differences in clinically significant behavior and includes marked variations in background features—such as genetic and environmental risk factors, course and duration of the disorder(s) in different people (notably males versus females), responses to treatment efforts, and the exceptionally wide range of outcomes these patients experience.

This chapter, then, will describe the pieces of the schizophrenia puzzle as they are currently known. It is important that you bear in mind from the outset that not all of the pieces or their presumed interconnections have been found, so the puzzle remains fragmented and incomplete—more so than perhaps in any other area of psychopathology.

DSM-IV-TR also identifies **delusional disorder,** a *nonschizophrenic* paranoid disorder whose main features were formerly included under the classic rubric *paranoia*, or *"true" paranoia* (to distinguish it from the paranoid subtype of schizophrenia). Like many individuals with schizophrenia, patients with delusional disorder nurture, give voice to, and sometimes take actions based on beliefs that are considered completely false and absurd by those around them. Unlike persons with schizophrenia, however, persons with delusional disorder may otherwise behave quite normally. Their behavior does not show the gross disorganization and performance deficiencies characteristic of schizophrenia; general behavioral deterioration is rarely observed with delusional disorder, even when it proves chronic.

Although the formal diagnosis of delusional disorder is rare in clinical and mental hospital populations, this ob-

schizophrenias Severe mental disorders characterized by the breakdown of integrated personality functioning, withdrawal from reality, emotional blunting and distortion, and disturbances in thought and behavior.

psychosis A significant loss of contact with reality, as when hallucinations or delusions are present.

delusional disorder A nonschizophrenic paranoid disorder in which a person nurtures, gives voice to, and sometimes takes action on beliefs that are considered completely false and absurd by others; formerly called *paranoia*.

To those around the schizophrenic person during an active phase of the disorder, he or she appears alien, incomprehensible, unpredictable, and often frightening.

servation provides a somewhat misleading picture of its actual prevalence. Many exploited inventors, fanatical reformers, self-styled prophets, morbidly jealous spouses, persecuted teachers, and other persons fall into this category. Unless they become a serious nuisance, these people are usually able to maintain themselves in the community and do not recognize their paranoid condition or seek help to alleviate it. Indeed, it is generally conceded that once a delusional system is well established, it is extremely difficult to dismantle. It is usually impossible to communicate with such individuals about their problems in a rational way. In addition, they are not likely to seek treatment, as many of them interpret that as an unacceptable admission of weakness, but are more likely to seek justice for all the wrong done to them. In some instances, they are potentially dangerous; in virtually all cases, they are inveterate "injustice-detectors," inclined to undertake retributive actions of one sort or another against their supposed tormenters.

A second type of nonschizophrenic paranoid disorder listed in DSM-IV-TR is **shared psychotic disorder,** in which two or more people, usually in the same family, develop persistent, interlocking delusional ideas. This condition was historically known as *folie à deux*.

Finally, brief episodes (i.e., lasting 1 month or less) of otherwise uncomplicated delusional thinking are included in the category **brief psychotic disorder.**

THE SCHIZOPHRENIAS

The disorders now called "schizophrenia" were at one time attributed to a type of mental deterioration beginning early in life. In 1860, the Belgian psychiatrist Benedict Morel described the case of a 13-year-old boy who had formerly been the most brilliant pupil in his school but who gradually lost interest in his studies, became increasingly withdrawn, lethargic, seclusive, and quiet, and appeared to have forgotten everything he had learned. He talked frequently of killing his father. Morel thought the boy's intellectual, moral, and physical functions had deteriorated as a result of brain degeneration of hereditary origin, and hence were irrecoverable. He used the term *démence précoce* (mental deterioration at an early age) to describe the condition and to distinguish it from the dementing disorders associated with old age.

Origins of the Schizophrenia Concept

The Latin form of this term—*dementia praecox*—was subsequently adopted in the late nineteenth century by the German psychiatrist Emil Kraepelin to refer to a group of conditions that all seemed to have the feature of mental deterioration beginning early in life. Actually, however, the term is somewhat misleading. There is no compelling evidence of progressive (i.e., worsening over time) brain degeneration in the natural course of the disorder (Cannon, 1998a, 1998b; Russell et al., 1997). Also, where progressive degeneration has been observed, it sometimes appears to have been treatment-induced as a result of excessive dosing with antipsychotic medication (Cohen, 1997; Gur et al., 1998). We will address this issue further in the section on neuroanatomical factors. Finally, schizophrenic symptoms sometimes make their first appearance well into middle age or beyond, although onset in adolescence or early adulthood is far more typical.

shared psychotic disorder A nonschizophrenic paranoid disorder in which two or more people, usually in the same family, develop persistent, interlocking delusional ideas; also known as *folie à deux*.

brief psychotic disorder A mental disorder characterized by brief episodes (lasting 1 month or less) of otherwise uncomplicated delusional thinking.

It remained for a Swiss psychiatrist, Eugen Bleuler, to introduce in 1911 a more acceptable descriptive term for this general class of disorders. He used "schizophrenia" (split mind) because he thought the condition was characterized primarily by disorganization of thought processes, a lack of coherence between thought and emotion, and an inward orientation away (split off) from reality. The splitting thus does not refer to multiple personalities, an entirely different form of disorder discussed in Chapter 7 (and now called *dissociative identity disorder*). Instead, in schizophrenia, there is a split within the intellect, between the intellect and emotion, and between the intellect and external reality. The subtitle of Bleuler's monograph on the subject (Bleuler, 1911/1950) was *The Group of Schizophrenias,* indicating his own belief that basic psychic splitting might be manifested in multiple forms.

Prevalence and Onset

Global prevalence rates for the schizophrenias are difficult to pin down because of substantial variations over time and place in the criteria for defining cases. In addition, cross-cultural research in psychopathology generally is fraught with many pitfalls for the unwary investigator. Among other problems, such research is subject to distorting biases arising when investigators apply the unexamined assumptions of their own culture to observations made about the behavior of members of cultures that may be very different (Tsai et al., in press; Lewis-Fernández & Kleinman, 1994). For example, in some cultures, the belief that one is in direct contact with a god who resides in a particular animal or tree is not considered to be divorced from reality, as it is in our culture. Problems of this sort are likely to be amplified where, as in the case of the schizophrenias, the essential nature of the disordered entity remains conceptually unclear.

Some believe that schizophrenia occurs at an approximately constant rate in most, if not all, societies. However, the pertinent epidemiological data (e.g., Eaton, 1985; Jablensky et al., 1992; Stevens & Hallick, 1992; Torrey, 1987) do not as a general rule support this uniformity assumption. One exception, discussed by Allen (1997), is that schizophrenia appears to be both rarer and of less severe quality in traditional, small-scale societies than it is in modern, well-developed ones. Accordingly, any sort of global assessment of prevalence rates for the schizophrenias is problematic.

We can be more certain of our ground if we concentrate on DSM-defined schizophrenia in the United States, where psychiatric epidemiology is relatively advanced. As was reported in Chapter 1, the *point prevalence* of schizophrenia in the United States is believed to be in the range of 0.2 to 2.0 percent of the population (American Psychiatric Association, 1994). *Lifetime prevalence* is estimated at 0.7 percent among persons not currently institutionalized (Kessler et al., 1994). During any given year, approximately 1 percent of adult U.S. citizens, over 2 million persons, meet diagnostic criteria for schizophrenia (Regier et al., 1993). The *incidence,* or cumulative occurrence rate of new cases, of schizophrenia in the United States could be as high as 0.2 percent per year (Tien & Eaton, 1992).

Schizophrenia has been the primary diagnosis for nearly 40 percent of all admissions to state and county mental hospitals, far outstripping all other diagnostic categories; it has been the second most frequent primary diagnosis (the first being either mood or alcohol-related disorders) for every other type of inpatient psychiatric admission, including private hospitals (Manderscheid et al., 1985). Forty-five percent of schizophrenic persons receiving hospital care during a given year receive that care in state and county mental hospitals, a proportion exceeded only by patients with severe cognitive impairments such as Alzheimer's dementia. During any given year, more than 1 million people in the United States receive outpatient care for a primary diagnosis of schizophrenia (Narrow et al., 1993). Because schizophrenic persons often require prolonged or repeated hospitalization, they have historically occupied about half of all available mental hospital beds in this country.

Although schizophrenic disorders sometimes first occur during childhood or old age, about three-fourths of all initial onsets occur between the ages of 15 and 45, with a median age in the mid-20s. The prevalence rate, overall, appears to be about the same for males and females, but males tend to have earlier onsets (early to mid-20s versus late 20s for females), and many investigators believe males develop more severe forms of these disorders (Iacono & Beiser, 1992; Marcus et al., 1993; Tien & Eaton, 1992). That belief is consistent with a brain-imaging study by Nopoulos, Flaum, and Andreasen (1997) showing schizophrenia-related anomalies of brain structure (discussed below) to be more severe in male than in female patients. Interestingly, the male-female difference in age of onset reverses with increasing age, and late-onset (35 and older) schizophrenia is significantly more common among women than men (Jeste & Heaton, 1994). Figure 12.1 depicts this reversal. There is also some evidence that this late-onset pattern in women is associated with a severe clinical presentation (Haffner et al., 1998). The schizophrenias, because of their complexity, their high rate of incidence (especially at the beginning of adult life), and their tendency to recur or become chronic are considered the most serious of all mental disorders, as well as among the most baffling.

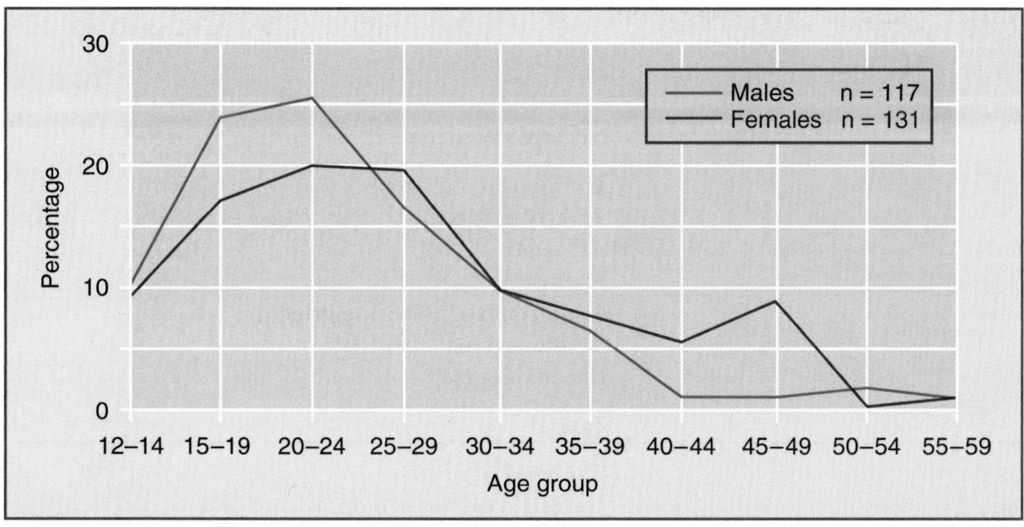

FIGURE 12.1
AGE DISTRIBUTION OF ONSET OF SCHIZOPHRENIA (FIRST SIGN OF MENTAL DISORDER) FOR MEN AND WOMEN
Source: Haffner et al. (1998).

IN REVIEW

- Why was the original name, *dementia praecox,* replaced with *schizophrenia?* Why is the latter name more accurate?
- What are some of the difficulties in determining the prevalence of the schizophrenias?
- When does initial onset of schizophrenia usually occur, and how does it vary by gender?

THE CLINICAL PICTURE IN SCHIZOPHRENIA

Since the days of Bleuler, two general symptom patterns, or syndromes, of schizophrenia have been differentiated. They are called **positive-** and **negative-syndrome schizophrenia** (e.g., Andreasen, 1985; Andreasen et al., 1995). *Positive signs and symptoms* are those in which something has been added to a normal repertoire of behavior and experience, such as marked emotional turmoil, motor agitation, delusional interpretation of events, or hallucinations. *Negative signs and symptoms,* by contrast, refer to an absence or deficit of behaviors normally present in a person's repertoire, such as emotional expressiveness, communicative speech, or reactivity to environmental events. A related differentiation that refers to essentially these same patterns but with more emphasis on biological variables and speed of onset calls them **Type I** and **Type II schizophrenia,** respectively (Crow, 1985). The two systems are compared in Table 12.1. Most patients exhibit both positive and negative signs during the course of their disorders (Breier et al., 1994; Guelfi, Faustman, & Csernansky, 1989). However, patients who exhibit a preponderance of negative symptoms have a more unfavorable prognosis than those who exhibit more positive symptoms (e.g., Fenton & McGlashan, 1994; McGlashan & Fenton, 1993).

It is important to keep in mind that the distinction of positive and negative is *not* dichotomous. In fact, it is not even necessarily a single dimension. Research evidence indicates that these polar terms would better be conceived as the end points of an uninterrupted continuum, or possibly as two separate and largely independent continua, both of which are for some reason involved in manifest schizophrenic behavior.

positive-syndrome schizophrenia Schizophrenia with a symptom pattern characterized by additions to normal behavior and experience, such as marked emotional turmoil, motor agitation, and/or delusions and hallucinations.

negative-syndrome schizophrenia Schizophrenia with a symptom pattern characterized by an absence or deficit of normal behaviors, such as emotional expressiveness, communicative speech, and/or reactivity to environmental events.

Type I schizophrenia Form of schizophrenia similar to the positive-syndrome type and thought to involve chiefly temporolimbic brain structures.

Type II schizophrenia Form of schizophrenia similar to the negative-syndrome type and thought to involve chiefly frontal brain structures.

TABLE 12.1 DIAGNOSTIC SIGNS DISTINGUISHING POSITIVE-SYNDROME OR TYPE I SCHIZOPHRENIA AND NEGATIVE-SYNDROME OR TYPE II SCHIZOPHRENIA

Positive-syndrome	Negative-syndrome
Hallucinations	Emotional flattening
Delusions	Poverty of speech
Derailment of associations	Asociality
Bizarre behavior	Apathy
Minimal cognitive impairment	Significant cognitive impairment
Sudden onset	Insidious onset
Variable course	Chronic course
Type I	**Type II**
The above plus:	*The above plus:*
Good response to drugs	Uncertain response to drugs
Limbic system abnormalities	Frontal lobe abnormalities
Normal brain ventricles	Enlarged brain ventricles

Positive signs and symptoms are those in which something has been added to normal behavior or experience–emotional turmoil, hallucinations, or motor agitation, for example. Negative symptoms, such as depicted here, refer to behavioral and emotional deficits and generally indicate a poorer prognosis.

Whatever the combination or relative proportion of positive and negative signs and symptoms in particular instances, schizophrenia encompasses many specific manifestations that vary greatly over time in an individual's life and from one person to another. Such largely unpredictable variations include the extent of development and rapidity of progression of negative signs (McGlashan & Fenton, 1993). The basic experience in schizophrenia, however, seems to be disorganization in perception, thought, and emotion to the extent that the affected person is no longer able to perform customary social roles in an adequate fashion. The DSM specifies in concrete terms a list of criteria for the diagnosis, reproduced in Table 12.2. What follows is a more in-depth examination of the schizophrenia construct as it has evolved to this point.

Disturbance of Associative Linking

Often referred to as *formal thought disorder,* associative disturbance is usually considered a prime indicator of a schizophrenic disorder. Basically, an affected person fails to make sense, despite seeming to conform to the semantic and syntactic rules governing verbal communication. The failure is not attributable to low intelligence, poor education, or cultural deprivation. Meehl (1962) aptly referred to the process as one of "cognitive slippage"; others have referred to it as "derailment" or "loosening" of associations or "incoherence." However labeled, the phenomenon is readily recognized by experienced clinicians: The patient seems to be using words in combinations that sound communicative, but the listener can understand little or nothing of what point he or she is trying to make. As an example from the files of one of the authors, consider

TABLE 12.2 THE DSM CRITERIA FOR THE DIAGNOSIS OF SCHIZOPHRENIA

A. *Characteristic symptoms:* Two (or more) of the following, each present for a significant portion of time during a 1-month period (or less if successfully treated):
   1. delusions
   2. hallucinations
   3. disorganized speech (e.g., frequent derailment or incoherence)
   4. grossly disorganized or catatonic behavior
   5. negative symptoms, i.e., affective flattening, alogia [little speech, or little substance of ideas contained in speech], or avolition [deficient or absence of "will"]

Note: Only one Criterion A symptom is required if delusions are bizarre or hallucinations consist of a voice keeping up a running commentary on the person's behavior or thoughts or two or more voices conversing with each other.

B. *Social/occupational dysfunction:* For a significant portion of the time since the onset of the disturbance, one or more major areas of functioning such as work, interpersonal relations, or self-care are markedly below the level achieved prior to the onset (or when the onset is in childhood or adolescence, failure to achieve expected level of interpersonal, academic, or occupational achievement).

C. *Duration:* Continuous signs of the disturbance persist for at least 6 months. This 6-month period must include at least 1 month of symptoms (or less if successfully treated) that meet Criterion A (i.e., active-phase symptoms) and may include periods of prodromal or residual symptoms. During these prodromal or residual periods, the signs of the disturbance may be manifested by only negative symptoms or two or more symptoms listed in Criterion A present in an attenuated form (e.g., odd beliefs, unusual perceptual experiences).

D. *Schizoaffective and Mood Disorder exclusion:* Schizoaffective Disorder and Mood Disorder With Psychotic Features have been ruled out because either (1) no Major Depressive, Manic, or Mixed Episodes have occurred concurrently with active-phase symptoms; or (2) if mood episodes have occurred during active-phase symptoms, their total duration has been brief relative to the duration of the active and residual periods.

E. *Substance/general medical condition exclusion:* The disturbance is not due to the direct physiologic effects of a substance (e.g., a drug of abuse, a medication) or a general medical condition.

F. *Relationship to a Pervasive Developmental Disorder:* If there is a history of Autistic Disorder or another Pervasive Developmental Disorder, the additional diagnosis of Schizophrenia is made only if prominent delusions or hallucinations are also present for at least a month (or less if successfully treated).

Source: American Psychiatric Association, 1994, pp. 285–286.

the following excerpt from a letter addressed to Queen Beatrix of the Netherlands by a highly intelligent man with schizophrenia.

Case Study **An Example of Cognitive Slippage** • I have also "killed" my ex-wife, [name], in a 2.5 to 3.0 hours sex bout in Devon Pennsylvania in 1976, while two Pitcairns were residing in my next room closet, hearing the event. Enclosed, please find my urology report, indicating that my male genitals, specifically my penis, are within normal size and that I'm capable of normal intercourse with any woman, signed by Dr. [name], a urologist and surgeon who performed a circumcision on me in 1982. *Conclusion:* I cannot be a nincompoop in a physical sense (unless Society would feed me chemicals for my picture in the nincompoop book).

This example has a relatively intact structure. In more extreme instances, communication becomes little more than gibberish, a "word salad."

Disturbance of Thought Content

Disturbances in the content of thought typically involve certain standard types of **delusions,** or false beliefs (Oltmanns & Maher, 1988). Prominent among these are beliefs that one's thoughts, feelings, or actions are being controlled by external agents; that one's private thoughts are being broadcast indiscriminately to others; that thoughts are being inserted into one's brain by alien forces; that some mysterious agency has robbed one of one's thoughts; or that some neutral environmental event (such as a TV program or a billboard) has an intended personal meaning, often termed an "idea of reference." Other absurd propositions, including delusions of grotesque bodily changes, are regularly observed.

Disruption of Perception

Major perceptual disruption often accompanies the criteria already indicated. The patient seems unable to sort out and process the great mass of sensory information to which all of us are constantly exposed. As a result, stimuli overwhelm the resources the person has for information processing. This point is illustrated in the following statements of people with schizophrenia: "I feel like I'm too alert... everything seems to come pouring in at once... I can't seem to keep anything out...." "My nerves seem supersensitive... objects seem brighter... noises are louder... my feelings are so intense... things seem so vivid and they come at me like a flood from a broken dam." "It seems like nothing ever stops. Thoughts just keep coming in and racing round in my head... and getting broken up... sort of into pieces of thoughts and images ... like tearing up a picture. And everything is out of control... I can't seem to stop it." It is estimated that approximately 50 percent of patients diagnosed as schizophrenic experience this breakdown of perceptual selectivity during the onset of their disorders. Other even more dramatic perceptual phenomena include **hallucinations**—false perceptions, such as voices that only the schizophrenic person can hear. Hallucinations of people with schizophrenia are most often auditory, although they can also be visual and even olfactory. The typical hallucination is one in which a voice (or voices) keeps up a running commentary on the person's behaviors or thoughts. Some investigators (e.g., Stern & Silbersweig, 1998) hypothesize that hallucinations in schizophrenia are the result of malfunctioning neural feedback connections between different brain regions.

delusions False beliefs about reality that are maintained in spite of strong evidence to the contrary.

hallucinations False perceptions, such as seeing or hearing things that are not real or present.

Emotional Dysfunction

The schizophrenias are often said to include elements of clearly inappropriate emotion, or affect. In the more severe or chronic cases, the picture is usually one of apparent *anhedonia* (inability to experience joy or pleasure) and emotional shallowness or "blunting" (lack of intensity or clear definition). The person may appear virtually emotionless, so that even the most compelling and dramatic events produce at most an intellectual recognition of what is happening. We must be cautious in interpreting this sign, however, because evidence suggests that the deficit is only one of expressiveness, not of feeling per se (Berenbaum & Oltmanns, 1992; Dworkin et al., 1998; Kring, 1998; Kring et al., 1993). In other instances, particularly in the acute phases, the person may show strong affect, but the emotion clashes with the situation or with the content of his or her thoughts. For example, the person may respond to news of a parent's death with gleeful hilarity.

Confused Sense of Self

Persons with schizophrenia may feel confused about their identity to the point of loss of a subjective sense of self or of personal agency. Delusional assumption of a new identity, including a unique one such as Jesus Christ or the Virgin Mary, is not uncommon. In other instances, the person may be perplexed about aspects of his or her own body, including its gender, or may be uncertain about the boundaries separating the self from the rest of the world. The latter confusion is often associated with frightening "cosmic" or "oceanic" feelings of being somehow intimately tied up with universal powers, including God or the Devil. These feelings appear to be related to ideas of external control and similar delusions.

Disrupted Volition

Goal-directed activity is almost universally disrupted in individuals with schizophrenia. The impairment always occurs in areas of routine daily functioning, such as work, social relations, and self-care, to the extent that observers note that the person is not himself or herself any more. The picture is thus one of deterioration from a previously mastered standard of performance in everyday affairs. For example, the person may no longer maintain minimal standards of personal hygiene or may evidence a profound disregard of personal safety and health. Many researchers attribute these disruptions of "executive" behavior to some sort of impairment in the functioning of the prefrontal region of the cerebral cortex (Lenzeweger & Dworkin, 1998).

Retreat to an Inner World

Ties to the external world are almost by definition loosened in the schizophrenic disorders. In extreme instances, the withdrawal from reality seems deliberate and involves active disengagement from the environment. This rejection of the external world may be accompanied by the elaboration of an inner world in which the person develops illogical and fantastic ideas, including the creation of strange beings who interact with the person in various self-directed dramas.

Disturbed Motor Behavior

Various peculiarities of movement are sometimes observed in the schizophrenias. These motor disturbances range from an excited sort of hyperactivity to a marked decrease in all movement or an apparent clumsiness. Also included here are various forms of rigid posturing, mutism, ritualistic mannerisms, and bizarre grimacing.

Continuing Problems in Defining Schizophrenia

In recent years, a third symptom pattern—*disorganized schizophrenia*—has been recognized as yet another cluster of schizophrenic signs that is partially independent of the other two (e.g., Ratakonda et al., 1998; Toomey et al., 1997). As the term implies, this is a pattern characterized chiefly by chaotic and seemingly directionless speech and behavior, and, in fact, it has been recognized as one of the classic subtypes of schizophrenia ("hebephrenia") over the past century. To complicate matters, Dolphus and colleagues (1996), employing the statistical technique of cluster analysis, recently suggested that there are at least *four* discriminable patterns of schizophrenia signs: (1) positive, (2) negative, (3) disorganized, and (4) mixed. Since most patients in fact display a "mixed" picture, especially over time, it is not clear that this proposal adds much to our understanding. It may also be noted that "disorganized" behavior was considered a *negative* sign in earlier formulations of the positive-negative distinction.

Thus, what we call "schizophrenia" in all probability encompasses a variety of disordered processes of varied etiology, developmental pattern, and outcome—perhaps more so than for any other psychiatric diagnosis. This leads to much heterogeneity at the clinical, observational level, which is the level at which DSM diagnoses are, with rare exception, designed to operate. Pinning down the essential features of "schizophrenic" behavior is therefore more than usually dependent on the judgments of acknowledged experts in the field, rather than on established and reliable scientific data. In fact, criteria for the diagnosis of schizophrenia have varied considerably over the past century (Hegarty et al., 1994). While no reasonable person doubts the reality of the behavioral phenomena described above, it has proved difficult to identify or to formulate in exact terms a common core for this presumed psychopathological entity.

Despite the dramatic quality of the associated clinical phenomena, therefore, it must be kept in mind that schizophrenia remains a *provisional construct* (Andreasen & Carpenter, 1993), one whose definition has evolved and changed over time—with substantial effects on incidence and prevalence rates relative to those of other disorders (Carson & Sanislow, 1993) and even, as we shall see, on observed clinical outcomes for persons assigned the diagnosis. Criteria for applying the diagnosis will almost certainly change in more than trivial ways with future changes in conceptualization.

IN REVIEW

- What are the main features distinguishing positive-syndrome schizophrenia from negative-syndrome schizophrenia?
- List the DSM criteria for the diagnosis of schizophrenia.
- What kinds of delusions and hallucinations are common in the schizophrenias?

THE CLASSIC SUBTYPES OF SCHIZOPHRENIA

Recent editions of the DSM have listed five subtypes of schizophrenia, based on the differing clinical pictures long thought to be variants of a common theme of disorder; they are summarized in Table 12.3. We will focus on four of these here: undifferentiated, catatonic, disorganized, and paranoid. Of these, the undifferentiated and paranoid types are the most common today. The fifth subtype—**schizophrenia, residual type**—is a category used for people who have experienced an episode of schizophrenia

schizophrenia, residual type Subtype of schizophrenia used as a diagnostic category for people who have experienced a schizophrenic episode from which they have recovered sufficiently so as to not show prominent symptoms, but who still manifest some mild signs of their past disorder.

TABLE 12.3 SUBTYPES OF SCHIZOPHRENIA

Type	Characteristics
Undifferentiated type	A pattern of symptoms in which there is a rapidly changing mixture of all or most of the primary indicators of schizophrenia. Commonly observed are indications of perplexity, confusion, emotional turmoil, delusions of reference, excitement, dream-like autism, depression, and fear. Most often this picture is seen in patients who are in the process of breaking down and becoming schizophrenic. It is also seen, however, when major changes are occurring in the adjustive demands impinging on a person with an already-established schizophrenic psychosis. In such cases, it frequently foreshadows an impending change to another primary schizophrenic subtype.
Paranoid type	A symptom picture dominated by absurd, illogical, and changeable delusions, frequently accompanied by vivid hallucinations, with a resulting impairment of critical judgment and erratic, unpredictable, and occasionally dangerous behavior. In chronic cases, there is usually less disorganization of behavior than in other types of schizophrenia, and less extreme withdrawal from social interaction.
Catatonic type	Often characterized by alternating periods of extreme withdrawal and extreme excitement, although in some cases one or the other reaction predominates. In the withdrawal reaction there is a sudden loss of all animation and a tendency to remain motionless for hours or even days in a single position. The clinical picture may undergo an abrupt change, with excitement coming on suddenly, wherein an individual may talk or shout incoherently, pace rapidly, and engage in uninhibited, impulsive, and frenzied behavior. In this state, an individual may be dangerous.
Disorganized type	Usually occurs at an earlier age than most other types of schizophrenia, and represents a more severe disintegration of the personality. Emotional distortion and blunting typically are manifested in inappropriate laughter and silliness, peculiar mannerisms, and bizarre, often obscene, behavior.
Residual type	Mild indications of schizophrenia shown by individuals in remission following a schizophrenic episode.

from which they have recovered sufficiently so as not to show prominent psychotic symptoms. They nevertheless still manifest some mild signs of their past disorder, such as odd beliefs, flat affect, or eccentric behavior.

Undifferentiated Type

As the term implies, the diagnosis of **schizophrenia, undifferentiated type,** is something of a wastebasket category. A person so diagnosed meets the usual criteria for schizophrenia—including (in varying combinations) delusions, hallucinations, disordered thoughts, and bizarre

schizophrenia, undifferentiated type Subtype of schizophrenia in which a person meets the usual criteria for schizophrenia—including (in varying combinations) delusions, hallucinations, disordered thoughts, and bizarre behavior—but does not clearly fit into one of the other types because of a mixed symptom pattern.

This painting was made by a male patient diagnosed as suffering from undifferentiated schizophrenia. Over a period of about 9 years, he did hundreds of paintings in which the tops of the heads of males were always missing, though the females were complete. Although the therapist tried several maneuvers to get him to paint a complete man's head, the patient never did.

behaviors—but does not clearly fit into one of the other types because of a mixed symptom pattern. People in the acute, early phases of a schizophrenic breakdown frequently exhibit undifferentiated symptoms, as do those who are in transitional phases from one to another of the standard subtypes.

Probably most instances of acute, rapid-onset schizophrenic breakdown occurring for the first time appear undifferentiated in type. However, current diagnostic criteria (that is, DSM-IV-TR) preclude the diagnosis of schizophrenia unless there have been signs of the disorder for at least 6 months, by which time a stable pattern may develop, consistent with a more definite indication of type. Some patients with schizophrenia, on the other hand, remain undifferentiated over long periods. The case of Rick Wheeler is illustrative of this course.

Case Study **He Thought He Could Move Mountains** • Rick Wheeler, 26 years old, neatly groomed, and friendly and cheerful in disposition, was removed from an airplane by airport police because he was creating a disturbance—from his own account probably because he was "on another dimension." On arrest, he was oriented to the extent of knowing where he was, his name, and the current date, but his report of these facts was embedded in a peculiar and circumstantial context involving science fiction themes. Investigation revealed that he had been discharged from a nearby state mental hospital 3 days earlier. He was brought to another hospital by police.

On admission, physical examination and laboratory studies were normal, but Rick claimed that he was Jesus Christ and he could move mountains. His speech was extremely difficult to follow because of incoherence and derailment. For example, he explained his wish to leave the city, "because things happen here I don't approve of. I approve of other things but I don't approve of the other things. And believe me, it's worse for them in the end." He complained that the Devil wanted to kill him and that his food contained "ground-up corpses." He was born, he claimed, from his father's sexual organs.

Background investigation revealed that Rick's difficulties began, after a successful academic start, in elementary school: "I could comprehend but I couldn't store . . . it's like looking at something but being unable to take it in." He thereafter maintained a D average until he dropped out halfway through his junior year of high school. He had never held a full-time job, and his social adjustment had always been poor. He showed no interest in women until he married, at age 19, a patient he'd met during one of the earliest of some 20 of his hospitalizations, beginning at age 16. A daughter was born from this match, but Rick had lost track of both her and his wife; he had shown no further interest in women. Rick himself was the eldest of five children; there was no known mental disorder in any of his first-degree relatives (that is, siblings and parents).

Unable to maintain employment, Rick had been supported mainly on federal disability welfare and by virtue of patienthood in public hospitals. His hospital admissions and discharges showed a substantial correlation with his varying financial status; that is, he tended to be released from the hospital around the first of the month, when his welfare check was due, and to be readmitted (or alternatively sent to jail) following some public altercation after his money had run out. Numerous attempts to commit Rick to the hospital indefinitely on an involuntary basis had failed because he was able to appear competent at court appearances. He had, however, been declared incompetent to receive his own checks, and various relatives had stepped forward to handle his finances. Now they are afraid to do so because Rick set his grandmother's house afire, having concluded (erroneously, as it turned out) that she was withholding some of his money. He had also threatened others and had been arrested several times for carrying concealed weapons.

In the latest hospitalization, two different antipsychotic medications were tried over a period of 5 weeks with no discernible improvement. Rick still claimed supernatural powers and special connections with several national governments, was still refusing food because of its contamination with ground-up corpses, and was still threatening bodily harm to people he found uncooperative. A further attempt was made to commit him and to place his affairs under legal guardianship. As Rick had rather boastfully predicted, this attempt failed because of his lucid defense of himself, and the court dismissed the action. He was discharged to a protected boarding house but disappeared 4 days later. (Adapted from Spitzer et al., 1983, pp. 153–155.)

Most patients who show this type of chaotic, undifferentiated pattern do not have the early and slowly developing, insidious onset—one associated with poor prognosis—that occurred in Rick's case. On the contrary, the breakdown erupts suddenly out of the context of a seemingly unremarkable life history, usually following a period of notable stress. The episode usually clears up in a matter of weeks or, at most, months. Recurrent episodes, however, are not uncommon, especially in the absence of vigorous follow-up treatment. Should the duration of this "schizophreniform" (see below) disturbance exceed 6 months, the disorder may qualify for the diagnosis of schizophrenia. In some few instances, treatment efforts are unsuccessful, and the mixed symptoms of the early undifferentiated disorder slide into a more chronic phase, with the person typically developing both the more specific symptoms of other subtypes as well as increasingly severe negative symptoms.

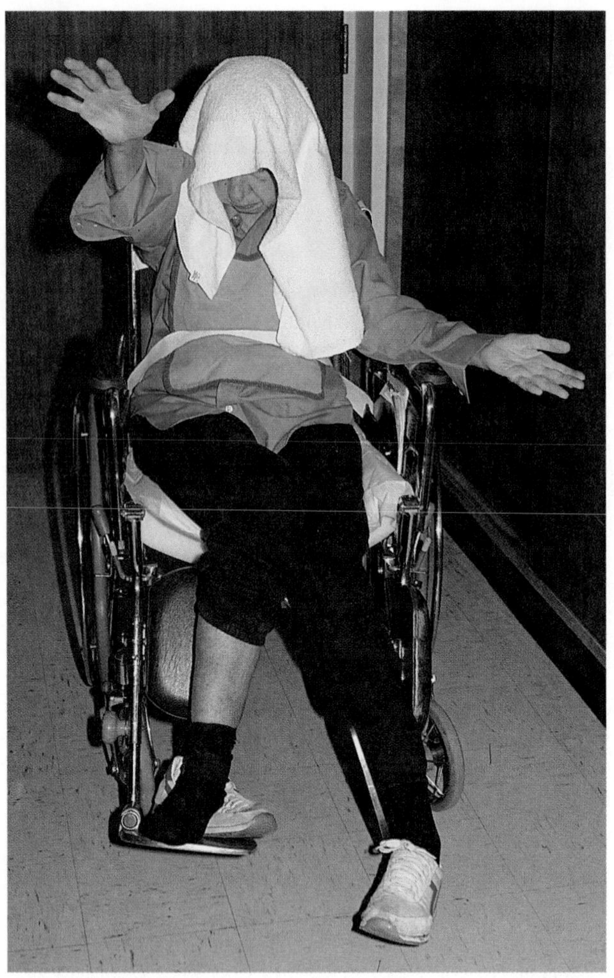

Peculiar posturing is a defining feature of catatonic-type schizophrenia.

Catatonic Type

The central feature of **schizophrenia, catatonic type,** is pronounced motor signs, either of an excited or a stuporous type, which sometimes make it difficult to differentiate this condition from a psychotic mood disorder. The clinical picture is often an early manifestation of a disorder that will become chronic and intractable unless the underlying process is somehow arrested. Though at one time common in Europe and North America, catatonic reactions have become less frequent in recent years.

Some of these patients are highly suggestible and will automatically obey commands or imitate the actions of others (*echopraxia*) or mimic their phrases (*echolalia*). If a patient's arm is raised to an awkward and uncomfortable position, he or she may keep it there for minutes or even hours. Ordinarily, patients in a catatonic stupor stubbornly resist any effort to change their position and may become mute, resist all attempts at feeding, and refuse to comply with even the slightest request. They pay no attention to bowel or bladder control and may drool. Their facial expression is typically vacant, and their skin appears waxy. Threats and painful stimuli have no effect, and they may have to be dressed and washed by nursing personnel.

Catatonic patients may pass suddenly from states of extreme stupor to great excitement, during which they seem to be under great "pressure of activity" and may become violent, being in these respects indistinguishable from some bipolar manic patients. They may talk or shout excitedly and incoherently, pace rapidly back and forth, openly indulge in sexual activities, attempt self-mutilation or even suicide, or impulsively attack and try to kill others. The suddenness and extreme frenzy of these attacks make such patients dangerous to both themselves and others. The following case illustrates some of the symptoms typical of catatonic reactions.

schizophrenia, catatonic type Subtype of schizophrenia in which the central feature is pronounced motor symptoms, either of an excited or stuporous type, which sometimes make it difficult to differentiate this condition from a psychotic mood disorder.

Case Study **Catatonia in a 16-Year-Old** • Todd Phillips, a 16-year-old high school student, was referred to a psychiatric hospital by his family physician. His family had been very upset by his increasingly strange behavior over the preceding 8 months and had consulted the family physician, who treated Todd with small doses of antipsychotic medication, without any improvement.

Although Todd has had many problems since he was a small child, there was a distinct change about 8 months ago. He began spending more and more time in his room and seemed uninterested in doing many of his usual activities. His grades dropped. He started stuttering. He used to weigh about 215 pounds, but began to eat less, and lost 35 pounds. For no apparent reason, he started drinking large quantities of water.

More recently, there was a change for the worse. A few months ago he began taking Tai Chi lessons and often stood for long periods in karate-like positions, oblivious to what was going on around him. He stopped doing his homework. He took an inordinately long time to get dressed, eat his meals, or bathe. Before getting dressed in the morning, he would go through an elaborate ritual of arranging his clothes on the bed before putting them on. When his parents asked him a question, he repeated the question over and over and did not seem to hear or understand what was said.

At school he received demerits for the first time for being late to class. His family began to lose patience with him when he eventually refused to go to school. When his father tried to get him out of bed in the morning, he lay motionless, sometimes having wet the bed during the night. It was at this point that his parents, in desperation, consulted their family physician.

When first seen in the hospital, Todd was a disheveled looking, somewhat obese adolescent, standing motionless in the center of the room with his head flexed forward and his hands at his sides. He appeared perplexed, but was correctly oriented to time and place. He was able to do simple calculations, and his recent and remote memory were intact. He answered questions slowly and in a peculiar manner. An example of his speech follows:

Q: Why did you come to the hospital?

A: Why did I come? Why did I come to the hospital? I came to the hospital because of crazy things with my hands. Sometimes my hands jump up like that... wait a minute... I guess it's happening.... Well, yes, see it's been happening. [Makes robotlike gestures with his hands.]

Q: What thoughts go through your head?

A: What thoughts go through my head? What thoughts go through my head? Well, I think about things... like... yes, well... I think thoughts... I have thoughts. I think thoughts.

Q: What thoughts?

A: What thoughts? What kinds of thoughts? I think thoughts.

Q: Do you hear voices?

A: Do I hear voices? I hear voices. People talk. Do I hear voices? No.... People talk. I hear voices. I hear voices when people talk.

Q: Are you sick?

A: Am I sick? No, I'm not sick... these fidgeting habits, these fidgeting habits. I have habits. I have fidgeting habits.

Throughout the examination Todd made repetitive chewing and biting motions. Occasionally, when questioned, he would smile enigmatically. He seemed unresponsive to much of what was going on around him. His infrequent movements were slow and jerky, and he often assumed the karate-like postures that his parents described, in which he would remain frozen. If the examiner placed Todd's hands in an awkward position, he remained frozen in that position for several minutes. (From Spitzer et al., 1983, pp. 139–140.)

Although the matter is far from settled, some clinicians interpret a catatonic patient's immobility as a way of coping with his or her reduced filtering ability and increased vulnerability to stimulation: It seems to provide a feeling of some control over external sources of stimulation, though not necessarily over inner ones. Freeman (1960) has cited the explanation advanced by one patient: "I did not want to move, because if I did everything changed around me and upset me horribly so I remained still to hold onto a sense of permanence" (p. 932).

Disorganized Type

Compared with the other subtypes of schizophrenia, **schizophrenia, disorganized type,** usually begins at an earlier age and represents a more severe disintegration of the personality. Fortunately, like the catatonic type, it is relatively uncommon. In pre-DSM-III classifications, this type was called *hebephrenic schizophrenia.*

Typically, an affected person has a history of oddness, overscrupulousness about trivial things, and preoccupation with obscure religious and philosophical issues. Frequently, he or she broods over the dire results of masturbation or minor infractions of social conventions. While schoolmates are enjoying normal play and social activities, this person gradually becomes more seclusive and more preoccupied with fantasies.

As the disorder progresses, the person becomes emotionally indifferent and infantile. A silly smile and inappropriate, shallow laughter after little or no provocation are common symptoms. If asked the reason for his or her laughter, the patient may state that he or she does not know or may volunteer some wholly irrelevant and unsatisfactory explanation. Speech becomes incoherent and may include considerable baby talk, childish giggling, a repetitious use of similar-sounding words, and a derailing of associated thoughts that may give a pun-like quality to speech. The patient may invent new words (neologisms). In some instances, speech becomes wholly incomprehensible.

Hallucinations, particularly auditory ones, are common. The voices heard by these patients may accuse them of immoral practices, "pour filth" into their minds, and call them vile names. Delusions are usually of a sexual, religious, hypochondriacal, or persecutory nature, and they are typically changeable, unsystematized, and fantastic. For example, one woman insisted not only that she was being followed by enemies but that she had already been killed a number of times. Another claimed that a long tube extended from the Kremlin directly to her uterus, through which she was being invaded by Russians.

In occasional cases, individuals become hostile and aggressive. They may exhibit peculiar mannerisms and other bizarre forms of behavior. These behaviors may take the

schizophrenia, disorganized type Subtype of schizophrenia that usually begins at an earlier age and represents a more severe disintegration of the personality than seen in the other subtypes.

form of odd facial grimaces; talking and gesturing to themselves; sudden, inexplicable laughter and weeping; and, in some cases, an abnormal interest in urine and feces, which patients may smear on walls and even on themselves. Obscene behavior and the absence of any modesty or sense of shame are characteristic. Although patients may exhibit outbursts of anger and temper tantrums in connection with fantasies, they are indifferent to real-life situations, no matter how horrifying or gruesome the latter may be. The clinical picture in disorganized schizophrenia is exemplified in the following interview.

Case Study **"I am a 'looner' . . . a bachelor"** • The patient was a divorcee, 32 years of age, who had come to the hospital with bizarre delusions, hallucinations, and severe personality disintegration. She had a record of alcoholism, promiscuity, and possible incestuous relations with a brother. The following conversation shows typical hebephrenic responses to questioning.

DOCTOR: How do you feel today?

PATIENT: Fine.

DOCTOR: When did you come here?

PATIENT: 1416, you remember, doctor [silly giggle].

DOCTOR: Do you know why you are here?

PATIENT: Well, in 1951 I changed into two men. President Truman was judge at my trial. I was convicted and hung [silly giggle]. My brother and I were given back our normal bodies 5 years ago. I am a policewoman. I keep a dictaphone concealed on my person.

DOCTOR: Can you tell me the name of this place?

PATIENT: I have not been a drinker for 16 years. I am taking a mental rest after a "carter" assignment or "quill." You know, a "penwrap." I had contracts with Warner Brothers Studios and Eugene broke phonograph records but Mike protested. I have been with the police department for 35 years. I am made of flesh and blood—see doctor [pulling up her dress].

DOCTOR: Are you married?

PATIENT: No. I am not attracted to men [silly giggle]. I have a companionship arrangement with my brother. I am a "looner"... a bachelor.

schizophrenia, paranoid type Subtype of schizophrenia in which a person is increasingly suspicious, has severe difficulties in interpersonal relationships, and experiences absurd, illogical, and often changing delusions.

The prognosis is generally poor if a person develops disorganized schizophrenia. At this stage of deterioration, no form of treatment intervention yet discovered has a high likelihood of effecting more than a modest recovery.

Paranoid Type

Formerly about one-half of all schizophrenic first admissions to hospitals were diagnosed as **schizophrenia, paranoid type.** In recent years, however, the prevalence of the paranoid type has shown a substantial decrease, while the undifferentiated type has shown a marked increase. The reasons for these changes are uncertain but may relate to the promptness with which newly diagnosed schizophrenic (or schizophreniform) patients are put on antipsychotic medication, which has an especially powerful effect in suppressing "positive" symptoms such as paranoid delusions.

Frequently, persons with paranoid-type schizophrenia show histories of increasing suspiciousness and of severe difficulties in interpersonal relationships. The eventual clinical picture is dominated by absurd, illogical, and often changing delusions. Persecutory delusions are the most frequent and may involve a wide range of bizarre ideas and plots. An individual may become highly suspicious of relatives or associates and may complain of being watched, followed, poisoned, talked about, or influenced by various tormenting devices rigged up by "enemies."

In addition to persecutory themes, themes of grandeur are also common in paranoid-type delusions. Persons with such delusions may, for example, claim to be the world's greatest economist or philosopher, or some prominent person of the past, such as Franklin Roosevelt, Joan of Arc, or even God. These delusions are frequently accompanied by vivid auditory, visual, and other hallucinations. Patients may hear singing, or God speaking, or the voices of their enemies, or they may see angels or feel damaging rays piercing their bodies at various points.

An individual's thinking and behavior become centered on the themes of persecution, grandeur, or both in a pathological "paranoid construction" that—for all its distortion of reality—provides a sense of identity and importance perhaps not otherwise attainable for the person. There thus tends to be a higher level of adaptive coping and of cognitive integrative skills with paranoid-type schizophrenia than with other types of schizophrenia, although these differences are not large and are not consistent across all cognitive domains (Zalewski et al., 1998).

Despite this modest relative "advantage" that individuals with paranoid-type schizophrenia enjoy, such people are far from easy to deal with. The weaving of delusions

A patient diagnosed as having paranoid-type schizophrenia was unable to respond at all when asked by a therapist to make an original drawing. Therefore, with the therapist's help, a picture (top left) was selected from a magazine for the patient to copy. One of his first attempts (top right) was a pencil drawing on manila paper showing great visual distortion, as well as an inability to use colors and difficulty in using letters of the alphabet. The evident visual distortion was a diagnostic aid for the therapist, who was able to learn from it that the patient, who was extremely fearful, saw things in this distorted way, aggravating his fear. In the picture at bottom left, the patient has shown obvious improvement, although it was not until a year after therapy began that he was able to execute a painting with the realism of the picture at bottom right.

and hallucinations into a paranoid construction results in a loss of critical judgment and in erratic, unpredictable behavior. In response to a command from a "voice," such a person may commit violent acts. Thus, patients with paranoid-type schizophrenia can sometimes be dangerous—for example, when they attack people they are convinced have been persecuting them. Somewhat paradoxically, such problems are exacerbated by the fact that such people show less bizarre behavior and less extreme withdrawal from the outside world than do individuals with other types of schizophrenia; as a consequence, they are less likely to be confined in protective environments.

The following conversation between a clinician and a man diagnosed as having chronic paranoid-type schizophrenia illustrates well the illogical, delusional symptom picture, together with continued attention to misinterpreted sensory data, that these individuals experience.

Case Study A Case of Paranoid Schizophrenia

DOCTOR: What's your name?

PATIENT: Who are you?

DOCTOR: I'm a doctor. Who are you?

PATIENT: I can't tell you who I am.

DOCTOR: Why can't you tell me?

PATIENT: You wouldn't believe me.

DOCTOR: What are you doing here?

PATIENT: Well, I've been sent here to thwart the Russians. I'm the only one in the world who knows how to deal with them. They got their spies all around here though to get me, but I'm smarter than any of them.

DOCTOR: What are you going to do to thwart the Russians?

PATIENT: I'm organizing.

DOCTOR: Whom are you going to organize?

PATIENT: Everybody. I'm the only man in the world who can do that, but they're trying to get me. But I'm going to use my atomic bomb media to blow them up.

DOCTOR: You must be a terribly important person then.

PATIENT: Well, of course.

DOCTOR: What do you call yourself?

PATIENT: You used to know me as Franklin D. Roosevelt.

DOCTOR: Isn't he dead?

PATIENT: Sure he's dead, but I'm alive.

DOCTOR: But you're Franklin D. Roosevelt?

PATIENT: His spirit. He, God, and I figured this out. And now I'm going to make a race of healthy people. My agents are lining them up. Say, who are you?

DOCTOR: I'm a doctor here.

PATIENT: You don't look like a doctor. You look like a Russian to me.

DOCTOR: How can you tell a Russian from one of your agents?

PATIENT: I read eyes. I get all my signs from eyes. I look into your eyes and get all my signs from them.

DOCTOR: Do you sometimes hear voices telling you someone is a Russian?

PATIENT: No, I just look into eyes. I got a mirror here to look into my own eyes. I know everything that's going on. I can tell by the color, by the way it's shaped.

DOCTOR: Did you have any trouble with people before you came here?

PATIENT: Well, only the Russians. They were trying to surround me in my neighborhood. One day they tried to drop a bomb on me from the fire escape.

DOCTOR: How could you tell it was a bomb?

PATIENT: I just knew.

Despite having considerable longevity, the formal subtyping scheme described above has never proved very productive either in improving diagnoses (e.g., patients frequently and apparently spontaneously change in subtype over time) or in shedding light on more basic issues such as the nature of a "common core," if any, of the schizophrenia experience.

Other Schizophrenic and Psychotic Patterns

As was noted in Chapter 6, the diagnosis of **schizoaffective disorder** (bipolar or depressive subtype) is applied to individuals who show features of both schizophrenia and severe mood disorder. In the DSM-IV-TR classification, this disorder is not considered to be a formal subtype of schizophrenia, although it is listed in the same section of the manual and shares the numerical code of the schizophrenias. Thus, although treated as a separate disorder, its status within the DSM system is left somewhat unclear—reflecting some continuing controversy in the field as to where it really belongs.

Schizophreniform disorder is a category reserved for schizophrenia-like psychoses of less than 6 months' duration. It may include any of the symptoms described in the preceding sections but is probably most often seen in an undifferentiated form. Brief psychotic states of this sort may or may not be related to subsequent psychiatric disorder (Strakowski, 1994). At present, however, all recent-onset cases of true schizophrenia presumably must first receive a diagnosis of schizophreniform disorder. Because of the possibility of an early and lasting remission from a first episode of schizophrenic breakdown, the prognosis for schizophreniform disorder (where it is a manifestation of recent-onset schizophrenic symptoms) is better than that for established forms of schizophrenia. Also, it appears likely that the potentially harmful effects of labeling may be reduced by keeping schizophreniform disorder out of the formal category of schizophrenias.

IN REVIEW

- What are the five major subtypes of schizophrenia listed in the DSM?
- Compare and contrast the time of onset, symptoms, and prognosis of the major subtypes.
- What distinguishes schizophreniform disorder from other schizophrenic disorders?

CAUSAL FACTORS IN SCHIZOPHRENIA

Despite an enormous research effort going back many years and continuing to the present, the causal factors un-

schizoaffective disorder Mental disorder in which a person shows features of both schizophrenia and severe mood disorder.

schizophreniform disorder Any schizophrenia-like psychosis of less than 6 months' duration.

derlying the schizophrenias remain unclear, particularly in their details. Primary responsibility has been attributed variously to (1) biological factors; (2) psychosocial factors, including pathogenic interpersonal and family patterns and decompensation under excessive stress; and (3) sociocultural factors, especially as influences on the local prevalence of various types of schizophrenic disorders. These three sets of factors are not mutually exclusive, of course, and it seems likely that each is involved in at least some cases. We will discuss biological factors first and in relatively greater detail because of the prominence they have attained in contemporary thinking about schizophrenia.

Biological Factors in Schizophrenia

Research relating to biological factors implicated in the causal pattern leading to schizophrenia has been concentrated on genetics and on various biochemical, neurophysiological, and neuroanatomical processes. Each of these research foci will be discussed in what follows.

Genetic Influences It has been known for many decades that disorders of the schizophrenic type tend to "run in families," giving rise to the notion of "tainted" genes as an important causal factor. In fact, the evidence for higher-than-expected rates of schizophrenia among biological relatives of "index" cases (that is, the diagnosed group of people who provide the starting point for inquiry, also called "probands") is overwhelming. Moreover, that evidence includes a strong correlation between closeness of the blood relationship (i.e., level of gene-sharing or consanguinity) and degree of concordance for the diagnosis, as depicted in Figure 12.2.

Of course, and as we have repeatedly emphasized, the interpretation of such familial concordance patterns is never completely straightforward, in part because of the strong relationship between the sharing of genes and the sharing of the environments in which those genes express themselves. As the genetic research reveals, individual environments (including prenatal ones) have a powerful effect in determining outcomes with respect to schizo-

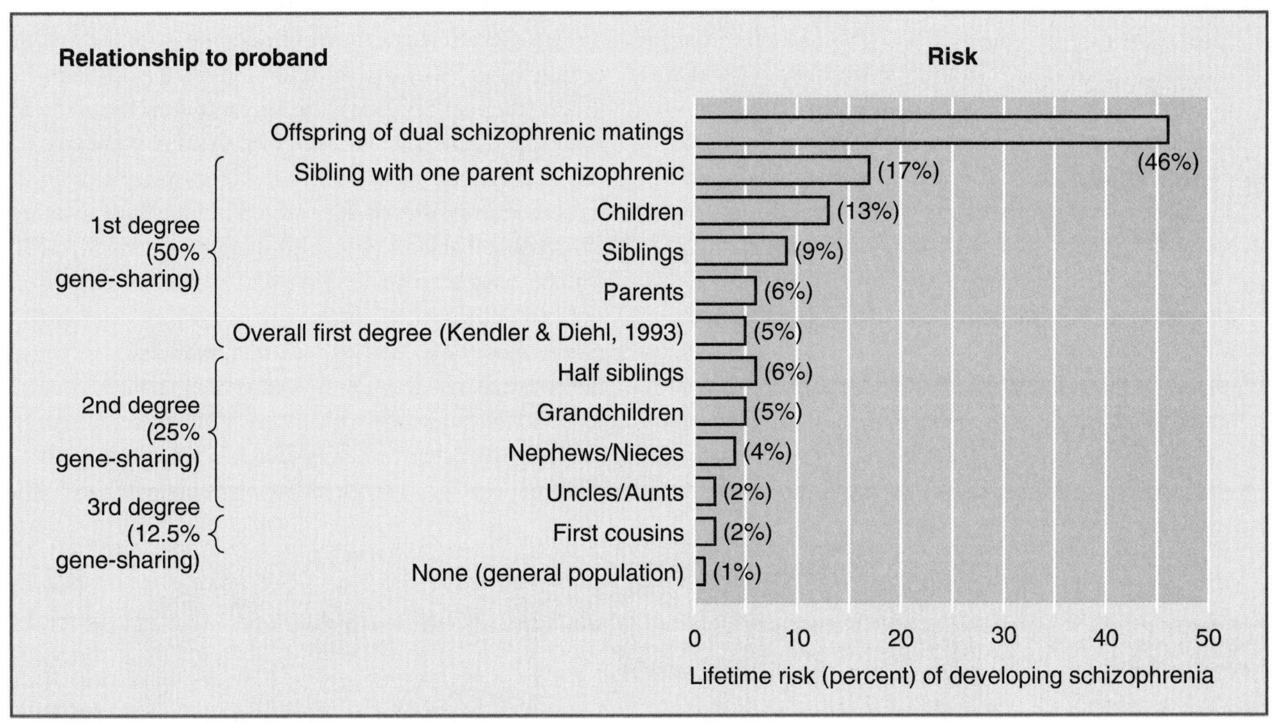

FIGURE 12.2
LIFETIME RISK OF DEVELOPING SCHIZOPHRENIA AS A FUNCTION OF CLOSENESS OF BLOOD RELATIONSHIP (CONSANGUINITY)

Included is a somewhat discrepant risk estimate derived from a thorough analysis of worldwide data on first-degree relatives of schizophrenic probands by Kendler and Diehl (1993). Discrepancies of this sort are not unusual in such "pedigree" research, reflecting differences in approach as well as biased observations. Twin concordance data are omitted here; see Figure 12.3.

Source: From *Schizophrenia Genesis* by Irving Gottesman, © 1991. Used by permission of W. H. Freeman and Company.

phrenia (Moldin & Gottesman, 1997). Thus, evidence of a shared family trait, while persuasive, remains incomplete because of the difficulty of figuring out where genetic influences end and environmental ones begin.

The still-open question of whether a tendency toward schizophrenia is directly inheritable would be easier to answer if we could (1) identify the exact mechanism whereby gene biochemical products (and those are the only immediate products genes have) could alter the probability of becoming schizophrenic and/or (2) isolate and identify the particular gene or genes involved. Unfortunately, and despite the dramatic progress of genetics research in re-

HIGHLIGHT 12.1

The Genain Quadruplets

Sometime in the early 1930s, the Genain quadruplets were born. Except for their low birth weights, ranging from Nora's 4 pounds, 8 ounces to Hester's 3 pounds (with Iris and Myra in between), the girls appeared to be reasonably normal babies, albeit premature. Hester had to be fitted with a truss (an abdominal compression device) because of a hernia but was nevertheless discharged from the hospital with her sisters as basically healthy some 6 weeks after the birth. Each of these genetically identical girls was to become schizophrenic before the age of 25, an outcome that would be expected to occur by chance only once in approximately 1.5 billion births. An intensive and lengthy on-site study of this family carried out by staff of the National Institute of Mental Health (Rosenthal, 1963) provides a window on the interacting influences operating in the schizophrenias.

Notwithstanding their genetic identity and physical similarity, the girls were treated as though they were two sets of twins: a superior and talented set consisting of Nora and Myra, and an inferior and problematic set consisting of Iris and Hester. Complying with parental attributions, the girls did in fact pair up for purposes of mutual support and intimacy; when threatened from the outside, however, they became a true foursome. Such threats were frequent because of the girls' celebrity status, causing them to become socially isolated. This isolation was encouraged by their parents.

Mr. Genain spent much of his time drinking and expressing his various fears and obsessions to his family. Fearing that the girls would get into sexual trouble or be raped unless he watched over them zealously, he imposed extreme restrictions and surveillance on them until their breakdowns. He was reported to have sexually molested at least two of his daughters; only Myra, who persistently distanced herself from him, was possibly not molested. When the girls complained to their mother about Mr. Genain's sexual approaches, she rationalized that he was merely testing their virtue; if they objected to his advances, then clearly all was well.

Hester had her first breakdown while still in high school, at age 18. Nora's breakdown followed, at age 20.

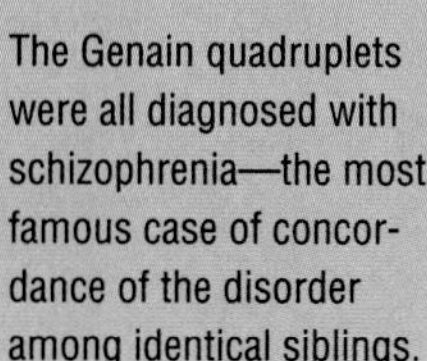

The Genain quadruplets were all diagnosed with schizophrenia—the most famous case of concordance of the disorder among identical siblings.

Iris "just went to pieces" at age 22. Myra, who had maintained the most independence from her disturbed parents, did not show signs of schizophrenia until age 24. It may be significant that in the cases of Nora, Iris, and Myra, deterioration began shortly after an incident in which a man had made rather insistent "improper advances."

Despite early clinical similarities displayed by the young women—undifferentiated and changing features and an abundance of "positive" signs—the courses and outcomes of their disorders differed markedly. The behavior of Hester and Iris was described in hospital records as persistently deteriorated. By contrast, Nora and Myra did not show the marked behavioral disorganization of their less functional sisters, although Myra's behavior was the more consistently appropriate over time. The quadruplets' outcomes show a corresponding pattern. At the time of Rosenthal's 1963 report, Myra was working steadily, married, and doing well. Nora was making a marginal adjustment outside the hospital. Iris was still fluctuating between periods of severe disturbance and relative lucidity in which she could manage brief stays outside the hospital. Hester remained continuously hospitalized in a condition of severe psychosis and was considered essentially a "hopeless case."

In a follow-up report some 20 years later, the relative adjustment of the sisters, then in their 50s, remained as it had been in the 1960s (DeLisi et al., 1984; Mirsky et al., 1984; Sargent, 1982a). Myra continued to do well and had had two children in the interim. The other three sisters were living at home with their mother, with Nora continuing to show a higher level of functioning than Iris or Hester. All of the sisters were on continuous medication, and even the beleaguered Hester appeared to have overcome to an extent her originally dismal prognosis.

It is of considerable interest that newly developed techniques of neurological assessment showed that Nora had impairments of the central nervous system similar to those of Hester, and yet her outcome seemed far better than that of Hester or even Iris. It is possible that the original pairing of Iris with Hester was destructive to Iris's development. In any event, despite their identical heredity, the Genain quadruplets array themselves along a considerable range of the possible outcomes associated with schizophrenic breakdown.

We have here, then, four genetically identical women, all of whom experienced schizophrenic disorders. The disorders, however, differed in severity, chronicity, and outcome. Obviously, these differences must be ascribed to differences in the environments the quads experienced, including their intrauterine environments, which presumably contributed to their modest variations detectable at birth. Clearly, Hester, possibly most compromised biologically and in relative parental disfavor from the beginning, faced the harshest environmental conditions, followed closely by her "twin," Iris. The outcome for these women has been grim. Myra was the most favored youngster and the one who experienced the least objectionable parental attention, partly owing to a greater independence and assertiveness than was displayed by her sisters. Nora was a close second in this respect but had the misfortune of being her incestuous father's "favorite." In the more recent assessments, Nora was also shown to have a compromised central nervous system (specifically, an imbalance of metabolic rates in different brain areas) comparable to that of Hester. Though Nora has not done as well as Myra, she has emerged as clearly superior in functioning to the other two sisters. We see here the considerable power of environmental forces in determining personal destiny, even in schizophrenia. ■

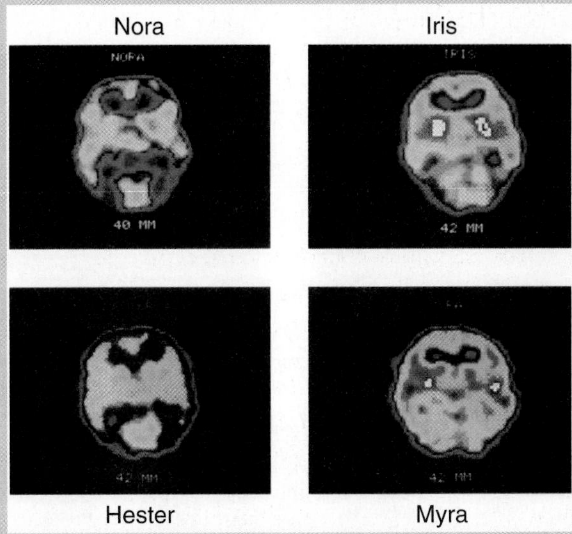

PET scans of the Genain quadruplets suggest a possible psychosocial impact resulting from the early matching of two pairs of co-twins. The scans indicate comparatively more severe brain impairment for Hester and Nora. The large areas of blue and yellow show that their brains consume lower levels of glucose, one indicator of lessened brain activity. The orange spots on the scans of Iris and Myra suggest more normal energy usage. Yet it is Iris, originally "matched" with Hester, who has had the poorer clinical outcome than either Nora or Myra (DeLisi et al., 1984).

cent years, neither of these seems at present an attainable goal. Although some investigators continue to hold the view that the genetic influence in schizophrenia is confined to one or at most a very few genes, the evidence points strongly toward *polygenic* involvement. That is, current expert thinking emphasizes the notion that a multiplicity of genes must somehow operate in concert to enhance the genetic schizophrenia risk (Gottesman, 1991; Kendler & Diehl, 1993; Moldin & Gottesman, 1997). If that proves to be the case, pinning down the genes involved will be a very difficult undertaking, as was confirmed by a study attempting to identify genes common to schizophrenia (Levinson et al., 1998).

It will be helpful to bear in mind these continuing uncertainties as we review the available data on twin and adoption studies of schizophrenia.

Twin Studies As with the mood disorders, concordance rates for schizophrenia for identical twins are routinely, and over very many studies, found to be significantly higher than those for fraternal twins or ordinary siblings.

Torrey and colleagues (1994) published a review of the major literature worldwide on twin studies in schizophrenia. Their findings are summarized in Figure 12.3. Noting in particular overall pairwise concordance rates of 28 and 6 percent in monozygotic and dizygotic twin pairs, respectively, we may conclude that a reduction in shared genes from 100 percent to 50 percent reduces the risk of schizophrenia nearly 80 percent. Also, 50 percent gene-sharing with a schizophrenic proband is associated with a lifetime risk (6 percent) that, while low in absolute terms, is markedly higher than that of the general population.

If schizophrenia were exclusively a genetic disorder, the concordance rate for identical twins would, of course, be 100 percent. In fact, however, there are more discordant than concordant identical pairs. On the other hand, concordance of significant magnitude clearly exists, and twin studies show us that predisposition for the disorder is associated with genetic variables.

The most thorough and searching of available investigations of discordant schizophrenia outcomes among monozygotic twins was reported by Torrey and colleagues (1994). The study involved 27 pairs of monozygotic twins who were discordant for the schizophrenia diagnosis. The researchers found that genetically identical individuals can manifest widespread biological differences, particularly in neurological integrity, that are associated with relative risk for the development of schizophrenia. It should be noted, however, that none of the findings was of sufficient magnitude to predict outcomes for individual cases. Also, there

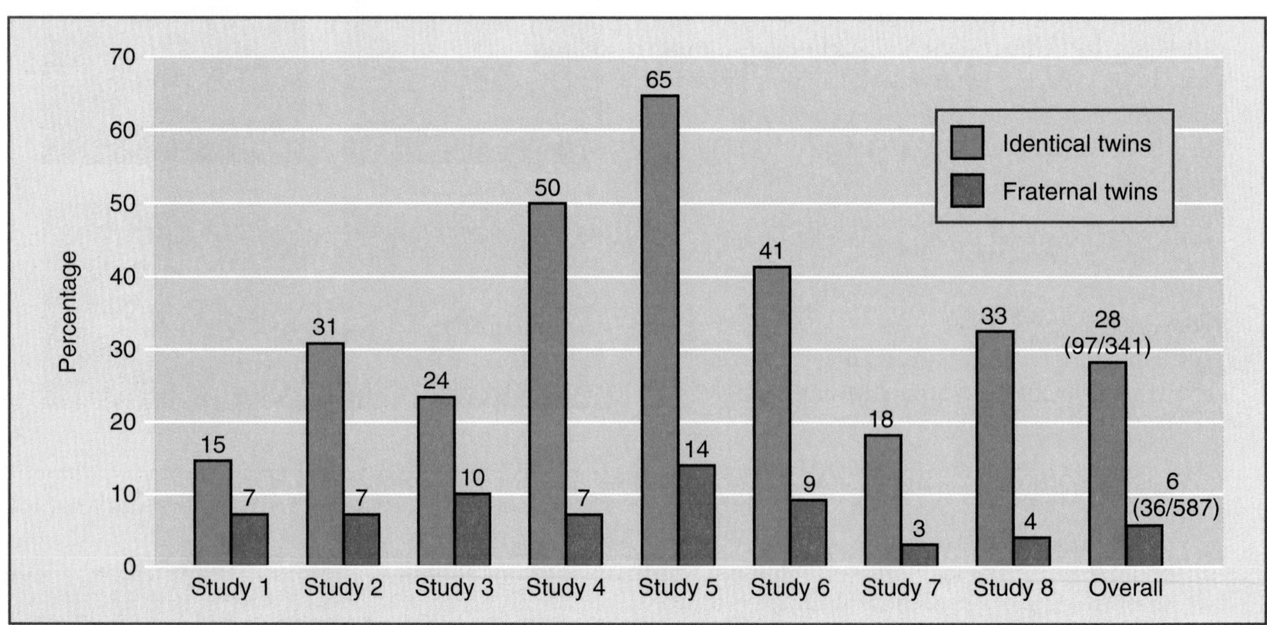

FIGURE 12.3
PAIRWISE TWIN CONCORDANCE RATES FOR SCHIZOPHRENIA FOUND IN EIGHT METHODOLOGICALLY ADEQUATE STUDIES
Source: From *Schizophrenia and Manic Depressive Disorder* by E. Fuller Torrey, Anne Bowler, Edward Taylor & Irving Gottesman. Copyright © 1994 by Basic Books, Inc.

were a few striking inconsistencies in the data; in a few cases, the well twin appeared more biologically compromised than his or her schizophrenic co-twin. As the researchers acknowledged, the results of this study, while intriguing, in themselves provide no clear resolution of basic questions concerning the ultimate source or sources of vulnerability to the development of schizophrenia. They do, of course, strongly implicate neurological anomalies as often playing a role in the causal pattern.

Returning to the specific issue of genetic influences, a clever investigative strategy employing discordant twins was pioneered by Fischer (1971, 1973). Reasoning that genetic influence, if present, would show up in the *offspring* of the *nonschizophrenic* twins of discordant monozygotic pairs, she found exactly that outcome in a search of official records in Denmark. Gottesman and Bertelsen (1989), in a follow-up of Fischer's subjects, reported an age-corrected schizophrenia incidence rate (that is, a rate taking into account predicted breakdowns for subjects not yet beyond the age of risk) of 17.4 percent for the offspring of the nonschizophrenic monozygotic twins. This rate, which far exceeds normal expectancy, was not significantly different from that for offspring of the schizophrenic members of discordant monozygotic pairs, or from that for offspring of schizophrenic dizygotic twins. Since exposure to schizophrenic aunts and uncles would presumably have, at most, limited etiological significance, these results give impressive support to the genetic hypothesis. They also, as the researchers noted, indicate that the implicated predisposition may remain "unexpressed" (as in the nonschizophrenic twins of discordant pairs) unless "released" by unknown environmental factors.

Adoption Studies Several studies have attempted to overcome the shortcomings of the twin method in achieving a true separation of hereditary from environmental influences by using what is called the *adoption method.* Here concordance rates for schizophrenia are compared for the biological and adoptive relatives of persons who have been adopted out of their biological families at an early age (preferably at birth) and have subsequently become schizophrenic. If concordance is greater among the patients' biological relatives than among their adoptive ones, a hereditary influence is strongly suggested; the reverse pattern would, of course, argue for environmental causation. There are several procedural variants to this basic method, as indicated in what follows.

A follow-up study of 47 people who had been born to schizophrenic mothers in a state mental hospital and placed with relatives or in foster homes shortly after birth found that 16.6 percent of these subjects were later diagnosed as schizophrenic. In contrast, none of the 50 control subjects selected from among residents of the same foster homes—whose biological mothers were not schizophrenic—later became schizophrenic. In addition to the greater probability of being diagnosed with schizophrenia, the offspring of schizophrenic mothers were more likely to be diagnosed as mentally retarded, neurotic, and psychopathic (that is, antisocial). They also were involved more frequently in criminal activities and spent more time in penal institutions (Heston, 1966). These findings suggest that any genetic liability conveyed by the mothers is not specific to schizophrenia but also includes a liability for other forms of psychopathology.

A large-scale and multifaceted adoption study was undertaken in Denmark with American investigators working in collaboration with Danish professionals (Kendler & Gruenberg, 1984; Kendler, Gruenberg, & Kinney, 1994a; Kety, 1987; Kety et al., 1968, 1978, 1994; Rosenthal et al., 1968; Wender et al., 1974). Based on a national sample of schizophrenic adoptees and their biological and adoptive relatives (together with suitable control cases), the data show a preponderance of schizophrenia and "schizophrenia spectrum" (which includes schizotypal and paranoid personality disorder) problems in the biological relatives of schizophrenic adoptees. By contrast, adoptive relatives of schizophrenic adoptees had an unremarkable incidence rate for schizophrenia.

The Danish adoption studies did not include independent assessments of the child-rearing adequacy of the adoptive families into which index (those who became schizophrenic) and control (those who did not) youngsters had been placed. It remained for Tienari and colleagues (Tienari et al., 1985, 1987; Tienari, 1991, 1994) to add this feature to their research plan. Their study, called the *Finnish Adoption Study,* is still in progress; it involves a follow-up of the adopted-away children of all women in Finland hospitalized for schizophrenia, beginning in 1960. As they grow into adulthood, these high-risk index children are compared to a control group of adoptees whose biological mothers were normal. The trend of the results is already clear, reaching high levels of statistical significance. There is the familiar finding that the index adoptees have developed more, and more serious (including schizophrenia), psychopathology than the controls. Most of this psychopathology, however, is concentrated in the index group reared by *poorly functioning adoptive parents*—for example, parents showing high levels of communication deviance (discussed later). Index adoptees reared by well-functioning adoptive parents had substantially less psychopathology, and control cases reared in disorganized adoptive families experienced more serious psychopathology as adults than did their counterparts raised in "healthy" families.

Supporting earlier work, these results show a moderate genetic effect—the differential "healthy" and disorder rates of index versus control adoptees irrespective of adoptive family context. However, parental inadequacy and disturbed communication have a substantial impact on outcome for both index and control cases. Further, the findings indicate a strong interaction between genetic vulnerability and an unfavorable family environment in the causal pathway leading to schizophrenia. Everything considered, the Finnish Adoption Study has provided strong confirmation of the diathesis-stress model as it applies to the origins of schizophrenia.

Summing up, the question as to whether there is genetic transmissibility of a predisposition to schizophrenia is not as easily answered as it appeared to be when first posed. Some genetic influence does make certain individuals abnormally vulnerable to schizophrenia. The data suggest that no such genetic contribution to etiology is sufficient in itself to produce schizophrenia, and they provide no basis for concluding that such a contribution is a necessary condition for a schizophrenic outcome. Indeed, most people who develop schizophrenia have no close relatives who are also known to have had the disorder—although, as we shall see, some of these normal relatives may share biological anomalies statistically associated with a schizophrenia diagnosis. Based on the best available studies, the aggregate average risk of schizophrenia for first-degree (sharing 50 percent genes) relatives of index cases is 4.8 percent, approximately nine times the rate for normal control cases (Kendler & Diehl, 1993).

Biochemical Factors The idea that serious mental disorders are due to "chemical imbalances" in the brain is now commonplace. To be useful to clinicians and researchers, however, such an idea must be reformulated into hypotheses that are as explicit and specific as possible. Researchers cannot effectively address the general question of what might be biochemically based contributions to the onset or maintenance of schizophrenic behaviors in the absence of clues that tell them where to look and what to look for. At present, as in the case of the severe mood disorders, the search is governed largely by attempts to discover the site and nature of central nervous system effects induced by drugs that diminish the behavioral expression of the disorder. In general, drugs that do so are ones found to alter (by up-regulation or down-regulation) the likelihood that a nerve impulse arriving at a synapse will cross the synapse and fire the next neuron in the chain.

In schizophrenia research, the most attractive of these specific ideas has been the dopamine hypothesis (Meltzer & Stahl, 1976), based on the observation that all of the early antischizophrenic drugs (called *neuroleptics*) had the common property of blocking dopamine-mediated neural transmission. Dopamine is a catecholamine neurotransmitter like norepinephrine, of which it is a chemical precursor. It appears to be the main neurotransmitter for perhaps a half-dozen identified brain pathways. According to the dopamine hypothesis, then, schizophrenia is the product of an excess of dopamine activity at certain synaptic sites. Variants of this view include hypotheses that a schizophrenic person has too many postsynaptic dopamine receptors or that these receptors have for some reason become supersensitive. However, the dopamine hypothesis has proved oversimplistic and inadequate as a general formulation of etiology (Carlsson, 1988; Csernansky & Grace, 1998; Grace & Moore, 1998; Koreen et al., 1994; Lieberman & Koreen, 1993).

Dopamine-blocking drugs, for example, are therapeutically nonspecific for schizophrenia (that is, they are also used effectively to treat psychotic symptoms associated with various other disordered states, such as neuropsychological disorders, some manias, and even drug-induced bad trips). Additionally, the receptor-blocking effect is accomplished too quickly (within hours) to be consistent with the clinical picture of a gradual improvement (often over several weeks) following initiation of neuroleptic drug therapy in schizophrenia. In other words, if only excess dopamine activity were the cause of schizophrenia, these drugs should have ameliorative effects almost immediately; they usually do not. Moreover, their therapeutic activity depends not so much on curtailing excessive dopaminergic activity as on reducing it to *abnormally* low levels, which creates additional problems of an often serious nature (e.g., tardive dyskinesia).

Research has shown the dopaminergic systems within the brain to be far more complicated than was originally thought. For example, we now know that several types of dopamine receptor sites exist on the dendrites of postsynaptic neurons (labeled D_2, D_4, etc.), that these are involved in differing biochemical processes, and that different antipsychotic drugs act on them in varying ways. The "second-generation" or "atypical" antipsychotic drugs, such as Clozaril (clozapine), Zyprexa (olanzapine), and Risperdal (risperidone), have a side-effect profile that is very different from (and generally more benign than) that of the original neuroleptics, one of several indications that their antipsychotic modes of action differ significantly from those of the "typical" drugs, such as Thorazine (chlorpromazine) and Haldol (haloperidol) (see Chapter 3). That is not to suggest that their principal effects necessarily involve something other than dopamine brain pathways, which continue to be seen as somehow generally implicated in the schizophrenias (O'Donnell & Grace, 1998). We just don't, as yet, know how.

Other biochemical theories of schizophrenia have been, and doubtless will continue to be, advanced, but to date no other such theory appears anywhere near as promising as the dopamine theory did (Lieberman & Koreen, 1993). The fact is that the brain chemistry of the schizophrenias remains very imperfectly understood. Ultimately, it seems likely that a complete understanding of the biochemistry of these disorders will have to include a sense of how other influences, such as aberrations of neural circuitry, may interact with whatever biochemical abnormalities are discovered to accompany schizophrenic behavior (Csernansky & Grace, 1998).

Neurophysiological Factors Much recent research has focused on the role of neurophysiological disturbances in schizophrenia, such as an imbalance in various neurophysiologic processes (e.g., those involved in eye movement control) and inappropriate autonomic arousal. Such disordered physiology would disrupt normal attentional and information-processing capabilities, and there seems to be a growing consensus that disturbances of this type underlie the cognitive and perceptual distortions characteristic of schizophrenia. Andreasen, Paradiso, and O'Leary (1998) refer to this process as one of "cognitive dysmetria," a type of "poor mental coordination" that results in "difficulty in prioritizing, processing, coordinating, and responding to information" (p. 203).

One aspect of this "dysmetria" is a highly reliable finding of a specific attentional difficulty in schizophrenia. A substantial proportion of schizophrenic persons are found to be deficient in their ability to track a moving target visually, a skill referred to as *smooth pursuit eye movement (SPEM)* (Holzman et al., 1988, 1998; Levy et al., 1983, 1993; Lieberman et al., 1993a). The deficiency is sometimes attributed to a disorder of nonvoluntary attention, one likely related to an impaired ability to detect the velocity of moving visual stimuli. Unfortunately, the potential significance of this clue is obscured by the fact that this type of speed discrimination is highly complex in organization and involves the participation of numerous widely disseminated brain processes (Holzman et al., 1998).

An impressive amount of evidence also indicates that many close relatives of schizophrenics share this SPEM deficit (e.g., Clementz et al., 1992; Iacono et al., 1992; Kuechenmeister et al., 1977; Levy et al., 1994), far more in fact than share the diagnosis (Levy et al., 1993). This would suggest an inherited source for the difficulty, while simultaneously ruling it out as a specific indicator for the disorder, a conclusion confirmed in a study by Keefe and colleagues (1997). As discussed below, much other evidence suggests the presence of widespread neurophysiologic risk factors for schizophrenia, ones that do not necessarily eventuate in the development of the disorder itself.

Numerous related findings indicate that persons who are merely at increased risk for schizophrenia for one or another reason, such as heredity, often experience difficulties in maintaining attention, in processing information, and in certain other indicators of deficit cognitive functioning, prior to any schizophrenic breakdown (Cornblatt & Keilp, 1994; Dworkin et al., 1993; Finkelstein et al., 1997; Fish et al., 1992; Green, Nuechterlein, & Breitmeyer, 1997; Kinney et al., 1997; Kwapil et al., 1997; Marcus et al., 1985, 1993; Roitman et al., 1997).

Also possibly related to attentional deficits in schizophrenia are certain anomalies shown by many schizophrenic persons in electroencephalographic (brain wave) reactions to momentary sensory stimulation (Friedman & Squires-Wheeler, 1994; Pritchard, 1986). This abnormal brain reaction to stimulation may also be characteristic of subjects merely at enhanced risk for the disorder (Stelmack, Houlihan, & McGarry-Roberts, 1993). Neurologic abnormalities, such as reflex hyperactivity and deficit performance in neuropsychological testing, have also been found to be shared by the nonpsychotic close relatives of schizophrenic individuals (Ismail, Cantor-Graae, & McNeil, 1998; Kinney, Woods, & Yurgelun-Todd, 1986; Kremen et al., 1994; Torrey et al., 1994).

We should also note the evidence that many persons diagnosed as having schizotypal personality disorder (see Chapter 9) show behavioral deficits, such as poor perceptual-motor coordination or distinctive anomalies in reaction-time performance, that are suggestive of subtle neurological impairment (Lenzenweger, 1994, 1998; Lenzenweger & Korfine, 1994; Rosenbaum, Shore, & Chapin, 1988; Siever, 1985). This schizotypal pattern is conceived as one manifestation of a general schizophrenia spectrum of disorder and is thought to render the person at risk for the full syndrome (Kwapil et al., 1997; Lenzenweger, 1994, 1998; Meehl, 1990a).

Additional research literature, going back many decades, documents an enormous variety of other ways in which attentional and cognitive processes seemingly dependent on intact neurophysiologic functioning are disrupted among schizophrenic persons. The disjointed array of findings reported remains baffling; as yet, there is no wholly satisfactory conceptual framework within which the pieces of the schizophrenia puzzle can be put together.

Indeed, an issue of the authoritative *Schizophrenia Bulletin* (vol. 24, no. 2, 1998) is devoted to the presentation of an array of "pathophysiologic models" purporting to integrate and explain many of the research findings reviewed in this section. While there are many instances of agreement on the facts, there is substantial divergence on how to interpret them.

Neuroanatomical Factors Abnormal neurophysiological processes in schizophrenia could be genetic in origin, but some at least could also be the product of biological deviations caused by other factors, as suggested by the discordant monozygotic twin data reviewed earlier. Problems of this sort could as likely arise from unknown intrauterine conditions or mechanical difficulties in the birth process as from faulty genes. In the histories of people who later become schizophrenic, obstetrical complications, such as an unduly short gestational period (premature birth) appear to be well above the norm (Cannon et al., 1993; Gureje, Bamidele, & Raji, 1994; Jones et al., 1998; Torrey et al., 1994), although it is possible that early brain injury contributes to schizophrenic outcomes only among genetically predisposed persons (see Marcus et al., 1993; Mednick et al., 1998). Such observations led to a resurgence of interest in an old issue—the anatomical intactness of the schizophrenic brain—to which we now turn.

Research on the structural properties of the brain in living subjects was largely unproductive until the development of modern computer-dependent technologies, such as computerized tomography (CT), positron emission tomography (PET), and magnetic resonance imaging (MRI). The use of these techniques in the study of the brains of people with schizophrenia has developed at an accelerating pace in recent years, with important results.

Brain Mass Anomalies Much evidence now indicates that in a minority of cases of schizophrenia, particularly among those of chronic, negative-symptom course, there is an abnormal enlargement of the brain's ventricles—the hollow areas filled with cerebrospinal fluid lying deep within the core (Andreasen et al., 1986; Carpenter et al., 1993; Gur & Pearlson, 1993; Gur et al., 1994; Marsh et al., 1997; Pearlson et al., 1989; Raz, 1993; Stevens, 1997). (See Figure 12.4 for MRI scans illustrating this enlargement.) Several other associated anatomical anomalies, such as enlarged sulci (the fissures in the surface of the cerebral cortex), are often reported as well. In fact, the same anomalies are sometimes found in the normal family members of schizophrenic patients (Cannon & Marco, 1994; DeLisi et al., 1986b) and in the high-risk offspring of schizophrenic mothers (Cannon et al., 1993, 1994). In the latter instance, they appear to be associated with low birth weight and the possibility of fetal damage from some unknown agent, possibly infectious (Lyon et al., 1989; Silverton et al., 1985).

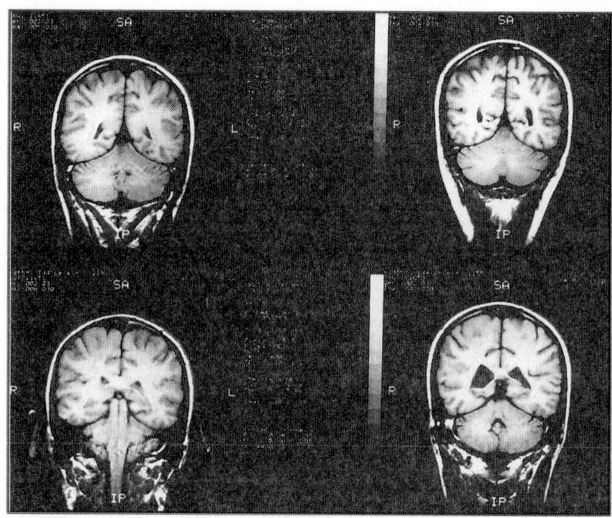

FIGURE 12.4
MRI SCANS OF DISCORDANT MONOZYGOTIC TWINS
In the schizophrenic twin (right), the brain's ventricles are larger than in the normal twin's brain (left).
Source: Max Aguilera/Hellweg

Because the brain normally occupies fully the rigid enclosure of the skull, enlarged ventricles imply a loss of brain tissue mass—possibly some type of atrophy or degeneration. Enlarged sulci have a similar significance. Some findings (e.g., Nestor et al., 1993) indicate deficient size of temporal lobe structures as well, but the evidence here is contradictory (Dwork, 1997). Bogerts (1993), in reviewing some 50 post-mortem studies of brains of individuals with schizophrenia, concluded that the findings are generally not consistent with the notion of *progressive degeneration* but favor the hypothesis of some type of anomaly in prenatal brain development that becomes manifest as schizophrenia (and as reduced brain volume) in young adulthood. Arnold and colleagues (1998) presented data in support of this conclusion from a sample of the brains of elderly schizophrenic patients. Additionally, data on neuropsychological test performance (Heaton et al., 1994) and an extensive review by Cannon and colleagues (1998) of the pertinent literature came to essentially the same conclusion of a static rather than a worsening anomaly.

These rather consistent findings relate to an ongoing controversy as to whether the supposed anatomical substrates of schizophrenia are best considered as due to a *neurodegenerative* or to a *neurodevelopmental* process (Buchanan, Stevens, & Carpenter, 1997; Csernansky & Bardgett, 1998). It should be noted that these are not mutually incompatible conceptions. The establishment of some type of static lesion would not rule out the possibility of later progressive changes in brain anatomy. In given instances, either or both might be true. However, little progress has been made in differentiating any such subgroups at the level of clinical observation (Buchanan & Carpenter, 1997; Stevens, 1997). The increasingly important neurodevelopmental conception is discussed below.

Deficit Localization Much research effort in recent years has focused on the question of what particular brain structures may be especially involved in contributing to the development of the symptoms common to schizophrenia. In an overall review of neuro-imaging studies in schizophrenia, Gur and Pearlson (1993) concluded that the evidence implicates primarily three brain regions: the frontal, the temporolimbic (i.e., the temporal lobes and the adjacent, interior limbic system structures such as the hippocampus), and the basal ganglia (subcortical neural centers chiefly involved in integrative functions). More recent reviews by Cannon and colleagues (1998) and Weinberger (1997) implicate the first two of these. Virtually all authorities agree, however, that few of the findings are specific for schizophrenia, having also been observed (usually in lesser degree) in other conditions, such as the severe mood disorders.

Concerning the frontal and prefrontal regions, many studies have demonstrated abnormally low frontal lobe activation—called *hypofrontality*—among schizophrenic persons when they engage in tasks supposedly requiring substantial frontal lobe involvement, such as the Wisconsin Card Sorting Test (WCST). Evidence of such hypofrontality has been reported for only the schizophrenic co-twins of discordant monozygotic twin pairs (Berman et al., 1992), for never-medicated patients (Buchsbaum et al., 1992), and especially for patients having high levels of negative versus positive symptoms (Andreasen et al., 1992; Wolkin et al., 1992). It should be cautioned, however, that the levels of hypofrontality observed among schizophrenic persons are often only marginally, albeit statistically significantly, different from levels observed in normal control subjects, with much overlap between the groups (e.g., Buchsbaum et al., 1992). Dysfunctional frontal lobes are believed to be especially important in accounting for *negative* signs and symptoms, and perhaps also attentional-cognitive deficits (Cannon et al., 1998; Goldman-Rakic & Selemon, 1997).

There is also considerable, though controversial, evidence relating to the special involvement of temporolimbic structures in schizophrenia (Cannon, 1998a; Bogerts, 1997; Haber & Fudge, 1997). The consensus appears to be that these centers, perhaps especially the left-side (i.e., for most people, dominant-side) ones, are somehow implicated, and that they have a particular role in the production of *positive* signs and symptoms (Bogerts, 1997; Cannon et al., 1998; Woodruff et al., 1997). The finding of temporolimbic involvement is consistent with the types of abnormal functioning observed in an extensive neuropsychological investigation of unmedicated, first-episode schizophrenic patients reported by Saykin and colleagues (1994).

Neurodevelopmental Issues Given all these findings, noted schizophrenia researcher Timothy Crow (1997) has voiced a persistent question that has quietly frustrated many of his colleagues around the world: "Where is the primary lesion in schizophrenia, and what is its nature?" He goes on to note this:

> The problem is that many changes in many different anatomical structures are reported. Which of these is reliably associated with the disease process? If, as seems likely, there is more than one such change, which is primary and which secondary? . . . We need to find changes characteristic at least of a subtype of psychopathology. . . . But there is an embarrassment of riches. (p. 521)

There are indeed very many reports of neuroanatomical differences between schizophrenic (or those at enhanced risk for it) and normal individuals; only the major ones have been reviewed here. And it is also true that reported findings point to no obvious candidate uniformly present in all cases of schizophrenia, or even in all cases of recognized subtypes of schizophrenia. Could it be the case that there is *no* "primary lesion" in schizophrenia or any of its subtypes? Increasing numbers of contemporary investigators are approaching an affirmative answer to that question.

The nature of this new thinking is by no means completely developed or uniformly expressed, but its essential kernel involves the idea that what we call "schizophrenia" may be due to a variable aberration in the basic circuitry, the basic wiring, of the brain itself. Most forms of the idea include the notion of an early, even prenatal, insult to the brain, one that may have detectable neurological effects in early childhood but will not necessarily result in the later development of schizophrenia. The latter arises when the initial injury somehow interferes with normal brain synapse development during a period of intensive synaptic reorganization, occurring for most people during adolescence or early adulthood. Conceivable candidates here include neuronal cell "pruning," cell migration, and programmed cell death, all processes known to occur normally during postnatal phases of brain development (see Weickert & Weinberger, 1998, for a useful overview).

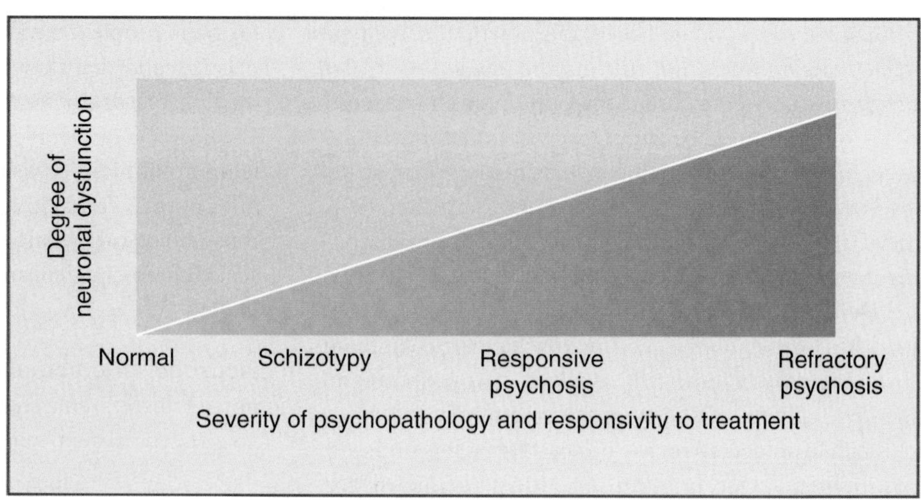

FIGURE 12.5 RELATIONSHIP BETWEEN INCREASING DAMAGE TO NEURONAL CIRCUITS AND CLINICAL PHENOMENOLOGY
Clinical psychopathology and the capacity to respond to typical antipsychotic drugs may occur on a physiological continuum in relationship to degree of neuropathology.
Source: From Csernansky & Bardgett (1998).

Fetuses or newborns sustaining the earlier insult, according to the developmental view, are at elevated risk for missing or misconnected circuitry arising during cell reorganization. They are thus more "vulnerable" (have an enhanced *diathesis*) to developing schizophrenia (e.g., see Walker & Diforio, 1997). The hypothesized relationship between such neurological involvement and clinical outcomes is depicted in Figure 12.5. Such deficiencies in "wiring" would not, of course, be directly observable by available methods of brain scanning. Certain research findings of recent years, some already described and more described below, appear consistent with this type of etiological scenario.

For a number of years, researchers have noted that people who become schizophrenic are more likely than people in general to have been born in the winter and early spring months—about an 8 percent deviation from the norm (DeLisi, Crow, & Hirsch, 1986a). This peculiar observation, which itself is now beyond dispute, has given rise to a variety of hypotheses involving what has come to

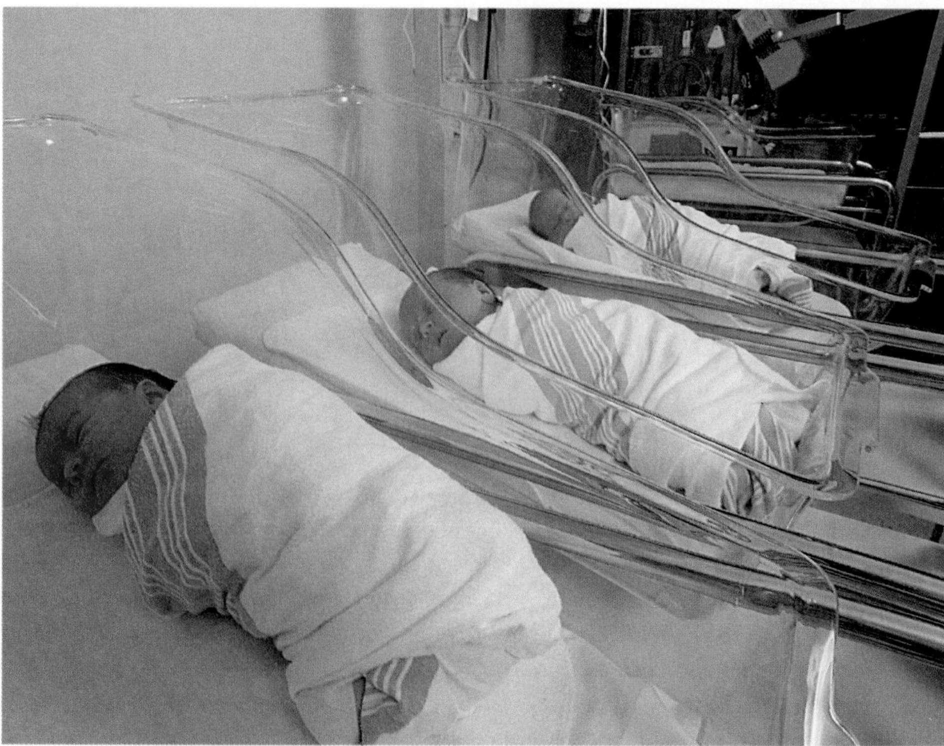

Early, even prenatal damage to the brain, whether through a mother's illness or other insult, is another of the diatheses associated with schizophrenia.

be called the "season of birth effect" in the development of schizophrenia. Some of these relate directly to the role of compromised brain integrity in schizophrenia, as was suggested early on by Bradbury and Miller (1985). Their best guess as to origin was some type of infectious process or obstetrical complications, or both.

Accumulating evidence suggests that Bradbury and Miller were on the right track. For example, Wright and colleagues (1995) found that maternal influenza in the second trimester of pregnancy is associated with impaired fetal growth, enhanced obstetrical complications, and later-developing schizophrenia. Several studies have suggested that, historically, influenza epidemics are associated at a higher-than-chance level with the gestation periods of fetuses who later became schizophrenic. Takei and colleagues (1997) identified the supposedly critical peak infectious period as the fifth gestational month. Here, risk of influenza exposure in the critical period was associated with enlarged ventricles and sulci among a group of 83 schizophrenic patients, relative to controls. Seemingly important and possibly related findings, reported by Torrey and colleagues (1993), establish a strong correlation between the occurrence of stillbirths and the live births of persons who become schizophrenic, both being elevated in winter months. The investigators suggest that there appears to be a common factor for both stillbirths and schizophrenia risk, presumably some infectious agent. In the one case, according to this hypothesis, it leads to death of the fetus; in the other, it produces brain changes that enhance vulnerability to schizophrenia.

An ingenious series of studies reported by Elaine Walker and her colleagues (Grimes & Walker, 1994; Walker, Savoie, & Davis, 1994; Walker et al., 1993) illustrates in compelling fashion the association between early neurodevelopmental deviation and schizophrenia risk. These investigators gathered family home movies made during the childhoods of 32 persons who eventually developed schizophrenia. From these movie clips, trained observers made "blind" (i.e., they were uninformed as to outcomes) ratings of certain dimensions of the emotional (Grimes & Walker, 1994) and facial expressions (Walker et al., 1993), motor skills, and neuromotor abnormalities (Walker et al., 1994) of these children and of their healthy-outcome siblings.

The facial and emotional expressions, and the motor competence, of the preschizophrenic children and the healthy-outcome children were found by the raters to differ significantly and in ways apparently disadvantageous to the former group. The preschizophrenic children showed less—and less positive than negative—emotionality, had poorer motor skills, and showed a higher rate of peculiar movements, such as tic-like muscle contractions, suggestive of neuromotor abnormalities. In other words, these children, in some instances before age two, were already showing behavioral abnormalities not unlike those already suggested. It is a reasonable hypothesis, therefore, that these preschizophrenic children as a group suffered from subtle neurological impairment of unknown origin. Once again, however, it is important to keep in mind that (1) these early-appearing subtle impairments are probably not progressive, (2) they do not inevitably eventuate in a diagnosis of schizophrenia, and (3) they will almost inevitably impact the child's social environment, probably often in negative ways—so, once again, an interaction with the environment is likely also to be a factor.

Interpreting the Biological Evidence: Diathesis and Stress The role of biological factors in the etiology of schizophrenia has been established. Impressive as the evidence is, however, we remain uncertain about precisely how biological factors, operating either singly or in combination, are implicated in inducing schizophrenic outcomes. Nor do we know which factors are most important—either in the aggregate or in individual cases.

In summary, then, biologically oriented research, particularly in recent years, has supplied a wealth of new insights regarding the nature of schizophrenia and some of the sources of vulnerability to it. However, it is likely that it will prove not to provide a complete answer to the riddle of schizophrenia—that is, biological findings will have to be supplemented by pertinent psychosocial and sociocultural research in order to provide a comprehensive understanding, and eventually control, of the problem. This is hardly an extraordinary conclusion; the general diathesis-stress model, whose origins largely derive from schizophrenia research, envisages exactly that sort of scenario (e.g., Walker & Diforio, 1997; Zubin & Spring, 1977). We turn now to an examination of the evidence relating to psychosocial influences in schizophrenia.

Psychosocial Factors in Schizophrenia

Some behavioral scientists (e.g., Whitaker, 1992) dispute the idea that schizophrenia is caused primarily by biological factors. It is unfortunate and counterproductive that biological and psychosocial research efforts are often conceived as mutually antagonistic and are rarely integrated (Carson & Sanislow, 1993). Although much lip service is paid to the evidence of interaction between biological and psychosocial variables in schizophrenia, studies that actually examine the interaction are rare. Hopefully, they will become better funded and so more common in coming years.

A good illustration of the potential of such interactionally oriented research is afforded by the home movie studies of Walker and colleagues, mentioned above. As was noted, it is extremely likely that the (presumably) neurologically based behavioral deficits of the preschizophrenic children would be noticed and responded to in negative ways by others coming in contact with them. The child who rarely manifests joy (even on celebratory family occasions such as birthdays), whose emotional expressiveness is prevailingly in the bland to negative range, who is motorically clumsy or awkward, and who may evidence peculiar involuntary movements is likely to have a far less stress-free early life than the child endowed with the opposite characteristics. Minimally, such a scenario suggests that the occurrence of challenging life events ("stress") that may affect social and personality development is not independent of a potentially pathogenic biological "diathesis." In fact, this idea has been a central element in the important contributions of psychologist Paul Meehl (1962, 1989, 1990a) in tracing the developmental course of schizophrenia outcomes. Berenbaum and Fujita (1994) have offered a similar conceptualization.

Notwithstanding its potential importance, research on psychosocial factors in the development of schizophrenia has been exceedingly sparse in recent years, especially as compared with research on biological correlates. As a result, much of the available psychosocially oriented research in schizophrenia is seriously dated. Much of it is also of questionable quality, in part because it was planned and carried out in an era of less rigorous standards, when, in fact, less was known about the proper design of research studies. It could also be argued that, as a general rule, research on psychosocial variables is inherently more complex and difficult than biologically oriented research. For these reasons, our discussion of psychosocial causal factors in schizophrenia will be relatively brief.

Damaging Parent-Child and Family Interactions

Studies of interactions in families having offspring with schizophrenia have focused on such factors as (1) schizophrenogenic (schizophrenia-causing) parents, (2) destructive parental interactions, and (3) faulty communication. The focus of research has shifted in recent years from parent-child to total family interactions. We will therefore deal here with the latter two of these foci. Before we proceed, however, let us take a moment to gain some perspective on this sensitive topic.

In the early years of attention to family variables in schizophrenia, beginning in the 1950s, parents were routinely assumed to have caused their children's disorders through hostility, deliberate rejection, or gross parental ineptitude. Many professionals blamed parents, and their feedback to them was often angry and insensitive, if not brutal. There is no evidence that could condone such attitudes. Most parents, whether or not they experience the "bad luck" (Meehl, 1978, 1989) of schizophrenia in a child, have done the best that could reasonably be expected, within the limits of their own situations, to foster their children's happiness and success. Some parents are cruel and abusive, but there is no evidence that such a pattern is especially associated with the development of schizophrenia. Apart from the fact that blaming parents does not help and may indeed worsen matters, blame could only be based on an oversimplified and erroneous notion of how people come to be schizophrenic.

One further caveat: Studies have shown a high incidence of emotional disturbances and conflict in the families from which persons with schizophrenia emerge (e.g., Hirsch & Leff, 1975). As we've repeatedly emphasized, however, we cannot reasonably assume that disturbance always passes from parent to offspring; it can work in the other direction as well. Whatever the original source of the difficulty, it appears that once it begins, the members of a family may stimulate each other to increasingly pathological behavior. For example, studies by Mishler and Waxler (1968) and Liem (1974) both found that parents' attempts to deal with the disturbed behavior of sons and daughters with schizophrenia had pathological effects on their own behavior and communication patterns. In fact, the bidirectionality of effects may be the single most robust finding gleaned from studying the families of people with schizophrenia.

Destructive Parental Interactions Of particular interest here is the work of Theodore Lidz and his associates, which continued over some two decades. In an initial intensive clinical study of 14 families with offspring who had schizophrenia, Lidz, Fleck, and Cornelison (1965) failed to find a single parental couple that functioned in a reasonably effective and well-integrated manner. Eight of the 14 couples lived in a state of severe chronic discord in which continuation of the marriage was constantly threatened. The other six couples in this study had achieved a state of equilibrium in which the relationship was maintained at the expense of a basic distortion in family relationships; in these cases, family members entered into a "collusion" in which the seriously disturbed behavior (e.g., a frankly delusional construction of some aspect of reality) of one or the other parent was redefined as normal and justified by consensual rationalization.

People with schizophrenia often have psychologically healthy siblings who were raised with them in the same families. How have these siblings escaped the presumed

Damaging patterns of interaction between family members have been shown to be correlated with the development of schizophrenia in those at risk and the relapse of discharged patients diagnosed with the disorder. Yet not all children in such families become schizophrenic. A possible reason for this discrepancy is that every child in a family experiences that family in his or her own way.

pathology of the family context? A possible answer is that they were not biologically predisposed. But it is also probably true, as emphasized by the Lidz group, that the subculture of a family is not constant—that every child raised within a family experiences a unique family pattern. Thus, a given child may experience a greater degree of exposure to family pathology, as through parental overinvolvement, than his or her more fortunate siblings.

Faulty Communication Gregory Bateson (1959, 1960) was one of the first investigators to emphasize the conflicting and confusing nature of communications among members of families in which at least one person had schizophrenia. He used the term *double-bind communication* to describe one such pattern. In this pattern, the parent presents to the child ideas, feelings, and demands that are mutually incompatible. For example, a mother may be verbally loving and accepting but emotionally anxious and rejecting; or she may complain about her son's lack of affection but freeze up or punish him when he approaches her affectionately. The mother subtly but effectively prohibits comment on such paradoxes, and the father is too ineffectual or distanced to intervene. In essence, according to Bateson's etiologic hypothesis, such a son is continually placed in situations where he cannot win, and he becomes increasingly anxious; presumably, such disorganized and contradictory communications in the family come to be reflected in his own thinking. However, no solid confirmation of the pathogenicity of double-bind communication has ever been reported.

Singer and Wynne (1963, 1965a, 1965b) linked the thought disorders in schizophrenia to two styles of thinking and communication in the family: amorphous and fragmented. The amorphous pattern is characterized by a failure in differentiation; here, attention toward feelings, objects, or people is loosely organized, vague, and drifting. Fragmented thinking involves greater differentiation but lowered integration, with erratic and disruptive shifts in communication. In their later research, Singer and Wynne (Singer, Wynne, & Toohey, 1978; Wynne, Toohey, & Doane, 1979) used the term *communication deviance* (or "transactional style deviance") to refer to these deficiencies of precision and coherence that they regarded as being at the heart of the purported negative effects parents have on their preschizophrenic children.

In a longitudinal study (Doane et al., 1981; Goldstein, 1985; Goldstein & Strachan, 1987; Goldstein et al., 1978; Lewis, Rodnick, & Goldstein, 1981), subjects who had been psychological clinic patients, but not schizophrenic, as adolescents were followed into adulthood. These researchers found that high parental communication deviance (as defined above), measured during their children's adolescence, did indeed predict the occurrence of adult schizophrenic spectrum disorders among these offspring. A family atmosphere of negative affect appeared to increase the likelihood of such outcomes. However, the study's design cannot rule out the possibility of a common genetic influence affecting both parents and offspring, one leading to odd communication in parents and (independently) to schizophrenia in offspring. That possibility is rendered unlikely by findings from the previously described Finnish Adoption Study, where (adoptive) parent communication deviance was associated with the development of serious psychopathology in adoptees (Tienari, 1994).

The Role of Excessive Life Stress and Expressed Emotion A marked increase in the severity of life stress has been found during the 10-week period prior to a person's schizophrenic breakdown (Brown, 1972). Problems typically centered on difficulties in intimate personal relationships, such as a breakup. Another study found interpersonal stressors to be significantly more common among people with schizophrenia than among members of a matched control group (Schwartz & Myers, 1977). Also, life stressors, like schizophrenia itself, have a higher co-occurrence rate in twins than in ordinary siblings (Kendler et al., 1993b), thus suggesting that some part of the elevated concordance for schizophrenia in twins may be due as much to shared stress as shared genes.

Whether or not poor relations with parents and family members is a cause of schizophrenia, *relapse* into schizophrenia following remission *is* associated with a certain type of negative communication, called **expressed emotion (EE),** directed at the patient by family members (Butzlaff & Hooley, 1998; Hooley & Hiller, 1998; Linszen et al., 1997; Miklowitz, Goldstein, & Falloon, 1983; Vaughn et al., 1984). Two components appear critical in the pathogenic effects of EE: emotional overinvolvement (intrusiveness) with the ex-patient, and excessive criticism of him or her. Interestingly, the quantitative review of pertinent research by Butzlaff and Hooley (1998) shows that the EE-relapse association is generally robust but strongest among patients having a chronic course. Expressed emotion may be especially intense where family members harbor the view that the disorder and its symptoms are under the voluntary control of the patient (Weisman et al., 1993). But here, too, the communication problems are likely to be two-way (Hooley & Hiller, 1998).

Some research shows EE to *predict* schizophrenia before its initial onset (Goldstein, 1985) and strongly suggests that EE's role in relapse is a directly causal one (Nuechterlein, Snyder, & Mintz, 1992). Also, attempts to reduce EE and associated behaviors in family members have been very impressive in terms of relapse prevention (Falloon et al., 1985; Hogarty et al., 1986; Leff et al., 1982; McFarlane et al., 1995). Familial EE has thus turned out to be a quite potent variable in the precipitation of schizophrenic episodes. As Hooley and Hiller (1998) suggest, it is now time to attempt to gain a fuller understanding of how it does this.

As noted earlier, the course of decompensation (deterioration, disorganization of thought and personality) in primarily positive-syndrome or Type I schizophrenia tends to be sudden, while that in primarily negative-syndrome or Type II schizophrenia tends to be gradual, though often finally more profound: The actual degree of decompensation may vary markedly, depending on the severity of stress and the makeup of the individual. The course of recovery or recompensation may also be relatively rapid or slow. Similarly, the degree of recovery may be complete, even leading to a better-adjusted person than before; it may be partial but sufficient for adequate independent living ("social recovery"); or it may be nonexistent, with some individuals eventually developing an intractable, chronic, prevailingly negative-syndrome schizophrenia (see Fenton & McGlashan, 1994).

expressed emotion (EE) Type of negative communication involving emotional overinvolvement and excessive criticism directed at a patient by family members.

Sociocultural Factors in Schizophrenia

As was noted earlier, prevalence rates for schizophrenia appear to vary substantially around the world. Granting the already acknowledged hazards of such cross-cultural comparisons, there is at least a twofold to threefold—and possibly considerably greater—variation in occurrence of the disorder in the various social groupings and geographic regions for which epidemiologic data are available (Gottesman, 1991; Stevens & Hallick, 1992). No satisfactory biological explanation for this variation has been identified (Kirch, 1993), and the possibility that the differences reflect intercultural social factors (e.g., religious beliefs and practices, family organization and values) that modify the schizophrenia risk cannot be ruled out (Torrey, 1987). If there are cultural factors that both enhance and diminish the risk for schizophrenia, it would obviously be of great value to understand how these operate. Unfortunately, little attention has been directed to this question, so we remain largely ignorant of any such influences.

It was also noted earlier that schizophrenia seems to occur less often and with diminished severity in traditional, less "well-developed" cultures (Allen, 1997). Systematic differences in the content and form of schizophrenia between cultures and even between subcultures have been documented by various investigators over many years. Often, cases within a particular subculture tend to have a distinctive form. For example, among the aborigines of West Malaysia, Kinzie and Bolton (1973) found the positive-syndrome type of schizophrenia to be by far the most common manifestation; they also noted that symptom content often had an obvious cultural overlay, such as "seeing a river ghost" or "men-like spirits or talking to one's soul" (p. 773).

With respect to sociocultural factors within the United States, there is a huge body of evidence going back to the 1930s indicating that the lower the socioeconomic status, the higher the prevalence of schizophrenia. Although it has quite reasonably been suggested (e.g., by Kohn, 1973) that the conditions of lower-class existence are themselves stressful and in addition impair an individual's ability to deal resourcefully with stress, there is also compelling evidence that lower-class membership can be a *result* of schizophrenia or its socially debilitating behavioral antecedents. Affected individuals often drift downward on the socioeconomic ladder because the early signs of impending disorder prevent them from finding jobs or developing human relationships that might otherwise provide economic stability (Gottesman, 1991).

Proportionally far more blacks than whites in the United States receive a diagnosis of schizophrenia. How-

Schizophrenia seems to occur less often and with less severity in traditional, nonindustrialized cultures. One study of the aborigines of West Malaysia found that the positive symptoms of schizophrenia were more common there than in other parts of the world and centered on cultural beliefs, such as hallucinations of a river ghost or male spirits who spoke to the person's soul.

ever, this imbalance appears to be primarily if not exclusively artifactual. Differences between African-American and Caucasian prevalence rates and clinical pictures for schizophrenia diminish markedly when social class, education, and related socioeconomic conditions are equated (Lindsey & Paul, 1989; Snowden & Cheung, 1990). Indeed, Brekke and Barrio (1997) report a diminished intensity of schizophrenic symptoms, relative to those of whites, among both black and Latino patients when socioeconomic class is controlled.

In general, then, there appears to be no one clinical entity or causal sequence in schizophrenia. Rather, we seem to be dealing with several types of psychologically maladaptive processes resulting from an interaction of biological, psychosocial, and sociocultural factors; the role of these factors undoubtedly varies for individual cases. Often the interaction appears to involve a vicious spiral that, once initiated, propels the person into a process of decreasing availability of coping resources in the face of increasing demands for performance adequacy. Some people panic and undergo a sort of psychobiological collapse; others appear to become gradually apathetic and demoralized, retreating from the unmanageable and perhaps (to them) unintelligible real world both physically and psychologically. Whatever the initial picture, outcomes are not at first notably predictable (Endicott et al., 1986; Strakowski, 1994; Vaillant, 1978) and typically become more so only after weeks, months, or, in some cases of rapidly altering clinical pictures, even years.

IN REVIEW

- What evidence from twin studies supports a genetic contribution to schizophrenia?
- What is the dopamine hypothesis? Explain the current view of this explanation for schizophrenia.
- What neuroanatomical anomalies differentiate people with schizophrenia from people who do not suffer from the disorder?
- Summarize the sociocultural factors that may contribute to the development of schizophrenia.

TREATMENTS AND OUTCOMES FOR SCHIZOPHRENIA

Before the 1950s, the prognosis for schizophrenia was generally considered extremely unfavorable, even hopeless. Patients receiving the diagnosis, unless their families were wealthy and could afford the expense of private psychiatric hospitalization, were routinely shuttled to remote, forbidding, overcrowded, and environmentally bleak public hospitals. Once "safely" incarcerated, they were treated—if at all—by poorly trained, overworked, demoralized staff with largely ineffective techniques that were often, in addition, objectively cruel (e.g., straitjackets) or predictably terrifying (e.g., electroconvulsive "shock" therapy, as it was originally called). As often as not, perhaps after a brief trial at one or more of the inadequate "therapies" offered, the patient was simply left to adjust to an institution he or she was never expected to leave (Deutsch, 1948). Such an adjustment in most instances ensured the erosion of capacities and skills essential to self-maintenance outside of the institution. Thus, complying with the self-fulfilling prophecies of their dismal prognoses, most admitted patients, in fact, did not ever leave.

The Effects of Antipsychotic Medication

For most schizophrenic persons, the outlook today is not nearly so bleak. Improvement came with dramatic suddenness when the phenothiazine class of drugs—then referred to as "major tranquilizers"—were introduced in the mid-1950s. Pharmacotherapy (treatment by drugs) with these potent compounds transformed the environment of mental hospitals practically "overnight" by virtually eliminating the ever-present threat of wild, dangerous, or otherwise anxiety-producing patient behaviors. Patients did indeed become "tranquil." These changes were so abrupt and compelling that it is difficult to convey the extent of their effects, particularly on the morale and optimism of hospital staffs. The latter seemingly gained the means to reliably normalize patient behavior, even to the extent of releasing many patients, who could be maintained on the drugs in outpatient facilities. With further advances in psychopharmacology, some even contemplated *curing* schizophrenia. A new and far more hopeful era had finally arrived.

Newer and better (mostly in the sense of reduced problematic side effects) antipsychotic drugs did in fact make their appearance in the interim, and they continue to be introduced at a high rate. A person with schizophrenia who enters a mental hospital or other facility as a first-time inpatient today has an 80 to 90 percent chance of being discharged within a matter of weeks or, at most, months. A minority of these early discharge patients recover permanently and without notable residual problems. Unfortunately, the rate of readmission remains extremely high, and many patients with schizophrenia experience repeated discharges and readmissions in what is commonly referred to as the "revolving door" pattern. Also, some persons who become schizophrenic—estimated to be about 10 percent of those diagnosed with schizophrenia—continue to be resistant to drug (or any other) treatment and undergo an irreversible negative-syndrome and/or disorganized deterioration.

In some relatively few instances, the progression of the disorder cannot be interrupted by any known intervention techniques. This deteriorating course can occur remarkably rapidly, reaching a stable state of profound dilapidation in a year or less. More typically, it develops over several years, normally stabilizing at a low functioning level within 5 years (Fenton & McGlashan, 1994; McGlashan & Fenton, 1993). The hope of a reliable "cure" for schizophrenia has not materialized, nor can it be discerned anywhere on the horizon. Antipsychotic medications are not a cure. Consider in this regard some remarks of Harvard social psychologist Roger Brown, who once attended a meeting of Schizophrenics Anonymous in order to familiarize himself with the problems of these people:

> [The group leader] began with an optimistic testimony about how things were going with him, designed in part to buck up the others. Some of them also spoke hopefully; others were silent and stared at the floor throughout. I gradually felt hope draining out of the group as they began to talk of their inability to hold jobs, of living on welfare, of finding themselves overwhelmed by simple demands. Nothing bizarre was said or done; there was rather a pervasive sense of inadequacy, of lives in which each day was a dreadful trial. Doughnuts and coffee were served, and then each one, still alone, trailed off into the Cambridge night.
>
> What I saw a little of at that meeting of Schizophrenics Anonymous is simply that there is something about schizophrenia that the antipsychotic drugs do not cure or even always remit on a long-term basis. (Brown & Herrnstein, 1975, p. 641)

What Brown saw as lacking in the club membership is what mental health professionals call **social recovery**—the ability to manage independently as an economically effective and interpersonally connected member of one's society. These members were not "psychotic," and most probably would not currently meet criteria for a schizophrenia diagnosis—excepting possibly the *residual* subtype. Antipsychotic drugs can usually resolve psychotic symptoms, and in their newer, "atypical" versions often without distressing side effects (Sheitman et al., 1998). Can they, by themselves, reverse that substantial part of the schizophrenia experience that so often leaves victims unable either to work or to love in satisfying and productive ways?

In a landmark study, Hegarty and colleagues (1994) did a quantitative analysis, on a decade-by-decade basis from 1895 through 1991, of worldwide clinical outcomes for patients treated for schizophrenia. Criteria employed for declaring a patient to be "improved" following treatment were essentially those defining the concept of social recovery. The results of the study, which involved 51,800 patients with schizophrenia and 311, 400 person-years of patient follow-up, are depicted in Figure 12.6. Note that there was, in fact, an increase in social recoveries following the introduction of antipsychotic medication (decades 1956–1975). That increase, however, was a quite modest one—going roughly from 40 to 50 percent socially recovered. It then evaporated, which the researchers argue was due to increased stringency in diagnostic criteria for schizophrenia—i.e., on average more seriously disturbed patients were included in these later years. A smaller-scale but similar study by Warner (1994) confirms the main findings reported here. Overall, these results are sobering and disappointing.

On a more optimistic note, the disappointing performance of the antipsychotic drugs in the above study relate only to the older "typical" compounds, such as chlorpromazine and haloperidol, and may conceivably be overcome with further advances in pharmacologic therapy. Sheitman and colleagues (1998) identify a number of

social recovery The ability to manage independently as an economically effective and interpersonally connected member of society.

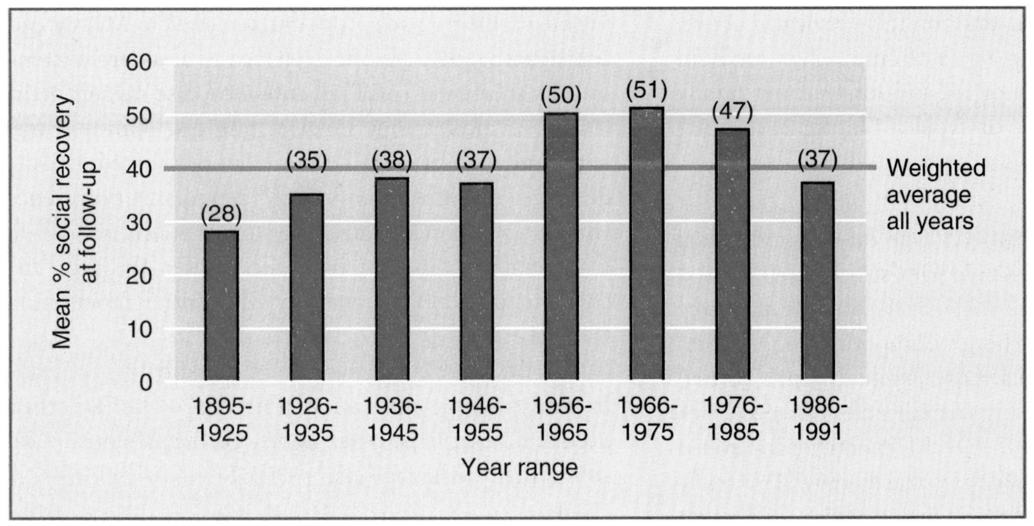

FIGURE 12.6
PERCENTAGE OF FOLLOWED-UP SCHIZOPHRENIC PATIENTS ATTAINING SOCIAL RECOVERY OVER MOST OF THE TWENTIETH CENTURY
Percentages have been rounded off to the nearest whole number.
Source: Adapted from Hegarty et al., 1994.

newer "atypical" antipsychotics in various stages of development and use, any of which might produce a better record in social recovery terms. Unfortunately, none has as yet been adequately evaluated with respect to this relatively demanding criterion.

In light of the limited success of the older antipsychotic drugs, it is somewhat disconcerting to realize that for several decades they were virtually the only treatment offered to many schizophrenic patients. That may now be changing, as described in what follows.

Psychosocial Approaches in Treating Schizophrenia

As a group, mental health professionals of the present era have only gradually come to realize the serious limitations of an exclusively pharmacological approach to the treatment of schizophrenia. In fact, so dominant was this viewpoint that some extremely promising alternative approaches appearing in the decades prior to the 1990s were quite simply ignored by the majority of the professional mental health community. Included here, for example, were a therapeutic community-based program of "self-help" for patients moved from the hospital to a commercially failed motel and given minimal professional oversight (Fairweather et al., 1969; Fairweather, 1980) and a rigorous token economy "social learning" program for chronic state hospital patients (Paul & Lentz, 1977). Neither of these involved extensive use of medication, and both produced exciting results in terms of patient progress. Also largely ignored was a report of a well-designed study demonstrating the superiority of specialized individual psychotherapy (by highly experienced therapists) versus antipsychotic medication in treating schizophrenia (Karon & VandenBos, 1981).

Perhaps the most notable indication of a changing perspective on the treatment of schizophrenia is the content of the American Psychiatric Association's (1997b) *Practice Guideline for the Treatment of Patients with Schizophrenia.* This document contains the expected comprehensive recommendations on managing the medication of patients in various phases and at differing severities of disorder, but it also makes a host of recommendations relating to the desirability of vigorous psychosocial intervention as well. In making these recommendations, the *Practice Guideline* takes notice of the development of a number of relatively new and demonstrably effective psychosocial initiatives in ameliorating the problems of patients with schizophrenia, particularly those problems that seem largely unresponsive to antipsychotic drugs (Kopelowicz & Liberman, 1998). Some of these initiatives, normally used in conjunction with medication, are briefly described below.

Family Therapy Although family therapy approaches are by no means new in the treatment of schizophrenia, there is a renewed emphasis on their importance—due in no small measure to research findings on the relapse hazards of familial expressed emotion (EE), reviewed above. Family therapy would appear to be an excellent medium for identifying instances of EE and for teaching family members how to control or avoid it (Tarrier & Barrowclough, 1990).

Individual Psychotherapy One-on-one individual psychotherapy for individuals with schizophrenia has a rich history but had largely fallen by the wayside under the onslaught of the antipsychotics, along with some reports that it (particularly in its more psychodynamic forms) made patients with schizophrenia worse. However, Hogarty and colleagues (1997a, 1997b) report on a controlled 3-year trial of what they call "personal therapy." This treatment was very effective in enhancing social adjustment and social role performance of discharged patients. Personal therapy is described as involving a staged, nonpsychodynamic approach oriented to the learning of coping skills for managing emotion and stressful events. It is not clear in what manner, if any, it differs from cognitive-behavioral therapy. In favorably commenting on this program, Fenton and McGlashan (1997) assert the need for a flexible individual psychotherapy component in virtually all treatment packages for schizophrenia.

Social-Skills Training and Community Treatment Training in social skills (e.g., see Bellack et al., 1997; Dilk & Bond, 1996; Halford & Haynes, 1991) is also a useful procedure for overcoming the embarrassment, ineptitude, awkwardness, and attentional "cluelessness" displayed in social situations by many persons who've undergone episodes of schizophrenia.

Somewhat belatedly, clinicians now understand that many patients with schizophrenia who are discharged into the community have great difficulty in marshaling resources and getting their lives organized (see Chapter 15). Included here is some propensity to become involved in substance abuse, often as self-medication for unpleasant antipsychotic drug side effects (Kosten & Ziedonis, 1997). There is therefore considerable need for persistent and vigorous community-based follow-up and aid in managing life problems. Such programs, reviewed by Mueser and colleagues (1998), are often referred to as **assertive community treatment (ACT)** or **intensive case management (ICM).** Typically, they involve multidisciplinary teams with limited caseloads to ensure that discharged patients don't get overlooked and "lost," a frequent occurrence where the local mental health system is poorly organized. In general, the more intensive the services, the larger the effect in clinical improvement and social functioning (Brekke et al., 1997).

Finally, there is the question of coordinating continuing antipsychotic medication, if needed, with these other, nonmedical services. When done well, the patient benefits substantially (Klerman et al., 1994; Kopelowicz, 1997).

A Problem: Overcoming Inertia Psychosocially based interventions to compensate for the shortcomings of antipsychotic medication in treating schizophrenia are not presently being used to their fullest. This may be due in part to the fact that mental health professionals and laypersons alike have continued to overestimate what the antipsychotic drugs can do and have consequently largely failed to take advantage of the opportunity these drugs provide to rebuild patients' resources through psychosocial therapies—in such a manner as to ensure their successful reentry into society's mainstream. An enormously expanded effort at the psychosocial level of intervention is needed to ease the massive personal, familial, and societal tragedies that the schizophrenias inflict.

To treat schizophrenia in the most effective way, as suggested by the currently available research, mental health professionals must overcome ideological prejudices that may prevent them from implementing what the research evidence supports. Further, we must all accept that effective treatment will require considerable highly trained personnel and resources, neither of which come cheap. However, the other side of this coin is the cost to society of supporting large numbers of economically dependent, unemployable adults who have high rates of utilization of expensive facilities—a cost estimated in the United States to be in excess of $70 billion annually (Wyatt et al., 1995). A literature review by Gabbard and colleagues (1997) emphasizes the economic "savings" realized where individual psychotherapy is employed in the treatment of severe mental disorders, including schizophrenia. It is a virtual certainty that "society"—that is, taxpayers—will pay one way or another. But the advantage of restoring lives in the process makes the economic investment in psychosocial interventions the obvious choice. The challenge of overcoming inertia is not trivial, but neither is it insurmountable.

assertive community treatment (ACT) Community-based psychosocial treatment program for helping people with schizophrenia manage life problems.

intensive case management (ICM) Community-based psychosocial treatment program that uses multidisciplinary teams with limited caseloads to ensure that discharged mental patients don't get overlooked and "lost" in the system.

IN REVIEW

- How did the introduction in the mid-1950s of pharmacotherapy with phenothiazines transform the environment of mental hospitals?
- What is the importance of social recovery in the prognosis of a person with schizophrenia?
- Describe the major psychosocial approaches to treating schizophrenia, including assertive community treatment (ACT) and intensive case management (ICM).

UNRESOLVED ISSUES: *The Overlooked Value of Psychosocial Intervention in the Schizophrenias*

The disorders we call the schizophrenias confront society with the massive problem of how to take care of people who seem unable, or unmotivated, to take care of themselves. Neither institutionalization nor deinstitutionalization has worked. And the traditional antipsychotic drugs have proved, as we have seen, insufficiently effective in promoting social recovery—though the newer ones show some greater promise. In overestimating their real properties, we have largely failed to take advantage of the ability the antipsychotic drugs have given us to rebuild patient resources and ensure their successful reentry into society's mainstream. A dispassionate analysis of the problem, as well as much pertinent research evidence, indicates that a vastly increased level of psychosocial intervention is needed to ease the massive personal, familial, and societal tragedies that result from the schizophrenias.

Merely identifying what is needed in a more comprehensive approach to the problem by no means ensures that these measures will be carried out. The main difficulty appears twofold: (1) professional inertia and (2) monetary expense. A potential third problem, that of patient noncompliance in taking prescribed medication, may be significantly eased with the development of new compounds having minimal noxious side effects.

We have already noted the failure of the professional community to pick up on promising treatment leads that deviated from standard practice. We need to find ways of overcoming the often ideologically based prejudices of professionals and institute a renewed respect for what the research evidence is actually telling us.

SUMMARY

THE SCHIZOPHRENIAS

- The schizophrenias are severe psychoses, and the group of related disorders includes some of the most extreme forms of psychopathology.
- Although they do differ in many clinical features, these disorders are characterized by a breakdown of integrated personality functioning, withdrawal from reality, emotional blunting and distortion, and disturbances in thought and behavior.
- The nonschizophrenic paranoid disorders include delusional disorder (formerly called *paranoia*), shared psychotic disorder (in which delusional ideas are shared by two or more people), and brief psychotic disorder (uncomplicated delusional thinking lasting 1 month or less).

THE CLINICAL PICTURE IN SCHIZOPHRENIA

- Modern research has tended to focus on positive-syndrome (e.g., hallucinations and delusions) or Type I schizophrenia versus negative-syndrome (e.g., emotional blunting, poverty of speech) or Type II schizophrenia.

THE CLASSIC SUBTYPES OF SCHIZOPHRENIA

- Subtypes of schizophrenia listed in the DSM include undifferentiated (mixed symptoms not fitting into other categories or moving rapidly among them), catatonic (involving chiefly motor symptoms), disorganized (incoherent, silly, or inappropriate affect and behavior), and paranoid (persistent ideas or hallucinations regarding persecution or grandiosity, or other themes).

- Several related disorders are schizoaffective disorder (with features of both schizophrenia and severe mood disorder) and schizophreniform disorder (with schizophrenia-like symptoms of less than 6 months' duration).

CAUSAL FACTORS IN SCHIZOPHRENIA

- The cluster of behaviors called the schizophrenias are baffling in their departure from the realities of common experience. Such behaviors have been correlated with biological, psychosocial, and sociocultural factors.
- There appears to be a hereditary component in the causal pattern, one that may or may not interact with other biological variables, such as early brain injury, to enhance the risk for developing the disorder.
- Current thinking about biological causes emphasizes a developmental view in which an early (including prenatal) brain anomaly results in a failure of the brain's circuitry to align itself properly during a later phase of synaptic reorganization.
- The weight of evidence indicates that biological factors alone cannot account for most instances of schizophrenia. Powerful, but as yet poorly understood, contributions come from psychosocial and sociocultural sources. Research suggests that complex interactions among numerous influences, which probably differ across patients, are involved.

TREATMENT AND OUTCOMES FOR SCHIZOPHRENIA

- Treatment of chronic cases of schizophrenia is currently difficult, at best. The treatment of schizophrenia in recent decades has probably relied too heavily on antipsychotic medications, which often do little to promote social recovery.

UNRESOLVED ISSUES: THE OVERLOOKED VALUE OF PSYCHOSOCIAL INTERVENTION IN THE SCHIZOPHRENIAS

- A variety of psychosocial treatment interventions for patients with schizophrenia have promising records. By and large, they have not been implemented at the levels required to serve the existing population of these patients.

KEY TERMS

schizophrenias (p. 396)
psychosis (p. 396)
delusional disorder (p. 396)
shared psychotic disorder (p. 397)
brief psychotic disorder (p. 397)
positive-syndrome schizophrenia (p. 399)
negative-syndrome schizophrenia (p. 399)
Type I schizophrenia (p. 399)
Type II schizophrenia (p. 399)
delusions (p. 402)
hallucinations (p. 402)
schizophrenia, residual type (p. 403)
schizophrenia, undifferentiated type (p. 404)
schizophrenia, catatonic type (p. 406)
schizophrenia, disorganized type (p. 407)
schizophrenia, paranoid type (p. 408)
schizoaffective disorder (p. 410)
schizophreniform disorder (p. 410)
expressed emotion (EE) (p. 424)
social recovery (p. 426)
assertive community treatment (ACT) (p. 428)
intensive case management (ICM) (p. 428)

CHAPTER THIRTEEN

Brain Disorders and Other Cognitive Impairments

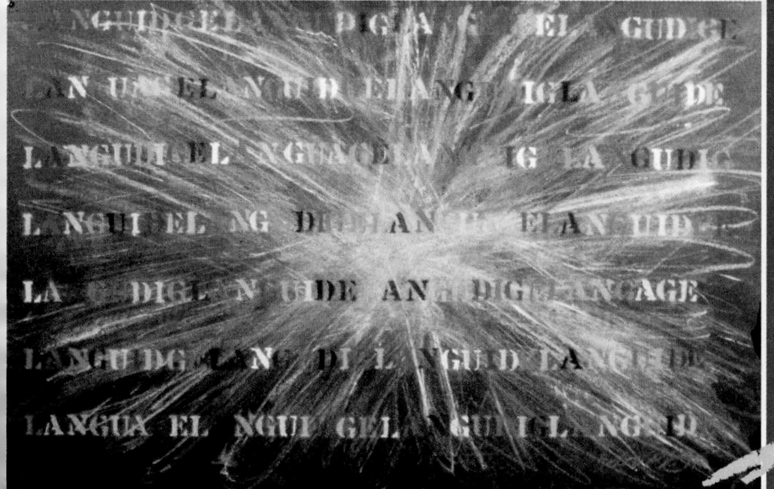

Robert V. P. Davis, *Untitled* (1990). Davis, who lives in Baltimore, Maryland, was 32 when he was diagnosed with dyslexia. In his art, he uses letters, words, and other symbols to communicate the feelings of loneliness, fear, and anxiety that arise from his struggle to understand and be understood. He hopes his art will broaden public awareness of dyslexia.

LEARNING OBJECTIVES

After reading this chapter, you should be able to:

- Describe the general clinical features and symptom patterns of neuropsychological disorders.
- List and characterize the major neuropsychological symptom syndromes.
- Differentiate between the two neuropsychological disorders associated with HIV-1 infection: AIDS dementia complex (ADC) and AIDS-related complex (ARC).
- Describe the clinical features of dementia of the Alzheimer's type (DAT), and summarize what is known about its causes and treatment.
- Compare and contrast vascular dementia (VAD) and DAT.
- Identify the ways in which traumatic brain injury can affect neuropsychological functioning, as well as the factors that determine prognosis.
- Explain what is meant by cultural-familial retardation, and review the major causal factors that have been suggested.
- Identify some problems in assessment of mental retardation, and describe various approaches to treatment and prevention.

Some psychological problems arise as a result of damage or defects in the brain tissue. The brain is the organ of behavior: It processes relevant available information from external and internal environments (including itself) and selects and executes action patterns stored in its memory banks. Damage to the brain may therefore disrupt effective thought, feeling, and behavior. The relationship between mental deficits associated with organic brain defects and abnormal behavior is complicated and often unclear, largely because the brain and its functions are so intertwined.

When structural defects in the brain are present before birth or occur at an early age, mental retardation may result. Its severity will depend to a large extent on the magnitude of the defect. Sometimes the intact brain sustains damage after it has completed normal biological development. A wide variety of injuries, diseases, and toxic substances may cause the functional impairment or death of neurons or their connections, which may lead to obvious deficits in psychological functioning. In some cases, such damage is associated with behavior that is not only impaired but also highly maladaptive—even psychotic. People who sustain serious brain damage after they have mastered the basic tasks of life are in a very different situation from those who start life with a deficit of this kind. When brain injury occurs in an older child or adult, there is a loss in established functioning. This loss—this deprivation of already acquired and customary skills—can be painfully obvious to the victim, adding an often pronounced psychological burden to the organic one. In other cases, the impairment may extend to the capacity for realistic self-appraisal, leaving these patients relatively unaware of their losses and thus poorly motivated for rehabilitation.

In this chapter, we will first discuss **neuropsychological disorders,** which entail behavioral and mental impairments that occur when the normal adolescent or adult brain has suffered significant organic damage. Then we will move to a consideration of mental retardation, compromised brain functioning that either is congenital or arises in the earliest phases of psychological development.

neuropsychological disorders Disorders entailing behavioral and mental impairments that occur when there has been significant organic damage to a normal adolescent or adult brain.

organic mental disorders Earlier term for mental disorders associated with brain damage; no longer used in the DSM.

NEUROPSYCHOLOGICAL DISORDERS AND BRAIN DAMAGE

Prior to DSM-IV, most of the disorders to be considered in this section were called **organic mental disorders,** an outmoded term that failed to distinguish between the direct *neurological* consequences of brain injury, including various cognitive deficits, and the *psychopathological* problems sometimes accompanying such injury, such as depression or paranoid delusions. Most people who have a neuropsychological disorder *do not* develop psychopathological symptoms, such as panic attacks, dissociative episodes, or delusions, although many will show at least mild deficits in cognitive processing and self-regulation. The psychopathological symptoms that do sometimes accompany brain impairment are less predictable than are the symptoms of a neuropsychological disorder and more likely to show individual nuances consistent with the prior personality and the total psychological situation confronting the patient. It is erroneous to assume that a psychological disorder—for example, a serious depression accompanying deficits produced by brain injury—is necessarily and completely explained by reference to the patient's brain damage; it might better be explained in terms of the psychological challenge presented by the patient's awareness of dramatically lessened competence.

HIGHLIGHT 13.1

Hardware and Software

When computers fail to do what we want and expect them to do for us, our troubleshooting speculations normally begin with two possibilities: (1) a hardware problem—perhaps a "sticky" chip, a deficient power supply, or a defective resistor or capacitor; or (2) a software problem, such as having a "bug" in a program or an error in the data we loaded into a machine that is in perfect working order.

By analogy, we may consider the intact human brain to be a highly programmable system of hardware, and psychosocial experience in both its developmental and current aspects to be functionally equivalent to software. Using our analogy, neuropsychological disorders, by definition, have hardware defects as their primary cause. In other words, in such situations, the brain cannot perform the necessary physical operations because of a breakdown in one or another (or several) of its components. The direct "symptoms" of such a breakdown should be predictable from a knowledge of how these components work. In general, knowledge of the direct effects of various types of brain damage is relatively advanced.

A breakdown in the brain's hardware will necessarily have pervasive effects on the processing of software, or past and present experience. Indeed, in the case of extensive hardware damage, much or perhaps most previously loaded information may be lost because the structural components in which it had been encoded are no longer operative; new information for the same reason fails to be adequately loaded. Such a condition is known clinically as *dementia*. With less extensive hardware damage, we see effects that depend to a considerable extent on the particular characteristics of the software that constitutes the record of an individual's life experience, which is unique. The delusion that one is Napoleon, rather common in the nineteenth century, would not have been seen in a patient who lived before Napoleon became famous. Such symptoms are at most only indirect manifestations of organic hardware breakdown; their content is obviously a product of life experience, and they sometimes occur in the absence of any demonstrable hardware breakdown at all. Such symptoms may be due entirely to serious flaws in the individual's personality, or (in our analogy) software. ■

The destruction of brain tissue may involve only limited behavioral deficits or a wide range of psychological impairments, depending on (1) the nature, location, and extent of neural damage; (2) the premorbid (predisorder) competence and personality of the individual; (3) the individual's total life situation; and (4) the amount of time since the first appearance of the condition. Although the degree of mental impairment is usually directly related to the extent of damage, impairment may have variable effects, depending on the individual. A well-functioning and resourceful personality can usually withstand brain damage (or any other stress) better than a rigid, immature, or otherwise psychologically handicapped one—except where brain damage is so severe or its location so critical as to destroy the integrity of the personality. Similarly, an individual who has a favorable life situation is likely to have a better prognosis than one who does not, a conclusion that extends to children suffering traumatic brain injuries (Yeates et al., 1997). In recent years, the concept of *brain reserve capacity* has been employed increasingly to account for the fact that intelligent, well-educated, mentally active people have enhanced resistance to mental and behavioral deterioration following significant brain injury (e.g., see Mori et al., 1997a; Schmand et al., 1997a). Because the brain is the center for the integration of behavior, however, there are limits to the amount of brain damage that anyone can tolerate or compensate for without exhibiting behavior that is decidedly abnormal.

General Clinical Features of Neuropsychological Disorders

The "mental" symptoms associated with neuropsychological disorders are considered to be the more or less direct product of the physical interruption of established neural pathways in the brain. The bases of these symptoms are relatively well understood, and the symptoms themselves have relatively constant features, which include the following:

1. *Impairment of memory:* The individual has notable trouble remembering recent events and less trouble remembering events of the remote past, with a ten-

dency in some patients to confabulate—that is, to invent memories to fill in gaps. In severe instances, no new experience can be retained for more than a few minutes.

2. *Impairment of orientation:* The individual is unable to locate himself or herself accurately, especially in time but also in space or in relation to the personal identities of self or others.
3. *Impairment of learning, comprehension, and judgment:* The individual's thinking becomes clouded, sluggish, and/or inaccurate. The person may lose the ability to plan with foresight or to understand abstract concepts and hence to process anything but the simplest of information, often described as "thought impoverishment."
4. *Impairment of emotional control or modulation:* The individual manifests emotional overreactivity and easy arousal to laughter, tears, rage, and other extreme emotions.
5. *Apathy or emotional blunting:* The individual shows little emotion, especially where deterioration is advanced.
6. *Impairment in the initiation of behavior:* The individual lacks self-starting capability and may have to be repeatedly reminded about what to do next, even when the behavior involved remains well within the person's range of competence. This is sometimes referred to as loss of "executive" function.
7. *Impairment of controls over matters of propriety and ethical conduct:* The individual may manifest a marked lowering of personal standards in appearance, personal hygiene, sexuality, language, and so on.
8. *Impairment of receptive and expressive communication:* The individual may be unable to comprehend written or spoken language or to express his or her own thoughts orally or in writing.
9. *Impaired visuospatial ability:* The individual has difficulty in coordinating motor activity with the characteristics of the visual environment, affecting performance in graphomotor (handwriting and drawing), constructional (e.g., assembling things), and other tasks dependent on such skills.

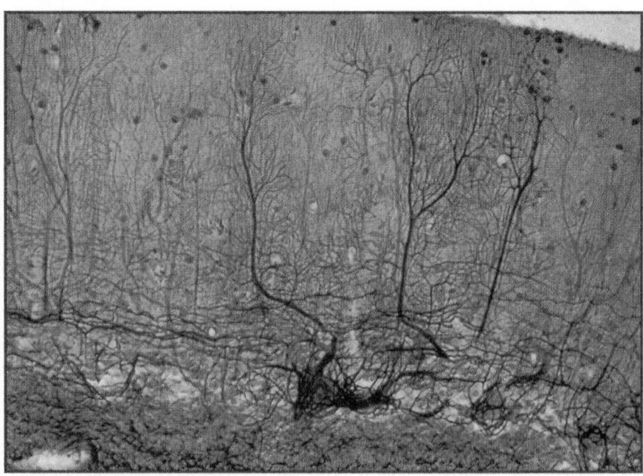

FIGURE 13.1
PHOTOMICROGRAPH OF NEURONS IN THE BRAIN
With possibly minor exceptions, cell bodies and neural pathways in the brain do not have the power of regeneration, which means that their destruction is permanent. In general, the greater the tissue damage, the greater the impairment.
Source: Leonard Lessin/Peter Arnold, Inc.

The Nature and Location of Neural Damage With possibly minor exceptions, cell bodies and neural pathways in the brain (see Figure 13.1) do not have the power of regeneration, which means that their destruction is permanent. Some functions lost as a result of actual brain damage may be relearned, typically at a compromised and less efficient level, or the injured person may develop techniques to compensate for what is missing. When recovery of function following brain injury is rapid, which often happens, much of the recovery is due to the resolution of temporary conditions, such as edema (swelling), produced in tissue spared from actual damage. In contrast, recovery from disabilities following an irreversible brain lesion may be relatively complete or limited, and it may proceed rapidly or slowly. Because there are limits to compensatory capacities of the brain, however, brain damage leads to more or less extensive permanent diminishment or loss of function over a wide range of physical and psychological abilities. In general, as already noted, the greater the amount of tissue damage, the greater the impairment of function.

The location of the damage may also play a significant role in determining a patient's ultimate neuropsychological status. The brain is highly specialized, each part—each cell, in fact—making a unique contribution to the functional whole of an organism's activity. The two hemispheres of the brain, while interacting intimately at many levels, are involved in somewhat different types of mental processing. For example, functions that are dependent on serial (i.e., ordered) processing of familiar information, such as using language or solving mathematical equations, take place mostly in the left hemisphere for nearly everyone. The right hemisphere is generally specialized for configurational or *gestalt* (i.e., appreciation of patterns) processing, which is best suited for grasping overall meanings in novel situations, reasoning on a nonverbal, intu-

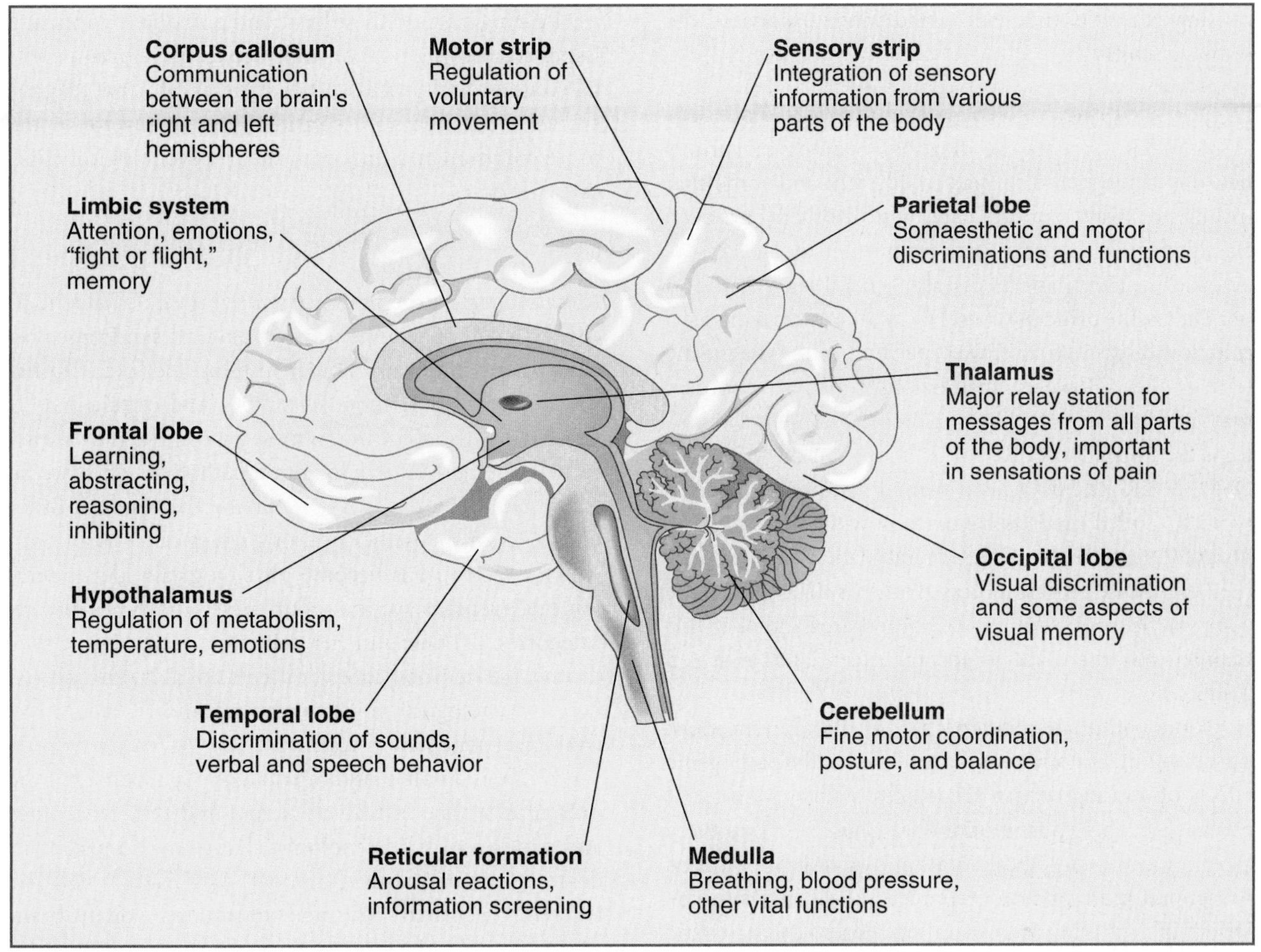

FIGURE 13.2
BRAIN STRUCTURES AND ASSOCIATED BEHAVIORS ON THE RIGHT CEREBRAL HEMISPHERE

itive level, and appreciation of spatial relations. Even within hemispheres, the various lobes and areas within them mediate specialized functions (see Figure 13.2).

Although none of these relationships between brain location and behavior can be considered constant or universal, it is possible to make broad generalizations about the likely effects of damage to particular parts of the brain. Damage to the frontal areas, for example, is associated with either of two contrasting clinical pictures: (1) behavioral inertia, passivity, apathy, and an inability to give up a given stream of associations or initiate a new one (perseverative thought); or (2) impulsiveness, distractibility, and insufficient ethical restraint. Damage to specific areas of the right parietal lobe may produce impairment of visual-motor coordination or distortions of body image, while damage to the left parietal area may impair certain aspects of language function, including reading and writing, as well as arithmetical abilities.

Damage to certain structures within the temporal lobes disrupts an early stage of memory storage. Extensive bilateral temporal damage can leave remote memory relatively intact but nothing new can be stored for later retrieval. Damage to other structures within the temporal lobes is associated with disturbances of eating, sexuality, and the emotions, probably by way of disrupting the functioning of the adjacent limbic system, a center deep in the brain that regulates these "primitive" functions, apparently by way of extensive communication with controlling frontal-lobe structures.

Occipital damage produces a variety of visual impairments and visual association deficits, the nature of the deficit depending on the particular site of the lesion. For example, a person may be unable to recognize familiar faces or to visualize and understand symbolic stimuli correctly. Unfortunately, many types of brain disease are general and therefore diffuse in their destructive effects, causing multiple and widespread interruptions of the brain's circuitry.

Diagnostic Issues in Neuropsychological Disorders

DSM-IV-TR presents the diagnostic coding of various neuropsychological disorders in different and somewhat inconsistent ways. Traditionally, these disorders have been classified by disease entity or recognizable medical disorder, such as Huntington's disease, general paresis, and so on. That is, the principal causal factor, the underlying neurological disease process, was specified in the diagnostic term applied. However, such basically medical disorders that may have various kinds of associated mental symptoms are normally coded not on Axis I but on Axis III of DSM-IV-TR. The associated mental conditions are then typically coded on Axis I, normally with the qualifying phrase "Due to [a specified General Medical Condition]" (i.e., the disease process indicated on Axis III). Many of the common neuropsychological disorders are handled in this manner, but there are important exceptions, as noted below.

Some pathological brain changes that may produce significant mental symptoms are related to the pathogenic effects of abusing certain substances, such as long-term, excessive alcohol consumption (see Chapter 10). In these cases, a specific etiological notation is included in the Axis I diagnosis, as in "Substance-Induced Persisting Amnestic Disorder" (referring to a circumscribed and characteristic type of memory impairment). DSM-IV also deals in a special way with certain conditions, often progressive, that result in pronounced and generalized cognitive deterioration, or *dementia*. Here the presumed underlying neurological disease process is sometimes included in the Axis I designation and on Axis III as well. Thus, notable cognitive impairment associated with cerebrovascular disease might have a DSM-IV-TR diagnostic code as follows:

Axis I: Vascular Dementia

Axis III: Occlusion, cerebral artery

There is a degree of redundancy here inasmuch as the Axis I term already implies the existence of cerebral artery blockage, or "occlusion." The important Axis I diagnosis "Dementia of the Alzheimer's Type" is managed in a similar way, with "Alzheimer's disease" being designated on Axis III.

delirium Neuropsychological symptom syndrome characterized by relatively rapid onset of widespread disorganization of the higher mental processes (perception, memory, and information processing) and by abnormal psychomotor activity; caused by a generalized disturbance in brain metabolism.

Bearing in mind these basic and potentially confusing issues concerning relationships between the brain, mental contents and processes, behavior, and formal diagnosis, we move now to a consideration of several of the more common and important neuropsychological clinical syndromes.

Neuropsychological Symptom Syndromes

A *syndrome* is a group of signs and symptoms that tend to cluster together. The neuropsychological syndromes include many indicators similar to those that occur in the schizophrenias, the mood disorders, and certain Axis II personality disorders, but in these syndromes they are assumed to reflect underlying brain pathology. The specific brain pathology may vary; it may be the result of brain disease or of the withdrawal of a chemical substance on which a person has become physiologically dependent. For our purposes, we will group these syndromes into six categories: (1) delirium, (2) dementia, (3) amnestic syndrome, (4) neuropsychological delusional syndrome, (5) neuropsychological mood syndrome, and (6) neuropsychological personality syndrome.

We should note that more than one syndrome may be present at a time in a given patient and that syndromes and patterns of syndromes may change over a particular disorder's course of development. As already noted, the behavior associated with some syndromes involving brain damage mimics the types of disorders described in previous chapters. Clinicians always need to be alert to the possibility that brain impairment itself may be directly responsible for the clinical phenomena observed. Failure to do so could result in serious diagnostic errors, as when a clinician falsely attributes a mood change to psychological causes and fails to consider what may actually be a neuropsychological origin, such as a brain tumor (Geschwind, 1975; Malamud, 1975; Purisch & Sbordone, 1997; Weinberger, 1984).

Delirium The syndrome called **delirium** is characterized by the relatively rapid onset of widespread disorganization of the higher mental processes; it is caused by a generalized disturbance in brain metabolism. Delirium may result from several conditions, including head injury, toxic or metabolic disturbances, oxygen deprivation, insufficient delivery of blood to brain tissues, or precipitous withdrawal from alcohol or other drugs in an addicted person. Information-processing capacities are impaired, affecting such basic functions as attention, perception, memory, and thinking; and the patient may have frightening hallucinations. The syndrome often includes abnormal psychomotor activity, such as wild thrashing about,

TABLE 13.1 DEMENTIA IN 417 FULLY EVALUATED PATIENTS

Diagnosis	Number	Percentage
Alzheimer's disease or dementia of unknown cause	199	47.7
Alcoholic dementia	42	10.0
Multi-infarct dementia [vascular dementia]	39	9.4
Normal pressure hydrocephalus	25	6.0
Intracranial masses [tumors]	20	4.8
Huntington's disease	12	2.9
Drug toxicity	10	2.4
Post-traumatic	7	1.7
Other identified dementing diseases*	28	6.7
Pseudodementias†	28	6.7
Dementia uncertain	7	1.7

*Including epilepsy, subarachnoid hemorrhage, encephalitis, amyotropic lateral sclerosis, Parkinson's disease, hyperthyroidism, syphilis, liver disease, and cerebral anoxia episode, all less than 1 percent incidence.

†Including depression (16), schizophrenia (5), mania (2), "hysteria" (1), and not demented (4).

Source: Based on Wells (1979).

and disturbance of the sleep cycle. Delirium reflects a breakdown in the functional integrity of the brain. In this respect, it may be seen as only one step above coma, and, in fact, it may lead to coma. A delirious person is essentially unable to carry out purposeful mental activity of any kind. Delirious states tend to be acute conditions that rarely last more than a week, terminating in recovery or, less often, in death due to the underlying injury or disease.

Dementia The essential feature of **dementia** is the normally progressive deterioration of brain functioning occurring after the completion of brain maturation (that is, after about 15 years of age). Early in the course of the disease, an individual is alert and fairly well attuned to events in the environment. Episodic (memory for events), but not necessarily semantic (language and concept), memory functioning is typically affected in the early stages, especially memory for recent events. Patients with dementia also show increasingly marked deficits in abstract thinking, the acquisition of new knowledge or skills, visuospatial comprehension, motor control, problem solving, and judgment. Personality deterioration and loss of motivation accompany these other deficits. Normally, dementia is also accompanied by an impairment in emotional control and in moral and ethical sensibilities; for example, the person may engage in crude solicitations for sex. Dementia may be progressive or static, more often the former; occasionally, it is even reversible. Its course depends to a large extent on its underlying causes.

The factors causing dementia are many and varied. They include degenerative processes that usually, but not always, affect older individuals. As Table 13.1 indicates, the most common cause of dementia is degenerative brain disease, particularly Alzheimer's disease. Other causes may be repeated cerebrovascular accidents (strokes); certain infectious diseases, such as syphilis, meningitis, and AIDS; intracranial tumors and abscesses; certain dietary deficiencies; severe or repeated head injury; anoxia (lack of oxygen); and the ingestion or inhalation of toxic substances.

The Amnestic Syndrome The essential feature of the **amnestic syndrome** is a striking deficit in the ability to recall ongoing events more than a few minutes after they have taken place. Immediate memory and, to a lesser extent, memory for events that occurred before the disorder's development may remain largely intact, as does

dementia Neuropsychological disorder characterized by progressive deterioration of brain functioning that occurs after the completion of brain maturation and that involves deficits in memory, abstract thinking, acquisition of new knowledge or skills, visuospatial comprehension, motor control, problem solving, and judgment.

amnestic syndrome Neuropsychological disorder characterized by a striking deficit in the ability to recall ongoing events more than a few minutes after they have taken place.

memory for words and concepts. An amnestic individual, then, is typically constrained to live for the most part only in the present or the remote past; the recent past is for most practical purposes unavailable. The question of whether the recent past is unavailable in some absolute sense is subject to differing interpretations, however. Some evidence suggests that these individuals may recognize or even recollect events of the recent past if given sufficient cues, which would indicate that the information has been acquired. Thus, some part of the memory difficulty may involve a defective retrieval mechanism rather than a failure of memory storage per se.

In contrast to the dementia syndrome, overall cognitive functioning in the amnestic syndrome may remain relatively intact. The affected person may thus be able to execute complex tasks if the nature of the task provides its own distinctive cues as to the stages of the task already completed. Theoretically, this disorder involves chiefly the relationship between the short-term and long-term memory systems; the contents of the former, always limited in scope and ephemeral in duration, are not stored in a way that permits ready accessibility or retrieval (Hirst, 1982).

In the most common forms of amnestic syndrome—those associated with alcohol or barbiturate addiction—the disorder may be irreversible; the person never regains the ability to acquire new information in a way that ensures its availability when needed. A wide range of other pathogenic factors, such as a correctable medical condition, may produce an amnestic syndrome. In these cases, depending on the nature and extent of damage to the affected neural structures and on the treatment undertaken, the syndrome may in time abate wholly, in part, or hardly at all. A wide range of techniques has been developed to assist the good-prognosis amnestic patient in remembering recent events (e.g., Gouvier et al., 1997).

The Neuropsychological Delusional Syndrome In **neuropsychological delusional syndrome,** false beliefs or belief systems arise in a setting of known or suspected brain impairment and are considered to be due primarily to the accompanying organic brain pathology. These delusions vary in content, depending to some extent on the particular etiology involved. For example, a distinctly paranoid, suspicious, and persecutory delusional system is commonly seen with long-standing abuse of amphetamine drugs, whereas grandiose and expansive delusions are more characteristic of the now fortunately rare advanced neurosyphilis (general paresis). Many early Alzheimer patients develop jealousy delusions, accusing their often elderly spouses of sexual infidelity. Other etiological factors in the neuropsychological delusional syndrome include head injury and intracranial tumors.

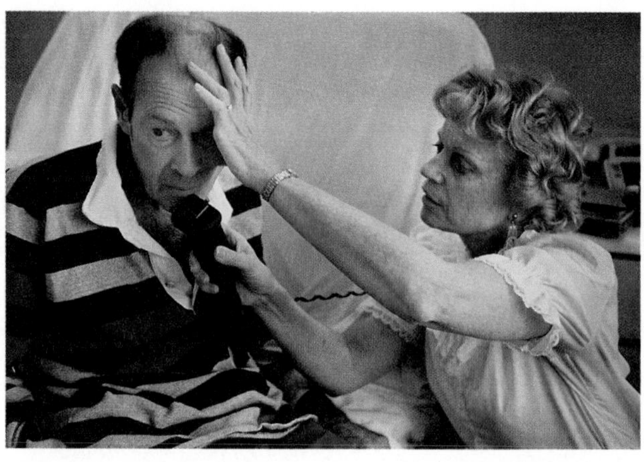

This man has Parkinson's disease, which may be associated with a neuropsychological mood syndrome, a cluster of symptoms that closely resembles those seen in either depressive or manic mood disorders.

Neuropsychological Mood Syndrome Some cases of serious mood disturbance appear to be caused by disruptions in the normal physiology of cerebral function. Such conditions may closely resemble the symptoms seen in either depressive or manic mood disorders. Severe depressive syndromes, whether or not associated with organic pathology, may on superficial examination appear as dementias, in which case the term *pseudodementia* is often applied. On the other hand, subjective complaints among the elderly of, for example, memory loss may be an accurate harbinger of developing dementia (Schmand et al., 1997b). The neuropsychological mood reaction may be minimal or severe, and the course of the disorder varies widely, depending on the nature of the organic pathology. **Neuropsychological mood syndromes** may be caused by cerebrovascular accidents (strokes), Parkinson's disease, head injury, withdrawal of certain drugs, intracranial tumors or tumors of the hormone-secreting organs, and excessive use of steroid (adrenocortical hormone) drugs or certain other medications. Of course, an awareness of lost function or a hopeless outlook might itself make a person depressed, so special care needs to be taken in the diagnostic process when there is reason to believe that the pa-

neuropsychological delusional syndrome Disorder characterized by false beliefs or belief systems arising from organic brain pathology.

neuropsychological mood syndromes Serious mood disturbances apparently caused by disruptions in the normal physiology of cerebral function.

tient harbors pessimistic thoughts about his or her clinical outcome (see Teri & Wagner, 1992; Teri et al., 1997).

Neuropsychological Personality Syndromes A notable change in an individual's general personality style or traits following brain injury of any kind is the essential feature of **neuropsychological personality syndromes.** Normally, the change is in a socially negative direction; it may include impaired social judgment, lessened control of emotions and impulses, diminished concern about the consequences of one's behavior, and an inability to sustain goal-directed activity. Many different causes are associated with the neuropsychological personality syndromes, and the course of the disorder depends on its etiology. Occasionally, as when it is induced by medication, the personality change may be transitory. Often, however, it is the first sign of impending deterioration, as when a kindly and gentle old man makes sexual advances toward a child or when a conservative executive suddenly begins to engage in unwise financial dealings. Much evidence indicates that a common organic feature in the personality syndromes may be damage to the frontal lobes (Bennett, Dittmar, & Ho, 1997; Sherwin & Geschwind, 1978; Stuss, Gow, & Hetherington, 1992), perhaps especially the right frontal (Borod, 1992).

We turn now to an examination of some longer-term disorders in which major, usually permanent, brain pathology occurs but in which an individual's emotional, motivational, and behavioral reactions to the loss of function also play an important role. Indeed, as was earlier suggested, it is often impossible to distinguish maladaptive behavior that is directly caused by neuropsychological dysfunction from that which is basically part of an individual's psychological reaction to the deficits and disabilities experienced (Bennett et al., 1997; Fabrega, 1981; Geschwind, 1975; Teri & Wagner, 1992).

The three types of neuropsychological mental disorder we will discuss in greater detail are (1) HIV-1 infection of the brain, (2) dementia of the Alzheimer's type, (3) and disorders involving traumatic head injury. Vascular (formerly multi-infarct) dementia will be briefly addressed following the section on Alzheimer's, chiefly as a contrast to that disease.

Neuropsychological Disorder With HIV-1 Infection

As we saw in Chapter 8, the devastating effects on the immune system produced by infection with the HIV-1 virus renders its victims susceptible to a wide variety of other infectious agents. In addition, the HIV-1 virus (or a mutant form of it) can itself result in the destruction of brain cells and the neuropsychological syndromes associated with such damage. Several different forms of such HIV-induced central nervous system pathology have been identified, some of which appear to be associated with the emergence of psychotic (e.g., delusional) phenomena (Sewell et al., 1994). To date, however, most attention has focused on the **AIDS dementia complex (ADC),** a generalized loss of cognitive functioning affecting a substantial proportion of AIDS patients.

The neuropathology of ADC involves various changes in the brain, among them generalized atrophy, edema, inflammation, and patches of demyelination (loss of the myelin sheath surrounding nerve fibers), as described by various investigators (Adams & Ferraro, 1997; Gabuzda & Hirsch, 1987; Gray, Gherardi, & Scaravilli, 1988; Price et al., 1988a; Sewell et al., 1994). No brain area may be spared, but the damage appears concentrated in subcortical regions, notably the central white matter, the tissue surrounding the ventricles, and deeper gray matter structures such as the basal ganglia and thalamus. Fully 90 percent of AIDS victims show evidence of such changes on autopsy (Adams & Ferraro, 1997).

Prominent Features The neuropsychological features of AIDS, which tend to appear as a late phase of HIV infection (although often before the full development of AIDS itself), usually begin with psychomotor slowing, diminished concentration, mild memory difficulties, and perhaps slight motor clumsiness. Progression is typically rapid after this point, with clear-cut dementia appearing in many cases within 1 year, although considerably longer periods have been reported. In general, and consistent with autopsy findings, the neuropsychological evidence points primarily to a disruption of brain function at the subcortical level; the most reliably reported finding is that of notably delayed reaction time (Law & Mapou, 1997). The later phases of ADC can be quite grim and include behavioral regression, confusion, psychotic thinking, apathy, and marked withdrawal, leading before death to an incontinent, bedridden state (Navia, Jordan, & Price, 1986; Price, Sidtis, & Rosenblum, 1988; Price et al., 1988).

Prevalence Studies Thirty-eight percent of 121 living AIDS patients studied by Navia and colleagues (1986) met

neuropsychological personality syndromes Disorders characterized by notable change in general personality style or personality traits following brain injury of any kind.

AIDS dementia complex (ADC) Generalized loss of cognitive functioning affecting a substantial proportion of AIDS patients.

DSM criteria for dementia. Patients with **AIDS-related complex (ARC),** a pre-AIDS manifestation of HIV infection involving minor infections, various nonspecific symptoms (such as unexplained fever), and blood cell count abnormalities, may also experience cognitive difficulty, although it may be too subtle to be readily detected on clinical observation or the more standard neuropsychological test batteries (Law & Mapou, 1997). In one study (Grant et al., 1987), 54 percent of ARC patients demonstrated definite impairment on a neuropsychological test battery. Significant numbers of HIV-infected persons were found to be neuropsychologically compromised in a cross-national study reported by Maj and colleagues (1994), although these investigators emphasize the subtlety of the deficits detected and their lack of substantial impact on social functioning in otherwise asymptomatic persons.

Clearly, infection with the HIV-1 virus poses a substantial threat to the anatomical integrity of the brain, in addition to having immune system effects. It is not yet known what protects the minority of AIDS patients who show no central nervous system involvement during the entire course of their illnesses.

Treatment The question of treatment for ADC is of course intimately tied to that involving control or eradication of the HIV-1 infection itself. Until fairly recently, it was impossible to feel confident about the prospects because of the enormous and unprecedented challenges presented by the complex structure and life cycle of this retrovirus (McCutchan, 1990). This picture improved with advances in antiviral therapy, and there is considerable evidence that these agents can improve cognitive and neurological functioning—although complete restoration is not a likely outcome (Adams & Ferraro, 1997; Law & Mapou, 1997). Unfortunately, experience with zidovudine (AZT) therapy indicates that this encouraging effect may prove temporary because the virus adapts over time to the presence of antiviral agents.

It remains true, therefore, that prevention of infection is the only certain defensive strategy, a circumstance not unlike the problem posed by neurosyphilis, another sexually transmitted and potentially dementing disease, in an earlier era. In general, humankind has not done well in controlling the spread of sexually transmitted diseases through cautious sexual behavior, and that pattern seems to be repeating itself with the HIV-1 virus.

Dementia of the Alzheimer's Type

While the dementia complicating many cases of HIV-1 infection is a very serious concern, especially for the family and friends of victims, it is dwarfed in magnitude by the problems our society faces in coping with the dementia that is the most salient aspect of Alzheimer's disease, officially (as on Axis I of DSM-IV-TR) termed **dementia of the Alzheimer's type (DAT).** DAT takes its name from Alois Alzheimer, a German neuropsychiatrist, who first described it in 1907.

It is a commonplace observation that the organs of the body deteriorate with aging. The cause or causes of this deterioration, however, remain largely obscure; science has not yet solved the riddle of aging. Of course, the brain—truly the master organ—is not spared in the aging process. Over time it too wears out, or degenerates. Mental disorders that sometimes accompany this brain degeneration and occur in old age have traditionally been called **senile dementias.** Unfortunately, a number of rare conditions result in degenerative changes in brain tissue earlier in life. Disorders associated with such earlier degeneration of the brain are known as **presenile dementias.**

Not only is the age of onset different for the presenile dementias, but they are also distinguished from the senile dementias by their different behavioral manifestations and brain tissue alterations. One important exception is Alzheimer's disease, which is a typical and common senile disorder but which can, in some people, occur well before old age. Alzheimer's disease is associated with a characteristic dementia syndrome having an imperceptible onset and a usually slow but progressively deteriorating course, terminating in delirium and death.

The Clinical Picture in DAT The diagnosis of DAT is often difficult and uncertain (Debettignles et al., 1997), a major reason being that it is not possible to confirm the presence of the distinctive Alzheimer neuropathology (described below) in living patients. The diagnosis is nor-

AIDS-related complex (ARC) Pre-AIDS manifestation of HIV infection, involving minor infections, various nonspecific symptoms (such as unexplained fever), blood cell count abnormalities, and sometimes cognitive difficulties.

dementia of the Alzheimer's type (DAT) Progressive dementia associated with Alzheimer's disease and ultimately terminating in death; onset may occur in middle or old age, and symptoms include memory loss, withdrawal, confusion, and impaired judgment.

senile dementias Mental disorders that sometimes accompany brain degeneration in old age.

presenile dementias Mental disorders resulting from brain degeneration occurring prior to old age.

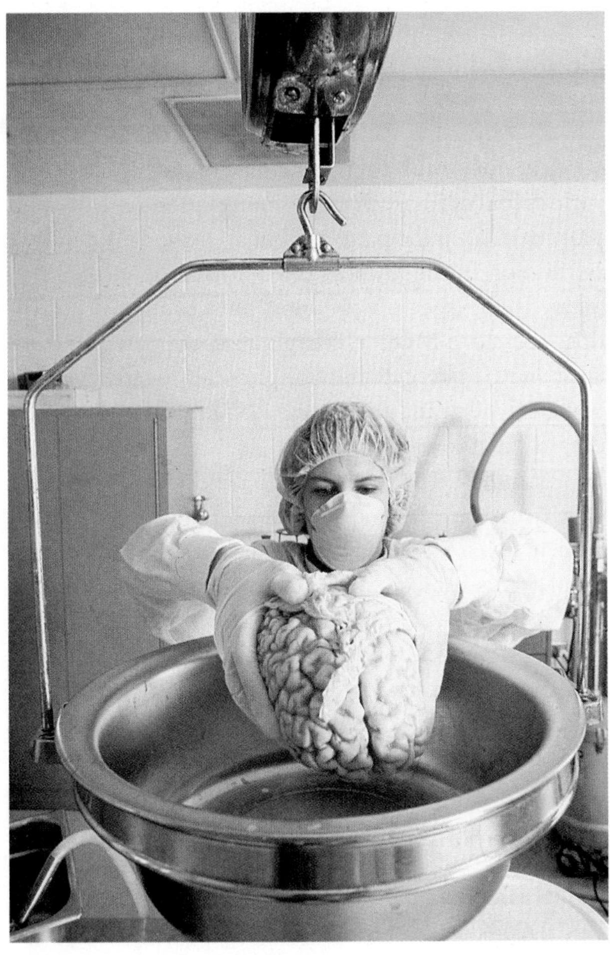

Some brain diseases, Alzheimer's among them, can be diagnosed with certainty only at autopsy. Clinicians must be conscientious in their diagnostic efforts with live patients because of the potentially serious consequences of error.

mally rendered only after all other potential causes of dementia are ruled out by case and family history, physical examination, and laboratory tests. Brain-imaging techniques, such as magnetic resonance imaging (MRI), may provide supportive evidence in showing enlarged ventricles or widening in the folds (sulci) of the cerebral cortex, indicating brain atrophy. Unfortunately, several other disease conditions, as well as normal aging, result in a similar type of atrophy—making it impossible at present to diagnose Alzheimer's definitively without an autopsy. Much contemporary research is therefore devoted to the discovery of valid antemortem (before death) criteria for the diagnosis of DAT.

The onset of Alzheimer's disease in older people is usually gradual, involving slow mental deterioration. In some cases a physical ailment or some other stressful event is a dividing point, but usually an individual passes into a demented state almost imperceptibly, so that it is impossible to date the onset of the disorder precisely. The clinical picture may vary markedly from one person to another, depending on the nature and extent of brain degeneration, the premorbid personality of the individual, the particular stressors present, and the degree of environmental support.

Signs often begin with the person's gradual withdrawal from active engagement with life. There is a narrowing of social activities and interests, a lessening of mental alertness and adaptability, and a lowering of tolerance to new ideas and changes in routine. Often thoughts and activities become self-centered and childlike, including a preoccupation with the bodily functions of eating, digestion, and excretion. As these changes—typical in a lesser degree of many older people—become more severe, additional symptoms, such as impaired memory for recent events, "empty" speech (in which grammar and syntax remain intact but vague and seemingly pointless expressions replace meaningful conversational exchange—e.g., "It's a nice day, but it might rain"), messiness, impaired judgment, agitation, and periods of confusion, make their appearance. Specific symptoms may vary considerably from patient to patient and from day to day for the same patient; thus, the clinical picture is by no means uniform until the terminal stages, when the patient is reduced to a vegetative level. There is also, of course, individual variation in the rapidity of the disorder's progression. In rare instances the symptoms may reverse and partial function may return, but in true DAT this reversal invariably proves temporary.

The end stages of Alzheimer's disease involve a depressingly similar pattern of reduction to a vegetative existence and ultimate death from some disease that overwhelms an affected person's limited defensive resources. Before this point, there is, as noted, some distinctiveness in patient behavior. Allowing for individual differences, a given victim is likely to show one of the several dominant behavioral manifestations described in the following paragraphs.

Approximately half of all DAT patients display a course of simple deterioration. That is, they gradually lose various mental capacities, typically beginning with memory for recent events and progressing to disorientation, poor judgment, neglect of personal hygiene, and loss of contact with reality to an extent precluding independent functioning as adults. Distinctly psychopathological symptoms (such as delusions), if they occur at all, are likely to be transitory and inconsistent over time. The following case—involving a man who had retired about 7 years prior to his hospitalization—is typical of simple deterioration resulting from DAT.

Case Study **An Engineer with DAT** • During the past 5 years, he had shown a progressive loss of interest in his surroundings and, during the last year, had become increasingly "childish." His wife and eldest son had brought him to the hospital because they felt they could no longer care for him in their home, particularly because of the grandchildren. They stated that he had become careless in his eating and other personal habits and was restless and prone to wandering about at night. He could not seem to remember anything that had happened during the day but was garrulous concerning events of his childhood and middle years.

After admission to the hospital, the patient seemed to deteriorate rapidly. He could rarely remember what had happened a few minutes before, although his memory for remote events of his childhood remained good. When he was visited by his wife and children, he mistook them for old friends; he could not recall anything about the visit a few minutes after they had departed.

The following brief conversation with the patient, which took place after he had been in the hospital for 9 months and about 3 months before his death, shows his disorientation for time and person:

DOCTOR: How are you today, Mr. ____?

PATIENT: Oh... hello [looks at doctor in rather puzzled way as if trying to make out who he is].

DOCTOR: Do you know where you are now?

PATIENT: Why yes... I am at home. I must paint the house this summer. It has needed painting for a long time but it seems like I just keep putting it off.

DOCTOR: Can you tell me the day today?

PATIENT: Isn't today Sunday?... why, yes, the children are coming over for dinner today. We always have dinner for the whole family on Sunday. My wife was here just a minute ago but I guess she has gone back into the kitchen.

In a less frequent manifestation of Alzheimer's disease, the patient develops a decidedly paranoid orientation to the environment, becoming markedly suspicious and often convinced that others are engaged in various injurious plots and schemes. Uncooperativeness and verbal abuse are common accompaniments, making the task of caregiving significantly more stressful. In the early phases of this reaction pattern, the cognitive deficits characteristic of Alzheimer's disease (memory loss, disorientation) may not be prominent, perhaps enabling the person to be quite observant and even logical in building the case for others' threatening activities. Though themes of victimization predominate in this form of the disorder, also common is the so-called jealousy delusion, in which the person persistently accuses his or her partner or spouse—who is often of advanced age and physically debilitated—of being sexually unfaithful. Family members may be accused of various foul deeds, such as poisoning the patient's food or plotting to steal the patient's funds. Fortunately, punitive retribution in the form of physical attacks on the "evildoers" is not especially common, but a combative pattern does occasionally occur, complicating the patient's management. In a recent study of physically aggressive DAT patients, Gilley and associates (1997) found that 80 percent of them were delusional.

Paranoid orientations tend to develop in people who have been sensitive and suspicious. Existing personality tendencies are apparently intensified by degenerative brain changes and the stress accompanying advancing age. As a general rule, advanced-stage Alzheimer's patients are unlikely to be aware of their own cognitive deficits (Vasterling, Seltzer, & Watrous, 1997; Wagner et al., 1997), and hence do not attribute negative events to this source.

When we picture a typical Alzheimer patient, we imagine a person of advanced age. Although most patients are older, for some, DAT is a presenile dementia that begins in their 40s or 50s; in such cases, the progress of the disease and its associated dementia is often rapid (Heyman et al., 1987). Considerable evidence suggests an especially substantial genetic contribution in early-onset DAT (Davies, 1986), although different genes may well be involved in different families (Breitner et al., 1993). These early-onset cases, occurring in comparatively young and vigorous patients, portray the tragedy of Alzheimer's disease in an especially stark light.

With appropriate treatment, which may include medication and the maintenance of a calm, reassuring, and unprovocative social milieu, many people with Alzheimer's disease show some symptom alleviation. In general, however, deterioration continues its downward course over a period of months or years. Eventually, patients become oblivious of their surroundings, bedridden, and reduced to a vegetative existence. Resistance to disease is lowered, and death usually results from pneumonia or some other respiratory or cardiac problem.

Prevalence of DAT The magnitude of the problem of DAT—often seriously underestimated—is already straining societal and family resources, both economic (Ernst et al., 1997; Max, 1993) and emotional (see below), and the future prospects are somewhat alarming as the population ages. As shown in Table 13.1 (see page 437), the disorder is believed to account for a large proportion of all cases of dementia of whatever cause. The ratio is doubtless considerably higher for older people. It is estimated that one of every six people in the United States over age 65 is clinically demented, and that one of every ten people in this age range suffers from DAT (Evans et al., 1989). The prevalence rate of DAT may approach 50 percent by age 85 (Fisher & Carstensen, 1990), and a United Kingdom study indicates that, in each 5-year interval from ages 75 to 89, there is an approximate doubling of the rate of new cases of DAT (Paykel et al., 1994). There are thus over 4 million living victims in the United States alone, and the number is increasing rapidly with the advancing age of the population. It is estimated that about 30 to 40 percent of nursing home residents are DAT patients. Some of these patients reside in mental hospitals or other types of institutional settings. Most, however, live in the community, typically with family members (Gurland & Cross, 1982), a circumstance that is often extremely stressful for caregivers (Brane, 1986; Fisher & Carstensen, 1990; Intrieri & Rapp, 1994; Shaw et al., 1997).

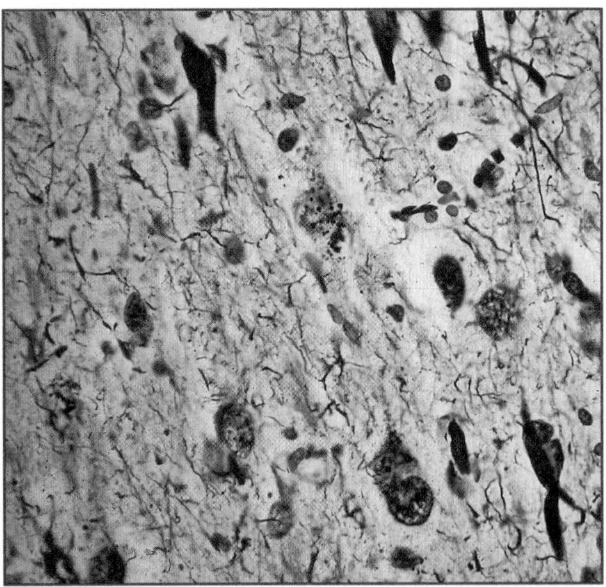

FIGURE 13.3
PHOTOMICROGRAPH OF BRAIN TISSUE FROM AN ALZHEIMER'S PATIENT
Note the characteristic plaques (dark patches) and neurofibrillary tangles (irregular patterns of strand-like fibers).
Source: Dr. Dennis J. Selkoe/Brigham and Women's Hospital, Harvard Medical School.

Causal Factors in DAT The quickening pace of research on Alzheimer's has already yielded many intriguing leads, as we shall see. It has also shown, however, that the etiology of the disease is complex and varying—not simply a matter of having been born with the wrong genes and getting on in years. We will focus our discussion on the known neuropathology of DAT and on the still puzzling genetic-environmental interaction that seems implicated in its causation.

Neuropathology The structural neuropathology of the brain associated with Alzheimer's has been known for some time. Readily determined by microscopic examination of tissue specimens (see Figure 13.3), it has three elements: (1) the widespread appearance of *senile plaques,* small areas of dark-colored matter that are in part the debris of damaged nerve terminals; (2) the tangling of the normally regular patterning of *neurofibrils* (strand-like protein filaments) within neuronal cell bodies; and (3) the abnormal appearance of small holes in neuronal tissue, called *granulovacuoles,* which derive from cell degeneration. Absolute confirmation of the diagnosis of DAT at present rests on observation of these changes in tissue samples, which is why it can normally be accomplished only after a patient has died. When sufficiently numerous, these microscopic alterations of the brain's substance lead to generalized brain atrophy, which as already noted may be visualized in live patients by brain-imaging techniques.

Another notable alteration in DAT concerns the neurotransmitter acetylcholine (ACh), which is known to be important in the mediation of memory. While there is widespread destruction of neurons in DAT, particularly in the area of the hippocampus (Adler, 1994; Mori et al., 1997b), evidence suggests that among the earliest and most severely affected are a cluster of cell bodies located in the basal forebrain and involved in the release of ACh (Whitehouse et al., 1982). This observation and related ones (e.g., Wester et al., 1988) have given rise to the ACh depletion theory of DAT etiology, the hypothesis being that a primary cause of the disease is insufficient availability of ACh in the brain. Although the evidence is not conclusive, the theory does integrate an impressive array of research data. For example, a temporary DAT-like syndrome may be produced in normal subjects who are given ACh-blocking drugs (Kopelman, 1986; Whitehouse, 1993).

Other investigators have tried to discover the sources of the primary DAT lesions, the neurofibrillary tangles and senile plaques. An important observation concerning the plaques is that at the core of the cell debris is a sticky protein substance called *beta amyloid.* This substance (and a chemical precursor to it) also occurs in abnormal abundance in other parts of DAT patients' brains (see Gajdusek, 1986; Hardy et al., 1986; Kang et al., 1987), and it is therefore believed to be somehow involved in the etiology of the disease. In fact, beta amyloid has been shown to be itself neurotoxic, causing cell death (Seppa, 1998). As yet, however, the source and the specific role of the abnormal accumulation of this protein in the DAT brain remain unclear.

Gene-Environment Interaction in DAT A general vulnerability to the development of DAT, even in very late-onset cases, may be inherited (Breitner, 1986; Breitner et al., 1993; Davies, 1986; Martin et al., 1997; Mohs et al., 1987; Sturt, 1986). Much of this evidence points to a genetic connection with Down syndrome (to be discussed later in this chapter), which is usually due to a trisomy (tripling) involving chromosome 21. Most people with Down syndrome who survive beyond about age 40 develop a DAT-like dementia (Bauer & Shea, 1986; Janicki & Dalton, 1993), with similar neuropathological changes (Schapiro & Rapoport, 1987). Anomalies of chromosome 21 have also been implicated in DAT (e.g., Van Broeckhoven et al., 1987), although it is clear that this chromosome cannot be the only site of origin for genetic influences in enhancing disease vulnerability (Breitner et al., 1993; Clark & Goate, 1993).

As in other varieties of psychopathology, it remains a puzzle as to how genetic influences manifest themselves in increasing risk of disorder. A partial answer to that puzzle in the case of DAT became available with the discovery that differing forms (genetic alleles) of a blood protein called *apolipoprotein-E (ApoE)* differentially predict risk for late-onset DAT. (e.g., see Katzman et al., 1997; Lopez et al., 1997; Martin et al., 1997; Plassman & Breitner, 1997). However, this discovery still does not account for all cases of DAT, not even all cases of late-onset DAT (e.g., see Bergem, Engedal, & Kringlen, 1997). Many people inheriting the most risky form of ApoE do not succumb to DAT, and some who do succumb to the disease have no such risk factor.

Substantial numbers of monozygotic twins are discordant for the disease (Bergem et al., 1997; Breitner et al., 1993). That important observation is most readily understood by positing some sort of critical environmental influence—such as significant prior head trauma—that may operate in concert with a genetic vulnerability to produce the pathological outcome. On this point, Gatz and associates (1994) note that many eventually fatal organ system failures, Alzheimer's disease among them, seem to be the product not of a single or even a limited array of specific causal factors. Rather, they are the result of an accumulation of risk factors, both genetic and environmental, that ultimately exceed some clinical threshold and produce disease. Advancing age, of course, increases exposure to risks. This view leaves open the possibility of reducing or delaying the occurrence of DAT through deliberately limiting exposure to risks—such as environmental toxins or excessive alcohol consumption—some of which are potentially controllable.

Treatments and Outcomes in DAT There is as yet no known treatment for DAT—medical, psychosocial, retraining-based, or rehabilitative, including attempts at preserving or replenishing brain ACh—that produces a sustained reversal or interruption of the deteriorating course. Until some means of accomplishing such an effect appears, treatment will consist mainly of palliative measures that diminish patient and caregiver distress and relieve as far as possible those complications of the disorder, such as combativeness, that increase the difficulties of management.

Several of the common problematic behaviors that are associated with DAT (and with other dementing disorders as well) include wandering off, incontinence, inappropriate sexual behavior, and inadequate self-care skills. These can be somewhat controlled using behavioral approaches, such as systematic contingent reinforcement. Such therapies need not be dependent on complex cognitive and communicational abilities, which are apt to be lacking in these patients. They may therefore be particularly appropriate for therapeutic intervention with this group. In general, reports of results are moderately encouraging in terms of reducing unnecessary frustration and embarrassment for the patient and difficulty for the caregiver (Fisher & Carstensen, 1990; Mintzer et al., 1997; Teri et al., 1997).

Treatment research has also been focused on the consistent findings of ACh depletion in DAT. The reasoning here is that it might be possible to improve functioning by administering drugs that enhance the availability of brain ACh. Currently, the most effective way of doing so is by inhibiting the production of acetylcholinesterase, the principal enzyme involved in the metabolic breakdown of ACh. This is the rationale for the drug tacrine (Cognex). The findings, however, indicate effects that are mostly quite limited and inconsistent (Rainer, 1997; Whitehouse, 1993). Rainer (1997) has suggested that a natural acetylcholinesterase inhibitor, galanthamine, derived from certain plant species, has more promise, but research on its use is as yet limited.

Other medications may be of some help for patients who experience difficulty in modulating their emotions and impulses. Some depressed DAT patients respond reasonably well to antidepressant or stimulant medication. Where medications are used, however, dosages must be carefully monitored because unanticipated effects are common and because the frequently debilitated state of these patients makes them susceptible to an exaggerated response.

As we have seen, neuronal cells that have died with the advance of Alzheimer's neuropathology are permanently lost; hence, even if some treatment were found to terminate a patient's progressive loss of brain tissue, he or she would still be left seriously impaired. The real key to effective intervention must therefore be preventive, or at least deployable at the first sign of Alzheimer's onset, sparing the bulk of the brain's neurons. Eventually, for example, we might be able to identify and reduce or eliminate the environmental hazards that play a role in stimulating the development of Alzheimer's (Gatz et al., 1994). Clearly, however, the most promising development in regard to prevention possibilities relates to the apolipoprotein (ApoE) research mentioned earlier. Conceivably, it will prove possible to fashion interventions—for example, by administering targeted drugs—that counteract pathogenic processes associated with inheritance of the highest-risk ApoE forms. That would truly be a momentous achievement.

Treating Caregivers In the meantime, any comprehensive approach to therapeutic intervention must consider the extremely difficult situation of caregivers. With advancing DAT, they are confronted not only with many challenging patient management problems but also with the "social death" of the patient as a person and their own "anticipatory grief" (Gilhooly et al., 1994). They are, as a group, at extraordinarily high risk for depression (Cohen & Eisdorfer, 1988), perhaps especially if they are husbands caring for impaired wives (Robinson-Whelen & Kiecolt-Glaser, 1997; Tower, Kasl, & Moritz, 1997). They tend to consume high quantities of psychotropic medication themselves and to report many stress symptoms (George, 1984; Hinrichsen & Niederehe, 1994). Because the basic problem usually seems to be one of high and sustained stress, any measures found successful in the reduction and management of stress and the enhancement of coping resources could be helpful in easing caregivers' burdens (Costa, Whitfield, & Stewart, 1989). Group support programs, for example, may produce measurable reductions in experienced stress and depression (e.g., Glosser & Wexler, 1985; Hebert et al., 1994; Kahan et al., 1985).

Whether or not, or at what point, to institutionalize a DAT patient whose requirements for care threaten to overwhelm his or her spouse or other family members can be a vexing and emotional decision (Cohen, Tyrrell, & Smith, 1993). It can also be one with significant financial implications because, on average, nursing home care is about twice as costly as home care (Hu, Huang, & Cartwright, 1986). Most DAT patients are cared for at home, mostly for emotional reasons, such as continuing love, loyalty, and a sense of obligation to the stricken parent or partner.

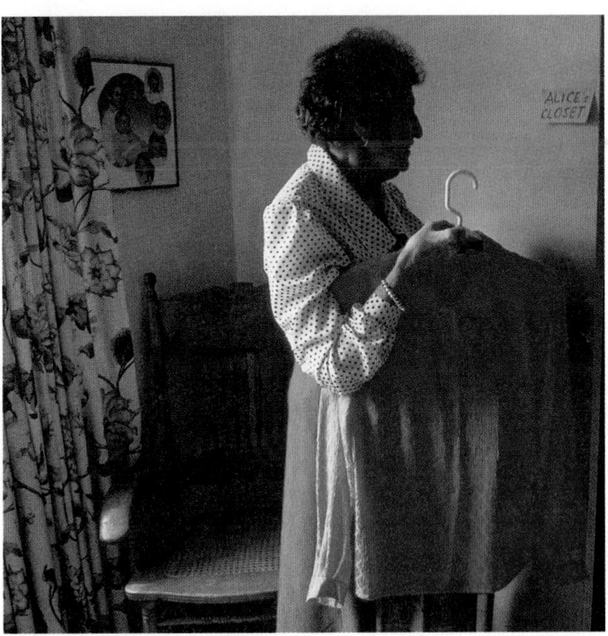

The stress on children or spouses of taking care of DAT patients is enormous. Group support programs can help reduce this stress and the depressive symptoms that may accompany it.

In one sense at least, the home care decision is a justifiable one; the move to an institution, particularly one lacking in social stimulation and support, may result in an abrupt worsening of symptoms and sometimes a markedly enhanced rate of deterioration—demonstrating once again the power of psychosocial influences, even in the case of widespread brain destruction. On the other hand, the emergence of marked confusion, gross and argumentative demeanor, stuporous depression, inappropriate sexual behavior, and disorientation for time, place, and person, not to mention possible sudden eruption of combative violence, can put an intolerable strain on caregivers. Because in all likelihood such conditions will worsen over time, wisdom dictates an early rather than a late removal to an institution, which in any event is where most DAT patients will have to spend their final weeks, months, or years.

Vascular Dementia

Vascular dementia (VAD), formerly *multi-infarct dementia,* is frequently confused with DAT because of its similar clinical picture of progressive dementia and its increasing incidence and prevalence rates with advancing age. It is

vascular dementia (VAD) Dementia resulting from a series of circumscribed cerebral infarcts (small strokes) that cumulatively destroy neurons over expanding regions of the brain, leading to brain atrophy and behavioral impairments that ultimately mimic those of DAT.

actually an entirely different disease in terms of its underlying neuropathology. In this disorder, a series of circumscribed cerebral infarcts—interruptions of the blood supply to minute areas of the brain because of arterial disease, commonly known as "small strokes"—cumulatively destroy neurons over expanding brain regions. The affected regions become soft and may degenerate over time, leaving only cavities. Although this disorder tends to have a more heterogeneous early clinical picture than DAT (Wallin & Blennow, 1993), the progressive loss of cells leads to brain atrophy and behavioral impairments that ultimately mimic those of DAT (Bowler et al, 1997). The decline, however, is less smooth for several reasons: (1) the discrete character of each infarct event; (2) variations over time in the volume of blood delivered by a seriously clogged artery, producing variations in the functional adequacy of cells that have not yet succumbed to oxygen deprivation; and (3) a tendency for vascular dementia to be associated with more severe behavioral complications, such as violence (Sultzer et al., 1993). VAD is far less common than DAT, accounting for only some 10 percent of dementia cases. One reason for this is that patients who suffer multiple small strokes have a high vulnerability to sudden death from a large infarct or one that affects vital centers. Occasionally, an unfortunate patient will be discovered to have both DAT and VAD, commonly referred to as "mixed" dementia (Cohen et al., 1997).

The medical treatment of VAD, while hazardous and complicated, offers slightly more hope at this time than that of DAT. Unlike DAT, the basic problem of cerebral arteriosclerosis can be medically managed to some extent, perhaps decreasing the likelihood of further strokes.

The psychological and behavioral aspects of the dementia caused by DAT and VAD are similar in many respects, and any management measure found useful in one is likely to be applicable in the other. Likewise, the maintenance of any gains achieved cannot be taken for granted because of the generally progressive nature of the underlying brain pathology. The daunting problems facing caregivers are also much the same in the two conditions, indicating the appropriateness of support groups, stress reduction techniques, and the like.

Disorders Involving Head Injury

Traumatic brain injuries (TBI) occur frequently, on the order of 7 to 8 million per year in the United States. Most of these are the result of motor vehicle crashes. A sizable number of cases are the result of penetration of the cranium by bullets or other objects. Significant brain damage is sustained in some 500,000 of these instances of TBI, and it is of sufficient severity in some 70,000 to 90,000 of those to preclude return to normal functioning (Bennett, Ditmar, & Ho, 1997). Nevertheless, relatively few people with TBIs find their way into mental hospitals because many head injuries do not involve appreciable damage to the brain, and even where they do, psychopathological complications are often not observed. In DSM-IV, brain injuries having notable, long-standing effects on adaptive functioning are coded on Axis I using the appropriate syndromal descriptive phrase, with the qualifier "due to head trauma."

traumatic brain injury (TBI) Any brain damage resulting from head trauma, such as in motor vehicle crashes or from gunshot wounds.

The Clinical Picture in Head Injury Disorders

Neuropsychologically significant head injuries usually give rise to immediate acute reactions, such as unconsciousness and disruption of circulatory, metabolic, and neurotransmitter regulation. Normally, if a head injury is sufficiently severe to result in unconsciousness, the person experiences *retrograde amnesia,* or inability to recall events immediately preceding the injury. Apparently, such trauma interferes with the brain's capacity to consolidate into long-term storage the events that were still being processed at the time of the trauma. *Anterograde amnesia* (also called post-traumatic amnesia) refers to an inability to effectively store in memory events happening during variable periods of time *after* the trauma. It is also frequently observed and is regarded by many as a negative prognostic sign.

A person rendered unconscious by a head injury usually passes through stages of stupor and confusion on the way to recovering clear consciousness. This recovery of consciousness may be complete in the course of minutes, or it may take hours or days. In rare cases, an individual may live for extended periods of time without regaining consciousness, a condition known as *coma.* In such cases, the prognosis for substantial improvement is poor. If the patient survives, coma may be followed by delirium, in which acute excitement is manifested, with disorientation, hallucinations, and generally agitated, restless, and confused activity. Often the patient talks incessantly in a disconnected fashion, with no insight into the disturbed condition. Gradually the confusion clears up, and the individual regains contact with reality.

The persistence and severity of post-trauma disruptions of brain function depend on the degree and type of injury. The disruptions may lead to early death or may clear up entirely. Quite often, as already noted, they develop into chronic disorders in which the individual's future cognitive and behavioral functioning is seriously compromised. In relatively severe but nonfatal brain injury, most of the recovery that will be experienced tends to occur in the earliest post-trauma phase, although sometimes return of function may occur after several years. Individual courses of recovery are highly variable (Crepeau & Scherzer, 1993; Powell & Wilson, 1994).

Fortunately, the brain, encased in the hard shell of the skull, is an extraordinarily well-protected organ. But even so, a hard blow on the head may result in a skull fracture in which portions of bone press on or are driven into the brain tissue. Even without a fracture, the force of the blow may result in small, pinpoint hemorrhages throughout the brain or in the rupturing of larger blood vessels in the brain. Some degree of bleeding, or *intracranial hemorrhage,* can occur with even relatively low-impact head injuries; while minute levels of bleeding are potentially serious, they may require no intervention. In severe injuries, there may be gross bleeding or hemorrhaging at the site of the damage. Enough blood may accumulate within the rigid confines of the skull that disruptive pressure is exerted on neighboring regions of the brain; a common form of this problem is the *subdural hematoma,* which, if not relieved by aspiration (drawing out) of the excess blood, may endanger vital brain functions or produce permanent neuronal damage.

When the hemorrhaging involves small spots of bleeding—often microscopic sleeves of red cells encircling tiny blood vessels—the condition is referred to as *petechial hemorrhages.* Professional boxers, for example, are likely to suffer this type of hemorrhaging from repeated blows to the head; they may develop a form of encephalopathy (characterized by an area or areas of permanently damaged brain tissue) from the accumulated damage of such injuries. Consequently, some former boxers suffer from impaired memory, slurred speech, inability to concentrate, involuntary movements, and other symptoms—a condition popularly referred to as being "punch-drunk."

Even when a traumatic brain injury seems relatively mild, with good return of function, careful neuropsychological assessment may reveal subtle residual impairment. Large numbers of relatively mild closed-head brain *concussions* (violent shock to tissues) and *contusions* (bruises) occur every year as a result of auto collisions, athletic injuries, falls, and other mishaps. Temporary loss of consciousness and postimpact confusion are the most common and salient immediate symptoms. There is considerable controversy about whether these mild brain injuries produce significant long-standing symptoms or impairments of various abilities (Brown, Fann, & Grant, 1994; Dikmen & Levin, 1993; Zasler, 1993).

Perhaps the most famous historical example of traumatic brain injury is the celebrated American crowbar case reported by Dr. J. M. Harlow in 1868. (Dr. Harlow's original report was reprinted in *History of Psychiatry,* 1993, Vol. 4, pp. 271–281.) Because it is of both historical and descriptive significance, it merits our attention.

Case Study **The Change in Phineas Gage** • The accident occurred in Cavendish, Vermont, on the line of the Rutland and Burlington Railroad, at that time being built, on the 13th of September, 1848, and was occasioned by the premature explosion of a blast, when this iron, known to blasters as a tamping iron, and which I now show you, was shot through the face and head.

The subject of it was Phineas P. Gage, a perfectly healthy, strong and active young man, twenty-five years of age... Gage was foreman of a gang of men employed in excavating rock, for the road way....

The missile entered by its pointed end, the left side of the face, immediately anterior to the angle of the lower jaw, and passing obliquely upwards, and obliquely backwards, emerged in the median line, at the back part of the frontal bone, near the coronal suture....

The iron which thus traversed the head, is round and rendered comparatively smooth by use, and is three feet seven inches in length, one and one fourth inches in its largest diameter, and weighs thirteen and one fourth pounds....

The patient was thrown upon his back by the explosion, and gave a few convulsive motions of the extremities, but spoke in a few minutes. His men (with whom he was a great favorite) took him in their arms and carried him to the road, only a few rods distant, and put him into an ox cart, in which he rode, supported in a sitting posture, fully three quarters of a mile to his hotel. He got out of the cart himself, with a little assistance from his men, and an hour afterwards (with what I could aid him by taking hold of his left arm) walked up a long flight of stairs, and got upon the bed in the room where he was dressed. He seemed perfectly conscious, but was becoming exhausted from the hemorrhage, which by this time, was quite profuse, the blood pouring from the lacerated sinus in the top of his head, and also finding its way into the stomach, which ejected it as often as every fifteen or twenty minutes. He bore his sufferings with firmness, and directed my attention to the hole in his cheek, saying, "The iron entered there and passed through my head."

Some time later, Dr. Harlow made the following report:

His physical health is good, and I am inclined to say that he has recovered. Has no pain in head, but says it has a queer feeling which he is not able to describe. Applied for his situation as foreman, but is undecided whether to work or travel. His contractors, who regarded him as the most efficient and capable foreman in their employ previous to his injury considered the change in his mind so marked that they could not give him his place again. The equilibrium or balance, so to speak, between his intellectual faculties and animal propensities, seems to have been destroyed. He is fitful, irreverent, indulging at times in the grossest profanity (which was not previously his custom), manifesting but little deference for his fellows, impatient of restraint or advice when it conflicts with his desires, at times pertinaciously obstinate, yet capricious and vacillating, devising many plans of future operations, which are no sooner arranged than they are abandoned in turn for others... his mind is radically changed, so decidedly that his friends and acquaintances said he was "no longer Gage."

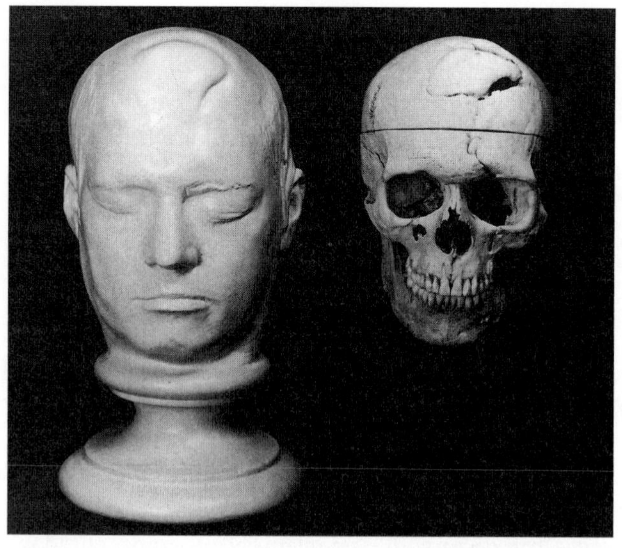

Though Phineas Gage survived when a tamping iron entered his face and shot through his head, his personality was so altered that his friends said that he was "no longer Gage."

It is evident from the above account that Gage acquired a severe frontal brain wound as well as a neuropsychological personality syndrome from his encounter with the tamping iron. As Stuss and colleagues (1992) have noted, Gage's persistent post-trauma difficulties are fairly characteristic for severe frontal-lobe damage; emotional dyscontrol and personality alterations, including impairment of self-reflective awareness, are often prominent features of behavior change due to this type of injury. In general, however, personality disturbances secondary to traumatic brain injury are somewhat unpredictable owing to the varied structural pathology apt to be involved in such injuries (Prigatano, 1992).

Treatments and Outcomes Immediate treatment for brain damage due to head injury is primarily a medical matter. Prompt treatment may prevent further injury or damage—for example, when pooled blood under pressure must be removed from the skull. In many instances, including some that may initially be considered "mild," immediate medical treatment may have to be supplemented by a long-range program of reeducation and rehabilitation.

Although many traumatic brain injury patients show few residual effects from their injury, particularly if they have experienced only a brief loss of consciousness, other patients sustain definite and long-lasting impairment. Common after-effects of moderate brain injury are chronic headaches, anxiety, irritability, dizziness, easy fatigability, and impaired memory and concentration. Where the brain damage is extensive, a patient's general intellectual level may be markedly reduced, especially if he or she has suffered severe temporal- or parietal-lobe lesions. Most victims have significant delays in returning to their occupations, and many are unable to return at all (Bennett, Dittmar, & Ho, 1997; Dikmen et al., 1994; Goran, Fabiano, & Crewe, 1997); other losses of adult social role functioning are also common (Hallett et al., 1994). In addition, various specific neurological and psychological defects may follow localized brain damage, as we have seen. Some 24 percent of traumatic brain injury cases, overall, develop post-traumatic epilepsy, presumably owing to the growth of scar tissue in the brain. Seizures usually develop within 2 years of the head injury, but sometimes much later.

In a minority of brain injury cases, notable personality changes occur, such as those described in the historic case of Phineas Gage. Other kinds of personality changes include passivity, loss of drive and spontaneity, agitation, anxiety, depression, and paranoid suspiciousness. Like cognitive changes, the kinds of personality changes that emerge in severely damaged people will depend, in large measure, on the site and extent of their injury (Prigatano, 1992).

The great majority of people suffering from mild concussions improve to a near normal status within a short time. With moderate brain injuries, it takes longer for patients to reach their maximum level of improvement, and many suffer from headaches and other symptoms for prolonged periods. A few develop chronic, incapacitating symptoms. In severe brain injury cases, the prognosis is less favorable (Jennet et al., 1976; Powell & Wilson, 1994). Many of these patients have to adjust to lower levels of occupational and social functioning (Bennett, Dittmar, & Ho, 1997; Dikmen et al., 1994), while others are so im-

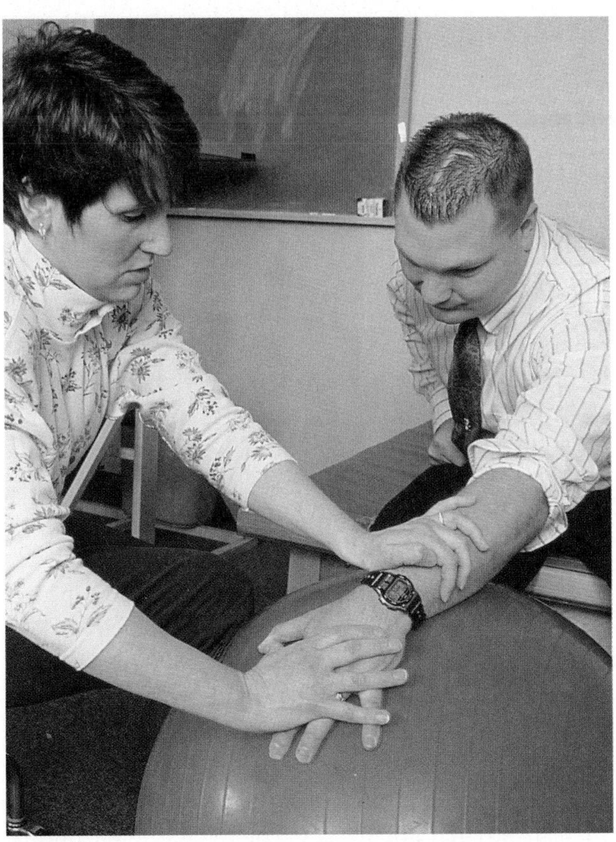

This police officer, who received a gunshot head wound in the line of duty, is receiving therapy to improve muscle tone and function in his left arm.

paired intellectually that they require continuing supervision and, sometimes, institutionalization. Even in cases where considerable amounts of brain tissue have been destroyed, however, some patients are able to become socially independent. In many cases, there is improvement with time, due largely to reeducation and to intact brain areas taking over new functions (Powell & Wilson, 1994).

Children who undergo significant traumatic brain injury are more likely to be adversely affected the younger they are at the time of injury and the fewer language, fine motor and other competencies they have. The severity of their injury and the degree to which their environment (such as parents) is accommodating or difficult will also affect the child's recovery (Anderson et al., 1997; Taylor & Alden, 1997; Yeates et al., 1997). When the injury is mild, most children emerge without lasting negative effects (Satz et al., 1997).

Treatment of traumatic brain injury beyond the purely medical phase is often difficult, protracted, and expensive. Its core is a careful and continuing assessment of neuropsychological functioning and the design of interventions intended to overcome remaining deficits. Many disciplines may become involved in the latter, such as neurology, psychology, neuropsychology, occupational therapy, physical therapy, speech/language therapy, cognitive rehabilitation, prevocational and vocational services, and recreational therapy. As often as not, treatment consists of providing patients with new techniques to compensate for losses that may well be permanent (Bennett, Dittmar, & Ho, 1997).

In general, outcomes in cases of traumatic brain injury are most favorable when there is (1) a short period of unconsciousness or post-traumatic anterograde amnesia; (2) no or minimal cognitive impairment; (3) a well-functioning pre-injury personality; (4) higher educational attainment; (5) a stable pre-injury work history; (6) motivation to recover or make the most of residual capacities; (7) a favorable life situation to which to return; (8) early intervention; and (9) an appropriate program of rehabilitation and retraining (Bennett, Dittmar, & Ho, 1997; Brooks, 1974; Dikmen et al., 1994; Diller & Gordon, 1981; Mackay, 1994).

The outlook for individuals who are also victims of alcoholism, drug dependence, or other medical problems may be unfavorable. Alcoholics, in particular, are prone to head injuries and other accidents and do not have good improvement records, possibly because many of them also have brain deficits related to excessive drinking (Mearns & Lees-Haley, 1993). Severe emotional problems sometimes appear to predispose an individual to car crashes and other violent events and also may delay recovery.

IN REVIEW

- What are nine symptoms generally associated with neuropsychological disorders?
- How is the location of brain damage related to a patient's neuropsychological symptoms?
- What are the key differences among delirium, dementia, and amnestic syndrome?
- What is the typical neuropsychological and neuropathological course of Alzheimer's disease?

MENTAL RETARDATION

The American Psychiatric Association (1994) in DSM-IV defined **mental retardation** as "significantly subaverage

mental retardation Significantly subaverage general intellectual functioning that is diagnosed before the age of 18 and is accompanied by significant limitations in adaptive functioning in skill areas such as self-care and safety.

general intellectual functioning . . . that is accompanied by significant limitations in adaptive functioning" (p. 39) in certain skill areas such as self-care, work, health, and safety. To qualify for the diagnosis, these problems must have begun before the age of 18. Mental retardation is thus defined in terms of level of performance as well as intelligence. The definition says nothing about causal factors, which may be primarily biological, psychosocial, sociocultural, or a combination of these. By definition, any functional equivalent of mental retardation that has its onset after age 17 must be considered a dementia rather than mental retardation. The distinction is an important one, because, as was pointed out early in the chapter, the psychological situation of a person who acquires a pronounced impairment of intellectual functioning after attaining maturity is vastly different from that of a person whose intellectual resources were subnormal throughout all or most of his or her development.

In contrast to other developmental disorders (see Chapter 14), mental retardation is coded on Axis II of the DSM, along with the personality disorders. Mental retardation, like other DSM diagnostic categories, is treated as a specific type of disorder, although it may occur in combination with other disorders appearing on either Axis I or Axis II. In fact, other psychiatric disorders, especially psychoses (Jacobson, 1990), occur at a markedly higher rate among retarded people than in the general population (Borthwick-Duffy, 1994; Sturmey & Sevin, 1993).

Mental retardation occurs among children throughout the world. In its most severe forms, it is a source of great hardship to parents as well as an economic and social burden on a community. The point prevalence rate of diagnosed mental retardation in the United States is estimated to be about 1 percent, which would indicate a population estimate of some 2.6 million people. In fact, however, prevalence is extremely difficult to pin down precisely because definitions of mental retardation vary considerably (Roeleveld, Zielhuis, & Gabreels, 1997). Most states have laws providing that persons with IQs below 70 who show socially incompetent or persistently problematic behavior can be classified as mentally retarded and, if judged otherwise unmanageable, may be placed in an institution. Informally, IQ scores between about 70 and 90 are often referred to as "borderline" or (in the upper part of the range) "dull-normal."

Initial diagnoses of mental retardation seem to occur very frequently at ages 5 to 6, to peak at age 15, and to drop off sharply after that. For the most part, these patterns in age of first diagnosis reflect changes in life demands. During early childhood, individuals with only a mild degree of intellectual impairment, who constitute the vast majority of the mentally retarded, often appear to be normal. Their subaverage intellectual functioning becomes apparent only when difficulties with schoolwork lead to a diagnostic evaluation. When adequate facilities are available for their education, children in this group can usually master essential school skills and achieve a satisfactory level of socially adaptive behavior. Following the school years, they usually make a more or less acceptable adjustment in the community and thus lose the identity of being mentally retarded.

The various levels of mental retardation, as defined in DSM-IV-TR, are listed in Table 13.2 and described in greater detail in the following sections.

Mild Mental Retardation Mildly retarded individuals constitute by far the largest number of those diagnosed as mentally retarded. Within the educational context, people in this group are considered "educable," and their intellectual levels as adults are comparable with those of average 8- to 11-year-old children. Statements such as the latter, however, should not be taken too literally. A mildly retarded adult with a mental age of, say, 10 (that is, intelligence test performance is at the level of the average 10-year-old) may not in fact be comparable to the normal 10-year-old in information-processing ability or speed (Weiss, Weisz, & Bromfield, 1986). On the other hand, he or she will normally have had far more experience in living, which would tend to raise the IQ score.

The social adjustment of mildly retarded people often approximates that of adolescents, although they tend to lack normal adolescents' imagination, inventiveness, and judgment. Ordinarily, they do not show signs of brain pathology or other physical anomalies, but often they require some measure of supervision because of their limited abilities to foresee the consequences of their actions. Individuals at a somewhat higher, "borderline" IQ level (about 71–84) may also need special services to maximize their potentials (Zetlin & Murtaugh, 1990). With early diagnosis, parental assistance, and special educational

TABLE 13.2 RETARDATION SEVERITY AND IQ RANGES

Diagnosed Level of Mental Retardation	Corresponding IQ Range
Mild retardation	50–55 to approximately 70
Moderate retardation	35–40 to 50–55
Severe retardation	20–25 to 35–40
Profound retardation	below 20–25

Mildly retarded individuals constitute the largest number of those labeled mentally retarded. With help, a great majority of these individuals can adjust socially, master simple academic and occupational skills, and become self-supporting citizens.

programs, the great majority of borderline and mildly retarded individuals can adjust socially, master simple academic and occupational skills, and become self-supporting citizens (Maclean, 1997; Schalock, Harper, & Carver, 1981).

Moderate Mental Retardation Moderately retarded individuals are likely to fall in the educational category of "trainable," which means that they are presumed able to master certain routine skills, such as cooking or minor janitorial work, if provided specialized instruction in these activities. In adult life, individuals classified as moderately retarded attain intellectual levels similar to those of average 4- to 7-year-old children. Although some can be taught to read and write a little and may manage to achieve a fair command of spoken language, their rate of learning is slow, and their level of conceptualizing extremely limited. Physically, they usually appear clumsy and ungainly, and they suffer from bodily deformities and poor motor coordination. Some of these moderately retarded people are hostile and aggressive; more typically, they present an affable, unthreatening personality picture. In general, with early diagnosis, parental help, and adequate opportunities for training, most moderately retarded individuals can achieve partial independence in daily self-care, acceptable behavior, and economic sustenance in a family or other sheltered environment.

Severe Mental Retardation Severely retarded individuals are sometimes referred to as "dependent retarded." In these individuals, motor and speech development are severely retarded, and sensory defects and motor handicaps are common. They can develop limited levels of personal hygiene and self-help skills, which somewhat lessen their dependence, but they are always dependent on others for care. However, many profit to some extent from training and can perform simple occupational tasks under supervision.

Profound Mental Retardation The term *life-support retarded* is sometimes used to refer to profoundly retarded individuals. Most of these people are severely deficient in adaptive behavior and unable to master any but the simplest tasks. Useful speech, if it develops at all, is rudimentary. Severe physical deformities, central nervous system pathology, and retarded growth are typical; convulsive seizures, mutism, deafness, and other physical anomalies are also common. These individuals must remain in custodial care all their lives. They tend, however, to have poor health and low resistance to disease and thus a short life expectancy.

Severe and profound cases of mental retardation can usually be readily diagnosed in infancy because of the presence of obvious physical malformations, grossly delayed development (e.g., taking solid food), and other obvious symptoms of abnormality. Although these individuals show a marked impairment of overall intellectual functioning, they may have considerably more ability in some areas than in others. It should also be noted that, despite their limitations, they can be rewarding, loyal, and affectionate social partners to understanding others.

Diagnosis Guidelines Until relatively recently, the American Psychiatric Association and the American Association on Mental Retardation (AAMR) generally agreed on definitions of mental retardation and specifications of levels or degrees of it. In 1992, the AAMR broke away from this tradition (Luckasson et al., 1992), adopting IQ 75 as the cutoff point for the diagnosis of mental retardation (thus expanding the pool of eligibles). In addition, the AAMR proposal substitutes the patterns and intensity of supports needed—intermittent, limited, extensive, and pervasive—for the levels of severity indicated above; the steps of the two systems for characterizing severity are not directly comparable. Several more technical revisions of standard diagnostic procedure are also called for in the AAMR approach. Many professionals have voiced criticism of the new AAMR-proposed guidelines and view this divergence of approaches as unfortunate and as increasing

TABLE 13.4 AVERAGE IQS OF 586 MILWAUKEE CHILDREN

	Age of Children in Years						
Maternal IQ	**1–3**	**3–5**	**5–7**	**7–9**	**9–11**	**11–14**	**14+**
80+ ($n = 48$)	95	93	90	94	87.5	94	90
< 80 ($n = 40$)	95	76	84	80	75	70	67.5

Source: From H. L. Garber, *The Milwaukee Project.* © 1988 American Association on Mental Retardation.

sive (and, after age 6, nonreversing) decline in IQ with advancing age, approaching the upper limits of the mental retardation range by age 14. Such a progressive loss is not easy to reconcile with a hereditary interpretation; it suggests, rather, the cumulative effects of a deficient environment, one that is associated with the mothers' IQ levels.

The effect may be due to the inadequacy of low IQ mothers in stimulating intellectual growth. Although this conclusion is consistent with most more recently acquired evidence (e.g., Camp et al., 1998), it would be tragic to convert such evidence to an assignment of blame against disadvantaged women. They need help, not blame, and when they get this help, the IQs of their children may be substantially elevated (Garber, 1988; Ramey & Haskins, 1981; Turkheimer, 1991; Zigler & Muenchow, 1992; Zigler & Styfco, 1994).

The causal pattern in cultural-familial mental retardation is believed to include an impoverished and intellectually deprived developmental history.

Whatever the specific etiology, children whose retardation is cultural-familial in origin are usually only mildly retarded. They show no identifiable brain pathology and are usually not diagnosed as mentally retarded until they enter school and have difficulties with their studies. As many investigators have pointed out, most of these children come from economically deprived, unstable, and often disrupted family backgrounds characterized by a lack of intellectual stimulation, an inferior quality of interaction with others, and general environmental deprivation (e.g., Birns & Bridger, 1977; Braginsky & Braginsky, 1974; Feuerstein, 1977):

> They are raised in homes with absent fathers and with physically or emotionally unavailable mothers. During infancy they are not exposed to the same quality and quantity of tactile and kinesthetic stimulations as other children. Often they are left unattended in a crib or on the floor of the dwelling. Although there are noises, odors, and colors in the environment, the stimuli are not as organized as those found in middle-class and upper-class environments. For example, the number of words they hear is limited, with sentences brief and most commands carrying a negative connotation. (Tarjan & Eisenberg, 1972, p. 16)

Since a child's current level of intellectual functioning is based largely on previous learning—and since schoolwork requires complex skills, such as being able to control one's attention, follow instructions, and recognize the meaning of a considerable range of words—these children are at a disadvantage from the beginning because they have not had an opportunity to learn requisite background skills or to be motivated toward learning. Thus, with each succeeding year, unless remedial measures are undertaken, they tend to fall further behind in school performance.

HIGHLIGHT 13.2

The Problem of Assessment

Because mental retardation is defined in terms of both intellectual (academic) and social competence, it is essential to assess both of these characteristics before labeling a person mentally retarded. Unfortunately, the assessment of social competence is subject to many of the same errors as the measurement of IQ. For example, if children are well adapted socially to life in an urban ghetto but not to the demands of a formal school setting, should they be evaluated as having a high, intermediate, or low level of social competence? Competence for what? It is doubtful that judgments of this kind can be made objectively—that is, without reference to particular value orientations.

To label a child mentally retarded is likely to have profound effects on both the child's self-concept and the reactions of others, and thus on his or her entire future life. Most immediately, it may lead to a disadvantaged upbringing by discouraged, demoralized parents (Richardson, Koller, & Katz, 1985), to say nothing of the likely effects on overburdened schoolteachers. Over the long term, such a label may become a self-fulfilling prophecy fueled by the tendency to behave in ways consistent with one's self-concept and others' expectations. Obviously, it is a label that has profound ethical and social implications. On the other hand, in many jurisdictions, the formal diagnosis admits the child and his or her family to a host of special services, including specialized education, that may well not otherwise be available. Clearly, the decision is one needing careful thought and a highly individualized approach. ■

Treatments, Outcomes, and Prevention

A number of programs have demonstrated that significant changes in the adaptive capacity of mentally retarded children are possible through special education and other rehabilitative measures. The degree of change that can be expected is related, of course, to an individual's particular situation and level of mental retardation.

Treatment Facilities and Methods One problem that causes anxiety for the parents of a mentally retarded child is whether to put the child in an institution. Most authorities agree that this should be considered a "last resort," in light of the unfavorable outcomes normally experienced—particularly in regard to the erosion of self-care skills (Lynch, Kellow, & Willson, 1997). In general, children who are institutionalized fall into two groups: (1) those who, in infancy and childhood, manifest severe mental retardation and associated physical impairment, and who enter an institution at an early age; and (2) those who have no physical impairments but show relatively mild mental retardation and a failure to adjust socially in adolescence, eventually being institutionalized chiefly because of delinquency or other problem behavior (see Stattin & Klackenberg-Larsson, 1993). In these cases, social incompetence is the main factor in the decision. The families of those in the first group come from all socioeconomic levels, whereas a significantly higher percentage of the families of those in the second group come from lower educational and occupational strata.

The effect of being institutionalized in adolescence depends heavily, of course, on an institution's facilities as well as on individual factors. For the many retarded teenagers who do not have families in a position to help them achieve a satisfactory adjustment, community-oriented residential care seems a particularly effective alternative (Alexander, Huganir, & Zigler, 1985; Landesman-Dwyer, 1981; Seidl, 1974; Thacher, 1978), although for maximum effectiveness great care must be taken in adequately assessing needs and in the recruitment of staff personnel (Petronko, Harris, & Kormann, 1994). Unfortunately, many neighborhoods resist the location of such facilities within their confines and reject integration of residents into the local society (Short, 1997).

For the mentally retarded who do not require institutionalization, educational and training facilities have historically been woefully inadequate. It still appears that a very substantial proportion of mentally retarded people in the United States are never reached by services appropriate to their specific needs (Luckasson et al., 1992; Tyor & Bell, 1984).

This neglect is especially tragic in view of the existing measures for helping these people. For example, classes for the mildly retarded, which usually emphasize reading and other basic school subjects, budgeting and money matters, and the development of occupational skills, have succeeded in helping many people become independent, productive community members. Classes for the moderately and severely retarded usually have more limited objectives, but they emphasize the development of self-care and other skills—e.g., toilet habits (Wilder et al., 1997)—that enable individuals to function adequately and to be of assistance in either a family (see, e.g., Heller, Miller, & Factor, 1997) or an institutional setting. Just mastering toilet training and learning to eat and dress properly may mean the difference between remaining at home or in a community residence and being institutionalized.

Today, there are probably under 80,000 individuals still in institutions for the retarded, less than half the number that were residents 30 years ago. Even many of these more seriously affected persons are being helped to be partly self-supporting in community-based programs (Brown, 1977; Landesman-Dwyer, 1981; Maclean, 1997; McDonnell et al., 1993; Robinson & Robinson, 1976; Thacher, 1978). These developments reflect both the new optimism that has come to prevail and also, in many instances, new laws and judicial decisions favorable to the rights of retarded people and their families. A notable example is Public Law 94–142, passed by Congress in 1975 and since modified several times (see Hayden, 1998, for an update). This statute, termed the Education for All Handicapped Children Act, asserts the right of mentally retarded people to be educated at public expense in the least restrictive environment possible.

During the 1970s, there was a rapid increase in alternate forms of care for the mentally retarded (Tyor & Bell, 1984). These included, but were not limited to, the use of decentralized regional facilities for short-term evaluation and training; small private hospitals specializing in rehabilitative techniques; group homes or halfway houses integrated into the local community; nursing homes for the elderly retarded; the placement of severely retarded children in more enriched foster-home environments; and varied forms of support to the family for own-home care. The last three decades, in short, have seen a marked enhancement of alternative modes of dealing with retarded citizens, rendering obsolete (and often leading to the closure of) many public institutions formerly devoted exclusively to this type of care.

Education and Mainstreaming Typically, educational and training procedures involve mapping out target areas of improvement, such as personal grooming, social behavior, basic academic skills, and (for retarded adults) simple occupational skills (see Forness & Kavale, 1993). Within each area, specific skills are divided into simple components that can be learned and reinforced before more complex behaviors are required. Training that builds on step-by-step progression can bring retarded individuals repeated experiences of success and lead to substantial progress even by those previously regarded as uneducable (see McDonnell et al., 1993).

For mildly retarded youngsters, the question of what schooling is best is likely to challenge both parents and school officials. Many such children fare better by attending regular classes for at least much of the day. Of course, this type of approach—called **mainstreaming**—does require careful planning, a high level of teacher skill, and facilitative teacher attitudes (Birns & Bridger, 1977; Borg & Ascione, 1982; Budoff, 1977; Hanrahan, Goodman, & Rapagna, 1990; Kozleski & Jackson, 1993; Stafford & Green, 1993).

Substantial research, however, suggests that mainstreaming is not the hoped-for panacea for retarded children (Gottlieb, 1981). Such programs are difficult to launch and to maintain (Lieberman, 1982); their success (or lack of it) seems to depend largely on such change-resistant influences as teacher attitudes and overall classroom climate (Haywood, Meyers, & Switzky, 1982; Miller, K. A., 1989; Schumm & Vaughn, 1992). Moreover, any educational gains may come at the expense of deficits in self-esteem suffered by handicapped children as they interact intensively with more cognitively advantaged peers (Haywood et al., 1982; Santich & Kavanagh, 1997). Gresham (1982) argues that such dangers may be decreased or eliminated if retarded children are given social skills training before they enter a mainstream classroom. Also, when the situation is sensitively managed, the normal classmates of mainstreamed children may themselves derive benefits from the experience (Lincoln et al., 1992). A variant of mainstreaming called the Parallel Alternate Curriculum program, which emphasizes specialized instruction in a regular classroom setting, has shown much promise. Even here, however, much attention must be given to teaching-staff development (Chandler, 1985; Smith & Smith, 1985).

Frontiers in Prevention Since the 1960s, programs geared toward preventing mental retardation have focused on reaching high-risk children early with the intensive cognitive stimulation believed to underlie the sound development of mental ability. Project Head Start is a well-known example that operates at the local community level, although its effectiveness is difficult to measure and

mainstreaming Placement of mentally retarded children in regular school classrooms for all or part of the day.

therefore subject to controversy (Gamble & Zigler, 1989; Zigler & Muenchow, 1992). Nevertheless, the available outcome data are clear in showing that well-managed Head Start programs have amassed a very creditable record in launching children on the path to educational and occupational accomplishment; considering the stakes in failed and socially costly lives, they appear to be an excellent community investment (Zigler & Styfco, 1994).

Somewhat sobering is the possibility that the educational performance of many Head Start children increases primarily because of temporarily enhanced motivation rather than higher rates of cognitive development (Zigler et al., 1982). Where the environment continues to be harmful over time, the gain for many youngsters exposed to short-term enrichment programs may be lost (Garber, 1988; Gray & Ramsey, 1982; Switsky, 1997). Obviously, much remains to be learned and done in the area of maintaining early gains. Where notable and sustainable gains have not been unequivocally demonstrated, the necessary financial investment may attract the kind of short-sighted political opposition commonly directed at expensive social programs (see Chafel, 1992). The irony is that the money is spent anyway, usually at compounded rates of increase, on such things as ADC (welfare-based aid to dependent children), chronic institutionalization, correctional facilities, and the "war on drugs."

IN REVIEW

- Define *mental retardation*. How is it classified in the DSM?
- Compare and contrast mild, moderate, severe, and profound mental retardation. How does the AAMR system differ from that of the APA?
- Describe five biological conditions that may lead to mental retardation.
- Describe some of the physical characteristics of children born with Down syndrome. What is its cause?
- What is the cause of and preventive treatment for phenylketonuria (PKU)?

SUMMARY

NEUROPSYCHOLOGICAL DISORDERS AND BRAIN DAMAGE

- The neuropsychological disorders are those in which behavioral and mental impairments are presumed to result from some malfunction of the brain's hardware, typically involving the destruction of brain tissue. These disorders are in some primary sense physical diseases and are accordingly coded on Axis III of the DSM, in addition to receiving descriptive Axis I coding that pertains to the nature of the mental symptoms. Neuropsychological disorders may be acute and transitory; in this case, brain functioning is only temporarily compromised.
- The DSM recognizes certain characteristic neuropsychological symptom syndromes whose precise organic etiology is unknown but is assumed to reflect underlying brain pathology. Examples are delirium, dementia, amnestic syndrome, and neuropsychological delusional, mood, and personality syndromes.
- Common primary causes of brain tissue destruction include certain infectious diseases such as the HIV-1 virus, brain tumors, physical trauma, degenerative processes, and cerebral infarcts (strokes).
- The correlation between brain injury and psychiatric disorder is not an especially strong one. Some people who have severe damage develop no severe mental symptoms, while others with slight damage have extreme reactions. It appears that an individual's premorbid personality and life situation are important in determining his or her reactions to brain damage.
- Elderly people are at fairly high risk for the development of chronic mental disorders, especially those related to brain degeneration caused by Alzheimer's disease.

MENTAL RETARDATION

- When serious organic brain impairment occurs before the age of 18, especially where it is congenital or is acquired shortly after birth, the cognitive and behavioral deficits experienced are referred to as *mental retardation*. Relatively common conditions associated with mental retardation include Down syndrome, phenylketonuria (PKU), and certain cranial anomalies.
- The large majority of cases of mental retardation are unrelated to obvious physical defects and are considered cultural-familial in origin, a term that acknowledges the difficulty of disentangling genetic and environmental causes of the disorder.
- Caution is warranted in labeling children as mentally retarded, in part because of the heavy reliance on IQ

scores to define the disorder. The IQ test is a measure of academic skill, not of ability to survive and even prosper in other areas of life. A variety of evidence points to the conclusion that cultural-familial retardation may be treatable and even preventable, if society can find the means of providing necessary cognitive stimulation to socially and economically deprived children.

KEY TERMS

neuropsychological disorders (p. 432)
organic mental disorders (p. 432)
delirium (p. 436)
dementia (p. 437)
amnestic syndrome (p. 437)
neuropsychological delusional syndrome (p. 438)
neuropsychological mood syndromes (p. 438)
neuropsychological personality syndromes (p. 439)
AIDS dementia complex (ADC) (p. 439)
AIDS-related complex (ARC) (p. 440)
dementia of the Alzheimer's type (DAT) (p. 440)
senile dementias (p. 440)
presenile dementias (p. 440)
vascular dementia (VAD) (p. 445)
traumatic brain injury (TBI) (p. 446)
mental retardation (p. 449)
Down syndrome (p. 453)
phenylketonuria (PKU) (p. 456)
macrocephaly (p. 456)
microcephaly (p. 456)
hydrocephalus (p. 457)
cultural-familial retardation (p. 457)
mainstreaming (p. 460)

CHAPTER FOURTEEN

Disorders of Childhood and Adolescence

James Hoyt, *Untitled.* Born in Aberdeen, Maryland, Hoyt started drawing as a child and studied painting and draftsmanship in school. In early adulthood, he was misdiagnosed as having schizophrenia. This diagnosis was later changed to bipolar disorder, which has been treated successfully, allowing him to enjoy a productive life.

LEARNING OBJECTIVES

After reading this chapter, you should be able to:

- Discuss how disorders of childhood and adolescence differ from adult disorders and identify some reasons why children are especially vulnerable to developing psychological problems.
- Describe the clinical features, causal factors, and treatment approaches for attention-deficit/hyperactivity disorder, conduct disorder and oppositional defiant disorder, anxiety disorders of childhood and adolescence, and childhood depression.
- Identify several symptom disorders that are common in children.
- Describe the clinical features, causal factors, and treatment of autism.
- List and explain the special factors that must be considered in treating mental health problems in children and adolescents.
- Discuss the use of play therapy in treating children with psychological problems.
- Describe the consequences of child abuse for development of the child.

Until the twentieth century, little account was taken of the special characteristics of psychopathology in children; maladaptive patterns considered relatively specific to childhood, such as autism, received virtually no attention at all. Only with the advent of the mental health movement and the availability of child guidance facilities have marked strides been made in assessing, treating, and understanding the maladaptive behavior patterns of children and adolescents. Still, progress in child psychopathology has lagged behind that in adult psychopathology.

In fact, initially, the problems of childhood were seen simply as downward extensions of adult-oriented diagnoses. The prevailing view was one of children as "miniature adults." But this view failed to take into account special problems, such as those associated with the developmental changes that normally take place in a child or adolescent. Only recently have clinicians come to realize that they cannot fully understand childhood disorders without taking into account these developmental processes. Today, even though great progress has been made in providing treatment for disturbed children, facilities are still woefully inadequate in relation to the magnitude of the task, and most children with problems do not receive psychological attention.

The numbers of children affected by psychological problems are considerable. Multisite studies in several countries have provided estimates of childhood disorder that range from 17 to 22 percent (Costello, 1989; Institute of Medicine, 1989; Verhulst & Koot, 1992; Zill & Schoenborn, 1990). In New Zealand, a group of 1600 birth cohort children (children born in the same time period, 1975–1976, at Queen Mary Hospital in Dunedin, N.Z.) were followed for over 21 years. The follow-up study was designed to obtain longitudinal data on such outcomes as health and behavioral problems and possible correlates of psychopathology. During the course of this longitudinal study, about one in four children developed a psychological disorder (McGee, Feehan, & Williams, 1995).

In most studies, maladjustment is found more commonly among boys than girls. In one survey of psychological disorder in children, Anderson and colleagues (1987) found that 17.6 percent of 11-year-old children studied had one or more disorders, with boys and girls diagnosed at a ratio of 1.7 boys to 1 girl. The most prevalent disorders were attention-deficit/hyperactivity disorder and separation anxiety disorders. Zill and Schoenborn (1990) reported that rates of childhood disorders varied by gender, with boys having higher rates of emotional problems over the childhood and adolescent years. However, for some diagnostic problems, such as eating disorders, rates for girls are higher than for boys.

In this chapter, we will first note some general characteristics of maladaptive behavior in children, compared with adult disorders. Then we will look at a number of important disorders of childhood and adolescence. Finally, we will give detailed consideration to some of the special factors involved in both the treatment and prevention of children's problems.

MALADAPTIVE BEHAVIOR IN DIFFERENT LIFE PERIODS

Psychological maturity is related to growth of the brain, which matures in stages, with growth occurring even in late adolescence (ages 17 to 21) (Hudspeth & Pribram, 1992). Many problematic behaviors and threats to adjustment emerge over the course of normal development (Kazdin, 1992). Indeed, several behaviors that characterize maladjustment or emotional disturbance are relatively common in childhood. Because of the manner in which personality develops, the various steps in growth and development, and the differing stressors people face in childhood, adolescence, and adulthood, we would expect to find some differences in maladaptive behavior in these periods. *Developmental science* (Hetherington, 1998) and,

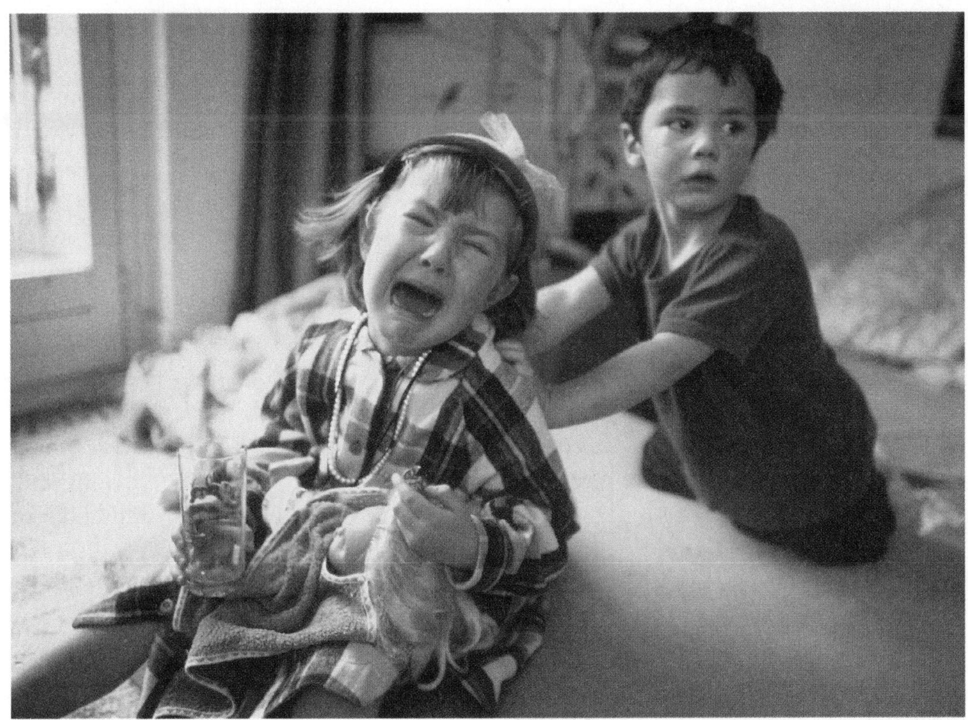

We cannot understand or consider a child's behavior as abnormal without considering the child's age and stage of development. Developmental psychopathology is devoted to studying the origins and course of maladaption in the context of normal growth processes.

more specifically, **developmental psychopathology** (Cicchetti & Rogosch, 1999) are two fields devoted to studying the origins and course of individual maladaptation in the context of normal growth processes.

It is important to view a child's behavior in reference to normal childhood development. We cannot understand or consider a child's behavior as abnormal without determining whether the behavior in question is appropriate for the child's age. Behavior such as temper tantrums or eating inedible objects might be viewed as symptoms of abnormal behavior at age 10 but not at age 2. Despite the somewhat distinctive characteristics of childhood disturbances at different ages, there is no sharp line of demarcation between the maladaptive behavior patterns of childhood and those of adolescence, or between those of adolescence and those of adulthood. Thus, although our focus in this chapter will be on the behavior disorders of children and adolescents, we will find some inevitable overlap with those of later life periods. In this context, it is useful to keep in mind that personality development is a continuous process over time—emotional problems of childhood can indeed surface later and plague a person into adulthood.

Varying Clinical Pictures

The clinical picture in childhood disorders tends to be distinct from those of other life periods. Some of the emotional disturbances of childhood may be relatively short-lived and less specific than those occurring in adulthood (Mash & Dozois, 1996). It should be kept in mind, however, that some childhood disorders severely affect future development. One study found that individuals who had been hospitalized as child psychiatric patients (between the ages of 5 and 17) showed excess mortality due to unnatural causes (about twice the rate of the general population) when followed up from 4 to 15 years later (Kuperman, Black, & Burns, 1988). Suicide accounted for most of these deaths, and the suicide rate was significantly greater than in the general population.

Special Vulnerabilities of Young Children

Young children are especially vulnerable to the development of psychological problems (Masten & Coatsworth, 1998). They do not have as complex and realistic a view of themselves and their world as they will have at a later age, they have less self-understanding, and they have not yet developed a stable sense of identity or a clear understanding of what is expected of them and what resources they might have to deal with them. Immediately perceived threats are tempered less by considerations of the past or

developmental psychopathology Field of psychology that focuses on determining the origins and course of development of individual maladaption in the context of normal growth processes.

future and thus tend to be seen as disproportionately important. As a result, children often have more difficulty in coping with stressful events than do adults (Compas & Epping, 1993; Keppel-Benson & Ollendick, 1993). For example, children are at risk for post-traumatic stress disorder after a disaster, especially if the family atmosphere is troubled, a circumstance that adds additional stress to the problems resulting from the natural disaster (Green et al., 1991).

Children's limited perspectives, as might be expected, lead them to use unrealistic concepts to explain events. For example, a child who commits suicide may be trying to rejoin a dead parent, sibling, or pet. For young children, suicide or violence against another person may be undertaken without any real understanding about the finality of death.

Children also are more dependent on other people than are adults. Though in some ways this dependency serves as a buffer against other dangers, because the adults around might "protect" a child against stressors in the environment, it also makes the child highly vulnerable to experiences of rejection, disappointment, and failure if these adults, because of their own problems, ignore the child. Also, children's lack of experience at dealing with adversity can make manageable problems seem insurmountable. On the other hand, although their inexperience and lack of self-sufficiency make them easily upset by problems that seem minor to the average adult, children typically recover more quickly from their hurts.

IN REVIEW

- Define *developmental psychopathology.*
- Why is it important to view children's behavior in reference to normal childhood development?
- What are several of the special psychological vulnerabilities of children?

DISORDERS OF CHILDHOOD

We discuss here several disorders of childhood as identified in the DSM-IV-TR classification system (see the endpapers of this book). We will focus on describing the clinical picture of each syndrome, while also surveying the possible causal factors and outlining treatment approaches that have proved effective.

The disorders that will be covered are attention-deficit/hyperactivity disorder, conduct disorder, anxiety disorders of childhood, depressive disorders, and several symptom disorders. Autism is covered in the following section. Some of these disorders are more transient than many of the abnormal behavior patterns of adulthood discussed in earlier chapters and are also perhaps more amenable to treatment. As we will see, if treatment is not received, childhood developmental problems sometimes merge almost imperceptibly into more serious and chronic disorders as the child passes into adulthood, or they manifest themselves later as different disorders (Gelfand, Jenson, & Drew, 1988).

Attention-Deficit/Hyperactivity Disorder

Attention-deficit/hyperactivity disorder (ADHD), often referred to as *hyperactivity,* is characterized by difficulties that interfere with effective task-oriented behavior in children—particularly impulsivity, excessive or exaggerated motor activity such as aimless or haphazard running or fidgeting, and difficulties in sustaining attention. Hyperactive children are highly distractible and often fail to follow instructions or respond to demands placed on them (Leung & Connolly, 1996). Impulsive behavior and a low frustration tolerance are also characteristic. Perhaps as a result of their behavioral problems, hyperactive children are often lower in intelligence, usually about 7 to 15 IQ points below average. Hyperactive children tend to talk incessantly and to be socially intrusive and immature. In a study of 916 youths in New Zealand, adolescents with ADHD and conduct disorder had higher rates of driving offenses than other adolescents (Nada-Raja, Langley, et al., 1997).

Children with ADHD generally affect the people around them negatively. Hyperactive children usually have great difficulties in getting along with their parents because they do not obey rules. Their behavior problems also result in their being viewed negatively by their peers. In general, however, hyperactive children do not appear to be anxious, although their overactivity, restlessness, and distractibility are often interpreted as indications of anxiety. They usually do poorly in school, commonly showing specific learning disabilities, such as difficulties in reading or in learning other basic school subjects. Hyperactive children also pose behavior problems in the elementary grades. The following case reveals a typical clinical picture.

attention-deficit/hyperactivity disorder (ADHD) Disorder of childhood characterized by difficulties that interfere with task-oriented behavior, such as impulsivity, excessive or exaggerated motor activity, and difficulties in sustaining attention; also known as *hyperactivity.*

Case Study **A Hyperactive 8-Year-Old Girl** • Gina was referred to a community clinic because of overactive, inattentive, and disruptive behavior. She was a problem to her teacher and to other students because of her hyperactivity and her uninhibited behavior. She would impulsively hit other children, knock things off their desks, erase material on the blackboard, and damage books and other school property. She seemed to be in perpetual motion, talking, moving about, and darting from one area of the classroom to another. She demanded an inordinate amount of attention from her parents and her teacher, and she was intensely jealous of other children, including her own brother and sister. Despite her hyperactive behavior, inferior school performance, and other problems, she was considerably above average in intelligence. Nevertheless, she felt stupid and had a seriously devaluated self-image. Neurological tests revealed no significant organic brain disorder.

The symptoms of ADHD are relatively common among children seen at child guidance centers. In fact, hyperactive children are the most frequent psychological referrals to mental health and pediatric facilities, and the disorder is thought to occur in about 3 to 5 percent of school-aged children (Goldman et al., 1998). However, one study reported a much higher prevalence rate of 16.1 percent for all types of ADHD (Wolrich, Hannah, et al., 1998). The disorder occurs most frequently among preadolescent boys—it is six to nine times more prevalent among boys than girls. ADHD occurs with the greatest frequency before age 8 and tends to become less frequent and involve briefer episodes thereafter. Some residual effects, such as attention difficulties, may persist into adolescence or adulthood (Odell, Warren, et al., 1997) although, as we will see, some authorities doubt the authenticity of this syndrome in adults (Bhandary, 1997). ADHD exists in other cultures—for example, among Chinese schoolboys (Leung, Luk, et al., 1996), who show an essentially similar pattern to that of hyperactive youngsters in the United States.

Causal Factors in Attention-Deficit/Hyperactivity Disorder The cause or causes of ADHD in children is debated (Breggin & Breggin, 1995). The extent to which the disorder results from environmental or biological factors remains unclear, although recent research points to both genetic (Nadder, Silberg, et al., 1998) and social environmental precursors (Hechtman, 1996a). Many researchers consider biological factors, such as genetic inheritance, to be likely important precursors in developing ADHD (Faraone, Biederman, & Milberger, 1994; Faraone et al., 1993b; Levy, Barr, & Sunohara, 1998). One early viewpoint that received a great deal of public attention suggested that hyperactivity in children may be produced by dietary factors, particularly food coloring (Feingold, 1977). However, this food-additive theory of hyperactivity has generally been discredited (Mattes & Gittelman, 1981; Stare, Whelan, & Sheridan, 1980). Firm conclusions as to the potential biological basis for ADHD must await further research.

Children with ADHD are described as overactive, impulsive, and having a low tolerance for frustration and an inability to delay gratification. Incessant talkers, they tend not to obey rules and often run the risk of a multitude of problems with schoolwork, teachers, and other students.

likelihood that a child will become enmeshed in this cycle (Capaldi & Patterson, 1994).

Treatments and Outcomes By and large, our society tends to take a punitive, rather than rehabilitative, attitude toward an antisocial, aggressive youth. Thus, the emphasis is on punishment and on "teaching the child a lesson." Such treatment, however, appears to intensify rather than correct the behavior.

Treatment for oppositional defiant disorder and conduct disorder tends to focus on the dysfunctional family patterns described above and on finding ways to alter the child's aggressive or otherwise maladaptive behaviors.

The Cohesive Family Model Therapy for a conduct-disordered child is likely to be ineffective unless some means can be found for modifying the child's environment. One interesting and often effective treatment strategy with conduct disorder is the *cohesive family model* (Patterson, Capaldi, & Bank, 1991; Webster-Stratton, 1991). In this family–group-oriented approach, parents of conduct-disordered children are viewed as lacking in parenting skills and as behaving in inconsistent ways, thereby reinforcing inappropriate behavior and failing to socialize the children. Children learn to escape or avoid parental criticism by escalating their negative behavior. This tactic, in turn, increases their parents' aversive interactions and criticism. The child observes the increased anger in his or her parents and models this aggressive pattern. The parental attention to the child's negative, aggressive behavior actually serves to reinforce that behavior instead of suppressing it. Viewing the genesis of conduct problems as emerging from such interactions places the treatment focus on the interaction between the child and the parents (Patterson et al., 1991).

Obtaining treatment cooperation from parents who are themselves in conflict with each other is a difficult process. Often, an overburdened parent who is separated or divorced and working simply does not have the time or inclination to learn and practice a more adequate parental role. In some cases, the circumstances may call for a child to be removed from the home and placed in a foster home or institution, with the expectation of a later return to the home if intervening therapy with the parent or parents appears to justify it.

Unfortunately, children who are removed to new environments often interpret this removal as further rejection, not only by their parents but by society as well. Unless the changed environment offers a warm, kindly, and accepting yet consistent and firm setting, such children are likely to make little progress. Even then, treatment may have only a temporary effect. Faretra (1981) followed up 66 aggressive and disturbed adolescents who had been admitted to an inpatient unit. She found that antisocial and criminal behavior persisted into adulthood, though with a lessening of psychiatric involvement. Many conduct-disordered children go on to have personality disorders as adults (Rutter, 1988; Zeitlin, 1986).

Behavioral Techniques The advent of behavior therapy techniques has made the outlook brighter for children who manifest conduct disorders (Kazdin, 1998). Teaching control techniques to the parents of such children is particularly important, so that they can function as therapists in reinforcing desirable behavior and modifying the environmental conditions that have been reinforcing maladaptive behavior. The changes brought about when parents consistently accept and reward their child's positive behavior and stop focusing attention on the negative behavior may finally change their perception of and feelings toward the child, leading to the basic acceptance that the child has so badly needed.

Though effective techniques for behavioral management can be taught to parents, they often have difficulty carrying out treatment plans. If this is the case, other techniques, such as family therapy or parental counseling, are used to ensure that the parent or person responsible for the child's discipline is sufficiently assertive to follow through on the program.

Anxiety Disorders of Childhood and Adolescence

In modern society, no one is totally insulated from anxiety-producing events or situations. Most children are vulnerable to fears and uncertainties as a normal part of growing up. Children with anxiety disorders, however, are more extreme in their behavior than those experiencing "normal" anxiety. These children appear to share many of the following characteristics: oversensitivity, unrealistic fears, shyness and timidity, pervasive feelings of inadequacy, sleep disturbances, and fear of school. Children diagnosed as suffering from an anxiety disorder typically attempt to cope with their fears by becoming overly dependent on others for support and help. In the DSM, anxiety disorders of childhood and adolescence are similar to anxiety disorders in adults (Albano, Chorpita, & Barlow, 1996).

Anxiety disorders are common among children. In fact, 9.7 percent of one community-based school sample clearly met diagnostic criteria for an anxiety-based disorder (Dadds, Spence, et al., 1997), and there is a greater preponderance of anxiety-based disorder in girls than in boys (Lewinsohn et al., 1998). Obsessive-compulsive disorders (OCD) are apparently not as rare in children as they were once thought to be but occur with a frequency between 0.5 and 2 percent (Thomsen, 1998). Two additional anxiety disorders of children and adolescence, separation anxiety disorder and selective mutism, will be described in more detail.

Separation Anxiety Disorder **Separation anxiety disorder** is the most common of the childhood anxiety disorders (Bernstein & Borchardt, 1991), reportedly occurring with a prevalence of 2.4 percent of children in a population health study (Bowen, Offord, & Boyle, 1990). Children with separation anxiety disorder are characterized by unrealistic fears, oversensitivity, self-consciousness, nightmares, and chronic anxiety. They lack self-confidence, are apprehensive in new situations, and tend to be immature for their age. Such children are described by their parents as shy, sensitive, nervous, submissive, easily discouraged, worried, and frequently moved to tears. Typically, they are overly dependent, particularly on their parents. The essential feature in the clinical picture of this disorder is excessive anxiety about separation from major attachment figures, such as mother, and from familiar home surroundings. In many cases, a clear psychosocial stressor can be identified, such as the death of a relative or a pet. The following case illustrates the clinical picture in this disorder.

Case Study **Separation Anxiety in a 6-Year-Old Boy •** Johnny was a highly sensitive 6-year-old who suffered from numerous fears, nightmares, and chronic anxiety. He was terrified of being separated from his mother, even for a brief period. When his mother tried to enroll him in kindergarten, he became so upset when she left the room that the principal arranged for her to remain in the classroom. After 2 weeks, however, this arrangement had to be discontinued, and Johnny had to be withdrawn from kindergarten because his mother could not leave him even for a few minutes. Later, when his mother attempted to enroll him in the first grade, Johnny manifested the same intense anxiety and unwillingness to be separated from her. At the suggestion of the school counselor, Johnny's mother brought him to a community clinic for assistance with the problem. The therapist, who initially saw Johnny and his mother, was wearing a white clinic jacket, which led to a severe panic reaction on Johnny's part. His mother had to hold him to keep him from running away, and he did not settle down until the therapist removed his jacket. Johnny's mother explained that he is terrified of doctors, and it is almost impossible to get him to a physician even when he is sick.

When children with separation anxiety disorder are actually separated from their attachment figures, they typically become preoccupied with morbid fears, such as the worry that their parents are going to become ill or die. They cling helplessly to adults, have difficulty sleeping, and they become intensely demanding. Separation anxiety is more common in girls (Majcher & Pollack, 1996), and the disorder is not very stable—44 percent of youngsters showed recovery at a 4-year follow-up (Cantwell & Baker, 1989). However, some children go on to exhibit *school refusal problems* (a fear of leaving home and parents to attend school) and continue to have adjustment difficulties over time.

Selective Mutism Another anxiety-based disorder sometimes found in children is **selective mutism**, a condition that involves the persistent failure to speak in specific social situations—for example, in school or in social groups—which is considered to interfere with educational or social adjustment. This disorder should be diagnosed only if the child actually has the ability to speak and knows the language. Moreover, in order for this disorder to be diagnosed, the condition must have lasted for a month and not be limited to the first month of school when many children are shy or inhibited.

Selective (formerly referred to as elective) mutism is apparently quite rare in clinical populations and most typically seen at preschool age. The disorder occurs in all social strata, and in about one-third of the cases studied, the child showed early signs of the problem such as shyness and internalizing behavior (Steinhausen & Juzi, 1996).

Both genetic and learning factors have been cited as possible causal factors underlying the disorder. Simmons, Goode, and Fombonne (1997) reported a case in which the mute child experienced a chromosomal abnormality. Steinhausen and Adamek (1997) reported some evidence that genetic factors play a part in selective mutism in that cases tend to occur more frequently in families in which taciturn behavior is prominent. Evidence for cultural or learning factors has also been presented. Black and Uhde (1995) found that the severity of mutism varied markedly in different environmental settings and reported that social anxiety was most commonly associated with mutism.

Selective mutism is treated much like other anxiety-based disorders. One study reported that the symptoms were reduced substantially with fluoxetine (Motavalli, 1995); however, family-based psychological treatment is

separation anxiety disorder Childhood disorder characterized by unrealistic fears, oversensitivity, self-consciousness, nightmares, and chronic anxiety.

selective mutism Anxiety-based disorder of childhood that involves the persistent failure to speak in specific social situations, which interferes with educational or social adjustment.

the most common therapeutic approach used (Tatem & DelCampo, 1995).

Causal Factors in Anxiety Disorders A number of causal factors have been emphasized in explanations of the childhood anxiety disorders. The more important appear to be the following:

1. Anxious children often manifest an unusual constitutional sensitivity that makes them easily conditionable by aversive stimuli. For example, they may be readily upset by even small disappointments—a lost toy or an encounter with an overeager dog. They then have a harder time calming down, a fact that can result in a build-up and generalization of surplus fear reactions.
2. The child can become anxious because of early illnesses, accidents, or losses that involved pain and discomfort. The traumatic effect of experiences such as hospitalization make such children feel insecure and inadequate. The traumatic nature of certain life changes, such as moving away from friends and into a new situation, can also have an intensely negative effect on a child's adjustment. Kashani and colleagues (1981a) found that the most common recent life event for children receiving psychiatric care was moving to a new school district.
3. Overanxious children often have the modeling effect of an overanxious and protective parent who sensitizes a child to the dangers and threats of the outside world. Often, the parent's overprotectiveness communicates a lack of confidence in the child's ability to cope, thus reinforcing the child's feelings of inadequacy (Dadds, Heard, & Rapee, 1991).
4. Indifferent or detached parents also foster anxiety in their children. Although the child is not necessarily rejected, neither is he or she adequately supported in mastering essential competencies and in gaining a positive self-concept. Repeated experiences of failure, stemming from poor learning skills, may lead to subsequent patterns of anxiety or withdrawal in the face of "threatening" situations. Other children may perform adequately but are overcritical of themselves and feel intensely anxious and devalued when they perceive themselves as failing to do well enough to earn their parents' love and respect.
5. The role that social-environmental factors might play in the development of anxiety-based disorders, though important, is not clearly understood. A cross-cultural study of fears (Ollendick et al., 1996) reported that significant differences were found among American, Australian, Nigerian, and Chinese children and adolescents. These authors suggested that cultures that favor inhibition, compliance, and obedience appear to increase the levels of fear reported. In another study in the United States, Last and Perrin (1993) reported that there were some differences between African-American and white children with respect to types of anxiety disorders. White children were more likely to present with school refusal than were African-American children, who showed more PTSD symptoms. This difference might result from differing patterns of referral for African-American and white families, or it might reflect differing environmental stressors placed on the children.
6. One study found a strong association between exposure to violence and a reduced sense of security and psychological well-being (Kliewer et al., 1998). The child's vulnerability to anxiety and depression may be set in place by his or her early experiences of feeling a lack of "control" over reinforcing environmental events (Chorpita & Barlow, 1998). Children who experience a sense of diminished control over negative environmental factors may become more vulnerable to the development of anxiety than those children who gain a sense of efficacy in managing stressful circumstances.

Treatments and Outcomes The anxiety disorders of childhood may continue into adolescence and young adulthood, leading first to maladaptive avoidance behavior and later to increasingly idiosyncratic thinking and behavior or an inability to "fit in" with a peer group. Typically, however, this is not the case. As affected children grow and have wider interactions in school and in peer-group activities, they often benefit from experiences such as making friends and succeeding at given tasks. Teachers who are aware of the needs of both overanxious and shy, withdrawn children are often able to ensure for them successful experiences that help alleviate anxiety.

Psychopharmacological treatment of anxiety disorders in children and adolescents is becoming more common today, although the effectiveness of drugs such as imipramine in treating these disorders is questionable. Moreover, one factor contributing to a need for caution in using medications for these disorders is the diagnostic uncertainty involved. Anxiety is often found to coexist with other conditions, particularly depression (Gittelman et al., 1985) and ADHD (Pliszka, 1989). Often, the diagnostic clarity required for cautious use of antianxiety medications is lacking.

Behavior therapy procedures, sometimes used in school settings, often help anxious children. Such procedures include assertiveness training, to provide help with mastering essential competencies, and desensitization, to reduce anxious behavior. One group of researchers reported the successful use of cognitive-behavioral treatment with 94 9- to 13-year-old children with anxiety disorders (Kendall, Flannery-Schroeder, et al. 1997). Behavioral treatment approaches such as desensitization must be explicitly tailored to a child's particular problem, and in vivo methods (using real-life situations graded in terms of the anxiety they arouse) tend to be more effective than having the child "imagine" situations.

An interesting and effective cognitive-behavioral anxiety prevention and treatment study was implemented in Australia. In an effort to identify and reduce anxiousness in young adolescents, Dadds, Spence, and colleagues (1997) identified 314 children who met the criteria for an anxiety disorder, out of a sample of 1786 7- to 14-year-olds in a school system in Brisbane, Australia. They contacted parents of these anxious children to engage them in the treatment intervention, and parents of 128 of the children agreed to participate. The treatment intervention involved holding group sessions with the children, in which they were taught to recognize their anxious feelings and deal with them more effectively than they otherwise would have. In addition, the parents were taught behavioral management procedures to deal more effectively with the child's behavior. Six months after therapy was completed, significant anxiety reduction was shown for the treatment group, compared with an untreated control sample.

Childhood Depression

Childhood depression includes behaviors such as withdrawal, crying, avoidance of eye contact, physical complaints, poor appetite, and even aggressive behavior and in some cases suicide (Pfeffer, 1996a, 1996b). One epidemiological study (Cohen et al., 1998) reported an association between somatic illness and childhood depressive illness, suggesting that there may be some common etiological factors.

Currently, childhood depression is classified according to the same DSM diagnostic criteria used for adults (Kovacs, 1996). The only modification for children is that irritability is often found as a major symptom and can be substituted for depressed mood, as seen in the following case.

Case Study A Case of Irritability as a Primary Symptom of Depression • Joey is a 10-year-old boy whose mother and teacher have shared their concerns about his irritability and temper tantrums displayed both at home and at school. With little provocation, he bursts into tears and yells and throws objects. In class he seems to have difficulty concentrating and seems easily distracted. Increasingly shunned by his peers, he plays by himself at recess, and at home he spends most of his time in his room watching TV. His mother notes that he has been sleeping poorly and has gained 10 pounds over the past couple of months from constant snacking. A consultation with the school psychologists has ruled out learning disabilities or attention-deficit disorder; instead, she says, he is a deeply unhappy child who expresses feelings of worthlessness and hopelessness—and even a wish that he would die. These experiences probably began about 6 months ago when his father, divorced from Joey's mother for several years, remarried and moved to another town, with the result that he spends far less time with Joey. (From Hammen & Rudolph, 1996, pp. 153–154.)

The use of adult diagnostic depressive categories with children is considered to be appropriate by many. Lobovits and Handel (1985), for example, found that adult diagnostic categories such as dysthymia or major depression could be reliably used with children. They conclude that the use of such criteria with children offers a useful starting point for untangling the confusion surrounding the diagnosis and prevalence rate of childhood depression (p. 52).

Depression in children and adolescents occurs with high frequency. The point prevalence (the rate at the time of the assessment) of major depressive disorder has been estimated to be between 0.4 and 2.5 percent for children and between 4.0 and 8.3 percent for adolescents (Birmaher, Ryan, et al., 1996). The lifetime prevalence for major depressive disorders in adolescence is between 15 and 20 percent (Harrington, Rutter, & Fombonne, 1996). A survey of 1710 high school students found that point prevalence was 2.9 percent, that lifetime prevalence was 20.4 percent, and that suicidal ideation at some time in life was high—19 percent—in this sample (Lewinsohn, Rohde, & Seeley, 1996). Before adolescence, rates of depression are somewhat higher in boys, but depression occurs at about twice the rate for adolescent girls as for adolescent boys (Hankin et al., 1998). Lewinsohn and colleagues (1993) also reported that 7.1 percent of the adolescents surveyed reported having attempted suicide in the past, and, in a more recent epidemiological study, Lewinsohn, Rohde, and Seeley (1994) pointed out that 1.7 percent of adolescents between 14 and 18 had made a suicide attempt.

Causal Factors in Childhood Depression The causal factors implicated in the childhood anxiety disorders are pertinent to the depressive disorders as well.

Biological Factors There appears to be an association between parental depression and behavioral and mood problems in children (Thapar & McGuffin, 1996). Children of parents with major depression were more impaired, received more psychological treatment, and had more psychological diagnoses than children of parents with no psychological disorders (Kramer, Warner, et al., 1998; Mufson, Weissman, & Warner, 1992). A controlled study of family history and onset of depression found that children from mood-disordered families had significantly higher rates of depression than those from nondisordered families (Kovacs, Devlin, et al., 1997). The suicide attempt rate has also been shown to be higher for children of depressed parents (7.8 percent) than for the offspring of control parents (Weissman et al., 1992). Children who have experienced past stressful events are susceptible to states of depression that make them vulnerable to suicidal thinking under stress (Brent, Moritz, & Liotus, 1996). All these correlations suggest a potential genetic component to childhood depression, but in each case learning could also be the causal factor.

Learning Factors Learning of maladaptive behaviors appears to be important in childhood depressive disorders (Kaslow, Deering, & Racusin, 1994). Children who are exposed to negative parental behavior or negative emotional states may develop depressed affect themselves. For example, childhood depression has been found to be more common in divorced families (Palosaari & Laippala, 1996).

Can children learn depressed mood from a depressed parent? One important area of research is focusing on the mother-child interaction in the transmission of depressed affect. Specifically, investigators have been evaluating the possibility that mothers who are depressed, through their interactions with their infants, transfer their low mood to them. Depression among mothers is not uncommon and can result from several sources. Of course, many women who are clinically depressed have children. Some women, however, become depressed during pregnancy or following the delivery of their child, in part because of exhaustion and hormonal changes that can affect mood. Several investigators have reported that marital distress, delivery complications, and difficulties with the infant are also associated with depression in mothers (Campbell et al., 1990; Sameroff, Seifer, & Zax, 1982).

Extensive research supports the view that the patterns of mother-infant behavior are critical to the development of attachment in a child and that depression in the mother can adversely affect the infant (Martinez, Malphurs, et al., 1996). Dysphoric mothers do not respond effectively to their children (Goldsmith and Rogoff, 1997). Depressed mothers tend to be less sensitively attuned to and more negative toward their infants than nondepressed mothers (Murray, Fiori-Cowley, et al., 1996). Other research has shown that negative (depressed) affect and constricted mood on the part of a mother, which shows up as unresponsive facial expressions and irritable behavior, can produce similar responses in her infant (Cohn & Tronick, 1983; Tronick & Cohn, 1989). Interestingly, the negative impact of depressed mothers' interaction style has also been studied at the physiological level. Infants have been reported to exhibit greater frontal brain electrical activity during the expression of negative emotionality by their mothers (Dawson, Panagiotides, et al., 1997).

Mothers who are depressed may transmit their depression to their children by their lack of responsiveness to the child as a result of their own depression. Unfortunately, depression among mothers is all too common. Exhaustion, marital distress as a result of the arrival of children in a couple's lives, delivery complications, and the difficulties of particular babies may all play a part.

The extent to which an infant's negative response to a caregiver's depressed, constricted mood results in later childhood depression has not been fully determined. This research is highly suggestive, however, and it may eventually lead to a fuller understanding of the possible link between a caregiver's mood and a child's behavior.

Another important line of research in childhood depression involves the cognitive-behavioral perspective. Considerable evidence has accumulated that depressive symptoms are positively correlated with the tendency to attribute positive events to external, specific, and unstable causes and negative events to internal, global, and stable causes (Hinshaw, 1992). For example, the child may learn to attribute peer rejection or teasing to a mistaken belief that he or she has some internal flaw. Hinshaw (1994) considers the tendency to develop distorted mental representations an important cause of disorders such as depression and conduct disorder. In addition, children who tend to show symptoms of depression tend to underestimate their self-competence over time (Cole et al., 1998).

Treatments and Outcomes The view that childhood and adolescent depression is like adult depression (Ryan et al., 1987) has prompted researchers to treat children displaying mood disorders, particularly adolescents who are viewed as suicidal (Greenhill & Waslick, 1997), with medications that have worked with adults. Research on the effectiveness of antidepressant medications with children is contradictory at best. Some recent studies using fluoxetine (Prozac) with depressed adolescents have shown the drug to be more effective than a placebo (DeVane & Sallee, 1996; Emslie, Rush, et al., 1997), although complete remission of symptoms was seldom obtained. However, another study by Sommers-Flannagan and Sommers-Flannagan (1996), an extensive evaluation of antidepressant medication treatment for children and adolescents, concluded that currently available antidepressant medications do not show improvement greater than a placebo. Antidepressant medications may have some undesirable side effects (i.e., nausea, headaches, nervousness, insomnia, and even seizures) in children and adolescents. Four accidental deaths with desipramine have been reported (Campbell & Cueva, 1995).

An important facet of psychological therapy with children, whether for depression or anxiety or other disorders, is providing a supportive emotional environment for them to learn more adaptive coping strategies and effective emotional expression. Older children and adolescents can often benefit from a positive therapeutic relationship in which they can discuss their feelings openly. Younger children or those with less developed verbal skills may benefit from play therapy. Controlled studies of psychological treatment with depressed adolescents have shown significantly reduced symptoms with cognitive-behavioral therapy (Brent, Holder, et al., 1997) derived from Beck's cognitive-behavioral approach (Ackerson et al., 1998), discussed in Chapter 6. Rawson and Tabb (1993) showed that short-term residential treatment was effective with depressed children aged 8 to 14.

Depressed mood has come to be viewed as an important risk factor in suicide among children and adolescents (Berman & Jobes, 1991; Ivarsson, Larsson, & Gillberg, 1998; Pfeffer, 1996a, 1996b). About 7 to 10 percent of adolescents report having made at least one suicide attempt (Safer, 1997b). Children who attempt suicide are at greater risk for subsequent suicidal episodes than are nonattempters, particularly within the first 2 years after their initial attempt (Pfeffer et al., 1994). Among the childhood disorders, then, depression especially merits aggressive treatment.

Symptom Disorders: Enuresis, Encopresis, Sleepwalking, and Tics

The childhood disorders we will deal with in this section—elimination disorders (enuresis and encopresis), sleepwalking, and tics—typically involve a single outstanding symptom rather than a pervasive maladaptive pattern.

Functional Enuresis The term **enuresis** refers to the habitual involuntary discharge of urine, usually at night, after the age of expected continence (age 5). In DSM-IV-TR, functional enuresis refers to bedwetting that is not organically caused. Children who have primary functional enuresis have never been continent; children who have secondary functional enuresis have been continent for at least a year but have regressed.

Enuresis may vary in frequency, from nightly occurrence to occasional instances when a child is under considerable stress or is unduly tired. It has been estimated that some 4 to 5 million children and adolescents in the United States suffer from the inconvenience and embarrassment of this disorder. Estimates of the prevalence of enuresis reported in DSM-IV were 7 percent for boys and 3 percent for girls at age 5; 3 percent for boys and 2 percent for girls at age 10; and 1 percent for boys and almost nonexistent for girls at age 18. Research has shown that there are clear sex differences in enuresis as well as age differences. In one extensive epidemiological study of enuresis in Holland, Verhulst and colleagues (1985) determined that between the ages of 5 and 8, enuresis is about two to three times more common among boys than among girls. The percentages for boys also diminish at a slower rate; the decline for girls between ages 4 and 6 is about 71 percent, while the decline for boys is only 16 percent. The researchers recommended that the upper age limit for diag-

enuresis Habitual involuntary discharge of urine, usually at night, after the age of expected continence (age 5).

nosing enuresis in boys be extended to age 8 because it is at about age 9 that approximately the same percentage of boys as girls reach "dryness"—that is, wetting the bed less than once a month.

Enuresis may result from a variety of organic conditions, such as disturbed cerebral control of the bladder (Kaada & Retvedt, 1981), neurological dysfunction (Lunsing et al., 1991), or other medical factors such as medication side effects (Took & Buck, 1996) or having a small functional bladder capacity and weak urethral sphincter (Dahl, 1992). One group of researchers reported that 11 percent of their enuretic patients had disorders of the urinary tract (Watanabe et al., 1994). However, most investigators have pointed to a number of other possible causal factors: (1) faulty learning, resulting in the failure to acquire inhibition of reflexive bladder emptying; (2) personal immaturity, associated with or stemming from emotional problems; (3) disturbed family interactions, particularly those that lead to sustained anxiety, hostility, or both; and (4) stressful events (Haug Schnabel, 1992). For example, a child may regress to bedwetting when a new baby enters the family and becomes the center of attention.

Medical treatment of enuresis typically centers on using medications, such as imipramine; the mechanism underlying the action of the drug is unclear, but it may simply decrease the deepest stages of sleep to light sleep enabling the child to recognize bodily needs more effectively (Dahl, 1992). An intranasal desmopressin (DDAVP) has also been used to help children manage urine more effectively. This medication, a hormone replacement, apparently increases urine concentration, decreases urine volume, and therefore reduces the need to urinate (Dahl, 1992). The use of this medication to treat enuretic children is no panacea. Disadvantages of its use are its high cost and the fact that it is effective only with a small subset of enuretic children, and then only temporarily. Bath, Morton, Uing, and Williams (1996) reported that treatment with desmopressin was disappointing but concluded that this treatment had some utility as a method to enable children to stay dry for brief periods of time—for example, at a camp or on a holiday. Moffatt (1997) suggested that DDAVP had an important place in treating nocturnal enuresis in youngsters who have not responded well to behavioral treatment methods. It is well to remember that medications by themselves do not cure enuresis and that there is frequent relapse when the drug is discontinued or the child habituates to the medication (Dahl, 1992).

Conditioning procedures have proved to be the most effective treatment of enuresis (Friman & Warzak, 1990). Mowrer and Mowrer (1938) introduced a procedure in which a child sleeps on a pad that is wired to a battery-operated bell. At the first few drops of urine, the bell is set off, thus awakening the child. Through conditioning, the child comes to associate bladder tension with awakening.

With or without treatment, the incidence of enuresis tends to decrease significantly with age, but many experts still believe that enuresis should be treated in childhood because no way currently exists to identify which children will remain enuretic into adulthood. In a comparison and evaluation of research on the treatment of bedwetting, Houts, Berman, and Abramson (1994) concluded that treated children were more improved at follow-up than nontreated children. They also found that the use of learning-based procedures was more effective in reducing bedwetting than were medications.

Functional Encopresis The term **encopresis** describes a symptom disorder of children who have not learned appropriate toileting for bowel movements after age 4. This condition is less common than enuresis; however, DSM-IV estimated that about 1 percent of 5-year-olds have encopresis. A study of 102 cases of encopretic children provided the following list of characteristics: The average age of children with encopresis was 7, with a range from ages 4 to 13. About one-third of encopretic children were also enuretic; and a large sex difference was found, with about six times more boys than girls in the sample. Many of the children soiled their clothing when they were under stress. A common time was in the late afternoon after school; few children actually had this problem at school. Most of the children reported that they did not know when they needed to have a bowel movement or were too shy to use the bathrooms at school.

Many encopretic children suffer from constipation; thus, an important element in the diagnosis of the disorder involves a physical examination to determine whether physiological factors are contributing to the disorder. The treatment of encopresis usually involves both medical and psychological aspects (Dawson, Griffith, & Boeke, 1990). One study found that of a sample of encopretic children treated by medical and behavioral procedures, more than half were cured—that is, no additional incidents occurred within 6 months following treatment. An additional 25 percent were improved (Levine & Bakow, 1975).

Sleepwalking (Somnambulism) Though the onset of sleepwalking disorder is usually between the ages of 6 and 12, the disorder is classified broadly under sleep dis-

encopresis Symptom disorder of children who have not learned appropriate toileting for bowel movements after age 4.

orders in DSM-IV-TR rather than under disorders of infancy, childhood, and adolescence. The symptoms of **sleepwalking disorder** involve repeated episodes in which a person leaves his or her bed and walks around without being conscious of the experience or remembering it later.

Statistics are meager but the incidence of sleepwalking reported for children in DSM is high for one episode—between 10 and 30 percent. However, the incidence for repeated episodes is low—from 1 to 5 percent. Children subject to this problem usually go to sleep in a normal manner but arise during the second or third hour of sleep. They may walk to another room of the house or even outside, and they may engage in complex activities. Finally, they return to bed and in the morning remember nothing that has taken place. While moving about, sleepwalkers' eyes are partially or fully open; they avoid obstacles, listen when spoken to, and ordinarily respond to commands, such as to return to bed. Shaking them will usually awaken sleepwalkers, and they will be surprised and perplexed at finding themselves in an unexpected place. Sleepwalking episodes usually last from 15 to 30 minutes. The causes of sleepwalking are not fully understood. Sleepwalking takes place during NREM (non–rapid eye movement) sleep. It appears to be related to some anxiety-arousing situation that has just occurred or is expected to occur in the near future (Klackenberg, 1987).

Little attention has been given to the treatment of sleepwalking. Clement (1970), however, reported on the treatment of a 7-year-old boy through behavior therapy. During treatment, the therapist learned that just before each sleepwalking episode, the boy usually had a nightmare about being chased by "a big black bug." After his nightmare began, he perspired freely, moaned and talked in his sleep, tossed and turned, and finally got up and walked through the house. He did not remember the sleepwalking episode when he awoke the next morning. Assessment data revealed no neurological or other medical problems and indicated that he was of normal intelligence. He was, however, found to be a very anxious, guilt-ridden little boy who avoided performing assertive and aggressive behaviors appropriate to his age and sex (p. 23). The therapist focused treatment on having his mother awaken the boy each time he showed signs of an impending episode. After washing his face with cold water and making sure he was fully awake, the mother would return him to bed, where he was to hit and tear up a picture of the big black bug. (At the start of the treatment program, he had made up several of these drawings.)

Eventually, the nightmare was associated with awakening, and he learned to wake up on most occasions when he was having a bad dream. Clement considered the basic behavior therapy model in this case to follow that used in the conditioning treatment for enuresis, where a waking response is elicited by an intense stimulus just as urination is beginning and becomes associated with, and eventually prevents, nocturnal bedwetting.

Tics A **tic** is a persistent, intermittent muscle twitch or spasm, usually limited to a localized muscle group. The term is used broadly to include blinking the eye, twitching the mouth, licking the lips, shrugging the shoulders, twisting the neck, clearing the throat, blowing the nose, and grimacing, among other actions. Tics occur most frequently between the ages of 2 and 14 (Evans, King, & Leckman, 1996). In some instances, as in clearing the throat, an individual may be aware of the tic when it occurs, but usually he or she performs the act habitually and does not notice it. In fact, many individuals do not even realize they have a tic unless someone brings it to their attention. A cross-cultural examination of tics found a similar pattern in research and clinical case reports from other countries (Staley, Wand, & Shady, 1997). Moreover, the age of onset (average 7 to 8 years) and predominant gender (male) of cases were reported to be similar across cultures.

The psychological impact tics can have on an adolescent is exemplified in the following case.

Case Study **An Adolescent's Facial Tic** • An adolescent who had wanted very much to be a teacher told the school counselor that he was thinking of giving up his plans. When asked the reason, he explained that several friends had told him that he had a persistent twitching of the mouth muscles when he answered questions in class. He had been unaware of this muscle twitch and even after being told about it could not tell when it took place. However, he became acutely self-conscious and was reluctant to answer questions or enter into class discussions. As a result, his general level of tension increased, and so did the frequency of the tic, which now became apparent even when he was talking to his friends. Thus, a vicious circle had been established. Fortunately, the tic proved amenable to treatment by conditioning and assertiveness training.

sleepwalking disorder Sleep disorder that usually appears between the ages of 6 and 12 and involves repeated episodes of leaving the bed and walking around without being conscious of the experience or remembering it later; also known as *somnambulism.*

tic Any persistent, intermittent muscle twitch or spasm, usually limited to a localized muscle group, often of facial muscles.

Tourette's syndrome is an extreme tic disorder involving multiple motor and vocal patterns. This disorder typically involves uncontrollable head movements with accompanying sounds, such as grunts, clicks, yelps, sniffs, or words. Some, possibly most, tics are preceded by an urge or sensation that seems to be relieved by the execution of the tic. Tics are thus often difficult to differentiate from compulsions—and they are sometimes referred to as "compulsive tics" (Jankovic, 1997). About one-third of individuals with Tourette's syndrome manifest *coprolalia,* which is a complex vocal tic involving the uttering of obscenities. The average age of onset for Tourette's syndrome is 7, and most cases have an onset before age 14. The disorder frequently persists into adulthood. It is about three times more frequent among males. Although the exact cause of Tourette's syndrome is undetermined, evidence suggests an organic basis. Because children with Tourette's syndrome can have substantial adjustment problems at school (Nolan & Gadow, 1997), interventions should be designed to aid their adjustment and to modify the reactions of peers to them. School psychologists can play an effective part in the social adjustment of the child affected with Tourette's syndrome (Walter & Carter, 1997) through behavioral intervention strategies that help to arrange the child's environment to be more accepting of such unusual behaviors.

There are many types of tics and many of these appear to be associated with the presence of other psychological disorders (Cardona et al., 1997), particularly obsessive-compulsive disorder (OCD). Most tics, however, do not have an organic basis but stem from psychological causes, such as self-consciousness or tension in social situations, and they are usually associated with severe behavioral problems (Rosenberg, Brown, & Singer, 1995). As in the case of the adolescent boy previously described, an individual's awareness of the tic often increases tension and the occurrence of the tic.

Of medications, neuroleptics are the most predictably effective tic-suppressing drugs (Kurlan, 1997). Clonazepam, clonidine, and tiapride have all shown effectiveness in reducing motor tics; however, tiapride has shown the greatest decrease in the intensity and frequency of tics (Drtikova et al., 1996). Campbell and Cueva (1995) reported that both haloperidol and pimozide reduced the severity of tics by about 65 percent but that haloperidol seemed the more effective of the two medications.

Behavioral intervention techniques have also been used successfully in treating tics. One successful program involved several sequential elements, beginning with awareness training, relaxation training, and the development of incompatible responses and then progressing to cognitive therapy and the modification of overall style of action. Finally, perfectionist expectations about self-image (often found in children and adolescents with tics) are addressed through cognitive restructuring (O'Connor et al., 1998).

IN REVIEW

- Which causal factors for ADHD have been supported by research, and which have been discredited?
- What are the key differences between the pharmacological and behavioral treatments of ADHD?
- Distinguish among conduct disorder, oppositional defiant disorder, and juvenile delinquency.
- Describe two common anxiety disorders found in children and adolescents.
- How do the symptoms associated with childhood depression relate to those seen in adult depression?
- Identify four common symptom disorders that can arise in childhood.

PERVASIVE DEVELOPMENTAL DISORDER: AUTISM

The **pervasive developmental disorders (PDD)** are a group of severely disabling conditions considered to be among the most difficult to understand and treat. They make up about 3.2 percent of cases seen in inpatient settings (Sverd, Sheth, Fuss, & Levine, 1995). They are considered to be the result of some structural differences in the brain that are usually evident at birth or become apparent as the child begins to develop (Siegel, 1996). There is fairly good diagnostic agreement in the determination of pervasive developmental disorders in children whether one follows the DSM-IV-TR or ICD-10 (the *International Classification of Disease* published by the World Health Organization), which have slightly different criteria for some disorders (Sponheim, 1996). There are several pervasive developmental disorders covered in DSM-IV-TR—for example, **Asberger's disorder,** which is a "severe and

Tourette's syndrome Extreme tic disorder involving multiple uncontrollable motor and vocal patterns.

pervasive developmental disorders (PDD) A group of severely disabling conditions considered to result from structural problems in the brain and usually evident at birth or in early childhood.

Asberger's disorder Severe and sustained impairment in social interaction that involves marked stereotypic behavior and inflexible adherence to routines, but usually appears later than autism.

sustained impairment in social interaction" that involves marked stereotypic (repetitive) behavior and inflexible adherence to routines (Gillberg, 1998). This pattern of behavior usually appears later than other pervasive developmental disorders such as autism but nevertheless involves substantial long-term psychological disability.

One of the most common and most puzzling and disabling of the pervasive developmental disorders and the one that we will address in more detail is *autistic disorder*, often referred to as **autism** or *childhood autism*. It is a developmental disorder that involves a wide range of problematic behaviors, including deficits in language, perceptual, and motor development; defective reality testing; and an inability to function in social situations. The following case illustrates some of the behaviors that may be seen in an autistic child.

Case Study **A Case of Autism** • The boy is 5 years old. When spoken to, he turns his head away. Sometimes he mumbles unintelligibly. He is neither toilet trained nor able to feed himself. He actively resists being touched. He dislikes sounds and is uncommunicative. He cannot relate to others and avoids looking anyone in the eye. He often engages in routine manipulative activities, such as dropping an object, picking it up, and dropping it again. He shows a pathological need for sameness. While seated, he often rocks back and forth in a rhythmic motion for hours. Any change in routine is highly upsetting to him.

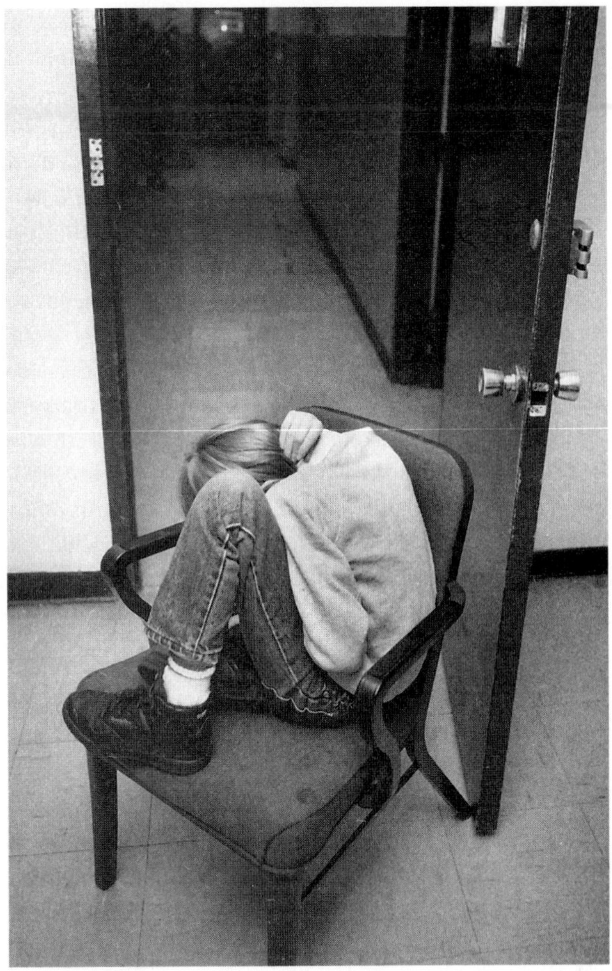

Extreme withdrawal from others is typical of autistic children.

Autism in infancy and childhood was first described by Kanner (1943). It afflicts some 80,000 American children—about 6.5 children in 10,000—and occurs about four or five times more frequently among boys than girls (Gillberg, 1995). A large epidemiological study of four regions of France reported similar rates, 4.9 per 10,000, with boys about two to one (Fombonne & du Mazaubrun, 1992). Autism is usually identified before a child is 30 months of age and may be suspected in the early weeks of life. One study found that autistic behavior such as lack of empathy, attention to others, and ability to imitate is shown as early as 20 months (Charman, Swettenham, Baron-Cohen, et al., 1997). Autistic children come from all socioeconomic levels.

The Clinical Picture in Autism Disorder

Autistic children show varying degrees of impairments and capabilities. In this section, we will discuss some of the behaviors that may be evident in autism. A cardinal and typical sign is that a child seems apart or aloof from others, even in the earliest stages of life (Adrien et al., 1992). Mothers often remember such babies as never being cuddly, never reaching out when being picked up, never smiling or looking at them while being fed, and never appearing to notice the comings and goings of other people.

A Social Deficit Typically, autistic children do not show any need for affection or contact with anyone, usually not even seeming to know or care who their parents are. Several studies, however, have questioned this view that autistic children are emotionally flat. These studies (Capps et al., 1993) have shown that autistic children do express emotions and should not be considered as having an apparent lack of emotional reaction as noted in traditional descriptions of the disorder. Instead, Sigman (1996)

autism A disabling pervasive developmental disorder that begins in infancy and involves a wide range of problematic behaviors, including deficits in language, perceptual, and motor development; defective reality testing; and an inability to function in social situations.

has characterized the seeming inability of autistic children to respond to others as a lack of social understanding—a deficit in the ability to attend to social cues from others. The autistic child is thought to have a "mind blindness," an inability to take the attitude of or to "see" things as others do. For example, an autistic child appears limited in the ability to understand where another person is pointing. Additionally, autistic children show deficits in attention and in locating and orienting to sounds in their environment (Townsend, Harris, & Courchesne, 1996).

The lack of social interaction among autistic children has been well described by numerous studies in the past. A behavioral observation study by Lord and Magill-Evans (1995) noted that autistic youngsters engaged in fewer social interactions than other children; however, this study also made the important observation that autistic children did not play—particularly did not show spontaneous play. In fact, much of the time nothing was going on.

An Absence of Speech The absence of or severely restricted use of speech is characteristic of autistic children, who have been considered to have an imitative deficit and do not effectively learn by imitation (Smith & Bryson, 1994). This dysfunction might explain the characteristic absence or limited use of speech by autistic children. If speech is present, it is almost never used to communicate except in the most rudimentary fashion, as by saying "yes" in answer to a question or by the use of **echolalia**—the parrotlike repetition of a few words. Although the echoing of parents' verbal behavior is found to a small degree in normal children as they experiment with their ability to produce articulate speech, persistent echolalia is found in about 75 percent of autistic children (Prizant, 1983).

The usual picture of an autistic child as lacking in language ability and being wholly withdrawn is probably oversimplified. Researchers have found that autistic children vary considerably in language skill and at least some autistic children do comprehend language, even though they may not use it to express themselves as other children do (Wetherby & Prizant, 1992).

Self-Stimulation Self-stimulation is often characteristic of autistic children, usually taking the form of such repetitive movements as head banging, spinning, and rocking, which may continue by the hour. Other bizarre as well as repetitive behaviors are typical. Such behavior is well described by Schreibman and Charlop-Christie (1998) and illustrated in the case of a young autistic boy.

Case Study Repetitive Behavior in an Autistic Boy • A. was described as a screaming, severely disturbed child who ran around in circles making high-pitched sounds for hours. He also liked to sit in boxes, under mats, and [under] blankets. He habitually piled up all furniture and bedding in the center of the room. At times, he was thought [to be] deaf, though he also showed extreme fear of loud noises. He refused all food except in a bottle, refused to wear clothes, chewed stones and paper, whirled himself, and spun objects.... He played repetitively with the same toys for months, lining things in rows, collected objects such as bottle tops, and insisted on having two of everything, one in each hand. He became extremely upset if interrupted and if the order or arrangement of things were altered. (From Gajzago & Prior, 1974, p. 264.)

Autistic children seem to actively arrange the environment on their own terms in an effort to exclude or limit variety and intervention from other people, preferring instead a limited and solitary routine. Autistic children often show an active aversion to auditory stimuli, crying even at the sound of a parent's voice. The pattern is not always consistent, however; autistic children may at one moment be severely agitated or panicked by a very soft sound and at another time be totally oblivious to loud noise.

Intellectual Ability Much has been learned in the last few years about the cognitive abilities of autistic children (Bennetto, Pennington, et al., 1996). Compared with other groups of children on cognitive or intellectual tasks, autistic children often show marked impairment. For example, autistic children are significantly impaired on memory tasks when compared with both normal and retarded children. Autistic children show a particular deficit in representing mental states—that is, they appear to have deficits in social reasoning but can manipulate objects (Scott & Baron-Cohen, 1996). Carpentieri and Morgan (1996) found that the cognitive impairment in autistic children is reflected in greater impairment in adaptive behaviors than is seen in mentally retarded children without autism. Whether this frequently observed cognitive impairment is the result of actual organic brain damage or of motivational deficits has not been clearly established. Koegel and Mentis (1985) raised the possibility that the deficits result at least partly from motivational differences; they found that autistic children can learn and perform tasks at a higher level if motivation for a task is found and appropriate reinforcement is provided.

Some autistic children are quite skilled at fitting objects together; thus, their performance on puzzles or form boards may be average or above. Even in the manipulation

echolalia Parrotlike repetition of a few words.

of objects, however, difficulty with meaning is apparent. For example, when pictures are to be arranged in an order that tells a story, autistic children show a marked deficiency in performance. Moreover, autistic adolescents, even those who are functioning well, have difficulty with symbolic tasks such as pantomime, in which they are asked to recall motor actions to imitate tasks (e.g., ironing) with imagined objects, yet they might perform the task well with real objects (Rogers, Bennetto, et al., 1996).

Some autistic children show markedly discrepant and relatively isolated abilities, such as astounding memory capabilities, like those Dustin Hoffman depicted in the movie *Rain Man*. In this context, Goodman (1989) described the case of an "autistic-savant" who showed unusual ability at an early age in calendar calculating (rapidly determining the day of the week of any calendar date in history) as well as in other areas, such as naming the capitals of most states and countries and rapid calculation that allowed him to win a lot of money in Las Vegas. Nevertheless, his language development was severely retarded, and he showed the indifference to others and related symptoms characteristic of autistic children.

Maintaining Sameness Many autistic children become preoccupied with and form strong attachments to unusual objects, such as rocks, light switches, film negatives, or keys. In some instances, the object is so large or bizarre that merely carrying it around interferes with other activities. When their preoccupation with the object is disturbed—for example, by its removal or by attempts to substitute something in its place—or when anything familiar in the environment is altered even slightly, these children may have a violent temper tantrum or a crying spell that continues until the familiar situation is restored. Thus, autistic children are often said to be "obsessed with the maintenance of sameness."

In summary, autistic children typically show difficulties in relationships to other people, in perceptual-cognitive functioning, in language development, and in the development of a sense of identity (L. K. Wing, 1976). They also engage in bizarre and repetitive activities, demonstrate a fascination with unusual objects, and show an obsessive need to maintain environmental sameness. This is indeed a heavy set of handicaps. Almost two-thirds of autistic patients will be dependent on others as adults (C. Gilbert, 1991).

Causal Factors in Autism

The precise cause or causes of autism are unknown. Most investigators now believe that autism begins with some type of inborn defect that impairs an infant's perceptual-cognitive functioning—the ability to process incoming stimuli and to relate to the world. Evidence has accumulated that defective genes or damage from radiation or other conditions during prenatal development may play a significant role in the etiological picture (Abramson et al., 1992; Rutter, 1991b; Waterhouse & Fein, 1997). Evidence for a genetic contribution to autism comes from examining the risk for autism in the siblings of autistic children. The best estimates are that families with one autistic child show a 3 to 5 percent risk of a sibling being autistic as well. Although this figure may seem low in an absolute sense, it is in fact extremely high, given the population frequency of autism in the population.

Twin studies have also consistently shown higher concordance rates among monozygotic than among dizygotic twins (Bailey, Le Couteur, & Gottesman, 1995). The conclusion from family and twin studies is that 80 to 90 percent of the variance in risk for autism is based on genetic factors, making it probably the most heritable of the various forms of psychopathology discussed in this text (Le Couteur et al., 1996; Rutter, 1991b). Nevertheless, the exact mode of genetic transmission is not yet understood, and it seems likely that relatives may also show an increased risk for other cognitive and social deficits that are milder in form than true autism (Smalley, 1991). In other words, there may be a spectrum of disorders related to autism.

It seems likely at this point that the disorder we call autism involves both multiple kinds of deficits (Howlin, 1998; Mesibov, Adams, & Klinger, 1997) and multiple causal pathways (Gillberg, 1990). Thus, it is not likely that researchers will find overall risk factors accounting for all autistic outcomes or even exceptional levels of consistency among studies where differing samples of autistic youngsters have been evaluated. Some investigators have pointed to the existence of a possible genetic defect, a fragile site on the X chromosome, referred to as *fragile X syndrome* (Brown, Jenkins, et al., 1986; Tsai & Ghaziuddin, 1992) that may occur in about 8 percent of autistic males (Smalley, 1991). In addition, 15 to 20 percent of males with the fragile X syndrome are also diagnosed with autism, further suggesting a link between the two syndromes. Nevertheless, there also appear to be some qualitative differences between autism and the fragile X syndrome (Smalley, 1991). Even subtler constitutional defects may also exist in autism. One case report noted an association of autism with pituitary deficiency (Gingell, Parmar, & Sungum-Paliwal, 1996).

Sociocultural factors have also been postulated as causal elements in autism. In his early studies of childhood autism, Kanner (1943) concluded that an innate disorder in a child is exacerbated by a cold and unresponsive mother, the first factor resulting in social withdrawal and the second tending to maintain this isolation. Most investigators, however, have failed to find the parents of autistic children to be "emotional refrigerators" (Schreibman & Charlop-Christie, 1998; Wolff & Morris, 1971), and Kanner's views have been generally discredited.

Clearly, much remains to be learned about the etiology of childhood autism. It appears most reasonable to suppose, however, that this disorder normally begins with an inborn defect or defects in brain functioning, regardless of what other causal factors may subsequently become involved.

Treatments and Outcomes of Autism

Treatment prognosis for autistic disorder is poor, and those diagnosed with autism, because of the severity of the problems, are often insufficiently treated (Wherry, 1996). Moreover, because of the typically poor response to treatment, autistic children are often subjected to a range of fads and "novel" approaches, which turn out to be equally ineffective.

Medical Treatment In the past, the use of medications to treat autistic children has not proven effective (Rutter, 1985). The drug most often used in the treatment of autism is haloperidol (Haldol), an antipsychotic medication (Campbell, 1987), but the data on its effectiveness do not warrant use unless a child's behavior is unmanageable by other means (Sloman, 1991). More recently, clonidine, an antihypertensive medication, has been used with reportedly moderate effects in reducing the severity of the symptoms (Fankhauser et al., 1992). If irritability and aggressiveness are present, the medical management of a case might involve use of medications to lower the level of aggression (Fava, 1997; Leventhal, Cook, & Lord, 1998). Although there are no surefire medications approved for this purpose, the drug clomipramine has had some observed beneficial effect. However, no currently available medication reduces the symptoms of autism enough to encourage general use. We will thus direct our attention to a variety of psychological procedures that have been more successful in treating autistic children.

Behavioral Treatment Behavior therapy in an institutional setting has been used successfully in the elimination of self-injurious behavior, the mastery of the fundamentals of social behavior, and the development of some language skills (Charlop-Christie et al., 1998). Ivar Lovaas (1987), a pioneer in behavioral treatment of autistic children, reported highly positive results from a long-term experimental treatment program of autistic children. Of the treated children, 47 percent achieved normal intellectual functioning and another 40 percent attained the mildly retarded level. In comparison, only 2 percent of the untreated control children achieved normal functioning and 45 percent attained mildly retarded functioning. These remarkable results did, however, require a considerable staffing effort, with well-qualified therapists working with each child at least 40 hours per week for 2 years. Interestingly, studies on the effectiveness of behavior therapy with institutionalized children have found that children who were discharged to their parents continued to improve, whereas those who remained in an institution tended to lose much of what they had gained (Lovaas, 1977).

Some of the other impressive results with autistic children have been obtained in projects that involve parents, with treatment in the home preferable to hospital-based therapy (Mesibov et al., 1997). Treatment contracts with parents specify the desired behavior changes in their child and spell out the explicit techniques for bringing about these changes. Such contracting acknowledges the value of the parents as potential agents of change (Huynen, Lutzker, et al., 1996). Perhaps the most favorable results are those of Schreibman and Koegel (1975), who reported successful outcomes in the treatment of 10 out of 16 autistic children. These investigators relied heavily on the use of parents as therapists to reinforce normal behavior in their children. They concluded that autism is potentially a "defeatable horror."

The Effectiveness of Treatment It is too early to evaluate the long-term effectiveness of the newer treatment

Some studies show that intensive behavioral treatment of autistic children, requiring a significant investment of time and energy on the part of therapist and parents, can bring improvement, particularly if this treatment continues at home rather than in an institution.

methods or the degree of improvement they actually bring about. The prognosis for autistic children, particularly for children showing symptoms before the age of 2, is poor. Commonly, the long-term results of autism treatments have been unfavorable. A great deal of attention has been given to high-functioning autistic children (children who meet the criteria for autism yet develop functional speech). Ritvo and colleagues (1988) studied 11 parents whom they believed met diagnostic criteria for autism (they were identified through having had children who were autistic). These individuals had been able to make modest adjustments to life, hold down jobs, and get married. The outcome in autism is often problematic, however.

One important factor limiting treatment success is the difficulty autistic children experience in generalizing behavior outside the treatment context (Handleman, Gill, & Alessandri, 1988). Children with severe developmental disabilities do not transfer skills across situations very well. Consequently, learned behavior in one situation does not appear to help them meet challenges in others. This important component needs to be addressed if training or treatment programs are to be successful.

In spite of a few remarkable cases of dramatic success, the overall prognosis for autistic children remains guarded. Less than one-fourth of the autistic children who receive treatment appear to attain even marginal adjustment in later life. Even with intensive long-term care in a clinical facility, where gratifying improvements in specific behaviors may be brought about, autistic children are a long way from becoming normal. Some make substantial improvement during childhood, only to deteriorate, showing symptom aggravation, at the onset of puberty (Gillberg & Schaumann, 1981).

Providing parental care to autistic children is more trying and stressful than providing it to normal or mentally retarded children (Kasari & Sigman, 1997). Parents of autistic children often find themselves in the extremely frustrating situation of trying to understand their autistic child, providing day-to-day care, and searching for possible educational resources for their child in the present health and educational environment. There are many more questions than answers, and parents of autistic children often find themselves in the dark about the best way to proceed to gain an understanding of their child's potential and the best means of helping him or her realize that potential. An unusually informative book on the topic of autism, *The World of the Autistic Child,* by Siegel (1996), provides a very valuable guide for understanding and dealing with the problems of educating and treating autistic children. She discusses the impact that having an autistic child can have on the family—both parents and siblings—and describes ways of dealing with the problems, including the possible need of psychological treatment for other family members. The book is particularly valuable in providing clues as to how parents can obtain available resources for educating and treating autistic children in the confusing educational environment. The question of residential placement, clearly a necessity in some situations and families, is also an important decision with which parents of many autistic children must come to terms. Efforts are being made to promote the development and growth of autistic people over their lifespans, in what has been referred to as the "Eden Model" (Holmes, 1998). In this approach, professionals and families recognize that autistic individuals may need to have different therapeutic regimes at different periods of their lives, and the available resources need to be structured to provide for their changing needs.

IN REVIEW

- Why is autistic disorder classified as a pervasive developmental disorder? Describe its clinical features.
- What is known about the causes and treatments of autistic disorder?

PLANNING BETTER PROGRAMS TO HELP CHILDREN AND ADOLESCENTS

The earlier discussion of several disorders of childhood and adolescence noted the wide range of treatment procedures available, as well as the marked differences in outcomes. In concluding the chapter, we will discuss certain special factors associated with the treatment of children and adolescents, the use of play therapy, and the problem of child abuse.

Special Factors Associated With Treatment for Children and Adolescents

Mental health treatment, psychotherapy, and behavior therapy have been found to be as effective with children and adolescents as with adults (Kazdin, 1998; Weisz, Weiss, & Donenberg, 1992), but treatments conducted in laboratory-controlled studies are more effective than "real-world" treatment situations (Weisz, Donenberg, et al., 1995). There are a number of special factors to consider in relation to treatment for children and adolescents.

The Child's Inability to Seek Assistance Most emotionally disturbed children who need assistance are not in a position to ask for it themselves or to transport themselves to and from child treatment clinics. Thus, unlike an adult, who can usually seek help, a child is dependent, primarily on his or her parents. Adults should realize when a child needs professional help and take the initiative in obtaining it. Sometimes, however, adults neglect this responsibility.

The law identifies four areas in which treatment without parental consent is permitted: (1) in the case of mature minors (those considered to be capable of making decisions about themselves); (2) in the case of emancipated minors (those living independently away from their parents); (3) in emergency situations; and (4) in situations in which a court orders treatment. Many children, of course, come to the attention of treatment agencies as a consequence of school referrals, delinquent acts, or parental abuse.

Vulnerabilities Placing Children at Risk for Developing Emotional Problems Many families provide an undesirable environment for their growing children (Ammerman et al., 1998). Studies have shown that up to a fourth of American children may be living in inadequate homes and 7.6 percent of American youth have reported spending at least one night in a shelter, public place, or abandoned building (Ringwalt, Greene, et al., 1998). Disruptive childhood experiences have been found to be a risk factor for adult problems. For example, one epidemiological study (Susser, Moore, & Link, 1993) reported that 23 percent of newly homeless men in New York City reported a history of out-of-home care as children, and another study by Caudill and colleagues (1994) reported that clients with a parental history of substance abuse were at over twice the risk for antisocial personality disorder.

Children growing up in troubled homes are at a double disadvantage. Not only are they deprived from the standpoint of environmental influences on their personality development (Crouch & Milner, 1993), but they also lack parents who will perceive their need for help and actively seek and participate in treatment programs. Inadequate or inattentive parenting can result in a failure to recognize serious signs of developing emotional problems.

High-risk behaviors or conditions need to be recognized and taken into consideration (Harrington & Clark, 1998). For example, there are a number of behaviors, such as engaging in sexual acts or delinquent behavior or using alcohol or drugs, that might place young people at great risk for developing later emotional problems. Moreover, there are situations that can "happen" to young people—physical or sexual abuse, parental divorce, family turbulence, and homelessness—that place them at great risk for emotional distress and subsequent maladaptive behavior. Dodge, Lochman, and colleagues (1997) found that children from homes with harsh discipline and physical abuse, for example, were more likely to be aggressive and conduct-disordered than those from homes with less harsh discipline and those from nonabusing families.

Need for Treating Parents as Well as Children Because many of the behavior disorders specific to childhood appear to grow out of pathogenic family interactions, it is often essential for the parents, as well as their child, to receive treatment. In some instances, in fact, the treatment program may focus on the parents entirely, as in the case of child abuse.

Increasingly, then, the treatment of children has come to mean family therapy, in which one or both parents, along with the child and siblings, may participate in all phases of the program. Many therapists have discovered that fathers are particularly difficult to engage in the treatment process. For working parents and for parents who basically reject the affected child, such treatment may be difficult to arrange (Gaudin, 1993), especially in the case of poorer families who lack transportation and money. Thus, both parental and economic factors help determine which emotionally disturbed children will receive assistance.

Possibility of Using Parents as Change Agents In essence, parents can be used as change agents by training them in techniques that enable them to help their child. Typically, such training focuses on helping the parents to understand the child's behavior disorder and to learn to reinforce adaptive behavior while withholding reinforcement for undesirable behavior. Encouraging results have been obtained with parents who care about their children and want to help (Forehand, 1993; Webster-Stratton, 1991). Kazdin, Holland, and Crowley (1997) described a number of barriers to parental involvement in treatment that resulted in dropout from therapy. Factors such as coming from a disadvantaged background, having parents who were antisocial, or having parents who were under great stress tended to result in premature treatment termination.

Problem of Placing a Child Outside the Family Most communities have juvenile facilities that, day or night, will provide protective care and custody for young victims of unfit homes, abandonment, abuse, neglect, and related conditions. Depending on the home situation and the special needs of the child, he or she will later be either

HIGHLIGHT 14.3

Family Therapy as a Means of Helping Children

To remedy a child's problems, it is often necessary to alter pathological family interaction patterns that produce or maintain the child's behavior (Sandberg, Johnson, et al., 1997).

Several family therapy approaches have been developed (Minuchin, 1974; Patterson, Capaldi, & Bank, 1991), each differing in some important ways—for example, in terms of how the family is defined (whether to include extended family members); what the treatment process will focus on (whether communications between the family members or the aberrant behavior of the problem family members is the focus); what procedures are used in treatment (analyzing and interpreting hidden messages in the family communications or altering the reward and punishment contingencies through behavioral assessment and reinforcement). Regardless of their differences, all family therapies view a child's problems, at least in part, as an outgrowth of pathological interaction patterns within the family, and they attempt to bring about positive change in family members through analysis and modification of the deviant family patterns (Carr, 1997).

Treatment outcome research strongly supports the effectiveness of family therapy in improving disruptive family relationships and promoting a more positive atmosphere for children (Hazelrigg, Cooper, & Borduin, 1987; Shadish et al., 1993). ■

returned to his or her parents or placed elsewhere. In the latter instance, four types of facilities are commonly relied on: (1) foster homes, (2) private institutions for the care of children, (3) county or state institutions, or (4) the homes of relatives. At any one time, more than a half-million children are living in foster-care facilities.

The quality of a child's new home is, of course, a crucial determinant of whether the child's problems will be alleviated or made worse. Although efforts are made to screen the placement facilities and maintain contact with the situation through follow-up visits, there have been too many reported cases of mistreatment in the new home. In cases of child abuse, child abandonment, or a serious childhood behavior problem that parents cannot control, it has often been assumed that the only feasible action was to take the child out of the home and find a temporary substitute. With such a child's own home so obviously inadequate, the hope has been that a more stable outside placement will be better. But when children are taken from their homes and placed in an institution (which promptly tries to change them) or in a series of foster homes (where they obviously do not really belong), they are likely to feel rejected by their own parents, unwanted by their new caretakers, rootless, constantly insecure, lonely, and bitter.

Accordingly, the trend today is toward permanent planning. First, every effort is made to hold a family together and to give the parents the support and guidance they need for adequate childrearing. If this is impossible, then efforts are made to free the child legally for adoption and to find an adoptive home as soon as possible. This, of course, means that the public agencies need specially trained staffs with reasonable caseloads and access to resources that they and their clients may need.

Value of Intervening Before Problems Become Acute

Over the last 25 years, a primary concern of many researchers and clinicians has been to identify and provide early help for children who are at special risk (Athey, O'Malley, et al., 1997). Rather than wait until these children develop acute psychological problems that may require therapy or major changes in living arrangements, psychologists are attempting to identify conditions in the children's lives that seem likely to bring about or maintain behavior problems and, where such conditions exist, to intervene before development has been seriously distorted (Cicchetti & Toth, 1998). An example of this approach is provided in the work of Steele and Forehand (1997). These investigators found that children of parents who have a chronic medical condition (fathers were diagnosed as having hemophilia, many were HIV-positive) were vulnerable to developing internalizing problems and avoidant behavior, particularly when the parent-child relationship was weak. These symptoms in the child were associated with depression in the parent. The investigators concluded that clinicians may be able to reduce the impact of parental chronic illness by strengthening the parent-child relationship and decreasing the child's use of avoidant strategies.

As described in Chapter 4, another type of early intervention has been developed in response to the special vulnerability children experience in the wake of a disaster or trauma such as a hurricane, accident, hostage-taking, or shooting. Children and adolescents often require considerable support and attention to deal with such a traumatic event, all too frequent in today's world. Individual and small-group psychological therapy might be implemented for victims of trauma (Gillis, 1993), support programs might operate through school-based interventions (Klingman, 1993), or community-based programs might be implemented to reduce the post-traumatic symptoms and prevent the occurrence of long-term maladjustment problems.

Early intervention has the double goal of reducing the stressors in a child's life and strengthening the child's coping mechanisms. If successful, it can effectively reduce the number and intensity of later problems, thus averting problems for both the individuals concerned and the broader society. It is apparent that children's needs can be met only if adequate preventive and treatment facilities exist and are available to the children who need assistance.

Using Play Therapy to Resolve Children's Psychological Problems

Even if a child's problems are viewed as primary and in need of specific therapeutic intervention, he or she may not be motivated for therapy or sufficiently verbal to benefit from psychotherapeutic methods that work with adults. Consequently, effective psychological treatment with children may involve using more indirect methods of therapy or providing individual psychological therapy for children in a less intrusive and more familiar way through play therapy (Sperling, 1997b).

As a treatment technique, play therapy emerged out of efforts to apply psychodynamic therapy to children. Because children are not able to talk about their problems in the way adults are, having not yet developed the self-awareness necessary, the applicability of traditional psychodynamic therapy methods to children is limited. Children tend to be oriented to the present and lack the capability for insight and self-scrutiny that therapy requires. Their perceptions of their therapist differ from those of adult patients, and they may have an unrealistic view that the therapist can magically change their environment (Wenar, 1990).

Through their play, children often express their feelings, fears, and emotions in a direct and uncensored fashion, providing a clinician with a clearer picture of problems and feelings. The activity of play has become a valuable source of personality and problem information about children, particularly when the sessions are consistent with their developmental level (Lewis, 1997).

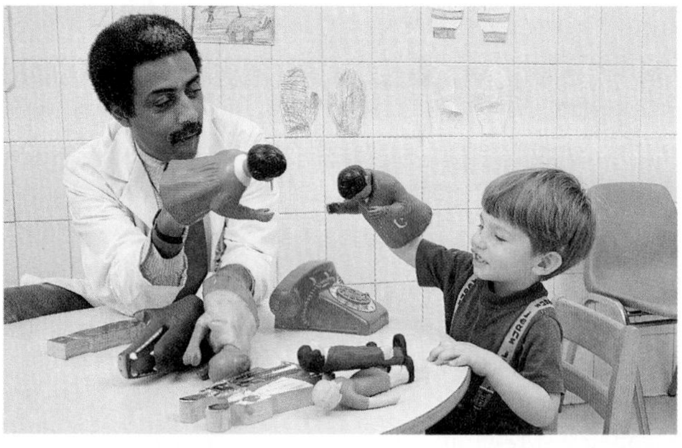

Children can often express their feelings more directly through play than in words, as shown in this play therapy session.

In a play therapy session, the therapist usually needs to provide some structure or to guide play activities so that the child can express pertinent feelings. This might mean that the therapist asks direct questions of the child during the play session, such as "Is the doll happy now?" or "What makes the doll cry?" In addition to being a means of understanding a troubled child's problems, play activity also provides a medium for bringing about change in the child's behavior. A central process in play therapy is that the therapist, through interpretation, provision of emotional support, and clarification of feelings (often by labeling them for the child), provides the child with a corrective emotional experience. That is, the therapist provides the child with an accepting and trusting relationship that promotes healthier personality and relationship development. The play therapy situation enables the child to reexperience conflict or problems in the safety of the therapy setting, thereby gaining a chance to conquer fears, to acclimate to necessary life changes, or to gain a feeling of security to replace anxiety and uncertainty.

How effective is play therapy in reducing a child's problems and promoting better adjustment? When compared with adult treatment studies, play therapy compares quite favorably. Casey and Berman (1985) conducted a careful study of treatment research with children and concluded that such treatment "appears to match the efficacy of psychotherapy with adults" (p. 395). Play therapy was found to be as effective as other types of treatment, such as behavior therapy. In another study, in which play therapy was integrated into an 8-week intervention program to treat conduct-disordered children, the subjects showed significant gain at a 2-year follow-up (McDonald, Bellingham, et al., 1997).

Child Abuse

Child abuse is an increasing concern in the United States (Lung & Daro, 1996). A survey of reported child abuse incidents in the United States found that child abuse reports increased 1.7 percent in 1995, with a total number of incidents exceeding 3.1 million. An estimated 1215 children were killed in 1995 in child abuse incidents (National Committee to Prevent Child Abuse, 1996). The excessive use of alcohol or drugs in a family appears to increase the risk of violent death in the home (Rivera, Muellar, et al., 1997). Some evidence suggests that boys are more often physically abused than girls. It is usually clear that many children brought to the attention of legal agencies for abuse have been abused before. Moreover, the significantly higher rates among psychiatric inpatients of having been abused as a child suggest the likely causal role such maltreatment has in the development of severe psychopathology (Read, 1997).

The seriousness of the child abuse problem in our society was not realized until the 1960s, when researchers began to report case after case like the following two.

Case Study **Two Cases of Child Abuse** • The mother of a 29-month-old boy claimed he was a behavior problem, beat him with a stick and screwdriver handle, dropped him on the floor, beat his head on the wall or threw him against it, choked him to force his mouth open to eat, and burned him on the face and hands. After she had severely beaten him, the mother found the child dead.

Because her 2½-year-old daughter did not respond readily enough to toilet training, the mother became indignant and in a fit of temper over the child's inability to control a bowel movement gave her an enema with near scalding water. To save the child's life, a doctor was forced to perform a colostomy (From Earl, 1965.)

Many abused children show impaired cognitive ability and memory when compared with control children (Friedrich, Einbender, & Luecke, 1983). In addition, abused children are likely to show problems in social adjustment and are particularly likely to feel that the outcomes of events are determined by external factors beyond their own control (Kinzl & Biebl, 1992; Toth, Manly, & Cicchetti, 1992). They are also more likely to experience depressive symptoms (Bushnell, Wells, & Oakley-Browne, 1992; Emery & Laumann-Billings, 1998). As a result, abused children are dramatically less likely to assume personal responsibility for themselves, and they generally demonstrate less interpersonal sensitivity than control children. Child abuse and neglect may initiate a chain of violence. Child abuse is also associated with delinquent and criminal behavior when the victim grows up. Maxfield and Widom (1996), in a follow-up study of 908 people who were abused as children, found that their arrest rate for nontraffic offenses was significantly higher than a control sample of people who had not been abused as children.

Abused children also tend to show more self-destructive behavior than nonabused children, and physically abused children may be more likely to abuse their own children when they become parents (Malinosky-Rummel & Hansen, 1993). Childhood victimization was also found to be significantly related to the number of lifetime symptoms of antisocial personality disorder and predictive of a diagnosis of that disorder (Luntz and Widom, 1994) and of psychosis (Read, 1997).

Sexual Abuse When the abuse involves a sexual component, such as incest or rape, the long-range consequences can be profound (Kendall-Tackett, Williams, & Finkelhor, 1993). Although some fairly recent analyses have questioned the impact of sexual abuse on child development (Rind, Tromovitch, & Bauserman, 1998), some research has suggested that people who have been sexually abused are more likely to develop substance abuse problems (Hernandez, 1992). Watkins and Bentovim (1992) reported that approximately 2 to 5 percent of men in the adult population have been sexually abused, often resulting in lifelong negative consequences, such as sexual problems (e.g., exhibitionism, homophobic behavior, depression, anxiety) and even a tendency to recapitulate this experience as an adult. Jackson and colleagues (1990) found that women who had experienced intrafamily sexual abuse had significantly poorer social adjustment, especially in dating relationships. The women also reported significantly lower sexual satisfaction, more sexual dysfunctions, and lower self-esteem than women in a control group. Adults who have been sexually abused as children often show serious psychological symptoms, such as a tendency to use dissociative defense mechanisms to excess, excessive preoccupation with bodily functions, lowered self-esteem (Nash et al., 1993), or a tendency to disengage as a means of handling stress as an adult (Coffey, Leitenberg, et al., 1996).

The role of sexual abuse in causing psychological problems has been the subject of several longitudinal studies. A large percentage of sexually abused children experience intense psychological symptoms following the incident (for example, 74 percent reported by Bentovim, Boston, & Van Elburg, 1987). At follow-up, however, the improvement often seems dramatic. Several studies have reported substantial improvement of sexually abused victims at follow-up (Bentovim et al., 1987; Conte, Berliner, & Schuerman, 1986). One study found that 55 percent of victims had substantially improved 18 months later, particularly in terms of sleeping problems, fears of the offender, and anxiety. However, 28 percent of the victims showed worsening behavior (Gomes-Schwartz, Horowitz, & Cardarelli, 1990).

Several investigators have conceptualized the residual symptoms of sexual abuse as a type of post-traumatic stress disorder (PTSD) because the symptoms experienced are similar, for example, nightmares, flashbacks, sleep problems, and feelings of estrangement (Donaldson & Gardner, 1985); also, PTSD symptoms are strongly associated with abuse (Koltek, Wilkes, & Atkinson, 1998). However, other investigators (e.g., Finkelhor, 1990) object to this explanation on grounds that viewing these symptoms as an example of PTSD will "lead us to miss some of [the] most serious effects" of the sexual abuse experience, such as prolonged depression or anxiety (p. 329).

Causal Factors in Child Abuse Since the 1960s, a great deal of research has been aimed at finding out which parents abuse their children and why, in the hope that these parents can ultimately be stopped or, better yet, prevented from abusing their children. It is important to realize that, in most cases, it is not possible to find a single cause of child abuse. As Jay Belsky (1993) pointed out, "There is no one pathway to these disturbances in parenting; rather, maltreatment seems to arise when stressors outweigh supports and risks are greater than protective factors" (p. 427). Rather, there are multiple pathways to abuse (Emery & Laumann-Billings, 1998). Parents who physically abuse their children tend to be young, with most under 30. In the majority of reported cases, they come from the lower socioeconomic levels (Peterson & Brown, 1994). An important common factor among families with abusing parents is a higher-than-average degree of frustration; many stressors are present in such parents' lives, including marital discord, unemployment, and alcohol abuse (Cicchetti & Toth, 1998). Evidence suggests that high levels of caregiver stress play an important part in child abuse and neglect (Hillson & Kuiper, 1994). Many incidents of physical abuse occur as parental reactions to a child's misbehavior in areas such as fighting, sexual behavior, aggression, and so on (Herrenkohl, Herrenkohl, & Egolf, 1983). Although no clear and consistent personality pattern emerges as typical of child-abusing parents, they seem to show a higher-than-average rate of psychological disturbance (Serrano et al., 1979). Some evidence from personality testing shows that they tend to be aggressive, nonconforming, selfish, and lacking in appropriate impulse control (Lund, 1975).

Treatment and Prevention of Child Abuse Because of complexities involved in the area of child abuse, interventions need to be implemented on multiple levels including individual, familial, and community (Becker, Alpert, et al., 1995). Practitioners and child protection agencies have attempted to reduce the amount and impact of child abuse. Their efforts include the following:

1. Community education programs have been developed to increase public awareness of the problem. Television advertisements have been especially effective at sensitizing parents and children to recognize abusive behavior and situations facilitating it.
2. Child protection teams have been organized by many state and county welfare departments to investigate and intervene in reported cases of child abuse. All states require physicians and other professionals to report cases of child abuse that come to their attention.
3. Teams of mental health specialists are working in many community mental health centers to evaluate and provide psychological treatment for both abused children and their parents.
4. Parent support groups, often made up of former child abusers, have been formed to offer parents who have abused their children or are at high risk for doing so alternative ways of behaving toward their children.

Unfortunately, child abuse all too frequently produces maladaptive social behavior in its victims. The treatment of abused children needs to address their problems of social adjustment, depression, and poor interpersonal skills. An interesting treatment approach for reducing the negative consequences of child abuse uses peers to help modify abused children's tendency to withdraw and improve their poor social skills. Fantuzzo and colleagues (1988) trained peer confederates to make play overtures to abused children. They found that peer-initiated efforts were more effective at increasing the social interaction of withdrawn children than were adult-initiated treatment efforts. Further work is needed on rehabilitative efforts to assist these unfortunate children in overcoming the psychologically disabling effects of being abused.

One of the most effective strategies for eliminating or reducing child abuse involves parent-focused interventions that include teaching parents clearly defined child training strategies aimed at improving childrearing skills (Wolfe & Wekerle, 1993). Research aimed at enabling early intervention with parents identified as likely to abuse their children has been promising. Wolfe and colleagues (1988) identified women who were at high risk for maltreatment of their children. They randomly assigned the women to either a treatment or a control group. The treatment consisted of behaviorally oriented parent training that provided child management skills; instruction in child care; modeling; rehearsal of instructions so as to give clear, concise demands; and the use of "time out" as a punishment. The study showed that this early intervention reduced the risk for child abuse among the mothers in the treatment group. Through such efforts on many levels, it is hoped that children will be spared abuse and that abusive or potentially abusive parents will be helped to be more effective and nurturant.

IN REVIEW

- What special factors must be considered in providing treatment for children and adolescents?
- Why is therapeutic intervention a more complicated process with children than with adults?
- Describe how play therapy works.
- What has been learned about parents at high risk for child abuse?

SUMMARY

MALADAPTIVE BEHAVIOR IN DIFFERENT LIFE PERIODS

- Children used to be viewed as "miniature" adults. It was not until the second half of the twentieth century that a diagnostic classification system focused clearly on the special problems of children.
- The DSM classification system provides clinical descriptions of a wide range of childhood mental and behavior problems.

DISORDERS OF CHILDHOOD

- Attention-deficit/hyperactivity disorder (ADHD) is one of the more frequent behavior problems of childhood. In this disorder, the child shows impulsive, overactive behavior that interferes with his or her ability to accomplish tasks.
- There is some controversy over the explicit criteria used to distinguish hyperactive children from "normal" children or from children who exhibit other behavior disorders, such as conduct disorders. This lack of clarity in defining ADHD increases the difficulty of determining its causal factors.
- The major approaches to treating children with ADHD are medication and behavior therapy. Using medications, such as amphetamines, with children is somewhat controversial. Behavior therapy, particularly the cognitive-behavioral type, has shown promise in modifying the behavior of hyperactive children.
- Other common disorders that involve behavior problems in children and adolescents are oppositional defiant disorder and conduct disorder. In these disorders, a child or adolescent engages in persistent aggressive or antisocial acts. In cases where the misdeeds involve illegal activities, the term *juvenile delinquency* may be applied.
- A number of potential causes for conduct disorder or delinquent behavior have been determined, ranging from biological factors to personal pathology to social conditions.
- Treatment of conduct disorders and delinquent behavior is often frustrating and difficult; it is likely to be ineffective unless some means can be found for modifying a child's environment.
- Other disorders, such as the childhood anxiety disorders and childhood depression, are quite different from the conduct disorders. Children who suffer from these disorders typically do not cause difficulty for others through their aggressive conduct. Rather, they are fearful, shy, withdrawn, insecure, and have difficulty adapting to outside demands.
- The childhood anxiety disorders may be characterized by extreme anxiety, withdrawal, or avoidance behavior. A likely cause for these disorders is early family relationships that generate anxiety and prevent the child from developing more adaptive coping skills. Behavior therapy approaches such as assertiveness training and desensitization may be helpful in treating this kind of disorder.
- Several other disorders that arise in childhood involve behavior problems centering on a single outstanding symptom rather than pervasive maladaptive patterns. These symptom disorders include enuresis, encopresis, sleepwalking disorder, and tics. Treatment of these disorders is generally more successful than for the other childhood disorders.

PERVASIVE DEVELOPMENTAL DISORDERS

- One of the most severe and inexplicable of childhood disorders is autism. In this disorder, extreme maladaptive behavior occurs during the early years and prevents the child from developing psychologically. Autistic children seem to remain aloof from others, not responding to and seemingly not caring about what goes on around them. Many never learn to speak.
- It is likely that autism has a genetic and biological basis. Neither medical nor psychological treatment has been able to normalize the behavior of autistic children, but newer instructional and behavior-modification techniques have sometimes significantly improved their ability to function. In general, the long-term prognosis for autistic children still appears guarded at best.
- Although genetic predisposition appears to be important in several disorders of childhood and adolescence, parental psychopathology, family disruption, and stressful circumstances, such as parental death or desertion or child abuse, can have an important causal influence. Recent research has underscored the importance of multiple risk factors in the development of psychopathology.

PLANNING BETTER PROGRAMS TO HELP CHILDREN AND ADOLESCENTS

- There are special problems, and special opportunities, involved in treating children and adolescents. The need for preventive and treatment programs for children is growing, and the concept of child advocacy has become a reality in recent years in some states.
- Child abuse is a serious problem that continues to drive both research and clinical efforts to find causes and devise preventive measures and treatment. Unfortunately, the financing and resources necessary for programs for improving psychological environments for children and adolescents are not always readily available, and the future remains uncertain.

KEY TERMS

developmental psychopathology (p. 465)
attention-deficit/hyperactivity disorder (ADHD) (p. 466)
Ritalin (p. 468)
Pemoline (p. 468)
conduct disorder (p. 470)
oppositional defiant disorder (p. 470)
juvenile delinquency (p. 470)
separation anxiety disorder (p. 475)
selective mutism (p. 475)
enuresis (p. 479)
encopresis (p. 480)
sleepwalking disorder (p. 481)
tic (p. 481)
Tourette's syndrome (p. 482)
pervasive developmental disorders (PDD) (p. 482)
Asberger's disorder (p. 482)
autism (p. 483)
echolalia (p. 484)

CHAPTER FIFTEEN

Contemporary Issues in Abnormal Psychology

Louise Dalip Bego, *Symphony,* acrylics. In 1973, Bego suffered a traumatic brain injury in a car accident. The long-term effects of this injury have been memory loss, inexplicable outbursts of anger, and a personality transformation. Bego turned to painting as an outlet for her feelings of depression, fear, and rage. She has won several citations for her work in her home state of Michigan.

LEARNING OBJECTIVES

After reading this chapter, you should be able to:

- Outline the commitment process, and identify the conditions that must be met for involuntary commitment.
- Explain the difficulty in assessing "dangerousness" and the legal basis of the therapist's duty to protect if a client is thought to be dangerous.
- Review the legal rulings relevant to the insanity defense, and describe the controversy associated with this plea.
- Summarize the arguments for and against deinstitutionalization.
- Differentiate among universal interventions, selective interventions, and indicated interventions, and give an example of each.
- Distinguish among the biological, psychosocial, and sociocultural types of universal interventions.
- List several national and international organizations involved in mental health efforts.
- Discuss the challenges facing mental health efforts now and in the future, and identify ways in which individuals can help.

This book has covered a great number of topics and issues pertinent to understanding abnormal behavior from a contemporary perspective. The final chapter has traditionally been somewhat of a forum for several important topics in abnormal psychology that have been noted only briefly in earlier chapters. These issues are very important to understanding the field of abnormal psychology and will give you a broader perspective on ways our society deals with, or in some cases fails to deal with, abnormal behavior.

We begin with several legal issues pertinent to psychiatric care and hospitalization of people with severe psychological problems: commitment, assessment of dangerousness, and deinstitutionalization. Closely related to these factors are the matters of (1) a therapist's duty to warn others if a client threatens violence and (2) the use—and some think abuse—of the insanity defense as a plea in capital crimes.

Next, we will explore the topic of prevention of mental disorders. Over the years, most mental health efforts have been largely restorative, geared toward helping people only after they have already developed serious problems. Seemingly, a more effective strategy would be to try to catch problems before they become severe or, better yet, to establish conditions in which psychological disorders will not occur. Unfortunately, the causes of many mental disorders are either not sufficiently understood or not specific enough to enable practitioners to initiate targeted preventive programs. As a result, prevention in the mental health field is still based largely on hypotheses about what works rather than on substantial empirical research. Nonetheless, many professionals believe that preventive mental health efforts are worthwhile.

Finally, we will close with a look at the challenges facing the field of mental health and consider what each of us can do to foster mental health.

CONTROVERSIAL LEGAL ISSUES AND THE MENTALLY DISORDERED

A number of important issues are related to the legal status of the mentally ill—the subject matter of **forensic psychology** or **forensic psychiatry**—and they center on the rights of mental patients and the rights of members of society to be protected from disturbed individuals and vice versa. Over the years, many legal rights have been gained for the mentally ill, including the right to treatment *and* the right to refuse treatment, the right to be free of custodial confinement if one is not dangerous to oneself or others and can safely survive outside of custody, the right to legal counsel at commitment hearings, and the right to live outside of mental institutions and be treated in the less restrictive environment of "adult homes" within a community (Hermann, 1990; Mental Health Law Project, 1987).

In spite of such hard-won legal rights, many issues related to the rights of the mentally ill continue to be controversial. In this section, we will consider a number of these. We will first review the procedures involved in involuntarily committing disturbed and dangerous individuals to psychiatric institutions. Next, we will turn to the assessment of "dangerousness" in disturbed persons; we will also discuss a related issue, which has become of key concern to psychotherapists—the court decision that psychotherapists have a duty to protect potential victims from any threatened violence by their patients even if this means ignoring their ethical and legal obligations to client confidentiality. In addition, we will examine the controversial insanity defense for capital crimes and the issue of deinstitutionalization, or what some have called the pre-

forensic psychology (psychiatry) Branch of psychology (or psychiatry) dealing with legal problems relating to mental disorders and the legal rights and protection of mental patients.

mature "dumping" of mental patients into the community. As you will see, in many cases, homeless shelters in metropolitan communities have become a "makeshift alternative" to inpatient mental health care (Haugland, Sigel, et al., 1997).

The Commitment Process

Persons with psychological problems or behaviors that are so extreme and severe as to pose a threat to themselves or others may require protective confinement. Individuals who commit crimes, whether or not they have a psychological disorder, are dealt with primarily through the judicial system—arrest, court trial, and, if convicted, possible confinement in a penal institution. Persons who are judged to be potentially dangerous because of their psychological state may, after civil commitment procedures, be confined in a mental institution. The steps in the commitment process vary slightly depending on state law (here we will use Minnesota as our model), the locally available community mental health resources, and the nature of the person's problem. For example, commitment procedures for a mentally retarded person will be different from those for a person with an alcohol-abuse problem.

A distinction should be made here between voluntary hospitalization and involuntary commitment. In most cases, people enter mental institutions without a court order; that is, they accept voluntary commitment or hospitalization. In these cases, they can, with sufficient notice, leave the hospital if they wish. In cases in which a person is believed to be dangerous or unable to provide for his or her own care, the need for involuntary commitment may arise.

Being mentally ill is not sufficient grounds for placing a person in a mental institution against his or her will. Although procedures vary somewhat from state to state, several conditions beyond mental illness usually must be met before formal commitment can occur (Simon & Aaronson, 1988). In brief, mentally ill individuals must also be judged to be as follows:

- Dangerous to themselves, or to others
- Incapable of providing for their basic physical needs
- Unable to make responsible decisions about hospitalization
- And/or in need of treatment or care in a hospital

The use of the "dangerousness" criterion as grounds for civil commitment has apparently increased (McNeil & Binder, 1986). Typically, filing a petition for a commitment hearing is the first step in the process of committing a person involuntarily. This petition is usually filed by a concerned person, such as a relative, physician, or mental health professional. When a petition is filed, a judge appoints two examiners to evaluate the "proposed patient." In Minnesota, for example, one examiner must be a physician (not necessarily a psychiatrist); the other can be a psychiatrist or a psychologist. The patient is asked to appear voluntarily for psychiatric examination before the commitment hearing. The hearing must be held within 14 days, which can be extended for 30 more days if good cause for the extension can be shown. The law requires that the court-appointed examiners interview the patient before the hearing.

If a person is committed to a mental hospital for treatment, the hospital must report to the court within 60 days as to whether the person needs to be confined even longer. If no report is given by the hospital, the patient must be released. If the hospital indicates that the person needs further treatment, then the commitment period becomes indeterminate, subject to periodic reevaluations.

Because the decision to commit a person is based on the conclusions of others about the person's capabilities and his or her potential for dangerous behavior, the civil commitment process leaves open the possibility of an unwarranted violation of a person's civil rights. As a consequence, most states have stringent safeguards in the procedures to ensure that any person who is the subject of a petition for commitment is granted due process, including rights to formal hearings with representation by legal counsel. If there is not time to get a court order for commitment or if there is imminent danger, however, the law allows emergency hospitalization without a formal commitment hearing. In such cases, a physician must sign a statement saying that an imminent danger exists. The patient can then be picked up (usually by the police) and detained under a "hold order," usually not to exceed 72 hours unless a petition for commitment is filed within that period.

Involuntary commitment in a psychiatric facility is, in large part, contingent on a determination that a person is dangerous and needs to be confined in order to protect him or her or society. Once committed, a patient may not consent to treatment—a situation that faces mental health professionals working in psychiatric facilities (Grisso & Appelbaum, 1998). We now turn to the important question of how to evaluate the potential dangerousness of patients.

The Assessment of "Dangerousness"

Although most disordered persons show no tendency toward violence (Lamberg, 1998), an increased risk of violence appears more likely among those who are *currently experiencing* psychotic symptoms (Tardiff, 1998). Several disorders that have an increased risk for violent behavior are schizophrenia, mania, personality disorder, substance abuse, and more rare conditions of organic brain injury and Huntington's disease. One study from Finland (Eronen, Hakola, & Tiihonen, 1996) reported that homicidal behavior among former patients was increased eightfold with the diagnosis of schizophrenia and tenfold with a diagnosis of antisocial personality or alcoholism. Violence among psychiatric patients is especially prominent for those who abuse alcohol (Steadman, Mulvey, et al., 1998).

Determining potential dangerousness is a crucial judgment for mental health professionals to make—not only from a therapeutic standpoint, to ensure that the most appropriate treatment is conducted, but also from the legal point of view of responsibility to the larger society. However, such a determination is often a difficult one to make (Heilbrun, 1997; Sigel & Kane, 1997). A 43-year-old homeless Cuban refugee, for example, who had only a few days earlier undergone a psychiatric evaluation and been released, stabbed two tourists to death on the Staten Island Ferry because "God told him to kill" (Triplett, 1986).

It is usually an easy matter to determine, after the fact, that a person has committed a violent act or acts and has demonstrated "dangerous behavior." The difficulty comes when one attempts to determine in advance whether a person is going to commit some particular violent act—a process referred to as "conducting a risk assessment" (Borum, 1996). Assessing a general state of "dangerousness" or appraising whether groups of offenders might be at risk for dangerous behavior is not the same thing as the far more formidable task of predicting whether a designated violent act will occur. How well do mental health professionals do in predicting the occurrence of dangerous acts? A general answer to this question would have to be "not as well as they or we would like."

Predicting who will become violent is very difficult. Mental health professionals typically err on the conservative side, considering some patients as more violence-prone than they actually are. At the same time, they have an obligation to integrate disordered individuals back into society, a move that has occasionally met with tragic results.

Violent acts are particularly difficult to predict because they are apparently determined as much by situational circumstances (for example, whether a person is under the influence of alcohol) as they are by an individual's personality traits or violent predispositions. It is, of course, impossible to predict with any great certainty what environmental circumstances are going to occur or what particular circumstances will provoke or instigate aggression for any given violently disposed person. One obvious and significantly predictive risk factor is a past history of violence (Megargee, 1993), but clinicians are not always able to unearth this type of background information.

As already noted, some types of patients, particularly actively schizophrenic and manic individuals (Binder & McNiel, 1988) or those with well-entrenched delusions (de Pauw & Szulecka, 1988), are far more likely to commit violent acts than the general population of mental patients, on average. Martell and Dietz (1992) reported a study of persons convicted of pushing or attempting to push unsuspecting victims, about half of whom were killed or seriously injured, into the paths of trains approaching subway stations in New York City. Most of the perpetrators of this gruesome crime were both psychotic and homeless at the time of the act.

Mental health professionals typically err on the conservative side when assessing "violence proneness" in a patient; that is, they overpredict violence. They consider some individuals more dangerous than they actually are and, in general, predict a greater percentage of clients to be dangerous, and thus to require protective confinement, than actually become involved in violent acts (Megargee, 1995). Such a tendency is of course quite understandable from the standpoint of the practitioner, considering the potentially serious consequences of a "false negative" judgment. It is likely, however, that many innocent patients thereby suffer a violation of their civil rights. Given a certain irreducible level of uncertainty in the prediction of violence, it is not obvious how this dilemma can be completely resolved.

Methods for Assessing Potential for Dangerousness

Evaluating a person's potential for committing violent acts

is difficult because only part of this equation is available for study:

$$\text{Predisposing personality} + \text{Environmental instigation} = \text{Aggressive act}$$

As we have noted, psychologists and psychiatrists usually do not know enough about the environmental circumstances the person will encounter to evaluate what the instigation to aggression will be. Predictions of dangerousness focus, then, primarily on aspects of the individual's personality.

The two major sources of personality information are data from personality tests and the individual's previous history. Personality testing can reveal whether an individual shows personality traits of hostility, aggressiveness, impulsiveness, poor judgment, and so on, but many individuals having these characteristics never do act on them. Facts about the person's previous history—such as having committed prior aggression, having verbalized threats of aggression, having an available means of committing violence (such as possession of a gun), and so on—are useful predictors (Monahan, 1981). Like personality testing, however, such data focus only on the individual factors and do not account for the situational forces that impinge on the person, which may include notably provocative behavior on the part of the victim (Megargee, 1995).

The prediction of violence is even more difficult in the case of an overcontrolled offender, one of whose more salient characteristics is a subaverage level of manifestly aggressive behavior prior to the commission of an aggressive act, very often an extremely violent one. Megargee (1970) studied extensively the "overcontrolled hostile" person who is the epitome of well-controlled behavior but who, typically on only one occasion, loses control and murderously attacks another person. Examples of this type of killer are dramatic: the high school honor student, reportedly civic-minded and fond of helping sick and old people, who is arrested for torturing and killing a 3-year-old girl in his neighborhood; or the mild, passive father of four who loses his temper over being cheated by a car dealer and beats the man to death with a tire iron. These examples illustrate the most difficult type of aggressive behavior to predict—the sudden, violent, impulsive act of a seemingly well-controlled and "normal" individual. However difficult, conducting risk assessment on individuals in forensic settings is often required of the mental health professional (Grisso & Tomkins, 1996).

The complex problem of risk assessment, or prediction of dangerousness, can be likened to the task of predicting the weather. "Ultimately, the goal of a warning system in mental health law is the same as the goal of a warning system in meteorology: to maximize the number of people who take appropriate and timely actions for the safety of life and property" (Monahan & Steadman, 1997, p. 937). In other words, both warning systems start with a detection of the dangerous event and culminate in taking actions to avoid the predicted problem.

The Duty to Protect: Implications of the Tarasoff Decision What should a therapist do on learning that a patient is planning to harm another person? Can the therapist violate the legally sanctioned confidence of the therapy contract and take action to prevent the patient from committing the act? Today, in most states, the therapist not only can violate confidentiality with impunity but may be required by law to do so—that is, to take action to protect persons from the threat of imminent violence against them. In its original form, this requirement was conceived as a duty to warn the prospective victim. The duty-to-warn legal doctrine was given a great deal of impetus in a California court ruling in 1976 in the case of *Tarasoff* v. *the Regents of the University of California et al.* (Mills, Sullivan, & Eth, 1987).

In this case, Prosenjit Poddar was being seen in outpatient psychotherapy by a psychologist at the university mental health facility. During his treatment, Mr. Poddar indicated that he intended to kill his former girlfriend, Tatiana Tarasoff, when she returned from vacation. The psychologist, concerned about the threat, discussed the case with his supervisors, and they agreed that Poddar was dangerous and should be committed for further observation and treatment. They informed the campus police, who picked up Poddar for questioning and subsequently judged him to be rational and released him after he promised to leave Ms. Tarasoff alone. Poddar then terminated treatment with the psychologist. About 2 months later, he stabbed Ms. Tarasoff to death. Her parents later sued the University of California and its staff involved in the case for their failure to hospitalize Poddar and their failure to warn Tarasoff about the threat to her life. In due course, the California Supreme Court in 1974 ruled that the defendants were not liable for failing to hospitalize Poddar; it did, however, find them liable for their failure to warn the victim. Ironically, Prosenjit Poddar, the criminal, was released on a trial technicality and returned home to India. In a later analysis of the case, Knapp (1980) said that the court ruled that difficulty in determining dangerousness does not exempt a psychotherapist from attempting to protect others when a determination of dangerousness exists. The court acknowledged that confidentiality was important to the psychotherapeutic relationship but stated that the protection privilege ends where the public peril begins (p. 610).

The duty-to-warn ruling—which has come to be known as the **Tarasoff decision**—while spelling out a therapist's responsibility in situations where there has been an explicit threat on a specific person's life, left other areas of application unclear. For example, does this ruling apply in cases where a patient threatens to commit suicide, and how might the therapist's responsibility be met in such a case? What, if anything, should a therapist do when the object of violence is not clearly named—for example, when global threats are made? Would the duty-to-warn ruling hold up in other states? In a subsequent ruling, the California Supreme Court ruled that the duty is to *protect*—rather than specifically to warn—the prospective victim, but that this duty is discharged if the therapist makes "reasonable efforts" to inform potential victims *and* an appropriate law enforcement agency of the pending threat. In other jurisdictions, however, rulings based on *Tarasoff* have been inconsistent and have been a source of much anxiety and confusion among mental health professionals, many of whom continue to believe on ethical and clinical grounds that strict confidentiality is an absolute and inviolable trust. A small minority of states—for example, Maryland and Pennsylvania—have explicitly affirmed the latter position, abandoning *Tarasoff* altogether (Mills et al., 1987). Official professional ethics codes, such as that of the American Psychological Association (1992), normally compel compliance with relevant law regardless of personal predilections to the contrary. Where the law is itself vague or equivocal, however, as it often is in this area, there is, of course, much room for idiosyncratic and biased interpretation.

The Insanity Defense

> The picture in the February 13, 1992, issue of *Time* said it all. The largest section offered Jeffrey Dahmer, on trial for the murder, dismemberment, and cannibalization of 15 men in Milwaukee. The top right-hand section pictured David Berkowitz, the "Son of Sam," who terrorized New York City for 13 months in 1976–1977 while killing six people and wounding seven others. The bottom right-hand frame showed John Hinckley, the would-be assassin of President Ronald Reagan in 1981. (Steadman et al., 1993, p. 1)

Tarasoff decision Ruling by a California court (1974) that a therapist has a duty to warn a prospective victim of any explicit threat made by a client in a therapy session.

insanity defense "Not guilty by reason of insanity" (NGRI) defense used in criminal trials.

NGRI defense The insanity defense or plea.

What linked the three infamous persons named here, apart from their murderous exploits, was their shared claim that they were in fact not legally responsible for their criminal acts. That is, each attempted to use the so-called **insanity defense**—also known as the **NGRI defense** ("not guilty by reason of insanity")—as a means of avoiding the legally prescribed consequences of their crimes. In technical legal terms, these men were invoking the ancient doctrine that their acts, while guilty ones (*actus rea*), lacked moral blameworthiness because they were unaccompanied by the corresponding (and, for a guilty judgment, legally mandated) intentional state of mind (*mens rea*)—the underlying assumption being that "insanity" somehow precludes or absolves the harboring of a guilty intent. Whatever the legal issues involved in this doctrine—and these on the face of it would appear to be legion—they were rendered moot in the Dahmer and Berkowitz cases because the planned insanity defenses proved unsuccessful, as is the usual outcome (Steadman et al., 1993).

The outcome of the Hinckley case was different in a number of important respects because the jury in this instance considered the defendant to be acting "outside of reason" and "not guilty by reason of insanity." At trial, in June 1982, Hinckley was acquitted on those grounds, a verdict that immediately unleashed a storm of public protest and of widespread, often unduly hasty attempts to reform the law pertaining to the NGRI defense so as to make it a less attractive option to capital case defendants and their attorneys. Hinckley himself was committed to the care of a federally operated high-security mental hospital, ostensibly to be involuntarily retained there until such time as his disorder remitted sufficiently that his release would not constitute a danger to himself or others. He remains incarcerated at this writing, and it seems doubtful that he will be declared sufficiently "well" to be "discharged" any time in the foreseeable future. His most recent petition for release (*Hinckley* v. *U.S.*, 1998) was denied, with the court finding that he was too dangerous to be released. Releasing him from custody would almost certainly bring forth another public outcry demanding abolition or limitation of the insanity defense. This view that "any and all" uses of the insanity defense should be suspect is unfortunate. This public outrage toward all insanity defense pleas unfortunately results from a persistent failure of legal scholars to examine critically and rigorously the guilt-absolving insanity construct and the *mens rea* doctrine from which it derives.

In any event, in recent years, the use of the NGRI defense in capital crime trials has been surrounded by controversy, largely owing to the uproar created by the outcome of the Hinckley trial (Steadman et al., 1993).

HIGHLIGHT 15.1

Can Altered Mind States Limit Responsibility in a Criminal Trial?

If a person commits a capital offense when his or her consciousness (and reason) is impaired, as in an altered state, should he or she be held responsible for the crime?

One criminal case, *Brancaccio* v. *State of Florida* (1997), provided some precedents on this issue. The defendant, a boy of 16, following an argument with his mother, took a walk in order to "cool down." On the walk, he encountered and beat to death an innocent bystander. Later, he attempted to cover up the crime by burning the body and by spray painting it (allegedly to remove his fingerprints from the victim). Although he was convicted of the crime at trial, this verdict was later overturned on appeal because the defendant was taking Zoloft and was believed to be suffering mental incapacitation as a result. The antidepressant is thought to produce "unexpected and intense agitation" in some people (Grinfeld & Wellner, 1998).

Courts have generally not considered altered states of consciousness, such as being intoxicated on drugs or alcohol, sufficient grounds for an insanity defense, because of the issue of volition—that is, the perpetrator of the crime consciously chose to become intoxicated in the first place. However, the question of being made toxic by drugs that were taken for the purpose of medication has added a new dimension to the defense that has not been fully resolved in the court system. ■

Some have contended that the objection to the insanity defense in capital crimes might reflect negative social attitudes toward the insane and that there is a "culture of punishment" that contributes to the reaction against the insanity plea (Perlin, 1996). There has been some concern, especially in cases of high visibility, that guilty (in the *actus rea* sense) defendants may feign mental disorder and fraudulently profit from this plea in avoiding criminal responsibility. Interestingly, the insanity defense is often *not* employed where it is appropriate, as it would have been, for example, in two high-visibility cases: one involving John Salvi (the abortion clinic assassin) and the other Theodore Kaczynski (the Unabomber). Apparently neither defendant wanted his mental state to be a part of the proceedings. In both cases, severe delusional disorder was likely to have played a significant role in the crime.

Despite some features that make it an appealing option to consider, especially where the undisputed facts are strongly aligned against the defendant, the NGRI defense has actually been employed quite rarely—in less than 2 percent of capital cases in the United States over time (Steadman et al., 1993). Studies have confirmed the fact, however, that persons acquitted of crimes by reason of insanity spend less time, on the whole, in a psychiatric hospital than persons who are convicted of crimes spend in prison (Kahn & Raifman, 1981; Pasewark, Pantle, & Steadman, 1982). In addition, states differ widely with respect to the amount of time that persons found not guilty by reason of insanity are confined. For example, one study by Callahan and Silver (1998) reported that in the states of Ohio and Maryland, nearly all persons acquitted by NGRI have been released within 5 years, whereas in Connecticut and New York, conditional release has been much more difficult to obtain.

Up to this point in the discussion, we have used the term "insanity defense" loosely, which is anathema to actual legal practice; we must be more attentive to the many precise legal nuances involved. Established precedents defining the insanity defense are as follows:

1. *The M'Naughten Rule (1843)*. Under this ruling, often referred to as the "knowing right from wrong" rule, people are believed to be sane unless it can be proved that, at the time of committing the act, they were laboring under such a defect of reason (from a disease of the mind) that they did not know the nature and quality of the act they were doing—or, if they did know that they were committing the act, they did not know that what they were doing was wrong.
2. *The irresistible impulse rule (1887)*. A second precedent in the insanity defense concerns the "irresistible impulse." This view holds that accused persons might not be responsible for their acts, even if they knew that what they were doing was wrong (according to the M'Naughten Rule), if they had lost the power to choose between right and wrong. That is, they could not avoid doing the act in question because they were compelled beyond their will to commit the act (Fersch, 1980).

3. *The Durham Rule.* In 1954, Judge David Bazelon, in a decision of the U.S. Court of Appeals, broadened the insanity defense further. Bazelon did not believe that the previous precedents allowed for a sufficient application of established scientific knowledge of mental illness and proposed a test that would be based on this knowledge. Under this rule, often referred to as the "product test," the accused is "not criminally responsible if his or her unlawful act was the product of mental disease or mental defect."
4. *The American Law Institute (ALI) standard (1962).* Often referred to as the "substantial capacity test" for insanity, this test combines the cognitive aspect of M'Naughten with the volitional focus of irresistible impulse in holding that the perpetrator is not legally responsible if at the time of the act he or she, owing to mental disease or defect, lacked "substantial capacity" either to appreciate its criminal character or to conform his or her behavior to the law's requirements.
5. *The Federal Insanity Defense Reform Act (IDRA).* Adopted by Congress in 1984 as the standard regarding the insanity defense to be applied in all federal jurisdictions, this act abolished the volitional element of the ALI standard and modified the cognitive one to read "unable to appreciate," thus bringing the definition quite close to M'Naughten. IDRA also specified that the mental disorder involved must be a severe one, and it shifted the burden of proof from the prosecution to the defense; that is, the defense must clearly and convincingly establish the defendant's insanity, as opposed to the prior requirement that the prosecution must clearly and convincingly demonstrate the defendant to have been sane when the prohibited act was committed.

This shifting of the burden of proof for the insanity defense, by the way, was an extremely common reform instituted by the states in the wake of protests of excessive laxity provoked by the Hinckley acquittal. Like the many other types of reform proposed at that time, the intent was to discourage use of the insanity defense and to make its success improbable if it *were* used. Unlike the average reform instituted, this one proved quite effective in altering litigation practices in the intended direction, according to the extensive data gathered by Steadman and colleagues (1993).

At the present time, most states and the District of Columbia subscribe to a version of either the ALI standard or the more restrictive M'Naughten Rule. New York is a special case. While it uses a version of M'Naughten to define insanity, with the burden of proof on the defense, an elaborate procedural code has been enacted, whose effect is to promote fairness in outcomes while ensuring lengthy and restrictive hospital commitment for defendants judged to be dangerous; it appears to have worked well (Steadman et al., 1993). In some jurisdictions, when an insanity plea is filed, the case is submitted for pretrial screening, which includes a psychiatric evaluation, review of records, and appraisal of criminal responsibility. In one study of 190 defendants who entered a plea of not criminally responsible, the following outcomes were obtained: 105 were judged to be criminally responsible; charges on 34 were dropped; 8 defendants were assessed by both the prosecution and defense to be insane and not responsible. A total of 134 withdrew their insanity pleas (Janofsky, Dunn, et al., 1996). The insanity defense was thought in this study to be somewhat of a "rich man's defense" in that such cases involved private attorneys rather than public defenders.

In another study, Silver (1995) found that the successful use of the NGRI defense varied widely between states. In addition, Silver reported that the length of confinement was related more to the judged seriousness of the crime than to whether the person was employing an NGRI defense. One study (Cirinclone, Steadman, & McGreevy, 1995) found that an NGRI plea was most likely to be successful if one or more of the following factors were present:

- The defendant had a diagnosed mental disorder, particularly a major mental disorder.
- The defendant was female.
- The violent crime was other than murder.
- There had been prior mental hospitalizations.

Three states—Idaho, Montana, and Utah—entirely abolished the attribution of insanity as an acceptable defense for wrongdoing, a somewhat draconian solution that compensates in clarity for what some feel it lacks in compassion. As expected, insanity acquittals did, in fact, decline in those states. However, in Montana, there was a corresponding rise in the use of "incompetent to stand trial" in which the charges were actually dismissed, in large part, negating the "desired result" of doing away with the insanity defense (Callahan, Robbins, et al., 1995).

As we have seen, with the expansion of the diagnostic classification of mental disorder, a broad range of behaviors can be defined as mental disease or defect. Which mental diseases serve to excuse a defendant from criminal responsibility? Generally, under the M'Naughten Rule, psychotic disorders were the basis of the insanity defense, although that would appear an arguable proposition; but under the Durham Rule or ALI standard, other conditions

HIGHLIGHT 15.2

Who Should Pay for the Crime—One or All?

Possibly the most bizarrely fascinating of controversial insanity pleas are those raised by the phenomenon of multiple personality disorder, now called *dissociative identity disorder* (DID), which we discussed in Chapter 7. The general nature of the problem can be stated quite succinctly: Within a legal system strongly oriented to the precise identification of *individual* responsibility for acts, what, if any, are the limits of the assignment of responsibility and the imposition of sanctions for infractions of the law when the same physical space and body are occupied at different times by more than one distinct and legally recognizable person? Should an individual, as the primary personality, be held legally accountable for, say, a capital crime that evidence suggests may have actually been committed surreptitiously, so to speak, by an alter personality?

The scenario just mentioned has rather often been the contention underlying an NGRI plea. Usually, as in the case of the Hillside Strangler, Kenneth Bianchi (convicted of 12 rapes and murders in California and Washington State), or in the case of a woman who kidnapped a newborn from a hospital and later claimed that an alter personality actually committed the crime (Appelbaum & Greer, 1994), it has failed. On a very few occasions, however, the NGRI plea in association with a claim that the actual criminal was a DID alter has worked, as in the well-publicized 1978 case of Ohio resident Billy Milligan, claiming to be host to ten personalities and accused of raping four women (*New York Times,* May 9, 1994).

The legal maneuvers inspired by the DID construct admittedly have a quality of whimsy about them. It is consequently difficult to convince most juries that the defendant was so taken over by an alter personality who perpetrated the crime that he or she should thereby be absolved of guilt and responsibility. ■

(such as personality disorder or dissociative disorder) might also apply.

How, then, is guilt or innocence determined? Many authorities believe that the insanity defense requires of the courts an impossible task—to determine guilt or innocence by reason of insanity on the basis of psychiatric testimony. Perlin (1996) reported that there is actually high agreement among experts as to the defendant's sanity; in a number of cases, conflicting testimony has resulted because both the prosecution and the defense have "their" panel of expert psychiatric witnesses, who are in complete disagreement (Fersch, 1980; Marvit, 1981).

It may well be that the notion "not guilty by reason of insanity," while defensible and humane in some abstract sense, is so flawed conceptually and procedurally that a serious rethinking of the entire matter is needed. Meanwhile, it would seem wise to employ stringent standards for the insanity defense, such as the federal IDRA rules or the relevant and carefully considered statutory procedures enacted in New York State (see Steadman et al., 1993, for details).

Finally, it should be noted that several states have adopted the optional plea/verdict of **guilty but mentally ill (GBMI).** In these cases, a defendant may be sentenced but placed in a treatment facility rather than in a prison. This two-part judgment serves to prevent the type of situation in which a person commits a murder, is found not guilty by reason of insanity, is turned over to a mental health facility, is found to be rational and in no further need of treatment by the hospital staff, and is unconditionally released to the community after only a minimal period of confinement. Under the two-part decision, such a person would remain in the custody of the correctional department until the full sentence was served. Marvit (1981) has suggested that this approach might "realistically balance the interest of the mentally ill offender's rights and the community's need to control criminal behavior" (p. 23). However, in Georgia, one of the states adopting this option, GBMI defendants received longer sentences and longer periods of confinement than those pleading NGRI and losing. Overall, outcomes from use of the GBMI plea, often employed in a plea-bargaining strategy, have been disappointing (Steadman et al., 1993).

guilty but mentally ill (GBMI) Optional guilty plea adopted by some states that allows a defendant to be sentenced but placed in a treatment facility rather than in a prison.

Deinstitutionalization

The population of psychiatric patients in the United States has shrunk considerably over the past 30 years. Between 1970 and 1992 alone, the number of state mental hospitals dropped from 310 to 273 and the patient population was reduced by 73 percent (Witkin, Atay, & Manderscheid, 1998). **Deinstitutionalization**—the movement to close mental hospitals and to treat persons with severe mental disorders in the community—has been the source of considerable controversy. Some authorities consider the emptying of the mental hospitals to be a positive expression of society's desire to free previously confined persons, while others speak of the "abandonment" of chronic patients to a cruel and harsh existence, which for many includes homelessness. Many citizens, too, complain of being harassed, intimidated, and frightened by obviously disturbed persons wandering the streets of their neighborhoods. The problems are real enough, but they have come about to a large extent because the planned community efforts to fill the gaps in service never really materialized at effective levels (Grob, 1994).

There was indeed a significant reduction in state and county mental hospital populations, from over a half million in 1950 (Lerman, 1981) to about 100,000 in the 1990s (Narrow et al., 1993); these figures are even more staggering when we consider that the U.S. population grew by nearly 100 million during the same period. A number of factors interacted to alter the pattern of mental hospital admissions and discharges over this period. As has been noted in previous chapters, the introduction of the antipsychotic drugs made it possible for many patients who would formerly have required confinement to be released into the community. The availability of these drugs led many to believe (falsely) that all mental health problems could be managed with medication. In addition, the changing treatment philosophy and the desire to eliminate mental institutions were accompanied by the belief that society wanted and could financially afford to provide better community-based care for chronic patients outside of large mental hospitals.

In theory, the movement to close the public mental hospitals seemed workable. According to plan, many community-based mental health centers would be opened and would provide continuing care to the residents of hospitals after their discharge. Residents would be given welfare funds (supposedly costing the government less than it takes to maintain large mental hospitals) and would be prescribed medication to keep them stabilized until they could obtain continuing care. Many patients would be discharged to home and family, while others would be placed in smaller, home-like board-and-care facilities or nursing homes.

deinstitutionalization Movement to close mental hospitals and to treat people with severe mental disorders in the community.

Some homeless people, casualties of indiscriminate deinstitutionalization, are seriously mentally disordered.

Many unforeseen problems arose, however. Many residents of mental institutions had no families or homes to go to; board-and-care facilities were often substandard; the community mental health centers were ill-prepared and insufficiently funded to provide needed services for chronic patients, particularly as national funding priorities shifted during the 1980s (Humphreys & Rappaport, 1993); many patients had not been carefully selected for discharge and were not ready for community living; and many of those who were discharged were not followed up sufficiently or with enough regularity to ensure their successful adaptation outside the hospital. One court case (*Albright* v. *Abington Memorial Hospital,* 1997) involved charges that the hospital failed to p rovide sufficient care for a seriously disturbed woman who later killed herself in a fire. Countless patients were discharged to fates that were even more harsh than the conditions in any of the hospitals (Westermeyer, 1987). The following case illustrates the situation.

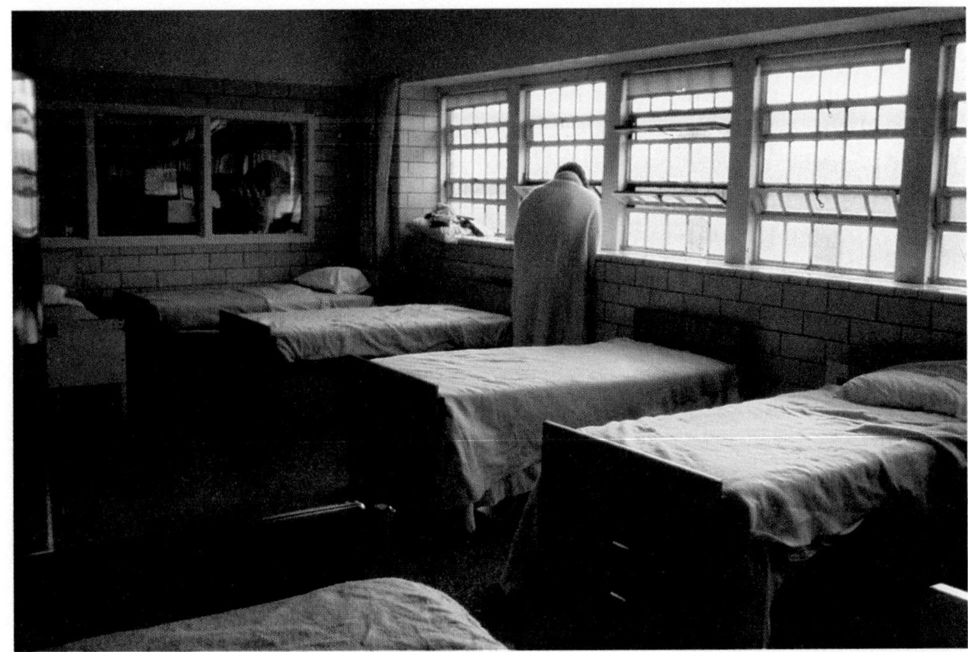

The extent of problems created by deinstitutionalization is not fully known, but some evidence suggests that the emptying of mental hospitals has contributed to the number of homeless people. Deinstitutionalization is not likely to be successful unless adequate continuing care is available in the community, and unless it allows for readmission to the hospital for short periods if necessary.

Case Study From Deinstitutionalization to Homelessness and Back • Dave B., 49 years old, had been hospitalized for 25 years in a state mental hospital. When the hospital was scheduled for phase-out, many of the patients, particularly those who were regressed or aggressive, were transferred to another state hospital. Dave was a borderline mentally retarded man who had periodic episodes of psychosis. At the time of hospital closing, however, he was not hallucinating and was "reasonably intact." Dave was considered to be one of the "less disturbed" residents because his psychotic behavior was less pronounced and he presented no problems of dangerousness.

He was discharged to a board-and-care facility (actually, an old hotel whose clientele consisted mostly of former inpatients). At first, Dave seemed to fit in well at the facility; mostly, he sat in his room or in the outside hallway, and he caused no trouble for the caretakers. Two weeks after he arrived, he wandered off the hotel grounds and was missing for several days. The police eventually found him living in the city dump. He had apparently quit taking his medication, and when he was discovered, he was regressed and catatonic. He was readmitted to a state hospital.

Homelessness By the early 1980s, cases like Dave's had become commonplace in large cities throughout the nation. Vagrants and "bag ladies" appeared in abundance on city streets and in transport terminals, and the virtually constantly overwhelmed shelters for homeless persons hastily expanded in futile efforts to contain the tide of recently discharged patients. Street crime soared, as did the death rate among these hapless persons, who were for the most part wholly lacking in survival resources for the harsh urban environment. As Westermeyer (1982a) noted:

> Patients are returned to the community, armed with drugs to control their illness. The worst aspects of their illnesses may be under control. But many of the patients are not ready to function in society. They need a gradual reintroduction—facilities where someone else can see that they take their drugs, see their psychiatrists, get food, clothing, and shelter. Such care is too often more than families can provide and such services are not generally available in a community. As a result, the numbers of bag ladies and men, vagrants and mentally disabled people, living in lonely hotels and dangerous streets, have burgeoned. (p. 2)

The full extent of problems created by deinstitutionalization is not precisely known. The ambiguity comes, in part, from the scarcity of rigorous follow-up data on patients who have been discharged from mental hospitals. There have not been a sufficient number of adequate research studies in this area. Moreover, such research investigations have tended to be difficult to conduct because the patients are transient and are hard to keep track of over time. Certainly, not all homeless people are former mental patients, but evidence suggests that deinstitutionalization has contributed substantially to the number of homeless people (Lamb, 1984) and to the number of mentally ill people in prison (Butterfield, 1998; Powell, Holt, & Fondacaro, 1997). Researchers have also demonstrated that a greater percentage of homeless people than of people with homes have significant psychopathology, as reflected in higher rates of hospitalization and felony convictions (see Fischer et al., 1986). More recently, Rossi (1990) estimated that 33 percent of homeless individuals suffer from chronic mental disorder. Goldfinger, Schutt, and colleagues (1996) reported that 84 percent of the homeless people in their study abused various substances.

In spite of the problems just described, some data on patient discharge and outcome status support the deinstitutionalization process (Braun et al., 1981) These same researchers, however, also concluded that deinstitutionalization is likely to be unsuccessful if continuing care in the community is not available or if it is inadequate.

The various approaches that have been implemented to circumvent patient failures to readjust to the community have not been particularly successful at reducing hospital readmissions and therefore at further reducing the average daily census in state hospitals. Nevertheless, advocates for deinstitutionalization continue to maintain that this is the most desirable approach to treating the chronically mentally ill. The controversy over deinstitutionalization is likely to continue, with advocates on both sides of the issue, until more definitive research is conducted.

Who Is Hospitalized? Meanwhile, the extent to which private (as opposed to publicly supported) mental health care, particularly private hospitalization, has expanded to fill at least part of the gap left by deinstitutionalization and inadequate funding for community mental health centers is not generally recognized. Deinstitutionalization notwithstanding, some 70 percent of all the dollars spent on mental health care are spent for hospitalization, much of it of the acute, short-term variety. These data, gathered by Kiesler and Simpkins (1993; Kiesler, 1993), indicate that the national investment in this relatively very costly type of approach is a huge one—constituting an "unnoticed majority" of the total mental health intervention effort of the nation. Many of these inpatient stays, moreover, occur in nonspecialized (i.e., nonpsychiatric) units of general hospitals, a setting whose overall effectiveness in dealing with mental patients is questionable.

Care in specialized, private mental hospitals or in specialized psychiatric units of private medical centers has long been an option for those families able to afford it. However, the mental health system appears to be undergoing considerable change at this time, due in large part to changes in funding for mental health care, with the result already noted. There has been some "privatization" of the mental health system (Dorwart et al., 1989), in cases where private insurance companies have agreed to cover the cost of inpatient mental health services. Several large private hospital corporations have, to some extent, filled the treatment void left by the public mental hospital cutbacks and are providing inpatient psychiatric care for a large number of patients currently receiving any type of formal treatment. **Health maintenance organizations (HMOs),** or companies that provide health care services for a fee from each patient (sometimes paid in full or in part by employers), tend to place limits on inpatient care as well as outpatient treatment. The demographics of the inpatient population have shifted in favor of a more socioeconomically advantaged group—that is, those who have medical insurance that contains provisions for psychiatric hospitalization. Because mental disorders are often chronic, this type of insurance tends to be very expensive (and hence aversive to employers), excluding many persons and families in less than affluent circumstances and limiting inpatient stays. With the continuing downsizing of public facilities, where do people with mental disorders go? Some of them, as we have seen, go into the streets.

Another related development in the care of chronic mental patients is the growth and expansion of private nursing home facilities, particularly for the elderly mentally disordered. Since the deinstitutionalization movement spurred the discharge of psychiatric patients into the community, alternative care facilities have expanded to fill the need for continued care (Morlock, 1989). This expansion of facilities for the elderly has been made possible through financial incentives provided by Medicare to fund treatment. Nursing homes have become the most common setting of care for the chronically mentally ill.

The federal government faces the problem of how to cope with the enormous costs involved in attempting to provide adequate and universal medical insurance coverage for all citizens. A huge part of the problem of needed health care reform is related to the escalating costs of hospitalization, felt by many to be out of control. It remains to be seen at this point whether the mental health sector will receive due consideration in whatever arrangements are finally enacted by Congress. A factor of considerable importance here is the possibility that private hospitalization has come to be overutilized, relative to other less expensive but at least equally effective forms of intervention (e.g., outpatient care), in the mental health and substance abuse arenas (Kiesler, 1993; Kiesler & Simpkins, 1993; VandenBos, 1993). Plausible alternatives that do not involve inpatient care include enhanced preventive intervention and rehabilitative psychotherapy (VandenBos, 1993).

health maintenance organization (HMO) A company that provides health care services to employers and individuals for a fixed prepaid fee.

IN REVIEW

- What conditions must be met before an individual can be involuntarily committed to a mental institution? Describe the legal process that follows.
- What is meant by the insanity or NGRI defense in criminal cases?
- Define *deinstitutionalization.* What factors drove this movement, and what problems have unfortunately resulted?

PERSPECTIVES ON PREVENTION

In the past, the concepts of primary, secondary, and tertiary prevention were widely used in public health to describe general strategies of disease prevention. These terms were derived from public health strategies employed for understanding and controlling infectious physical diseases, and were thought to provide a useful perspective in the mental health field as well.

However, for years, there was a relative lack of progress in prevention (Albee, 1996). Heller (1996), for example, noted: "Until the last decade anything approaching a true prevention science did not exist" (p. 1124). In the early 1990s, the U.S. Congress directed the National Institute of Mental Health (NIMH) to work with the Institute of Medicine (IOM) to develop a report detailing a long-term prevention research program. Among other things, the IOM report provided a new conceptualization that clarified the definitions of "prevention" so as to focus attention on the distinction between prevention and treatment efforts (Munoz, Mrazek, & Haggerty, 1996). Prevention efforts are now classified into three subcategories:

1. *Universal interventions:* Efforts that are aimed at influencing the general population.
2. *Selective interventions:* Efforts that are aimed at a specific subgroup of the population considered at risk for developing certain mental health problems—for example, adolescents or ethnic minorities.
3. *Indicated interventions:* Efforts that are directed to high-risk individuals who are identified as having minimal but detectable symptoms of mental disorder but who do not meet criteria for clinical diagnosis—for example, individuals forced from their homes due to a flood or some other disaster.

As shown in Figure 15.1, preventive efforts are clearly differentiated from treatment and maintenance interventions.

Universal Interventions

Universal interventions are concerned with two key tasks: (1) altering conditions that can cause or contribute to mental disorders (risk factors) and (2) establishing conditions that foster positive mental health (protective factors). Epidemiological studies (as discussed in Chapter 1) are particularly important in this area because they help investigators obtain information about the incidence and distribution of various maladaptive behaviors needing prevention efforts (Dohrenwend, 1998). These findings can then be used to suggest preventive efforts that might be most appropriate. For example, various epidemiological studies and reviews have shown certain groups to be at high risk for mental disorders: recently divorced people (Bloom, Asher, & White, 1978); the physically disabled (Freeman, Malkin, & Hastings, 1975); elderly people living alone (Neugarten, 1977); physically abused children (Malinosky-Rummel & Hansen, 1993); and people who have been uprooted from their homes (Westermeyer, Williams, & Nguyen, 1991). Although findings such as these may be the basis for immediate selective or indicated preventions, they may also aid in universal preventions by revealing what to look for and where to look—in essence, by focusing efforts in the right direction. Universal preventions include biological, psychosocial, and sociocultural efforts. Virtually any effort that is aimed at improving the human condition, at making life more fulfilling and meaningful, is considered to be part of universal prevention of mental disorder.

Biological Measures Biologically based strategies for universal prevention begin with developing adaptive lifestyles. Many of the goals of health psychology (see Chapter 8) can be viewed as universal prevention strategies. Such efforts geared toward improving diet, establishing a routine of physical exercise, and developing overall good health habits can do much to improve physical well-being. To the extent that physical illness always produces some sort of psychological stress that can result in such problems as depression, good health is preventive with respect to mental health problems.

Psychosocial Measures Viewing normality as optimal development and high functioning rather than the mere absence of pathology as the goal implies that people need

universal interventions Prevention efforts aimed at influencing the general population and intended to reduce risk factors and enhance protective factors

propriate information and having practice at resisting others around them, adolescents can make stick a decision *not* to use alcohol or drugs. The visible success of these programs has come to the attention of educators in other school districts, and a number of efforts are under way to "export" these programs for broader use in U.S. schools. Recently, the Northland approach has been adapted for a prevention project in Russia as a means of fighting alcohol abuse—one of the most serious health problems in that country (Grechanaia, Romanova, et al., 1997).

Indicated Interventions

Indicated interventions emphasize the early detection and prompt treatment of maladaptive behavior in a person's family and community setting. In some cases—for example, in a crisis or after a disaster—indicated prevention consists of immediate and relatively brief intervention to prevent any long-term behavioral consequences. We will later examine in some depth an indicated prevention effort after an airplane crash.

Crisis Intervention Often, people in crisis are in a state of acute turmoil and feel overwhelmed and incapable of dealing with the stress by themselves. They do not have time to wait for the customary initial therapy appointment, nor are they usually in a position to continue therapy over a sustained period of time. They need immediate assistance. Crisis intervention has emerged in response to a widespread need for immediate help for individuals and families confronted with especially stressful situations—whether disasters or family situations that have become intolerable (Butcher & Dunn, 1989; Everly, 1995; Greenfield, Hechtman, & Tremblay, 1995; Morgan, 1995). Two approaches are widely used for crisis intervention: (1) short-term crisis therapy, involving face-to-face discussion, and (2) telephone hotlines, which are usually handled either by professional mental health personnel or by paraprofessionals—laypersons who have been trained for this work.

Short-Term Crisis Intervention **Short-term crisis therapy,** as the name implies, is of brief duration and focuses on the immediate problem of an emotional nature with which an individual or family is having difficulty. In crisis situations, a therapist is usually very active, helping to clarify the problem, suggesting plans of action, providing reassurance, and otherwise giving needed information and support. In essence, the therapist tries to provide as much help as the individual or family will accept. If the problem involves psychological disturbance in one of the family members, emphasis is usually placed on mobilizing the support of other family members. Often, this enables the person to avoid hospitalization and a disruption of family life. Short-term crisis intervention may also involve bringing other mental health or medical personnel into the treatment picture. Most individuals and families who come for short-term crisis therapy do not continue in treatment for more than one to six sessions.

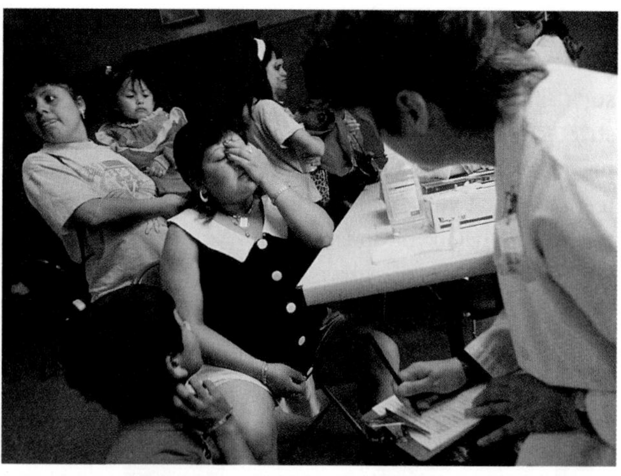

The provision of crisis counseling during the aftermath of a disaster—in this case, the Los Angeles earthquake—has been shown to reduce long-term maladaptive reactions.

indicated interventions Prevention efforts directed toward individuals already showing maladaptive behavior and intended to keep it from becoming a long-term problem.

short-term crisis therapy Brief treatment that focuses on the immediate emotional problem with which an individual or family is having difficulty.

Telephone Hotline The telephone hotline has become a common approach to dealing with people undergoing crises. Today, all major cities in the United States and most smaller ones have some form of telephone hotline to help people undergoing periods of severe stress. Although the threat of suicide is the most dramatic example, the range of problems that people call about is virtually unlimited—from breaking up with someone to being on a bad drug trip. In addition, there are specific hotlines in many communities for rape victims and for runaways who need assistance.

As in other crisis interventions, a person handling hotline calls is confronted with the problem of rapidly assessing what is wrong and how bad it is. Even if an accurate assessment is possible and the hotline worker does everything within his or her power to help the caller, a distraught person may hang up without leaving any name, telephone number, or address. This can be a deeply disturbing experience for the hotline counselor—particularly if, for example, the caller has announced that he or she has just swallowed a lethal dose of sleeping pills. Even in less severe cases, of course, the hotline worker may never learn whether the caller's problem has been solved. In other instances, however, the caller may be induced to come in for counseling, making more personal contact possible.

For a therapist or volunteer counselor, crisis therapy can be the most discouraging of any intervention approach that we have discussed in this book. The urgency of the intervention and the frequent inability to provide any therapeutic closure or follow-up are probably key factors in this discouragement. Free clinics and crisis centers have reported that their counselors—many of whom are volunteers—tend to burn out after a short period of time. Despite the high frustration level of this work, however, crisis intervention counselors fill a crucial need in the mental health field, particularly for the young people who make up most of their clients. This need is recognized by the many community mental health centers and general hospitals that provide emergency psychological services, through either hotlines or walk-in services. For thousands of people in desperate trouble, an invaluable social support is provided by the fact that there is somewhere they can go for immediate help or someone they can call who will listen to their problems and try to help them. Thus, the continuing need for crisis intervention services and telephone hotlines is evident.

An Illustration of Indicated Prevention The immediate consequences of an air crash are devastating. Survivors typically have traumatic responses to the accident that impair their immediate functioning and place great demands on their psychological adjustment for weeks after the disaster. Family members of victims often experience extensive psychological trauma after the accident; they may need to make extensive changes during their loved one's lengthy recovery period or to make major life changes to adjust to their loved one's death. Even rescue personnel caught up in dealing with the aftermath of an airline disaster may suffer from post-traumatic stress disorder.

In many respects, the emotional responses of and adjustive demands placed on air crash victims are similar to those of victims of natural disasters, such as hurricanes, floods, earthquakes, and volcanic eruptions (McFarlane, Clayer, & Bookless, 1997). A number of special considerations, however, influence the intensity of the problems that are seen following airplane crashes: Typically, airplane crashes are sudden and unexpected; they are usually quite chaotic in terms of their destruction; and they usually occur away from one's familiar settings. Consequently, the sense of community that characterizes response to many disasters is lacking. In addition, the impact of an air disaster affects a larger number of people than those immediately involved in the accident itself.

Air disasters differ from natural disasters in another important respect—they usually involve considerable blame and anger that can aggravate or intensify the emotional reactions of survivors even months after the crash. Most airports are required to have a disaster plan that includes rescue and evacuation procedures to deal with an airplane crash. Some airport disaster plans have incorporated a psychological support program to provide emergency mental health services to survivors and the family members of crash victims as well as to rescue workers (Butcher & Dunn, 1989; Carlier, Lambert, & Gersons, 1997).

These programs are viewed as indicated prevention efforts in that they are aimed at providing emergency psychological services in order to prevent the development of psychological disorders or to reduce the severity of such problems if they occur. Three types of indicated prevention have been shown to be effective in dealing with the psychological problems related to air disasters: (1) immediate crisis intervention services to crash survivors and surviving family members; (2) crisis telephone hotline services to provide information and referrals to victims who lack crisis intervention services; and (3) post-disaster debriefing sessions for secondary victims, such as rescue personnel, affected by the disaster. We will look at each of these services briefly.

Immediate Crisis Intervention Services Timing is critical to crisis intervention, which, when supplied in the immediate aftermath of a disaster, can reduce the emotional distress experienced and can result in a more effective future psychological adjustment (Butcher & Hatcher, 1988). Crisis intervention treatment involves providing a victim with an opportunity to express his or her intense feelings about the incident to a supportive, understanding specialist.

First of all, a crisis counselor provides objective emotional support and tries to provide a long-term perspective—to allow victims to see that there is hope of surviving psychologically. A crisis counselor also serves as a source of information and a buffer against misinformation coming from rumor. Disasters are always followed by periods of confusion, misinformation, and negative emotional states. One important role of the mental health professional in disaster response efforts is to obtain, decipher, and clearly communicate to victims the most accurate picture of the situation obtainable at the moment.

Finally, a crisis counselor provides practical suggestions to promote adaptation. In an extreme crisis, people often lose perspective and "forget" that they are usually quite effective in dealing with life problems. An important facet of the mental health professional's role in dealing with disaster victims is to guide them through the difficult times by providing a perspective on the problems being faced and by offering valuable guidance for alleviating those problems.

Telephone Hotline Crisis Counseling Services After an air disaster, confusion prevails, as does considerable psychological turmoil among passengers and crew members. Inaccurate information and anxiety-producing doubts can create a state of tension that results in demoralization and negative behavior, such as absenteeism from work, excessive drinking, and morale problems.

An effective way to deal with this psychological uncertainty and reduce the negative atmosphere following an air disaster is to provide telephone counseling services—an informational hotline of sorts—for all those who feel the need to discuss their concerns, whether airline employees or the families of passengers. For example, a 24-hour telephone hotline crisis counseling service was established shortly after the crash of an airliner in Detroit, Michigan, in 1987 in which 156 people died; it continued in operation for 4 weeks. This service was staffed by psychologists qualified in crisis management, who provided counseling, information, and referral services.

Post-disaster Debriefing Sessions Those who appear to function well at the disaster site may experience difficulties after the immediate crisis has subsided, and they have returned to family and normal duties. Even experienced disaster workers who are well trained and effective at the site can be affected later by the pressures and problems experienced during the disaster.

The desire to "unwind" in a psychologically safe environment and to share one's experience of the disaster are universal needs of people following a traumatic situation. Debriefing sessions are designed to provide those who might be directly affected by the accident an opportunity to relate their experiences and to express their feelings and concerns about the disaster. Chemtob and colleagues (1997), for example, have explored the use of debriefing sessions—sessions designed to allow victims to describe their experiences and learn about the reactions of others—and found this approach to be effective in reducing the emotional reactions to traumatic events.

Immediate crisis intervention, telephone hotline counseling services, and debriefing programs have become standard efforts following major disasters to help victims and emergency workers return more quickly and effectively to normal functioning. By reducing the impact of a tragedy, these programs attempt to prevent the development of more severe psychological disorders.

IN REVIEW

- What are the three subcategories of prevention efforts that arose from the IOM redefinition of "prevention"?
- What are some strategies for biological, psychosocial, and sociocultural universal interventions?
- Define *selective intervention.* What are some selective intervention programs that have shown promise in prevention of teenage alcohol and drug abuse?
- What is meant by *indicated intervention*?

CHALLENGES FOR THE FUTURE

Public awareness of the magnitude and severity of the contemporary mental health problem and the interest of government, professional, and lay organizations have prompted programs directed at better understanding, more effective treatment, and long-range prevention. Efforts to improve mental health are apparent not only in the United States but also in many other countries; they involve a maze of local, national, and international organizations and efforts. To name but a few, in the United States, federal agencies such as the National Institute of Mental Health (NIMH), the National Institute on Drug Abuse (NIDA), and the National Institute on Alcohol Abuse and Alcoholism (NIAAA) are devoted to promoting varied research, training, and service. State and county government agencies may focus their efforts on the delivery of mental health services to residents on an inpatient or outpatient basis.

Mental health programs in the United States are also the concern of several professional organizations, many corporations, and a number of voluntary mental health organizations. In addition, international organizations, such as the World Health Organization (WHO) and the World Federation for Mental Health, have contributed to mental health programs worldwide.

Through the efforts of these organizations and others, more and more mental health problems can be expected to yield to scientific analysis their causes and thus their treatment and prevention. The 1990s witnessed an amazing openness and a diminishing of previously impassable borders. Along with this increased interchange of ideas and greater cooperation will come a broader collaboration on mental health problems. Reductions in international tension and a greater international cooperation in the sciences and in health planning will likely promote more sharing of information on mental health. The greatest future challenge may be not in making vast strides in understanding mental health problems, but more in using the discoveries to help people in need.

The Crisis in Mental Health Care

We have seen in this chapter that mental health treatment is valuable for preventing as well as easing mental disorders. Yet getting such treatment can be difficult, if not impossible, for many. Over the past decade, as costs for general health care have risen dramatically (Giles, 1993; O'Connor, 1996), mental health treatment has become less readily available and less often reimbursed (Glazer & Gray, 1996; Resnick et al., 1994).

Managed health care has resulted in programs that differ widely in the type and quality of mental health services provided. Although their stated intention is to provide the most effective treatments available, decisions about treatment provision are often based more on business factors than on treatment considerations. HMOs that are overly cost-conscious have come to be viewed by many in the field as tending to business to the neglect of patients' needs (Hoyt & Austad, 1992; Karon, 1995; Schreter, Sharfstein, & Schreter, 1994). Unfortunately, mental health treatment can often be a target for cost-cutting—its urgency does not seem as great as repairing a ruptured appendix or a blocked artery.

The mental health services typically covered by HMOs tend to be the less expensive and less labor-intensive treatment approaches. As might be expected, pharmacotherapy is the most frequent mental health treatment provided by HMOs. About 10 percent of the U.S. population is prescribed some psychoactive medication each year (Klerman et al., 1994). Interestingly, more psychoactive medication is now prescribed by primary care physicians than by psychiatrists. Some HMOs have advocated the expanded use of somatic therapies in an attempt to contain costs. Psychosocial interventions such as individual psychotherapy are discouraged or limited to relatively few sessions. Long-term psychotherapy has been virtually eliminated for all but a small number of wealthy private clients (Lazarus, 1996). On the other hand, group psychotherapy is often promoted and encouraged because it is thought of as being cost-effective.

Most managed health care corporations have adopted the model of providing focused, brief, intermittent mental health treatment for most problems (Cummings, 1995; Hoyt & Austad, 1992). Patients who require longer treatments or need inpatient hospitalization are typically not well served by such organizations (Gabbard, 1994). In fact, long-term mental health treatment is typically discouraged by managed health care organizations. For example, most such organizations approve only short inpatient stays (less than 10 days) and four to six sessions of outpatient mental health treatment at a time. Few if any of the decisions regarding the amount and type of services provided are directly guided by empirical criteria. Decisions as to whether to cover 8 or 20 sessions of psychotherapy, for example, are arbitrary and often seem capricious both to the practitioner and to the patient (Harwood et al., 1997).

A clear divide has developed between mental health service providers and managers. Available services are often governed more by financial concerns than by the judgments of mental health professionals. Practitioners, as a result, are expressing outrage over the situation. One psychologist (Sank, 1997) suggested that ethics charges be filed against mental health professionals who violate patient-therapist confidentiality agreements by disclosing the process of therapy to HMOs. Lawsuits have been directed at HMOs for failing to provide appropriate and needed service. Managed health care organizations are likely to face claims of negligence as a result of their legal exposure and obligation to provide services (Benda & Rozovsky, 1997). It appears likely that conflict will be prominent over the next few years as managed health care corporations assume more control over the mental health system. Some independent psychologists and psychiatrists have left the field because they could no longer earn a livable income from conducting psychotherapy.

Critics of managed care argue that there is no convincing evidence that current efforts are actually controlling costs (Gabbard, 1994; Harwood et al., 1997) and no scientific support for the limited benefit options currently being exercised (England, 1994). Some have pointed out that the administrative costs for managed care (including high salaries for HMO executives) are exorbitant. Gabbard (1994), for example, estimated that about one-fourth of the health care expenditures in the United States go for managed care administration.

managed health care System for securing health care services from hospitals, physicians, and other providers for a designated population, with the goal of holding down costs.

The revolution in health care has clearly created controversy in the field of psychotherapy. The mental health field is being drastically altered by economic considerations. These problems are likely to continue as society attempts to come to terms with the cost of health care and the need to provide care for citizens who desperately need help. One thing appears to be certain: The nature of the mental health professions is changing. Whether these changes are for better or for worse is yet to be determined.

The Need for Planning

Beyond the need for better individual care, it seems imperative that more effective planning be done at community, national, and international levels if mental health problems are going to be reduced or eliminated. Many challenges must be met to create a better world for ourselves and future generations. Without slackening efforts to meet mental health needs at home, the United States will probably find it increasingly essential to participate more broadly in international measures toward reducing group tensions and promoting mental health and a better world for people everywhere. At the same time, measures undertaken to reduce international conflict and improve the general condition of humankind should make their contribution to this nation's social progress and mental health. Both kinds of measures will require understanding and moral commitment from concerned citizens.

Within the United States, as well as the rest of the industrialized world, progress in prolonging life has brought with it burgeoning problems in the prevalence of disorders associated with advanced age, particularly the dementing conditions such as Alzheimer's disease. As was noted in Chapter 13, there can be no assurance the means of eradicating or arresting this threat will be found before it has become overwhelming in terms of the numbers of people affected. Planning and preparation would seem the only rational hope of forestalling a potential disaster of unprecedented yet predictable magnitude; we need to make a beginning.

The Individual's Contribution

> Each man can make a difference, and each man should try.
> —John F. Kennedy

The history of abnormal psychology provides clear examples of individuals whose efforts were instrumental in changing thinking about problems. Philippe Pinel took off the chains, Dorothea Dix initiated a movement to improve the conditions of asylums, and Clifford Beers inspired the modern mental health movement with his autobiographical account of his own experience with mental illness. Who may lead the next revolution in mental health is anyone's guess. What is clear is that a great deal can be accomplished by individual effort.

When students become aware of the tremendous scope of the mental health problem, both nationally and internationally, and the woefully inadequate facilities for coping with it, they often ask, "What can I do?" Thus, it seems appropriate to suggest a few of the lines of action interested individuals can profitably take.

Many opportunities in mental health work are open to trained personnel, both professional and paraprofessional. Social work, clinical psychology, psychiatry, and other mental health occupations are rewarding in terms of personal fulfillment. In addition, many occupations, ranging from law enforcement to teaching and the ministry, can and do play key roles in the mental health and well-being of many people. Training in all these fields usually offers individuals opportunities to work in community clinics and related facilities, to gain experience in understanding the needs and problems of people in distress, and to become familiar with community resources.

Citizens can find many ways to be of direct service if they are familiar with national and international resources and programs, and if they invest the effort necessary to learn about their community's special needs and problems. Whatever one's role in life—student, teacher, police officer, lawyer, homemaker, business executive, or trade unionist—one's interests are directly at stake. For although the mental health of a nation may be manifested in many ways—in its purposes, courage, moral responsibility, scientific and cultural achievements, and quality of daily life—its health and resources derive ultimately from the individuals within it. In a participatory democracy, it is they who plan and implement the nation's goals.

Besides accepting some measure of responsibility for the mental health of others through the quality of one's own interpersonal relationships, there are several other constructive courses of action open to each citizen, including (1) serving as a volunteer in a mental hospital, community mental health center, or service organization; (2) supporting realistic measures for ensuring comprehensive health services for all age groups; and (3) working toward improved public education, responsible government, the alleviation of group prejudice, and the establishment of a more sane and harmonious world.

All of us are concerned with mental health for personal as well as altruistic reasons, for we want to overcome the harassing problems of contemporary living and find our share of happiness in a meaningful and fulfilling life. To do so, we may sometimes need the courage to admit that our problems are too much for us. When existence seems futile or the going becomes too difficult, it may help to remind ourselves of the following basic facts, which have been emphasized throughout this text: From time to time, each of us has serious difficulties in coping with the problems of living. During such crisis periods, we may need psychological and related assistance. Such difficulties are not a disgrace; they can happen to anyone if the stress is sufficiently severe. The early detection and correction of maladaptive behavior is of great importance in preventing the development of more severe or chronic conditions. Preventive measures—primary, secondary, and tertiary—are the most effective long-range approach to the solution of both individual and group mental health problems.

Recognizing these facts is essential because statistics show that almost all of us will at some time in our lives have to deal with severely maladaptive behavior or mental disorder either in ourselves or in someone close to us. Our interdependence and the loss to us all, individually and collectively, when any one of us fails to achieve his or her potential are eloquently expressed in the famous lines of John Donne (1624):

> No man is an island, entire of itself; every man is a piece of the continent, a part of the main. If a clod be washed away by the sea, Europe is the less, as well as if a promontory were, as well as if a manor of thy friends or of thine own were: any man's death diminishes me, because I am involved in mankind, and therefore never send to know for whom the bell tolls; it tolls for thee.

IN REVIEW

- Discuss the controversy over the effects of managed health care on the treatment and prevention of mental illness.
- Describe several ways in which individuals can contribute to the advancement of mental health.

SUMMARY

CONTROVERSIAL LEGAL ISSUES AND THE MENTALLY DISORDERED

- Being "mentally ill" is not considered sufficient grounds for commitment to a hospital. There must be, in addition, evidence that the individual is dangerous either to himself or herself or to society. It is not an easy matter, even for trained professionals, to determine in advance if a person is "dangerous" and likely to cause harm to self or others. Nevertheless, professionals must, at times, make such judgments.
- Court rulings have found mental health professionals liable when patients they were treating caused harm to others. The Tarasoff decision held that a therapist has a duty to protect potential victims if a patient has threatened to harm them.
- Another controversial issue in forensic psychology is the use of the insanity defense, or the NGRI defense, for capital crimes. The original legal precedent for such a defense, the M'Naughten Rule, held that, at the time of committing the act, the accused must have been laboring under such a defect of reason that he or she did not know the nature and quality of the act or that what he or she was doing was wrong. More recently, the American Law Institute (ALI) standard opened the possibility of valid NGRI pleas by persons who have not been diagnosed as psychotic. This broadening of the insanity plea led to its use in more and more cases.
- The successful use of the NGRI defense by John Hinckley, attempted assassin of President Reagan, set off a storm of protest, resulting ultimately in widespread tightening of the laws. One effective and widely adopted reform was to shift the burden of proof to the defense.
- There has also been a great deal of controversy over deinstitutionalization—the release of patients from public mental hospitals—and the subsequent failure to provide adequate follow-up of these patients in the community. In closing large psychiatric institutions, many administrators underestimated the amount of care that would be needed after discharge and overestimated communities' abilities to deal with patients with chronic problems. The result was that some patients were released to situations that required more adaptive abilities than they possessed.
- Recent work in the area of aftercare for former mental patients has provided clearer guidelines for discharge and therapeutic follow-up. Meanwhile, there has been a burgeoning use of private hospitalization in psychiatric care, an expensive alternative not normally available to the less than affluent.

PERSPECTIVES ON PREVENTION

- Increasingly, mental health professionals are trying not only to cure mental health problems but also to prevent them, or at least reduce their effects.

- Prevention can be viewed as occurring on three levels: (1) universal interventions attempt to reduce risk factors and enhance protective factors by influencing the general population; (2) selective interventions are aimed at reducing the possibility of mental disorder and fostering positive mental health efforts in subpopulations that are considered at special risk; and (3) indicated interventions attempt to reduce the impact or duration of a mental health problem that has already occurred.

CHALLENGES FOR THE FUTURE

- A large number of organizations are involved in organized efforts for treatment and prevention of mental disorders. Several federal government agencies have mental health as their primary mission. For example, the National Institute of Mental Health (NIMH), the National Institute on Drug Abuse (NIDA), and the National Institute on Alcohol Abuse and Alcoholism (NIAAA) are devoted to promoting research, training, and service in this field. State and county government agencies focus their efforts on the delivery of mental health services to residents on an inpatient or outpatient basis.
- Mental health efforts in the United States are also the concern of several professional organizations, many corporations, and a number of voluntary organizations. In addition, international organizations, such as the World Health Organization (WHO) and the World Federation for Mental Health, have established mental health programs worldwide.
- Changes in the health care industry have created many complex issues regarding who should determine the amount and type of treatment for mental health problems and who should be responsible for deciding how long treatment should continue.

KEY TERMS

forensic psychology (psychiatry) (p. 496)
Tarasoff decision (p. 500)
insanity defense (p. 500)
NGRI defense (p. 500)
guilty but mentally ill (GBMI) (p. 503)
deinstitutionalization (p. 504)
health maintenance organization (HMO) (p. 506)
universal interventions (p. 507)
selective interventions (p. 509)
indicated interventions (p. 512)
short-term crisis therapy (p. 512)
managed health care (p. 515)

REFERENCES

JOURNAL ABBREVIATIONS

Acta Neurol. Scandin.—*Acta Neurologica Scandinavica*
Acta Psychiatr. Scandin.—*Acta Psychiatrica Scandinavica*
Aggr. Behav.—*Aggressive Behavior*
Alcoholism: Clin. Exper. Res.—*Alcoholism: Clinical and Experimental Research*
Am. J. Community Psychol.—*American Journal of Community Psychology*
Amer. J. Clin. Nutri.—*American Journal of Clinical Nutrition*
Amer. J. Drug Alcoh. Abuse—*American Journal of Drug and Alcohol Abuse*
Amer. J. Epidemiol.—*American Journal of Epidemiology*
Amer. J. Geriatr. Psychiat.—*American Journal of Geriatric Psychiatry*
Amer. J. Med. Genet.—*American Journal of Medical Genetics*
Amer. J. Med. Sci.—*American Journal of the Medical Sciences*
Amer. J. Ment. Def.—*American Journal of Mental Deficiency*
Amer. J. Ment. Retard.—*American Journal of Mental Retardation*
Amer. J. Nurs.—*American Journal of Nursing*
Amer. J. Occup. Ther.—*American Journal of Occupational Therapy*
Amer. J. Orthopsychiat.—*American Journal of Orthopsychiatry*
Amer. J. Psychiat.—*American Journal of Psychiatry*
Amer. J. Psychoanal.—*American Journal of Psychoanalysis*
Amer. J. Psychother.—*American Journal of Psychotherapy*
Amer. J. Pub. Hlth.—*American Journal of Public Health*
Amer. Psychol.—*American Psychologist*
Ann. Behav. Med.—*Annals of Behavioral Medicine*
Ann. Int. Med.—*Annals of Internal Medicine*
Ann. Neurol.—*Annals of Neurology*
Ann. NY Acad. Sci.—*Annals of the New York Academy of Science*
Ann. Sex Res.—*Annals of Sex Research*
Annu. Rev. Med.—*Annual Review of Medicine*
Annu. Rev. Psychol.—*Annual Review of Psychology*
Annu. Rev. Sex Res.—*Annual Review of Sex Research*
App. Prev. Psychol.—*Applied and Preventive Psychology*
Arch. Clin. Neuropsychol.—*Archives of Clinical Neuropsychology*
Arch. Gen. Psychiat.—*Archives of General Psychiatry*
Arch. Gerontol. Geriatr.—*Archives of Gerontology and Geriatrics*
Arch. Int. Med.—*Archives of Internal Medicine*
Arch. Neurol.—*Archives of Neurology*
Arch. Sex. Behav.—*Archives of Sexual Behavior*
Austral. N.Z. J. Psychiatr.—*Australian and New Zealand Journal of Psychiatry*
Behav. Gen.—*Behavior Genetics*
Behav. Mod.—*Behavior Modification*
Behav. Res. Ther.—*Behavior Research and Therapy*
Behav. Ther.—*Behavior Therapy*
Behav. Today—*Behavior Today*
Biol. Psychiat.—*Biological Psychiatry*
Brit. J. Addict.—*British Journal of Addiction*
Brit. J. Clin. Psychol.—*British Journal of Clinical Psychology*
Brit. J. Dev. Psychol.—*British Journal of Developmental Psychology*
Brit. J. Learn. Dis.—*British Journal of Learning Disabilities*
Brit. J. Psychiat.—*British Journal of Psychiatry*
Brit. Med. J.—*British Medical Journal*
Bull. Amer. Acad. Psychiatr. Law—*Bulletin of the American Academy of Psychiatry and Law*
Canad. J. Behav. Sci.—*Canadian Journal of Behavioral Science*
Canad. J. Psychiat.—*Canadian Journal of Psychiatry*
Child Ab. Negl.—*Child Abuse and Neglect*
Child Adoles. Psychiat.—*Child and Adolescent Psychiatry*
Child Adoles. Psychiatr. Clin. N. Amer.—*Child and Adolescent Psychiatric Clinics of North America*
Child Develop.—*Child Development*
Child Psychiat. Human Devel.—*Child Psychiatry and Human Development*
Clin. Neuropharmac.—*Clinical Neuropharmacology*
Clin. Pediat.—*Clinical Pediatrics*
Clin. Pharm.—*Clinical Pharmacy*
Clin. Psychol. Rev.—*Clinical Psychology Review*
Clin. Psychol. Sci. Prac.—*Clinical Psychology: Science and Practice*
Clin. Psychol.—*The Clinical Psychologist*
Clin. Res. Dig. Suppl. Bull.—*Clinical Research Digest Supplemental Bulletin*
Cog. Ther. Res.—*Cognitive Therapy and Research*
Coll. Stud. J.—*College Student Journal*
Comm. Ment. Hlth. J.—*Community Mental Health Journal*
Compr. Psychiat.—*Comprehensive Psychiatry*
Contemp. Psychol.—*Contemporary Psychology*
Counsel. Psychol.—*Counseling Psychologist*
Crim. Just. Behav.—*Criminal Justice and Behavior*
Cult. Med. Psychiatr.—*Culture, Medicine, and Psychiatry*
Cultur. Psychiatr.—*Cultural Psychiatry*
Curr. Dirs. Psychol. Sci.—*Current Directions in Psychological Science*
Develop. Med. Child Neurol.—*Developmental Medicine & Child Neurology*
Develop. Psychol.—*Developmental Psychology*
Develop. Psychopath.—*Development and Psychopathology*
Deviant Behav.—*Deviant Behavior*
Dis. Nerv. Sys.—*Diseases of the Nervous System*
Eat. Dis.—*Eating Disorders*
Eur. Arch. Psychiat. Clin. Neurosci.—*European Archives of Psychiatry and Clinical Neuroscience*
Except.—*Exceptionality*
Exper. Neurol.—*Experimental Neurology*
Fam. Hlth.—*Family Health*
Fam. Plann. Perspect.—*Family Planning Perspectives*
Fam. Process—*Family Process*
Fed. Proc.—*Federal Proceedings*
Hlth. Psychol.—*Health Psychology*
Hosp. Comm. Psychiat.—*Hospital and Community Psychiatry*
Human Behav.—*Human Behavior*
Human Develop.—*Human Development*
Human Genet.—*Human Genetics*
Inf. Behav. Develop.—*Infant Behavior and Development*
Int. J. Clin. Exp. Hypn.—*International Journal of Clinical and Experimental Hypnosis*
Int. J. Eat. Dis.—*International Journal of Eating Disorders*
Int. J. Epidemiol.—*International Journal of Epidemiology*
Int. Rev. Psychiat.—*International Review of Psychiatry*
Integr. Psychiat.—*Integrative Psychiatry*
Inter. J. Addict.—*International Journal of Addictions*
Inter. J. Ment. Hlth.—*International Journal of Mental Health*
Inter. J. Psychiat.—*International Journal of Psychiatry*
Inter. J. Psychoanal.—*International Journal of Psychoanalysis*
Inter. J. Soc. Psychiat.—*International Journal of Social Psychiatry*
J. Abn. Psychol.—*Journal of Abnormal Psychology*
J. Abnorm. Child Psychol.—*Journal of Abnormal Child Psychology*
J. Abnorm. Soc. Psychol.—*Journal of Abnormal and Social Psychology*
J. Affect. Dis.—*Journal of Affective Disorders*
JAMA—*Journal of the American Medical Association*
J. Amer. Acad. Adoles. Psychiat.—*Journal of the American Academy of Adolescent Psychiatry*
J. Amer. Acad. Child Adoles. Psychiat.—*Journal of the American Academy of Child and Adolescent Psychiatry*
J. Amer. Acad. Child Psychiat.—*Journal of the American Academy of Child Psychiatry*
J. Amer. Coll. Hlth.—*Journal of American College Health*
J. Amer. Geriat. Soc.—*Journal of the American Geriatrics Society*
J. Anxiety Dis.—*Journal of Anxiety Disorders*
J. Appl. Beh. Anal.—*Journal of Applied Behavior Analysis*
J. Autism Devel. Dis.—*Journal of Autism and Developmental Disorders*
J. Behav. Assess.—*Journal of Behavioral Assessment*
J. Behav. Med.—*Journal of Behavioral Medicine*
J. Behav. Ther. Exper. Psychiat.—*Journal of Behavior Therapy and Experimental Psychiatry*
J. Chem. Depen. Treat.—*Journal of Chemical Dependency Treatment*
J. Child Fam. Stud.—*Journal of Child and Family Studies*
J. Child Psychol. Psychiat.—*Journal of Child Psychology and Psychiatry.*
J. Child Clin. Psychol.—*Journal of Child Clinical Psychology*

J. Clin. Geropsychol.—*Journal of Clinical Geropsychology*
J. Clin. Psychiat.—*Journal of Clinical Psychiatry*
J. Clin. Psychol. in Med. Set.—*Journal of Clinical Psychology in Medical Settings*
J. Clin. Psychol.—*Journal of Clinical Psychology*
J. Clin. Psychopharm.—*Journal of Clinical Psychopharmacology*
J. Cog. Neurosci.—*Journal of Cognitive Neuroscience*
J. Cog. Rehab.—*Journal of Cognitive Rehabilitation*
J. Coll. Stud. Psychother.—*Journal of College Student Psychotherapy*
J. Comm. Psychol.—*Journal of Community Psychology*
J. Cons. Clin. Psychol.—*Journal of Consulting and Clinical Psychology*
J. Couns. Psychol.—*Journal of Counseling Psychology*
J. Edu. Psychol.—*Journal of Educational Psychology*
J. Exper. Psychol.—*Journal of Experimental Psychology*
J. Fam. Pract.—*Journal of Family Practice*
J. Gen. Psychol.—*Journal of General Psychology*
J. Gerontol.—*Journal of Gerontology*
J. Head Trauma Rehab.—*Journal of Head Trauma Rehabilitation*
J. His. Behav. Sci.—*Journal of the History of the Behavioral Sciences*
J. Int. Neuropsycholog. Soc.—*Journal of the International Neuropsychological Society*
J. Intell. Develop. Dis.—*Journal of Intellectual Developmental Disability*
J. Intell. Dis. Res.—*Journal of Intellectual Disability Research*
J. Interpers. Violen.—*Journal of Interpersonal Violence*
J. Learn. Dis.—*Journal of Learning Disabilities*
J. Marit. Fam. Ther.—*Journal of Marital and Family Therapy*
J. Marr. Fam.—*Journal of Marriage and the Family*
J. Ment. Deficien. Res.—*Journal of Mental Deficiency Research*
J. Ment. Hlth. Couns.—*Journal of Mental Health Counseling*
J. Ment. Sci.—*Journal of Mental Science*
J. Nerv. Ment. Dis.—*Journal of Nervous and Mental Diseases*
J. Neurol. Neurosurg. Psychiat.—*Journal of Neurology, Neurosurgery, & Psychiatry*
J. Neuropsychiat. Clin. Neurosci.—*Journal of Neuropsychiatry and Clinical Neurosciences*
J. Off. Rehab.—*Journal of Offender Rehabilitation*
J. Pediat. Psychol.—*Journal of Pediatric Psychology*
J. Pers. Assess.—*Journal of Personality Assessment*
J. Pers. Soc. Psychol.—*Journal of Personality and Social Psychology*
J. Personal. Dis.—*Journal of Personality Disorders*
J. Personal.—*Journal of Primary Prevention*
J. Psychiat. Res.—*Journal of Psychiatric Research*
J. Psychiat.—*Journal of Psychiatry*
J. Psychoact. Drugs—*Journal of Psychoactive Drugs*
J. Psychohist.—*Journal of Psychohistory*
J. Psychol.—*Journal of Psychology*
J. Psychopath. Behav. Assess.—*Journal of Psychopathology and Behavioral Assessment*
J. Psychopharm.—*Journal of Psychopharmacology*
J. Psychosom. Res.—*Journal of Psychosomatic Research*
J. Sex Marit. Ther.—*Journal of Sex and Marital Therapy*
J. Sex. Res.—*Journal of Sex Research*
J. Speech Hear. Dis.—*Journal of Speech and Hearing Disorders*
J. Stud. Alcoh.—*Journal of Studies on Alcohol*
J. Subst. Abuse—*Journal of Substance Abuse*
J. Trauma. Stress.—*Journal of Traumatic Stress*
Monogr. Soc. Res. Child. Develop.—*Monographs of the Society for Research in Child Development*
Neurobiol. Aging—*Neurobiology of Aging*
Neurosci. Lett.—*Neuroscience Letters*
N. Engl. J. Med.—*New England Journal of Medicine*
Personal. Indiv. Diff.—*Personality and Individual Differences*
Personal. Soc. Psychol. Bull.—*Personality and Social Psychology Bulletin*
Personal. Soc. Psychol. Rev.—*Personality and Social Psychology Review*
Profess. Psychol.—*Professional Psychology*
Prog. Neuropsychopharmacol. Biol. Psychiatry—*Progress in Neuropsychopharmacology & Biological Psychiatry*
Psych. Today—*Psychology Today*
Psychiat. Ann.—*Psychiatric Annals*
Psychiat. Clin. N. Amer.—*Psychiatric Clinics of North America*
Psychiat. News—*Psychiatric News*
Psychiat. Res.—*Psychiatric Research*
Psychiatr. Q.—*Psychiatric Quarterly*
Psychiatr. Serv.—*Psychiatric Services*
Psychol. Aging—*Psychology and Aging*
Psychol. Assess.—*Psychological Assessment*
Psychol. Bull.—*Psychological Bulletin*
Psychol. Inq.—*Psychological Inquiry*
Psychol. Med.—*Psychological Medicine*
Psychol. Meth.—*Psychological Methods*
Psychol. Rep.—*Psychological Reports*
Psychol. Rev.—*Psychological Review*
Psychol. Sci.—*Psychological Science*
Psychopharm. Bull.—*Psychopharmacology Bulletin*
Psychosom. Med.—*Psychosomatic Medicine*
Psychother. Psychosom.—*Psychotherapy and Psychosomatics*
Q. J. Exp. Psych. [A]—*Quarterly Journal of Experimental Psychology: [A] Human Experimental Psychology*
Schizo. Bull.—*Schizophrenia Bulletin*
School Psychol. Rev.—*School Psychology Review*
Sci. News—*Science News*
Scientif. Amer.—*Scientific American*
Soc. Psychiat.—*Social Psychiatry*
Soc. Psychiat. Psychiatr. Epidemiol.—*Social Psychiatry and Psychiatric Epidemiology*
Soc. Sci. Med.—*Social Science and Medicine*
Transcult. Psychiat.—*Transcultural Psychiatry*

Abel, E. L. (1988). Fetal alcohol syndrome in families. *Neurotoxicology and Teratology, 10,* 1–2.

Abel, E. L. (1990). *Fetal alcohol syndrome.* New York: Plenum.

Abel, E. L. (1998). Fetal alcohol syndrome: The "American Paradox." *Alcohol & Alcoholism, 33*(3), 195–201.

Abel, G. G., & Rouleau, J. L. (1990). The nature and extent of sexual assault. In W. L. Marshall, D. R. Laws, & H. E. Barbaree (Eds.), *Handbook of sexual assault: Issues, theories, and treatment of the offender.* (pp. 9–22). New York: Plenum.

Abraham, H. D., & Wolf, E. (1988). Visual function in past users of LSD: Psychophysical findings. *J. Abn. Psychol., 97,* 443–47.

Abraham, K. (1960a). Notes on the psychoanalytic treatment of manic depressive insanity and allied conditions. In *Selected papers on psychoanalysis.* New York: Basic Books. (Original work published 1911.)

Abraham, K. (1960b). The first pregenital stage of libido. In *Selected papers on psychoanalysis.* New York: Basic Books. (Original work published 1916.)

Abrahamson, D. J., Barlow, D. H., Sakheim, D. K., Beck, J. G., & Athanasiou, R. (1985). Effects of distraction on sexual responding in functional and dysfunctional men. *Behav. Ther., 16,* 503–15.

Abrams, R. (1996). ECT stimulus parameters as determinants of seizure quality. *Psychiat. Ann., 26,* 701–4.

Abramson, L., Alloy, L., & Metalsky, G. (1995). Hopelessness depression. In G. Buchanan & M. Seligman (Eds.), *Explanatory style.* (pp. 113–134). Hillsdale, NJ: Erlbaum.

Abramson, L. Y., Metalsky, G. I., & Alloy, L. B. (1989). Hoplelessness depression: A theory-based subtype of depression. *Psychol. Rev., 96,* 358–372.

Abramson, L. Y., & Seligman, M. E. P. (1977). Modeling psychopathology in the laboratory: History and rationale. In M. Maser & M. E. P. Seligman (Eds.), *Psychopathology: Experimental models.* San Francisco: Freeman.

Abramson, L. Y., Seligman, M. E. P., & Teasdale, J. D. (1978). Learned helplessness in humans: Critique and reformulation. *J. Abn. Psychol.,* 87, 49–74.

Abramson, R. K., Wright, H. H., Cuccaro, M. L., & Lawrence, L. G. (1992). Biological liability in families with autism. *J. Amer. Acad. Child Adoles. Psychiat., 31,* 370–71.

Achenbach, T. M., & Howell, C. T. (1993). Are American children getting worse? A 13-year comparison. *J. Amer. Acad. Child Adoles. Psychiat., 32,* 1145–54.

Ackerson, J., Scogin, F., McKendree–Smith, N., & Lyman, R. (1998). Cognitive bibliotherapy for mild and moderate adolescent depressive symptomatology. *J. Cons. Clin. Psychol., 66*(4), 685–90.

ACSF Investigators. (1992). AIDS and sexual behaviour in France. *Nature, 360,* 407–9.

Adam, B. S., Everett, B. L., & O'Neal, E. (1992). PTSD in physically and sexually abused psychiatrically hospitalized children. *Child Psychiat. Human Develop., 23,* 3–8.

Adams, H. E., & McAnulty, R. D. (1993). Sexual disorders: The paraphilias. In P. Sutker & H. Adams (Eds.), *Comprehensive handbook of psychopathology.* (pp. 563–79). New York: Plenum.

Adams, M. A., & Ferraro, F. R. (1997). Acquired immunodeficiency syndrome dementia complex. *J. Clin. Psychol., 53*(7), 767–78.

Ader, R., & Cohen, N. (1984). Behavior and the immune system. In W. D. Gentry (Ed.), *Handbook of behavioral medicine.* (pp. 117–73). New York: Guilford.

Adler, T. (1994). Alzheimer's causes unique cell death. *Sci. News, 146*(13), 198.

Adrien, J. L., Perrot, A., Sauvage, D., & Leddet, I. (1992). Early symptoms in autism from family home movies: Evaluation and comparison between 1st and 2nd year of life using I.B.S.E. scale. *Acta Paedopsychiatrica International Journal of Child and Adolescent Psychiatry, 55,* 71–75.

Affleck, G., Tennen, H., Urrows, S., & Higgins, P. (1994). Person and contextual features of daily stress reactivity: Individual differences in relations of undesirable daily events with mood disturbance and chronic pain intensity. *J. of Pers. Soc. Psychol., 66*(2), 329–40.

Agnew, J. (1985). Man's purgative passion. *Amer. J. Psychother., 39*(2), 236–46.

Agras, S. W., Telch, C. F., Arnow, B., Eldredge, K., et al. (1997). One-year follow–up of cognitive-behavioral therapy for obese individuals with binge eating disorder. *J. Cons. Clin. Psychol., 65*(2), 343–47.

Agras, W. S. (1982). Behavioral medicine in the 1980's: Nonrandom connections. *J. Cons. Clin. Psychol., 50*(6), 820–40.

Aiken, L. R. (1996). *Rating scales and checklists.* New York: Wiley.

Akiskal, H. S. (1979). A biobehavioral approach to depression. In R. A. Depue (Ed.), *The psychobiology of depressive disorders: Implications for the effects of stress.* New York: Academic Press.

Akiskal, H. S. (1997). Overview of chronic depressions and their clinical management. In H. S. Akiskal & G. B. Cassano (Eds.), *Dysthymia and the spectrum of chronic depressions.* (pp. 1–34). New York: Guilford.

Akiskal, H. S., Maser, J. D., Zeller, P. J., Endicott, J., Coryell, W., Keller, M., Warshaw, M., Clayton, P., & Goodwin, F. (1995). Switching from 'unipolar' to bipolar II. *Arch. Gen. Psychiat., 52,* 114–123.

Albano, A. M., Chorpita, B. F., & Barlow, D. H. (1996). Childhood anxiety disorders. In E. J. Mash & R. A. Barkley (Eds.), *Child psychopathology* (pp. 196–241). New York: Guilford.

Albee, G. W. (1996). Revolutions and counterrevolutions in prevention. *Amer. Psychol., 51*(11), 1130–33.

Albertsons' Inc. v. Workers' Compensation Board of the State of California, 131, Cal App 3d, 182 Cal Reptr 304, 1982.

Albright v. Abington Memorial Hospital, 696 A.2d 1159 (Pa 1997).

Alden, L., & Capp, R. (1988). Characteristics predicting social functioning and treatment response in clients impaired by extreme shyness: Age of onset and the public/private shyness distinction. *Canad. J. Behav. Sci., 20,* 40–49.

Alexander, F. (1946). Individual psychotherapy. *Psychosom. Med., 8,* 110–15.

Alexander, F. (1950). *Psychosomatic medicine.* New York: Norton.

Alexander, G. M., & Sherwin, B. B. (1993). Sex steroids, sexual behavior, and selective attention for erotic stimuli in women using oral contraceptives. *Psychoneuroendocrinology, 18,* 91–102.

Alexander, J. F., Holtzworth-Munroe, A., & Jameson, P. B. (1994). The process and outcome of marital and family therapy: Research review and evaluation. In A. E. Bergin & S. L. Garfield (Eds.), *Handbook of psychotherapy and behavior change* (4th ed., pp. 595–630). New York: Wiley.

Alexander, K., Huganir, L. S., & Zigler, E. (1985). Effects of different living settings on the performance of mentally retarded individuals. *Amer. J. Ment. Def., 90,* 9–17.

Alison, N. G. (1994). Fetal alcohol syndrome: Implications for psychologists. *Clin. Psychol. Rev., 14,* 91–111.

Al-Issa, I. (1982). Does culture make a difference in psychopathology? In I. Al-Issa (Ed.), *Culture and psychopathology.* Baltimore: University Park Press.

Allen, B., & Skinner, H. (1987). Lifestyle assessment using microcomputers. In J. N. Butcher (Ed.), *Computerized psychological assessment: A practitioner's guide.* New York: Basic Books.

Allen, J. S. (1997). At issue: Are traditional societies schizophrenogenic? *Schizo. Bull., 23*(3), 357–64.

Allerton, W. S. (1970). Psychiatric casualties in Vietnam. *Roche Medical Image and Commentary, 12*(8), 27.

Allodi, F. A. (1994). Posttraumatic stress disorder in hostages and victims of torture. *Psychiat. Clin. of N. Amer., 17,* 279–88.

Alloy, L. B., Abramson, L. Y., Whitehouse, W. G., Hogan, M. E., Tashman, N. A., Steinberg, D. L., Rose, D. T., & Donovan, P. (1999). Depressogenic cognitive styles: Predictive validity, information processing and personality characteristics, and developmental origins. *Behav. Res. Ther., 37,* 503–531.

Alloy, L. B., Kelly, K. A., Mineka, S., & Clements, C. M. (1990). Comorbidity in anxiety and depressive disorders: A helplessness/hopelessness perspective. In J. D. Maser & C. R. Cloninger (Eds.), *Comorbidity in anxiety and mood disorders,* (pp. 499–543). Washington, DC: American Psychiatric Press.

Alloy, L., Reilly-Harrington, N. A., & Fresco, D. M. (1997). *Cognitive styles and life events as predictors of bipolar and unipolar episodes.* Paper presented at the meeting of the Association for the Advancement of Behavior Therapy.

Alloy, L. B., & Tabachnick, N. (1984). Assessment of covariation by humans and animals: The joint influence of prior expectations and current situational information. *Psychol. Rev., 91,* 112–149.

Alpert, J. E., Maddocks, A., Nierenberg, A. A., O'-Sullivan, R., Pava, J. A., Worthington, J. J., Biederman, J., Rosenbaum, J. F., & Fava, M. (1996). Attention-deficit hyperactivity disorder in childhood among adults with major depression. *Psychiat. Res., 62,* 213–19.

Alpert, J. E., Uebelacker, L. A., McLean, N. E., Nierenberg, A. A., Pava, J. A., Worthington III, J. J., Tedlow, J. R., Rosenbaum, J. F., & Fava, M. (1997). Social phobia, avoidant personality disorder and atypical depression: Co-occurrence and clinical implications. *Psychol. Med., 27,* 627–633.

Alterman, A. I. (1988). Patterns of familial alcoholism, alcoholism severity, and psychopathology. *J. Nerv. Ment. Dis., 176,* 167–75.

Alterman, A. I., McDermott, P. A., Cacciola, J. S., Rutherford, M. J., Boardman, C. R., McKay, J. R., & Cook, T. G. (1998). A typology of antisociality in methadone patients. *J. Abn. Psychol., 107*(2), 412–22.

Alterman, A. I., Searles, J. S., & Hall, J. G. (1989). Failure to find differences in drinking behavior as a function of familial risk for alcoholism: A replication. *J. Cons. Clin. Psychol., 98,* 50–53.

Amato, P. R., & Keith, B. (1991a). Parental divorce and the well-being of children: A meta-analysis. *Psychol. Bull., 110,* 26–46.

Amato, P. R., & Keith, B. (1991b). Parental divorce and adult well-being: A meta-analysis. *Journal of Marriage and the Family, 53,* 43–58.

American Medical Association Committee on Human Sexuality. (1972). *Human Sexuality.* (p. 40). Chicago: American Medical Association.

American Psychiatric Association. (1968). *Diagnostic and statistical manual of mental disorders* (2nd ed.). Washington, DC: Author.

American Psychiatric Association. (1972). Classification of mental retardation. *Supplement to the Amer. J. Psychiat., 128*(11), 1–45.

American Psychiatric Association. (1994). *Diagnostic and statistical manual of mental disorders (DSM-IV)* (4th ed.). Washington, DC: Author.

American Psychiatric Association. (1997a). Practice guideline for the treatment of patients with Alzheimer's disease and other dementias of late life. *Amer. J. Psychiat., Supplement, 154*(5), 1–39.

American Psychiatric Association. (1997b). Practice guideline for the treatment of patients with schizophrenia. *Amer. J. Psychiat.* (Supplement), *154*(4), 1–63.

American Psychiatric Association. (2000). *Diagnositc and statistical manual of mental disorders* (4th ed., rev.). Washington, DC: Author.

American Psychological Association. (1992). Ethical principles of psychologists and code of conduct. *Amer. Psychol., 47*(12), 1597–611.

Ammerman, R. T., Kane, V. R., Slomka, G. T., Reigel, D. H., Franzen, M. D., & Gadow, K. D. (1998). Psychiatric symptomatology and family functioning in children and adolescents with spina bifia. *J. Clin. Psychol. Med. Set., 5*(4), 449–65.

Anand, K. J. S., & Arnold, J. H. (1994). Opioid tolerance and dependence in infants and children. *Critical Care Medicine, 22,* 334–42.

Andersen, A. E., Bowers, W., & Evans, K. (1997). Inpatient treatment of anorexia nervosa. In D. M. Garner & P. E. Garfinkel (Eds.), *Handbook of treatment for eating disorders.* (pp. 327–353). New York: Guilford.

Andersen, B. L. (1983). Primary orgasmic dysfunction: Diagnostic considerations and review of treatment. *Psychol. Bull., 93,* 105–36.

Andersen, B. L., & Cyranowski, J. M. (1995). Women's sexuality: Behaviors, responses, and individual differences. *J. Cons. Clin. Psychol., 63, 891–906.*

Anderson, B. L., Kiecolt-Glaser, J. K., & Glaser, R. (1994). A biobehavioral model of cancer stress and disease course. *Amer. Psychol., 49*(5), 389–404.

Anderson, C., Krull, D., & Weiner, B. (1996) Explanations: Processes and consequences. In E.T. Higgins & A. Kruglanski (Eds.), *Social Psychology: Handbook of Basic Principles.* (pp. 271–296). New York: Guilford.

Anderson, G., Yasenik, L., & Ross, C. A. (1993). Dissociative experiences and disorders among women who identify themselves as sexual abuse survivors. *Child Ab. Negl., 17,* 677–86.

Anderson, J. C., Williams, S., McGee, R., & Silva, P. A. (1987). DSM III disorders in preadolescent children. *Arch. Gen. Psychiat., 44,* 69–80.

Anderson, K., & Lehto, J. (1995). *Young people and alcohol, drugs and tobacco: European action plan.* Geneva: World Health Organization.

Anderson, N. B., & Jackson, J. S. (1987). Race, ethnicity, and health psychology: The example of essential hypertension. In G. C. Stone (Ed.), *Health psychology: A discipline and a profession.* (pp. 265–84). Chicago: University of Chicago Press.

Anderson, N. B., & McNeilly, M. (1993). Autonomic reactivity and hypertension in blacks: Toward a contextual model. In J. C. S. Fray & J. G. Douglas (Eds.), *Pathophysiology of hypertension in blacks.* (pp. 107–139). New York: Oxford.

Anderson, V. A., et al. (1997). Predicting recovery from head injury in young children: A prospective analysis. *J. Int. Neuropsychologic. Soc., 3*(6), 568–80.

Andreasen, N. C. (1985). Positive vs. negative schizophrenia: A critical evaluation. *Schizo. Bull., 11,* 380–89.

Andreasen, N. C., & Carpenter, W. T., Jr. (1993). Diagnosis and classification of schizophrenia. *Schizo. Bull., 19*(2), 199–214.

Andreasen, N. C., et al., (1995). Symptoms of schizophrenia: Methods, meanings, and mechanisms. *Arch. Gen. Psychiat., 52*(5), 341–51.

Andreasen, N. C., Nasrallah, H. A., Dunn, V., Olson, S. C., & Grove, W. M. (1986). Structural abnormalities in the frontal system in schizophrenia: A magnetic resonance imaging study. *Arch. Gen. Psychiat. 43,* 136–44.

Andreasen, N. C., Paradiso, S., & O'Leary, D. S. (1998). "Cognitive dysmetria" as an integrative theory of schizophrenia: A dysfunction in cortical-subcortical-cerebellar circuitry? *Schizo. Bull., 24*(2), 203–67.

Andreasen, N. C., Rezai, K., Alliger, R., Swayze, V. W., Flaum, M., Kirchner, P., Cohen, G., & O'Leary, D. S. (1992). Hypofrontality in neuroleptic-naive patients and in patients with chronic schizophrenia. *Arch. Gen. Psychiat., 49*(12), 959–65.

Andreasson, S., & Brandt, L. (1997). Mortality and morbidity related to alcohol. *Alcohol and Alcoholism, 32*(2), 173–78.

Andrews, G., & Harvey, R. (1981). Does psychotherapy benefit neurotic patients? A reanalysis of the Smith, Glass, and Miller data. *Arch. Gen. Psychiat., 38,* 1203–8.

Anton, R. F. (1996). New methodologies for pharmacological treatment trials for alcohol dependence. *Alcoholism: Clin. Exper. Res., 20*(7), 3A–9A.

Antoni, M. H., Schneiderman, N., Fletcher, M. A., & Goldstein, D. A. (1990). Psychoneuroimmunology and HIV-1. *J. Cons. Clin. Psychol., 58,* 38–49.

Antony, M. M., & Barlow, D. H. (1996). Emotion theory as a framework for explaining panic attacks and panic disorder. In R. M. Rapee (Ed.), *Current controversies in the anxiety disorders.* (pp. 55–76). New York: Guilford.

Antony, M., Downie, F. , & Swinson R. (1998). Diagnostic issues and epidemiology in obsessive-compulsive disorder. In R. Swinson, M. Antony, S. Rachman, & M. Richter (Eds.), *Obsessive-compulsive disorder: Theory, research, and treatment.* (pp. 3-32). New York: Guilford.

Appelbaum, P. S., & Greer, A. (1994). Who's on trial? Multiple personalities and the insanity defense. *Hosp. Comm. Psychiat., 45*(10), Spec Issue 965–66.

Appelbaum, P. S., Jick, R. Z., Grisso, T., Givelber, D., Silver, E., & Steadman, H. J. (1993). Use of posttraumatic stress disorder to support an insanity defense. *Amer. J. Psychiat., 150,* 229–34.

Arango, V., & Underwood, M. D. (1997). Serotonin chemistry in the brain of suicide victims. In R. W. Maris, M. M. Silverman, & S. S. Canetton (Eds.), *Review of Suicidology, 1997.* (pp. 237–50). New York: Guilford.

Archer, R., Griffin, R., & Aiduk, R. (1995). MMPI-2: Clinical correlates for ten common code types. *J. Pers. Assess., 65,* 391–408.

Aring, C. D. (1974). The Gheel experience: Eternal spirit of the chainless mind! *JAMA, 230*(7), 998–1001.

Aring, C. D. (1975a). Gheel: The town that cares. *Fam. Hlth., 7*(4), 54–55, 58, 60.

Armstrong, J. (1995). Psychological assessment. In J. L. Spira (Ed.), *Treating dissociative identity disorder.* (pp. 3–37). San Francisco: Jossey-Bass.

Arndt, I. O, McLellan, A. T., Dorozynsky, L., Woody, G. E., & O'Brien, C. P. (1994). Desipramine treatment for cocaine dependence: Role of antisocial personality disorder. *J. Ner. Ment. Dis., 182,* 151–56.

Arnett, P. A., Fischer, M., & Newby, R. F. (1996). The effects of Ritalin on response to reward and punishment in children with ADHD. *Child Study Journal, 26*(1), 51–70.

Arnold, S. E., et al. (1998). Absence of neurodegeneration and neural injury in the cerebral cortex in a sample of elderly patients with schizophrenia. *Arch. Gen. Psychiat., 55,* 225–32.

Ashton, A. K., Hamer, R., & Rosen, R. C. (1997). Serotonin reuptake inhibitor-induced sexual dysfunction and its treatment: A large-scale retrospective study of 596 psychiatric outpatients. *J. Sex and Marit. Ther., 23,* 165–175.

Athey, J. L., O'Malley, P., Henderson, D. P., & Ball, J. W. (1997). Emergency medical services for children: Beyond lights and sirens. *Profess. Psychol., 28*(5), 464–70.

Atkinson, D. R. (1983). Ethnic similarity in counseling psychology: A review of research. *Counsel. Psychol, 11,* 79–92.

Atkinson, D. R., Furlong, M. J., & Poston, W. C. (1986). Afro-American preferences for counselor characteristics. *J. Couns. Psychol., 33,* 326–30.

Attie, I. & Brooks-Gunn, J. (1995). The development of eating regulation across the life span. In D. Cicchetti & D. J. Cohen (Eds.), *Developmental psychopathology: Vol. 2. Risk, disorder, and adaptation.* (pp. 332–368). New York: Wiley.

Ayllon, T., & Azrin, N. H. (1968). *The token economy: A motivational system for therapy and rehabilitation.* New York: Appleton-Century-Crofts.

Azari, N. P., Horwitz, B., Pettigrew, K. D., & Grady, C. L. (1994). Abnormal pattern of glucose metabolic rates involving language areas in young adults with Down syndrome. *Brain & Language, 46*(1), 1–20.

Babiak, P. (1995) When psychopaths go to work. *International Journal of Applied Psychology, 44,* 171–188.

Babor, T. F. (1996). The classification of alcoholics: Typology theories from the nineteenth century to the present. *Alcohol, Health, & Research World, 20*(1), 6–14.

Bach, M., & Bach, D. (1995). Predictive value of alexithymia: A prospective study in somatizing patients. *Psychother. Psychosom., 64,* 43–48.

Bailey, A., Le Couteur, A., & Gottesman, I. (1995). Autism as a strongly genetic disorder: Evidence from a British twin study. *Psychol. Med., 25*(1), 63–77.

Bailey, J. M. & Pillard, R. C. (1991). A genetic study of male sexual orientation. *Arch. Gen. Psychiat., 48,* 1089–96.

Bailey, J. M., Pillard, R. C., Neale, M. C., & Agyei, Y. (1993). Heritable factors influence female sexual orientation. *Arch. Gen. Psychiat., 50,* 217–23.

Bailey, J. M. & Shriver, A. (1999). Does childhood sexual abuse cause borderline personality disorder? *J. Sex Marit. Ther., 25,* 45–57.

Bailey, J. M., & Zucker, K. J. (1995). Childhood sex-typed behavior and sexual orientation: A conceptual analysis and quantitative review. *Develop. Psychol., 31,* 43–55.

Baldwin, A. L., Baldwin, C., Cole, R. E. (1990). Stress-resistant families and stress-resistant children. In J. Rolf, A. S. Masten, D. Cicchetti, K. H. Nuechterlein, & S. Weintraub (Eds.), *Risk and protective factors in the development of psychopathology.* New York: Cambridge University Press.

Ballenger, J. C. (1996). An update on pharmacological treatment of panic disorder. In H. G. Westenberg, J. A. Den Boer, & D. L. Murphy (Eds.), *Advances in the neurobiology of anxiety disorders.* (pp. 229–246). Chichester, England: Wiley.

Bandura, A. (1964). *Principles of behavior modification.* New York: Holt, Rinehart & Winston.

Bandura, A. (1969). *Principles of behavior modification.* New York: Holt, Rinehart & Winston.

Bandura, A. (1974). Behavior theory and the models of man. *Amer. Psychol., 29*(12), 859–69.

Bandura, A. (1977a). Self-efficacy: Toward a unifying theory of behavioral change. *Psychol. Rev., 84*(2), 191–215.

Bandura, A. (1977b). *Social learning theory.* Englewood Cliffs, NJ: Prentice-Hall.

Bandura, A. (1986). *Social foundations of thought and action: A social cognitive theory.* Englewood Cliffs, NJ: Prentice-Hall.

Barbaree, H. E. (1990). Stimulus control of sexual arousal: Its role in sexual assault. In W. L. Marshall, D. R. Laws, & H. E. Barbaree (Eds.), *Handbook of sexual assault.* (pp. 115–42). New York: Plenum.

Barbaree, H. E., Seto, M., Serin, R., Amos, N., & Preston, D. (1994). Comparisons between sexual and nonsexual rapist subtypes: Sexual arousal to rape, offense precursors, and offense characteristics. *Crim. Just. Behav., 21,* 95–114.

Barlow, D. H. (1988). *Anxiety and its disorders: The nature and treatment of anxiety and panic.* New York: Guilford.

Barlow, D. H. (Ed.). (1993). *Clinical handbook of psychological disorders* (2nd ed.). New York: Guilford.

Barlow, D. H., Brown, T. A., & Craske, M. G. (1994). Definitions of panic attacks and panic disorder in the DSM-IV: Implications for research. *J. Abn. Psychol., 103*(3), 553–64.

Barlow, D. H., Chorpita, B., & Turovsky, J. (1996). Fear, panic, anxiety, and disorders of emotion. In D. Hope (Ed.), *Perspectives on anxiety, panic, and fear.* 43rd Annual Nebraska Symposium on Motivation. (pp. 251–328). Lincoln: University of Nebraska Press.

Barlow, D. H., & Craske, M. G. (1994). *Mastery of your anxiety and panic-II.* San Antonio, TX: Harcourt Brace.

Barlow, D. H., Gorman, J. M., Shear, M. K., & Woods, S. W. (2000). Cognitive-behavioral therapy, imipramine, or their combination for panic disorder: A randomized control trial. *JAMA, 283,* 2529–2536.

Barlow, D. H., Sakheim, D. K., & Beck, J. G. (1983). Anxiety increases sexual arousal. *J. Abn. Psychol., 92,* 49–54.

Barnard, K., Morisset, C., & Spieker, S. (1993). Preventative interventions: Enhancing parent-infant relationships. In C. H. Zeanah, Jr. (Ed.), *Handbook of infant development.* New York: Guilford.

Barnes, G. E., & Prosen, H. (1985). Parental death and depression. *J. Abn. Psychol., 94,* 64–69.

Baron, I. S., & Goldberger, E. (1993). Neuropsychological disturbances of hydropcephalic children with implications for special education and rehabilitation. *Neuropsychological Rehabilitation, 3*(4), 389–410.

Barry, H., III. (1982). Cultural variations in alcohol abuse. In I. Al-Issa (Ed.), *Culture and psychopathology.* Baltimore: University Park Press.

Barsky, A. J., et al. (1998). A prospective 4- to 5-year study of DSM-III-R Hypochondriasis. *Arch. Gen. Psychiat., 5 5(8), 737–44.*

Barsky, A. J., Wool, C., Barnett, M. C., & Cleary, P. D. (1994). Histories of childhood trauma in adult hypochondriacal patients. *Amer. J. Psychiat., 151*(3), 397–401.

Barsky, A. J., Wyshak, G., & Klerman, G. L. (1992). Psychiatric comorbidity in DSM-III-R hypochondriasis. *Arch. Gen. Psychiat., 49*(2), 101–8.

Başoğlu, M., & Mineka, S. (1992). The role of uncontrollable and unpredictable stress in post-traumatic stress responses in torture survivors. In M. Başoğlu (Ed.), *Torture and its consequences: Current treatment approaches.* (pp. 182–225). Cambridge: Cambridge University Press.

Başoğlu, M., Mineka, S., Paker, M., Aker, T., Livanou, M., & Gok, S. (1997). Psychological preparedness for trauma as a protective factor in survivors of torture. *Psychol. Med., 27,* 1421–33.

Başoğlu, M., Paker, M., Paker, O., Ozmen, E., Marks, I., Sahin, D., & Sarimurat, N. (1994). Psychological effects of torture: A comparison of tortured with nontortured political activists in Turkey. *Amer. J. Psychiat., 151,* 76–81.

Bass, E., & Davis, L. (1988). *The courage to heal.* New York: Harper & Row.

Bateson, G. (1959). Cultural problems posed by a study of schizophrenic process. In A. Auerback (Ed.), *Schizophrenia: An integrated approach.* New York: Ronald Press.

Bateson, G. (1960). Minimal requirements for a theory of schizophrenia. *Arch. Gen. Psychiat., 2,* 477–91.

Bath, R., Morton, R., Uing, A., & Williams, C. (1996). Nocturnal enuresis and the use of desmopressin: Is it helpful? *Child: Care, Health & Development, 22*(22), 73–84.

Baucom, D. H. (1983). Sex role identity and the decision to regain control among women: A learned helplessness investigation. *J. Pers. Soc. Psychol., 44,* 334–43.

Bauer, A. M., & Shea, T. M. (1986). Alzheimer's disease and Down syndrome: A review and implications for adult services. *Education and Training of the Mentally Retarded, 21,* 144–50.

Baum, A., Gatchel, R. J., & Schaeffer, M. A. (1983). Emotional, behavioral, and physiological effects of chronic stress at Three Mile Island. *J. Cons. Clin. Psychol., 51,* 565–72.

Baumeister, R. F. (1990). Suicide as escape from self. *Psychol. Rev., 97,* 90–113.

Baumeister, R. F. & Butler, J. L. (1997). Sexual masochism: Deviance without pathology. In D. R. Laws & W. O'Donohue (Eds.), *Sexual deviance: Theory, assessment, and treatment.* New York: Guilford.

Baumrind, D. (1967). Child care practices anteceding three patterns of preschool behavior. *Genetic Psychology Monographs, 75,* 43–88.

Baumrind, D. (1971). Current patterns of parental authority. *Develop. Psychol., 4*(1), 1–103.

Baumrind, D. (1975). *Early socialization and the discipline controversy.* Morristown, NJ: General Learning Press.

Baumrind, D. (1991). Effective parenting during the early adolescent transition. In P. A. Cowan & E. M. Hetherington (Eds.), *Family transitions.* (pp. 111–164). Hillsdale, NJ: Erlbaum.

Baumrind, D. (1993). The average expectable environment is not good enough: A response to Scarr. *Child Develop., 64,* 1299–1317.

Bayer, R. (1981). *Homosexuality and American psychiatry.* New York: Basic Books.

Beach, S. R. H., & O'Leary, K. D. (1992). Treating depression in the context of marital discord: Outcome and predictors of response of marital therapy versus cognitive therapy. *Behav. Ther., 23,* 507–28.

Beal, A. L. (1995). Post-traumatic stress disorder in prisoners of war and combat veterans of the Dieppe raid: A 50 year follow-up. *Canad. J. Psychiat., 40*(4), 177–84.

Bebbington, P., Brugha, T., McCarthy, B., Potter, J., Sturt, E., Wykes, T., Katz, R., & McGuffin, P. (1988). The Camberwell collaborative depression study I. Depressed probands: Adversity and the form of depression. *Brit. J. Psychiat., 152,* 754–65.

Beck, A. T. (1967). *Depression: Causes and treatment.* Philadelphia: University of Pennsylvania Press.

Beck, A. T. (1983). Cognitive therapy of depression: New perspectives. In P. J. Clayton & J. E. Barrett (Eds.), *Treatment of depression: Old controversies and new approaches.* (pp. 265–90). New York: Raven Press.

Beck, A. T., & Emery, G., (with) Greenberg, R. L. (1985). *Anxiety disorders and phobias: A cognitive perspective.* New York: Basic Books.

Beck, A. T., Freeman, A., and Associates (1990). *Cognitive therapy of personality disorders.* New York: Guilford.

Beck, A. T., Hollon, S. D., Young, J. E., Bedrosian, R. C., & Budenz, D. (1985). Treatment of depression with cognitive therapy and amitriptyline. *Arch. Gen. Psychiat., 42,* 142–48.

Beck, A. T., Rush, A. J., Shaw, B., & Emery, G. (1979). *Cognitive therapy of depression: A treatment manual.* New York: Guilford.

Beck, A. T., Steer, R. A., Kovacs, M., & Garrison, B. (1985) Hopelessness and eventual suicide: A 10-year prospective study of patients hospitalized with suicidal ideation. *Amer. J. Psychiat., 142,* 559–63.

Beck, A. T., & Ward, C. H. (1961). Dreams of depressed patients: Characteristic themes in manifest content. *Arch. Gen. Psychiat. (Chicago), 5,* 462–67.

Beck, A. T., & Weishaar, M. (1989). Cognitive therapy. In A. Freeman, K. M. Simon, L. E. Beutler, & H. Arkowitz (Eds.), *Comprehensive handbook of cognitive therapy.* (pp. 21–36). New York: Plenum.

Beck, J. G. (1992) Behavioral approaches to sexual dysfunction. In S. Turner, K. Calhoun, & H. Adams (Eds.), *Handbook of clinical behavior therapy* (2nd ed.). New York: Wiley.

Beck, J. G. (1995). Hypoactive sexual desire disorder: An overview. *J. Cons. Clin. Psychol., 63,* 919–27.

Beck, J. G., and Barlow, D. H. (1984). Unraveling the nature of sex roles. In E. A. Blechman (Ed.), *Behavior modification with women.* (pp. 34–59). New York: Guilford.

Becker, E., Rinck, M., & Margraf, J. (1994). Memory bias in panic disorder. *J. Abn. Psychol., 103,* 396–9.

Becker, J. V., Alpert, J. L., BigFoot, D. S., Bonner, B. L., et al. (1995). Empirical research on child abuse treatment: Report by the Child Abuse and Neglect Treatment Working Group: American Psychological Association. *J. Child Clin. Psychol., 24,* 23–46.

Becker, J. V., & Kaplan, M. S. (1991). Rape victims: Issues, theories, and treatment. *Ann. Rev. Sex Res., 2,* 267–92.

Beech, H. R., Burns, L. E., & Sheffield, B. F. (1982). *A behavioral approach to the management of stress.* New York: Wiley.

Beers, C. (1970). *A mind that found itself* (rev. ed.). New York: Doubleday. (Original work published 1908.)

Bekker, M. H. (1996). Agoraphobia and gender: A review. *Clin. Psychol. Rev., 16*(2), 129–46.

Belar, C. D. (1997). Clinical health psychology: A specialty for the 21st century. *Hlth. Psychol., 16*(5), 411–416.

Bell, A. P., Weinberg, M. S., & Hammersmith, S. K. (1981). *Sexual preference: Its development in men and women.* Bloomington, IN: Indiana University Press.

Bell, E., Jr. (1958). The basis of effective military psychiatry. *Dis. Nerv. Sys., 19,* 283–88.

Bellack, A. S., Mueser, K. T., Gingerich, S., & Agresta, J. (1997). *Social skills training for schizophrenia.* New York: Guilford.

Bellerson, K. J. (1997). *The complete and updated fat book.* New York: Avery Publishing.

Belsky, J. (1993). Etiology of child maltreatment: A developmental-ecological analysis. *Psychol. Bull., 114,* 413–34.

Belter, R. W., & Shannon, M. P. (1993). Impact of natural disasters on children and families. In C. F. Saylor (Ed.), *Children and disasters.* (pp. 85–104). New York: Plenum.

Benda, C. G., & Rozovsky, F. A. (1997). *Managed care and the law: Liability and risk management, a practical guide.* Boston: Little, Brown.

Benjamin, L. S. (1982). Use of structural analysis of social behavior (SASB) to guide intervention in psychotherapy. In J. C. Anchin & D. L. Kiesler (Eds.), *Handbook of interpersonal psychotherapy.* New York: Pergamon.

Benjamin, L. S. (1993). *Interpersonal diagnosis and treatment of personality disorders.* New York: Guilford.

Benjamin, L. S. (1996a). An interpersonal theory of personality disorders. In J. F. Clarkin & M. F. Lenzenweger (Eds.), *Major theories of personality disorder.* (pp. 141–220). New York: Guilford.

Benjamin, L. S. (1996b). *Interpersonal diagnosis and treatment of personality disorders* (2nd ed.). New York: Guilford.

Benjamin, L. S., & Wonderlich, S. A. (1994). Social perceptions and borderline personality disorder: The relation to mood disorders. *J. Abn. Psychol., 103*(4), 610–624.

Bennett, A. E. (1947). Mad doctors. *J. Nerv. Ment. Dis., 106,* 11–18.

Bennett, J. B., & Lehman, W. E. K. (1996). Alcohol, antagonism, and witnessing violence in the workplace: Drinking climates and social alienation-integration. In G. R. Vandenbos & E. Q. Bulatao (Eds.), *Violence in the workplace.* (pp. 105–52). Washington: American Psychological Association.

Bennett, T. L., Dittmar, C., & Ho, M. R. (1997). The neuropsychology of traumatic brain injury. In A. M. Horton, D. Wedding, & J. Webster (Eds.), *The neuropsychology handbook* (Vol. 2). (pp. 123–72). New York: Springer.

Bennetto, L., Pennington, B. F., & Rogers, S. J. (1996). Intact and impaired memory functions in autism. *Child Develop., 67*(4), 1816–35.

Ben-Porath, Y. S. (1997). Use of personality assessment instruments in empirically guided treatment planning. *Psychol. Assess., 9*(4), 361–68.

Bentovim, A., Boston, P., & Van Elburg, A. (1987). Child sexual abuse—children and families referred to a treatment project and the effects of intervention. *Brit. Med. J., 295,* 1453–57.

Berenbaum, H., & Connelly, J. (1993). The effects of stress on hedonic capacity. *J. Abn. Psychol., 102*(3), 474–81.

Berenbaum, H., & Fujita, F. (1994). Schizophrenia and personality: Exploring the boundaries and connections between vulnerability and outcome. *J. Abn. Psychol., 103*(1), 148–58.

Berenbaum, H., & Oltmanns, T. F. (1992). Emotional experience and expression in schizophrenia and depression. *J. Abn. Psychol., 101*(1), 37–44.

Bergem, A. L. M., Engedal, K., & Kringlen, E. (1997). The role of heredity in late-onset Alzheimer disease and vascular dementia. *Arch. Gen. Psychiat., 54*(3), 264–70.

Bergner, R. M. (1997). What is psychopathology? And so what? *Clin. Psychol. Sci. Pract., 4* (3), 235–48.

Berlin, F. S. (1994, May). The case for castration, part 2. *Washington Monthly, 26,* 28–29.

Berman, A. L., & Jobes, D. A. (1991). *Adolescent suicide.* Washington, DC: American Psychological Association.

Berman, A. L., & Jobes, D. A. (1992). Suicidal behavior of adolescents. In B. Bongar (Ed.), *Suicide: Guidelines for assessment, management and treatment.* New York: Oxford University Press.

Berman, K. F., Torrey, E. F., Daniel, D. G., & Weinberger, D. R. (1992). Regional cerebral blood flow in monozygotic twins discordant and concordant for schizophrenia. *Arch. Gen. Psychiat., 49*(12), 927–34.

Bernstein, D. P., Useda, D., Siever, L. J. (1995). Paranoid personality disorder. In W. J Livesley (Ed), *The DSM-IV personality disorders. Diagnosis and treatment of mental disorders.* (pp. 45–57). New York: Guilford.

Bernstein, E. M., & Putnam, F. W. (1986). Development, reliability, and validity of a dissociation scale. *J. Nerv. Men. Dis., 174,* 727–35.

Bernstein, G. A., & Borchardt, C. M. (1991). Anxiety disorders of childhood and adolescence: A critical review. *J. Amer. Acad. Adoles. Psychiat., 30,* 519–32.

Bertelsen, A., Harvald, B., & Hauge, M. (1977). A Danish twin study of manic depressive disorders. *Brit. J. Psychiat., 130,* 330–51.

Besharov, D. J. (1992, July). Yes: Consider chemical treatment. *ABA Journal, 78,* 42.

Beutler, L. E. (1992). Systematic treatment selection. In J. C. Norcross & M. R. Goldfried (Eds.), *Psychotherapy integration.* New York: Basic Books.

Beutler, L. E., Machado, P. P., & Neufeldt, S. A. (1994). Therapist variables. In A. E. Bergin & S. L. Garfield (Eds.), *Handbook of psychotherapy and behavior change* (4th ed.). (pp. 229–69). New York: Wiley.

Bhandary, A. N. (1997). The chronic attention deficit syndrome. *Psychiat. Ann., 27*(8), 543–44.

Bickel, W. K., Amass, L., Higgins, S. T., Badger, G. J., & Esch, R. A. (1997). Effects of adding behavioral treatment in opioid detoxification with Buprenophrine. *J. Cons. Clin. Psychol., 65*(5), 803–10.

Bieber, I., Dain, H. J., Dince, P. R., Drellich, M. G., Grand, H. G., Gundlach, R. H., Kremer, M. W., Rifkin, A. H., Wilbur, C. B. & Bieber, T. B. (1962). *Homosexuality: A psychoanalytic study of male homosexuals.* New York: Basic Books.

Biederman, J., Faraone, S. V., Milberger, S., Jetton, J. G., Chen, L., Mick, E., Greene, R. W., & Russell, R. L. (1996). Is childhood oppositional defiant disorder a precursor to adolescent conduct disorder? Finding from a four-year follow-up of children with ADHD. *Child Adoles. Psychiat. 35*(9), 1193–1204.

Biederman, J., Rosenbaum, J. F., Hirschfeld, D. R., Faraone, S., Bolduc, E., Gersten, M., Meminger, S., Kagan, J., Snidman, N. & Reznick, J. S. (1990). Psychiatric correlates of behavioral inhibition in young children of parents with and without psychiatric disorders. *Arch. Gen. Psychiat., 47,* 21–26.

Bifulco, A. T., Brown, G. W., & Harris, T. O. (1987). Childhood loss of parent, lack of adequate parental care and adult depression: A replication. *J. Affect. Dis., 12,* 115–28.

Bigler, E. D. (1996). *Neuroimaging.* New York: Plenum.

Billet, E., Richter, J., & Kennedy, J. (1998). Genetics of obsessive-compulsive disorder. In R. Swinson, M. Antony, S. Rachman, & M. Richter (Eds.), *Obsessive-compulsive disorder: Theory, research, and treatment.* (pp.181–206). New York: Guilford.

Billy, J. O. G., Tanfer, K., Grady, W. R., & Klepinger, D. H. (1993). The sexual behavior of men in the United States. *Fam. Plann. Perspect., 25,* 52–60.

Binder, R. L., & McNiel, D. E. (1988). Effects of diagnosis and context of dangerousness. *Amer. J. Psychiat., 145,* 788–92.

Birmaher, B., Ryan, S. W., Williamson, D., Brent, D., Kaufman, J., Dahl, R., Perel, J., & Nelson, B. (1996). Childhood and adolescent depression: A review of the past 10 years. Part I. *J. Amer. Acad. Child Adoles. Psychiat. 35,* 1427–39.

Birns, B., & Bridger, W. (1977). Cognitive development and social class. In J. Wortis (Ed.), *Mental retardation and developmental disabilities* (Vol. 9). (pp. 203–33). New York: Brunner/Mazel.

Bishop, E. R., Mobley, M. C., & Farr, W. F., Jr. (1978). Lateralization of conversion symptoms. *Compr. Psychiat., 19,* 393–96.

Black, A. (1974). The natural history of obsessional neurosis. In H. R. Beech (Ed.), *Obsessional states.* London: Methuen.

Black, B., & Uhde, T. W. (1995). Psychiatric characteristics of children with selective mutism: A pilot study. *J. Amer. Acad. Child Adoles. Psychiat., 34*(7), 847–56.

Black, D. W., Yates, W., Petty, F., Noyes, R., & Brown, K. (1986). Suicidal behavior in alcoholic males. *Compr. Psychiat., 273*(3), 227–33.

Blaine, J. D. (1992). Introduction. In J. D. Blaine (Ed.), *Buprenorphine: An alternative treatment for opioid dependence.* (pp. 1–4). Washington, DC: U.S. Department of Health and Human Services.

Blair, R. J. R., Jones, L., Clark, F., & Smith, M. (1997). The psychopathic individual: A lack of responsiveness to distress cues? *Psychophysiology, 34,* 192–198.

Blais, M. A., Hilsenroth, M. J., & Castlebury, F. D. (1997). Content validity of the DSM-IV borderline and narcissistic personality disorder criteria sets. *Compr. Psychiat., 38*(1), 31–37.

Blanchard, E. B. (1992). Psychological treatment of benign headache disorders. *J. Cons. Clin. Psychol., 60*(4), 537–51.

Blanchard, E. B. (1994). Behavioral medicine and health psycholgy. In A. E. Bergin & S. L. Garfield (Eds.), *Handbook of psychotherapy and behavior change.* (pp. 701–33). New York: Wiley.

Blanchard, E. B., & Andrasik, F. (1982). Psychological assessment and treatment of headache: Recent developments and emerging issues. *J. Cons. Clin. Psychol., 50*(6), 859–79.

Blanchard, E. B., Andrasik, F., Ahles, T. A., Teders, S. J., & O'Keefe, D. (1980). Migraine and tension headache: A meta-analytic review. *Behav. Ther., 11,* 613–31.

Blanchard, E. B., Appelbaum, K. A., Radnitz, C. L., Michultka, D., Morrill, B., Kirsch, C., Hillhouse, J., Evans, D. D., Guarnieri, P., Attanasio, V., Andrasik, F., Jaccard J., & Dentinger, M. P. (1990a). Placebo-controlled evaluation of abbreviated progressive muscle relaxation and of relaxation combined with cognitive therapy in the treatment of tension headache. *J. Cons. Clin. Psychol., 58,* 210–15.

Blanchard, E. B., Appelbaum, K. A., Radnitz, C. L., Morrill, B., Michultka, D., Kirsch, C., Gaurinieri, P., Hillhouse, J., Evans, D. D., Jaccard, J., & Barron, K. D. (1990b). A controlled evaluation of thermal biofeedback and thermal biofeedback combined with cognitive therapy in the treatment of vascular headache. *J. Cons. Clin. Psychol., 58,* 216–24.

Blanchard, E. B., & Epstein, L. H. (1978). *A biofeedback primer.* Reading, MA: Addison-Wesley.

Blanchard, E. B., Hickling, E. J., Barton, K., & Taylor, A. E. (1996). One-year prospective follow-up of motor vehicle accident victims. *Behav. Res. Ther., 34*(10), 775–86.

Blanchard, E. B., Miller, S. T., Abel G. G., Haynes, M. R., & Wicker, R. (1979). Evaluation of biofeedback in treatment of borderline essential hypertension. *J. Appl. Beh. Anal., 12,* 99–109.

Blanchard, E. B., & Young, L. D. (1973). Self-control of cardiac functioning: A promise as yet unfulfilled. *Psychol. Bull., 79,* 145–63.

Blanchard, E. B., & Young, L. D. (1974). Clinical applications of biofeedback training: A review of evidence. *Arch. Gen. Psychiat., 30,* 573–89.

Blanchard, R. (1985). Typology of male-to-female transsexualism. *Arch. Sex. Behav., 14,* 247–61.

Blanchard, R. (1989). The classification and labeling of nonhomosexual gender dysphorias. *Arch. Sex. Behav., 18.,* 315–34.

Blanchard, R. (1991). Clinical observations and systematic study of autogynephilia. *J. Sex Marit. Ther., 17,* 235–51.

Blanchard, R. (1992). Nonmonotonic relation of autogynephilia and heterosexual attraction. *J. Abnorm. Psych., 101,* 271–76.

Blanchard, R. (1993). Varieties of autogynephilia and their relationship to gender dysphoria. *Arch. Sex. Behav., 22,* 241–51.

Blanchard, R. (1994). A structural equation model for age at clinical presentation in nonhomosexual male gender dysphorics. *Arch. Sex. Behav., 23,* 311–32.

Blanchard, R., & Hucker S. J. (1991). Age, transvestitism, bondage, and concurrent paraphilic activities in 117 fatal cases of autoerotic asphyxia. *Brit. J. Psychiat., 159,* 371–77.

Blatt, S. J., Sanislow, C. A., Zuroff, D. C., & Pilkonis, P. A. (1996). Characteristics of effective therapists: Further analyses of the NIMH Treatment of Depression Collaborative Research Program. *J. Cons. Clin. Psychol., 64*(6), 1276–84.

Blatt, S. J., Zuroff, D. C., Quinlan, D. M., & Pilkonis, P. A. (1996). Interpersonal factors in brief treatment of depression: Further analyses of the NIMH Treatment of Depression Collaborative Research Program. *J. Cons. Clin. Psychol., 64*(1), 162–71.

Bleeker, E. (1968). Many asthma attacks psychological. *Sci. News, 93*(17), 406.

Bleuler, E. (1950). *Dementia praecox or the group of schizophrenias.* New York: International Universities Press. (Originally published in 1911.)

Bloch, H. S. (1969). Army clinical psychiatry in the combat zone—1967–1968. *Amer. J. Psychiat., 126,* 289.

Bloom, B. L., Asher, S. J., & White, S. W. (1978). Marital disruption as a stressor: A review and analysis. *Psychol. Bull., 85,* 867–94.

Bobashev, G. V., & Anthony, J. C. (1998). Clusters of marijuana use in the United States. *Amer. J. Publ. Hlth., 148*(12), 1168–73.

Bockhoven, J. S. (1972). *Moral treatment in community mental health.* New York: Springer.

Bogerts, B. (1993). Recent advances in the neuropathology of schizophrenia. *Schizo. Bull., 19*(2), 431–45.

Bogerts, B. (1997). The temporolimbic system theory of positive schizophrenic symptoms. *Schizo. Bull., 23*(3), 423–36.

Bohn, M. J. (1993). Alcoholism. *Psychiat. Clin. N. Amer., 16,* 679–92.

Bolles, R. C., & Fanselow, M. S. (1982). Endorphins and behavior. *Annu. Rev. Psychol., 33,* 87–101.

Booth, B. M., Cook, C. L., & Blow, F. C. (1992). Comorbid mental disorders in patients with AMA discharges from alcoholism treatment. *Hosp. Comm. Psychiat., 43,* 730–31.

Booth, B. M., Russell, D. W., Soucek, S., & Laughlin, P. R. (1992a). Social support and outcome of alcoholism treatment: An exploratory analysis. *Amer. J. Drug Alcoh. Abuse, 18,* 87–101.

Booth, B. M., Russell, D. W., Yates, W. R., & Laughlin, P. R. (1992b). Social support and depression in men during alcoholism treatment. *J. Subst. Abuse, 4,* 57–67.

Booth-Kewley, S., & Friedman, H. S. (1987). Psychological predictors of heart disease: A quantitative review. *Psychol. Bull., 101,* 343–62.

Borg, W. R., & Ascione, F. R. (1982). Classroom management in elementary mainstreaming classrooms. *J. Educ. Psychol., 74,* 84–95.

Borkman, T. J., Kaskutas, L. A., Room, J., et al. (1998). An historical and developmental analysis of social model programs. *J. Subst. Abuse, 15*(1), 7–17.

Borkovec, T. D. (1985). The role of cognitive and somatic cues in anxiety and anxiety disorders: Worry and relation-induced anxiety. In A. H. Tuma & J. D. Maser (Eds.), *Anxiety and the anxiety disorders.* (pp. 463–78). Hillsdale, NJ: Erlbaum.

Borkovec, T. D. (1994). The nature, functions, and origins of worry. In G. L. C. Davey & F. Tallis (Eds.), *Worrying, perspectives on theory, assessment, and treatment.* (pp. 5–34). Sussex, England: Wiley.

Borkovec, T. D. (1997). On the need for a basic science approach to psychotherapy research. *Psychol. Sci., 8*(3), 145–47.

Borkovec, T. D., Abel, J. L., & Newman, H. (1995). Effects of psychotherapy on comorbid conditions in generalized anxiety disorder. *J. Cons. Clin. Psychol., 63*(3), 479–83.

Bornstein, R. F. (1992). The dependent personality: Developmental, social, and clinical perspectives. *Psychol. Bull., 112,* 3–23.

Bornstein, R. F. (1995). Comorbidity for dependent personality disorder and other psychological disorders: An integrative review. *J. Person. Dis., 9(4), 286–303.*

Bornstein, R.F. (1997). Dependent personality in the DSM-IV and beyond. *Clin. Psychol.: Sci. Prac., 4,* 175–187.

Borod, J. C. (1992). Interhemispheric and intrahemispheric control of emotion: A focus on unilateral brain damage. *J. Cons. Clin. Psychol., 60*(3), 339–48.

Borthwick-Duffy, S. A. (1994). Epidemiology and prevalence of psychopathology in people with mental retardation. *J. Cons. Clin. Psychol., 62*(1), 17–27.

Borum, R. (1996). Improving the clinical practice of violence risk assessment. *Amer. Psychol., 51, 945–56.*

Boscarino, J. A. (1996). Posttraumatic stress disorder, exposure to combat, and lower plasma cortisol among Vietnam veterans: Findings and clinical implications. *J. Cons. Clin. Psychol., 64(1), 191–201.*

Botvin, G. J. (1983). Prevention of adolescent substance abuse through the development of personal and social competence. *National Institute on Drug Abuse Research Monograph Series, 47,* 115–40.

Botvin, G. J., Baker, E., Dusenbury, L., Tortu, S., & Botvin, E. M. (1990). Preventing adolescent drug abuse through a multimodal cognitive-behavioral approach: Results of a 3 year study. *J. Cons. Clin. Psychol., 58,* 437–57.

Botvin, G. J., & Botvin, E. M. (1992). Adolescent tobacco, alcohol, and drug abuse: Prevention strategies, empirical findings, and assessment issues. *J. Devel. Behav. Pediat., 13*(4), 290–301.

Bourne, P. G. (1970). Military psychiatry and the Vietnam experience. *Amer. J. Psychiat., 127*(4), 481–88.

Bouton, M. E. (1994). Conditioning, remembering, and forgetting. *J. Exper. Psychol.: Animal Behavior Processes, 20,* 219–231.

Bouton, M., Mineka, S., & Barlow, D. H. (2001). A modern learning theory perspective on the etiology of panic disorder. *Psychol. Rev.*

Bouton, M. E., & Nelson, J. B. (1997). The role of context in classical conditioning: Some implications for cognitive behavior therapy. In W. T. O'Donohue (Ed.), *Learning theory and behavior therapy.* (pp. 59-84). Boston, MA: Allyn & Bacon, Inc.

Bowen, R. C., Offord, D. R., & Boyle, M. H. (1990). The prevalence of overanxious disorder and separation anxiety disorder: Results from the Ontario Child Health Study. *J. Amer. Acad. Child Adoles. Psychiat., 29,* 753–58.

Bowlby, J. (1960). Separation anxiety. *Inter. J. Psychoanal., 41,* 89–93.

Bowlby, J. (1969). *Attachment and loss* (Vol. 1). New York: Basic Books.

Bowlby, J. (1973). *Separation: Anxiety and anger. Psychology of attachment and loss series* (Vol. 3). New York: Basic Books.

Bowlby, J. (1980). *Attachment and loss, III: Loss, sadness, and depression.* New York: Basic Books.

Bowler, J. V., et al. (1997). Comparative evolution of Alzheimer disease, vascular dementia, and mixed dementia. *Arch. Neurol., 54*(6), 697–703.

Boyd, J. H., Burke, J. D., Gruenberg, E., Holzer, C. E., Rae, D. S., George, L. K., Karno, M., Stoltzman, R., McEvoy, L., & Nestadt, G. (1984). Exclusion criteria of DSM-III: A study of co-occurrence of hierarchy-free syndromes. *Arch. of Gen. Psychiat., 41,* 983–89.

Boyd, J. H., & Weissman, M. M. (1985). Epidemiology of major affective disorders. In R. Michels, J. O. Cavenar, H. K. H. Brodie, A. M. Cooper, S. B. Guze, L. L. Judd, G. L. Klerman, & A. J. Solnit (Eds.), *Psychiatry* (Vol. 3). Philadelphia: Lippincott.

Bradbury, T. N., & Miller, G. A. (1985). Season of birth in schizophrenia: A review of evidence, methodology, and etiology. *Psychol. Bull., 98,* 569–94.

Bradford, J. M. (1990). The antiandrogen and hormonal treatment of sex offenders. In W. L. Marshall, D. R. Laws, & H. E. Barbaree (Eds.), *Handbook of sexual assault: Issues, theories, and treatment of the offender.* (pp. 363–85). New York: Plenum.

Bradley, L. A., & Prokop, C. K. (1982). Research methods in contemporary medical psychology. In P. C. Kendall & J. N. Butcher (Eds.), *Handbook of research methods in clinical psychology.* New York: Wiley Interscience.

Bradley, S. J., & Zucker, K. J. (1997). Gender identity disorder: A review of the past 10 years. *J. Amer. Acad. Child Adoles. Psychiat., 36,* 872–880.

Braginsky, B. M., & Braginsky, D. D. (1974). The mentally retarded: Society's Hansels and Gretels. *Psych. Today, 7*(10), 18, 20–21, 24, 26, 28–30.

Brancaccio* v. *State of Florida. (1997). 69850.2d 597 (Fla. App. 4 Dist).

Brandsma, J. M., Maultsby, M. C., & Welsh, R. J. (1980). *Outpatient treatment of alcoholism: A review and comparative study.* Baltimore: University Park Press.

Brane, G. (1986). Normal aging and dementia disorders: Coping and crisis in the family. *Prog. in Neuropsychopharmacol. Biol. Psychiatry, 10,* 287–95.

Braun, B. G., & Sachs, R. G. (1985). The development of multiple personality disorder: Predisposing, precipitating, and perpetuating factors. In R. P. Kluft (Eds.), *Childhood antecedents of multiple personality disorder.* (pp. 37–64). Washington, DC: American Psychiatric Press.

Braun, P., Kochansky, G., Shapiro, R., Greenberg, S., Gudeman, J. E., Johnson, S., & Shore, M. (1981). Overview: Deinstitutionalization of psychiatric patients, a critical review of outcome studies. *Amer. J. Psychiat., 138*(6), 736–49.

Braun, S. (1996). *Buzz.* (1) New York: Oxford University Press.

Breggin, P. R., & Breggin, G. R. (1995). The hazards of treating "attention deficit/hyperactivity disorder" with methylphenidate (Ritalin). *J. Coll. Stud. Psychother., 10*(2), 55–72.

Breier, A., Buchanan, R. W., Kirkpatrick, B., Davis, O. R., Irish, D., Summerfelt, A., & Carpenter, W. T. (1994). Effects of clozapine on positive and negative symptoms in outpatients with schizophrenia. *Amer. J. Psychiat., 151*(1), 20–26.

Breitner, J. C. S., (1986). On methodology and appropriate inference regarding possible genetic factors in typical, late-onset AD. *Neurobiol. Aging, 7,* 476–77.

Breitner, J. C. S., Gatz, M., Bergem, A. L. M., Christian, J. C., Mortimer, J. A., McClearn, G. E., Heston, L. L., Welsh, K. A., Anthony, J. C., Folstein, M. F., & Radebaugh, T. S. (1993). Use of twin cohorts for research in Alzheimer's disease. *Neurology, 43,* 261–67.

Brekke, J. S., & Barrio, C. (1997). Cross-ethnic symptom differences in schizophrenia: The influence of culture and minority status. *Schizo. Bull., 23*(2), 305–16.

Brekke, J. S., Long, J. D., Nesbitt, N., & Sobel, E. (1997). The impact of service characteristics on functional outcomes from community support programs for persons with schizophrenia: A growth curve analysis. *J. Cons. Clin. Psychol., 65*(3), 464–75.

Bremner, J. D., Southwick, S. M., & Charney, D. S. (1995). Etiological factors in the development of posttraumatic stress disorder. In C. M. Mazure (Ed.), *Does stress cause psychiatric illness?* Washington, DC: American Psychiatric Association.

Brems, C. (1995). Women and depression: A comprehensive analysis. In E. E. Beckham & W. R. Leber (Eds.), *Handbook of depression* (2nd ed.). (pp. 539–66). New York: Guilford.

Brems, C., & Lloyd, P. (1995). Validation of the MMPI-2 low self-esteem scale. *J. Pers. Assess., 65*(3), 550–56.

Brent, D. A., Holder, D., Kolko, D., Birmaher, B., Baugher, M., Roth, C., Iyengar, S., & Johnson, B. A. (1997). A clinical psychotherapy trial for adolescent depression comparing cognitive, family, and supportive. *Arch. Gen. Psychia., 54,* 877–85.

Brent, D. A., Moritz, G., & Liotus, L. (1996). A test of the diathesis-stress model of adolescent depression in friends and acquaintenances of suicide victims. In C. Pfeffer (Ed.), *Severe stress and mental disturbance in children.* (pp. 347–60). Washington: American Psychiatric Press.

Breslau, N., Davis, G. C., Andreski, P., Peterson, E. L., & Schultz, L. R. (1997). Sex differences in posttraumatic stress disorder. *Arch. Gen. Psychiat., 54,* 1044–48.

Bretschneider, J. G., & McCoy, N. L. (1988). Sexual interest and behavior in healthy 80- to 102-year-olds. *Arch. Sex. Behav., 17,* 109–29.

Brewer, R. D., Morris, P. D., Cole, T. B., Watkins, S., Patetta, M. J., & Popkin, C. (1994). The risk of dying in alcohol-related automobile crashes among habitual drunk drivers. *New Engl. J. Med., 331*(8), 523–17.

Bridges, F. A., & Cicchetti, D. (1982). Mothers' ratings of the temperament characteristics of Down's Syndrome infants. *Develop. Psychol., 18,* 238–44.

Brodsky, B. S., Cloitre, M., & Dulit, R. A. (1995). Relationship of dissociation to self-mutilation and childhood abuse in borderline personality disorder. *Amer. J. Psychiat., 152*(12), 1788–92.

Brody, A. L., & Baxter L. (1996). Neuroimaging in obsessive compulsive disorder: Advances in understanding the mediating neuroanatomy. In H. G. Westenberg, J. A. Den Boer, & D. L. Murphy (Eds.), *Advances in the neurobiology of anxiety disorders.* (pp. 313–31). Chichester, England: Wiley.

Brom, D., Kleber, R. J., & Defares, P. B. (1989). Brief psychotherapy for posttraumatic stress disorders. *J. Cons. Clin. Psychol., 57,* 607–12.

Brookoff, D., Cook, C. S., Williams, C., & Mann, C. S. (1994). Testing reckless drivers for cocaine and marijuana. *New Engl. J. Med., 331,* 518–22.

Brooks, D. N. (1974). Recognition, memory, and head injury. *J. Neurol. Neurosurg. Psychiatry, 37*(7), 794–801.

Brown, G. W. (1972). Life-events and psychiatric illness: Some thoughts on methodology and causality. *J. Psychosom. Res., 16,* 311–20.

Brown, G. W., & Harris, T. O. (1978). *Social origins of depression.* London: Tavistock.

Brown, G. W., Harris, T. O., & Bifulco, P. M. (1985). Long-term effects of early loss of parent. In M. Rutter, C. E. Izard, & P. B. Read (Eds.), *Depression in young people: Clinical and developmental perspectives.* (pp. 251–96). New York: Guilford.

Brown, P. (1994). Toward a psychobiological model of dissociation and posttraumatic stress disorder. In S. J. Lynn & J. W. Rhue (Eds.), *Dissociation: Clinical and theoretical perspectives.* (pp. 94–122). New York: Guilford.

Brown, R. & Herrnstein, R. J. (1975). *Psychology.* Boston: Little Brown.

Brown, R. A., Evans, D. M., Miller, I. W., Burgess, E. S., & Mueller, T. L. (1997). Cognitive-behavioral treatment for depression in alcoholism. *J. Cons. Clin. Psychol., 65*(5), 715–36.

Brown, R. I. (1977). An integrated program for the mentally handicapped. In P. Mittler (Ed.), *Research to practice in mental retardation* (Vol. 2). (pp. 387–88). Baltimore: University Park Press.

Brown, S. J., Fann, J. R., & Grant, I. (1994). Postconcussional disorder: Time to acknowledge a common source of neurobehavioral morbidity. *J. Neuropsychiat. & Clin. Neurosci., 6*(1), 15–22.

Brown, T. A. (1996). Validity of the DSM-III-R and DSM-IV classification systems for anxiety disorders. In R. M. Rapee (Ed.), *Current controversies in the anxiety disorders.* (pp. 21–45). New York: Guilford.

Brown, T. A., Chorpita, B. F., & Barlow, D. H. (1998). Structural relationships among dimensions of the DSM-IV anxiety and mood disorders and dimensions of negative affect, positive affect, and autonomic arousal. *J. Abn. Psychol., 107*(2), 179–92.

Brown, T. A., O'Leary, T. A., & Barlow, D. H. (1993). Generalized anxiety disorder. In D. H. Barlow (Ed.), *Clinical handbook of psychological disorders.* New York: Guilford.

Brown, W. T., Jenkins, E. C., Cohen, I. L., Fisch, G. S., WolfSchein, E. G., Gross, A., Fein, D., Mason-Brothers, A., Ritvo, E., Ruttenberg, B. A., Bentley, W., & Castell, S. (1986). Fragile x and autism: A multicenter survey. *Amer. J. Med. Genet., 23,* 341–52.

Browne, A., & Finkelhor, D. (1986). Impact of child sexual abuse: A review of the research. *Psychol. Bull. 99,* 66–77.

Brownmiller, S. (1975). *Against our will: Men, women, and rape.* New York: Simon & Schuster.

Bruch, H. (1986). Anorexia nervosa: The therapeutic task. In K. D. Brownell & J. P. Foreyt (Eds.), *Handbook of eating disorders.* (pp. 328–32). New York: Basic Books.

Bruch, M. A. (1989). Familial and developmental antecedents of social phobia: Issues and findings. Special Issue: Social phobia. *Clin. Psychol. Rev., 9*(1), 37–47.

Bry, B. H., McKeon, P., & Pandina, R. J. (1982). The extent of drug use as a function of number of risk factors. *J. Abn. Psychol., 91*(4), 273–79.

Bryan, A. D., Aiken, L. S., & West, S. G. (1997). Young women's condom use: The influence of acceptance of sexuality, control over sexual encounter, and perceived susceptibility to common STDs. *Hlth. Psychol., 16*(5), 468–479.

Buchanan, G., & Seligman, M. E. P. (Eds.). (1995). *Explanatory style.* Hillsdale NJ: Erlbaum.

Buchanan, G. M., & Seligman, M. E. P. (1995). Afterword: The future of the field. In G. M. Buchanan & M. E. P. Seligman (Eds.), *Explanatory style.* (pp. 247–52). Hillsdale, NJ: Erlbaum.

Buchanan, R. W., & Carpenter, W. T., Jr. (1997). The neuroanatomies of schizophrenia. *Schizo. Bull., 23*(3), 367–72.

Buchanan, R. W., Stevens, J. R., & Carpenter, W. T., Jr. (1997). The neuroanatiomy of schizophrenia: Editors' introduction. *Schizo. Bull., 23*(23), 365–66.

Buchsbaum, M. S., Haier, R. J., Potkin, S. G., Nuechterlein, K., Bracha, H. S., Katz, M., Lohr, J., Wu, J., Lottenberg, S., Jerabek, P. A., Trenary, M., Tafalla, R., Reynolds, C., & Bunney, W. E., Jr. (1992). Frontostriatal disorder of cerebral metabolism in never-medicated schizophrenics. *Arch. Gen. Psychiat., 49*(12), 935–41.

Buckley, P., Thompson, P., Way, L., & Meltzer, H. Y. (1994). Substance abuse among patients with treatment-resistant schizophrenia: Characteristics and implications for clozapine therapy. *Amer. J. Psychiat., 151,* 385–89.

Buckner, H. T. (1970). The transvestic career path. *Psychiatry, 3*(3), 381–89.

Budoff, M. (1977). The mentally retarded child in the mainstream of the public school: His relation to the school administration, his teachers, and his agemates. In P. Mittler (Ed.), *Research to practice in mental retardation* (Vol. 2). (pp. 307–13). Baltimore: University Park Press.

Bullard, D. M., Glaser, H. H., Heagarty, M. C., & Pivcheck, E. C. (1967). Failure to thrive in the neglected child. *Amer. J. Orthopsychiat., 37,* 680–90.

Bullman, T. A., & Kang, H. K. (1997). Posttraumatic stress disorder and the risk of traumatic deaths among Vietnam veterans. In C. S. Fullerton & R. J. Ursano (Eds.), *Posttraumatic stress disorders.* (pp. 175–89). Washington: American Psychiatric Press.

Burgess, A. W., & Holmstrom, L. (1974). Rape trauma syndrome. *Amer. J. Psychiat., 131,* 981–86.

Burks, V. S., Dodge, K. A., & Price, J. M. (1995). Models of internalizing outcomes of early rejection. *Develop. Psychopath., 7,* 683–95.

Burman, B., & Margolin, G. (1989). Marriage and health. *Advances, 6*(4), 51–58.

Bushnell, J. A., Wells, J. E., & Oakley-Browne, M. A. (1992). Long-term effects of intrafamilial sexual abuse in childhood. *Acta Psychiatr. Scandin., 85,* 136–42.

Buss, D. M. (1989). Sex differences in human mate preferences: Evolutionary hypotheses tested in 37 cultures. *Behavioral and Brain Sciences, 12,* 1–49.

Butcher, J. N. (1996a). Understanding abnormal behavior across cultures: The use of objective personality assessment methods. In J. N. Butcher (Ed.), *International adaptations of the MMPI-2.* (pp. 3–25). Minneapolis: University of Minnesota Press.

Butcher, J. N. (Ed.). (1996b). *International applications of the MMPI-2: A handbook of research and clinical applications.* Minneapolis, MN: University of Minnesota Press.

Butcher, J. N., Dahlstrom, W. G., Graham, J. R., Tellegen, A., & Kaemmer, B. (1989). *Minnesota Multiphasic Personality Inventory: MMPI-2: Manual for administration and scoring.* Minneapolis: University of Minnesota Press.

Butcher, J. N., & Dunn, L. (1989). Human responses and treatment needs in airline disasters. In R. Gist and B. Lubin (Eds.), *Psychosocial aspects of disaster.* New York: Wiley.

Butcher, J. N., & Hatcher, C. (1988). The neglected entity in air disaster planning: Psychological services. *Amer. Psychol., 43,* 724–29.

Butcher, J. N., Rouse, S., & Perry, J. (1998). Empirical description of psychopathology in therapy clients: Correlates of MMPI-2 scales. In J. N. Butcher (Ed.), *Foundation sources for the MMPI-2.* Minneapolis: University of Minnesota Press.

Butcher, J. N., Williams, C. L., Graham, J. R., Archer, R., Tellegen, A., Ben-Porath, Y. S., & Kaemmer,

B. (1992). *MMPI-A: Manual for administration, scoring, and interpretation.* Minneapolis: University of Minnesota Press.

Butler, L. D., et al. (1996). Hypnotizability and traumatic experience: A diathesis-stress model of dissociative symptomatology. *Amer. J. of Psychiat., Festschrift Supplement, 153*(7), 42–63.

Butow, P., Beumont, P., & Touyz, S. (1993). Cognitive processes in dieting disorders. *Int. J. Eat Dis., 14,* 319–330.

Butterfield, F. (1998). Prisons replace hospitals for the nation's mentally ill. *New York Times,* pp. 1–17.

Butzlaff, R. L., & Hooley, J. M. (1998). Expressed emotion and psychiatric relapse: A meta-analysis. *Arch. Gen. Psychiat., 55*(6), 547–52.

Cacioppo, J. T. (1994). Social neuroscience: Autonomic, neuroendocrine, and immune response to stress. *Psychophysiology, 31,* 113–28.

Cacioppo, J. T., et al. (1998). Cellular immune responses to acute stress in female caregivers of dementia patients and matched controls. *Hlth. Psychol., 17,* 182–89.

Cadoret, R. J., O'Gorman, T. W., Troughton, E., & Heywood, E. (1985). Alcoholism and antisocial personality: Interrelationships and environmental factors. *Arch. Gen. Psychiat., 42,* 161–67.

Caetano, R. , Clark, C. L., & Tam, T. (1998). Alcohol consumption among racial/ethnic minorities, *Alcohol World: Health and Research, 22* (4), 233–42.

Callahan, L. A., & Silver, E. (1998). Factors associated with the conditional release of persons acquitted by reason of insanity: A decision tree approach. *Law and Human Behavior, 22*(2), 147–63.

Camp, B. W., et al. (1998). Maternal and neonatal risk factors for retardation: Defining the "at risk" child. *Early Human Development, 50*(2), 159–73.

Campbell, D. (1926). *Arabian medicine and its influence on the Middle Ages.* New York: Dutton.

Campbell, M. (1987). Drug treatment of infantile autism: The past decade. In H. Meltzer (Ed.), *Psychopharmacology: The third generation of progress.* (pp. 1225–31). New York: Raven Press.

Campbell, M., & Cueva, J. E. (1995). Psychopharmacology in child and adolescent psychiatry: A review of the past seven years. Part 1. *J. Amer. Acad. Child Adoles. Psychiat. 34*(9), 1124–32.

Campbell, S. B., Cohn, J. F., Ross, S., Elmore, M., & Popper, S. (1990, April). *Postpartum adaptation and postpartum depression in primiparous women.* International Conference of Infant Studies, Montreal.

Canetto, S. S. (1997). Gender and suicidal behavior: Theories and evidence. In R. W. Maris, M. M. Silverman, & S. S. Canetton (Eds.), *Review of Suicidology, 1997.* (pp. 138–67). New York: Guilford.

Cannon, T. D. (1998a). Genetic and perinatal influences in the etiology of schizophrenia: A neurodevelopmental model. In M. F. Lenzenweger & R. H. Dworkin (Eds.), *Origins and development of schizophrenia.* (pp. 67–92). Washington: American Psychological Association.

Cannon, T. D. (1998b). Neurodevelopmental influences in the genesis and epigenesis of schizophrenia: An overview. *App Prev. Psychol., 7*(1), 47–62.

Cannon, T. D., et al. (1998). The genetic epidemiology of schizophrenia in a Finnish twin cohort. *Arch. Gen Psychiat., 55*(1), 67–74,

Cannon, T. D., & Marco, E. (1994). Structural brain abnormalities as indicators of vulnerability to schizophrenia. *Schizo. Bull., 20*(1), 89–102.

Cannon, T. D., Mednick, S. A., Parnas, J., Schulsinger, F., Praestholm, J., & Vestergaard, A. (1993). Developmental brain abnormalities in the offspring of schizophrenic mothers: I. Contributions of genetic and perinatal factors. *Arch. Gen. Psychiat., 50*(7), 551–64.

Cannon, T. D., Mednick, S. A., Parnas, J., Schulsinger, F., Praestholm, J., & Vestergaard, A. (1994). Developmental brain abnormalities in the offspring of schizophrenic mothers: II. Structural brain characteristics of schizophrenia and schizotypal personality disorder. *Arch. Gen. Psychiat., 51*(12), 955–62.

Cannon, W. B. (1915). *Bodily changes in pain, hunger, and rage* (1st ed.). New York: D. Appleton.

Cannon, W. B. (1929). *Bodily changes in pain, hunger, fear and rage.* New York: Appleton.

Cantwell, D. P., & Baker, L. (1989). Stability and natural history of DSM III childhood diagnoses. *J. Amer. Acad. Child Adoles. Psychiat. 28,* 691–700.

Capaldi, D. M., & Patterson, G. R. (1994). Interrelated influences of contextual factors on antisocial behavior in childhood and adolescence for males. In D. C. Fowles, P. Sutker, & S. H. Goodman (Eds.), *Progress in experimental personality and psychopathology research.* New York: Springer.

Capps, L., Kasari, C., Yirmiya, N., & Sigman, M. (1993). Parental perception of emotional expressiveness in children with autism. *J. Cons. Clin. Psychol., 61,* 475–84.

Cardona, F., Camillo, E., Casini, M. P., Luchetti, A., & Muscetta, A. (1997). Tic disorders in childhood: A retrospective study. *Giornale di Neuropsichiatria dell'Eta Evolutiva, 17*(2), 120–26.

Carey, G., & DiLalla, D. L. (1994). Personality and psychopathology: Genetic perspectives. *J. Abn. Psychol., 103,* 32–43.

Carey, G., & Goldman, D. (1997). The genetics of antisocial behavior. In D. M. Stoff, J. Breiling, & J. D. Maser (Eds.), *Handbook of antisocial behavior.* (pp. 243–254). New York: Wiley.

Carey, M. P., Maisto, S. A., Kalichman, S. C., Forsyth, A. D., & Wright, E. M. (1997). Enhancing motivation to reduce the risk of HIV infection for economically disadvantaged urban women. *J. Cons. Clin. Psychol., 65*(4), 531–541.

Carlier, I. V., & Gersons, B. P. (1997). Stress reactions in disaster victims following the Bijlmermeer plane crash. *J. Trauma. Stress, 10*(2), 329–35.

Carlier, I. V., Lambert, R. D., & Gersons, B. P. (1997). Risk factors for post-traumatic stress symptomatology in police officers: A prospective analysis. *J. Nerv. Ment. Dis. 185*(8), 498–506.

Carlat, D. J., Camargo, C. A., Jr., & Herzog, D. B. (1997). Eating disorders in males: A report on 135 patients. *Amer. J. Psychiat., 154*(8), 1127–1132.

Carlson R. (1997, April). *Sildenafil: An effective oral drug for impotence. Inpharma, 1085: 11-12.* Annual Meeting of the American Urological Association, New Orleans.

Carlson, C. L., & Bunner, M. R. (1993). Effects of methylphenidate on the academic performance of children with Attention Deficit Hyperactivity Disorder and learning disabilities. *School Psychol. Rev., 22,* 184–98.

Carlson, C. R., & Hoyle, R. H. (1993). Efficacy of abbreviated progressive muscle relaxation training: A quantitative review of behavioral medicine research. *J. Cons. Clin. Psychol., 61*(6), 1059–67.

Carlson, E. A., & Sroufe, L. A. (1995). Contribution of attachment theory to developmental psychopathology. In D. Cicchetti & D. J. Cohen (Eds.), *Developmental Psychopathology: Vol. 1 Theory and Methods.* (pp. 581–617). New York: Wiley.

Carlson, E. B., & Armstrong, J. (1994). The diagnosis and assessment of dissociative disorders. In S. J. Lynn & J. W. Rhue (Eds.), *Dissociation: Clinical and theoretical perspectives.* (pp. 159–74). New York: Guilford.

Carlson, E. B., & Rosser-Hogan, R. (1993). Mental health status of Cambodian refugees ten years after leaving their homes. *Amer. J. Orthopsychiat., 63,* 223–31.

Carlson, M. (1990, Jan. 29). Six years of torture. *Time, 135,* 26–27.

Carlsson, A. (1988). The current status of the dopamine hypothesis of schizophrenia. *Neuropsychopharmacology, 1,* 179–86.

Carpenter, W. T., Buchanan, R. W., Kirkpatrick, B., Tamminga, C., & Wood, F. (1993). Strong inference, theory testing, and the neuroanatomy of schizophrenia. *Arch. of Gen. Psychiat., 50*(10), 825–31.

Carpentieri, S., & Morgan, S. B. (1996). Adaptive and intellectual functioning in autistic and nonautistic retarded children. *J. Autism and Devel. Diso., 26*(6), 611–20.

Carr, A. (1997). Positive practice in family therapy. *J. Marit. Fam. Ther., 23*(3), 271–93.

Carroll, K. M., Ball, S. A., & Rounsaville, B. J. (1993). A comparison of alternate systems for diagnosing antisocial personality disorder in cocaine abusers. *J. Nerv. Ment. Dis., 181,* 436–43.

Carroll, K. M., & Rounsaville, B. J. (1993). History and significance and childhood attention deficit disorder in treatment-seeking cocaine abusers. *Compr. Psychiat., 34,* 75–82.

Carskadon, M. A. (1990). Patterns of sleep and sleepiness in adolescents. *Pediatrician, 17,* 5–12.

Carson, R. C. (1979). Personality and exchange in developing relationships. In R. L. Burgess & T. L. Huston (Eds.), *Social exchange in developing relationships.* New York: Academic Press.

Carson, R. C. (1982). Self-fulfilling prophecy, maladaptive behavior, and psychotherapy. In J. C. Anchin & D. J. Kiesler (Eds.), *Handbook of interpersonal psychotherapy.* (pp. 64–77). New York: Pergamon.

Carson, R. C. (1989). Personality. *Ann. Rev. Psychol.* (Vol. 40). (pp. 227–48). Palo Alto, CA: Annual Reviews.

Carson, R. C. (1996b). Seamlessness in personality and its derangements. *J. Personal. Assess., 66*(2), 240–247.

Carson, R. C. (1997). Costly compromises: A critique of the diagnostic and statistical manual of mental disorders. In S. Fisher & R. P. Greenberg (Eds.), *From placebo to panacea: Putting psychiatric drugs to the test.* (pp. 98–112). New York: Wiley.

Carson, R. C., & Sanislow, C. A. (1993). The schizophrenias. In P. B. Sutker & H. E. Adams (Eds.), *Comprehensive handbook of psychopathology.* (pp. 295–333). New York: Plenum.

Carson, T. P., & Carson, R. C. (1984). The affective disorders. In H. E. Adams & P. B. Sutker (Eds.), *Comprehensive handbook of psychopathology.* New York: Plenum.

Carstairs, G. M., & Kapur, R. L. (1976). *The great universe of Kota: Stress, change and mental disorder in an Indian village.* Berkeley, CA: University of California Press.

Carter, C. S., Servan-Schreiber, D., & Perlstein, W. M. (1997). Anxiety disorders and the syndrome of chest pain with normal coronary arteries: Prevalence and pathophysiology. *J. Clin. Psychiat., 58*(3), 70–73.

Casey, R. J., & Berman, J. S. (1985). The outcome of psychotherapy with children. *Psychol. Bull., 98,* 388–400.

Caspi, A., & Moffitt, T. E. (1995). The continuity of maladaptive behavior: From description to understanding in the study of antisocial behavior. In D. Cicchetti & C. Cohen (Eds.), *Developmental psychopathology.* Vol 2: Risk, disorder and adaptation. (pp. 472–511). New York: Wiley.

Cassidy, F., Forest, K., Murry, E., & Carroll, B. J. (1998). A factor analysis of the signs and symptoms of mania. *Arch. Gen. Psychiat., 55*(1), 27–32.

Caudill, B. D., Hoffman, J. A., Hubbard, R. L., Flynn, P. M., & Luckey, J. W. (1994). Parental history of substance abuse as a risk factor in predicting crack smokers' substance use, illegal activities, and psychiatric status. *Amer. J. Drug Alcoh. Abuse, 20,* 341–54.

Ceci, S. J. (1995). False beliefs: Some developmental and clinical considerations. In D. Schacter (Ed.), *Memory distortions: How minds, brains and societies reconstruct the past. (pp. 91–125).* New York: Harvard University Press.

Chafel, J. A. (1992). Funding Head Start: What are the issues? *Amer. J. Orthopsychiat., 62*(1), 9–21.

Chambers, R. E. (1952). Discussion of "Survival factors. . ." *Amer. J. Psychiat., 109,* 247–48.

Chambless, D. L., et al. (1998). Update on empirically validated therapies, II. *Clin. Psychol., 51*(1), 3–16.

Chandler, H. N. (1985). The kids-in-between: Some solutions. *J. Learn. Dis. 18,* 368.

Charlop-Christie, M. H., Schreibman, L., Pierce, K., & Kurtz, P. F. (1998). Childhood autism. In R. J. Morris, T. R. Kratochwill, et al. (Eds.), *The practice of child therapy.* (pp. 271–302). Boston: Allyn & Bacon.

Charman, T., Swettenham, J., Baron–Cohen, S., Cox, A., Baird, G., & Drew, A. (1997). Infants with autism: An investigation of empathy, pretend play, joint attention, and imitation. *Develop. Psychol., 33*(5), 781–89.

Charney, D., Grillon, C., & Bremner J. D. (1998). The neurobiological basis of anxiety and fear: Circuits, mechanisms, and neurochemical interactions (Part I). *The Neuroscientist, 4,* 35–44.

Chase-Lansdale, P. L., Cherlin, A. J., & Kieran, K. E. (1995). The long-term effects of parental divorce on the mental health of young adults: A developmental perspective. *Child Develop., 66,* 1614–34.

Chassin, L., Curran, P. J., Hussong, A. M., & Colder, C. R. (1996). The relation of parent alcoholism to adolescent substance use: A longitudinal follow-up. *J. Abn. Psychol., 105*(1), 70–80.

Chassin, L., Pillow, D. R., Curran, P. J., Molina, B. S., & Barrera, M. (1993). Relation of parental alcoholism in early adolescent substance use: A test of three mediating mechanisms. *J. Abn. Psychol., 102,* 3–19.

Chassin, L., Rogosch, F., & Barrera, M. (1991). Substance use and symptomatology among adolescent children of alcoholics. *J. Abn. Psychol., 100,* 449–463.

Checkley, S. (1992). Neuroendocrinology. In E. S. Paykel (Ed.), *Handbook of affective disorders* (2nd ed.). New York: Guilford.

Chemtob, C. M., Hamada, R. S., Roitblat, H. L., & Muraoka, M. Y. (1994). Anger, impulsivity, and anger control in combat-related post-traumatic stress disorder. *J. Cons. Clin. Psychol., 62,* 827–32.

Chemtob, C. M., Novaco, R. W., Hamada, R. S., & Gross, D. M. (1997). Cognitive–behavioral treatment for severe anger in posttraumatic stress disorder. *J. Cons. Clin. Psychol., 65*(1), 184–89.

Chemtob, C. M., Tomas, S., Law, W., & Cremniter, D. (1997). Postdisaster psychosocial intervention: A field study of the impact of debriefing on psychological distress. *Amer. J. Psychiat., 154*(3), 415–17.

Chen, C. C., & Yeh, E. K. (1997). Population differences in ALDH levels and flushing response. In G. Y. San (Ed.), *Molecular mechanisms of alcohol.* New York: Humana.

Chesney, M. (1996). New behavioral risk factors for coronary heart disease: Implications for intervention. In K. Orth-Gomer & N. Schneiderman (Eds.), *Behavioral medicine approaches to cardiovascular disease prevention.* (pp. 169–182). Mahwah, NJ: Lawrence Erlbaum.

Chic, J., Gough, K., Falkowski, W., & Kershaw, P. (1992). Disulfiram treatment of alcoholism. *Brit. J. Psychiat., 161,* 84–89.

Chorpita, B. F., & Barlow, D. H. (1998). The development of anxiety: The role of control in the early environment. *Psychol. Bull., 124*(1), 3–21.

Chowdhury, A. (1996) The definition and classification of Koro. *Cult., Med. Psychiat.,* 20,41–65.

Christensen, A. & Heavey, C. L. (1999). Interventions for couples. In J. T. Spence, J. M. Darley, & D. J. Foss (Eds.), *Annual Review of Psychology.* (pp. 165–190). Palo Alto., CA: Annual Review.

Christensen, A., & Jacobson, N. S. (1994). Who (or what) can do psychotherapy: The status and challenge of nonprofessional therapies. *Psychol. Sci., 5*(1), 8–14.

Christiansen, B. A., Smith, G. T., Roehling, P. V., & Goldman, M. S. (1989). Using alcohol expectancies to predict adolescent drinking behavior after one year. *J. Cons. Clin. Psychol., 57,* 93–99.

Chrousos, G. B., & Gold, P. W. (1992). The concepts of stress and stress system disorders: Overview of physical and behavioral homeostasis. *JAMA, 267,* 1244–52.

Chu, J. A., & Dill, D. L. (1990). Dissociative symptoms in relation to childhood physical and sexual abuse. *Amer. J. Psychiat., 147,* 887–92.

Cicchetti, D., & Lynch, M. (1995). Failures in the expectable environment and their impact on individual development: The case of child maltreatment. In D. Cicchetti & D. J. Cohen (Eds.), *Developmental psychopathology: Vol. 2. Risk, disorder, and adaptation.* (pp. 32–72). New York: Wiley.

Cicchetti, D., & Rogosch, F. (1999). Conceptual and methodological issues in developmental psychopathological research. In P. C. Kendall, J. N. Butcher, & G. Holmbeck (Eds.), *Research methods in clinical psychology* (2nd ed.). (pp. 433–65). New York: Wiley.

Cicchetti, D., & Toth, S. L. (1995a). A developmental psychopathology perspective on child abuse and neglect. *J. Amer. Acad. Child Adoles. Psychiat., 34*(5), 541–565.

Cicchetti, D., & Toth, S. L. (1995b). Developmental psychopathology and disorders of affect. In D. Cicchetti & D. J. Cohen (Eds.), *Developmental psychopathology Vol. 2: Risk, disorder, and adaptation.* (pp. 369–420). New York: Wiley.

Cicchetti, D., & Toth, S. L. (1998). The development of depression in children and adolescents. *Amer. Psychol., 53*(2), 221–41.

Cigrang, J. A., Pace, J. V., & Yasuhara, T. T. (1995). Critical incident stress intervention following fatal aircraft mishaps. *Aviation, Space, and Environmental Medicine, 66*(9), 880–82.

Clark, C. R. (1987). Specific intent and diminished capacity. In A. Hess and I. Weiner (Eds.), *Handbook of forensic psychology.* New York: Wiley.

Clark, D. A., Beck, A. T., & Beck, J. S. (1994a). Symptom difference in major depression, dysthymia, panic disorder, and generalized anxiety disorder. *Amer. J. Psychiat., 151,* 205–9.

Clark, D. A., & Steer, R. A. (1996). Empirical status of the cognitive model of anxiety and depression. In P. M. Salkovskis (Ed.), *Frontiers of cognitive therapy.* (pp. 75–96). New York: Guilford.

Clark, D. A., Steer, R. A., & Beck, A. T. (1994b). Common and specific dimensions of self-reported anxiety and depression: Implications for the cognitive and tripartite models. *Amer. J. Psychiat., 103,* 645–54.

Clark, D. C. (1995). Epidemiology, assessment, and management of suicide in depressed patients. In E. E. Beckham & W. R. Leber (Eds.), *Handbook of depression* (2nd ed.). (pp. 526–38). New York: Guilford.

Clark, D. C., & Fawcett, J. (1992). Review of empirical risk factors for evaluation of the suicidal patient. In B. Bongar (Ed.), *Suicide: Guidelines for assessment, management and treatment.* New York: Oxford University Press.

Clark, D. M. (1986). A cognitive approach to panic. *Behav. Res. Ther., 24,* 461–70.

Clark, D. M. (1988). A cognitive model of panic attacks. In S. Rachman & J. D. Maser (Eds.), *Panic: Psychological perspectives.* Hillsdale, NJ: Erlbaum.

Clark, D. M. (1996). Panic disorder: From theory to therapy. In R. M. Rapee (Ed.), *Current controversies in the anxiety disorders.* (pp. 318–44). New York: Guilford.

Clark, D. M. (1997). Panic disorder and social phobia. In D. M. Clark & C. G. Fairburn (Eds.), *Science and practice of cognitive behaviour therapy.* (pp. 119–54). Oxford University Press.

Clark, L. A. (1992). Resolving taxonomic issues in personality disorders: The value of large-scale analyses of symptom data. *J. Pers. Dis., 6,* 360–76.

Clark, L. A., & Livesley, W. J. (1994). Two approaches to identifying dimensions of personality disorder. Convergence on the five-factor model. In P. T. Costa, Jr., & T. A. Widiger (Eds.), *Personality disorders and the five-factor model of personality.* Washington, DC: American Psychological Association.

Clark, L. A., & Watson, D. (1991a). Theoretical and empirical issues in differentiating depression from anxiety. In J. Becker & A. Kleinman (Eds.), *Psychosocial aspects of depression.* Hillsdale, NJ: Erlbaum.

Clark, L. A., & Watson, D. (1991b). Tripartite model of anxiety and depression: Psychometric evidence and taxonomic implications. *J. Abnor. Psychol., 100,* 316–36.

Clark, L. A., Watson, D., & Mineka, S. (1994). Temperament, personality, and the mood and anxiety disorders. *J. Abn. Psychol., 103, 103–16.*

Clark, L. A., Watson, D., & Reynolds, S. (1995). Diagnosis and classification of psychopathology: Challenges to the current system and future directions. *Annu. Rev. Psychol., 46,* 121–53.

Clark, M. E. (1996). MMPI-2 negative treatment indicators content and content component scales: Clinical correlates and outcome prediction for men with chronic pain. *Psychol. Assess., 8,* 32–47.

Clark, R. F., & Goate, A. M. (1993). Molecular genetics of Alzheimer's disease. *Arch. Neurol., 50*(11), 1164–72.

Clarke, A. M., Clarke, A. D. B., & Berg, J. M. (Eds.). (1985). *Mental deficiency: The changing outlook* (4th ed.). London: Methuen.

Clarke, G. N., Sack, W. H., & Goff, B. (1993). Three forms of stress in Cambodian adolescent refugees. *J. Abnor. Child Psychol., 21,* 65–77.

Clayton, P. J. (1982). Bereavement. In E. S. Paykel (Ed.), *Handbook of affective disorders.* New York: Guilford.

Cleckley, H. M. (1941). *The mask of sanity* (1st ed.). St. Louis, MO: Mosby.

Cleckley, H.M. (1982). *The mask of sanity* (rev. ed.). New York: Plume.

Clement, P. (1970). Elimination of sleepwalking in a seven-year-old boy. *J. Cons. Clin. Psychol.,* 34(1), 22–26.

Clementz, B. A., Grove, W. M., Iacono, W. G., & Sweeney, J. A. (1992). Smooth-pursuit eye movement dysfunction and liability for schizophrenia: Implications for genetic modeling. *J. Abn. Psychol., 101*(1), 117–29.

Cloitre, M., Heimberg, R. G., Liebowitz, M. R., & Gitow, A. (1992). Perceptions of control in panic disorder and social phobia. *Cog. Ther. Res., 16* (5), 569–77.

Cloninger, C. R., Bayon, C., & Przybeck, T. R. (1997). Epidemiology and Axis I comorbidity of antisocial personality. In D. M. Stoff, J. Breiling, & J. D. Maser (Eds.), *Handbook of antisocial behavior.* (pp. 12–21). New York: Wiley.

Cloninger, C. R., Reich, T., Sigvardsson, S., von Knorring, A. L., & Bohman, M. (1986). The effects of changes in alcohol use between generations on the inheritance of alcohol abuse. In *Alcoholism: A medical disorder.* Proceedings of the 76th Annual Meeting of the American Psychopathological Association.

Cloninger, R., Sigvardsson, S., Von Knorring, A. L., & Bohman, M. (1984). An adoption study of somatoform disorders: II. Identification of two discrete somatoform disorders. *Arch. Gen. Psychiat., 41,* 863–71.

Clum, G. A., Clum, G. A., & Surls, R. (1993). A meta-analysis of treatments for panic disorder. *J. Con. Clin. Psychol., 61*(2), 317–26.

Coffey, P., Leitenberg, H., Henning, K., Turner, T., & Bennett, R. T. (1996). The relation between methods of coping during adulthood with a history of childhood sexual abuse and current psychological adjustment. *J. Cons. Clin. Psychol., 64*(5), 1090–93.

Cohen, C. I., et al. (1997). "Mixed dementia": Adequate or antiquated? A critical review. *Amer. J. Geriatr Psychiat., 5*(4), 279–83.

Cohen, D. (1997). A critique of the use of neuroleptic drugs in psychiatry. In S. Fisher & R. P. Greenberg (Eds.), *From placebo to panacea: Putting psychiatric drugs to the test.* (pp. 173–228). New York: Wiley.

Cohen, D., & Eisdorfer, C. (1988). Depression in family members caring for a relative with Alzheimer's disease. *J. Amer. Geriat. Soc., 36,* 885–89.

Cohen, S., Tyrrell, D. A. J., & Smith, A. P. (1993). Negative life events, perceived stress, negative affect, and susceptibility to the common cold. *J. Pers. Soc. Psychol., 64*(1), 131–40.

Cohler, B. J., Stott, F. M., & Musick, J. S. (1995). Adversity, vulnerability, and resilience: Cultural and developmental perspectives. In D. Cicchetti & D. J. Cohen (Eds.), *Developmental psychopathology: Vol. 2. Risk, disorder, and adaptation.* (pp. 753–800). New York: Wiley.

Cohn, J. F., & Tronick, E. Z. (1983). Three months infant's reaction to simulated maternal depression. *Child Develop. 54,* 185–93.

Coie, J. D. (1996). Effectiveness trials: An initial evaluation of the FAST track program. Paper presented at the Fifth National Institute of Mental Health Conference on Prevention Research, Washington.

Coie, J. D., & Cillessen, A. H. N. (1993). Peer rejection: Origins and effects on children's development. *Curr. Dir. Psychol. Sic., 2,* 89–92.

Coie, J. D., & Lenox, K. F. (1994). The development of antisocial individuals. In D. C. Fowles, P. Sutker, & S. H. Goodman (Eds.), *Progress in experimental personality and psychopathology research.* New York: Springer.

Cole, D. A., Martin, J. M., Peeke, L. G., Seroczynski, A., & Hoffman, K. (1998). Are cognitive errors of underestimation predictive or reflective of depressive symptoms in children: A longitudinal study. *J. Abn. Psychol. 107*(3), 481–96.

Cole, G., Neal, J. W., Fraser, W. I., & Cowie, V. A. (1994). Autopsy findings in patients with mental handicap. *J. Intell. Dis. Res., 38*(1), 9–26.

Collacott, R. A., & Cooper, S.-A. (1997). The five-year follow-up study of adaptive behavior in adults with Down syndrome. *J. Intell. Develop. Dis., 22*(3), 187–97.

Collacott, R. A., et al. (1998). Behavior phenotype for Down's syndrome. *Brit. J. Psychiat., 172,* 85–89.

Columbus, M., Allen, J. P., & Fertig, J. B. (1995). Assessment in alcoholism treatment: An overview. In NIAAA (Ed.), *Assessing alcohol problems: A guide for clinicians and researchers.* (pp. 1–11). Washington: Department of Health and Human Services.

Compas, B. E., & Epping, J. E. (1993). Stress and coping in children and families: Implications for children coping with disaster. In C. F. Saylor (Ed.), *Children and disasters.* (pp. 11–28). New York: Plenum.

Comstock, B. S. (1992). Decision to hospitalize and alternatives to hospitalization. In B. Bongar (Ed.), *Suicide: Guidelines for assessment, management and treatment.* New York: Oxford University Press.

Cone, J. D. (1999). Observational assessment: Measure development and research issues. In P. C. Kendall, J. N. Butcher, & G. Holmbeck (Eds.), *Research methods in clinical psychology* (2nd ed.). (pp. 183–223). New York: Wiley.

Connors, G. J., Carroll, K. M., DiClemente, C. C., Longabaugh, R., & Donovan, D. M. (1997). The therapeutic alliance and its relationship to alcoholism treatment participation and outcome. *J. Cons. Clin. Psychol., 65,* 588–98.

Connors, G. J., Maisto, S. A., & Derman, K. H. (1994). Alcohol-related expectancies and their applications to treatment. In R. R. Watson (Ed.), *Drug and alcohol abuse reviews: Vol. 3. Alcohol abuse treatment.* (pp. 203–31). Totowa, NJ: Humana Press.

Conrod, P. J., Pihl, R. O., & Vassileva, J. (1998). Differential sensitivity to alcohol reinforcement in groups of men at risk for distinct alcoholism subtypes. *Alcoholism: Clin. Exper. Res., 22*(3), 585–97.

Conte, J., Berliner, L., & Schuerman, J. (1986). *The impact of sexual abuse on children* (Final Report No. MH 37133). Rockville, MD: National Institute of Mental Health.

Cook, M., & Mineka, S. (1990). Selective associations in the observational conditioning of fear in monkeys. *J. Exper. Psychol.: Animal Behavior Processes, 16,* 372–89.

Cooke, D. J. (1996). Psychopathic personality in different cultures: What do we know? What do we need to find out? *J. Person. Dis., 10*(1), 23–40.

Cookerly, J. R. (1980). Does marital therapy do any lasting good? *Journal of Marital and Family Therapy, 6*(4), 393–97.

Coombs, R. H., Paulson, M. J., & Palley, R. (1988). The institutionalization of drug use in America: Hazardous adolescence, challenging parenthood. *J. Chem. Depen. Treat., 1*(2), 9–37.

Coons, P. M. (1986a). Child abuse and multiple personality disorder: Review of the literature and suggestions for treatment. *Child Abuse and Neglect, 10,* 455–62.

Coons, P. M., & Millstein, V. (1992). Psychogenic amnesia: A clinical investigation of 25 cases. *Dissociation, 5,* 73–79.

Cordova, J. V., & Jacobson, N. S. (1993). Couple distress. In D. H. Barlow (Ed.), *Clinical handbook of psychological disorders* (2nd ed.). (p. 481–512). New York: Guilford.

Cornblatt, B. A., & Keilp, J. G. (1994). Impaired attention, genetics, and the pathophysiology of schizophrenia. *Schizo. Bull., 20*(1), 31–46.

Coryell, W. (1997). Do psychotic, minor, and intermittent depressive disorders exist on a continuum? *J. Affect. Dis., 45,* 75–83.

Coryell, W., Endicott, J., & Keller, M. (1987). The importance of psychotic features to major depression: Course and outcome during a 2-year follow-up. *Acta Psychiatr. Scandin., 75,* 78–85.

Coryell, W., Endicott, J., Keller, M., Andreasen, N., Grove, W., Hirschfeld, R. M. A., & Scheftner, W. (1989). Bipolar affective disorder and high achievement: A familial association. *Amer. J. Psychiat., 146,* 983–88.

Coryell, W., Endicott, J., Maser, J. D., Mueller, T., Lavori, P., & Keller, M. (1995). The likelihood of recurrence in bipolar affective disorder: The importance of episode recency. *J. Affect. Dis., 33,* 201–206.

Coryell, W., & Winokur, G. (1982). Course and outcome. In E. S. Paykel (Ed.), *Handbook of affective disorders.* New York: Guilford.

Coryell, W., & Winokur, G. (1992). Course and outcome. In E. S. Paykel (Ed.), *Handbook of affective disorders* (2nd ed.). New York: Guilford.

Coryell, W., Winoker, G., Keller, M. B., & Scheftner, W. (1992). Alcoholism and primary major depression: A family study approach to co-existing disorders. *J. Affect. Dis., 24,* 93–99.

Costa, P. T., Jr., & McCrae, R. R. (1987). Neuroticism, somatic complaints, and disease: Is the bark worse than the bite? *J. Personal., 55,* 299–316.

Costa, P. T., Jr., Whitfield, J. R., & Stewart, D. (Eds.). (1989). *Alzheimer's disease: Abstracts of the psy-*

chological and behavioral literature. Washington, DC: American Psychological Association.

Costa, P. T., Jr., & Widiger, T. A. (Ed.). (1994). *Personality disorders and the five-factor model of personality.* Washington, DC: American Psychological Association.

Costello, E. J. (1989). Developments in child psychiatric epidemiology. *J. Amer. Acad. Child Adoles. Psychiat., 28,* 836–41.

Cotton, N. S. (1979). The familial incidence of alcoholism. *J. Stud. Alcoh., 40,* 89–116.

Cottraux, J., & Gérard, D. (1998). Neuroimaging and neuroanatomical issues in obsessive-compulsive disorder: Toward an integrative model-perceived impulsivity. In R. Swinson, M. Antony, S. Rachman, & M. Richter (Eds.), *Obsessive-compulsive disorder: Theory, research, and treatment.* (pp. 154–180). New York: Guilford.

Cox, B. J. (1996). The nature and assessment of catastrophic thoughts in panic disorder. *Behav. Res. Ther., 34*(4), 363–74.

Cox, D. J., Freundlich, A., & Meyer, R. G. (1975). Differential effectiveness of electromyographic feedback, verbal relaxation instructions, and medication placebo with tension headaches. *J. Cons. Clin. Psychol., 43,* 892–98.

Coyne, J. C. (1976). Depression and the response of others. *J. Abn. Psychol., 55*(2), 186–93.

Coyne, J. C. (1994). Self-reported distress: Analog or ersatz depression? *Psychol. Bull., 116*(1), 29–45.

Craighead, W. E., Craighead, L. W., & Ilardi, S. S. (1998). Psychosocial treatments for major depressive disorder. In P. E. Nathan & J. M. Gorman (Eds.), *A guide to treatments that work.* (pp. 226–39). New York: Oxford University Press.

Craske, M. G., & Barlow, D. H. (1993). Panic disorder and agoraphobia. In D. H. Barlow (Ed.), *Clinical handbook of psychological disorders.* (pp. 1–47). New York: Guilford.

Craske, M. G., & Rowe, M. K. (1997). A comparison of behavioral and cognitive treatments of phobias. In G. C. L. Davey, (Ed.), *Phobias: A handbook of theory, research and treatment.* (pp. 247–80). Chichester, England: Wiley.

Crepeau, F., & Scherzer, P. (1993). Predictors and indicators of work status after traumatic brain injury: A meta-analysis. *Neuropsychological Rehabilitation, 3*(1), 5–35.

Crews, F. (1995). *The memory wards: Freud's legacy in dispute.* New York: Granta.

Crits-Christoph, P. (1992). The efficacy of brief dynamic psychotherapy: A meta-analysis. *Amer. J. Psychiat., 149*(2), 151–58.

Crits-Christoff, P., & Connolly, M. B. (in press). Empirical bases of supportive-expressive psychodynamic psychotherapy. In R. F. Bornstein & J. M. Masling (Eds.), *Empirical research on the psychoanalytic process.* Washington: American Psychological Association.

Crits-Christoph, P. (1998). Psychosocial treatments for personality disorders. In P. E. Nathan & J. M. Gorman (Eds.), *A guide to treatments that work.* (pp. 544–53). New York: Oxford University Press.

Crittenden, P. M., & Ainsworth, M. D. S. (1989). Child maltreatment and attachment theory. In D. Cicchetti & V. Carlson (Eds.), *Child maltreatment: Theory and research on the causes and consequences of child abuse and neglect.* (pp. 432–63). Cambridge: Cambridge University Press.

Crouch, J. L., & Milner, J. S. (1993). Effective intervention with neglected families. *Crim. Just. Behav., 20,* 49–65.

Crow, T. J. (1985). The two syndrome concept: Origins and current status. *Schizo. Bull., 11,* 471–86.

Crow, T. J. (1997). Temporolimbic or transcallosal connections: Where is the primary lesion in schizophrenia and what is its nature? *Schizo. Bull., 23*(3), 521–24.

Csernansky, J. G., & Bardgett, M. E. (1998). Limbic-cortical neuronal damage and the pathophysiology of schizophrenia. *Schizo. Bull., 24*(2), 231–48.

Csernansky, J. G., & Grace, A. A. (1998). New models of the pathophysiology of schizophrenia: Editors' introduction. *Schizo Bull., 24*(2), 185–87.

Cummings, N. (1995). Impact of managed care on employment and training: A primer for survival. *Professional Psychology: Research and Practice, 26,* 10–15.

Dadds, M. R., Heard, P. M., & Rapee, R. M. (1991). Anxiety disorders in children. *Int. Rev. Psychiat., 3,* 231–41.

Dadds, M. R., Spence, S. H., Holland, D. E., Barren, P. M., & Laurens, K. R. (1997). Prevention and early intervention for anxiety disorders: A controlled study. *J. Cons. Clin. Psychol., 65*(4), 627–35.

Dahl, R. E. (1992). The pharmacologic treatment of sleep disorders. *Psychiat. Clin. N. Amer., 15,* 161–78.

Dalgleish, T., Rosen, K., & Marks, M. (1996). Rhythm and blues: The theory and treatment of seasonal affective disorder. *Brit. J. Clini. Psychol., 35,* 163–82.

Dare, C., & Eisler, I. (1997). Family therapy for anorexia nervosa. In D. M. Garner & P. E. Garfinkel (Eds.), *Handbook of treatment for eating disorders.* (pp. 307–24). New York: Guilford.

Darke, J. L. (1990). Sexual aggression: Achieving power through humiliation. In W. L. Marshall, D. R. Laws, & H. E. Barbaree (Eds.), *Handbook of sexual assault.* (pp. 55–72). New York: Plenum.

Davey, G. C. L. (1997). A conditioning model of phobias. In G. C. L. Davey, (Ed.), *Phobias: A handbook of theory, research and treatment.* (pp. 301–22). Chichester, England: Wiley.

Davidson, K., & Prkachin, K. (1997). Optimism and unrealistic optimism have an interacting impact on health-promoting behavior and knowledge changes. *Personal Soc. Psychol. Bull., 23*(6), 617–625.

Davidson, K. M., & Tyrer, P. (1996). Cognitive therapy for antisocial and borderline personality disorders: Single case study series. *Brit. J. Clin. Psychol., 35,* 412–429.

Davidson, R. J. (1998). Affective style and affective disorders: Perspectives from affective neuroscience. *Cognition and Emotion, 12,* 307–330.

Davies, P. (1986). The genetics of Alzheimer's disease: A review and discussion of the implications. *Neurobiol. Aging, 7,* 459–66.

Davies, P. T., & Windle, M. (1997). Gender-specific pathways between maternal depressive symptoms, family discord, and adolescent adjustment. *Develop. Psychol., 33*(4), 657–68.

Davila, J., Hammen, C., Burge, D., Paley, B., & Daley, S. E. (1995). Poor interpersonal problem solving as a mechanism of stress generation in depression among adolescent women. *J. Abn. Psychol., 104*(4), 592–600.

Dawe, S., & Richmond, R. (1997). Controlled drinking as a treatment goal in Australian alcohol treatment agencies. *J. Subst. Abuse, 14*(1), 81–6.

Dawkins, M. P. (1997). Drug use and violent crime among adolescents. *Adolescence, 32,* 395–405.

DAWN Project (1996). Heroin: Abuse and addiction. NIDA Research Report. Washington: National Household Survey on Drug Abuse.

Dawson, D. A., Harford, T. C., & Grant, B. F. (1992). Family history as a predictor of alcohol dependence. *Alcoholism: Clin. Exper. Res., 16,* 572–75.

Dawson, G., Panagiotides, H., Klinger, L. G., & Spieker, S. (1997). Infants of depressed and nondepressed mothers exhibit differences in frontal brain electrical activity during the expression of negative emotions. *Develop. Psychol., 33*(5), 650–56.

Dawson, P. M., Griffith, K., & Boeke, K. M. (1990). Combined medical and psychological treatment of hospitalized children with encopresis. *Child Psychiat. Human Devel., 20,* 181–290.

Deale, A., Chalder, T., Marks, I., & Wessely, S. (1997). Cognitive behavior therapy for chronic fatigue syndrome. *Amer. J. Psychiat., 154*(3), 408–14.

Deas-Nesmith, D., Brady, K. T., & Campbell, S. (1998). Comorbid substance use and anxiety disorders in adolescents. *J. Psychopath. Behav. Assess., 20*(2), 139–48.

Debettignles, B. H., Swihart, A. A., Green, L. A., & Pirozzolo, F. J. (1997). The neuropsychology of normal aging and dementia: An introduction. In J. A. M. Horton, D. Wedding, & J. Webster (Eds.), *The neuropsychology handbook* (Vol. 2). (pp. 173–210). New York: Springer.

DeFazio, V. J., Rustin, S., & Diamond, A. (1975). Symptom development in Vietnam era veterans. *Amer. J. Orthopsychiat., 45*(1), 158–63.

DeLisi, L. E., Crow, T. J., & Hirsch, S. R. (1986a). The third biannual winter workshops on schizophrenia. *Arch. Gen. Psychiat., 43,* 706–11.

DeLisi, L. E., Goldin, L. R., Hamovit, J. R., Maxwell, E., & Kuritz, D. (1986b). A family study of the association of increased ventricular size with schizophrenia. *Arch. Gen. Psychiat., 43,* 148–53.

DeLisi, L. E., Mirsky, A. F., Buchsbaum, M. S., van Kammen, D. P., Berman, K. F., Phelps, B. H., Karoum, F., Ko, G. N., Korpi, E. R., et al. (1984). The Genain quadruplets 25 years later: A diagnostic and biochemical followup. *Psychiat. Res., 13,* 59–76.

Delk, E. W., & Meilman, P. W. (1996). Alcohol use among college students in Scotland compared with norms from the United States. *J. Amer. Coll. Hlth, 44,* 274–81.

DeMarsh, J., & Kumpfer, K. L. (1985). Family-oriented interventions for the prevention of chemical dependency in children and adolescents. Special Issue: Childhood and Chemical Abuse: Prevention and Intervention. *J. Child. Contem. Soc., 18*(1–2), 117–51.

Deming, M. P., Chase, N. D., & Karesh, D. (1996). Parental alcoholism and perceived levels of family health among college freshmen. *Alcoholism Treatment Quarterly, 14*(1), 47–56.

Den Boer, J. A., Vilet, I. M., & Westenberg, H. G. M. (1996). Advances in the psychopharmacology of social phobia. In H. G. Westenberg, J. A. Den Boer, & D. L. Murphy (Eds.), *Advances in the neurobiology of anxiety disorders.* (pp. 401–418). Chichester, England: Wiley.

de Pauw, K. W., & Szulecka, T. K. (1988). Dangerous delusions: Violence and misidentification syndromes. *Brit. J. Psychiat., 152,* 91–96.

Depue, R. A. (1996). A neurobiological framework for the structure of personality and emotion: Implications for personality disorders. In J. F. Clarkin & M. F. Lenzenweger (Eds.), *Major the-*

ories of personality disorder. (pp. 347–390). New York: Guilford.

Derr, R. F., & Gutmann, H. R. (1994). Alcoholic liver disease may be prevented with adequate nutrients. *Medical Hypotheses, 42,* 1–4.

DeRubeis, R. (1997, May). *Cognitive therapy IS as effective as medication for severe depression: A mega-analysis.* Paper presented at the meeting of the Amercian Psychological Society, Washington.

DeRubeis, R. J., Gelfand, L. A., Tang, T. Z., & Simons, A. D. (1999). Medications versus cognitive behavior therapy for severely depressed outpatients: Mega-analysis of four randomized comparisons. *Amer. J. Psychiat., 156,* 1007–1013.

De Silva, P., Rachman, S. J., & Seligman, M. E. P. (1977). Prepared phobias and obsessions: Therapeutic outcomes. *Behav. Res. Ther., 15,* 65–78.

De Silva, R. A. (1993). Cardiac arrhythmias and sudden cardiac death. In A. Stoudemire & B. Fogel (Eds.), *Medical-psychiatric practice* (vol 2, p. 199). Washington, DC: American Psychiatric Press.

Deutsch, A. (1948). *The shame of the states.* New York: Harcourt, Brace.

Devanand, D. P., et al. (1994). Does ECT alter brain structure? *Amer. J. Psychiat., 151,* 957–70.

DeVane, C. L., & Sallee, F. R. (1996). Serotonin selective reuptake inhibitors in child and adolescent psychopharmacology: A review of published experience. *J. Clin. Psychiat., 57*(2), 55–66.

de Vries, L. B. A., Halley, D. J. J., Oostra, B. A., & Niermeijer, M. F. (1994). The fragile-X syndrome: A growing gene causing familial intellectual disability. *J. Intellect. Dis. Res., 38*(1), 1–8.

Dew, M. A., Penkower, L., & Bromet, E. J. (1991). Effects of unemployment on mental health in the contemporary family. *Behav. Mod., 15,* 501–544.

De Young, M. (1982) Innocent seducer and innocently seduced? The role of the child incest victim. *J. Clin. Child. Psychol, 11,* 56–60.

Diamond, M. C. (1988). *Enriching heredity: The impact of the environment on the anatomy of the brain.* New York: Free Press.

Di Clemente, C. C. (1993). Changing addictive behaviors: A process perspective. *Curr. Dir. Psychol. Sci., 2,* 101–6.

Dikmen, S. S., & Levin, H. S. (1993). Methodological issues in the study of mild head injury. *J. Head Trauma Rehab., 8*(3), 30–37.

Dikmen, S. S., Temkin, N. R., Machamer, J. E., & Holubkov, A. L. (1994). Employment following traumatic head injuries. *Arch. Neurol., 51*(2), 177–86.

Dilk, M. N., & Bond, G. R. (1996). Meta-analytic evaluation of skills training research for individuals with severe mental illness. *J. Cons. Clin. Psychol., 64*(6), 1337–46.

Diller, L., & Gordon, W. A. (1981). Interventions for cognitive deficits in brain-injured adults. *J. Cons. Clin. Psychol., 49,* 822–34.

Diokno, A. C., Brown, M. B., & Herzog, A. R. (1990). Sexual function in the elderly. *Arch. Int. Med., 150,* 197–200.

Dishion, T. P, & Patterson, G. R. (1997). The timing and severity of antisocial behavior: Three hypotheses within an ecological framework. In D. M. Stoff, J. Breiling, & J. D. Maser (Eds.), *Handbook of antisocial behavior.* (pp. 205–217). New York: Wiley.

Doane, J. A., West, K., Goldstein, M. J., Rodnick, E., & Jones, J. (1981). Parental communication deviance and affective style as predictors of subsequent schizophrenia spectrum disorders in vulnerable adolescents. *Arch. Gen. Psychiat., 38,* 679–85.

Dodd, B., & Leahy, J. (1989). Facial prejudice. *Amer. J. Ment. Retard., 94,* 111.

Dodge, K. A. (1980). Social cognition and children's aggressive behavior. *Child Develop., 51,* 162–70.

Dodge, K. A., Lochman, J. E., Harnish, J. D., Bates, J. E., & Pettit, G. S. (1997). Reactive and proactive aggression in school children and psychiatrically impaired chronically assaultive youth. *J. Abn. Psychol., 106*(1), 37–51.

Dodge, K. A., Pettit, G. S., & Bates, J. E. (1994). Socialization mediators of the relation between socioeconomic status and child conduct problems. *Child Develop., 65,* 649–65.

Dohrenwend, B. P. (1998). A psychosocial perspective on the past and future of psychiatric epidemiology. *Amer. J. Epidemiol., 147*(3), 222–29.

Dohrenwend, B. P., Dohrenwend, B. S., Gould, M. S., Link, B., Neugebauer, R., & Wunsch-Hitzig, R. (1980). *Mental illness in the United States: Epidemiological estimates.* New York: Praeger.

Dohrenwend, B. P., Shrout, P. E., Link, B. G., Skodol, A. E., & Martin, J. L. (1986). Overview and initial results from a risk factor study of depression and schizophrenia. In J. E. Barrett (Ed.), *Mental disorders in the community: Progress and challenge.* New York: Guilford Press.

Dohrenwend, B. P., Shrout, P. E., Link, B. G., Skodol, A. E., & Stueve, A. (1995). A case-control study of life events and other possible psychosocial risk factors for episodes of schizophrenia and major depression. In C. M. Mazure (Ed.), *Does stress cause psychiatric illness?* Washington, DC: American Psychiatric Press.

Dolberg, O. T., Iancu, I., Sasson, Y., & Zohar, J. (1996a). The pathogenesis and treatment of obsessive-compulsive disorder. *Clin. Neuropharmac., 19*(2), 129–147.

Dolberg, O. T., Sasson, Y., Marazziti, D., Kotler, M., Kindler, S., & Zohar, J. (1996b). New compounds for the treatment of obsessive-compulsive disorder. In H. G. Westenberg, J. A. Den Boer, & D. L. Murphy (Eds.), *Advances in the neurobiology of anxiety disorders.* (pp. 299–311). Chichester, England: Wiley.

Dolphus, S., et al., (1996). Identifying subtypes of schizophrenia by cluster analysis. *Schizo Bull., 22*(3), 545–55.

Donaldson, M. A., & Gardner, R., Jr. (1985). Diagnosis and treatment of traumatic stress among women after childhood incest. In C. R. Filley (Ed.), *Trauma and its wake: The study and treatment of posttraumatic stress disorder.* (pp. 356–77). Newbury Park, CA: Sage.

Donne, J. (1624). Meditation XVII. *Devotions upon emergent occasions.* London.

Dooley, D., & Catalano, R. (1980). Economic change as a cause of behavioral disorder. *Psychol. Bull., 87,* 450–68.

Dorwart, R. A., Schlesinger, M., Horgan, C., & Davidson, H. (1989). The privatization of mental health care and directions for mental health services research. In C. A. Taube, D. Mechanic, & A. A. Hohmann (Eds.), *The future of mental health services research.* (pp. 139–54). Washington, DC: U.S. Department of Health and Human Services.

Drtikova, I., Balastikova, B., Lemanova, H., & Zak, J. (1996). Clonazepam, clonidine and tiapride in children with tic disorder. *Homeostasis in Health & Disease, 37*(5), 216.

DuFour, M. C., Stinson, F. S., & Cases, M. F. (1993). Trends in cirrhosis morbidity and mortality. *Seminars in Liver Disease, 13*(2), 109–25.

Dunbar, F., (1943). *Psychosomatic diagnosis.* New York: Harper & Row.

Duncan, G. J., Brooks-Gunn, J., & Klebanov, P. K. (1994). Economic deprivation and early childhood development. *Child Develop., 65,* 296–318.

Dunne, E. J. (1992). Following a suicide: Postvention. In B. Bongar (Ed.), *Suicide: Guidelines for assessment, management and treatment.* New York: Oxford University Press.

Dunner, D. L. (1993). *Psychiatric clinics of North America.* Philadelphia: Saunders.

DuPaul, G. I., & Barkley, R. A. (1990). Medication therapy. In R. A. Barkley (Ed.), *Attention deficit hyperactivity disorder: A handbook for diagnosis and treatment.* (pp. 573–612). New York: Guilford.

Durkheim, E. (1951). *Suicide: A study in sociology* (J. A. Spaulding & G. Simpson, Trans., G. Simpson, Ed.). New York: Free Press. (Originally published 1897.)

Dwork, A. J. (1997). Postmortem studies on the hippocampal formation in schizophrenia. *Schizo. Bull., 23*(3), 385–402.

Dworkin, R. H., et al. (1998). Affective expression and affective experience in schizophrenia. In M. F. Lenzenweger & R. H. Dworkin (Eds.) *Origins and development of schizophrenia.* (pp. 385–426). Washington: American Psychological Association.

Dworkin, R. H., Cornblatt, B. A., Friedman, R., Kaplansky, L. M., Lewis, J. A., Rinaldi, A., Shilliday, C., & Erlenmeyer–Kimling, L. (1993). Childhood precursors of affective vs. social deficits in adolescents at risk for schizophrenia. *Schizo. Bull., 19*(3), 563–77.

Earl, H. G. (1965). 10,000 children battered and starved: Hundreds die. *Today's Health, 43*(9), 24–31.

Earlywine, M., & Finn, P. R. (1990, March). *Personality, drinking habits, and responses to cues for alcohol.* Paper presented at the 5th Congress of the International Society for Biomedical Research on Alcoholism and the Research Society on Alcoholism, Toronto, Canada.

Eaton, W. W. (1985). Epidemiology of schizophrenia. *Epidemiological Reviews,* 7, 105–26.

Eaton, W. W., Kessler, R. C., Wittchen, H. U., & Magee, W. J. (1994). Panic and panic disorder in the United States. Amer. *J. Psychiat., 151*(3), 413–20.

Eaton, W. W., & Keyl, P. M. (1990). Risk factors for the onset of Diagnostic Interview Schedule/DSM-III agoraphobia in a prospective, population based study. *Arch. Gen. Psychiat., 47,* 819–24.

Ebert, D., & Martus, P. (1994). Somatization as a core symptom of melancholic type depression. *J. Affect. Dis., 32*(4), 253–256.

Ebigo, P. O. (1982). Development of a culture specific (Nigeria) screening scale of somatic complaints indicating psychiatric disturbance. *Culture, Medicine and Psychiatry, 6,* 29–43.

Egeland, B. & Sroufe, L. A. (1981). Attachment and early maltreatment. *Child Develop., 52,* 44–52.

Egendorf, A. (1986). *Healing from the war.* Boston: Houghton Mifflin.

Ehlers, A. (1993). Somatic symptoms and panic attacks: A retrospective study of learning experiences. *Behav. Res. Ther., 31*(3), 269–278.

Ehlers, A. (1995). A 1-year prospective study of panic attacks: Clinical course and factors associated with maintenance. *J. Abn. Psychol.*, 104.

Ehlers, A., & Breuer, P. (1996). How good are patients with panic disorder at perceiving their heartbeats. *Biol. Psychol., 42,* 165–82.

Eich, E., Macaulay, D., Loewenstein, R. J., & Dihle, P. H. (1997). Memory, amnesia, and dissociative identity disorder. *Psychol. Sci., 8,* 417–422.

Eisenberg, H. M. (1990). Behavioral changes after closed head injury in children. *J. Cons. Clin. Psychol., 58,* 93–98.

Ellason, J. W., & Ross, C. A. (1997). Two-year follow-up of inpatients with dissociative identity disorder. *Amer. J. Psychiat., 154*(6), 832–839.

Ellicott, A., Hammen, C., Gitlin, M., Brown, G., & Jamison, K. (1990). Life events and the course of bipolar disorder. *Amer. J. Psychiat., 147,* 1194–98.

Ellis, A. (1958). Rational psychotherapy. *J. Gen. Psychol., 59,* 35–49.

Ellis, A. (1970). *Reason and emotion in psychotherapy.* New York: Lyle Stuart.

Ellis, A. (1973). Rational-emotive therapy. In R. J. Corsini (Ed.), *Current psychotherapies.* Itasca, IL: Peacock Publishers.

Ellis, A. (1975). Creative job and happiness: The humanistic way. *The Humanist, 35*(1), 11–13.

Ellis, A. (1989). The history of cognition in psychotherapy. In A. Freeman, K. M. Simon, L. E. Beutler, & H. Arkowitz (Eds.), *Comprehensive handbook of cognitive therapy.* (pp. 5–19). New York: Plenum.

Ellis, A., & Dryden, W. (1997). *The practice of rational emotive behavior therapy* (2nd ed.). New York: Springer.

Ellis, L. (1989). *Theories of rape: Inquiries into the causes of sexual aggression.* New York: Hemisphere Publishing.

Ellison, K. (1977). Personal communication.

Emery, R. E., & Kitzmann, K. M. (1995). The child in the family: Disruptions in family functions. In D. Cicchetti & D. J. Cohen (Eds.), *Developmental psychopathology: Vol. 2. Risk, disorder, and adaptation.* (pp. 3–31). New York: Wiley.

Emery, R. E., & Laumann-Billings, L. (1998). An overview of the nature, causes, and consequences of abusive relationships: Toward differentiating maltreatment and violence. *Amer. Psychol., 53*(2), 121–35.

Emmelkamp, P. M. G. (1994). Behavior therapy with adults. In A. E. Bergin & S. L. Garfield (Eds.), *Handbook of psychotherapy and behavior change* (4th ed.). (pp. 379–427). New York: Wiley

Emslie, G. J., Rush, A. J., Weinberg, W. A., Kowatch, R. A., Hughes, C. W., Carmody, T., & Rintelmann, J. (1997). A double-blind, randomized, placebo-controlled trial of fluoxetine in children and adolescents with depression. *Arch. Gen. Psychiat., 54,* 1031–37.

Endicott, J., et al. (1986). Diagnosis of schizophrenia: Predictions of short-term outcome. *Arch. Gen. Psychiat.*, 43, 13–19.

Engdahl, B. E., Harkness, A. R., Eberly, R. E., & Bielinski, J. (1993). Structural models of captivity trauma, resilence, and trauma response among former prisoners of war 20 and 40 years after release. *Soc. Psychiat. Psychiat. Epidemiol., 28,* 109–15.

Englander-Golden, P., Elconin, J., Miller, K. J., & Schwarzkopf, A. B., (1986). Brief SAY IT STRAIGHT training and follow-up in adolescent substance abuse prevention. *J. Prim. Preven., 6*(4), 219–30.

Epstein, R. S., Fullerton, C. S., & Ursano, R. J. (1998). Posttraumatic stress disorder following an air disaster: A prospective study. *Amer. J. Psychiat., 155*(7), 934–38.

Epstein, S. (1994). Integration of the cognitive and the psychodynamic unconscious. *Amer. Psychol., 49*(8), 709–24.

Erickson, S. J., Feldman, S., Shirley, S., & Steiner, H. (1996). Defense mechanisms and adjustment in normal adolescents. *Amer. J. Psychiat., 153*(6), 826–28.

Eriksen, W. (1994). The role of social support in the pathogenesis of coronary heart disease. A literature review. *Fam. Pract., 11,* 201–209.

Ernst, R. L., et al. (1997). Cognitive function and the costs of Alzheimer disease: An exploratory study. *Arch. Neurol., 54*(6), 687–93.

Eron, L. D., Huesmann, L. R., Lefkowitz, M. M., & Walder, L. O. (1974). How learning conditions in early childhood—including mass media—relate to aggression in late adolescence. *Amer. J. Orthopsychiat., 44*(3), 412–23.

Eronen, M., Hakola, P., & Tiihonen, J. (1996). Mental disorders and homicidal behavior in Finland. *Arch. Gen. Psychiat., 53*(6), 497–501.

Errico, A. L., Parsons, O. A., & King, A. C. (1991). Assessment of verbosequential and visuospatial cognitive abilities in chronic alcoholics. *Psychol. Assess., 3,* 693–96.

Evans, D. A., Funkerstein, H., Albert, M. S., Scherr, P. A., Cook, N. R., Chown, M. J., Hebert, L. E., Hennekens, C. H., & Taylor, J. O. (1989). Prevalence of Alzheimer's disease in a community population of older persons. *JAMA, 262,* 2551–56.

Evans, D. W., King, R. A., & Leckman, J. F. (1996). Tic disorders. In E. J. Mash & R. A. Barkley (Eds.), *Child psychopathology.* (pp. 436–56). New York: Guilford.

Everly, G. S. (1995). The role of the Critical Incident Stress Debriefing (CISD) process in disaster counseling. Special Issue: Disasters and crises: A mental health counseling perspective. *J. Ment. Hlth. Couns., 17*(3), 278–90.

Everson, S. A., et al. (1997). Hopelessness and 4-year progression of carotid atherosclerosis: The Kuopio ischemic heart disease risk factor study. *Arteriosclerosis, Thrombosis, and Vascular Biology, 17,* 1490–1495.

Exner, J. E. (1993). *The Rorschach: A comprehensive system. Vol. 1: Basic foundations.* New York: Wiley.

Exner, J. E. (1995). Why use personality tests? A brief historical view. In J. N. Butcher (Ed.), *Clinical personality assessment: Practical considerations* (10th ed.). (pp. 10–18). New York: Oxford University Press.

Eyman, J. R., & Eyman, S. K. (1992). Psychological testing for potentially suicidal individuals. In B. Bongar (Ed.), *Suicide: Guidelines for assessment, management and treatment.* New York: Oxford University Press.

Eysenck, H. J. (1965). Extroversion and the acquisition of eyeblink and GSR conditioned responses. *Psychol. Bull., 63,* 258–70.

Eysenck, M. W., Mogg, K., May, J., Richards, A., & Mathews, A. (1991). Bias in interpretation of ambiguous sentences related to threat in anxiety. *J. Abn. Psychol., 100,* 144–50.

Fabrega, H. (1981). Cultural programming of brain-behavior relationships. In J. R. Merikangas (Ed.), *Brain-behavior relationships.* Lexington, MA: Heath.

Faigel, H., & Heiligenstein, E. (1996). Medication for attention deficit hyperactivity disorder: Commentary and response. *J. Amer. Coll. Hlth, 45,* 40–42.

Fairbank, J. A., Schlenger, W. E., Caddell, J. M., & Woods, M. G. (1993). Posttraumatic stress disorder. In P. Sutker & H. E. Adams (Eds.), *Comprehensive handbook of psychopathology* (2nd ed.). (pp. 145–65). New York: Plenum.

Fairburn, C. G., & Carter, J. C. (1997). Self-help and guided self-help for binge-eating problems. In D. M. Garner & P. E. Garfinkel (Eds.), *Handbook of treatment for eating disorders.* (pp. 494–499). New York: Guilford.

Fairburn, C. G., Jones, R., Peveler, R. C., Hope, R. A., & O'Connor, M. (1993). Psychotherapy and bulimia nervosa: Long-term effects of interpersonal psychotherapy, behavior therapy, and cognitive behavior therapy. *Arch. Gen. Psychiat., 50*(6), 419–28.

Fairburn, C. G., Welch, S. L., Doll, H. A., Davies, B. A., & O'Connor, M. E. (1997). Risk factors for bulimia nervosa: A community-based case-control study. *Arch. Gen. Psychiat., 54*(6), 509–517.

Fairweather, G. W. (Ed.). (1980). *The Fairweather Lodge: A twenty-five year retrospective.* San Francisco: Jossey Bass.

Fairweather, G. W., Sanders, D. H., Maynard, H., & Cressler, D. L. (1969). *Community life for the mentally ill: An alternative to institutional care.* Chicago: Aldine.

Fallon, A. E., & Rozin, P. (1985). Sex differences in perceptions of desirable body shape. *J. Abn. Psychol., 94,* 102–5.

Falloon, I. R. H., Boyd, J. L., McGill, C. W., Williamson, M., & Razani, J. (1985). Family management in the prevention of morbidity of schizophrenia: Clinical outcome of a two-year longitudinal study. *Arch. Gen. Psychiat., 42,* 887–96.

Falsetti, S. A., Kilpatrick, D. G., Dansky, B. S., Lydiard, R. B., & Resnick, H. S. (1995). Relationship of stress to panic disorder: Cause or effect? In C. M. Mazure (Ed.), *Does stress cause psychiatric illness?* (pp. 111–47). Washington, DC: American Psychiatric Association.

Fals-Stewart, W., O'Farrell, T. J., & Birchler, G. R. (1997). Behavioral couples therapy for male substance-abusing patients: A cost outcomes analysis. *J. Cons. Clin. Psychol., 65*(5), 789–802.

Famy, C., Streissguth, A. P., & Unis, A. S. (1998). Mental illness in adults with fetal alcohol syndrome or fetal alcohol effects. *Amer. J. Psychiat., 155*(4), 552–34.

Fankhauser, M. P., Karumanchi, V. C., German, M. L., & Yates, A. (1992). A double-blind, placebo-controlled study of the efficacy of transdermal clonidine in autism. *J. Clin. Psychiat., 53,* 77–82.

Faraone, S. V., Biederman, J., Lehman, B. K., & Keenan, K. (1993a). Evidence for the independent familial transmission of attention deficit hyperactivity disorder and learning disabilities: Results from a family genetic study. *Amer. J. Psychiat. 150*(6), 891–95.

Faraone, S. V., Biederman, J., & Milberger, S. (1994). An exploratory study of ADHD among second-degree relatives of ADHD children. *Biol. Psychiat., 35,* 398–402.

Faretra, G. (1981). A profile of aggression from adolescence to adulthood: An 18-year follow-up of psychiatrically disturbed and violent adolescents. *Amer. J. Orthopsychiat., 51,* 439–53.

Fava, M. & Rosenbaum, J. F. (1995). Pharmacotherapy and somatic therapies. In E. E. Beckham & W. R. Leber (Eds.), *Handbook of depression* (2nd ed.). (pp. 280–301). New York: Guilford.

Fava, M. (1997). Psychopharmacologic treatment of pathologic anger. *Psychiat. Clin. N. Amer., 20,* 427–52.

Fawzy, F. I., Fawzy, N. W., Hyun, C. S., Elashoff, R., Guthrie, D., Fahey, J. L., & Morton, D. L. (1993). Malignant melanoma: Effects of an early structured psychiatric intervention, coping, and affective state on recurrence and survival 6 years later. *Arch. Gen. Psychiat., 50*(9), 681–89.

Feingold, B. F. (1977). Behavioral disturbances linked to the ingestion of food additives. *Delaware Medical Journal, 49,* 89–94.

Feldman, L. (1992). *Integrating individual and family therapy.* New York: Brunner/Mazel.

Feldman, L. B., & Feldman, S. L. (1997). Conclusion: Principles for integrating psychotherapy and pharmocotherapy. *In Session: Psychotherapy in Practice, 3*(2), 99–102.

Felsman, J. K., & Valliant, G. E. (1987). Resilient children as adults: A 40-year study. In E. J. Anthony & B. J. Cohler (Eds.), *The invulnerable child.* (pp. 289–314). New York: Guilford.

Fenna, D., et. al. (1971). Ethanol metabolism in various racial groups. *Canadian Medical Association Journal, 105,* 472–75.

Fennell, M. J. V. (1989). Depression. In K. Hawton, P. M. Salkovskis, J. Kirk, & D. M. Clark (Eds.), *Cognitive behaviour therapy for psychiatric problems: A practical guide.* Oxford, UK: Oxford University Press.

Fenton, W. S., & McGlashan, T. H. (1994). Antecedents, symptom progression, and long-term outcome of the deficit syndrome in schizophrenia. *Amer. J. Psychiat., 151*(3), 351–56.

Fenton, W. S., & McGlashan, T. H. (1997). We can talk: Individual psychotherapy for schizophrenia. *Amer. J. Psychiat.,* 154(11), 1493–95.

Fersch, E. A., Jr. (1980). *Psychology and psychiatry in courts and corrections.* New York: Wiley.

Feuerstein, R. (1977). Mediated learning experience: A theoretical basis for cognitive modifiability during adolescence. In P. Mittler (Ed.), *Research to practice in mental retardation* (Vol. 2). (pp. 105–16). Baltimore: University Park Press.

Fichter, M. M., et al. (1991). Fluoxetine versus placebo: A double-blind study with bulimic inpatients undergoing intensive psychotherapy. *Pharmacopsychiatry, 24,* 1–7.

Fields, J. Z., Turk, A., Durkin, M., Ravi, N. V., & Keshavarzian, A. (1994). Increased gastrointestinal symptoms in chronic alcoholics. *American Journal of Gastroenterology, 89,* 382–86.

Fierman, E. J., Hung, M. F., Pratt, L. A., Warshaw, M. G., Yonkers, K. A., Peterson, L. G., Epstein-Kaye, T. M., & Norton, H. S. (1993). Trauma and posttraumatic stress disorder in subjects with anxiety disorders. *Amer. J. Psychiat., 150,* 1872–74.

Figueroa, E., & Silk, K. (1997). Biological implications of childhood sexual abuse in borderline personality disorder. *J. Person. Dis., 11* (1), 71–92.

Fillmore, K. M., Golding, J. M., Leino, E. V., Ager, C. R., & Ferrer, H. P. (1994). Societal-level predictors of groups' drinking patterns: A research synthesis from the Collaborative Alcohol-Related Longitudinal Project. *Amer. J. Pub. Hlth., 84,* 247–53.

Finkelhor, D. (1984). *Child sexual abuse.* New York: Free Press.

Finkelhor, D. (1990). Early and long term effects of child sexual abuse: An update. *Profess. Psychol.: Research and Practice, 21,* 325–30.

Finkelstein, J. R. J., Cannon, T. D., Gur, R. E., Gur, R. C., & Moberg, P. (1997). Attentional dysfunctions in neuroleptic-naive and neuroleptic-withdrawn schizophrenic patients and their siblings. *J. Abn. Psychol., 106*(2), 203–12.

Finn, P. R. (1990, Mar.). *Dysfunction in stimulus-response modulation in men at high risk for alcoholism.* Paper presented at a symposium on the Genetics of Alcoholism: Recent Advances. Satellite Symposium of the Annual Meeting of the Research Society on Alcoholism, Montreal, Canada.

Finn, P. R., & Pihl, R. O. (1987). Men at high risk for alcoholism: The effect of alcohol on cardiovascular response to unavoidable shock. *J. Abn. Psychol., 96,* 230–36.

Finn, P. R., Sharkansky, E. J., Viken, R., West, T. L., Sandy, J., & Bufferd, S. (1997). Heterogeneity in the families of sons of alcoholics: The impact of familial vulnerability type on offspring characteristics. *J. Abn. Psychol., 106*(1), 26–36.

Finn, S. E., & Tonsager, M. E. (1997). Information–gathering and therapeutic models of assessment: Complementary paradigms. *Psychol. Assess., 9*(4), 374–85.

First, M. B., Williams, J. B. W., & Spitzer, R. L. (1997). *DTREE: The DSM-IV Expert.* Toronto: Multi-Health Systems.

Fischer, M. (1971). Psychoses in the offspring of schizophrenic monozygotic twins and their normal co-twins. *Brit. J. Psychiat., 118,* 43–52.

Fischer, M. (1973). Genetic and environmental factors in schizophrenia: A study of schizophrenic twins and their families. *Acta Psychiatr. Scandin.,* Suppl. No. 238.

Fischer, P. J., Shapiro, S., Breakey, W. R., Anthony, J. C., & Kramer, M. (1986). Mental health and social characteristics of the homeless: A survey of mission users. *Amer. J. Pub. Hlth., 76*(5), 519–24.

Fish, B., Marcus, J., Hans, S. L., Auerbach, J. G., & Perdue, S. (1992). Infants at risk for schizophrenia: Sequelae of a genetic neurointegrative defect: A review and replication analysis of pandysmaturation in the Jerusalem Infant Development Study. *Arch. Gen. Psychiat., 49*(3), 221–35.

Fisher, J. D., & Fisher, W. A. (1992). Changing AIDS-risk behavior. *Psychol. Bull., 111*(3), 455–74.

Fisher, J. E., & Carstensen, L. L. (1990). Behavior management for the dementias. *Clin. Psychol. Rev., 10,* 611–30.

Fisher, S., & Greenberg, R. P. (1997a). The curse of the placebo: Fanciful pursuit of a pure biological therapy. In S. Fisher & R. P. Greenberg (Eds.), *From placebo to panacea: Putting psychiatric drugs to the test.* (pp. 3–56). New York: Wiley.

Fiske, S., & Taylor, S. (1991). *Social cognition,* 2nd ed. New York: McGraw Hill.

Flier, J. S., Underhill, L. H., & Lieber, C. S. (1995). Medical disorders of alcoholism. *New Engl. J. Med., 333*(6), 1058–65.

Flor, H., & Birbaumer, N. (1993). Comparison of the efficacy of electromyographic biofeedback, cogntive-behavior therapy, and conservative medical interventions in the treatment of chronic musculoskeletal pain. *J. Cons. Clin. Psychol., 61*(4), 653–58.

Foa, E., Franklin, M., & Kozak, M. (1998). Psychosocial treatments for obsessive-compulsive disorder: Literature review. In R. Swinson, M. Antony, S. Rachman, & M. Richter (Eds.), *Obsessive-compulsive disorder: Theory, research, and treatment.* (pp. 258–76). New York: Guilford.

Foa, E., & Kozak, M. J. (1986). Emotional processing of fear: Exposure to corrective information. *Psychol. Bull., 99,* 20–35.

Foa, E. B., Zinbarg, R., & Rothbaum, B. O. (1992). Uncontrollability and unpredictability in post-traumatic stress disorder: An animal model. *Psychol. Bull., 112*(2), 218–238.

Foley, M. A. Santini, C., & Sopasakis, M. (1989). Discriminating between memories: Evidence for children's spontaneous elaboration. *Journal of Experimental Child Psychology. 48,* 146–69.

Foltin, R. W., & Fischman, M. W. (1997). A laboratory model of cocaine withdrawal in humans: Intravenous cocaine. *Experimental and Clinical Pharmacology, 5*(4), 404–11.

Fombonne, E., & du Mazaubrun, C. (1992). Prevalence of infantile autism in four French regions. *Soc. Psychiat. Psychiat. Epidemiol., 27,* 203–10.

Forehand, R. (1993). Twenty years of research on parenting: Does it have practical implications for clinicians working with parents and children? *Clin. Psychol., 46,* 169–76.

Forehand, R., Wierson, M., Frame, C. L., & Kempton, T. (1991). Juvenile firesetting: A unique syndrome or an advanced level of antisocial behavior? *Behav. Res. Ther., 29,* 125–28.

Forgac, G. E., & Michaels, E. J. (1982). Personality characteristics of two types of male exhibitionists. *J. Abn. Psychol., 91,* 287–93.

Forness, S. R., & Kavale, K. A. (1993). Strategies to improve basic learning and memory deficits in mental retardation: A meta-analysis of experimental studies. *Education and Training in Mental Retardation, 28*(2), 99–110.

Fowles, D. C. (1980). The three arousal model: Implications of Gray's two-factor learning theory for heart rate, electrodermal activity, and psychopathy. *Psychophysiology, 17,* 87–104.

Fowles, D. C. (1993). Electrodermal activity and antisocial behavior: Empirical findings and theoretical issues. In J.-C. Roy, W. Boucsein, D. Fowles, & J. Gruzelier (Eds.), *Progress in electrodermal research.* London: Plenum.

Fowles, D. C., & Missel, K. A. (1994). Electrodermal hyporeactivity, motivation, and psychopathy: Theoretical issues. In D. C. Fowles, P. Sutker, & S. H. Goodman (Eds.), *Progress in experimental personality and psychopathology research.* New York: Springer.

Frances, A. J., et al. (1991). An A-to-Z guide to DSM-IV communications *J. Abn. Psychol., 100,* 907–12.

Frank, E., Anderson, C., & Rubenstein, D. (1978). Frequency of sexual dysfunction in normal couples. *New Engl. J. Med., 299,* 111–15.

Frank, E., Kupfer, D. J., Perel, J. M., Cornes, C., Jarett, D. B., Mallinger, A. G., Thase, M. E., McEachran, A. B., & Grochocinski, V. J. (1990). Three-year outcomes for maintenance therapies in recurrent depression. *Arch. Gen. Psychiat., 47,* 1093–99.

Frank, E., Prien, R. F., Jarrett, R. B., Keller, M. B., Kupfer, D. J., Lavori, P. W., Rush, A. J., & Weissman, M. M. (1991). Conceptualization and rationale for consensus definitions of terms in major depressive disorder: Remission, recovery, relapse, and recurrence. *Arch. Gen. Psychiat., 48,* 851–55.

Frank, E., & Spanier, C. (1995). Interpersonal psychotherapy for depression: Overview, clinical efficacy, and future directions. *Clin. Psychol. Sci. Pract., 2,* 349–69.

Frank, J. D. (1978). *Persuasion and healing* (2nd ed.). Baltimore: Johns Hopkins University Press.

Frasure-Smith, N., Lesperance, F., & Talajic, M. (1993). Depression following myocardial infarction: Impact on 6-month survival. *JAMA, 270,* 1819–25.

Frasure-Smith, N., Lesperance, F., & Talajic, M. (1995). Depression and 18-month prognosis following myocardial infarction. *Circulation, 91,* 999.

Fray, J. C. S., & Douglas, J. G. (Eds.). (1993). *Pathophysiology of hypertension in blacks.* New York: Oxford University Press.

Frayser, S. G. (1985). *Varieties of sexual experience: An anthropological perspective on human sexuality.* New Haven, CT: HRAF Press.

Frazier, M., & Merrill, K. W. (1998). Issues in behavioral treatment of attention-deficit/hyperactivity disorder. *Education & Treatment of Children, 20*(4), 441–61.

Frazier, P., & Burnett, J. (1994). Immediate coping strategies among rape victims. *J. Couns. Devel. 72,* 633–39.

Frazier, P., & Schauben, L. (1994). Causal attributions and recovery from rape and other stressful life events. *J. Soc. Clin. Psychol., 14,* 1–14.

Frederick, C. J. (1985). An introduction and overview of youth suicide. In M. L. Peck, N. L. Farberow, & R. E. Litman (Eds.), *Youth Suicide.* (pp. 1– 6). New York: Springer.

Freeman, R. D., Malkin, S. F., & Hastings, J. O. (1975). Psychosocial problems of deaf children and their families: A comparative study. *Amer. Ann. Deaf, 120,* 391–405.

Freeman, T. (1960). On the psychopathology of schizophrenia. *J. Ment. Sci., 106,* 925–37.

Freeman, W. (1959). Psychosurgery. In S. Arieti (Ed.), *American handbook of psychiatry* (Vol. 2). (pp. 1521–40). New York: Basic Books.

Fremouw, W. J., de Perczel, M., & Ellis, T. E. (1990). *Suicide risk: Assessment and response guidelines.* Elmsford, NY: Pergamon.

Freud, A. (1946). *Ego and the mechanisms of defense.* New York: International Universities Press.

Freud, S. (1917). Mourning and Melancholia. In W. Gaylin (Ed.), *The meaning of despair: Psychoanalytic contributions to the understanding of depression.* New York: Science House.

Freud, S. (1935). Letter to an American mother. Reprinted in Paul Friedman (1959), Sexual deviations, in S. Arieti (Ed.), *American Handbook of Psychiatry* (Vol. 1). (pp. 606–7). New York: Basic Books.

Freund, K., & Blanchard, R. (1993). Erotic target location errors in male gender dysphorics, paedophiles, and fetishists. *Brit. J. Psychiat., 162,* 558–63.

Freund, K., & Kuban, M. (1993). Deficient erotic gender differentiation in pedophilia: A followup. *Arch. Sex. Behav., 22,* 619–28.

Freund, K., Langevin, R., Zajac, Y., Steiner, B., & Zajac, A. (1974). The transsexual syndrome in homosexual males. *J. Nerv. Ment. Dis., 158,* 145–53.

Frick, P. J. (1998). *Conduct disorders and severe antisocial behavior.* New York: Plenum.

Friedman, D., & Squires-Wheeler, E. (1994). Event-related potentials (ERPs) as indicators of risk for schizophrenia. *Schizo. Bull., 20*(1), 63–74.

Friedman, H. S., & Booth-Kewley, S. (1987b). The "disease-prone" personality: A meta-analytic view of the construct. *Amer. Psychol., 42, 539–55.*

Friedman, H. S., Hawley, P. H., & Tucker, J. S. (1994). Personality, health, and longevity. *Curr. Dir. Psychol. Sci., 3*(2), 37–41.

Friedman, M., & Rosenman, R. H. (1959). Association of specific overt behavior pattern with blood and cardiovascular findings. *JAMA, 169,* 1286.

Friedman, M., & Ulmer, D. (1984). *Treating Type A behavior and your heart.* New York: Knopf.

Friedman, M. J., & Yehuda, R. (1995). Post-traumatic stress disorder and comorbidity: Psychobiological approaches to differential diagnosis. In M. J. Friedman, D. S. Charney, et al., *Neurobiological and clinical consequences of stress: From normal adaptation to post-traumatic stress disorder.* (pp. 429–45). Philadelphia: Lippincott-Raven.

Friedman, R., & Iwai, J. (1976). Genetic predisposition and stress-induced hypertension. *Science, 193,* 161–92.

Friedrich, W., Einbender, A. J., & Luecke, W. J. (1983). Cognitive and behavioral characteristics of physically abused children. *J. Cons. Clin. Psychol., 51*(2), 313–14.

Friman, P. C., & Warzak, W. J. (1990). Nocturnal enuresis: A prevalent, persistent, yet curable parasomnia. *Pediatrician, 17,* 38–45.

Fruzzetti, A. E. (1996). Causes and consequences: Individual distress in the context of couple interactions. *J. Consult. Clin. Psychol., 64,* 1192–201.

Fulmer, R. H., & Lapidus, L. B. (1980). A study of professed reasons for beginning and continuing heroin use. *Inter. J. Addictions, 15,* 631–45.

Futterman, A., Thompson, L., Gallagher-Thompson, D., & Ferris, R. (1995). Depression in later life: Epidemiology, assessment, etiology, and treatment. In E. E. Beckham & W. R. Leber (Eds.), *Handbook of depression* (2nd ed.). (pp. 494–525). New York: Guilford.

Fyer, A. J., Chapman, S., T. F., Martin, L. Y., & Klein, D. F. (1995). Specificity in familial aggregation of phobic disorders. *Arch. Gen. Psychiat., 52, 564–73.*

Gabbard, G. O. (1994). Inpatient services: The clinician's view. In R. K. Schreter, S. S. Sharfstein, C. A. Schreter (Eds.), *Allies and adversaries.* (pp. 22–30). Washington, DC: American Psychiatric Press.

Gabbard, G. O., Lazar, S. G., Hornberger, J., & Spiegel, D. (1997). The economic impact of psychotherapy: A review. *Amer. J. Psychiat.,* 154(2), 147–55.

Gabuzda, D. H., & Hirsch, M. S. (1987). Neurologic manifestations of infection with human immunodeficiency virus: Clinical features and pathogenesis. *Ann. Int. Med., 107,* 383–91.

Gagnon, J., & Simon, W. (1973). *Sexual conduct: The social origins of human sexuality.* Chicago: Aldine.

Gajdusek, D. C. (1986). On the uniform source of amyloid in plaques, tangles, and vascular deposits. *Neurobiol. Aging, 7,* 453–54.

Gajzago, C., & Prior, M. (1974). Two cases of "recovery" in Kanner syndrome. *Arch. Gen. Psychiat., 31*(2), 264–68.

Galin, D., Diamond, R., & Braff, D. (1977). Lateralization of conversion symptoms: More frequent on the left. *Amer. J. Psychiat., 134,* 578–80.

Galler, J. R. (Ed.) (1984). *Human nutrition: A comprehensive treatise: Vol. 5. Nutrition and Behavior.* New York: Plenum Press.

Gamble, T. J., & Zigler, E. (1989). The head start synthesis project: A critique. *J. App. Devel. Psychol., 10,* 267–74.

Garb, H. N. (1989). Clinical judgment, clinical training, and professional experience. *Psychol. Bull., 105,* 387–96.

Garber, H. L. (1988). *The Milwaukee Project: Preventing mental retardation in children at risk.* Washington, DC: American Association on Mental Retardation.

Gardner, E. L. (1997). Brain reward mechanisms. In J. H. Lowinson, P. Ruiz, R. B. Millman, & J. G. Langrod (Eds.), *Substance abuse: A comprehensive textbook.* Baltimore: Williams & Wilkins.

Gardner, M. (1993, Summer). The false memory syndrome. *Skeptical Inquirer, 17,* 370–75.

Garner, D. M. (1997). Psychoeducational principles in treatment. In D. M. Garner & P. E. Garfinkel (Eds.), *Handbook of treatment for eating disorders* (pp. 145–177). New York: Guilford.

Garner, D. M., & Garfinkel, P. E. (Eds.). (1997) *Handbook of treatment for eating disorders.* (2nd ed.). New York: Guilford.

Garner, D. M., Garfinkel, P. E., Schwartz, D. M., & Thompson, M. M. (1980). Cultural expectations of thinness in women. *Psychol. Rep., 47,* 483–91.

Garner, D. M., Vitousek, K. M., & Pike, K. M. (1997). Cognitive-behavioral therapy for anorexia nervosa. In D. M. Garner & P. E. Garfinkel (Eds.), *Handbook of treatment for eating disorders.* (pp. 94–144). New York: Guilford.

Garrison, C. Z., Weinrich, M. W., Hardin, S. B., Weinrich, S., & Wang, L. (1993). Post-traumatic stress disorder in adolescents after a hurricane. *Amer. J. Epidemiol., 138,* 522–30.

Gatchel, R. J., & Turk, D. C. (Eds.). (1996). *Psychological approaches to pain management: A practitioner's handbook.* New York: Guilford.

Gatz, M., Lowe, B., Berg, S., Mortimer, J., & Pedersen, N. (1994). Dementia: Not just a search for the gene. *The Gerontologist, 34,* 251–55.

Gaudin, J.M., Jr. (1993). Effective intervention with neglectful families. *Crim. Just. Behav., 20,* 66–89.

Gawin, F. H., & Kleber, H. D. (1986). Abstinence symptomatology and psychiatric diagnosis in cocaine abusers. *Arch. Gen. Psychiat., 43,* 107–13.

Gebhard, P. H., Gagnon, J. H., Pomeroy, W. B., & Christenson, C. V. (1965). *Sex offenders: An analysis of types.* New York: Harper & Row.

Geisz, D., & Steinhausen, H. (1974). On the "psychological development of children with hydrocephalus." (German) *Praxis der Kinderpsychologie und Kinderpsychiatrie, 23*(4), 113–18.

Gelehrter, T. D., Collins, F. S., & Ginsburg, D. (1998). *Principles of Medical Genetics.* Baltimore: Williams and Wilkins.

Gelfand, D. M., Jenson, W. R., & Drew, C. J. (1988). *Understanding child behavior disorders* (2nd ed.). New York: Holt, Rinehart & Winston.

Gelfand, D. M., & Teti, D. M. (1990). The effects of maternal depression on children. *Clin. Psychol. Rev., 10,* 329–53.

Gentry, W. D. (1984). Behavioral medicine: A new research paradigm. In W. D. Gentry (Ed.), *Handbook of behavioral medicine.* (pp. 1–12). New York: Guilford.

Gentry, W. D., Chesney, A. P., Gary, H. G., Hall, R. P., & Harburg, E. (1982). Habitual anger-coping styles: I. Effect of mean blood pressure and risk for essential hypertension. *Psychosom. Med., 44,* 195–202.

George, L. K. (1984). *The burden of caregiving.* Center Reports of Advances in Research. Durham, NC: Duke University Center for the Study of Aging and Human Development.

Geschwind, N. (1975). The borderland of neurology and psychiatry: Some common misconceptions. In D. F. Benson & D. Blumer (Eds.), *Psychiatric aspects of neurological disease.* (pp. 1–9). New York: Grune & Stratton.

Gest, S. D. (1997). Behavioral inhibition: Stability and associations with adaptation from childhood to early adulthood. *J. Pers. Soc. Psychol., 72*(2), 467–75.

Giannetti, R. A. (1987). The GOLPH Psychosocial History: Response contingent data acquisition and reporting. In J. N. Butcher (Ed.), *Computerized psychological assessment: A practitioners guide.* New York: Basic Books.

Gibbs, N. A. (1996). Nonclinical populations in research on obsessive-compulsive disorder: A critical review. *Clin. Psychol. Rev., 16*(8), 729–73.

Gilbert, C. (1991). Outcome in autistic-like conditions. *J. Amer. Acad. Child Adoles. Psychiat. 30,* 375–82.

Gilbert, N. (1992, May). Realities and mythologies of rape. *Society,* 4–11.

Giles, T. R. (1993). *Managed mental health care: A guide to practitioners, employees, and hospital administrators.* Boston: Allyn & Bacon.

Gilhooly, M. L. M., Sweeting, H. N., Whittick, J. E., & McKee, K. (1994). Family care of the dementing elderly. *Inter. Rev. Psychiat., 6*(1), 29–40.

Gillberg, C. (1995). The prevalence of autism and autism spectrum disorders. In F. C. Verhulst & H. M. Koot (Eds.), *The epidemiology of child and adolescent psychopathology.* (pp. 227–57). New York: Oxford University Press.

Gillberg, C., & Schaumann, H. (1981). Infantile autism and puberty. *J. Autism Develop. Dis., 11*(4), 365–71.

Gillberg, C. U. (1998). Asperger syndrome and high–functioning autism. *Brit. J. Psychiat., 172,* 200–209.

Gillberg, C. U. (1990). Autism and pervasive developmental disorders. *J. Child Psychol. Psychiatry, 31,* 99–119.

Gilley, D. W., et al. (1997). Psychotic symptoms and physically aggressive behavior in Alzheimer's disease. *J. Amer. Geriat. Soc., 45*(9), 1074–79.

Gillis, H. M. (1993). Individual and small-group psychotherapy for children involved in trauma and disaster. In C.F. Saylor (Ed.), *Children and disasters.* (pp. 165-186). New York: Plenum

Gingell, K., Parmar, R., & Sungum-Paliwal, S. (1996). Autism and multiple pituitary deficiency. *Develop. Med. Child Neuro., 38,* 545–53.

Gitlin, M. J. (1996). *The psychotherapist's guide to psychopharmacology* (2nd ed.). New York: Free Press.

Gittelman, R., Mannuzza, S., Shenker, R., & Bonagura, N. (1985). Hyperactive boys almost grown up. *Arch. Gen. Psychiat., 42,* 937–47.

Glaser, R., Kiecolt-Glaser, J. K., Speicher, C. E., & Holliday, J. E. (1985). Stress, loneliness, and changes in herpes virus latency. *J. Behav. Med., 8,* 249–60.

Glaser, R., Rice, J., Sheridan, J., Fertel, R., Stout, J., Speicher, C., Pinsky, R., Kotur, M., Post, A., Beck, M., & Kiecolt-Glaser, J. (1987). Stress-related immune suppression: Health implications. *Brain, Behavior, and Immunity, 1,* 7–20.

Glassman, A. H., & Shapiro, P. A. (1998). Depression and the course of coronary artery disease. *Amer. J. Psychiat., 155*(1), 4–11.

Glatt, M. M. (1995). Controlled drinking after a third of a century. *Addiction, 90*(9), 1157–60.

Glazer, W. M., & Gray, G. V. (1996). How effective is utilization review? In A. Lazarus et al. (Ed.), *Controversies in managed mental health care.* (pp. 179–194). Washington, DC: American Psychiatric Press.

Gleaves, D. L., & Eberenz, K. (1993). The psychopathology of anorexia nervosa: A factor analytic investigation. *J. Psychopath. Behav. Assess., 15*(2), 141–52.

Glitz, D. A., & Balon, R. (1996). Serotonin-selective drugs in generalized anxiety disorder: Achievements and prospects. In H. G. Westenberg, J. A. Den Boer, & D. L. Murphy (Eds.), *Advances in the neurobiology of anxiety disorders.* (pp. 335–58). Chichester, England: Wiley.

Glosser, G., & Wexler, D. (1985). Participants' evaluation of education/support groups for families of patients with Alzheimer's disease and other dementias. *Gerontologist, 25,* 232–36.

Goddard, A. W., Woods, S. W., & Charney, D. S. (1996). A critical review of the role of norepinephrine in panic disorder: Focus on its interaction with serotonin. In H. G. Westenberg, J. A. Den Boer, & D. L. Murphy (Eds.), *Advances in the neurobiology of anxiety disorders.* (pp. 107–137). Chichester, England: Wiley.

Gold, E. R. (1986). Long-term effects of sexual victimization in childhood: An attributional approach. *J. Cons. Clin. Psychol., 54,* 471–75.

Gold, J., & Stricker, G. (Ed.). (1993). *Comprehensive handbook of psychotherapy integration.* New York: Plenum.

Goldberg, C. (1997, October 1). A drinking death rattles elite M.I.T. *New York Times,* p. A10

Goldberg, J., True, W. R., Eisen, S. A., & Henderson, W. G. (1990). A twin study of the effects of the Vietnam War on posttraumatic stress disorder. *JAMA, 263,* 1227–32.

Goldfinger, S. M., Schutt, R. K., Seidman, L. J., Turner, W. M., et al. (1996). Self report and observer measures of substance abuse among homeless mentally ill persons in the cross-section and over time. *J. Nerv. Ment. Dis., 184*(11), 667–72.

Goldfried, M. R., & Merbaum, M. (Eds.). (1973). *Behavior change through self control.* New York: Holt, Rinehart & Winston.

Goldfried, M. R., Greenberg, L. S., & Marmar, C. (1990). Individual psychotherapy: Process and outcome. *Annu. Rev. Psychol.* (Vol. 41). (pp. 659–88). Palo Alto, CA: Annual Reviews.

Golding, J. M. (1994). Sexual assault history and physical health in randomly selected Los Angeles women. *Hlth. Psychol., 13*(2), 130–38.

Golding, J. M., Cooper, M. L., & George, L. K. (1997). Sexual assault history and health perceptions: Seven general population studies. *Hlth. Psychol., 16*(5), 417–25.

Goldman, L. S., Genel, M., Bezman, R. J., & Slanetz, P. J. (1998). Diagnosis and treatment of attention-deficit/hyperactivity disorder in children and adolescents. *JAMA, 279*(14), 1100–07.

Goldman-Rakic, P. S., & Selemon, L. D. (1997). Functional and anatomical aspects of prefrontal pathology in schizophrenia. *Schizo. Bull., 23,* 437–58.

Goldsmith, D. F., & Rogoff, B. (1997). Mother's and toddler's coordinated joint focus of attention: Variations with maternal dysphoric symptoms. *Develop. Psychol., 33,* 113–19.

Goldsmith, W., & Cretekos, C. (1969). Unhappy odysseys: Psychiatric hospitalization among Vietnam returnees. *Amer. J. Psychiat., 20,* 78–83.

Goldstein, A., et al. (1974, Mar. 4). Researchers isolate opiate receptor. *Behav. Today, 5*(9), 1.

Goldstein, A. J., & Chambless, D. (1978). A reanalysis of agoraphobia. *Behav. Ther., 9,* 47–59.

Goldstein, I., Lue, T. F., Padma-Nathan, H., Rosen, R. C., Steers, W. D., & Wicker, P. A. (1998). Oral sildenafil in the treatment of erectile dysfunction. *N. Engl. J. of Med., 338,* 20, 1397–1404.

Goldstein, M. J. (1985). Family factors that antedate the onset of schizophrenia and related disorders: The results of a fifteen year prospective longitudinal study. *Acta Psychiatr. Scandin.* (Suppl. No. 319), *71,* 7–18.

Goldstein, M. J., Rodnick, E. H., Jones, J. E., McPherson, S. R., & West, K. L. (1978). Family precursors of schizophrenia spectrum disorders. In L. C. Wynne, R. L. Cromwell, & S. Matthysse (Eds.), *The nature of schizophrenia: New approaches to research and treatment.* New York: Wiley.

Goldstein, M. J., & Strachan, A. M. (1987). The family and schizophrenia. In T. Jacob (Ed.), *Family interaction and psychopathology: Theories, methods, and findings.* (pp. 481–508). New York: Plenum.

Goldstein, S., & Goldstein, M. (1998). *Managing attention-deficit hyperactivity disorder in children: A guide for practitioners (2nd ed.).* New York: Wiley.

Golomb, M., Fava, M., Abraham, M., & Rosenbaum, J. F. (1995). Gender differences in personality disorders. *Amer. J. Psychiat., 152*(4), 579–82.

Gomes-Schwartz, B., Horowitz, J., & Cardarelli, A. (1990). *Child sexual abuse: The initial effects.* Newbury Park, CA: Sage.

Good, B. J., & Kleinman, A. M. (1985). Culture and anxiety: Cross-cultural evidence for the patterning of anxiety disorders. In A. H. Tuma & J. D. Master (Eds.), *Anxiety and the anxiety disorders.* Hillsdale, NJ: Erlbaum.

Goode, E. (1994, Sept. 19). Battling deviant behavior. *U.S. News and World Report,* 74–75.

Goodman, R. (1989). Infantile autism: A syndrome of multiple primary deficits? *J. Autism Devel. Dis., 19,* 409–24.

Goodwin, D. K. (1988). *The Fitzgeralds and the Kennedys: An American saga.* New York: St. Martin's Press.

Goodwin, D. W., Schulsinger, F., Hermansen, L., Guze, S. B., & Winokur, G. (1973). Alcohol problems in adoptees raised apart from alcoholic biological parents. *Arch. Gen. Psychiat., 28*(2), 238–43.

Goodwin, D. W., Schulsinger, F., Moller, N., Hermansen, L., Winokur, G., & Guze, S. B. (1974). Drinking problems in adopted and nonadopted sons of alcoholics. *Arch. Gen. Psychiat., 31*(2), 164–69.

Goodwin, F. K., & Ghaemi, S. N. (1998). Understanding manic-depressive illness. *Arch. Gen. Psychiat., 55*(1), 23–25.

Goodwin, F. K., & Jamison, K. R. (1990). *Manic-depressive illness.* New York: Oxford University Press.

Goodwin, L. (1992). Alcohol and drug use in fraternities and sororities. *Journal of Alcohol and Drug Education, 37*(2), 52–63.

Goran, D. A., Fabiano, R. J., & Crewe, N. (1997). Employment following severe traumatic brain injury: The utility of the Individual Ability Profile System (IAP). *Arch. Clin. Neuropsychol., 12*(7), 691–98.

Gordis, E. (1997). Patient-treatment matching. *Alcohol Alert, 36,* 1–4.

Gordis, E., DuFour, M. C., Warren, K. R., Jackson, R. J., Floyd, R. L., & Hungerford, D. W. (1995). Should physicians counsel patients to drink alcohol? *JAMA, 273,* 1–12.

Gorenstein, E. E. (1992). *The science of mental illness.* San Diego: Academic Press.

Gorlick, D. A. (1993). Overview of pharmacologic treatment approaches for alcohol and other drug addiction. *Psychiat. Clin. N. Amer., 16,* 141–56.

Gorman, J. M., Battista, D., Goetz, R. R., Dillon, D. J., Liebowitz, M. R., Fyer, A. J., Kahn, J. P., Sandberg, D., & Klein, D. F. (1989). A comparison of sodium bicarbonate and sodium lactate infusion in the induction of panic attacks. *Arch. Gen. Psychiat., 46,* 145–50.

Gorman, J. M., & Coplan, J. D. (1996). Comorbidity of depression and panic disorder. *J. Clin. Psychiat., 57*(10), 34–41.

Gortner, E. T., Gollan, J. K., & Jacobson, N. S. (1997). Psychological aspects of perpetrators of domestic violence and their relationships with the victims. *Psychiat. Clin. N. Amer., 20*(2), 327–52.

Gospodinoff, M. L. (1989). Premature ejaculation: Clinical subgroups and etiology. *J. Sex Marit. Ther., 15,* 130–34.

Gotlib, I. H., & Avison, W. (1993). Children at risk for psychopathology. In C. Costello (Ed.), *Basic issues in psychopathology.* (pp. 271–319). New York: Guilford.

Gotlib, I. H., & Hammen, C. L. (1992). *Psychological aspects of depression: Toward a cognitive-interpersonal integration.* Chichester, UK: Wiley.

Gottesman, I. I. (1991). *Schizophrenia genesis: The origins of madness.* New York: Freeman.

Gottesman, I. I., & Bertelsen, A. (1989). Confirming unexpressed genotypes for schizophrenia: Risks in the offspring of Fischer's Danish identical and fraternal discordant twins. *Arch. Gen. Psychiat., 46,* 867–72.

Gottlieb, G. (1992) *Individual development and evolution: The genesis of novel behavior.* New York: Oxford University Press.

Gottlieb, G., Wahlsten, D., & Lickliter, R. (1998). The significance of biology for human development: A developmental psychbiological systems view. In W. Damon & R. Lerner (Eds.), *Handbook of child psychology (5th ed.): Vol. 1: Theoretical models of human development.* (pp. 233–73). New York: Wiley.

Gottlieb, J. (1981). Mainstreaming: Fulfilling the promise? *Amer. J. Ment. Def., 86,* 115–26.

Gouvier, W. D., et al. (1997). Cognitive retraining with brain-damaged patients. In A. M. Horton, W. D. & J. Webster (Eds.), *The neuropsychology handbook* (Vol. 2). (pp. 3–46). New York: Springer.

Grace, A. A., & Moore, H. (1998). Regulation of information flow in the nucleus accumbens: A model for the pathophysiology of schizophrenia. In M. F. Lenzenweger & R. H. Dworkin (Eds.), *Origins and development of schizophrenia.* (pp. 123–60). Washington: American Psychological Association.

Grady, K., Gersick, K. E., & Boratynski, M. (1985). Preparing parents for teenagers: A step in the prevention of adolescent substance abuse. *Family Relations Journal of Applied Family and Child Studies, 34*(4), 541–49.

Grant, B. F. (1997). Prevalence and correlates of alcohol use and DSM-IV alcohol dependence in the United States: Results of the National Longitudinal Alcohol Epidemiologic Survey. *J. Stud. Alcoh., 58*(5), 464–73.

Grant, B. F., & Dawson, D. A. (1997). Age at onset of alcohol use and its association with DSM–IV alcohol abuse and dependency: Results from the National Longitudinal Alcohol Epidemiologic Survey. *J. Subst. Abuse, 9,* 103–10.

Grant, I., & Adams, K. M. (1996). Neuropsychological assessment of neuropsychiatric disorders. New York: Oxford University Press.

Grant, I., Atkinson, J. H., Hesselink, J. R., Kennedy, C. J., Richman, D. D., Spector, S. A., & McCutchan, J. A. (1987). Evidence for early central nervous system involvement in the acquired immunodeficiency syndrome (AIDS) and other human immunodeficiency virus (HIV) infections. *Ann. Int. Med., 107,* 828–36.

Grant, S. J., & Sonti, G. (1994). Buprenorphine and morphine produce equivalent increases in extracellular single unit activity of dopamine neurons in the ventral tegmental area in vivo. *Synapse, 16,* 181–87.

Grant, V. W. (1953). A case study of fetishism. *J. Abnorm. Soc. Psychol., 48,* 142–49.

Gray, F., Gherardi, R., & Scaravilli, F. (1988). The neuropathology of the acquired immune deficiency syndrome (AIDS). *Brain, 111,* 245–66.

Gray, J. A. (1987). *The psychology of fear and stress* (2nd edition). New York: Cambridge University Press.

Gray, J. A. (1991). Fear, panic, and anxiety: What's in a name? *Psycho. Inq., 2,* 77–78.

Gray, J. A., & McNaughton, N. (1996). The neuropsychology of anxiety: Reprise. In D. A. Hope (Ed.), *Perspectives on anxiety, panic, and fear, Vol. 43 of the Nebraska Symposium on Motivation.* (pp. 61–134). Lincoln: University of Nebraska Press.

Gray, W. W., & Ramsey, B. K. (1982). The early training project: A lifespan view. *Human Develop., 25,* 48–57.

Gray-Little, B. (1995). The assessment of psychopathology in racial and ethnic minorities. In J. N. Butcher (Ed.), *Clinical personality assessment: Practical considerations.* (pp. 141–157). New York: Oxford University Press.

Grechanaia, T., Romanova, O., Williams, C. L., Perry, C. L., & Murray, P. (1997, Oct.). *Russian-American research project partners for prevention: Implementation of slick Tracey Home Team Program in Russia.* National Institute of Alcohol And Alcoholism. Washington: U.S. Government Printing Office.

Greeley, A. M. (1993, Mar. 20). How serious is the problem of sexual abuse by clergy? *America, 168,* 6–10.

Green, B. L., Korol, M., Grace, M. C., Vary, M. G., Leonard, A. C., Gleser, G. C., & Smitson Cohen, S. (1991). Children and disaster: Age, gender, and parental effects on PTSD symptoms. *J. Amer. Acad. Child Adoles. Psychiat., 30,* 945–51.

Green, B. L., & Lindy, J. D. (1994). Post traumatic stress disorder in victims of disasters. *Psychiat. Clin. N. Amer., 17,* 301–10.

Green, M. F., Nuechterlein, K. H., & Breitmeyer, B. (1997). Backward masking performance in unaffected siblings of schizophrenic patients: Evidence for a vulnerability indicator. *Arch. Gen. Psychiat., 54*(5), 465–72.

Green, R. (1987). *The "sissy boy syndrome" and the development of homosexuality.* New Haven: Yale University Press.

Green, R. (1992). *Sexual science and the law.* Cambridge: Harvard University Press.

Green, R., & Fleming, D. (1990). Transsexual surgery followup: Status in the 1990's. In J. Bancroft, C. Davis, & H. Ruppel (Eds.), *Annual review of sex research.* Mt. Vernon, IA: Society for the Scientific Study of Sex.

Greenberg, L. S., Elliott, R. K., & Lietaer, G. (1994). Research on experiential psychotherapies. In A. E. Bergin & S. L. Garfield (Eds.), *Handbook of psychotherapy and behavior change.* (pp. 509–52). New York: Wiley.

Greenfield, B., Hechtman, L., & Tremblay, C. (1995). Short-term efficacy of interventions by a youth crisis team. *Canad. J. Psychiat., 40,* 320–24.

Greenhill, L. L. (1992). Pharmacologic treatment of attention deficit hyperactivity disorder. *Psychiat. Clin. N. Amer., 15,* 1–28.

Greenhill, L. L., & Waslick, B. (1997). Management of suicidal behavior in children and adolescents. *Psychiat. Clin. N. Amer., 20*(3), 641–66.

Greenough, W. T., & Black, J. E. (1992). Induction of brain structure by experience: Substrates for cognitive development. In M. R. Gunnar & C. A. Nelson (Eds), *Minnesota Symposia on Child Psychology: Developmental Neuroscience* (Vol. 24). (pp. 155–200). Hillsdale, NJ: Erlbaum.

Greenspan, S. (1997). Dead manual walking? Why the AAMR definition needs redoing. *Education & Training in Mental Retardation & Developmental Disabilities, 32*(3), 179–90.

Greer, S. (1964). Study of parental loss in neurotics and sociopaths. *Arch. Gen. Psychiat., 11*(2), 177–80.

Gresham, F. M. (1982). Misguided mainstreaming: The case for social skills training with handicapped children. *Exceptional Children, 48,* 422–33.

Griffin, D., & Bartholomew, K. (1994). Models of the self and other: Fundamental dimensions underlying measures of adult attachment. *J. Pers. Soc. Psychol., 67,* 430–45.

Grilo, C. M., Becker, D. F., Fehon, D. C., Edell, W. S., & McGlashan, T. H. (1996). Conduct disorder, substance use disorders, and coexisting conduct and substance use disorders in adolescent inpatients. *Amer. J. Psychiat., 153*(7), 914–20.

Grimes, K., & Walker, E. F. (1994). Childhood emotional expressions, educational attainment, and age at onset of illness in schizophrenia. *J. Abn. Psychol., 103*(4), 784–90.

Grinfeld, M. J., & Wellner, M. (1998). Pill poisoned: The seasoning of medication defenses. *Forensic Echo, 2*(3), 4–10.

Grisso, T., & Appelbaum, P. S. (1998). *Assessing competence to consent to treatment.* New York: Oxford University Press.

Grisso, T., & Tomkins, A. J. (1996). Communicating violence risk assessments. *Amer. Psychol., 51*(9), 928–30.

Grob, G. N. (1994). Mad, homeless, and unwanted: A history of the care of the chronically mentally ill in America. *Psychiat. Clin. N. Amer., 17*(3), 541–58.

Gross, R., Sasson, Y., Chopra, J., & Zohar, J. (1998). Biological models of obsessive-compulsive disorder: The serotonin hypothesis. In R. Swinson, M. Antony, S. Rachman, & M. Richter (Eds.), *Obsessive-compulsive disorder: Theory, research, and treatment.* (pp. 141–53). New York: Guilford.

Groth, N. A. (1979). *Men who rape.* New York: Plenum.

Guelfi, G. P., Faustman, W. O., & Csernansky, J. G. (1989). Independence of positive and negative symptoms in a population of schizophrenic patients. *J. Nerv. Ment. Dis., 177,* 285–90.

Guerra, F. (1971). *The pre-Columbian mind.* New York: Seminar Press.

Gunderson, J. G., & Phillips, K. A. (1991). A current view of the interface between borderline personality disorder and depression. *Amer. J. Psychiat., 148,* 967–75.

Gunderson, J. G., Ronningstam, E., & Smith, L. E. (1995). Narcissistic personality disorder. In W. J. Livesley (Ed.), *The DSM-IV personality disorders.* (pp. 201–212). New York: Guilford.

Gunderson, J. G., Zanarini, M. C., Kisiel, C. L. (1995). Borderline personality disorder. In W. J. Livesley (Ed.), *The DSM-IV personality disorders.* (pp. 141–157). New York: Guilford.

Gunn, J. (1993). Castration is not the answer. *Brit. Med. J., 307,* 790–91.

Gur, R. E., et al. (1998). A follow-up magnetic resonance imaging study of schizophrenia: Relationship of neuroanatomical changes to clinical and neurobehavioral measures. *Arch. Gen. Psychiat., 55*(2), 145–52.

Gur, R. E., Mozley, P. D., Shtasel, D. L., Cannon, T. D., Gallacher, F., Turetsky, B., Grossman, R., & Gur, R. C. (1994). Clinical subtypes of schizophrenia: Differences in brain and CFS volume. *Amer. J. Psychiat., 151*(3), 343–50.

Gur, R. E., & Pearlson, G. D. (1993). Neuroimaging in schizophrenia research. *Schizo. Bull., 19*(2), 337–53.

Gureje, O., et al. (1997). Somatization in cross-cultural perspective: A World Health Organization study in primary care. *Amer. J. Psychiat., 154*(7), 989–995.

Gureje, O., Bamidele, R., & Raji, O. (1994). Early brain trauma and schizophrenia in Nigerian patients. *Amer. J. Psychiat., 151*(3), 368–71.

Gurland, B. J., & Cross, P. S. (1982). Epidemiology of psychopathology in old age. In L. F. Jarvik & G. W. Small (Eds.), *Psychiatric clinics of North America.* Philadelphia: Saunders.

Gurman, A. S., & Kniskern, D. P. (1978). Research on marital and family therapy: Progress, perspective and prospect. In S. L. Garfield & A. E. Bergin (Eds.), *Handbook of psychotherapy and behavior change.* New York: Wiley.

Gurman, A. S., Kniskern, D. P., & Pinsof, W. M. (1986). Research on marital and family therapies. In S. L. Garfield & A. E. Bergin (Eds.), *Handbook of psychotherapy and behavior change* (3rd ed.) (pp. 565–626). New York: Wiley.

Guze, S. B., (1995). Review of DSM-IV (no title). Amer. J. Psychiat., 152, 1228.

Guze, S. B., Cloninger, C. R., Martin, R. L., & Clayton, P. J. (1986). A follow-up and family study of Briquet's Syndrome. *Brit. J. Psychiat., 149,* 17–23.

Haaga, D. A., & Davison, G. C. (1989). Outcome studies of rational-emotive therapy. In M. Bernard & R. DeGiuseppe (Eds.), *Inside rationale-motive therapy.* New York: Academic Press.

Haaga, D. A., & Davison, G. C. (1992). Disappearing differences do not always reflect healthy integration: An analysis of cognitive therapy and rational-emotive therapy. *Journal of Psychotherapy Integration, 1,* 287–303.

Haaga, D. A. F., Dyck, M. J., & Ernst, D. (1991). Empirical status of cognitive theory of depression. *Psychol. Bull., 110* (2), 215–36.

Haas, G. (1997). Suicidal behavior in schizophrenia. In R. W. Maris, M. M. Silverman, & S. S. Canetton (Eds.), *Review of Suicidology, 1997.* (pp. 202–35). New York: Guilford.

Haber, S. N., & Fudge, J. L. (1997). The interface between dopamine neurons and the amygdala: Implications for schizophrenia. *Schizo. Bull., 23*(3), 471–82.

Hafen, B. Q., Karren, K. J., Frandsen, K. J., & Smith, N. L. (1996). *Mind/body health: The effects of attitudes, emotions, and relationships.* Needham Heights, MA: Allyn & Bacon.

Haffner, H., et al. (1998). Causes and consequences of the gender difference in age at onset of schizophrenia. *Schizo. Bull., 24*(1), 99–114.

Halberstam, M. (1972). Can you make yourself sick? A doctor's report on psychosomatic illness. *Today's Health, 50*(12), 24–29.

Haley, S. A. (1978). Treatment implications of post-combat stress response syndromes for mental health professionals. In C. R. Figley (Ed.), *Stress disorders among Vietnam veterans.* New York: Brunner/Mazel.

Halford, W. K., & Haynes, R. (1991) Psychosocial rehabilitation of chronic schizophrenic patients: Recent findings on social skills training and family psychoeducation. *Clin. Psychol. Rev., 11,* 23–44.

Hall, G. (1994). Pavlovian conditioning: Laws of association. In N. J. Mackintosh (Ed.), *Animal learning and cognition.* (pp. 15–43). San Diego, CA: Academic Press.

Hallett, J. D., Zasler, N. D., Maurer, P., & Cash, S. (1994). Role change after traumatic brain injury in adults. *Amer. J. Occup. Ther., 48*(3), 241–46.

Halmi, K. A., et al. (1991). Comorbidity of psychiatric diagnoses in anorexia nervosa. *Arch. Gen. Psychiat., 48,* 712–718.

Hamer, D. H., Hu, S., Magnuson, V. L., Hu, N., & Pattatucci, A. M. L. (1993). A linkage between DNA markers on the X chromosome and male sexual orientation. *Science, 261,* 321–27.

Hammen, C. L. (1991). Generation of stress in the course of unipolar depression. *J. Abnorm. Psychol., 100,* 555–61.

Hammen, C. L. (1995). Stress and the course of unipolar disorders. In C. M. Mazure (Ed.), *Does stress cause psychiatric illness?* Washington, DC: American Psychiatric Press.

Hammen, C., & Gitlin, M. (1997). Stress reactivity in bipolar patients and its relation to prior history of disorder. *Amer. J. Psychiat., 154*(6), 856–857.

Handleman, J. S., Gill, M. J., & Alessandri, M. (1988). Generalization by severely developmentally disabled children: Issues, advances, and future directions. *The Behavior Therapist, 11,* 221–23.

Hankin, B. L., Abramson, L. Y., Moffitt, T. E., Silva, P. A., McGee, R., & Angell, K. E. (1998). Development of depression from preadolescence to young adulthood: Emerging gender differences in a 10-year longitudinal study. *J. Abn. Psychol., 107*(1), 128–40.

Hannigan, J. H. (1996). What research with animals is telling us about alcohol-related neurodevelopmental disorder. *Pharmacology, Biochemistry & Behavior, 55*(4), 489–500.

Hanrahan, J., Goodman, W., & Rapagna, S. (1990). Preparing mentally retarded students for mainstreaming: Priorities of regular class and special school teachers. *Amer. J. Ment. Retard., 94,* 470–74.

Happe, F., & Frith, U. (1996). Theory of mind and social impairment in children with conduct disorder. *Brit. J. Develop. Psychol., 14,* 385–98.

Hardy, J. A., Mann, D. M., Wester, P., & Winblad, B. (1986). An integrative hypothesis concerning the pathogenesis and progression of Alzheimer's disease. *Neurobiol. of Aging, 7,* 489–502.

Hardy, K. V., & Laszloffy, T. A. (1995). Therapy with African Americans and the phenomenon of rage. *In Session, 1*(4), 57–70.

Hare, E. H. (1962). Masturbatory insanity: The history of an idea. *J. Ment. Sci., 108,* 1–25.

Hare, R. D. (1970). *Psychopathy: Theory and research.* New York: Wiley.

Hare, R. D. (1978). Electrodermal and cardiovascular correlates of psychopathy. In R. D. Hare & D. Schalling (Eds.), *Psychopathic behavior: Approaches to research.* (pp. 107–43). Chichester, UK: Wiley.

Hare, R. D. (1980). A research scale for the assessment of psychopathy in criminal populations. *Personal. Indiv. Diff., 1,* 111–19.

Hare, R. D. (1991). *The Hare psychopathy checklist—Revised.* Toronto: Multi-Health systems.

Hare, R. D. (1998). Psychopathy, affect and behavior. In D. J. Cooke, A. E. Forth, & R. D. Hare (Eds.), *Psychopathy: Theory, research, and implications for society.* (pp. 105–37). Dordrecht, Netherlands: Kluwer Academic Publishers.

Hare, R. D., Hart, S. D., & Harpur, T. J. (1991). Psychopathy and DSM-IV criteria for antisocial personality disorder. *J. Abn. Psychol., 100,* 391–98.

Hare, R. D., McPherson, L. M., & Forth, A. E. (1988). Male psychopaths and their criminal careers. *J. Cons. Clin. Psychology, 56,* 710–14.

Harford, T. C., & Parker, D. A. (1994). Antisocial behavior, family history, and alcohol dependence symptoms. *Alcoholism (NY), 18,* 265–68.

Harkness, A. R., & Lilienfeld, S. O. (1997). Individual differences science for treatment planning: Personality traits. *Psychol. Assess., 9*(4), 349–60.

Harlow, J. M. (1868). Recovery from the passage of an iron bar through the head. *Publication of the Massachusetts Medical Society, 2,* 327.

Harlow, J. M. (1993). Recovery from the passage of an iron bar through the head. *History of Psychiatry, 4,* 271–81.

Harpur, T. J., & Hare, R. D. (1994). Assessment of psychopathy as a function of age. *J. Abn. Psychol., 103,* 604–9.

Harrington, R., & Clark, A. (1998). Prevention and early intervention for depression in adolescence and early adult life. *Eur. Arch. Psychiat. Clin. Neurosci., 248*(1), 32–45.

Harrington, R., Rutter, M., & Fombonne, E. (1996). Developmental pathways in depression: Multiple meanings, antecedents, and end points. *Develop. Psychopath., 8,* 601–16.

Harris, T., Brown, G. W., & Bifulco, A. (1986). Loss of parent in childhood and adult psychiatric disorder: The role of lack of adequate parental care. *Psychol. Med., 16,* 641–59.

Hart, S. D. (1998). Psychopathy and risk for violence. In D. J. Cooke, A. E. Forth, & R. D. Hare (Eds.), *Psychopathy: Theory, research, and implications* *for society.* (pp. 355–373). Dordrecht, Netherlands: Kluwer Academic Publishers.

Hart, S. D., & Hare, R. D. (1997). Psychopathy: Assessment and association with criminal conduct. In D. M. Stoff, J. Breiling, & J. D. Maser (Eds.), *Handbook of antisocial behavior.* (pp. 22–35). New York: Wiley.

Harwood, T. M., Beutler, L. E., Fisher, D., Sandowicz, M., Albanese, A. L., & Baker, M. (1997). Clinical decision making in managed health care. In J. N. Butcher (Ed.), *Personality assessment in managed health care: Using the MMPI-2 in treatment planning.* (pp. 15–41) New York: Oxford University Press.

Hasegawa, S., et al. (1997). Physical aging in persons with Down syndrome: Bases on external appearance and diseases. *Japanese Journal of Special Education, 35*(2), 43–49.

Hatta, S. M. (1996) A Malay cross cultural worldview and forensic review of amok. *Austral. NZ J. Psychiat., 30,* 505–10.

Hauff, E., & Vaglum, P. (1994). Chronic posttraumatic stress disorder in Vietnamese refugees. *J. Nerv. Ment.Dis., 182,* 85–90.

Haug Schnabel, G. (1992). Daytime and nighttime enuresis: A functional disorder and its ethological decoding. *Behaviour, 120,* 232–61.

Haugland, G., Sigel, G., Hopper, K., & Alexander, M. J. (1997). Mental illness among homeless individuals in a suburban county. *Psychiat. Serv., 48*(4), 504–09.

Hawkins, J. D., Arthur, M. W., & Olson, J. J. (1997). Community interventions to reduce risks and enhance protection against antisocial behavior. In D. M. Stoff, J. Breiling, & J. D. Maser (Eds.), *Handbook of antisocial behavior.* (pp. 365–374). New York: Wiley.

Hawton, K. (1992). Suicide and attempted suicide. In E. S. Paykel (Ed.), *Handbook of affective disorders* (2nd ed.). New York: Guilford.

Hayden, M. F. (1998). Civil rights litigation for institutionalized persons with mental retardation: A summary. *Mental Retardation, 36*(1), 75–83.

Haynes, S. N., Leisen, M. B., & Blaine, D. D. (1997). Design of individualized behavioral treatment programs using function analytic clinical case methods. *Psychol. Assess., 9*(4), 334–48.

Haywood, H. C., Meyers, C. E., & Switsky, H. N. (1982). Mental retardation. *Ann. Rev. Psychol., 33.,* 309–342.

Hazelrigg, M., Cooper, H., & Bordoin, C. (1987). Evaluating the effectiveness of family therapies: An integrative review and analysis. *Psychol. Bull., 101,* 428–42.

Healy, D., & Williams, J. M. G. (1988). Dysrhythmia, dysphoria, and depression: The interaction of learned helplessness and circadian dysrhythmia in the pathogenesis of depression. *Psychol. Bull., 103,* 163–78.

Heather, J. (1995). The great controlled drinking consensus. Is it premature? *Addiction, 90*(9), 1160–63.

Heatherton, T. F., Mahamedi, F., Striepe, M., Field, A. E., & Keel, P. (1997). A 10-year longitudinal study of body weight, dieting, and eating disorder symptoms. *J. Abn. Psychol., 106*(1), 117–125.

Heatherton, T. F., Nichols, P., Mahamedi, F., & Keel, P. K. (1995). Body weight, dieting, and eating disorder symptoms among college students 1982 to 1992. *Amer. J. Psychiat., 152,* 1623–1629.

Heaton, R., Paulsen, J. S., McAdams, L. A., Kuck, J., Zisook, S., Braff, D., Harris, M. J., & Jesta, D. V. (1994). Neuropsychological deficits in schizophrenics: Relationship to age, chronicity, and dementia. *Arch. Gen. Psychiat., 51*(6), 469–76.

Hebert, R., Leclerc, G., Bravo, G., & Girouard, D. (1994). Efficacy of a support group programme for caregivers of demented patients in the community: A randomized control trial. *Arch. Gerontol. Geriatr., 18,* 1–14.

Hechtman, L. (1996a). Attention-deficit hyperactivity disorder. In L. Hechtman (Ed.), *Do they grow out of it?* (pp. 17–38). Washington: American Psychiatric Press.

Hegarty, J. D., Baldessarini, R. J., Tohen, M., Waternaux, C., & Oepen, G. (1994). One hundred years of schizophrenia: A meta-analysis of the outcome literature. *Amer. J. Psychiat., 151*(10), 1409–16.

Heider, F. (1958). *The psychology of interpersonal relations.* New York: Wiley.

Heilbrun, K. (1997). Prediction versus management models relevant to risk assessment: The importance of legal decision-making context. *Law and Human Behavior, 21*(4), 347–59.

Heiman, J. R. (1980). Female sexual response patterns. Interactions of physiological, affective, and contextual cues. *Arch. Gen. Psychiat., 37,* 1311–16.

Heller, K. (1996). Coming of age of prevention science: Comments on the 1994 National Institute of Mental Health–Institute of Medicine Prevention Reports. *Amer. Psychol., 51*(11), 1123–27.

Heller, T., Miller, A. B., & Factor, A. (1997). Adults with mental retardation as supports to their parents: Effects on parental caregiving appraisal. *Mental Retardation, 35*(5), 338–46.

Helzer, J. E., Canino, G. J., Yeh, E. K., Bland, R., et al. (1990). Alcoholism—North America and Asia: A comparison of population surveys with the Diagnostic Interview Schedule. *Arch. Gen. Psychiat., 47*(4), 313–19.

Hemphill, J. F., Hart, S. D., & Hare, R. D. (1994). Psychopathy and substance use. *J. Person. Dis., 8,* 139–70.

Henriques, J. B., & Davidson, R. J. (1990). Regional brain electrical asymmetries discriminate between previously depressed and healthy control subjects. *J. Abn. Psychol., 99,* 22–31.

Henriques, J. B., & Davidson, R. J. (1991). Left frontal hypoactivation in depression. *J. Abn. Psychol., 100,* 535–45.

Henry, W. P., Strupp, H. H., Schacht, T. E., & Gaston, L. (1994). Psychodynamic approaches. In A. E. Bergin & S. L. Garfield (Eds.), *Handbook of psychotherapy and behavior change* (4th ed.) (pp. 467–508). New York: Wiley.

Herbert, T. B., & Cohen, S. (1993). Depression and immunity: A meta-analytic review. *Psychol. Bull., 113*(3), 472–86.

Herd, J. A. (1984). Cardiovascular disease and hypertension. In W. D. Gentry (Ed.), *Handbook of behavioral medicine.* (pp. 222–81). New York: Guilford.

Herdt, G., & Stoller, R. G. (1990). *Intimate communications: Erotics and the study of a culture.* New York: Columbia University Press.

Herman, J. L. (1993, March/April). The abuses of memory. *Mother Jones, 18,* 3–4.

Herman, J. L. (1994, Spring). Presuming to know the truth. *Nieman Reports, 48,* 43–46.

Herman, J. L., Perry, J. C., & van der Kolk, B. A. (1989). Childhood trauma in borderline personality disorder. *Amer. J. Psychiat., 146,* 490–95.

Hermann, D. H. J. (1990). Autonomy, self determination, the right of involuntarily committed persons to refuse treatment, and the use of substituted judgment in medication decisions involving incompetent persons. *International Journal of Law and Psychiatry, 13,* 361–85.

Hernandez, J. T. (1992). Substance abuse among sexually abused adolescents. *Journal of Adolescent Health, 13,* 658–62.

Herrenkohl, R. C., Herrenkohl, E. C., & Egolf, B. P. (1983). Circumstances surrounding the occurrence of child maltreatment. *J. Cons. Clin. Psychol., 51*(3), 424–31.

Herzog, W., Schellberg, D., & Deter, H.-C. (1997). First recovery in anorexia nervosa patients in the long-term course: A discrete-time survival analysis. *J. Cons. Clin. Psychol., 65*(1), 169–177.

Hester, R. K., & Delaney, H. D. (1997). Behavioral self-control program for Windows: Results of a controlled clinical trial. *J. Cons. Clin. Psychol., 65*(4), 686–93.

Heston, L. (1966). Psychiatric disorders in foster home reared children of schizophrenic mothers. *Brit. J. Psychiat., 112,* 819–25.

Hetherington, E. M. (1991). The role of individual differences and family relationships in children's coping with divorce and remarriage. In P.S. Cowan & E. M. Hetherington (Eds.), *Family transitions.* (pp. 165–194). Hillsdale, NJ: Erlbaum.

Hetherington, E. M. (1998). Relevant issues in developmental science: Introduction to the special series. *Amer. Psychol., 53*(2), 93–5.

Hetherington, E. M., Bridges, M., & Insabella, G. (1998) What matters? What does not? Five perspectives on the association between marital transitions and children's adjustment. *Amer. Psychol., 53,* 167–84.

Hetherington, E. M. & Parke, R. D. (1993). *Child psychology: A contemporary viewpoint,* (4th ed.). New York: McGraw Hill.

Hetherington, E. M., Stanley-Hagan, M., & Anderson, E. R. (1989). Marital transitions: A child's perspective. *Amer. Psychol., 44,* 303–312.

Heyman, A., Wilkinson, W. E., Hurwitz, B. J., Helms, M. J., et al. (1987). Early-onset Alzheimer's disease: Clinical predictors of institutionalization and death. *Neurology, 37,* 980–84.

Higuci, S. S., Matsushita, H., Imazeki, T., Kinoshita, T., Takagi, S., & Kono, H. (1994). Aldehyde de hydrogenase genotypes in Japanese alcoholics. *Lancet, 343,* 741–42.

Hijii, T., et al. (1997). Life expectancy and social adaptation in individuals with Down syndrome with and without surgery for congenital heart disease. *Clin. Pediat., 36*(6), 327–32.

Hilgard, E. R. (1977). *Divided consciousness: Multiple controls in human thought and action.* New York: Wiley.

Hillson, J. M., & Kuiper, N. A. (1994). A stress and coping model of child treatment. *Clin. Psychol. Rev., 14,* 261–85.

Hinckley v. U.S. (1998). 140 F.3d 277 (D.C. Cir., 1998).

Hinrichsen, G. A., & Niederehe, G. (1994). Dementia management strategies and adjustment of family members of older patients. *Gerontologist, 34*(1), 95–102.

Hinshaw, S. F., & Anderson, C. A. (1996). Conduct and oppositional disorders. In E. J. Mash & R. A. Barkley (Eds.), *Child psychopathology.* (pp. 113–49). New York: Guilford.

Hinshaw, S. F., Zupan, B. A., Simmel, C., & Nigg, J. T. (1997). Peer status in boys with and without attention-deficit hyperactivity disorder: Predictions from overt and covert antisocial behavior, social isolation, and authoritative parents. *Child Develop., 68*(5), 880–96.

Hinshaw, S. P. (1992). Externalizing behavior problems and academic underachievement in childhood and adolescence: Causal relationships and underlying mechanisms. *Psychol. Bull., 111,* 127–55.

Hinshaw, S. P. (1994). Conduct disorder in childhood: Conceptualization, diagnosis, comorbidity, and risk status for antisocial functioning in adulthood. In D. C. Fowles, P. Sutker, & S. H. Goodman (Eds.), *Progress in experimental personality and psychopathology research.* New York: Springer.

Hinton, W. L., Tiet, Q., Giaouyen, C., & Chesney, M. (1997). Predictors of depression among refugees from Vietnam: A longitudinal study of new arrivals. *J. Nerv. Ment. Dis., 185*(1), 39–45.

Hiroto, D. S., & Seligman, M. E. P. (1975). Generality of learned helplessness in man. *J. Pers. Soc. Psychol., 31*(2), 311–27.

Hirsch, S. R., & Leff, J. P. (1975). *Abnormalities in parents of schizophrenics.* London: Oxford University Press.

Hirschfeld, R. M. A. (1996). Panic disorder: Diagnosis, epidemiology, and clinical course. *J. Clin. Psychiat., 57*(10), 3–8.

Hirschfeld, R. M. A., Shea, M. T., & Weise, R. (1995). Dependent personality disorder. In W. J. Livesley (Ed.), *The DSM-IV personality disorders.* (pp. 239–256). New York: Guilford.

Hirshfeld, D. R., Rosenbaum, J. F., Biederman, J., Bolduc, E. A., Faraone, S. V., Snidman, N., Reznick, J. S., Kagan, J. (1992). Stable behavioral inhibition and its association with anxiety disorder. *J. Amer. Acad. Child Adoles. Psychiat., 31,* 103–111.

Hirst, W. (1982). The amnesic syndrome: Descriptions and explanations. *Psychol. Bull., 91,* 435–60.

Hobfoll, S., Ritter, C., Lavin, J., & Hulsizer, M. et al. (1995). Depression prevalence and incidence among inner-city pregnant and postpartum women. *J. Cons. Clin. Psychol.,* 3, 445–453.

Hoffman, P. L., & Tabakoff, B. (1996). Alcohol dependence: A commentary on mechanisms. *Alcohol & Alcoholism, 31*(4), 333–40.

Hogarty, G. E., et al. (1997a). Three-year trials of personal therapy among schizophrenic patients living with or independent of family: I. Description of study and effects on relapse rate. *Amer. J. Psychiat., 154*(11), 1504–13.

Hogarty, G. E., et al. (1997b). Three-year trials of personal therapy among schizophrenic patients living with or independent of family, II: Effects on adjustment of patients. *Amer. J. Psychiat., 154*(11), 1514–24.

Hogarty, G. E., Anderson, C. M., Reiss, D. J., Kornblith, S. J., & Greenwald, D. P. (1986). Family psychoeducation, social skills training, and maintenance chemotherapy in the aftercare treatment of schizophrenia: 1. One-year effects of a controlled study. *Arch. Gen. Psychiat., 43,* 633–42.

Holder, H. D., Longabaugh, R., Miller, W. R., & Rubonis, A. V. (1991). The cost effectiveness of treatment for alcohol problems: A first approximation. *J. Stud. Alcoh., 52,* 517–40.

Holland, H. C. (1974). Displacement activity as a form of abnormal behavior in animals. In H. R. Beech (Ed.), *Obsessional states.* (pp. 161–73). London: Methuen.

Hollander, E., DeCaria, C. M., Nitescu, A., Gully, R., Suckow, R. F., et al. (1992). Serotonergic function in obsessive-compulsive disorder: Behavioral and neuroendocrine responses to oral m-chlorophenylpiperazine and fenfluramine in patients and healthy volunteers. *Arch. Gen. Psychiat., 49,* 21–28.

Hollander, E., Stein, D. J., Decaria, C. M., Cohen, L., Saoud, J. B., Skodol, A., Kellman, D., Rosnick, L., & Oldham, J. M. (1994). Serotonergic sensitivity in borderline personality disorder: Preliminary Findings. *Amer. J. Psychiat., 151*(2), 277–280.

Hollon, S., & Beck, A. T. (1978). Psychotherapy and drug therapy: Comparisons and combinations. In S. L. Garfield & A. E. Bergin (Eds.), *Handbook of psychotherapy and behavior change.* (pp. 437–90). New York: Wiley.

Hollon, S. D., & Beck, A. T. (1994). Cognitive and cognitive-behavioral therapies. In A. E. Bergin & S. L. Garfield (Eds.), *Handbook of psychotherapy and behavior change* (4th ed.). (pp. 428–66). New York: Wiley.

Hollon, S. D., DeRubeis, R. J., & Evans, M. D. (1987). Causal mediation of change in treatment for depression: Discriminating between nonspecificity and noncausality. *Psychol. Bull., 102,* 139–49.

Hollon, S. D., DeRubeis, R. J., & Evans, M. D. (1996). Cognitive therapy in the treatment and prevention of depression. In P. M. Salkovskis (Ed.), *Frontiers of cognitive therapy.* (pp. 293–317). New York: Guilford.

Hollon, S. D., DeRubeis, R. J., Evans, M. D., Wiemer, M. J., Garvey, M. J., Grove, W. M., & Tuason, V. B. (1992). Cognitive therapy and pharmacotherapy for depression: Singly and in combination. *Arch. Gen. Psychiat., 49*(10), 774–81.

Hollon, S. D., Evans, M., & DeRubeis, R. (1990). Cognitive mediation of relapse prevention following treatment for depression: Implications of differential risk. In R. Ingram (Ed.), *Psychological aspects of depression.* New York: Plenum.

Holmes, D. L. (1998). *Autism through the lifespan: The Eden Model.* Bethesda, MD: Woodbine House.

Holmes, V. F., & Rich, C. L. (1990). Suicide among physicians. In S. J. Blumenthal & D. J. Kupfer (Eds.), *Suicide over the life cycle: Risk factors, assessment, and treatment of suicidal patients.* (pp. 599–618). Washington, DC: American Psychiatric Press.

Holohan, C. J., & Moos, R. H. (1991). Life stressors, personal and social resources, and depression: A 4-year structural model. *J. Abn. Psychol. 100,* 31–38.

Holroyd, K. A., & Andrasik, F. (1978). Coping and the self-control of chronic tension headache. *J. Cons. Clin. Psychol., 46,* 1036–45.

Holroyd, K. A., Andrasik, F., & Westbrook, T. (1977). Cognitive control of tension headache. *Cog. Ther. Res., 1,* 121–33.

Holsboer, F. (1992). The hypothalmic-pituitary-adrenocortical system. In E. S. Paykel (Ed.), *Handbook of affective disorders* (2nd ed.). New York: Guilford.

Holt, C. S., Heimberg, R. G., & Hope, D. A. (1992). Avoidant personality disorder and the generalized subtype of social phobia. *J. Abn. Psychol., 101,* 318–25.

Holvey, D. N., & Talbott, J. H. (Eds.). (1972). *The Merck manual of diagnosis and therapy* (12th ed.). Rahway, NJ: Merck, Sharp, & Dohme Research Laboratories.

Holzbeck, E. (1996). Thiamine absorption in alcoholic delirium patients. *J. Stud. Alcoh., 57*(6), 581–84.

Holzman, P. S., et al. (1998). How are deficits in motion perception related to eye-tracking dysfunction in schizophrenia. In M. F. Lenzenweger & R. H. Dworkin (Eds.), *Origins and development of schizophrenia.* (pp. 161–84). Washington: American Psychological Association.

Holzman, P. S., Kringlen, E., Matthysse, S., Flanagan, S. D., Lipton, R. B., Cramer, G., Levin, S., Lange, K., & Levy, D. L. (1988). A single dominant gene can account for eye tracking dysfunctions and schizophrenia in offspring of discordant twins. *Arch. Gen. Psychiat., 45,* 641–47.

Hook, E. B. (1980). Genetic counseling dilemmas: Down's syndrome, paternal age, and recurrence risk after remarriage. *Amer. J. Med. Genet., 5,* 145–51.

Hooker, E. (1957). The adjustment of the male overt homosexual. *Journal of Projective Techniques, 21,* 18–30.

Hooley, J. M. (1998). Expressed emotion and locus of control. *J. Nerv. Ment. Dis. 186,* 374–78.

Hooley, J. M., & Hiller, J. B. (1998). Expressed emotion and the pathogenesis of relapse in schizophrenia. In M. F. Lenzenweger & R. H. Dworkin (Eds.), *Origins and development of schizophrenia.* (pp. 447–68). Washington: American Psychological Association.

Hooley, J. M., & Teasdale, J. D. (1989). Predictors of relapse in unipolar depressives: Expressed emotion, marital distress, and perceived criticism. *J. Abn. Psychol., 98,* 229–35.

Hoon, P. W., Wincze, J. P., & Hoon, E. F. (1977). A test of reciprocal inhibition: Are anxiety and sexual arousal in women mutually inhibitory? *J. Abn. Psychol. 86,* 65–74.

Hope, D. A., & Heimberg, R. G. (1993). Social phobia and social anxiety. In D. H. Barlow (Ed.), *Clinical handbook of psychological disorders.* (pp. 99–136). New York: Guilford.

Hops, H., Duncan, T. E., Duncan, S. C., & Stoolmiller, M. (1996). Parent substance use as a predictor of adolescent use: A six-year lagged analysis. *Ann. Behav. Med., 18*(3), 157–64.

Horevitz, R., & Loewenstein, R. J. (1994). The rational treatment of multiple personality disorder. In S. J. Lynn & J. W. Rhue (Eds.), *Dissociation: Clinical and theoretical perspectives.* (pp. 289–316). New York: Guilford.

Hornig, C. D., & McNally, R. J. (1995). Panic disorder and suicide attempt: A reanalysis of data from the Epidemiologic Catchment Area study. *Brit. J. Psychiat. 67,* 76–77.

Horowitz, L. M. (1996). The study of interpersonal problems: A Leary legacy. *J. Pers. Assess., 66*(2), 283–300.

Horowitz, M. J., & Solomon, G. F. (1978). Delayed stress response syndromes in Vietnam veterans. In C. R. Figley (Ed.), *Stress disorders among Vietnam veterans: Theory, research, and treatment.* New York: Brunner/Mazel.

Horvath, A. O., & Greenberg, L. S. (Eds.). (1994). *The working alliance: Theory, research, and practice.* New York: Wiley.

Houts, A. C., Berman, J. S., & Abramson, H. (1994). Effectiveness of psychological and pharmacological treatments for nocturnal eneurisis. *J. Cons. Clin. Psychol., 62,* 737–45.

Howes, M. J., Hokanson, J. E., & Loewenstein, D. A. (1985). Induction of depressive affect after pro-

Kraepelin, E. (1883). *Compendium der psychiatrie.* Leipzig: Abel.

Kraepelin, E. (1899). *Psychiatrie. Ein lehrbuch fur studierende und aerzte* (6th ed.). Leipzig: Barth.

Kramer, P. D. (1993). *Listening to Prozac: A psychiatrist explores antidepressant drugs and the remaking of the self.* New York: Viking Penguin.

Kramer, R. A., Warner, V., Olfson, M., Ebanks, C. M., Chaput, F., & Weissman, M. M. (1998). General medical problems among the offspring of depressed parents: A 10-year follow-up. *J. Amer. Acad. Child & Adoles. Psychiat., 37*(6), 602–11.

Krantz, D. S., & Glass, D. C. (1984). Personality, behavior patterns, and physical illness: Conceptual and methodological issues. In W. D. Gentry (Ed.), *Handbook of behavioral medicine.* (pp. 38–86). New York: Guilford.

Kranzler, H. R., Del Boca, F. K., & Rounsaville, B. (1997). Comorbid psychiatric diagnosis predicts three-year outcomes in alcoholics: A posttreatment natural history study. *J. Stud. Alcoh., 57*(6), 619–26.

Kreitman, N., Sainsbury, P., Pearce, K., & Costain, W. R. (1965). Hypochondriasis and depression in outpatients at a general hospital. *Brit. J. Psychiat., 3,* 607–15.

Kremen, W. S., Seidman, L. J., Pepple, J. R., Lyons, M. J., Tsuang, M. T., & Faraone, S. V. (1994). Neuropsychological risk indicators for schizophrenia: A review of family studies. *Schizo. Bull., 20*(1), 103–19.

Kriechman, A. M. (1987). Siblings with somatoform disorders in childhood and adolescence. *J. Amer. Acad. Child Adoles. Psychiat., 26,* 226–31.

Kring, A. M. (1998, May 22). Emotion disturbance in schizophrenia. In Ann M. Kring (Chair), American Psychological Society, (p. 41). Washington.

Kring, A. M., Kerr, S. L., Smith, D. A., & Neale, J. M. (1993). Flat affect in schizophrenia does not reflect diminished subjective experience of emotion. *J. Abn. Psychol., 102*(4), 507–17.

Krippner, S. (1994). Cross-cultural treatment perspectives on dissociative disorders. In S. J. Lynn & J. W. Rhue (Eds.), *Dissociation: Clinical and theoretical perspectives.* (pp. 338–64). New York: Guilford.

Krupnick, J. L., et al. (1996). The role of therapeutic alliance in psychotherapy and pharmacotherapy outcome: Findings in the NIMH TDCRP. *J. Cons. Clin. Psychol., 64*(3), 532–39.

Kuch, K. (1997). Accident phobia. In G. C. L. Davey, (Ed.), *Phobias. A handbook of theory, research and treatment.* (pp. 153–62). Chichester, England: Wiley.

Kuechenmeister, C. A., Linton, P. H., Mueller, T. V., & White, H. B. (1977). Eye tracking in relation to age, sex, and illness. *Arch. Gen. Psychiat., 34,* 578–79.

Kuhn, T. S. (1962). *The structure of scientific revolutions.* Chicago: University of Chicago Press.

Kulka, R. A., Schlenger, W. E., Fairbank, J. A., Hough, R. L., Jordan, B. K., Marmar, C. R., & Weiss, D. S. (1990). *Trauma and the Vietnam War generation: Report of findings from the National Vietnam Veterans Readjustment Study.* NY: Brunner/Mazel.

Kuperman, S., Black, D. W., & Burns, T. L. (1988). Excess mortality among formerly hospitalized child psychiatric patients. *Arch. Gen. Psychiat., 45,* 277–82.

Kupersmidt, J. B., Coie, J. D., & Dodge, K. A. (1990). The role of poor peer relationships in the development of disorder. In S. R. Asher & J. D. Coie (Eds.), *Peer rejection in childhood.* (pp. 274–308). New York: Cambridge University Press.

Kurlan, R. (1997). Treatment of tics. *Neurologic Clinics, 15*(2), 403–409.

Kushner, M. (1968). The operant control of intractable sneezing. In C. D. Spielberger (Ed.), *Contributions to general psychology: Selected readings for introductory psychology.* New York: Ronald Press.

Kwapil, T. R. (1996). A longitudinal study of drug and alcohol use by psychosis-prone and impulsive-nonconforming individuals. *J. Abn. Psychol., 105*(1), 114–23.

Kwapil, T. R., Miller, M. B., Zinser, M. C., Chapman, J., & Chapman, L. J. (1997). Magical ideation and social anhedonia as predictors of psychosis proneness: A partial replication. *J. Abn. Psychol., 106*(3), 491–95.

Kwon, S. M., & Oei, T. P. (1994). The roles of two levels of cognitions in the development, maintenance, and treatment of depression. *Clin. Psychol. Rev., 14*(5), 331–58.

Laan, E., & Everaerd, W. (1995). Determinants of female sexual arousal: Psychophysiological theory and data. *Annu. Rev. Sex Res., 6,* 32–76.

La Greca, A. M., Silverman, W. K., Vernberg, E. M., & Prinstein, M. J. (1996). Symptoms of posttraumatic stress disorder in children after Hurricane Andrew: A prospective study. *J. Cons. Clin. Psychol., 64*(4), 712–23.

Lahey, B. B., Loeber, R., Quay, H. C., Frick, P. J., & Grimm, S. (1992). Oppositional defiant and conduct disorders: Issues to be resolved for DSM-IV. *J. Amer. Acad. Child Adoles. Psychiat., 29,* 620–26.

Lamb, H. R. (1984). Deinstitutionalization and the homeless mentally ill. *Hosp. Comm. Psychiat., 35,* 899–907.

Lambe, E. K., Katzman, D. K., Mikulis, D. J., Kennedy, S. H., & Zipursky, R. B. (1997). Cerebral gray matter volume deficits after weight recovery from anorexia nervosa. *Arch. Gen. Psychiat., 54*(6), 537–542.

Lamberg, L. (1998). Mental illness and violent acts: Protecting the patient and the public. *JAMA, 280,* 407–08.

Lambert, M. J. (1989). The individual therapist's contribution to psychotherapy process and outcome. *Clin. Psychol. Rev., 9,* 469–85.

Lambert, M. J., & Bergin, A. E. (1994). The effectiveness of psychotherapy. In A. E. Bergin & S. L. Garfield (Eds.), *Handbook of psychotherapy and behavior change* (4th ed.). (pp. 143–89). New York: Wiley.

Lambert, M. J., Shapiro, D. A., & Bergin, A. E. (1986). The effectiveness of psychotherapy. In S. L. Garfield & A. E. Bergin (Eds.), *Handbook of psychotherapy and behavior change.* New York: Wiley.

Landesman-Dwyer, S. (1981). Living in the community. *Amer. J. Ment. Def., 86,* 223–34.

Lang, A. R., & Kidorf, M. (1990). Problem drinking: Cognitive behavioral strategies for self control. In M. E. Thase, B. A. Edelstein, & M. Hersen (Eds.), *Handbook of outpatient treatment of adults.* (pp. 413–42). New York: Plenum.

Lang, P. (1970). Autonomic control. *Psych. Today, 4*(5), 37–41.

Lang, P. J. (1968). Fear reduction and fear behavior: Problems in treating a construct. In J. M. Shlien (Ed.), *Research in psychotherapy* (Vol. 3). Washington DC: American Psychological Association.

Lang, P. J. (1971). Application of psychophysiological methods to the study of psychotherapy and behavior modification. In A. E. Bergin & S. L. Garfield (Eds.), *Handbook of psychotherapy and behavior change.* New York: Wiley

Lang, P. J. (1985). The cognitive psychophysiology of emotion: Fear and anxiety. In A. H. Tuma & J. D. Maser (Eds.), *Anxiety and the anxiety disorders.* Hillsdale, NJ: Erlbaum.

Lange, W. R., Cabanilla, B. R., Moler, G., Bernacki, E. J., & Frankenfield, D. (1994). Preemployment drug screening at the Johns Hopkins Hospital, 1989 and 1991. *Amer. J. Drug Alcoh. Abuse, 20,* 35–46.

Langevin, R., Handy, L., Day, D., & Russon, A. (1985). Are incestuous fathers pedophilic, aggressive, and alcoholic? In R. Langevin (Ed.), *Erotic preference, gender identity, and aggression.* (pp. 161–80). Hillsdale, NJ: Erlbaum.

Last, C. G., & Perrin, S. (1993). Anxiety disorders in African-American and white children. *J. Abnorm. Child Psychol., 21,* 153–64.

Lauer, C. J., Schreiber, W., Holsboer, F., & Krieg, J.-C. (1995). In quest of identifying vulnerability markers for psychiatric disorders by all-night polysomnography. *Arch. Gen. Psychiat., 52,* 145–53.

Lauer, J., Black D. W., & Keen, P. (1993) Multiple personality disorder and borderline personality disorder: Distinct entities or variations on a common theme? *Annals of Clinical Psychiatry, 5,* 129–134.

Laufer, R. S., Brett, E., & Gallops, M. S. (1985). Dimensions of posttraumatic stress disorder among Vietnam veterans. *J. Nerv. Ment. Dis., 173*(9), 538–45.

Laumann, E. O., Gagnon, J. H., Michael, R. T., & Michaels, S. (1994). *The social organization of sexuality: Sexual practices in the United States.* Chicago: The University of Chicago Press.

Law, W. A., & Mapou, R. L. (1997). Neuropsychological findings in HIV-1 disease and AIDS. In A. M. Horton, D. Wedding, & J. Webster (Eds.), *The neuropsychology handbook* (Vol. 2). (pp. 267–308). New York: Springer.

Lazarus, A. A. (1981). *The practice of multimodal therapy.* New York: McGraw-Hill.

Lazarus, A. A. (Ed.). (1985). *Casebook of multimodal therapy.* New York: Guilford.

Lazarus, A. A. (1989). Dyspareunia: A multimodal psychotherapeutic perspective. In S. R. Leiblum & R. C. Rosen (Eds.), *Principles and practice of sex therapy* (2nd ed.). (pp. 89–112). New York: Guilford.

Lazarus, A. A. (Ed.). (1996). *Controversies in managed mental health care.* Washington, DC: American Psychiatric Press, Inc.

Lazarus, A. A. (1997a). Through a different lens: Commentary on "Behavior Therapy: Distinct but Acculturated." *Behav. Ther., 28*(4), 573–75.

Lazarus, A. A. (1997b). *Brief but comprehensive psychotherapy: The multimodal way.* New York: Springer.

Leal, J., Ziedonis, D., & Kosten, T. (1994). Antisocial personality disorder as a prognostic factor for pharmacotherapy of cocaine dependence. *Drug and Alcohol Dependence, 35,* 31–35.

Lease, C. A., & Ollendick, T. H. (1993). Development and psychopathology. In A. S. Bellack & M. Hersen (Eds.), *Psychopathology in adulthood.* Needham, MA: Allyn and Bacon.

Lebedev, B. A. (1967). Corticovisceral psychosomatics. *Inter. J. Psychiat., 4*(3), 241–46.

Le Couteur, A., Bailey, A., Goode, S., Pickles, A., Robertson, S., Gottesman, I., & Rutter, M. (1996). A broader phenotype of autism: The clinical spectrum in twins. *J. Child Clin. Psychiat., 37*(7), 785–801.

Lee, J. R., & Goodwin, M. E. (1987). Deinstitutionalization: A new scenario. *Journal of Mental Health Administration, 14,* 40–45.

Lees-Haley, P. R., Smith, H. H., Williams, C. W., & Dunn, J. T. (1996). Forensic neuropsychological test usage: An empirical survey. *Arch. Clin. Neuropsychol., 11,* 45–51.

Lees-Roitman, S. E., Cornblatt, B. A., Bergman, A., Obuchowski, M., Mitropoulou, V., Keefe, R. S. E., Silverman, J. M., & Siever, L. J. (1997). Attentional functioning in schizotypal personality disorder. *Amer. J. Psychiat., 154*(5), 655–660.

Leff, J., Kuipers, L., Berkowitz, R., & Sturgeon, D. A. (1982). A controlled trial of social intervention in the families of schizophrenic patients. *Brit. J. Psychiat., 141,* 121–34.

le Grange, D., Telch, C. F., & Tibbs, J. (1998). Eating attitudes and behaviors in 1,435 South African Caucasian and Non-Caucasian college students. *Amer. J. Psychiat., 155*(2), 250–254.

Lehto, J. (1995). *Approaches to alcohol control policy: European alcohol action plan.* Geneva: World Health Organization.

Leibenluft, E. (1996). Women with bipolar illness: Clinical and research issues. *Amer. J. Psychiat., 153*(2), 163–173.

Leiblum, S. R., Pervin, L. A., & Campbell, E. H. (1989). The treatment of vaginismus: Success and failure. In S. R. Leiblum & R. C. Rosen (Eds.), *Principles and practice of sex therapy* (2nd ed.). (pp. 113–40). New York: Guilford.

Leichtman, M. (1995). Behavioral observations. In J. N. Butcher (Ed.), *Clinical personality assessment: Practical considerations.* (pp. 251–66). New York: Oxford University Press.

Leichtman, M. D. & Ceci, S. J. (1995). The effects of stereotypes and suggestions on preschoolers' reports. *Develop. Psychol., 31,* 568–78.

Leitenberg, H., et al. (1994). Comparison of cognitive-behavior therapy and desipramine in the treatment of bulimia nervosa. *Behav. Res. Ther., 32,* 37–46.

Lelliott, P., Marks, I., McNamee, G., & Tobena, A. (1989). Onset of panic disorder with agoraphobia. *Arch. Gen. Psychiat., 46,* 1000–4.

Lencz, T., Raine, A., Scerbo, A., Redmon, M., Brodish, S., Holt, L., & Bird, L. (1993). Impaired eye tracking in undergraduates with schizotypal personality disorder. *Amer. J. Psychiat., 150,* 152–54.

Lenzenweger, M. F. (1994). Psychometric high-risk paradigm, perceptual aberrations, and schizotypy: An update. *Schizo. Bull., 20*(1), 121–35.

Lenzenweger, M. F. (1998). Schizotypy and schizotypic psychopathology: Mapping an alternative expression of schizophrenia liability. In M. F. Lenzenweger & R. H. Dworkin (Eds.), *Origins and development of schizophrenia.* (pp. 93–122). Washington: American Psychological Association.

Lenzenweger, M. F., & Dworkin, R. H. (Ed.). (1998). *Origins and development of schizophrenia: Advances in experimental psychopathology.* Washington: American Psychological Association.

Lenzenweger, M. F., & Korfine, L. (1994). Perceptual aberrations, schizotypy, and the Wisconsin Card Sorting Test. *Schizo. Bull., 20*(2), 345–56.

Leon, G. R., Keel, P. K., Klump, K. L., & Fulkerson, J. A. (1997). The future of risk factor research in understanding the etiology of eating disorders. *Psychopharm. Bull., 33*(3), 405–411.

Leonard, K. E., & Senchak, M. (1996). Prospective prediction of husband marital aggression within newlywed couples. *J. Abn. Psychol., 105,* 369–80.

Leor, W., Poole, W., & Kloner, R. (1996). Sudden cardiac death triggered by an earthquake. *New Engl. J. Med., 334,* 413.

Lerman, P. (1981). *Deinstitutionalization: A cross-problem analysis.* Rockville, MD: U.S. Department of Health and Human Services.

Lerner, P. M. (1995). Assessing adaptive capacities by means of the Rorschach. In J. N. Butcher (Ed.), *Clinical personality assessment: Practical considerations.* (pp. 317–25). New York: Oxford University Press.

Lesch, K.-P., Bengel, D., Heils, A., Sabol, S., Greenburg, B., Petri, S., Benjamin, J., Muller, C., Hamer, D., & Murphy, D. (1996). Association of anxiety-related traits with a polymorphism in the serotonin transporter gene regulatory region. *Science, 274,* 1527–31.

Lester, D. (1988). Youth suicide: A cross-cultural perspective. *Adolescence, 23,* 955–58.

Leung, P. W., & Connolly, K. (1996). Distractibility in hyperactive and conduct disordered children. *J. Child Psychol. Psychiat., 37*(3), 305–12.

Leung, P. W., Luk, S. L., Ho, T. P., Taylor, E., Mak, F. L., & Bacon-Shone, J. (1996). The diagnosis and prevalence of hyperactivity in Chinese boys. *Brit. J. Psychiat., 168,* 486–496.

LeVay, S. (1991). A difference in hypothalamic structure between heterosexual and homosexual men. *Science, 253,* 1034–37.

LeVay, S. (1993). *The sexual brain.* Cambridge, MA: MIT Press.

Leventhal, B. L., Cook, E. H., & Lord, C. (1998). The irony of autism. *Arch. Gen. Psychiat., 55,* 643–44.

Leventhal, H., Patrick–Muller, L., & Leventhal, E. A. (1998). It's long-term stressors that take a toll: Comment on Cohen et al. (1988). *Hlth. Psychol., 17*(3), 211–13.

Levine, M. D., & Bakow, H. (1975). Children with encopresis: A study of treatment outcomes. *Pediatrics, 58,* 845.

Levinson, D. F., et al., (1998). Genome scan of schizophrenia. *Amer. J. Psychiat., 155*(6), 741–50.

Levor, R. M., Cohen, M. J., Naliboff, B. D., & McArthur, D. (1986). Psychosocial precursors and correlates of migraine headache. *J. Cons. Clin. Psychol., 54,* 347–53.

Levy, D. L., Holzman, P. S., Matthysse, S., & Mendell, N. R. (1993). Eye tracking dysfunction and schizophrenia: A critical perspective. *Schizo. Bull., 19*(3), 461–536.

Levy, D. L., Holzman, P. S., Matthysse, S., & Mendell, N. R. (1994). Eye tracking and schizophrenia: A selective review. *Schizo. Bull., 20*(1), 47–62.

Levy, D. L., Yasillo, N. J., Dorcus, E., Shaughnessy, R. Gibbons, R. D., Peterson, J., Janicak, P.G., Gaviria, M., & Davis, J. M. (1983). Relatives of unipolar and bipolar patients have normal pursuit. *Psychiat. Res., 10,* 285–93.

Levy, F., Barr, C., & Sunohara, G. (1998). Directions of aetiologic research on attention deficit hyperactivity disorder. *Austral. N.Z. J. Psychiatr., 32*(1), 97–103.

Lewinsohn, P. M. (1974). A behavioral approach to depression. In R. J. Friedman & M. M. Katz (Eds.), *The psychology of depression: Contemporary theory and research.* New York: Halstead Press.

Lewinsohn, P. M., & Gotlib, I. H. (1995). Behavioral theory and treatment of depression. In E. E. Beckham & W. R. Leber (Eds.), *Handbook of depression* (2nd ed.). (pp. 352–75). New York: Guilford.

Lewinsohn, P. M., Gotlib, I. H., Lewinson, M., Seeley, J. R., & Allen, N. B. (1998). Gender differences in anxiety disorders and anxiety symptoms in adolescents. *J. Abn. Psychol. 107*(1), 109–17.

Lewinsohn, P. M., Hoberman, H. M., & Rosenbaum, M. (1988). A prospective study of risk factors for unipolar depression. *J. Abn. Psychol., 97,* 251–64.

Lewinsohn, P. M., Hoberman, H. M., Teri, L., & Hautzinger, M. (1985). An integrative theory of depression. In S. Reiss & R. Bootzin (Eds.), *Theoretical issues in behavior therapy.* (pp. 331–59). San Diego: Academic Press.

Lewinsohn, P. M., Hops, H., Roberts, R. E., Seeley, J. R., & Andrews, J. A. (1993). Adolescent psychopathology: I. Prevalence and incidence of depression and other DSM-III-R disorders in high school students. *J. Abn. Psychol., 102,* 133–44.

Lewinsohn, P. M., Rohde, P., & Seeley, J. R. (1994). Psychosocial risk factors for future adolescent suicide attempts. *J. Cons. Clin. Psychol., 62,* 297–305.

Lewinsohn, P. M., Rohde, P., & Seeley, J. R. (1996). Epidemiology of adolescent suicide. *Clin. Psychol. Sci. Prac., 3,* 25–46.

Lewis, C. F., & Ednie, K. (1997) Koro and homicidal behavior. *Amer. J. Psychiat., 154,* 1169.

Lewis, D. O., Yeager, C. A., Swica, Y., Pincus, J. H., & Lewis, M. (1997). Objective documentation of child abuse and dissociation in 12 murderers with Dissociative Identity Disorder. *Amer. J. of Psychiat., 154*(12), 1703–1710.

Lewis, J. M., Rodnick, E. H., & Goldstein, M. J. (1981). Intrafamilial interactive behavior, communication deviance, and risk for schizophrenia. *J. Abn. Psychol., 90,* 448–57.

Lewis, J. W., & Walter, D. (1992). Buprenorphine: Background to its development as a treatment for opiate dependence. In J. D. Blaine (Ed.), *Buprenorphine: An alternative treatment for opioid dependence.* (pp. 5–11). Washington, DC: U.S. Department of Health and Human Services.

Lewis, O. (1997). Integrated psychodynamic psychotherapy with children. *Child Adoles. Psychiat. Clin. N. Amer., 6*(1), 53–68.

Lewis-Fernández, R., & Kleinman, A. (1994). Culture, personality, and psychopathology. *J. Abn. Psychol., 103*(1), 67–71.

Licavoli, L. T., & Orland, R. M. (1997). Psychotherapy, pharmacotherapy and nutritional therapy in the treatment of eating disorders. *In Session: Psychotherapy in Practice, 3*(3), 57–78.

Lidz, T. (1994). To the Editor. *Amer. J. Psychiat., 151,* 458–59.

Lidz, T., Fleck, S., & Cornelison, A. R. (1965). *Schizophrenia and the family.* New York: International Universities Press.

Lieberman, J. A., Jody, D., Alvir, J. M. J., Ashtari, M., Levy, D. L., Bogerts, B., Degreef, G., Mayerhoff, D. I., & Cooper, T. (1993a). Brain morphology, dopamine, and eyetracking abnormalities in first-episode schizophrenia: Prevalence and clinical correlates. *Arch. Gen. Psychiat., 50*(5), 357–68.

Lieberman, J. A., & Koreen, A. R. (1993). Neurochemistry and neuroendocrinology of schizophrenia: A selective review. *Schizo. Bull., 19*(2), 371–429.

Lieberman, L. M. (1982). The nightmare of scheduling. *J. Learn. Dis., 15,* 57–58.

Liebman, J. M., & Cooper, S. J. (1989). *The neuropharmacological basis of reward.* New York: Clarendon Press.

Liem, J. H. (1974). Effects of verbal communications of parents and children: A comparison of normal and schizophrenic families. *J. Cons. Clin. Psychol., 42,* 438–50.

Lilienfeld, S. O. (1992). The association between antisocial personality and somatization disorders: A review and integration of theoretical models. *Clin. Psychol. Rev., 12,* 641–662.

Lilienfeld, S. O., & Marino, L. (1995). Mental disorder as a Roschian concept: A critique of Wakefield's harmful dysfunctionanalysis. *J. Abn. Psychol., 104*(3), 411–420.

Lincoln, J., Batty, J., Townsend, R., & Collins, M. (1992). Working for greater inclusion of children with severe learning difficulties in mainstream secondary schools. *Educational & Child Psychology, 9*(4), 46–51.

Lindman, R. E., & Lang, A. R. (1994). The alcohol-aggression stereotype: A cross-cultural comparison of beliefs. *Inter. J. Addict., 29,* 1–13.

Lindsey, K. P., & Paul, G. L. (1989). Involuntary commitments to public mental institutions: Issues involving the overrepresentation of blacks and the assessment of relevant functioning. *Psychol. Bull., 106,* 171–83.

Linehan, M. M. (1987). Dialectical behavioral therapy: A cognitive behavioral approach to parasuicide. *J. Personal. Dis., 1,* 328–33.

Linehan, M. M. (1993). *Cognitive-behavioral treatment of borderline personality disorder: The dialectics of effective treatment.* New York: Guilford.

Linehan, M. M., Armstrong, H. E., Suarez, A., Allmon, D., & Heard, H. L. (1991). Cognitive-behavioral treatment of chronically parasuicidal borderline patients. *Arch. Gen. Psychiat., 48,* 1060–64.

Linehan, M. M., Heard, H. L., & Armstrong, H. E. (1993) Naturalistic follow-up of a behavioral treatment for chronically parasuicidal borderline patients. *Arch. Gen. Psychiat., 50,* 971–74.

Linehan, M. M., Tutek, D. A., Heard, H. L., & Armstrong, H. E. (1994). Interpersonal outcome of cognitive behavioral treatment for chronically suicidal borderline patients. *Amer. J. Psychiat., 151*(12), 1771–76.

Link, B. G., Cullen, F. T., Frank, J., & Wozniak, J.F. (1987). The social rejection of former mental patients: Understanding why labels matter. *American Journal of Sociology, 92,* 1461–1500.

Linszen, D. H., et al. (1997). Patient attributes and expressed emotion as risk factors for psychotic relapse. *Schizo. Bull., 23*(1), 119–30.

Lintzeris, N., Holgate, F., & Dunlop, A. (1996). Addressing dependent amphetamine use: A place for prescription. *Drug and Alcohol Review, 15*(2), 189–95.

Lipowski, Z. J. (1988). Somatization: The concept and its clinical application. *Amer. J. Psychiat., 145,* 1358–68.

Lipton, D. N., McDonel, E. C., & McFall, R. M. (1987) Heterosocial perception in rapists. *J. Cons. Clin. Psychol., 55,* 17–21.

Lishman, W. A. (1990). Alcohol and the brain. *Brit. J. Psychiat., 156,* 635–44.

Lishman, W. A., Jacobson, R. R., & Acker, C. (1987). Brain damage in alcoholism: Current concepts. *Acta Medica Scandinavica* (Suppl. 717), 5–17.

Litz, B. T., King, L. A., King, D. W., Orsillo, S. M., & Friedman, M. J. (1997). Warriors as peacekeepers: Features of the Somalia experience and PTSD. *J. Cons. Clin. Psychol., 65*(6), 1001–1010.

Litz, B. T., Orsillo, S. M., Friedman, M., Ehlich, P., et al. (1997). Post-traumatic stress disorder associated with peacekeeping duty in Somalia for U.S. military personnel. *Amer. J. Psychiat., 154*(2), 178–84.

Livesley, W. J. (1995). Past achievements and future directions. In W. J. Livesley (Ed.), *The DSM-IV personality disorders.* (pp. 497–506). New York: Guilford.

Livesley, W. J., Schroeder, M. L., Jackson, D. N., & Jang, K. L. (1994). Categorical distinctions in the study of personality disorder: Implications for classification. *J. Abn. Psychol., 103,* 6–17.

Loeber, R., Green, S. M., Lahey, B. B., Crist, M. A., & Frick, P. J. (1992). Developmental sequences in the age of onset of disruptive child behaviors. *Journal of Child and Family Studies, 1,* 21–41.

Loftus, E. F. (1993). The reality of repressed memories. *Amer. Psychol., 48*(5), 518–537.

Loftus, E. F., Feldman, J., & Dashiell, R. (1995). The reality of illusory memories. In D. Schacter, J. Coyle, L. Sullivan, M. Mesulam, & G. Fischbach (Eds.), *Memory distortions: Interdisciplinary perspectives.* Cambridge: Harvard University Press.

Loftus, E. F., & Ketchum, K. (1994). *The myth of repressed memory: False memories and allegations of sexual abuse.* New York: St Martin's.

Lohr, B. A., Adams, H. E., & Davis, J. M. (1997). Sexual arousal to erotic and aggressive stimuli in sexually coercive and noncoercive men. *J. Abn. Psychol., 106,* 230–42.

Loosen, P. T. (1986). Hormones of the hypothalmic-pituitary thyroid axis: A psychoneuroendocrine perspective. *Pharmacopsychiatry, 19,* 401–15.

Lopez, O. L., et al. (1997). The apoliproprotein E e4 allele is not associated with psychiatric symptoms or extra-pyramidal signs in probable Alzheimer's disease. *Neurology, 49*(3), 794–97.

Lopez, S. R., Lopez, A. A., & Fong, K. T. (1991). Mexican Americans' initial preferences for counselors: The role of ethnic factors. *J. Couns. Psychol., 38,* 487–96.

Lord, C., & Magill-Evans, J. (1995). Peer interactions of autistic children and adolescents. *Develop. Psychopath., 7,* 611–26.

Lorr, M., & Klett, C. J. (1968). Crosscultural comparison of psychotic syndromes. *J. Abn. Psychol., 74*(4), 531–43.

Lösel, F. (1998). Treatment and management of psychopaths. In D. J. Cooke, A. E. Forth, & R. D. Hare (Eds.), *Psychopathy: Theory, research, and implications for society.* (pp. 303-354). Dordrecht, Netherland: Kluwer Academic Publishers.

Lovaas, O. I. (1977). *The autistic child: Language development through behavior modification.* New York: Holsted Press.

Lovaas, O. I. (1987). Behavioral treatment of normal educational and intellectual functioning in young autistic children. *J. Cons. Clin. Psychol., 44,* 3–9.

Lozoff, B. (1989). Nutrition and behavior. Special issue: Children and their development: Knowledge base, research agenda, and social policy application. *Amer. Psychol., 44,* 231–236.

Luchins, A. S. (1991). Moral treatment in asylums and general hospitals in 19th century America. *J. Psychol., 123,* 585–607.

Luckasson, R., Coulter, D. L., Polloway, E. A., Reiss, S., Schalock, R. L., Snell, M. E., Spitalnik, D. M., & Stark, J. A. (1992). *Mental retardation: Definition, classification, and systems of supports* (9th ed.). Washington, DC: American Association on Mental Retardation.

Lukas, C., & Seiden, H. M. (1990). *Silent grief: Living in the wake of suicide.* New York: Bantam Books.

Lund, S. N. (1975). *Personality and personal history factors of child abusing parents.* Unpublished doctoral dissertation, University of Minnesota.

Lung, C. T., & Daro, D. (1996). *Current trends in child abuse reporting and fatalities: The results of the 1995 annual 50-state survey.* Chicago: National Committee to Prevent Child Abuse.

Lunsing, R. J., Hadders Algra, M., Touwen, B. C., & Huisjes, H. J. (1991). Nocturnal enuresis and minor neurological dysfunction at 12 years: A follow-up study. *Develop. Med. Child Neurol., 33,* 439–45.

Luntz, B. K., & Widom, C. S. (1994). Antisocial personality disorder in abused and neglected children grown-up. *Amer. J. Psychiat., 151,* 670–74.

Luten, A., Ralph, J., & Mineka, S. (1997). Depressive attributional style: Is it specific to depression vs. anxiety vs. negative affect? *Behav. Res. Ther., 35,* 703–719.

Lykken, D. T. (1957). A study of anxiety in the sociopathic personality. *J. Abn. Soc. Psychol., 55*(1), 6–10.

Lykken, D. T. (1995). *The Antisocial Personalities.* Hillsdale, NJ: Erlbaum.

Lynam, D. R. (1996). Early identification of chronic offenders: Who is the fledgling psychopath? *Psychol. Bull., 120*(2), 209–234.

Lynam, D. R. (1997). Pursuing the psychopath: Capturing the fledgling psychopath in a nomological net. *J. Abn. Psychol., 106*(3), 425–438.

Lynch, J. J. (1977). *The broken heart.* New York: Basic Books.

Lynch, J. P. (1996). Clarifying divergent estimates of rape from two national surveys. *Public Opinion Quarterly, 60,* 410–30.

Lynch, P. S., Kellow, J. T., & Willson, V. L. (1997). The impact of deinstitutionalization on the adaptive behavior of adults with mental retardation. *Education & Training in Mental Retardation & Developmental Disabilities, 32*(3), 255–61.

Lynd-Stevenson, R. M. (1996). A test of the hopelessness theory of depression in unemployed young adults. *Brit. J. of Clin. Psych., 35,* 117–32.

Lyness, S. A. (1993). Predictors of differences between Type A and B individuals in heart rate and blood pressure reactivity. *Psychol. Bull., 114*(2), 266–95.

Lyon, M., Barr, C. E., Cannon, T. D., Mednick, S. A., & Shore, D. (1989). Fetal neural development and schzophrenia. *Schizo. Bull., 15,* 149–61.

Lyons-Ruth, K. (1996). Attachment relationships among children with aggressive behavior problems: The role of disorganized early attachment patterns. *J. Cons. Clin. Psychol., 64*(1), 64–73.

Lyubomirsky, S., & Nolen-Hoeksema, S. (1995). Effects of self-focused rumination on negative thinking and interpersonal problem solving. *J. Pers. Soc. Psychol., 69*(1), 176–190.

Lyubomirsky, S., Caldwell, N. D., & Nolen-Hoeksema S. (1998). Effects of ruminative and distracting responses to depressed mood on retrieval of autobiographical memories. *J. Pers. Soc. Psychol., 75* 166–77.

McBride, W. J., Murphy, J. M., Gatto, G. J., et al. (1992). CNS mechanisms of alcohol drinking in genetically selected lines of rats. *Alcohol and Alcoholism, 27* (supplement 2).

McBurnett, K. & Pfiffner, L. (1998). Comorbidities and biological correlates of conduct disorder. In D. J. Cooke, A. E. Forth, & R. D. Hare (Eds.), *Psychopathy: Theory, research, and implications for society.* (pp. 189–204). Dordrecht, Netherlands: Kluwer Academic Publishers.

McCann, I. L., Sakheim, D. K., & Abrahamson, D. J. (1988). Trauma and victimization: A model of psychological adaptation. *Counsel. Psychol., 16,* 531–94.

McCarroll, J. E., Ursano, R. J., & Fullerton, C. S. (1995). Symptoms of PTSD following recovery of war dead: 13–15-month follow-up. *Amer. J. Psychiat., 152*(6), 939–41.

McCarthy, B. W. (1989). Cognitive-behavioral strategies and techniques in the treatment of early ejaculation. In S. R. Leiblum & R. C. Rosen (Eds.), *Principles and practice of sex therapy* (2nd ed.). (pp. 141–67). New York: Guilford.

McClelland, D. C. (1979). Inhibited power motivation and high blood pressure in men. *J. Abn. Psychol., 88*(2), 182–90.

McDonald, L., Bellingham, S., Conrad, T., Morgan, A., et al. (1997). Families and schools together (FAST): Integrating community development with clinical strategies. *Families in Society, 78*(2), 140–55.

MacDonald, M. R., & Kuiper, N. A. (1983). Cognitive-behavioral preparations for surgery: Some theoretical and methodological concerns. *Clin. Psychol. Rev., 3,* 27–39.

McDonnell, J., Hardman, M. L., Hightower, J., & Keifer-O'Donnel, R. (1993). Impact of community-based instruction on the development of adaptive behavior of secondary-level students with mental retardation. *Amer. J. Ment. Retard., 97*(5), 575–84.

McFall, M. E., Murburg, M. M., Grant, N., Veith, R. C. (1990). Autonomic responses to stress in Vietnam combat veterans with posttraumatic stress disorder. *Biol. Psychia., 27(1), 1165–75.*

McFall, R. M. (1990). The enhancement of social skills: An information-processing analysis. In W. L. Marshall, D. R. Laws, & H. E. Barbaree (Eds.), *Handbook of sexual assault: Issues, theories, and treatment of the offender.* (pp. 311–30). New York: Plenum.

McFarlane, A. C., Clayer, J. R., & Bookless, C. L. (1997). Psychiatric morbidity following a natural disaster: An Australian bushfire. *Soc. Psychiat. Psychiatr. Epidemiol., 32*(5), 261–68.

McFarlane, W. R., et al. (1995). The multiple family group and psychoeducation in the treatment of schizophrenia. *Arch. Gen. Psychiat., 54,*679–87.

McGee, R., Feehan, M., & Williams, S. (1995). Long-term follow-up of a birth cohort. In F. C. Verhulst & H. M. Koot (Eds.), *The epidemiology of child and adolescent psychopathology.* (pp. 366–84). New York: Oxford Medical.

McGlashan, T. H., & Fenton, W. S. (1993). Subtype progression and pathophysiologic deterioration in early schizophrenia. *Schizo. Bull., 19*(1), 71–84.

McGue, M. (1998). Behavioral genetic models of alcoholism and drinking. In K. E. Leonard & H. T. Blane (Eds.), *Psychological theories of drinking and alcoholism.* New York: Guilford.

McGue, M., Pickens, R. W., & Svikis, D. S. (1992). Sex and age effects on the inheritance of alcohol problems: A twin study. *J. Abn. Psychol., 101*(1), 3–17.

McGuffin, P., & Gottesman, I. I. (1985). Genetic influences on normal and abnormal development. In M. Rutter & L. Hersov (Eds.), *Child and adolescent psychiatry: Modern approaches* (2nd ed.). Oxford: Blackwell Scientific.

McHugh, P. R. (1992). Psychiatric misadventures. *American-Scholar, 61,* 497–510.

McHugh, P. R. (1995). Resolved: Multiple personality disorder is an individually and socially created artifact. Affirmative. *J. Amer. Acad. Child Adoles. Psychiat.* 34, 957–959; 962–963.

McIntosh, J. L. (1992). Suicide of the elderly. In B. Bongar (Ed.), *Suicide: Guidelines for assessment, management and treatment.* New York: Oxford University Press.

McIvor, R. J., & Turner, S. W. (1995). Assessment and treatment approaches for survivors of torture. *Brit. J. Psychiat., 166,* 705–11.

MacKinnon, A., & Foley, D. (1996). The genetics of anxiety disorders. In H. G. Westenberg, J. A. Den Boer, & D. L. Murphy (Eds.), *Advances in the neurobiology of anxiety disorders.* (pp. 39–59). Chichester, England: Wiley.

McLellan, A. T., Arndt, I. O., Metzger, D. S., Woody, G. E., & O'Brien, C. P. (1993). The effects of psychosocial services in substance abuse treatment. *JAMA, 269,* 1953–59.

McLoyd, V. C. (1998) Socioeconomic disadvantage and child development. *Amer. Psychol., 53,* 185–204.

MacMillan, D. L., Gresham, F. M., & Siperstein, G. N. (1993). Conceptual and psychometric concerns about the 1992 AAMR definition of mental retardation. *Amer. J. Ment. Retard., 98*(3), 325–35.

McNally, R. J. (1994). *Panic disorder: A critical analysis.* New York: Guilford.

McNally, R. J. (1996). Cognitive bias in anxiety disorders. In D. Hope (Ed.), *Perspectives on anxiety, panic and fear,* (pp. 211–50). Lincoln: University of Nebraska Press.

McNeil, D. E., & Binder, R. L. (1986). Violence, civil commitment, and hospitalization. *J. Nerv. Ment. Dis., 174*(2), 107–11.

McReynolds, P. (1996). Lightner Witmer: Little-known founder of clinical psychology. *Amer. Psychol., 51,* 237–240.

McReynolds, P. (1997). Lightner Witmer: The first clinical psychologist. In W. G. Bringmann, H. E. Luck, R. Miller, & C. E. Early (Eds.), *A pictorial history of psychology.* (pp. 465–470). Chicago: Quintessence Books.

Maccoby, E. E., & Martin, J. A. (1983). Socialization in the context of the family: Parent-child interaction. In E. M. Hetherington (Ed.), *Socialization, personality, and social development: Vol. 4. Handbook of child psychology.* New York: Wiley.

Mackay, L. E. (1994). Benefits of a formalized traumatic brain injury program within a trauma center. *J. Head Trauma Rehab., 9*(1), 11–19.

Mackintosh, N. J. (1983). *Conditioning and associative learning.* Oxford: Clarendon.

Maclean, W. E., Jr. (Ed.). (1997). *Ellis' handbook of mental deficiency: Psychological theory and research.* Mahwah, NJ: Erlbaum.

Maddux, J. F., Vogtsberger, K. N., Prihoda, T. J., Desmond, D. F., Watson, D. D., & Williams, M. L. (1994). Illicit drug injectors in three Texas cities. *Intern. J. Addict., 29,* 179–94.

Magee, W. J., Eaton, W. W., Wittchen, H., McGonagle, K. A., & Kessler, R. C. (1996). Agoraphobia, simple phobia, and social phobia in the National Comorbidity Survey. *Arch. Gen. Psychiat., 53,* 159–68.

Maher, J. J. (1997). Exploring effects on liver function. *Alcohol Health & Research, 2*(1), 5–12.

Mahler, M. (1976). *On human symbiosis and the vicissitudes of individuation.* New York: Library of Human Behavior.

Mahoney, G., Glover, A., & Finger, I. (1981). Relationship between language and sensorimotor development of Down's syndrome and nonretarded children. *Amer. J. Ment. Def., 86,* 21–27.

Mahoney, M., & Arnkoff, D. (1978). Cognitive and selfcontrol therapies. In S. Garfield & A. Bergin (Eds.), *Handbook of psychotherapy and behavior change: An empirical analysis.* New York: Wiley.

Maier, S. F., & Watkins, L. R. (1998). Cytokines for psychologists: Implications of bidirectional immune-to-brain communication for understanding behavior, mood, and cognition. *Psychol. Rev., 105*(1), 83–107.

Maier, S. F., Watkins, L. R., & Fleshner, M. (1994). Psychoneuroimmunology: The interface between behavior, brain, and immunity. *Amer. Psychol., 49*(12), 1004–17.

Maier, S., Seligman, M., & Solomon, R. (1969). Pavlovian fear conditioning and learned helplessness. In B. A. Campbell & R. M. Church (Eds.), *Punishment and aversive behavior.* New York: Appleton-Century-Crofts.

Main, M. B., & Weston, D. R. (1981). Security of attachment to mother and father: Related to conflict behavior and the readiness to establish new relationships. *Child Develop., 52,* 932–940.

Maisch, H. (1972). *Incest.* New York: Stein & Day.

Maisto, S. A., & McKay, J. R. (1995). Diagnosis. In National Institute of Alcohol And Alcoholism, *Assessing alcohol problems: A guide for clinicians and researchers.* (pp. 41–54). Washington: U.S. Department of Health and Human Services.

Maiuro, R. D., Cahn, T. S., Vitaliano, P. P., Wagner, B. C., & Zegree, J. B. (1988). Anger, hostility, and depression in domestically violent versus generally assaultive men and nonviolent control subjects. *J. Consult. Clin. Psychol., 56,* 17–23.

Maj, M., Satz, P., Janssen, R., Zaudig, M., Starace, F., D'Elia, L., Sughondhabirom, B., Mussa, M., Naber, D., Ndetei, D., Schulte, G., & Sartorius, N. (1994). WHO neuropsychiatric AIDS study, cross sectional Phase II: Neuropsychological and neurological findings. *Arch. Gen. Psychiat., 51*(1), 51–61.

Majcher, D., & Pollack, M. (1996). Childhood anxiety disorders. In L. Hechtman (Ed.), *Do they grow out of it?* (pp. 139–70). Washington: American Psychiatric Press.

Major, B., Zubek, J. M., Cooper, M. L., Cozzarelli, C., et al. (1997). Mixed messages: Implications of social conflict and social support within close relationships for adjustment to a stressful life event. *J. Pers. Soc. Psychol. 72*(6), 1349–63.

Malamud, N. (1975). Organic brain disease mistaken for psychiatric disorder: A clinicopathologic study. In D. F. Benson & D. Blumer (Eds.), *Psychiatric aspects of neurological disease.* (pp. 287–307). New York: Grune & Stratton.

Malatesta, V. J., & Adams, H. (1993) The sexual dysfunctions. In P. Sutker & H. Adams (Eds.), *Comprehensive textbook of psychopathology.* New York: Plenum.

Maletsky, B. M. (1998). The paraphilias: Research and treatment. In P. E. Nathan & J. M. Gorman (Eds.), *A guide to treatments that work.* (pp. 472–500). New York: Oxford University Press.

Malinosky-Rummell, R., & Hansen, D.J. (1993). Long-term consequences of childhood physical abuse. *Psychol. Bull., 114,* 68–79.

Manderscheid, R. W., Witkin, M. J., Rosenstein, J. J., Milazzo-Sayre, L. J., Bethel, H. E., & MacAskill, R. L. (1985). In C. A. Taube & S. A. Barrett (Eds.), *Mental Health, United States, 1985.* Washington, DC: National Institute of Mental Health.

Manfro, G. G., Otto, M. W., McArdle, E. T., & Worthington, J. J. (1996). Relationships of antecedent stressful life events to childhood and family history of anxiety and the course of panic. *J. Affect. Dis., 41*(2), 135–39.

Mann, L. M., Chassin, L., & Sher, K. J. (1987). Alcohol expectancies and risk for alcoholics. *J. Cons. Clin. Psychol., 55,* 411–17.

Mannuzza, S., Klein, R., Bessler, A., Malloy, P., & LaPadula, M. (1993). Adult outcome of hyperactive boys: Educational achievement, occupational rank, and psychiatric status. *Arch. Gen. Psychiat., 50,* 565–76.

Manuck, S. B., et al. (1991). Individual differences in cellular immune response to stress. *Psychol. Sci., 2*(2), 111–115.

Marangell, L. B., Ketter, T. A., George, M. S., Pazzaglia, P. J., Callahan, A. M., Parekh, P., Andreason., P. J., Horwitz, B., Herscovitch, P., & Post, R. (1997). Inverse relationship of peripheral thyrotropin-stimulating hormone levels to brain activity in mood disorder. *Amer. J. Psychiat., 145*(2), 224–30.

Marans, S., & Cohen, D. (1993). Children and inner–city violence: Strategies for intervention. In L. Leavitt & N. Fox (Eds.), *Psychological effects of war and violence on children.* (pp. 281–302). Hillsdale, NJ: Erlbaum.

March, J., & Leonard, H. (1998). Obsessive-compulsive disorder in children and adolescents. In R. Swinson, M. Antony, S. Rachman, & M. Richter (Eds.), *Obsessive-compulsive disorder: Theory, research, and treatment.* (pp. 367–94). New York: Guilford.

Marcus, J., Hans, S. L., Auerbach, J. G., & Auerbach, A. G. (1993). Children at risk for schizophrenia: The Jerusalem infant development study: II. Neurobehavioral deficits at school age. *Arch. Gen. Psychiat., 50*(10), 797–809.

Marcus, J., Hans, S. L., Mednick, S. A., Schulsinger, F., & Michelson, N. (1985). Neurological dysfunctioning in offspring of schizophrenics in Israel and Denmark: A replication analysis. *Arch. Gen. Psychiat., 42,* 753–61.

Marcus, M. D. (1997). Adapting treatment for patients with binge-eating disorder. In D. M. Garner & P. E. Garfinkel (Eds.), *Handbook of treatment for eating disorders.* (pp. 484–493). New York: Guilford.

Margolin, G., & Wampold, B. E. (1981). Sequential analysis of conflict and accord in distressed and non-distressed marital partners. *J. Cons. Clin. Psychol., 49*(4), 554–67.

Margolis, R. D., & Zweben, J. E. (1998). *Treating patients with alcohol and other drug problems: An integrated approach.* Washington: American Psychological Association.

Margraf, J., Ehlers, A., & Roth, W. T. (1986a). Sodium lactate infusions and panic attacks: A review and critique. *Psychosom. Med., 48,* 23–51.

Margraf, J., Ehlers, A., & Roth, W. (1986b). Biological models of panic disorder and agoraphobia—A review. *Behav. Res. Ther., 24,* 553–67.

Margraf, J., & Schneider, S. (1991). *Outcome and active ingredients of cognitive-behavioral treatment for panic disorders.* Paper presented at AABT, New York.

Maris, R. W. (1997). Social forces in suicide: A life review, 1965–1995. In R. W. Maris, M. M. Silverman, & S. S. Canetton (Eds.), *Review of Suicidology, 1997,* (pp. 42–60). New York: Guilford.

Marks, I. M. (1969). *Fears and phobias.* New York: Academic Press.

Marks, I. M. (1982). Toward an empirical clinical science: Behavioral psychotherapy in the 1980's. *Behav. Ther., 13,* 63–81.

Marks, I. M. (1987). *Fear, phobias, and rituals: Panic, anxiety, and their disorders.* New York: Oxford University Press.

Marks, I., & Nesse, R. M. (1991). Fear and fitness: An evolutionary of anxiety disorders. Paper presented at the Eleventh National Conference on Anxiety Disorders. Chicago, IL.

Marks, I., Swinson, R. P., Başoğlu, M., & Kunch, K. (1993). Alprazolam and exposure alone and combined in panic disorder with agoraphobia: A controlled study in London and Toronto. *Brit. J. Psychiat., 162,* 776–787.

Marlatt, G. A. (1985). Cognitive assessment and intervention procedures for relapse prevention. In G. A. Marlatt & J. R. Gordon (Eds.), *Relapse prevention.* New York: Guilford.

Marlatt, G. A., Baer, J. S., Kivahan, D. R., Dimeoff, L. A., Larimer, M. E., Quigley, L. A., Somers, J. M., & Williams, E. (1998). Screening and brief intervention for high-risk college student drinkers: Results from a 2-year follow up assessment. *J. Cons. Clin. Psychol., 66*(4), 604–15.

Marlatt, G. A., & Vandenbos, G. R. (Eds.) (1997). *Addictive behaviors: Readings on etiology, prevention, and treatment.* Washington, DC: American Psychological Association.

Marsella, A. J. (1980). Depressive experience and disorder across cultures. In H. C. Triandis & J. Draguns (Eds.), *Handbook of cross-cultural psychology* (Vol. 6). Boston: Allyn & Bacon.

Marsella, A. J., Sartorius, N., Jablensky, A., & Fenton, F. R. (1985). Cross-cultural studies of depressive disorders: An overview. In A. Kleinman & B. Good (Eds.), *Culture and depression.* Berkeley, CA: University of California Press.

Marsh, L., et al. (1997). Structural magnetic resonance imaging abnormalities in men with severe chronic schizophrenia and an early age at clinical onset. *Arch. Gen. Psychiat., 54*(12), 1104–12.

Marshall, W. L. (1993). The treatment of sex offenders: What does the outcome data tell us? A reply to Quinsey, Harris, Rice, and Lalumiere. *J. Interpers. Viol., 8,* 524–30.

Marshall, W. L. (1997). Pedophilia: Psychopathology and theory. In D. R. Laws & W. O'Donohue (Eds.), *Sexual deviance: Theory, assessment, and treatment.* (pp. 152–74). New York: Guilford.

Marshall, W. L., & Barbaree, H. E. (1990a). An integrated theory of the etiology of sexual offending. In W. L. Marshall, D. R. Laws, & H. E. Barbaree (Eds.), *Handbook of sexual assault.* (pp. 257–69). New York: Plenum.

Marshall, W. L., & Barbaree, H. E. (1990b). Outcome of comprehensive cognitive-behavioral treatment programs. In W. L. Marshall, D. R. Laws, & H. E. Barbaree (Eds.), *Handbook of sexual assault: Issues, theories, and treatment of the offender.* (pp. 363–85). New York: Plenum.

Marshall, W. L., Barbaree, H. E., & Christophe, D. (1986). Sexual offenders against female children: Sexual preferences for age of victim and type of behavior. *Canad. J. Behav. Sci., 18,* 424–39.

Marshall, W. L., Jones, R., Ward, T., Johnston, P., & Barbaree, H. E. (1991). Treatment outcome with sex offenders. *Clin. Psychol. Rev., 11,* 465–85.

Marshall, W. L., & Pithers, W. D. (1994). A reconsideration of treatment outcome with sex offenders. *Crim. Just. Behav., 21,* 10–27.

Marshall, R. D., & Klein, D. F. (1995). Pharmacotherapy in the treatment of posttraumatic stress disorder. *Psychiat. Ann., 23*(10), 588–89.

Martell, D. A., & Dietz, P. E. (1992). Mentally disordered offenders who push or attempt to push victims onto subway tracks in New York City. *Arch. Gen. Psychiat., 49*(6), 472–75.

Martin, E. S., et al. (1997). Studies in a large family with late-onset Alzheimer disease (LOAD). *Alzheimer Disease and Associated Disorders, 11*(3), 163–70.

Martin, S. E. (1992). The epidemiology of alcohol-related interpersonal violence. *Alcohol Health & Research World, 16*(2), 230–37.

Martinez, A., Malphurs, J., Field, T., Pickens, J., et al. (1996). Depressed mothers and their infants' interactions with nondepressed partners. *Infant Mental Health Journal, 17*(1), 74–80.

Marvit, R. C. (1981). Guilty but mentally ill—an old approach to an old problem. *Clin. Psychol., 34*(4), 22–23.

Mash, E. J., & Dozois, D. J. A. (1996). Child psychopathology: A developmental perspective. In E. J. Mash & R. A. Barkley (Eds.), *Child psychopathology.* (pp. 3–60). New York: Guilford.

Mason, B. J., & Ownby, R. L. (1998). Alcohol. In P. J. Goodnick et al. (Eds.), *Mania: Clinical and research perspectives.* (pp. 63–80). Washington: American Psychiatric Press.

Mason, F. L. (1997). Fetishism: Psychopathology and theory. In D. R. Laws & W. O'Donohue (Eds.) *Sexual deviance: Theory, assessment, and treatment.* (pp. 75–91). New York: Guilford.

Masten, A. S., & Coatsworth, J. D. (1995). Competence, resilience, and psychopathology. In D. Cicchetti & D. J. Cohen (Eds.), *Psychopathology: Vol. 2. Risk, disorder, and adaptation.* (pp. 715–52). New York: Wiley.

Masten, A. S, & Coatsworth, J. D. (1998) The development of competence in favorable and unfavorable environments: Lessons from research on successful children. *Amer. Psychol., 53,* 205–20.

Masters, W. H., & Johnson, V. E. (1966). *Human sexual response.* Boston: Little, Brown.

Masters, W. H., & Johnson, V. E. (1970). *Human sexual inadequacy.* Boston: Little, Brown.

Masters, W. H., & Johnson, V. E. (1975). *The pleasure bond: A new look at sexuality and commitment.* Boston: Little, Brown.

Masters, W. H., Johnson, V. E., & Kolodny, R. C. (1992). *Human sexuality.* New York: HarperCollins.

Mathew, R. J., Wilson, W. H., & Melges, F. T. (1992). Temporal disintegration and its psychological and physiological correlates: Changes in the experience of time after marijuana smoking. *Annals of Clinical Psychiatry, 4,* 235–45.

Mathews, A. M., & MacLeod, C. (1994). Cognitive approaches to emotion and emotional disorders. *Ann. Rev. Psychol., 45,* 25–50.

Matier, K., Halperin, J. M., Sharma, V., & Newcorn, J. H. (1992). Methylphenidate response in aggressive and non-aggressive ADHD children: Distinctions on laboratory measures of symptoms. *J. Amer. Acad. Child Adoles. Psychiat., 31,* 219–25.

Matsunaga, E., Tonomura, A., Hidetsune, O., & Yasumoto, K. (1978). Reexamination of paternal age effect in Down's syndrome. *Human Genet., 40,* 259–68.

Mattes, J. A., & Gittelman, R., (1981). Effects of artificial food colorings in children with hyperactive symptoms: A critical review and results of a controlled study. *Arch. Gen. Psychiat., 38*(6), 714–18.

Mattson, M. E., Allen, J. P., Longabaugh, R., Nickless, C. J., et al. (1994). A chronological reivew of empirical studies matching alcoholic clients to treatment. *J. Stud. Alcoh. 12,* 16–29.

Mattson, S. N., Jernigan, T. L., & Riley, E. P. (1994). MRI and prenatal alcohol exposure. *Alcohol Health & Research World, 18*(1), 49–52.

Mattson, S. N., Riley, E. P., Gramling, L., Delis, D. C., & Jones, K. L. (1998). Neuropsychological comparison of alcohol–exposed children with or without physical features of fetal alcohol syndrome. *Neuropsychology, 12*(1), 146–53.

Mattson, M. E., & Riley, E. P. (1998). A review of the neurobehavioral deficits in children with fetal alcohol syndrome or prenatal exposure to alcohol. *Alcoholism: Clin. Exper. Res., 22*(2), 279–94.

Max, W. (1993). The economic impact of Alzheimer's disease. *Neurology, 43*(8, Suppl. 4), S6–S10.

Maxfield, M. G., & Widom, C. S. (1996). The cycle of violence: Revisited six years later. *Archives of Pediatric and Adolescent Medicine, 150,* 390–95.

Mays, J. A. (1974, Jan. 16). High blood pressure, soul food. *Los Angeles Times,* II, 7.

Mazure, C. M., & Druss, B. G. (1995). An historical perspective on stress and psychiatric illness. In C. M. Mazure (Ed.), *Does stress cause psychiatric illness?* Washington, DC: American Psychiatric Association.

Means* v. *Baltimore County [Abstract], Court of Appeals of Maryland, 344 Md 661 2d 1238. (1997).

Mearns, J., & Lees-Haley, P. R. (1993). Discrimination of neuropsychological sequelae of head injury from alcohol-abuse-induced deficits: A review and analysis. *J. Clin. Psychol., 49*(5), 714–20.

Medical Council on Alcoholism (1997). *Alcohol-related liver disease.* London: Author.

Mednick, S. A., et al. (1998). A two-hit working model of the etiology of schizophrenia. In M. F. Lenzenweger & R. H. Dworkin (Eds.), *Origins and development of schizophrenia.* (pp. 27–66). Washington: American Psychological Association.

Meehl, P. E. (1962). Schizotaxia, schizotypy, schizophrenia. *Amer. Psychol., 17,* 827–38.

Meehl, P. E. (1978). Theoretical risks and tabular asterisks: Sir Karl, Sir Ronald, and the slow progress of soft psychology. *J. Cons. Clin. Psychol., 46,* 806–34.

Meehl, P. E. (1989). Schizotaxia revisited. *Arch. Gen. Psychiat., 46,* 935–44.

Meehl, P. E. (1990a). Toward an integrated theory of schizotaxia, schizotypy, and schizophrenia. *J. Personal. Dis., 4,* 1–99.

Megargee, E. I. (1970). The prediction of violence with psychological tests. In C. D. Spielberger (Ed.), *Current topics in clinical and community psychology* (Vol. 2). New York: Academic Press.

Megargee, E. I. (1995a). Assessing and understanding aggressive and violent patients. In J. N. Butcher (Ed.), *Clinical personality assessment: Practical considerations.* (pp. 395–409). New York: Oxford University Press.

Megargee, E. I. (1995b). Use of the MMPI-2 in correctional settings. In Y. S. Ben-Porath, J. R. Graham, G. N. Hall, R. D. Hirschman, & M. S. Zaragoza (Eds.), *Forensic applications of the MMPI-2.* (pp. 127–59) Thousand Oaks, CA: Sage.

Mehlum, L., Friis, S., Irion, T., Johns, S., Karterud, S., Vaglum, P., & Vaglum, S. (1991). Personality disorders 2–5 years after treatment: A prospective follow-up study. *Acta Psychiatr. Scandin., 84,* 72–77.

Meichenbaum, D. (1974). *Cognitive behavior modification.* General Learning Corporation, 16.

Meichenbaum, D. (1985). *Stress inoculation training.* New York: Pergamon.

Meichenbaum, D. (1993). Changing conceptions of cognitive behavior modification: Retrospect and prospect. *J. Cons. Clin. Psychol., 61,* 202–204.

Meichenbaum, D., & Cameron, R. (1983). Stress inoculation training: Toward a general paradigm for training coping skills. In D. Meichenbaum & M. E. Jaremko (Eds.), *Stress reduction and prevention.* (pp. 115–54). New York: Plenum.

Meichenbaum, D., & Jaremko, M. E. (1983). *Stress reduction and prevention.* New York: Plenum.

Meltzer, H. Y., & Stahl, S. M. (1976). The dopamine hypothesis of schizophrenia: A review. *Schizo. Bull., 2*(1), 19–76.

Mendelson, J. H., & Mello, N. (1992). Human laboratory studies of buprenorphine. In J. D. Blaine (Ed.), *Buprenorphine: An alternative treatment for opiate dependence.* (pp. 38–60). Washington, DC: U.S. Department of Health and Human Services.

Mental Health Law Project. (1987, October). Court decisions concerning mentally disabled people confined in institutions. *MHLP Newsletter.* Washington, DC.

Merbaum, M. (1977). Some personality characteristics of soldiers exposed to extreme war stress: A follow-up study of post-hospital adjustment. *J. Clin. Psychol.,* 33, 558–62.

Merbaum, M., & Hefez, A. (1976). Some personality characteristics of soldiers exposed to extreme war stress. *J. Cons. Clin. Psychol., 44*(1), 1–6.

Merikangas, K. R., & Swendsen, J. D. (1997). Genetic epidemiology of psychiatric disorders. *Epidemiological Reviews, 19*(1), 144–55.

Merikangas, K. R., Wicki, W., & Angst, J. (1994). Heterogeneity of depression: Classification of depressive subtypes by longitudinal course. *Brit. J. Psychiat., 164,* 342–48

Mesibov, G. B., Adams, L. W., & Klinger, L. G. (1997). *Autism: Understanding the disorder.* New York: Plenum.

Meston, C. M. & Gorzalka, B. B. (1996) Differential effects of sympathetic activation on sexual arousal in sexually dysfunctional and functional women. *J. Abn. Psychol., 105,* 582–91.

Metalsky, G. I., Abrason, L. Y., Seligman, M. E. P., Semmel, A., & Peterson, C. R. (1982). Attributional styles and life events in the classroom: Vulnerability and invulnerability to depressive mood reactions. *J. Pers. Soc. Psychol., 43,* 612–17.

Metz, M. E., Pryor, J. L., Nesvacil, L. J., Abuzzahab, F., & Koznar, J. (1997). Premature ejaculation: A psychophysiological review. *J. Sex Marit. Ther., 23,* 3–23.

Meyer, C. B., & Taylor, S. E. (1986). Adjustment to rape. *J. Pers. Soc. Psychol., 50,* 1226–34.

Meyer, J. K. (1995) Paraphilias. In H. I. Kaplan & J. B. Sadock (Eds.), *Comprehensive textbook of psychiatry. (6th ed.).* (pp. 1334–47). Baltimore: Williams and Wilkins.

Meyer, R. E., & Mirin, S. M. (1979). *The heroin stimulus: Implications for a theory of addiction.* New York: Plenum.

Middleton, W., Burnett, P., Raphael, B., & Martinek, P. (1996). The bereavement response: A cluster analysis. *Brit. J. Psychiat., 169,* 167–71.

Miklowitz, D. J. (1996). Psychotherapy in combination with drug treatment for bipolar disorder. *J. Clin. Psychopharm., 16* (Suppl 1), 56S–66S.

Miklowitz, D. J., Goldstein, M. J., & Falloon, I. R. (1983). Premorbid and symptomatic characteristics of schizophrenics from families with high and low levels of expressed emotion. *J. Abn. Psychol. 92,* 359–67.

Miles, C. (1977). Conditions predisposing to suicide: A review. *J. Nerv. Ment. Dis.,* 164, 232–46.

Miller, F. T., Abrams, T., Dulit, R., & Fyer, M. (1993b). Substance abuse in borderline personality disorder. *Amer. J. Drug Alcoh. Abuse, 19,* 491–97.

Miller, K. A. (1989). Enhancing early childhood mainstreaming through cooperative learning: A brief literature review. *Child Study Journal, 19,* 285–92.

Miller, R. (1970). Does Down's syndrome predispose children to leukemia? *Roche Report, 7*(16), 5.

Miller, S. D. (1989). Optical differences in cases of multiple personality disorder. *J. Nerv. Ment. Dis., 177,* 480–486.

Miller, S. D., et al. (1991). Optical differences in multiple personality disorder. A second look. *J. Nerv. Ment. Dis., 179,* 132–135.

Miller, W. R., Benefield, R. G., Tonigan, J. S. (1993). Enhancing motivation for change in problem drinking: A controlled comparison of two therapist styles. *J. Cons. Clin. Psychol. 61*(3), 455–61.

Miller, W. R., Brown, J. M., Simpson, T. L., Handmaker, N. S., Bien, T. H., Luckie, L. F., Montgomery, H. A., Hester, R. K., & Tonigan, J. S. (1995). What works? A methodological analysis of the alcohol treatment outcome literature. In R. K. Hester & W. R. Miller (Eds.), *Handbook of alcoholism treatment approaches: Effective alternatives.* (pp. 12–44). Needham, MA: Allyn & Bacon.

Miller, W. R., Leckman, A. L., Tinkcom, M., & Rubenstein, J. (1986). *Longterm follow-up of controlled drinking therapies.* Paper given at the Ninety-fourth Annual Meeting of the American Psychological Association, Washington, DC.

Miller, W. R., & Rollnick, S. (1991). Using assessment results. In W. R. Miller & S. Rollnick (Eds.), *Motivational interviewing.* (pp. 89–99). New York: Guilford.

Millon, T. (1981). *Disorders of personality: DSM-III, Axis II.* New York: Wiley.

Millon, T., & Davis, R. D. (1995). The development of personality disorders. In D. Cicchetti & D. J. Cohen (Eds.), *Developmental psychopathology: Vol. 2. Risk, disorder, and adaptation.* (pp. 633–76). New York: Wiley.

Millon, T. & Davis, R. D. (1996). An evolutionary theory of personality disorders. In J. F. Clarkin & M. F. Lenzenweger (Eds.), *Major theories of per-*

sonality disorder. (pp. 221–346). New York: Guilford.

Millon, T. & Martinez, A. (1995). Avoidant personality disorder. In W. J. Livesley (Ed.), *The DSM-IV personality disorders.* (pp. 218–233). New York: Guilford.

Mills, M. J., Sullivan, G., & Eth, S. (1987). Protecting third parties: A decade after Tarasoff. *Amer. J. Psychiat., 144*(1), 68–74.

Mindus, P., Nyman, H., Lindquist, C., & Meyerson, B. A. (1993). *Neurosurgery for intractable obsessive-compulsive disorder, an update.* Paper presented at the International Workshop on Obsessive Disorder, Vail, Co.

Mindus, P., Rasmussen, S. A., & Lindquist, C. (1994). Neurosurgical treatment for refractory obsessive-compulsive disorder: Implications for understanding frontal lobe function. *J. Neuropsychiat. Clin. Neurosci., 6,* 467–77.

Mineka, S. (1985a). Animal models of anxiety-based disorders: Their usefulness and limitations. In A. H. Tuma & J. D. Maser (Eds.), *Anxiety and the anxiety disorders.* Hillsdale, NJ: Erlbaum.

Mineka, S. (1985b). The frightful complexities of the origins of fears. In F. R. Brush & J. B. Overmier (Eds.), *Affect, conditioning, and cognition: Essays on the determinants of behavior.* Hillsdale, NJ: Erlbaum.

Mineka, S. (1992). Evolutionary memories, emotional processing and the emotional disorders. In D. Medin (Ed.), *The psychology of learning and motivation,* (Vol. 28). (pp. 161–206). New York: Academic Press.

Mineka, S., & Cook, M. (1986). Immunization against the observational conditioning of snake fear in monkeys. *J. Abn. Psychol., 95,* 307–18.

Mineka, S., & Cook, M. (1993). Mechanisms underlying observational conditioning of fear in monkeys. *J. Exper. Psychol.: General, 122,* 23–38.

Mineka, S., Davidson, M., Cook, M., & Keir, R. (1984). Observational conditioning of snake fear in Rhesus monkeys. *J. Abn. Psychol. 93*(4), 355–72.

Mineka, S., Gunnar, M., & Champoux, M. (1986). Control and early socioemotional development: Infant rhesus monkeys reared in controllable versus uncontrollable environments. *Child Develop. 57,* 1241–56.

Mineka, S., & Nugent, K. (1995). Mood-congruent memory biases in anxiety and depression. In D. Schacter (Ed.), *Memory distortions: How minds, brains and societies reconstruct the past.* (pp. 173–93).Cambridge: Harvard University Press.

Mineka, S., Rafaeli-Mor, E., & Yovel, I. (in press). Cognitive biases in emotional disorders: Social-cognitive and information processing perspectives. In R. Davidson, H. Goldsmith, and K. Scherer (Eds.), *Handbook of Affective Science.*

Mineka, S., & Thomas, C. (1999). Mechanisms of change during exposure treatments for anxiety disorder. In T. Dagleish & M. Power (Eds.), *Handbook of cognition and emotion.* (pp. 747–64). Chichester, England: Wiley.

Mineka, S., Watson, D., & Clark, L. A. (1998). Comorbidity of anxiety and unipolar mood disorders. In J. T. Spence, J. M. Darley, & D. J. Foss (Eds.), *Annual review of psychology.* (pp. 377–412). Palo Alto. (A: Annual Reviews. *Annu. Rev. Psychol., 49,* 377–412.

Mineka, S., & Zinbarg, R. (1991). Animal models of psychopathology. In C. E. Walker (Ed.), *Clinical psychology: Historical and research foundations* (pp. 51–86. New York: Plenum.

Mineka, S., & Zinbarg, R. (1995). Conditioning and ethological models of social phobia. In R. Heimberg, M. Liebowitz, D. Hope, & F. Schneier (Eds.), *Social phobia: Diagnosis, assessment, and treatment.* New York: Guilford.

Mineka, S., & Zinbarg, R. (1996). Conditioning and ethological models of anxiety disorders: Stress-in-Dynamic Context Anxiety Models. In D. Hope (Ed.), *Perspectives on Anxiety, Panic, and Fear: Nebraska Symposium on Motivation.* Lincoln: University of Nebraska Press.

Mineka, S., & Zinbarg, R. (1998). Experimental approaches to the anxiety and mood disorders. In J. Adair & D. Blanger (Eds.), *Advances in psychological science: (Vol. 1): Social, personal and cultural aspects.* (pp. 429–454). Hove, England UK: Psychology Press/Erlbaum.

Mintzer, M. Z., Guarino, J., Kirk, T., Roache, J. D., & Griffiths, R. R. (1997). Ethanol and Pentobarbital: Comparison of behavioral and subjective effects in sedative drug abusers. *Experimental and Clinical Psychopharmacology, 5*(3), 203–15.

Minuchin, S. (1974). *Families and family therapy.* Cambridge, MA: Harvard University Press.

Minuchin, S., Baker, L., Rosman, B., Liebman, R., Milman, L., & Todd, T. (1975). A conceptual model of psychosomatic illness in children. *Arch. Gen. Psychiat., 32,* 1031–38.

Mirsky, A. F., DeLisi, L. E., Buchsbaum, M. S., Quinn, O. W., Schwerdt, P., Siever, L. J., Mann, L., Weingartner, H., Zec, R., et al. (1984). The Genain quadruplets: Psychological studies. *Psychiat. Res., 13,* 77–93.

Mischel, W. (1990). Personality dispositions revisited and revised: A view after three decades. In L. A. Pervin (Ed.), *Handbook of personality: Theory and research.* (pp. 111–135). New York: Guilford.

Mischel, W. (1993). *Introduction to personality* (5th ed.). Fort Worth, Texas: Harcourt, Brace & Jovanovich.

Mishler, E. G., & Waxler, N. E. (1968). *Interaction in families: An experimental study of family processes and schizophrenia.* New York: Wiley.

Mitchell, J. E., Pomeroy, C., & Adson, D. E. (1997). Managing medical complications. In D. M. Garner & P. E. Garfinkel (Eds.), *Handbook of treatment for eating disorders* (pp. 383–393). New York: Guilford.

Miyakawa, T., Yagi, T., Kitazawa, H., Yasuda, M., Kawai, N., Tsuboi, K., & Niki, H. (1997). Fyn-Kinase as a determinant of ethanol sensitivity: Relation to NMDA receptor function. *Science, 278,* 698.

Moffatt, M. E. (1997). Nocturnal enuresis: A review of the efficacy of treatments and practical advice for clinicians. *Developmental and Behavioral Pediatrics, 18*(1), 49–56.

Moffitt, T. (1993a) Adolescence-limited and life-course-persistent antisocial behavior: A developmental taxonomy. *Psychological Review, 100,* 674–701.

Moffitt, T. E. (1993b). The neuropsychology of conduct disorder. *Development and Psychopathology, 5,* 135–51.

Moffitt, T. E., & Lyman, D. (1994). The neuropsychology of conduct disorder and delinquency: Implications for understanding antisocial behavior. In D. C. Fowles, P. Sutker, & S. H. Goodman (Eds.), *Progress in experimental personality and psychopathology research.* New York: Springer.

Mohr, D. C., & Beutler, L. E. (1990). Erectile dysfunction: A review of diagnostic and treatment procedures. *Clin. Psychol. Rev., 10,* 123–50.

Mohs, R. C., Breitner, J. C., Siverman, J. M., & Davis, K. L. (1987). Alzheimer's disease: Morbid risk among first-degree relatives approximates 50% by 90 years of age. *Arch. Gen. Psychiat., 44,* 405–8.

Moldin, S. O., & Gottesman, I. I. (1997). Genes, experience, and chance in schizophrenia—Positioning for the 21st century. *Schizo. Bull., 23*(4), 547–61.

Monahan, J. (1981). *Predicting violent behavior: An assessment of clinical techniques.* Beverly Hills, CA: Sage.

Monahan, J., & Steadman, H. J. (1997). Violent storms and violent people: How meteorology can inform risk communication in mental health law. *Amer. Psychol., 51*(9), 931–38.

Money, J. (1985). *The destroying angel.* (pp. 17–31, 51–52, 61–68, 83–90, 107–20, 137–48) Buffalo, NY: Prometheus Books.

Money, J. (1986). Lovemaps: Clinical concepts of sexual/erotic health and pathology, paraphilia, and gender transposition. New York: Irvington.

Money, J. (1988). *Gay, straight, and in-between.* (p. 77). New York: Oxford University Press.

Monroe, S. M., & Simons, A. D. (1991). Diathesis-stress theories in the context of life stress research: Implications for the depressive disorders. *Psychol. Bull., 110,* 406–25.

Moolchan, E. T., & Hoffman, J. A. (1994). Phases of treatment: A practical approach to methadone maintenance treatment. *Inter. J. Addict., 151,* 165–68.

Mora, G. (1967). Paracelsus' psychiatry. *Amer. J. Psychiat., 124,* 803–14.

Morey, L. C. (1988a). Personality disorders in DSM-III and DSM-III-R: Convergence, coverage, and internal consistency. *Amer. J. Psychiat., 145,* 573–77.

Morey, L. C., Skinner, H. A., & Blashfield, R. K. (1984). A typology of alcohol abusers: Correlates and implications. *J. Abn. Psychol., 93,* 408–17.

Morgan, J. (1995). American Red Cross disaster mental health services: Implementation and recent developments. Special Issue: Disasters and stress: A mental health counseling perspective. *J. Ment. Hlth. Couns., 17*(3), 291–300.

Morganstern, J., Labouvie, E., McCrady, B. S., Kahler, C. W., & Frey, R. M. (1997). Affiliation with Alcoholics Anonomyous after treatment: A study of its therapeutic effects and mechanisms of action. *J. Cons. Clin. Psychol., 65*(5), 768–77.

Morganstern, J., Langenbucher, J., Labouvie, E., & Miller, K. J. (1997). The comorbidity of alcoholism and personality disorders in a clinical population. *J. Abn. Psychol., 106*(1), 74–84.

Mori, E., et al. (1997a). Medial temporal structures relate to memory impairment in Alzheimer's disease: An MRI volumetric study. *J. Neurol. Neurosurg. Psychiat., 63*(2), 214–21.

Mori, E., et al. (1997b). Premorbid brain size as a determinant of reserve capacity against intellectual decline in Alzheimer's Disease. *Amer. J. Psychiat., 154*(1), 18–24.

Morlock, L. L. (1989). Recognition and treatment of mental health problems in the general health care sector. In C. A. Taube, D. Mechanic, & A. A. Hohmann (Eds.), *The future of mental health services research.* (pp. 39–62). Washington, DC: U.S. Department of Health and Human Services.

Morrison, J. (1980). Adult psychiatric disorders in parents of hyperactive children. *Amer. J. Psychiat., 137*(7), 825–27.

Mosbascher, D. (1988). Lesbian alcohol and substance abuse. *Psychiat. Ann., 18,* 47–50.

Moscato, B. S., Russell, M., Zielezny, M., Bromet, E., Egri, G., Mudar, P., & Marshall, J. R. (1997). Gender differences in the relation between depressive symptoms and alcohol problems: A longitudinal perspective. *Amer. J. Epidemiol., 146*(11), 966–74.

Moser, P. W. (1989 January). Double vision: Why do we never match up to our mind's ideal? *Self,* pp. 51–52.

Motavalli, N. (1995). Fluoxetine for (s)elective mutism. *J. Amer. Acad. Child Adoles. Psychiat., 34*(6), 701–02.

Mowrer, O. H. (1947). On the dual nature of learning: A reinterpretation of "conditioning" and "problem solving."*Harvard Educational Review, 17,* 102–148.

Mowrer, O. H., & Mowrer, W. M. (1938). Enuresis—a method for its study and treatment. *Amer. J. Orthopsychiat., 8,* 436–59.

Mrazek, P. J., & Haggerty, R. J. (1994). *Reducing risks for mental disorders: Frontiers for prevention intervention research.* Washington: National Academy Press.

Mueser, K. T., et al. (1998). Models of community care for severe mental illness: A review of research on case management. *Schizo. Bull., 24*(1), 37–74.

Mufson, L., Weissman, M. M., & Warner, V. (1992). Depression and anxiety in parents and children: A direct interview study. *J. Anxiety Dis., 6,* 1–13.

Mukherjee, S., Sackeim, H. A., & Schnur, D. B. (1994). Electroconvulsive therapy of acute manic episodes: A review of 50 years' experience. *Amer. J. Psychiat., 151,* 169–76.

Munoz, R. F., Mrazek, P. J., & Haggerty, R. J. (1996). Institute of Medicine report on prevention of mental disorders: Summary and commentary. *Amer. Psychol., 51*(11), 1116–22.

Murphy, C. M., Meyer, S-L, & O'Leary, K. D. (1994). Dependency characteristics of partner assaultive men. *J. Abn. Psychol., 103,* 729–35.

Murphy, D. L., Greenburg, B., Altemus, M., Benjamin, J., Grady, T., & Pigott, T. (1996). The neuropharmacology and neurobiology of obsessive-compulsive disorder: An update on the serotonin hypothesis. In H. G. Westenberg, J. A. Den Boer, & D. L. Murphy (Eds.), *Advances in the neurobiology of anxiety disorders.* (pp. 279–97). Chichester, England: Wiley.

Murphy, J. M. (1976). Psychiatric labeling in cross-cultural perspective. *Science, 191* (4231), 1019–28.

Murphy, W. D. (1997). Exhibitionism: Psychopathology and theory. In D. R. Laws & W. O'Donohue (Eds.) *Sexual deviance: Theory, assessment, and treatment.* (pp. 22–39). New York: Guilford.

Murray, C. J. L., & Lopez, A. D. (1996). *The global burden of disease.* Cambridge, MA: Harvard University Press.

Murray, L. & Cooper, P. (1997). Postpartum depression and child development. *Psychol. Med., 27,* 253–60.

Murray, L., Fiori–Cowley, A., Hooper, R., & Cooper, P. (1996). The impact of postnatal depression and associated adversity on early mother-infant interactions and later infant outcomes. *Child Develop., 67*(5), 2512–26.

Myers, H. F., & McClure, F. H. (1993). Psychosocial factors in hypertension in blacks: The case for an interactional perspective. In J. C. S. Fray & J. G. Douglas (Eds.), *Pathophysiology of hypertension in blacks.* (pp. 90–106). New York: Oxford.

Myers, J. K., Weissman, M. M., Tischler, G. L., Holzer, C. E., Leaf, P. J., & Stoltzman, R. (1984). Six-month prevalence of psychiatric disorders in three communities: 1980 to 1982. *Arch. Gen. Psychiat., 41,* 959–67.

Nada-Raja, S., Langley, J. D., McGee, R., Williams, S. M., Begg, D. J., & Reeder, A. I. (1997). Inattentive and hyperactive behaviors and driving offenses in adolescence. *J. Amer. Acad. Child Adoles. Psychiat. 36*(4), 515–22.

Nadder, T. S., Silberg, J. L., Eaves, L. J., Maes, H. H., & Meyer, J. M. (1998). Genetic effects on ADHD symptomatology in 7- to 13-year-old twins: Results from a telephone survey. *Behav. Gen., 28*(2), 83–99.

Narby, J. (1982). The evolution of attitudes towards mental illness in preindustrial England. *Orthomolecular Psychiatry, 11,* 103–10.

Narrow, W. E., Regier, D. A., Rae, D. S., Manderscheid, R. W., & Locke, B. Z. (1993). Use of services by persons with mental and addictive disorders: Findings from the National Institute of Mental Health Epidemiologic Catchment Area Program. *Arch. Gen. Psychiat., 50,* 95–107.

Nash, M. R., Hulsey, T. L., Sexton, M. C., Harralson, T. L., & Lambert, W. (1993). Long-term sequelae of childhood sexual abuse: Perceived family environment, psychopathology, and dissociation. *J. Cons. Clin. Psychol., 61*(2), 276–83.

Nathan, P. E., & Gorman, J. M. (Eds.). (1998). *A guide to treatments that work.* New York: Oxford University Press.

National Committee to Prevent Child Abuse. (1996). *Study of the national incidence and prevalence of child abuse and neglect.* Washington D.C.: Author.

National Highway Safety Administration. (1990). *Transportation statistics.* Department of Transportation. Washington, DC.

National Institute of Drug Abuse (1998). *Director's report:* 1997. Washington: Author.

National Institute of Drug Abuse. (1994). Washington, DC: U.S. Department of Health and Human Services.

National Institute of Mental Health. (1976, Apr. 20). Rising suicide rate linked to economy. Los Angeles Times, VIII, 2, 5.

Navia, B. A., Jordan, B. D., & Price, R. W. (1986). The AIDS dementia complex: I. Clinical features. *Ann. Neurol., 19,* 517–24.

Neale, M. C., Walters, E. E., Eaves, L. J., & Hermine, M. H. (1994). Mutivariate genetic analysis of twin-family data on fears: Mx models. *Behavior Genetics, 24*(2), 119–39.

Neisser, U. (1967). *Cognitive psychology.* New York: Appleton Century Crofts.

Neisser, U. (Ed.) (1982). *Memory observed: Remembering in natural contexts.* San Francisco: Freeman.

Nelson, C. A., & Bloom, F. E. (1997) Child development and neuroscience. *Child Develop., 68,* 970–87.

Nelson, L. D., & Adams, K. M. (1997). Challenges for neuropsychology in the treatment rehabilitation of brain-injured patients. *Psychol. Assess., 9*(4), 368–73.

Nelson, Z. P., & Mowry, D. D. (1976). Contracting in crisis intervention. *Comm. Ment. Hlth. J., 12,* 37–43.

Nemeroff, C. B., & Schatzberg, A. F. (1998). Pharmacological treatment of unipolar depression. In P. E. Nathan & J. M. Gorman (Eds.), *A guide to treatments that work.* (pp. 212–25). Oxford, England: Oxford University Press.

Nesdale, D., Rooney, R., & Smith, L. (1997). Migrant ethnic identity and psychological distress. *Journal of Cross-Cultural Psychology, 28*(5), 569–88.

Nestor, P. G., Shenton, M. E., McCarley, R. W., Haimson, J., Smith, S., O'Donnell, B., Kimble, M., Kikinis, R., & Jolesz, F. A. (1993). Neuropsychological correlates of MRI temporal lobe abnormalities in schizophrenia. *Amer. J. Psychiat., 150*(12), 1849–55.

Neufeld, R. W. (1990). Coping with stress, coping without stress, and stress with coping: In interconstruct redundencies. *Stress Medicine, 6,* 117–25.

Neugarten, B. L. (1977). Personality and aging. In J. E. Birren & K. W. Schaie (Eds.), *Handbook of the psychology of aging.* New York: Van Nostrand.

Newman, J. P. (1997). Conceptual models of the nervous system: Implications for antisocial behavior. In D. M. Stoff, J. Breiling, & J. D. Maser (Eds.), *Handbook of antisocial behavior.* (pp. 324–335). New York: Wiley.

Newman, L., Henry, P. B., DiRenzo, P., & Stecher, T. (1988–89). Intervention and student assistance: The Pennsylvania model. Special Issue: Practical approaches in treating adolescent chemical dependency: A guide to clinical assessment and intervention. *J. Chem. Depen. Treat., 2*(1), 145–62.

Newman, M. L., & Greenway, P. (1997). Therapeutic effects of providing MMPI-2 test feedback to clients in a university counseling service. *Psychol. Assess., 9,* 122–31.

New York Times (1994, May 9). Multiple personality cases perplex legal system. pp. 143.

Niederehe, G. & Schneider. (1998). Treatments for depression and anxiety in the aged. In P. E. Nathan & J. M. Gorman (Eds.), *A guide to treatments that work.* (pp. 270–87). New York: Oxford University Press.

Nigg, J. T., & Goldsmith, H. H. (1994). Genetics of personality disorders: perspectives from personality and psychopathology research. *Psychol. Bull., 115,* 346–80.

Nijenhuis, E. R. S., et al. (1998). Somatoform dissociative symptoms as related to animal defensive reactions to predatory imminence and injury. *J. Abn. Psychol., 107*(1), 63–73.

Nisbett, R. E., & Wilson, T. D. (1977). Telling more than we can know: Verbal reports on mental processes. *Psychol. Rev., 84,* 231–59.

Noia, G., De Santis, M., Fundaro, C., Mastromarino, C., Trivellini, C., Rosati, P., Caruso, A., Segni, G., & Mancuso, S. (1994). Drug addiction in pregnancy: 13 years of experience. *Fetal Diagnosis and Therapy, 9,* 116–24.

Nolan, E. E., & Gadow, K. D. (1997). Children with ADHD and tic disorder and their classmates: Behavioral normalization with methylphenidate. *J. Amer. Acad. Child Adoles. Psychiat. 36*(5), 597–604.

Nolen-Hoeksema, S. (1990). *Sex differences in depression.* Stanford, CA: Stanford University Press.

Nolen-Hoeksema, S., & Girgus, J. S. (1994). The emergence of gender differences in depression during adolescence. *Psychol. Bull., 115*(3), 424–43.

Nolen-Hoeksema, S., Morrow, J., & Fredrickson, B. L. (1993). Response styles and the duration of episodes of depressed mood. *J. Abn. Psychol., 102*(1), 20–28.

Nopoulos, P., Flaum, M., & Andreasen, N. C. (1997). Sex differences in brain morphology in schizophrenia. *Amer. J. Psychiat., 154*(12), 1648–54.

Norcross, J. C., & Goldfried, M. R. (Ed.). (1992). *Handbook of psychotherapy integration.* New York: Basic Books.

Norton, K., & Hinshelwood, R. D. (1996). Severe personality disorder. Treatment issues and selection for in-patient psychotherapy. *Brit. J. Psychiat., 168,* 723–731.

Novy, D. M., Blumentritt, T. L., Nelson, D. V., & Gaa, A. (1997). The Washington University Sentence Completion Test: Are the two halves alternate forms? Are the female and male forms comparable? *J. Pers. Assess., 68*(3), 616–27.

Noyes, R., Kathol, R. G., Fisher, M. M., Phillips, B. M., Suelzer, M. T., & Holt, C. S. (1993). The validity of DSM-III-R hypochondriasis. *Arch. Gen. Psychiat., 50*(12), 961–70.

Nuechterlein, K. H., Snyder, K. S., & Mintz, J. (1992). Paths to relapse: Possible transactional processes connecting patient illness onset, expressed emotion, and psychotic relapse. *Brit. J. Psychiat., 161* (Suppl. 18), 88–96.

Nunes, E. V., Frank, K. A. S., & Kornfield, D. S. (1987). Pyschological treatment for the Type A behavior pattern and for coronary artery disease: A meta-analysis of the literature. *Psychosom. Med., 48,* 159–173.

O'Connor, S. J. (1996). Who will manage the managers? In A. Lazarus (Ed.), *Controversies in managed mental health care.* (pp. 383–401). Washington, DC: American Psychiatric Press, Inc.

O'Connor, B. P., McGuire, S., Reiss, D., Hetherington, E. M., & Plomin, R. (1998). Co-occurence of depressive symptoms and antisocial behavior in adolescence: A common genetic liability. *J. Abn. Psychol., 107*(1), 27–37.

Odell, J. D., Warren, R. P., Warren, W., Burger, R. A., & Maciulis, A. (1997). Association of genes within the major histocompatibility complex with attention-deficit hyperactivity disorder. *Neuropsychobiology, 35*(4), 181–86.

O'Donnell, C. R. (1995). Firearm deaths among children and youth. *Amer. Psychol., 50*(9), 771–76.

O'Donnell, I., & Farmer, R. (1995). The limitations of official suicide statistics. *Brit. J. Psychiat., 166,* 458–61.

O'Donnell, I., Farmer, R., & Catalan, J. (1996). Explaining suicide: The views of survivors of serious suicide attempts. *Brit. J Psychiat., 168,* 780–86.

O'Donnell, P., & Grace, A. A. (1998). Dysfunctions in multiple interrelated systems as the neurobiological bases of schizophrenic symptom clusters. *Schizo. Bull., 24*(2), 267–84.

Office of Technology Assessment. (1993). *Biological components of substance abuse and addiction.* Washington, DC: United States Congress, Office of Technology Assessment.

Offord, D. R., & Bennett, K. J. (1996). Conduct disorder. In L. Hechtman (Ed.), *Do they grow out of it?* (pp. 77–100). Washington: American Psychiatric Press.

Ogata, S. N., Silk, K. R., Goodrich, S., Lohr, N. E., & Hill, E. M. (1990). Childhood sexual and physical abuse in adult patients with borderline personality. *Amer. J. Psychiat., 147,* 1008–13.

O'Hara, M., Schlecte, J., Lewis, D., & Varner, M. (1991). Controlled prospective study of postpartum mood disorders: Psychological, environmental, and hormonal variables. *J. Abn. Psychol., 100,* 63–73.

O'Hara, M., Zekoski, E., Philipps, L., & Wright, E. (1990). Controlled prospective study of postpartum mood disorders: Comparison of childbearing and nonchildbearing women. *J. Abn. Psychol., 99,* 3–15.

Öhman, A. (1996). Perferential preattentive processing of threat in anxiety: Preparedness and attentional biases. In R. M. Rapee (Ed.), *Current controversies in the anxiety disorders.* (pp. 253–90). New York: Guilford.

Öhman, A., Dimberg, U., & Esteves, F. (1989). Preattentive activation of aversive emotions. In T. Archer & L. G. Nilsson (Eds.), *Aversion, avoidance, and anxiety: Perspectives on aversively motivated behavior.* (pp. 169–99). Hillsdale, NJ: Erlbaum.

Öhman, A., Dimberg, U., & Öst, L. G. (1985). Animal and social phobias: Biological constraints on learned fear responses. In S. Reiss & R. Bootzin (Eds.), *Theoretical issues in behavior therapy.* (pp. 123–75). New York: Academic Press.

Öhman, A., & Mineka, S. (2001). *Revisiting preparedness: Toward an evolved module of fear learning.*

Ohtsuka, K., Bruton, E., DeLuca, L., & Borg, V. (1997). Sex differences in pathological gambling using gaming machines. *Psychol. Rep., 80*(3), 1051–57.

Okura, K. P. (1975). Mobilizing in response to a major disaster. *Community Health Journal, 2*(2), 136–44.

Olds, D. L., Henderson, C., & Tatelbaum, R. (1994). Prevention of intelletual impairment in children of women who smoke cigarettes during pregnancy. *Pediatrics, 93,* 228–233.

Olds, D. L., Henderson, C., Tatelbaum, R., & Chamberlin, R. (1986). Improving the delivery of prenatal care and outcomes of pregnancy: A randomized trial of nurse home visitation. *Pediatrics, 77,* 16–28.

O'Leary, A. (1985). Self-efficacy and health. *Behav. Res. Ther., 23,* 437–51.

O'Leary, K. D. (1995). Assessment and treatment of partner abuse. *Clin. Res. Dig. Suppl. Bull, 12, 13,* 1–2.

Ollendick, T. H., Yang, B., King, N. J., Dong, Q., et al. (1996). Fears in American, Australian, Chinese, and Nigerian children and adolescents: A cross-cultural study. *Journal of Child Psychology & Psychiatry & Allied Sciences, 37*(2), 213–20.

Oltmanns, T. F., & Maher, B. A. (Eds.). (1988). *Delusional beliefs.* New York: Wiley.

O'Malley, S. S., Jaffe, A. J., Rode, S., & Rounsaville, B. (1996). Experience of a "slip" among alcoholics treated with naltrexone or placebo. *Amer. J. Psychiat., 153*(2), 281–83.

Oren, D. A., & Rosenthal, N. E. (1992). Seasonal affective disorders. In E. S. Paykel (Ed.), *Handbook of affective disorders* (2nd ed.). (pp. 551–67). New York: Guilford.

Orford, J. (1985). Excessive appetites: A psychological view of addiction. New York: Wiley.

Orne, M. T., Dinges, D. F., & Orne, E. C. (1984). On the differential diagnosis of multiple personality in the forensic context. *Int. J. Clin. Exp. Hypn., 32,* 118–69.

Osborn, A. F. (1992). Social influences on conduct disorder in mid-childhood. *Studia Psychologica, 34,* 29–43.

Oscar-Berman, M., Shagrin, B., Evert, D. L., & Epstein, C. (1997). Impairments of brain and behavior. *Alcohol Health and Research World, 21*(1), 65–75.

Osgood, C. E., & Luria, Z. (1954). A blind analysis of a case of multiple personality using the semantic differential. *J. Abnorm. Soc. Psychol., 49,* 579–591.

Öst, L. G. (1987). Age of onset of different phobias. *J. Abn. Psychol., 96,* 223–9.

Öst, L. G. (1997). Rapid treatment of specific phobias. In G. C. L. Davey, (Ed.), *Phobias. A handbook of theory, research and treatment* (2nd ed.). (pp. 227–46). Chichester, England: Wiley.

Öst, L. G., & Hellström, K. (1997). Blood-injury-injection phobia. In G. C. L. Davey, (Ed.), *Phobias. A handbook of theory, research and treatment.* (pp. 63–80). Chichester, England: Wiley.

Öst, L. G., & Hugdahl, K. (1985). Acquisition of blood and dental phobia and anxiety response patterns in clinical patients. *Behav. Res. Ther., 23*(1), 27–34.

Öst, L. G., & Hugdahl, K.(1981). Acquisition of phobias and anxiety response patterns in clinical patients. *Behav. Res. Ther., 19,* 439–47.

Otto, M. W., Fava, M., Penava, S. J., Bless, E., et al. (1997). Life event, mood, and cognitive predictors of perceived stress before and after treatment for major depression. *Cog. Ther. Res., 21*(4), 403–20.

Overmier, J. B., & Seligman, M. E. P. (1967). Effects of inescapable shock upon subsequent escape and avoidance learning. *Journal of Comparative and Physiological Psychology, 63,* 23–33.

Page, A. C. (1994). Blood-injury phobia. *Clin. Psychol. Rev., 14*(5), 443–61.

Page, A. C., & Martin, N. G. (1998). Testing a genetic structure of blood-injury-injection fears. *Am. J. Med. Genet., 81* 377–84.

Page, W. F., Engdahl, B. E., & Eberly, R. E. (1997). Persistence of PTSD in former prisoners of war. In C. S. Fullerton & R. J. Ursano (Eds.), *Posttraumatic stress disorder.* (pp. 147–58). Washington: American Psychiatric Press.

Palace, E. M. (1995). Modification of dysfunctional patterns of sexual response through autonomic arousal and false feedback. *J. Cons. Clin. Psychol., 63,* 604–15.

Palace, E. M., & Gorzalka, B. B. (1990). The enhancing effects of anxiety on arousal in sexually dysfunctional and functional women. *J. Abn. Psychol., 99,* 403–11.

Palmer, C. T. (1988). Twelve reasons why rape is not sexually motivated: A skeptical examination. *J. Sex Res., 25,* 512–30.

Palosaari, U., & Laippala, P. (1996). Parental divorce and depression in young adulthood: Adolescents' closeness to parents and self-esteem as mediating factor. *Acta Psychiat. Scandin., 93*(1), 20–36.

Pan, H. S., Neidig, P. H., & O'Leary, K. D. (1994). Predicting mild and severe husband-to-wife physical aggression. *J. Consult. Clin. Psychol., 62,* 975–81.

Paris, J., Zweig-Frank, H., & Guzder, J. (1994a). Psychological risk factors for borderline personality disorder in female patients. *Compr. Psychiat., 35*(4), 301–305.

Paris, J., Zweig-Frank, H., & Guzder, J. (1994b). Risk factors for borderline personality disorders in male outpatients. *J. Nerv. Ment. Dis., 182,* 375–80.

Parker, G., Hadzi-Pavlovic, D., Roussos, J., Wilhelm, K., Mitchell, P., Austin, M.-P., Hickie, I., Gladstone, G., Eyers, K. (1998) Non-melancholic depression: The contribution of personality, anxiety and life events to subclassification. *Psychological Medicine, 28,* 1209–19.

Parker, J. G., Rubin, K. H., Price, J. M., & DeRossier, M. E. (1995). Peer relationships, child development, and adjustment: A developmental psychopathology perspective. In D. Cicchetti & D. J. Cohen (Eds.), *Developmental psychopathology: Vol. 2. Risk, disorder, and adaptation.* (pp. 96–161). New York: Wiley.

Parsons, O. A. (1998). Neurocognitive deficits in alcoholics and social drinkers: A continuum? *Alcoholism: Clin. Exper. Res. 22*(4), 954–61.

Pasewark, R. A., Pantle, M. L., & Steadman, H. J. (1982). Detention and rearrest rates of persons found not guilty by reason of insanity and convicted felons. *Amer. J. Psychiat., 139*(7), 892–97.

Paternite, C. E., & Loney, J. (1980). Childhood hyperkinesis: Relationships between symptomatology and home environment. In C. K. Whelan & B. Henker (Eds.), *Hyperactive children: The social ecology of identification and treatment.* New York: Academic Press.

Patterson, G. R. (1979). Treatment for children with conduct problems: A review of outcome studies. In S. Feshbach & A. Fraczek (Eds.), *Aggression and behavior change: Biological and social processes.* New York: Praeger.

Patterson, G. R. (1996). Characteristics of developmental theory for early onset delinquency. In M. F. Lenzenweger & J. L. Haugaard (Eds.), *Frontiers of developmental psychopathology* (pp. 81–124). New York: Oxford University Press.

Patterson, G. R., Capaldi, D., & Bank, L. (1991). An early starter model for predicting deliquency. In D. Pepler & K. H. Rubin (Eds.), *The development and treatment of childhood aggression.* (pp. 139–168). Hillsdale, NJ: Erlbaum.

Paul, G. L., & Lentz, R. J. (1977). *Psychosocial treatment of chronic mental patients: Milieu versus social-learning programs.* Cambridge, MA: Harvard University Press.

Pauls, D. L., Alsobrooke, J. P., Goodman, W., Rasmussen, S., & Leckman, J. F. (1995). A family study of obsessive-compulsive disorder. *Amer. J. Psychiat., 152*(1), 76–84.

Pavlov, I. P. (1927). *Conditioned reflexes.* London: Oxford University Press.

Pavone, L., Meli, C., Nigro, F., & Lisi, R. (1993). Late diagnosed phenylketonuria patients: Clinical presentation and results of treatment. *Developmental Brain Dysfunction, 6*(1–3), 184–87.

Paykel, E. S., Brayne, C., Huppert, F. A., Gill, C., Barkley, C., Gehlhaar, E., Beardsall, L., Girling, D. M., Pollitt, P., & O'Connor, D. (1994). Incidence of dementia in a population older than 75 years in the United Kingdom. *Arch. Gen. Psychiat., 51*(4), 325–32.

Pearlson, G. D., Kim, W. S., Kubos, K. L., Moberg, P. J., Jayaram, G., Bascom, M. J., Chase, G. A., Goldfinger, A. G., & Tune, L. E. (1989). Ventricle-brain ratio, computed tomographic density, and brain area in 50 schizophrenics. *Arch. Gen. Psychiat., 46,* 690–97.

Pelham, W. E., Carlson, C., Sams, S. E., Vallano, G., Dixon, M. J., & Hoza, B. (1993). Separate and combined effects of methylphenidate and behavior modification on boys with attention-deficit hyperactivity disorder in the classroom. *J. Cons. Clin. Psychol., 61,* 506–15.

Pelham, W. E., Murphy, D. A., Vannatta, K., Milich, R., Licht, B. G., Gnagy, E. M., Greenslade, K. E., Greiner, A. R., & Vodde-Hamilton, M. (1992). Methylphenidate and attributions in boys with attention-deficit hyperactivity disorder. *J. Cons. Clin. Psychol., 60,* 282–92.

Pelham, W. E., Jr., Swanson, J. M., Furman, M., & Schwindt, H. (1996). Pemoline effects on children with ADHD: A time response by dose-response analysis on classroom measures. *Annual Progress in child Psychiatry & Child Development, 1996,* 473–93.

Pennebaker, J. W. (1997). *Opening up: The healing power of expressing emotions.* New York: Guilford.

Penrose, L. S. (1963). *Biology of mental defect* (3rd ed.). New York: Grune & Stratton.

Pentz, M. A. (1983). Prevention of adolescent substance abuse through social skill development. *National Institute on Drug Abuse Research Monograph Series, 47,* 195–232.

Perlberg, M. (1979, Apr.). Adapted from Trauma at Tenerife: The psychic aftershocks of a jet disaster. *Human Behav.,* 49–50.

Perlin, M. L. (1996). Myths, realities, and the political world: The anthropology of insanity defense attitudes. *Bull. Amer. Acad. Psychiat. Law, 24*(1), 5–25.

Perls, F. S. (1967). Group vs. individual therapy. *ETC: A Review of General Semantics, 34,* 306–12.

Perls, F. S. (1969). *Gestalt therapy verbatim.* Lafayette, CA: Real People Press.

Perris, C. (1992). Bipolar-unipolar distinction. In E. S. Paykel (Ed.), *Handbook of affective disorders* (2nd ed.). New York: Guilford.

Perry, C. L., Williams, C. L., Forster, J. L., Wolfson, M., Wagenaar, A. C., Finnegan, J. R., McGovern, P. G., Veblen-Mortensen, S., Komro, K. A., & Anstine, P. S. (1993). Background, conceptualization, and design of a community-wide research program on adolescent alcohol use: Project Northland. *Health Education Research: Theory and Practice, 8*(1), 125–36.

Pert, C. B., & Snyder, S. H. (1973, Mar. 9). Opiate receptor: Demonstration in nervous tissue. *Science, 179*(4077), 1011–14.

Peterson, C., et al. (1998). Catastrophizing and untimely death. *Psychol. Sci., 9*(2), 127–130.

Peterson, C., Maier, S. F., & Seligman, M. E .P. (1993). *Learned helplessness: A theory for the age of personal control.* New York: Oxford University Press.

Peterson, C., Seligman, M. E. P., & Vaillant, G. E. (1988). Pessimistic explanatory style is a risk factor for physical illness: A thirty-five-year longitudinal study. *J. Pers. Soc. Psychol., 55,* 23–27.

Peterson, L., & Brown, D. (1994). Integrating child injury and abuse-neglect research: Common histories, etiologies, and solutions. *Psychol. Bull., 116*(2), 293–315.

Peterson, R. A., & Reiss, S. (1987). *Test maual for the anxiety sensitivity index.* Orland Park, IL: International Diagnostic Systems.

Petraitis, J., Flay, B. R., Miller, T. Q. et al. (1998). Illicit substance use among adolescents: A matrix of prospective predictors. *Substance Use & Misuse, 33*(13) 2661–604.

Petronko, M. R., Harris, S. L., & Kormann, R. J. (1994). Community-based behavioral training approaches for people with mental retardation and mental illness. *J. Cons. Clin. Psychol., 62*(1), 49–54.

Pfeffer, C. R. (1996a). Suicidal behavior in response to stress. In C. R. Pfeffer (Ed.), *Severe stress and mental disturbance in children.* (pp. 327–46). Washington: American Psychiatric Association.

Pfeffer, C. R. (1996b). Suicidal behavior. In L. Hechtman (Ed.), *Do they grow out of it?* (pp. 121–38). Washington: American Psychiatric Press.

Pfeffer, C. R., Hurt, S. W., Kakuma, T., Peskin, J., Siefker, C. A., & Nagbhairava, S. (1994). Suicidal children grow up: Suicidal episodes and effects of treatment during followup. *J. Amer. Acad. Child Adoles. Psychiat., 33,* 225–30.

Pfohl, B., & Blum, N. (1995). Obsessive-compulsive personality disorder. In W. J. Livesley (Ed.), *The DSM-IV personality disorders.* (pp. 261–276). New York: Guilford.

Phillips, K. (1996). *The broken mirror: Understanding and treating body dysmorphic disorder.* New York: Oxford University Press.

Piccinelli, M., & Wilkinson, G. (1994). Outcome of depression in psychiatric settings. *Brit. J. Psychiat., 164,* 297–304.

Pickworth, W. B., Rohrer, M. S., & Fant, R. V. (1997). Effects of abused drugs on psychomotor performance. *Experimental and Clinical Psychopharmacology, 5*(3), 235–41.

Pigott, T., & Seay, S. (1998). In R. Swinson, M. Antony, S. Rachman, & M. Richter (Eds.), *Obsessive-compulsive disorder: Theory, research, and treatment.* (pp. 298–326). New York: Guilford.

Pigott, T. M., Myers, K. R., & Williams, D. A. (1996). Obsessive-compusive disorder: A neuropsychiatric perspective. In R. M. Rapee (Ed.), *Current controversies in the anxiety disorders.* (pp. 134–60). New York: Guilford.

Pillard, R. C. (1988). Sexual orientation and mental disorder. *Psychiatr. Ann., 18,* 52–56.

Pine, D. S., Cohen, P., Brook, J., & Coplan, J. D. (1997). Psychiatric symptoms in adolescence as predictors of obesity in early adulthood: A longitudinal study. *Amer. J. Pub. Hlth., 87,* 1303–10.

Pinsof, W. M. (1995). *Integrative problem-centered therapy: A synthesis of family, individual, and biological therapies.* New York: Basic Books.

Plassman, B. L., & Breitner, J. C. (1997). The genetics of dementia in late life. *Psychiat. Clin. N. Amer., 20*(1), 59–76.

Pliszka, S. R. (1989). Effect of anxiety on cognition, behavior, and stimulant response in ADHD. *J. Amer. Acad. Child Adoles. Psychiat., 28*(6), 882–87.

Pliszka, S. R. (1991). Antidepressants in the treatment of child and adolescent psychopathology. Special issue: Child psychopharmacology. *J. Clin. Child Psychol., 20,* 313–20.

Plomin, R. (1986). *Development, genetics and psychology.* Hillsdale, NJ: Erlbaum.

Plomin, R. (1990). The role of inheritance in behavior. *Science, 248,* 183–188.

Plomin, R. (1998). Using DNA in health psychology. *Hlth. Psychol., 17*(1), 53–55.

Plomin, R., & Daniels, D. (1987). Why are children in the same family so different from one another? *Behavioral and Brain Sciences, 10,* 1–15.

Plomin, R., DeFries, J. C., McClearn, G. E., & Rutter, M. (1997). *Behavior genetics* (3rd ed.). New York: W. H. Freeman.

Polich, J. M., Armor, D. J., & Braiker, H. B. (1981). *The course of alcoholism: Four years after treatment.* New York: Wiley Interscience.

Polivy, J., Zeitlin, S., Herman, P., & Beal, L. (1994). Food restriction and binge eating: A study of former prisoners of war. *J. Abn. Psychol., 103,* 409–411.

Pollard, C. A., Pollard, H. J., & Corn, K. J. (1989). Panic onset and major events in the lives of agoraphobics: A test of contiguity. *J. Abn. Psychol., 98,* 318–21.

Ponce, F. Q., & Atkinson, D. R. (1989). Mexican-American acculturation, counselor ethnicity, counseling style, and perceived counselor credibility. *J. Couns. Psychol., 36,* 203–208.

Pope, K. S. (1996). Memory, abuse, and science: Questioning claims about the false memory syndrome epidemic. *Amer. Psychol., 51,* 957–74.

Pope, K. S., Sonne, J. L., & Holroyd, J. (1993). *Sexual feelings in psychotherapy: Explorations for therapists and therapists-in-training.* Washington, DC: American Psychological Association.

Popkin, J. (1994, Sept. 19). Sexual predators. *U.S. News and World Report,* 65–73.

Post, R. M. (1992). Transduction of psychosocial stress into the neurobiology of recurrent affective disorder. *Amer. J. Psychiat., 149*(8), 999–1010.

Post, R. M., Weiss, S. R. B., & Smith, M. A. (1995). Sensitization and kindling: Implications for the evolving neural substrates of post-traumatic stress disorder. In M. J. Friedman, D. S. Charney, et al., *Neurobiological and clinical consequencies of stress: From normal adaptation to post-traumatic stress disorder.* (pp. 203–24). Philadelphia: Lippincott-Raven.

Potts, N. L., & Davidson., J. R. T. (1995). Pharmacological treatments: Literature review. In R. G. Heimberg, M. R. Liebowitz, D. A. Hope, & Schneier, F. R. (Eds.), *Social phobia: Diagnosis, assessment, and treatment* (pp. 334–65). New York: Guilford.

Powell, G. E., & Wilson, S. L. (1994). Recovery curves for patients who have suffered very severe brain injury. *Clinical Rehabilitation, 8*(1), 54–69.

Powell, T. A., Holt, J. C., & Fondacaro, K. M. (1997). The prevalence of mental illness among inmates in a rural state. *Law & Human Behavior, 21*(4), 427–38.

Prasher, V. P., et al. (1997). ApoE genotype and Alzheimer's disease in adults with Down syndrome: Meta-analysis. *Amer. J. Ment. Retard., 102*(2), 103–10.

Prasher, V. P., & Kirshnan, V. H. (1993). Age of onset and duration of dementia in people with Down syndrome: Integration of 98 reported cases in the literature. *International Journal of Geriatric Psychiatry, 8*(11), 915–22.

Pratt, L., Ford, D., Crum, R., Armenian, H., Galb, J., & Eaton, W. (1996). Depression, psychotropic medication, and risk of myocardial infarction. *Circulation, 94,* 3123–3129.

Preskorn, S. H., and Burke, M. (1992). Somatic therapy for major depressive disorder: Selection of an antidepressant. *J. Psychiat., 53,* 5–18.

Pretzer, J. L., & Beck, A. T. (1996). A cognitive theory of personality disorders. In J. F. Clarkin & M. F. Lenzenweger (Eds.), *Major theories of personality disorder.* (pp. 36–105). New York: Guilford.

Pribor, E. F., Yutzy, S. H., Dean, J. T., & Wetzel, R. D. (1993). Briquet's syndrome, dissociation, and abuse. *Amer. J. Psychiat., 150*(10), 1507–11.

Price, R. W., Brew, B., Sidtis, J., Rosenblum, M., Scheck, A. C., & Cleary, P. (1988). The brain in AIDS: Central nervous system HIV-1 infection and the AIDS dementia complex. *Science, 239,* 586–92.

Price, R. W., Sidtis, J., & Rosenblum, M. (1988). The AIDS dementia complex: Some current questions. *Ann. Neurol.,* Suppl., *23,* 27–33.

Prichard, J. C. (1835). *A treatise on insanity.* London: Sherwood, Gilbert, & Piper.

Prigatano, G. P. (1992). Personality disturbances associated with traumatic brain injury. *J. Cons. Clin. Psychol., 60*(3), 360–68.

Pritchard, W. S. (1986). Cognitive event-related potential correlates of schizophrenia. *Psychol. Bull., 100*(1), 43–66.

Prizant, B. M. (1983). Language acquisition and communicative behavior in autism: Toward an understanding of the "whole" of it. *J. Speech Hear. Dis., 46,* 241–49.

Project Match Group. (1997). Project MATCH: Rationale and methods for a multisite clinical trial matching patients to alcoholism treatment. *Alcoholism: Clin. Exper. Res., 17*(6), 1130–45.

Psychological Corporation. (1997a). *WAIS-III manual.* San Antonio, TX: Author.

Psychological Corporation. (1997b). *Wechsler Memory Scale III manual.* San Antonio, TX: Author.

Puig-Antich, J., Goetz, D., Davies, M., Kaplan, T., Davies, S., Ostrow, L., Asnis, L., Twomey, J., Iyengar, S., & Ryan, N. D. (1989). A controlled family history study of prepubertal major depressive disorder. *Arch. Gen. Psychiat., 46,* 406–18.

Puri, B. K., Baxter, R., & Cordess, C. C. (1995). Characteristics of fire–setters: A study and proposed multiaxial psychiatric classification. *Brit. J. Psychiat., 166,* 393–96.

Purisch, A. D., & Sbordone, R. J. (1997). Forensic neuropsychology: Clinical issues and practice. In A. M. Horton, D. Wedding, & J. Webster (Eds.), *The neuropsychology handbook* (Vol. 2). (pp. 309–56). New York: Springer.

Putnam, F. W., Zahn, T. P., & Post, R. M. (1995). Differential autonomic nervous system activity in multiple personality disorder. *Psychiatry Research, 31,* 251–260.

Quinsey, V. L., & Earls, C. M. (1990). The modification of sexual preferences. In W. L. Marshall, D. R. Laws, & H. E. Barbaree (Eds.), *Handbook of sexual assault: Issues, theories, and treatment of the offender.* (pp. 279–95). New York: Plenum.

Quinsey, V. L., Harris, G. T., Rice, M. E., & Lalumiere, M. L. (1993). Assessing treatment efficacy in outcome studies of sex offenders. *J. Interpers. Viol., 8,* 512–23.

Quinton, D., & Rutter, M. (1988). *Parenting breakdown: The making and breaking of intergenerational links.* Aldershot, Hants: Avebury.

Rabow, J., & Duncan-Schill, M. (1995). Drinking among college students. *Journal of Alcohol & Drug Education, 40*(3), 52–64.

Rachman, J. G., & Hodgson, R. (1980). *Obsessions and compulsions.* Englewood Cliffs, NJ: Prentice-Hall.

Rachman, S. J. (1990). *Fear and courage.* New York: Freeman.

Rachman, S. J. (1997). Claustrophobia. In G. C. L. Davey, (Ed.), *Phobias: A handbook of theory, research and treatment.* (pp. 163–181). Chichester, England: Wiley.

Rachman, S., & Shafran, R. (1998). Cognitive and behavioral features of obsessive-compulsive disorder. In R. Swinson, M. Antony, S. Rachman, & M. Richter (Eds.), *Obsessive-compulsive disorder: Theory, research, and treatment.* (pp. 51–78). New York: Guilford.

Rado, S. (1956). *Psychoanalysis and behavior.* New York: Grune & Stratton.

Rado, S. (1962). *Psychoanalysis of behavior II,* (p. 96). New York: Grune & Stratton.

Rainer, M. (1997). Galanthamine in Alzheimer's disease: A new alternative to tacrine? *CNS Drugs,* 7(2), 89–97.

Ramey, C. T., & Haskins, R. (1981). The causes and treatment of school failure: Insights from the Carolina Abecedarian Project. In M. J. Begab, H. C. Haywood, & H. L. Garber (Eds.), *Psychosocial influences in retarded performance* (Vol. II). Baltimore: University Park Press.

Rapee, R. M. (1996). Information-processing views of panic disorder. In R. M. Rapee (Ed.), *Current controversies in the anxiety disorders.* (pp. 77–93). New York: Guilford.

Rapee, R. M., & Barlow, D. H. (1993). Generalized anxiety disorder, panic disorder, and the phobias. In P. B. Sutker & H. E. Adams (Eds.), *Comprehensive handbook of psychopathology* (2nd ed.). New York: Plenum.

Raskin, V. D. (1993). Psychiatric aspects of substance use disorders in childbearing populations. *Psychiatr. Clin. N. Amer., 16,* 157–65.

Rasmussen, S., & Eisen, J. L. (1991). Phenomenology of OCD: Clinical subtypes, heterogeneity and coexistence. In J. Zohar, T. Insel, & S. Rasmussen (Eds.), *The psychobiology of obsessive-compulsive disorder.* New York: Springer.

Ratakonda, S., et al. (1998). Characterization of psychotic conditions: Use of the domains of psychopathology model. *Arch. Gen. Psychiat., 55*(1), 75–81.

Ratti, L. A., Humphrey, L. L., & Lyons, J. S. (1996). Structural analysis of families with a polydrug-dependent, bulimic, or normal adolescent daughter. *J. Cons. Clin. Psychol., 64*(6), 1255–1262.

Rauch, S. L., & Jenike, M. A. (1998) Pharmacological treatment of obsessive-compulsive disorder. In P. E. Nathan & J. M. Gorman (Eds.), *A guide to treatments that work* (pp. 358–76). Oxford, England: Oxford University Press.

Rawson, H. E., & Tabb, C. L. (1993). Effects of therapeutic intervention on childhood depression. *Child and Adolescent Social Work Journal, 10,* 39–52.

Ray, O. & Ksir, C. (1995). Drugs, society and human behavior. New York: McGraw-Hill.

Raz, S. (1993). Structural cerebral pathology in schizophrenia: Regional or diffuse? *J. Abn. Psychol., 102*(3), 445–52.

Read, J. (1997). Child abuse and psychosis: A literature review and implications for professional psychology. *Profess. Psychol., 28*(5), 448–56.

Redmond, D. E., Jr. (1985). Neurochemical basis for anxiety and anxiety disorders: Evidence from drugs which decrease human fear of anxiety. In A. H. Tuma & J. D. Maser (Eds.), *Anxiety and the anxiety disorders.* Hillsdale, NJ: Erlbaum.

Rees, T. P. (1957). Back to moral treatment and community care. *J. Ment. Sci., 103,* 303–13. In H. B. Adams "Mental illness" or interpersonal behavior? *Amer. Psychologist,* 1964, 19, 191–97.

Regier, D. A., Boyd, J. H., Burke, J. D., Rae, D. S., Myers, J. K., Kramer, M., Robins, L. N., George, L. K., Karno, M., & Locke, B. Z. (1988). One-month prevalence of mental disorders in the United States. *Arch. Gen. Psychiat., 45,* 877–986.

Regier, D. A., Narrow, W. E., Rae, D. S., Manderscheid, R. W., Locke, B. Z., & Goodwin, F. K. (1993). The de facto US mental and addictive disorders service system: Epidemiologic Catchment Area prospective 1-year prevalence rates of disorders and services. *Arch. Gen. Psychiat., 50,* 85–94.

Rehm, L. P., & Tyndall, C. I. (1993). Mood disorders: Unipolar and bipolar. In P. B. Sutker & H. E. Adams (Eds.), *Comprehensive handbook of psychopathology* (2nd ed.). New York: Plenum.

Reich, J., Noyes, R., & Troughton, E. (1987). Dependent personality disorder associated with phobic avoidance in patients with panic disorder. *Amer. J. Psychiat., 144,* 323–6.

Reid, A. H. (1985). Psychiatric disorders. In A. M. Clarke, A. B. D. Clarke, & J. M. Berg (Eds.), *Mental deficiency: The changing outlook* (4th ed.). (pp. 291–325). London: Methuen.

Reid, J. B., & Eddy, J. M. (1997). The prevention of antisocial behavior: Some considerations in the search for effective interventions. In D. M. Stoff, J. Breiling, & J. D. Maser (Eds.), *Handbook of antisocial behavior.* (pp. 343–356). New York: Wiley.

Reilley, P., Clark, H., & Shopshire, M. (1994). Anger management and temper control: Critical components of post–traumatic stress disorder and substance abuse treatment. *Psychoactive Drugs, 26,* 401–07.

Reisman, J. M. (1991). *A history of clinical psychology.* New York: Hemisphere Press.

Reiss, S., & McNally, R. J. (1985). Expectancy model of fear. In S. Reiss & R. R. Bootzin (Eds.), *Theoretical issues in behavior therapy.* (pp. 107–121). San Diego, CA: Academic Press.

Reitan, R. M., & Wolfson, D. (1985). *The Halstead-Reitan Neuropsychological Test Battery: Theory and clinical interpretation.* Tuscon, AZ: Neuropsychology Press.

Rescorla, R. A., (1988). Pavlovian conditioning: It's not what you think it is. *Amer. Psychol., 43,* 151–160.

Resnick, H. S., Kilpatrick, D. G., Dansky, B. S., Saunders, B., & Best, C. L. (1993). Prevalence of civilian trauma and posttraumatic stress disorder in a representative national sample of women. *J Cons. Clin. Psychol., 61,* 984–991.

Resnick, R. J., Bottinelli, R., Puder-York, M., Harris, H. B., & O'Keffe, B. E. (1994). Basic issues in managed mental health services. In R. L. Lowman & R. J. Resnick (Eds.), *The mental health professional's guide to managed care.* Washington, DC: American Psychological Association.

Reynaud, M., Leleu, X., Bernoux, A., Meyer, L., Lery, J. F., & Ruch, C. (1997). Alcohol use disorders in French hospital patients. *Alcohol and Alcoholism, 32*(6), 749–55.

Ricciuti, H. N. (1993). Nutrition and mental development. *Curr. Dir. Psychol. Sci., 2*(2), 43–46.

Rice, M. E., & Harris, G. T. (1997). The treatment for adult offenders. In D. M. Stoff, J. Breiling, & J. D. Maser (Eds.), *Handbook of antisocial behavior.* (pp. 425–435). New York: Wiley.

Rice, M. E., Quinsey, V. L., & Harris, G. T. (1991). Sexual recidivism among child molesters released from a maximum security psychiatric institution. *J. Cons. Clin. Psychol., 59,* 381–86.

Richardson, S. A., Koller, H., & Katz, M. (1985). Relationship of upbringing to later behavior disturbance of mildly mentally retarded young people. *Amer. J. Ment. Def., 90,* 18.

Riggs, D. S., & Foa, E. B. (1993). Obsessive compulsive disorder. In D. H. Barlow (Ed.), *Clinical handbook of psychological disorders.* (pp. 189–239). New York: Guilford.

Rind, B., Tromovitch, P., & Bauserman, R. (1998). A meta-analytic examination of assumed properties of child sexual abuse using college samples. *Psychol. Bull., 124*(1), 22–53.

Ringwalt, C. L., Greene, J. M., Robertson, M., & McPheeters, M. (1998). The prevalence of homelessness among adolescents in the United States. *Amer. J. Pub. Hlth., 88*(9), 1325–29.

Rittson, B. (1995). *Community and municipal action on alcohol: European alcohol action plan.* Geneva: World Health Organization.

Ritvo, E. R., Freeman, B. J., Pingree, C., Mason-Brothers, A., Jorde, L., Jenson, W. R., McMahon, W. M., Peterson, P. B., Mo, A., & Ritvo, A. (1989). The UCLA-University of Utah epidemiologic survey of autism: Prevalence. *Amer. J. Psychiat., 146,* 194–99.

Rivera, F. P., Muellar, B. A., Somes, G., Mendoza, C. T., Rushforth, N. B., & Kellerman, A. L. (1997). Alcohol and illicit drug abuse and the risk of violent death in the home. *JAMA, 278*(7), 569–75.

Roberts, J. E., Gotlib, I. H., & Kassel, J. D. (1996). Adult attachment security and symptom of depression. The mediating told of dysfunctional attitudes and low self-esteem. *J. Pers. Soc. Psychol., 70,* 301–20.

Robins, L. N. (1978). Aetiological implications in studies of childhood histories relating to antisocial personality. In R.D. Hare & D. Schalling (Eds.), *Psychopathic behavior: Approaches to research.* (pp. 255–71). Chichester, UK: Wiley.

Robins, L. N. (1991). Conduct disorder. *J. Child Psychol. Psychiat., 32,* 193–212.

Robins, L. N., Helzer, J. E., Weissman, M. M., Orvaschel, H., Gruenberg, E., Burke, J. D., & Regier, D. (1984). Lifetime prevalence of specific psychiatric disorders in three sites. *Arch. Gen. Psych., 41,* 949–58.

Robins, L. N., & Price, R. (1991). Adult disorders predicted by childhood conduct problems: Results from the NIMH Epidemiologic Catchment Area Project. *Psychiatry, 54,* 116–32.

Robins, L. N., & Regier, D. A. (Eds.). (1991). *Psychiatric disorders in America.* New York: Free Press.

Robinson R. G., & Downhill, J. E. (1995). Lateralization of psychopathology in response to focal brain injury. In R. J. Davidson & K. Hugdahl (Eds.), *Brain asymmetry.* (pp. 693–711). Cambridge, MA: MIT Press.

Robinson, N. M., & Robinson, H. B. (1976). *The mentally retarded child* (2nd ed.). New York: McGraw-Hill.

Robinson-Whelen, S., & Kiecolt-Glaser, J. (1997). Spousal caregiving: Does it matter if you have a choice? *J. Clin. Geropsychol., 3*(4), 283–89.

Rodin, J. (1993). *Body traps.* New York: Norton.

Roeleveld, N., Zielhuis, G. A., & Gabreels, F. (1997). The prevalence of mental retardation: A critical review of recent literature. *Develop. Med. Child Neurol., 39*(2), 125–32.

Roemer, L., Molina, S., & Borkovec, T. D. (1997). An investigation of worry content among generally anxious individuals. *J. Nerv. Ment. Dis., 185*(5), 314–19.

Rogers, C. R. (1951). *Client-centered therapy.* Boston: Houghton Mifflin.

Rogers, C. R. (1959). A theory of therapy, personality, and interpersonal relationships as developed in the client-centered framework. In S. Koch (Ed.), *Psychology: A study of a science* (Vol. 3). (pp. 184–256). New York: McGraw-Hill.

Rogers, C. R. (1961). *On becoming a person: A client's view of psychotherapy.* Boston: Houghton Mifflin.

Rogers, C. R. (1966). Client-centered therapy. In S. Arieti et al. (Eds.), *American handbook of psychiatry* (Vol. 3). New York: Basic Books.

Rogers, C. R., Gendlin, G. T., Kiesler, D. J., & Truax, C. B. (1967). *The therapeutic relationship and its impact: A study of psychotherapy with schizophrenics.* Madison: University of Wisconsin Press.

Rogers, M. P. (1989). The interaction between brain, behavior, and immunity. In S. Cheren (Ed.), *Psychosomatic medicine: Theory physiology, and practice.* (pp. 279–330). Madison, CT International Universities Press.

Rogers, S. J., Bennetto, L., McEvoy, R., & Pennington, B. F. (1996). Imitation and pantomine in high-functioning adolescents with autism spectrum disorders. *Child Develop., 67*(5), 2060–73.

Rohde, P., Lewinsohn, P. M., Seeley, J. R. (1990). Are people changed by the experience of having an episode of depression? A further test of the scar hypothesis. *J. Abn. Psychol., 99,* 264–71.

Roitman, S. E. L., et al. (1997). Attentional functioning in schizotypal personality disorder. *Amer. J. Psychiat., 154*(5), 655–60.

Romach, M. K., & Sellers, E. M. (1998). Alcohol dependency: Women, biology, and pharmacotherapy. In E. F. McCance-Katz & T. R. Kosten (Eds.), *New treatments for chemical addictions.* Washington, American Psychiatric Press.

Ronningstam, E., & Gunderson, J. G. (1989). Descriptive studies on narcissistic personality disorder. *Psychiat. Clin. N. Amer., 12,* 585–601.

Roose, S. P., Galssman, A. H., Attia, E., & Woodring, R. N. (1994). Comparative efficacy of selective serotonin reupatke inhibitors and tricyclics in the treatment of melancholia. *Amer. J. Psychiat., 151*(12), 1735–39.

Rorvik, D. M. (1970, Apr. 7). Do drugs lead to violence? *Look,* 58–61.

Rosen, R. C. (1996). Erectile dysfunction: The medicalization of male sexuality. *Clin. Psychol. Rev., 16,* 497–519.

Rosen, R. C., & Leiblum, S. J. (1995). Treatment of sexual disorders in the 1990s: An integrated approach. *J. Cons. Clin. Psychol., 63,* 877–90.

Rosen, R. C., & Leiblum., S. J. (1987). Current approaches to the evaluation of sexual desire disorders. *J. Sex Res., 23,* 141–62.

Rosenbaum, G., Shore, D. L., & Chapin, K. (1988). Attention deficit and schizotypy: Marker versus symptom variables. *J. Abn. Psychol., 97,* 41–47.

Rosenbaum, J. F., Biederman, J., Pollock, R. A., & Hirshfeld, D. R. (1994). The etiology of social phobia. *J. Clin. Psychiat., 55*(6), 10–16.

Rosenberg, L. A., Brown, J., & Singer, H. S. (1995). Behavioral problems and severity of tics. *J. Clin. Psychol., 51*(6), 760–67.

Rosenthal, D. (Ed.). (1963). *The Genain quadruplets.* New York: Basic Books.

Rosenthal, D., Wender, P. H., Kety, S. S., Schulsinger, F., Welner, J., & Ostergaard, L. (1968). Schizophrenics' offspring reared in adoptive homes. In D. Rosenthal & S. S. Kety (Eds.), *The transmission of schizophrenia.* (pp. 377–92). New York: Pergamon.

Rosenthal, R. J. (1992). Pathological gambling. *Psychiat. Ann., 22,* 72–78.

Rosler, A., & Witztum, E. (1998). Treatment of men with paraphilia with a long-acting analogue of gonadotropin-releasing hormone. *New Engl. J. Med., 338,* 416–22.

Ross, C. A. (1989). *Multiple personality disorder: Diagnosis, clinical features, and treatment.* New York: Wiley.

man, & S. S. Canetton (Eds.), *Review of Suicidology, 1997.* (pp. 251–70). New York: Guilford.

Segal, Z. V., & Stermac, L. E. (1990). The role of cognition in sexual assault. In W. L. Marshall, D. R. Laws, & H. E. Barbaree (Eds.), *Handbook of sexual assault.* (pp. 161–75). New York: Plenum.

Segraves, R. T., & Althof, S. (1998) Psychotherapy and pharmacotherapy of sexual dysfunctions. In P. Nathan & J. Gorman (Eds.), *A Guide to treatments that work.* (pp. 447–71). New York: Oxford University Press.

Segraves, R. T., & Segraves, K. B. (1991). Diagnosis of female arousal disorder. *Sex. Marit. Ther., 6,* 9–13.

Seidl, F. W. (1974). Community oriented residential care: The state of the art. *Child Care Quarterly, 3*(3), 150–63.

Seligman, M. E. P. (1971). Phobias and preparedness. *Behav. Ther., 2,* 307–20.

Seligman, M. E. P. (1974). Depression and learned helplessness. In R. J. Friedman & M. M. Katz (Eds.), *The psychology of depression: Contemporary theory and research.* Washington, DC: Hemisphere.

Seligman, M. E. P. (1975). *Helplessness: On depression, development, and death.* San Francisco: Freeman.

Seligman, M. E. P. (1990). Why is there so much depression today? The waxing of the individual and the waning of the commons. In R. E. Ingram (Ed.), *Contemporary psychological approaches to depression.* New York: Plenum.

Seligman, M. E. P. (1995). The effectiveness of psychotherapy: The Consumer Reports study. *Amer. Psychol., 50,* 965–74.

Seligman, M. E. P. (1998). Afterword—A plea. In P. E. Nathan & J. M. Gorman (Eds.), *A guide to treatments that work* (pp. 568–71). New York: Oxford University Press.

Seligman, M. E. P., & Binik, Y. (1977). The safety signal hypothesis. In H. Davis & H. M. B. Hurwitz (Eds.), *Operant-Pavlovian interactions.* (pp. 165–88). Hillsdale, NJ: Erlbaum.

Sell, R. L., Wypij, D., & Wells, J. A. (1995). The prevalence of homosexual behavior and attraction in the United States, the United Kingdom, and France: Results of national population-based samples. *Arch. Sex. Behav., 24,* 235–48.

Selye, H. (1956). *The stress of life.* New York: McGraw-Hill.

Selye, H. (1976a). *Stress in health and disease.* Woburn, MA: Butterworth.

Selye, H. (1976b). *The stress of life* (2nd ed.). New York: McGraw-Hill.

Seppa, N. (1998). Amyloid can trigger brain damage. *Sci. News, 154*(July 4), 4.

Serrano, A. C., Zuelzer, M. B., Howe, D. D., & Reposa, R. E. (1979). Ecology of abusive and nonabusive families, *J. Amer. Acad. Child Psychiat., 18,* 167–75.

Seto, M. C., & Barbaree, H. E. (1995). The role of alcohol in sexual aggression. *Clin. Pscyhol. Rev., 15*(6), 545–66.

Sewell, D. W., Jeste, D. V., Atkinson, J. H., Heaton, R. K., Hesselink, J. R., Wiley, C., Thal, L., Chandler, J. L., & Grant, I. (1994). HIV-associated psychosis: A study of 20 cases. *Amer. J. Psychiat., 151*(2), 237–42.

Shadish, W. R., Montgomery, L. M., Wilson, P., Wilson, M. R., Bright, I., & Okwumabua, T. (1993). Effects of family and marital psychotherapies: A metaanalysis. *J. Cons. Clin. Psychol., 61*(6), 992–1002.

Shadish, W. R., et al. (1997). Evidence that therapy works in clinically representative conditions. *J. Cons. Clin. Psychol., 65*(3), 355–65.

Shaley, A. Y., Bonne, O., & Eth, S. (1996). Treatment of posttraumatic stress disorder: A review. *Psychosom. Med., 58,* 165–82.

Shapiro, A. K., & Morris, L. A. (1978). The placebo effect in medical and psychological therapies. In S. L. Garfield & A. E. Bergin (Eds.), *Handbook of psychotherapy and behavior change* (2nd ed.). (pp. 369–410). New York: Wiley.

Shapiro, F. (1996). Eye movement desensitization and reprocessing (EMDR): Evaluation of controlled PTSD research. *J. Behav. Ther. Exper. Psychiat., 27,* 209–18.

Sharkey, J. (1997, Sept. 28). You're not bad, you're sick. It's in the book. *New York Times,* pp. 1, 5.

Shaw, W. S., et al. (1997). Longitudinal analysis of multiple indicators of health decline among spousal caregivers. *Ann. Behav. Med., 19*(2), 101–109.

Shea, M. T. (1995). Interrelationships among categories of personality disorders. In W. J. Livesley (Ed.), *The DSM-IV personality disorders.* (pp. 397–406). New York: Guilford.

Shedler, J., Mayman, M., & Manis, M. (1993). The *illusion* of mental health. *Amer. Psychol., 48*(11), 1117–31.

Sheehan, D. Z. (1982). Panic attacks and phobias. *New Engl. J. Med., 307,* 156–8.

Sheehan, D. Z. (1983). *The anxiety disease.* New York: Bantum Books.

Sheitman, B. B., Kinon, B. J., Ridgway, B. A., Lieberman, J. A. (1998). Pharmacological treatments of schizophrenia. In P. E. Nathan & J. M. Gorman (Eds.), *A guide to treatments that work.* (pp. 167–89). Oxford, England: Oxford University Press.

Shelby, J. S., & Tredinnick, M. G. (1995). Crisis intervention with survivors of natural disaster: Lessons from Hurricane Andrew. *Journal of Counseling and Development, 73*(5), 491

Shelton, R. C., Hollon, S. D., Purdon, S. E., Loosen, P. T. (1991). Biological and psychological aspects of depression. *Behav. Ther., 22,* 201–28.

Shepher, J. (1971). Mate selection among second generation kibbutz adolescents and adults. *Arch. Sex. Behav., 1,* 293–307.

Shepherd, J., & Brickley, M. (1996). The relationship between alcohol intoxication, stressors, and injury in urban violence. *British Journal of Criminology, 36*(4), 546–66.

Sher, K. J., Frost, R. O., & Otis, R. (1983). Cognitive deficits in compulsive checkers: An exploratory study. *Behav. Res. Ther., 21,* 357–64.

Sher, K. J., Frost, R. O., Kushner, M., Crews, T. M., & Alexander, J. E. (1989). Memory deficits in compulsive checkers: A replication and extension in a clinical example. *Behav. Res. Ther., 27,* 65–69.

Sher, K. J., & Trull, T. J. (1994) Personality and disinhibitory psychopathology: Alcoholism and antisocial personality disorder. *J. Abn. Psychol., 103,* 92–102.

Sher, K. J., Wood, M. D., Wood, P. D., & Raskin, G. (1996). Alcohol outcome expectancies and alcohol use: A latent variable cross–lagged panel study. *J. Abn. Psychol., 105*(4), 561–74.

Sherwin, B. B. (1988). A comparative analysis of the role of androgen in human male and female sexual behavior: Behavioral specificity, critical thresholds, and sensitivity. Special Issue: Sexual differentiation and gender-related behaviors. *Psychobiology, 16,* 416–25.

Sherwin, I., & Geschwind, N. (1978). Neural substrates of behavior. In A. M. Nicholi (Ed.), *The Harvard guide to modern psychiatry.* (pp. 59–80). Cambridge, MA: Harvard University Press.

Sheung-Tak, C. (1996) A critical review of Chinese koro. *Cult., Med. Psychiat., 20,* 67–82.

Short, C. (1997). The myth of community care: A historical review for people with mental handicap. *Italian Journal of Intellective Impairment, 9*(2), 219–29.

Short, K. H., & Johnston, C. (1997). Stress, maternal distress, and children's adjustment following immigration: The buffering role of social support. *J. Cons. Clin. Pscyhol., 65*(3), 494–503.

Short, R. H., & Hess, G. C. (1995). Fetal alcohol syndrome: Characteristics and remedial implications. *Developmental Disabilities Bulletin, 23*(1), 12–29.

Siegel, B. (1996). *The world of the autistic child.* New York: Oxford University Press.

Siegel, B. S. (1986). *Love, medicine, and miracles.* New York: Harper and Row.

Siegel, R. K. (1984). Hostage hallucinations: Visual imagery induced by isolation and life-threatening stress. *J. Nerv. Ment. Dis., 172*(5), 264–72.

Siegelman, M. (1979). Adjustment of homosexual and heterosexual women: A cross-national replication. *Arch. Sex. Behav., 8,* 121–26.

Siever, L. J. (1985). Biological markers in schizotypal personality disorder. *Schizo. Bull., 11,* 564–75.

Siever, L. J., Bernstein, D. P., & Silverman, J. M. (1995). Schizotypal personality disorder. In W. J. Livesley (Ed.), *The DSM-IV personality disorders.* (pp. 71–90). New York: Guilford.

Siever, L. J., & Davis, K. L. (1991). A psychobiological perspective on the personality disorders. *Amer. J. Psychiat., 148,* 1647–58.

Sigal J. J., Silver, D., Rakoff, V., & Ellin, B. (1973, Apr.). Some second-generation effects of survival of the Nazi persecution. *Amer. J. Orthopsychiat., 43*(3), 320–27.

Sigel, G. S., & Kane, R. J. (1997). Violence prediction reconsidered. *The Forensic Examiner, 6*(11–12), 21–4.

Sigman, M. (1996). Behavioral research in childhood autism. In M. F. Lenzenweger & J. L. Haugaard (Eds.), *Frontiers of developmental psychopathology.* (pp. 190–208). New York: Oxford University Press.

Sigvardsson, S., Von Knorring, A. L., Bohman, M., & Cloninger, C. R. (1984). An adoption study of somatoform disorders: I. The relationship of somatization to psychiatric disability. *Arch. Gen. Psych., 41,* 853–59.

Silberman, E. K., et al. (1985). Dissociative states in multiple personality disorder: A quantitative study. *Psychiatr. Res., 15,* 253–260.

Silk, K. R., Eisner, W., Allport, C., DeMars, C., Miller, C., Justice, R. W., & Lewis, M. (1994). Focused time-limited inpatient treatment of borderline personality disorder. *J. Person. Dis., 8*(4), 268–278.

Silver, E. (1995). Punishment or treatment? Comparing the lengths of confinement of successful and unsuccessful insanity defendants. *Law and Human Behavior, 19*(4), 375–88.

Silverman, K., Higgins, S. T., Brooner, R. K., & Montoya, I. D. (1996). Sustained cocaine abstinence in methadone maintenance patients through voucher-based reinforcement therapy. *Arch. Gen. Psychiat., 53*(3), 409–15.

Silverman, M. M. (1997). Current controversies in suicidology. In R. W. Maris, M. M. Silverman, &

S. S. Canetton (Eds.), *Review of Suicidology, 1997.* (pp. 1–21). New York: Guilford.

Silverman, P. R., & Klass, D. (1996). Introduction: What's the problem? In D. Klass, P. R. Silverman, & S. L. Nickman (Eds.), *Continuing bonds: New understandings of grief.* (pp. 3–27). Washington: Taylor & Francis.

Silverman, W. H., & Silverman, M. M. (1987). Comparison of key informants, parents, and teenagers for planning adolescent substance abuse prevention programs. *Psychology of Addictive Behaviors, 1*(1), 30–37.

Silverstein, A. B., Legutki, G., Friedman, S. L., & Takayama, D. L. (1982). Performance of Down's syndrome individuals on the Stanford-Binet Intelligence Scale. *Amer. J. Ment. Def., 86,* 548–5.

Silverton, L., Finello, K. M., Schulsinger, F., & Mednick, S. A. (1985). Low birth weight and ventricular enlargement in a high-risk sample. *J. Abn. Psychol., 94,* 405–9

Simeon, D., et al. (1997). Feeling unreal: 30 cases of DSM-III-R depersonalization disorder. *Amer. J. Psychiat., 154*(8), 1107–1113.

Simeon, D., Hollander, E., Stein, D., Cohen, L., et al. (1995). Body dysmorphic disorders in the DSM-IV field trial for obsessive compulsive disorder. *Amer. J. Psychiat., 152,* 1207–1209.

Simmons, D., Goode, S., & Fombonne, E. (1997). Elective mutism and chromosome 18 abnormality. *Eur. Child Adoles. Psychiat., 6*(2), 112–14.

Simon, R. J., & Aaronson, D. E. (1988). *The insanity defense.* New York: Praeger.

Simons, A. D., Angell, K. L., Monroe, S. M., & Thase, M. E. (1993). Cognition and life stress in depression: Cognitive factors and the definition, rating, and generation of negative life events. *J. Abn. Psychol., 102,* 584–91.

Simons, R. C., & Hughes, C. C. (Eds). (1985). *The culture bound syndromes.* Boston: Reidel.

Singer, J. E. (1980). Traditions of stress research: Integrative comments. In I. G. Sarason & C. D. Spielberger (Eds.), *Stress and anxiety* (Vol. 7). (pp. 3–10). Washington, DC: Hemisphere.

Singer, M., & Wynne, L. C. (1963). Differentiating characteristics of the parents of childhood schizophrenics, childhood neurotics and young adult schizophrenics. *Amer. J. Psychiat., 120,* 234–43.

Singer, M., & Wynne, L. C. (1965a). Thought disorder and family relations of schizophrenics. III. Methodology using projective techniques. *Arch. Gen. Psychiat., 12,* 182–200.

Singer, M., & Wynne, L. C. (1965b). Thought disorder and family relations of schizophrenics. IV. Results and implications. *Arch. Gen. Psychiat., 12,* 201–12.

Singer, M. T., Wynne, L. C., & Toohey, M. L. (1978). Communication disorders and the families of schizophrenics. In L. C. Wynne, R. L. Cromwell, & S. Matthysse (Eds.), *The nature of schizophrenia: New approaches to research and treatment.* (pp. 499–511). New York: Wiley.

Skinner, B. F. (1990). Can psychology be a science of mind? *Amer. Psychol. 45,* 1206–10.

Skodol, A. E., et al. (1993). Comorbidity of DSM-III-R eating disorders and personality disorders. *Int. J. Eat. Dis., 14,* 403–416.

Skodol, A. E., Oldham, J. M., Hyler, S. E., Stein, D. J. (1995). Patterns of anxiety and personality disorder comorbidity. *J. Psychiat. Res., 29*(5), 361–74.

Skodol, A. E., Rosnick, L., Kellman, H. D., Oldham, J. M., & Hyler, S. E. (1991). Development of a procedure for validating structured assessments of Axis II. In J. Oldham (Ed.), *Personality disorders: New perspectives on diagnostic validity.* Washington DC: American Psychiatric Press.

Slater, E., & Meyer, A. (1959). Contributions to a pathology of the musicians: Robert Schumann. *Confina Psychiatrica, 2,* 65–94.

Sloman, L. (1991). Use of medication in pervasive developmental disorders. *Psychiat. Clin. N. Amer. 14,* 165–82.

Sloper, P., Turner, S., Knussen, C., & Cunningham, C. C. (1990). Social life of school children with Down's syndrome. *Child: Care, Health, and Development, 16,* 235–51.

Slovenko, R. (1994). Legal aspects of post-traumatic disorder. *Psychiat. Clin. N. Amer., 17,* 439–46.

Slutsky, W. S., Heath, A. C., Dinwiddie, S. H., Madden, P. A., & Bucholz, K. K. (1998). Common genetic risk factors for conduct disorder and alcohol dependence. *J. Abn. Psychol., 107*(3), 363–74.

Slutsky, W., Heath, A. C., Dunne, M. P., Statham, D. J., Dinwiddie, S. H., Madden, P. A. F., Martin, N. G., & Bucholz, K. K. (1997). Modeling genetic and environmental influences in the etiology of conduct disorder: A study of 2,682 adult twin pairs. *J. Abn. Psychol., 100*(2), 266–79.

Smalley, S. L. (1991). Genetic influences in autism. *Psychiat. Clin. N. Amer., 14,* 125–39.

Smith G., & Smith, D. (1985). A mainstreaming program that really works. *J. Learn. Dis., 18,* 369–72.

Smith, I. M. & Bryson, S. (1994). Imitation and action in autism: A critical review. *Psychol. Bull., 116*(2), 259–73.

Smith, M. L., Glass, G. V., & Miller, T. I. (1980). *The benefits of psychotherapy.* Baltimore: Johns Hopkins University Press.

Smith, W. (1989). *A profile of health and disease in America.* New York: Facts on File.

Smithyan, S. D. (1978). *The undetected rapist.* Ph.D. Dissertation, Claremont Graduate School. University Microfilms International: Ann Arbor, MI.

Smyth, J. M. (1998). Written emotional expression: Effect sizes, outcome types, and moderating variables. *J. Cons. Clin. Psychol., 66*(1), 174–84.

Snowden, K. R., & Cheung, F. K. (1990). Use of inpatient mental health services by members of ethnic minority groups. *Amer. Psychol., 45,* 347–55.

Snyder, D. K., & Wills, R. M. (1989). Behavioral versus insight-oriented marital therapy: Effects on individual and interspousal functioning. *J. Cons. Clin. Psychol. 57,* 39–46.

Sobell, M. B., & Sobell, L. C. (1995). Controlled drinking after 25 years: How important was the great debate? *Addiction, 90*(9), 1149–53.

Sokol, M. S., & Pfeffer, C. R. (1992). Suicidal behavior of children. In B. Bongar (Ed.), *Suicide: Guidelines for assessment, management and treatment.* New York: Oxford University Press.

Soloff, P. H., Cornelius, J., George, A. (1991). The depressed borderline: One disorder or two? *Psychopharma. Bull., 27,* 23–30.

Soloff, P. H., Lis, J. A., Kelly, T., Cornelius, J., & Ulrich, R. (1994). Risk factors for suicidal behavior in borderline personality disorder. *Amer. J. Psychiat., 151*(9), 1316–23.

Solomon, Z., & Kleinhauz, M. (1996). War-induced psychic trauma: An 18-year follow-up of Israeli veterans. *Amer. J. Orthopsychiat., 66*(1), 152–60.

Sommers-Flannagan, J., & Sommers-Flannagan, R. (1996). Efficacy of antidepressant medication with depressed youth: What psychologists should know. *Profess. Psychol., 27*(2), 145–53.

Sonnenberg, S. M. (1988). Victims of violence and post-traumatic stress disorder. *Psychiat. Clin. N. Amer., 11,* 581–90.

Southwick, S. M., Yehuda, R., & Charney, D. S. (1997). Neurobiological alterations in PTSD: Review of the clinical literature. In *Posttraumatic stress disorder.* (pp. 241–66). Washington: American Psychiatric Press.

Southwick, S. M., Yehuda, R., & Morgan, C. A. (1995). Clinical studies of neurotransmitter alterations in post-traumatic stress disorder. In M. Friedman & D. S. Charney, et al. (Eds.), *Neurobiological and clinical consequences of stress: From normal adaptation to post-traumatic stress disorder.* (pp. 335–49). Philadelphia: Lippincott-Raven.

Spanos, N. P. (1996). *Multiple identies and false memories: A sociocognitive perspective.* Washington, DC: American Psychological Association.

Spanos, N., & Burgess, C. (1994). Hypnosis and multiple personality disorder: A sociocognitive perspective. In S. J. Lynn & J. W. Rhue (Eds.), *Dissociation: Clinical and theoretical perspectives.* (pp. 136–58). New York: Guilford.

Speer, D. C. (1992). Clinically significant change: Jacobson and Truax (1991) revisited. *J. Cons. Clin. Psychol., 60*(3), 402–08.

Speier, P. L., Sherak, D. L., Hirsch, S., & Cantwell, D. P. (1995). Depression in children and adolescents. In E. E. Beckham & W. R. Leber (Eds.), *Handbook of depression* (2nd ed.). (pp. 467–493). New York: Guilford.

Sperling, E. (1997a). The collateral treatment of parents with children and adolescents in psychotherapy. *Child Adoles. Psychiatr. Clin. N. Amer., 6*(1), 81–95.

Sperling, E. (1997b). The role of play in child psychotherapy. *Child Adoles. Psychiat. Clin. N. Amer., 6*(1), 68–79.

Spiegel, D. (1991). A psychosocial intervention and survival time of patients with metastatic breast cancer. *Advances, 7*(3), 10–19.

Spielberger, C. D., Johnson, E. H., Russell, S. F., Crane, R. J., & Worden, T. J. (1985). The experience and expression of anger. In M. A. Chesney & R. H. Rosenman (Eds.), *Anger and hostility in cardiovascular and behavioral disorders.* New York: Hemisphere.

Spiess, W. F. J., Geer, J. H., & O'Donohue, W. T. (1984). Premature ejaculation: Investigation of factors in ejaculatory latency. *J. Abn. Psychol., 93,* 242–45.

Spitzer, R. L., Gibbon, M., Skodol, A. E., Williams, J. B. W., & First, M. B. (1989). *DSM-III-R casebook.* Washington, DC: American Psychiatric Press.

Spitzer, R. L., Gibbon, M., Skodol, A. E., Williams, J. B. W., & First, M. B. (Ed.). (1994). *DSM-IV casebook* (4th ed.). Washington: American Psychiatric Press.

Spitzer, R. L., Skodol, A. E., Gibbon, M., & Williams, J. B. W. (1981). *DSM-III casebook.* Washington, DC: American Psychiatric Association.

Spitzer, R. L., Skodol, A. E., Gibbon, M., & Williams, J. B. W. (1983). *Psychopathology: A casebook.* New York: McGraw-Hill.

Sponheim, B. (1996). Changing criteria for autistic disorders: A comparison of the ICD-10 research criteria and DSM-IV with DSM-IIIR, CARS, and ABC. *J. Autism Devel. Dis., 26*(5), 513–25.

Spoont, M. R. (1992). Modulatory role of serotonin in neural information processing: Implications for human psychopathology. *Psychol. Bull., 112*(2), 330–50.

Spreen, O., & Strauss, E. (1998). *A compendium of neuropsychological tests.* New York: Oxford University Press.

Spunt, B., Goldstein, P., Brownstein, H., & Fendrich, M. (1994). The role of marijuana in homicide. *Inter. J. Addict., 29,* 195–213.

Squires-Wheeler, E., Friedman, D., Amminger, G. P., Skodol, A., Looser-Ott, S., Roberts, S., Pape, S., & Erlenmeyer-Kimling, L. (1997). Negative and positive dimensions of schizotypal personality disorder. *J. Personal. Dis., 11*(3), 285–300.

Stafford, S. H., & Green, V. P. (1993). Facilitating preschool mainstreaming: Classroom strategies and teacher attitude. *Early Child Development & Care, 91,* 93–98.

Staley, D., Wand, R., & Shady, G. (1997). Tourette Disorder: A cross-cultural review. *Compr. Psychiat., 38*(1), 6–16.

Stanton, M. D., & Todd, T. C. (1976, June). *Structural family therapy with heroin addicts: Some outcome data.* Paper presented at the Society for Psychotherapy Research. San Diego.

Starck, L. C., Branna, S. K., & Tallen, B. J. (1994). Mesoridazine use and priapism. *Amer. J. Psychiat., 151,* 946.

Stare, F. J., Whelan, E. M., & Sheridan, M. (1980). Diet and hyperactivity: Is there a relationship? *Pediatrics, 6*(4), 521–25.

Stattin, H., & Klackenberg-Larsson, I. (1993). Early language and intelligence development and their relationship to future criminal behavior. *J. Abn. Psychol., 102*(3), 369–78.

Steadman, H. J., McGreevy, M. A., Morrissey, J. P., Callahan, L. A., Robbins, P. C., & Cirincione, C. (1993). *Before and after Hinckley: Evaluating insanity defense reform.* New York: Guilford.

Steadman, H. J., Mulvey, E. P., Monahan, J., Robbins, P. C., Appelbaum, P. S., Grisso, T., Roth, L. H., & Silver, E. (1998). Violence by people discharged from acute psychiatric inpatient facilities and by others in the same neighborhoods. *Arch. Gen. Psychiat., 55,* 393–401.

Steele, R. G., & Forehand, R. (1997). The role of family processes and coping strategies in the relationship between parental chronic illness and childhood internalizing problems. *J. Abnorm. Child Psychol., 25,* 83–94.

Steer, R. A., Clark, D., Beck, A. T., & Ranieri, W. F. (1995). Common and specific dimensions of self-reported anxiety and depression: A replication. *J. Abn. Psychol., 104*(3), 542–45.

Stein, J. (1970). *Neurosis in contemporary society: Process and treatment.* Belmont, CA: Brooks/Cole.

Steinhausen, H. C., & Adamek, R. (1997). The family history of children with elective mutism: A research report. *Eur. Child Adoles. Psychiat., 6*(2), 107–11.

Steinhausen, H. C., & Juzi, C. (1996). Elective mutism: An analysis of 100 cases. *J. Amer. Acad. Child Adoles. Psychiat., 35*(5), 606–14.

Steketee, G. S. (1993). *Treatment of obsessive-compulsive disorder.* New York: Guilford.

Stelmack, R. M., Houlihan, M., & McGarry-Roberts, P. A. (1993). Personality, reaction time, and event-related potentials. *J. Pers. Soc. Psychol., 65*(2), 399–409.

Stene, J., Stene, E., Stengel-Rutkowski, S., & Murken, J. D. (1981). Paternal age and Down's syndrome, data from prenatal diagnoses (DFG). *Human Genet., 59,* 119–24.

Stephens, R. S., Roffman, R. A., & Simpson, E. E. (1994). Treating adult marijuana dependence: A test of the relapse prevention model. *J. Cons. Clin. Psychol., 62,* 92–99.

Stermac, L., Hall, K., & Henskens, M. (1989). Violence among child molesters. *J. Sex Res., 26,* 450–59.

Stermac, L. E., Segal, Z. V., & Gillis, R. (1990). Social and cultural factors in sexual assault. In W. L. Marshall, D. R. Laws, & H. E. Barbaree (Eds.), *Handbook of sexual assault.* (pp. 143–60). New York: Plenum.

Stern, D. B. (1977). Handedness and the lateral distribution of conversion reactions. *J. Nerv. Ment. Dis., 164,* 122–28.

Stern, E. & Silbersweig, D. A. (1998). Neural mechanisms underlying hallucinations in schizophernia: Theole of abnormal fronto-temporal interactions. In M. F. Lenzenweger & R. H. Dworkin (Eds.), *Origins and development of schizophrenia: Advances in experimental psychopathology.* (pp. 235–46). Washington, DC: American Psychologocial Association.

Stevens, J. R. (1997). Anatomy of schizophrenia revisited. *Schizo. Bull., 23*(3), 373–373.

Stevens, J. R., & Hallick, L. M. (1992). Viruses and schizophrenia. In S. Specter, M. Bendinelli, & H. Friedman (Eds.), *Viruses and immunity.* (pp. 303–16). New York: Plenum.

Stewart, J. B., Hardin, S. B., Weinrich, S., & McGeorge, S. (1992). Group protocol to mitigate disaster stress and enhance social support in adolescents exposed to Hurricane Hugo. *Issues in Mental Health Nursing, 13,* 105–19.

Stewart, S. H., Finn, P. R., & Pihl, R. O. (1990, Mar.). *The effects of alcohol on the cardiovascular stress response in men at high risk for alcoholism: A dose response study.* Paper presented at the annual meeting of the Canadian Psychological Association, Ottawa.

Stice, E., Killen, J. D., Hayward, C., & Taylor, C. B. (1998). Support for the continuity hypothesis of bulimic pathology. *J. Cons. Clin. Psychol., 66*(5), 784–790.

Stokes, P. E., & Sikes, C. R. (1987). Hypothalamic-pituitary-adrenal axis in affective disorders. In H. Y. Meltzer (Ed.), *Psychopharmacology: A third generation of progress.* (pp. 589–607). New York: Raven Press.

Stone, G. C., Weiss, S. M., Matarazzo, J. D., Miller, N. E., Rodin, J., Belar, C. D., Follick, M. J., & Singer, J. E. (Eds.), (1987). *Health psychology: A discipline and a profession.* Chicago: University of Chicago Press.

Storandt, M., & Vanden Bos, G. (1994). *Neuropsychological assessment of dementia and depression in older adults.* Washington: American Psychological Association.

Strakowski, S. M. (1994). Diagnostic validity of schizophreniform disorder. *Amer. J. Psychiat., 151*(6), 815–24.

Strange, R. E., & Brown, D. E., Jr. (1970). Home from the wars. *Amer. J. Psychiat., 127*(4), 488–92.

Strauman, T. J., Lemieux, A. M., & Coe, C. L. (1993). Self-discrepancy and natural killer cell activity: Immunological consequences of negative self-evaluation. *J. Pers. Soc. Psychol., 64*(6), 1042–52.

Strean, H. S. (1985). *Resolving resistances in psychotherapy.* New York: Wiley Interscience.

Streiner, D. L., & Norman, G. R. (1995). *Health measurement scales.* New York: Oxford University Press.

Strober, M. (1995). Family-genetic perspectives on anorexia nervosa and bulimia nervosa. In C. G. Fairburn & K. Brownell (Eds.), *Comprehensive textbook of eating disorders and obesity.* (pp. 212–218). New York: Guilford.

Strober, M. (1997). Consultation and therapeutic engagement in severe anorexia nervosa. In D. M. Garner & P. E. Garfinkel (Eds.), *Handbook of treatment for eating disorders.* (pp. 229–247). New York: Guilford.

Stroebe, M. S., & Stroebe, W. (1983). Who suffers more? Sex differences in health risks of the widowed. *Psychol. Bull., 93*(2), 279–301.

Sturmey, P., & Sevin, J. (1993). Dual diagnosis: An annotated bibliography of recent research. *J. Intell. Dis. Res., 37*(5), 437–48.

Sturt, E. (1986). Application of survival analysis to the inception of dementia. *Psychol. Med., 16,* 583–93.

Stuss, D. T., Gow, C. A., & Hetherington, C. R. (1992). "No longer Gage": Frontal lobe dysfunction and emotional changes. *J. Cons. Clin. Psychol., 60*(3), 349–59.

Sue, S., Fujino, D. C., Hu, L., Takeuchi, D. T., & Zane, N. W. S. (1991) Community mental health services for ethnic minority groups: A test of the cultural responsiveness hypothesis. *J. Cons. Clin. Psychol., 59,* 533–40.

Sue, S., Zane, N., & Young, K. (1994). Research on psychotherapy with culturally diverse populations. In A. E. Bergin & S. L. Garfield (Eds.), *Handbook of psychotherapy and behavior change.* (pp. 783–820) New York: Wiley.

Sulkunen, P. (1976). Drinking patterns and the level of alcohol consumption: An international overview. In R. I. Gibbons et al. (Eds.), *Research advances in alcohol and drug problems* (Vol. 3). New York: Wiley.

Sullivan, H. S. (1953). In H. S. Perry & M. L. Gawel (Eds.), *The interpersonal theory of psychiatry.* New York: Norton.

Sullivan, P. F. (1995). Mortality in anorexia nervosa. *Amer. J. Psychiat., 152,* 1073–1074.

Sultzer, D. L., Levin, H. S., Mahler, M. E., High, W. M., & Cummings, J. L. (1993). A comparison of psychiatric symptoms in vascular dementia and Alzheimer's disease. *Amer. J. Psychiat., 150*(12), 1806–12.

Summerfelt, L., Huta, V., & Swinson, R. (1998). In R. Swinson, M. Antony, S. Rachman, & M. Richter (Eds.), *Obsessive-compulsive disorder: Theory, research, and treatment.* (pp. 79–119). New York: Guilford.

Surwit, R. S., Shapiro, D., & Good, M. L. (1978). Comparison of cardiovascular biofeedback, neuromuscular biofeedback, and meditation in the treatment of borderline essential hypertension. *J. Cons. Clin. Psychol., 46,* 252–53.

Susser, E., Moore, R., & Link, B. (1993). Risk factors for homelessness. *Amer. J. Epidemiol., 15,* 546–66.

Sutker, P. B. & Allain, A. N. (1995). Psychological assessment of aviators captured in World War II. *Psychol. Assess., 7,* 66–68.

Sutker, P. B., Allain, A. N., Johnson, J. J., & Butters, N. M. (1992). Memory and learning performances in POW survivors with history of malnutrition and combat veteran controls. *Archives of Clinical Neuropsychology, 7,* 431–44.

Sutker, P. B., Galina, H., & West, J. A. (1990). Trauma-induced weight loss and cognitive deficits among former prisoners of war. *J. Cons. Clin. Psychol., 58,* 323–28.

Sverd, J., Sheth, R., Fuss, J., & Levine, J. (1995). Prevalence of pervasive developmental disorder in a sample of psychiatrically hospitalized children and adolescents. *Child Psychiat. Human Devel., 25*(4), 221–40.

Swadi, H., & Zeitlin, H. (1988). Peer influence and adolescent substance abuse: A promising side? *Brit. J. Addiction, 83*(2), 153–57.

Swain, R. A., Armstrong, K. E., Comery, T. A., Humphreys, A. G., Jones, T. A., Klein, J. A., & Greenough, W. T. (1995). Speculations on the fidelity of memories stored in synaptic connections. In D. Schactern (Ed.), *Memory distortions: How minds, brains, and societies reconstruct the past* (pp. 274–297). Cambridge: Harvard University Press.

Swendsen, J., Hammen, C., Heller, T., Gitlin, M. (1995). Correlates of stress reactivity in patients with bipolar disorder. *Amer. J. Psychiat., 152*(5), 795–97.

Swenson, C. C., Powell, P., Foster, K. Y., & Saylor, C. E. (1991). *The long-term reactions of young children to natural disaster.* Paper presented at the annual convention of the American Psychological Association, San Francisco.

Switzky, H. N. (1997). Mental retardation and the neglected construct of motivation. *Education & Training in Mental Retardation & Developmental Disabilities, 32*(3), 194–200.

Szapocznik, J., Perez-Vidal, A., Brickman, A. L., Foote, F. H., Santisteban, D., Hervis, O., & Kurtines, W. M. (1988). Engaging adolescent drug abusers and their families in treatment: A strategic structural systems approach. *J. Cons. Clin. Psychol., 56,* 552–57.

Szasz, T. (1974). *The myth of mental illness* (rev. ed.). (pp. 17–80). New York: Harper & Row.

Tacke, U. (1990). Fluoxetine: An alternative to the tricyclics in the treatment of major depression. *Amer. J. Med. Sci., 298,* 126–29.

Takei, N., et al. (1997). Prenatal exposure to influenza and increased cerebrospinal fluid spaces in schizophrenia. *Schizo. Bull., 22*(3), 521–34.

Takeshita, T. K., Morimoto, X., Mao, Q., Hashimoto, T., & Furyuama, J. (1993). Phenotypic differences in low Km Aldehyde de hydrogenase in Japanese workers. *Lancet, 341,* 837–38.

Talamini, J. T. (1982). *Boys will be girls: The hidden world of the heterosexual male transvestite.* Washington, DC: University Press of America.

Talley, P. F., Strupp, H. H., & Morey, L. C. (1990). Matchmaking in psychotherapy: Patient-therapist dimensions and their impact on outcome. *J. Cons. Clin. Psychol., 58,* 182–88.

Tardiff, K. (1998). Unusual diagnoses among violent patients. *Psychiat. Clin. N. Amer., 21*(3), 567–76.

Tardiff, K., Marzuk, P. M., Leon, A. C., Hirsch, C. S., Stajic, M., Portera, L., & Hartwell, N. (1994). Homicide in New York City: Cocaine use and firearms. *JAMA, 272,* 43–46.

Tarjan, G., & Eisenberg, L. (1972). Some thought on the classification of mental retardation in the United States of America. *Amer. J. Psychiat., Suppl., 128*(11), 14–18.

Tarrier, M., & Barrowclough, C. (1990) Family interventions for schizophrenia. *Behav. Mod., 14,* 408–40.

Tasto, D. L., & Hinkle, J. E. (1973). Muscle relaxation treatment for tension headaches. *Behav. Res. Ther., 11,* 347–50.

Tatem, D. W., & DelCampo, R. L. (1995). Selective mutism in children: A structural family therapy approach to treatment. *Contemporary Family Therapy: An International Journal, 17*(2), 177–94.

Tavel, M. E. (1962). A new look at an old syndrome: Delirium tremens. *Arch. Int. Med., 109,* 129–34.

Taylor, C., & Meux, C. (1997). Individual cases: The risk, the challenge. *Int. Rev. Psychiat., 9*(2), 285–302.

Taylor, H. G., & Alden, J. (1997). Age-related differences in outcomes following childhood brain insults: An introduction and overview. *J. Int. Neuropsychologic. Soc., 3*(6), 555–67.

Taylor, S. (1995). Anxiety sensitivity: Theoretical perspectives and recent findings. *Behav. Res. Ther., 33*(3), 243–58.

Taylor, S. E., & Brown, J. (1988). Illusion and well-being: A social psychological perspective on mental health. *Psychol. Bull., 103,* 193–210.

Teasdale, J. (1988). Cognitive vulnerability to persistent depression. *Cognition and Emotion, 2,* 247–74.

Teasdale, J. D. (1996). Clinically relevant therapy: Integrating clinical insight with cognitive science. In P. M. Salkovskis (Ed.), *Frontiers of cognitive therapy.* (pp. 26–47). New York: Guilford.

Teicher, M. H., Glod, C. A., Magnus, E., Harper, D., Benson, G., Krueger, K., & McGreenery, C. E. (1997). Circadian rest-activity disturbances in seasonal affective disorder. *Arch. Gen. Psychiat., 54,* 124–30.

Telch, C. F., & Stice, E. (1998). Psychiatric comorbidity in women with binge eating disorder: Prevalence rates from a non-treatment-seeking sample. *J. Cons. Clin. Psychol., 66*(5), 768–776.

Telch, M. (1995, July). *Singular and combined efficacy of in vivo exposure and CBT in the treatment of panic disorder with agoraphobia.* Paper presented at the World Congress of Behavioural and Cognitive Therapies, Copenhagen, Denmark.

Telch, M. J. (1981). The present status of outcome studies: A reply to Frank. *J. Cons. Clin. Psychol., 49*(3), 472–75.

Telch, M. J., Schmidt, N. B., LaNae Jaimez, T., Jacquin, K. M., & Harrington, P. J. (1995). Impact of cognitive-behavioral treatment on quality of life in panic disorder patients. *J. Cons. Clin. Psychol., 63*(5), 823–30.

Tellegen, A. (1985). Structures of mood and personality and their relevance to assessing anxiety, with an emphasis on self-report. In A. H. Tuma & J. Maser (Eds.), *Anxiety and the anxiety disorders.* Hillsdale, NJ: Erlbaum.

Teri, L., et al. (1997). Behavioral treatment of depression in dementia patients: A controlled clinical trial. *J. Gerontol.,* Series B, 52B, P159–P166.

Teri, L., & Wagner, A. (1992). Alzheimer's disease and depression. *J. Cons. Clin. Psychol., 60*(3), 379–91.

Thacher, M. (1978, Apr.). First steps for the retarded. *Human Behav.*

Thapar, A., & McGuffin, P. (1996). The genetic etiology of childhood depressive symptoms: A developmental perspective. *Develop. Psychopath., 8*(4), 751–60.

Tharp, R. G. (1991) Cultural diversity and treatment of children. *J Cons. Clin. Psychol., 59,* 799–812.

Thase, M. E., Frank, E., & Kupfer, D. J. (1985). Biological processes in major depression. In E. E. Beckham & W. R. Leber (Eds.), *Handbook of depression: Treatment, assessment, and research.* (pp. 816–913). Homewood, IL: Dorsey Press.

Thase, M. E., & Howland, R. H. (1995). Biological processes in depression: An updated review and integration. In E. E. Beckham & W. R. Leber (Eds.), *Handbook of depression* (2nd ed.). (pp. 213–279). New York: Guilford.

Thase, M. E., Simons, A. D., Cahalane, J. F., & McGeary, J. (1991). Cognitive behavior therapy of endogenous depression: Part 1: An outpatient clinical replication series. *Behav. Ther., 22,* 457–68.

Thompson-Pope, S. K., & Turkat, I. D. (1993). Schizotypal, schizoid, paranoid, and avoidant personality disorders. In P. B. Sutker & H. E. Adams (Eds.), *Comprehensive handbook of psychopathology* (2nd ed.). New York: Plenum.

Thomsen, P. H. (1998). Obsessive-compulsive disorder in children and adolescents: Clinical guidelines. *Eur. Chid Adoles. Psychiat., 7*(1), 1–11.

Thoreson, C. E., & Powell, L. H. (1992). Type A behavior pattern: New perspectives on theory, assessment, and intervention. *J. Cons. Clin. Psychol., 60*(4), 595–604.

Tien, A. Y., & Anthony, J. C. (1990). Epidemiological analysis of alcohol and drug use as risk factors for psychotic experiences. *J. Nerv. Ment. Dis., 178,* 473–80.

Tien, A. Y., & Eaton, W. W. (1992). Psychopathologic precursors and sociodemographic risk factors for the schizophrenia syndrome. *Archi. Gen. Psychiat., 49*(1), 37–46.

Tienari, P. (1991). Interaction between genetic vulnerability and family environment: The Finnish adoptive family study of schizophrenia. *Acta Psychiatr. Scandin., 84,* 460–65.

Tienari, P. (1994). The Finnish adoption study of schizophrenia. Implications for family research. *Brit. J. Psychiat., 164,* 20–26.

Tienari, P., Lahti, I., Sorri, A., Naarala, M., Moring, J., Wahlberg, K.-E., & Wynne, L. C. (1987). The Finnish adoptive family study of schizophrenia. *J. Psychiat. Res., 21,* 437–45.

Tienari, P., Sorri, A., Lahti, I., Naarala, M., Wahlberg, K.-E., Pohjola, J., & Moring, J. (1985). Interaction of genetic and psychosocial factors in schizophrenia. *Acta Psychiatr. Scandin.* (Suppl. No. 319), *71,* 19–30.

Time. (1966, June 17). From shocks to stop sneezes, p. 72.

Tomarken, A., Sutton, S., & Mineka, S. (1995). Fear-relevant illusory correlations: What types of associative linkages promote judgmental bias? *J. Abn. Psychol., 104,* 312–26.

Tomarken, A. J., Simien, C., & Garber, J. (1994). Resting frontal brain asymmetry discriminates adolescent children of depressed mothers from low-risk controls. *Psychophysiology, 31,* 97–98.

Tomes, N. (1994). Feminist histories of psychiatry. In M. Micale & R. Porter (Eds.), *Discovering the history of psychiatry.* (pp. 348–383). New York: Oxford University Press.

Tonigan, J. S., Toscova, R., & Miller, W. R. (1995). Meta-analysis of the literature on Alcoholics Anonymous. *J. Stud. Alcoh., 57*(1), 65–72.

Took, K. J., & Buck, B. L. (1996). Enuresis with combined risperidone and SSRI use. *J. Acad. of Child Adoles. Psychiat. 35*(7), 840–41.

Toomey, R., et al. (1997). Revisiting the factor structure for positive and negative symptoms: Evidence from a large heterogeneous group of psychiatric patients. *Amer. J. Psychiat., 154*(3), 371–77.

Torgersen, S. (1993). Genetics. In A. S. Bellack & M. Hersen (Eds.), *Psychopathology in adulthood.* Needham Heights, MA: Allyn and Bacon.

Torrey, E. F. (1987). Prevalence studies in schizophrenia. *Brit. J. Psychiat.*, 150, 598–608.

Torrey, E. F., Bower, A. E., Taylor, E. H., & Gottesman, I. I. (1994). *Schizophrenia and manic-depressive disorder: The biological roots of mental illness as revealed by the landmark study of identical twins.* New York: Basic Books.

Torrey, E. F., Bowler, A. E., Rawlings, R., & Terrazas, A. (1993). Seasonality of schizophrenia and stillbirths. *Schizo. Bull., 19*(3), 557–62.

Toth, S. L., Manly, J. T., & Cicchetti, D. (1992). Child maltreatment and vulnerability to depression. *Develop. Psychopath., 4,* 97–112.

Tower, R. B., Kasl, S. V., & Moritz, D. J. (1997). The influence of spouse cognitive impairment on respondents' depressive symptoms: The moderating role of marital closeness. *J. Gerontol.*, Series B, 52B(5), S270–S278.

Townsend, J., Harris, N. S., & Courchesne, E. (1996). Visual attention abnormalities in autism: Delayed orienting to location. *J. Int. Neuropsycholog. Assoc., 2,* 541–50.

Townsley, R., Turner, S., Beidel, D., & Calhoun, K. (1995). Social phobia: An analysis of possible developmental factors. *J. Abn. Psychol., 104,* 526–31.

Trasler, G. (1978). Relations between psychopathy and persistent criminality-methodological and theoretical issues. In R. D. Hare & D. Schalling (Eds.), *Psychopathic behavior: Approaches to research.* New York: Wiley.

Tremble, J., Padillo, A., & Bell, C. (1994). *Drug abuse among ethnic minorities, 1987:* Washington, DC: U.S. Department of Health and Human Services.

Trickett, P. K., & Putnam, F. W. (1993). Impact of child sexual abuse on females: Toward a developmental, psychobiological integration. *Psychological Science, 4*(2), 81–87.

Trinder, H., & Salkovskis, P. M. (1994). Personally relevant intrusions outside the laboratory: Long-term suppression increases intrusion. *Behav. Res. Ther., 32*(8), 833–42.

Triplett, F. (1986, July 21). The madman on the ferry; Released from a hospital, a mental patient kills two people. *Time,* p. 28.

Trivedi, M. H. (1996). Functional neuroanatomy of obsessive-compulsive disorder. *J. Clin. Psychiat., 57*(8), 26–36.

Tronick, E. Z., & Cohn, J. F. (1989). Infant-mother face-to-face interaction: Age and gender differences in coordination and miscoordination. *Child Develop., 59,* 85–92.

Tryer, P. (1995). Are personality disorders well classified in DSM-IV? In W. J. Livesley (Ed.), *The DSM-IV personality disorders.* (pp. 29–42). New York: Guilford.

Tsai, J. L., Butcher, J. N., Munoz, R. F., & Vitousek, K. (in press). Culture, ethnicity, and psychopathology. In H. E. Adams & P. B. Sutker (Eds.), *Comprehensive handbook of psychopathology.* New York: Plenum.

Tsai, L. Y., & Ghaziuddin, M. (1992). Biomedical research in autism. In D. M. Berkell (Ed.), *Autism.* (pp. 53–76). Hillsdale: Erlbaum.

Tseng, W., Asai, M., Kitanishi, K., McLaughlin, D. G., & Kyomen, H. (1992). Diagnostic patterns of social phobia: Comparison in Tokyo and Hawaii. *J. Nerv. Ment. Dis., 180,* 380–5.

Tucker, G. J. (1998). Editorial: Putting DSM-IV in perspective. *Amer. J. Psychiat., 155*(2), 159–161.

Tuckman, J., Kleiner, R., & Lavell, M. (1959). Emotional content of suicide notes. *Amer. J. Psychiat. 116,* 59–63.

Tulving, E. (1993). What is episodic memory? *Curr. Dir. Psychol. Sci., 2*(3), 67–70.

Tuomisto, M. T. (1997). Intra-arterial blood pressure and heart rate reactivity to behavioral stress in normotensive, borderline, and mild hypertensive men. *Hlth. Psychol., 16*(6), 554–565.

Turkheimer, E. (1991). Individual and group differences in adoption studies of IQ. *Psychol. Bull., 110*(3), 392–405.

Turner, J. R. (1994). *Cardiovascular reactivity and stress: Patterns of physiological response.* New York: Plenum.

Turner, S. M., Beidel, D. C., & Townsley, R. M. (1992). Social phobia: A comparison of specific and generalized subtypes and avoidant personality disorder. *J. Abn. Psychol., 101,* 326–31.

Tyor, P. L., & Bell, L. V. (1984). *Caring for the retarded in America: A history.* Westport, CT: Greenwood Press.

Uecker, A., Mangan, P. A., Obrzut, J. E., & Nadel, L. (1993). Down syndrome in neurobiological perspective: An emphasis on spatial cognition. *J. Clin. Child Psychol., 22*(2), 266–76.

Ullmann, L. P., & Krasner, L. (1975). *Psychological approach to abnormal behavior* (2nd ed.). Englewood Cliffs, NJ: Prentice Hall.

United Press International. (1982, Oct. 24). "Tylenol hysteria" hits 200 at football game. *Chicago Tribune,* Sec. 1, p. 4.

Ursano, R. J., Boydstun, J. A., & Wheatley, R. D. (1981). Psychiatric illness in U.S. Air Force Vietnam prisoners of war: A five-year follow-up. *Amer. J. Psychiat., 138*(3), 310–14.

USDHHS. (1994). Preventing tobacco use among young people: A report of the Surgeon General. *U.S. Department of Health and Human Services.*

Uva, J. L. (1995). Autoerotic asphyxiation in the United States. *Journal of Forensic Sciences, 40,* 574–81.

Vaillant, G. E. (1978). The distinction between prognosis and diagnosis in schizophrenia: A discussion of Manfred Bleuler's paper. In L. C. Wynne, R. L. Cromwell, & S. Matthysse (Eds.), *The nature of schizophrenia: New approaches to research and treatment.* (pp. 637–40). New York: Wiley.

Valentiner, D. B., Foa, E. B., Riggs, D. S., & Gershuny, B. S. (1996). Coping strategies and posttraumatic stress disorder in female victims of sexual and nonsexual assault. *J. Abn. Psychol., 105*(3), 455–58.

Valleni-Basile, L. A., Garrison, C. Z., Jackson, K. I., Waller, J. L., McKeown, R. E., Addy, C. I., & Cuffe, S. P. (1994). Frequency of obsessive-compulsive disorder in a community sample of young adolescents. *J. Amer. Acad. Child Adoles. Psychiat., 33,* 782–91.

Van Broeckhoven, C., Genthe, A. M., Vandenberghe, A., Horsthemke, B., et al. (1987). Failure of familial Alzheimer's disease to segregate with the A4-amyloid gene in several European families. *Nature, 329,* 153–55.

VandenBos, G. R. (1986). Psychotherapy research: A special issue. *Amer. Psychol., 41,* 111–12.

VandenBos, G. R. (1993). U. S. Mental Health Policy: Proactive evolution in the midst of health care reform. *Amer. Psychol., 48*(3), 283–90.

van den Hout, M. A. (1988). The explanation of experimental panic. In S. Rachman & J. D. Maser (Eds.), *Panic: Psychological perspectives.* Hillsdale, NJ: Erlbaum.

van der Kolk, B. A., et al. (1996). Dissociation, somatization, and affect dysregulation: The complexity of adaptation to trauma. *Amer. J. Psychiat., Festschrift Supplement, 153*(7), 83–93.

van der Kolk, B. A., & Saporta, J. (1993). Biological responses to psychic trauma. In J. P. Wilson, B. Raphael et al., *International handbook of traumatic stress syndromes.* (pp. 25–33). New York: Plenum.

van der Sande, R., Van Rooijen, L., Buskens, E., Allart, E., Hawton, K., VanDer Graaf, Y., & Van Engeland, H. V. (1997). Intensive in-patient and community intervention versus routine care after attempted suicide. *Brit. J. Psychiat., 171,* 35–41.

Van Ree, J. M. (1996). Endorphins and experimental addiction. *Alcohol, 13*(1), 25–30.

Van Velzen, C. J. M., & Emmelkamp, P. M. G. (1996). The assessment of personality disorders: Implications for cognitive and behavior therapy. *Behav. Res. Ther., 34*(8), 655–668.

Vargas, M. A., & Davidson, J. (1993). Posttraumatic stress disorder. *Psychiat. Clin. N. Amer., 16,* 737–48.

Vasiljeva, O. A., Kornetov, N. A., Zhankov, A. I., & Reshetnikov, V. I. (1989). Immune function in psychogenic depression. *Amer. J. Psychiat., 146,* 284–85.

Vasterling, J. J., Seltzer, B., & Watrous, W. (1997). Longitudinal assessment of deficit unawareness in Alzheimer's disease. *Neuropsychiatry, Neuropsychology, & Behavioral Neurology, 10*(3), 197–202.

Vaughn, C. E., Snyder, K. S., Jones, S., Freeman, W. B., & Falloon, I. R. H. (1984). Family factors in schizophrenic relapse: Replication in California of British research on expressed emotion. *Arch. Gen. Psychiat., 41,* 1169–77.

Veale, D., Gournay, K., Dryden, W., Boocock, A. et al. (1996) Body dysmorphic disorder: A cognitive behavioral model and pilot randomized control trial. *Behav. Res. & Ther., 34,* 717–29.

Vega, W. A., & Rumbaut, R. G. (1991). Reasons of the heart: Ethnic minorities and mental health. *Annual Review of Sociology, 17.*

Vega, W. A., Zimmerman, R. S., Warheit, G. J., Apospori, E., & Gil, A. G. (1993). Risk factors for early adolescent drug use in four ethnic and racial groups. *Amer. J. Pub. Hlth., 83,* 185–89.

Velting, D. M., & Gould, M. S. (1997). Suicide contagion. In R. W. Maris, M. M. Silverman, & S. S. Canetton (Eds.), *Review of Suicidology, 1997.* (pp. 96–137). New York: Guilford.

Verhulst, F. C., & Achenbach, T. M. (1995) Empirically based assessment and taxonomy of psychopathology: Cross cultural applications. A review. *Eur. Child Adoles. Psychiat., 4,* 61–76.

Verhulst, F. C., & Koot, H. M. (1992). *Child psychiatric epidemiology: Concepts, methods, and findings.* Beverly Hills, CA: Sage.

Verhulst, J. H., Van Der Lee, J. H., Akkerhuis, G. W., Sanders-Woudstra, J. A. R., Timmer, F. C., & Donkhorst, I. D. (1985). The prevalence of nocturnal enuresis: Do DSM-III criteria need to be changed: A brief research report. *J. Child Psychol. Psychiat., 26*(6), 983–93.

Vinokur, A. D., Price, R. H. & Caplan, R. D. (1996). Hard times and hurtful partners: How financial strain affects depression and relationship satisfaction of unemployed persons and their spouses. *J. Pers. Soc. Psychol., 71,* 166–79.

Vitousek, K., & Manke, F. (1994). Personality variables and disorders in anorexia and bulimia nervosa. *J. Abn. Psychol., 103*(1), 137–47.

Volkow, N. D., Ding, Y. S., Fowler, J. S., Ashby, C., Liebermann, J., Hitzemann, R., & Wolf, A. P.

(1995). Is methylphenidate like cocaine? Studies on their pharmacokinetics and distribution in the human brain. *Arch. Gen. Psychiat., 52,* 456–63.

Von Korff, M., Ormel, J., Katon, W., & Lin, E. H. B. (1992). Disability and depression among high utilizers of health care: A longitudinal analysis. *Archi. Gen. Psychiat., 49*(2), 91–100.

Vredenbrug, K., Flett, G. L., & Krames, L. (1993). Analogue versus clinical depression: A critical reappraisal. *Psychol. Bull., 113* (2), 327–44.

Wachtel, E. F. (1994). *Treating troubled children and their families.* New York: Guilford.

Wachtel, P. L. (1977). *Psychoanalysis and behavior therapy: Toward an integration.* New York: Basic Books.

Wachtel, P. L. (1993). *Therapeutic communication: Principles and effective practice.* New York: Guilford.

Wachtel, P. L. (1997). *Psychoanalysis, behavior therapy, and the relational world.* Washington: American Psychological Association.

Wadden, T. A., Luborsky, L., Greer, S., & Crits-Christopher, P. (1985). The behavioral treatment of essential hypertension: An update and comparison with pharamacological treatment. *Clin. Psychol. Rev., 4,* 403–29.

Wagenaar, A. C., & Perry, C. L. (1995). Community strategies for the reduction of youth drinking: Theory and application. In G. M. Boyd, J. Howard, & R. A. Zucker (Eds.), *Alcohol problems among adolescents.* (pp. 197–223). Hillsdale, NJ: Erlbaum.

Wagner, B. M. (1997). Family risk factors for child and adolescent suicidal behavior. *Psychol. Bull., 121*(2), 246–98.

Wagner, M. T., et al. (1997). Unawareness of cognitive deficit in Alzheimer disease and related dementias. *Alzheimer Disease & Associated Disorders, 11*(3) 125–31.

Wakefield, J. C. (1992a). Disorder as harmful dysfunction: a conceptual critique of DSM-III-R's definition of mental disorder. *Psychol. Rev., 99*(2), 232–247.

Wakefield, J. C. (1992b). The concept of mental disorder: On the boundary between biological facts and social values. *Amer. Psychol., 47*(3), 373–388.

Wakefield, J. C. (1997). Normal inability versus pathological disability: Why Ossorio's definition of mental disorder is not sufficient. *Clin. Psychol. Sci. Prac., 4*(3), 249–258.

Walker, E., Katon, W., Harrop-Griffiths, J., Holm, L., Russo, J., & Hickok, L. R. (1988). Relationship of chronic pelvic pain to psychiatric diagnoses and childhood sexual abuse. *Amer. J. Psychiat., 145,* 75–80.

Walker, E. F., & Diforio, D. (1997). Schizophrenia: A neural diathesis-stress model. *Psychol. Rev., 104*(4), 667–85.

Walker, E. F., Grimes, K. E., Davis, D. M., & Smith, A. J. (1993). Childhood precursors of schizophrenia: Facial expressions of emotion. *Amer. J. Psychiat., 150*(11), 1654–60.

Walker, E. F., Savoie, T., & Davis, D. (1994). Neuromotor precursors of schizophrenia. *Schizo. Bull., 20*(3), 441–51.

Wallace, J. (1996). Theory of 12 step-oriented treatment. In F. Rotgers, D. S. Keller, et al. (Eds.), *Treating substance abuse: Theory and technique.* (pp. 13–26). New York: Guilford.

Wallace, R. A. (1987). *Biology: The world of life.* Glenview, IL: Scott, Foresman.

Waller, G. (1994). Childhood sexual abuse and borderline personality disorder in the eating disorders. *Child Ab. Negl., 18,* 97–101.

Waller, N. G., & Ross, C. A. (1997). The prevalence and biometric structure of pathological dissociation in the general population: Taxometric and behavioral genetic findings. *J. Abn. Psychol., 106*(4), 499–510.

Wallerstein, R. S. (1989). The psychotherapy research project of the Menninger Foundation: An overview. *J. Cons. Clin. Psychol., 57,* 195–205.

Wallin, A., & Blennow, K. (1993). Heterogeneity of vascular dementia: Mechanisms and subgroups. *Journal of Geriatric Psychiatry and Neurology, 6*(3), 177–88.

Walsh, B. T., & Garner, D. M. (1997). Diagnostic issues. In D. M. Garner & P. E. Garfinkel (Eds.), *Handbook of treatment for eating disorders* (pp. 25–33). New York: Guilford.

Walter, A. L., & Carter, A. S. (1997). Gilles de la Tourette's syndrome in childhood: A guide for school professionals. *School Psychol. Rev., 26*(1), 28–46.

Warner, R. (1994). Recovery from schizophrenia: Psychiatry and political economy (2nd ed.). New York: Routledge-Kegan Paul.

Warnes, H. (1973). The traumatic syndrome. *Ment. Hlth. Dig., 5*(3), 33–34.

Warren, J. I., Dietz, P. E., & Hazelwood, R. R. (1996). The sexually sadistic serial killer. *Journal of Forensic Sciences, 41,* 970–74.

Warshaw, M. G., Massion, A. O., Peterson, L. G., Pratt, L. A., & Keller, M. B. (1995). Suicidal behavior in patients with panic disorder: Retrospective and prospective data. *J. Affect. Dis., 34,* 235–47.

Watanabe, H., Kawauchi, A., Kitamori, T., & Azuma, Y. (1994). Treatment system for nocturnal enuresis according to an original classification system. *European Urology, 25,* 43–50.

Waterhouse, L., & Fein, D. (1997). Genes tPA, Fyn, and FAK in autism? *J. Autism Devel. Dis., 27*(3), 220–23.

Watkins, B., & Bentovim, A. (1992). The sexual abuse of male children and adolescents: A review of current research. *J. Child Psychol. Psychiat., 33,* 197–248.

Watson, D., Clark, L. A., Weber, K., Assenheimer, J. S., Strauss, M. E., & McCormick, R. A. (1995a). Testing a tripartite model: I. Evaluating the convergent and discriminant validity of anxiety and depression symptom scales. *J. Abn. Psychol., 104,* 3–14.

Watson, D., Clark, L. A., Weber, K., Assenheimer, J. S., Strauss, M. E., & McCormick, R. A. (1995b). Testing a tripartite model: II. Exploring the symptom structure of anxiety and depression in student, adult, and patient samples. *J. Abn. Psychol., 104,* 15–25.

Watson, J. (1924). *Behaviorism.* The People's Institute Publishing Co., Inc.

Watten, R. G. (1995). Negative affectivity and consumption of alcohol: A general population study. *Journal of Community & Applied Social Psychology, 5*(3), 173–81.

Webster-Stratton, C. (1991). Annotation: Strategies for helping families with conduct disordered children. *J. Child Psychol. Psychiat., 32,* 1047–62.

Wechsler, H., Davenport, A., Dowdall, G., Moeykens, M. S., & Castillo, S. (1994). Health and behavioral consequences of binge drinking in college. *JAMA, December,* 1672–77.

Wechsler, H., Dowdall, G. W., Maenner, G., Gledhill-Hoyt, J., Lee, H. (1998). Changes in binge drinking and related problems among American college students between 1993 and 1997. *J. Amer. Coll. Hlth., 47*(2), 57–68.

Wegner, D. M. (1994). Ironic processes of mental control. *Psychol. Rev., 101*(1), 34–52.

Wehr, T. A., & Goodwin, F. K. (1987). Can antidepressants cause mania and worsen the course of affective illness? *Amer. J. Psychiat., 144,* 1403–11.

Wehr, T. A., Jacobsen, F. M., Sack, D. A., Arendt, J., Tamarkin, L., & Rosenthal, N. E. (1986). Phototherapy of seasonal affective disorder. *Arch. Gen. Psychiat., 43,* 870–75.

Weickert, C. S., & Weinberger, D. R. (1998). A candidate molecule approach to defining developmental pathology in schizophrenia. *Schizo. Bull., 24*(2), 303–316.

Weinberg, M. S., Williams, C. J., & Pryor, D. W. (1994). *Dual Attraction.* New York: Oxford University Press.

Weinberger, D. R. (1984). Brain disease and psychiatric illness: When should a psychiatrist order a CAT scan? *Amer. J. Psychiat., 141,* 1521–27.

Weinberger, D. R. (1997). On localizing schizophrenic neuropathology. *Schizo. Bull., 23*(3), 537–40.

Weiner, R. D., & Krystal, A. D. (1994). The present use of electroconvulsive therapy. *Annu. Rev. Med., 45,* 273–81.

Weinrot, M. R., & Riggan, M. (1996). *Vicarious sensitization: A new method to reduce deviant arousal in adolescent offenders.* Manuscript submitted for publication.

Weisbeck, G. A., Schuckit, M. A., Kalmijn, J. A., Tipp, J. A., et al. (1996). An evaluation of the history of marijuana withdrawal syndrome in a large population. *Addiction, 91*(10), 1469–1478.

Weisenberg, M. (1977). Pain and pain control. *Psychol. Bull., 84,* 1008–44.

Weisman, A., Lopez, S. R., Karno, M., & Jenkins, J. (1993). An attributional analysis of expressed emotion in Mexican-American families with schizophrenia. *J. Abn. Psychol., 102*(4), 601–6.

Weiss, B., Weisz, J. R., & Bromfield, R. (1986). Performance of retarded and nonretarded persons on information-processing tasks: Further tests of the similar structure hypothesis. *Psychol. Bull., 100,* 157–75.

Weisse, C. S. (1992). Depression and immunocompetence: A review of the literature. *Psychol. Bull., 111*(3), 475–89.

Weissman, M. M. (1993). The epidemiology of personality disorders: A 1990 update. *J. Personal. Dis., Supplement,* 44–62.

Weissman, M. M., Fendrich, M., Warner, V., & Wickramaratne, P. (1992). Incidence of psychiatric disorder in offspring at high and low risk for depression. *J. Amer. Acad. Child Adoles. Psychiat., 31,* 640–48.

Weisz, J. R., Donenberg, G. R., Han, S. S., & Weiss, B. (1995). Bridging the gap between laboratory and clinic in child and adolescent psychotherapy. *J. Cons. Clin, Psychol., 63*(5), 688–701.

Weisz, J. R., McCarty, C. A., Eastman, K. L., Chaiyasit, W., & Suwanlert, S. (1997) Developmental psychopathology and culture: Ten lessons from Thailand. In S. Luthar, J. Burack, D. Cicchetti, and J. Weisz (Eds.), *Developmental psychopathology: Perspectives an adjustment, risk, and disorder* (pp. 568–92) Cambridge, England: Cambridge University Press.

Weisz, J. R., Suwanlert, S., Chaiyasit, W., & Walter, B. R. (1987). Over and undercontrolled clinic-referral problems among Thai and American children and adolescents: The wat and wai of cultural differences. *J. Cons. Clin. Psychol., 55,* 719–726.

Weisz, J. R., Suwanlert, S., Chaiyasit, W., Weiss, B., Achenbach, T. M., & Eastman, K. L. (1993). Behavior and emotional problems among Thai and American adolescents: Parent reports for ages 12–16. *J. Abn. Psychol., 102,* 395–403.

Weisz, J. R., & Weiss, B. (1991) Studying the referability of child clinical problems. *J. Cons. Clin. Psychol., 59,* 266–73.

Weisz, J. R., Weiss, B., & Donenberg, G. R. (1992). The lab versus the clinic: Effects of child and adolescent psychotherapy. *Amer. Psychol., 47,* 1578–85.

Weizman, R., Laor, N., Barber, Y., Selman, A., Schujovizky, A., Wolmer, L., Laron, Z., & Gil-Ad, I. (1994). Impact of the Gulf war on the anxiety, cortisol, and growth hormone levels of Israeli civilians. *Amer. J. Psychiat., 151,* 71–75.

Wekstein, L. (1979). *Handbook of suicidology: Principles, problems, and practice.* New York: Brunner/Mazel.

Wells, A., & Butler, G. (1997). Generalized anxiety disorder. In D. M. Clark & C. G. Fairburn (Eds.), *Science and practice of cognitive behaviour therapy.* (pp. 155–178). Oxford University Press.

Wells, A., & Clark, D. M. (1997). Social phobia: A cognitive perspective. In G. C. L. Davey (Ed.), *Phobias: A handbook of description, treatment, and theory.* Chicherster, England: Wiley.

Wells, C. E. (1979). Diagnosis of dementia. *Psychosomatics, 20,* 517–22.

Wenar, C. (1990). *Developmental psychopathology: From infancy through adolescence* (2nd ed.). New York: McGraw-Hill.

Wender, P. H., Kety, S. S., Rosenthal, D., Schulsinger, F., Ortmann, J., & Lunde, I. (1986). Psychiatric disorders in the biological and adoptive families of adopted individuals with affective disorders. *Arch. Gen. Psychiat., 43,* 923–29.

Wender, P. H., Rosenthal, D., Kety, S. S., Schulsinger, F., & Weiner, J. (1974). Cross-fostering: A research strategy for clarifying the role of genetic and experimential factors in the etiology of schizophrenia. *Arch. Gen. Psychiat., 30*(1), 121–28.

Wenzlaff, R. M., Wegner, D. M., & Klein, S. B. (1991). The role of thought suppression in the bonding of thought and mood. *J. Pers. Soc. Psychol., 60 (4),* 500–8.

Wester, P., Eriksson, S., Forsell, A., Puu, G., & Adolfsson, R. (1988). Monoamine metabolite concentrations and cholinesterase activities in cerebrospinal fluid of progressive dementia patients: Relation to clinical parameters. *Acta Neurol. Scandin., 77,* 12–21.

Westermeyer, J. (1982a). Bag ladies in isolated cultures, too. *Behav. Today, 13*(21), 1–2.

Westermeyer, J., (1987). Public health and chronic mental illness. *Amer. J. Pub. Hlth., 77*(6), 667–68.

Westermeyer, J. (1989). Paranoid symptoms and disorders among 100 Hmong regfugees: A longitudinal study. *Acta psychiatr. Scandin. 80,*(1), 47–59.

Westermeyer, J., & Janca, A. (1997) Language, culture and psychopathology: Conceptual and methodological issues. *Transcult. Psychiatry, 34,* 291–311.

Westermeyer, J., Neider, J., & Callies, A. (1989). Psychosocial adjustment of Hmong refugees during their first decade in the United States. A longitudinal study. *J. Nerv. Ment. Dis., 177,* 132–39.

Westermeyer, J., Williams, C. L., & Nguyen, N. (Eds.). (1991). *Mental health and social adjustment: A guide to clinical and prevention services.* Washington, DC: U.S. Government Printing Office.

Wetherby, A. M., & Prizant, B. M. (1992). Facilitating language and communication development in autism: Assessment and intervention guidelines. In D. E. Berkell (Ed.), *Autism.* (pp. 107–34). Hillsdale, NJ: Erlbaum.

Wherry, J. S. (1996). Pervasive developmental, psychotic, and allied disorders. In L. Hechtman (Ed.), *Do they grow out of it?* (pp. 195–223). Washington: American Psychiatric Press.

Whitaker, L. C. (1992). *Schizophrenic disorders: Sense and nonsense in conceptualization, assessment, and treatment.* New York: Plenum.

White, J., Moffitt, T. E., & Silva, P. A. (1989). A prospective replication of the protective effects of IQ in subjects at high risk for juvenile delinquency. *J. Clin. Cons. Psychol., 57,* 719–24.

Whitehouse, P. J. (1993). Cholinergic therapy in dementia. *Acta Neurol. Scandin., 88* (Suppl. 149), 42–45.

Whitehouse, P. J., et al. (1982). Alzheimer's disease and senile dementia: Loss of neurons in the basal forebrain. *Science, 215,* 1237–39.

Whybrow, P. C. (1997). *A mood apart.* New York: Basic Books.

Widiger, T. A. (1992). Categorical versus dimensional classification: Implications from and for research. *J. Personal. Dis., 6,* 287–300.

Widiger, T. A. (1993). The DSM-III-R categorical personality disorder diagnoses: A critique and alternative. *Psychol. Inq., 4,* 75–90.

Widiger, T. A. & Corbitt, E. M. (1995). Antisocial personality disorder. In W. J. Livesley (Ed.), *The DSM-IV personality disorders.* (pp. 103–126). New York: Guilford.

Widiger, T. A., & Frances, A. (1985). Axis II personality disorders: Diagnostic and treatment issues. *Hosp. Comm. Psychiat., 36,* 619–27.

Widiger, T. A., & Frances, A. J. (1994). Toward a dimensional model for the personality disorders. In P. T. Costa, Jr., & Widiger (Eds.), *Personality Disorders and the Five-Factor Model of Personality.* (pp. 19-39). Washington: American Psychological Association.

Widiger, T., & Rogers, J. (1989). Prevalence and comorbidity of personality disorders. *Psychiat. Ann., 19,* 132–36.

Widiger, T. A., Frances, A. J., Pincus, H. A., Davis, W. W., & First, M. B. (1991). Toward an empirical classification for the DSM-IV. *J. Abn. Psychol., 100* (3), 280–88.

Widiger, T. A., Frances, A., Warner, L., & Bloom, C. (1986). Diagnostic criteria for the Borderline and Schizotypal Personality Disorders. *J. Abn. Psychol., 95*(1), 43–51.

Widiger, T. A., & Sanderson, C. J. (1995). Toward a dimensional model of personality disorders. In W. J. Livesley (Ed.), *The DSM-IV personality disorders.* (pp. 433–458). New York: Guilford.

Widiger, T., & Trull, T. J. (1993) Borderline and narcissistic personality disorders. In P. B. Sutker & H. E. Adams (Eds.), *Comprehensive handbook of psychopathology* (2nd ed.). New York: Plenum.

Widom, C. S. (1977). A methodology for studying noninstitutionalized psychopaths. *J. Cons. Clin. Psychol., 45,* 674–83.

Wiggins, J. S. (1982). Circumplex models of interpersonal behavior in clinical psychology. In P. C. Kendall & J. N. Butcher (Eds.), *Handbook of research methods in clinical psychology.* New York: Wiley Interscience.

Wilbur, R. S. (1973, June 2). In S. Auerbach (Ed.), POWs found to be much sicker than they looked upon release. *Los Angeles Times,* Part I, p. 4.

Wilder, D. A., et al. (1997). A simplified method of toilet training adults in residential settings. *J. Behav. Ther. Exper. Psychiat., 28*(3), 241–46.

Wille, R. & Beier, K. M. (1989). Castration in Germany. *Ann. Sex Res., 2,* 103–133.

Williams, J. M., Watts, F. N., MacLeod, C., & Mathews, A. (1997). *Cognitive psychology and emotional disorders.* Chichester, Engalnd: Wiley.

Williams, L. M., & Finkelhor, D., (1990). The characteristics of incestuous fathers: A review of recent studies. In W. L. Marshall, D. R. Laws, & H. E. Barbaree (Eds.), *Handbook of sexual assault.* (pp. 231–56). New York: Plenum.

Williams, R. B., Jr., Barefoot, J. C., & Shekelle, R. B. (1985). The health consequences of hostility. In M. A., Chesney, S. E., Goldston, & R. H. Rosenman, (Eds.), *Anger, hostility, and behavioral medicine.* (pp. 173–85). New York: Hemisphere/McGraw-Hill.

Williams, R. B., Jr., & Gentry, W. D. (Eds.). (1977). *Behavioral approaches to medical treatment.* Cambridge, MA: Ballinger.

Williams, R. B., Jr., Haney, T. L., Lee, K. L., Kong, V., & Blumenthal, J. A. (1980). Type A behavior, hostility, and coronary atherosclerosis. *Psychosom. Med., 42,* 529–38.

Wilson, G. T., & Fairburn, C. G. (1993). Cognitive treatments for eating disorders. *J. Cons. Clin. Psychol., 61*(2), 261–69.

Wilson, G. T., & Fairburn, C. G. (1998). Treatments for eating disorders. In P. E. Nathan & J. M. Gorman (Eds.), *A guide to treatments that work.* (pp. 501–30). New York: Oxford University Press.

Wilson, G. T., Fairburn, C. G., & Agrus, W. S. (1997). Cognitive-behavioral therapy for bulimia nervosa. In D. M. Garner & P. E. Garfinkel (Eds.), *Handbook of treatment for eating disorders.* (pp. 67–93). New York: Guilford.

Wilson, M. (1993). DSM-III and the transformation of American psychiatry: A history. *Amer. J. Psychiat., 150,* 399–410.

Wilson, M. I., & Daly, M. (1996). Male sexual proprietariness and violence against wives. *Curr. Dir. Psychol. Sci., 5,* 2–7.

Wing, L. K. (1976). Diagnosis, clinical description and prognosis. In L. Wing (Ed.), *Early childhood autism.* London: Pergamon.

Winokur, G., & Tsuang, M. T. (1996). *The natural history of mania, depression, and schizophrenia.* Washington: American Psychiatric Press.

Winslow, J. T., & Insel, T. R. (1991). Neuroethological models of obsessive-compulsive disorder. In J. Zohar, T. Insel, & S. Rasmussen (Eds.), *The psychobiology of obsessive-compulsive disorder.* New York: Springer.

Winston, A., Laikin, M., Pollack, J., Samstag, L.W., McCullough, L., & Muran, C. (1994). Short-term psychotherapy of personality disorders. *Amer. J. Psychiat., 151,* 190–94.

Wise, R. A. (1996). Addictive drugs and brain stimulation reward. *Annual Review of Neuroscience, 19,* 319–40.

Wise, R. A., & Munn, E. (1995). Withdrawal from chronic amphetamine elevates baseline intracranial self-stimulation thresholds. *Psychopharmacology, 117*(2), 130–36.

Wiseman, C. V., Gray, J. J., Mosimann, J. E., & Ahrens, A. (1992). Cultural expectations of thinness in woman: An update, *Int. J. Eat. Dis., 11,* 85–89.

Witkin, M. J., Atay, J., & Manderscheid, R. W. (1998). Trends in state and county mental hospitals in the U.S. from 1970 to 1992. *Psychiat. Serv., 47*(10), 1079–81.

Wittchen, H., Zhao, S., Kessler, R. C., Eaton, W. W. (1994). DSM-III-R generalized anxiety disorder in the National Comorbidity Survey. *Arch. Gen. Psychiat., 51,* 355–64.

Wolf, M., Risley, T., & Mees, H. (1964). Application of operant conditioning procedures to the behavior problems of an autistic child. *Behav. Res. Ther., 1,* 305–12.

Wolfe, B. E., & Maser, J. D. (1994). Treatment of panic disorder: Consensus statement. In B. E. Wolfe & J. D. Maser (Eds.), *Treatment of panic disorder. A consensus development conference.* (pp. 237–255). Washington, DC: American Psychiatric Press.

Wolfe, D. A., Edwards, B., Manion, I., & Koverola, C. (1988). Early intervention for parents at risk of child abuse and neglect: A preliminary investigation. *J. Cons. Clin. Psychol., 56,* 34–39.

Wolfe, D. A., & Wekerle, C. (1993). Treatment strategies for child physical abuse and neglect: A critical progress report. *Clin. Psychol. Rev., 13,* 473–500.

Wolfe, V. V., Gentile, C., & Wolfe, D. A. (1989). The impact of sexual abuse on children: A PTSD formulation. *Behav. Ther., 20,* 215–28.

Wolff, H. G. (1960). Stressors as a cause of disease in man. In J. M. Tanner (Ed.), *Stress and psychiatric disorder.* London: Oxford University Press.

Wolff, P. H. (1972). Ethnic differences in alcohol sensitivity. *Science, 175,* 449–50.

Wolff, W. M., & Morris, L. A. (1971). Intellectual personality characteristics of parents of autistic children. *J. Abn. Psychol., 77*(2), 155–61.

Wolkin, A., Sanfilipo, M., Wolf, A. P., Angrist, B., Brodie, J. D., & Rotrosen, J. (1992). Negative symptoms and hypofrontality in chronic schizophrenia. *Arch. Gen. Psychiat., 49*(12), 959–65.

Wolpe, J. (1958). *Psychotherapy by reciprocal inhibition.* Stanford, CA: Stanford University Press.

Wolpe, J. (1988). *Life with out fear. Anxiety and its cure.* Oakland, CA: New Harbinger Publications, Inc.

Wolpe, J. (1993). Commentary: The cognitivist oversell and comments on symposium contributions. *J. Behav. Ther. Exper. Psychiat., 24*(2), 141–47.

Wolrich, M. L., Hannah, J. N., Baumgaertel, A., & Feurer, I. D. (1998). Examination of DSM-IV criteria for attention deficit disorder in a countywide sample. *Journal of Developmental & Behavioral Pediatrics, 19*(3), 162–68.

Wonderlich, S., Klein, M. H., & Council, J. R. (1996). Relationship of social perceptions and self-concept in bulimia nervosa. *J. Cons. Clin. Psychol., 64*(6), 1231–1237.

Wood, C. (1986). The hostile heart. *Psych. Today, 20,* 10–12.

Woodruff, P. W. R., et al. (1997). Auditory hallucinations and the temporal cortical response to speech in schizophrenia: A functional magnetic resonance imaging study. *Amer. J. Psychiat., 154*(12), 1676–82.

Woody, G. E., McLellan, A. T., Luborsky, L., & O'Brien, C. P. (1987). Twelve month follow-up of psychotherapy for opiate dependence. *Amer. J. Psychiat., 144,* 590–96.

Woo-Ming, A. & Siever, L. (1998). Psychopharmacological treatment of personality disorders. In P. Nathan & J. Gorman (Eds.), *A guide to treatments that work.* (pp. 554–567). New York: Oxford University Press.

World Health Organization. (1997). *World Health Organization Report, 1997: Conquering suffering, furthering humanity.* Geneva: Author.

Worthington, E. R. (1978). Demographic and preservice variables as predictors of post-military adjustment. In C. R. Figley (Ed.), *Stress disorders among Vietnam veterans.* New York: Brunner/Mazel.

Wright, P., Takei, N., Rifkin, L., & Murray, R. M. (1995). Maternal influenza, obstetric complications, and schizophrenia. *Amer. J. Psychiat., 152*(12), 1714–20.

Wynne, L. C., Toohey, M. L., & Doane, J. (1979). Family studies. In L. Bellak (Ed.), *The schizophrenic syndrome.* New York: Basic Books.

Yang, B., & Clum, G. A. (1996). Effects of early negative life experience on cognitive functioning and risk for suicide: A review. *Clin. Psychol. Rev., 16*(3), 177–95.

Yapko, M. D. (1994). *Suggestions of abuse: True and false memories of childhood sexual trauma.* New York: Simon & Schuster.

Yeates, K. O., et al. (1997). Preinjury family environment as a determinant of recovery from traumatic brain injuries in school-age children. *J. Int. Neuropsychologic Soc., 3*(6), 617–30.

Yeh, M., Takeuchi, D. T., & Sue, S. (1994) Asian-American children treated in the mental health system: A comparison of parallel and mainstream outpatient service centers. *J. Clin. Child Psychol., 23,* 5–12.

Yehuda, R. (1998). *Psychological trauma.* Washington: American Psychiatric Press.

Yehuda, R., Resnick, H., Schmeidler, J., Yang, R. K., & Pitman, R. K. (1998). Predictors of cortisol and 3-Methoxy-4-hydroxy-penylglycol responses in the acute aftermath of rape. *Biol. Psychiat., 43*(11), 855–59.

Yehuda, R., Southwick, S. M., Giller, E. L., et al. (1992). Urinary catecholamine excretion and severity of PTSD symptoms in Vietnam combat veterans. *J. Nerv. Ment. Dis., 180,* 321–25.

Yehuda, R., Teicher, M. H., Trestman, R. L., Levengood, R. A., & Siever, L. J. (1996). Cortisol regulation in posttraumatic stress disorder and major depression: A chronobiological analysis. *Biological Psychiatry, 40,* 79–88.

Zalewski, C., et al. (1998). A review of neuropsychological differences between paranoid and nonparanoid schizophrenia patients. *Schizo. Bull., 24*(1), 127–46.

Zametkin, A., & Liotta, W. (1997). The future of brain imaging in child psychiatry. *Child Adoles. Psychiat. Clin. N. Amer., 6*(2), 447–60.

Zanarini, M. C., Williams, A. A., Lewis, R. E., Reich, R. B., Vera, S. C., Marino, M. F., Levin, A., Yong, L., & Frankenburg, F. R. (1997). Reported pathological childhood experiences associated with the development of borderline personality disorder. *Amer. J. Psychiat., 154*(8), 1101–06.

Zasler, N. D. (1993). Mild traumatic brain injury: Medical assessment and intervention. *J. Head Trauma Rehab., 8*(3), 13-29.

Zeidner, M. (1993). Coping with disaster: The case of Israeli adolescents under threat of missile attack. *Journal of Youth and Adolescence, 22,* 89–108.

Zeitlin, H. (1986). *The natural history of psychiatric disorder in childhood.* New York: Oxford University Press.

Zelikovsky, N., & Lynn, S. J. (1994). The aftereffects and assessment of physical and psychological abuse. In S. J. Lynn & J. W. Rhue (Eds.), *Dissociation: Clinical and theoretical perspectives.* (pp. 190–214). New York: Guilford.

Zellner, D. A., Harner, D. E., & Adler, R. L. (1989). Effects of eating abnormalities and gender on perceptions of desirable body shape. *J. Abn. Psychol., 98,* 93–96.

Zetlin, A., & Murtaugh, M. (1990). Whatever happened to those with borderline IQs? *Amer. J. Ment. Retard., 94,* 463–69.

Zetzer, H. A., & Beutler, L. E. (1995). The assessment of cognitive functioning and the WAIS-R. In L. E. Beutler and M. R. Berren (Eds.), *Integrative assessment of adult personality.* (pp. 121–186). New York: Guilford.

Zigler, E., Abelson, W. D., Trickett, P. K., & Seitz, V. (1982). Is an intervention program necessary in order to improve economically disadvantaged children's IQ scores? *Child Develop., 53,* 340–48.

Zigler, E., & Muenchow, S. (1992). *Head Start: The inside story of America's most successful educational experiment.* New York: Basic Books.

Zigler, E., & Styfco, S. J. (1994). Head Start: Criticisms in a constructive context. *Amer. Psychol., 49*(2), 127–32.

Zill, N., & Schoenborn, G. A. (1990). Developmental, learning, and emotional problems: Health of our nation's children. *Advance data: National Center for Health Statistics* (Number 190).

Zimmerman, M., & Coryell, W. (1990). Diagnosing personality disorders in the community. A comparison of self report and interview measures. *Arch. Gen. Psychiat., 47,* 527–31.

Zinbarg, R. E., & Barlow, D. H. (1996). Structure of anxiety and the anxiety disorders: A hierarchical model. *J. Abn. Psychol., 105,* 181–93.

Zoccolillo, M., Meyers, J., & Assiter, S. (1997). Conduct disorder, substance dependence, and adolescent motherhood. *Amer. J. Orthopsychiat., 67*(1), 152–57.

Zoccolillo, M., Pickles, A., Quinton, D., & Rutter, M. (1992). The outcome of conduct disorder: Implications for defining adult personality disorder and conduct disorder. *Psychol. Med., 22,* 971–86.

Zubin, J., & Spring, B. J. (1977). Vulnerability: A new view of schizophrenia. *J. Abn. Psychol., 86,* 103–26.

Zucker, K. J. & Blanchard, R. (1997). Transvestic fetishism: Psychopathology and theory. In D. R. Laws & W. O'Donohue (Eds.), *Sexual deviance: Theory, assessment, and treatment.* (pp. 253–79). New York: Guilford.

Zucker, K. J., & Bradley, S. J. (1995). *Gender identity disorder and psychosexual problems in children and adolescents.* New York: Guilford.

Zucker, K. J., Sanikhani, M., & Bradley, S. J. (1997). Sex differences in referral rates of children with gender identity disorder: Some hypotheses. *J. Abnorm. Child Psychol., 25,* 217–27.

Zweben, J. E., & O'Connell, K. (1992). Strategies for breaking marijuana dependence. *J. Psychoact. Drugs, 24,* 165–71.

PHOTO CREDITS

Chapter 1

Page 1: *Untitled.* George Widener is a participating artist of VSA arts, *http://www.vsarts.org/*; 2: Lee Snider/The Image Works; 4: Bettmann/Corbis; 6: Tony Freeman/Photo Edit; 9: AP/Wide World Photos; 10: Christopher Morrow/Stock Boston; 13: Granger Collection; 14: Granger Collection; 15L: Granger Collection; 15R: Granger Collection; 16: Sven Nackstrand/Liaison Agency, Inc.; 17: Réunion de Musées Nationaux/Art Resource; 18: Granger Collection; 19: Stock Montage; 20: Brown Brothers; 22: The Wellcome Library; 23: Bettmann/Corbis; 25T: Bettmann/Corbis; 25B: Bettmann/Corbis; 27: Reuters Newmedia Inc/Corbis; 28: Robert Brenner/PhotoEdit; 30: Hank Morgan/Rainbow

Chapter 2

Page 36: *Spaghetti #2.* Gale L. Bell is a participating artist of VSA arts, *http://www.vsarts.org/*; 38: Mike Massaschi/Stock Boston; 40: Mark Richards/Photo Edit; 45L: D. Gorten/TimePix; 45R: D. Gorten/TimePix; 48: Corbis/Reuters; 52: Laura Dwight/Peter Arnold, Inc.; 54: Bettmann/Corbis; 55: Elizabeth Crews/The Image Works; 60: Dr. Albert Bandura; 61: Aaron T. Beck M.D./Center for Cognitive Therapy; 62: Christopher Bissell/Stone Images; 63: Chuck Savage/Uniphoto; 65: Mark Elias/AP/Wide World Photos; 68: Lawrence Migdale/Stock Boston; 70: J. Greenberg/The Image Works; 71: Mimi Forsyth/Monkmeyer; 74: Michael O'Brien

Chapter 3

Page 79: *Bulgarian Series: January Protest.* George Widener is a participating artist of VSA arts, *http://www.vsarts.org/*; 82: Frank Siteman/Rainbow; 83: Hank Morgan/Rainbow; 85: Will & Deni McIntyre/Photo Researchers, Inc.; 86: Bob Daemmrich/Stock Boston; 87: Peter Vandermark/Stock Boston; 88: Merrim/Monkmeyer; 94: Will McIntyre/Photo Researchers, Inc.; 100: Peter Simon/Stock Boston; 102: Tony Freeman/Photo Edit; 103: S. Agricola/The Image Works; 105: Richard Hutchings/Photo Researchers, Inc.; 107: Courtesy of Dr. Joseph Wolpe; 108: Jacques Chenet/Woodfin Camp & Associates; 109: Alan Carey/The Image Works; 112: David K. Crow/PhotoEdit; 117: Joseph Nettis/Photo Researchers, Inc.

Chapter 4

Page 122: *Illumination.* Joan Bowman is a participating artist of VSA arts, *http://www.vsarts.org/*; 124L: Thomas Friedman/Photo Researchers, Inc.; 124R: F. Hoffmann/The Image Works; 126: R. Maiman/Corbis Sygma; 128: Bob Daemmrich/Stock Boston; 134: Okoniewski/The Image Works; 136: United States Coast Guard; 137: K. Bernstein/Spooner/Liaison Agency; 139: Larry Burrows/TimePix; 142: Sipa Press

Chapter 5

Page 149: *August Day of 1998.* Nicole Aimee Macaluso is a participating artist of VSA arts, *http://www.vsarts.org/*; 151: Peter Winmann/Animals, Animals; 153: Michael Okoniewski/The Image Works; 154: David Wells/The Image Works; 156L: Susan Mineka; 156R: Michael Newman/PhotoEdit; 157: Billy Horsman/Stock Boston; 163: David Gifford/Science Photo Library/Photo Researchers, Inc.; 168: Hattie Young/Science Photo Library/Photo Researchers, Inc.; 174: Christopher Bissell/Stone Images; 177: Scott Foresman Library; 180L: Andy Schwartz/Photofest; 180R: Andy Schwartz/Photofest

Chapter 6

Page 188: *Portrait.* James Hoyt is a participating artist of VSA arts, *http://www.vsarts.org/*; 193: Bob Daemmrich/Stock Boston; 195: Sheila Terry/Science Photo Library/Photo Researchers, Inc.; 199: Beringer-Dratch/The Image Works; 203: Peter Turnley/Corbis; 206: John Bellissimo/Corbis; 210: Snider/The Image Works; 211: Richard Hutchings/Photo Researchers, Inc.; 213: Penny Tweedie/Woodfin Camp & Associates; 216L: Austrian Archives/Corbis; 216R: AP/Wide World

Chapter 7

Page 237: *Starving Madonna and Children #2.* Carole Eskridge is a participating artist of VSA arts, *http://www.vsarts.org/*; 240: Martin/Custom Medical Stock Photo; 242: Bob Daemmrich/Stock Boston; 247: Grantpix/Photo Researchers; 249: Susan Greenwood/Liaison Agency; 253: Dennis Budd Gray/Stock Boston

Chapter 8

Page 260: *A Tree of Suppression.* Sue E. Clancy is a participating artist of VSA arts, *http://www.vsarts.org/*; 264L: Leinwand/Monkmeyer; 264R: Frank Siteman/Stock Boston; 266: The Incredible Machine/Boehringer Ingelheim Zentrale GmbH; 267: David Young-Wolff/Photo Edit; 270: Robert Frerck/Odyssey Productions; 274: Jeff Greenberg/Stock Boston; 277: David Lissy/Index Stock; 279: William Thompson/Index Stock; 280: Sipa Press; 283: Lawrence Schwartswald/Liaison Agency; 286: Dorothy Littell/The Image Works

Chapter 9

Page 290: *Self Portrait.* Louise Dalip Bego is a participating artist of VSA arts, *http://www.vsarts.org/*; 293: Frank Siteman/Stock Boston; 296: M. Antman/The Image Works; 298: Joel Gordon Photography; 302: M. Bridwell/PhotoEdit; 306: Frank Siteman/PhotoEdit; 307L: Courtesy Otto F. Kernberg; 307R: Norton Professional Books; 313: Bettmann/Corbis; 316: Louis Fernandez/Black Star

Chapter 10

Page 324: *Self Pity Transmuted into True Talent.* Jay Kyle Peterson is a participating artist of VSA arts, *http://www.vsarts.org/*; 327: Paul Conklin/PhotoEdit; 332: George Steinmetz; 336: A. Farnsworth/The Image Works; 339: Serge Attal/The Image Bank; 343: R. Lord/The Image Works; 348: D & I MacDonald/Index Stock

Chapter 11

Page 358: *The Shadow Gang.* George Widener is a participating artist of VSA arts, *http://www.vsarts.org/*; 359: Will & Deni McIntyre/Photo Researchers, Inc.; 364: A. Ramey/PhotoEdit; 367: Peter Yates/Mercury; 370: Barry Yee/Liaison Agency; 373L: AP/Wide World Photos; 373R: Bettmann/Corbis; 375: Mary Ellen Mark; 379L: Courtesy the survivors living and deceased of convicted pedophile, former priest James Porter; 379R: Corbis/Reuters; 382: Maynard/Sipa Press; 388: Bill Bachmann/Stock Boston; 389: Scott Camazine/Photo Researchers, Inc.

Chapter 12

Page 395: *Vision.* Jane A. Gerus is a participating artist of VSA arts, *http://www.vsarts.org/*; 397: Barbara J. Feigles/Stock Boston; 400: Alfred Gescheidt/The Image Bank; 404: Al Vercoutere, Malibu, CA.; 406: Monkmeyer; 409: Al Vercoutere, Malibu, CA; 412: The Genain Quadruplets. Courtesy the Genain Family; 413: NIMH; 420: Larry Mulvehill/Photo Researchers; 423: Billy E. Barnes/PhotoEdit; 425: David Alan Harvey/Woodfin Camp & Associates

Chapter 13

Page 431: *Untitled.* Robert V. P. Davis is a participating artist of VSA arts, *http://www.vsarts.org/*; 438: Lynn Johnson/Black Star; 441: Custom Medical Stock Photo; 445: R. Sidney/The Image Works; 448: The Warren Anatomical Museum, Francis A. Countway Library of Medicine, Harvard Medical School; 449: Hank Morgan/Photo Researchers, Inc.; 451: Lawrence Migdale/Stock Boston; 453: David Woo/Stock Boston; 455: Elaine Rebman/Photo Researchers, Inc.; 458: Guy Gillette/Photo Researchers, Inc.

Chapter 14

Page 463: *Untitled.* James Hoyt is a participating artist of VSA arts, *http://www.vsarts.org/*; 465: Ursula Markus/Photo Researchers, Inc.; 467: Aurora; 472: Frank Siteman/Stock Boston; 473: Stewart Cohen/Stone Images; 478: Laura Dwight/PhotoEdit; 483: Abraham Menashe; 486: Will & Deni McIntyre/Photo Researchers, Inc.; 490: Heron/Monkmeyer

Chapter 15

Page 495: *Symphony.* Louise Dalip Bego is a participating artist of VSA arts, *http://www.vsarts.org/*; 498: Robert Brenner/PhotoEdit; 504: Joseph Schuyler/Stock Boston; 505: Eric Roth/Index Stock; 510: Bob Daemmrich/Stock Boston; 512: AP/Wide World Photos

NAME INDEX

SUBJECT INDEX